The Selected Papers of JOHN JAY

THE SELECTED PAPERS

of

JOHN JAY

Volume 6   1794–1798

Elizabeth M. Nuxoll, *Editor*

Mary A. Y. Gallagher, Robb K. Haberman,

Jennifer E. Steenshorne, and Brant M. Vogel,

Associate Editors

University of Virginia Press
Charlottesville and London

The preparation of this volume was made possible by grants from the National Historical Publications and Records Commission and the National Endowment for the Humanities, with additional support from the Columbia University Libraries.

The publication of this volume has been supported by the Columbia University Libraries.

University of Virginia Press

First published 2020

1 3 5 7 9 8 6 4 2

♾ The paper used in this publication meets the minimum requirements of ANSI/NISO Z39.48-1992 (R 1997) (Permanence of Paper).

LIBRARY OF CONGRESS CATALOGING-IN-PUBLICATION DATA

Jay, John, 1745–1829.
    The selected papers of John Jay / Elizabeth M. Nuxoll, editor ; Mary A. Y. Gallagher, Robb K. Haberman, Jennifer E. Steenshorne, and Brant M. Vogel associate editors.
        v.   cm.
    Revision of: John Jay / edited by Richard B. Morris. New York : Harper & Row, 1975.
    Includes bibliographical references and index.
    Contents: v. 1. 1760–1779—v. 6. 1794–1798.
    ISBN 978-0-8139-2804-3 (v. 1 : cloth : alk. paper)
    1. Jay, John, 1745–1829—Archives. 2. Statesmen—United States—Archives. 3. United States—Politics and government—1775–1783—Sources. 4. United States—Politics and government—1783–1809—Sources. 5. New York (State)—Politics and government—1775–1865—Sources. I. Nuxoll, Elizabeth Miles, 1943– II. Gallagher, Mary A. Y. III. Haberman, Robb K. IV. Steenshorne, Jennifer E. V. Vogel, Brant M. VI. Jay, John, 1745–1829. John Jay. VII. Title.
    E302.J422 2010
    973.3—dc22

                                                                                          2009023614

ISBN 978-0-8139-2804-3 (vol. 1)
ISBN 978-0-8139-4381-7 (vol. 6)

Frontispiece: John Jay, by John Trumbull, 1794. Oil on canvas. (John Jay Homestead State Historic Site, Katonah, N.Y.; New York State Office of Parks, Recreation, and Historic Preservation)

Contents

Illustrations

Introduction

Volume 6 of the Selected Papers of John Jay opens as John Jay departs for England in May 1794 to begin what is to prove the most controversial mission of his career—the negotiation of the treaty that now bears his name. Barrels of ink have been consumed then and later discussing the merits of Jay's negotiating skills, the options available to him, and the short- and long-term results of the treaty. In this volume the editors seek to publish the most significant Jay documents related to the treaty's negotiation, ratification, and implementation. The volume then covers Jay's first three years in office as New York governor, which followed immediately the negotiation of the Jay Treaty.

In many ways the volume portrays a different experience than Jay's earlier diplomatic endeavors. Unlike his first trip to Europe in 1779, Jay's voyage went smoothly—with no imminent danger of being lost at sea. This time he was not accompanied by his beloved wife Sally who remained in New York caring for his home and young children. Travelling with him at Sally's insistence was his oldest son, Peter Augustus Jay, the child left behind in the care of grandparents during Jay's earlier European missions. Rather than being burdened by the equivalent of William Carmichael, the duplicitous secretary hoping to take over his job who traveled with him to Spain in 1779, Jay brought as his secretary the artist John Trumbull, a loyal, astute, personable, and well-connected assistant.

No longer an unknown and unwelcome emissary as he was in Spain, Jay reached London as an experienced diplomat, perhaps the most knowledgeable American about foreign affairs at the time, following his mission to Spain, his role as peace negotiator in France, and his four-year term as secretary for foreign affairs. Furthermore, he brought with him his prestige as first chief justice of the United States Supreme Court.[1] Moreover, with his long history of resistance to French influence over, and interference in, American political affairs, he was regarded by the British as favorable to improving Anglo-American relations, and probably their best hope for fruitful negotiations and for weaning the United States from the French alliance. For all these reasons, unlike John Adams and Thomas Pinckney, who were often disrespected or ignored by British officials, Jay was greeted warmly by them. He was also cultivated by those seeking American favors or connections, ranging from Loyalists seeking to recover confiscated property to creditors seeking repayment of American prewar debts, merchants seeking trade, and scientists, clergymen, and reformers seeking to unite Americans to their causes.

Jay was anxious to return home as soon as possible, and his negotiations were often arduous and stressful. During this mission Jay was no longer isolated, reserved, and wary as he often was earlier in his career, but, apparently modelling his diplomacy on Benjamin Franklin's, was sociable and interacted with many aspects of life in Britain, the details of which were often recorded in diaries and correspondence of Peter Augustus Jay and John Trumbull, as well as in his own papers.[2] While remaining aware that his favorable treatment was generally not inspired by him personally but derived from his position as special emissary to Great Britain, Jay forged what seemed to be a genuinely cordial relationship with British foreign minister William Grenville, and, to a lesser extent, with other British officials. Although Grenville was at the time of Jay's arrival preoccupied with European affairs and the reorganization of the cabinet, once negotiations finally started they proceeded expeditiously and smoothly, as Jay and Grenville worked their way through various treaty drafts, while Grenville consulted with the requisite cabinet officials and legal authorities, and responded to various British political pressures on the issues at stake.[3]

Jay's instructions primarily directed him to secure compensation for American ships and cargoes seized by the British in disregard of American neutrality and to resolve unfulfilled agreements made under the peace treaty with Britain of 1783, notably the British evacuation of frontier posts on American soil, the compensation for slaves removed by the British during the war of independence, and the removal of legal obstacles to American payment of prewar debts to British creditors. He was also authorized to negotiate a treaty of commerce. Avoidance of war was the main objective, but Jay was strictly barred from agreeing to anything that contradicted the terms of the treaties with France.[4]

Negotiations with Grenville began in earnest at the end of July 1794, by which time Jay had received some of the documentation needed of American ships seized by the British, primarily in the West Indies. On 30 July, Jay presented an official note complaining about irregular captures, improper condemnation of vessels, and the hard treatment and impressment of American seamen. Grenville countered with the complaints of British creditors, but then concentrated on maritime issues. He refused to modify British policies on the rights of neutral commerce and the definitions of neutrality violations. He agreed not to impress bona fide American seamen who could prove their citizenship, but defined as Americans only those who were citizens at the time of the peace in 1783, not anyone who was naturalized after that date. Irritated by the frequent issuance of false papers to non-Americans, the British also retained high standards of proof of citizenship. Jay and Grenville then began to negotiate on issues related to the peace treaty. They agreed not to press the question of which country had first violated the treaty, but to seek possible reciprocal concessions. On 6 August Jay presented a draft convention and treaty of commerce. He focused first on the primary issues related to the peace treaty—boundaries and the British retention of western posts. He then took up the rights of neutral commerce, spoliations, and debts, before moving on to commercial issues, including admission to trade with the British West Indies, reciprocal duties, access to the carrying trade, and commodities to be allowed in trade between the two nations. Finally, he took up issues applicable in time of war, particularly the use of privateers, the handling of prizes, and protection for citizens of one nation owning property in the other nation. He also proposed bans on the future sequestration or confiscation of debts of citizens of the other nation during wartime.

At the end of August Grenville delivered a counter proposal, in which he agreed to evacuate the western posts but not before 1 June 1796. He proposed preservation of property rights and a free flow of goods across borders for British traders, and Indians involved in the fur trade, but without offering equivalent privileges for American traders. Although Jay had proposed resolving boundary disputes by arbitration commissions, Grenville sought to extend the northwestern boundary far enough south to give British traders direct access to the headwaters of the Mississippi River. After Jay challenged such a boundary proposal, Grenville reconsidered the appointment of boundary commissioners, and set a meeting date for the discussion of all issues threatening the success of the negotiations. He also expressed willingness to consider an article officially admitting American vessels into the British East Indies. Detailed comparisons of variations between these two proposals and later ones can be found in the notes to those documents.

By the end of September Jay presented a new draft treaty which varied enough from Grenville's proposal as to require another round of negotiations. At the end of October, Grenville submitted a new draft. Jay objected to a proposal that goods in the Indian trade enter from Canada duty-free, and to proposals for removing all alien tonnage duties and imposts. Grenville agreed to settle the northwest boundary by commission but would not advance the date for withdrawal from the western posts.[5]

After further negotiations in November, both sides agreed to sign the treaty, as the best that could be obtained at that time. Progress on the question of neutral rights had been handicapped by the fact that the British had never accepted the interpretation of the law of nations on which the Americans and other neutral nations based their claims, and would suffer a great military disadvantage with France should they do so, given Britain's stronger navy, and much smaller army compared to that of France. Lacking sufficient naval strength to enforce its claims the United States could not insist on incorporating its interpretations of neutral rights, though Jay did secure agreement for compensation for illegal seizures. The British would not agree to compensation for slaves removed from the United States. Britain further insisted on the repayment of prewar debts to British creditors, but agreed to submit the claims facing legal impediments to a commission. It did agree to open East Indian trade and to some trade with the British West Indies, the latter only in ships no larger than seventy tons, and demanded a ban on reshipping West Indian products to Europe. Such stipulations, particularly the lack of true reciprocity in trade relations, set the stage for the battles over ratification of the treaty.

Once the treaty was signed on 19 November, Jay sought to convey copies of the treaty to America in time to reach Congress before the end of its session in March 1795, but efforts were foiled by the French capture of the English packet carrying two texts, and adverse sailing conditions confronting the ship bearing a third text. Anxious to recover his health after the arduous negotiations, and wishing to avoid a dangerous winter passage, Jay determined to remain in England until the spring. He wished to learn the American response to the treaty and to be available to renegotiate if necessary, but had assured his supporters in New York who were waging his campaign for the governorship that he would return before his term would begin should he be elected. Aware of the delays in receipt of the treaty, he set sail for New York in April 1795 and arrived in New York to a warm reception that was quickly followed by news of his election.

Jay traveled to Philadelphia to brief Washington and Secretary of State Randolph, and probably some of the senators, on the details of his negotiations at the time of the opening of the special senate session held in June 1795 to consider ratification of the treaty. Despite the reservations of most American leaders, the prospects for the treaty were good, as the Federalist Party controlled the Senate and was anxious to avoid war. The discussions were all kept secret, along with the details of the treaty, until after the Senate agreed to ratify, though it suspended Article 12 regarding the West Indian trade.

Once the terms of the treaty became known at the end of June, the political response, led by Republican politicians and journalists, as well as by the French and their supporters, was explosive. Jay was hung in effigy, copies of the treaties were burned, and assemblies protesting it, and petitioning Washington not to sign the treaty, sometimes turned violent. In New York the opposition was led by Jay's former friend Robert R. Livingston,[6] and much of the Livingston clan, while Alexander Hamilton and Rufus King penned the most important writings in support of the treaty under the pseudonym "Camillus." Jay supported Hamilton's efforts behind the scenes but took no direct role in the defense of the treaty until after ratification. Most damaging to the treaty's prospects was the arrival of news of the numerous British ship seizures of American vessels under a secret British Order in Council of 25 April 1795 that went into effect just after Jay's departure from England, which led Washington to postpone signing the treaty and return home to Virginia. However, cabinet members called for his return after the British minister, George Hammond, revealed intercepted French dispatches that seemed to indicate that Secretary of State Edmund Randolph had sought payment from the French in exchange for his support. Irritated by French interference and by the political pressures being placed on him with regard to the treaty, Washington decided to sign the treaty on 14 August 1795 and forwarded it to England for the exchange of ratifications. Again a series of mishaps delayed the exchange, and Washington was unable to inform Congress of the ratification until the end of February 1796.

The Republicans then had one last chance to obstruct the treaty: Republicans who controlled the House of Representatives sought to block appropriations for implementation of the treaty. Federalists, playing on the fear of war and the economic consequences of the failure to fulfill the treaty, mobilized popular opposition to the congressional efforts and gradually secured enough votes to approve the necessary appropriations.

Over the next few years, various commissions mandated by the treaty to settle unresolved disputes related to debts, spoliations, and boundaries eventually reached satisfactory conclusions on those issues. Jay remained in correspondence with officials involved in these efforts throughout his governorship, and periodically gave advice on these and other issues to Washington, Secretary of State Timothy Pickering and other cabinet members, and minister to Great Britain Rufus King. As governor Jay also was active in defense efforts in New York,[7] particularly during the Quasi-War with France that resulted from French anger at the terms of the Jay Treaty and American fury at French refusal to receive American diplomats, and over the XYZ affair, when members of the French government sought bribes as the price for re-opening negotiations.[8] The Jay Treaty, and its consequences remained a force in New York politics and led to continued attacks on Jay throughout his terms as governor, but particularly during his reelection campaign in 1798.[9]

Despite its continued unpopularity, particularly among Republicans, the Jay Treaty accomplished its primary goal of avoiding war with Great Britain, if not quite for the twenty years Washington anticipated, at least long enough for the United States to strengthen its finances and its defense before con-fronting the world's strongest naval power. It also set precedents for effective international use of arbitration commissions to resolve boundaries and other seemingly intractable and complicated issues.

In contrast to the well-documented and widely-debated Treaty of 1794, Jay's subsequent duties as chief executive of New York State remain under-studied and little understood. Jay's reputation as a principled, hardworking, and experienced statesman secured his selection as the Federalist candidate in the 1795 gubernatorial election. Moreover, Federalist leaders—and un-doubtedly many voters as well—recalled that Jay had suffered a narrow defeat in the previous contest for the governorship after state authorities upheld the controversial decision to disqualify ballots cast in three counties.[10]

The current contest pitted Jay and his running mate Stephen Van Rens-selaer against state Chief Justice Robert Yates and former state representative William Floyd. News of Jay's arrival in New York on 28 May was well received by his political supporters, who feared that his lengthy absence in London would have a negative impact on the election's outcome. In the week follow-ing Jay's return, newspaper accounts pointed to a Federalist victory as ballots were counted from the towns and counties that comprised New York's four districts (Southern, Middle, Eastern, and Western). The final tally showed that Jay's strong performance in the Southern and Western Districts enabled him to surpass his opponent by a margin of 13,511 to 11,880 votes.[11] The elec-tion results were confirmed on 6 June, and Jay was duly sworn in less than a month later on 1 July.[12]

Throughout his two terms as governor (1795–1801), Jay displayed the same political acumen and cautious temperament that had served him so well during his previous two decades of public service. When faced with a series of administrative challenges, ranging from commercial expansion, western settlement, and demographic growth to epidemics, threats of French invasion, and intense partisanship, Jay carried out a consistent course of governance guided by the principles of prudence and efficiency.

Jay laid out a comprehensive agenda soon after taking office that focused on military preparation, yearly yellow fever outbreaks, legal reform, and Indian negotiations. Jay publicly outlined his vision for New York's future when he addressed the state legislature at its opening session in January 1796. Jay identified the four key policy issues in his speech and urged that the assembled lawmakers also make them a top priority.[13]

Jay had the foresight to realize that even though his recent treaty with Britain had defused the threat of immediate war, the United States could eventually become enmeshed in European conflicts and fight against revolutionary France. Fearing that this development would devastate New York's mercantile-based economy, he advocated that legislators adopt a series of defensive measures for the purpose of fortifying the city and port of New York, amassing an adequate supply of arms and military stores, and improving the status of the state militia.[14]

Yellow fever posed an even more immediate danger than did foreign conflict. When Jay became governor in the summer of 1795 outbreaks of the disease had already beset New York City, as well as other towns and ports along the eastern seaboard. In the course of the decade, these epidemics would continue to ravage New York and claim over 3,300 lives. Convinced that active governance and increased regulations provided the most effective means of combating the scourge of yellow fever, Jay requested that lawmakers commit more resources, and used his own authority to learn more about the disease and raise public awareness of prevention methods. As part of this campaign, he oversaw the appointment of health officials and commissioners, declared a national day of thanksgiving, and approved several pieces of legislation for the construction of a new lazaretto, the quarantine of ships, the cleaning of public spaces and buildings, and the inspection of provisions. Collectively, these public health policies, which accommodated conflicting medical theories, transformed how New York responded to outbreaks of disease.[15]

As the most prominent magistrate in New York, and indeed the nation, Jay emphasized the need for perfecting the state's administration of justice. To this end, he recommended improved compensation for those sitting on the supreme court of judicature and the hiring of more personnel to assist the attorney general.[16] However, Jay's most ambitious plan for reforming the judicial system involved the state's management of convicted criminals. Jay called for the construction of a state penitentiary in order to have more direct oversight of prisoners. He also sought to amend the state's harsh penal code by both diminishing the number of felonies punishable by death and by making judicious use of the governor's power to pardon.[17]

Since the end of the war of independence, the government of New York held frequent talks with the Haudenosaunee and other Indian groups that either resided within the current state boundaries or had migrated to British Canada during or soon after the conflict. These negotiations centered on issues of sovereignty and land ownership, and they continued during Jay's tenure as governor. It was Jay's duty to appoint the agents who would represent New York's interests at these conferences, and he also often met with Indian delegations in person when they visited New York City and Albany. The resulting treaties included extensive purchases at greatly reduced prices of Haudenosaunee territories by state officials and private individuals. Whereas Jay did sometimes intercede on behalf of Indian communities when he believed that they were being treated unfairly, he nonetheless approved of such transactions, as they furthered the twin goals of landed settlement and commercial development in the state interior.[18]

Nevertheless, the critical developments that unsettled New York in 1798 posed the greatest challenges that Jay had yet faced as governor. In that year, the Adams administration and Congress rescinded the Treaty of Alliance with France that had been signed two decades earlier. With the subsequent outbreak of the Quasi-War between the United States and France, Jay became increasingly more concerned about the potential destruction of New York City and its maritime trade.[19] He responded to the diplomatic crisis by convening an early session of the New York legislature that met in August.[20] In the months that followed, Jay focused his labors on coordinating the planning, funding, and implementation of defense policies among municipal, state, and federal authorities.

Jay's worry about the welfare of New York City and its residents was compounded by the return of yellow fever in the late summer of 1798. By the time the disease had subsided in November, it had claimed the lives of over two thousand people. The suffering was intensified by labor and food shortages, as several citizens, including some who held positions of authority, fled the metropolis. Despite the efforts of Jay and his subordinates to provide the best medical, hygiene, and sanitation services, the epidemic of that year proved the worst in magnitude and virulence that New York had experienced to date.

Jay had the good fortune to work alongside a Federalist-dominated legislature during his first three years in office and could therefore rely on the support of a political majority for his administrative initiatives. Moreover, Jay's

Federalist colleagues acknowledged the popularity of his leadership by again selecting him to stand as governor for the 1798 election.[21]

Jay may have served as the titular leader of the Federalists in New York, yet it would be a mistake to view his political program as representing the values and interests of only his party. Many aspects of his agenda, including his emphasis on penal reform, defensive preparation, and combating yellow fever, were, in fact, a continuation of the policies endorsed and implemented by his Republican predecessor George Clinton. Moreover, Jay was able to blunt the impact of party divisiveness by appointing and working alongside Republicans, and endorsing men of merit and ability, regardless of their political affiliations.[22] Jay therefore displayed a commitment to administering the state in a manner that was both judicious and efficient. Carrying out this practice, particularly in 1798, surely tested Jay's mettle, for he did so in a political climate marked by rabid partisanship and at a time when his Clintonian opponents gradually gained ground in New York City and the northern sections of the state.[23]

Notes

1. For JJ's mission to Spain, see *JJSP*, 2. For his role as peace negotiator in France, and his first private visit to Britain following completion of the treaty negotiations, see *JJSP*, 3. For JJ's role as Secretary for Foreign Affairs, see *JJSP*, 4 and 5. For his actions as Chief Justice, see *JJSP*, 5.

2. See generally PAJ Diary, Parts A, B, and C, AD, NNC; Trumbull, *Autobiography*; JT Lbks, NHi.

3. See the editorial notes "Negotiating the Jay Treaty," and "John Jay's Mission to London," both below.

4. See the editorial note "The Jay Treaty: Appointment and Instructions"; and AH to JJ; and ER to JJ, both 6 May 1794, and notes, *JJSP*, 5: 609–21, 631–47.

5. For the details of the progress of the negotiations, see JJ's Draft for a Convention and Treaty of Commerce of 6 Aug., Grenville's Draft Treaties of 30 Aug., JJ's letters to Grenville of 1 and 4 Sept., JJ's Objections to Grenville's Draft Treaty Proposals, [6 Sept.], and JJ's Project for a Treaty of 30 Sept. 1794, and notes, all below.

6. Although JJ's former friend, and now political opponent, RRL, had reached out to JJ before his departure, he was one of the strongest opponents of the treaty on JJ's return. See RRL to JJ, 11 May 1794, *JJSP*, 5: 647–48; and the editorial note "Aftermath of the Jay Treaty: Responses, Ratification, and Implementation," below.

7. See the editorial note "Defending New York," below.

8. See the editorial note, "John Jay and the Response to the XYZ Affair in New York," below.

9. See the editorial note "John Jay Wins Reelection as Governor in 1798," below.

10. See the editorial note, "The Disputed Election of 1792," *JJSP*, 5: 353–59.

11. *A New Nation Votes*, https://elections.lib.tufts.edu/catalog/9p290b39d (accessed Aug. 2018).

12. *Argus, Greenleaf's New Daily Advertiser* (New York), 2 July 1795.

13. See JJ's Address to the New York State Legislature, [6 Jan. 1796], below.

14. For the legislative response and subsequent defensive policies implemented during JJ's administration, see the editorial notes, "Defending New York," and "Militia Matters in New York State," both below.

15. See the editorial note "John Jay and the Yellow Fever Epidemics," below.

16. For the legislation passed in response to Jay's recommendations, see "An ACT making provision for the more due and convenient conducting public prosecutions at the Courts of Oyer and Terminer and Gaol delivery, and General Sessions of the Peace," [12 Feb. 1796], and "An ACT for the payment of certain officers of government and other contingent expenses," [12 Apr. 1796], *N.Y. State Laws*, 19th sess. (1796), 6–7, 45.

17. See the editorial note "Crime and Punishment in Federalist New York," below.

18. See the editorial note "Indian Affairs under Jay's Governorship," below.

19. See the editorial note "John Jay and the Response to the XYZ Affair in New York," below.

20. See Proclamation Summoning an Early Session of the New York State Legislature, [2 July 1798], and JJ's Address to the New York State Legislature, [9 Aug. 1798], both below.

21. See the editorial note "John Jay Wins Reelection as Governor in 1798," below.

22. Militia appointments and promotions proved a notable exception to Jay's willingness to work in harmony with his Clintonian opponents. See the editorial note "Militia Matters in New York State," below.

23. For the shift of power to upstate New York, see the editorial note "The Capital Moves to Albany," below.

Publication Objectives

Although drawing to some degree on work done by the late Professor Richard B. Morris and his staff for the planned volume 3 of his unfinished edition of Jay's unpublished papers, our volume 6, like *The Selected Papers of John Jay* as a whole, presents a more complete selection of Jay materials, edited and updated to conform to the standards of modern documentary editions as described below. Like the volumes of the earlier edition, this is a selective rather than comprehensive volume, but it is not restricted to previously unpublished texts. The former policy left readers without ready access to many of Jay's most important documents, forcing them to rely primarily on early, often outmoded, unreliable, or unannotated texts, or texts widely scattered through multiple modern editions, for documents essential for evaluating Jay, his work, and his times. In addition, many unpublished texts previously selected under the former guidelines have since appeared within other documentary editions, rendering decisions made by the former editors obsolete.

This edition seeks to include all of Jay's most significant writings and correspondence, and a representative cross section of his remaining texts, including both incoming and outgoing correspondence. Greater weight is given to unpublished texts, but they are not included if they are routine or otherwise insignificant. Foreign language texts are generally transcribed literally in the original language and accompanied by an English translation, either composed at the time or prepared by later editors. Most earlier editions presented the texts only in translation. In general, items not written to or from Jay or his immediate family are excluded, but records of public bodies in which he participated or important texts documenting his ideas and actions that are otherwise not recorded are sometimes included. The table of contents identifies the documents appearing in the volume as well as the related editorial notes.

This volume includes texts selected from manuscripts related to John Jay held at the Rare Book and Manuscript Library at Columbia University as well as thousands of photocopies collected from other repositories and private collections not only in the United States but in other countries, especially Spain, France, the Netherlands, and Great Britain. Many of the texts from foreign repositories were made available on microfilm from copies on deposit at the Library of Congress.

The Columbia University Libraries, to the extent possible, placed abstracts and images of all the Jay texts and portions of the related background material into the online image database. The editorial apparatus and annotation of the documents selected for print publication serve as a guide to the overall content of Jay's papers, and coordinate the texts with, and cross reference them to, the handwritten documents viewable online. The editorial apparatus, annotations, and indexes furnish the reader with the background needed to identify the persons and subjects treated in all the documents and such other data essential to an understanding of their contents and the relationships among the various documents, published and unpublished. Persons and subjects identified in earlier volumes are not further identified unless their status or circumstances have changed during the years covered by the present volumes. The location of such earlier identifications is indicated in the index, and, in the case of major figures in the volumes, in the biographical directory.

Personal and family texts related to public affairs are also included in the volume, as well as documents presenting major themes related to social and family history found within the large body of personal papers that, for the most part, are previously unpublished.

Editorial Guidelines

The editorial aim in transcription is to render texts as literally as possible. Thus, spelling and capitalization are retained as in the manuscripts. If it is impossible to tell whether the writer intended to use an upper- or lowercase letter, modern usage governs. Grammar and syntax are retained as in the originals, and the use of [*sic*] is avoided. Paragraph indentations are standardized to the customary indentation. When an author has chosen not to indent the first line of new paragraphs, however, that format is respected.

The author's salutation is retained, and no punctuation added to supply the author's omission. Dashes used in place of periods or semicolons in modern punctuation are retained. Dashes used to fill up a line are silently omitted. A blank space left in the manuscript by the author is so depicted and the fact mentioned in an endnote.

The place of writing and the date always appear at the head of the letter. When placed elsewhere in the original, or when both the date and place of writing, or any part of them, have been omitted, the information is supplied, if possible, within square brackets. Generally, canceled matter is ignored unless it is of special significance. However, because John Jay so often suppressed sensitive information within texts, and because he often extensively reworked texts to get the impact he desired, in draft and autograph documents, all legible substantive or stylistically significant canceled matter is indicated; minor excisions of spelling and grammatical errors or slips of the pen are, however, omitted. When canceled matter is included, it is struck through and placed before the revised passage. Excisions within longer deletions are indicated by double strike-through lines. Interlineations are shown within caret symbols. Complex revisions not easily depicted in the text are explained in endnotes. When their importance warrants it, variant readings derived from the collation of multiple texts of a document with the master text are entered in endnotes.

Where a portion of a word is missing from a manuscript and there is no doubt about the missing letters, the proper letters are inserted in brackets. Passages that are not conjecturable are indicated by the editorial insertion of an italicized explanatory phrase in square brackets, such as [*illegible*], [*torn*] or [*mutilated*].

Abbreviations are retained. When a period or colon is part of the abbreviation or indicates that letters were written above the line, it is printed at the end of the abbreviation (e.g., "4th."). Unfamiliar and archaic abbreviations are sometimes expanded, or explained in the table of abbreviations used in the edition. The thorn is rendered as "th" ("ye" is thus transcribed as "the"); the "tailed *p*" is rendered as "per" or "pro". The ampersand used as an abbreviation for "and" (as in "& Co." for "and Company") and in "&c" (for "etc.") is retained. Unless otherwise noted pounds (£) are pounds sterling.

In many instances a document may be represented by an ALS, a Dft, an LbkC, and so forth. The most authentic text is published—that is, the ALS or LS, or if that does not exist, the Dft. Contemporary copies take precedence over LbkCs, which in turn take precedence over later transcripts or extracts. The existence of the variant copies is cited in the source note.

Coded passages are decrypted whenever possible and printed in small caps. The method of decryption and special problems involved are explained in the source note; the general use by John Jay of ciphers and codes is explained in the editorial note in *JJSP*, 2: 7–13.

All manuscripts are located in the Papers of John Jay, Rare Book and Manuscript Library, Columbia University Libraries, unless otherwise noted. When reference is made to letters in the online edition of The Papers of John Jay, the designation EJ is used and the manuscript identification number added.

Editorial notes providing relevant background information and linking the texts included in the volume with related documents that were not selected for publication are placed as head notes above the first or most significant document on a particular subject. Their location is indicated in the table of contents.

Manuscript Designations

AD	Autograph document
ADS	Autograph document signed
AL	Autograph letter
ALS	Autograph letter signed
AL[S]	Autograph letter, signature cropped
C	Contemporary copy

D	Document
Dft	Draft (in author's hand unless otherwise noted)
DftS	Draft signed
DS	Document signed
E	Extract
FC	File copy (in author's hand unless otherwise noted)
L	Letter
LbkC	Letterbook copy (not in author's hand unless so stated)
LS	Letter signed
PrC	Press copy
PtD	Printed document
PtDS	Printed document signed
PtL	Printed letter
RC	Recipient's copy
SR	Sales Record
Tr	Transcript (made at a much later date)

Abbreviations

AH	Alexander Hamilton
BF	Benjamin Franklin
CT	Charles Thomson
EJ	Digital Edition of the Papers of John Jay
ER	Edmund Randolph
GW	George Washington
Inst.	Instant, the current month
JA	John Adams
JJ	John Jay
JM	James Madison
JQA	John Quincy Adams
JT	John Trumbull
l.t.	livres tournois (French monetary unit)
NYMS	New-York Manumission Society
PAJ	Peter Augustus Jay
PJM	Peter Jay Munro
RK	Rufus King
RRL	Robert R. Livingston
SLJ	Sarah Livingston Jay
TJ	Thomas Jefferson

| TP | Timothy Pickering |
| Ult. or Ult°. | Ultimo, the previous month |

Textual Symbols

∧∧	inserted text
∧∧·····∧∧	text inserted within an insertion
[roman]	Insertion, or conjectural reading, in roman text, in brackets
[*illegible*]	insertion noting illegible word or passage, in italics, in brackets
[~~*illegible*~~]	insertion noting illegible excised word or passage, in italics, in brackets
SMALL CAPS	encoded text decoded in the manuscript, in small cap
[SMALL CAPS]	encoded text decoded by the editors, in small caps, in brackets

Sources

The bulk of the original material drawn on for this publication is in the Papers of John Jay in the Columbia University Libraries. The rest comes from various public and private collections in the United States and abroad.

Public Collections in the United States

Abbreviations are as they appear in the National Union Catalog of the Library of Congress.

CSmH	Henry E. Huntington Library, Art Collections and Botanical Gardens
CSt	Stanford University Library
Ct	Connecticut State Library, Hartford
CtY-BR	Yale University, Beinecke Rare Book and Manuscript Library
DLC	Library of Congress
DNA	National Archives
DNDAR	Daughters of the American Revolution, Washington, D.C.
DUSC	United States Supreme Court, Washington, D.C.
ICHi	Chicago Historical Society
MB	Boston Public Library
MH	Harvard College Library

MHi	Massachusetts Historical Society
MiU-C	William L. Clements Library, Ann Arbor
MWA	American Antiquarian Society
N	New York State Library
NcU	University of North Carolina
NHi	New-York Historical Society
NHyF	Franklin D. Roosevelt Library, Hyde Park, N.Y.
NjP	Princeton University
NN	New York Public Library
NNC	Columbia University
NNGL	Gilder Lehrman Collection, N.Y.
NNMus	Museum of the City of New York
NNPM	Pierpont Morgan Library, N.Y.
NNYSL	New York Society Library
NTucW	Westchester County Historical Society, Tuckahoe N.Y.; now listed as at Elmsford, N.Y.
NyKaJJH	John Jay Homestead State Historic Site, Katonah, N.Y.
NyRyJHC	Jay Heritage Center, Rye, N.Y.
OCHP	Cincinnati Historical Society
PHi	Pennsylvania Historical Society
PPAmP	American Philosophical Society
PPFAR	United States Federal Archives and Records Center, Philadelphia
PPIn	Independence Hall National Historical Park
PU	University of Pennsylvania, Philadelphia
RPB	Brown University Library, Providence
ScHi	South Carolina Historical Society, Charleston
ViMtvL	Mount Vernon Ladies' Association of the Union

Private Collections in the United States

PC	Private Collection (not identified)

Foreign Collections

CO	Colonial Office, National Archives, Kew
FO	Foreign Office, National Archives, Kew
SpMaAHN	Archivo Histórico Nacional, Madrid
StedNL-M	National Library of Scotland, Edinburgh
UK-BL	British Library
UK-KeNA	National Archives, Kew

UkDhU	Durham University, Library
UkLPR	Public Record Office, National Archives, Kew
UkOxU	Oxford University, Bodleian Library
UkWC-A	Royal Archives, Windsor Castle

Short Titles of Works Frequently Cited

A New Nation Votes
A New Nation Votes: American Election Returns 1787–1825 https://elections.lib.tufts
.edu/

Adams Family Correspondence
Margaret Hogan et al., eds., *Adams Papers: Adams Family Correspondence* (13 vols. to
date; Cambridge, Mass., 1963–

AHR
American Historical Review

Ammon, *Genet Mission*
Harry Ammon, *The Genet Mission* (New York, 1973)

ANBO
American National Biography Online

Anderson, *Physician heal thyself*
Marynita Anderson, *Physician heal thyself: medical practitioners of eighteenth-century
New York* (New York, 2004)

Annals
Annals of the Congress of the United States (42 vols.; Washington, D.C., 1834–56)

ASP
*American State Papers: documents, legislative and executive, of the Congress of the United
States selected and edited under the authority of Congress* (38 vols.; Washington, D.C.,
1832–61). This series is divided into ten classes: *Foreign Relations, Indian Affairs,
Finance, Commerce and Navigation, Military Affairs, Naval Affairs, Post-Office Depart-
ment, Public Lands, Claims,* and *Miscellaneous*

Barrett, *Old Merchants of N.Y.*
Walter Barrett, *Old Merchants of New York City* (New York, 1870)

Bayley, *Letters*
Richard Bayley, *Letters from the Health-Office submitted to the Common Council of the
City of New-York* (New York, 1799; *Early Am. Imprints*, series 1, no. 35161)

Belknap and Morse, "Report on Oneida and Mohekunuh Indians"
Jeremy Belknap and Jedidiah Morse, "The report of a committee of the board of correspondents of the Scots Society for propagating Christian knowledge, who visited

the Oneida and Mohenkunuh Indians in 1796," *Collections of the Massachusetts Historical Society, for the year M,DCC,XCVIII* (Boston, 1798; *Early Am. Imprints*, series 1, no. 34082), 12–32

Bemis, *Jay's Treaty*
Samuel Flagg Bemis, *Jay's Treaty: A Study in Commerce and Diplomacy* (New Haven and London, 1962)

Bird, *Press and Speech under Assault*
Wendell Bird, *Press and Speech under Assault: The Early Supreme Court Justices, the Sedition Act of 1798, and the Campaign against Dissent* (New York, 2016)

Brooke, *Columbia Rising*
John L. Brooke, *Columbia Rising: Civil Life on the Upper Hudson from the Revolution to the Age of Jackson* (Chapel Hill, N.C., and Williamsburg, Va., 2010)

Burrows and Wallace, *Gotham*
Edwin G. Burrows and Mike Wallace, *Gotham: A History of New York City to 1898* (New York and Oxford, 1999)

Carey, *American Remembrancer*
Mathew Carey, ed., *The American Remembrancer; or An Impartial Collection of Essays, Resolves, Speeches, &c., Relative or Having Affinity to the Treaty with Great Britain* (3 vols.; Philadelphia, 1795–1796; *Early Am. Imprints*, series 1, no. 28389)

Childs, *Debates*
Francis Childs, *The Debates and Proceedings of the Convention of the State of New-York, Assembled at Poughkeepsie, on the 17th June, 1788. To Deliberate and Decide on the Form of Federal Government Recommended by the General Convention at Philadelphia, on the 17th September, 1787. Taken in Short Hand* (New York, 1788; *Early Am. Imprints*, series 1, no. 21310)

Clarfield, "Postscript to the Jay Treaty"
Gerard Clarfield, "Postscript to the Jay Treaty: Timothy Pickering and Anglo-American Relations, 1795–1797," *WMQ* 23 (January 1966): 106–20

Cobbett, *Parliamentary History of England*
William Cobbett, *Parliamentary History of England, from the Earliest Period to the Year 1803* (36 vols.; London, 1806–1820)

Combs, *Jay Treaty*
Jerald A. Combs, *The Jay Treaty* (Berkeley, 1970)

Convention Journal
Journal of the Convention of the State of New-York Held at Poughkeepsie, in Dutchess County, the 17th of June, 1788 (Poughkeepsie, 1788; *Early Am. Imprints*, series 1, no. 21313)

Currie and Hosack, *Sketch of the yellow fever*
William Currie, David Hosack, et al., *A sketch of the rise and progress of the yellow fever, and of the proceedings of the Board of Health, in Philadelphia, in the year 1799: to which is*

added, a collection of facts and observations respecting the origin of the yellow fever in this country; and a review of the different modes of treating it (Philadelphia, 1800; *Early Am. Imprints*, series 1, no. 37274)

Davis, *Brief Account*
> Davis, Matthew L., *A brief account of the epidemical fever which lately prevailed in the city of New York; with the different proclamations, reports and letters of Gov. Jay, Gov. Mifflin, the Health Committee of New York, &c, upon the subject. To which is added, an accurate list of the names of those who have died of the disease from July 29, to Nov. 1* (New York, 1795; *Early Am. Imprints*, series 1, no 28538)

DHSC
> Maeva Marcus et al., eds., *The Documentary History of the Supreme Court of the United States, 1789–1800* (8 vols.; New York, 1985–2007)

DNA: Domestic Letters
> Domestic Letters of the Department of State, 1784–1906, RG 59, item 120, National Archives (M40). Accessed on Fold3.com

Duffy, *History of Public Health*
> John Duffy, *A History of Public Health in New York City 1625–1866* (New York, 1968)

Early Am. Imprints
> *Early American Imprints*, series 1: Evans, 1639–1800 [microform; digital collection], edited by American Antiquarian Society, published by Readex, a division of Newsbank, Inc. Accessed: Columbia University, New York, N.Y., 2006–19, http://infoweb .newsbank.com/
> *Early American Imprints*, series 2: Shaw-Shoemaker, 1801–1819 [microform; digital collection], edited by American Antiquarian Society, published by Readex, a division of Newsbank, Inc. Accessed: Columbia University, New York, N.Y., 2006–19, http:// infoweb.newsbank.com/

Eddy, *Account of the State Prison*
> Thomas Eddy, *An account of the state prison or penitentiary House, in the city of New-York* (New York, 1801; *Early Am. Imprints*, series 2, no. 431)

Elkins and McKitrick, *Age of Federalism*
> Stanley Elkins and Eric McKitrick, *The Age of Federalism* (New York and Oxford, 1993)

Executive Journal
> *Journal of Executive Proceedings of the Senate* (Washington, D.C., 1828)

Fewster, "British Ship Seizures"
> Joseph M. Fewster, "The Jay Treaty and British Ship Seizures: The Martinique Cases," *WMQ* 45 (July 1988): 426–52

Furstenberg, *When the U.S. Spoke French*
> Francois Furstenberg, *When the United States Spoke French: Five Refugees Who Shaped a Nation* (New York, 2014)

Gellman, *Emancipating New York*
David N. Gellman, *Emancipating New York: The Politics of Slavery and Freedom, 1777–1827* (Baton Rouge, 2006)

Graymont, "New York State Indian Policy"
Barbara Graymont, "New York State Indian Policy after the Revolution," *New York History* 57 (Oct. 1976): 438–74

Hardie, *Account of the Malignant Fever*
James Hardie, *An Account of the Malignant Fever, La[t]ely Prevalent in the City of New-York* (New York, 1799)

Hastings and Noble, *Military Minutes*
Hugh Hastings and Henry H. Noble, eds., *Military Minutes of the Council of Appointment of the State of New York, 1783–1821* (4 vols.; Albany, 1901)

Heaton, "Yellow Fever"
Claude Edwin Heaton, "Yellow Fever in New York City," *Bulletin of the Medical Library Association* 34 (April 1946), 67–78

Hist. Mss. Comm., *Fortescue Manuscripts*
Historical Manuscripts Commission, *Report on the Manuscripts of J.B. Fortescue, Esq., Preserved at Dropmore* vols. 3–4 (London, 1899)

HPJ
Henry P. Johnston, ed., *The Correspondence and Public Papers of John Jay* (4 vols.; New York, 1890–93)

Humphrey, *Land and Liberty*
Thomas J. Humphrey, *Land and Liberty: Hudson Valley Riots in the Age of Revolution* (Dekalb, Ill., 2004)

JCC
Worthington C. Ford et al., eds., *Journals of the Continental Congress, 1774–1789* (34 vols.; Washington, D.C., 1904–37)

JJSP
Elizabeth M. Nuxoll et al., eds., *The Selected Papers of John Jay* (6 vols. to date; Charlottesville, Va., 2010–)

Journal of the House, vols. 1–3
Journal of the House of Representatives of the United States (Washington, D.C., 1826)

JQA Diaries Digital
The Diaries of John Quincy Adams: A Digital Collection http://www.masshist.org/jqa diaries/php/

King, *Life and Correspondence of Rufus King*
Charles R. King, M. D., ed., *The life and correspondence of Rufus King; comprising his letters, private and official, his public documents, and his speeches* (6 vols.; New York, 1894–1900)

Lillach, "Jay Treaty Commissions"
Richard B. Lillach, "The Jay Treaty Commissions," *St. John's Law Review* 37 (May 1963): 260–83

Longworth's American Almanack
Longworth's American almanack, New-York register, and city directory for the twenty-second year of American independence. Containing most things useful in a work of this kind. Embellished with a view of the new theatre (New York, 1797; Early Am. Imprints, series 1, no. 32386)

LPAH
Julius Goebel Jr. and Joseph Smith, et al., eds., *The Law Practice of Alexander Hamilton* (5 vols.; New York: 1964–81)

Marcus, *Origins of the Federal Judiciary*
Maeva Marcus, ed., *Origins of the Federal Judiciary: Essays on the Judiciary Act of 1789* (New York, 1992)

MCCNYC
Minutes of the Common Council of the City of New York, 1784–1831 (19 vols.; New York, 1917)

McCullough, *Adams*
David McCullough, *John Adams* (New York, 2001)

Monaghan, *Murrays of Murray Hill*
Charles Monaghan, *The Murrays of Murray Hill* (Brooklyn, 1998)

Monroe Papers
Daniel Preston, ed., *The Papers of James Monroe* (6 vols. to date; Westport, Conn., 2003–)

Moore, *International Adjudications*
John Bassett Moore, ed., *International Adjudications, ancient and modern; history and documents, together with mediatorial reports, advisory opinions, and the decisions of domestic commissions, on international claims* (4 vols.; New York, 1929–36)

Moore, *International Arbitrations*
John Basset Moore, ed., *History and digest of the international arbitrations to which the United States has been a party: together with appendices containing the treaties relating to such arbitrations, and historical and legal notes on other international arbitrations ancient and modern, and on the domestic commissions of the United States for the adjustment of international claims* (6 vols.; Washington, D.C., 1898)

Murphy, *Building the Empire State*
Brian P. Murphy, *Building the Empire State: Political Economy in the Early Republic* (Philadelphia, 2015)

N.Y. Assembly Journal, 19th sess. (1796)
[New York State], *Journal of the Assembly, of the state of New-York. At their nineteenth session, begun and held at the city-hall, of the city of New-York, on Wednesday, the sixth*

of January, one thousand seven hundred and ninety-six (New York, 1796; *Early Am. Imprints,* series 1, no. 47862)

N.Y. Assembly Journal, 20th sess. (1796–97)
[New York State], *Journal of the Assembly, of the State of New-York; at their twentieth session, the first meeting begun and held at the City of New-York, the first day of November, 1796, and the second at the city of Albany, the third Day of January, 1797* (Albany, [1797]; *Early Am. Imprints,* series 1, no. 32553)

N.Y. Assembly Journal, 21st sess. (January 1798)
[New York State], *Journal of the Assembly of the state of New-York; at their twenty-first session, began and held at the city of Albany, the second day of January, 1798* (Albany, [1799]; *Early Am. Imprints,* series 1, no. 34210)

N.Y. Assembly Journal, 22nd sess. (August 1798)
[New York State], *Journal of the Assembly of the state of New-York; at their twenty-second session, began and held at the city of Albany, the ninth day of August, 1798* (Albany, [1798]; *Early Am. Imprints,* series 1, no. 34212)

N.Y. Assembly Journal, 22nd sess., 2nd meeting (1799)
[New York State], *Journal of the Assembly of the state of New-York; at their twenty-second session, second meeting, begun and held at the city of Albany, the second day of January, 1799* (Albany, [1799]; *Early Am. Imprints,* series 1, no. 35924)

N.Y. Assembly Journal, 23rd sess. (1800)
[New York State], *Journal of the Assembly of the state of New-York; at their twenty-third session, began and held at the city of Albany, the twenty-eighth day of January, 1800* (Albany, [1800]; *Early Am. Imprints,* series 1, no. 38084)

N.Y. Assembly Journal, 24th sess. (1800–1801)
[New York State], *Journal of the Assembly of the state of New-York: at their twenty-fourth session, began and held at the city of Albany, the fourth day of November, 1800* (Albany, [1801]; *Early Am. Imprints,* series 2, no. 1037)

N.Y. Civil List
Franklin B. Hough, *The New-York Civil List* (Albany, N.Y., 1855–63)

NYGM
State of New York, *Messages from the Governors comprising Executive Communications to the Legislature and other Papers relating to Legislation from the Organization of the First Colonial Assembly in 1683 to and including the Year 1906* vol. 2 1777–1822 (Albany, 1909)

"N.Y. Hibernian Volunteers"
"New-York Hibernian Volunteers, 1796 Jan.–Mar.," New-York Historical Society Manuscript Collection

N.Y. Senate Journal, 17th sess. (1794)
[New York State], *Journal of the Senate, of the state of New-York, at their seventeenth session, begun and held at the city of Albany, the seventh day of January, 1794* (Albany, [1794]; *Early Am. Imprints,* series 1, no. 27398)

N.Y. Senate Journal, 18th sess. (1795)
[New York State], *Journal of the Senate of the state of New-York. At their eighteenth session, begun at the town of Poughkeepsie, in the county of Dutchess, on Tuesday, the sixth of January: and held by adjournment, at the city of New York, Tuesday, January 20, 1795* (New York, [1795]; *Early Am. Imprints*, series 1, no. 29188)

N.Y. Senate Journal, 19th sess. (1796)
[New York State], *Journal of the Senate of the state of New-York. At their nineteenth session, begun and held at the City-Hall, of the city of New-York, on Wednesday, the sixth of January, one thousand seven hundred and ninety-six* (New York, 1796; *Early Am. Imprints*, series 1, no. 30871)

N.Y. Senate Journal, 20th sess. (1796–97)
[New York State], *Journal of the Senate, of the state of New-York; at their twentieth session, the first meeting began and held at the city of New-York, the first day of November, 1796; and the second, at the city of Albany, the third day of January, 1797* (Albany, [1797]; *Early Am. Imprints*, series 1, no. 32554)

N.Y. Senate Journal, 21st sess. (January 1798)
[New York State], *Journal of the Senate, of the state of New-York; at their twenty-first session, began and held at the city of Albany, the second day of January, 1798* (Albany, [1798]; *Early Am. Imprints*, series 1, no. 34211)

N.Y. Senate Journal, 22nd sess. (August 1798)
[New York State], *Journal of the Senate of the state of New-York; at their twenty-second session, began and held at the city of Albany, the ninth day of August, 1798* (Albany, [1798]; *Early Am. Imprints*, series 1, no. 34213)

N.Y. Senate Journal, 22nd sess., 2nd meeting (1799)
[New York State], *Journal of the Senate of the state of New-York; at their twenty-second session, second meeting, began and held at the city of Albany, the second day of January, 1799* (Albany, [1799]; *Early Am. Imprints*, series 1, no. 35925)

N.Y. Senate Journal, 23rd sess. (1800)
[New York State], *Journal of the Senate of the state of New-York; at their twenty-third session, began and held at the city of Albany, the twenty-eighth day of January, 1800* (Albany, [1799]; *Early Am. Imprints*, series 1, 38085)

N.Y. State Laws, (1777–97), 1
[New York State], *Laws of the state of New-York, comprising the Constitution, and the acts of the Legislature, since the Revolution, from the first to the twentieth session, inclusive in three volumes*, vol. 1, 2nd ed. (New York, 1798; *Early Am. Imprints*, series 1, no. 34214)

N.Y. State Laws, (1777–97), 2
[New York State], *Laws of the state of New-York, comprising the Constitution, and the acts of the Legislature, since the Revolution, from the first to the twentieth session, inclusive in three volumes*, vol. 2, 2nd ed. (New York, 1798; *Early Am. Imprints*, series 1, no. 48545)

N.Y. State Laws, (1777–97), 3

[New York State], *Laws of the state of New-York, comprising the Constitution, and the acts of the Legislature, since the Revolution, from the first to the twentieth session, inclusive in three volumes,* vol. 3 (New York, 1797; *Early Am. Imprints,* series 1, no. 32555)

N.Y. State Laws, 18th sess. (1795)

[New York State], *Laws of the state of New-York. Eighteenth session* (New York, 1795; *Early Am. Imprints,* series 1, no. 29189)

N.Y. State Laws, 19th sess. (1796)

[New York State], *Laws of the state of New-York. Nineteenth session* (New York, 1796; *Early Am. Imprints,* series 1, no. 30876)

N.Y. State Laws, 20th sess. (1797)

[New York State], *Laws of the state of New-York, passed at the twentieth session of the Legislature, begun at the city of New-York, and held by adjournment at the city Albany* (New York, 1797; *Early Am. Imprints,* series 1, no. 32556)

N.Y. State Laws, 21st sess. (January 1798)

[New York State], *Laws of the state of New-York, passed at the twenty-first session of the Legislature, begun and held at the city of Albany, the second day of January, 1798* (Albany, 1798; *Early Am. Imprints,* series 1, no. 34215)

N.Y. State Laws, 22nd sess. (August 1798)

[New York State], *Laws of the state of New-York, passed at the twenty-second session of the Legislature, begun and held at the city of Albany, the ninth day of August, 1798* (Albany, 1798; *Early Am. Imprints,* series 1, no. 34216)

N.Y. State Laws, 22nd sess., 2nd meeting (1799)

[New York State], *Laws of the state of New-York. Passed at the twenty-second session, second meeting, of the Legislature, begun and held at the city of Albany, the second day of January, 1799* (Albany, 1799; *Early Am. Imprints,* series 1, no. 35926)

N.Y. State Laws, 23rd sess. (1800)

[New York State], *Laws of the state of New-York, passed at the twenty-third session of the Legislature, begun and held at the city of Albany, the twenty-eighth day of January, 1800* (Albany, 1800; *Early Am. Imprints,* series 1, no. 38087)

ODNBO

Oxford Dictionary of National Biography Online

OED

Oxford English Dictionary

PAB

Mary-Jo Kline et al., eds., *Political Correspondence and Public Papers of Aaron Burr* (2 vols.; Princeton, N.J., 1983)

PAH

Harold C. Syrett et al., eds., *The Papers of Alexander Hamilton* (27 vols.; New York, 1961–87)

Perkins, *First Rapprochement*

Bradford Perkins, *The First Rapprochement: England and the United States, 1795–1805* (Berkeley and Los Angeles, 1967)

Perkins, "Hawkesbury"

Bradford Perkins, "Lord Hawkesbury and the Jay-Grenville Negotiations," *Mississippi Valley Historical Review* 40 (Sept. 1953): 291–304

PGW: PS

Dorothy Twohig et al., eds., *The Papers of George Washington, Presidential Series* (19 vols. to date; Charlottesville, Va., 1987–)

PGW: RS

W. W. Abbot et al., eds., *The Papers of George Washington, Retirement Series* (4 vols.; Charlottesville, Va., 1998–99)

PJA

Robert J. Taylor, Gregg L. Lint, et al., eds., *Papers of John Adams* (19 vols. to date; Cambridge, Mass., 1977–)

PJM

William T. Hutchinson, William M. E. Rachal, Robert A. Rutland et al., eds., *The Papers of James Madison, Congressional Series* (17 vols.; Chicago and Charlottesville, 1962–91)

Princetonians

N.J. Wesley F. Craven and Ruth L. Woodward, *Princetonians 1784–1790: A Biographical Dictionary*, vol. 4 (Princeton, N.J., 1991)

PTJ

Julian T. Boyd, Charles T. Cullen et al., eds., *The Papers of Thomas Jefferson* (43 vols. to date; Princeton, N.J., 1950–)

PWL

Carl E. Prince et al., eds., *The Papers of William Livingston* (5 vols.; New Brunswick, N.J., 1979–88)

Ritcheson, "Pinckney's London Mission"

Charles R. Ritcheson, "Thomas Pinckney's London Mission, 1792–1796, and the Impressment Issue," *The International History Review* 2 (Oct. 1980): 523–41

Scattergood, *Memoirs*

William and Thomas Evans, *Memoirs of Thomas Scattergood, late of Philadelphia. A minister of the Gospel of Christ. Compiled for the American Friends' Library, chiefly from his notes and letters* (London, 1845)

Schaeper, *Bancroft*
Thomas J. Schaeper, *Edward Bancroft: Scientist, Author, Spy* (New Haven and London, 2011)

Shrady, "Medical Items"
George F. Shrady, ed., "Medical Items," *The Medical Record* (New York) 23 (14 Apr. 1883): 419–20

Smith, *Diary*
Elihu Hubbard Smith, *The Diary of Elihu Hubbard Smith: 1771–1798.* Edited by James E. Cronin (Philadelphia, 1973)

Stahr, *John Jay*
Walter Stahr, *John Jay: Founding Father* (New York, 2005)

Stat.
The Public Statutes at Large of the United States, vols. 1–17 (Boston, 1845–73)

Statement of the Officers of Artillery
A statement, explanatory of the resignation of the officers of the Regiment of Artillery, of the City & County of New-York (New York, 1797; *Early Am. Imprints*, series 1, no. 32568)

Sterling, "Letters of Samuel Bayard"
David L. Sterling, "A Federalist Opposes the Jay Treaty: The Letters of Samuel Bayard," *WMQ* 18 (July 1961): 408–24

Stinchcombe, *XYZ Affair*
William Stinchcombe, *The XYZ Affair* (Westport, Conn., 1980)

Taylor, *Divided Ground*
Alan Taylor, *The Divided Ground: Indians, Settlers, and the Northern Borderland of the American Revolution* (New York, 2006)

Trumbull, *Autobiography*
John Trumbull, *The Autobiography of Colonel John Trumbull, Patriot-Artist, 1756–1843.* Edited by Theodore Sizer (New Haven, Conn., 1953)

Vattel, *Law of Nations*
Emmer de Vattel, *The law of nations; or, Principles of the law of nature; applied to the conduct and affairs of nations and sovereigns. By M. de Vattel. A work tending to display the true of interest of powers. Translated from the French* (London, 1759)

Wilkinson, "The Pitt-Portland Coalition of 1794"
David Wilkinson, "The Pitt-Portland Coalition of 1794 and the Origins of the 'Tory' Party," *History* 83 (April 1988): 249–64

WJ
William Jay, ed., *The Life of John Jay: With Selections from His Correspondence and Miscellaneous Papers* (2 vols.; New York, 1833)

WMQ
   William and Mary Quarterly, 3rd series (1944–)

Young, *Democratic Republicans*
   Alfred F. Young, *The Democratic Republicans of New York: The Origins, 1763–1797*
   (Chapel Hill, N.C., and Williamsburg, Va., 1967)

Acknowledgments

The *Selected Papers of John Jay* builds on the work of collecting, transcribing, and annotating John Jay documents previously done at Columbia University from the 1950s to the 1990s by Richard B. Morris and the staff of the John Jay project. Acknowledgments of the contributions made to that project appear in volume 1 of this series, and in *John Jay: The Making of a Revolutionary: Unpublished Papers, 1745–1780* (New York, 1975). Portions of the unfinished manuscript for volumes 3 and 4 of that series, edited by Richard B. Morris and Ene Sirvet, were included in revised form in this volume.

Since the completion of the original two volumes of the *Unpublished Letters of John Jay* in 1980, the John Jay project benefited from continued work under Richard B. Morris and Ene Sirvet until the project's closing in 1996, and subsequently from the work of the Digital Library staff on the online edition. Since the opening of the new publication project late in 2004 to produce the new edition of *The Selected Papers of John Jay*, the editors have incurred new debts that are acknowledged below.

Work on the new volumes has been funded by grants from the National Historical Publications and Records Commission, the National Endowment for the Humanities, and the Florence J. Gould Foundation, with additional support from the Columbia University Libraries, the Columbia University Law School, the Peck Stacpoole Foundation, the Gilder Lehrman Institute for American History, the Richard Gilder Foundation, and Suzanne Clary, President of the Jay Heritage Center, Rye, New York. The advice and administrative assistance of the NHPRC staff, especially Timothy Connelly and Darrell Meadows, have also been invaluable.

Reopening of the project resulted especially from the efforts of Jean W. Ashton, then director of the Rare Book and Manuscript Library and project director of the Jay Papers; of "transition team" Barbara Oberg and Herbert E. Sloan; of Mary Jo Kline, editor during the project's planning stages; of then–University Librarian Elaine Sloan; and the members of the project's advisory board: Richard L. Bushman, Patricia Bonomi, Herbert E. Sloan, Barbara Black, Barbara Oberg, John Jay Iselin, Jeffrey B. Morris, Carol Berkin, and Jack N. Rakove, and later members Christopher Brown, Evan Haefeli, Sean M. Quimby, Michael T. Ryan, Eric T. Wakin, and John Witt. Special thanks to Jeffrey B. Morris for rights to incorporate into the new and revised edition material from the two volumes of John Jay papers published by Richard B. Morris.

The staff of the project has included at various times an admirable group of editorial assistants, interns, and student aides. This volume reflects the work of editorial assistants Jennifer Milne Turner, Benjamin Hellwege, and Monique Politowski; aides Sidhya Balakrishnan, Katie Dunn, Anna Gedal, Alexandra Gross, Jennifer Miller, Cody Nager, and Lena Rubin; and interns Kristin Ng, Susan Rucano, Rochelle Haughton, Allison de Sève, David James, Jeff Johnson-Kaiserling, Andrew Kordik, and Alexander Maltezos, of Fordham University, and Stephanie Schmeling of New York University. The project wishes to thank Professor Elaine F. Crane of Fordham University for facilitating the project internship program with Fordham University and Peter Wosh, Director of the Archives Program at New York University, for establishing an internship program with the project at NYU. The support of the administration of the Columbia University Libraries, especially James G. Neal, former Vice President for Information Services and University Librarian; Ann D. Thornton, Vice Provost and University Librarian; Kristine Kavanaugh, Associate Vice President for Planning; Damon E. Jaggars, former Associate University Librarian for Collections and Services; and Chris Cronin, Associate University Librarian for Collections, has been essential for sustaining the project. The editors have relied on assistance from the staff of the Rare Book and Manuscript Library under the direction of Michael T. Ryan, Barbara A. Rockenbach, and Sean M. Quimby.

The editors also continue to benefit from the work of Steven P. Davis, Roberta L. Blitz, and the staff of Columbia University Libraries Digital Program both for their assistance in providing us with electronic versions of previously published transcriptions and for updating and improving access to the existing scanned document database (Papers of John Jay (http://dlc.library.columbia.edu/jay). The Development Office, especially Karen G. Kapp, Cynthia Goldstein, Talia Jimenez, and Deborah Farre, has assisted in securing and managing project grants. Additional thanks go to the Library Systems Office, especially Robert D. Castro, for technical support; and to the Human Resources and Finance & Payroll Departments, especially Mary Beth

Figueroa and Joel E. Fine, for assistance with personnel, budgetary, and payroll issues. At the University of Virginia Press, planning, design, and implementation of the production of the *Selected Papers of John Jay*, particularly the efforts of Penny Kaiserlian, Ellen Satrom, Mark Mones, Ellen Barber, Mark Mastromarino, and Angie Hogan, are reflected in this volume.

Documents, illustrations, and research information for this volume above and beyond what was initially secured by the Jay project and acknowledged in volume 1 were obtained from the following institutions and individuals: Adams Papers Editorial Project, Massachusetts Historical Society, Boston, Massachusetts; Albany Institute of History and Art, New York; British Library, London, England; Connecticut Historical Society, Hartford; Documentary History of the Ratification of the Constitution Project, Madison, Wisconsin; Friends Historical Library, Swarthmore, Pennsylvania; Gilder Lehrman Collection, Gilder Lehrman Institute for American History, New York, New York; Harlan Crow Library, Dallas, Texas; Henry Francis du Pont Winterthur Museum, Delaware; Independence Hall National Historical Park, Philadelphia, Pennsylvania; Jay Heritage Center, Rye, New York; Jay Homestead State Historic Site, Katonah, New York; John Jay College, New York, New York; Massachusetts Historical Society, Boston, Massachusetts; Moravian Archives, Moravian Historical Society, Nazareth, Pennsylvania; Museum of the City of New York, New York; National Archives, Kew, England; National Archives and Records Administration, College Park, Maryland; National Portrait Gallery, London, England; New York Public Library, New York, New York; New-York Historical Society, New York, New York; New York State Archives, Albany; New York State Bureau of Historic Site and Park Services, Division for Historic Preservation, Peebles Island State Park; Papers of Benjamin Franklin, Yale University, New Haven, Connecticut; Papers of George Washington, University of Virginia, Charlottesville; Westchester County Historical Society, Elmsford, New York; Yale University Art Gallery, New Haven, Connecticut; Rhonda Barlow; Richard B. Bernstein; Mark D. Boonshoft; Trevor Coombs; Celia Caust-Ellenbogen; Jenny M. Davidson; Andrew J. Fagal; William Ferraro; Craig Friend; Francois Furstenberg; Adrina M. Garbooshian-Huggins; David Hancock; Doina G. Harsanyi; Benjamin L. Huggins; Thomas Keefe; Larry Kidder; Mary Jo Kline; Andrew Knight; Nathan Kozunskanich; John Kralevich; Valerie LaRobardier; James P. McClure; Thomas J. McCullough; Neal Millikan; Christopher F. Minty; Louise V. North; Jamie Paxton; Patricia and John Roberts; David Sewell; Constance B. Schulz; Mary Sherrer; Diane Shewchuk; Barbara Strong; Sallie Sypher; Susan J. Thompson; Mark Whatford; and Jocelyn K. Wilk.

The sources of all documents published herein that do not form a part of the Papers of John Jay in the Columbia University Libraries are indicated in the respective source notes, and permission to publish these papers is gratefully acknowledged.

Chronology, 1794–1798

1794

12–13 May	Jay sails for England on the *Ohio*
8 June	Jay arrives in England
June–Aug.	Conferences between Jay and Grenville
11 July	Grenville and Jay decide to maintain *status quo* in Northwest during negotiations
30 July	Jay presents Grenville with a note on irregular captures and condemnation of American vessels
3 Aug.	Hammond tells Grenville that the U.S. is not interested in armed neutrality
6 Aug.	Jay sends Grenville his first treaty draft
30 Aug.	Grenville sends counter-proposals for commercial and general treaties
Sept.	Monroe's friendly reception in France puts a damper on negotiations
6 Sept.	Jay and Grenville continue discussion of treaty drafts
30 Sept.	Jay writes a second treaty draft with a more comprehensive statement on neutral rights
10 Oct.	Jay meets Loughborough to discuss the Lord Chancellor's recommendations for additions to the treaty
Oct.–15 Nov.	Further discussions held, and alterations made to the treaty
19 Nov.	Treaty signed by Jay and Grenville

1795

10 Apr.	Jay departs London
28 May	Jay arrives in New York
6 June	Jay's election as Governor of New York certified
8 June	Jay leaves for Philadelphia to explain the treaty
	Washington sends treaty to Senate for ratification

17 June	Jay returns to New York
24 June	Senate approves treaty
29 June	Philadelphia *Aurora* publishes summary of treaty
	Jay resigns as Chief Justice of the U.S. Supreme Court
July	First cases of yellow fever are reported in New York City
July–Aug.	Anti-treaty writings appear, and protests against treaty held in several cities
1 July	Jay sworn in as Governor
22 July–	
9 Jan. 1796	Hamilton, King, and Jay collaborate on "The Defence," a series of 38 pro-treaty essays under pen-name "Camillus"
27–28 July	Treaty of Cayuga Ferry signed between Cayuga and Onondaga and state of New York
8 Aug.	Health Committee calls for quarantine center and hygiene measures to combat yellow fever
13 Aug.	Quarantine Proclamation issued
14 Aug.	Washington signs the Jay Treaty
19 Aug.	Randolph resigns as Secretary of State
9 Sept.	Jay asks Governor Mifflin to reopen trade between New York and Philadelphia
Oct.–Nov.	Health Committee reports 732 deaths from yellow fever
28 Oct.	Treaty ratifications exchanged in London
11 Nov.	Day of Thanksgiving Proclamation issued for 26 Nov.

1796

6 Jan.	Jay delivers opening address before the 19th session of the state legislature
Feb.	Richard Bayley appointed as Health Officer of the Port of New York
Feb.–Mar.	Robert Goodloe Harper's address defending treaty is published in New York and Philadelphia
29 Feb.	Washington declares treaty in effect
11 Mar.	Proclamation issued regarding protest at the state assembly
1 Apr.	State legislature passes law establishing a new health commission and quarantine procedures

26 Apr.	At Jay's urging, state legislature passes penal reform law
28 Apr.	House of Representatives votes to implement Jay Treaty by vote of 51–48
31 May	Akwesasne and Kahnawake Mohawks and state of New York sign treaty in New York City
4 Oct.	Commission to settle boundary with Canada first meets in New Brunswick
1 Nov.	Jay delivers opening address before the 20th session of the state legislature, the date selected for choosing presidential electors
9 Dec.	Massive fire devastates Wall Street area

1797

10 Feb.	State legislature amends infectious disease law of 1 Apr. 1796
17 Feb.	State legislature passes bill appointing a state comptroller
4 Mar.	Adams delivers presidential inaugural address
10 Mar.	State legislature passes bill making Albany de facto state capital
Apr.	Mohawk of Upper Canada and state of New York sign treaty
27 Apr.	Proclamation issued ordering quarantine of ships from the Mediterranean and West Indies
23–24 June	Congress passes laws expanding state militias and improving harbor defenses
17 Aug.	Proclamation issued ordering quarantine of ships from Philadelphia
20 Sept.	Jay family moves to Albany and occupies new Governor's House
Oct.–Mar. 1798	XYZ Affair causes breakdown of relations between the United States and France
25 Oct.	Commissioners determine that Schoodic River is intended boundary with Canada
25 Nov.	Proclamation issued on completion of the state prison

1798

2 Jan.	Jay delivers opening address before the 21st session of the state legislature

1 Mar.	Proclamation issued in response to the Livingston land riots
3 May	Congress passes bill for additional maritime defenses
1 June	Oneida Mohawk and state of New York sign treaty at Kanonwalohale
8 June	Several committees meet in City Hall for the purpose of improving harbor defenses
12 June	Jay's reelection as Governor confirmed
14 June	Congress passes bill for the creation of a Provisional Army; Hamilton appointed inspector-general of American Army
18 June–14 July	Congress passes the Alien and Sedition Acts
2 July	Special early session of the state legislature called for the purpose of responding to hostilities with France
7 July	Congress annuls the Treaty of Alliance with France
July–Sept. 1800	France and the United States engage in maritime hostilities during the Quasi-War
Aug. –Nov.	New York City's greatest yellow fever epidemic leaves over 2,000 dead
9 Aug.	Jay's address to a special session of state legislature on emergency defense spending
17 Aug.	State legislature sends President Adams a message of support
27 Aug.	State legislature passes appropriation bill of $150,000 for defensive purposes
Sept.	Washington appointed commander-in-chief of American Army; Hamilton takes command of defensive efforts for the port and harbor of New York
16 Nov.–24 Dec.	State legislatures in Kentucky and Virginia pass resolutions denying the legality of the Federalist Alien and Sedition Acts

The Selected Papers of JOHN JAY

JOHN JAY'S MISSION TO LONDON

After a crossing of twenty-five days, Jay arrived at Falmouth on the evening of 8 June 1794.[1] Accompanying Jay was his secretary, the painter John Trumbull; his eighteen-year-old son, Peter Augustus Jay; and his enslaved manservant, Peter (or Peet) Williams. Each played an important role. Trumbull, who had served under Washington, was the son of Connecticut Governor Jonathan Trumbull Sr. He had important connections with Benjamin West, with whom he had studied, and Edmund Burke, who sponsored his parole after Trumbull was arrested as a spy. Peter Augustus, who was about to start studying law, proved to be charming and popular, a way for people to do favors for Jay by looking after his son. Peter Williams, much as he had done when Jay was riding circuit as Chief Justice, took care of Jay's day-to-day needs and managed the household.[2]

In Jay's absence, his nephew Peter Jay Munro attended to his business in New York, aided by Sarah Livingston Jay, both of whom were given power of attorney for legal matters, real estate, and Jay's private banking. Munro, Sally, and daughter Maria Jay kept Jay abreast of family, political, and business dealings via numerous letters. They also all corresponded with Peter Augustus Jay, who kept them informed of how he and his father fared in London.[3]

Awaiting Jay in London was the American Minister to Great Britain, Thomas Pinckney. Jay was sensitive to the fact that Pinckney may have resented his mission and made sure to consult Pinckney throughout the negotiation. Also consulted was the young John Quincy Adams, who arrived in London in October 1794 on his way to his mission at The Hague. Jay advanced the young Adams money enough to live on.[4]

Jay's mission and his presence in London were immediately noted by both the government and the opposition press, usually to promote their respective political positions. He was described in a variety of ways, of varying accuracy;[5] the most amusing perhaps as "a Gentleman of about 60 years old, and received great part of his education in this country; he was formerly of the University of Cambridge; and, having from early attachment to us, as well as from a knowledge of the true interests of his country, a wish to see matters settled in an amicable way." Many reported that as soon as he had resolved the negotiations with Great Britain, he would go on to Paris to negotiate a peace between Great Britain and France.[6]

The standard accounts of the Jay Treaty negotiations depict a sporadic series of private one-on-one meetings with British Foreign Secretary William

Grenville, resulting in the signing of the treaty on 19 November 1794.[7] However, Jay's letters and dispatches, his son Peter Augustus's diary and letters,
invitations and calling cards, newspaper accounts, and John Trumbull's memoirs, reveal a more complicated series of events. Jay was reunited with the
Shelburne circle, courted by both the radical opposition and the cabinet, and
entertained by bankers, merchants, and aristocrats. While they tried to cultivate Jay to press their own interests, Jay strategically mined these contacts for
American interests.[8]

Jay took the unusual step of renting rooms at the Hotel Royal in Pall Mall
instead of renting a house. With an understanding that his expense account
would in all likelihood be criticized, Jay explained to Edmund Randolph that
he had four options for his London accommodations: take a house and purchase furniture, take a house and rent furniture, take lodgings, or reside in a
hotel. The first two he dismissed as being too expensive for a lengthy duration, and the third would not offer him a suitable place to entertain. "To go
into Lodgings I soon found was out of the Question, there being none of a
proper class, where a Table would be provided—" "The Expences of living
in an Hotel are well known to be extravagantly high, but they are simple—
many Servants would not be necessary." The details of entertaining, which
he clearly expected to do, could be handled by the hotel staff. In addition,
residing in the hotel would give the appearance of impermanency, something
to be desired as Jay wished the negotiations to be concluded as quickly as
possible.[9]

Life in London

Peter Augustus Jay's diary and memorandum book, as well as his letters to
his family, offer the fullest account of their life in London. He records lists of
people visited and the active social life the Jays had, with both English Whigs
and American expatriates. Peter gained entrée to many places and events via
these new and old friends, touring the British Museum (where he handled
a pair of Roman dice, noting that they were loaded) and private collections,
attending trials (notably Warren Hastings's trial for treason, as well as the
gratuitous trial of John Horne Tooke), the opera (which he disliked), and the
theater, seeing Mrs. Siddons perform numerous times.[10]

Surviving calling cards; invitations to play cards, attend the theater, and
dine; and lists of calls made and received show the mixture of business and
pleasure in their socializing. John Julius Angerstein, John Sinclair, Jeremy and
Samuel Bentham,[11] Joseph Banks, Richard and Mary Penn, Charles Blagden, Benjamin West, John Singleton Copley, Thomas Brand Hollis, Eliza-

beth Montagu, Baron and Lady Inchiquin, John and Lucy Paradise, Edmund Burke, Ralph Payne and Lady Frances Payne make frequent appearances,[12] as well as Lord Amherst and Lady Amherst.[13] Cabinet ministers and the international diplomatic corps are represented. And, of course, the merchants and bankers with an interest in the outcome of the treaty and the American trade predominate:[14] merchants such as John and Alexander Anderson (West Indies, slave trade), John Blackburn, John Brickwood, Patrick Colquhoun; Alderman Harvey Christian Combe and Joseph Delafield, brewers; the Murray family, Effingham Lawrence, James Bourdieu, and William Manning; bankers, such as David Barclay, Alexander and Francis Baring, Thomas Coutts, William Curtis, Robert Herries, and representatives of Hope & Co. and Bird, Savage, & Bird.[15] These companies would play key roles in the treaty implementation.

Soon after Jay's arrival in Falmouth, he notified the Foreign Secretary William Grenville and the American Minister, Thomas Pinckney, and began the trip to London, which he reached on 15 June. Three days later, he presented his commission to Grenville, who received him without hesitation and quickly arranged an audience with the king and queen on 2–3 July.[16] On 20 June, Jay presented Grenville his general power, after which the two men arranged a meeting on 27 June.[17]

Of the small number of official meetings recorded, very little of the discussion has survived. John Trumbull reported in his autobiography that Jay and Grenville held tête-à-têtes without even the presence of secretaries. However, the social record makes clear that Pitt and his fellow ministers were involved in the negotiations.

On 18 July, Jay wrote Hamilton: "Shortly after my arrival I dined with Lord Grenville; the cabinet Minister were present, but not a Single Foreigner. On Monday next I am to dine with the Lord Chancellor, & on next Friday with Mr. Pitt. I mention these Facts to explain what I mean by favorable appearances. I think it best that they should remain *unmentioned* for the present and they make no part of my Communications to Mr. Randolph or others. This is not the Season for such communications—they may be misinterpreted, tho' not by you."[18] Peter's diary makes mention of multiple dinners with Pitt and other cabinet members, both during the treaty negotiations and afterward.[19]

Mid-September 1794 proved a crucial point in the negotiations, as the treaty was at this time two separate treaties—one to settle differences of the Treaty of Peace and the other to resolve commercial issues. Peter Augustus recorded in his diary that on 12 Sept., "We dined with Mr. Dundas at Wimbleton in company with Mr. Pitt, the Lord Chancellor [Lord Loughborough],

John Jay, by John Trumbull, 1793.
(Yale University Art Gallery)

& Lord Macartney who has lately arrived from China, & who told us many interesting facts relating to that country".[20] A week later, Jay and his son spent the weekend at Grenville's seat at Dropmore. Among those who dined with them there were Loughborough, Lord Mornington, Lord and Lady Inchiquin, Lord and Lady Boston, Count Starhemberg, and a Miss Eardley. Shortly thereafter, the plan for the conjoined treaty appears to have been made.[21]

October brought about another critical juncture. The issues of legal rights and the introduction of evidence from one nation to the other would be important in the arbitration of the claims cases. Loughborough invited Jay to dine, with Peter and Trumbull, asking that he arrive early in order to discuss the matter on the 11th. Pitt was also in attendance. Jay would discuss the resulting article in advance of the signing with John Quincy Adams and Thomas Pinckney, in a meeting on the 20th, and again during implementation, with Washington.[22]

Old Friends and Radical Politics

Among the Jays's first visitors on their arrival in London were John and Angelica Schuyler Church.[23] Angelica, now famous as the sister-in-law of Alexander Hamilton, was a daughter of General Philip Schuyler, a friend and kinsman of Jay (their mothers were cousins), and one of his chief political supporters. She was known for her kindness to Americans in London. However, her hospitality to Jay during the negotiations appears more significant when considering John Church's career. The English-born Church had made his fortune during the Revolution and was at this time a member of Parliament and a member of the Radical Whigs, who opposed the war with France. Through the Churches, the Jays—as is recorded in Peter's diary—socialized with Charles James Fox and Richard Brinsley Sheridan.[24]

Shortly after his arrival, Jay received a letter from Sarah Vaughan, the wife of politician Benjamin Vaughan. Jay became friends with the Vaughans during the peace negotiations. In her letter, she invited the Jays to visit, commenting on her husband's absence: "You are too sensible of my husband's respect & esteem for you, to doubt a moment, that nothing but indispensable business which detains him out of town would have prevented him from immediately on your arrival renewing those attentions which have always been so pleasing to him".[25] However, Sarah Vaughan did not know the whereabouts of her husband. As a member of the radical opposition in Parliament, Benjamin Vaughan was very critical of Pitt's administration and, particularly, the war with France. This, his contacts with French agents (including an Irish revolutionary), and some indiscreet correspondence, led him to be interrogated before the Privy Council on 8 May 1794, along with Lord Lauderdale and members of Parliament Sheridan, William Smith, and Thomas Maitland.[26] Vaughan feared arrest despite Pitt's assurances otherwise; he was determined to immigrate to America. Under unclear circumstances, he landed in France on 19 May, where he was arrested and eventually sent to Carmes Prison in Paris, where he was held in seclusion from 1 June to 30 July. He was eventually cleared and ordered to go to Switzerland. Vaughan's letters to his wife and friends were confiscated, and Sarah did not hear from him until he reached Geneva, sometime in early August. At the time of her letter to Jay, she had followed her husband's directions and had informed only her brother William Manning, her attorney, and Lord Shelburne of her situation.[27]

Breakfast with Wilberforce

Politics, personal interests, and official business often overlapped. In his diary of 7 July 1794, William Wilberforce records dining at the home of Quaker merchant banker Samuel Hoare Jr.[28] Hoare shared Wilberforce's political and ethical beliefs. An independently minded Whig, Wilberforce was a member of Parliament and intimate ally of Pitt's, and had become increasingly critical of the British war with France—despite his relationship with Pitt—while his evangelicalism and opposition to the slave trade grew. The dinner was held specifically to introduce Jay and Wilberforce. He found the Jay party to have "Simplicity of manners—" and to be "very pleasing well inform'd Men—". Peter's diary records dining with Wilberforce several times, and the two men continued to meet in other circumstances. On 22 December, Wilberforce records having breakfast with Jay "tête–à–tête" and "heard openly his opinion in Politics Friend to Peace— Many American War Anecdotes— He *swore* when grew more easy—."[29] The two would continue to correspond on social issues well into the nineteenth century.

Aside from entertaining, Jay made sure to perform favors and dispense advice to his acquaintances, old and new. Peter's diary records numerous dinners and theater visits with the Penns and Lord Amherst, and Jay offered advice to both parties on the status of the properties that they had possessed in North America.

Jay had been familiar with Richard Penn and his family, including his aunt, Lady Juliana Penn, since his previous stay in London, as well as, presumably, through their Pennsylvania connections. Jay had counselled the Penns on their land claims presumably lost in the American Revolution during the 1780s and continued to do so during his current mission in London.

Similarly, Lord and Lady Amherst initiated a social relationship with the Jays through invitations and the gift of a well-known engraving that depicted Lord Amherst as commander-in-chief of British forces during the Seven Years' War. Amherst held an interest in Tyron County in Jay's home state. As with the Penns, Jay—and subsequently Peter Augustus—advised the Amhersts on matters of landed property for several decades.[30]

Jay was also asked to assist with persons whose relatives and friends were caught up in the dangerous affairs of revolutionary France. One of the first letters Jay received on his arrival in London was from Edward Newenham, the Irish Protestant reform politician who had met Jay in Paris in 1782 and who was also a correspondent with Washington and Franklin. Newenham confided to Jay his concern for the whereabouts and safety of his daughter, who was married to the Swedish Consul in Marseilles. Doubtless moved by such entreaties, Jay promised to make suitable and discreet inquiries after her.[31]

Later that year, the London press remarked on the possibility that Jay would use his influence to free Lafayette, then imprisoned by Prussian forces. Opposition papers thought America's diplomat capable of pushing the British government to intervene in international and humanitarian affairs. One such newspaper, for instance, reported in December 1794, "We have heard, and we hope it is true, that Mr. JAY, the Minister Extraordinary from the United States of America, has received instructions to request the good offices of our Cabinet with the Court of Vienna for the release of M. DE LA FAYETTE and the companions of his misfortunes."[32]

The United States' diplomatic relationship with France and the presence of James Monroe as minister there put Jay in the position to help those seeking information on missing friends and relatives and to aid in returning them to England. For example, Richard Wellesley, the Earl of Mornington, soon to be Governor-General of India, enlisted Jay's service in an attempt to bring home his sister Anne Fitzroy (1775–1844) and brother Henry Wellesley (1773–1847), who had been captured by the French when attempting to return from Portugal. In an effort to release the pair, Jay apparently offered informal advice to Mornington and also passed along letters—though not in an official capacity. These endeavors were seemingly successful, as Mornington's siblings managed to return to England in January 1795.[33]

While Jay was engaged in diplomacy and personal favors, his son spent much of his time conducting family business and shopping for family and friends. Peter Augustus procured such luxury items in London as books, jewelry, and fine cups and saucers. He also attended to legal matters, acting as Peter Jay Munro's agent in Edinburgh, witnessing the transfer of some of Munro's father's property. During this excursion to Scotland, Peter Augustus managed to tour the environs and take in the cultural sights as he did in London.[34] Like the Jays, John Trumbull also mixed business with leisure. He took the opportunity to travel to France, ostensibly on art business, but also to undertake diplomatic activities.[35]

Jay's hopes for a quick return to America were not realized as two developments thwarted any hope of a speedy settlement: the first being the creation of a coalition between Pitt and the Portland Whigs in July and the second being the ongoing war with France. The Treaty would not be signed until 19 November 1794. Jay decided against a dangerous winter voyage[36] and spent the rest of his stay in London setting up the Spoliation Commission with Samuel Bayard and John Trumbull, all the while continuing a busy social schedule. Jay would not be able to leave London until April 1795.[37]

1. See JJ to Grenville, 8 and 15 June 1794, below; JJ to Thomas Pinckney, 8 June 1794, ALS, NNC (EJ: 09467); JJ to ER, 9 June 1794, C, DNA: Jay Despatches, 1794–95 (EJ: 04268); C, NHi: King (EJ: 04413); ASP: FR, 1: 475; and Grenville to JJ, 16 and 19 June 1794, both below. For a description of the voyage from Falmouth to London, see PAJ to PJM, 22 June 1794, below. The arrival was anticipated and noted in the London press, despite some confusion about Jay's title and mission, e.g.,

"Sir John Jay is coming over vested with full powers from Congress to confer with the Ministers of this country," *Whitehall Evening Post*, 7–10 June 1794; "FALMOUTH, June 8. This evening arrived in this Port, John Jay, Esq. in the American Ship Ohio, in 19 days, from New York," *St. James Chronicle or British Evening Post*, 10–12 June 1794; and "Mr. Jay, a Member of Congress . . . has arrived at Falmouth," *Sun*, 11 June 1794.

2. See the editorial note, "The Jay Treaty: Appointment and Instructions," *JJSP*, 5: 609–21. On Peter Williams, see Circuit Court Diary, [11 Oct.–16 Dec. 1791] note 42, *JJSP* 5, 345; JJ to SLJ, 22 Apr. 1794, *JJSP*, 5: 625–26; JJ to SLJ, 16 Aug. 1794, and 13 Mar. 1795, both below. See also Account Book of JJ's Mission to London, 1794, D, NNC.

3. On Jay family business, see PJM to JJ, 15 June 1794, and notes; PAJ to SLJ, 13 May 1794 (first and second letters); SLJ to JJ, 29 May 1794; Maria Jay to JJ, 13 June 1794; PAJ to SLJ, 29 June 1794; JJ to SLJ, 4 July 1794; JJ to SLJ, 6–8 July 1794; PAJ to SLJ, 1 Aug. 1794; SLJ to JJ, 2 Aug. 1794; JJ to PJM, 14 Sept. 1794; PJM to JJ, 16 Oct. 1794; SLJ to JJ, 11 Nov. 1794; RK to SLJ, 17 Nov. 1794; JJ to SLJ, 21 Nov. 1794; PJM to PAJ, 28 Dec. 1794; PAJ to SLJ, 2 Jan. 1795; JJ to SLJ, 3–6 Feb. 1795; JJ to SLJ, 6 Mar. 1795; and PAJ to SLJ, 7 Mar. 1795, all below.

4. JJ to Thomas Pinckney, 31 Aug. 1794; JJ to JA, 21 Nov. 1794; JQA to JJ, 21 Nov. 1794; JJ to JA, 24 Nov. 1794; and JJ to JQA, 24 Nov. 1794, all below.

5. The *General Evening Post* of 7–10 June described the "Chief Justice" who arrived on a "brig [out of] Charleston" as "a man of blunt manners, and the most decided character" before giving a description of the actual mission; The *London Chronicle* of 12–14 June reported: "Yesterday Mr. Jay, the American Commissioner to our Ministry, arrived in town. We have little doubt but that misunderstandings between the two countries will be arranged to the perfect satisfaction of both." The above newspapers also reported that "Mr. Jefferson, the American Minister, is gone to France," meaning James Monroe. The *Oracle and Public Advertiser* of 12 June, on noting Jay's arrival from "Philadelphia," reported that "a Gentleman took *ten guineas* to return a *hundred*, if hostilities, be commenced on the part of the Americans on or before that day, 9th June, against this country."

6. *Whitehall Evening Post*, 28 June–1 July 1794; *General Evening Post*, 1–3 July 1794. These rumors were pervasive enough to cause member of Parliament and Pitt partisan George Canning (1770–1827) to write in November 1794 that "All the vulgar notion of a Treaty with France having been opened, or even thought to be opened, is nonsense. Mr. Jay, the American Ambassador, is no more gone, or going, to Paris than I am." George Canning, *Letter-Journal of George Canning, 1793–1795*, ed. Peter Jupp (London, 1991), 149–50.

7. For the details of the negotiations between JJ and Grenville, see the editorial note, "Negotiating the Jay Treaty," below.

8. PAJ Diary, Parts A, B, and C, AD, NNC (Diary B, EJ: 90476); London Calling List of Government Officials and Foreign Ministers, 15 June 1794–March 1795, below; PAJ's Addresses of London Residents, Including Americans, c. July 1794, AD, NNC (EJ: 09207); PAJ's Addresses of London Residents, c. July 1794, AD, NNC (EJ: 09209); JJ's List of Cabinet Members Addresses, AD, NNC (EJ: 09192); and Calling Cards, D, NNC.

9. For JJ's explanations of his expenses while in England and the documents on the settlement of his accounts in 1795 and 1796, see To the Public, 25 Apr. 1797, below. See also JJ's Account Book of the Jay Treaty Mission, NNC. JJ was indeed criticized by opponents of the Treaty for his extravagance. JJ to ER, 5 Mar. 1795, LS DNA: Jay Despatches, 1794–95 (EJ: 04293).

10. For the British Museum, see 23 June 1794, PAJ Diary A, AD, NNC; for the Hastings trial and for the opera, see 17 June 1794, PAJ Diary A, AD, NNC; for the Horne Tooke trial, see 17 Nov. 1794, PAJ Diary A, AD, NNC; and JJ to SLJ, 21 Nov. 1794, below; for Sarah Siddons's performances, see 1, 7, and 10 Mar. 1795, PAJ Diary B, AD, NNC (EJ: 90476). Warren Hastings (1732–1818), former

Governor-General of Bengal, underwent a lengthy impeachment trial that was tried in the House of Commons from 1787–95, for which Hastings received a verdict of acquittal. Sarah Siddons (1755–1831) was the preeminent actress of the time, known for her Shakespearian work.

11. John Julius Angerstein (1736–1823), London financier, Lloyd's underwriter, and art collector; Jeremy Bentham (1748–1832), philosopher and reformer, founder of utilitarianism, helped to establish University College London; his brother Samuel Bentham (1757–1831), was an engineer and naval architect. Jeremy and Samuel Bentham were introduced to the Jays by John Sinclair. In a letter to Philip Metcalfe of 14 Sept. 1794, Jeremy Bentham described Peter as "a young Jay, little more than fledged," and his father as "Chief-justice Jay is a good chief-justice-like looking man, of a sensible, shrewd countenance, rather reserved, but not unpleasantly so." Both Jeremy and Samuel determined to "cultivate them all." Alexander Taylor Milne, ed., *The Correspondence of Jeremy Bentham* vol. 5 *January 1794 to December 1797* (London: 1981), 75–76. See also JJ to John Sloss Hobart, 12 Aug. 1794, below.

12. Joseph Banks, baronet (1743–1820), President of the Royal Society of London (1778–1820), explorer and naturalist; Mary Penn (1756–1829), daughter of William Masters of Philadelphia, moved to London with her husband Richard Penn Jr. in 1775; Charles Brian Blagden, FRS (1748–1820), Secretary of the Royal Society (1784–97); Benjamin West, American-born artist, moved to London in 1763 and succeeded Joshua Reynolds (1723–92) as president of the Royal Academy; John Singleton Copely (c. 1738–1815), American-born artist working in London; Thomas Brand Hollis, FRS (1719–1804), British radical and supporter of the American Revolution; Murrough O'Brien, 10th Baron of Inchiquin (1726–1808), well-connected member of the Irish peerage; Mary Palmer, Lady Inchiquin (1750–1820), Baron Inchiquin's second wife and Joshua Reynolds's niece; Edmund Burke (1729/30–1797), Irish-born politician, author and controversialist; Ralph Payne, 1st Baron Lavington (1739–1807), born in St. Kitts, Governor of the Leeward Islands (1768–71, 1799–1807), member of Parliament elevated to the Irish peerage (1795), and supporter of Fox; his wife Françoise Lambertine Christiana Charlotte Harriet Theresa de Kolbel, Lady Lavington (1767—1807). See Lucy Paradise to SLJ, 12 Nov. 1794, ALS, NNC (EJ: 07036); Richard Penn to JJ, 26 Jan. 1795, ALS, NNC (EJ: 07050); Mrs. Montagu to JJ, 5 Mar. 1795, ALS, NNC (EJ: 06950); JJ to Lucy Paradise, 8 Apr. 1795, Dft, NNC (EJ: 08941); Lucy Paradise to JJ, 8 Apr. 1795, AL, NNC (EJ: 07037); and Thomas Pinckney to JJ, 10 Apr. 1795, ALS, NNC (EJ: 09463).

13. Jeffrey Amherst (1717–97), first Baron Amherst, career soldier who successfully commanded British forces in North America during the Seven Years' War. A supporter of Pitt the Younger, he served as commander-in-chief in 1793–95. Elizabeth Cary (1739/40–1830), Lady Amherst, was Amherst's second wife.

14. See note 8, above. See also the longer list kept by PAJ that includes female members of these merchant and banker families, confirming the social nature of the mission throughout. PAJ Memoranda & Statement of Accounts, [11 May 1794–9 Apr. 1795], AD, NNC.

15. John William Anderson, baronet (c. 1736–1813), slave trader, member of Parliament, and Lord Mayor of London (1797–98), involved in the West India Docks; his brother Alexander Anderson, a slave-trade advocate, with whom he owned John and Alexander Anderson & Co. of Eastcheap and Bance Island, Sierra Leone; John Blackburn (1766–1824), son of wealthy merchant, member of Parliament for Aldborough; John Brickwood, merchant and shipowner; Patrick Colquhoun (1745–1820), Scottish-born merchant, economist, and magistrate for the East End, who later formed the Thames River Police in consultation with Jeremy Bentham; Harvey Christian Combe (1752–1818), politician and brewer; Combe with his brother-in-law Joseph Delafield, owned Combe Delafield & Co. brewery in Long Acre; Effingham Lawrence (1735–1806), New York-born London merchant; James Bourdieu Jr. (1763–1835), Huguenot merchant, partner in Bourdieu, Chollet & Bourdieu;

David Barclay of Youngsbury (1729–1809), Quaker merchant and banker of Barclay, Bevan & Co.; Thomas Coutts (1735–1822), Scottish banker and founder of Coutts & Co.; William Curtis, baronet (1752–1829), politician, banker, and provisioner to the Royal Navy, Lord Mayor of London (1795–96); and Robert Herries (1730–1813), merchant who founded the London Exchange Banking Company, former member of Parliament, and former partner in John Coutts and Co. See JJ to Lindley Murray, 22 Aug. 1794, below; Robert Herries to JJ, 16 Sept. 1794, AL, NNC (EJ: 05673); JJ to Herries, 17 Sept. 1794, Dft, NNC (EJ: 08905); Patrick Colquhoun to JJ, 20 Dec. 1794, AL, NNC (EJ: 05527); Lindley Murray to JJ, 11 Dec. 1794, ALS, NNC (EJ: 09613); JJ to Colquhoun, 21 Dec. 1794, Dft, NNC (EJ: 08924); Colquhoun to JJ, 16 Jan. 1795, AL, NNC (EJ: 05529); and Colquhoun to JJ, 20 Jan. 1795, AL, NNC (EJ: 05528). On the Baring brothers, see Lansdowne to JJ, 31 July 1795, below.

16. See Grenville to JJ, and JJ to Grenville, both 19 June 1794, below. See also George III to Grenville, [8 Apr. 1794], Hist. Mss. Comm., *Fortescue Manuscripts* 3: 49.

17. See Grenville to JJ (private), 24 June 1794 and note 1, below; and the editorial note "Negotiating the Jay Treaty," and note 1, below.

18. JJ to AH, 18 July 1794, ALS, DLC (EJ: 10766); *PAH* 16: 608–9. The first Grenville dinner was on 26 June, and Lord Chancellor Loughborough's was on 27 July 1794.

19. PAJ notes dinners with Pitt on 26 June at Grenville's; 12 Sept. at Dundas's; 11 Oct. 1794 at Loughborough's; 14 Jan. with Pinckney; and 17 Jan. 1795 hosted by the Speaker of the House of Commons Henry Addington, with the Dukes of Portland and Richmond, the Earl Spencer, Lords Grenville, Amherst, Hawkesbury, Camden, and Mornington in attendance. A newspaper reports that "the Merchants trading to North America" feted Jay on 17 Dec. 1794, at Free Mason's Tavern with Pitt, Grenville, Loughborough, Dundas, Portland, Pinckney, and other dignitaries offering numerous toasts. *Oracle and Public Advertiser* (London), 24 Dec. 1794.

20. George Macartney, 1st Earl Macartney, KB (1737–1806), colonial administrator in the East and West Indies and Africa, headed the Macartney Embassy to China.

21. Frederick Irby, 2nd Baron Boston (1749–1825), courtier, Lord of the Bedchamber to George III and George IV; Christian (Methuen) Irby, Lady Boston (d. 1832); Count Ludwig von Starhemberg (1762–1833), ambassador from Austria. For invitations, see note 8, above.

22. See note 8, above; and the editorial note "Aftermath of the Jay Treaty: Responses, Ratification, and Implementation," and note 38, below; JQA Diaries, 20 Oct. 1794, vol. 21, MHi: Adams; *JQA Diaries Digital*, http://www.masshist.org/jqadiaries/php/doc?id=jqad21_40 (accessed Aug. 2019).

23. See PAJ to SLJ, 29 June 1794, and 7 Mar. 1795, both below; and JT to JJ, 24 Mar. 1795, below. The Jays dined with Mr. Church or Mrs. Church on 15, 17, 19 (with Fox), 23, 29, and 30 June (breakfast with Mrs. Church), 18 Aug., 7 Sept., 7 and 27 Nov. 1794, 25 Jan., 21 Feb., 3 and 10 March 1795 (dined and theater with Mrs. Church). Other social events mentioned in PAJ's Diary include: "Mrs. Church introduces Madam Flairault" on 3 July 1794; tour of Sheridan's Drury Lane Theater with Mr. Church on 1 Oct. 1794; attendance at after-dinner 15th birthday party for Miss Church on 4 Nov. 1794; attendance at after-dinner dance at Mrs. Church's on 6 Jan. 1795; attendance at home theatricals at Mrs. Church's on 7 Feb. 1795; PAJ accompanies Mrs. Church to a nursery in Hammersmith for trees on 5 Mar. 1795. PAJ Diary A, B, and C, Ds, NNC (Diary B, EJ: 90476).

24. Richard Brinsley Sheridan (1751–1816), Dublin-born playwright and radical Whig, member of Parliament for Stafford. JT also knew Sheridan from Church's dinner table in 1784. Trumbull, *Autobiography*, 94.

25. Sarah Vaughan to JJ, 11 July 1794, ALS, NNC (EJ: 08147). For JJ's reply, see his letter of 19 July 1794, below.

26. William Smith (1756–1835), member of Parliament for Camelford, Dissenter, and abolitionist; Thomas Maitland (1760–1824), member of Parliament for Haddington Burghs, army officer.

27. William Manning (1763–1835). Sarah Vaughan, her sister-in-law Harriet, and her seven children left for America in late August 1794. Benjamin Vaughan joined them in 1797. For more on Benjamin Vaughan's situation, see JJ to James Monroe, 31 Oct. 1794, below; and Mary Vaughan Marvin, *Benjamin Vaughan, 1751–1835* (Hallowell, Me., 1979), 30–45. See also JJ to Benjamin Vaughan, 31 Aug. 1797, below.

28. William Wilberforce (1759–1833), grandson of wealthy merchant William Wilberforce (1690–1776), member of Parliament for Hull (1780–84), Yorkshire (1784–1812), and Bramber (1812–25), had an evangelical conversion experience in 1785, leading him to promote Christianity and peace, and become deeply involved in abolitionism and ending of the West Indies slave trade. Although of high moral conviction, he continued to work with Pitt, and was considered a highly sociable man of the world. *ODNBO*; "Wilberforce, William," *The History of Parliament: The House of Commons 1790–1820*, ed. R. Thorne, (London, 1986) https://www.historyofparliamentonline.org/volume/1790–1820/member/wilberforce-william-1759–1833 (accessed Oct. 2018); Samuel Hoare Jr. (1751–1825), London merchant, Quaker, and founder of the Society for the Abolition of the Slave Trade. Hoare was involved in planning for the settlement of Sierra Leone with formerly enslaved persons.

29. William Wilberforce Diary, UkOxU: Wilberforce.

30. See note 13, above; and JJ to Lady Elizabeth Amherst, 20 Feb. 1795, below.

31. Edward Newenham to JJ, 15 June 1794, ALS, NNC (EJ: 09589); and JJ to Newenham, 26 June 1794, Dft, NNC (EJ: 09591).

32. *Morning Chronicle* (London), 11 Dec. 1794.

33. See JJ to Mornington, 22 Sept. 1794, Dft, NNC (EJ: 08906); Mornington to JJ, 25 Sept. 1794, ALS, UkWC-A (EJ: 00044); JJ to Mornington, 26 Sept. 1794, Dft, NNC (EJ: 08908); Mornington to JJ, 30 Sept. 1794, ALS, NNC (EJ: 06954); Lady Hyacinthe Gabrielle Mornington (mother of Lord Mornington) to JJ, 2 Oct. 1794, ALS, NNC (EJ: 06955); and JJ to Lady Mornington, 2 Oct. 1794, Dft, NNC (EJ: 08909). See also JJ's memorandum to JT of people who sought lost friends and relatives, 5 Feb. 1795, below. For similar requests to JJ, see David Hartley to JJ, 5 Jan. 1795, below; JJ to Hartley, 8 Jan. 1795, below; and JT to JJ, 24 Mar. 1795, below.

34. See PJM to JJ, 16 Oct. 1794, below; PAJ to SLJ, 2 Jan. 1795, below; NNC: PAJ Diary B, AD, NNC (EJ: 90476); and PAJ Memoranda & Statement of Accounts, [11 May 1794–9 Apr. 1795], AD, NNC.

35. Trumbull, *Autobiography*, 184–88.

36. See JJ to SLJ, 21 Nov. 1794, below.

37. See JJ to Samuel Bayard, 5 Jan. (first and second letters), and 5 Mar. 1795, all below; and Bayard to JJ, 31 Mar. 1795, below; JJ to Bayard, 20 Jan. 1795, Dft, NNC (EJ: 12836); Crickitt and Townley to JJ, 20 Jan. 1795, ALS, NNC (EJ: 07380); Bayard to JJ, 27 Jan. 1795, ALS, DNA (EJ: 04352); JJ to Bayard, 27 Jan. 1795, ALS, DNA (EJ: 04353); and Dft, NNC (EJ: 12837).

Peter Augustus Jay to Sarah Livingston Jay (First Letter)

[Aboard ship *Ohio*, New York harbor] May 13th. 1794

Dr Mama,

We lay still at the same place where Mr. Munro left us last night—[1] we made an attempt this morning to get out but the wind obliged us to return—

Peter Augustus Jay, by James Sharples Sr., 1797. Pastel and charcoal on blue paper. (Luce Collection, object no. 1952.353, New-York Historical Society)

A Boat which has just come along side & brought letters for M[r]. Scattergood[2] gives us this opportunity of writing to you.

I was sick for an hour or two yesterday, but since that I have been perfectly well— Papa too has not been incommoded he is now writing to you— Be so good as to give my love & bid good bye again to my Sisters & Uncle & Aunt Jay & M[rs]. Munro— we feared M[r]. Munro would have had a long disagreable passage up, but were very ~~disagreably~~ disappointed to find that he had returned to town with ~~ease~~ pleasure & expedition— We live very well on board at least as yet— our ducks lay, & the goat gives a large quantity of milk— & tho' our Cook is none of the cleanest yet Pete[3] makes up the deficiency & together with the steward dresses *our* victuals—

My dear Mama I again bid you adieu— may that all-merciful being upon whom we depend for preservation give you every blessing & happiness— I am Your very affectionate son

Peter Augustus Jay

M[rs]. Sarah Jay

ALS, NNC (EJ: 06047).

1. The *Ohio*, Kemp, was probably moored in the Lower Harbor. See *Daily Advertiser* (New York), 12 May 1794. On JJ's departure and voyage from New York, see the editorial note "The Jay Treaty: Appointment and Instructions," and notes 53–54, *JJSP*, 5: 616–17, 621.

2. Among the passengers aboard the *Ohio* was Thomas Scattergood (1748–1814), Quaker minister and reformer of the treatment of the mentally ill, who was travelling to London on religious business. In a letter written on the 22 May 1794, Scattergood wrote of the comfort that his "kind friend John Jay" gave him in the face of his loneliness on the journey. Scattergood, *Memoirs*, 133. See Scattergood to JJ, 6 May 1794, ALS, NNC (EJ: 07107); 9 May 1794, ALS, NNC (EJ: 07108); SLJ to JJ, 29 May 1794, below; JJ to Scattergood, 19 June 1794, Dft, NNC (EJ: 08888); and JJ to SLJ, 6 July 1794, ALS, NNC (EJ: 08057).

3. Peter Williams, JJ's enslaved manservant, who had previously accompanied JJ in that capacity on his circuit court travels. See *JJSP*, 5: 345n42; and the editorial note, "John Jay's Mission to London" and note 2, above.

Peter Augustus Jay to Sarah Livingston Jay (Second Letter)

[Aboard ship] Ohio 13th May 1794— 10 oClock at night

Dr. Mama

The wind so long unfavorable has at length become propitious— The Moon is near full ∧&∧ gives us a sufficiency of light & we are under weigh in order to get to sea— As I find the motion increases I have determined at least to begin a letter to go by the Pilot, & to bid you for the Voyage a final adieu— We were ashore this afternoon & bought two additional Sheep and a very large Quantity of fresh fish, so that we shall be in no danger of starving— every thing now is in the best order & promises a prosperous passage—[1] I am your very affectionate son

Peter Augustus Jay

Mrs. Sa Jay

ALS, NNC (EJ: 06046).

1. See PAJ to SLJ, 13 May 1794 (first letter) above.

From Sarah Livingston Jay

New York 29th. May 1794

My dear Mr. Jay,

I did myself the pleasure of writing to you on the 26th. by the Belvedere Captn. Depeyster which Vessel still remains in Port— The Factor he said will soon sail, & your brother takes charge of my letters— I would wish not to omit a single opportunity of letting you know we are all well— It was with inexpressible pleasure I heard the Ohio had been met on the 18th. ins^t. & that all was well—[1] how rejoiced should I be to hear similar intelligence after the storm which now prevails— Oh! my dear M^r. Jay how greatly does circumstance alter our ideas of things— I've known the time when in your company I have enjoyed a storm like this, perhaps because it seem'd to secure to me the sole enjoyment of that pleasure— at present I cannot, nor would ~~I would~~ I wish to describe the painful fancies it gives birth to— I know you disapprove the anticipation of evils, but indeed my best of husbands such a storm as this is enough to prostrate one's Reason. At this season of the year it is so unusual— the poplars this morning were on the ground & the Cherries though still unripe were blown from the tree before the dining room window into the stable Yard— Frank has raised the poplars— When I droop who Shall raise me if the wide Ocean should swallow up my husband & my Child— don't Chide me, I'll recover myself instantly, it was a slip of my pen— When one has their all at Stake a little solicitude demands pity rather than censure— The Children are ignorant of my anxiety & undesignedly increase my sensibility— they are washing the little prints that ornament their Chimney, & in taking them down for that purpose, a tender contest ensued about which should have the pleasure at improving the appearance of yours. Maria had first taken it down & nothing from Nan could persuade her to relinquish her charge— I was silent but the affection it discovered for the Original, in the present state of my mind, affected me— They call me to take Coffee. I hope to recover my spirits before I resume my pen—

There is at present a meeting of the Friends in this City— M^r. Shotwell called upon me the day before yesterday to request permission to introduce to my acquaintance two gentlemen who were connected with M^r. Scattergood by being parents of the first & second wives of that gentleman— they expressed great sensibility of your politeness to their Son in-Law & great cordiality for me— they had not heard the circumstance of your having been met by the Atlas, & the progress you had then made, so that I had the satisfaction of informing them of it— If you see M^r. Scattergood you can tell him his wife & family are well; those gentlemen desired me to mention ˄it˄ in my letter to you—[2]

Your brother Fady has been very friendly, he came through the rain to give me the pleasing intelligence above related a few hours after the Vessel arrived that brought the tidings— M^r. Neilson[3] who owned the Vessel wrote me a polite card informing me of it, & D^r. Charlton[4] call'd upon the like Errand— I mention those attentions because I know you'll receive as much pleasure from the motive that induced them as I did myself—

Our Connections and intimate friends are well— The Children join in Love to their Papa & brother— I am my dear M[r]. Jay Your very affectionate Wife

Sa. Jay

ALS, NNC (EJ: 06556). Addressed: "The honble M[r]. Jay". Endorsed: "... rec[d]. 5 July / an[d]. 6 July 1794".

1. For JJ's departure on 12–13 May on board the *Ohio*, see the editorial note "The Jay Treaty: Appointment and Instructions," *JJSP*, 5: 616–17 and 621nn53–54. SLJ to JJ, 26 May, not found.

2. Both Scattergood and Shotwell were prominent Quakers. Thomas Scattergood was a fellow-passenger of JJ's on the voyage. See PAJ to SLJ, 13 May 1794, note 2, above. In JJ's reply to SLJ of 6 July 1794, below, he wrote that he gave Scattergood "the pleasing Information" and that he was an agreeable companion. William Shotwell (c. 1760–1837) was a New York–based merchant and member of the NYMS. Elizabeth Bacon (c. 1752–80), who married Scattergood in 1772, was the daughter of Philadelphia hatter and Quaker elder David Bacon (1729–1809). In 1783, he married Sarah Hoskins (1751–1832), daughter of Quaker elder John Hoskins (1727–1814), of Burlington, N.J., who also attended the Philadelphia Yearly Meeting. Scattergood, *Memoirs*, 3, 12. The New York Yearly Meeting met 26–31 May 1794 in New York City. Email, Celia Caust-Ellenbogen, Friends Historical Library, Swarthmore College, 21 Sept. 2017.

3. William Neilson, merchant, 80 Pearl St., owner of the ship *Atlas*. His second wife was Lady Kitty Duer, widow of William Duer, whom he married in 1801. See also Maria Jay to JJ, 13 June 1794, below. Barrett, *Old Merchants of New York*, 142–43.

4. John Charlton, JJ's family physician. He would be an adviser to JJ during the yellow fever epidemics during his governorship. See the editorial note, "John Jay and the Yellow Fever Epidemics," below.

From Alexander Hamilton

Philadelphia June 4th 1794

My Dear Sir

The session of Congress is about to close much better than I expected— All mischievous measures have been prevented and several good ones have been established. Among these additional provisions of revenue & some of force are not the least important.

But as more immediately connected with the objects of your mission you will learn with satisfaction that the bill which had passed the senate before you left this for punishing and preventing practices contrary to neutrality has ~~passed~~ become a law, with only one material alteration, the rejection of the clause which ∧forbade the∧ selling of prizes.[1] I now consider the Executive and the Judiciary as armed with adequate means of repressing the fitting out of Privateers, the taking commissions, or enlisting in foreign service, the unauthorised undertaking of military expeditions &[c].

At Charlestown some considerable irregularities have lately happened. But means have been taken and are in train which will no doubt arrest their progress & correct the evil.[2]

I believe it would be useful for you to collect ∧and communicate exact∧ information with regard to the usage of Europe as to permitting the sale of prizes in neutral countries. If this should be clearly against the toleration of the practice, the Executive might still perhaps disembarrass itself.

Men's minds have gotten over the irritation by which they were some time since possessed, and if G Britain is disposed to justice peace and conciliation [*illegible*] the two countries may still arrive at a better understanding than has for some time subsisted between them. Is there not a crisis which she ought not to suffer to pass without laying a solid foundation for future harmony? I think there is— Adieu My Dear Sir. Not knowing how far any press of business on the Department of State might delay its communication I thought a ∧few∧ hasty lines would not be unacceptable. Y^{rs} truly

A: Hamilton

John Jay Esqr. Chief Justice

ALS, NNC (EJ: 05628). Endorsed. *PAH*, 16: 456–57.

1. On the sale of prizes, see Art. 21 of JJ's Project for a Treaty with Great Britain, 30 Sept. 1794, below.

2. Charleston had become a safe haven for French privateers, with ships sponsored and outfitted there, as well as prizes sold, thus violating U.S. neutrality. This was done with the full knowledge, or even cooperation, of the South Carolina state government and leading merchants. See AH to Isaac Holmes, 2 June 1794, *PAH*, 16: 446–47. A notable example was the *Sans Cullotes* (one of the illegal privateers mentioned on the Hammond list referred to in TJ's letter appended to Art. 7 of the Jay Treaty), which captured the British ship *Fanny*, the case of which was dismissed as pre-treaty by JT in his role as commissioner in 1798. See Opinion in the Case of the Fanny—Pile Master, LbkC, NHi: JT Lbk. 1796–1802, 133–147.

To Grenville

Falmouth 8. June 1794

My Lord

I landed here this Evening with a Commission from the President of the United States, constituting me their Envoy to his majesty—[1]

The State of my Health not permitting me to travel rapidly, I transmit the enclosed Packet for your Lordship, with one for the marquis of Buckingham, by the Post— They were committed to my Care by Sir John Temple—[2] it appears to me more proper to deny myself the Honor of delivering them in person than, for that purpose to detain them from your Lordships untill my

William Wyndham Grenville,
1st Baron Grenville, by John
Hoppner, c. 1800. Oil on canvas.
(© National Portrait Gallery,
London)

arrival in London—[3] I have the Honor to be with great Respect my Lord Your Lordship's most obed[t]. & most h'ble Serv[t]—

John Jay

The Right Honorable Lord Grenville one of his majesty's Principal Secretaries of State—

ALS, UK-KeNA: FO 95/512 (EJ: 04968). Dft, NNC (EJ: 90243, EJ: 08487); LbkC, NNC: JJ Lbk. 8; *HPJ*, 4: 22.

1. On JJ's appointment as envoy extraordinary to Britain, see the editorial note "The Jay Treaty: Appointment and Instructions," *JJSP*, 5: 609–21.

2. On Temple, British consul general, see "Consuls *De Gratia*: The Role of British Consuls," *JJSP*, 4: 245–50.

3. For JJ's arrival in London, see JJ to Grenville, 15 June 1794, below.

From Tench Coxe

Philadelphia June 9th. 1794

Sir

I have had the honor to write you twice since your departure from the United States.[1]

Congress have risen this day, and no act has been passed to interfere with the maintenance of peace at this Juncture. The new penal law, which was sincerely intended to restrain our citizens from conduct injurious to foreign nations, will no doubt be considered by them as a new proof of the reasonable and pacific dispositions of this Government.

We have not recurred to a land tax, nor are any of the interior revenues imposed during this Session of an inconvenient nature. Licences on the Sales of foreign spirits & wines—carriages for pleasure—snuff & manufactured Tobacco, Sales at auction, and loaf sugar are the Objects from which they are to be drawn— Some further import duty has been laid, which is a fresh exemplification of the fact, that whenever foreign circumstances force us into expences a large share of them take such a course as to encourage domestic manufactures. It is important to good Government, that our unexceptionable mode of excising spirits and stills has produced a revenue equal to the Estimates, & has been confirmed by a wise amendatory law instead of that repeal which two or three prejudiced Counties had vainly expected—[2]

It is worthy of remark that ˄the˄ existing belief on the continuance of peace has produced very little rise in our funds; from which it is obvious that the fall which occured sometime since, did not arise from the prospect of war so much as from other Causes. These I take to have been the diversion of foreign Capital from our funds by the tempting opportunities offered in Europe to the Money holders—and the sales of stock by many of the great holders to purchase our unimproved lands— The fall was about 12PC^t, the rise has been about 10 PCent— Our funds and Bank Stocks have been much diffused by the Sales of the great holders, which more and more strengthens the solid basis of that description of property. It was however not in the least danger before. The discontent that is alledged by some of our gazettes on this Subject does not exist; tho there may be some liveliness of feeling from the unlucky circumstance that a part of the debt of the U.S. was sold before its appreciation by holders in one quarter to holders in another— But this will be a shortlived Sensation, & will produce no danger of any kind, much less will it induce any real injury. I mention this because our news paper paragraphists say much upon the Subject. The freedom of the press in this Country is often more fully evinced by such publications, than the judgment of any influential or even numerous body of men.

The fatigue duly incidental to the last week of the Session will be received as an Apology for concluding myself with perfect respect, Sir your most obedient & most humble servant

Tench Coxe

My two letters were p^r Mr Wm Penn, and Geo. Barclay.—
John Jay, Esquire

ALS, NNC (EJ: 09822).

1. Tench Coxe, author of reports and articles on economic subjects, assistant secretary of the treasury from 1789 to 1792, and currently commissioner of revenue, wrote letters to JJ on 3, 4, 7 and 8 (2 letters), and 25 May 1794. Presumably he is referring to his letters of 8 May and/or 25 May. See Coxe Papers, PHi.

2. On 5 June 1794, Congress passed "An Act making further provision for securing and collecting the Duties on foreign and domestic Spirits, Wines and Teas," *Stat.*, 1: 378–81. Despite opposition from the affected manufacturers, on 5 June, Congress adopted "An Act laying certain duties upon Snuff and refined Sugar," *Stat.*, 1: 384–90. On 9 June Congress passed "An Act laying duties on property sold at Auction," *Stat.*, 1: 397–400. See *PAH*, 16: 397–99; *PGW: PS*, 16: 478–508. For background on the earlier response to excise taxes on whiskey and spirits, see the editorial note "John Jay's Moderate Response to the Whiskey Rebellion," *JJSP*, 5: 447–49. For the suppression of violent opposition to the excise taxes later in the year, see the notes in Coxe to JJ, 8 Nov. 1794, below, and, for JJ's response, JJ to Coxe, 18 Dec. 1794, ALS, PHi: Coxe; Dft, NNC (EJ: 09819).

From Maria Jay

[New York June 13th. 1794.]

My Dear Papa

Nothing can exceed our wishes to hear of the health & safe arrival of yourself & Brother. Since we had the pleasure of hearing of you by the atlas,[1] I have search'd the papers in vain in hopes some other Vessels might have been equally fortunate, but now I believe we must await letters from yourself & brother, announcing your arrival, which we flatter ourselves has been the case before this— You my dear papa I suppose will be too much engaged in business to favor us with accounts of England but from Brothers pen we dare hope that pleasure. As Mama & ‿Nancy‿ are both writing I fancy what little of news there is they communicate. For myself I am with Mama's approbation studying french & I hope will [be] able to give you satisfaction on your return. Little William & Sally do not by your absence or distance forget the affection & tenderness they have ever experienced from you, but on the contrary shew interesting marks of tenderness for you which pleases us all & delights Mama— please to remember ‿me‿ to Brother & be assured my dear papa that in duty & affection the little folks shall never rival Your dutiful daughter

Maria Jay

ALS, NNC (EJ: 09693).

1. See SLJ to JJ, 29 May 1794, above.

Maria Jay, by Charles B. J. Févret de Saint-Mémin, 1798. (From *The St.-Mémin Collection of Portraits* [New York, 1862]; Rare Book & Manuscript Library, Columbia University in the City of New York)

To Grenville

Pall Mall—Royal Hotel—15 June 1794

My Lord

You have doubtless recieved a Letter which I had the Honor of writing to you from Falmouth.[1] I arrived here this morning. The Journey has given me some Health, and much pleasure; nothing having occurred on the Road to induce me to wish it shorter.

col. Trumbull does me the favor of accompanying me as Secretary; and I have brought with me a Son, who I am anxious should form a right Estimate of whatever may be interesting to our Country—[2] will you be so obliging my Lord! as to permit me to present them to You, and to inform me of the Time when it will be most agreable to your Lordship, that I should wait upon you,[3] and assure you of the Respect with which I have the Honor to be my Lord Your Lordships most obedient & most h'ble Servant

John Jay

The Right Honorable Lord Grenville

ALS, UK-KeNA: FO 95/512 (EJ: 04969); Dft, NNC (EJ: 08488); LbkC, NNC: JJ Lbk. 8; *WJ*, 1: 323; *HPJ*, 4: 23.

1. See JJ to Grenville, 8 June 1794, above.

2. On JJ's travelling companions, JT, PAJ, and Peter Williams, see the editorial notes "The Jay Treaty: Appointment and Instructions," *JJSP*, 5: 616, 621nn51–52, and "John Jay's Mission to London," above.

3. Grenville received JJ on 18 June. See the editorial note "Negotiating the Jay Treaty," below.

PAJ's diary entry for this day notes, "This Morning at 11 oClock Papa, Colonel Trumbull & myself were according to appointment introduced to Lord Grenville by M^r. Pinkney. The interviews lasted but a short time & gave rise to little conversation." PAJ Diary A, AD, NNC.

From Peter Jay Munro

New York 15th. June 1794

Dear Sir,

Being at Bedford, when the Embargo expired, my Absence deprived me of the Pleasure of writing to you, by the vessels which then sailed for England— While at Bedford, I visited the Major, but could not find, that he had made, or was making, any Preparation for Stone wall— Indeed, every Thing seemed to be more at a Stand than ever, and convinced me, that for this Year at least, you will not be a great Gainer by the Farm— The work at the Mill appeared to be Substantial and good— the workmen informed me, they should raise it within ten days, but doubtless the weather, (which has been uncommonly bad) must have occasioned some delay.— John was from home, & as I had informed him of the Time, when I should be at his house, his Absence lead me to conclude, his acc^{ts}. were not in readiness for settlement.— The major did not appear more prepared— On my coming away, I took Occasion to say, that I sh^d. see him in about a fortnight, & w^d. *then* settle his acc^t.—

A M^r. Grant is arrived from Jamaica, who offers to pay, the principal & Interest due on the Bonds from Nathl. Grant, provided the Obligees will assign those Bonds, and the Mortgage to some Gentlemen in England.— You may recollect that the Bonds are payable in Bills of Exchange, which at present, are 8 perCent above par, and consequently the Obligees, by accepting the Principal and Interest in money, will not be benefited by the Advance upon Bills— M^r. V. Horn's Eagerness to receive his Money, prevented all Treaty with M^r. Grant, upon this Subject, who perhaps, might have been induced, to have offered an Advance of three, or four per Cent, upon the amount of the Debt, to have obtained our acceptance of it in Money.—[1]

The Power of Atty you left me, does not comprehend this Business, but the one given to Aunt Jay, authorises the discharge, tho' not the assignment of the mortgage.—[2] After an attentive Consideration of this Subject, I advised her, to accept the principal & Interest in money and not to insist upon a payment in Bills, And I am persuaded, that considering all the Circumstances of the Case, a payment in money, notwithstanding the present high rate of exchange, is preferable, to a payment in such Bills, as we should have been obliged to have rec^d. from M^r. Grant.— Aunt Jay having acquiesced in

this Opinion, the only remaining Difficulty arose from the power of Atty—
I objected to an Assignment of the Mortgage, to the Persons proposed by
M^r. Grant, because they were absent, and ignorant of the Deficiency in the
Power— After much Conversation, w[hic]^h. it w^d. be useless to detail, I told
M^r. VHorn that as he had seen the power of Atty. and knew of its Defects, I
w^d. agree to an Assignm^t. of the Mortgage being made *to him*, and w^d. also
give him my bond, that upon your Return to America, you sh^d. ratify the
sale— To this he agreed, and M^r. Grant consented, to accepted M^r. VHorn's
assignm^t. of the whole— The first of July, is the day appointed for the payment of the money, your Share of w^h. amounts to about £1760.—

Remember me affectionately to Peter— They were well at Rye a few Days
ago— Both our families are in Health.— I am D^r. Sir Your aff^{te}. Nephew,

P. Jay Munro

P.S. I apprehend some Difficulty with M^r. Post, who pretends that previous
to your departure, you settled with him the acc^t. of materials purchased.—
I have not disputed this fact as yet, being desirous to obtain all the proceeds
of the Sales, before we entered into any Questions of this Kind.[3]

ALS, NNC (EJ: 09371). Dft, dated 14 June, containing excessive deletions and interlineations not
noted here, NNMus (EJ: 00423).

1. JJ and his cousin Augustus Van Horne apparently were due money deriving from an inheritance claim due Augustus's wife Anne Van Horne (d. 1790). She was an heir of her first husband,
Nathaniel Marston (1730–56), and his father Nathaniel Marston (1704–78), who left a legacy that
included bonds payable by the heirs of the late Jamaican merchant Nathaniel Grant (d. 1776). The
executor of the Grant estate, whom JJ met in London, was Richard Grant, Esq. (c. 1747–1820), of
8 Russell Place, Fitzroy Square, former proctor to George III for Jamaica, who acted as solicitor
to Jamaican land interests, and had dealings with Samuel Vaughan. His nephew in New York may
have been John Grant, merchant, at 220 Pearl Street. The Grants were likely also distant relatives of
the Jays and Van Hornes. See William Duncan, *The New-York directory, and register, for the year 1795*
(New York, 1795; *Early Am. Imprints*, series 1, no. 28598), 89; and New-York Historical Society, *Abstracts of Wills on File in the Surrogate's Office: City of New York* (New York, 1901), 33(9): 50–53. See
also SLJ to JJ, 7 July, below; JJ to SLJ, 17 July, ALS, NNC (EJ: 08059); JJ to SLJ, 18 July, below; JJ to
PJM, 18 July, ALS, NNMus: Jay (EJ: 00425); SLJ to JJ, 2 Aug., below; JJ to SLJ, 16 Aug., below; PJM
to JJ, 30 Aug., Dft, NNMus: Jay (EJ: 00426); PJM to JJ, 18 Sept., Dft, NNMus: Jay (EJ: 00428); PJM
to JJ, 1 Oct., Dft, NNMus: Jay (EJ: 00429); SLJ to JJ, 11 Oct., C, NNC (EJ: 06561); JJ to SLJ, 13 Oct.,
Dft, NNC (EJ: 08063); JJ to PJM, 29–30 Oct., ALS, NNMus: Jay (EJ: 00431); and JJ to PJM, 17 Nov.
1794, ALS, NNMus: Jay (EJ: 00432). For PJM's management of JJ's business affairs, see also the
editorial note, "John Jay's Mission to London," above.

2. See PJM to JJ, 19 Nov. 1794, below; Robert Morris to JJ, 21 Nov., ALS, NNC (EJ: 07025); PJM
to JJ, 4 Dec. 1794, Dft, NNMus: Jay (EJ: 00435); and JJ to PJM, 22 Feb. 1795, ALS, NNMus: Jay (EJ:
00445).

3. See also JJ to SLJ, 6 July, C, NNC (EJ: 08057); and JJ to PJM, 14 Dec. 1794, ALS, NNMus: Jay
(EJ: 00438).

London Calling List of Government Officials and Foreign Ministers

[London, 15 June 1794–March 1795]

1. Lord Spencer— S^t. James's Place[1]
2. Baron de Kutzleben— 6 Jermyn S^t.[2] x
3. Duke of Portland— Piccadilly x
4. Lord Grenville— Dover Street x
5. M^r. Windham— Hill Street— x
6. Chev[alie]^r. d'Almeida— 72 South Audley S^t. x
7. Lord Cornwallis— Lower Grosvenor S^t.[3] x
8. M^r. Bukaty— 8 Upper Berkley St. Edgware Road
9. M^r. Pinckney— Cumberland place—
10. Chev[alie]^r d'Engestrom— 3 d^o. x
11. Comte de Bruhl— 20 d^o. x
12. Lord Chatham— d^o. x
13. Lord Hawksbury— Hertford Street— x
14. Baron Jacobi Klost— 3 Glo'[uce]ster place— x
   ∧Comte de Lavezzari— 5 Somerset S^t. (Port[ma]^n. Sq— x∧
15. M^r. Dundas— Somerset place—
16. Marq. del Campo— Manchester House x
17. Comte de Starhemberg— 8 Cavendish Sq. x
18. Comte de Wedel Jarlsburg 4 Wimpole S^t. x
19. Comte de Haslang— 46 Harley S^t. x
20. Comte Woronzow— 36 d^o. x
21. Marq. Circello— 7 Mansfield S^t., Port[lan]^d. Place x
22. Marq. Spinola— 2 Dutchess S^t. d^o. x
23. Baron de Nagell 14 Portland Place—
24. Lord Mansfield— Portland Place— x
25. Lord Chancellor— Bedford Square— x
26. Comte de S^t. Martin de Frons, Lincoln's inn fields
27. Turkish Ambassador, 4 Robt. S^t. Adelphi—

AD, NNC (EJ: 09206). An "x" next to a name may indicate a completed visit.

1. The following were members of Pitt's cabinet: George John Spencer, 2nd Earl Spencer (1758–1834), Lord Privy Seal; William Henry Cavendish-Bentinck, 3rd Duke of Portland; William Grenville; William Windham (1750–1810); John Pitt, 2nd Earl of Chatham (1756–1835), older brother of William Pitt, the Younger, cousin (via his mother) of William Grenville, First Lord of the Admiralty (1788–94); Charles Jenkinson, 1st Earl of Liverpool (1727–1808), known as Baron Hawkesbury,

William Pitt the Younger, "Ministerial Eloquence," by James Gillray, published by Hannah Humphrey, hand-colored etching, published 6 January 1795. (© National Portrait Gallery, London)

President of the Board of Trade; Henry Dundas, 1st Viscount Melville (1742–1811), Home Secretary (see Dundas to JJ, 9 Sept. 1794, below); David Murray, 7th Viscount Stormont and 2nd Earl of Mansfield, diplomat and politician who opposed Pitt during the 1780s but joined with him at outbreak of the French war; and Lord Loughborough, Lord Chancellor. *ODNBO.* For changes in the cabinet in 1794, see JJ to GW, 21 July 1794, below.

2. The following were members of the foreign diplomatic corps: Christian Moritz, Baron de Kutzleben (1749–98), envoy extraordinary and minister plenipotentiary from the Landgrave of Hesse Cassel; João d'Almeida de Mello e Castro (1756–1814), Portugal's minister to Great Britain, 1792–1801; Franciszek Bukaty (1747–97), Polish chargé d'affaires and later envoy extraordinary and minister plenipotentiary; Count Lars von Engeström (1751–1826), Swedish envoy, 1793–95; Aloys Friedrich, Graf von Brühl (1739–89), privy councilor and envoy of the Elector of Savoy; Baron de Jacobi Klost, envoy and minister plenipotentiary from the King of Prussia; Comte de Lavezzari, resident from the Republic of Venice; Bernardo del Campo (Bernardo del Campo y Perez de la Serna), Spanish ambassador. The English-speaking Del Campo had been Floridablanca's secretary when JJ was in Spain (*JJSP,* 2: 803); Ludwig von Starhemberg; Count Frederik Christian Wedel-Jarlsberg (1757–1831), minister extraordinary from the Kingdom of Denmark and Norway;

Count de Haslang, envoy extraordinary from Bavaria and the Elector Palatine; Count Semyon Romanovich Vorontsov (Woronzow) (1744–1832), Russian ambassador to Great Britain, 1785–1800, and to the United Kingdom, 1801–6; Marquis de Circello, envoy extraordinary and plenipotentiary from the Kingdom of the Two Sicilies; Marchese Cristoforo Vincenzo de Spinola, envoy extraordinary and minister plenipotentiary from the Republic of Genoa; Anne Willem Carel, Baron van Nagell van Ampsen (1756–1851), ambassador extraordinary and plenipotentiary from the States-General (Netherlands); Count de St. Martin de Front, envoy extraordinary from the King of Sardinia; and Yusuf Agah Efendi (1744–1824) first Turkish ambassador to Great Britain. Robert Beatson, *A Political Index to the Histories of Great Britain & Ireland* (London, 1806), 181.

3. Charles Cornwallis, first Marquess Cornwallis (1738–1805), British general in the American Revolution, and Governor General of India, 1786–94. He returned to Great Britain in 1794, becoming Master-General of the Ordnance. *ODNBO*.

From Grenville

Dropmore June 16. 1794.

Sir

I have this Evening[1] received your letter announcing your arrival in London on which I beg leave to congratulate you, and to express at the same time my best acknowledgments for the trouble you have taken with respect to the letters you were so good as to forward to me from Falmouth.[2]

I am very sorry that it will not be possible for me to have the honour of seeing you tomorrow, but if Wednesday morning at Eleven o'clock would suit you I shall be very happy at that time to receive you Sir & the other Gentlemen whom you mention to me in your letter, at my office in Downing Street. I have the honour to be with great respect Sir Your most dutiful & most obedient huble Servt

Grenville

ALS, NNC (EJ: 08517); CS, UK-KeNA: FO 95/512 (EJ: 04973); LbkC, NNC: JJ Lbk. 8.

1. The CS version reads "morning".

2. See JJ to Grenville, 8 and 15 June, above.

From Grenville

[Downing Street 19th. June 1794.]

Lord Grenville presents his Compliments to M^r. Jay. He had the honor to lay before the King yesterday the Copy of Mr Jay's letter of Credence.[1] As Wednesday is the usual day for His Majesty's giving Audience to foreign Ministers, and as there will be no Levee next Wednesday on account of

His Majesty's journey to Portsmouth, His Majesty has fixed Wednesday sev'nnight[2] for receiving Mr Jay. But if Mr Jay, under the circumstances of his Special Commission should be desirous of having his Audience sooner, His Majesty has been graciously pleased to authorize Lord Grenville to say that His Majesty will permit Lord Grenville to introduce Mr Jay after the Levee tomorrow— In that Case Lord Grenville would wish to see Mr Jay in the morning at Eleven instead of Twelve as they had before fixed.[3]

AL, NNC (EJ: 08518); C, UK-KeNA: FO 95/512 (EJ: 04974); C, in JJ's hand, DLC: Washington; LbkC, NNC: JJ Lbk. 8; *HPJ*, 4: 23–24.

1. See "Letter of Credence to His Britannic Majesty," 5 May 1794, *ASP: FR*, 1: 470, captioned as George Washington to King of England, DS, UK-KeNA: FO 95/512 (EJ: 04972); C, UK-KeNA: FO 95/512 (EJ: 04963).

2. Sev'nnight or Se'nnight: archaic contraction of seven night, meaning a week. *OED*.

3. On JJ's introduction to George III, see the editorial note "Negotiating the Jay Treaty," below.

To Grenville

[Pall Mall—Royal Hotel 19 June 1794]

Mr Jay presents his respectful compliments to Lord Grenville. His Majesty's having been graciously pleased to permit Lord Grenville to introduce Mr Jay tomorrow, is a mark of Friendship and Attention to the United States, which they will recieve with Sensibility, and acknowledge with Gratitude. Wednesday Sev'nnight being, for the Reason mentioned by Lord Grenville, the Day most *convenient* to his Majesty for recieving Mr. Jay, he thinks he ought rather to submit to the Delay of that Honor, than omit this occasion of manifesting his Respect and Attention to whatever may be interesting to his majestys Convenience or wishes. Mr. Jay percieves, and thanks Lord Grenville for, his kindness on this occasion—[1] By a Gentleman who expects to set out on Sunday next for Falmouth and thence to Philadelphia, Mr. Jay will communicate these agreable Circumstances to the President—[2]

AL, UK-KeNA: FO 95/512 (EJ: 04970). Endorsed. C, in JJ's hand, DLC: Washington (EJ: 12422); LbkC, NNC: JJ Lbk. 8.

1. See Grenville to JJ, 19 June 1794, above; and the editorial note "Negotiating the Jay Treaty," below.

2. See JJ to GW (private), 23 June 1794, below.

From Jacob Read

Charleston 19th June 1794

Sir

I beg leave to assure You that the Intelligence of your appointment & Mission to the Court of great Britain was Received here with the utmost possible Satisfaction by every person in this Community whose Opinions merited consideration or who possessed a Shilling—[1] That Success may attend your negociations is our Sincere wish & that Yourself may enjoy health & a Speedy & happy Return to Your Country among our frequent & fervent prayers— We Consider Peace of the Utmost importance to America in General & to this Country in particular. There are here however Clamourers for Reprisal Confiscation & War— these people do not Recollect our Situation, that we have more to lose, less to gain, are the most Exposed & the weakest & State in the Union— The Sensible & Reasoning part of the Community are however of a Very different Opinion from those Enragéés

A Mr William Greenwood[2] a Merchant from this State whom you will find a very humble shrewd Man will I dare Say make a point of paying you his Respects, he will give you much & perhaps useful Information from this Country—

My Present Letter will I hope be delivered You by Mr James Bond Read[3] my Brother who is in Europe pursuing the study of Medicine he will I hope ~~have~~ before the Receipt of this have paid his Respects to you (unless his absence from London prevents) or he certainly will do so on Receipt of my Letters accompanying the Present

Mrs Read[4] desires me to present her most respectful regards to you with every good wish for your own welfare & success

We have not lately heard from New York there having been no arrivals from the prevalence of the Southerly winds

Our summer has Commenced with Intollerable hot weather but prospects are flattering if we can have peace[5] With Very great respect & Esteem I beg leave to subscribe myself Your most obedient Humble Servant

Jacob Read

His Excel^{cy} / John Jay / London

ALS, NNC (EJ: 07071). Addressed: "His Excellency / John Jay / Envoy Extraordinary & Minister / Plenipotentiary for the / United States at the Court / of Great Britain / London". Endorsed: "... an[swere]d —14 Aug 1794".

1. Jacob Read, Federalist, of the South Carolina House of Representatives, would be elected to

the U.S. Senate later in 1794. On JJ's mission, see the editorial note "The Jay Treaty: Appointment and Instructions," *JJSP*, 5: 609–21.

2. William Greenwood (d. 1822), a British-born merchant who settled in 1767 in Charleston and established the firm of Leger & Greenwood. A Loyalist officer during the war of independence, he fled South Carolina in 1782. After his claim for compensation from the British government failed, he returned to America in an effort to recover his confiscated property. Wilbur Henry Siebert, *Loyalists in East Florida* (2 vols.; DeLand, 1929), 2: 103; J. G. Braddock Sr., "Will the Real William Greenwood Stand Up," *Southern Genealogist's Exchange Society Quarterly* 46 (Sept. 2005): 195.

3. In his response of 14 Aug., JJ reported he met frequently with James Bond Read, who had since gone to Scotland. James Bond Read (1766–c. 1841), son of James and Rebecca Bond Read of South Carolina. Jacob Read was his eldest brother and guardian after the death of their parents. James Bond Read attended Princeton and studied medicine at the University of Leiden in the Netherlands. He practiced first in South Carolina and then settled in Savannah. There is no record of James Bond Read's meetings with the Jays in London. Dft, NNC (EJ: 08896); *Princetonians*, 219–21.

4. Catherine Van Horne Read, daughter of New York merchant David Van Horne.

5. In his response, cited above in note 3, JJ asserted: "Peace my ~~good Friend~~ ₍Dr Sir₎ was formerly thought a good Sort of Thing, but within these few Years past it seems to have been going fast out of Fashion— but to be serious—there seems to be something more than common at work in ₍or on₎ the human mind, and urging it to Enterprizes ~~whi~~ tending to introduce a new State of Things— Symptoms of it appear ₍more or less &₎ in different Degrees in all parts of Europe, even in Spain where Quiescency in every sense has ₍long₎ been cherished. Geneva is at this moment undergoing another Revolution— where next, no one can tell— ~~we live in an Eventful Period, and~~ our Country may catch the Flame— ₍we live in an eventful season₎ we have Nothing to do but our Duty, and one part of it is to prepare for every Event— Let us preserve peace while it can be done with Propriety, and if ~~it~~ in that we fail let us wage war not in newspapers and ₍~~rudely~~₎ impotent Sarcasms but with Manly Firmness & unanimous and vigorous Efforts—"

Peter Augustus Jay to Peter Jay Munro

London 22ᵈ. June 1794

Dr. Cousin

We arrived here on Sunday after a weeks journey from Falmouth, tho' the Newspapers had brought us to town several days before, they had likewise had the goodness to shorten our passage to 19 days, the ignorance of the London editors of Papers is really extraordinary; The *Times* of the other morning informed the public that Papa had already had a conference with Mr. *Dundas*,[1] The Chronicle of the next day very wisely declares that this paragraph was premature, but that it was supposed Mr. Jay would soon return, as the Ohio (which at the same time was advertised as taking in her cargo at the iron Gate) was waiting for him at Falmouth—[2]

The country and the Towns thro' which we passed on our journey are really delightful & exhibit no symptoms of that poverty misery and decline of which we hear so much— The country is cultivated in the highest degree

& the people are generally well clothed— The small villages however are not to be compared with our own— The walls of the houses are for the most part built of clay mixed with straw & gravel, & which after sometime become exceeding hard and the roofs are universally of thatch— in the towns & cities they are of Slate and flat tile— Untill we approached London we saw no large or even thrifty trees, the soil or the climate seems unfriendly to them— [3]

Ever since we have been in the country there has been a succession of great events which awaken the attention while they pain the feelings on account of the quantities ˄of blood˄ with which they have been accompanied— It is computed that not less than eighty thousand men have perished since the opening of the campaign, ˄&˄ yet it is but opened— The Battle between the french & english fleets must have been one of the ˄most˄ desperate that has been fought in modern times— Tho' the English have taken six ships of the line yet not one of them struck their colors, the "Le Vengeur" which was sunk fired the upper tier of guns while the water was rushing in the lower ports, & "Le Jacobin" went down the men shouting Vive la Republic, tis said that not a man of either was saved— However glorious this Victory may be to the British, its consequences have not been so important as might have been supposed, their own ˄fleet˄ was so shattered in the action as to be under the necessity of returning to port, & affording a safe passage into L'Orient to near 300 vessels from America loaded with provisions— [4] The Rejoicings in London were not over when the news arrived of a compleat defeat suffered by Gen[l]. Clarifayt,[5] & the consequent retreat of the allies the taking a town in Spain with 7000 men,[6] & the imminent danger of Ypres which was beseiged by the french. Again on Friday a Gazette extraordinary announced announced a victory gained by the Prince of Orange over the French with the loss of 7,000 men & 20 peices of cannon— & there is a rumor this morning that in consequence of another battle, Ypres has been relieved— [7]

It is surprising what great sans culottes the young Americans have become, most of them have been at Paris and de[scribe] the horrid scenes of which they were Spectators with a coo[lness and] want of emotion which astonishes & disgusts— one of them who you are acquainted with told us the other day that Hebert[8] had been very polite to him, & that after he had been condemned he went to see him & the other deputies executed, & praised the adroitness with which they were beheaded, he said he held his watch in his hand during the whole time & that the sixteen heads were in the basket in eighteen minutes. For my own part I think that the man who can view such scenes as these & yet endeavour not only to excuse but to justify them must want either common humanity or common sense—

As I grow more acquainted with this town I shall soon set ~~about~~ about executing my commissions, some small impositions I have met with have shewn me that I ought not to be in too great a hurry— With my best respects to M^rs. Munro, I am Your affectionate Cousin,

Peter Augustus Jay

ALS, NNMus (EJ: 00424). Addressed: "Peter Jay Munro Esqr. / *New York*". Endorsed.

1. On 16 June 1794 *The World and Fashionable Advertiser* (London) similarly reported, "Mr. JAY, the American Plenipotentiary, has had his first interview with Mr. DUNDAS. We are happy to find, and every man of humanity and intelligence will be proud to hear, that the tone of this Negotiation is completely pacific. Every thing that honour or policy will permit us to concede, is to be given up, for the purpose of averting that aggravated addition to our calamities—another AMERICAN WAR!" For JJ's arrival in England, newspaper coverage, and relations with the British cabinet, see the editorial note, "John Jay's Mission to London," above. On Dundas, see JJ to GW, 21 July 1794, below.

2. On the Jays' voyage from the United States on the *Ohio*, see the editorial note "The Jay Treaty: Appointment and Instructions," *JJSP*, 5: 616–17, 621nn53–54.

3. "Thrifty trees" is an archaic usage meaning strong and healthy. *OED*. For PAJ's less-flattering description of London, see PAJ to SLJ, 1 Aug. 1794, below.

4. The naval battle known as the "Glorious First of June," the result of which was accurately described by PAJ. See *PGW: PS*, 16: 292–93n5. Although the French Atlantic Fleet lost ships in the encounter, more than three hundred fifty ships carrying desperately needed supplies of grain from the French West Indies slipped by the British fleet and made port. The French merchant vessels had gathered in the Chesapeake after the arrival of the joint British military and naval expedition, which successfully forced the surrender of a number of French colonies. The French fleet, which arrived at Hampton Roads in early February, had brought refugees from Saint-Domingue to the Chesapeake and then convoyed the merchant vessels to Europe.

5. François Sébastien Charles Joseph de Croix, Count of Clerfayt (1733–98), Austrian general, was forced to retreat by French forces in the Flanders campaign in the spring of 1794.

6. The French achieved victory in the second battle of Boulou, 29 April–1 May 1794.

7. Ypres surrendered to the French on 18 June.

8. Jacques-René Hébert (1757–94), radical French journalist and editor of *Le Père Duchesne*, was executed on 24 March 1794 by order of the Revolutionary Tribunal.

To Edmund Randolph

London 23^d. June 1794.

Sir

I had the Honor to write to you a few Lines at Falmouth on the 9th. instant[1] mentioning my having arriv'd there the preceeding evening:— that Letter was committed to the care of our Consul M^r. Fox:—[2] He expected to forward it by the Active Capt. Blair who was soon to sail for Phil[adelphi]^a. but whose departure has been unexpectedly prolong'd to this time.[3]

On the 15th. I arriv'd here, and the same day mention'd it by Letter to Lord

Grenville.—[4] He appointed the 18th. for my reception, & I then communicated to him my first commission,[5] left with him a Copy of it. This was a Visit of Ceremony, and nothing pass'd between us relative to the Objects of my mission.— The next Day I sent Him copies of my Letters of Credence.[6]

On the 20th. I had an interview with Him by his appointment, and I communicated to Him my general Power, of which I have since sent him a Copy.—[7] much general conversation took place, and the principal Topics were touch'd upon.— His Lordship did not commit himself on any point:— He heard me very patiently & politely. He promis'd to ~~name~~ ^appoint^ a short day for another conference, and I took my leave impress'd with Sentiments favorable to his Character & Manners.— If his disposition be hostile He conceals it admirably.— What will be the Decision of the Court, I will not venture even to conjecture.— As yet I have no Reason to be dissatisfied or to consider appearances as being unfavorable.— No Delays or Arts to procrastinate have been practis'd.[8]

It is to be wish'd that no Intelligences of an irritating Nature may arrive from America.—[9] I do not regard Preparations for War as of that Nature. They ought not in my Opinion to be neglected or delay'd in the most profound State of Peace.

I shall not omit any opportunity of giving you such information as will enable you to see precisely the State of the negotiation: and shall endeavour to avoid deceiving you or myself by delusive Hopes or groundless Fears. I have the Honor to be with great Respect Sir Your most Obedient and very Humble Servant

John Jay

The Honble. Edmd. Randolph Esqr. Secretary of the U.S. for the department of State.

LS, body in JT's hand, DNA: Jay Despatches, 1794–95 (EJ: 04272). C, NHi: King (EJ: 04414); LbkC, NNC: JJ Lbk. 8; *ASP: FR*, 1: 476; *HPJ*, 4: 28–29.

1. JJ to ER, 9 June 1794, C, NHi: King (EJ: 04413); C, DNA: Jay Despatches, 1794–95 (EJ: 04268). For ER's response to JJ's correspondence of 9 and 23 June, see his letter of 18 Aug. 1794, ALS, DNA: Jay Despatches, 1794–95 (EJ: 04306); C, NHi: King (EJ: 04438).

2. Robert Were Fox (1754–1818), Quaker shipping agent in Falmouth who served as U.S. consul for that port. See *PTJ*, 26: 231.

3. The *Active* was an American ship captured by a British privateer while transporting a cargo of sugar, coffee, and cotton from Philadelphia to Nantes in 1793. See *PTJ*, 26: 646.

4. See JJ to Grenville, 15 June 1794, above.

5. See ER to JJ, 6 May 1794, *JJSP*, 5: 636–47.

6. See JJ to Grenville, and Grenville to JJ, both 19 June 1794, above.

7. For the letter of credence of 5 May and JJ's "general power" of 6 May, see ER to JJ, 6 May 1794, *JJSP*, 5: 636–47.

8. The two preceding sentences were paraphrased in an unsigned article published on JJ's mission to date that appeared in the *Philadelphia Gazette*, 20 Sept. 1794. For further quotations from JJ's correspondence that appeared in this piece, see JJ to GW (private), 23 June 1794, and JJ to ER, 12 July 1794, both below.

9. For JJ's concern about the reception in Britain of news about ER's harsh exchange with Hammond, see JJ to ER, 6–8 July 1794, below.

To George Washington (private)

London 23 June 1794—

Dear Sir

On Sunday the 15th. of this month I arrived here. The next Day I made Inquiries for Mr Lear,[1] and was informed that he had gone to Liverpool to embark for america. I asked whether it was probable that Letters sent by the post would find him still there— the answer was that it was highly improbable. Under these Circumstances & well knowing the jealous attention now paid to Letters passing through the post office, I thought it most adviseable to forbear making the Experiment, and to return that Letter to You.

My Letter of this Date to Mr Randolph contains an exact Account of the present State of the affairs of my mission here.[2] I shall be disappointed if *no* good should result; as yet the minister stands entirely uncommitted. From some light Circumstances I incline to believe that our mercantile Injuries will be redressed, but how, or how far, I cannot conjecture. My next Conference will doubtless place Things in more particular, and in clearer points of view.[3]

Doct^r. Gordon[4] has Information which he *relies* upon, that the Posts will not be surrendered, and he authorizes me to tell you so in Confidence. His Information does not make so strong an Impression on my mind, as it does on his— it merits attention, but in my opinion is not *conclusive.*[5]

The Observations I have hitherto made induce me to believe that the war with France is popular: and that a War with us would be unpopular. The Word *Jacobin* is here a Term of Reproach, & used as such among the common people— They who wish the Reform of this Government do I apprehend wish a certain Degree of Success to the present French Cause, not because they like it, but because they think such Success would promote their favorite objects. I often hear Gentlemen converse on these Subjects but think it prudent to be reserved— as to their internal Parties and Divisions, I make it a Rule to remain Silent.

Your administration is greatly commended.[6] The Idea ₍entertained by some₎ of applying private Debts to compensate public Injuries, alarms and disgusts, and impairs Credit.[7] ~~The Condemnation & Sale of Prizes~~ [re-mains?],~~[illegible]~~ I am anxious to have it in my power to communicate something decisive. As yet I am entirely satisfied with the minister— I ought to add, that M[r]. Pinckney's Conduct relative to me, corresponds with my Ideas of Delicacy and propriety—[8] With perfect Respect Esteem and attach-ment I am Dear Sir your obliged and obed[t]. Serv[t]

John Jay

P.S. The enclosed Copies of a Note of the 19th Inst: from Lord Grenville and of my answer, afford Indications of his present Temper, that will not escape you.[9] It is always useful to communicate such papers, but seldom useful to publish them.[10] Publications unnecessarily and frequently made must natu-rally encrease Reserve and Circumspection to such a Degree, as in great Mea-sure to exclude of Confidence and Conversation, and to confine negociation to the slow and wary mode of written Communications,—written too under the Impression & Expectation of publication—

ALS, DLC: Washington (EJ: 10613). Marked: "private". Dft, NNC (EJ: 08448); *WJ*, 2: 216–18; *HPJ*, 4: 26–28; *PGW: PS*, 16: 264–66.

1. Tobias Lear.

2. For this letter, see above.

3. JJ reported on his next conference with Grenville in his letter to ER, 6–8 July 1794, below.

4. William Gordon (1728–1807), English clergyman who had settled in the United States, author of *The history of the rise, progress, and establishment of the independence of the United States of America* (London, 1788).

5. For JJ's subsequent fears regarding the necessity of resolving the issue of the frontier posts, see JJ to AH, 18 July–[5 Aug.] 1794, ALS, DLC: Hamilton (EJ: 10766); *PAH*, 16: 608–10.

6. The *Philadelphia Gazette* of 20 Sept. 1794 carried an unsigned article reporting on JJ's recep-tion by Grenville, which noted that "the character of the President was spoken of in terms of the highest respect." For further quotations from JJ's correspondence published in this piece, see JJ to ER, 12 July 1794, below.

7. On the efforts of some members of Congress to withhold payment of American debts to Brit-ish merchants to force Britain to return the posts and slaves, see the editorial note "The Jay Treaty: Appointment and Instructions," *JJSP*, 5: 609–21.

8. For concerns about Pinckney's reaction to JJ's appointment, see ibid.

9. See Grenville to JJ, and JJ to Grenville, both 19 June 1794, above. JJ reported on his reception by the king and the queen in JJ to ER, 6–8 July 1794, below.

10. In the draft, JJ initially wrote: "~~they ought not to be published~~ ˄these papers sh[d] I think re-main private˄".

From Grenville (private)

Dropmore June 24. 1794—

Sir

I am much obliged to you for the communication of the papers which you have been so good as to send me.[1] I shall be desirous of an opportunity of conversing with you again on Friday morning at Eleven, if that hour should suit you— In the mean time I can only assure you of my sincere desire to contribute to the object of cordiality & friendship between the two countries, & of the real pleasure which I feel in having to treat for that purpose with a minister whose former conduct, as well as his personal character are so much calculated to inspire esteem & confidence. I have the honor to be Sir Your most obedient & most humble Serv[t]

Grenville

The Hon[ble] John Jay &c &c &c

ALS, NNC (EJ: 08519). Marked: "*Private*".

1. Probably JJ's credentials, which JJ sent him under cover of JJ to Grenville, 18 and 21 June 1794, both AL, UK-KeNA: FO 95/512 (EJ: 04971; EJ: 04975).

Peter Augustus Jay to Sarah Livingston Jay

London 29th June 1794

D[r]. Mama

It is with much mortification that we learn, that the Ship which carries our letters ∧&∧ which was to have sailed a week ago, will still be detained several days before she can get to sea. A gentleman who is going in her to settle in America has offered to take our letters, & we have accepted his offer— We have experienced very great attentions at this place every body *seems* at least to wish us well, the merchants in particular,— M[r]. & M[rs]. Church[1] have been profuse in their civility, we are to dine with them to day for the fourth time since our arrival— M[rs]. Low[2] begs to be remembered to you & to M[rs]. Munro— M[rs]. White[3] & her family is in the country— D[r]. Hays is with Lord Moira,[4] & I suppose by this time at Ostend, & M[rs]. Whites son[5] on board the Nymph at Portsmouth—

The Count Moustier & the Marchioness ᵃ le de Brehan are here and I believe in a good deal of distress— we saw them the other day. Little count Louis is in the Austrian service, & the count's son Edward in France, but where, or under what circumstances is unknown to his Father— as yet he has been unable to escape from ~~his~~ the country—[6] M^rs. Paradise[7] & Doct^r. Bancroft[8] present their respects to you, they have both shewn us all the attentions in their power— Tell little Wig[9] that Papa has not forgot his picture with a Cow in it we were talking of it this morning— Ask him what we shall bring for his dear little treker, how does she do? Maria & Nancy would in all probability like this place less than New York— here are no young misses whom it would be easy for them to get acquainted ~~it~~ with, & ∧it∧ would be impossible for them to walk on the flatstones or even in the park without danger of being ran over. M^r. Pinkney's family & almost all the genteel people & now in the country— Please give my love to Aunt Ridley who I suppose is with you— and believe me my dear mama to be Your affectionate son.

Peter Augustus Jay

M^rs. Jay

ALS, NNC (EJ: 06049).

1. John Barker Church, then a member of Parliament for Wendover, and Angelica Schuyler Church. PAJ recorded in his diary that they previously dined with the Churches on 15, 17, and 19 June. PAJ Diary A, AD, NNC. On 29 June, also in attendance at the Churches' were two allies of Charles James Fox, Lord Robert Spencer (1747–1831) member of Parliament, and "the celebrated Colonel Tarlton—", Banastre Tarleton (1754–1833), who gained notoriety in the war of independence for his brutal actions in the southern campaign, particularly at the Battle of the Waxhaws. *ODNBO*. For the Jays' relationship with the Churches and others mentioned in this letter, see the editorial note, "John Jay's Mission to London," above.

2. Possibly Margarita Cuyler Low (1738–1802), widow of the loyalist Isaac Low.

3. Mrs. White is Eva Van Cortlandt White, daughter of JJ's aunt Frances Jay Van Cortlandt, widow of loyalist Henry White, and mother of Peter Jay Munro's wife Margaret.

4. Francis Rawdon Hastings, first marquess of Hastings and second earl of Moira (1754–1826), served as an army officer and politician. In June 1794, he led 7,000 men to Ostend in Flanders in support of the Duke of York. *ODNBO*.

5. The son mentioned is the future Sir John Chambers White (c. 1770–1845), who had joined the British navy shortly after the family's removal to London in 1783, and was about to take command of the *Nymph*. Cuyler Reynolds, *Genealogical and family history of Southern New York and the Hudson River Valley: a record of the achievements of her people in the making of a commonwealth and the building of a nation* (3 vols.; New York, 1914), 3: 1409.

6. Eléonore-François-Elie, marquis de Moustier, and Anne Flore Millet, the marquise de Bréhan. After Moustier's recall in 1790, he obtained posts in Berlin and Constantinople. In 1793, the couple managed to take refuge under reduced circumstances in London, where Moustier acted as a liaison between the British military and Émigré troops. Moustier's son Clément-Édouard (1779–1830), later succeeded him as the 4th marquis. The marquise's son was Armand-Louis-Fidèle de Bréhan (1770–1828), who had accompanied his mother and Moustier to the United States. Moustier would attempt to use his connection to JJ to aid a fellow refugee and transmit letters to France. See Moustier to JJ, 18 Dec. 1794, ALS, NNC (EJ: 07028); JJ to Moustier, 18 Dec. 1794, Dft, NNC (EJ: 08922); and *JJSP*, 4: 50n25, 55, 119n24, 136, 137n5, 248n3, 446n6, 547, 558–60, 566–68, 597, 601, 603n3, 648, 651, 676, 714, 716, and 733.

7. Lucy Ludwell Paradise.
8. Edward Bancroft.
9. William Jay.

From William Bayard

[Greenwich House S⁰. Hampton June 29 1794]

Dear Sir

My Son William[1] in his last Letter to me from Dear New York, mentioned the business You was comeing to this Country About. And I was not a Little happy When I heard of Your Safe Arrival, As such I hope the business between the two Country's will prove benefitial, and Lasting to both, for no Man Alive Loves, Nor Wishes better, to his Darling Native Country than I do. My brother Who had the pleasure of Seeing You in London Informed me the handsome Manner In Which You Expressed Your Self of my Dear William be Ass[ure]ᵈ Mʳ Jay their is No Love Lost As In all his letters to me. he Mentions You In Equal Terms of Regard & Esteem, my Old Natural Friend mʳ Wallace passed Last Sunday With me When he Mentioned he had Seen You & that he Should Again as Soon as he Returned to Town When I Requested of him to present You my Compᵗˢ. And to Say how happy I Should be to see You Under my Roof,[2] he by Letter Writes me he had Seen You and deliver'd my Message which You kindly Recᵈ. with an Assurance, that when You Came to Portsmouth You would take a bed with me In Your Way which I shall be doubly ₐhappyₐ aᵇᵗ. As I wish from my Soul to Speak in the Language of the natives of our Own Country to Bury the Hatchet to Shake hands & be friends, That being done, come direct from London to Greenwich House at S⁰ Hampton, then Will I shew You the Country About go With You to Portsmouth, the Isle of White my brothers Genˡ. Shirrely,[3] &ᶜ. making my house Yʳ head Quarters While You stay In the neighbourhood, I shall say No more at present. than to Assure You that I am Dʳ Sir Very Sincerely Yours

Wᵐ. Bayard

P.S. should I have made any mistake In Your Address—It's from a Want of Not Knowing the Proper one.

The Honᵇˡᵉ John Jay Esqʳ &ᶜ &ᶜ

ALS, NNC (EJ: 08361). "John Jay Esqʳ." in top left corner. Tr, NNC (EJ: 12527). The Bayards were a prominent New York family of Huguenot descent. William Bayard Sr. (1720–1804), a Loyalist, had sailed for England in 1783; he and JJ had passed each other in London in 1783 as "perfect Strangers". *JJSP*, 3: 489, 534, 535n5.

1. William Bayard Jr. (1761–1826) was a partner in the prominent New York City mercantile firm of LeRoy and Bayard. *PAH*, 25: 96; *PTJ: RS*, 9: 579–80.

2. In his reply of 1 July, JJ promised to visit if he had the leisure, passed along compliments to Bayard's family, and noted "I cordially concur in wishing that not only Peace but Friendship may be established between the two Countries; and am happy in observing that a Similar Disposition seems to prevail very generally among the people here." Dft, NNC (EJ: 08889). See also William Bayard to JJ, 16 Aug. 1794, ALS, NNC (EJ: 08362); JJ to William Bayard, 24 Aug. 1794, below.

3. Thomas Shirley, 1st Baronet (1727–1800), the son of William Shirley, colonial governor of Massachusetts. The younger Shirley was promoted to lieutenant-general in 1793 and full general in 1798. *ODNBO*.

To Sarah Livingston Jay

London 4 July 1794

my dear Sally

This will be delivered to you by the Chev.^r Frieré,[1] who with his Lady, expects to sail next Sunday for new York, from whence they will pass on to Phil.^a where he is to reside in Quality of minister from Portugal to the U.S.— Mrs Church speakes handsomely of the Lady with whom I have not the pleasure of being acquainted— I have seen the Chev.^r and am pleased with him— he speakes English and seems an agreable man— I expect to write you another Letter[2] by this Vessel vizt the Frances & Mary Capt Reed—[3] Adieu— Yours most affectionately

John Jay

ALS, NNC (EJ: 90244: EJ: 08056). Addressed: "Mrs Jay / Broadway / New York". Note: "Honored by / Chev.^r Friere / & Madame de Friere". Endorsed.

1. Ciprião Ribeiro, chevalier de Freiré (1749–1824), formerly the Portuguese chargé d'affaires in London. He served as the resident minister from Portugal to the United States from 1794 to 1799. *PTJ*, 31: 54.

2. Probably JJ to SLJ, 6–8 July 1794, below.

3. The *Frances and Mary*, Captain Reed, embarked from Gravesend on 13 July and arrived in New York on 1 September. *Oracle and Public Advertiser* (London), 16 July; *Daily Advertiser* (New York), 15 Sept. 1794.

To Edmund Randolph

London 6.th [–8] July 1794

Sir

The Letters which since my arrival I have had the Honor of writing to you, are as follows.— 9.th June at Falmouth,[1] left with our Consul[2] there to transmit by the Active Cap.^tn Blair for Phil.^a—[3] & the 23.^d June[4] by Mr Francis, of which I also sent a Duplicate by the Mohawk. Cap.^tn Allan to New York,[5] & 26 June by the same—[6]

On the 27th. June I had a conference with Lord Grenville, in the course of which all the Topics of Difference between the two Nations were touch'd.— This Conference I considered as intended for more particular discussions: It amounted ∧however∧ only to a friendly and informal conversation on these subjects:— He appeared to be liberal, candid & temperate, but did not commit himself or say any thing decisive on any point.— He observ'd that He wish'd first to be inform'd of the Extent of our Views and Objects, and that a consultation with the rest of the Kings Ministers would be necessary to enable him to be more explicit.—[7] This appear'd to me to be perfectly fair and proper.

In conversing on the subject of Captures and Spoliations I was surpris'd that not a single case under the instructions of November had been laid before him—[8] He requested me to furnish him with some of the strongest of those cases; and remarked that an accurate knowledge of facts should precede any measures on that Head:— He said very frankly that there might be such a state of things as to render the interposition of Government proper and necessary to satisfy Justice; and that He, was desirous of having such exact information as would enable Him to judge whether & how far the Captures in question were under that Predicament.[9]

On applying to M[r]. Pinckney I learned that no such cases had been transmitted to him from America.

M[r]. Crafts, a Gentleman from Boston, has furnished me with the case of the Charlotte decided at Antigua & from which decision an appeal was made.— it unfortunately happens that this is not among the strongest of those cases.—M[r]. Crafts took the Opinion of Council on the subject. That Opinion is as follows.

The Charlotte—Coffin.
appeal from Antigua

D[r]. Nicholl is requested to peruse the Proceedings and evidence contained in the process herewith left and advise whether it is expedient for the Claimants to prosecute this Appeal:—

"I have perus'd the proceedings and evidence contain'd in the process transmitted, by which it appears that the Cargo of this Ship being the Produce of the French West India Colonies, and coming directly from thence to France was consider'd as liable to confiscation, although it should be the property of Americans.

In the war before the last Great Britain condemn'd Neutral Vessells and their cargoes trading to the French Islands, upon the Ground that the trade was not permitted in times of peace and that the Permission was given by the

French during the distress of War, as an expedient to protect their Property against British Captors: which occasional protection neutral nations were held to have no right to afford them.[10] In the last war, neutral Vessells trading to the French Islands: were not condemn'd but the former principle was not thereby considered to be abandon'd, inasmuch as the French had open'd their Colonial Ports *before the commencement* of Hostilities.— No such Step (as far as I am inform'd) was taken by the French previous to the present Hostilities: And as the Americans and other Neutrals were not permitted *before the War* to purchase the produce of the French Islands and carry it in their own Vessells from thence to France, and as the Instructions of the 8th. January 1794 (revoking those of the 6th. November 1793) still direct the Siezure of "all Vessells with their Cargoes; that are loaden with goods the produce of the French West India Islands, and coming directly from any part of the Said Islands, to any Port in Europe" [I] should apprehend that the sentence of condemnation [will] be affirmed.[11] However, it being understood that a negotiation between Great Britain & America is now pending, in which it is probable that the legality of this Trade will undergo some discussion and settlement, it will at all events be expedient on the part of the Appellant, so far to proceed, as to preserve his right of bringing the sentence to a revision; more especially as no decision upon the point has yet taken place by the Lords of Appeal: but the Expediency of finally bringing the Cause to a hearing may depend upon the result of the pending negotiation or upon some decision to be given by the Appellant Court.

J. Nicholl[12]

["]2d. July 1794"

The list of Captures with which I was furnished does not state the Principles or Pretexts on which the [con]demnations mention'd in it were grounded, & consequently is of little use on the present Occasion.— The Case of Marston Watson, which I rec'd from you before my departure, is a very strong one; but then it asserts only the *Expectation*, but not the *certainty* of condemnation.[13]

No Dispatches from Mr. Higginson (of whose instructions I have a Copy) have as yet reach'd me:— Those instructions are in my Opinion well devised, and if as well executed, will furnish me with all the Information which it seems has become so requisite.[14]

On the 3d. of this Month, I was in the usual form presented to the King, & the next day to the Queen.[15] The reception I receiv'd from them both was affable & satisfactory; and perfectly calculated to create an opinion of the good will of this Government to the United States: The King seem'd to be well prepar'd for the occasion: He express'd his confidence in the assurances I gave him of the disposition of the United States to cultivate Peace and Harmony:— He intimated (but without any direct application) that it was expedient for all Nations who respected Order, good Government, morality and Religion, to be Friends:— on this topic He expressed many general sentiments that were liberal & proper:— How far these appearances will correspond with *future Facts*, Time only can decide:— they certainty afford *some*, tho' not *conclusive* Evidence of a friendly disposition.

By the Arrival of the William Penn, your late correspondence with M^r. Hammond became known to the public.— what impression it has made on the Government here, I have not as yet been able to judge.[16]

In the conduct of this Negotiation, I shall proceed with as much Expedition as Prudence will permit: It appears to me expedient to be guided by Occasions & circumstances, and to give every conciliatory application a fair Experiment:— Conceiving it to be adviseable to afford the Minister an opportunity of increasing the Evidence of a friendly disposition, I prepared a Letter to him, which after having well considered I sent to him the next day:— it is in these words, viz.

Pall Mall, Royal Hotel, 3^d: July 1794

My Lord,

Such various and important affairs must necessarily demand and employ your Time & Attention, that I really feel a Reluctance to add to their number— and yet, circumstanced as I am, & circumstanced as my Country is, I find myself irresistably impelled to submit to your Lordship's Consideration, the expediency of my being authorized to convey to the President (by the Vessels which sail next week) such assurances as may tend to compose his, and the public mind in America.

I can find but few authenticated Cases of the Captures in Question, which have as yet arrived here, and they shall speedily be laid before your Lordship.— would it not for the present consist with your Ideas on that subject to say, that if those Captures, on being investigated, should appear to be of such Extent and Magnitude, as to merit the Attention & Interposition of Government, that then &c. &c.

Would it not also be right and proper to open the Door for appeals: and to instruct his Majestys Officers in America to promote by their conduct, that Friendship & mutual good will, which the Governments of both Countries desire to establish & perpetuate:— Delay is often hazardous:— pardon my anxiety lest new difficulties should arise:— to prevent, is generally more easy than to remedy.[17]

I cannot conclude this Letter without expressing to your Lordship how sensibly I feel and am gratified by the friendly disposition of his Majesty towards the United States, manifested by the very gracious reception with which I have been honored by their Majesties, and the magnanimity of the Sentiments which the King condescended to express on the Occasion.

It is my Duty, and I shall perform it with the most cordial satisfaction, to make known to the President these pleasing circumstances:[18] they perfectly harmonize with the liberality & candour, and with the obliging attentions I have experience'd from your Lordship: & if these representations should be accompanied with correspondent *official assurances,* a promising foundation would be laid for the Establishment & Duration of that Friendship and Cordiality between our Two Countries, which I pray God may speedily take place, & become perpetual.[19] With very Sincere Respect & Esteem I have the Honor to be my Lord Your Lordship's &c &c &c

J.J.

P.S As yet, I have rec[d]. no official Letters by the late arrivals from America.[20] The Right Hon[ble]. Lord Grenville one of his Majesty's principal secretaries of State &c &c &c

To this letter I have not as yet receivd an Answer.[21] nor did I expect one so early.— You will readily perceive that before it can be answer'd, the Administration will probably think it necessary to decide on their line of Conduct towards our Country.— whatever the Answer may be, it will unavoidably contain indications, either of Evasions or Suspence, or Irritation, or fair & liberal Conduct:— what the complexion will be, I cannot predict: as yet I have every reason to be satisfied, & it is but just and right that I should say it without Reserve.

I shall persevere in my Endeavors to acquire the Confidence & Esteem of the Government, not by improper Compliances, but by that Sincerity, Candor, Truth & Prudence, which in my opinion will always prove to be more wise & more effectual than Finesse & Chicane.

Formal discussions of disputed points should in my Judgement be postponed untill the case becomes desperate.— my present object is to accommodate rather than to convict or convince:— Men who sign their names to agreements seldom retract.

If however, my present plan should fail, and I am far from being certain that it will not, I shall then prepare and present such formal, & at the same time such temperate & *firm* Representations as may be necessary to place the Claims & Conduct of the two Governments in their proper points of View

On the 5th. July I receiv'd the following letter from M[r]. Henry Waddell viz

July 5th. 1794.

Sir,

By the advice of Thos. Pinckney Esqr. I have called upon you to state the particulars of the capture & detention of the American Ship Amsterdam Packet, but not having the Honor of a personal interview permit me to do it in this way.

The American Ship Amsterdam Packet (Henry Waddell master) of New York, owned by Messrs. Dan[ie]^l. Ludlow & Co., laden with Sugar, Cotton, Coffee, Pot & Pearl ashes, Oil & Tobacco, left said Port on the *28th. of Octr. last*, bound for the port of Havre de Grace. But on the 29th. Novr. following, was forcibly taken by the Privateer Princess Elizabeth Cutter, & carried into Liverpool, where the Vessel as well as Cargo are still detained, without any other reason assign'd, than that the Captors say they are indemnified by the Order of the 6th. November, (which no doubt you ₐareₐ acquainted with) & for which she must wait the *adjudication*. It is now *seven* months since the Vessel was taken, & if we have to wait our turn for the adjudication of the Admiralty court, it will be *Three or Four* months more, before we can hope for a Releasement.—

Any services render'd by you will be thankfully acknowledg'd by Sir &c &c &c

Henry Waddell

Hon^e. John Jay Esqr. Envoy Extra: &c &c[22]

I immediately sent ~~that~~ ₐitₐ to Lord Grenville enclos'd in the following Letter. viz

Pall Mall July 5th. 1794

My Lord

I am persuaded your Sensibility will be hurt by the Delay mention'd in the enclos'd Letter to me from M^r. Waddell— the impressions which it must naturally make, even on the most liberal minds, are to be regretted.— It will be sensibly felt by the owner, whose nearest connexions have, to my knowledge, done and suffer'd much from their attachment to this Country.

I forbear to add any thing, except very sincere assurances of the Respect and Esteem with which I have the Honor to be &c &c &c

JJ

The Right Honble. Lord Grenville &c &c &c.[23]

This Letter needs no comment, it will probably lead the Minister to observe, that all Descriptions of Persons among us are affected by the injuries of which we complain, and will naturally participate in the Resentments which those injuries cannot fail to excite— it is for the sake of this Idea, that I mention this Transaction: which in other respects may not be deem'd of sufficient importance to find a place in this Letter.

I have seen many respectable & influential characters here, and from their sentiments & conversation there certainly is reason to believe, that War with us would be an unpopular measure; provided nothing should occur, to fix the imputation of aggression on us.

In a late conversation with certain persons attached to the administration, and of weight in that Scale, the general Conduct of our Government receiv'd the most unreserved approbation, and the Character of the President was spoken of in terms of the highest respect.[24]

I have not heard that Carltons Speech[25] or Simcoe's Interference were defended by anybody, as yet I have neither heard or seen anything that looks like a hostile Disposition in the mass of this Nation towards ours, but the contrary.[26]

What designs may be or have been in the *Cabinet* is another matter:— information of that kind is not readily acquir'd, but I shall not be inattentive to it. Men are prone to suspect, sometimes too much and sometimes too little:—and to avoid both Extremes is more proper than it is easy.

On the Subject of the Affairs committed to me I have nothing further to add at present.

I have receiv'd a Letter from M^r. Bourne, which, together with my answer to it, should, I think be communicated to you.— they are as follows, viz.

Amsterdam June 27th. 1794

Sir,

I am made happy by the opportunity of tendering to you my congratulations on your safe arrival in Europe which I beg you to accept of, accompanied with my Cordial Wishes for the success of your mission, as involving the most important interests of our Country.

I am sorry to observe that the conduct of this Government of late (tho perhaps more equivocal than that which has been pursued by G. Britain) must operate very serious injury to the Commerce of America.— In the face of express stipulation of Treaty, they have prohibited us from taking away nearly all the Articles for which we have a demand, & many others unless on condition of giving heavy Bonds that they shall be landed in America, or rather not in France:— in short such are the troubles & vexations which burthen our intercourse with them, that our Vessells are generally oblig'd to depart in Ballast.

We have no Friend or Assistant here, cloth'd with public Authority, to whom we can resort for advice or protection on the points elluded to, but should it be within the Latitude of your powers to remonstrate, I doubt not, the Issue would be favorable.

Persuaded that you will not ask an apology for what has been prompted by a sense of duty to my Country, I forbear to make one for the trouble I give you by this communication, and pray you to be assur'd of those sentiments of profound Respect & Esteem, with which I have the Honor to be &c &c &c

S: Bourne

Hon^e. John Jay Esqr. &c &c &c[27]

London 5th. July 1794

Sir

I have been favor'd with yours of the 27th. of last Month, accept my thanks for the friendly congratulations contained in it.

That the President may be inform'd of the Facts you mention, I shall take the liberty of transmitting ~~an Extract from~~ ∧copy of∧ your letter to the Secretary of State.

Not being within the limits of my Commission I cannot with Propriety interfere by making any representations on these Subjects.

With the best wishes for your Health & Happiness I am Sir &c &c &c

J.J.

Sylvanus Bourne Esqr Amsterdam[28]

8 July 1794. Nothing new has occurred since the aforegoing Letter was written— I have the Honor to be with great Respect Sir Your most ob^t. & h'ble Servt

John Jay[29]

The Honb. Edm. Randolph Esqr. Secretary of State &^c.—[30]

LS, DNA: Jay Despatches, 1794–95 (EJ: 04274); C, NHi: King (EJ: 04416).

1. JJ to ER, 9 June, C, DNA: Jay Despatches, 1794–95 (EJ: 04268), and C, NHi: King (EJ: 04413).

2. Robert Were Fox.

3. The *Active*, Captain Blair, arrived in Philadelphia on 15 Aug. after a 44-day voyage from Falmouth. *Philadelphia Gazette*, 16 Aug. 1794.

4. JJ to ER, 23 June 1794, above.

5. The sloop *Mohawk*, Captain Allen, arrived in New York on 27 Aug. following a 56-day passage from London. *Daily Advertiser* (New York), 27 Aug; *Philadelphia Gazette*, 28 Aug. 1794.

6. JJ to ER, 26 June 1794, ALS, DNA: Jay Despatches, 1794–95 (EJ: 04273), and C, NHi: King (EJ: 04415).

7. For the influence exercised by other cabinet ministers on the negotiations, see JJ's Project for a Treaty with Great Britain, 30 Sept., and the editorial note "Negotiating the Jay Treaty," both below. On the reorganization of the cabinet, then in progress, see JJ to GW, 21 July 1794, below.

8. For an explanation as to why this information had not reached Britain, see ER to JJ, 20 Sept. 1794, LS, DNA: Jay Despatches (EJ: 04324); C, NHi: King (EJ: 04455); and *ASP: FR*, 1: 497.

9. For Grenville's response to JJ's representations about captures and impressment, see JJ to Grenville, 30 July 1794, and the editorial note "Negotiating the Jay Treaty," both below.

10. On Britain's "Rule of 1756," see *JJSP*, 5: 610, 617n4.

11. On the Orders in Council of 6 Nov. 1793 and 8 Jan. 1794, see the editorial note "The Jay Treaty: Appointment and Instructions," *JJSP*, 5: 609–21. On the desperate need in France for grain, see PAJ to PJM, 22 June 1794, above.

12. As instructed by ER, JJ had hired Nicholl to advise him on the prize cases. See ER to JJ, 6 May 1794, *JJSP*, 5: 645n17.

13. On this list, not found, see ER to JJ, 6 May 1794, *JJSP*, 5: 637, 644n9. On the list subsequently provided by ER, which JJ presented to Grenville on 28 July, see JJ to Grenville, 30 July 1794, below. ER enclosed a short statement (not found) on the case of Marston Watson in ER to JJ, 20 Sept. 1794, cited in note 19, below.

14. On Higginson, see the editorial note "Negotiating the Jay Treaty," below.

15. For the letters of credence to the king and queen, see ER to JJ, 6 May 1794, *JJSP*, 5: 642, 647n49.

16. The *William Penn* brought ER's letters to JJ of 27 May 1794 [C, DNA: Jay Despatches, 1794–95 (EJ: 04263); C, NHi: King (EJ: 04408); C, NNC (EJ: 07069); and C, partially encoded, NNC (EJ: 08632)], in which ER transmitted more information on spoliations and commented on a sharp exchange with Hammond, whose conduct he described as that of a minister foreseeing the outbreak of war between the United States and England; and of 28 May 1794 [C, NHi: Jay (EJ: 00622); C, NHi: King (EJ: 04409); and C, DNA: Jay Despatches, 1794–95 (EJ: 04264)], covering a list and a box of documents on spoliations. The ship's captain did not, however, discover these materials until 14 July, when he delivered them to JJ. In his letter of 16 July, JJ remarked that, while some of the papers were not useful, he was glad to have the cases and would present them to Grenville when the opportunity arose. See JJ to ER, 16 July, ALS, DNA: Jay Despatches, 1794–95 (EJ: 04279); C, NHi: King (EJ: 04426); and *ASP: FR*, 1: 479–80. In his letter of 8 June, ER notified JJ that he would be receiving more documentation on spoliations by the *Atlantic*. See LS, DNA: Jay Despatches, 1794–95 (EJ: 04266); C, NHi: Jay (EJ: 00603); C, NHi: King (EJ: 04411); and *ASP: FR*, 1: 475. Also on board were the letters of ER to Hammond, 20 May, and Hammond to ER, 22 May, debating the hostile actions perpetrated by each side against the other; and ER to JJ, 29 May 1794, C, NHi: Jay (EJ: 00629); NHi: King (EJ: 04410); and DNA: Jay Despatches, 1794–95 (EJ: 04265), covering documentation related to Hammond's complaints, and to Maryland's claim to stock in the Bank of England; *ASP: FR*, 1: 461–63, and 474–75; and *PGW: PS*, 16: 105–7, 190, 409–11.

17. On the procedural irregularities that characterized the proceedings of the admiralty courts that condemned American vessels in the West Indies and prolonged a final settlement of the cases, see Fewster, "British Ship Seizures," 426–52.

18. See JJ to GW, 21 July 1794, below.

19. For GW's approval of this letter, see ER to JJ, 20 Sept. 1794, ALS, DNA: Jay Despatches, 1794–95 (EJ: 04324); LbkC, NHi: King (EJ: 04455); *ASP: FR*, 1: 497.

20. See JJ to Grenville, 3 July 1794, ALS, UK-KeNA: FO 95/512 (EJ: 04977); C, unknown repository, formerly PRO (EJ: 03988); NHi: King (EJ: 04417); DNA: Jay Despatches, 1794–95 (EJ: 04361).

21. No response has been found.

22. Henry Waddell to JJ, 5 July 1794, C, DNA: Jay Despatches, 1794–95 (EJ: 04360), and LbkC, NHi: King (EJ: 04418).

23. JJ to Grenville, 5 July 1794, C, DNA: Jay Despatches, 1794–95 (EJ: 04359); C, unknown repository, formerly PRO (EJ: 03989); LbkC, NHi: King (EJ: 04419).

24. This paragraph was closely paraphrased in an unsigned article that appeared in the *Philadel-*

phia Gazette of 20 Sept. 1794, the same date on which ER acknowledged receipt of this letter, on which, see note 29, below. For quotations from other correspondence from JJ in this piece, see JJ to GW (private), 23 June, above, and JJ to ER, 12 July 1794, below.

25. In his speech in February 1794, to a delegation from western Indian tribes, Dorchester had informed the Indians that Americans had no interest in peace and would soon be at war with Britain, thus enabling Britain and the Indians to fix a boundary line to their mutual satisfaction. Simcoe had anticipated that the United States would attempt to seize the frontier posts and was actively preparing for war. See Bemis, *Jay's Treaty*, 229–33, 239–40.

26. For his report on an informal discussion of Simcoe with Grenville, see JJ to ER, 12 July 1794, below. For his view that Dorchester and Simcoe believed there would be war with the United States, see JJ to GW, 21 July 1794, below.

27. Sylvanus Bourne to JJ, 27 June 1794, C, DNA: Jay Despatches, 1794–95 (EJ: 04362), and LbkC, NHi: King (EJ: 04420).

28. JJ to Bourne, 5 July 1794, C, DNA: Jay Despatches, 1794–95 (EJ: 04062), and LbkC, NHi: King (EJ: 04421).

29. For his response to the above letter, see ER to JJ, 20 Sept. 1794, cited in note 19, above. In an earlier letter, ER noted that he had already received JJ's letter of 9 July [ALS, DNA: Jay Despatches, 1794–95 (EJ: 04275); C, NHi: King (EJ: 04423)], in which JJ had mentioned having sent "a long and particular letter" of 6 July. ER then speculated that this letter might have been brought by the Portuguese minister, said to have arrived at New York from London, on 15 Sept. See ER to JJ, 17 Sept., ALS, DNA: Jay Despatches, 1794–95 (EJ: 04323); and C, NHi: King (EJ: 04453).

30. The last paragraph, closing, signature, and ER's name and title are in JJ's hand.

To Sarah Livingston Jay

London— Sunday Evᵍ. 6[–8] July 1794

my dear Sally,

All this Day have I constantly been employed in writing Letters. The Number of applications made to me on Subjects unconnected with public or private affairs, have consumed more Time than I could with any convenience spare. Vessels will sail in the Course of this Week to america, and it is necessary and proper that I should write by them. You have seen me in similar Situations before; and how little Leisure I had for the pleasure of writing to my particular Friends. I am happy however in having a Degree of Health which enables me to dispatch these incidental affairs with so much[1] Expedition as to prevent their accumulating upon me—

Yesterday I had the Satisfaction of recievᵍ. your kind Letter of the 29 May:[2] I thank you for it very cordially: it is the first of your's that has reached me since my arrival; it has added to my Consolation. To be assured that you were all well, is a pleasing Circumstance. God grant that You may all continue so. I am anxious for a Leisure moment to write to Maria and Nancy, Fœdy & Mʳ. Munro, but fear it will not be in my power by this vessel.

Peter is very well and will write to You. His conduct is such as to meet with my approbation— He at present enjoys advantages which few of his age and Country meet with. I hope and believe he will not neglect them.[3]

Your[4] Description of the violent Storm and the apprehensions which it excited in your mind,[5] occasion Emotion not easily described. I think it providential that we hastened away as we did.[6] On the 29 May we were beyond its Reach.[7] But God governs on the Ocean, as well as on the Land; and no Events take place without his Permission or appointm.[t]

Has M[r]. Munro concluded with Col. Post— do you know how Things go on at Bedford. You know how to write to me in such a Manner as that if the Letters miscarry no Inconveniences will happen— I wrote to you from Falmouth, and twice from Hence—[8] I hope some of those Letters will soon reach You. I know how anxious you must[9] be to hear of our safe arrival— and I am equally so[10] that Intelligence of it may soon reach You.

I have given M[r]. Scattergood the pleasing Information you mention— I found him an agreable Companion— he is still here. M[rs]. Low is gone out of Town. M[r]. Johnson[11] talks of carrying his Family to the fœderal city, and settling there. M[r]. Vaughan's Family have been very friendly and attentive. How my Mission will terminate I cannot yet decide— There is Room[12] for Hope, and also some for doubts. I wish it was finished, that I may again take my place in our little domestic Circle— never I hope to leave it again[13] while I live— however, being in the Way of my Duty I must resign and be composed—

when you write, mention the Dates of such Letters as you may recieve from me.

8 July— nothing new has occurred— Be so good as to forward the Letter herewith enclosed—[14] Kiss all our dear little ones for me

M[rs]. Jay

AL, NNC (EJ: 08057). Closing and signature excised. Dft, PC: Kenneth W. Rendell, Inc. Enclosure not found.

1. Here in the Dft JJ excised "a Degree of" before interlining "so much".

2. SLJ to JJ, 29 May 1794, above.

3. Here in the Dft JJ excised the following paragraph: "So you have had a sad Storm and the poplars are blown down— I feel more affected by the apprehensions it excited in your mind than for any Damage it may have done to our Trees— I hear also you had a severe Frost and that much Injury has been done by it— These are disagreable Circumstances—but our Country still has many Blessings."

4. Before this word JJ excised in the Dft "I feel vio".

5. Here in the Dft JJ excised "affect me very".

6. Here in the Dft JJ excised "Had we sailed two or three days later".

7. Here in the Dft JJ excised "of the Storm wh. then prevailed".

8. Letter from Falmouth not found, but see JJ to SLJ, 23 June, ALS, NNC (EJ: 08055); and 4 July 1794, above.

9. Here in the Dft JJ excised "happy" and "will", and interlined "anxious" and "must".

10. Here in the Dft JJ excised "anxious" and interlined "equally so".

11. Joshua Johnson, whose son Thomas Johnson attended Princeton College. See JJ to SLJ, 23 June, ALS, NNC (EJ: 08055).

12. Here in the Dft JJ excised "Reason", before interlining "Room".

13. Here in the Dft JJ excised "until I bid it a fin".

14. Letter not identified. This 8 July postscript does not appear in the Dft.

From John Sinclair

[Whitehall.—next door to Park Ln. Sunday.—6 July 1794]

Sir John Sinclair presents his Compliments to Mr Jay.— Has the honour of sending the agricultural account of Middlesex, and of some of the other Counties in England, in case Mr Jay might wish to see the nature of the extensive inquiries now going forward, respecting the present state of this country, and the means of its improvement.— Will be very happy to be of any service to Mr Jay during his residence in London.—[1]

AL, NNC (EJ: 07139). Endorsed: ". . . an^d. 8 July 1794." JJ replied on 8 July 1794, Dft, NNC (EJ: 08890).

1. John Sinclair (1754–1835), Scottish agricultural reformer, promoter of practical knowledge, and politician. Sinclair was the founder and head of the Board (or Society) for the Encouragement of Agriculture and Internal Improvement, known as the Board of Agriculture (1793). The Jays met Sinclair on 1 July at a dinner party where he introduced them to members of his circle, including Joseph Banks and the Bentham brothers, Jeremy and Samuel. *ODNBO.* The work Sinclair sent JJ was probably Thomas Baird's *General view of the agriculture of the County of Middlesex: with observations on the means of its improvement: drawn up for the consideration of the Board of Agriculture and Internal Improvement* (London, 1793). For more on the JJ–Sinclair correspondence, see the editorial note "John Jay's Mission to London," above.

From Sarah Livingston Jay

New York, 7th July 1794

My d^r. M^r. Jay

M^r. Le Roy tells me that a ship will sail for Amsterdam tomorrow, & as I cannot hear of any destined for England, I have determined to write you a few lines being sensible how grateful it will be to you to hear of the continued health & welfare of your family & friends— Maria Ann & William have been ten days at Rye with their Uncle & Aunt— little Sarah & myself are alone, sister Ridley not being yet arrived— Johnny Lyon came to Town today—

he has not told me yet what sum he'll want tho' I believe it will be pretty considerable— The Mill is raised & about under cover— the freshets which have been the last month excessive have not injured it in the least— He is very sanguine about the importance of your Mill & thinks that when it is completed it will be very beneficial to the Country & lucrative to you— Your opinion of M^rs. Lyon's death I believe was but too well founded her loss to her husband & the farm will not be soon or easily repaired— He seems to think his Father too much Abroad & domestic concerns too much neglected—[1]

M^r. Grant's business is not yet settled, when it is it will give me pleasure to inform you of it—[2]

I will inclose a piece of intelligence from the Minerva of the 6th. ins^t. that may perhaps be useful to you—[3] Remember me most affectionately to Peter & be assured the best wishes & ₐmost ardentₐ prayers for your health, happiness & success & for your safe & speedy return to your Country, family & friends shall be unceasingly offered by your affectionate wife

Sa. Jay

Via Amsterdam—

DftS, NNC (EJ: 06557). Endorsed. Notation on final page: "M^rs. Jay accepts with / Pleasure M^r. & M^rs. Bayarrd's polite invitation / to dinner on Tuesday next.— / Wednesday 2d. July—" Enclosure not found.

1. John Lyon, son of Samuel Lyon. Which Mrs. Lyon is referred to is unclear. The first Mrs. Samuel Lyon, Mary Lounsberry Lyon, is listed as dying in January 1792. The date of the death of the second Mrs. Lyon, Elizabeth Fleming Lyon, is not indicated. Nor is a death date given for the wife of John Lyon, Sally Smith Lyon, but it is after his death in 1820. See *North Castle History*, 13 (1986): 17.

2. For the business with the Grants, see PJM to JJ, 15 June 1794, above, and the editorial note "John Jay's Mission to London," above.

3. The New York–based *American Minerva* was edited by Federalist Noah Webster Jr. However, it was not published on 6 July 1794, a Sunday. Possibly the issue referred to, is that for 5 July, which recorded toasts regarding JJ's negotiations given at Fourth of July events in New York.

From William Jackson

Amsterdam, July 8th. 1794

Dear Sir,

Believing that the enclosed paper might be interesting to you, I prevailed upon the Person, in whose hands I saw it at the Hague, to let me make a hasty translation of it, which, nevertheless, faithfully renders the sense of the original.

It is said here that both the Emperor and the King of Prussia are much dissatisfied, and I am inclined to believe that the discontents of both, though for different reasons, have a part of their source in these resolutions of the States of Friesland.

It is even said that the Emperor not only meditates a separate negociation with France—but is about to revive his claim to Silesia, which he is expected to invade.

The rapid success of the french arms has greatly alarmed the people here, who consider the invasion of Holland near at hand.

I think it a duty to state to you that in such an event the american property in this country will be greatly exposed. Mr. Short is absent— M^r. Dumas is not only a foreigner but superannuated— and there is no Person to represent the United States, or to vindicate the rights of our Citizens in Holland.

It is with great deference I presume to suggest to yourself and M^r. Pinck-ney the propriety of requesting M^r. Johnson to come for a short time to this Country to watch over the interests of the US.— I cannot help thinking that the impending crisis authorises M^r. Pinckney and yourself to appoint that Gentleman to this trust, for which his Knowledge of business and consular character are additional qualifications.

In any determination I persuade myself that you will excuse the zeal which has prompted this freedom—and that you will believe me to be, most re-spectfully, Dear Sir, Your faithful, obedient Servant

W Jackson

To John Jay Esquire London

ALS, NNC (EJ: 08636). Enclosure not found. William Jackson (1759–1828), formerly an officer in the Continental Army and secretary to the Constitutional Convention, had served as GW's secre-tary from 1789 to 1792. In 1793, Jackson went to Europe as William Bingham's agent. He married Ann Willing Bingham's sister Elizabeth in 1795. *PGW: PS*, 9: 312–13.

To Edmund Randolph

London 12th: July 1794

Sir

I had yesterday the Honor of seeing Lord Grenville— He assured me that no unnecessary Delays should retard a full Discussion of the points in Ques-tion; and observed that the new arrangement of the ministry involved the ne-cessity of Time for their being all informed and consulted.[1] In this assurance I have perfect confidence.[2]

we had an informal Conversation relative to Simcoe's hostile measure—[3] we concurred in opinion[4] that, during the present negociation, and untill the conclusion of it, all Things ought to remain and be preserved in Status quo — that therefore both Parties should continue to hold their Possessions, and that all encroachments on either Side should be done away — That all hostile measures (if any such should have taken place) shall cease, and that in case it should unfortunately have happened that Prisoners or Property should have been taken, the Prisoners shall be released, and the Property restored. And we have agreed that both Governments shall immediately give orders & Instructions accordingly.[5]

This Agreement appears to me so perfectly reasonable and so conducive to the Preservation of mutual Confidence and good Temper, that I flatter myself it will meet with the Presidents approbation; and I have given Lord Grenville explicit assurances (which he has reciprocated) that on the Part of the united States, it will be faithfully observed and fulfilled —[6] I have the Honor to be with great Respect Sir Your most obedient and h'ble Serv

John Jay

The Hon'ble Edm: Randolf Esqʳ Secʸ of State &c. &c.

ALS, DNA: Jay Despatches, 1794–95 (EJ: 04278); C, NHi: King (EJ: 04425); LbkC, NNC: JJ Lbk. 8; E, NN: Bancroft (EJ: 02749); E, PHi (EJ: 01176); E, NhHi: Josiah Bartlett.

1. For the changes to the ministry, which had been announced on 11 July, see JJ to GW, 21 July 1794, below. On receipt of this news, ER remarked that he did not believe that the "interweavaing of parties" in the new government would produce anything favorable to the United States. ER's reservations may have stemmed from the position of Lord Loughborough, a vocal and energetic opponent of the American Revolution, as Lord Chancellor. See ER to JJ, 17 Sept., ALS, DNA: Jay Despatches, 1794–95 (EJ: 04323); C, NHi: King (EJ: 04453), and ASP: FR, 1: 496. On consultations with the cabinet, see the editorial note "Negotiating the Jay Treaty," below.

2. JJ here may have had in mind the endless delays experienced by JA as minister to Great Britain, on which see the editorial note "Anglo-American Relations," JJSP, 4: 33–41, especially, 35–37.

3. On Simcoe, see JJ to ER, 6–8 July 1794, above.

4. On 20 Sept. 1794, the Philadelphia Gazette carried an unsigned article beginning "We are authorized to say, that it has been agreed between Mr. Jay and Lord Grenville" thereafter quoting the remainder of the paragraph with minor variations in capitalization and punctuation.

5. At the conclusion of this paragraph, the Philadelphia Gazette added the following sentence: "Arrangements have been accordingly taken on both sides." In a subsequent letter to ER, JJ enclosed Grenville's instructions to Hammond to this effect. See JJ to ER, 16 July, ALS, DNA: Jay Despatches, 1794–95 (EJ: 04279); C, NHi: King (EJ: 04426); ASP: FR, 1: 479–80. For other instructions from British officials to Carleton and Simcoe about the agreement, see PGW: PS, 16: 398–401.

6. In his response, ER informed JJ that GW had agreed to allow all things to remain in status quo, and that the War and State Departments had been instructed to issue appropriate orders to their subordinates. See ER to JJ, 20 Sept. 1794, ALS, DNA: Jay Despatches, 1794–95 (EJ: 04324); C, NHi: King (EJ: 04455); ASP: FR, 1: 497.

To Sarah Livingston Jay

London 18 July 1794

my dear Sally

I have written to you more than one Letter by the Ohio Capt. Kemp—they will inform you that three Letters from you have arrived— the latest of them is dated the 13th. June— I have also written by him a few Lines to the Girls with whose Letters I am much pleased.[1]

Mr. Roche expects to sail in a few Days for Boston, and thinking it probable that Letters by him will reach you sooner than those by the Ohio, I write you this in Haste, that you may have every chance of hearing that we are well, and may have the pleasure which I am persuaded these marks of attention will give you. I entirely approve of your arrangement with Mr. Grant— I mention this in the enclosed Letter to Mr. munro— when that Business shall be completed give me the earliest Advice of it— If concluded as we have Reason to expect, it will afford me much Satisfaction.[2]

Take good Care of your Health— mine continues as usual— Let our Friends at Rye hear from You— assure them of my affection— Health & Happiness attend you and our dear little Flock— Yours affecty

John Jay

Mrs. Jay

ALS, N (EJ: 04021; EJ: 05301). Addressed: "Mrs. Jay / Broadway / New York / Care of Mr. / Wm. Roch / to Boston". Stamped: "BOSTON"; in circular "2D/SE". Endorsed.

1. JJ wrote two letters dated 17 July 1794, ALS, NNC (EJ: 08058); ALS, NNC (EJ: 08059). He also wrote an additional letter dated 18 July 1794, ALS, NNC (EJ: 08060). Of the three letters he mentions receiving, JJ names only two, 26 May and 13 June 1794, both not found. The third is most likely SLJ to JJ, 29 May 1794, above. Of the correspondence from his children, Maria Jay's letter to JJ, 13 June 1794, survives, above.

2. For the business with the Grants, see PJM to JJ, 15 June 1794, above.

To Sarah Vaughan

London 19 July 1794

Dear Madam

Had it not been for an old Rule long confirmed by Habit, of dis-~~pensing~~∧patching∧ Business before I accept the Invitations of pleasure, I Should not for a Moment have delayed that of ~~immediately answering~~ ∧thanking∧ You for the very friendly Letter with which you have honored me[1] ~~among the pleasing Circumstances~~ The necessity I have since been under of writing a number of public and private Letters to america, ~~together with~~ & ˄the˄ variety of applications ~~to~~ which ~~it was necessary to attend~~ ˄constantly required my attention˄, have ~~since~~ given me unceasing Employment

I look forward with pleasure to some ~~moment~~ Season of Leisure when it will be in ˄my˄ power to accept your kind Invitation, and pass a few Days with a Family for whom I have ~~always~~ entertained the most cordial Esteem and Regard— My Son shall [soon] be with me— I am sollicitous that he should know, and should love his Fathers Friends— ~~I Shall [would it]~~ an Introduction to your little Groupe ~~as~~ ˄will be˄ a pleasing Circumstance— I am indebted to such a Groupe for a great Deal of domestic Satisfaction, ~~and shall be happy in an opportunity of~~ our Sons may lay a foundation for future Friendship ˄that may be˄ agreable and ~~perhaps~~ useful to ˄them˄ both—[2] ~~Farewell~~ ˄adieu˄ my dear Madam— assure Mr Vaughan of my Attachmt and believe to be with great and sincere Respect & Esteem Yr most obt. & very hble Servt.

Mrs ˄Sarah˄ Vaughan Rottendean[3]

Dft, NNC (EJ: 08148).

1. Sarah Vaughan to JJ, 11 July 1794, ALS, NNC (EJ: 08147). Sarah Manning Vaughan (1754–1834), the daughter of London merchant William Manning (1729–91), was Benjamin Vaughan's wife.

2. In her letter, Sarah Vaughn wrote "I wish much to present my little group to your notice, particularly the one who was not many hours old when his father presented him to you in Jeffries Square." This probably refers to William Oliver Vaughan (1783–1826). For the friendship between the Vaughans and the Jays, see the editorial note "John Jay's Mission to London," above.

3. Rottingdean, on the Sussex coast.

To George Washington

London 21 July 1794

Dear Sir

In a Packet last week to Mr. Randolph was enclosed directed to You a Book which the author, a Mr. Miles of this City, requested me to forward to You.[1] I was then so pressed for Time as not to have Leisure to write to you.

You will recieve herewith enclosed a Note or Memoir which Messrs. Lameth and Duport have given me for the purpose of laying it before you.[2] These Gentlemen express an extreme Sollicitude & anxiety about their Families, and they doubtless have great Reason. This war has produced, and will probably continue to produce more misery to Individuals than any other in modern Times.

Among my Letters to Mr Randolph is one stating an agreem^t. between L^d. Grenville and myself for preserving things in a pacific and unaltered State between us and the British on the Side of Canada and the Frontiers: and M^r. Simcoe will soon recieve orders to retire from the Miami to his former Position.[3]

Some Cabinet Councils have lately been held, and it is probable that the manner of settling their Differences with us has been among the Subjects of their Deliberations. From the Silence and Circumspection of Lord Grenville I apprehend that the Cabinet has not yet ultimately concluded on their Plan. This Delay is unpleasant, but I do not think it unnatural. The Opposition Members lately come in,[4] have so frequently held a Language friendly to America, that it is probable they find it necessary in order to be consistent, to adhere to Sentiments not agreable to *some* of the others.

I am led by several little Circumstances, not easily detailed or explained, to believe that the late Administration looked upon a war with us as inevitable, and I am of opinion that the Instructions of the 6 Novr. were influenced by that Idea.[5] I also believe that Lord Dorchester was instructed to act conformable to that Idea; and that Simcoe was governed by it.[6] I am *certain* that Intelligence (which made some Impression) was conveyed to the Ministry that our Army if successful against the Indians, had orders to attack and take the posts. There is also Room to believe that the indiscreet Reception given to the late french minister—the unnecessary Rejoicings about french Successes,[7] and a Variety of similar Circumstances did impress this Government with strong apprehensions of an unavoidable War with us, and did induce them to entertain a Disposition hostile to us.

I have given L^d. Grenville positive assurances that no attack pending the negociation will be made on the posts held by them at the Conclusion of the war; but I also told him that I thought it highly probable that every new advanced Post, and particularly the one said to be taken by M^r. Simcoe on the miami would be attacked. I must do him the Justice to say that hitherto I have found him fair and candid, and apparently free from asperity or Irritation.

So far as personal attentions to the Envoy may be regarded as Symptoms of good will to his Country, my Prospect is favorable. These Symptoms however are never decisive— they justify Expectation, but not Reliance.

I most heartily wish the Business over, and myself at home again. But it would not be prudent to urge and press unceasingly, lest ill Humour should result; and ill Humour will mar any Negociation. On the other Hand much Forbearance and seeming Inactivity invite Procrastination and neglect. The Line between these Extremes is delicate— I will endeavour to find and observe it,[8] with perfect Respect Esteem and Attachment I am Dear Sir Your obliged & obed.^{t.} Servt.

John Jay

This Gov.^{t.} seems determined to prosecute the War with France— Lord Spencer[9] is gone to the Emperor, instructed, as is said, to fix him in the same System—

Presid.^{t.} of the U.S.

ALS, DNA: Jay Despatches, 1794–95 (EJ: 04281). Dft, NNC (EJ: 08449), lacks postscript; *WJ*, 2: 218–19; *HPJ*, 4: 33–34; *PGW: PS*, 16: 398–401.

1. On the book sent by William Augustus Miles, *A letter to the Duke of Grafton, with notes, including a complete exculpation of M. De La Fayette, from charges indecently urged against him by Mr. Burke in the House of Commons, on 17 March 1794* (London, 1794), see *PGW: PS*, 16: 334–35.

2. For this undated memoire, written by Adrien-Jean-François Duport and either Charles-Malo-François, comte de Lameth, or Théodore, comte de Lameth, see *PGW: PS*, 16: 404–9. It solicited American intervention on behalf of women held in France following the passage of decrees of 12 Aug. and 17 Sept. 1793, ordering the arrest of suspect persons. It requested that instead of detention the women, their female children, and male children under the age of 14 be allowed exile in Switzerland or America.

3. See JJ to ER, 12 July 1794, above. For the instructions given by Grenville to Hammond, and by the Duke of Portland to Dorchester and to Simcoe, see *PGW: PS*, 16: 400–401.

4. Changes in William Pitt's cabinet were announced on 11 July, and reflected a coalition with the so-called Portland Whigs. The Portland Whigs, under the leadership of the William Henry Cavendish-Bentinck, Duke of Portland, broke with Fox's radical Whigs over their support for the French Revolution. The Portland Whigs supported the continuance of the war with France and wished to preserve America's neutrality. The Duke of Portland became Home Secretary. Portlandites William Wentworth-Fitzwilliam, 4th Earl Fitzwilliam (1748–1833), became Lord President of the Council, replacing Charles Pratt, 1st Earl Camden, after his death in April; George John Spencer, became Lord Privy Seal; and William Windham became Secretary at War. Henry Dundas, Pitt's "man of action," became the first Secretary of State for War, and had a major role in planning and overseeing the joint British military and naval expedition to the West Indies. The Order of 6 Nov. 1793 had been issued under his signature. However, he would prove surprisingly open to American trade, particularly in the East Indies. Hawkesbury, a staunch supporter of the ideas of Sheffield who favored strict limitations on the American carrying trade, remained as President of the Board of Trade. The Earl of Mansfield replaced Fitzwilliam as Lord President of the Council on 17 December 1794. Also in December, John Pitt would be moved to the position of Lord Privy Seal (1794–98), trading positions with Lord Spencer, who took over at the Admiralty. *ODNBO*. See Perkins, *First Rapprochement*, 18–20; Elkins and McKitrick, *Age of Federalism*, 379–80; and Wilkinson, "The Pitt-Portland Coalition of 1794," 249–64. See also London Calling List of Government Officials and Foreign Ministers, [15 June 1794–March 1795] note 1, above; and the editorial notes "John Jay's Mission to London," above, and "Negotiating the Jay Treaty," below.

5. On the Order of 6 Nov., see the editorial note "The Jay Treaty: Appointment and Instructions," *JJSP*, 5: 611–12, 618n14. For the suggestion that the American embargo may have contributed to this impression, see Ritcheson, "Pinckney's London Mission," 524.

6. On Dorchester and Simcoe, and on ER's belief that they and Hammond anticipated a war between the two nations, see JJ to ER, 6–8 July 1794, note 16; and JJ to GW, 21 July 1794, both above.

7. Genet, on whom see the editorial note "John Jay and the Genet Affair," *JJSP*, 5: 546–61.

8. Here in the Dft, JJ wrote, then excised, the following: "I will faithfully do my best to bring Things to a satisfactory Settlement— If I fail my Mind shall not reproach me— If I succeed an addition will be made to those pleasing Reflections which cannot be taken from me."

9. This postscript does not appear in the Dft. For the significant setbacks suffered earlier in the year by the First Coalition, of which Britain was the leading member, see PAJ to PJM, 22 June 1794, above. George John Spencer was named ambassador extraordinary to Vienna on 17 July to encourage the Austrians to increase their efforts against the French. See *PGW: PS*, 16: 401.

To Grenville

[London 30th. July 1794—]

The undersigned envoy of the united States of America has the honor of representing to the Right Honorable Lord Grenville his britannic Majesty's Secretary of State for the Department of foreign affairs.[1]

That a very considerable number of american vessels have been irregularly captured, and as improperly condemned by certain of His Majesty's officers and Judges.

That in various Instances, these captures & condemnations were so conducted, and the captured placed under such unfavorable circumstances, as that, for want of the Securities required, and other obstacles, no appeals were made in some Cases, nor any Claims in others.

The undersigned presumes that these Facts will appear from the Documents which he has had the honor of submitting to his Lordship's Consideration; and that it will not be deemed necessary at *present*, to particularize these cases and their merits, or detail the Circumstances which discriminate some from others.[2]

The great and extensive injuries having thus, under color of His Majesty's Authority and Commissions, been done to a numerous class of American merchants, the united States can for Reparation have Recourse only to the Justice Authority and Interposition of his Majesty.

That the Vessels and Property taken and condemned, have been chiefly sold, and the Proceeds divided among a great number of Persons; of whom some are dead—some unable to make Retribution—and others, from frequent Removals and their particular Circumstances, not easily reached by civil Process.

That as, for these Losses and Injuries, adequate compensation by means of judicial Proceedings, has become impracticable, and considering the causes which combined to produce them, the united States confide in his majesty's Justice and magnanimity to cause such Compensation to be made to these innocent Sufferers as may be consistent with equity; and the undersigned flatters himself that such Principles may without difficulty be adopted, as will serve as Rules whereby to ascertain the Cases and the Amount of Compensation.

So grievous are the Expenses and Delays attending litigated Suits, to Persons whose Fortunes have been so materially affected and so great is the Distance of Great Britain from America, that the undersigned thinks he ought to express his anxiety, that a mode of Proceeding as summary and little expensive may be devised, as Circumstances and the peculiar Hardship of these Cases may appear to permit and require.

And as (at least in some of these Cases) it may be expedient and necessary as well as just, that the Sentences of the Courts of Vice admiralty should be revised and corrected by the Court of appeals here, the undersigned hopes it will appear reasonable to his majesty to order, that the captured in question, who have not already so done, be there admitted to enter both their appeals and their claims.[3]

The undersigned also finds it to be his Duty to represent that the Irregularities before mentioned, extended not only to the Capture and Condemnation of american Vessels and Property, and to unusual personal Severities, but even to the Impressment of american Citizens to serve on board of armed Vessels. He forbears to dwell on the injuries done to these unfortunate Individuals, or on the emotions which they must naturally excite, either in the Breast of the nation to whom they belong, or of the just and humane of every Country. His Reliance on the Justice and Benevolence of his Majesty, leads him to endulge a pleasing Expectation that orders will be given, that Americans so circumstanced be immediately liberated, and that Persons honored with his Majesty's Commissions, do in future abstain from similar Violences—[4]

It is with cordial Satisfaction that the undersigned reflects on the Impressions which such equitable and conciliatory measures would make on the minds of the United States; and how naturally they would inspire and cherish those Sentiments & Dispositions, which never fail to preserve, as well as to produce, Respect Esteem and Friendship—[5]

John Jay

ADS, UK-KeNA: FO 95/512 (EJ: 04984). Dft, originally dated 27 July and redated 30 July 1794, NHi: Jay (EJ: 00631); Dft, enclosed in JJ to Grenville, 27 July 1794, and endorsed as received on 28 July 1794, UK-KeNA: FO 95/512 (EJ: 04980); C, unknown repository, formerly PRO (EJ: 03990); C, in JJ's hand, DNA: Jay Despatches, 1794–95 (EJ: 04284); C, NHi: King (EJ: 04432); C, in Spanish, SpMaAHN (EJ: 04064); LbkC, in JJ to ER, 2 Aug. 1794, NNC: JJ Lbk. 8; *HPJ*, 4: 38–41.

1. JJ sent Grenville a draft of this representation on 27 July, noting that "The Subject as relative to both the Governments is delicate—" The Dft text does not vary from the above. JJ to Grenville, 27 July 1794, UK-KeNA: FO 95/512 (EJ: 04980).

2. On 28 July 1794, JJ submitted to Grenville a "General Statement by Captains of Vessels seized at Martinique," signed on 29 Apr. by 40 American shipowners, masters, and consignees stating that all had been seized in February and condemned under one "indistinguishable sentence," as "Bad Men supplying the wants of Bad Men, in a Bad Cause." The list names the ship, its port of origin, and the signators. It was probably the list JJ received from ER on 14 July. See D, UK-KeNA (EJ: 04982); JJ to ER, 6–8 July, above. A copy of the document can also be found in the Earl Grey Papers, 382c, UkDhU. See Fewster, "British Ship Seizures," 431n18.

3. For JJ's instructions to press the British government to assume responsibility for compensating American shippers because of the irregular court proceedings in the West Indies, see the editorial note "The Jay Treaty: Appointment and Instructions," *JJSP*, 5: 609–21, and ER to JJ, 6 May 1794, *JJSP*, 5: 636–47. On the British government's disavowal of the court erected by Charles Grey, commander of the British armed forces, on his own authority; on the refusal of the American captains to pay the security demanded; and on their resultant failure to appeal verdicts against them within the specified time, see Fewster, "British Ship Seizures," 431–35.

4. The British had previously impressed American seamen during the Anglo-French crisis in 1787 and Nootka Sound controversy in 1790. Impressment first surfaced as an issue in the present war when the combined British military and naval expedition reached the West Indies at the end of 1793 (on which see the editorial note "The Jay Treaty: Appointment and Instructions," *JJSP*, 5: 609–21), and again in May 1794, when the governor of Rhode Island removed 6 American seamen from the British sloop *Nautilus* at Newport, and temporarily detained its commanding officers. Hammond complained about the latter incident in his letter to ER of 22 May, on which see JJ to ER, 6–8 July 1794, above; and *PGW: PS*, 16: 377. For the requirement that British ships and officers be hospitably received in American ports, see Art. 22 of JJ's Project for a Treaty with Great Britain, 30 Sept. 1794, below.

Since TJ had previously instructed Pinckney to discuss impressment with Grenville, ER did not charge JJ to do so in his instructions of 6 May. JJ raised it here on his own initiative, and apparently obtained from Grenville an order restraining impressments that was published in an unidentified British gazette on 6 Sept. 1794, a copy of which JJ enclosed in his letter to ER of 13 Sept. 1794, below. Nevertheless, JJ's efforts, like Pinckney's before and after, failed to persuade Britain to abandon a practice it considered essential to its ability to station a naval force in the West Indies, and to increase its force from 16,000 sailors by tens of thousands more, especially since it considered the practice an extension of its right to search vessels for enemy goods and thus defensible under the law of nations. For his disappointment that Grenville did not prohibit impressment in his draft proposal, see JJ's Objections to Grenville's Draft Treaty Proposals of 30 Aug., [6 Sept. 1794], below. On Pinckney's efforts to address this intractable issue, see Samuel F. Bemis, "The London Mission of Thomas Pinckney, 1792–1796," *American Historical Review* 28 (Jan. 1923): 233–41; Denver Brunsman, "Subjects vs. Citizens: Impressment and Identity in the Anglo-American Atlantic," *Journal of the Early Republic* 30 (Winter 2010): 564–66, 571–72; and Ritcheson, "Pinckney's London Mission," 523–41.

5. For his reply, see Grenville to JJ, 1 Aug. 1794, below, which JJ transmitted, along with his representation, under cover of JJ to ER, 2 Aug. 1794, ALS, DNA: Jay Despatches, 1794–95 (EJ: 04286); C, King: NHi (EJ: 04431), all of which, along with the Order in Council of 6 Aug. 1794, JJ subsequently advised should be published. See JJ to ER, 23 Aug. 1794, ALS, DNA: Jay Despatches (EJ: 04308); C, NHi: King (EJ: 04439); *ASP: FR*, 1: 484. For other reports on the negotiations, see

JJ to ER, 31 July 1794, ALS, DNA: Jay Despatches, 1794–95 (EJ: 04289); C, NHi: King (EJ: 04430); and JJ to ER, 8 Aug. 1794, ALS, DNA: Jay Despatches, 1794–95 (EJ: 04288); JJ to ER, 9 Aug. 1794, ALS, DNA: Jay Despatches, 1794–95 (EJ: 04303); C, NHi: King (EJ: 04435); and *ASP: FR*, 1: 480–82, receipt of which was acknowledged in ER to JJ, 11 Oct. In a postscript to that letter, dated 18 Oct., ER announced that he would immediately publish the communications as recommended in JJ's letter of 23 Aug., in which JJ had also suggested that agents should be appointed to manage the claims and appeals of American merchants and shippers. Subsequently, however, he decided not to publish JJ to ER, 2 Aug., because it might be considered a means of preparing the public "for yieldings and sacrifices," because nothing was said of the posts, and, since he had read it to those who "alone" were interested, he and JJ would be "more the masters of the whole matter at its winding up." In a subsequent letter, ER announced that, after consultation with the merchants, Samuel Bayard would soon depart for London to execute this function and that, although reluctant because they believed the government should accept primary responsibility for procuring redress, the merchants had agreed to form a committee to act in concert with ER. In a second postscript to his letter of 11 Oct., dated 19 Oct., ER indicated that five merchants would constitute the committee, to be chaired by Thomas Fitzsimons. See ER to JJ, 11, 13, 18, and 19 Oct. 1794, LS, DNA: Jay Despatches, 1794–95 (EJ: 04326); C, NHi: King (EJ: 04457); 20 Oct. 1794, LS, DNA: Jay Despatches, 1794–95 (EJ: 04327); C, NHi: King (EJ: 04458); C, NHi: Jay (EJ: 00610); and 29 Oct. 1794, LS, DNA: Jay Despatches, 1794–95 (EJ: 04328); C, NHi: King (EJ: 04459); C, NHi: Jay (EJ: 00612); *ASP: FR*, 1: 498–500. See also JJ to ER, 21 Aug. 1794, ALS, DNA: Jay Despatches, 1794–95 (EJ: 04307); C, NHi: King (EJ: 04440).

JJ's representation to Grenville appeared, sometimes in conjunction with Grenville's reply, in the *Daily Advertiser* (New York), 23 Oct.; *Baltimore Daily Intelligencer*, 24 Oct.; *Delaware Gazette* (Wilmington), 25 Oct.; *Washington Spy* (Elizabethtown, Md.), 28 Oct.; *New-Jersey State Gazette* (Trenton), 29 Oct.; *American Apollo* (Boston), 30 Oct.; *Massachusetts Mercury* (Boston), 31 Oct.; *Impartial Herald* (Newburyport), 31 Oct.; *Catskill Packet* (New York), 1 Nov.; *Oracle of the Day* (Portsmouth), 1 Nov. 1794. Both appeared in the London press through mid-December: *The Sun*, 9 Dec.; *True Briton*, 9 Dec.; *Courier and Evening Gazette*, 10 Dec.; *Morning Chronicle*, 10 Dec.; *Morning Post and Fashionable World*, 10 Dec.; *Oracle and Public Advertiser*, 10 Dec.; *Star*, 10 Dec.; *General Evening Post*, 9–11 Dec.; *London Chronicle*, 9–11 Dec.; *St. James's Chronicle or the British Evening Post*, 9–11 Dec. 1794.

In a letter of 30 July 1794, JJ had informed ER that he believed British military setbacks in the Flanders campaign had prevented the cabinet from giving more attention to American affairs. He reported further that Grenville was "besieged by our British creditors," and that he had heard that Virginia had passed new legislation making it more difficult for their claims to be satisfied. Having read all of ER's correspondence with Hammond, JJ praised him for handling the situation well and advised him to continue to be temperate. He also noted that he was to meet with Grenville on 31 July, and notified ER in a letter of that day that the meeting had occurred and that Grenville had promised him a written response the next day. See JJ to ER, 30 July 1794, ALS, DNA: Jay Despatches, 1794–95 (EJ: 04282); C, NHi: King (EJ: 04428); 31 July 1794, ALS, DNA: Jay Despatches, 1794–95 (EJ: 04289); C, NHi: King (EJ: 04430); *ASP: FR*, 1: 480–81. These letters were probably sent under cover of JJ to GW (private), 5 Aug. 1794, below.

From Grenville

[Downing Street 1st. August 1794.]

The Undersigned Secretary of State has had the honour to lay before the King the Ministerial note which he has received from Mr. Jay, Envoy Extraordinary and Minister Plenipotentiary from the United States of America, respecting the alleged irregularity of the capture and condemnation of several American Vessels, and also respecting the circumstances of personal severity by which those proceedings are stated to have been accompanied in some particular instances.[1]

The undersigned is authorized to assure Mr. Jay, that it is His Majesty's Wish that the most complete and impartial justice should be done to all the Citizens of America, who may in fact have been injured by any of the proceedings above-mentioned. All experience shews that a Naval War extending over the four Quarters of the Globe must unavoidably be productive of some inconveniences to the Commerce of Neutral Nations, and that no care can prevent some irregularities in the course of those proceedings which are universally recognized as resulting from the just rights incident to all Belligerent Powers.[2] But the King will always be desirous that these inconveniences and irregularities should be so much limited as the nature of the case will admit, and that the fullest opportunity should be given to all to prefer their complaints, and to obtain redress and compensation where they are due.

In Mr. Jay's Note, mention is made of several Cases where the Parties have hitherto omitted to prefer their claims, and of others where no appeals have been made from the sentences of condemnation pronounced in the first instance.

As to the cases of the first description, Lord Grenville apprehends that the regular course of Law is still open to the Claimants; and that by preferring appeals to the Commissrs. of Prize Causes here against the sentence of the Courts below the whole merits of those cases may be brought forward, and the most complete justice obtained.[3]

In the cases of the second description the proceeding might in some instances be more difficult from the lapse of the time usually allotted for preferring appeals. But His Majesty being anxious that no temporary or local circumstances, such as those to which Mr. Jay refers in His Note should impede the course of substantial justice has been pleased to refer it to the Proper Officers to consider of a Mode of enlarging the time for receiving the appeals in those cases,[4] in order to admit the claimants to bring Their complaints before the regular Court appointed for that purpose.

The Undersigned has no doubt that in this manner a very considerable part of the injuries alledged to have been suffered by the Americans may, if the complaints are well founded, be redressed in the usual course of judicial proceeding, at a very small expense to the Parties, and without any other interposition of His Majesty's Government than is above stated. Until the result and effect of these proceedings shall be known, no definitive judgment can be formed respecting the nature and extent of those cases (if any such shall ultimately be found to exist) where it shall not have been practicable to obtain substantial redress in this mode. But he does not hesitate to say beforehand that, if cases shall then be found to exist to such an extent as properly to call for the interposition of Government, where, without the fault of the Parties complaining, they shall be unable, from whatever circumstances, to procure such redress in the ordinary course of Law, as the justice of their cases may entitle them to expect, His Majesty will be anxious that justice should at all events be done, and will readily enter into the discussion of the measures to be adopted, and the principles to be established for that purpose.[5]

With respect to all Acts of personal severity and violence, as the King must entirely disapprove every such transaction, so His Majesty's Courts are always open for the punishment of offences of this nature, and for giving redress to the sufferers in every case where the fact can be established by satisfactory proof, nor does it appear that any Case of that nature can exist, where there would be the smallest difficulty of obtaining in that mode substantial and exemplary justice.

On the Subject of the Impress, Lord Grenville has only to assure M[r]. Jay, that if in any instance American Seamen have been impressed into The King's Service, it has been contrary to the King's desire, tho' such cases may have occasionally arisen from the difficulty of discriminating between British and American Seamen, especially where there so often exists an interest and intention to deceive. Whenever any representation has been made to Lord Grenville on this subject, he has never failed to receive His Majesty's Commands for putting it in a proper course, in order that the facts might be enquired into and ascertained; and to the intent that the Persons in question might be released, if the facts appeared to be satisfactorily established.

With respect to the desire expressed by M[r]. Jay, that new orders might be given with a view to prevent, as far as it is possible, the giving any just ground of complaint on this head, Lord Grenville has no reason to doubt that His

Majesty's intentions respecting this point are already sufficiently understood by His majesty's Officers employed on that service, but he has nevertheless obtained His Majesty's Permission to assure M^r. Jay, that Instructions to the effect desired will be renewed in consequence of His application.[6]

The Undersigned avails himself with pleasure of this opportunity to renew to M^r. Jay his assurances of his sincere Esteem and Consideration.[7]

Grenville

ALS, NHi: Jay (EJ: 04466). C, enclosed in JJ to ER, 2 Aug. 1794, LS (EJ: 04286); C, DNA: Jay Despatches, 1794–95 (EJ: 02667); C, NHi: King (EJ: 04433); C, in Spanish, SpMaAHN (EJ: 04065); C, UK-KeNA: FO 95/512 (EJ: 04986); LbkC, in JJ to ER, 2 Aug. 1794, NNC: JJ Lbk. 8; *HPJ*, 4: 41–44.

1. See JJ to Grenville, 30 July 1794, above.

2. For a similar articulation of Britain's position by Hammond, see the editorial note "The Jay Treaty: Appointment and Instructions," *JJSP*, 5: 609–21.

3. The prize courts established by the British military commander, Lieutenant General Charles Grey, in the West Indies were unauthorized and later disavowed by the British government. See Fewster, "British Ship Seizures," 431–34.

4. On the limited time allowed to make an appeal and on the securities captains were required to post, see ibid., 432, 435, 436.

5. An order from the king and council of 6 Aug. 1794 extended the time allotted for appealing sentences of condemnation. See JJ to ER, 9 Aug. 1794, ALS, DNA: Jay Despatches, 1794–95 (EJ: 04303); C, NHi: King (EJ: 04435); and *ASP: FR*, 1: 482, in which he enclosed a copy of the order. It was published in *Oracle of the Day* (Portsmouth), 18 Oct.; *Hartford Gazette*, 20 Oct., *Connecticut Journal* (New Haven), 22 Oct.; *United States Chronicle* (Providence), 23 Oct.; and *Greenfield Gazette*, on 30 Oct. 1794.

The American claims were finally settled only after the commission established under Art. 7 of the Jay Treaty concluded its work in 1804. Total awards to Americans amounted to $10,345,200. See Bemis, *Jay's Treaty*, 441. On the very complicated settlement of these cases and on the degree to which the British government took responsibility for settling the American claims and compensating both captors and claimants, see ER to JJ, 6 May 1794, *JJSP*, 5: 636–47, especially 645n17, and Fewster, "British Ship Seizures," 437–51.

6. On the suggestion by Gouverneur Morris that American seamen be given identification papers, on its rejection by TJ, and on discussions about an alternative, see Ritcheson, "Pinckney's London Mission," 529–36. On the matter of impressments, and the order restraining them, see JJ to Grenville, 30 July 1794, above.

7. The above document was printed in *Philadelphia Gazette*, 20 Oct.; *Dunlap and Claypoole's American Daily Advertiser* (Philadelphia), 21 Oct.; *Columbian Gazetteer* and *Gazette for the Country* (both New York), 23 Oct.; *Greenleaf's New York Journal*, 25 Oct.; *Connecticut Courant* and *American Mercury* (both Hartford), 27 Oct.; *Albany Register*, 27 Oct.; *New-Jersey State Gazette* (Trenton), 29 Oct.; *Connecticut Journal* (New Haven), 29 Oct.; *Federal Orrery* (Boston), 30 Oct.; *Massachusetts Mercury* (Boston), 31 Oct.; *Catskill Packet*, 1 Nov.; *Oracle of the Day* (Portsmouth), 1 Nov.; *Middlesex Gazette* (Middletown, Conn.), 1 Nov.; *Eastern Herald* (Portland), 3 Nov. 1794. It appeared along with JJ's representation of 30 July in the London papers in December: *Sun* and *True Briton*, both 9 Dec.; *Courier and Evening Gazette, Morning Chronicle, Morning Post and Fashionable World, Oracle and Public Advertiser*, and *Star*, all 10 Dec.; and *General Evening Post, London Chronicle, St. James's Chronicle or the British Evening Post*, all 9–11 Dec. 1794.

A commentator writing in *General Advertiser* (Philadelphia), 25 Oct., reprinted in *United States Chronicle* (Providence), on 6 Nov., described JJ's representation to Grenville as "spirited and manly," but with no hint of "servility or fear, or a disposition to crouch to the imperious pride" of the British. The piece characterized Grenville's answer as "evasive and circumlocutory", the "common style of Courts," and "calculated to give us very little satisfaction. "A." writing in *Greenleaf's New York Journal*, 29 Oct. 1794, declared that JJ's representation evinced "gross adulation and submission," and asserted that, though "cunning, Jay had in this instance certainly been outwitted," and that Grenville had, by granting a "shadow or something worse," guaranteed that Britain would never be "called upon for the substance." A vastly inflated account of JJ's achievements to date, claiming that JJ and Grenville had settled "the preliminaries of an honourable negotiation," and that British vessels had received orders "not to molest American vessels," appeared in the *Massachusetts Spy* (Worcester), on 15 Oct. 1794. For JJ's assessment of progress in the negotiations, see JJ to GW (private), 5 Aug. 1794, below.

Peter Augustus Jay to Sarah Livingston Jay

London 1st. August 1794

Dear Mama

We have for some time past been in daily expectation of hearing from you, by the numerous vessels from America which constantly arrive— we hope however that it will be but a short time before we experience that pleasure— Maria & Nancy wish me to give them a description of London; they will perceive perhaps how impossible it is for me to comply with the request when I tell them that such a description fills five octavo volumns which they may find in the city Library— I have been in this place near two months & have seen but a very small part of it indeed— the house in which we lodge is 5 miles from the place where the American Ships lye at Anchor, & the town extends considerably beyond each of those places— A fire broke out some days ago which destroyed 630 houses, many of the Inhabitants who are of the poorer class are reduced to very great distress; they now live in tents pitched in the church yards by order of Government— A Subscription is opened for their releif which will probably amount to a very considerable sum— The Salt-petre ware houses of the East India company first fell a sacrifice to the flames—& the explosions and torrents of fire produced from this drug were the principle means of spreading the conflagration— Those who were spectators of this dreadful scene, say that a stream of melted nitre almost resembling the Volcanic Lava flowed down into the Thames and continued burning even amid the water—[1]

An Eruption of Mount Vesuvius too has lately happened which has destroyed the Town of Porto Greco containing about 18,000 inhabitants together with several adjoining villages— But it is said that a very small proportion of lives were lost— This eruption has had the effect of ~~several~~ lowering the mountain several hundred feet, the conic summit has fallen in & a new crater opened on the side—[2]

Your Chairs are in the hands of a workman he says that from the shape of the work he will not be able to make them so fashionable as he would wish, & he equally laments your prohibition of gilding— Aunt Jay's bracelets are[?] doing, they are to cost twelve guineas. Papa has not yet had leisure to sit for his picture but I shall not cease to remind him of it, & as soon as it is finished I will have it set & a companion made to it according to your directions—[3]

Be so good as to give my love to Maria & Nancy. Tell little Wig ~~to~~ not to forget me, & to kiss sally for me— I am my dear Mama your Affect^te. Son

Peter Augustus Jay

M^rs. S. Jay—

ALS, NNC (EJ: 06050).

1. The Ratcliffe Fire was the largest such fire in London between the Great Fire of 1666 and the aerial bombings of the Second World War. Ratcliffe, a riverside district in East London, was a center of shipbuilding and warehouses. The fire began on 23 July 1794 when a kettle of pitch boiled over, spreading to a barge containing saltpetre, causing an explosion. The resultant fire destroyed 453 houses and displaced 1,400 people. See *Lloyd's Evening Post* (London), 23–25 July 1794.

2. The massive eruption of Mt. Vesuvius began on 13 June 1794.

3. For PAJ's shopping lists and errands, see the editorial note "John Jay's Mission to London," above, and PAJ's Memoranda & Statement of Accounts, [11 May 1794–9 Apr. 1795], AD, NNC. In the Memoranda, PAJ notes: "I am to request M^rs. Johnson to get for Mama two chairs seated with the seats given Mama by the Marchioness LaFayette in the most elegant fashion so as to serve as patterns for others but they are not to be *gilt*".

"Aunt Jay" refers to Mary Duyckinck Jay (1736–1824), wife of JJ's brother Peter. For more on the bracelets, see JJ to SLJ, 16 Aug. 1794, and note 4, below.

To Edmund Randolph

London 2 Augt 1794

Sir

I had the Honor of writing to you on the 31 ult:[1] That Letter was sent to Falmouth in Hopes it would reach Doct^r. Edwards before he sailed from Hence for Boston. He went from here on Tuesday last. I enclose a copy—

That Letter mentioned my having presented an official Representation to Lord Grenville on the Subject of Spoliations &c^a. to which his Lordship had given me Reason to expect an answer in a Day or two. I have accordingly rec^d. it,[2] and now take the first opportunity which has since offered, of transmitting to you (herewith enclosed) copies of them both.

The footing on which the answer places compensation by Government affords Scope for Delay— much will depend on the good Faith with which the Business may be conducted— the present administration does not appear to me to be hostile to us, but the contrary— as to Lord Grenville it is doing him no more than Justice to say that from the commencement of the Negociation I have observed no change in his Conduct, which has been uniform, candid and conciliating. From hence however no Inferences are to be drawn, that in my opinion an ultimate Settlement, satisfactory to either party, can or will take place. To such a Settlement (speaking in general Terms) I do believe that this Country as well as ours is disposed [but]³ there are real Difficulties, as well as some Prejudices which [stand] in the way.⁴ I am not without Hopes that such a Settlement will be effected, but am not sanguine in my Expectations; [for] in all *accommodations* there must be Yieldings, and questions relative to the due Degree and Reciprocity of such Yieldings by one side or the other, may produce great and per[haps] insuperable Obstacles.

It is very desirable that the negociation may not suffer from useless and improper asperities, of any kind, on either Side [and] that the conduct of our fellow citizens may constantly har[monize] with that of their Government— By wisdom and moderation endeavouring to preserve and cultivate peace and Friend[ship] and yet preparing to meet hostile Events with Compos[ure] Firmness and Vigour—⁵ I have the Honor to be with great Respect Sir Your most obedᵗ. & h'ble. [Servᵗ.]

John Jay

The Hon'ble Edm. Randolph Esqʳ Secʸ of State &cᵃ.

LS, DNA: Jay Despatches, 1794–95 (EJ: 04286). C, NHi: King (EJ: 04431); LbkC, NNC: JJ Lbk. 8.

1. JJ to ER, 31 July 1794, ALS, DNA: Jay Despatches, 1794–95 (EJ: 04289); C, NHi: King (EJ: 04430).

2. See Grenville to JJ, 1 Aug. 1794, above.

3. Material in brackets here and below supplied from the NHi copy.

4. For a repetition of these sentiments, see JJ to ER, 21 Aug., ALS, DNA: Jay Despatches, 1794–95 (EJ: 04307); C, NHi: King (EJ: 04440); and *ASP: FR*, 1: 483–84.

5. This letter was probably sent under cover of JJ to GW, 5 Aug. 1794, below.

From Sarah Livingston Jay

N York Augˢᵗ. 2ᵈ. 1794

My dʳ Mʳ Jay,

This mornᵍ. Genˡ. Clarkson inform'd me that a Vessel wᵈ. sail for Liverpool to-morrow, & as a long time has elaps'd since an opportunity has offered by which I could write I recᵈ. the intelligence with pleasure— As I am well convinced that you are more interested in the health & comfort of myself & children than any other circumstance, it heightens the satisfaction I feel in having it in my power to assure you we still enjoy those blessings— all our near connections are well— The three Children pass'd a fortnight at y^r. brother's, & it is now a fortnight since they return'd. I've not had the pleasure of seeing either Peter or Polly since you left me— At present Peggy Munro & her little Son are at Rye & to-day M^r. Munro is gone there & leaves it on Monday for Albany— I suppose he writes you as he tells me he does, of the business he transacts for you— mess^{rs}. W. & B.[1] have each paid him 100£ on their respective Notes & he has delivered it to me— Since you went away I have advanced to John Lyon 156£ for the Mill & besides that have paid 62£ for a pair of Mill stones which M^r. Greene bought here at N York— He thinks that in about 6 weeks he shall be able to begin to grind—[2] I have rec^d. from M^r. A. Van Horne on Acc^{nt}. one thousand three hundred & eighty pounds for you, & other sums which added to that makes upwards of 200£ Not a farthing of which can M^r. Munro or myself improve. M^r. Grant delayed the payment so long that stock of every kind is too high to purchase nor indeed is it for sale.[3] The situation of affairs in Europe & discontent in Canada lead people here with full Confidence to anticipate peace & indeed the extreme prosperity of the Country is such that your Mission is much more popular & I have heard from good Authority that many who wish'd for war & were disaffected to the public measures are now as desirous of Peace—& success to your Mission is become an Universal toast— Money is so plenty that a friend of ours told me he had taken ∧it∧ up on Long Island at 6 p^r. Cent & could have as much as he wanted at that rate— a friend of ours has not been able to put out any upon good security— The Waggon you engaged has not yet arrived— M^{rs}. Ridley has sold her house at B[altimore] & Thinking she sh^d. be ready to leave that place by the ~~25th.~~ ∧beginning∧ July promised possession the 25th., but not having finished her business she was obliged to stay with a friend & Susan came here this week on a visit— Judge Symes is to fetch her in a fortnight to Carry her to Morris Town from whence in Sept^{br}. she sets out for the Westward— M^r. Smith's Lot next to us was sold at Auction for 4450£ & the Auctioneer by M^r. Smith's order informed the bidders that your house extended 2 feet on his ground & that for those 2 feet you had offered 200£, which had been refused— M^r. Henderson who purchased it said he would not be hard with you but that he would not say he would accept the 200£ for the 2 feet— ~~at first I thought~~ Cousin Peter who was alarm'd at that assertion came here to examine your Deed & thinking their Claim groundless, wrote M^r. Henderson that he believ'd it so, & that he never had heard you express an Apprehension of the kind— M^r. Henderson still thinks you have made some mistake as it is endorsed in the handwriting of the late Chief Justice on his Deed— at first I did not intend to trouble you with a relation of this malicious transaction as I am sure your mind must be sufficiented employed with public business to require an exemption ~~of~~ ₐfromₐ private vexations ₐbut M^r. M[unro] thought it best you sh^d. be informed of it—ₐ I think it was best M^r. Munro pursued the measure he did least the silence of your friends should be misconstrued into an acknowledgement of the Claim—[4] I have endeavored tho' in haste to recollect what I thought ₐtheₐ most interesting circumstances in our affairs to communicate to you tho' in doing so I've done violence to my inclinations which would have led me to the choice of very different subjects— three pages have I written without expressing one anxious desire of seeing you or even of hearing from you or our d^r. Son— Would you believe that Stewart has not yet sent me y^r. picture? I call upon him often, I have not hesitated to tell him it was in his power to contribute infinitely to my gratification by indulging me with y^r. portrait— he has at length resumed the pencil & Munro has been sitting with your robe for him— It is your very self, it is an inimitable picture & I am all impatience to have it to myself— There is an excellent engraver here & Stewart has been solicited by a respectable number of Citizens to permit an Engraving to be taken of that picture for which he has asked & obtained my consent he begs me to remind you of the promise you made him the day ~~you~~ he breakfasted with you—[5] be so kind as to enquire where Characci resides—[6] Susan & the Children &^c. &^c.

Genl. Clarkson call'd for my letter before I had finished Copying it a great deal of it is therefore from memory & copied to preserve facts only—

FC, NNC (EJ: 06558). Endorsed: "Letter to M^r. Jay 2^d. / Aug^st. Via Liverpool".

1. Watson and Buchanan. See PJM to JJ, 30 Aug. 1794, Dft, NNMus: Jay (EJ: 00426).

2. For the labor completed and negotiated by Samuel and John Lyon on the Bedford farmstead, see JJ to SLJ, 13 Mar. 1795, and note 5, below.

3. For the financial dealings involving JJ, Augustus Van Horne, and Richard Grant, see PJM to JJ, 15 June 1794, and note 1, above.

4. Henderson may refer to Samuel Henderson, listed in the 1800 census in the 1st Ward, or William Henderson, merchant.

5. Gilbert Stuart first painted JJ in London, in 1783/84. In March 1793, after a time in Dublin, Stuart sailed to the United States, accompanied by the Irish miniaturist and engraver Walter Robertson. Through JJ's recommendations, Stuart gained many sitters, including GW. *JJSP*, 3: 491, 561–62; Carrie Reborm Barratt and Ellen G. Miles, *Gilbert Stuart* (New Haven and London, 2004), 120–23.

SLJ's frustration in obtaining the portrait reflects Stuart's practice of not finishing his work and leaving it to others. However, SLJ was more persistent than most, complaining to JJ on several occasions that Stuart had not delivered the painting. SLJ to JJ, 27 Sept., ALS, NNC (EJ: 06560); 11 Oct., ALS, NNC (EJ: 06561); and 12 Nov. 1794, ALS, NNC (EJ: 06564).

Finally, SLJ received the portrait in mid-November. She remarked to PAJ that "I believe it is to my own credit I owe his Portrait for Stewart has been [*illegible*] but to yield it to my importunities—", and notified JJ that "it hangs in the dining-room where the two small prints used to hang, & you cannot imagine how much I am gratifyed by having it—". SLJ to PAJ, 15 Nov. 1794, ALS, NNC (EJ: 13700); SLJ to JJ, 5–15 Dec. 1794, ALS, NNC (EJ: 06566).

The earlier portraits of JJ by Stuart were retrieved in London and finished by JT. These were later made available to Walter Robertson for an engraving, in lieu of JJ sitting for him. The portrait of JJ in the black silk suit was engraved and published in London in April 1795 by the New Yorker, Cornelius Tiebout, who was studying in London with engraver James Heath. Robertson to JJ, 15 Apr. 1796, below; JJ to Robertson, 15 Apr. 1796, below.

6. Characci is the Italian sculptor Giuseppe Ceracchi (1751–1801). He visited the United States in 1790–92 and 1794–95 in hopes of gaining commissions from Congress to sculpt a monument to liberty and from individuals to sculpt portrait busts in the Roman style. He sculpted GW, Madison, TJ, BF, and JJ. JJ's portrait bust is located at the Supreme Court in Washington, D.C. See JJ to Egbert Benson, 31 Mar. 1792, *JJSP*, 5: 372–74.

From Grenville (private)

St. James's Square August 5th. 1794

Private

Since Lord Grenville had last the honour of seeing Mr Jay[1] he has looked more particularly into the grounds on which Mr Jefferson in the Paper communicated to Lord Grenville by Mr Jay accuses great Britain of the first violation of treaty by her conduct respecting the Posts.[2] He now sends Mr Jay a Note on that subject[3] which he does not communicate to Him as an official Paper because He has the satisfaction to think that the course their negotiation is taking is such as to preclude the necessity of any ministerial discussion on the question of prior infraction. But as Mr Jay himself seemed not to be fully in possession of the facts, Lord G. wishes to state them to him, having no doubt of their effect on a mind as open & candid as he has found that of Mr Jay to be. Lord G. does not wish to trouble Mr Jay for any answer to this Note which is merely a private communication.

C, UkLPR: FO 95/512 (EJ: 04988). Marked: "*Private*".

1. On the meeting of 31 July, see JJ to Grenville, 30 July 1794, above.

2. See TJ to Hammond, 29 May 1792, in which TJ had argued that the United States had complied in all essentials with the Treaty of 1783, and that violations of it should be counted from the time news of it had arrived in the United States in March 1783. *PTJ*, 23: 551–612. JJ had earlier argued that the United States had been the first to violate the treaty, and was, thus compelled to present the case as developed by TJ. See JJ's Report to Congress, 13 Oct. 1786, *JJSP*, 4: 417–33.

3. See Grenville's Notes Respecting the Posts, 5 Aug. 1794, below.

Grenville's Notes Respecting the Posts

[St. James's Square] August 5th. 1794

The Provisional Articles were signed at Paris Novr. 30th. 1782. They were to constitute the Treaty of Peace to be concluded between Great Britain and the United States; but that Treaty was not to be concluded, 'till Terms of Peace with France were settled.[1] Even these Articles were not ratified in America 'till the 15 April 1783. There is therefore no Pretence to say that the Treaty of Peace ought to have been executed by His Majesty in America early in April 1783 several months before that Treaty was signed and when even the Provisional Articles were not mutually ratified. The Treaty of Peace was in fact not signed 'till Septr. 3rd: 1783. It was not ratified in America 'till the 14th of Jany. 1784, and that Ratification was not exchanged in Europe till the End of May 1784 nor received in London till the 28th of that month.

'Till that period, no order for evacuating the Forts cou'd with propriety be sent from hence. In the beginning of Mr Jeffersons letter[2] He quotes from Vattel the indisputable doctrine of the Law of Nations as to the Time when a treaty begins to bind the contracting Parties, namely that when it had received its whole form which certainly is not 'till after the mutual exchange of the ratifications of the Powers in whose name it is concluded. That Gentleman's subsequent Allegations in p. 61 of a Breach of the Treaty by the non-Execution of the Article respecting those Posts at the several periods which he mentions prior to July 1784 are therefore wholly & evidently unfounded, and the Statement of them could only be calculated to inflame animosities.

On 13 July 1784, there had barely been time for the arrival of orders at Quebec on that subject, supposing those Orders had been given immediately after the Exchange of the Ratifications.

But, in the intermediate time, Measures had been taken in America which are incontestible infractions of the Treaty.

Measures not merely resulting from the continuance of a Status Quo agreeably to reason & to the Practice of all nations during the Suspension of Hostilities and 'till the final Exchange of Ratifications, but new legislative acts adopted after the knowledge of the Terms agreed upon, avowedly intended to defeat the Execution of those Terms, when the Treaty shou'd be concluded & ratified and in their operation necessarily producing that Effect.

On the bare Statement of these Dates, there can be no doubt from which side the first violation of the Treaty proceeded if that Discussion were now necessary or usefull.[3]

C, UK-KeNA: FO 95/512 (EJ: 04989). Endorsed: "Notes regarding the / Posts." C, NNC (EJ: 08523).

1. For France's demand that the Anglo-American peace treaty should not be signed in advance of treaties among the European powers, see *JJSP*, 3: 420.

2. See TJ to Hammond, 29 May 1792, *PTJ*, 23: 551–612, in which he argues that treaties come into effect the moment of its notification to the country at large (ibid., 552–53, 601–2), and that therefore Britain was the first to violate the peace treaty by carrying off enslaved persons and refusing to hand over the posts. Because JJ had previously concluded, in the report described below, for which he had been publicly criticized, that the United States had been the first to violate the treaty, he evidently chose, as his instructions implicitly ordered him to do by providing him with a copy of TJ's letter, to present TJ's argument that Britain was the first to violate the treaty. See the editorial note "The Jay Treaty: Appointment and Instructions," *JJSP*, 5: 609–21, especially 614.

3. In his report to Congress of 13 Oct. 1786, *JJSP*, 4: 426–27, JJ had stated the following:

> As to the detention of our posts, your Secretary thinks that Britain was not bound to surrender them until we had ratified the treaty. Congress ratified it 14th. January 1784 and Britain on the 9th. April following. From that time to this, the 4th. and 6th. Articles of the treaty have been constantly violated on our part by legislative Acts then and still existing and operating—
>
> Under such circumstances, it is not a matter of surprize to your Secretary that the posts are detained, nor in his opinion would Britain be to blame in continuing to hold them, until America shall cease to impede her enjoying every essential right secured to her, and her people and adherents by the treaty.

For a summary of a subsequent discussion between JJ and Grenville about which nation first violated the peace treaty, see JJ to ER, 13 Sept. 1794, below.

To George Washington (private)

London 5 Augt. 1794

Dear Sir

On the 2^d. Inst: I wrote to M^r. Randolph, and sent him Copies of my Representation relative to Captures, and of the answer to it.[1]

I am this moment returned from a long Conference with Lord Grenville— our Prospects become more and more promising as we advance in the Business— The Compensation Cases (as described in the answer) and the amount of Damages, will I have Reason to hope be referred to the Decision of Commissioners mutually ₐto beₐ appointed ₐby the two Governm^ts.ₐ and the money paid without Delay on their Certificates; and the Business closed as speedily as may be possible.[2] The Question of admitting our Vessells into the Islands under certain Limitations, is under Consideration; and will soon be decided— A Treaty of Commerce is on the Carpet— all other things being agreed the posts will be included. They contend that the article about the *Negroes*, does not extend to those who came in on their Proclamations;

to whom (being vested with the Property in them by the Rights of War) they gave Freedom; but *only* to those who were *bona fide* the property of americans when the war ceased. They will I think insist that british Debts, so far as *injured* by lawful Impediments, should be *repaired* by the U. S. by Decision of mutual Commissioners— These things have passed in *Conversation*, but no Commitments on either Side: and not to have any official weight or use whatever.

The King observed to me the other Day— ["]Well Sir! I imagine you begin to see that your mission will probably be successful"— "I am happy may it please your majesty to find that you entertain that Idea"— "Well but dont you percieve that it is like to be so?" "There are some recent circumstances (the *Answer* to my Representation &cᵃ.) which induce me to flatter myself that it will be so" He nodded with a Smile—signifying—that it was to those circumstances that he alluded— The Conversation then turned to indifferent Topics— This was at the drawing Room.

I have never been more unceasingly employed than I have been for some Time past, and still am— I hope for Good—but God only knows. The Wᵐ. Penn³ sails in the Morning. I write these few Lines in Haste to let you see that the Business is going on as fast as can reasonably be expected: and that it is very *important* that Peace and Quiet should be preserved for the present

on hearing last night that one of our Indiamen had been carried into Halifax, I mentioned it to Lᵈ. Grenville— He will write immediately by the Packet on the Subject—⁴ Indeed I believe they are endeavouring to restore a proper Conduct towards us *every where*— but it will take some Time before the Effects will be visible. I write all this to You in *Confidence*, and for your own *private* Satisfaction— I have not Time to explain my Reasons, but they are *cogent*.

I could fill some Sheets with interesting communications, if I had Leisure— but other Matters press and must not be postponed; for "there is a Tide in human affairs"⁵ of which every moment is precious— whatever may be the Issue, nothing in my power to ensure Success, shall be neglected or delayed, with Sincere Respect Esteem and Attachment I am Dear Sir Your obliged and obᵗ. Servᵗ.

John Jay

Presidᵗ of U.S

P.S. I shall enclose with this my Dispatches to Mʳ Randolph—⁶ If the Wᵐ. Penn should be stopped by a *belligerent* vessel—they will respect a Letter directed to You more than one directed to him—

ALS, DLC: Washington (EJ: 10630). Marked: *"Private"*. FC, NNC (EJ: 08450); Tr, MH: Sparks (EJ: 05347); *WJ*, 2: 200–22; *HPJ*, 4: 44–46; *PGW*, 16: 510–13.

1. See JJ to ER, 2 Aug. 1794, above, enclosing JJ's representation to Grenville, 30 July 1794, and Grenville to JJ, 1 Aug. 1794, both above.

2. On settlement of the claims, see Grenville to JJ, 1 Aug. 1794, above. JJ may also have sent a letter to AH under cover of the present letter. See JJ to AH, 16 Aug. 1794, below.

3. The *William Penn*, Captain Josiah, sailed from Gravesend for Philadelphia on 12 Aug. 1794. *Oracle and Public Advertiser* (London), 14 Aug. 1794.

4. On the capture of the *Pigou*, see *PGW: PS*, 16: 512.

5. JJ's reference to tides and human affairs originates from a line in Shakespeare's *Julius Caesar*, act 4, scene 3, lines 218–21: "There is a tide in the affairs of men. / Which taken at the flood, leads on to fortune; / Omitted, all the voyage of their life / Is bound in shallows and in miseries." JJ had used variations of this reference in his writings at least twice before, in his letter to JA, 14 Oct. 1785, and in *The Federalist* 64, [5 Mar. 1788], *JJSP*, 4: 200, 201n2, 664.

6. Cited at JJ to Grenville, 30 July 1794, above.

NEGOTIATING THE JAY TREATY

On 20 June, Jay presented Grenville his general power, after which the two men arranged a meeting on 27 June.[1] Unusually, Jay proposed that no secretaries (John Trumbull and James Bland Burges) should be present, and that anything committed to paper be considered informal, with each party able to retract or change their opinion with liberty. As Trumbull recorded in his autobiography, Jay emphasized to Grenville "that this was not a trial of skill in the science of diplomatic fencing, but a solemn question of peace or war between two people, in whose veins flowed the blood of a common ancestry, and on whose continued good understanding might perhaps depend the future freedom and happiness of the human race." Grenville agreed.[2]

Although Jay had hoped to begin broad and substantive discussions then, Grenville informed him that he would first have to confer with the cabinet, soon to be reorganized. Pitt was about to form a coalition with the prowar opposition Whigs surrounding the Duke of Portland.[3] Jay was able, however, to use the opportunity to press for an end to British attacks on American shipping and to claim compensation for depredations that had already occurred. Handicapped by his own lack of proper evidence about them, he discovered, to his great surprise, that neither Grenville nor Pinckney had received any information on British captures of American vessels under the Order in Council of 6 November 1793. Documentation from Randolph did not begin to arrive until early July nor did the promised reports from Nathaniel Higginson, who had been sent to the West Indies to provide them.[4] Nevertheless, on 3 July, Jay appealed to Grenville to issue temporary orders to reduce the number of captures and speed the flow of appeals. Although Grenville did not respond immediately, in letters to Rufus King, to Randolph, and to Washington, Jay cautiously expressed his satisfaction with the manner in which his discussions were proceeding.[5] His plan, Jay told Randolph, was to accommodate, not to convict or convince, since men who signed their names to arguments could not easily retract them.[6]

Changes in the British ministry were announced on 11 July. They and setbacks for the British-led coalition in the European conflict claimed Grenville's attention and brought a temporary halt to substantive discussions. Nevertheless, Grenville found time that day to listen to Jay's concerns about Simcoe's fortification of Fort Miamis at Detroit and British incitement of Indians.[7] He pledged that British attacks on American territory would cease, that the status quo would be maintained, and that any prisoners or territory taken by British forces would be returned. On 15 July, Grenville gave Jay a letter of instructions he had written to Hammond codifying their agreement to end the unauthorized hostilities from Canada for Jay to enclose in his dispatches to Randolph for delivery to Hammond.[8]

By the end of July, Grenville was ready to engage with Jay on the principal objects of his mission. Jay prepared carefully. Having received some documentation on spoliations from Randolph, on 23 July, Jay informed Grenville that he was forwarding complete case files on some of the captures. On 27 July, he sent Grenville a draft of his planned representation, followed the next day by a letter covering a "General Statement by Captains of Vessels seized at Martinique" signed on 29 April, which he had inadvertently omitted from his letter of the previous day. During their meeting on 30 July, Jay presented the "official note on the object of his mission" in which he complained about the irregular captures, the improper condemnations of American vessels, and the "unusual personal severities" and impressment Americans had suffered at the hands of British forces in the West Indies. Grenville countered that he was besieged by British creditors, leading Jay to anticipate that resolution of the debt issue would be difficult. In his written response to Jay's representation of 1 August, Grenville chose to concentrate on the maritime issues. Although he implied that Britain would not make concessions on what it considered legally defensible principles regarding the rights of neutral commerce and the definition of contraband, concessions for which the United States could offer nothing of comparable value, he stated that it was prepared to correct abuses. In a naval war of global proportions, he noted, some "inconveniences" to neutral commerce were inevitable, but added Americans would be given every opportunity to present their claims and that it was the king's wish to do *"complete and impartial justice"* to all American citizens.[9] Having addressed with relative success one of the primary objectives of his mission, Jay immediately dispatched copies of his representation and Grenville's reply to Randolph.[10]

Next on the agenda were treaty issues. In advance of a meeting on 5 August, Grenville sent Jay an unofficial note indicating that he had reviewed Jefferson's claim that Britain's retention of the North American posts constituted the first treaty violation, thereby giving American acts complained of by Britain the cloak of legitimacy,[11] a claim Grenville unequivocally rejected. He was, no doubt, aware that Jay had previously and publicly stated as secretary for foreign affairs that impediments various states had placed in the way of British creditors had constituted the first violation of the treaty. Although Jay did not explicitly agree to Grenville's conclusion, he could not effectively contest it.[12] Grenville, on his part, chose not to end negotiations before they began by pressing his case. Instead, the two men agreed to try to identify reciprocal concessions and to preface the treaty by stating that they had decided to terminate their differences without drawing their merits into question.[13]

Jay immediately followed up on this conference by presenting Grenville with a preliminary draft convention and treaty of commerce on 6 August.[14] He first considered issues related to the peace treaty: identifying which river was the St. Croix River the peace negotiators intended as the northeastern boundary between the United States and New Brunswick; settling the northwestern boundary if the headwaters of the Mississippi River did not extend far enough north to meet a line passing through the Lake of Woods; and return of the western posts still held by the British. Here, Jay's intimate knowledge of the intent of the treaty's negotiators gave him an advantage. Furthermore, concessions on these matters would not diminish Britain's ability to wage war against France, and would give the United States reason to remain neutral in the conflict. Jay concluded the convention portion of his draft with items on the rights of neutral commerce, spoliations, and debts. He then took up issues to be included in the treaty of commerce: in peace, admission of the United States to trade with the British West Indies, reciprocal duties, the carrying trade and commodities allowed in regular trade between the two nations;[15] and in war, prizes when one of two nations was neutral, privateers when at war with one another; and finally, protection for citizens owning lands in the opposite nation, and a prohibition against sequestration or confiscation of debts.[16]

As he had led Jay to expect, Grenville did not respond immediately.[17] Jay remained cautiously optimistic. On 8 August, he informed Randolph that his prospects were "not discouraging," and, a day later, announced that he had hired William Scott, an eminent jurist with expertise on prize cases, to advise him on management of American appeals of prize court verdicts and claims for compensation.[18] Jay also enclosed a copy of an Order in Council of 6 August that he had just received from Grenville instructing the king's vice admiralty courts in the West Indies to admit appeals of condemnations of American vessels even if the time limit for so doing had lapsed.[19] In mid-month, Jay politely tried to elicit a response on the draft that he had submitted to Grenville ten days earlier. Grenville, as politely, indicated that pressing business prevented him from giving it his full attention.[20]

Reassured by Grenville's initial response on spoliations and impressments, on 21 August, Jay informed Randolph that he anticipated that his next conference with Grenville would produce something decisive, "at least on *some* of the great points," even though affairs had come to a temporary halt.[21] The numerous calls on Grenville's attention had occasioned some delays, he reported, but he had no reason to think they could have been avoided. In this letter, Jay also noted that Monroe, the newly appointed American minister to France, had arrived at Paris.[22]

On 30 August Grenville delivered his two-part counter-proposal, significantly more developed than Jay's original draft, with apologies for not having been able to send it sooner. His carefully chosen opening was an agreement to evacuate the posts. The concession, long-demanded by the United States, was not totally satisfactory, since Grenville specified that Britain would hold the posts until 1 June 1796. In place of the barrier state along the northern border Britain had long aspired to erect,[23] Grenville added provisions that preserved property rights and provided for the free flow of goods and unimpeded cross-border access for British traders and Indians involved in the fur trade.[24] He did not, however, provide an equivalent privilege for Americans, an omission Jay quickly called to his attention. Jay challenged these unequal privileges conceded to British traders without parallel benefits to Americans, and proposed additions that would have demilitarized the frontier.[25]

Grenville's second article took up both of the border issues created by the unavoidably vague and erroneous maps on which the peace negotiators had had to depend. Two issues were still unresolved: boundaries related to the St. Croix River and the northern boundary west of Lake Superior. Where Jay's draft of 6 August had proposed leaving both disputes to be resolved by commissions, Grenville's solution to the northwestern boundary was a carefully couched demand to extend the boundary far enough south to give the British direct access to the headwaters of the Mississippi.[26]

The very next day Jay notified Grenville that several items in his draft, especially the article on the northwest boundary line might constitute "parting points," and asked for a meeting to discuss them. When Grenville did not respond immediately, Jay wrote again on 4 September to emphasize the need for a meeting and enclosed a series of remarks on the boundary question for Grenville's consideration. Grenville answered the next day. While he did not concede that his interpretation of the treaty was incorrect, he made a discreet retreat from it by allowing that Jay's proposal for appointing commissioners, did *not* appear "ill adapted" to reaching a just solution to the dilemma, and set a meeting on 6 September to discuss all the issues that threatened the success of the negotiations.[27] In advance of it, Jay sent a list of other points in Grenville's draft he believed were in need of revision. The observations and alterations Grenville sent Jay under cover of a note of 7 September[28] predicted that the discussion would be wide-ranging and substantive. A meeting to continue it was scheduled for several days later.[29] Grenville balanced his conciliatory retreat on the boundary matter by calling Jay's attention to what he and others considered the inappropriate professions of affection for France found in Monroe's first address to the French National Convention of 15 August and in Randolph's earlier correspondence with the Committee of Public Safety. Jay took this matter very seriously and so advised Randolph in a private letter accompanying his lengthy public report on the negotiations with Grenville.[30]

During their next meeting, sometime in mid-September, Jay presented Grenville with his proposal for resolving the Lake of the Woods controversy.[31] The conversation that followed, Jay said, was "temperate and candid." Grenville also indicated he would be willing to consider an article officially admitting American vessels to the British East Indies, and, in the spirit of reciprocity, offered to postpone payments awarded by the commissioners to British creditors until the posts were evacuated.[32] It was probably in the course of this meeting that the decision was made to consolidate the two treaties into a single document.[33]

During the remainder of the month, Jay worked diligently to present a new draft, including, as he later reported to Randolph, most of the articles in Grenville's two drafts as well as several additional articles he proposed for their "mutual consideration." Jay presented his draft to Grenville on 30 September. Eager for a response, he wrote Grenville on 7 October to ask whether he would be able to tell Washington that progress toward a treaty was being made by the time the next packet departed in several weeks. Anticipating Grenville's response, he noted that, having reviewed his draft, he had concluded that some of the articles he had suggested would have to be revised. Grenville promptly agreed. Jay's "Contre projet," he said, varied so much from the substance of the articles he had proposed that it would take more time than he had anticipated to resolve the differences and bring their negotiation to a satisfactory conclusion. He then invited Jay to meet with him the next day so he could identify the "leading points" that, if Jay insisted on them, would create "insurmountable obstacles" to the conclusion of the treaty.[34] Shortly thereafter, Jay reviewed the draft of the treaty with Pinckney and with John Quincy Adams, then on his way to assume his position as minister to the Netherlands. None of them were enthusiastic about it, but they considered it preferable to war.[35]

Negotiations continued throughout the month. Jay met with Grenville on 24 and 28 October.[36] The next day, Jay informed Randolph that Grenville had created a new draft[37] that omitted some articles from Jay's draft of 30 September and added others, removing some obstacles and lessening others, although some still remained. Grenville, he said, wanted goods for the Indian trade to enter the United States from Canada *duty free*, and to this he could not agree.[38] He did not know whether the strong objections he had raised to Grenville's attempt to remove alien tonnage and an impost would be sustained.[39] On the positive side, Jay reported, Grenville had finally agreed to settle the northwest boundary by a survey and commission and would probably agree to admit American traders to Canada and its Indian trade, although he would not allow them to navigate the St Lawrence to the sea.[40] He would not agree to advance the 1796 date set for evacuation of the posts,[41] but had added a clause allowing the United States to extend its settlements anywhere within the treaty boundaries other than within the precincts of the posts.[42] Jay also informed Grenville that Washington had expressed satisfaction with Jay's reception by the king and confidence that the negotiations would result in a mutually beneficial treaty that he pledged to support.[43] It would soon be decided, Jay thought, whether a treaty was possible or not.[44]

When discussion resumed on 30 October, Grenville presented an article on the Indian trade, and then proposed a substitute for it the next day. This, Jay immediately accepted and asked for a meeting during which he hoped they could complete the negotiation. He wrote Randolph on 5 November to say that it was "almost certain" that the treaty would soon be finished.[45] After reading the copy of the treaty Grenville sent him on 10 November, Jay discovered one more problem that he did not specify in correspondence, but which was evidently resolved in person on the 11th. On 17 November, George III issued a formal commission to Grenville to conclude the treaty, and Jay sent Randolph a brief note to indicate that it had been agreed upon, would be signed either that day or the next, and sent by the packet.[46] It was Grenville's and Jay's intent that the treaty should speed its way to the United States, and the packet had been held accordingly. Its departure was, however, delayed and the treaty did not arrive in the United States until 7 March 1795.

Jay and Grenville had both worked intensely and exhaustively to bring the treaty to a point where they could both accept it. Well aware from long experience that treaties recognize or codify reality but do not often enlarge it, Jay realistically anticipated that the treaty would not meet American expectations when it arrived in the United States.[47] In his cover letter to Randolph he noted tersely that his opinion of the treaty could be deduced from the fact he had signed it. No better treaty, he said, could have been obtained. There followed an explanation of some of the difficulties and controversies he knew would arise: the agreement not to identify a first violator of the peace treaty; the delay in evacuating the posts; the Indian trade; some of the other commercial terms that he knew had already come in for criticism, actually by Hamilton though relayed through Randolph; the commissions; debts and sequestration; the West Indies trade; the definition of contraband; and Britain's determination to insure that her vessels would not again be preyed upon by French privateers in American waters as they had been during the ministry of Genet.[48] To King, he wrote that though he believed the treaty beneficial on the whole, he would be surprised if he entirely escaped censure; to Hamilton he wrote that, if this treaty were not ratified, he did not believe another could be negotiated. He told Washington who, unknown to Jay had already indicated his displeasure with some clauses, that the treaty must speak for itself and that confidence in Washington's character had been important to the success of the negotiation.[49]

Uppermost in Jay's mind, but understated in the long list of items in his instructions, was maintaining peace between the two nations.[50] He had, he told Randolph, made room for conciliation by doing "*essential* Justice," acknowledging to the British as he had already done to Americans the possibility that the United States could not always clearly claim that it had had right on its side, especially with regard to first violation of the treaty and British creditors. In the matters of the British removal of slaves, the degree to which neutral rights and definitions of contraband had been established in the law of nations, and the speed and terms under which British withdrawal from the posts could be expected, he had also admitted that the case made by Grenville was defensible, if not unassailable. He realized what others were reluctant to accept, that hopes for improvement of the conditions of trade between the United States and Britain had to be measured against Britain's maritime and economic power and Americans' lack of it; that concessions simply could not be forced. Jay was at his best when dealing with ambiguities in the peace treaty, where his involvement as negotiator gave him some authority, but even here, realities on the ground, the interests of British fur traders and their Indian allies, made it essential for him to accept terms that diminished the luster of the substantial benefits Americans realized from evacuation of the posts. The treaty was made possible by Britain's recent setbacks in the war against France and its determination to continue it until victory was achieved. It came to pass because both nations had an interest in not going to war with one another, not because Jay or the United States had a strong hand to play. American potential, so strongly believed in by Americans, did not weigh heavily in Britain's scale.

1. For JJ's reports on his initial interactions with Grenville and on his meeting with George III and Charlotte of Mecklenburg-Strelitz, see JJ to ER, 23 June, and 6–8 July 1794, both above; JJ to GW (private), 23 June 1794, above. On JJ's earlier experience as American minister attempting to negotiate unresolved treaty issues, see the editorial note "Anglo-American Relations," *JJSP*, 4: 33–41.

2. Trumbull, *Autobiography*, 181. James Bland Burges (1752–1824) was under-secretary of state in the Foreign Office.

3. On the cabinet reorganization and consultation with its members, see JJ to ER, 12 July 1794, above; JJ to GW, 21 July 1794, above; and JJ to Grenville, 30 July 1794, above; and the notes on various articles in JJ's Project for a Treaty with Great Britain, 30 Sept. 1794, below. For a complete discussion, see David Wilkinson, "The Pitt–Portland Coalition of 1794," 249–64.

4. Higginson found it difficult to find ships to carry his dispatches and soon succumbed to yellow fever. ER notified JJ of his death in a letter of 11 Aug., and subsequently informed him that some of the documentation he had collected, then in the possession of his widow, was being withheld from ER because it had come in a ship infected with yellow fever. ER later commented that Higginson's death had been "no small embarrassment to us," that his expenses had amounted to "no inconsiderable sum," that the results of his efforts had been "small," and that, because of the raging yellow fever epidemic in the West Indies, it had been impossible to find a suitable replacement for him. See ER to JJ, 11 Aug. 1794, ALS, DNA: Jay Despatches, 1794–95 (EJ: 04304); C, NHi: Jay (EJ: 00606); C, NHi: King (EJ: 04436); ER to JJ, 20 Sept. 1794, LS, DNA: Jay Despatches, 1794–95 (EJ: 04324); C, NHi: King (EJ: 04455); ER to JJ, 11, 13, 18, and 19 Oct. 1794, LS, DNA: Jay Despatches, 1794–95 (EJ: 04326); C, NHi: King (EJ: 04457); and *ASP: FR*, 1: 482–83, 497, 499.

5. See JJ to RK, 8 July 1794, ALS, NHi: King (EJ: 00758); King, *Life and Correspondence of Rufus King*, 1: 568–69; JJ to ER, 9 July 1794, LS, DNA: Jay Despatches, 1794–95 (EJ: 04275); C, NHi: King (EJ: 04423); *ASP: FR*, 1: 478–79, in which JJ reported that he had received correspondence containing acts of Congress but no information on ER's dealings with Hammond or on the expiration of the embargo Congress had imposed. JJ reported a meeting with Grenville on 11 July that addressed the hostilities perpetrated by Simcoe in JJ to ER, 12 July 1794, above; and JJ to GW, 21 July 1794, above.

In addition to the documentation sent under cover of ER's previous letters of 27 and 29 May 1794, ER continued to supply JJ with information on British spoliations. See ER to JJ, 9 June 1794, C, DNA: Jay Despatches, 1794–95 (EJ: 04267); C, NHi: King (EJ: 04412); 10 July 1794, C, DNA: Jay Despatches, 1794–95 (EJ: 04277); LS, NHi: Jay (EJ: 00604); C, NHi: King (EJ: 04424); C, NHi: Jay (EJ: 10076); 18 July 1794, C, NHi: Jay (EJ: 00605); C, NHi: King (EJ: 04427); C, DNA: Jay Despatches, 1794–95 (EJ: 04280); 15 Aug. 1794, ALS, DNA: Jay Despatches, 1795–95 (EJ: 04305); C, NHi: Jay (EJ: 00607); C, NHi: King (EJ: 04437); and 18 Aug. 1794, ALS, DNA: Jay Despatches, 1794–95 (EJ: 04306); C, NHi: Jay (EJ: 00624); NHi: King (EJ: 04438); *ASP: FR*, 1: 476–80, 482–83.

6. See JJ to ER, 6–8 July 1794, above.

7. For ER's continued complaints about the hostile activities of Lord Dorchester and Lieutenant Governor Simcoe, see ER to JJ, 18 Aug. 1794, ALS, DNA: Jay Despatches, 1794–95 (EJ: 04306); C, NHi: Jay (EJ: 00624); C, NHi: King (EJ: 04438); 30 Aug. 1794, ALS, DNA: Jay Despatches, 1794–95 (EJ: 04309); C, NHi: King (EJ: 04441); 5 Sept. 1794, C, NHi: King (EJ: 04442), which JJ transmitted to Grenville on 13 Oct. 1794, Hist. Mss. Comm., *Fortescue Manuscripts*, 3: 528–29 (EJ: 02683); 12 Sept. 1794, DNA: Jay Despatches, 1794–95 (EJ: 04310); C, NHi: King (EJ: 04443); C, NHi: Jay (EJ: 00608); 17 Sept. 1794, DNA: Jay Despatches, 1794–95 (EJ 04323); C, NHi: King (EJ: 04453); *ASP: FR*, 1: 483, 484, 485, 496.

8. See JJ to ER, 9 July 1794, ALS, DNA: Jay Despatches, 1794–95 (EJ: 04275); C, NHi: King (EJ: 04423), in which he acknowledged receipt of information on the events leading to ER's correspondence with Hammond and the expiration of the embargo. JJ informed ER that documentation on British attacks on American commerce and other relevant matters sent under cover of ER's letters of 27, 28, and 29 May and 8 June had arrived. JJ to ER, 12 July 1794, above; and 16 July, ALS, DNA: Jay Despatches, 1794–95 (EJ: 04279); C, NHi: King (EJ: 04426); *ASP: FR*, 1: 479–80. JJ acknowledged receipt of "thirty odd papers" to, from, and respecting Hammond, and announced he had a meeting with Grenville on 30 July. JJ to GW, 21 July 1794, above; JJ to ER, 30 July 1794, ALS, DNA: Jay Despatches, 1794–95 (EJ: 04282); C, NHi: King (EJ: 04428); *ASP: FR*, 1: 480.

9. In his instructions to JJ, ER held that provisions were never contraband. ER to JJ, 6 May, *JJSP*, 5: 640. While JJ could protest the practice of British depredations on American commerce, his ability to argue against the principle of Britain's definition of contraband, and her captures and confiscations of neutral shipping engaged in voyages to France or her colonies, was limited by the fact that Britain had never agreed to the interpretation of the law of nations that would have forbidden them. Present circumstances made it even more difficult for JJ to alter Britain's determination to hold to her interpretation of the law of nations with regard to neutral commerce and her broad definition of contraband, on which see Grenville to JJ, enclosing Responses to Queries, 7 Sept. 1794, below. The only means open to Britain, a naval power with a small army, to gain a military advantage over France's large army at a time when it was achieving considerable success in the Flanders campaign, was to exploit her dominant weakness, a dire shortage of supplies for the French army and population, somewhat alleviated recently in the course of the Glorious First of June, a naval battle in the course of which French merchant vessels loaded with provisions from the Chesapeake had slipped by the battling navies and made port. See PAJ to PJM, 22 June 1794, above.

10. See JJ to ER, 2 Aug. 1794, above.

11. See Grenville to JJ, 4 Aug. 1794, AL, NNC (EJ: 08522); 5 Aug. 1794, above, with the enclosed notes, where TJ to Hammond, 29 May 1792, the letter Grenville refers to here, is discussed. ER had enclosed it in JJ's instructions.

12. See Extracts from JJ's Report on Violations of the Treaty of Peace, 13 Oct. 1786, *JJSP*, 4: 417–33; and the editorial note, "The Jay Treaty: Appointment and Instructions," *JJSP*, 5: 609–21. For his report on this discussion, see JJ to ER, 13 Sept. 1794, below.

13. For the first statement of the decision to end discussion about first violations, later reiterated in the preface to JJ's Project for a Treaty with Great Britain, 30 Sept., below, see JJ's Draft for a Convention and Treaty of Commerce of 6 Aug. 1794, below. ER was very critical of this decision, especially since he believed it absolved the British from compensating American planters for slaves taken by the British. See JJ to ER, 13 Sept. 1794, below; ER to JJ, 3 Dec., LS (Duplicate), NHi: Jay (EJ: 00619); and 15 Dec. 1794, C, NHi: Jay (EJ: 00620); *ASP: FR*, 1: 509–12.

14. See JJ to Grenville, 6 Aug. 1794, below.

15. JJ did not delineate two separate treaties in his draft of 6 Aug., although his cover letter to Grenville of that date describes his presentation as an outline for a convention and a treaty of commerce. His instructions authorized him to conclude a treaty of commerce, but only if its conditions were sufficiently favorable and included the right of American vessels to participate in the carrying trade with the British West Indies. See ER to JJ, 6 May 1794, *JJSP*, 5: 636–47, especially 639–41. For JJ's involvement in earlier attempts to negotiate a treaty of commerce with Britain after negotiations for the peace treaty were concluded, see *JJSP*, 3: 373–88.

16. See JJ's Draft for a Convention and Treaty of Commerce, 6 Aug. 1794, below.

17. For his attempt to elicit a response, see JJ to Grenville, 16 Aug. 1794, below; and Grenville to JJ, 17 Aug. and 30 Aug. 1794, both below.

18. For his instructions to this effect, see ER to JJ, 6 May 1794, *JJSP*, 5: 636–47, esp. 638.

19. On 8 Aug., Grenville also ordered Hammond to improve his antagonistic relations with ER. See Perkins, "Hawkesbury," 291.

20. See Grenville to JJ, 8 Aug. 1794, ALS, NNC (EJ: 08529); and JJ to ER, 8 Aug. 1794, ALS, DNA: Jay Despatches, 1794–95 (EJ: 04288); C, NHi: King (EJ: 04434); and *ASP: FR*, 1: 482; JJ to Grenville, 16 Aug. 1794, below; and Grenville to JJ, 17 Aug. 1794, below. On the Order in Council, see JJ to Grenville, 30 July 1794, above.

21. For his suggestion that it would be desirable to have a treaty ready for Congress to consider in the session opening at the beginning of November, see JJ to Grenville, 6 Aug. 1794, below.

22. See JJ to ER, 23 Aug. 1794, ALS, DNA: Jay Despatches, 1794–95 (EJ: 04308); C, NHi: King (EJ: 04439). On the repercussions caused by Monroe's address to the French National Convention, and the presentation of letters from ER to the Committee of Public Safety, see ER to JJ (private), 12 Nov. 1794, below.

23. See Bemis, *Jay's Treaty*, 147–82.

24. For earlier concerns to maintain access for fur traders to the portages and to navigation on the lakes, see Mary A. Giunta et al., eds., *The Emerging Nation: A Documentary History of the Foreign Relations of the United States under the Articles of Confederation, 1780–1789* (3 vols.; Charlottesville and London, 1996), 2: 106, 474, 484. For pressures on Grenville to protect fur-trading interests, see Perkins, "Hawkesbury," 292.

25. See JJ's Objections to Grenville's Draft Treaty Proposals of 30 Aug., [6 Sept. 1794], below. None of these suggestions were incorporated into the Treaty of Amity, Commerce, and Navigation of 19 Nov. 1794.

26. See JJ's Draft for a Convention and Treaty of Commerce of 6 Aug., and Grenville's draft of a general treaty in his Draft Treaties of 30 Aug. 1794, both below.

27. See JJ to Grenville, 1 and 4 Sept. 1794, both below; and Grenville to JJ, 5 Sept. 1794, below.

28. See JJ's Objections to Grenville's Draft Treaty Proposals of 30 Aug., [6 Sept. 1794], below; and Grenville to JJ (private), 7 Sept. 1794, below.

29. Several days later, JJ informed ER that he thought the business of the northwestern boundary could be managed so as not to be an obstacle to an agreement, as indeed it was managed. See JJ to ER, 14 Sept. 1794, ALS, DNA: Jay Despatches, 1794–95 (EJ: 04320); C, NHi: King (EJ: 04452);

ASP: FR, 1: 496; and JJ's Project for a Treaty with Great Britain, 30 Sept. 1794, below, at Art. 3; and note 33, below.

30. See Grenville to JJ (private), 7 Sept. 1794, below; JJ to Grenville (private), 7 Sept. 1794, below; and JJ to ER (private), 13 Sept. 1794, below.

31. See Art. 3 of JJ's Project for a Treaty with Great Britain, 30 Sept. 1794, below.

32. See JJ to ER, 18 Sept. 1794, ALS, DNA: Jay Despatches, 1794–95 (EJ: 04322); C, NHi: King (EJ: 04454); *ASP: FR*, 1: 496–97; and Art. 6 of JJ's Project for a Treaty with Great Britain, 30 Sept. 1794, below. A lively American trade with the East Indies was already under way, but without official sanction. See Art. 14 of JJ's Project for a Treaty with Great Britain, 30 Sept., below. On Dundas's approval of the concessions made on the East India trade, see Perkins, "Hawkesbury," 292.

33. No explanation for this decision has been found. JJ informed ER of it in JJ to ER, 2 Oct. 1794, ALS, DNA: Jay Despatches, 1794–95 (EJ: 04325); C, NHi: King (EJ: 04456); and *ASP: FR*, 1: 498. In the midst of these discussions, JJ and PAJ spent the weekend of 19–21 September at Grenville's seat at Dropmore, outside of London. Also in attendance were Loughborough (the Lord Chancellor), and other notables. See PAJ Diary A, AD, NNC; and the editorial note "John Jay's Mission to London," above.

34. For the text of a report from Hawkesbury, which, since it objects to some of the new articles JJ proposed, was probably given to Grenville between 30 Sept. and 7 Oct., see Perkins, "Hawkesbury," 291–304.

35. See JJ to Grenville, 7 Oct. 1794, ALS, UK-KeNA: FO 95/512 (EJ: 05007); Dft, NNC (EJ: 08501); and Grenville to JJ, 7 Oct. 1794, ALS, NNC (EJ: 08534). For the new material introduced by JJ, see Arts. 12 through 22 of his Project for a Treaty with Great Britain, 30 Sept. 1794, below. On review of the treaty draft by JQA and Pinckney, see JQA Diaries, 20–22 Oct. 1794, vol. 21, MHi: Adams; *JQA Diaries Digital*, http://www.masshist.org/jqadiaries/php/doc?id=jqad21_40 (accessed Aug. 2019). JQA recorded his assessment of the Treaty as reported to JJ and noted on 22 Oct.: "It is far from being satisfactory to those Gentlemen; it is much below the standard which I think would be advantageous to the Country, but with some alterations, which are marked down, and to which it seems there is a probability they will consent it is in the opinion of the two plenipotentiaries, preferable to a War."

36. See JJ to ER, 29 Oct. 1794, DNA: ALS, Jay Despatches, 1794–95 (EJ: 04329); and C, NHi: King (EJ: 04460). The *Morning Post* of London reported cabinet meetings on 20 and 22 Oct. to discuss the treaty negotiations. See Perkins, "Hawkesbury," 292n4.

37. This draft has not been found, but was probably based on decisions made in the cabinet meetings noted above.

38. See Art. 1 of Grenville's draft of a general treaty in his Draft Treaties, 30 Aug. 1794, and Art. 9 of JJ's Project for a Treaty with Great Britain, 30 Sept. 1794, both below. Art. 3 of the Treaty of Amity, Commerce, and Navigation of 19 Nov. 1794 provided that duties paid by British subjects would be no higher than those paid by American citizens. Peltries and Indians' goods were to be exempt from duties.

39. See Art. 3 of Grenville's draft of a commercial treaty in his Draft Treaties, 30 Aug. 1794, and Art. 11 of JJ's Project for a Treaty with Great Britain, 30 Sept. 1794, both below. These matters were discussed on 24 and 28 October.

40. See Art. 3 of JJ's Project for a Treaty with Great Britain, 30 Sept. 1794, below.

41. For Grenville's reasons for refusing to advance the date, see JJ to ER, 19 Nov. 1794, below.

42. See Art. 2 of JJ's Project for a Treaty with Great Britain, 30 Sept. 1794, below.

43. See JJ to Grenville, 27 Oct. 1794, ALS, UK-KeNA: FO 95/512 (EJ: 05008); Dft, UKWC-A (EJ: 00046); C, DNA: Jay Despatches, 1794–95, two copies (EJ: 04330; EJ: 04336); C, NHi: King

(EJ: 04461); and Tr, NNC (EJ: 08503); *ASP: FR*, 1: 500. For his acknowledgment of this letter, see Grenville to JJ, 30 Oct. 1794, LS, NNC (EJ: 08535); C, UK-KeNA: FO 95/512 (EJ: 05009); C, DNA: Jay Despatches, 1794–95 (EJ: 04337).

44. See JJ to ER, 29 Oct. 1794, ALS, DNA: Jay Despatches, 1794–95 (EJ: 04329); C, NHi: King (EJ: 04460); and *ASP: FR*, 1: 500.

45. See Grenville to JJ, 31 Oct. 1794, ALS, NNC (EJ: 08536); C, UK-KeNA: FO 95/512 (EJ: 05010); and JJ to Grenville, 1 Nov. 1794, ALS, UK-KeNA: FO 95/512 (EJ: 05011). JJ to ER, 5 Nov. 1794, ALS, DNA: Jay Despatches, 1794–95 (EJ: 04331)

46. See Grenville to JJ, 10 Nov. 1794, AL, NNC (EJ: 08537); JJ to Grenville, 11 Nov. 1794, ALS, UK-KeNA: FO 95/512 (EJ: 05013); JJ to ER, 17 Nov. 1794, ALS, partially encoded, marked duplicate, DNA: Jay Despatches, 1794–95 (EJ: 04335); and George III, Commission to Grenville to Treat and Conclude a Treaty with JJ, 17 Nov. 1794, C, NHi.

47. The treaty did not reach Philadelphia until 7 Mar. 1795, several days after Congress had adjourned. GW kept its terms secret until Congress convened on 8 June, by which time JJ himself had returned. See the editorial note "Aftermath of the Jay Treaty," below.

48. See Grenville's Draft Treaties of 30 Aug. 1794, and JJ's Project for a Treaty with Great Britain, 30 Sept. 1794, both below; harsher criticism of the draft treaties would later arrive in ER to JJ, 15 Dec. 1794, C, NHi: (EJ: 00620); and *ASP: FR*, 1: 509–12. See also JJ to ER, 19 Nov. 1794, below.

49. See JJ to RK, 19 Nov. 1794, below; JJ to AH, 19 Nov. 1794, UkWC-A (EJ: 00049); JJ to GW, 19 Nov. 1794, ALS, DNA: Jay Despatches, 1794–95 (EJ: 10638); Dft, NNC (EJ: 08454); ER to JJ, 15 Dec. 1794, C, NHi: (EJ: 00620); and *ASP: FR*, 1: 509–12.

50. ER did not instruct JJ to strive to establish friendly relations with Britain. Instead, he described one of the purposes of JJ's mission as "to repel war," for which the United States was "not disposed," but to which it might be driven by the need to vindicate its honor. See ER to JJ, 6 May 1794, *JJSP*, 5: 636–47.

To Grenville

[[Royal Hotel, London] 6 Augt. 1794]

M^r. Jay presents his respectful Compliments to Lord Grenville and encloses some Outlines for a Convention & Treaty of Commerce.[1] Some of them appear to him questionable— more mature Reflection and the Light which usually springs from mutual Discussions may occasion alterations— Many of the *common* articles are omitted—& will be inserted of course. It is very desireable that it may be concluded in Season to arrive about the 1st. of Nov^r—[2]

ALS, UK-BL: Dropmore, Ms 59049. Endorsed: ". . . Incl^{re}—". Dft, NNC (EJ: 08493); C, DNA: Jay Despatches, 1794–95 (EJ: 04313); C, NHi: King (EJ: 04445).

1. See JJ's Draft for a Convention and Treaty of Commerce, 6 Aug. 1794, below.

2. The date on which JJ anticipated the next session of Congress to open. See JJ to Grenville, 16 Aug. 1794, below.

John Jay's Draft for a Convention and Treaty of Commerce

[London, 6 August 1794]

Whereas between His Majesty the King of G. Britain and the united States of America, there do exist mutual Complaints and consequent Claims, originating as well in certain articles of their Treaty of Peace, as in the Laws of Nations relative to the respective Rights of belligerent and neutral nations.

And whereas both the said Parties being sincerely desirous to establish permanent Peace & ~~Harmony &~~ Friendship, by a Convention that may be so satisfactory and reciprocally advantageous, have respectively empowered their undersigned Ministers to treat of and conclude the same

And whereas the said Ministers find it impossible, to admit the said mutual complaints and Claims of the *first Description*, to be well founded, in their existing Extent— and to the End that the obstacles to concord and agreement which thence arise, may be done away.

They have agreed that all the said complaints and Claims, shall be forever merged and sunk in the following articles vizt.[1]

The Boundaries of the united States as delineated in the said Treaty of Peace, and every Article in the said Treaty contained, are hereby recognized ratified and forever confirmed. But inasmuch as the Parties differ as to which is the River intended by the Treaty, and therein called the River S^t. Croix It is agreed that the said Question shall be referred to the final Decision of Commissioners to be appointed and empowered as follows vizt.[2]

Whereas it is doubtful whether the River Missisippi extends so far to the Northward, as to be intersected by the west Line, from the Lake of the Woods, which is mentioned in the said Treaty— It is agreed that [~~if on Examin?~~] the actual Extent of the said River to the northward shall be explored & ascertained by Commissioners for that purpose to be appointed and authorized as follows vizt.[3]

It is agreed that if from the Report of the said commissioners it shall appear that the said River does not extend so far to the Northward as to be intersected by the West Line aforesaid, ~~that~~ by Reason whereof the Boundary Lines of the united States in that Quarter would not close, that then and forthwith thereupon such a closing Line shall be established as shall be adjudged and determined to be most consistant with the true Intent and meaning of the said Treaty by Commissioners to be appointed and authorized in the manner prescribed in the article relative to those who are to decide which is the River S^t. Croix intended by the said Treaty—with these Differences only vizt.

It is agreed that his Majesty shall withdraw all his Troops and Garrisons from every Post and Place within the Limits of the united States,[4] by the first Day of June next;[5] And that all settlers & Traders within the Precincts or Commands of the said Posts and Garrisons, shall continue to have and enjoy unmolested all their Property of every kind and Shall be protected therein — and may either remain and become Citizens of the united States, or may sell their Land ~~and~~ ∧or∧ other property, and remove with their Effects, at any Time within two Years from the *first* Day of June next.[6]

It is agreed that his Majesty will cause full and compleat Satisfaction and Compensation for all Vessels and Property of American Citizens which have been ~~illegally~~ or during the Course of the present War shall be illegally captured and condemned under Colour of Authority and Commissions derived from him,[7] and that, in all Cases where it shall be apparent full Justice and Compensation cannot be obtained and actually had in the ordinary Course of judicial proceedings— and for this purpose Commissioners Shall be appointed and empowered in manner following vizt.[8]

And whereas Debts bona fide contracted before the peace, and remaining unpaid by american Debtors to British Creditors, have probably in some Instances been prejudiced and rendered more precarious by the lawful Impediments which after the peace did for some Time exist to their being prosecuted and recovered.

It is agreed that in all Cases where it shall be apparent that the said Creditors by the operation of the said Impediments on the Security & Value of their Debts, have sustained Damage ~~the united States will render full and compleat Satisfaction and Compensation to the said Creditors for the~~ for which adequate Reparation cannot now be ~~had in the ordin~~ obtained and actually had in the ordinary course of judicial proceedings, (it being understood that in these Damages Interest shall be encluded only in Cases where according to Equity & good Conscience all things being considered, it ought to be allowed and paid) the united States will make full and compleat satisfaction and Compensation to the said Creditors for the same. And for this purpose Commissioners shall be appointed and authorized in the manner prescribed in the preceeding Article with these Differences only vizt.[9]

It is agreed that ~~further~~ it shall and may be lawful for the ∧said∧ united States and their Citizens, to carry in their own Vessels of the Burden of 100 Tons or under, from the said united States any Goods Wares and Merchandizes, which [~~illegible~~] ∧British∧ Vessels ~~to~~ ∧now∧ carry from the united States, ∧[*in margin*] and also∧ to any of his Majestys Islands and Ports in the West Indies, and shall pay in the said Islands and ports only such Rate of

Tonnage as british Vessels do or shall be liable to ∧pay∧ in the united States, and only such other charges Imposts and Duties as British Vessels and Cargoes ∧laden in &∧ arriving from the united States, now are or hereafter shall be lawfully liable to in the said Islands and ports. And that it shall and may be lawful for the said american Vessels to ~~lade~~ purchase lade and carry away from the said Islands and ports all such of the Productions and manufactures of the said Islands as they may think proper, & paying only such Duties and charges ~~as british~~ ∧on Exportation∧ as such vessels and cargoes if british would be liable to Provided always that they carry and land the same in the united States only, and at no place whatever out of the same It being expressly agreed and declared that West India Productions or Manufactures shall not be transported in american Vessels, either from his Majestys said Islands, or from the united States, to any part of the world except the united States— reasonable Sea Stores excepted and excepting also Rum made in the united States from West India Molasses.[10]

It is agreed, that all the ∧other∧ Ports ~~of~~ ∧&∧ Territories of his Majesty ∧whatsoever & wheresoever∧ (not comprehended within ∧[~~the west In~~?]∧ the Limits of his chartered trading Companies) shall be free and open to the citizens ∧~~and vess~~∧ of the united States, and that they and their Vessels and cargoes shall therein enjoy all the commercial Rights and pay only the same Duties & charges either on Importation or Exportation as if they were British ~~Subjects~~ ∧Merchants∧ vessels and Cargoes, except that they shall pay the same Rate of Tonnage ∧as may be∧ charged on British Vessels in the united States—[~~illegible~~] and on the other Hand It is agreed that all the Ports and Territories of the united States without Exception shall be free and open to British Merchants and Subjects, and that they and their Vessels and Cargoes shall therein enjoy all the commercial Rights and pay only the same Duties and Charges (Tonnage excepted) as if they were american Merchants ∧Vessels &∧ Cargoes— It being the Intention of this article that in his Majestys Territories (except as before excepted) american Merchants ~~and~~ and Merchant Vessels shall be exactly on the same footing with British merchants and merchant Vessels, and that British Merch^ts and merch^t Vessels shall in all the [~~form~~?] Territories of the U.S. be exactly on the same Footing with American Merch^ts. & merch^t Vessels[11] (~~Tonnage only excepted~~)

~~With Respect to~~

The Trade between the united States and the british west Indies shall be considered as regulated and explained by the preceeding Article, and therefore as being excluded from the operation of the following articles—

It is agreed that all the Productions and Manufactures of his Majestys Dominions in any part of the world [~~illegible~~] may freely be imported in British or american Vessels into the united States, subject equally ∧and alike∧ to the Duties on Importation which may there be established and that all the Productions & Manufactures of the united States may be freely imported in American or british Vessels into any of the said Dominions of his majesty subject equally to the [same?] Duties on Importation which may there be established—

And to the End that these Duties may be made reciprocal It is agreed that additional Articles for that purpose shall be negociated and added to this Convention as soon as may be conveniently done—

1st It is agreed that when Great Britain is at war and the united States neutral, no Prizes taken from or by Great Britain shall be sold in the united States and that when the united States are at War and *the united States*[12] neutral, no Prizes Taken from or by the united ∧States∧ shall be sold in his majestys Dominions.[13]

It is agreed that if it should unfortunately happen that Great Britain and the United States ∧should be at war∧, there shall be no Privateers commissioned by them against each other,[14] and that the merchants and others residing in each other Countries shall be allowed nine months to retire with the Effects, and ~~the vessels in which~~ shall not be liable to capture in there way Home to their respective Countries

It is agreed that British Subjects who now hold Lands in ~~America~~ the United States, and american Citizens who now hold Lands in His Majestys Dominions shall continue to hold them according to the Nature and Tenure of their Estates & Titles therein, and may grant ~~Leas~~ and sell and devise the same ~~in li~~ as, and to whom, they please, in like manner as if they were natives; and that neither they nor their Heirs or assigns shall so far as may respect the said Lands and the legal Remedies incident thereto, be regarded as aliens—

It is agreed that ∧neither∧ Debts due from Individuals of the one Nation to Individuals of the other, nor shares or monies which they may have in the funds or in the public or private Banks, shall ever in any Event of War or national Differences be sequestered or confiscated— except that in Case of War ∧and only during its Continuance∧ payment may be suspended— it being both unjust and impolitic that Debts and Engagements contracted and made by Individls having Confidence in each other and in their respective Governments, should ever be ~~a~~ destroyed or impaired by national Authority on account of national Differences and Discontents[15]—

AD, UK-KeNA: FO 95/512 (EJ: 04990). CS, DNA: Jay Despatches, 1794–95 (EJ: 04313); NHi: King (EJ: 04445); UK-BL: Liverpool Papers, xi; C, unknown repository, formerly PRO (EJ: 03991); LbkC, in JJ to ER, 13 Sept. 1794, NNC: JJ Lbk. 8.

1. On the implications of this decision, see the editorial note "Negotiating the Jay Treaty," above.

2. As secretary for foreign affairs JJ had previously proposed settling this boundary by commission to Congress. See JJ's Report on the Eastern Boundary of the United States, 21 Apr. 1785, *JJSP*, 4: 74–77. Grenville's draft of a general treaty in his Draft Treaties of 30 Aug. 1794, below, also provided for determining which river was the intended St. Croix by commission. JJ did not here discuss how the commissioners were to be appointed and empowered. The first part of Art. 2 of Grenville's draft of a general treaty detailed how the commissioners were to be appointed and specified that their final decision was to be made "in *London*." For revisions to this decision, see Art. 3 of JJ's Project for a Treaty with Great Britain, 30 Sept. 1794, below.

3. See the second part of Art. 2 of Grenville's draft of a general treaty in his Draft Treaties of 30 Aug. 1794, which delineated a boundary designed to ensure that the British had direct access to the Mississippi River. For his response, see JJ to Grenville, 1 and 4 Sept. 1794, both below; Grenville to JJ, 5 Sept. 1794, below; and Art. 3 of JJ's Project for a Treaty with Great Britain, 30 Sept. 1794, below.

4. For the decision to end discussion about whether British retention of the posts constituted the first violation of the Treaty of 1783, a charge rejected in Grenville to JJ (private), and note 2, and Grenville's Notes Respecting the Posts, and note 2, both 5 Aug. 1794, both above.

5. Grenville's draft of a general treaty in his Draft Treaties of 30 Aug. 1794 specified that withdrawal would occur by 1 June 1796, by which time, he anticipated, the treaty would have been ratified by both parties. He specified that measures to evacuate the posts and deliver them to the Americans would be jointly agreed upon. For discussion of this issue, see Art. 1 of JJ's Project for a Treaty with Great Britain, 30 Sept. 1794, below.

6. See Art. 1 of Grenville's draft of a general treaty in his Draft Treaties of 30 Aug. 1794, and Art. 2 of JJ's Project for a Treaty with Great Britain, 30 Sept. 1794, both below; neither of which set a limit on the amount of time to be allowed for selling property or removing effects. Grenville's draft did not discuss the issue of citizenship.

7. On the unauthorized establishment of admiralty courts in the West Indies by the commander of the British expedition, see ER to JJ, 6 May 1794, *JJSP*, 5: 636–47; and Fewster, "British Ship Seizures," 431–32.

8. See Art. 4 of Grenville's draft of a general treaty in his Draft Treaties of 30 Aug. 1794, and Art. 5 of JJ's Project for a Treaty with Great Britain, 30 Sept. 1794, both below.

9. See Art. 3 of Grenville's draft of a general treaty in his Draft Treaties of 30 Aug. 1794, and Art. 6 of JJ's Project for a Treaty with Great Britain, 30 Sept. 1794, both below.

10. For Britain's rejection of the possibility of reciprocal trade and admission of American vessels to trade with the West Indies during negotiations for a commercial treaty in 1783, in which JJ was involved, see *JJSP*, 3: 373–88. For development of an article on admitting the United States to trade with the British West Indies, see Art. 10 of JJ's Project for a Treaty with Great Britain, 30 Sept. 1794, below.

11. JJ's instructions supposed a treaty to deal with compensation for British depredations on American trade and issues still outstanding from the peace treaty of 1783 and a separate treaty of commerce if the above issues could be satisfactorily resolved. Grenville's Draft Treaties of 30 Aug. 1794 also presented commercial issues as in a separate treaty. On the decision to merge the two treaties, see JJ's Project for a Treaty with Great Britain, 30 Sept. 1794, below.

12. In margin, in another hand: "Great Britain".

13. On the sale of prizes, see Art. 23 of JJ's Project for a Treaty with Great Britain, 30 Sept. 1794, below.

14. For objections to this provision, see ER to JJ, 12 Nov. 1794, *ASP: FR*, 1: 502; and 15 Dec. 1794, C, NHi: Jay (EJ: 00620); *ASP: FR*, 1: 510.

15. For AH's suggestion that banning sequestration of debts might be an incentive for Britain to conclude a treaty, see AH to JJ, 6 May 1794, *JJSP*, 5: 632. For inclusion of this provision in subsequent drafts of the treaty, see Art. 10 of Grenville's draft of a general treaty in his Draft Treaties of 30 Aug. 1794, below; and Art. 8 of JJ's Project for a Treaty with Great Britain, 30 Sept. 1794, below.

To George Washington

London, 11 Augt. 1794

Dear Sir

The Letter herewith enclosed from M^r. Wangenheim[1] came to me enclosed from him, requesting me to transmit it to You— it was and now is, without a cover— of this Gentleman I have no Knowledge or information but from these Letters. I have written to him, that the Issue of his application to You could not be foreseen; but that as the united States interposed no Impediments to Emigrants, so on the other Hand, their Governm^t. offered no particular Gratifications or Inducements. many applications of the like kind are almost daily made, some by Frenchmen & others here. I uniformly give them the same answer. The spirit of Emigration to our Country becomes more and more diffused. Certain Resolutions from N. Carolina and Kentucky are here— they do no Good.

The Sentiments expressed by M^r. Fox relative to your administration are not singular here—[2] I have frequently heard the same from important Characters opposed to him in Politics— A War with us would be very unpopular, unless we provoked it— I expect soon to write to You again. I have the Honor to be with perfect Respect Esteem and Attachm^t. Dear Sir Your Obligated & ob^t. Servt

John Jay

Presid. of U.S.—

ALS, DLC: Washington (EJ: 10631). Dft, NNC (EJ: 08451); *PGW: PS*, 16: 548–49.

1. On Karl August Freiherr von Wangenheim (1773–1850) and his letter to GW of 10 Feb. 1794, see *PGW: PS*, 15: 209–13; for GW's response to JJ, see GW to JJ, 1–4 Nov. 1794, ALS, NNC (EJ: 07256); Dft, DLC: Washington (EJ: 10637); *PGW: PS*, 17: 125–29.

2. A speech given in Parliament by Charles James Fox on 21 Jan. 1794. See *PGW: PS*, 16: 549.

To John Sloss Hobart

London 12 Aug[t]. 1794

my good Friend

I wrote you by Cap[t]. Kemp,[1] and by him returned a cask of your bottled ~~Red streake~~ ∧cyder∧, which I hope you will recieve in good order.[2]

I passed this morning in a visit to S[r]. John Sinclair Presid[t]. of the Board of Agriculture,[3] and Col. Bentham[4] who is preparing for the Establishm[t]. of a panopticon agreable to the plan delineated in a publication which I once communicated to You—[5]

The agricultural Society is incorporated with a yearly allowance by Gov[t]. of three thousand pounds a Year— Their plans are extensive they have been singularly industrious, and much has ~~already~~ been done— I enclose you the proposed Plan of their general Report—[6] if executed in the Extent and in the Manner intended, it will be the most interesting work of the kind respecting Husbandry which has appeared in any Country—

S[r]. John shewed us Sheep of ~~the~~ different Breeds stuffed and prepared in the highest Degree of Perfection— of these drawings are making— models are collecting of the most useful, ∧~~utensils &~~∧ Machines— among them is one for cleaning Grain from the Straw, which by the help of two Horses a Man and a Boy will ~~compleat~~ ∧do∧ 70 or 80 Bushells p[r] Day— They begin to be in use among the Farmers, which I consider as a Proof of their answering the Purpose—

Among the Sheep the Teasewater[7] is the largest— S[r]. John shewed me a Fleece presented to the Board which weighs twenty odd pounds— He tells me they frequently weigh sixty pounds a Quarter—

~~Advice~~ from ~~Switzerland~~ ∧Saxony∧ ∧he is∧ inform[d]. ~~him~~ that the Spanish Breed had been imported there—that they succeeded well, and did not degenerate— They sent him a sample of the Wool— I enclose ~~you~~ a Lock of it— ~~I think~~ this fact ~~interesting it~~ shews that the Fineness of wool depends not less on Breed than on management.[8]

S[r] John has a Farm in Scotland which rented for £300 a Year— it was employed in raising store Cattle, which were ∧usually∧ sold into England and fattened for the London Market— He ~~swept off~~ ∧dismissed∧ the Cattle and introduced Sheep— it proved ~~so~~ profitable ~~that~~ ∧&∧ he is now offered £1200 a Year for it— his flock is 3000—

the Progress of Husbandry in this Country is astonishing— the King patronizes it, and is himself a great Farmer— He has been doing ~~great Things~~ ∧much∧ in that Way at Windsor

Col. Bentham[9] has invented a Number of curious and very useful Machines intended to be introduced into the Panopticon— He shewed us a Model of the Building— it seems admirably calculated for its purposes—

He has a Machine for sawing at once ∧from a plank∧ the Felley[10] of a Wheel to its Form— ∧~~from a plank~~∧ another ∧Contrivance∧ for cutting it to its proper Length & angle— another for finishing ~~at one Operation~~ the Spoke— another for boring and morticing the Hub— another for driving the Spokes— He has one for turning a circular Saw, for ~~fine~~ ∧small∧ work— another for making the Mouldings if they may be so called, ∧the pieces∧ on ~~Sash work~~ ∧was wʰ.∧ form Sashes— others for working different kinds of Saws∧ ~~another~~ ∧one∧ for sawing Stone ∧into many Slabs at once∧— another for polishing them— another for plaining boards and taking a Shaving of its full width from one End to the other— &ᶜ &ᶜ &ᶜᵃ He has patents for these Machines, but as yet they cannot be ~~had~~ ∧purchased∧— he has ~~a useful~~ one for cutting Corks with incredible Expedition

~~I dined lately with~~ Govʳ. Hunter[11] from Norfolk Island ∧with whom I was last Week in Company∧ speaking of its Productions ~~he~~ mentioned that among ~~its~~ ∧the∧ Birds there were swans that were black, having only a few white Feathers in the wings— They are plenty— one stuffed and well preserved I am told is here— as yet I have not seen it— He also mentioned a wild Flax growing on ~~dry Ground~~ ∧upland∧ to about ~~near four~~ ∧three∧ feet high, and good— I do not yet learn that any of the Seed of it is here—

They who have Leisure and a Turn for these things might here acquire much ~~interesting~~ ∧entertaining & some useful∧ Information— want of Time represses my Curiosity and will not allow me to pay much attention to objects unconnected with those of my Mission— I am Dʳ Sir Your affecᵗᵉ. Friend & Servᵗ.

John Jay

Remember me to Mʳˢ Hobart— & yʳ. Neighbours at Throggs Neck Judge Hobart

Dft, NNC (EJ: 08895). *WJ,* 2: 222–24; *HPJ,* 4: 46–49.

1. Letter not found.

2. PAJ wrote to Hobart about apples and grating on 13 Mar. 1795, Dft, NyRyJHC.

3. The Jays dined with Sinclair at Robert Herries's on 9 Aug. 1794. Sinclair invited both Jays to see "a great number of curious machines", but only JJ was able to make the visit. PAJ Diary A, AD, NNC. See also Sinclair's formal invitation to JJ, 11 Aug. 1794, ALS, NNC (EJ: 07140), and JJ's reply of the same date, Dft, NNC (EJ: 08894).

4. Samuel Bentham, already involved in engineering steam mills, was involved in realizing his brother's design, see note 5, below. Financial considerations prevented Samuel and Jeremy from achieving completion. See Alexander Taylor Milne, ed., *The Correspondence of Jeremy Bentham* vol. 5 *January 1794 to December 1797* (London: 1981), 74–76; and the editorial note John Jay's Mission to London, note 11, above.

5. Letter not found. Probably referring to Jeremy Bentham, *Panopticon: or, the inspection-house. Containing the idea of a new principle of construction applicable to any sort of establishment, in which persons . . . are to be kept . . . and in particular to penitentiary–houses, prisons. . . . In a series of letters, written in . . . 1787* (Dublin, 1791).

6. Enclosure not found. In his note to Sinclair of 11 Aug., JJ commented that he had read the plan of the General Report of the Board of Agriculture and that "To see one of the most useful of the arts of peace making such Progress in the Course of such a war, is uncommon as well as pleasing.—"

7. Teeswater is a breed of long-wool sheep also raised for meat. *OED.*

8. In his reply of 16 Oct. 1794, Hobart commented that "Your visit to Sʳ. John Sinclair was truly a feast!" ALS, NNC (EJ: 05676).

9. PAJ and JT would also see Samuel Bentham's inventions during a day visit on 11 Sept., followed that evening by dinner with both Bentham brothers, with JJ present, but leaving early. Viewing Bentham's inventions led PAJ to remark that "their effects are so surprizing that one would think it almost impossible to be produced by Machinery, yet when you see the very simple principles upon which they act you are angry with yourself for not discovering them at once." PAJ Diary A, AD, NNC. JJ and PAJ would also dine with Jeremy Bentham on 20 March 1795. PAJ Diary C, AD, NNC.

10. Felly refers to the curved pieces of wood which, joined together, form the circular rim of a wheel. *OED.*

11. John Hunter (1728–93), naval officer and colonial governor. In 1786, Hunter was the second captain under Arthur Phillip of the *Sirius*, the frigate that accompanied the first fleet of convict transports to Botany Bay. The ship did not return to England as originally planned. In 1790, Hunter was sent with a company of marines and convicts to Norfolk Island, where it was hoped they could support themselves. He returned to England in 1792. In 1794, he was appointed governor of New South Wales, leaving in February 1795 and returning in 1800. *ODNBO.* The Jays met Hunter at a dinner at Grenville's on 8 Aug. 1794. PAJ Diary A, AD, NNC.

To Grenville

Royal Hotel— pall Mall 16 Augᵗ. 1794—

My Lord

Circumstanced as I am, and as my Country is, it cannot be easy, nor would it be right, if possible, entirely to exclude from my mind the Sollicitude which naturally results from the very delicate and responsible Situation in which I am placed— it is delicate and responsible, not only with Respect to myself, but to those who placed me in it—

The Average Length of Voyages from hence to Philadelphia & New York, I understand, is between six and Seven Weeks. The Congress meets the first Monday in november; and of their punctuality there is no Room for Doubt.

The President must be exceedingly anxious to insert in his *Speech* something satisfactory and decisive relative to our negociation— it will be expected from him. The Effects of a Disappointment appear to me in a Point of Light, which fills my Mind with anxiety to obviate it.

Will not the Materials contained in the informal Notes which I had the Honor of enclosing to your Lordship, enable us to come to a speedy Conclusion? It gives me pain to press your Lordship— I have no other appology for it, but the Motives which impell me; and which I flatter myself will not appear less cogent to your Lordship, than they do to me[1]— with sincere Respect and Esteem I have the Honor to be My Lord Your Lordships most obed[t]. & h'ble Servant

John Jay

The Right Honorable Lord Grenville

ALS, UK-KeNA: FO 95/512 (EJ: 04991). C, UK-KeNA: FO 95/512 (EJ: 03992).

1. For JJ's previous request for a response by 1 Nov., see his letter to Grenville and Draft for a Convention and Treaty of Commerce, both 6 Aug. 1794, both above. For his reply, see Grenville to JJ, 17 Aug. 1794, below.

To Alexander Hamilton

London 16 Aug[t]. 1794

Dear Sir

I am happy to find by a new York paper, that the Result of the late Inquiry into your official conduct is perfectly consistent with the Expectations of your Friends. it is there represented as being voluminous, and in a variety of Respects interesting— Be so good as to send me a copy.[1] I wrote to you lately a confidential Letter, under Cover to the President. my Dispatches to M[r] Randolph were under the same cover.[2] I presumed that if the Vessel should be examined by some rude privateer, more Respect would be paid to a Letter directed to the President, than to others.

Nothing very important has since occurred— Things are in a Train that *looks* promising; but the Issue is of Course uncertain. The Resolutions from Kentucky[3] and N. Carolina are here;[4] and make disagreable Impressions. Incivilities as often produce Resentment as Injuries do—

Affairs in Europe wear a serious Aspect— The french continue Successful, and the English decided— it is thought the Dutch will resign to their Fate without very strenuous Opposition. Geneva is undergoing another Revolution. News of Robespierres [vio]lent Death, has arrived and gains Credit.[5] If

true, the [Impo]rtance of it to France or the allies cannot yet be calculated—
[Such] Events have hitherto been more common than influencial— Yours
Sincerely

John Jay

ALS (torn), DLC: Hamilton (EJ: 10767). DftS, from which a conjectural reading was made to supplement ALS, NNC (EJ: 05647). *PAH*, 17: 97–99.

1. On the congressional investigation of AH on charges that he had procured discounts or credits
for himself or others from the Bank of the United States or the Bank of New York on the basis of
public monies deposited there under his direction, and that he had illegally drawn on monies bor-
rowed in Europe to the United States, see *PAH*, 16: 494–95.

2. See JJ to AH, 18 July–[5 Aug.] 1794, ALS, DLC: Hamilton (EJ: 10766); *PAH*, 16: 608–9, probably sent with other dispatches under cover of JJ to GW, 5 Aug. 1794, above. In it JJ commented
"appearances continue to be singularly favorable; but appearances merit only a certain degree of
circumspect Reliance." He had much reason to expect, he added, that the outcome of his negotiations would be satisfactory, but admitted he was apprehensive that "certain points not by us to be
yeilded will occasion Difficulties hard to surmount."

3. A meeting of citizens from Kentucky on 24 May 1794, had resolved "That the injuries and insults done and offered by Great Britain to America, call loudly for redress. That the recent appointment of the enemy of the Western country to negotiate with that nation, and the tame submission
of the general government, when we alone were injured by Great Britain, make it highly necessary,
that we should at this time state our just demands to the President and Congress." The resolution
was published in *Gazette of the United States* (Philadelphia), 23 June 1794. See also *PAH*, 16: 588–89.

4. The North Carolina resolution condemned British spoliations on American trade with the
West Indies, demanded that Britain should immediately surrender the western posts, commended
the policy of sequestering debts, cheered French victories, and threatened to attack the British-held
posts in the west. See *PAH*, 17: 97–98.

5. Robespierre was guillotined on 28 July 1794.

To Sarah Livingston Jay

London 16 aug^t. 1794

my dear Sally,

By the Hope Capt. Haley[1] I have written to You, to Peter, and to Gussy—
these Letters were all under one Cover directed to you, I also wrote by the
same Vessel to Judge Hobart[2]

This is intended to go by the Belvedere Capt. Depeyster—[3] It is uncertain
which of the two vessels will arrive first, & therefore I write by both—

M^{rs}. Johnson has sent to me two Bracelets and two pins which Peter by
~~your~~ ʌPolly'sʌ Desire requested her to have made— I think them neat, and
am at a Loss whether to send them now, or bring them with me— for the
present I believe I will keep them, and wait upon orders, which shall be punctually executed—[4]

I heard a few Days ago that our Friend Grand had removed into Switzerland— I wish it may be true—for Peace and Tranquility are best adapted to his Age and delicate Health— If I should learn where he resides, I purpose to write to him—[5]

Tell M[r] Munro that a Letter[6] for him from me is on the way, so that in Case it should miscarry, he may percieve that I have not been unmindful of the one he wrote to me—

M[r]. Grant of Jamaica (the Executor) resides here— Soon after my arrival, he paid me a visit, which I returned— and since that he has made no advances to Sociability— He must feel that all has not been right. I hope you have settled with his nephew in New York;[7] and yet I should not be surprized if some new Delays and Difficulties had interposed—

Peet[8] begins at times to wish himself Home again. the novelty is a good deal over— I wish we were all ~~entering~~ entering the Street ˄Door,˄ and you and the Children and Servants running to meet us. God grant that this wish may be realized, and in the mean Time preserve and bless us all. adieu my Dear Sally— my Love to the Children— Yours Sincerely and affect[y]

John Jay

M[rs]. Jay—

ALS, NNC (EJ: 08062).

1. The *Hope*, Nathan Haley, arrived in New York from London on 13 Oct. *Columbian Gazetteer* (New York), 13 Oct. 1794.

2. See JJ to SLJ, 13 Aug. 1794, ALS, NNC (EJ: 08061); and JJ to Hobart, 12 Aug. 1794, above. The other letters have not been found.

3. The *Gazette of the United States* (Philadelphia), of 24 Oct. 1794, reported that the *Belvedere*, Captain Depeyster, had recently arrived in New York from London.

4. "Polly" refers to Mary Duyckinck Jay, the wife of JJ's brother Peter. PAJ's Memoranda and Statement of Accounts, notes on 16 Aug.: "Sent Mrs. P. Jay's Bracelets & Mrs. Munro's breast pins by Captain DePeyster to Mama on the 16th. Aug." PAJ describes the pins as "Two breast pins are to be made of Aunt Munro's hair— the hair to be plaited enameled settings the letters E. M. engraved on the back— & by direction of Mrs. M. Munro." See the editorial note, "John Jay's Mission to London," above; PAJ to SLJ, 1 Aug. 1794, above.

5. On Ferdinand Grand's move to Switzerland, see JJ to Grand, 31 Dec. 1793, and note 1, *JJSP*, 5: 581–82.

6. Possibly JJ to PJM, 15 July 1794, ALS, NNMus (EJ: 00425), which was acknowledged in PJM to JJ, 18 Sept. 1794, Dft, NNMus (EJ: 00428).

7. For more on the financial transactions involving the Jays and the Grants, see PJM to JJ, 15 June 1794, and note 1, above.

8. Peter Williams, JJ's enslaved manservant. See the editorial note, "John Jay's Mission to London," and note 2, above.

From Grenville (private)

Dropmore Aug. 17. 1794.

Sir

I yesterday received your letter[1] & can with truth assure you that I am not less desirous than you naturally are to expedite the conclusion of our negotiation, & that I feel the force of the reasons you mention for wishing to avoid unnecessary delay. You cannot on the other hand but be sensible of the multitude & urgency of other business at the present moment which makes it impossible to me to give to our negotiation as entire & undivided an attention as I should wish to be enabled to do— I have however been working on the hints of which you sent me the copy agreably to my desire, & have been endeavouring to frame from them & from such suggestions as occur to me a regular projet[2] which I trust I shall soon be able to communicate to you, & which may tend as I hope to bring the whole business within a tolerably narrow compass— I have the honor to be with very sincere respect & esteem Sir Your Most faithful Humble Servant

Grenville

ALS, NNC (EJ: 08530). Marked: "*Private*". C, UK-KeNA: FO 95/512 (EJ: 04992). For JJ's reply, see his letter of 18 Aug. 1794, ALS, UkLPR (EJ: 04993).

1. JJ to Grenville, 16 Aug. 1794, above.

2. Diplomatic term from the French. Draft of a proposed treaty of agreement, *OED*.

To Lindley Murray

Royal Hotel— Pall Mall 22 aug^t. 1794

Dear Sir

I thank you very sincerely for the kind Letter you was so obliging as to write to me on the 15th. of this month.[1] The Sentiments of Esteem and Regard which are expressed in it, afford additional Enducements to my Endeavours to deserve them.

To see things as being what they are, to estimate them aright, and to act accordingly, are of all attainments, the most important—circumstanced as we are, it is exceedingly difficult to acquire either of these ∧and especially the last∧ in any eminent Degree; but in proportion to our Progress, so will be our wisdom, and our Prospect of Happiness. I perceive that we concur in ~~testament~~ ∧thinking∧, that we must go Home to be happy, and that our Home is not in this world. Here we have nothing to do but our Duty, and by it to regulate our Business and our Pleasures: for there are innocent as well as vicious Pleasures, and Travellers thro' the World (as we all are) may without Scruple gratefully enjoy the good Roads, pleasant Scenes and agreable accommodations, with which Providence may be pleased to render our Journey more chearful and comfortable, but in search of these we are not to deviate from the main Road, nor when they occur should we permit them to detain or retard us. The theory of Prudence is sublime, and in many Respects simple,— The Practice is difficult; and it necessarily must be so, or this would cease to be a State of Probation.

The Sentiments diffused thro' your Book[2] are just striking and useful— but my good Friend! our opinions are oftener right than our Conduct; and among the strange things of the world, nothing seems more strange, than that men pursuing Happiness, should knowing ˄ly˄ quit the right & take a wrong Road; and frequently do what their Judgments neither approve or nor prefer. Yet so is the fact: and this Fact points strongly to the necessity of our being healed, or restored or regenerated by a power more energetic than any of those which belong properly belong to the human mind. We percieve that a great Breach has been made in the moral and physical Systems, by the Introduction of moral and physical Evil— how, or why, we know not—so however it is— & it certainly seems proper that this Breach sh^d. be closed, and order restored. For this purpose only one adequate plan has ever appeared in the world, and that is the Christian Dispensation— in this ˄plan˄ I have full faith.— Man in his natural present state is but appears to be a degraded creature—his best Gold is mixed with Dross, and his best Motives ˄are˄ very far from being pure and free from Earth & Impurity—

I mention these things that you may see the State of my Mind relative to these interesting Subjects; and to relieve yours from Doubts w^h. your friendship for me might render disagreable.

I regret your want of Health, and the bodily afflictions with w^h. you are visited— God only knows what is best— Many will have Reason to rejoice in the End for the Days wherein they have seen adversity. Your Mind is in full Strength & vigour and that is an inestimable Blessing.

It really w^d. give me great pleasure to see ˄visit˄ you before I return, ˄but˄ I dare not promise myself that Satisfaction being so much and so constantly under the Direction of Circumstances w^h. I cannot controul

As to the Wars now waging— They appear to me to be of a different Description from ordinary ones— They are in my opinion as unlike common Wars, as the great plague in London was unlike common Sicknesses. I think

we are just entering on the Age of Revolutions; and that the Impurities of our moral *atmosphere* (if I may use the Expression) are about to be purified by a Succession of political Storms. I sincerely wish for general peace and good will among Men, but I shall be mistaken if (short Intervals excepted) the Season for those Blessings is not at some Distance— If any Country escapes I am inclined to think it will be our own; and I am led to this opinion by general Principles & Reasoning, and not by particular Facts or Occurrences, some of which ~~certainly~~ ∧so strongly∧ favor a contrary Idea, as to produce in my Mind much Doubt & Apprehensions— I am Dear Sir your aff^te. Friend
Lindley Murray Esqr.

Dft, NNC (EJ: 09607). Endorsed: ". . . in an^r. 15 [Aug.] 1794". *WJ*, 1: 344–46; *HPJ*, 4: 50–53.

1. Lindley Murray to JJ, 15 July 1794, ALS, NNC (EJ: 09606). Murray (1745–1826) and JJ became friends when they both clerked for Benjamin Kissam. See *JJSP*, 1: 28–29, 50–51. Murray was the son of Robert Murray, a wealthy Quaker merchant and shipowner, nephew of John Murray (the Presbyterian) and brother of John Murray Jr., all of whom had been members of the NYMS. See *JJSP*, 4: 30. The Murrays were also in partnership with London merchant Philip Sansom. During the American Revolution, Lindley Murray spent the early part of the conflict on Long Island, returning to occupied New York City in 1779 as a merchant. Murray maintained that he was neutral in the conflict, although the Murray family had a mixed reputation politically. In December 1784, citing the health problems that would continue the rest of his life, Murray and his wife Hannah departed for England, settling in York. However, he remained an American citizen, refrained from socializing with other exiles, and continued to own property in New York. In England, he began his second, very successful career as a writer and grammarian. His *English Grammar, Adapted to the Different Classes of Learners* (London, 1795), for example, sold an estimated million copies in both the United States and Great Britain. *ANBO.*

In his letter to JJ, Murray invited him to visit in York, apologizing for not being able to go to London because of his health. He congratulated JJ on his appointment, writing, "When I first heard of the commission of my much esteemed Friend, John Jay, as Envoy Extraordinary to the British Court, I rejoiced in the prospect which his known abilities, integrity, and benevolence afforded, of a speedy and happy dispersion of those clouds of hostility, which have been for some time gathering, and which seemed of late ready to involve the two countries in confusion and distress." He also expressed the wish that once JJ had successfully completed his mission, he would negotiate a peace with France. Newspapers had reported rumors to this effect beginning in early July. See, for example, *Morning Post and Fashionable World* (London), 2 July 1794. See also the editorial note "John Jay's Mission to London," above.

2. The expanded edition of *The power of religion on the mind, in retirement, sickness, and at death; exemplified in the testimonies and experience of persons, distinguished by their greatness, learning, or virtue* (London, 1793). Murray had sent JJ a copy of the first edition in 1787. See JJ to Murray, 17 Oct. 1787, Dft, NNC (EJ: 12420).

To William Bayard

London 24 Aug[t] 1794

D[r] Sir

I am greatly obliged by y[r]. kind Letter of the 16 of this month; and your friendly Invitation to my Son to pass some time with you at y[r]. Seat.[1]

It is a Maxim with me my d[r]. Sir, that young Folks should be employed, and in such a regular Manner, as that they may have something to do every Day at fixed Hours— Early Habits of order and Punctuality you know, have an Influence on a Man's Conduct thru' Life. I have communicated ~~to him~~ your Letter to him, and he is much gratified by the Attention with which you honor him. He shall not be disappointed in his wishes to accompany me, ~~as soon as~~ a Season of Liesure may arrive, and put it in my power to make you a Visit.

It certainly is very desireable that peace and Harmony may subsist between great Britain and America; but what the Issue of the Negociation may be, cannot be known untill it shall be finished. Conjectures may prove ill founded & mislead— it is not adviseable therefore to hazard them— with the best Wishes for the Health & Happiness of M[rs]. Bayard yourself & Family I am D[r]. S[r]. y[r]. most ob[t]. & hble Serv[t]

W[m]. Bayard Esq[r]

Dft, NNC (EJ: 08900).

1. In Bayard to JJ, 16 Aug. 1794, ALS, NNC (EJ: 08362), he repeated his invitation of 29 June 1794 (above), and noted that he had not previously known that PAJ accompanied his father.

To James Monroe

London 28 Aug[st]. 1794

Sir

In July 1792 Miss Bainslow, a young Lady now of 17, and whose Family reside near this City, was placed at Boulogne Sur Mer, under the Care, and in the House of Madame Delseux, a respectable widow Lady there, for the Benefit of Education. In September last she was (together with her Friend and fellow-pensioner, Miss *Hornblow*) arrested, and confined in a convent. In January following they were removed back to Madame Delseux's House, where they still remain confined, in the Manner prescribed by the Decree—[1]

Miss Bainslows Friends are exceedingly sollicitous to interest your kind offices in favor of these young Ladies— They entreat me to lay these Facts before you, and convey their most earnest Request that you will be so good as to endeavour to obtain Permission for them to return Home.

When I consider what my Feelings would be had I a Daughter of that age so circumstanced, I find it impossible to resist their application. I know by Experience that Business not connected with the objects of one's mission, can seldom be pleasant. The Business of Humanity however, seems to be attached to opportunities of doing it. I will not enlarge on this Subject— every Remark incident to it, will occur to you. For my part, I am not apprized of any objection to permitting these foreign *Children* to ˄go˄ Home to their Parents; and should such a general Permission be effected by your Means, the Remembrance of it would be sweet to you forever—[2] I had the honor of writing a few Lines to you on the Instant, and remain Sir your most obᵗ. & h'ble Servᵗ

John Jay

The Hon'ble Mʳ. Munro

ALS, PHi (EJ: 01178). C, DLC: Monroe (EJ: 10625); Dft and Tr, NNC (EJ: 09619); *WJ*, 1: 350; *HPJ*, 4: 53–54. No reply has been found.

1. The fate of the Misses Bainslow and Hornblow is unknown.

2. See the editorial note "John Jay's Mission to London," above; and JJ's memorandum to JT of people who sought lost friends and relatives, 5 Feb. 1795, below.

From Grenville, enclosing Draft Treaties of Amity and Commerce

[London] Aug. 30. 1794

Sir

I have now the honour to transmit to you two projets the one for regulating all points in dispute between His Majesty and the United States, the other for the establishment of commercial regulations. You will perceive that I have proceeded in forming these projets on the foundation of the paper you communicated to me,[1] but that I have occasionally made such variations as seemed to me to be just & expedient. I have thought that some time might be saved by communicating them to you in this manner. Whenever you shall have sufficiently considered them to be enabled to converse either on the whole or on any distinct branches of so extensive a subject I shall be very much at your order, having very sincerely at heart the speedy and favourable conclusion of our negotiation.[2]

It would have been more satisfactory to me if I had found it practicable to send you these projets sooner, but you will I am sure be sensible of the circumstances which must at this conjuncture have interfered with the preparation of an arrangement intended to comprehend so extensive a Subject and to lay the foundation of lasting harmony & friendship between our two Countries. Even in the state in which I now send you these Papers I am apprehensive that some verbal corrections may occur as necessary to give full effect to the objects intended to be provided for, supposing those objects to be mutually consented to. And I think there are one or two other points on which we have occasionally touched in our conversations for which no provision is made in these projets— But I have preferred making the Communication in its present shape rather than that any further delay should be created, & I trust with real confidence to your candour respecting Such further suggestions as I may occasionally see ground to State to You. I have the honor to be with very sincere esteem & respect Sir Your most faithful & most obedient Humble servant

(signed) Grenville

Preamble.[3]
Article 1st.

It is agreed that there shall be between the Dominions of His Britannic Majesty in *Europe*[4] and the Territories of the United States a reciprocal & perfect liberty of Commerce & navigation[5] and a free admission of all Ships belonging to either party whether the same be Ships of War[6] or Merchant Vessels; and that the Subjects & Inhabitants of the two Countries respectively shall have Liberty freely and Securely, & without hinderance or molestation of any kind, to come with their said Ships & their Cargoes to the Lands Countries, Cities, Ports, Places & Rivers within the Dominions & Territories aforesaid, to enter into the same, to resort thereto, and to remain and reside there without any limitation of time; also to hire, purchase & possess Houses & Warehouses for the purposes of their Commerce and generally that the Merchants and traders on each side shall enjoy the most complete protection and Security for their Commerce; but subject always as to what respects this Article to the general Laws and Statutes of the Two Countries respectively.[7]

Article 2d:

It shall be free for the two Contracting Parties respectively to appoint Consuls for the protection of Trade, to reside in the Dominions & Territories aforesaid, the same being *of the Nation* on whose behalf they shall be so appointed, & not otherwise: And such Consuls shall enjoy those Liberties & rights which belong to them by reason of their Functions;—[8] But either Party may except from the general liberty of residence of such Consuls, such particular places as such Party shall judge proper to be so excepted.[9]

The map of North America Grenville proposed as authoritative, "The United States of North America: with the British territories and those of Spain according to the treaty of 1784," William Faden, published 1793. (Map image courtesy of the Norman B. Leventhal Map Center at the Boston Public Library)

Article 3ᵈ.

The Vessels of the two contracting Parties respectively coming to the Dominions or Territories aforesaid, shall enjoy the same liberty in Respect of the Entry & Discharge of their lawful cargoes, and all other Regulations which respect the general convenience and advantage of Commerce, as now are, or shall at any time be enjoyed by any other Foreign Nation, which shall be the most favor'd in that respect: and no distinction shall exist of Tonnage or other Duties (such light house Duties excepted, as are levied for the Profit of Individuals or of Corporations,) by which the Vessells of the one party shall pay in the Ports of the other, any higher or other Duties than shall be paid in similar Circumstances by the Vessells of the foreign nation the most favored in that respect; or by the vessells of the Party into whose Ports they shall come.[10]

Article 4th.

No Article being of the growth, produce or Manufacture of any of the Dominions or Territories of the one party shall pay on being imported directly
from the said territories or Dominions into the Ports of the other, any higher
or other duties than shall be there paid for the like Articles on importation
from any other foreign Country.

Article 5th:

No new Prohibition shall be laid in any of the territories or Dominions
aforesaid, by one of the contracting Parties, on the importation of any Article
being of the Growth produce or Manufacture of the Territories or Dominions of the other. Nor shall article being of the growth produce or manufacture of any other Country be prohibited to be imported into the Dominions
of one of the contracting Parties by the Vessells of the other, except such Articles only as are now so prohibited.[11]

Article 6th.

With respect to the territories and Dominions of his Britannic Majesty in
the West Indies, the following arrangements have been agreed to by the Contracting Parties.

His Majesty consents that it shall & may be lawfull, during the time herein
after limited for the Citizens of the United States of America, to carry to any
of His Majesty's Islands & Ports in the West Indies from the United States,
in their own Vessells, not being above the burthen of Seventy Tons,[12] any
Goods or Merchandize being of the growth or produce of the said States,
which it is or *may* be lawfull to carry to the said Islands and Ports from the
said States in British Vessels, and that the said American Vessels and their
Cargoes shall pay there no other or higher Duties than shall be payable by
British vessels in similar circumstances: And that it shall be lawfull to the said
American Citizens to purchase, load, and carry away in their said Vessels to
the United States, from the said Islands and Ports all such articles being of the
growth & Produce of the sd. Islands, as may by Law be carried from thence
to the said States in British Vessells: and subject only to the same duties and
Charges on exportation, to which British Vessells are or shall be ~~liable~~ subject
in similar circumstances.[13]

Provided always that they carry and land the same in the United States
only, it being expressly agreed and declared, that during the continuance
of this Article The United States will prohibit the carrying any West India
productions or manufactures in American Vessels, either from his Majesty's
Islands, or from the United States, to any part of the World except the United

States:— reasonable Sea Stores excepted, and excepting also Rum made in the United States from West India Molasses.[14]

It is agreed that this Article and every matter & thing therein contained, shall continue to be in force, during the Continuance of the War in which His Majesty is now engaged, and also for two years from and after the day of the signature of the preliminary Articles of Peace by which the same may be terminated.

And it is further agreed that at the expiration of the said term, the Two contracting parties will treat further concerning the arrangement of their Commerce in this respect, according to the situation in which his Majesty may then find himself as with respect to the West Indies; and with a view to the mutual advantage and extension of Commerce[15]

Article 7th:

This Treaty, and all the Matters therein contained, except the Sixth Article, shall Continue to be in force for twelve years from the day of the Exchange of the ratifications thereof; and if during the continuance of this treaty, there shall arise on either side, any complaint of the infraction of any Article thereof, it is agreed that neither the whole treaty nor any Article thereof shall on that account be suspended until representation shall have been made to the Government by the Minister of the Party Complaining; and even if re- dress shall not then be obtain'd, four Months notice shall be given previous to such suspension.

Preamble.[16]

Article 1.[17]

It is agreed that His Majesty will withdraw all His Troops and Garrisons from the Posts within the Boundary Line assigned it by the Treaty of Peace to the United States. This evacuation shall take place on, or before the first of June 1796,[18] and all the proper measures shall in the interval be taken by concert between His Majesty's Governor General in America and the Government of the United States for settling the previous arrangements which may be necessary respecting the delivery of the said Posts. All Settlers and Traders within the precincts or jurisdiction of the said Posts shall continue to have and to enjoy unmolested all their property of every kind and shall be pro- tected therein so long as they shall think proper to remain there, and shall be at full liberty to remove at such times as they shall think proper, and to sell their Lands, Houses, or Effects, or to retain the property thereof.[19]

It shall at all times be free to His Majesty's Subjects and to the Indians who are to the Southward and Westward of the Lakes,[20] to pass and repass with their Goods and Merchandizes and to carry on their commerce within or without the jurisdiction of the Said Posts, in the manner hitherto accustomed, and without any hindrance or molestation from the Officers or Citizens of the United States. The several waters, carrying Places, and roads adjacent to the Lakes, or communicating with them, shall continue to be free and open to His Majesty's Subjects, and to the Indians for that purpose, and no impediment or obstacle shall be given to the passage of goods or merchandize of any kind, nor shall any duty be attempted to be levied upon them.[21]

Article 2.

In order to remove all uncertainty with respect to the said Boundary Line assigned to the United States by the said Treaty of Peace, [in margin: Arrangements] the following ~~agreement~~ ˄arrangements˄ ~~has~~ ˄have˄ been agreed upon between the Two Contracting Parties to the said Treaty, and are to be considered as forming a part thereof.[22]

First, That whereas doubts have arisen what River[23] was truly intended under the name of the River S^{te}. Croise[24] mentioned in the said Treaty and forming a part of the boundary—therein described, that Question shall be referred to the final decision of Commissioners in London,[25] to be appointed in the following manner, viz, That One Commissioner shall be named by His Majesty, and one by the United States and that the said Two Commissioners shall agree on the choice of a third, or if they cannot so agree that they shall each propose one Person, and that of the two names so proposed one shall be drawn by lot in the presence of the Two Original Commissioners. And that the Three Commissioners so appointed shall be sworn impartially to examine and decide the said Question, according to such documents as shall respectively be laid before them on the part of the British Government and of the United States.[26]

Secondly, that whereas it is now understood that the River Missisippi would at no point thereof be intersected by such Westward Line as is described in the said Treaty,[27] and whereas it was stipulated by the said Treaty that the navigation of the Missisippi should be free to both parties, it is agreed that the boundary line shall run in the manner described by the said Treaty from the Lake Huron [in the body: (to the northward of the Isle Phillippeaux in Lake Superior[,]^{28} and that from thence the said Line shall proceed to the bottom of West Bay in the said Lake and from thence in a due West Course to the River of the Red Lake or Eastern branch of the Missisippi,[29] and down the said Branch to the main River of the Missisippi and that as well on the said Branch as on)] [in margin: Or (thro' Lake Superior and from thence to the Water communication between the said Lake and the Lake of the Woods to the point where the said Water communication shall be intersected by a Line running due North from the Mouth of the River S^{te}. Croix which falls into the Missisippi below the falls of S^{t}. Anthony; and that the boundary shall proceed from such point of intersection in a due Southerly Course along the said Line to the Missisippi; and that as well on the said Water communication as on)] every part of the Missisippi where the same bounds the Territories of the United States, the Navigation shall be free to both Parties, and His Majestys Subjects shall always be admitted to enter freely into the Bays, Ports and Creeks on the American side, and to land and dwell there for the purposes of their commerce,[30] and for greater Certainty, The Undersigned Ministers have annexed to each of the Copies of this Treaty a copy of the Map made use of by them, with the boundaries as marked thereon agreeably to this Article.[31]

And the Boundaries of the United States as fixed by the said Treaty of Peace and by this Treaty, together with all the other Articles of the said Treaty are hereby recognized, ratified and forever confirmed.[32]

Article 3.[33]

Whereas it is alledged by divers British Merchants and others His Majesty's Subjects that debts to a considerable amount which were bonâ fide contracted before the Peace still remain owing to them by Citizens or Inhabitants of the United States,[34] and that by the operation of various lawful impediments since The Peace not only the full recovery of the said Debts has been delayed, but also the security and value thereof has been impaired and lessened and that in many instances the British Creditors cannot now obtain by the Ordinary course of judicial proceedings full and just relief for the loss and damage so sustained by them, it is agreed that in all cases where such relief cannot, for whatever reason, be now had by British Creditors in the ordinary course of justice, The United States of America will make full and complete satisfaction to the said Creditors; and that, for this purpose, Commissioners shall be appointed and authorized to act in America, in manner following; that is to say Two Commissioners shall be named by His Majesty, and Two by the United States, and a fifth by the unanimous choice of the other four. But if they shall not agree in such choice, then one name shall be proposed by the British Commissioners and one by the Commissioners of the United States, and one of the two names so proposed shall be drawn by Lot in the presence of the said Original Commissioners. And in case of death, sickness, or necessary absence the places of the said Commissioners shall be respectively supplied in the same manner as such Commissioners respectively were first appointed. The said five Commissioners shall be sworn to hear all such complaints as shall within the space of eighteen months from their first sitting [in margin: or within such further time as they shall see cause to allow for that purpose,] be preferred to them by British Creditors or their Representatives in virtue of this Article, and impartially to determine the same accordingly to the true intent of this Article, and of the Treaty of Peace. And the said Commissioners in awarding such Sums as shall appear to them to be due to the said Creditors by virtue of this Article are empowered to take into their consideration and to determine all claims on account either of principal or interest in respect of the said Debts and to decide respecting the same according to the merits of the several cases due regard being had to all the circumstances thereof and as equity and justice shall appear to them to require. And the said Commissioners shall be [illegible] empowered to examine all Persons on oath touching the Premises, and also to receive in evidence at their discretion, and according as they shall think most consistent with equity and justice, all written depositions, or Books, or Papers, or Copies, or Extracts thereof, every such deposition, book, paper, copy, or extract being duly authenticated, according to the legal forms now respectively existing in the Two Countries, or in such other manner as the said Commissioners shall see cause to prescribe and require.

Three of the said Commissioners shall constitute a board, and be empowered to do any Act appertaining to the said Commission, provided that in every such case, one of the Commissioners— named on each side, and the fifth Commissioner chosen as above shall be present, and all decisions shall be made by the majority of voices of the Commissioners then present.

The award of the said Commissioners, or of any three of them as aforesaid shall in all cases be final and conclusive both as to the justice of the claim, and to the amount of the Sum to be paid to the Claimant, and the United States undertake to cau[se] the same to be paid to such Claimants without deduction, in Sterling Money and in such Place, or Places, and at such time or times, as shall be awarded by the said Commissioners: and on condition of such releases to be given by the Claimant of his demands against individuals as to them shall appear just and reasonable.[35]

Article 4.

Whereas Complaints have been made by divers Merchants and others, Citizens of the United States, that during the course of the War in which His Majesty is now engaged they have sustained considerable loss and damage by reason of irregular or illegal captures, and condemnations of their vessels under colour of authority or commission from His Majesty; and that from various Circumstances belonging to the said cases adequate compensation for the said losses cannot now be obtained by the ordinary course of judicial proceedings, it is agreed that in all such cases where adequate compensation cannot, for whatever reason, be now had by the said Merchants and others, full and complete satisfaction will be made by the British Government to the said Complainants; and that for this purpose Commissioners shall be appointed and authorized to act in London in the same manner and with the same Powers and authorities, and subject to the same restrictions as the Commissioners named in the Third Article of this Treaty; and that the award of the said Commissioners shall in like manner be final and conclusive in all respects. And His ~~British~~ ‸Britannic‸ Majesty engages to cause to be paid to such Complainants respectively the Amount of all Sums so awarded, without deduction, in ~~Sterling Money~~ [in margin: specie], and at such time or times & in such place or places as shall be awarded by the said Commissioners, and on condition of such releases on the part of the Complainants of their demands against individuals as to the said Commissioners shall appear just and reasonable.[36]

And it is further agreed that if it shall appear that in the course of the War loss and Damage has been sustained by His Majesty's Subjects by reason of the capture of their Vessels and Merchandize, such capture having been made either within the limits of the jurisdiction of the Said States, or by Vessels armed in the Ports of the said States, or by Vessels commanded or owned by the Citizens of the said States, the said United States will make full satisfaction for such loss or damage [in margin: when complete satisfaction &c &c] the same being to be ascertained by Commissioners in the manner already mentioned in this Article.[37]

Article 5.

It is agreed that with respect to the Neutral Commerce which One Party may carry on with the European Enemies of the Other, [in margin: Indian] when engaged in War, the principles to be observed by Great Britain towards The United States and reciprocally by The United States towards Great Britain shall always, and in all points, be the same as those which shall at that time be observed by the Said Parties respectively towards the most favored Neutral Nations of Europe with the Exception of such particular privileges as may, before the commencement of the War to which the same shall apply, have been granted by special Treaty to particular European Nations, and with such extensions or modifications as may occasionally be established by special treaty between Great Britain and the United States for their mutual convenience.[38]

Article 6.

It is agreed that in all cases where Vessels shall be captured or detained on just suspicion of having on board Enemies property, or of carrying to the Enemy any of the Articles which *are Contraband* of War, [in margin: 2. Enumeration Gain—indemnify &c] the said Vessels shall be brought to the nearest or most Convenient Port; and that all proper measures shall be taken to prevent delay in deciding the case of Ships so brought in for adjudication, and in the payment or recovery of any indemnification adjudged or agreed to be paid to the Masters or Owners of such Ships.—[39]

Article 7.

When one of the Contracting Parties is engaged in War, and the other remains Neutral, the said Neutral Power shall not suffer the Ships, Vessels, Goods, or Merchandise of the other which may be taken at Sea or elsewhere by the Enemy to be brought into any of It's Ports or Dominions and much less to be there sold, or exchanged but shall publicly forbid any thing of that kind to be done:[40] And if any Ships, Vessels, Goods or Merchandize of either of the Contracting parties or their People or Subjects so taken at Sea or elsewhere, shall be carried into the Ports or Countries of the other by the Enemy, neither the same, nor any part thereof shall be allowed to be sold or exchanged in that Port, or ₐinₐ any other Place in the Dominion of the said neutral Party. The Master of the Ship or Vessel so taken, as also the Mariners and Passengers of every Description shall as soon as they arrive, be immediately set at Liberty; and the said Ship or Vessel so brought shall not be permitted to stay in that harbour, but shall be obliged immediately to leave the Port with her goods, merchandize and lading, and without being allowed to return to the same, or to any other Port in the dominions of the said Neutral Party. Provided nevertheless that nothing in this Article shall be construed to derogate from the public treaties which have already been entered into by either of the contracting Parties with other nations but, in so far as such Treaties do not interfere, and in all cases to which they do not apply; the above Article shall remain in full force, and shall be executed accordingly. And the contracting Parties will not in future conclude any treaty in derogation of this Article.[41]

Article 8.

It is agreed that the subjects and Inhabitants of the Kingdoms, Provinces, and Dominions of the contracting Parties shall exercise no Acts of hostility or violence against each other, either by Sea or by Land, or in Rivers Streams, Ports or Havens, under any Colour or pretence whatsoever; ~~or~~ ₐand particularlyₐ that the Subjects or People of either Party shall not receive any Patent

Commission or Instruction, for arming ~~and~~ and acting at Sea as Privateers, or any Letters of Reprisal, as they are called, from any Princes or States, Enemies to the other Party; neither shall they arm ships in such manner as is above said, nor go out to Sea therewith [in margin: for the purpose of exercising any act of violence against the Subjects or People of the other Contracting Party:] nor shall they in any manner molest or disturb the ₐsaidₐ Subjects or People ~~of the other contracting Party~~ To which end [in margin: sufficient Laws & regulations shall if necessary, be provided and] as often as it is required by either Party, strict and express prohibitions shall be renewed and published in all the territories countries and dominions of each Party wheresoever, that no one shall in any wise use such Commissions or Letters of reprisal, or engage in any such acts of hostility as aforesaid, under the pain of severe punishment to be inflicted on the transgressors, besides their being liable to make full restitution and satisfaction to those to whom they have done any damage. Neither shall any Letters of Reprisal be hereafter granted by either of the said contracting Parties to the prejudice or detriment of the Subjects of the other, except only in such case wherein justice is denied or delayed; which denial or delay of Justice shall not be regarded as verified, unless the petition of the Person who desires the said Letters of Reprisal be communicated to the Minister residing there on the part of the Government against whose Subjects or People they are granted, that within the space of 4 months, or sooner, if it be possible they may manifest the contrary, or procure the satisfaction which may be justly due.[42]

Article 9.

Neither of the said contrac[ting] Parties shall permit the Ships or goods belonging to the Subjects of the other to be taken within the Limits of their respective Jurisdictions on their coasts, nor in the Ports or Rivers of their Dominions by Ships of War or others having commission from any Prince, Republic, or City whatsoever; but in case it should so happen, Both Parties shall employ their united force to obtain reparation of the damage thereby occasioned.[43]

Article 10.

If it should unfortunately happen that a war should break out between Great Britain and the united States all merchants and others residing in the two Countries respectively shall be allowed Nine Months to retire with their effects; and shall be protected from capture in their way home, provided always that this favour is not to extend to those who shall act contrary to the established Laws.[44] And it is further agreed that neither debts due from Individuals of the one nation to Individuals of the other, nor shares or monies which they may have in the public Funds, or in the public, or private Banks shall ever in any Event of War or National differences be sequestered or confiscated[45] it being both unjust and impolitic that debts and engagements contracted and made by Individuals having Confidence in each other and in their respective Governments should ever be destroyed or impaired by national Authority on account of national differences and discontents.[46]

Article 11.

It is agreed that British Subjects, who now hold Lands in the ᴧterritories of theᴧ United States, and American Citizens who now hold Lands in His Majesty's dominions shall continue to hold them, according to the nature and tenure of their Estates and Titles therein, and may grant and sell and devise the same as, and to whom they please, in like manner as if they were natives; and that neither they nor their Heirs or Assigns shall so far as may respect the said Lands, and the legal remedies incident thereto, be regarded as Aliens.[47]

Commercial Projet.[48]

Article 2.   Omit these Words, "the same being of the Nation on whose behalf they shall be so appointed and not otherwise" And insert in lieu thereof "The same being first approved by the Government of the Country in which they shall be so appointed to reside and not otherwise.["]

Article 3.   The last sentence to run thus;
"by which the Vessels of the one Party shall pay in the Port of the other any higher or other Duties than shall be paid in similar Circumstances by the Vessels of the Foreign Nation the most favoured in that Respect, or any higher or other Duties than shall be paid in similar Cases by the Vessels of the Party itself into whose Port they shall come."

ALS, with enclosures, NNC (EJ: 08525; EJ: 08531), used for transcription for the commercial treaty section; C, UK-KeNA: FO 95/512 (EJ: 04996; EJ: 04997), used for transcription for the general treaty section; Dft of articles without cover letter, UK-BL: Dropmore, Ms 59049, contains general treaty only; C, in the hand of JT, with enclosures, DNA: Jay Despatches, 1794–95 (EJ: 04314), contains the general treaty followed by the commercial treaty, enclosed in JJ to ER, 13 Sept. 1794, below; C, NHi: King (EJ: 04446), contains the general treaty followed by the commercial treaty; LbkC, enclosed in JJ to ER, 13 Sept. 1794, NNC: JJ Lbk. 8, contains the general treaty followed by the commercial treaty.

1. See JJ's Draft for a Convention and Treaty of Commerce, 6 Aug. 1794, above.

2. For JJ's immediate reaction to Grenville's draft, see JJ to Grenville, 1 and 4 Sept. 1794, below; and the editorial note "Negotiating the Jay Treaty," above.

3. Although commercial matters follow discussion of disputes about the treaty of 1783, JJ's draft of 6 Aug. is not formally separated into two distinct treaties. JJ had, no doubt, informed Grenville

that he was authorized to negotiate a commercial treaty if the other matters he had been instructed to address were satisfactorily resolved and if it did not violate American treaties with France. See AH to JJ, and ER to JJ, both 6 May 1794, *JJSP*, 5: 631–47. For the decision to merge the two treaties delineated here into a single treaty of amity and commerce, see JJ's Project for a Treaty with Great Britain, 30 Sept. 1794, below.

4. JJ's draft of 6 Aug. specified reciprocity covering trade with "any part of the world." Art. 11 of JJ's Project of 30 Sept. accepted Grenville's restriction of this trade to Europe.

5. Art. 11 of JJ's Project for a Treaty with Great Britain of 30 Sept. replicates this statement exactly. Art. 11 of the Treaty of Amity, Commerce, and Navigation of 19 Nov. 1794 follows it closely, adding "between their respective People, in the Manner, under the Limitations, and on the Conditions specified in the following Articles." Art. 14 of the Treaty of Amity, Commerce, and Navigation of 19 Nov. 1794 repeats it.

6. Art. 11 of JJ's Project for a Treaty with Great Britain of 30 Sept. did not provide for the admission of warships.

7. The NHi copy of this text (EJ: 04446) contains an expanded version of this clause: "and with a view to such arrangements, as may best conduce to the mutual advantage and extension of commerce."

Art. 11 of JJ's Project for a Treaty with Great Britain of 30 Sept. follows the wording of this paragraph closely. When he reviewed this article, ER commented that it represented nothing more than a courtesy nations commonly granted to one another unless its meaning extended to the point where each legislature could define it. See ER to JJ, 15 Dec. 1794, LS, NHi: Jay (EJ: 00620); *ASP: FR*, 1: 511.

8. JJ's draft of 6 Aug. made no mention of consuls. JJ's Project for a Treaty with Great Britain of 30 Sept. agrees with Grenville's to this point. ER commented that the tone of this article was more suitable to the American temper, which made every effort to prevent foreign governments from seducing American citizens by the lure of office. He then asked if consular powers would be further delineated in the course of negotiations. See ER to JJ, 15 Dec. 1794, LS, NHi: Jay (EJ: 00620); *ASP: FR*, 1: 511. For the terms on which the United States had, in the absence of a commercial treaty, admitted consuls from Britain, see the editorial note "*Consuls De Gratia:* The Role of British Consuls," *JJSP*, 4: 245–50. After this sentence, Art. 13 of JJ's Project for a Treaty with Great Britain of 30 Sept. added a provision specifying actions the receiving government might take in the event of inappropriate behavior by a consul. Art. 16 of the Treaty of Amity, Commerce, and Navigation of 19 Nov. 1794 closely follows JJ's text.

9. Art. 13 of JJ's Project for a Treaty with Great Britain of 30 Sept. replicates this statement.

10. JJ's draft of 6 Aug. had asked for reciprocity. Grenville here provides a "most favored nation" formula. For his further revisions, see Art. 11 of JJ's Project for a Treaty with Great Britain, 30 Sept., below. ER submitted Grenville's draft to AH for comment. Following AH's confidential response, ER then noted that American merchants would be reluctant to have the distinctions that currently existed between their vessels and foreign vessels abolished unless there was a very obvious equivalent. Their reluctance would be even stronger, he added, if the "distinction in the *duties on goods*" brought to the United States in British vessels was eliminated. He also remarked that JJ had no doubt considered that the United States would have to extend privileges he might concede to Britain to other nations to whom the United States had granted most favored nation commercial status. See *PAH*, 17: 409–11; and ER to JJ, 15 Dec. 1794, LS, NHi: Jay (EJ: 00620); *ASP: FR*, 1: 511.

11. ER here repeats AH's comment that this article "wanted reciprocity," and gave claim to "some very considerable equivalent;" that if the equivalent was supposed to have been Art. 6, opening the

West Indies trade, the term allowing it was extremely limited, and since restrictions on the reexportation of West Indian commodities would deprive the United States of a valuable trade it currently enjoyed, it had little value as an offset. See ER to JJ, 15 Dec. 1794, cited above; and *PAH*, 17: 409–11.

12. JJ's draft of 6 Aug. had proposed limiting the burden of ships to 100 tons or under. Art. 10 of JJ's Project for a Treaty with Great Britain of 30 Sept. left blank the number of tons.

13. Grenville's draft of this paragraph differs in words but agrees in substance with JJ's draft of 6 Aug. Art. 10 of JJ's Project for a Treaty with Great Britain of 30 Sept. follows the wording suggested by Grenville here.

14. Grenville's draft of this paragraph differs in wording from but agrees in substance with JJ's draft of 6 Aug. Art. 10 of JJ's Project for a Treaty with Great Britain of 30 Sept. mentioned specifically that American vessels could carry sugar, coffee, and cotton, reasonable sea stores excepted, only to the United States, and specified the term when the article would be in force.

15. Art. 10 of JJ's Project for a Treaty with Great Britain of 30 Sept. provides the same term when the article would be in force and for further negotiations thereafter.

16. This version is taken from the UK-KeNA: FO 95/512 copy (EJ: 04996). It contains two corrections to the commercial projet at the end of the document; only one of these corrections was made in the copy which JJ received.

JJ's draft of 6 Aug. includes a preface which referenced the two nations' "mutual complaints and Claims" and expressed the hope that they should be "forever merged and sunk" in the articles that followed. JJ's Project for a Treaty with Great Britain of 30 Sept. also provided a preface articulating this sentiment.

17. Where JJ began his draft with articles dealing with the two boundary issues, both of which, it was finally decided, had to be resolved in the indefinite future by commissioners, Grenville here chose to begin his draft by agreeing to a demand long urged by the United States.

18. In his draft of 6 Aug., JJ had specified 1 June 1795, by which time it was unlikely that the treaty would have been ratified.

19. See the first of JJ's Objections to Grenville's Draft Treaty Proposals of 30 Aug., [6 Sept. 1794], below. In his draft of 6 Aug., JJ specified that settlers and traders within the precincts of the posts could either choose to remain, hold their property, and become American citizens, or sell their lands and other property and remove with their effects within two years. In his response to JJ's first objection, Grenville accepted the substance of JJ's comment. See Grenville to JJ, 7 Sept. 1794, below.

20. For Grenville's attempt to claim a significant portion of this territory for Britain, see the second item of Art. 2.

21. JJ's draft of 6 Aug. did not discuss access to American traders for either Indians or British subjects. Although the British and American commissioners had discussed the degree of access to and protection for traders in the area south of the boundaries to be conceded to the United States, the Treaty of 1783 omitted all reference to these issues. Fur traders had been among those most displeased with the territorial cessions Britain made then. See *JJSP*, 3: 401, 464. Thereafter, the British government made determined efforts to establish a "neutral Indian barrier state" to safeguard the interests of its Indian allies and British fur traders. See Bemis, *Jay's Treaty*, 147–82.

The second, third, and fourth objections JJ offered to Grenville's draft challenged Grenville's attempt to secure preferential status to Britain's clients without parallel privileges for American citizens. In his response of 7 Sept., Grenville reserved Articles 2, 3, and 4 for further consideration. See JJ's Objections to Grenville's Draft Treaty Proposals of 30 Aug., [6 Sept. 1794]; Grenville to JJ, 7 Sept.; and Art. 9 of JJ's Project for a Treaty with Great Britain, 30 Sept. 1794, all below.

22. Grenville's draft here repositions to the end of the article a statement from JJ's draft of 6 Aug., that the boundaries of the United States delineated in the Peace Treaty were "recognized, ratified and forever confirmed," thereby enabling Britain to lay claim to a significant amount of territory south and west of the line claimed by the United States. JJ repositioned his statement to the beginning of the fourth article of his Project for a Treaty with Great Britain, 30 Sept., below. The Treaty of Amity, Commerce, and Navigation of 19 Nov. 1794 omits any statement to this effect.

23. For the peace commissioners' discussion of the northeastern boundary, see *JJSP*, 3: 182, 209nn3, 5.

24. JJ's draft of 6 Aug. positioned the Lake of the Woods dispute ahead of the St. Croix. By reversing their order, Grenville positioned himself to begin with a dispute more easily resolved before making his proposal for the Lake of the Woods boundary, on which see below. The Treaty of Amity, Commerce, and Navigation of 19 Nov. 1794 considered the Lake of the Woods issue first.

25. In his fifth objection, JJ questioned why the commissioners should meet in London. See JJ's Objections to Grenville's Draft Treaty Proposals of 30 Aug., [6 Sept. 1794]; Grenville to JJ: Responses to Queries, 7 Sept.; and Art. 4 of JJ's Project for a Treaty with Great Britain, 30 Sept. 1794, all below.

26. JJ's draft of 6 Aug. did not suggest how the commissioners were to be appointed, authorized, or salaried.

27. JJ's draft of 6 Aug. had specified that it was doubtful whether the Mississippi extended far enough north to intersect with the west line from the Lake of the Woods.

28. The line hereafter suggested by Grenville would move the northern boundary significantly to the south by the time it met the headwaters of the Mississippi River as depicted on the map engraved by William Faden, on which see JJ to Grenville, 4 Sept., below, and the maps prepared by JT, *ASP: FR*, 1: 492.

29. For JJ's immediate and unequivocal rejection of Grenville's suggestion that the treaty provision granting free navigation of the Mississippi implied that British territory should extend to its headwaters, and for his refusal to consider ceding the considerable territory involved, see JJ to Grenville, 1 Sept., below. JJ further questioned Grenville's attempt to secure British access to the river in his sixth and seventh objections of 6 Sept., to which Grenville replied on 7 Sept., below. See Art. 3 of JJ's Project for a Treaty with Great Britain, 30 Sept., below.

30. See JJ's Objections to Grenville's Draft Treaty Proposals of 30 Aug., [6 Sept.]; Grenville to JJ, Responses to Queries, 7 Sept.; and JJ's Project for a Treaty with Great Britain, 30 Sept., note 9, all below.

31. For AH's suggestion that it might be possible to persuade Britain to guarantee the American right to navigate the river by pledging mutual enjoyment and trade on the same terms as with U.S. Atlantic ports, see AH to JJ, 6 May, *JJSP*, 5: 633–34.

32. See note 9, above.

33. In JJ's draft of 6 Aug., compensation for American losses and damages resulting from British spoliations on American commerce preceded his discussion of repayment of debts to British creditors. The Treaty of Amity, Commerce, and Navigation of 19 Nov. 1794 preserved Grenville's order, addressing the debts first.

34. For his initial suggestion on remedies to be provided to British creditors, see JJ's Draft for a Convention and Treaty of Commerce of 6 Aug., above; and, for his comments on Grenville's proposal, see the eighth through the eleventh of JJ's Objections to Grenville's Draft Treaty Proposals of 30 Aug., [6 Sept.], below. For his response, see Grenville to JJ, Responses to Queries, 7 Sept., below.

35. For the final arrangement, see Art. 4 of JJ's Project for a Treaty with Great Britain, 30 Sept., below.

36. JJ's draft of 6 Aug. did not specify that compensation should be provided by the British government.

37. JJ's draft of 6 Aug. made no reference to British claims for compensation for loss or damage to their vessels or merchandise resulting from French privateers, on which see the editorial note "John Jay and the Genet Affair," *JJSP*, 5: 546–61. See also JJ's Objections to Grenville's Draft Treaty Proposals of 30 Aug., [6 Sept.], below, where JJ suggested putting these captures on the same footing as British captures of American vessels; Grenville to JJ, Responses to Queries, 7 Sept.; and Art. 5 of JJ's Project for a Treaty with Great Britain, 30 Sept., both below. For discussion within GW's cabinet of the need to compensate British merchants for prizes taken by the French, see *PAH*, 16: 511–15, 559–61.

38. See the thirteenth of JJ's Objections to Grenville's Draft Treaty Proposals of 30 Aug., [6 Sept.]; and Art. 11 of JJ's Project for a Treaty with Great Britain, 30 Sept., both below.

39. JJ noted the lack of a definition of contraband in the fourteenth of his objections to Grenville's Draft Treaty Proposals of 30 Aug., [6 Sept.], below. JJ subsequently put forth the American position that free ships made free goods. See Arts. 15 and 17 of JJ's Project for a Treaty with Great Britain, 30 Sept., below.

40. In passing the Neutrality Act of 4 June 1794, the House had struck out the clause that forbade the sale of prizes taken by an enemy from a nation with whom the United States was at peace. See *PAH*, 16: 457.

41. For his response to this article, see the fifteenth of JJ's Objections to Grenville's Draft Treaty Proposals of 30 Aug., [6 Sept.]; and Art. 24 of JJ's Project for a Treaty with Great Britain, 30 Sept., both below.

42. JJ's draft of 6 Aug. did not raise this issue, strongly complained about by the British during the Genet ministry, on which see the editorial note "John Jay and the Genet Affair," *JJSP*, 5: 546–61. For his subsequent discussion of the matter, see Art. 20 of JJ's Project for a Treaty with Great Britain, 30 Sept., below, which Art. 19 of the Treaty of Amity, Commerce, and Navigation of 19 Nov. 1794 closely follows.

43. See the seventeenth of JJ's Objections to Grenville's Draft Treaty Proposals of 30 Aug., [6 Sept.]; Grenville to JJ: Responses to Queries, 7 Sept.; and Art. 24 of JJ's Project for a Treaty with Great Britain, 30 Sept., all below.

44. See Art. 24 of JJ's Project for a Treaty with Great Britain, 30 Sept., below. There is no equivalent statement in JJ's draft of 6 Aug. 1794.

45. See the final article in JJ's draft of 6 Aug.; the seventeenth of JJ's Objections to Grenville's Draft Treaty Proposals of 30 Aug., [6 Sept.]; and Art. 8 of JJ's Project for a Treaty with Great Britain, 30 Sept., both below.

46. Beginning with "And it is further agreed" there is substantial agreement between the present text, JJ's draft of 6 Aug., above, and Art. 8 of JJ's Project for a Treaty with Great Britain, 30 Sept., below.

47. Grenville here follows exactly the wording of JJ's draft of 6 Aug., which remained unchanged in Art. 7 of JJ's Project for a Treaty with Great Britain, 30 Sept., below.

48. See note 16, above.

To Thomas Pinckney

Royal Hotel—pall mall—31 aug^t. 1794

my Dr Sir

I sympathize with you most sincerely in the ~~late calamity~~ Distress you experience; and [~~would wi~~] ∧really∧ wish to relieve you from ~~much official~~ ∧as much as possible∧ ~~attentions~~ to public affairs[1]

When I ~~rec^d. from~~ ∧yesterday rec^d∧ the papers relative to the Copper, I was at Liesure to take up that Business—[2] I ~~have~~ ∧am∧ this Moment [*illegible*] ∧become so circumstanced as to∧ find it absolutely necessary to devote my whole time to the Business of my Mission,[3] in order to avail myself of the Prospect there now is of my being ~~en~~ enabled to write decidedly ∧on the Subject∧ to ~~the president~~ Mr Randolph ~~on the Subject,~~ in Season for my Letter to reach Ph[iladelphi]^a. before ∧or by∧ the ~~meeting~~ ∧sitting∧ of Congress.—[4] This ∧circumstance∧ constrains me to return the Papers relative to the Copper, ~~and will oblige me to devote all my Time to the Business in Question~~ ∧to Mr Dias∧ & I return them with regret and Reluctance; for on every occasion, & particularly on the Present, I am sollicitous to manifest the real Esteem and Regard with w^h. I am D^r. Sir y^r. most obt & hble Servt

The Honb. Mr Pinckney

Dft, NNC (EJ: 09470).

1. JJ refers to the death of Pinckney's wife, Elizabeth "Betsey" Motte Pinckney (1762–94) on 24 Aug. 1794. PAJ wrote in his diary on 25 Aug., "This day we were exceedingly shocked at the unexpected account of M^rs. Pinkney's death—" PAJ Diary A, AD, NNC.

2. The copper refers to copper and other materials AH charged Pinckney with obtaining, as supplies for building six frigates. Pinckney was given a draft of 180,000 guilders, with instructions to first try to obtain the materials in Great Britain, or, if unsuccessful, Gothenburg, Copenhagen, and Amsterdam. See AH to Thomas Pinckney, 25 June 1794, *PAH*, 16: 527–29.

3. JJ had just received Grenville's Draft Treaties of Amity and Commerce, 30 Aug. 1794, above.

4. JJ wrote to ER on 13 Sept. 1794, below. Congress next met on 19 Nov. 1794.

To Grenville

Royal Hotel. Pall Mall. 1 Septr. 1794

my Lord

I was Yesterday honored with your Lordship's Letter of the 30th. of August, with the Projects & map,[1] which accompanied it.— I consider the articles in these Projects, like those in our conversations, as being merely for *mutual* consideration—

In these Projects several parting points present themselves— some of them I presume may be easily accommodated; but there are others which create in my mind serious apprehensions. one of these articles, being without the Limits of my authority, I think I ought now to particularize— it is the one which respects a cession of Territory in the northwestern corner of the united States. It is proper also that I should say with Frankness, that in my opinion many circumstances and considerations, which shall be submitted to your Lordship, will restrain the united States from such a cession.[2]

This article would entirely frustrate my Hopes, if I had not Reason to persuade myself, that the enlarged and enlightened Policy of excluding *secondary*, from a competition with *primary* objects, will always harmonize with your Lordship's mind.

The present occasion is great, and tho' critical, yet auspicious to the Establishment of confidence and Friendship between the two Countries: with the magnitude and Importance of these objects, the Projects in question really do not appear to me to be commensurate. I am aware that in forming them, your Lordship had many Difficulties growing out of the Subject, and probably some others, to encounter; and that your attention was constantly divided between a multitude of great and pressing affairs. As soon as I shall have more maturely considered these Projects, I shall take the Liberty of requesting the favor of your Lordship to name a Day for me to communicate the Result of my Reflections—

The negociation now becomes delicate, and I should experience more than proportionate Embarrassments, were it not for my confidence in your Lordship's candor and Liberality, and for those Sentiments of Esteem, as well as Respect, with which I have the Honor to be my Lord Your Lordship's most obedient & most h'ble Servant,

John Jay

The Right Honorable Lord Grenville

ALS, UK-KeNA: FO 95/512 (EJ: 04998); Dft, NNC (EJ: 08495); FC, with corrections, NNC (EJ: 12779); C, unknown repository, formerly PRO (EJ: 03993); C, DNA: Jay Despatches, 1795–96 (EJ: 04315); C, NHi: King (EJ: 04447); LbkC, in JJ to ER, 13 Sept. 1794, NNC: JJ Lbk. 8.

1. On Faden's map, see JJ to Grenville, 4 Sept. 1794, below.

2. See Grenville's Draft Treaties of Amity and Commerce, 30 Aug. 1794, above; and JJ to Grenville, 4 Sept. 1794, below.

To Grenville

[Royal Hotel—pall mall, 4 Septr. 1794—]

M^r. Jay presents his respectful Compliments to Lord Grenville, and requests the favor of his Lordship to name a Time for recieving M^r. Jay, on the Subject of the proposed Treaties. In the mean time, M^r. Jay has the Honor of submitting the Remarks herewith enclosed, to His Lordships Consideration—[1]

> Remarks on that Part of the second Article of the Project of a Treaty for terminating all Differences between Great Britain and the united States of America, which purports a Cession or Dereliction, by the latter, of the Country lying to the westward and northward of either of the two Lines therein proposed & described.

For this cession or Dereliction two Reasons are assigned, vizt.

1st. That it is now understood that the River Mississippi would in no part thereof, be intersected by a west Line from the Lake of the Woods.—[2]

2dly. That it was stipulated by the Treaty of Peace, that the navigation of the River Missisippi should be free to both Parties—

Admitting the Fact mentioned in the *first* of these Reasons, to be well founded, it shews *only* that the northern and western Lines of the United States do not meet and close—and therefore, that it is necessary to fix on a Line for closing them. But no argument thence results, that either Great Britain or the united States, ought to cede or acquire any Territory further than what such closing Line may possibly render unavoidable.

That the Missisippi would in no point thereof be intersected by a west Line from the Lake of the Woods, is a Fact involved in too much uncertainty to be assumed as a Foundation for national Stipulations; for however it may be conjectured or supposed, yet it still remains to be ascertained.

The map sent to M^r. Jay by Lord Grenville—vizt. Faden's, published in 1793—[3] informs us, that the River Missisippi has been ascended only as far up as about the 45 Degree of north Latitude, that is about a Degree above the Falls of S^t. Anthony— so that its further Extent and Course towards the north, are *yet to be discovered.*

On the same map, Faden lays down a Stream connected with the marshy Lake, near the 45 Degree of Latitude; and thus denominates it "*The Missisippi by Conjecture.*"

He also lays down on the same map a Stream connected with the white Bear Lake, near the Latitude 46, and thus denominates it "*The missisippi by Conjecture.*"

He also lays down on the same map a Stream connected with the Red Lake, in Latitude 47, and thus denominates it "Red Lake River, or *Lahontan's Missisippi.*"

Inasmuch therefore as *three* different Streams found in the immense wilderness above Latitude 45, are *conjectured* to be the *Missisippi*, it is plain, that so far from being *certain* how far that River runs to the north, we really are yet to learn where it does run, and which of the Rivers in that wilderness it is. How then can it be assumed as a Fact, resting on good Evidence, that the Missisippi would at no Point thereof, be intersected by a west Line from the Lake of the Woods?

Individuals differing about Boundaries depending on the course and Extent of Brooks or Streams, settle questions of that kind by actual Surveys. States usually and with good Reason do the same— Why be content with delusive conjectures and Probabilities, when absolute certainty can easily be had. Let a Survey be accurately made by joint Commissioners, and at joint Expence. The united States are ready to adopt that measure, and to enter into the necessary Stipulations and arrangements—

If it should appear on such a Survey that the West Line would intersect the Missisippi, no Room for further questions or Dispute will remain— but if the contrary should prove to be the Case; then, as the northern and western Lines of the united States would not close, the manner of closing them will naturally and necessarily come under Consideration. Several modes of closing them may be devised; neither of which may be altogether agreable to both Parties— unless they shall be able to agree, let joint commissioners at joint Expence, and upon oath, fix a closing Line, in the manner which they shall judge most consonant with the true Intent & meaning of the Treaty of Peace.— The united States are ready to enter into such eventual Stipulations as may be necessary for that Purpose.

The second Reason assigned for this cession is "that it was stipulated by the Treaty of Peace, that the Navigation of the Missisippi should be free to both Parties."— From this Stipulation it is argued, as a natural and necessary Inference, that it was in the Expectation and Intention of the Parties that they should and would both border, not only on the River, but also on the *navigable* part of it—

This Inference seems to be violent. a Right freely to navigate a Bay, a Straight, a Sound, or a River is perfect without, and does not *necessarily* presuppose, the Dominion and Property of Lands adjacent to it.

But altho from a Right to navigate the River Missisippi, a Right to adjacent Lands cannot be inferred, yet when that Right is connected with the

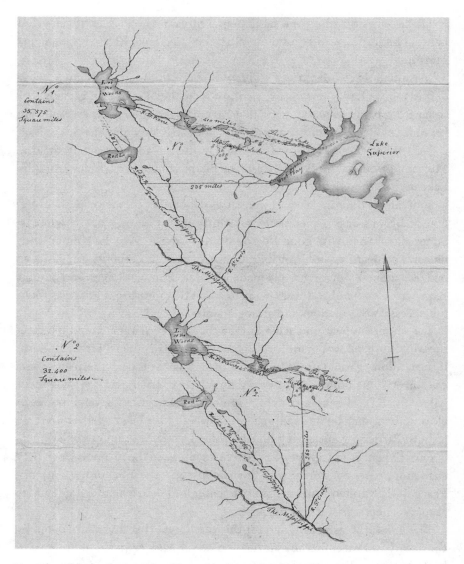

Two maps of the northwestern boundary of the United States accompanying JJ's 4 September 1794 objections to Grenville's projets of 30 August 1794, draft or file copy by John Trumbull. (Rare Book & Manuscript Library, Columbia University in the City of New York)

Circumstance that both Parties were to be bounded by a Line terminating at the River; it is thought to be thence presumable that the Parties expected and intended that the said Line would and should terminate at a navigable Part of it.—

They might, or they might not, have expected & intended it.— whether they did or not, can only be discovered from their concomitant words and actions.

On looking into the Treaty for *words* indicating such Intention our Search proves fruitless— there are no such *words* in it; not the least Shadow of a Stipulation or Declaration on the Point.

If we review the Plan and manifest Design of the Treaty relative to Boundaries, we find the Idea of such Intention uniformly contradicted.

The Treaty in delineating the Boundaries of the United States, passes from the northwest angle of Nova Scotia, to the Head of Connecticut River— then down that River to the 45 Degree of Latitude—then on that Line of Latitude to the River Iroquois, there (quitting that Line of Latitude) to Lake Ontario—then from Lake to Lake, thro' their connecting waters, untill it arrives at the *Lake of the Woods*, and passing thro' it, to the north westernmost point thereof, proceeds on a *due West* course to the Missisippi &c. &c^a.

now it was always well known, and the maps shew it, that the *Lake of the woods* is situated at a great Distance in the North above the Latitude of the Falls of S^t. Anthony, which interrupt the navigation of the Missisippi; and consequently that a *due west* Line from the Lake of the Woods, must of *necessity* strike the River above those Falls; & as *far* above them, as the Latitude of the Lake, is above the Latitude of the Falls.—

Again—It was not then known, nor is it yet known, how far the Missisippi runs navigable beyond those Falls— nor whether any, or how many other Falls intervene between them and its Source. The Parties therefore, being entirely ignorant of the Extent, and of the course, and of the character of the River high above the Falls, could not possibly have judged, or divined or guessed, whether the Place or Part of the River, at which the west Line would strike it, was navigable or not— How then could they expect or intend any thing about it?— nothing could be more obvious, than that a *due* west Line *might* terminate on the River at a Place *not* navigable; and had Navigation been in View, it seems strange that the Treaty should not contain a Provision, that if the said west Line, on being actually run, should strike the River at a Place where it was not navigable, that then the said Line should be inclined so many Degrees Southerly, as might be necessary to bring it to the first navigable water of the River. Yet nothing like this is to be found in the Treaty—

It is not difficult to discern from the Treaty, and so was the Fact, that other Ideas and Views governed the Direction of the Boundary Lines.

The Question then was, where would it be most *convenient* to both Parties; and all Things considered, where would it be most wise & prudent that the Boundaries between them should be fixed?

Two Lines were proposed and considered, one from the Point before mentioned on Connecticut River and running straight on the Line of the ~~of~~ 45ᵗʰ. Degree of Latitude, west to the Mississippi— The other was the one adopted and established by the Treaty—

The official Papers of the ∧british ministers∧ which respect that Negociation will probably shew, that Great Britain had the choice of these two Lines, and that she preferred the latter— this choice and Preference gives no Support to the Idea that she *then* contemplated *navigable* water in that part of the Missisippi which was supposed to penetrate into Canada. The *first* Line if adopted would have favored it, and fair Presumption might have classed *that* among the Reasons of Preference. But notwithstanding this Great Britain did not prefer it— on the contrary, as the waters would form a Line which could never be mistaken, and afforded great conveniences to both Parties, the Line of the waters was preferred by both.

This water Line was by mutual consent terminated at the northwesternmost Point of the Lake of the Woods. It was agreed that the Missisippi should bound the United States on the *west*— nothing then remained but to agree on the course, which the closing Line from that Lake to the River should run; and a *due west* course was agreed upon, without any Expectation or Design that it would or should there meet with *navigable* water.—

The Truth is, that the Stipulation respecting the navigation of the River being free to both Parties, was an after thought; & gave Occasion to a new and Subsequent article, vizᵗ. the 8ᵗʰ.—

Even on the drawing that article, when the navigation of the River became an object of Contemplation; no Connection was introduced between the Right mentioned in that article, and the Boundaries designated in the second article— no Facilities were asked or proposed or stipulated for a water or any other Communication between Canada & the navigable water of the Missisippi; which doubtless would have been the Case, had such a communication been then in View; especially considering the absolute uncertainty, and extreme Improbability, of that River's being navigable above the high Latitude of the Lake of the woods.

From the beforementioned Circumstances and Considerations it seems fairly to result that the *two* Reasons assigned for the cession in question as a matter of Equity and Right, do not afford it a solid Foundation—

If this conclusion be just, it precludes, the necessity of shewing at large, that none of the Inferences ascribed to the said two Reasons, involve a Claim to Tracts of Country so extensive as either of the two proposed and marked on the map— each of which includes more than thirty thousand square *miles*—and that without taking into the Computation the extensive Country lying between (what in the subjoined Diagrams are for the purpose of computation regarded as) the West Sides of these Tracts and the Missisippi, and to the Southward of the West Line from the Lake of the Woods, and which Country would on either of the proposed Plans, also become annexed to Canada—[4]

AD, with two maps by JT, UK-KeNA: FO 95/512 (EJ: 05000). Endorsed. C, in JT's hand, with maps, DNA: Jay Despatches, 1794–95 (EJ: 04316); C, unknown repository, formerly PRO (EJ: 03994); C, NHi: King (EJ: 04448); LbkC, in JJ to ER, 13 Sept. 1794, NNC: JJ Lbk. 8.

1. For JJ's immediate rejection of what he considered Grenville's proposed cession of a significant area north and west of the headwaters of the Mississippi, see JJ to Grenville, 1 Sept. 1794, above; and Grenville to JJ, 5 Sept. 1794, below.

2. In the course of peace negotiations with Richard Oswald in 1782, JJ had claimed that there was water carriage from Canada to the mouth of the Mississippi. See *JJSP*, 3: 184.

3. See William Faden, "The United States of North America with the British Territories and those of Spain according to the Treaty of 1784" (London, 1793). *American Memory* http://hdl.loc .gov/loc.gmd/g3300.ct001218 (accessed Oct. 2018). Faden (1749–1836), a cartographer, served as royal geographer to George III.

4. For his report on this issue, see JJ to ER, 13 Sept. 1794, below.

From Grenville

[Downing Street 5th. Septr. 1794]

Lord Grenville presents his Compliments to Mr. Jay— He has receiv'd Mr. Jay's note,[1] with the enclos'd remarks, and will be glad to see him at his Office Tomorrow at Twelve o'Clock.[2]

Lord Grenville has in the mean time the Honor to enclose to Mr. Jay, some observations which have occurr'd to him, on the perusal of the Paper which he receiv'd from Mr. Jay.

Observations respecting the North Western Boundary of the United States of America.

It cannot for a moment be admitted, that the proposed arrangement on the subject of the northwestern boundary is properly to be consider'd in the manner in which it is spoken of by Mr. Jay, namely, as a Cession or Dereliction of Territory on the part of the United States,

This Boundary to the north West, as fix'd by the Treaty, is a Line "to be drawn from the Lake of the Woods, in a due west course to the Missisipi." There are in this agreement Two distinct parts.

1st. That the Boundary Line should be drawn, in a due Westerly course, from the Lake of the Woods;— And

2ᵈ. That it should likewise be drawn, in a due westerly course, to the Missisipi.[3]

If such a Line cannot in fact be drawn between those points, there can be no ground for considering one part of this stipulation as more permanently fixed than the other, or as affording a more equitable ground for any future arrangement; and it would be quite as reasonable for this Country to consider as a Cession of Territory on our part the adoption of any other boundary, than that of a due Westerly Line striking the Missisipi; as for the United States to urge that such a Cession exists on their part, if such a Line is not drawn from the Lake of the Woods.

To this consideration must be added, that which so plainly results from the Article respecting future Navigation of the Missisipi, on which head it seems sufficient for the present to remark that such a right evidently and necessarily implies the possibility of access to that River, without passing thro' a foreign Territory.[4]

Little objection occurs to the making an actual Survey, except that of Delay. If, on that Survey, the stipulations in the Treaty should be found to be compatible with the real Geography of the Country, it is certain that no further dispute could exist on that point.

But, if we have from the best information on the subject sufficient reason to believe that no such line can be drawn as is mentioned in the Treaty, it cannot be desireable, when all the interests of the Two Countries with relation to each other are under discussion, with a view to lasting friendship, to leave unsettled so material a ground of difference, as that of an unascertain'd Boundary— The mode of settling that point is necessarily connected with the general result of the present negotiation.— If no more can be accomplished on any other point, than the doing strict justice between the Parties, according to existing Treaties and the Laws of Nations, the appointment of Commissaries, as proposed by Mʳ. Jay, does not appear ill adapted to obtain the same object as to this point; provided that those Commissaries are distinctly enabled to take into their consideration the 8ᵗʰ. Article, and to give to that stipulation such effect, as they shall think it ought in justice to have, in the formation of a new Boundary line.[5]

But, if the negotiation should lead to new Stipulations of mutual advantage, no Subject appears more proper for the application of that Principle, than one in which there exist two Doubtfull & contradictory Claims, founded on an Agreement which cannot by any possibility be executed: especially if it be true, as it is considered here, that this is a point, where any Advantage whatever it should be, which Great Britain might acquire, would, under all circumstances, be found at least equally beneficial to the United States.

C, DNA: Jay Despatches, 1794–95 (EJ: 04317); C, UK-KeNA: FO 95/512 (EJ: 03985); C, NNC (EJ: 08526, EJ: 08532); C, NHi: King (EJ: 04449); C of observations, UK-KeNA: FO 95/512 (EJ: 05002); LbkC, in JJ to ER, 13 Sept. 1794, NNC: JJ Lbk. 8.

1. See JJ to Grenville, 4 Sept. 1794, above.

2. For a summary of this meeting, see JJ to ER, 13 Sept. 1794, below.

3. Article 2 of the Treaty of 1783 reads: ". . . thence through Lake Superior northward of the Isles Royal and Phelipeaux to the Long Lake; thence through the middle of said Long Lake and the water communication between it and the Lake of the Woods, to the said Lake of the Woods; thence through the said lake to the most northwesternmost point thereof, and from thence on a due west course to the river Mississippi; thence by a line to be drawn along the middle of the said river Mississippi until it shall intersect the northernmost part of the thirty-first degree of north latitude."

4. See Art. 2 of Grenville's draft of a general treaty in his Draft Treaties of Amity and Commerce, 30 Aug. 1794, above.

5. Art. 4 of the Treaty of Amity, Commerce, and Navigation of 19 Nov. 1794, much as JJ suggests here, committed the two parties to make a joint survey of the area and, if the survey established that the river did not intersect the line specified in the Treaty of 1783, to engage in amicable negotiation to settle the issue conformable to the intent of the Treaty of 1783. No survey was undertaken at the time. The boundary in this area was finally settled in Art. 2 of the Webster-Ashburton Treaty of 1842, which conferred the territory Grenville claimed to the United States. Art. 4 of this treaty confirmed all land grants made by Britain as well as all "equitable possessory claims arising from a possession and improvement" of lands held more than six years before the date of the treaty. Art. 7 opened sections of the St. Lawrence, Detroit, and St. Clair rivers to navigation by both parties.

From George Washington

Philadelphia 5th. Sepr. 1794

My dear Sir

This encloses a copy of my last—written,[1] as you will readily perceive, with much haste as one indication of it, I omitted the stamp of privacy, but you would not, I am well persuaded, consider it as official nor in any other light than as the private sentiments very hastily thrown together of Your obedient and Affectionate

Go: Washington

ALS, DLC (EJ: 10633). LbkC, DLC: Washington.

1. In this letter of 30 Aug. 1794, GW makes observations on the intrigues by Simcoe and other British officers on the frontier, particularly to sow dissent among the Indians. He believed that unless the British withdrew from the forts, trade between the nations would suffer and war would be inevitable. For the copy enclosed with this letter, see C, marked: "Duplicate," NNC (EJ: 07255). For the original letter, see ALS, UkWC-A (EJ: 00043).

John Jay's Objections to Grenville's
Draft Treaty Proposals of 30 August

[London, 6 September 1794]

1. In what capacity are they to remain? As British Subjects or American Citizens? If the First, a Time to make this Election should be assigned.

2. If His Majesty's Subjects are to pass into the American Territories for the purposes of Indian Trade—ought not American Citizens to be permitted to pass into His Majesty's Territories for the like purpose?

3. If the American Indians are to have the privilege of trading with Canada—ought not the Canada Indians to be privileged to trade with the United States?

4. If Goods for Indian Trade shall be introduced *Duty Free* by British Traders—how is the Introduction of other Goods with them to be prevented?— And, for this Privilege operating a loss to the American Revenue, what Reciprocal Benefit is to be allowed?[1]

5. Why should the Commissioners for ascertaining the River S[t]. Croix meet and decide in London? Is it not probable that actual Views and Surveys, and the Testimony and Examination of Witnesses on the spot, will be necessary?[2]

6. Why confine the Mutual Navigation of the Mississipi to where the same bounds the Territory of the *United States*?

7. Why should *perpetual* commercial privileges be granted to Great Britain on the *Mississipi* when She declines granting *perpetual* Commercial Privileges to the United States *any where*?[3]

III Art:

8. This Preamble, connected with the Silence of the Treaty as to the Negroes carried away, implies that the United States have been Aggressors—[4] It also unnecessarily impeaches these[5] Judicial Proceedings.

9. On no principle ought more to be asked than that the United States indemnify Creditors for Losses and Damages caused by the Impediments mentioned.

10. The Word *had* is not sufficiently definite— the Object being not only Sentence, Decree or Judgment, but Payment and Satisfaction.[6]

11. Sterling Money fluctuates according to Exchange. This should be *fixed*.[7]

12. Why not place these Captures on the footing with the others, and charge the United States only in Cases where Justice and compleat Compensation cannot be had from Judicial Proceedings?

13. Why provide only for *Neutral* Commerce with *European* Enemies?—What difference does the complexion or Colour of Enemies make in neutral Right?

The whole of this Article is so indefinite as to be useless.[8]

14. What are or shall be deemed Contraband in the sense of this Article?[9]

15. As the United States have permitted the French to sell Prizes in the United States, the restriction not to do it in future should commence at the Expiration of the *present* War.[10]

16. There should be an Article against the Impressment of each other's people.[11]

17. This united Force should be confined to the *moment* of aggression.[12]

18. The Confiscation of Debts &ca.— This Article should be in the Treaty of Commerce—not in this.[13]

Conduct in case of Indian wars.

AD, UK-KeNA: FO 95/512 (EJ: 05001). C, labeled "Communications from Mr. Jay Septr 6th 1794", unknown repository, formerly PRO (EJ: 03995); Dft and Tr, PC, Kenneth W. Rendell, Inc., and SR, incomplete, Rendell Catalog 54 1970/71 (EJ: 12972); C, enclosed in JJ to ER, 13 Sept. 1794, DNA: Jay Despatches, 1794–95 (EJ: 04312); C, NHi: King (EJ: 04444); LbkC, NNC: JJ Lbk. 8; *ASP: FR*, 1: 492; *HPJ*, 4: 97–99.

1. On the above items, see Art. 1 of Grenville's draft of a general treaty in his Draft Treaties of 30 Aug. 1794, above. For his response to the first item, see Grenville to JJ, Responses to Queries, 7 Sept. 1794, below.

2. See Art. 2 of Grenville's draft of a general treaty in his Draft Treaties of 30 Aug. 1794, above.

3. See Art. 2, item 2, of Grenville's draft of a general treaty in his Draft Treaties of 30 Aug. 1794, above.

4. For Grenville's reasons for excluding from his draft of a general treaty the issue of enslaved persons carried away, see JJ to ER, 13 Sept. 1794, below.

5. This reads as "their" in other versions.

6. Art. 3 of Grenville's draft of a general treaty in his Draft Treaties of 30 Aug. 1794, above, contains the following: "in all Cases where such relief cannot, for whatever reason, be now had by British Creditors in the ordinary Course of justice, the United States of America will make full and Complete satisfaction to the said Creditors;" Art. 6 of JJ's Project for a Treaty with Great Britain, 30 Sept. 1794, below, reads: "be actually obtained, had and received by the said creditors in the ordinary course of justice. . . ."

7. JJ's comments on this issue relate to Art. 3 of Grenville's draft of a general treaty in his Draft Treaties of 30 Aug. 1794, above.

8. See Art. 5 of Grenville's draft of a general treaty in his Draft Treaties of 30 Aug. 1794, above.

9. See Art. 6 of Grenville's draft of a general treaty in his Draft Treaties of 30 Aug. 1794, above.

10. See Art. 7 of Grenville's draft of a general treaty in his Draft Treaties of 30 Aug. 1794, above.

11. See Art. 8 of Grenville's draft of a general treaty in his Draft Treaties of 30 Aug. 1794, above. For his attempt to include impressment in the treaty, see Art. 22 of JJ's Project for a Treaty with Great Britain, 30 Sept. 1794, below.

12. See Art. 9 of Grenville's draft of a general treaty in his Draft Treaties of 30 Aug. 1794, above.

13. See Art. 10 of Grenville's draft of a general treaty in his Draft Treaties of 30 Aug. 1794, above; and, for his responses to all of JJ's objections, see Grenville to JJ, Responses to Queries, 7 Sept. 1794, below.

From Grenville (private)

St. James's Square Sept[r] 7, 1794.

Dear Sir,

I send You the inclosed Paper[1] as containing what you perhaps may not have seen, & what cannot fail to be interesting to you, as I will not deny that it has been to me. I will beg you to return the paper as I preserve the series.

I do not believe that you personally will much envy M[r] Monroe the honour of the paternal kiss which he has received; and if such an exhibition is thought not to degrade an American Minister I know not why it should become matter of complaint on the part of the British Government.[2]

But with the same openness which you shall always find in me You must allow me as an Individual, feeling a strong interest in the maintenance of good order and morality in every civilized Country to say to you, as to one whom I believe to be actuated by the same principles, & whom I know to be a Person of distinguished abilities & character & of a very deserved weight in the Government of Your Country that in my opinion neither honor nor advantage will result from what is now done, even omitting the contrast which it makes with the language & conduct which you have been authorized to hold here.

I have hitherto been inclined to think the Government of the United States sincere in the desire to cultivate among the People of that Country the dispositions of neutrality, of peace, and of good understanding with Great Britain, because such was their evident and unquestionable interest to which I could not believe them blind. But it is not consistent with neutrality to make Ministerial declarations of favour and preference, nor can it lead to the maintenance of good order in any Country that its Government should give official sanction and adherence to acts at which all Religion & all Humanity revolt. I know what may be said of the allowance to be made for circumstances, particularly as operating on the deliberations of Congress; but it will not escape you that the Letters of the Secretary of State[3] go far beyond the resolutions of either House of Congress, & that by a singular contrast, their language will be found scarcely to exceed the usual bounds of diplomatic caution & reserve, while that of the Minister for Foreign Affairs is such as might be expected from the most zealous & eager partizan, heated by popular discussion.[4]

The purpose with which I make these observations to you in this unofficial form cannot be mistaken. I seriously & much apprehend the effect of this transaction both here & in America. We shall continue to labour with the same desire to preserve between the two nations a friendly disposition to each other; but such a declaration as this will be taken to be, of the sentiments & views of Your Government is ill calculated to produce that effect in either Country. It will afford matter of Offence & sincere regret to all well disposed Persons here, & matter of triumph & encouragement there to all who wish external War or domestic confusion.

I have felt it very much due to the candour & openness which I have always found on your part to speak to you in this undisguised manner, on a point which has given me much concern from the desire I felt of being in some degree the instrument of a permanent friendship and intimate union between the two Countries, & from the hope I entertained of the accomplishment of this object. I do not allow myself to despair of it, nor do I even yet bring myself to think that the dispositions of your Government can be such as this transaction taken by itself should seem to announce. But I lament the circumstance, & I believe that in so doing my sentiment upon it will not be very different from yours. Have the honour to be, & & &

Grenville.

C, UK-KeNA: FO 95/512 (EJ: 05003). Marked: *"Private"*. Endorsed: "Honble Mr Jay, & & &"; C, unidentified collection, formerly PRO (EJ: 03987).

1. Enclosure not found.

2. For a satirical comment contrasting the traditional kiss of the monarch's hand JJ bestowed when received by George III with Monroe's "fulsome complimentary Address" to a government "just about to drive away the legal Representatives of the U. S.," which the author described as Monroe's readiness to deliver a more debasing kiss, see "Anecdotes, [For Politicians, not for the Ladies.]," *Rising Sun* (Keene), 2 May 1797.

3. For the text of ER's two letters of 10 June 1794 to the Committee of Public Safety, see *ASP: FR*, 1: 674; *Monroe Papers*, 3: 30–32.

4. For Monroe's Address to the French National Convention of 15 Aug. 1794 on the occasion of his recognition as American minister to France, in which he asserted his belief that "Republicks should approach near to each other," proclaimed the affection of American citizens for France, and his own hopes to promote the interests of both nations, and for his presentation of ER's two letters to the Committee of Public Safety, and for the Convention's response, see *Monroe Papers*, 3: 30–32.

To Grenville (private)

Sunday night, 7 Sepr. 1794

Accept my thanks my Lord! for the Paper you was so obliging as to communicate in your Letter of to Day.[1] it is returned herewith enclosed. I have been anxious to learn the Manner of M^r. Munro's Introduction, and the circumstances which attended his Reception. I find some Things to regret— none that occasion Surprize Indeed, I have been so long conversant with Men, and human affairs, that few occurrences surprize me.

Had I been in M^r. Randolph's place, I should not have written exactly such a Letter. Strictures unnecessarily offensive, might have been avoided— good and sincere wishes for the Establishment of a Government founded on rational Liberty; might have been added; and every Inference of approbation or Disapprobation relative to the Principles and Conduct of the Revolution might easily have been obviated.

M^r. Randolph doubtless participated in the general Irritation of his Country, and permitted his Feelings to have, in my opinion, an undue Influence on his Pen; for there certainly is a Distinction between the Proprieties of official, and of personal or private Correspondence.[2]

Some allowances are always to be made for human nature— It is more easy and pleasant to give oneself to the Stream, than to oppose it. Characters exceedingly firm, and self possessed, and estimable; and characters exceedingly otherwise, are rare. The great mass of mankind are placed between these Extremes— some nearer to the one Extremity—some to the other. We must take men and Things as they are; and act accordingly. This I know is moralizing more than may become a Letter from me to your Lordship, but I constantly feel myself so much at my Ease in speaking or writing to those in whom I have confidence, that I am apt on such occasions to think loud.

If it was not vain to look back, I could trace all these Effects to their causes, and mark the Mistakes which Britain & America have committed relative to each other; for as the falling of little Sparks often causes great Conflagrations, so little Errors usually generate greater, and those, greater still— but *cui bono*?[3] what is passed, is passed— the *future* is a field in which good cultivation may keep down weeds and reap a Harvest according to the Seed sown— that as we sow, so we shall reap, is as true in politics as it is in Religion. The Seed of [*illegible*] of Thorns and Nettles will not produce Grapes and Figs.[4] Even of good Seed, there must be a *quantum*, if the Field be only half seeded, too much Room will be left for Weeds to shoot, and for such Tares to take Root as Mischief may incline to cast into it.

Let us go on, my Lord! and having done all that dispassionate Reason may indicate as wise and prudent, leave the Issue to Providence— modern Philosophers may say what they please, God does and *will* govern the World.

All that we have to do is, to do our Duty—that is, to do what is right and prudent— It is an obvious Rule of Prudence never, with one's Eyes open, to walk into a Snare spread for our Feet. It is natural for France to produce, if possible, a War between our two Countries— To avoid it, will require management— I might have been more particular on this point than I have been, but was affraid to urge Considerations that might be misinterpreted— the more I become acquainted with your Lordship, the more these apprehensions subside.

on reading over this Letter I think it a singular ∧one∧ to send to you; and yet I will send it, and rely on the opinions which excited the Esteem and Regard with which I have the Honor to be my Lord your Lordship's most obed^t. and most h'ble Servant

John Jay

The Right Honorable Lord Grenville

ALS, UK-KeNA: FO 95/512 (EJ: 05005). Marked: *"private"*. C, unknown repository, formerly PRO (EJ: 03996).

1. See Grenville to JJ (private), of this date, above; enclosure not found.

2. On ER's letters, see Grenville to JJ (private), of this date, above, and JJ to ER (private), 13 Sept., below. For his comments on ER's correspondence and Monroe's address, see JJ to AH, 11 Sept. 1794, below.

3. Who does it benefit?

4. An amalgam of Biblical imagery taken from Galatians 6: 7; Matthew 7: 15–20; and Luke 6: 43–45.

From Grenville

S^t. James's Square, Sep^{tr}. 7th: 1794.

Sir

In Order to narrow as much as possible the Objects of our Discussions, I have stated in the enclosed paper what occurs to me on the different points to which your notes[1] apply, except the 2^d: 3^d: & 4th: Articles of those Notes, which I have reservd for further examination and inquiry;— I expect that by tuesday or wednesday at furthest I shall be able to converse further with you on those points as well as with respect to what you suggested on the subject of the East Indies.[2]— The Points in Discussion will then be reduced within a small compass, but they certainly do not relate to the least important parts of our Negotiation.— with respect to them I can only say that you shall continue to find in me the same openness of discussion and the same desire to state to you without reserve what I think may be conceded to the object of speedy consideration, & what the Interest & Honor of my Country & the Duty which I owe to the King oblige me to insist upon as necessary for that object.

It is with sentiments of very real Esteem & Respect that I have the Honor to be &c &c &c

Sign'd Grenville

P.S. I also send a note of two Alterations to be made in the commercial Projet in consequence of our conversation of yesterday.

G.

[Grenville's Responses to Jay's Queries]

To the Hon^b. M^r. Jay &c &c &c

Observations — enclos'd with the above Letter

N°.1. In consequence of the observation contain'd in the first remark, Lord Grenville proposes to add in the first Article of the Projet, after the words "property thereof" at the end of the first paragraph these words: "And such of them as shall continue to reside there for the purposes of their Commerce shall not be compell'd to become Subjects of the United States or to take any Oath of Allegiance to the Government thereof, but they shall be at full Liberty so to do (if they think proper) within One Year after the evacuation of the Posts, which period is hereby assigned to them for making their choice in this respect."

Considering the length of the first Article, now encreased by this addition it may be better to divide it into Two; the second beginning with the Words, "It shall at all times be free" &c &c &c[3]

Articles 2. 3. & 4.} Reserved for further Examination.

5. The meeting of the Commissioners respecting the River St Croix is proposed to be in London, because it is supposed that the great mass of evidence on the subject is here:— A Power may be given to them either to direct a local survey, or to adjourn to America, but it seems very unlikely that this could become necessary.[4]

6. No idea was entertain'd of confining the mutual Navigation of the Missisipi to that part of the River where it bounds the Territory of the United States,— that qualification was intended only to have reference to the free admission of British Merchants Ships, into the Bays Ports and Creeks of the United States on the Missisipi, nor would it have been propos'd at all to repeat in this Article what is so distinctly stipulated in The Treaty of Peace respecting the free Navigation of the Missisipi, except for the purpose of expressly extending that stipulation to every part of the Waters now propos'd to form a part of the Boundary.

7. The Right of Admission into Ports &c. for the purposes of trade, and the general liberty of Commerce spoken of in the Article, are not consider'd as Commercial privileges, such as are usually made the subject of temporary regulation by special Treaties of Commerce—. Great Britain by no means declines to give the same rights permanently to America, as with respect to those parts of Her Dominions which are open to foreign commerce.

These rights are indeed now generally acknowledged to be incident to a state of Amity and good correspondence, and if it is proposed, to particularize them, as with respect to the Missisipi;— this is done only with the view of removing the possibility of such doubts as were formerly raised here on the subject[5]

8. On the fullest reconsideration of this Preamble Lord Grenville sees no ground to think it liable to the objection made by Mr Jay, particularly when compar'd with the Preamble propos'd for the Fourth Article;— The Proceedings in both Articles are grounded on the allegations of Individuals:— The Truth of those Allegations is referred to the decision of the Commissioners.— Lord Grenville's opinion respecting the prior aggression of the United States, as well as His reasons for that opinion are well known to M^r. Jay;— but He has no wish to introduce into the propos'd treaties any discussion of that point.[6]— He is therefore very ready to consider any form of words which M^r. Jay may suggest for those articles as better suited to the two Objects to which they are directed, those of Justice to Individuals, & conciliation between the Governments:— And this applies equally to the remarks N°s. 9 & 10.

11. The substitution of the word *Specie* as suggested by M^r. Jay seems fully to meet the object here mentiond.

12. What M^r. Jay here desires was intended to be done, and was indeed conceiv'd to be implied in the general words at the end of the Article.— But Lord Grenville sees no objection to the insertion of express words for the purpose.

13. Lord Grenville explain'd to M^r. Jay this morning the reason of the insertion of the word *European* in the place here referrd to:— The Subject is connected with the larger consideration to which their conversation led, & from the further discussion of which Lord Grenville is inclin'd to hope that mutual advantage may arise. M^r. Jay will observe that the subject to which his remark N°. 15 applies is one instance among many which might be brought to shew that this Article would not be inefficient.

14. To meet the object which was this morning suggested in conversation on this Article, Lord Grenville would propose the adoption of the following

additional Article to come in immediately after the eighth.— Lord Grenville has in conformity to what was mentioned by M^r. Jay, used the words of *Vattell*.

"In Order to regulate what is in future to be esteemed contraband, it is agreed, that under the said denomination shall be comprized all Arms and Implements serving in the purpose of War by Land or Sea, such as Cannon, Musquets, Mortars, Petards, Bombs, Grenades, Carcasses, Saucisses, Carriages for Cannon, musquet rests, Bandileers, Gunpowder, Match, Saltpetre, Ball, Pikes, Swords, Headpieces, Cuirasses, Halberds, Lances, Javelins, Horses, Horse furniture, Holsters, Belts, and generally all other implements of War["]; as also Timber for Shipbuilding, Tar or Rosin, Sheet Copper, Sails, Hemp & Cordage, and generally whatever may serve directly to the equipment of Vessels;— unwrought Iron and Fir planks only excepted:— And all the above Articles are hereby declar'd to be just objects of confiscation, whenever they are attempted to be carried to an Enemy.

And whereas Corn, Grain or Provisions can be consider'd as contraband in certain cases only, namely when there is an expectation of reducing the Enemy by the want thereof,[7] it is agreed that in all such cases, the said Articles shall not be confiscated; but that the Captors, or in their default the Government under whose Authority they act, in this respect, shall pay to the Masters or owners of such Vessels, the full value of all such Articles, together with a reasonable mercantile profit thereon, and also the Freight and Demurrage incident to their Detention.[8]

15. It seems by no means unreasonable that the effect of this Stipulation should be extended to the existing War, as a natural consequence of the good understanding to be established by this Negotiation, and by the removal of all existing differences.

And it would tend to prevent so many occasions of acrimony and dispute, on both sides, that Lord Grenville thinks it highly desirable to maintain this Article in its present form.[9]

16. Lord Grenville sees no reason whatever to object to this Article.[10]

17. This remark seems also perfectly just, and will best be met by omitting the concluding part of this Article.[11]

18. Lord Grenville rather thinks this Article ought to be permanent, for the mutual interest of both Countries; but He is content to leave this point to the decision of M^r. Jay, who is much too enlighten'd not to see the effect which a contrary conduct to that here prescribd must produce as with respect to America.[12]

Commercial Projet.—Observations.

Article 2ᵈ. Omit these words, "the same being of the Nations on whose behalf they shall be so appointed not otherwise;" And insert in lieu thereof— "The same being first approv'd by the Government of the Country in which they shall be so appointed to reside, and not otherwise."

3ᵈ: The last sentence to run thus, "— by which the Vessels of the One party shall pay in the Ports of the other, any higher or other duties than shall be paid in the similar circumstances by the Vessels of the Foreign Nation the most favor'd in that respect, or any higher or other duties than shall be paid in similar cases by the Vessels of the Party itself into whose Ports they shall come."

ALS, with enclosed observations, DNA: Jay Despatches, 1794–95 (EJ: 04318); C, UK-KeNA: FO 95/512 (EJ: 05004); C, unknown repository, formerly PRO (EJ: 03986); C, NNC (EJ: 08527); C, NHi: King (EJ: 04450); LbkC, in JJ to ER, 13 Sept. 1794, NNC: JJ Lbk. 8; C, NNC (EJ: 12780), cover letter only.

1. See JJ's Objections to Grenville's Draft Treaty Proposals of 30 Aug., [6 Sept. 1794], above.

2. A suggestion JJ perhaps made in the course of his conversation with Grenville on 6 Sept., on which see Grenville to JJ, 5 Sept. 1794, above. See JJ's Project for a Treaty with Great Britain, 30 Sept. 1794, note 52, below, which discusses Art. 13 of the Treaty of Amity, Commerce, and Navigation of 19 Nov. 1794.

3. See Art. 2 of JJ's Project for a Treaty with Great Britain, 30 Sept. 1794, below.

4. See Art. 4 of JJ's Project for a Treaty with Great Britain, 30 Sept., below.

5. See Art. 9 of JJ's Project for a Treaty with Great Britain, 30 Sept., below.

6. For a summary of Grenville's rebuttal of TJ's contention that Britain's evacuation of enslaved persons after the preliminary treaty had been announced in the United States constituted the first violation of the Treaty of 1783, see JJ to ER, 13 Sept. 1794, below.

7. Vattel, *Law of Nations*, bk. 3, chap. 7, sec. 112, which reads in part: "Commodities particularly *useful* in war, and the importation of which to an enemy is prohibited, are called *contraband goods.* Such are *arms, ammunition, timber for ship-building, every kind of naval stores, horses,*—and even provisions, in certain junctures, when we have hopes of reducing the enemy by famine." See also Art. 16 of JJ's Project for a Treaty with Great Britain, 30 Sept., below.

8. See Vattel, *Law of Nations*, bk. 3, chap. 7, sec. 113; Art. 16 of JJ's Project for a Treaty with Great Britain, 30 Sept., below.

9. See Art. 23 of JJ's Project for a Treaty with Great Britain, 30 Sept., below, in which JJ sustained Grenville's position.

10. See Art. 22 of JJ's Project for a Treaty with Great Britain, 30 Sept., below.

11. See Art. 9 of Grenville's draft of a general treaty in his Draft Treaties of 30 Aug. 1794, above.

12. JJ covered this issue in Art. 8 of his Project for a Treaty with Great Britain, 30 Sept., below. As Art. 10 of the Treaty of Amity, Commerce, and Navigation of 19 Nov., it was one of those articles whose term was agreed to be permanent.

From Henry Dundas

Horse Guards Monday 9th. Sept. 1794

Sir

you was so obliging as to say you would do me the honour of taking a quiet Dinner with me at my retreat at Wimbledon. If Thursday next is agreable to you, and your Son and Mr Trumbull, I shall be very happy of your Company that day. I dine soon after four o clock,[1] and I have the honour to remain, with great Respect Sir your most obedient and humble Servant

Henry Dundas

ALS, NNC (EJ: 05436). Endorsed: ". . . an^d. 9 sep^r. 1794".

1. PAJ records in his diary that on 12 Sept., "We dined with M^r. Dundas at Wimbleton in company with M^r. Pitt, the Lord Chancellor, & Lord Macartney who has lately arrived from China, & who told us many interesting facts relating to that country". PAJ Diary A, AD, NNC. A scheduling conflict delayed this meeting as JJ and his two secretaries had plans on the appointed day, so Dundas wrote back on the 10th proposing the following Friday, which JJ accepted. JJ to Dundas, 9 and 10 Sept., both Dft, NNC (EJ: 08901; EJ: 05436); Dundas to JJ, 10 Sept. 1794, ALS, NNC (EJ: 05573).

On Dundas, see JJ to GW, 21 July 1794, above. For JJ's sense that a majority of the British cabinet was disposed to settle differences with the United States, see JJ to ER, 13 Sept. 1794, below. See also the editorial notes "John Jay's Mission to London," and "Negotiating the Jay Treaty," both above.

From William Scott

[Commons Sepr. 10. 1794]

Sir

I have the Honor of sending the Paper drawn up by Dr Nicholl & myself—[1] It is longer and more particular than perhaps you meant—but it appeared to be an Error on the better Side rather to be too minute than to be ⌃too⌃ reserved in the Information We had to give— And it will be in your Excellency's Power either to apply the whole or such Parts as may appear more immediately pertinent to the Objects of your Inquiry.

I take the Liberty of adding that I shall at all times think myself much honored by any Communications from you, either during your Stay here or after your Return, on any Subject in which you may suppose that my Situation can give me the Power of being at all useful to the joint Interests of both Countries— If they should ever turn upon Points in which the Duties of my official Station appear ⌃to me⌃ to impose upon me an Obligation of Reserve, I shall have no Hesitation in saying, that I feel them to be such— on any other Points, on which you may wish to have an Opinion of mine, you may depend on receiving one that is formed with as much Care as I can use, and delivered with all possible Frankness & Sincerity.[2] I have the Honor to be, with great Respect and Consideration, Your Excellency's most obedient & very humble Servant

W[m]. Scott

ALS, NNC (EJ: 07134). Endorsed: ". . . with Instructions on case of Appeals and Claims". C, NHi: King (EJ: 04451); C, enclosure in JJ to ER, 13 Sept. 1794, below; LbkC, DNA: Jay Despatches, 1794–95 (EJ: 04319); LbkC, JJ: Lbk. 8; ASP: FR, 1: 494–96.

1. Encloses William Scott and John Nicholl to JJ, 10 Sept., below. JJ enclosed both to ER in his letter of 13 Sept., below. ER subsequently informed JJ that these documents had been presented to the Philadelphia committee of merchants and that efforts would be made to give the instructions their full effect. See ER to JJ, 12 Nov. 1794, ASP: FR, 1: 502.

Both the letter and the instructions were published in the *Daily Advertiser* (New York), 29 Nov.; *Federal Intelligencer* (Baltimore), 3 Dec.; *Greenleaf's New York Journal*, 6 Dec.; *Albany Gazette*, 11 Dec.; *Mercury* (Boston), 12–16 Dec.; *Columbian Centinel* (Boston), 13 Dec.; *Aurora General Advertiser* (Philadelphia), 18 Dec.; *Oracle of the Day* (Portsmouth), 20 Dec.; *American Mercury* (Hartford), 22 Dec.; *Norwich Packet*, 25 Dec.; *United States Chronicle* (Providence), 25 Dec.; *Eastern Herald* (Portland), 29 Dec. 1794; *Herald of the United States* (Warren, R.I.), 3 Jan.; and *Eagle: Or, Dartmouth Centinel* (Hanover, N.H.), 2 Nov. 1795. They were also printed by Francis Childs and John Swaine as *A letter and instructions from Sir William Scott and Doctor John Nicholl, prepared at the instance of Mr. Jay* (Philadelphia, 1794; *Early Am. Imprints*, series 1, no. 47283). In London, they were published in the *Courier and Evening Gazette*, 23 and 25 Feb. 1795.

2. For JJ's reply acknowledging receipt of the instructions, see JJ to Scott, 12 Sept. 1794, Dft, NNC (EJ: 90056; EJ: 08902).

From William Scott and John Nicholl

[Commons Sep[r]. 10. 1794]

Sir

We have the Honor of transmitting, agreeably to your Excellencys Request a Statement of the general Principles of Proceeding in Prize Causes in British Courts of Admiralty and of the Measures proper to be taken when a Ship and Cargo are brought in as Prize within their Jurisdictions.

The general Principles of Proceeding cannot, in our Judgment, be stated more correctly or succinctly than we find them laid down in the following Extract from a Report made to His late Majesty in the year 1753 by Sir George Lee then Judge of the Prerogative Court, D[r]. Paul His Majestys Advocate General, Sir Dudley Rider His Majestys Attorney General and M[r]. Murray (afterwards Lord Mansfield) His Majestys Solicitor General.[1]

"When two Powers are at War, they have a Right to make Prizes of the Ships, Goods, and Effects, of each other, upon the High Seas: Whatever is the

Property of the Enemy, may be acquired by Capture at Sea; but the Property of a Friend, cannot be taken, provided he observes his Neutrality.

Hence, the Law of Nations has established;

That the Goods of an Enemy, on Board the Ship of a Friend, may be taken.

That the lawful Goods of a Friend, on Board the Ship of an Enemy, ought to be restored.

That Contraband Goods, going to the Enemy, tho' the Property of a Friend, may be taken as Prize; because supplying the Enemy, with what enables him better to carry on the War, is a Departure from Neutrality.

By the Maritime Law of Nations, universally and immemorially received, there is an established method of Determination, whether the Capture be, or be not, lawful Prize.

Before the Ship, or Goods, can be disposed of by the Captor, there must be a regular judicial Proceeding wherein both Parties may be heard, and Condemnation thereupon as Prize, in a Court of Admiralty, judging by the Law of Nations and Treaties.

The proper and regular Court, for these Condemnations, is the Court of that State to whom the Captor belongs.

The Evidence to acquit or condemn, with, or without, Costs and Damages, must, in the first Instance, come merely from the Ship taken, vizt. the Papers on Board, and the Examination on *Oath* of the Master and other Principal Officers; for which Purpose, there are Officers of Admiralty in all the considerable Sea Ports of every Maritime Power at War, to examine the Captains, and other Principal Officers of every Ship, brought in as a Prize, upon General and Impartial Interrogatories: If there do not appear from thence Ground to condemn, as Enemys Property, or Contraband Goods going to the Enemy, there must be an Acquittal, unless from the aforesaid Evidence, the Property shall appear so doubtful, that it is reasonable to go into further Proof thereof.

A Claim of Ship, or Goods, must be supported by the Oath of some body, at least as to Belief.

The Law of Nations requires good Faith: Therefore every Ship must be provided with complete and genuine Papers; and the Master at least should be privy to the Truth of the Transaction.

To enforce these Rules, if there be false or colourable Papers; if any Papers be thrown over-board; if the Master and Officers examined in Preparatorio grossly prevaricate; if proper Ship's Papers are not on Board; or if the Master and Crew can't say, whether the Ship or Cargo be the Property of a Friend or Enemy, the Law of Nations allows, according to the different Degrees of Misbehavior, or Suspicion, arising from the Fault of the Ship taken, and other Circumstances of the Case, Costs to be paid, or not to be received, by the Claimants, in Case of Acquittal and Restitution. On the other Hand, if a Seizure is made without probable Cause the Captor is adjudged to pay Costs and Damages: For which Purpose all Privateers are obliged to give Security for their good Behaviour; and this is referred to; and expressly stipulated, by many Treaties.

Tho' from the Ships Papers, and the preparatory Examinations, the Property does not sufficiently appear to be Neutral, the Claimant is often indulged with Time to send over Affidavits to supply that Defect: If he will not shew the Property, by sufficient Affidavits, to be Neutral it is presumed to belong to the Enemy. Where the Property appears from Evidence not on board the Ship, the Captor is justified in bringing her in, and excused paying Costs, because he is not in Fault; or, according to the Circumstances of the Case, may be justly intitled to receive his Costs.

If the Sentence of the Court of Admiralty is thought to be erroneous, there is, in every Maritime Country a superior Court of Review, consisting of the most considerable Persons, to which the Parties who think themselves aggrieved, may Appeal; and this superior Court judges by the same Rule which governs the Court of Admiralty, vizt. The Law of Nations, and the Treaties subsisting with that neutral Power, whose Subject is a Party before them.

If no Appeal is offered, it is an Acknowledgment of the Justice of the Sentence by the Parties themselves, and conclusive.

This Manner of Tryal and Adjudication is supported, alluded to, and inforced, by many Treaties.

In this Method, all Captures at Sea were try'd, during the last War, by Great Britain, France and Spain, and submitted to by the neutral Powers.

—In this method, by Courts of Admiralty acting according to the Law of Nations, and particular Treaties, all Captures at Sea have immemorially been judged of, in every Country of Europe. Any other method of Tryal would be manifestly unjust, absurd, and impracticable".

Such are the Principles which govern the Proceedings of the Prize Courts

The following are the Measures which ought to be taken by the Captor and by the neutral Claimant, upon a Ship and Cargo being brought in as Prize

The Captor immediately upon bringing his Prize into Port sends up or delivers upon Oath to the Registry of the Court of Admiralty all Papers found on board the captured Ship.— In the course of a few days the Examinations in Preparatory of the Captain and some of the Crew of the captured Ship are taken upon a set of standing Interrogatories, before the Commissioners of the Port to which the Prize is brought and which are also forwarded to the Registry of the Admiralty as soon as taken. A monition[2] is extracted by the Captor from the Registry, and served upon the Royal Exchange notifying the Capture and calling upon all Persons interested to appear and shew cause, why the Ship and Goods should not be condemned. At the expiration of twenty days the monition is returned into the Registry with a Certificate of its service, and if any Claim has been given the Cause is then ready for hearing upon the evidence arising out of the Ships Papers and preparatory Examinations.

The Measures taken on the part of the neutral Master or Proprietor of the Cargo are as follows:

Upon being brought into Port, the Master usually makes a Protest which he forwards to London as Instructions (or with such further directions as he thinks proper) either to the Correspondent of his Owners or to the Consul of his Nation in order to Claim the Ship and such parts of the Cargo as belong to his Owners or with which he was particularly entrusted. Or the Master himself as soon as he has undergone his examination goes to London to take the necessary Steps.

The Master, Correspondent, or Consul applies to a Proctor who prepares a Claim supported by an Affidavit of the Claimant stating briefly to whom, as he believes, the Ship and Goods claimed belong, and that no Enemy has any Right or Interest in them. Security must be given to the Amount of sixty Pounds to answer Costs, if the Case should appear so grossly fraudulent on the Part of the Claimant as to subject him to be condemned therein.

If the Captor has neglected in the mean time to take the usual Steps (but which seldom happens as he is strictly enjoined both by his Instruction and by the Prize Act to proceed immediately to Adjudication) a Process issues against him on the application of the Claimants Proctor to bring in the Ships Papers and preparatory Examinations, and to proceed in the usual way.

As soon as the Claim is given, Copies of the Ships Papers and Examinations are procured from the Registry, and upon the return of the monition the Cause may be heard. It however seldom happens, (owing to the great pressure of business especially at the commencement of a War) that Causes can possibly be prepared for hearing immediately upon the expiration of the time for the return of the monition. In that case each Cause must necessarily take its regular turn;— Correspondent measures must be taken by the neutral Master if carried within the Jurisdiction of a Vice Admiralty Court by giving a Claim supported by his Affidavit, and offering Security for Costs if the Claim should be pronounced grossly fraudulent.

If the Claimant be dissatisfied with the Sentence his Proctor enters an Appeal in the Registry of the Court where the Sentence was given or before a Notary Public (which ∧regularly∧ should be enter'd within fourteen days after the Sentence) and he afterwards applies at the Registry of the Lords of Appeal in Prize Causes (which is held at the same place as the Registry of the High Court of Admiralty) for an Instrument called an Inhibition and which should be taken out within three months, if the Sentence be in the High Court of Admiralty and within nine months, if in a Vice Admiralty Court but may be taken out at later Periods if a reasonable Cause can be assigned for the delay that has intervened. This Instrument directs the Judge, whose Sentence is appealed from to proceed no further in the Cause, it directs the Registrar to transmit a Copy of all the Proceedings of the inferior Court, and it directs the Party who has obtained the Sentence to appear before the superior Tribunal to answer to the Appeal. On applying for this Inhibition Security is given on the part of the Appellant to the amount of Two hundred Pounds to answer Costs in case it should appear to the Court of Appeals that the Appeal is merely vexatious. The Inhibition is to be served upon the Judge, the Registrar, and the adverse Party and his Proctor by shewing the Instrument under Seal and delivering a Note or Copy of the Contents. If the Party cannot be found and the Proctor will not accept the service the Instrument is to be served "viis et modis" that is, by affixing it to the door of the last place of residence or by hanging it upon the Pillars of the Royal Exchange. That Part of the Process above described which is to be executed abroad may be performed by any Person to whom it is committed, and the formal Part at Home is executed by the Officer of the Court. A Certificate of the Service is endorsed upon the back of the Instrument, sworn before a Surrogate of the superior Court, or before a Notary Public if the service is abroad.

If the Cause be adjudged in a Vice Admiralty court, it is usual upon entering an Appeal there, to procure a Copy of the proceedings which the Appellant sends over to his Correspondent in England who carries it to a Proctor and the same Steps are taken to procure and serve the Inhibition as where the Cause has been adjudged in the High Court of Admiralty. But if a Copy of the Proceedings cannot be procured in due time, an Inhibition may be obtained, by sending over a Copy of the Instrument of Appeal or by writing to the Correspondent an Account only of the time and substance of the Sentence.

Upon an Appeal fresh Evidence may be introduced, if upon hearing the Cause the Lords of Appeal shall be of Opinion, that the case is of such doubt as that further Proof ought to have been ordered by the Court below.

Further Proof usually consists of Affidavits made by the asserted Proprietors of the Goods in which they are sometimes joined by their Clerks and others acquainted with the transaction and with the real property of the Goods claimed. In corroboration of these Affidavits may be annexed original Correspondence, Duplicates of Bills of Lading, Invoices, Extracts from books &.ᶜ. These Papers must be proved by the Affidavits of Persons who can speak to their authenticity.— And if Copies or Extracts, they should be collated and certified by public Notaries. The Affidavits are sworn before the Magistrates or others competent to administer Oaths in the Country where they are made, and authenticated by a Certificate from the British Consul.

The degree of Proof to be required depends upon the degree of suspicion and doubt that belongs to the Case. In Cases of heavy suspicion and great importance the Court may order, what is called "Plea and proof" that is, instead of admitting Affidavits and Documents introduced by the Claimants only, each Party is at liberty to alledge in regular pleadings such circumstances as may tend to acquit or condemn the Capture and to examine Witnesses in support of the Allegations, to whom the adverse Party may administer interrogatories. The Depositions of the Witnesses are taken in Writing. If the Witnesses are to be examined abroad, a Commission issues for that purpose. But in no case is it necessary for them to come to England. These solemn proceedings are not often resorted to.

Standing Commissions may be sent to America for the *general* Purpose of receiving Examinations of Witnesses in all Cases where the Court may find it necessary for the purposes of Justice to decree an Inquiry to be conducted in that Manner

With respect to Captures and Condemnations at Martinico which are the Subjects of another Inquiry contained in your Note, we can only answer in general, that we are not informed of the Particulars of such Captures and Condemnations, but as we know of no legal Court of Admiralty established at Martinico, we are clearly of Opinion that the legality of any Prizes taken there must be tryed in the High Court of Admiralty of England upon Claims given, in the Manner above described, by such Persons as may think themselves aggrieved by the said Captures.

We have the Honor to be, Sir Your Excellency's most obedient & very humble Servants

Wᵐ. Scott

John Nicholl

DS, NNC (EJ: 08533). Closing in Scott's hand; signed by Scott and Nicholl. Endorsed: "Sʳ. Wᵐ. Scott & Dʳ. / Nicoll's Instructions". Enclosed in Scott to JJ, same date, above. C, NHi: King (EJ: 04451); C, enclosure in JJ to ER, 13 Sept. 1794, below; LbkC, DNA: Jay Despatches, 1794–95 (EJ:

04319); LbkC, JJ Lbk. 8; *ASP: FR*, 1: 494–96. For periodical and pamphlet publications, see Scott to JJ, same date, note 1, above.

1. George Lee (c. 1700–1758) dean of arches and judge of the Prerogative Court of Canterbury, 1751–54; Dudley Ryder (1691–1756), attorney general, 1734–54; William Murray, later first earl of Mansfield, solicitor general, 1742–54; George Paul (d. 1763), advocate general. *ODNBO*. "Report of the Committee Nominated by his Britannic Majesty to Reply to the Statement of Reasons Formulated by the Court of Berlin, 18 Jan. 1753," in Thomas Baty, ed., *Prize law and continuous voyage* [London, 1915], 116–34. The report was a response to the suspension of repayment of a debt to Great Britain in 1744 by Frederick II of Prussia, after Britain captured ostensibly neutral Prussian vessels that were allegedly carrying contraband supplies to France, then at war with Great Britain. See *PAH*, 19: 342n30.

2. Monition: in maritime law, "similar to a writ of summons, commencing a cause for the condemnation of a ship as prize." *OED*.

To Alexander Hamilton

London, 11 Sept[r] 1794

Dear Sir

I had last week the Pleasure of recieving from You a few Lines by M[r]. Blaney.[1] You will recieve this Letter by the Hands of M[r]. Morris—[2] He will also be the Bearer of my Dispatches to M[r] Randolph. they will be voluminous, particular, and in many Respects interesting.[3] It should not be forgotten that there is Irritation here, as well as in America—and that our *party* Processions, Toasts, Rejoicings &[c] &[c]. have not been well calculated to produce Good Will and good Humour. The Government nevertheless distinguishes between national acts, and these party Effusions, and have entertained hitherto an opinion and Belief that the Presid[t] and our Governm[t]. and Nation in general, were really desirous of an amicable Settlement of Differences, and of laying a Foundation for Friendship as well as peace between the two Countries.

The Secretary's Letters by M[r]. Munro, and his Speech on his Introduction to the Convention have appeared in the English papers. Their Impression in this Country may easily be conjectured— I wish they had both been more guarded. The Language of the United States at Paris and at London, should correspond with their neutrality. These things are not favorable to my Mission.[4]

A speedy Conclusion to the Negociation is problematical, tho not highly improbable. If I should be able to conclude the Business on admissible Terms, I shall do it, and risque Consequences; rather ∧than∧ by the Delays of waiting for, and covering myself by opinions & Instructions hazard a Change in the Disposition of this Court— for it seems our Country, or rather some parts of it, will not forbear Asperities. I hear that Virg[ini]ᵃ. is taking british property by Escheat; and other things which in the present Moment are unseasonable, are here reported.[5]

As the proposed Articles are under Consideration—as they have already undergone some Alterations,[6] and as I am not without Hopes of other and further Amendments, I really think they ought not to be published in their present crude State; especially as in the Course of a few Weeks I expect to be able to communicate their *ultimate* Form. If *then*, they should not appear to me to be such as I ought to sign, I will transmit them, and wait for further Instructions—[7] I am Dear Sir Yours Sincerely—

John Jay

Col. Hamilton

ALS, DLC: Hamilton (EJ: 10768); Dft, NNC (EJ: 05648); *WJ*, 2: 229–30; *PAH*, 17: 221–23.

1. David Blaney, a Virginian, was recommended to JJ by Henry Lee, and would eventually deliver the treaty to ER on 7 Mar. 1795. See Henry Lee to JJ, 6 July 1794, ALS, NNC (EJ: 12815); JJ to ER, 19 and 21 Nov. 1794, below; and *PAH*, 17: 221–22.

2. Robert Morris Jr.

3. See JJ to ER, 13 Sept. (two letters, one of which was private), and 14 Sept. 1794, all below.

4. On ER's two letters (one written in the name of the Senate and the other, the House of Representatives) to the Committee of Public Safety, 24 June 1794, and on Monroe's speech to the French National Assembly, see *PGW: PS*, 16: 676–79; *Monroe Papers*, 3: 30–32; and *ASP: FR*, 1: 673–74. For remarks on ER's letters and Monroe's speech, see Grenville to JJ (private), 7 Sept., and JJ to Grenville (private), 7 Sept. 1794, both above. For ER's instructions to JJ on discussions with the British ministry about the U.S. attitude toward France, see JJ to ER (private), 13 Sept. 1794, below.

5. Escheat: based on common law, "the reversion of land or property to the state upon the death of an owner when there are no qualified heirs or when property goes unclaimed." *OED*.

Specifically, at this time, states used this principle to confiscate property owned by British citizens in order to repay British debts.

6. See Grenville's Draft Treaties of 30 Aug. 1794; JJ to Grenville, 1, 4, and [6 Sept. 1794]; and Grenville to JJ, 5 and private letter of 7 Sept. 1794, all above.

7. JJ wrote to GW on much the same topics in his letter of 13 Sept. 1794, ALS, DLC: Washington (EJ: 10634); C, NNC (EJ: 08463); *PGW: PS*, 16: 176–80.

To Edmund Randolph

London 13ᵗʰ. Septʳ. 1794.—

Sir.

Hitherto my Letters have communicated to you but little information of much importance, except on one point;— Altho all the general objects of my Mission were opened at once, & were received with every indication of the same Candor & Disposition to Agreement with which they were stated, yet the Nature of the Business turned the imediate & more particular Attention of both parties to the Affairs of the Captures,— the result has been communicated to you.[1]

A number of informal conversations on the other Points then took place, & every Difficulty which attended them, came into View, & was discussed with great fairness & Temper,— the Inquiry naturally led to the Fact, which constituted the first violation of the Treaty of Peace;—[2] The carrying away of the Negroes contrary to the 7th: Article of the Treaty of Peace,[3] was insisted upon as being the *first* aggression;— To this it was answered in substance,— That Great Britain understood the Stipulation contained in that Article in the obvious sense of the Words which expressed it, vist; as an engagement not to cause any Destruction, nor to carry away *any Negroes or other Property* of the American Inhabitants, or in other words, that the Evacuation should be made without Depredation: That no alteration in the actual State of Property was operated or intended by that Article:— That every Slave like every Horse which escap'd or stray'd from within the American lines, & came into the Possession of the British Army, became by the Laws & Rights of War *British* Property;—and therefore ceasing to be *American* Property, the exportation thereof was not inhibited by the Stipulation in question;— That to extend it to the Negroes who under the Faith of Proclamations, had come in to them, of whom they thereby acquir'd the Property. and to whom, according to promise, Liberty had been given; was to give to the Article a greater Latitude than the Terms of it would warrant, & was also *unnecessarily* to give it a construction which being *Odious*, could not be supported by the known & established rules for construing Treaties;— To this was replied the several remarks and considerations which are mentioned at large in a Report which I once made to Congress on this Subject, & which for that reason, it would be useless here to repeat;—[4] On this point we could not agree.[5]

I then brought into View another circumstance as affording us just cause of Complaint, antecedent to any of those urged against us, Vizt: that from the Documents recited & stated in Mr. Jefferson's letter to Mr. Hammond, it appears that the Posts were not only not evacuated within the reasonable time stipulated by Treaty, but also, that no order for the purpose had at least within that time, if ever, been given.

To this it was answered, That the Provisional Articles were sign'd at Paris on the 30th: Novr. 1782, That those Articles were to constitute the Treaty of Peace proposed to be concluded between Great Britain & the United States, but which Treaty was not to be concluded till the Terms of Peace should be agreed upon between Great Britain & France;— That the Treaty of Peace was not concluded untill the 3ᵈ: September 1783;— That it was not ratified in America untill the 14ᵗʰ: January 1784, and that the Ratification was not receiv'd in London untill the 28ᵗʰ: May 1784; nor exchangd untill the End of that Month: That, according to the Laws of Nations, Treaties do not oblige the Parties to begin to execute the Engagements contained in them, untill they have receiv'd their whole Form, that is, untill after they shall [have] been ratified by the respective Sovereigns that are Parties to them, & untill after those Ratifications shall have been exchanged;— That therefore it was not untill the end of May 1784 that Great Britain was bound to give any Orders to evacuate the Posts;— That such orders could not arrive at Quebec, untill in July 1784, and consequently that the allegations of a Breach of the Treaty by the non execution of the Article respecting the Posts, grounded on circumstances prior to the 13ᵗʰ: July 1784 are evidently unfounded:— That in the interval between the arrival & publication in America of the provisional Articles and the month of July 1784, by which time, at soonest, orders (issued after the Exchange of the ratifications of the Treaty of Peace, the last of May) could reach Quebec; incontestable Violations of the Treaty had taken place in the United States.

That Reason and the Practise of Nations warrant during a suspension of Hostilities *only* such measures as result from a continuance of the *Status quo*, untill the *final* Exchange of Ratifications.— That in opposition to this, new legislative acts had, in the interval before mentioned, been passed; which were evidently calculated to be beforehand with the Treaty, and to prevent its having its full and fair operation on certain points and objects, when it should be ratified and take Effect:— That these acts were the first Violations of the Treaty, and justified Great Britain in detaining the Posts untill the Injuries caused by their Operation, should be compensated.—

That Britain was not bound to evacuate the Posts, nor to give any Orders for the purpose, untill after the Exchange of the Ratifications, does appear to me to be a proposition that cannot be reasonably disputed;[6]

That certain legislative acts did pass in the United States, in the interval aforesaid, which were inconsistent with the Treaty of Peace is equally certain; But it does not thence ₐnecessarilyₐ follow, that those Acts were without Justice even as relative to the Treaty, for precedent Violations on the part of Great Britain, would justify subsequent retaliation on the part of the United States:— Here again the ~~affair of the~~ Affair of the Negroes emerg'd;—and was insisted upon;—and was answered as before:— I confess however that his Construction of that Article has made an impression upon my Mind, &

induc‸e‸d me to suspect that my former opinion on that Head may not be well founded.

Thus it became evident that admissions of Infractions of the Treaty of Peace, and that this or that Party committed the first aggression were not to be expected, & that such Discussions would never produce a Settlement:—[7]

It then became adviseable to quit those Topics, and to try to agree on such a sett of reciprocal concessions as (ballancing each other) might afford Articles for a Treaty, as beneficial to both parties, as to induce them to bury in it all former Questions and Disputes;— This Idea gave occasion to a variety of propositions of different kinds, which it would be tedious and useless to enumerate, and of which you will readily conceive there were some that could not meet with mutual approbation;— Among those ‸which‸ were mentioned was one for altering essentially our Boundaries in the Northwestern corner of the United States;—[8] This I regarded as inadmissable, & hoped would not be persisted in;— One for doing us complete justice respecting the Captures;— One for partially opening to us a Trade with the West India Islands; One for our paying the Damages sustained by British Creditors by lawfull impediments;— this was strongly insisted on;— I did not think it utterly inadmissable, in case we receiv'd proper justice and priviledges under other Articles, for then, in my judgement, it would not be adviseable to part and separate on that point, & various reasons convinced me it would be adhered to;— One for putting the Ships & Merchants of both parties on an equal footing:— In short, in order to bring the whole subject comprehensively into view, nothing that occurr'd was omitted to be mentioned;— These were free conversations, neither of us considering the other as being committed by any thing that was said or propos'd.[9]

It was necessary then to select points for mutual consideration, and quitting desultory Discussions, to fix our attention on certain propositions, each being at Liberty to propose what he pleas'd, and again to retract his proposition, if on mature reflection He should be so inclin'd: with this view, after returning home, I selected the following, and having reduc'd them to writing, sent them to Lord Grenville for his consideration; in the mean time employing myself in reflecting & endeavoring to decide in my own mind how far, & with what modifications or omissions it would be proper to adopt them.

[*Here Jay embedded a copy of his letter to Grenville of 6 Aug. 1794, above.*]

The paper that was enclosed, is in these words. vizt:

[*Here Jay embedded a copy of the enclosed Draft for a Convention and Treaty of Commerce, 6 Aug. 1794, above.*]

From the 6th: to the 30th: of August nothing of importance occurred;—

On the 30th: day of August Lord Grenville wrote me a Letter and enclosed Two Drafts or Projects of Treaties; The Letter is in these words. Viz^t.

[*Here Jay embedded a copy of Grenville's letter of 30 Aug. 1794, above.*]

The Drafts or Projets are as follows. Viz^t—[10]

[*Here Jay embedded a copy of Grenville's Draft Treaties of 30 Aug. 1794, above.*]

To the beforementioned Letter, I return'd the following Answer, Viz^t.[11]

[*Here Jay embedded a copy of his letter to Grenville of 1 Sept. 1794, above.*]

The proposed alterations in our North Western boundary and the consequential Cession and Dereliction of Territory, appeard to me to be a point, which I ought without delay to state to his Lordship, in the Light in which it appeared to me;— I therefore prepared and sent him inclosed in a Note the following Remarks, Viz^t.

[*Here Jay embedded a copy of his letter to Grenville of 4 Sept. 1794, above.*]

In order that you may have an accurate idea of the Lines proposed by Lord Grenville, I here insert copies of the Diagrams mentioned in the foregoing Remarks—[12]

On the 5th: Septr. Lord Grenville wrote me the following Note, Viz^t.

[*Here Jay embedded a copy of Grenville's letter of 5 Sept. 1794, above.*]

The Observations enclos'd with this Note, were as follows, Viz^t.

[*Here Jay embedded a copy of Grenville's Observations respecting the North Western Boundary of the United States of America, above.*]

Expecting that, when we met, the first of the above Projects, would, as first in the Order of things, be first considered, my attention was more immediately confin'd to it;— But the Time consum'd in preparing the remarks beforementioned, left me very little leisure to employ in forming satisfactory opinions on the different parts of this Projet;— several however occurred to me, of which I made short notes;— They are as follows;— You will find the numbers mark'd in the margin of the project.

[*Here Jay embedded a copy of his Objections to Grenville's Draft Treaty Proposals of 30 Aug., [6 Sept. 1794], above.*][13]

On the 6th: of September agreeable to Lord Grenville's appointment, I waited upon Him;— We spent several hours in discussing the several topics which arose from these Notes, and some others which in the course of the conversation occurred— He promised to take what I had offered into consideration, and manifested throughout the Conversation every Disposition to accommodate, that could be wish'd:— We may not finally be able to agree;— If we should not, it would in my opinion occasion *mutual* regret, for I do believe that the greater part of the Cabinet,[14] & particularly Lord Grenville, are really disposed and desirous not only to settle all Diferences amicably, but also to establish permanent Peace, Good Humour, and Friend-ship between the Two Countries.

On the 8th: of September I receiv'd from Lord Grenville the following let-ter enclosing the Papers mention'd in it.—Viz^t.—

[*Here Jay embedded a copy of Grenville's letter of 7 Sept. 1794, with his enclosed observations, above.*]

Thus Sir![15] I have given you a very particular and correct account of the negociation. Many observations & explanatory Remarks might be added. I might also inform you, that I had strenuously urged the Justice of Compen-sation for the Detention of the Posts; and that ∧I consider∧ the Priviledge of trading to the west Indies as providing for ∧claims of that kind.∧[16] On this Priviledge, and the Probability of its being revived after the Expiration of the Term assigned for its Duration,[17] I could enlarge,— but it does not strike me as necessary to go into further Details; nor indeed could I at present find Time for the Purpose.

It will not escape you, that the Articles now under Consideration will doubtless undergo many Alterations, before they assume that final Form, in which they will either be accepted or rejected; and *therefore* that it would not be proper to publish them at present. I think that in the Course of a few Weeks, the Questions now under Discussion will be decided. No Time shall be lost in communicating to you the Result.

Another Subject remains to be mentioned. It appeared to me adviseable that our People should have precise and plain Instructions relative to the Prosecution of appeals and Claims in Cases of Capture. For that purpose I applied to Sir William Scott, and requested him, in concert with Doct^r. Nicholl, to prepare them. We conversed on the Subject, and I explained to him my views and Objects—.

On the 10th: of Septr. I received them, enclosed with the following Let-ter from Sir William, which I insert on Account of the friendly Disposition towards our Country which it manifests, and which appears to me to be less uncommon here than we generally suppose—vizt.

[*Here Jay embedded a copy of William Scott's letter to JJ of 10 Sept. 1794, with an enclosed paper of that date signed by Scott and John Nicholl, above.*][18]

I take the Liberty of advising that these Instructions with a proper Title prefix'd, be printed in a Pamphlet and published for general Information.[19]

You will find herewith enclosed a Copy of the Instructions of the King and Council revoking the order to Capture neutral vessels, laden with Corn &c^a. bound to France— A Gazette of the 6th. September, containing an order re-straining Impressments &c.— and a Gazette of the 9th September[20] containing a Copy of the order of the 6th of August relative to Appeals and Claims, of which Copies have already been sent to you.[21] I have the Honor to be with great Respect, Sir, Your most obedt. & humble Servant,

John Jay

"The Honble Edm: Randolph Esqr. / Secretary of State &c. &c. &c."

LS, DNA, with several paragraphs in JJ's hand including the closing pages, DNA: Jay Despatches, 1794–95 (EJ: 04312); C, NHi: King (EJ: 04444); LbkC, NNC: JJ Lbk. 8; HPJ, 4: 60–114.

1. See JJ to ER, 2 Aug. 1794, above.

2. See Grenville's Notes Respecting the Posts, 5 Aug. 1794, above, where TJ's letter to Hammond, 29 May 1792 (PTJ, 23: 551–613), is discussed.

3. For Art. 7, see PTJ, 23: 568–69.

4. JJ's Report on Violations of the Treaty of Peace, 13 Oct. 1786, JJSP, 4: 417–33.

5. The Treaty of Amity, Commerce, and Navigation of 19 Nov. 1794 contained no provision on the return of enslaved persons or compensation for them.

6. See Grenville to JJ (private), and Grenville's Notes on Posts, both 5 Aug. 1794, both above.

7. See the opening statement to this effect in the preamble to JJ's Project for a Treaty with Great Britain, 30 Sept. 1794, below, replicated in the Treaty of Amity, Commerce, and Navigation of 19 Nov. 1794. In his initial reply to this letter, ER remarked that Grenville's reasoning on the "negroes" and the "*first* aggression" was so new to him that it should not be assented to without the "fullest reflection." ER also questioned whether JJ had incorrectly reported the date proposed for the evacuation of the posts in the forthcoming treaty (1796 instead of 1795), an interval ER considered "unnecessarily long" and designed to give the British opportunities for more injurious trade relations with the Indians than they could arrange if Americans were their neighbors at Detroit. See ER to JJ, 12 Nov. 1794, ASP: FR, 1: 501–2.

8. For JJ's rejection of Grenville's attempt to alter this boundary, see JJ to Grenville, 1 and 4 Sept. 1794, above.

9. ER considered JJ's acceptance of Grenville's reasoning about enslaved persons unsatisfactory. Art. 7 of the peace treaty specified that British forces should withdraw without carrying away "any Negroes, or other Property" of Americans. ER argued that since the treaty used the word "negroes" rather than "slaves," the intent was that they should be returned whether or not they had become property of the British by capture or freed by them. While he admitted that enemies could justly claim property that they had captured, rights so acquired could and had been renounced by the treaty. He so argued that loss of their enslaved persons had made it impossible for planters to pay their debts to British creditors. He particularly objected to Grenville's suggestion that returning the enslaved persons would be "odious," given that Britain had established slavery in the United States and continued importing enslaved persons against the will of most of them. In a later letter, he criticized JJ for removing the issue of "first violation" because it gave the United States no claim to retaliate by impeding British creditors from collecting their debts. See ER to JJ, 15 Dec. 1794, LS, NHi: Jay (EJ: 00620); ASP: FR, 1: 509–12. In his reply, JJ tartly observed that it took two to make a bargain, stated that he and Grenville could not agree, and asked whether this item would have been a good reason for breaking off negotiations. See JJ to ER, 6 Feb. 1795, below.

During peace negotiations enslaved persons were treated as property, losses of which were to be documented so they could be used to offset claims for restitution of confiscated Loyalist property. Britain subsequently assumed the obligation of compensating many Loyalists. Congress and the American commissioners assumed, however, that Art. 7 expressly stipulated that no enslaved persons should be carried off. The British, however, claimed from the onset that the stipulation did not apply to enslaved persons who had accepted freedom in return for service to the British. See *JJSP*, 3: 215n7, 266–67n8, 286n14, 343, 413, 414–15n2, 426.

ER also stated that GW believed that allowing the British to retain the posts until 1796 would be injurious to the United States. For opposition to JJ's appointment on grounds he would be willing to sacrifice western lands and compensation for enslaved persons in return for commercial privileges, see the editorial note "The Jay Treaty: Appointment and Instructions," *JJSP*, 5: 614. ER then remarked that, in making these observations and others on Grenville's draft of a commercial treaty, he had guided himself by two ideas, the first that JJ's preliminary discussions with Grenville might have resulted in an understanding from which, even if not formalized, it might be difficult to retreat. Secondly, he said, JJ's instructions had left him "at such full liberty as to render it improper to seem to get rid of some share of responsibility, by passing too minute strictures on what has been done." See ER to JJ, 3 Dec. 1794, LS, marked "Duplicate", NHi: Jay (EJ: 00619); and 15 Dec., LS, NHi: Jay (EJ: 00620); *ASP: FR*, 1: 509–12. For ER's observations on Grenville's draft of a commercial treaty, see ER to JJ, 15 Dec. 1794, LS, NHi: Jay (EJ: 00620).

10. This line is from the LbkC version; it does not appear in either the DNA or NHi versions.

11. This line appears out of sequence in the DNA version. It is located as it appears in the LbkC version.

12. This line is supplied from the LbkC version.

13. The objections appear in the DNA and the LbkC versions.

14. For the dinner invitation from a key member of the cabinet, see Dundas to JJ, 9 Sept. 1794, above.

15. The following four paragraphs appear in JJ's hand.

16. Since Britain considered itself justified in holding the posts because of American violations of the peace treaty, and since it had stood firmly against opening the West Indies to many American products and to American vessels in the failed negotiations for a commercial treaty in 1783, JJ was certainly aware of the weakness of his position. On these negotiations, in which JJ participated, see *JJSP*, 3: 380–81, 445. On the support of Hawkesbury, current President of the Board of Trade, for Sheffield's policy of closing the West Indies trade to American vessels, see JJ to GW, 21 July 1794, and note 4, above.

17. Art. 12 of the Treaty of Amity, Commerce, and Navigation of 19 Nov. 1794 was to have been in force for the duration of Britain's war against France until two years after the signing of preliminaries to end it.

18. See Scott to JJ, and Scott and Nicholl to JJ, 10 Sept. 1794, both above; and JJ to Scott, 12 Sept. 1794, Dft, NNC (EJ: 08902; EJ: 90056), acknowledging receipt of the instructions. ER subsequently informed JJ that these documents had been presented to the Philadelphia committee of merchants and that efforts would be made to give the instructions their full effect. See also William Scott to JJ, 10 Sept. 1794, note 1, above.

19. The following two paragraphs are not found in the DNA version, but are located in the NHi and LbkC versions.

20. Neither of these gazettes has been found.

21. The next day JJ informed ER that Robert Morris Jr. would deliver the above letter to him. He added that he now had reason to hope that Grenville would agree to postpone the northwest boundary issue until accurate surveys of the area were made at joint expense, so that it would no longer be an obstacle to agreement. Several days later, JJ informed ER that he expected to hear soon whether Grenville would accept JJ's proposal to have the northwestern boundary issue decided by a commission and whether or not he would give American ships facilities in the East

Indies. Grenville, he said, was also considering other "interesting matters." Payment on the debts, he thought, would be postponed until after the posts were evacuated, and it seemed increasingly possible that they could agree on a treaty, since the cabinet and public opinion seemed to hold a favorable opinion of the United States. One of two things, he concluded, would "result from it, either peace, or, if war, union." Prepare for war, he advised, but avoid indications of ill will. See JJ to ER, 14 Sept. 1794, below; and 18 Sept. 1794, ALS, DNA: Jay Despatches, 1794–1795 (EJ: 04322); and C, NHi: King (EJ: 04454); *ASP: FR*, 1: 496–97. For his acknowledgement of the dispatches and his expression of concern that commissioners meeting after a peace might "sow the seeds of war," see ER to JJ, 12 Nov. 1794, *ASP: FR*, 1: 502.

To Edmund Randolph (private)

London 13 Sept*r*. 1794

Sir

I have had the pleasure of recieving yours by M*r* Fisher.[1] He called when I was from Home. Then directly afterwards I was so engaged in public Business, that I could not return his visit immediately. The moment I could find Liesure for the purpose, I called with Col. Trumbull at his Lodgings; and was mortified to learn that he had just gone to Liverpool. I hope on his Return to see him, and then to have an opportunity of shewing him those Civilities and Attentions which I shall always think due to your Recommendations.

In my *public* Letter to you by this opportunity,[2] I thought it most delicate to omit mentioning that your Letter by M*r* Munro, and his Speech to the Convention is regarded here as not being consistant with the neutral Situation of the U.S.— An uneasy Sensation has thereby been made here in the public Mind, and probably in that of the Cabinet. It is not pleasant for me to say these Things. but so is the fact, and it is proper that you should know it.[3]—

I enclose two pamphlets—[4] How far the Ideas they convey may be useful in our Country I cannot say.[5] with the best Wishes for your Health & Happiness I am Sir your most ob*t*. and hble serv*t*.

John Jay

Honb. Edm. Randolph Esq*r*.

ALS, DNA: Jay Despatches, 1794–95 (EJ: 04311). Marked: *"Private"*.

1. Possibly ER to JJ, 18 Aug. 1794, ALS, DNA: Jay Despatches, 1794–95 (EJ: 04306); C, NHi: Jay (EJ: 00624); C, NHi: King (EJ: 04438).

2. See JJ to ER, 13 Sept. 1794, above.

3. See Grenville to JJ, and JJ to Grenville, both 7 Sept. 1794, (both private), both above. JJ also reported the British reaction to Monroe's address and ER's letters to the Committee for Public Safety to GW in a letter of this same date. See *PGW: PS*, 16: 677. For ER's instruction to JJ to "stop the progress" of any hints made by the British Ministry that the United States had any "supposed

predilection" for the French nation, as "irrelative to the question in hand," see ER to JJ, 6 May 1794, *JJSP*, 5: 638.

4. Enclosures not found.

5. For his reply, see ER to JJ (private), 12 Nov. 1794, below.

To Edmund Randolph

London 14 Septr. 1794

Sir

M^r. Morris will, together with this, deliver to you a long Letter from me dated Yesterday—[1]

The Negociation proceeds: and I now have some Reason to hope, that the Business of the north western Corner will be so managed as to cease to be an obstacle to agreement—

I have proposed that the further Discussion of that Matter be postponed until accurate Surveys of the River be made, by joint Commissioners at joint Expence; and I do flatter myself that this Proposition will be adopted— Of this I cannot yet be certain, but it is however my present *opinion* that it will[2]— I have the Honor to be with great Respect Sir Your most ob^t. & hble Servt.

John Jay

Honb. Edm^d Randoph Esqr Sec^y of State &c &c

P.S. I wrote to you (n°. 14) 23 Augt. last by Cap^n. Scott to Boston—[3] my Letter of Yesterday is n°. 15—

ALS, DNA: Jay Despatches, 1794–95 (EJ: 04320). Marked: "n^o. *16*". C, NHi: King (EJ: 04452); LbkC, NNC: JJ Lbk. 8; *ASP: FR*, 1: 496.

1. JJ to ER, 13 Sept. 1794, above.

2. See Art. 3 of JJ's Project for a Treaty with Great Britain, 30 Sept. 1794, below.

3. JJ to ER, 23 Aug. 1794, C, DNA: Jay Despatches, 1794–95 (EJ: 04308).

To Peter Jay Munro

London 14 Septr. 1794

Dear Peter

As yet I have rec^d. but one Letter from you:[1] which by the next vessel that sailed I answered.[2] I was disappointed in not recieving a Line either from your Aunt or you or any of the Family by the *Sansom* Capt. Smith who sailed from N York—[3]

When we arrived here M^rs. White was at Southhampton, from whence she very lately Return^d.— just before she left it, John came to Town & made us a visit— He made Enquiries about you and his Sister in a friendly Manner— expressed his wishes for a Reconciliation and that I would enterpose to bring it about with the old Lady— I observed to him that Interpositions of that kind were seldom useful; and that I believed it was best to leave it to Time— He thereupon intimated that his Mother wished that all Differences might be terminated; and that she would be glad to see me when she came to Town— I told him, I should certainly make her an early visit—[4]

on hearing that she had returned; I went with Col. Trumbull and Peter to pay our Respects to her— we were rec^d. in a friendly Manner— nothing very interesting passed on the occasion— nothing but general Inquiries and Conversation took Place— Peter has been there since— last week M^r. Mongan, now Dean Warburton,[5] was in Town— he had seen M^rs. White— she expressed a wish to have him and me to dine with her, and asked me when I should be disengaged— I told him any Day in the next week— some Days ago I rec^d. an Invitation to me and Col. Trumbull & Peter to dine there next Thursday, which I accepted—[6]

When next you write to me, dont be sparing of Details— I mean such only, as may *prudently* be trusted to a Letter

You can tell me about the Farm and the Mills, and the Mares & Colts &^c. &^c. without Risque of Inconveniencies in Case the Letter should miscarry—[7]

I should like to know also who talks fastest— my Sally, or your Peter— cæteris paribus,[8] I should lay on the former.

Before I left you, I requested your particular attention to Old Mary, and desired you to make her comfortable (in Case those who ought to do it, should not) at my Expence. I am anxious to be informed on that Head: for if she should suffer I should be hurt and mortified— I know you have a great Deal to do and to think of—and so have I, and many others— The Claims of Humanity however must always be primary Objects of attention— I make this Remark not from apprehensions of your having neglected my Request, but from the Sollicitude I experience about her. She has been so good to my Father and Mother, and to their Children—& for so long a Course of Years been a faithful ready and affectionate Servant, that in my Opinion she has laid us all under Obligations which her subsequent Faults and Errors can never cancel—and we should never think of her after her Death without Compunction & Remorse, if we permitted her latter Days to wear away in want and misery. —as to the sum I would be willing to advance—it may be best to remove Doubts— advance and charge me with whatever her necessities may require— of those Necessities it is not difficult to judge—[9] my Love to Peggy & your Mother Yours sincerely

John Jay

Peter Jay Munro Esq[r]

ALS, NNMus (EJ: 00427). Addressed. Endorsed: ". . . rec[d]. 17th. nov."

1. Probably PJM to JJ, 15 June 1794, above.

2. Probably JJ to PJM, 18 July 1794, ALS, NNMus (EJ: 00425).

3. New York papers announced that the *Sansom*, John Smith, would sail from New York to London on 23 June. *New-York Daily Gazette*, 16 June 1794.

4. Eve Van Cortlandt White and John White, mother and brother of PJM's wife Margaret "Peggy" White Munro. See PAJ to SLJ, 29 June 1794, above, and PJM to JJ, 19 Nov. 1794, below. The feud with "the old lady" may have stemmed from PJM's elopement with Peggy White, as well as political differences.

5. Terrance Charles Mongan (1754–1826), an Irish Catholic turned Anglican cleric, who had served in America as a military chaplain. He adopted the surname of Warburton by royal warrant in 1792 and served as the Dean of Ardagh (1790–1800); later Anglican bishop of Limerick.

6. PAJ noted on 18 Sept. in his diary, "We dined with Mrs. White of New York—". PAJ Diary A, AD, NNC.

7. For PJM's handling of JJ's business affairs, see PJM to JJ, 15 June 1794, and the editorial note, "John Jay's Mission to London," both above, and PJM's reply to JJ of 19 Nov. 1794, below.

8. "cæteris paribus": All other things being equal. See PJM to JJ, 19 Nov. 1794, below. PJM confirmed JJ's belief that his daughter would talk faster.

9. "Old Mary" refers to an elderly enslaved woman who had belonged to JJ's father Peter, and who, under the terms of his will in 1782, was free to choose her subsequent master. JJ was apparently offering to provide for her proper care if the later owner was not doing so. JJ was still contributing to her support in 1824. See *JJSP*, 2: 721; JJ to PAJ, 4 Nov. 1824, ALS, NNC (EJ: 06284); FC, NyKaJJH (EJ: 09993).

To Alexander Hamilton

London 17 Sept[r]. 1794

Dear Sir

There is something very pleasant in the Reflection that while war discord and oppression triumph in so many parts of Europe, their Domination does not extend to our Country. I sometimes flatter myself that Providence in compassion to the afflicted in these Countries, will continue to leave America in a proper State to be an azylum to them.—

Among those who have suffered severely from these Evils, is Mons[r]. De Rochefoucauld Liancourt, formerly President of the National Assembly of France— His Rank and Character are known to you.— He will be the

Bearer of this Letter, and I am persuaded that his Expectations from it will be realized.—[1] Yours sincerely

John Jay

The Hon'ble Col. Hamilton

ALS, DLC: Hamilton (EJ: 10769). Endorsed. *WJ*, 2: 231; *HPJ*, 4: 115–16; *PAH*, 17: 240–41. JJ sent similar letters of the same date to John Langdon, ALS, J.G.M. Stone Collection, Annapolis, microfilm in DNA; and to Jeremiah Wadsworth, Dft, NNC (EJ: 12528). See also JJ's farewell note to La Rochefoucauld-Liancourt of 22 Sept. 1794, Dft, NNC (EJ: 08907).

1. François Alexandre Frédéric, Duc de La Rochefoucauld-Liancourt (1747–1827), a French social reformer, was elected to the Estates General in 1789, and became president of the General Assembly on 18 July 1789; he fled to England in 1792. He arrived in Philadelphia in November 1794 and toured the United States and Canada. La Rouchefoucauld returned to Europe in 1797 and published his accounts of travels in North America. *Voyages dans les Etats-Unis d'Amerique, fait in 1795 et 1797* (8 vols., Paris, 1799; translated, 2 vols., London, 1799).

To Grenville

Royal Hotel Pall—Mall 30 Sep[r]. 1794

My Lord

I have endeavoured to incorporate the Two Treaties in the enclosed Project, and added some articles, ∧chiefly borrowed∧ from the Treaty between great Britain and France

An article to comprehend the Provisions contemplated by the Lord Chancellor is still wanting. While the others are under Examination it may be prepared.

~~whenever~~ ∧~~as soon as~~ when∧ your Lordship ~~may~~ ∧shall∧ be ready to Converse with me on the Subject do me the Honor to name a Time most convenient to your Lordship.

So mutable are human affairs especially in these mutable Times, that ~~it seems very expedient to put~~ ∧the sooner∧ the peace & Friendship of our two Countries ∧are put∧ out of Hazard, ~~as soon as possible~~ ∧the better∧ ~~If the next Packet could carry the pleasing Tidings, it would be a happy Circumstance~~— With very sincere Respect and Esteem I have the Honor to be my Lord Your Lordships most obedient and most h'ble Servant

John Jay

The Right Honorable Lord Grenville

Dft, UkWC-A (EJ: 00048); C, NNC (EJ: 08499); Hist. Mss. Comm., *Fortescue Manuscripts*, 3: 516–17. With this letter, JJ enclosed his Project for a Treaty with Great Britain of this date, below.

John Jay's Project for a Treaty with Great Britain

[Royal Hotel, Pall Mall, 30 September 1794]

Treaty of Amity and Commerce made and concluded by and between His Britannic Majesty; and the President of the United States of America, on the part and behalf of the said States, by and with the advice and consent of the Senate thereof—

His Britannic Majesty and the United States of America, being desirous by a Treaty of Amity and Commerce, to terminate their differences in such a manner, as without drawing the merits of them into question, shall produce mutual content and good understanding—[1] And also to regulate the Commerce between their respective countries, territories, and inhabitants, in such manner, as to render the same reciprocally beneficial and satisfactory— They have *respectively* named their Plenipotentiaries, and given them full powers to treat of and conclude the said Treaty— That is to say— His Britannic Majesty has named for His Plenipotentiary and the President of the said United States, by and with the advice and consent of the Senate thereof, hath appointed for their Plenipotentiary who have agreed on and concluded the following Articles vizt.[2]

1st. There shall be a firm, inviolable and universal Peace, and a true and sincere Friendship, between His Britannic Majesty his Heirs and Successors, and the United States of America; and between their respective Countries, Territories, Cities, Towns and People, and Inhabitants of every degree, without exception of Persons or Places—[3]

2d. His Majesty will withdraw all his Troops and Garrisons from all Posts and Places[4] within the boundary lines assigned by the Treaty of Peace to the United States. This Evacuation shall take place on or before the first day of June 1796, and all the proper measures shall in the interval be taken by concert between the Government of the United States, and His Majesty's Governor General in America, for settling the previous arrangements which may be necessary respecting the delivery of the said Posts.[5]

All Settlers and Traders within the Precincts or jurisdiction of the said Posts shall continue to enjoy unmolested, all their property of every kind, and shall be protected therein— They shall be at full liberty to remain there, or to remove with all their effects, and also to sell their Lands, Houses, or Effects, or to retain the property thereof.[6] Such of them as shall continue to reside there for the purposes of their Commerce, shall not be compelled to become citizens of the United States, or to take any Oath of allegiance to the

Government thereof, but they shall be at full liberty so to do, if they think proper; and they shall make and declare their election within one year after the evacuation aforesaid—[7] All the other Settlers who shall continue there after the expiration of the said year, shall be considered as having elected to become citizens of the United States—[8]

It[9] shall at all times be free to the Indians dwelling within the Boundaries of either of the parties, to pass and repass with their own proper goods and effects, and to carry on their commerce within or without the jurisdiction of either of the said parties, without hindrance or molestation;[10] or being subjected to any imposts whatever— but goods in bales (Peltries excepted) shall not be considered as goods belonging bona fide to Indians—[11] Provided however that this priviledge shall be suspended with respect to those Tribes, who may be at war and while they may be at war, with the party within whose Jurisdiction they may either dwell, or attempt to come— But neither of the contracting Parties will form any political connexions, nor hold any Treaties with Indians dwelling within the boundaries of the other— They will with good faith endeavour to restrain *their respective* Indians from war, and the better to prevent it, they will make every future indian war a common cause so far as to prohibit and prevent any supplies of am∧m∧unition or arms being given or sold even by indian traders to the belligerent tribe or tribes or to any individuals of them—

In case it should happen (which God forbid) that war should exist between the said parties, they mutually engage to abstain not only from inviting, but also from permitting any Indians to join in it; but on the contrary, will reject their offers of aid and *receive* no assistance from them; nor shall they be allowed under any pretence or in any capacity, to attend or resort to the armies or detachments of either of the said parties—[12]

No armed vessels shall be kept by either of the parties on the lakes and waters thro' which the boundary line between them passes— It being their earnest desire to render mutual justice, confidence and good will, a sufficient Barrier against encroachment and aggression—

Under the influence of these motives, they will as soon as circumstances shall render it seasonable, enter into arrangements for diminishing or wholly withdrawing all military force from the Borders[13]—

3ᵈ. Whereas it is questioned and uncertain, whether the River Mississippi does extend so far to the northward, as to reach or intersect the due west line from the Lake of the Woods, which is mentioned in the Treaty of Peace, and consequently whether the northern and western lines of the United States do or do not close in that corner; and in the latter case how they ought to be closed; which questions it would be premature to discuss and endeavour to settle, while the parties remain uninformed of the actual extent and other material circumstances of the said River.

Wherefore it is agreed that all discussions on these subjects shall be postponed, untill an accurate survey of the said River shall be made— Such a survey of the River Mississippi, beginning at the distance of one degree of Latitude below and from the Falls of St. Anthony, and proceeding thence to its source or head, shall be made. The said survey shall comprehend the course, width & depth of the said River, the Falls and Rapids which may be found therein; and an account of the intervals where it may be navigable, and for what Vessels; and of all such other matters and things, as it may be interesting to both or either of the said parties to be informed of. It shall also comprehend similar surveys and accounts of all the principal Branches or Streams, which empty into the said River, above the said place of beginning. The Lake of the Woods shall also be surveyed— the most northwestern point thereof shall be ascertained and described; and the Latitude and Longitude thereof, as well as the Latitude and Longitude of the Head or Source of the Mississippi, and of the said principal Branches or Streams, shall be correctly taken and fixed— [14]

This work shall be performed and executed by, and under the direction of three Commissioners, whereof one shall be appointed by his Majesty one by the President of the United States with the advice and consent of the Senate, and the *third* by those two. In case those two should not be able to agree in such appointment, then each of them shall propose a person, and of the two so proposed, one shall be taken by lot in the presence of both the proposers, and the one so taken shall be the *third* commissioner.— [15]

The said *two first appointed* Commissioners shall as soon as may be after *being duly notified*, meet ^at^ Philadelphia, and before they proceed to execute any part of their commission shall take the following Oath or Affirmation before any one of the National or State Judges viz[t].

"I A.B. one of the Commissioners appointed to make the surveys directed in and by the Article of the Treaty of Amity & Commerce between his Britannic Majesty and the United States of America, do solemnly swear (or affirm) that I have no personal interest in the issue of those surveys, and that I will faithfully and diligently, impartially and carefully make the said surveys, according to the directions of the said article, and to the best of my skill and understanding— And I do also solemnly swear (or affirm) that I will sincerely endeavour to agree with my colleague in the appointment of a third Commissioner— that I will propose only such person or persons as I shall judge to be qualified for that place, and that I will not oppose but will favor the appointment of that one among those whom we shall propose, whom I shall really think the best qualified for the same."

When the said third Commissioner shall be appointed, he shall before he proceeds to act, take the Oath or Affirmation first above mentioned—

The said third Commissioner shall always preside, and every question that may come before the board, shall be decided by plurality of voices, openly given, *that is not by Ballot*—

They shall appoint one chief clerk, and also such assistant clerks as they may judge from time to time to be necessary, each of whom before he does any act in that capacity, shall take the following oath or affirmation before any one of the said commissioners who are hereby severally authorized to administer the same, vizt.

"I A.B. appointed clerk (or assistant clerk) to ‸the‸ Commissioners appointed in pursuance of the article of the Treaty of Amity and Commerce between His Britannic Majesty and the United States of America, to make the surveys therein directed, do solemnly swear (or affirm) that I am not personally interested in the said surveys and ‸that‸ I will do the duties of the said place with fidelity care and diligence according to the best of my skill and understanding."

The said Commissioners shall appoint such Astronomers and Surveyors, as they shall judge necessary; and shall administer to them respectively an Oath or Affirmation purporting that they have no personal interest in the said surveys, and that they will respectively perform the duties to be assigned to them by the said Commissioners, with fidelity care and diligence—

The said Commissioners shall decide on the allowances and compensation to be made to the several persons whom they shall employ as aforesaid, and to all others whom they may occasionally employ; but these compensations or allowances shall be confined to the time or times during which the said persons shall be in actual service.—

When their Business shall be finished, the said Commissioners shall deliver to the Minister of His Majesty at Philadelphia for the use of his Majesty, a Chart representing the said surveys, a statement of their accounts, and a journal of their proceedings, which shall contain such remarks, facts and circumstances, as shall tend to explain the said chart, and as shall in their opinion be necessary to ~~preserve and~~ convey ‸and preserve‸ the information intended to be acquired by the execution of their commission. They shall also on the same day, deliver exact duplicates of the said Chart statement and journal, for the use of the United States, to their Secretary of State of his Office—

Arrangements shall be taken by concert between the Government of the United States and His Majesty's Governor General in America, to afford proper protection, facilities and supplies to the said Commissioners—

The whole expence of executing this Commission shall be paid in equal moieties by his Majesty and the United States— Necessary advances of money shall from time to time be made, and his Majesty's Minister at Philadelphia, and the Secretary of the Treasury of the United States, shall be respectively authorized and enabled to make such advances, in equal proportions—

Whenever any one of the said Commissioners shall die, or in the opinion of the other two signified by writing under their hands, become disqualified by sickness or otherwise for service, the place of such Commissioner shall be supplied by another to be appointed in the same manner that he was, and to take the same Oaths that he did, and to perform the same duties that were encumbent on him— And his Majesty will authorize his Minister with the United States, to make such appointments as this Treaty assigns to his Majesty—

The said Commissioners shall be paid for their services at the rate of   per annum while on actual service. They shall also be provided with necessary supplies while actually on service, but while absent from the said surveys or service they shall bear their own expences, and receive no Salary nor Compensation.

And to the end that this survey may not be interrupted by the Indian Tribes in the vicinity, the Government of the United States will by concert with His Majesty's Governor of upper Canada, take the necessary measures for explaining the object of the same to those Indians; and unite their efforts in composing their apprehensions and in restraining them from interrupting the progress and completion of the work—[16]

4th. Altho' the Boundaries of the United States as delineated by the Treaty of Peace are hereby recognized and admitted, yet as the Parties differ as to which is the River intended by the said Treaty, and therein called the River St. Croix, which forms a part of the Boundary therein described—

It is agreed that the said question shall be referred to the final decision of three Commissioners to be appointed exactly in the same manner, and to take the same oaths (mutatis mutandis) before any *respectable* Magistrate, as is prescribed in the preceeding Article relative to the Commissioners therein mentioned— They shall meet at *Quebec, Halifax,* &c.[17]

They shall appoint a clerk, and if necessary, assistant clerks, Astronomers and Surveyors— They shall in like manner administer to them the same

Oaths (mutatis mutandis) they shall make them allowances and compensations on the like principle of actual service, and they themselves shall receive the same compensations with those Commissioners, and while actually on duty shall be allowed their reasonable Expences—

They shall direct such surveys as they shall judge proper, and may adjourn to such place or places as they may think expedient. They shall hear and receive whatever Testimony and Evidences shall be offered to them by the parties, and without improper precipitation or delay, shall by writing under their hands, attested by their Clerk decide which is the River S^t. Croix intended by the Treaty— The said written decision shall contain a description of the said River, and the Latitude and Longitude of its mouth and of its source— They shall deliver duplicates of this writing and of statements of their accounts and of the journal of their proceedings, to the agent of his Majesty and to the Agent of the United States, who shall be respectively appointed and authorized to manage the business on their respective parts and behalf—

The expence of executing this Business shall be paid in equal moieties by both parties, and the necessary advances shall be made in like manner as the advances mentioned in the preceeding Article are provided for— And the said Commissioners shall be authorized to employ all such persons as they shall deem necessary and proper in the Business committed to them by this Article—

5th.[18] Whereas complaints have been made by divers Merchants and other citizens of the United States, that during the course of the war in which his Majesty is now engaged, they have sustained considerable losses and damage, by reason of irregular ~~and~~ ∧or∧ illegal captures[19] and condemnations of their Vessels and other property under colour of authority or commissions from his Majesty, and that from various circumstances belonging to the said cases, adequate compensation for the said losses and damages, cannot now be actually obtained,[20] had and received by the ordinary course of judicial proceedings. It is agreed that in all such cases where adequate compensation cannot for whatever reason or cause be now actually obtained had and received by the said Merchants and others, for the said losses and damages, full and complete satisfaction for the same will be made by the British Government to the said Complainants.

That for this purpose five Commissioners shall be appointed and authorized (to meet and act in *London*) in manner following vizt. Two of them shall be appointed by his Majesty, two of them by the President of the United States by and with the advice and consent of the Senate, and the fifth by the unanimous voice of the other four.

When the said first four Commissioners shall meet, they shall before they proceed to act, respectively take the following Oath or Affirmation vizt.—

"I A.B. one of the Commissioners appointed in pursuance of the   article of the Treaty of amity and commerce between His Britannic Majesty and the United States of America do solemnly swear (or affirm) that I will honestly diligently impartially and carefully hear, and according to justice and equity and the best of my judgement decide, all such complaints as under the said article shall be preferred to the said commissioners, and that I will forbear to act as a commissioner in any case in which I may be personally interested. And I do further solemnly swear (or affirm) that I will sincerely endeavour to agree with my colleagues in appointing a proper person to be the fifth Commissioner."

In case the said four Commissioners should not agree in such choice, then the said fifth Commissioner shall be appointed by lot in the manner directed in the third Article of this Treaty and when appointed shall take the first of the before mentioned Oaths or Affirmations.

Three of the said Commissioners shall constitute a Board, and have power to do any act appertaining to the said commission provided that one of the commissioners named on each side, and the fifth commissioner shall be present, and all decisions shall be made by the majority of the voices of the Commissioners then present.

In case of death sickness or necessary absence, the places of such Commissioners respectively shall be supplied in the same manner as such Commissioners were first appointed and the new ones shall take the same Oath or Affirmation and do the same duties.

They shall appoint a Clerk and administer to him an Oath (or Affirmation) faithfully and impartially and diligently to do his duty[21]—

Eighteen months from the day on which the said Commissioners shall form a Board and be ready to proceed to Business are assigned for the reception of complaints & applications but they are nevertheless authorized for *once* to prolong that term to a further period in case it shall appear to them to be reasonable and proper.[22]

The said Commissioners in awarding such sums as shall appear to them to be justly and equitably due to the said complainants, in pursuance of the true intent and meaning of this article, are impowered to take into their consideration, and to determine all claims according to the merits of the several cases, due regard being had to all the circumstances thereof, and as equity and justice shall appear to them to require, and the said commissioners shall have power to examine all persons on Oath touching the premisses, and also to receive in evidence according as they think most consistent with equity and justice all written depositions, or books or copies, or papers or ˄or Copies or˄ extracts thereof— Every such Deposition, book, paper, copy, or extract being duly authenticated according to the legal forms now respectively existing in the two countries, or in such other manner as the said Commissioners shall see cause to prescribe and require.

The award of the said Commissioners or of any three of them as aforesaid, shall in all cases be final and conclusive, both as to the justice of the claim, and to the amount of the sum to be paid to the complainant or claimant— And his Majesty undertakes to cause the same to be paid to such claimants without deductions in specie, and at such time or times and at such place or places as shall be awarded by the said commissioners, and on condition of such releases to be given by the claimant of his demands against individuals as by the said Commissioners may be directed.

And whereas certain merchants and others his Majesty's subjects complain that in the course of the war they have sustained loss and damage by reason of the capture of their Vessels and Merchandize within the limits and jurisdiction of the said States or by vessels armed in ports of the said States,

It is agreed that all such cases shall be, and hereby are referred to the Commissioners before mentioned, and they are authorized to proceed in like manner relative to those as to the other cases committed to them. And the United States undertake to pay to the complainants or claimants in specie without deductions, the amount of the sum to be awarded to them respectively by the said Commissioners, at the times and places which in such awards shall be specified, and on condition of such releases to be given by the Claimant of his demands against individuals, as the said awards may direct.

And it is further agreed that not only existing cases of both descriptions, but also all such as shall exist at the time of exchanging the Ratifications of this Treaty shall be considered as being within the provisions, intent and meaning of this article[23]—

6th. Whereas it is alledged by divers british merchants and others his Majesty's subjects that debts to a considerable amount which were bona fide contracted before the peace, still remain owing to them by citizens or inhabitants of the United States, and that by the operation of various lawful impediments since the peace, not only the full recovery of the said debts, has been delayed, but also the security[24] thereof has been in several instances impaired and lessened; so that by the ordinary course of judicial proceedings the British creditors cannot obtain and actually have and receive full and adequate compensation for the losses and damages which they have thereby sustained[25]

It is agreed that in all such cases where full compensation for such losses and damages cannot for whatever reason (other than insolvency not imputable to the said impediments and delays)[26] be actually obtained had and received by the said creditors in the ordinary course of justice, the United States will make full and complete satisfaction for the same to the said creditors And that for this purpose five commissioners shall be appointed & authorized exactly in the manner directed with respect to those mentioned in the preceeding article, and shall take the same Oaths or Affirmations (mutatis mutandis) and proceed as is therein directed. The same term of eighteen months is also assigned for the reception of claims and they are in like manner authorized for once to prolong it to a more distant period. They shall receive testimony books, papers and evidence in the same latitude and exercise the like discretion and powers respecting that subject, and shall decide the claims in question whether they respect principal or interest, or ballances of either, according to the merits of the several cases, and to justice equity and good conscience, having due regard to all the circumstances thereof—

The award of the said Commissioners shall in all cases be final and conclusive, both as to the justice of the claim, and to the amount of the sum to be paid to the claimant, and the United States undertake to cause the same to be paid to such claimants without any deductions, in specie, at such place or places and at such Time or times, after the first day of June 1796[27] as shall be awarded by the said Commissioners and on condition of such assignments by the said claimants of their demands against individuals to the United States, or of such releases of their said demands against ∧to∧ individuals, as the said Commissioners may think proper to direct—

The said Commissioners shall meet at Philadelphia, but shall have power to adjourn at their discretion to any other place or places in the United States—

It is further agreed that the Commissioners mentioned in this and in the preceeding article shall be paid at the rate of   per annum for the first eighteen months and at the rate of   per annum for the residue of the time they may sit— No allowances whatever shall be made to them on account of expences— Their Clerks shall each be paid at the rate of   per annum for the whole time of their service—

These expenses shall be paid in equal shares by both the parties, and they will provide that the said salaries shall be paid quarterly to be computed from the day of the first meeting to do business. They will also provide that on the said first day of meeting one hundred pounds sterling be paid in advance and on account to each of the said Commissioners, and fifty pounds sterling to each of the clerks—[28]

7th. It is agreed that British Subjects who now hold lands in the Territories of the United States, and American Citizens who now hold lands in the Dominion of his Majesty shall continue to hold them according to the nature and tenure of their respective Estates and Titles therein, and may grant and sell and devise the same, as, and to whom they please, in like manner as if they were *natives*— And that neither they nor their heirs or assigns shall, so far as may respect the said lands and the legal remedies incident thereto, be regarded as aliens—[29]

8th. Neither the debts due from individuals of the one nation to individuals of the other, nor shares or monies, which they may have in the public funds, or in the public or private Banks, shall ever in any event of war or national differences, be sequestered or confiscated— it being both unjust and consequently impolitic that debts and engagements contracted and made by individuals having confidence in each other, and in their respective Governments, should ever be destroyed or impaired by national authority, on account of national differences and discontents—

It is agreed between His said Majesty and the United States of America that there shall be a reciprocal and entirely perfect liberty of navigation and commerce between their respective people in the manner, under the limitations, and on the conditions specified in the following Articles vizt.[30]

9th. It shall be free to his Majesty's subjects and to the citizens of the United States,[31] to pass and repass into their respective Territories and Countries *on the continent of America* (the country within the limits of the Hudson's Bay company only excepted) and to navigate all the Lakes, Rivers and waters thereof, and freely to carry on trade and commerce with each other, and with the Indians dwelling within the boundaries of the said contracting parties. But the navigation of His Majesty's Rivers to or from the Sea shall not be open to vessels of the United States, Nor shall the Rivers of the United States be open to british vessels from the Sea further than to the usual ports near the sea into which they have heretofore been admitted. But the River Mississippi shall according to the treaty of peace continue to be open to both parties, and all the Ports and Places on its eastern side may freely be resorted to and used by both parties, in as ample a manner as any of the Atlantic ports or places of the United States or any of the ports or places of his Majesty in Great Britain[32]—

All Goods and Merchandizes, (whose importation into his Majesty's said American dominions[33] shall not be *entirely* prohibited) may freely for the purposes of Commerce be carried into the same, by american citizens, in any manner except by sea,[34] and shall be subject only to the same duties as in like cases would be payable by his Majesty's subjects. And, on the other hand, all Goods and Merchandizes (whose importation into the United States shall not be entirely prohibited) may freely for the purposes of commerce, be carried into the same from his Majesty's *said* Territories, by British subjects, in any manner except by Sea,[35] and shall be subject only to the same duties as in like cases would be payable by american Citizens.[36] Peltries may always be freely carried (except by sea) from one side to the other without paying any duty or impost, and so also may all other goods whose exportation may not be entirely prohibited ∧may also be freely carried paying Duties as∧ aforesaid.

No higher or other Tolls, or Rates of Ferriage than what are or shall be payable by natives, shall be executed or demanded ∧or executed∧ on either side.[37]

As this Article is particularly intended and calculated to render in a great degree the local advantages of each common to both, And thereby to promote a disposition favorable to friendship and good neighbourhood, it is agreed that the respective Governments will constantly promote this amicable intercourse, by causing speedy and impartial justice and necessary protection to be done and extended to all who may be concerned therein[38]—

10th. His Majesty consents that it shall and may be lawful, during the time herein after limited, for the citizens of the United States, to carry to any of his Majesty's Islands and Ports in the West Indies, from the United States in their own vessels, not being above the burthen of   tons,[39] any Goods or Merchandizes being of the growth, manufacture[40] or produce of the said States, which it is, or may be lawful to carry to the said islands or ports from the said States in british vessels— And that the said American vessels and their cargoes shall pay there no other or higher duties or charges than shall be payable by british vessels in similar circumstances. And that it shall be lawful for the said american citizens to purchase load and carry away in their said vessels to the United States from the said islands and ports all such articles, being of the growth manufacture or produce of the said islands, as may by law be carried from thence to the said States in british vessels, and subject only to the same duties and charges on Exportation, to which British vessels are or shall be subject in similar circumstances— It is his Majesty's intention that american vessels shall, as to the articles which may lawfully [be] exported or imported to or from the said ∧Islands∧ and the united States, as well as with respect to duties and charges, shall be exactly on the same footing on which British vessels now are and that any extension or ampli∧fi∧cation of the priviledges of the latter shall immediately extended to the former.[41] Provided always that the said american vessels do carry and land their cargoes in the United States *only*— it being expressly agreed and declared that during the continuance of this article, the United States will prohibit[42] the carrying any Sugar Coffee or Cotton in American vessels,[43] either from his Majesty's islands or from the United States to any part of the world except the United States, reasonable sea-stores excepted—

It is agreed that this article and every matter and thing therein contained, shall continue to be in force during the continuance of the war in which his Majesty is now engaged and also for two years from and after the day of the signature of the preliminary Articles of peace by which the same may be terminated.

And it is further agreed that at the expiration of the said term, the two contracting will treat further concerning their commerce in this respect, according to the situation in which his Majesty may then find himself with respect to the West Indies, and with a view to such arrangements as may best conduce to the mutual advantage and extension of commerce—[44]

11th. There shall be between all the dominions of his Majesty in Europe and the Territories of the United States, a reciprocal and perfect liberty of commerce and navigation[45] And it is agreed that this navigation and commerce shall continue to be exactly on the same footing in every respect on which they now stand, except that in cases where any other nation or nations now are or hereafter shall be admitted by either party to greater priviledges or favors, the same shall immediately become common to the other party, who shall enjoy the same priviledge or favor *freely*, if the concession was gratuitously made, or on allowing the same equally valuable compensation if the concession was made in consideration of compensation— Neither of the parties will in future lay any other or higher duties or imposts on each others vessels and merchandizes, than what they shall lay on the like vessels and merchandizes of all other nations— nor shall they lay any prohibitions on any kind of merchandize without extending it to the same kind of merchandize to whatever nation belonging.

The people and inhabitants of the two countries respectively, shall have liberty freely and securely, and without hindrance or molestation to come with their ships and cargoes to the lands countries cities ports places and rivers within the dominions and territories aforesaid— to enter into the same, to resort thereto, and to remain and reside there without any limitation of time— also to hire and possess houses and warehouses for the purposes of their commerce, and generally that the merchants and traders on each side shall enjoy the most complete protection and security for their commerce,

but subject always as to what respects this article to the general laws and statutes of the two countries respectively—[46]

12th. In consideration that the United States agree not to lay any duties or
imposts on the exportation [in margin: N.B. The Constitution forbids Duties on Exportation][47] of any of their commodities produce or manufactures
in british vessels, His Majesty agrees that masts ship-timber staves, board
plank and spars may be imported into his said dominions, duty free, from the
United States in American vessels— and also that the duty on the importation of Rice from the United States shall be reduced to   per hundred and that on whale oil to   and that Salt may be imported into
the United States in their vessels from Turks Island duty free—[48]

13th. It shall be free for the two contracting parties respectively, to appoint
Consuls for the protection of Trade, to reside in the dominions and territories aforesaid,[49] and who shall enjoy those liberties and rights which belong
to them by reason of their function— But before any consul shall act as such,
he shall be in the usual forms approved and admitted by the party to whom
he is sent, and it is hereby declared to be lawful and proper that in case of illegal or improper conduct towards the laws and government, a consul may
either be punished according to law if the laws will reach the case, or be dismissed or even sent back, the offended Government assigning to the other
their reasons for the same—[50]

Either of the parties may except from the residence of Consuls such particular places as such party shall judge proper to be so excepted—[51]

14th. His Majesty consents that american vessels trading to Asia shall be hospitably received and treated, in all his Asiatic Ports and Dominions; and may
freely import into the same any of the productions and manufactures of the
United States, and purchase and carry from thence any of the productions
and ∧or∧ manufactures of those countries directly from ∧to∧ the United
States, but not directly to any part of Europe. This Article shall be of the same
duration with the Article respecting the West Indies.[52]

15th. It shall be lawful for all the subjects of his Majesty, and the citizens of
the United States, to sail with their ships with perfect security and liberty, no
distinction being made who are the proprietors of the merchandizes laden
thereon, from any port whatever, to the countries which are now or shall be
hereafter at war with His Majesty, or the United States. It shall likewise be
lawful for them respectively to sail and traffic with their ships and merchandizes, with the same liberty and security, from the countries ports and places
of those who are enemies of both, or of either party, and to pass directly, not

only from the places of the enemy aforementioned, to neutral places, but also from one place belonging to an Enemy to another place belonging to an enemy, whether they be under the jurisdiction of the same or of several Sovereigns or Governments. And as every thing shall be deemed to be free which shall be found on board the Ships belonging to the said subjects or citizens aforesaid, altho' the whole lading or part thereof should belong to the enemies of the contracting parties, (contraband Goods always excepted) so it is also agreed that the same liberty be extended to persons who are on board a free ship, to the end, that altho' they be enemies to both or to either party, they may not be taken out of such free ship, unless they are soldiers actually in the service of the enemies and on their voyage for the purpose of being employed in a military capacity in their fleets or armies.

This liberty of navigation and Commerce shall extend to all kinds of merchandizes, excepting those only which are specified in the following article, and which are described under the name of contraband—[53]

16th. Under the name of contraband or prohibited goods shall be comprehended Arms, cannon, Harquebusses, Mortars, Petards, Bombs, Grenades, Saucisses, Carcasses, carriages for cannon, Musket Rests, Bandoleers, Gun powder, Match, Salt Petre, Ball, Pikes, Swords, Head pieces, Helmets, Cuirasses, Halberds, Javelins, Holsters, Belts, Horses and Harness, and all other like kinds of arms and warlike Implements fit for the use of Troops.

These Merchandizes which follow shall not be reckoned among Contraband Goods— That is to say, All sorts of cloth, and all other manufactures of Wool, Flax, Silk, Cotton, or any other materials, all kinds of wearing apparel, together with the articles of which they are usually made— Gold, Silver coined or uncoined—Tin, Iron, Lead, Copper, Brass, Coals—as also Wheat and Barley and Flour, and every kind of Corn and Pulse—Tobacco and all kinds of Spices,—Salted and Smoked Flesh, Fish, Cheese, Butter, Beer, Cyder, Oil, Wines, Sugar, Salt, and all kinds of provisions whatever which serve for sustenance and food to mankind. All kinds of Cotton, Flax, Hemp, Cordage Cables, Sails, Sail-cloth— Tallow, Pitch, Tar, Rosin, Anchors and any parts of Anchors, Ship masts, Planks, Timber of all kinds of Trees, and all other things proper either for building or repairing Ships. Nor shall any other Goods whatever which have not been worked into the form of any Instrument of Furniture for warlike use, by land or by sea, be reputed contraband, much less such as have been already wrought and made up for any other purpose. All which things shall be deemed goods not contraband, As likewise all others which are not herein before and particularly enumerated and described as contraband. So that they may be freely carried by the respective subjects and citizens of the contracting parties even to places belonging to an enemy excepting only such places as are besieged blocked or invested, and whereas it[54] frequently happens that vessels sail for a Port or place belonging to an Enemy, without knowing that the same is either besieged blockaded or invested It is agreed that every vessel so circumstanced may be turned away from such port or place, but she shall not be detained, nor her cargo, if not contraband, be confiscated, unless after notice she shall again attempt to enter— but she shall be permitted to go to any other Port or place she may think proper. Nor shall any vessel or Goods of either party, that may have entered ~~or be found in~~ ˄into˄ such port or place, before the same was besieged blockaded or invested by the other, and be found therein after the Reduction or Surrender of such place, be liable to Confiscation, but shall be restored to the owners or Proprietors thereof. And whereas corn Grain or other Provisions can only be considered as contraband on occasions and in Cases when a well founded Expectation exists of reducing an Enemy by the Want thereof It is agreed that in all such Cases, the said articles shall not be confiscated; but that the Captors, or in their Default, the Government under whose Authority they act, shall pay to the Masters or owners of such Vessels, the full value of all such articles, with a reasonable mercantile Proffit thereon, together with the Freight, and also the Demurrage incident to their Detention—[55]

17th. To the end that all manner of dissentions and quarrels may be avoided and prevented on both sides— It is agreed that in case either of the contracting parties should be engaged in war, the vessels belonging to the subjects or citizens of the other, shall be furnished with Sea Letters or Passports, expressing the name, property and bulk of the Ship or Vessel— and also the name and place of abode of the Master or Commander, that it may appear thereby, that the said Ship really belongs to ˄such˄ subjects or citizens— Which passports shall be made out and granted according to the form annexed to the present Treaty. They shall likewise be renewed every year, if the Ship happens to return home within the space of a year.

It is also agreed that such Ships when laden, are to be provided not only with passports as abovementioned but also with certificates containing the several particulars of the cargo, the place from whence the Ship sailed, and whither she is bound; so that it may be known whether she carries any of the prohibited or contraband goods specified in the preceeding article— which certificates shall be prepared by the officers of the place from whence the Ship set sail in the accustomed form— and if any one shall think fit to express in the said certificates the name of the person to whom the Goods belong, he may freely do so—[56]

18th. The Merchant Ships of either of the parties, coming to any of the coasts of either of them, but without being willing to enter into port, or being entered, yet not willing to land their cargoes or break bulk, shall not be obliged to give an account of their lading; unless suspected on sure evidence, of carrying contraband goods to the enemies of either of the contracting parties—

In case the said Merchant Ships shall meet with any Men of War or Privateers of either of the contracting parties, either on the coast or on the High Seas, the said men of War & Privateers are to remain out of Cannon shot, and to send their boats to the Merchant Ship which may be met with, and shall enter her to the number of two or three men only, to whom the master or commander of such ship or vessel, shall show his passport containing the proof of the property of the ship, made out according to the form annexed to this present Treaty; And the Ship which shall exhibit the same, shall have liberty to continue her voyage, and it shall be wholly unlawful to molest or search her, or to chase or compel her to alter her course.

But such of the said merchant Ships as may be bound for a port at enmity with the other contracting party, concerning whose voyage, and the sort of goods on board, there may be just cause for suspicion, shall be obliged to exhibit, as well on the high seas as in the Ports and Havens, not only her passports, but also her Certificates expressing that the goods are not of the kind which are contraband as specified in the   article of this Treaty.

If on exhibiting the above mentioned Certificates, containing a list of the Cargo, the other party should discover any goods of that kind which are declared contraband or prohibited by this treaty, and which are designed for a port subject to the enemy of the said party, it shall be unlawful to break up or open the Hatches, Chests, Bales or other Vessels found on board such Ship, or to remove even the smallest parcel of Goods, unless the lading be brought on shore, in the presence of the Officers of the Court of Admiralty, and an inventory made by them of the said goods. Nor shall it be lawful to sell, exchange or alienate the same in any manner, unless after lawful process shall have been had against such prohibited goods, and the Judges of the Admiralty shall, by sentence pronounced, have confiscated the same Saving always as well the Ship itself, as all the other goods ˄found˄ therein, which by this Treaty are accounted free; neither may they be detained on pretence of their being mixed with prohibited goods, much less shall they be confiscated as lawful prize. And if when only part of the cargo shall consist of contraband goods, the master of the Ship shall consent and offer to deliver them to the captor who has discovered them; in such case the captor, having received those goods as lawful prize, shall forthwith release the ship and not hinder her by any means from prosecuting her voyage to the place of her destination.[57]

19th. It is agreed that whatever ~~may~~ ₍shall₎ be found to be laden by the respective subjects or citizens of either of the said parties on any ship belonging to the enemies of the other, altho' the same be not contraband goods, shall be confiscated in the same manner as if it belonged to the enemy himself. Excepting always those goods which were put on board such ship before the declaration of war, or the general order for reprizals, or even after such declaration or order, if it were done within the times following, that is to say, if they were put on board such ship in any port or place, within the space of two months after such declaration, or order for Reprizals, between Archangel, St. Petersburg, and the Scilly Islands, and between the said Islands and the City of Gibraltar—of ten weeks in the Mediterranean Sea, and of eight months in any other country or place in the world. So that the goods whether contraband or not, which were put on board any Ship belonging to an enemy as aforesaid before the war, or after the declaration of the same or of the general order for reprizals, within the times and limits above mentioned shall not be liable to confiscation, but shall be restored without delay to the proprietors demanding the same. Provided nevertheless that if the said Merchandizes be contraband, it shall not be any ways lawful to carry them after being so restored, to the ports belonging to the enemy—[58]

20th. And that more abundant care may be taken for the security of the respective subjects and citizens of the contracting parties, and to prevent their suffering injuries by the men of war or privateers of either party, all commanders of ships of war and privateers, and all other the said subjects and citizens shall forbear doing any damage to those of the other party, ₍or committing any outrage against them₎ and if they act to the contrary, they shall be punished, and shall also be bound in their persons and estates to make satisfaction and reparation for all damages and the interest thereof, of whatever nature the said damages may be.—

For this cause all commanders of privateers, before they receive their commissions, shall hereafter be obliged to give before a competent judge, sufficient security by at least two responsible sureties who have no interest in the said privateer, each of whom together with the said commander shall be jointly and severally bound in the sum of fifteen hundred pounds sterling, or if such ship be provided with above one hundred and fifty Seamen or Soldiers, in the sum of three thousand pounds sterling, to satisfy all damages and injuries which the said privateer or her officers or men or any of them may do or commit during their Cruize contrary to the tenor of this Treaty, or to the laws ~~or~~ ˄and˄ instructions for regulating their conduct and further that in all cases of aggressions thereof, the said commissions shall be revoked and annulled—

It is also agreed that whenever a judge of a Court of Admiralty of either of the parties, shall pronounce sentence against any vessel or goods or property belonging to the subjects or citizens of the other party, a formal and duly authenticated copy of all the proceedings in the cause, and of the said sentence, shall be delivered gratis to the commander of the said vessel before the said sentence shall be executed— And this the said judge shall do on pain of forfeiting his commission—[59]

21st. When the Quality of the Ship Goods and Master shall sufficiently appear, from such passports and certificates, it shall not be lawful for the commanders of men of war or privateers, to exact any farther proof, under any pretext whatever. But if any merchant Ship shall not be provided with such passports or certificates, then it may be examined by a proper judge, but in such manner as, if it shall be found, from other proofs and documents, that it truly belongs to the subjects or citizens of one of the contracting parties, and does not contain any contraband goods designed to be carried to the enemy of the other, it shall not be liable to confiscation, but shall be released together with its cargo, in order to proceed on its voyage— If the master of the ship named in the passports, should happen to die, or be removed by any other cause, and another put in his place, the Ships and Goods laden thereon, shall nevertheless be equally secure, and the passport ˄shall˄ remain in full force—[60]

22d. It is further agreed that both the said contracting parties shall not only refuse to receive any Pirates into any of their ports, havens, or towns, or permit any of their inhabitants to receive protect harbour conceal or assist them in any manner, but will bring to condign punishment all such Inhabitants as shall be guilty of such acts or offences. And all their ships with the goods or merchandizes taken by them and brought into the ports of either of the said parties, shall be seized, as far as they can be discovered, and shall be restored to the owners or their factor's or agents duly deputed and authorized in writing by them, (proper evidence being first given in the court of admiralty for proving the property) even in case such effects should have passed into other hands by sale, if it be proved that the buyers knew, or might have known that they had been piratically taken.[61]

It is likewise agreed and concluded that the subjects and citizens of the two nations, shall not do any acts of hostility or violence against each other; nor accept commissions or instructions so to act from any foreign Prince or State, enemies to the other party, nor shall the enemies of one of the parties be permitted to invite or endeavour to enlist in their military Service, any of the subjects or citizens of the other party; and the laws against all such offences and aggressions shall be punctually executed— And if any subject or citizen of the said parties respectively shall accept any foreign commission or letters of marque for arming any vessel to act as a privateer against the other party, and be taken by the other party, it is hereby declared to be lawful for the said party to treat and punish the said subject or citizen having such commission or letters of marque, as a pirate—[62]

It is expressly stipulated that neither of the said contracting parties will order or authorize any acts of reprizal against the other on complaints of injuries or damages until the said party shall first have presented to the other a statement thereof, verified by competent proof and evidence and demanded justice, and satisfaction, and the same shall either have been refused, or unreasonably delayed—[63]

Not only the merchant ships but also the ships of war of either of the contracting parties shall be hospitably received in the ports of the other, and their Officers shall be treated with that decorum and respect which friendly nations owe to each other. But the said officers as well as all others shall be amenable to the laws of the land, and shall take care so to govern and regulate the conduct of the men under their command, as that they behave peaceably and inoffensively;[64] and particularly that a Habeas Corpus issued by the proper magistrate directed to any of the said officers, commanding him forthwith to bring any particular person duly described by his name or otherwise, before such magistrate, shall be punctually obeyed by such officer.—

And all magistrates duly authorized to issue such writs, on complaint that any subject or citizen of either of the said parties, other than the one to whom the said man of war belongs, hath been impressed and is unlawfully detained on board thereof, shall issue a Habeas Corpus to the officer having the command of the said man of war, and thereby order him to have such person or persons so said to have been impressed, before the said Magistrate, at a time and place therein to be specified, which writ shall be obeyed— And the said Magistrate shall then proceed to enquire into the merits of the case, and shall do therein as to him shall appear to be just and right, either remanding the said person or persons or persons, if the complaint be groundless, or discharging him, if it be well founded. And in the latter case, the said Officer shall deliver forthwith to the said person or persons, whatever arrears of wages may be due, and whatever Effects or Property he or they may have on board— All which shall be done uprightly and with good faith—[65]

23d. It shall not be lawful for any foreign Privateer,(not being subjects or citizens of either of the said parties) who have commissions from any other prince or state, in enmity with either nation, to arm their Ships in the ports of either of the said parties, nor to sell what they have taken, nor in any other manner to exchange the same, nor shall be allowed to purchase more provisions, than shall be necessary for their going to the nearest port of that prince or state from whom they obtained their commissions.[66]

It shall be lawful for the Ships of war and privateers belonging to the said parties respectively so far and so far only as shall not be repugnant to former treaties made in this respect with other sovereigns or states,[67] to carry whithersoever they please the ships and goods taken from their enemies without being obliged to pay any fee to the officers of the admiralty or to any Judges whatever— nor shall the said prizes when they arrive at and enter the ports of the said parties, be detained or seized— neither shall the searchers or other officers of those places, visit or take cognizance of the validity of such prizes, nor shall the said prizes be unladen or break bulk, but they shall hoist sail and depart as speedily as may be and ∧carry∧ their said prizes to ∧the∧ place mentioned in their Commissions or patents, which the Commanders of the said ships of war or Privateers shall be obliged to shew. No shelter or refuge shall be given in their ports to such as have made a prize upon the subjects or citizens of either of the said parties, but if forced by stress of weather, or the dangers of the sea to enter therein, particular care shall be taken to hasten their departure, and to cause them to retire as soon as possible. And further that while the said parties continue in amity, neither of them will in future make any Treaty that shall be inconsistant with this article—[68]

24th. Neither of the said parties shall permit the ships or goods belonging to the subjects or citizens of the other to be taken within cannon shot of the coast, nor in any of the bays, ports or rivers of their territories, by ships of war or others having commission from any prince republic or state whatever. But in case it should so happen, the party whose territorial rights shall thus have been violated, shall make full and ample satisfaction for the vessel or vessels so taken, whether the same be vessels of war or merchant vessels—[69]

If at any time a Rupture should take place (which God forbid) between His Majesty and the United States, the merchants and others of the two nations, residing in the dominions of the other, shall have the priviledge of remaining and continuing their trade therein so long as they behave peaceably and commit no offence against the laws; and in case their conduct should render them suspected, and the respective Governments should think proper to order them to remove, the term of twelve months from the publication of the order shall be allowed them for that purpose to remove with their families effects and property, but this favor shall not be extended to those who shall act contrary to the established laws. And for greater certainty it is declared, that such rupture shall not be deemed to exist while negociations for accomodating differences shall be depending, nor until the respective Ambassadors or Ministers shall be recalled or sent home on account of such differences, and not on account of personal misconduct, according to the nature and degrees of which, both parties retain their right either to request the recall or immediately to send home the Ambassador or Minister of the other, and that without prejudice to their mutual Friendship and Good understanding—[70]

25th. It is further agreed that his Majesty and the United States on mutual requisitions, by them respectively or ∧by∧ their respective ministers or officers authorized to make the same, will deliver up to justice all persons who being charged with Murder or Forgery committed within the jurisdiction of either, shall seek an asylum within ∧any∧ [of] the countries of the other, and that on such evidence of criminality, as according to the laws of the place where the fugitive or person so charged shall be found, would justify his apprehension and commitment for Tryal, if the offence had there been committed. The expence of such apprehension and delivery shall be born and defrayed by those who make the requisition and receive the fugitive—[71]

26th. It is agreed that the first Eight Articles of this Treaty shall be permanent And that all the subsequent articles shall be limited in their duration to twelve years, to be computed from the day on which this Treaty shall be ratified by the President of the United States by and with the advice and consent of the Senate thereof[72] But whereas the tenth Article will expire by its own limitation at the end of two years from the signing the preliminary articles of the peace which are to terminate the present war in which his Majesty is engaged,[73] It is agreed that proper measures shall by concert be seasonably taken for bringing the subject of that article into amicable treaty and discussion, so early before the expiration of the said term, as that new arrangements on that head at ∧may, by∧ that time, be perfected and ready to take place. But if it should unfortunately happen that His Majesty and the United States should not be able to agree on such new arrangements, in that case all the Articles of this Treaty except the first Eight shall then cease and expire together.[74]

D, with minor corrections and an added paragraph in JJ's hand, UK-KeNA: FO, 95/512 (EJ: 05006). This document was enclosed in JJ's letter to Grenville of 30 Sept. 1794, above.

1. Grenville's Draft Treaties of 30 Aug., above, lacked a preface. JJ's draft of 6 Aug. had specified that the two negotiators had found it impossible to admit the "mutual complaints and Claims of the *first Description* to be well founded." For Grenville's assertion that he had no desire to assess blame for the tensions that had arisen between the two countries, see item 8, Grenville to JJ, Responses to Queries, 7 Sept. 1794, above. For ER's reaction, see JJ to ER, 13 Sept. 1794, note 7, above; and ER to JJ, 12 Nov. 1794, *ASP: FR*, 1: 501–2.

2. The Treaty of Amity, Commerce, and Navigation of 19 Nov. 1794 adds the names of the plenipotentiaries and otherwise closely follows the wording of this preface.

3. The Treaty of Amity, Commerce, and Navigation of 19 Nov. 1794 closely follows JJ's wording of this article. On JJ's instructions with regard to peace, see the editorial note "Negotiating the Jay Treaty," and note 50, above.

4. In his draft of a general treaty in his Draft Treaties of 30 Aug., above, Grenville specified only posts.

5. Although his draft of 6 Aug. had specified 1 June 1795 as the deadline for the evacuation of British forces, JJ here accepted the modification given in Art. 1 of Grenville's draft of a general treaty in his Draft Treaties of 30 Aug., above. Art. 2 of the Treaty of Amity, Commerce, and Navigation of 19 Nov. 1794 incorporated this modification and further specified that, in the meantime, the United States could extend its settlements in any part within the boundary line except within the precincts and jurisdiction of the posts. JJ and Grenville had agreed to this change on 28 Oct. See the editorial note "Negotiating the Jay Treaty," above. For his reason for accepting the change, see JJ to ER, 19 Nov. 1794, below. For ER's concerns about the complications that might arise from prolonging the evacuation, see ER to JJ, 15 Dec. 1794, LS, NHi: Jay (EJ: 00620); *ASP: FR*, 1: 509–12.

6. JJ's draft agrees in substance with Grenville's draft of a general treaty to this point. For ER's suggestion that the protection accorded British subjects on territories to be evacuated was too generous, see ER to JJ, 15 Dec. 1794, LS, NHi: Jay (EJ: 00620); *ASP: FR*, 1: 511.

7. Grenville's draft of a general treaty in his Draft Treaties of 30 Aug., above, did not take up the issue of citizenship discussed in the remainder of this article. See JJ's Objections to Grenville's Draft Treaty Proposals of 30 Aug., [6 Sept. 1794], above.

8. Art. 2 of the Treaty of Amity, Commerce, and Navigation of 19 Nov. 1794 closely follows JJ's draft from "All settlers . . ." for the remainder of this paragraph.

9. Art. 3 of the Treaty of Amity, Commerce, and Navigation of 19 Nov. 1794 begins at this point. Grenville's draft of a general treaty in his Draft Treaties of 30 Aug., above, specified that passage was to be free not only to Indians but to his Majesty's subjects. See his draft and JJ's Objections to Grenville's Draft Treaty Proposals, cited above. JJ considered free passage for British subjects and American citizens in Art. 9, below. Art. 3 of the Treaty of Amity, Commerce, and Navigation of 19 Nov. 1794 gave the right of passage to British subjects as well as to American citizens into the respective territories of the two parties, the Hudson Bay Company territory excepted. It excluded American vessels from the inland waters of Canada except for small vessels trading between Quebec and Montreal, but reaffirmed Britain's right to navigate the Mississippi and to resort to ports on its eastern bank. It also regulated goods allowed in the trade and specified that duties on it would be equal for both parties. Indians and furs traded in inland commerce were to be exempt from duties. Terms for this article were finally agreed to on 1 Nov. 1794. For his comments on this article, see JJ to ER, 19 Nov. 1794, below. For Hawkesbury's insistence that Americans not be allowed to use the St. Lawrence to the sea, see Perkins, "Hawkesbury," 294.

10. For his demand that Indians on both sides of the border should have equal privileges to trade with either party to the treaty, see JJ's Objections to Grenville's Draft Treaty Proposals of 30 Aug., [6 Sept. 1794], above. For ER's concern that allowing British subjects and Indians to carry on

trade on the American side of the border would "produce great embarrassment, and all the heart-burnings of rivalship," see ER to JJ, 12 Nov. 1794, *ASP: FR*, 1: 501–2.

11. Art. 3 of the Treaty of Amity, Commerce, and Navigation of 19 Nov. 1794 retained the provisions about peltries and bales.

12. Art. 3 of the Treaty of Amity, Commerce, and Navigation of 19 Nov. 1794 did not include any of JJ's specific suggestions about restraining Indian warfare. Instead, it charged the two governments to promote amicable relations.

13. The Treaty of Amity, Commerce, and Navigation of 19 Nov. 1794 did not include any provision for a demilitarized border. For Hawkesbury's comments on protecting the British traders, and insistence that Britain be allowed to maintain a naval force on the lakes, see Perkins, "Hawkesbury," 294.

14. Art. 2 of Grenville's draft of a general treaty goes over the two boundary controversies. While Grenville agreed there that the St. Croix controversy should be resolved by a commission, he put forward an interpretation of the peace treaty that allowed Britain to claim a significant portion of territory south of the present northwest border on grounds that the peacemakers intended the line to extend as far south as the headwaters of the Mississippi River, a claim JJ emphatically denied. See Grenville's Draft Treaties, 30 Aug., and JJ to Grenville, 1 and 4 Sept. 1794, all above. In his letter of 18 Sept., JJ informed ER that he had discussed his draft of this article with Grenville and that he expected a response within a few days. Grenville's decision was not finalized until the end of October. See JJ to ER, 18 Sept. 1794, ALS, DNA: John Jay Despatches, 1794–95 (EJ: 04324); C, NHi: King (EJ: 04455); and *ASP: FR*, 1: 496–97; and the editorial note "Negotiating the Jay Treaty," above. Art. 4 of the Treaty of Amity, Commerce, and Navigation of 19 Nov. 1794 provided for a survey of the area, after which the two parties were committed to amicable negotiation of a boundary conformable to the intent of the peace treaty.

15. The manner of choosing commissioners is essentially the same as Grenville's proposal in his draft of a general treaty for choosing commissioners to settle the disputed northeastern boundary and prescribed for the settlement of this dispute in Art. 5 of the Treaty of Amity, Commerce, and Navigation of 19 Nov. 1794.

Art. 4 of the Treaty of Amity, Commerce, and Navigation of 19 Nov. 1794 required the two parties to make a joint survey of the northern Mississippi and stipulated that, if the river did not intersect a line drawn due west of the Lake of the Woods, they should use "amicable negotiation" to settle the boundary according to justice, mutual convenience and conformably to the intent of the peace treaty. On the settlement of this disputes in 1842 by the Webster-Ashburton Treaty, see Grenville to JJ, 5 Sept. 1794, note 5, above.

16. JJ's detailed description of how the three-man boundary commissions described here and below should operate and how they should be sworn in, staffed, and compensated were not incorporated into the Treaty of Amity, Commerce, and Navigation of 19 Nov. 1794.

17. JJ had protested Grenville's suggestion that this commission should meet in London. See Grenville's draft of a general treaty in his Draft Treaties of 30 Aug., and JJ's Objections to Grenville's Draft Treaty Proposals of 30 Aug., [6 Sept. 1794], both above. Art. 5 of the Treaty of Amity, Commerce, and Navigation of 19 Nov. 1794 adopted JJ's suggestion that the commissioners should meet in Halifax. For his comments on settlement of the St. Croix river issue, see JJ to ER, 19 Nov. 1794, below. ER subsequently informed JJ that GW approved of the arrangements made to settle both the St. Croix and northwestern boundary issues. See ER to JJ, 15 Dec. 1794, LS, NHi: Jay (EJ: 00620); *ASP: FR*, 1: 511.

On the commission that convened at St. Andrew's, New Brunswick, in 1796, see David Demeritt, "Representing the 'True' St. Croix: Knowledge and Power in the Partition of the Northeast," *WMQ* 54 (July 1997): 515–48; and R. D. Tallman and J. I. Tallman, "The Diplomatic Search for the

St. Croix River, 1796–1798," *Acadiensis* 1 (Spring 1972): 59–71. The three commissioners chosen at this time were Thomas Barclay, by the British, David Howell, by the Americans, and Egbert Benson, by the two commissioners. Barclay, a New York Loyalist, had studied law with JJ. Tallman and Tallman, "Diplomatic Search," 61. This dispute was also finally resolved by the Webster-Ashburton treaty.

18. Grenville's draft of a general treaty in his Draft Treaties of 30 Aug., above, considered the claims of British creditors before those of American merchants for compensation for losses experienced under the Order in Council of 6 Nov. 1793. This reversal of order accounts for differences in where the selection and function of the commissioners is described.

19. For ER's concern that the terms "irregular" and "illegal" were not sufficient to ensure compensation for Americans, see ER to JJ, 12 Nov. 1794, *ASP: FR*, 1: 502.

20. To this point, JJ's draft closely replicates the text of Art 4 of Grenville's draft of a general treaty in his Draft Treaties of 30 Aug., above. Thereafter, the substance of the provisions is similar, except that Grenville did not prescribe an oath. Art. 6 of the Treaty of Amity, Commerce, and Navigation of 19 Nov. 1794 provided the text of an oath to be taken by both sets of commissioners that closely follows the text JJ here provides, except that it does not include the pledge to try to agree with colleagues on the appointment of the fifth commissioner. For his comment that Art. 6 was a sine qua non, see JJ to ER, 19 Nov. 1794, below.

21. Art. 8 of the Treaty of Amity, Commerce, and Navigation of 19 Nov. 1794 provided that the two parties should agree on the payment of salaries and expenses for both sets of commissioners when the treaty was ratified. It further specified that replacement of commissioners by reason of death or illness should follow the manner of their original appointment. For his comments on this article, see JJ to ER, 19 Nov. 1794, below.

22. One of the abuses most complained about by American merchants was the unreasonable time set by the unauthorized admiralty courts in the West Indies that was allowed for appealing decisions, on which see JJ's representation to Grenville, 30 July 1794, above.

23. See Art. 4 of Grenville's draft of a general treaty in his Draft Treaties of 30 Aug. 1794, above. Art. 7 of the Treaty of Amity, Commerce, and Navigation of 19 Nov. 1794 specifies that all cases involving British merchants who had sustained loss or damage within the limits or jurisdiction of the United States, where restitution had not been made according to the tenor of a letter from TJ to Hammond of 5 Sept. 1793, would be referred to the commission handling merchant complaints. The treaty's text closely follows the text of this paragraph. For his comments on Art. 7 and the agent to be appointed to represent American merchants, see JJ to ER, 19 Nov. 1794, below. For notice that GW approved this clause, see ER to JJ, 15 Dec. 1794, LS, NHi: Jay (EJ: 00620); *ASP: FR*, 1: 511.

24. To this point JJ's draft closely replicates Art. 3 of Grenville's draft of a general treaty, which here adds "and value." Grenville's draft also stipulates that the commissioners should be appointed and should act in America. As does JJ's draft, the Treaty of Amity, Commerce, and Navigation of 19 Nov. 1794 specified that they should meet in Philadelphia, but have the power to adjourn from place to place as need arose.

25. For Hawkesbury's comment that juries composed of debtors would be unlikely to return justice to British creditors and that therefore it was necessary to make the American government responsible for insuring equitable compensation to them, see Perkins, "Hawkesbury," 296–97.

26. This parenthetical phrase is not present in Grenville's draft of a general treaty. Art. 6 of the Treaty of Amity, Commerce, and Navigation of 19 Nov. 1794 stipulates that the United States would compensate British creditors for losses and damages they experienced from legal impediments, but not to those resulting from the insolvency of the debtors or those experienced by the manifest delay or negligence, or willful omission of the claimant.

27. For Grenville's suggestion that payments on the debts should be delayed until the posts were evacuated, see the editorial note "Negotiating the Jay Treaty," above. Art. 6 of the Treaty of Amity, Commerce, and Navigation of 19 Nov. 1794 specified that the commissioners could not require payment to take place sooner than twelve months from the day of the exchange of ratifications of the treaty. Under Art. 5 of this draft, payments to American merchants were to be made as determined by the commissioners who awarded the damages.

28. Art 8. of the Treaty of Amity, Commerce, and Navigation of 19 Nov. 1794 governed payment of the commissioners and their staffs, as described in note 21, above.

29. For his concern that the treaty should provide explicitly for future as well as present inheritances, see ER to JJ, 12 Nov. 1794, *ASP: FR*, 1: 502. On Grenville's proposal to abolish alienism between the two nations, see JJ to ER, 19 Nov. 1794, below; and Art. 9 of the Treaty of Amity, Commerce, and Navigation of 19 Nov. 1794. For Grenville's communication, before and immediately following the conclusion of treaty negotiations, of dossiers related to loyalist estates confiscated in the United States, whose owners wished to be considered as British creditors, see Grenville to JJ, 1 Nov. 1794, C, UkLPR: FO: 95/512 (EJ: 05012), and 19 Nov. 1794, below. See also JJ to Loughborough, 9 Oct. 1794, below, and notes.

30. Grenville's Draft Treaties of 30 Aug., above, here begins a separate treaty of commerce consisting of seven articles. The text of this paragraph from JJ's draft closely follows the text of Art. 1 of Grenville's draft of a commercial treaty and of Art. 11 of the Treaty of Amity, Commerce, and Navigation of 19 Nov. 1794, which, like JJ's draft, does not separate the content into two treaties. JJ subsequently informed ER that he and Grenville were incorporating Grenville's two treaties into a single treaty of amity and commerce. He also stated that he had proposed several additional articles, probably articles 15, 17, 18, 19, 21, 22, and 25 of the present draft. He added that, while he still hoped for agreement on a treaty, the outcome remained uncertain. See JJ to ER, 2 Oct. 1794, ALS, DNA: Jay Despatches, 1794–1795 (EJ: 04325); and C, NHi: King (EJ: 04456).

31. Art. 3 of the Treaty of Amity, Commerce, and Navigation of 19 Nov. 1794, which follows a discussion of the posts to be evacuated, here adds "and also to the Indians dwelling on either side of the said boundary line." It otherwise closely follows JJ's text.

32. For Hawkesbury's assertion that British merchants currently had a considerable share of the trade up the Mississippi and that it should be protected, see Perkins, "Hawkesbury," 294–95.

33. Art. 3 of the Treaty of Amity, Commerce, and Navigation of 19 Nov. 1794 here substitutes "said Territories in America."

34. Art. 3 of the Treaty of Amity, Commerce, and Navigation of 19 Nov. 1794 omits this exception. Following the word "subjects" it adds "on the importation of the same from Europe into the said Territories."

35. Art. 3 of the Treaty of Amity, Commerce, and Navigation of 19 Nov. 1794 omits this exception.

36. Art. 3 of the Treaty of Amity, Commerce, and Navigation of 19 Nov. 1794 here adds an additional clause. As does JJ, this draft exempts peltries and incorporates his provisions on "bales" of goods from Art. 2, above. It further exempts the "proper Goods and Effects" of Indians and goods merely carried over portages and then immediately re-embarked.

37. Art. 3 of the Treaty of Amity, Commerce, and Navigation of 19 Nov. 1794 incorporates this provision.

38. Art. 3 of the Treaty of Amity, Commerce, and Navigation of 19 Nov. 1794 concludes with this statement.

39. Art. 12 of the Treaty of Amity, Commerce, and Navigation of 19 Nov. 1794 contained a limit of 70 tons. For AH's advice about a preexisting act of Parliament that allowed foreign European vessels of 70 tons or less to engage in the carrying trade with the British West Indies under certain restric-

tions, see AH to JJ, 6 May 1794, *JJSP*, 5: 633. For earlier suggested limits, see Art. 6 of Grenville's draft of a commercial treaty in his Draft Treaties of 30 Aug. 1794, above. JJ previously stated that admission to the West Indies trade was considered compensation for Britain's retention of the posts. See JJ to ER, 13 Sept. 1794, above. He subsequently stated that he could not obtain better terms for the West Indies article unless he was willing to agree to abolish all "alien duties" between the two nations. See JJ to ER, 19 Nov. 1794, below. For ER's assertion that the "*douceur*" of trading with the West Indies would not make having to pay their debts to British creditors palatable to half of the nation, that the limited term of the grant and other restrictions on the trade made it of little value, and for his accurate prediction of the reaction to this article, see ER to JJ, 15 Dec. 1794, LS, NHi: Jay (EJ: 00620); *ASP: FR*, 1: 511–12.

40. Here and below, Art. 6 of Grenville's draft of a commercial treaty of 30 Aug. did not provide for the admission of American or West Indian "manufacture." Art. 12 of the Treaty of Amity, Commerce, and Navigation of 19 Nov. 1794, however, did. Otherwise, JJ's draft closely follows Grenville's Art. 6 to the end of the paragraph. JJ's draft to this point agrees in substance with Art. 12 of the Treaty of Amity, Commerce, and Navigation of 19 Nov. 1794.

41. This sentence does not appear either in Art. 6 of Grenville's draft of a commercial treaty of 30 Aug. or in Art. 12 of the Treaty of Amity, Commerce, and Navigation of 19 Nov. 1794.

42. Here Art. 12 of the Treaty of Amity, Commerce, and Navigation of 19 Nov. 1794 adds "and restrain."

43. Art. 6 of Grenville's draft of a commercial treaty of 30 Aug. prohibits the carrying of "any West India productions in American vessels" except to the United States, and excepting rum made in the United States from West India Molasses. Art. 12 of the Treaty of Amity, Commerce, and Navigation of 19 Nov. 1794 adds molasses and cocoa to the products listed here by JJ.

44. The preceding two paragraphs of JJ's draft closely follow Art. 6 of Grenville's draft of a commercial treaty of 30 Aug., as does Art. 12 of the Treaty of Amity, Commerce, and Navigation of 19 Nov. 1794, which, however, adds an additional clause. For Hawkesbury's concern to preserve the growth in British shipping and his opposition to concessions to the United States in the West Indies trade, see Perkins, "Hawkesbury," 301–4.

45. This sentence closely follows the opening sentence of Art. 1 of Grenville's draft of a commercial treaty of 30 Aug. which, however, adds that all ships belonging to either party, including both warships and merchant vessels should be admitted. Art. 14 of the Treaty of Amity, Commerce, and Navigation of 19 Nov. 1794 does not include this provision.

46. JJ's draft and Art. 14 of the Treaty of Amity, Commerce, and Navigation of 19 Nov. 1794 closely follow the remainder of Art. 1 of Grenville's draft of a commercial treaty of 30 Aug.

47. Marginal note in JJ's hand.

48. There is no equivalent to this article either in Grenville's draft of a commercial treaty of 30 Aug. or in the Treaty of Amity, Commerce, and Navigation of 19 Nov. 1794. For his remark that he and Grenville could not agree on several articles they had considered, see JJ to ER, 19 Nov. 1794, below.

49. Here Art. 2 of Grenville's draft of a commercial treaty of 30 Aug. provided that consuls must be citizens of the nation they represented. This provision was not carried into Art. 16 of the Treaty of Amity, Commerce, and Navigation of 19 Nov. 1794.

50. Grenville's draft of a commercial treaty of 30 Aug. did not contain an equivalent of this provision, which the Treaty of Amity, Commerce, and Navigation of 19 Nov. 1794 closely follows. For JJ's insistence, while Secretary for Foreign Affairs, that consuls be duly accredited by Congress before they began to exercise their functions, see JJ's Report to Congress on Richard Soderstrom, *JJSP*, 4: 61–62. For complications that had arisen when Britain appointed consuls to the United States

before it concluded a commercial treaty, see the editorial note "Consuls *de Gratia*: The Role of British Consuls," *JJSP*, 4: 245–49.

51. This provision closely followed Art. 2 of Grenville's draft of a commercial treaty of 30 Aug. and carried into Art. 16 of the Treaty of Amity, Commerce, and Navigation of 19 Nov. 1794.

52. There is no equivalent in Grenville's draft of a commercial treaty of 30 Aug. for this provision. Art. 13 of the Treaty of Amity, Commerce, and Navigation of 19 Nov. 1794 provided that "Vessels belonging to the Citizens of the United States" should be hospitably received in British territories in the East Indies. For previous American penetration into the trade with British East India, and for the use of American ships as a means for British personnel to evade British East India Company restrictions on remittances, see the editorial note "Americans Engage in the China Trade"; and JJ's "Report on a Letter from John O'Donnell," 5 Aug. 1786, *JJSP*, 4: 91–95, 387–90.

53. Grenville's draft of a commercial treaty of 30 Aug. contained no equivalent for this article. Art. 17 of the Treaty of Amity, Commerce, and Navigation of 19 Nov. 1794 rejected the notion of free ships making free goods and replaced it with a restatement of the Order in Council of 8 June 1793, as observed in ER to JJ, 12 Nov. 1794, *ASP: FR*, 1: 501–2.

JJ later informed ER that he had assumed responsibility for merging Grenville's two draft treaties of 30 Aug. into a single treaty of amity and commerce—the present draft. In it, he said, he had omitted several of Grenville's proposals but included most of them to which he had added several of his own "for mutual consideration." Thereafter, Grenville, in turn, had extracted several, omitted some, and added others, forming a new draft (not identified). Difficulties appeared: some articles were removed, some were modified, and a few still remained. Discussions were continuing, JJ reported, and would soon be concluded either in a treaty or in certainty that amicable settlement was "impracticable." See JJ to ER, 29 Oct. 1794, ALS, DNA: Jay Despatches, 1794–1795 (EJ: 04329); C, NHi: King (EJ: 04460); *ASP: FR*, 1: 500–501.

54. The following section through the end of the paragraph is in JJ's hand.

55. Grenville's Draft Treaties of 30 Aug. do not define contraband. However, Grenville supplied the definition of contraband incorporated in part into Art. 18 of the Treaty of Amity, Commerce, and Navigation of 19 Nov. 1794 in [Grenville to JJ, Responses to Queries, 7 Sept. 1794], above, perhaps after receiving Hawkesbury's comments opposing any concessions on the rights of neutral commerce and his insistence that provisions might be considered contraband. He also, however, recommended ending the disputes caused by the Order of 6 Nov. and establishing a commission to settle them. See Perkins, "Hawkesbury," 297–99. Art. 18 also stated that when provisions were seized, owners should be compensated for them. It also provided protection for neutral ships that unknowingly approached a blockaded port. For JJ's comments on Britain's refusal to accept the American interpretation of the law of nations while engaged in the current war, see JJ to ER, 19 Nov. 1794, below.

56. Neither Grenville's draft of a commercial treaty of 30 Aug. nor the Treaty of Amity, Commerce, and Navigation of 19 Nov. 1794 contains an equivalent for this article.

57. Grenville's draft of a commercial treaty of 30 Aug. contains no equivalent for this article. Art. 18 of the Treaty of Amity, Commerce, and Navigation of 19 Nov. 1794 provides that, in cases when provisions and other articles not generally contraband were regarded as such and had been seized, owners or masters of the vessel should be completely indemnified, and the vessel released without undue delay.

58. Neither Grenville's draft of a commercial treaty of 30 Aug. nor the Treaty of Amity, Commerce, and Navigation of 19 Nov. 1794 contains an equivalent for this article.

59. Art. 8 of Grenville's draft of a general treaty of 30 Aug. prohibited the subjects of either party from accepting privateering commissions from an enemy to the other party. ER relayed GW's con-

cern that the present article might be understood to restrict the use of privateers against Britain in the event that the United States went to war with her, although he observed that treaties were usually dissolved by a declaration of war. See ER to JJ, 12 Nov. 1794, *ASP: FR*, 1: 501–2. Art. 19 of the Treaty of Amity, Commerce, and Navigation of 19 Nov. 1794 follows the present article closely except that it requires the authenticated copy of the proceedings to be delivered to the commander of the vessel without the smallest delay on payment of all fees and demands for the same. There is no provision under which the judge forfeits his commission. For his note that it was based on the Anglo-French treaty of commerce, see JJ to ER, 19 Nov. 1794, below.

60. Neither Grenville's draft of a commercial treaty of 30 Aug. nor the Treaty of Amity, Commerce, and Navigation of 19 Nov. 1794 carries an equivalent for this article.

61. Grenville's draft of a commercial treaty of 30 Aug. contains no equivalent for this article. Art. 20 of the Treaty of Amity, Commerce, and Navigation of 19 Nov. 1794 closely follows JJ's text to this point. For his note that the clause forbidding natives commanding privateers against the other party was derived in part from the United States' treaty with Holland, see JJ to ER, 19 Nov. 1794, below. Art. 19 of this treaty prohibited natives of either nation from taking privateering commissions from nations with which the opposite partner was at war. For ER's concern that the treaty would prohibit the United States from employing privateers against the British in the event of an Anglo-American war, see ER to JJ, 12 Nov. 1794, *ASP: FR*, 1: 501–2; and 3 Dec. 1794, C, NHi: Jay (EJ: 00619).

62. Art. 8 of Grenville's draft of a general treaty of 30 Aug. emphatically forbids the subjects of either party from accepting commissions to act against the other. Art. 21 of the Treaty of Amity, Commerce, and Navigation of 19 Nov. 1794, however, closely follows JJ's text.

63. Grenville's draft of a commercial treaty of 30 Aug. contains no equivalent for this paragraph. Art. 22 of the Treaty of Amity, Commerce, and Navigation of 19 Nov. 1794, however, closely follows JJ's text.

64. Grenville's draft of a commercial treaty of 30 Aug. contains no equivalent for this text. The first paragraph of Art. 23 of the Treaty of Amity, Commerce, and Navigation of 19 Nov. 1794 specifies that the officers should be treated with the respect due their commissions and that both officers and crews should pay due respect to the laws and government of the country. It provides further that those who insult these officers should be punished as disturbers of the peace and amity of the two nations. For Hammond's recent complaints about the treatment of British forces in Rhode Island, see ER to GW, 18 July 1794, *PGW: PS*, 16: 377–79.

65. Although his draft of a general treaty of 30 Aug. did not contain a prohibition against impressment, Grenville indicated that he would not object to one. Nevertheless, there was no provision in the Treaty of Amity, Commerce, and Navigation of 19 Nov. 1794 prohibiting impressment. See JJ's Objections to Grenville's Draft Treaty Proposals of 30 Aug., [6 Sept. 1794]; and Grenville to JJ, Responses to Queries, 7 Sept. 1794, both above. For his sense that Britain was unlikely to make concessions on impressment, see JJ to GW (private), 3 Sept. 1795, below.

66. JJ here allowed Grenville to overrule his attempt to insure that Art. 7 of Grenville's draft of a general treaty of 30 Aug. which barred the admission and sale of prizes taken by an enemy into the ports of the neutral party, would not go into effect until the conclusion of the present war. See item 15 of JJ's Objections to Grenville's Draft Treaty Proposals of 30 Aug., [6 Sept. 1794], above. For the rejection by the House of Representatives of a clause forbidding the sale of prizes, see AH to JJ, 4 June 1794, above. JJ's text here is closely followed in Art. 24 of the Treaty of Amity, Commerce, and Navigation of 19 Nov. 1794. See Grenville to JJ, Responses to Queries, 7 Sept., above. For problems that arose with Genet's commissioning of privateers, see the editorial note "John Jay

and the Genet Affair," *JJSP*, 5: 546–61. ER claimed that the correspondence between TJ and Hammond that JJ had carried with him proved that the United States was not accountable for captures made by French vessels armed in American ports and subsequently stated that GW approved this position. See ER to JJ, 12 Nov. 1794, *ASP: FR*, 1: 501–2; and 15 Dec. 1794, C, NHi: Jay (EJ: 00620); *ASP: FR*, 1: 509–12.

67. ER's concern that Grenville's successors might insist that the Franco-American treaty was no longer in force because of changes in the French government may apply to this passage. See ER to JJ, 12 Nov. 1794, *ASP: FR*, 1: 502.

68. The text of this article follows Art. 7 of Grenville's draft of a commercial treaty of 30 Aug. and is closely replicated in Art. 25 of the Treaty of Amity, Commerce, and Navigation of 19 Nov. 1794.

69. The text of this article, which elaborates on Art. 9 of Grenville's draft a general treaty of 30 Aug., is closely followed in the concluding paragraph of Art. 25 of the Treaty of Amity, Commerce, and Navigation of 19 Nov. 1794. For problems of this nature that arose during Genet's ministry, see the editorial note "John Jay and the Genet Affair," *JJSP*, 5: 546–61.

70. Art. 10 of Grenville's draft of a general treaty of 30 Aug. briefly addresses protections for merchants in the event of war between the United States and Britain. This paragraph in JJ's draft is closely followed in Art. 26 of the Treaty of Amity, Commerce, and Navigation of 19 Nov. 1794.

71. Grenville's draft of a general treaty of 30 Aug. contains no equivalent for this article, which is closely followed in Art. 27 of the Treaty of Amity, Commerce, and Navigation of 19 Nov. 1794.

72. Grenville's draft of a general treaty of 30 Aug. did not make any of its articles permanent. It provided a term of twelve years for all articles except Art. 6, which governed the West Indies trade. Art. 28 of the Treaty of Amity, Commerce, and Navigation of 19 Nov. 1794 made the first ten articles permanent, and gave all subsequent articles a term of twelve years, with the exception of the article governing the West Indies trade, which Congress rejected because it restrained Americans from carrying West Indian products to any ports except those in the United States. See Bemis, *Jay Treaty*, 355.

73. Art. 6 in Grenville's draft of a general treaty of 30 Aug. and Art. 12 in the Treaty of Amity, Commerce, and Navigation of 19 Nov. 1794 carry identical limitations.

74. The text of Art. 28 of the Treaty of Amity, Commerce, and Navigation of 19 Nov. 1794 closely follows JJ's draft.

From Grenville

St James's Sqr. Octr. 7. 1794.

Sir

It shall certainly be my object to hasten as much as possible the examination & consideration of the Contre projet which I have received from you.[1] But on such attention as I have hitherto been able to give to it I find so much new matter, and so much variation in the form & substance of the Articles proposed in the projet, that I am very apprehensive the discussion of these points will of necessity consume more time than I had flattered myself might have been sufficient to bring our negotiation to a satisfactory issue.— If you can conveniently call in St James's Square tomorro morning at Eleven I will mention to you a few of the leading points which must if insisted upon on your part create as I fear ~~was~~ insurmountable obstacles to the conclusion of the treaty proposed, but the extent & delicacy of these subjects will require more detailed & particular examination in every part where a departure is proposed from the terms of the projet delivered to you.

I flatter myself that it is unnecessary for me to repeat the assurances of my sincere desire to bring the business to a speedy & satisfactory conclusion— I have the honour to be with great respect & esteem Sir Your most faithful & obedient humble Servt

Grenville—

J. Jay Esq[r] &c &c &c

ALS, NNC (EJ: 08534). C, unknown repository, formerly PRO (EJ: 01606). Hist. Mss. Comm., *Fortescue Manuscripts*, 3: 517.

1. See JJ to Grenville, and the Project for a Treaty with Great Britain, both 30 Sept. 1794, above.

To Loughborough

R.H. P.M. 9 Oct[r] 1794

my Lord

The Expediency of the article[1] ~~hinted to me~~ Suggested by your Lordship to facilitate the ~~admission~~ ₍Introduction₎ of Evidence from the one to the other of our Countries, has not ceased to engage my attention; ~~and has been~~ ₍since₎ ~~delayed for no other Reason~~ but I doubted the Propriety of giving ~~yourself~~ Lordship any ~~Trou~~ Trouble on that Subject, while ~~the~~ ₍there was less₎ Probability of a Treaty ~~appeared to be~~ ₍than I flatter₎ myself there now is— The few Difficulties ~~that~~ ₍w^h that₎ remain will I think be surmounted by the ₍candor &₎ liberal Policy which in the ~~Progress~~ ₍course₎ of the Negociation I have had occasions to observe.

~~I should I sh Instead of~~

Your Talents & Experience my Lord would give advantages to this article which it could not ~~receive from me~~ ₍derive from mine₎. Its object being common ~~Good~~ ₍& public Utility₎, I venture to request your Lordship to ~~undertake~~ ₍prepare₎ it— I would do myself the Honor to wait on you and ~~communicate~~ ₍mention₎ some Ideas and Information relative to the ~~american p~~ arrangements ~~most expedient in~~ ₍w^h. w^d. best₎ in my opinion be best accommodated to₎ America, but ~~even with~~ considering ~~how much your Lordship must necessarily be occupied occupations might~~ ₍that the Time most convenient₎ to your Lordship ought first to be known, ~~I I~~ I think it more proper to wait for ~~& be directed by~~ your orders on that Head[2]

186

I have the honor to be my Lord with great Respect & Consideration Your Lordships most ob^t. & most hble. Servt

The R^t. Honble the Lord Chancellor

Dft, NNC (EJ: 08910).

1. For the text of the proposed clause concerning the admission of evidence, see Article Proposed by the Lord Chancellor (Loughborough), [c. 9 Oct. 1794], below. See also JJ to ER, 19 Nov. 1794, below; JJ to GW (private), 3 Sept., and (private), 4 Sept. 1795, both below; and JJ to TP, 6 June 1796, below.

2. On 10 Oct., Loughborough invited JJ, with PAJ and JT, to dine the following day at his house in Hampstead. He requested that JJ arrive early to discuss the matter, remarking that "I flatter myself we should very easily manage the article proposed." ALS, NNC (EJ: 06913). See also JJ's acceptance of the same date, Dft, NNC (EJ: 08911). PAJ recorded in his diary that "We dined with the Lord Chancellor at Hamstead in company with M^r. Pitt, M^r. Windham— The Master of the Rolls (Pepper Arden) The Advocate General (Sir W. Scott) & Lord Mansfield." 11 Oct. 1794, PAJ Diary A, AD, NNC.

Article Proposed by the Lord Chancellor (Loughborough)

[London, [c. 9 Oct. 1794]]

1. That the Native Subjects of the united States & those of H[is]. B[rittanic]. M[ajesty]. shall not be considered in either Country as Aliens in respect of any legal disability.[1]

[in lighter ink] But This stipulation is not to extend to ~~any to repeal annul~~ any points of navigation, those being already settled by the other Articles of this Treaty.[2]

[in lighter ink] Q[uery]. Is ~~that~~ this practicable under the present Constitution of Canada or applicable to that Country?

The Consequences of this Article to the American in the British Dominions would be

1. That He could take to his own use by descent or purchase any Interest in Land

2. That He could exercise any trade or occupation, from many of which Aliens are excluded by particular acts.

3. That He would not be liable to alien duties of any sort even Light House & anchorage dues

4. That He could become a Member of any Corporation, and entitled to all the priviledges of It.

5. That He could hold any Office by Election or Commission from the Crown & could become a Member of Parl[iamen]^t. or of the privy Council.

=not knowing how far the Disabili-
tys of Alienage extend in America,
It cannot be accurately stated what
would be the Effect of the Article
wh. respect to the British Subject
in America. Supposing the Law
to be the same in both Countrys,
the First consequence would be
reciprocal;— But the Advantage
from it is evidently on the side of
America. For It is more likely that
British Capital would be attracted
to the cultivation of American
Land, than that any American
Capital sh^d. be transferred to
Britain—

as to all the other consequences
It is probable that the advantage is
solely on the side of America

But there is an Advantage, common to both Countrys, by which
ₐeachₐ gains what It gives— That
the connections of both ₐwould
be soₐ interwoven— That the
Subjects of each would find themselves at home in the other, and
their Union would be cemented by
kindness as well as by Policy—

2nd: That Wills made in either Country
affecting real Estates in both, remaining ₐ(as they must)ₐ in that Country
where they are made, An Exemplification of the Will (which as the British
dominions wo[ul]^d. be under the Great
Seal & probably in America under
that of the fœderal Court) should be
allowed to have the same effect as the
Will Itself.

Observation

The Copy of a Will of personal Estate duely authenticated from America is admitted here & ~~probate~~ ₐAdministrationₐ granted upon It— A Probate of a Will here would probably be equally regarded in America. All therefore that is required in this case is to settle the Mode of authenticating the Copy, which belongs to a subsequent Head.

3d: All Deeds conveying any real Estate or Interest in Land or any personal property ₐin Americaₐ, of the value of £100 ₐexecuted in Englandₐ should be enrolled in one of the Courts of West[minster] Hall upon the acknowledgement of one of the Partys ₐbefore a Judgeₐ & also an Affidavit filed of the Witnesses of the Execution of ₐbyₐ the other Partys— The Deed with an office Copy of the affidavit being Transmitted to America should be there received as proved & in case of its Loss an Exemplification from the Roll should supply its place.
It would still be necessary to add another guard; As the Signature of the Judge to the order on the Deed when the deed ₐitselfₐ is sent, or of the officer who attests the will Copy could not be proved abroad, & therefore an Affidavit should be made of that fact, before the Mayor ₐannexed to the Instrumentₐ & certified under the Seal of the City—
The forgery of any Signature or counterfeiting the Seal (if they are not

The Regulation which w^{od}. be necessary as to this Article in America must be submitted to M^r. Jay.

already subject to Punishment) should
be subjected to the same that is provided in like cases.[3]

4. The preceding Article w^od. likewise
extend to the office Copys of the Judgments of all Courts that have no known
Seal viz. that the Handwriting of the
officer delivering out the Copy sh^d. be
proved by affidavit ∧&∧ certified under
the City Seal

The Court of Admiralty has a Seal
as well as the Court for the probate of
Wills

5. The Mode of taking Evidence under
Commissions is extremely defective
& a great embarrassment to Justice I
should think it a great advancement
of Justice if the Chancellor instead of
leaving to the Partys the carriage &
the Execution of their own Commission were enabled to address the Cheif
Justice of the fœderal Court & request
Him to interpose His authority by appointing Commissioners to examine
the Witnesses on the Interrogatories
transmitted, to administer the oath
to them, & cause their Answers to be
taken down in their presence & then to
return the whole sealed up, and authenticated under the Seal of the Court.
The same thing might be done here &
I should add to It a Qualification that
no Person shd. be appointed a Commissioner ∧here∧ who had not been a
Barrister of at least five Years standing.

It would be inconvenient to appoint
a Standing Commission here, because
in each case convenience would require

that the Time & place of executing It
should be considered; But in Effect It
would be inconvenient to appoint a
Standing Commission here, because in
each case convenience would require
that the Time & place of executing It
should be considered; But in Effect
there would be very little change in the
Commissioners.[4]

The greater part of these Articles
would require the Sanction of
Parl[iamen]t: for what respects the
British dominions; But if the outline I
have attempted to draw meets M^r. Jay's
Approbation, I think it would not be
difficult to frame one or two articles
expressive of the general principles that
govern them, which might find their
place without impropriety in a diplo-
matick act, and which would soon be
developed in a Legislative Act.[5]

AD, in JJ's hand, n.d., NHi: Jay Papers (EJ: 00892, images 9–16), entitled "Lord Chancellor's proposed *Article*". In file entitled: "Papers connected with the Negociation of the British Treaty, 1794".
LbkC, in JT's hand, enclosed in JJ to ER, 19 Nov. 1794, NNC: JJ Lbk. 8.

1. Loughborough proposed this article to JJ on or shortly before 9 Oct. 1794. They met to discuss
it on 10–11 October. See JJ to Loughborough, 9 Oct. 1794, above. JJ's instructions regarding alienage issues stated "The intercourse with England make it necessary that the disabilities, arising from
alienage in case of inheritance, should be put upon a liberal footing or rather abolished." ER to JJ,
6 May 1794, *JJSP*, 5: 640.

2. This and the next comment are by Grenville.

3. On JJ's legal difficulties regarding securing evidence needed for settling Jay family inheritances
from the Peloquin estate in England, see *JJSP*, 3: 361–62, 491–92. Alienage, however, was not among
the obstacles in that case.

4. On the use of commissions to collect evidence for court cases involving parties abroad, see
the notes on the Van Staphorst case, and the Minutes of the Supreme Court, 1–3 Aug. 1792, *JJSP*,
5: 184, 329, 331.

5. On this proposal, see also JJ to GW (private), 3 Sept., and (private), 4 Sept. 1795, below.
JQA noted in his diary: "The Article proposed by Lord Loughborough, the Chancellor, is certainly extremely liberal, although Mr Jay thinks it best to leave it as a subject for future consideration. It is that in either Country the subjects or citizens of the other shall be exempted from *all
the disability of alienage*. Such an article would certainly tend to promote the friendly intercourse

between the nations; and I do not know that it could produce any material ~~intercourse with~~ inconveniences to either. But it would be necessary to have an Act of parliament to confirm the stipulation here, which his Lordship says may be obtained without difficulty. A more material obstacle arises from the Constitution of the United States, with one clause of which, such an article would certainly militate."

JQA Diaries, 22 Oct. 1794, vol. 21, MHi: Adams; *JQA Diaries Digital*, http://www.masshist.org /jqadiaries/php/doc?id=jqad21_44 (accessed Aug. 2019).

To Grenville

Royal Hotel—Pall Mall—13 Oct[r]. 1794

My Lord

I rec[d]. last Evening, by a Vessel in 21 Days from New York, Dispatches from the Secretary of State. They contain much Information, respecting the then present State of affairs in the united States.

Among other interesting circumstances, the Transaction of Governor Simcoe relative to an american Settlement at the Great Soders, is stated, and accompanied with Copies of the Papers respecting it.

Extracts from these Papers, and from M[r]. Randolph's Letter to me of the 30 Aug[t]., I have now the Honor of laying before your Lordship— a subsequent Letter from M[r]. Randolph of the 5 Sept[r]. inclosed a copy of one he had written to M[r]. Hammond on the Subject, and also a copy of M[r]. Hammonds answer, expressing his Intention of transmitting them to Gov[r]. Simcoe, and to His Majesty's Ministers—[1]

Those Papers were sent to me, not merely for my Information, but to enable me to make proper Representations on the Subject.

Considering the present promising State of the negotiation, I cannot think it necessary to make any formal applications to your Lordship respecting these painful occurrences.

It is to be regretted that the same Disposition to Conciliation which animates your Lordship, does not appear to be entertained and seconded by His Majesty's officers and agents in America and the West Indies. I flatter myself however, that Instructions tending to produce a Conduct conformable to that Disposition, have been sent, and that it will not be long before their Effects will become visible, and relieve the Presidents mind from apprehensions, which I find have taken strong hold of it.

These Considerations restrain me from troubling your Lordship with Details and Remarks concerning an Opinion, which has become general and fixed, of unfriendly measures with the Indians.[2]

The treaty now preparing will I hope be such as to remove every Cause of Complaint, and produce Sentiments & Sensations of a different kind.—

I saw the Capt. of the Philadelphia Ship last night— he told me he expects to sail next *Sunday*. In case a few Days more should happen to be necessary to complete the Treaty I will endeavour to detain him at the Expense of the united States— I have the Honor to be with great Respect & Esteem Your Lordship's most obed^t. & most hble Servt

John Jay

The right Honorable Lord Grenville

ALS, UK-BL: Dropmore, Ms, 59049. Enclosures: extract of ER to JJ, 30 Aug. 1794; Captain Williamson to ER, 19 Aug. 1794; Lt. R. H. Sheaffe to Captain Williamson, 16 Aug. 1794. Dft, NNC (EJ: 08174). PtD, with enclosures, Hist. Mss. Comm., *Fortescue Manuscripts*, 3: 528–30.

1. For ER's letter of 30 Aug., see C, DNA: Jay Despatches, 1794–95 (EJ: 04309); LbkC, NHi: King (EJ: 04441); E, Hist. Mss. Comm., *Fortescue Manuscripts*, 3: 529 (EJ: 00066). For ER's letter of 5 Sept., enclosing his letter to Hammond of 1 Sept. and Hammond's reply of 3 Sept. 1794, see LbkC, NHi: King (EJ: 04442).

2. On complaints regarding Lieutenant Governor Simcoe's efforts to block American settlement and to encourage Indian attacks, see JJ to GW (private), 29 Oct. 1794, below.

From Peter Jay Munro

New York 16th. Octr. 1794

Dear Sir,

I had the pleasure of writing to you & Cousin Peter, upon the 10th. Instant,[1] and being now ready to set off for Albany, I leave this Letter, to be forwarded to you, in Case an opportunity should offer during my absence. I have also left a Letter for my father, which will be sent by the same Conveyance— In his Letter to me, he states many reasons, why he supposes the Lands above Albany, are not his, and he then adds, "If you think the recovery of them possible, or even probable, you have my full consent and permission, to begin immediately, without loss of Time, and endeavour to recover them, for the use & benefit of yourself and family." And again "I do not wish, to appropriate any of these Lands to my self, *if* I have any right to them, I am willing to grant, make over, and resign them. to you and your Children forever, and to divest my self of them, as soon as you please." In Consequence of this Letter, I have enclosed him, a very short Instrument adapted to the purpose, and which I have no Question he will be willing to execute— the only Difficulty will be, to procure *proper* witnesses.—

I have suggested to him, two ways, in which in my opinion, this might be effected.— The one executing the paper, in the presence of a master of some vessel, coming to this Port.— the other, the obtaining your Consent, that Cousin Peter, might visit Edinburgh— but at the same time I informed him, that I prefered the last method, if it should be agreeable to you, to him & to Peter.

I advised him, in case he concured with me in Sentiment, to write to you, and request a visit from my Cousin. If he should follow my advice, permit me to request the Favor, of your and of Peter['s] Acquiesence in the Measure.— I will chearfully be at the expence of his the Journey, of himself & servant.— The object is of magnatude, to me, the attaining it or not, will differ me several thousand pounds.[2]

If Peter goes, be so kind as to put him upon his guard, as to the Disposition of my father— I think I understand him, & am certain, that it would be improper, that Peter should let him perceive, that before his arrival at Edinburgh, the true object of his visit was known— My Situation in life, I *wish* him to represent, *exactly as it is*— but in regard to my Mother, he must be *totally silent*— I learn from my father, that he is very infirm, and daily apprehends another Stroke of the Palsy.—

We are all is good health— I remain Dear Sir Your aff^te. Nephew,

P. Jay Munro

The Hon. John Jay Esqr.

ALS, NNC (EJ: 09375). Dft, NNMus (EJ: 00430).

1. Probably PJM to JJ, 11 Oct., Dft, NNMus (EJ: 00429), and PJM to PAJ, 11 Oct. 1794, Dft, NNMus (EJ: 04052).

2. The lands still owned by the Reverend Harry Munro were located in New York State. JJ approved of PJM's request in letters of 9 Dec. 1794 [ALS, NNMus: Munro (EJ: 00436)], and 14 Dec. 1794 [ALS, NNMus: Munro (EJ: 00438)]. PAJ left for Scotland on 12 Dec., reaching Edinburgh five days later. He dined with the Rev. Harry Munro several times and successfully completed their business on 23 Dec. PAJ spent Christmas with Munro and left the city on 27 Dec., reaching London on 31 Dec. On 24 Dec., Munro wrote JJ, thanking him for allowing PAJ to make the journey. "I have had much pleasure and satisfaction, since he came here, in his agreeable company and Conversation. His ingaging Manners, good Sense and polite Behaviour must endear him to all his acquaintance; and I sincerely congratulate you Sir, in having so promising a Son." For the rest of PAJ's journey, see PAJ Diary A, AD, NNC; PAJ to SLJ, 2 Jan. 1795, below, and the editorial note "John Jay's Mission to London," above.

To George Washington (private)

London 29 October 1794

Dear Sir

I have been honored with your's of the 5th. of September.[1] Want of Liesure constrains me to be concise— I am authorized by Lord Grenville to assure you in the most explicit Terms, that no Instructions to stimulate or promote Hostilities by the Indians against the United States have been sent to the King's officers in Canada. I am preparing an official Representation to him on this Subject, and he will give me an official answer to it; but as this cannot be done in Season to forward by this Vessel (for Letters after this Day will be too late to go by her) His Lordship has permitted me to make this *informal* Communication to you, for your Satisfaction. I am to lay before him a Statement of the Evidence relative to the Interferences complained of, to the End that it may be sent to Canada, and Enquiry made into the Truth of the Alligation & Facts in question. This would have been done sooner, but for Reasons which shall be explained to You.—

The Treaty is drawing towards a Conclusion, & unless some Difficulties yet to be removed, should prove *insuperable*, will speedily be compleated. My Letter to Mr Randolph will contain all the Information which I can find Time at present to communicate.— Be assured my Dear Sir of the perfect Respect Esteem and attachment with which I am Your obliged & obt. Servt

John Jay

The President of U.S.

ALS, DLC: Washington (EJ: 10636). Marked: *"private".* HPJ, 4: 122–23; PGW: PS, 17: 115–16.

1. This letter was a cover letter for GW to JJ, 30 Aug., in which GW complained strenuously about the conduct of John Graves Simcoe (1752–1806), Lieutenant Governor of Canada, who had insisted that the United States refrain from occupying lands ceded by Britain in 1783 and far from the posts Britain still retained. GW held the British responsible for inciting the Indians against American settlers, and argued that it was vain for the British government to disavow such actions while not punishing the agents who perpetrated them. See PGW: PS, 16: 613–16, 641; and JJ to Grenville, 13 Oct. 1794, above. Art. 2 of the Treaty of Amity, Commerce, and Navigation of 19 Nov. 1794 specified that the United States might extend settlements to any part within the 1783 boundary line except within jurisdiction of the occupied posts prior to British evacuation of them by 1 June 1796. This provision did not figure in JJ's Project for a Treaty with Great Britain, 30 Sept. 1794, above.

In his letter to GW of 19 Nov., JJ reported he had not completed the representation to Grenville because his time was occupied by the completion of the treaty. JJ to GW, C, DLC: Washington (EJ: 10638); Dft, NNC (EJ: 08454); PGW: PS, 17: 173–75.

To James Monroe

London 31 Octr. 1794

Sir

Altho' you are not personally acquainted with Benjn. Vaughan Esqr., a Member of Parliamt—an amiable & a worthy Gentln. yet I am persuaded that his character and attachmt. to our Country are known to You.

In the Correspondence between Mr. Jefferson & Mr. Hammond, his agency respecting the Negociations ∧for the Treaty∧ of Peace, became more prominent, than could be agreable or useful to him; & there is Reason to apprehend that certain Transactions in this Country, have led the Governm^t. to regard him in an unfavorable Light— He is now in   ¹ It is possible that circumstances may occur to render the good offices of his Friends expedient. Considering the Zeal of his Family for the Welfare of our Country, and that he has been particularly useful, I think he has a just Claim to our Friendship, and to such marks of it, as may be requisite and proper.

Mr Pinckney has written or will write to You on this Subject—² I have the Honor to be with great Respect Sir Your most ob^t. & hble Servt.

The Honb. James. Munro Esqr Minister of the united States at Paris—

Dft, NNC (EJ: 09620). *Monroe Papers*, 3: 136.

1. Space left blank in manuscript. Benjamin Vaughan was at this time in exile in Switzerland. See JJ to Sarah Vaughan, 19 July 1794, above.

2. Thomas Pinckney wrote Monroe about Vaughan's situation on 4 Nov. 1794. Monroe wrote Vaughan on 23 Nov. and 4 Dec. 1794. See also Vaughan to James Monroe, 29 Jan. 1795. *Monroe Papers*, 3: 213–16.

From Tench Coxe

[Philadelphia Novr 8 1794]

Dear Sir,

I have the honor to send you by way of letter a recent publication, which contains among other matter some of my ideas on the *present* state of our public affairs. If you can find time for a perusal of the work or even of all the text that follows the 379th. page, and an inspection of the documents inserted in that part of the work, so far as you have not seen them, or the text, it may be of some use.¹ The 16th Chapter of the 1st. Book,² and the 9th. Chapter of the 2^d Book³ are the most interesting. Some of the notes on the reply to L^d. Sheffield are interesting.—

I can assure you Sir, with the utmost pleasure and with truth, that the insurgency in the Western parts of Pennsylvania is crushed— Those people had trifled with the Government of Pennsy[lvani]ᵃ. in the times of the Province and in the times of the commonwealth— They will never trifle again with this Government. The operation has been expensive, but the incidental & immediate advantages of it *fully* compensate us. The confidence of our own people & of impartial foreigners now here is prodigiously increased—⁴ You will see the remarks I have made upon it in the 508th—& 509th pages.

The Revenues of 1792 & 1793 have proved to be 5,400,000 dollars, and 7,150,000 Dollars.—

The astonishing demand for our produce and abundance of Money have raised flour to eight dollars per bble—.

Our public funds and bank stocks are very saleable, and at favorable prices. There is no appearance of declension—but the reverse.

Be pleased to inspect the comparative view of the taxables of Pennsylvania on page 481 which contains a precise exhibition upon the subject of our population in the middle States.

The reflexions on the state of the Union were written for the special purpose of convincing those in the Southern states, who complain of the operations of the Government, and who entertain fears about the balance of trade &c. that they are really mistaken.— Our Imports are *now* vastly beyond what they appear to have been in the Ch. 12. book 1.[5]

A distinct view of the Encouragement to Manufactures resulting from our impost, is given in Ch: 3 book 2.—[6] I recommend, Sir, to your most particular attention the view of our fisheries given in page 345 as relative to our capacity to injure the trade of those who may unnecessarily make War upon us.

Being very much engaged, I have only time to add that I have the honor to be with great respect.—[7] Sir, Your most Obedient Servant

Tench Coxe

ALS, NNC (EJ: 09823). Endorsed: "Rec^d 11 Decr. 1794 by Mr / Bayard / . . . an^d.18 Dec. 1794". Enclosure: *A view of the United States of America, in a series of papers, written at various times, between the years 1787 and 1794, by Tench Coxe, of Philadelphia; interspersed with authentic documents: the whole tending to exhibit the progress and present state of civil and religious liberty, population, agriculture, exports, imports, fisheries, navigation, ship-building, manufactures, and general improvement.* (Philadelphia, 1794; *Early Am. Imprints*, series 1, no. 26829). C, PHi: Coxe. By the time JJ received Coxe's material, he had already signed the treaty with Great Britain.

1. For the reply, see JJ to Coxe, 18 Dec. 1794, ALS, PHi: Coxe; Dft, NNC (EJ: 09819); *WJ*, 2: 240–41; *HPJ*, 4: 152–53.

2. This chapter is titled "Containing a summary statement of the principal facts, which characterize the American people, and their country or territory, in 1793".

3. This chapter is titled "Miscellaneous reflections upon certain important facts and considerations, which occur, at this time, in the affairs of the United States; intended as a conclusion to this collection".

4. In his reply to Coxe, JJ asserted "The manner in which the Insurrection has been dissipated, gives me pleasure; and there is Reason to hope that the Arts and Counsels which produced it, will not be able to operate such another—". JJ to Coxe, 18 Dec. 1794, citation in note 1, above.

The insurgency in western Pennsylvania stemmed from an excise on distilled spirits promoted by AH and enacted into law in 1791. A presidential proclamation issued by GW on 15 Sept. 1792 failed to quell the protests against the "whiskey tax," and matters came to a head in the summer of

1794 with an armed clash between protesters and federal troops south of Pittsburgh. GW adopted a dual approach to the crisis, appointing commissioners to meet with the rebels while also issuing a proclamation on 7 Aug. 1794 that called for the mobilization of the militia. The insurrection soon collapsed following a military expedition into the troubled region. For JJ's views of the earlier stages of the protest, see the editorial note "John Jay's Moderate Response to the Whiskey Rebellion," *JJSP*, 5: 447–49.

While in London, JJ regularly received reports of the events in western Pennsylvania from ER. GW also contacted JJ about the Whiskey Rebellion, commenting that "self-created Societies" were responsible for fomenting dissent against the national government and that other nations approved that his administration had suppressed the uprising. JJ shared these sentiments, assuring GW that the British government looked favorably on the outcome; "their confidence in your Wisdom Decision and Energy has been confirmed by the Event." ER to JJ, 11 Aug. 1794, C, DNA: Jay Despatches, 1794–95 (EJ: 04304); C, NHi: King (EJ: 04436); Duplicate, NHi: Jay (EJ: 00606); 18 Aug. 1794, C, DNA: Jay Despatches, 1794–95 (EJ: 04306); C, NHi: King (EJ: 04438); 30 Aug. 1794, C, DNA: Jay Despatches, 1794–95 (EJ: 04309); C, NHi: King (EJ: 04441); C, marked "Duplicate", NHi: Jay (EJ: 00611); 12 Sept. 1794, C, DNA: Jay Despatches, 1794–95 (EJ: 04310); C, NHi: King (EJ: 04443); C, marked "Duplicate", NHi: Jay (EJ: 00608); 15 Sept. 1794, C, DNA: Jay Despatches, 1794–95 (EJ: 04321); 17 Sept. 1794, C, DNA: Jay Despatches, 1794–95 (EJ: 04323); C, NHi: King (EJ: 04453); C, marked "Duplicate", NHi: Jay (EJ: 00609); 20 Oct. 1794, C, DNA: Jay Despatches, 1794–95 (EJ: 04327); C, NHi: King (EJ: 04458); C, marked "Duplicate", NHi: Jay (EJ: 00610); GW to JJ, 1[–4] Nov. 1794, ALS, NNC (EJ: 07256); DftS, DLC: Washington (EJ: 10637); LbkC, DLC: Washington; C (extract), NHi: O'Reilly (EJ: 00688); *HPJ*, 4: 128–32; *WJ*, 2: 231–35; *PGW: PS*, 17: 125–29; GW to JJ, 18 Dec. 1794, ALS, NNC (EJ: 07257); DftS, DLC: Washington (EJ: 10639); LbkC, DLC: Washington (EJ: 12656); *HPJ*, 4: 150–52, *WJ*, 2: 238–40; *PGW: PS*, 17: 286–89; JJ to GW, 25 Feb. 1795, ALS, DLC: Washington (EJ: 10642); Dft, NNC (EJ: 08455); C (extract), NHi: O'Reilly (EJ: 00691); *HPJ*, 4: 160–62; *WJ*, 2: 243–45; *PGW: PS*, 17: 577–80.

5. This chapter is titled "Abstract of goods, wares and merchandize, exported from each of the United States of America, (with the aggregate of the whole) from the 1st October, 1791, to 30th September, 1792, being one year".

6. This chapter is titled "Containing the tariff of the United States, for the information of merchants and manufacturers".

7. In his reply, JJ contended, "Our Affairs relative to this County have a promising aspect— The best Disposition towards us prevails here, and Indications & Proofs of it daily increase. I do really believe that this Gov^t. mean to give conciliatory measures with the U. S. a full and fair Tryal— it never can be wise to cast ourselves into the Arms and Influence of any nation but certainly it is wise and proper to cherish the good will of those who wish to be on Terms of Friendship and Cordiality with us. It may seem strange, and yet I am convinced, that next to the King, our President is more popular in this County than any Man in it—." JJ to Coxe, 18 Dec. 1794, ALS, PHi: Coxe; Dft, NNC (EJ: 09819); *WJ*, 2: 241; *HPJ*, 4: 152–53.

Coxe was convinced the data he supplied JJ conclusively demonstrated that the U.S., Britain's best customer and natural commercial ally, was in a strong bargaining position, and he had high hopes for the Jay Treaty. When details of the treaty arrived, he wrote four lengthy articles excoriating it under the pseudonym "Juriscola." He condemned the restrictions imposed on trade with the West Indies by Art. 12 of the treaty, and adopted southern arguments that failure to win compensation for slaves removed by the British during the war left the South unable to repay prewar debts to British merchants. Coxe, alienated by AH's failure to designate him acting secretary of the treasury while AH was on military duty during the Whiskey Rebellion, and holding Anglophobic foreign policy views more closely aligned with TJ than with AH, soon switched allegiance to the Republican party. Jacob E. Cooke, *Tench Coxe and the Early Republic* (Chapel Hill, N.C., and Williamsburg, Va., 1978), 274–79.

From Sarah Livingston Jay

New Y. 11th. Novbr. 1794

My dr. Mr. Jay,

I was mortified by seeing in this morning's Paper that Mr. Bayard had sailed the 8th. for London—[1] had I been informed of his going, with what pleasure wd. I have written to you by him— By the same Paper I see advertised the Departure of a Vessel about the middle of the present month for London— it shall not be my fault if you do not hear from me by that— The last letter I've had the pleasure of receiving from you was dated the 24th. Augst.[2] The Septbr. Mail is arrived in Town, but unfortunately there are no letters for me—nor have I heard of any letters that mention you— You know by experience my best beloved! how painful are the sensations of suspense, but let the causes of delay be what they will, never will I imagine your silence to proceed from indifference; too frequent have been the proofs to the Contrary for me ever to doubt yr. love or attention— A few days ago Mrs. Smith from B[edford]. call'd here to pay me a visit, I found her sociably disposed & listen'd to her information— she told me things were sadly neglected at the house upon the hill— The tenant of it living in an very improper manner with a young woman in the Neighbourhood, spending some times 2 or 3 days with her at her house & receiving visits from her as unsuitable at his own— the young woman (she told me) had kept one of the farm-horses all Summer at her father's for her use & that the neighbours censure them both very much— With a great number of Cows, some of which are excellent he makes no butter but for his own use— & a number of annecdotes which I think discover inattention to business which I cannot but regret— I wrote to the Old Woman's Son-in-law lately about flour &:, & in my letter dropt a hint that I fear'd in the hurry of business he had forgot his promise of writing to you, suggesting that it was not yet too late— Munro has not yet return-d from Albany, as he means to take B—[edfor]d in his way home, he will be able to tell you how your affairs there are conducted—

Your brother Fady is I believe offended with me— about a month ago he sent his Clerk here to ask me for the money for the tierce[3] of spirits; I told the young man I would with pleasure pay for it, and asked for the Order—

he told me he had none, but w^d. give me his rec^t. I declined paying without the Order— half an hour after Moncrieffe call'd upon me & in like manner offer'd his rec^t. for the Money. I told Tommy that in his Uncle's letter from M^r. Hilton he was requested by that gentleman to pay the money to M^rs. Hilton his Mother, & I s[ai]^d. I was ready to pay it to her Order— A few days after Fady call'd here for his wife— his Countenance indicated displeasure— so you refused to pay for the Spirits says he— by no means sir I replyed, I only requested to have M^rs. Hilton's order as an indemnification— Very well said y^r. brother, I've p^d. for it & shall charge my brother interest on the sum— I asked if that would not be rather hard as I had both money & inclination to pay & only wished to do y^r. business regularly— from that time I've not seen him— I sent for your Nephew & acquainting him with what had pass'd, he approv'd my Conduct & advised that I should let it rest 'till he sent me M^rs. Hilton's rec^t. or 'till you return'd— I received a beautiful letter to-day from Maria, written just before she left Morris-Town— I long for her next letter which will be from Bethlehem— her poor Aunt Symmes will have a disagreeable journey—[4] M^rs. Ridley has not yet reached NYork— I have had some hopes that you would have re-cross'd the Atlantic before she had travel'd from Baltimore to this City— but an Advertisment in to-day's paper relative to M^r. Bayard's business in England, seems to suggest an Expectation of the President's that M^r. Bayard will find you in Europe—[5] If that should be the case, for Heaven's sake my d^r. M^r. Jay don't risque a winter's passage— At least don't let any considerations about me & the family induce you to hazard what you do not approve, but do that only which you think best after consulting able Mariners— You must be convinced that it will give me infinite pleasure to re-embrace you & your son; but you may be assured that should your business demand your still longer detention, no exertion shall be omitted on my part to bear with fortitude the seperation, nor any thing neglected in my power to perform to lessen the injury your family & affairs might sustain from y^r. absence— the 2^d. of Nov^br. I wrote you by Cap^tn. Kemp & likewise sent you duplicates of 2 other letters—[6] I sincerely hope he'll arrive safe, & that letters from my dear son & yourself will e'er long inspire with new fortitude your ever affectionate wife—

Nothing new has taken place in our domestic arrangements, myself, the Children & servants enjoy health. All our particular friends are well— M^r. Kemp call'd in last evening— he requested to be particularly remembered to you— I ask'd him if he would not write, but he said he dar'd not take that liberty—

RC, NNC (EJ: 06563). Endorsed.

1. Samuel Bayard of Philadelphia, formerly clerk to the Supreme Court, was appointed agent to deal with claims for British spoliations on American commerce in Oct. 1794. He had previously applied for the position of JJ's secretary, taken by JT. See Samuel Bayard to AH, 23 Apr. 1794, *PAH*, 16: 313–15. The *New-Jersey Journal* (Elizabethtown), of 12 Nov. 1794, reported, "On Friday morning last sailed from Philadelphia, bound for London, the ship *Adriana*, Capt. Fitzpatrick, with whom went passengers, Samuel Bayard, Esq. agent of claims and appeals for the United States, and family". See John Sloss Hobart to JJ, 20 Nov. 1794, below. Bayard arrived in London on 11 Dec., and JJ reported his arrival in Falmouth to ER in a letter of 10 Dec. 1794, LS, DNA: Jay Despatches, 1794–95 (EJ: 04343).

2. Letter not found.

3. A tierce is defined as "an old measure of capacity equivalent to one third of a pipe; also a cask or vessel holding this quantity, usually of wine." A pipe is "typically equal to two hogsheads or 63 wine gallons." *OED*.

4. Maria Jay to SLJ, 9 Nov. 1794, ALS, NNC (EJ: 09694). On 1 Oct. 1794, SLJ wrote JJ of Maria Jay's desire to attend the Moravian Seminary at Bethlehem. SLJ to JJ, 1 Oct. 1794, ALS, NNC (EJ: 06561): "Maria has a long time had a great inclination to go to Bethlehem & has solicited me to write for admission for her— I told her that I had been inform'd the school was full & that they had the names of 60 Children who wished admission when vacancies occurred— When Judge Symmes was here, Bethlehem being mentioned in conversation Maria express'd her regret for the impossibility of gaining admission into the school there— the Judge told her that her Aunt, his daughter, & himself were to pass thro' that place in their way to Cincinati & that if she would permit him to have the pleasure of introducing her to the directress of the society, he did not doubt being able to procure admission for her as the society were indebted to him for acts of friendship during the war, for which they had often expressed their gratitude & a desire of evincing it— upon this Maria renewed her intreaties, telling me she wished to make a greater proficiency in her studies than in her present situation she was able, & that she hoped by answering your expectations, to justify me to you for consenting— As You my dear Mr. Jay the guardian & Protector of our little flock, was too distant to be consulted in time for this only prospect of admission, I enquired of those most able to inform me what was best & was almost unanimously advised to embrace the proposal— I have done so, & sincerely hope it will meet your approbation— she is discreet, has a great desire to improve, & there I am told they have every opportunity. Mr. & Mrs. Arden have two daughters there to whom they mean to pay a visit about the time Maria is to go, & they have promised to take her under their protection in case they refuse to admit her—". "Judge Symmes" is John Cleves Symmes (1742–1814), who had just married SLJ's sister Susannah "Susan" Livingston in September [SLJ to JJ, 27 Sept. 1794, C, marked "Duplicate", NNC (EJ: 06560)]. Symmes was a member of the Continental Congress from New Jersey, judge, and land speculator. He was also a friend of William Livingston. The Symmeses were on their way to his lands in Ohio. The Moravian Seminary (later Academy) was founded in 1742 as an all-female school by the Countess Benigna von Zinzendorf. After the Revolution, the school was opened to non-Moravians. The curriculum was rigorous, including academic subjects as well as needlework, with an emphasis on music and Christian piety. In addition to Maria and Louisa Arden, Maria's classmates included Walter Livingston's daughters, Kitty, Cornelia, and Harriet, as well as Catharine and Ann Livingston Reade. Maria was accepted in October [SLJ to JJ, 25 Oct. 1794, ALS, NNC (EJ: 06538); and PJM to JJ, 4 Dec. 1794, Dft, NNMus (EJ: 00435)]. Ann Jay followed her sister to Bethlehem in 1796. William C. Reichel, *A history of the Moravian Seminary for young ladies, at Bethlehem, Pa. With a catalogue of its pupils, 1785–*

1870 (Lancaster, Pa., 1901), 20–99, 346–50, 352. See also SLJ to Maria Jay, 12 Nov. 1794, ALS, NNC (EJ: 06384); SLJ to Catharine Livingston Ridley, 25 Nov. 1794, ALS, NNC (EJ: 06470); JJ to Maria Jay, 9 Dec. 1794, ALS, NNC (EJ: 05939); and JJ to SLJ, 6 Mar. 1795, below.

5. See "For the Information of Merchants." *Daily Advertiser* (New York), 11 Nov. 1794.

6. Probably SLJ to JJ, 1 Nov. 1794, ALS, NNC (EJ: 06562).

From Edmund Randolph (private)

Philadelphia November 12th. 1794

Sir,

In my public Letter of this date,[1] you will find every thing of an official Nature, which we are able to communicate at present.

Your private favor of the 13th. of September[2] last brings with it the satisfactory conviction, that I have not misplaced my confidence in your candor. You may be assured, that, as in the whole of our diplomatic connection hitherto, I have arrived at every demonstration of sincerity; so shall I not depart from it in what remains.

In one sense I learn with regret that my letter to the Committee of public Safety in France[3] should create any uneasy emotions in the Breast of the British Ministry. I should regret, that I have been made the instrument of weakening the good disposition, which the majority of them appear to bear towards us. For I was among the first, who expressed a solicitude for the appointment of an Envoy to Great Britain;[4] I am second to no man, in believing that harmony with that Country is of immense value to the United States; in my small sphere I have laboured to avert a war with it; my efforts in the Line of my Department have been directed to the maintenance of perfect neutrality; and you will therefore credit me, when I say, that I shall rejoice in your Success.[5] The British Minister here, and some other British Agents have taught their correspondents on your side of the water to expect from me acts, not consistent with the impartiality, which we profess[6] But surely I may appeal to the intercourse between us, for a refutation of such a suspicion.

And yet, under the influence of even these Sentiments, my tranquillity is in no manner disturbed by an apprehension that the British Government, if pure in their views, would be checked in their spirit of Amity; when they have before them the most striking example of amity on our part, in your mission, which was instituted in the moment of the most aggravating injury and insult.

But, Sir, notwithstanding these considerations, I should hold myself to blame, if in my letter I had overleaped the degree of strength, intended by the House of Representatives. For it is not enough, that a public Officer should merely suppress the vehemence of any predilection or prejudice, which he may entertain; but he ought also to be watchful lest they should steal from his Pen. Conscious as I am, that I restrained my affections, and was upon my guard against their impulse, when *that letter was written*; I have this morning compared it with the Resolution, on which it was founded; with that calm attention, arising from the persuasion, that, if an error has been committed, it was no more.[7] But I frankly own, that I discover no error. The House did not mean, that the resolution only should be transmitted. They gave it as the Text of the Letter. This text required the draft, to contain terms expressive of *sensibility* for the *friendly* and *affectionate* manner, in which the Committee had addressed Congress; and *an unequivocal* assurance, that the House have much *interest* in the *happiness* and *prosperity* of the French *Republic*. The address of the Committee was naturally adverted to, and it became my duty to make a response to the matter of it. The word *unequivocal* imposed the necessity of a pointed development of Sensation. The happiness and prosperity of the French Republic implied a defeat of the allied powers; and that the happiness and prosperity of the French people was connected with the Republic, in contradistinction to monarchy. If a scope was not presented here for much more than was said; censure would have been liberally bestowed (and probably not without cause) if less had been said. I could, indeed, have reduced the Language to the coldness of death. But this would have been hardly expressive of Sensibility. I could have made it lukewarm; but this would not have amounted to an *unequivocal* assurance. In short, it is after all not easy, to form a scale for graduating one set of words to the precise fervor of another. All, which can be undertaken with certainty, is, not to transgress wilfully the Standard, which is proposed. My conclusion therefore, is, that if a fault has existed any where, it belongs to the House of Representatives.[8] With best wishes for your Health and Happiness, and with true respect and esteem, I have the honor to be, Sir, Your most obedient Servant

Edm: Randolph

Since my public letter of the 8th. instant we have received no intelligence of consequence from the Army. But it is impossible that Things should be otherwise than right.

The Honble John Jay Esqr. &c. &c.

LS, NHi: Jay (EJ: 00618). Marked: "*Duplicate* (Private)".

1. ER to JJ, 12 Nov. 1794, *ASP: FR*, 1: 501–2, in which ER acknowledged receiving JJ to ER, 13 Sept. 1794, above, and JJ to ER, 14 Sept. 1794, ALS, DNA: Jay Despatches, 1794–95 (EJ: 04320); C, NHi: King (EJ: 04452); and *ASP: FR*, 1: 496, a brief letter in which JJ indicated his hope that difficulties over the Lake of the Woods boundary issue could be managed.

2. See Grenville to JJ (private), 7 Sept.; JJ to Grenville (private), 7 Sept.; and JJ to ER (private), 13 Sept. 1794, all above.

3. See *ASP: FR*, 1: 674.

4. For ER's claim, see the editorial note, "The Jay Treaty: Appointment and Instructions," *JJSP*, 5: 609–21.

5. ER had previously expressed concern that the British believed it was an American violation of neutrality when the French violated an American passport given during the American embargo allowing its vessel *L'Aimable Gentille* to sail from the United States in ballast and instead shipped gunpowder aboard. He contended that his correspondence with British officials was well calculated to demonstrate the government's sincerity, and stated that he would send all documents related to the incident to the British government. See ER to JJ, 9 July 1794, ALS, DNA: Jay Despatches, 1794–95 (EJ: 04276); and C, NHi: King (EJ: 04422); and JJ to ER, 21 Aug., ALS, DNA: Jay Despatches, 1794–95 (EJ: 04307); and C, NHi: King (EJ: 04440); and *ASP: FR*, 1: 478, 483.

6. For his assertion that the hostility between ER and Hammond was the responsibility of the former, see Grenville to JJ (private), 21 Nov. 1794, below.

7. The resolution of the House of Representatives of 25 Apr. 1794 read as follows: "Resolved, unanimously, That the letter of the Committee of Public Safety of the French Republic, addressed to Congress, be transmitted to the President of the United States, and that he be requested to cause the same to be answered on behalf of this House, in terms expressive of their sensibility for the friendly and affectionate manner in which they have addressed the Congress of the United States, with an unequivocal assurance that the Representatives of the People of the United States have much interest in the happiness and prosperity of the French Republic." *Journal of the House*, 2: 132.

8. ER had previously speculated that the British government would almost certainly attempt to separate the United States from France, and enjoined JJ to ensure that nothing in any treaty signed with Britain should derogate from American obligations to her. ER later resigned as Secretary of State on the suggestion that he had had improper relations with Fauchet, the French minister. See ER to JJ, 6 May 1794; and the editorial note "The Jay Treaty: Appointment and Instructions," *JJSP*, 5: 636–47, 609–21.

From John Quincy Adams

The Hague November 14. 1794.

Dear Sir.

M^r. Vall-travers informs me that he intends going to London, where he purposes paying his respects to you. I have therefore requested him to take charge of a packet for the Secretary of State, which I have taken the Liberty of enclosing to your care, according to the permission, you were pleased to give me on the day of my departure from London. The opportunities of sending to America from England are so much more frequent than from hence, that in all probability this will be the most expeditious conveyance for my Letters at present.[1]

We had a tolerable passage from London here, which took us only three days. I have been received and acknowledged by the States General, and had this day a gracious Audience of the Stadtholder to whom I delivered my credentials for him.

The french troops in this Quarter continue their career of victory. Every thing here however is yet quiet. The effort at Amsterdam has terminated in disarming the petitioners. M^r. Van Staphorst I hear is at Hamburg.

I am very anxious to receive intelligence from America. There must be I think by this time some arrivals in England. We have none here. Our credit and reputation suffers here as well as in England, from the Western Insurrection. I hope and believe it will eventually be serviceable to both. Participating in the cordial wishes of every friend to our Country, for the successful accomplishment of your mission, I remain with Sentiments of the most respectful Attachment, Dear Sir, your very humble & obedient Servant

John Q. Adams.

His Excellency John Jay,

ALS, UkWC-A (EJ: 00047).

1. Rodolph Vall-travers (1723–c. 1815) was a Swiss-born writer and sometime diplomat. He corresponded with JA, TJ, BF, and GW, and proposed many plans to aid the United States and attempted to involve himself in American business, with little effect. See, for example, Vall-travers to GW, 20 Mar. 1791, *PGW: PS*, 7: 606–8. On 28 Oct. 1794, he requested that JJ "graciously" honor him "with the Character of your private Secretary, with, or without a Salary; and entitling me thereby to the Protection enjoyed by Individual of the Corps diplomatic" so that he might travel to England and avoid a trap by his late wife's family. ALS, NNC (EJ: 07214). JJ appears not to have replied directly to Vall-travers, but instead sent his negative response via JQA. See JJ to JQA, 24 Nov. 1794; and JQA to JJ, 21 Nov. 1794, both below.

Rufus King to Sarah Livingston Jay

Philadelphia 17 Nov 1794

dear Madam,

M^rs. Ridley has not yet arrived, I will take care that she receives the letter immediately on her coming to Town— I understand that the last dispatches from M^r. Jay are very satisfactory, and that at this date he had expectations of closing his Negotiation in the course of a few ~~Days~~ Weeks.[1] With Sincere Esteem I am Dear Madam Your ob^t. Servt.

Rufus King

M^rs. Jay

ALS, NNC (EJ: 12817).

1. RK was JJ's first choice for secretary, but RK declined, feeling it was his duty to remain in the Senate. RK to JJ, 2 May 1794, *JJSP*, 5: 628–29. RK was one of the people JJ wrote on 19 Nov. immediately after the treaty was signed. JJ to RK, 19 Nov. 1794, below.

To Edmund Randolph

London 19ᵗʰ. November 1794.

Sir,

The long expected Treaty accompanies this letter;— a probability of soon concluding it has caused the Packet to be detained for more than a week;— The difficulties which retarded its accomplishment, frequently had the appearance of being insurmountable; they have at last yielded to modifications of the Articles in which they existed, and to that mutual disposition to Agreement which reconciled Lord Grenville and myself to an unusual degree of Trouble and Application.[1]— They who have levelled uneven Grounds know how little of the work afterwards appears.

Since the Building is finished, it cannot be very important to describe the scaffolding, or go into all the details which respected the Business.— Explanatory remarks on certain Articles might be useful by casting Light on governing principles which in some instances, are not so obvious as to be distinctly seen on the first view.— Feeling the want of Liesure and Relaxation, I cannot undertake it in this moment of Haste;— I must confine myself to a few cursory Observations, & hope allowances will be made for Inaccuracies and Omissions.

My Opinion of the Treaty is apparent from my having signed it; I have no reason to believe or conjecture, that one more favorable to us is attainable.

Perhaps it is not very much to be regretted that all our differences are merged in this Treaty, without having been decided. disagreeable imputations are thereby avoided, and the Door of Conciliation is fairly and widely opened, by the *essential* Justice done, and the conveniencies granted to each other by the Parties.[2]

The Term limited for the evacuation of the Posts, could not be restricted to a more early day:— that point has been pressed. The Reasons which caused an inflexible adherence to that term, I am persuaded, were these, vizᵗ.— That the Traders have spread through the Indian Nations, Goods to a great amount. That the Returns for those Goods cannot be drawn into Canada at an earlier Period;— That the Impression which the Surrender of all the Posts to American Garrisons will make on the minds of the Indians cannot be foreseen:— On a former Occasion it was intimated to them (not very delicately) that they had been forsaken, & given up to the United States:— That the protection promised on our part, however sincere and however in other Respects competent, cannot entirely prevent those Embarrassments which without our fault may be occasioned by the War.— That, for these reasons, the Traders ought to have time to conclude their Adventures which were calculated on the Existing state of things.— they will afterwards calculate on the new State of Things:— but that in the mean time the care of Government should not be withdrawn from them.[3]

The 3[d]. Article will I presume appear to you in a favorable light— a number of Reasons which in my Judgement are solid support it:— I think they will on consideration become obvious. It was proposed and urged that the commercial Intercourse opened by this Article ought to be exempted from all Duties whatever on either side. The inconveniencies which we should experience from such a measure were stated and examined. It was finally agreed to subject it to native Duties:[4]— in this compromise, which I consider as being exactly right, that difficulty terminated;— But, for this compromise the whole Article would have failed, and every expectation of an amicable Settlement been frustrated: A continuance of Trade with the Indians was a decided ultimatum;— much Time and Paper, and many Conferences were employed in producing this Article. that part of it which respects the Ports and places on the Eastern side of the Missisipi, if considered in connexion with the Article in the Treaty of Peace, and with the Article in this Treaty which directs a Survey of that River to be made, will I think appear unexceptionable.[5]

In discussing the question about the River S[t]. Croix, before the Commissioners,[6] I apprehend the old French claims will be revived— we must adhere to Mitchell's Map;[7]— the Vice President perfectly understands this Business.

The 6th. Article was a *sine qua non*, and is intended as well as calculated to afford that Justice and Equity which judicial proceedings may on trial be found incapable of affording;— That the Commissioners may do exactly what is right they are to determine according to the merits of the several cases, having a due regard to all the Circumstances, and as Justice and Equity shall appear to them to require.[8]

It is very much to be regretted that a more summary Method than the one indicated in the Seventh Article could not have been devised and agreed upon for settling the Capture cases.— Every other Plan was perplexed with Difficulties which frustrated it:— Permit me to hint the expediency of aiding the Claimants, by employing a Gentleman at the public Expence to oversee and manage the Causes of such of them as cannot conveniently have Agents of their own hire; and whether in some cases pecuniary assistance might not be proper;— I do not consider myself at liberty to make such an appointment nor to enter into ₐanyₐ such pecuniary engagements. It would probably be more easy to find a proper person on your side of the Water, than on this— here there are few fit for the Business & willing to undertake it, who (having many affairs of their own to attend to) would not be tempted to consider the Business of the Claimants in a secondary light. Several objections to giving him a fixed Salary are obvious; in my opinion a moderate Commission on the sums to be recovered and received would be a more eligible method of compensating him for his Services.[9]— Our Consul here talks and I believe in earnest of returning to America or I should expect much advantage from his Zeal and Endeavours to serve such of the Claimants as might commit their Business to his management.[10]

You will find in the 8th. Article a Stipulation which in effect refers the manner of paying the Commissioners very much to our Election:— I prefer paying them *jointly*:— the Objection to it is, that the English pay high:— I have always doubted the Policy of being *Penny-wise*.[11]

The Lord Chancellor has prepared an Article respecting the mutual admission of evidence &ca—which we have not had time fully to consider and decide upon: it contains a Clause to abolish *Alienism* between the two Countries;— His Lordships conduct and conversation indicate the most friendly disposition towards us;— a Copy of his Article shall be sent and I wish to receive precise instructions on that Head.[12]

The Credit of some of the States having to my knowledge suffered by appearances of their being favorable to the Idea of sequestrating British Debts on certain occasions—the 10th. Article will be useful.— Persons wishing to invest their Property in our Funds and Banks, have frequently applied to me to be informed whether they might do it without risque of confiscation or Sequestration.— my answer has been uniform, Vizt. That in my opinion such measures would be improper, and therefore that in my Opinion they would not be adopted; some pressed me for Assurances, but I have declined giving any:[13]

The 12th. Article admitting our Vessels of Seventy Tons and under into the British Islands in the West Indies affords occasion for several explanatory Remarks;— It became connected with a proposed Stipulation for the Abolition of all Alien Duties of every kind between the Two Countries:— This Proposition was pressed, but strong objections opposed my agreeing to it.— A Satisfactory statement of the Negotiation on this point, would be prolix;— at present I cannot form a very concise one, for that would not require less time.— the Selection and arrangement necessary in making abridgements cannot be hastily performed. The Duration of this Article is short, but if we meet the disposition of this Country to Good Humour and Cordiality,

I am much inclined to believe it will be renewed.— the Duration of the Treaty is connected with the renewal of that Article, and an opportunity will then offer for discussing and Settling many important matters.[14]

The Articles which opens the British Ports in the East Indies to our Vessels and Cargoes, needs no comment. It is a manifestation and Proof of Good-will towards us.

The Questions about the Cases, in which alone Provisions become contraband, and the Question whether and how far Neutral Ships protect Enemy's Property, have been the subjects of much Trouble and many fruitless discussions.— That Britain at this Period and involved in War should not admit principles which would impeach the Propriety of her Conduct, in siezing Provisions bound to France, and Enemy's property on board of Neutral Vessels does not appear to me extraordinary.— The Articles as they now stand, secure compensation for Siezures, and leave us at liberty to decide whether they were made in such cases as to be warranted by the *existing* Law of Nations; —[15] As to the Principles we contend for, you will find them saved in the conclusion of the 12th. Article, from which it will appear that we still adhere to them.[16]

The Two Articles about Privateers,[17] were taken from the Treaty of Commerce between Great Britain and France, and the One for treating Natives, commanding Privateers, as Pirates, in certain cases, was partly taken from our's with Holland.[18]

The Prohibition to Sell Prizes in our Ports, had its use; and we have no reason to regret that your Instructions to me admitted of it.[19]

Various Articles which have no place in this Treaty, have from time to time been under consideration, but did not meet with mutual approbation and Conduct.—

I must draw this letter to a Conclusion;— Lord Grenville is anxious to dismiss the Packet as soon as possible;— [*illegible*] ~~authorized exchange Ratifications[?]~~

There is reason to hope that occasions for complaint on either side will be carefully avoided:— Let us be just and friendly to all Nations.

I ought not to omit mentioning the acknowledgements due from me to M[r]. Pinckney, with whom I have every reason to be satisfied, and from whose Advice and Opinions I have derived light and Advantage in the course of the negotiation:— His approbation of the Treaty gives me pleasure, not merely because his Opinion corresponds with my own, but also from the Sentiments I entertain of his Judgement and Candor.[20]

It is desireable that I should have the earliest advice of the ratification, and be enabled to finish whatever may be expected of me in season to return in one of the first Spring Vessels. My Health is not competent to a Winter's Voyage, or I should be the Bearer of the Treaty:— This Climate does not agree with me, and the less so on account of the Application and Confinement to which it was necessary for me to submit.

I had almost forgotten to mention, that on finishing and agreeing to the Draft of the Treaty, I suggested to Lord Grenville, as a measure that would be very acceptable to our Country, the interposition of his Majesty with Algiers and other States of Barbary that may be hostile to us:— This Idea was favorably received, and it is my opinion that this Court would in good Earnest undertake that Business, in case nothing should occur to impeach the Sincerity of that mutual Reconciliation which it is to be hoped will now take place.[21]

It will give you pleasure to hear that great reserve and Delicacy has been observed respecting our Concerns with France:— The Stipulations in favor of existing Treaties was agreed to without hesitation: not an Expectation nor even a wish has been expressed that our conduct towards France should be otherwise than fair and friendly:— In a word:—I do not know how the negotiation could have been conducted on their part, with more Delicacy, Friendliness, and Propriety than it has been from first to last.[22] I have the Honor to be Sir your most obt. & hble Servt.

John Jay

To the Honble. Edmund Randolph Esqr.
Secry. of State &c &c &c

C, DNA: Jay Despatches, 1794–95 (EJ: 04338). Marked: "*No. 22 Duplicate*". Endorsed by clerk: "... recorded page 120." C, NHi: King (EJ: 04465); LbkC, NNC: JJ Lbk. 8; *WJ*, 1: 334 (extract); *HPJ*, 4: 137–44; *ASP: FR*, 1: 503–4. Enclosures: For the copy of the Jay Treaty, [19 Nov. 1794], see below; for the Article Proposed by Lord Chancellor (Loughborough), [c. 9 Oct. 1794], see above.

1. See the editorial note "Negotiating the Jay Treaty," above.

2. On the decision to refrain from deciding which of the two nations was the first to violate the peace treaty, see the preface to JJ's Project for a Treaty with Great Britain, 30 Sept. 1794, above. ER first described the decision not to identify the first violator, as well as that regarding enslaved persons, as so new to him that he could not agree to their accuracy without the fullest reflection. In a subsequent letter, he expressed strong concern that JJ's failure to fix the blame for the first violation on Britain might have serious adverse effects on American claims. See JJ to ER, 13 Sept. 1794, above; ER to JJ, 12 Nov. 1794, *ASP: FR*, 1: 501–2; and ER to JJ, 15 Dec. 1794, C, NHi: Jay (EJ: 00620); *ASP: FR*, 1: 509–12.

3. See Art. 2 of the Treaty of Amity, Commerce, and Navigation, 19 Nov. 1794, below. For British criticism of the peace treaty of 1783 for its failure to defend the interest of British traders, see *JJSP*, 3: 397n. In his letter of 15 Dec. 1794, cited above, ER remarked that the passage of time had increased GW's repugnance to the extension of time, which, he thought, would prolong the time needed to establish peaceful relations with the Indians, and would counteract the development of an American fur trade.

4. That is, American duties. See Art. 3 of the Treaty of Amity, Commerce, and Navigation, 19 Nov. 1794, below.

5. See the editorial note "Negotiating the Jay Treaty," above; and Art. 3 of the Treaty of Amity, Commerce, and Navigation, 19 Nov. 1794, below.

6. On the St. Croix boundary commission of 1796, see JJ's Project for a Treaty with Great Britain, 30 Sept. 1794, above; and the editorial note "Aftermath of the Jay Treaty: Responses, Ratification, and Implementation, below. ER informed JJ that GW approved his reasoning and conduct on the boundary issues as very judicious. See ER to JJ, 15 Dec. 1794, cited above.

7. See Richard Oswald to Thomas Townsend, 8 Oct. 1782, *JJSP*, 3: 185–86.

8. On this article, regarding debts owed to British creditors, see Art. 6 of the Treaty of Amity, Commerce, and Navigation, 19 Nov. 1794, below.

9. On this article, see Articles 7 and 8 of the Treaty of Amity, Commerce, and Navigation, 19 Nov. 1794, below.

10. Joshua Johnson (1742–1802), served as American consul in London from 1790–97. ER had announced the appointment of Samuel Bayard as agent for the American merchants. See ER to JJ, 29 Oct. 1794, C, DNA: Jay Despatches, 1794–95 (EJ: 04328); C, NHi: Jay (EJ: 00612); C, NHi: King (EJ: 04459); and *ASP: FR*, 1: 499–500.

11. See Art. 8 of the Treaty of Amity, Commerce, and Navigation, 19 Nov. 1794, below.

12. See Article Proposed by the Lord Chancellor (Loughborough), [c. 9 Oct. 1794], above. On alienage, see also Art. 9 of the Treaty of Amity, Commerce, and Navigation, 19 Nov. 1794, below.

13. On sequestration, see Art. 10 of the Treaty of Amity, Commerce, and Navigation, 19 Nov. 1794, below.

14. On the West Indies article, see Art. 6 of Grenville's Draft of a commercial treaty in his Treaties of 30 Aug., and note 13, and Art. 10 of JJ's Project for a Treaty with Great Britain, 30 Sept. 1794, and notes 39–44, both above.

15. See Grenville to JJ, 7 Sept. 1794, above.

16. See the final clause of the 10th Art. in JJ's Project for a Treaty with Great Britain of 30 Sept. 1794, which was subsequently incorporated into Art. 12 of the Treaty of Amity, Commerce, and Navigation of 19 Nov. 1794, and ultimately rejected by the United States. JJ had also attempted to concede practice while saving the principle in his negotiations with Gardoqui for use of the Mississippi, which he was willing to concede for ten years while establishing the principle that the United States had the right to it. See the editorial note "Negotiations with Gardoqui Reach an Impasse," *JJSP*, 4: 364–78.

17. Arts. 19 and 21 of the Treaty of Amity, Commerce, and Navigation of 19 Nov. 1794. Arts. 19 through 25 of this treaty, which closely follow Arts. 20, 22, and 23 of JJ's Project for a Treaty with Great Britain, 30 Sept. 1794, above, were designed by JJ to respond to Britain's complaints about infractions of American neutrality perpetrated by Genet, no doubt as a result of conversations with Grenville, since, for the most part, there are no equivalents for them in Grenville's Draft Treaties of 30 Aug. 1794, above. On Genet's breaches of American neutrality, see the editorial note "John Jay and the Genet Affair," *JJSP*, 5: 546–61

18. Art. 8 of the Dutch-American Treaty of 1782 and Art. 20 of the Treaty of Amity, Commerce, and Navigation, 19 Nov. 1794, below.

19. See item 11 of ER's instructions to JJ, 6 May 1794, *JJSP*, 5: 640, and Art. 24 of the Treaty of Amity, Commerce, and Navigation, 19 Nov. 1794, below.

20. See JJ to Pinckney, 19 Nov. 1794, Dft, NNC (EJ: 09471); and Pinckney to JJ, 20 Nov. 1794, ALS, ScHi (EJ: 03483).

21. This had been suggested in ER to JJ, 6 May 1794, *JJSP*, 5: 642.

22. For his injunction to repulse any attempts by Britain to detach the United States from France, see ER to JJ, 6 May 1794, *JJSP*, 5: 638, 642.

Treaty of Amity, Commerce, and Navigation, between His Britannick Majesty, and the United States of America, by Their President, with the Advice and Consent of Their Senate

[[London], 19 November 1794]

His Britannick Majesty and The United States of America, being desirous by a Treaty of Amity Commerce and Navigation, to terminate their differences in such a manner, as, without reference to the merits of their respective Complaints and Pretensions may be the best calculated to provide mutual satisfaction and good understanding: And also to regulate their Commerce and Navigation between their respective Countries, Territories and People, in such a manner as to render the same reciprocally beneficial and satisfactory; They have respectively named their Plenipotentiaries, and given them full Powers to treat of and conclude the said Treaty; That is to say, His Britannick Majesty has named for his Plenipotentiary, The Right Honourable William Wyndham Baron Grenville of Wotton, One of His Majesty's Privy Council, and His Majesty's principal Secretary of State for Foreign Affairs;— And the President of the said United States, by and with the Advice and consent of the Senate thereof, hath appointed for their Plenipotentiary the Honourable John Jay, Chief Justice of the said United States, and their Envoy Extraordinary to His Majesty, who have agreed on and concluded the following Articles.

Article 1st:

There shall be a firm, inviolable and universal Peace, and a true and sincere Friendship between his Britannick Majesty, His Heirs and Successors, and the United States of America, and between their respective Countries, Territories, Cities, Towns and People, of every degree, without Exception of Persons or Places.

Article 2nd:

His Majesty will withdraw all his Troops and Garrisons from all Posts and Places, within the Boundary-lines assigned by the Treaty of Peace to the United States;— This Evacuation shall take place on or before the 1st. day of June 1796; and all the proper measures shall in the interval be taken by Concert between the Government of the United States, and His Majestys Governor General in America, for settling the previous arrangements which may be necessary respecting the Delivery of the said Posts;— The United States in the mean time, at their Discretion, extending their Settlements to any part within the said Boundary Line, except within the said Precincts or Jurisdiction of any of the said Posts.— All Settlers and Traders, within the Precincts or Jurisdiction of the said Posts, shall continue to enjoy, unmolested, all their Property of every kind, and shall be protected therein:— They shall be at full liberty to remain there, or to remove with all or any Part of their Effects; and it shall also be free to them to sell their Lands, Houses or Effects, or to retain their Property thereof at their discretion; such of them as shall continue to reside within the said Boundary Lines, shall not be compelled to become Citizens of the United States, or to take any Oath of Allegiance to the Government thereof, but they shall be at full liberty so to do, if they think proper, and They shall make and declare their Election within One Year after the Evacuation aforesaid:— And All Persons who shall continue there after the Expiration of the said Year, without having declared their Intention of remaining Subjects of His Britannick Majesty, shall be considered as having elected to become Citizens of the United States.

Article 3ᵈ:

It is Agreed, that it shall at all times be free to His Majesty's Subjects, and to the Citizens of the United States, and also to the Indians dwelling on either side of the said Boundary-line, freely to pass and repass, by Land or inland Navigation, into the respective Territories and Countries of the Two Parties on the Continent of America, (the Country within the limits of the Hudson's Bay Company only excepted,) and to Navigate all the Lakes, Rivers and Waters thereof, and freely to carry on Trade and Commerce with each other:— But it is understood, that this Article does not extend to the admission of the Vessels of the United States, into the Sea Ports, Harbours, Bays or Creeks of His Majesty's said Territories, nor into such parts of the Rivers of his Majesty's said Territories, as are between the Mouth thereof and the highest Port of Entry from the Sea, except in small Vessels, trading, bona fide, between Montreal and Quebec, under such regulation as shall be established to prevent the possibility of any Frauds in this respect:— nor to the Admission of British Vessels from the Sea, into the rivers of the United States, beyond the highest Ports of Entry for Foreign Vessels from the Sea.— The River Missisipi shall however, according to the Treaty of Peace, be entirely open to both Parties; And it is further agreed, That all the Ports and Places on its Eastern Side, to whichsoever of the Parties belonging, may freely be resorted to, and used by both Parties, in as ample a manner as any of the Atlantic Ports of the United States, or any of the Ports or Places of His Majesty in Great Britain.

All Goods and Merchandize whose Importation into his Majesty's said Territories in America, shall not be entirely prohibited, may freely, for the purpose of Commerce be carried into the same, in the manner aforesaid, by the Citizens of the United States, and such Goods and Merchandize shall be subject to no higher or other Duties than would be payable to His Majesty's Subjects on the Importation of the same from Europe into the said Territories:— And in like manner, All Goods and Merchandize, whose Importation in to the United States, shall not be wholly prohibited, may, freely for the purposes of Commerce, be carried into the same, in the manner aforesaid, by His Majesty's Subjects, and such Goods and Merchandize shall be subject to no higher or other Duties than would be payable by the Citizens of the United States on the importation of the same in American Vessels, into the Atlantic Ports of the said States.— And all goods not prohibited to be exported from the said Territories respectively, may in like manner, be carried out of the same, by the Two Parties respectively, paying Duty as aforesaid.

No Duty of Entry shall ever be levied by either Party on Peltries, brought by Land or Inland Navigation into the said Territories respectively, nor shall the Indians passing or repassing with their own proper Goods and Effects, of whatever nature, pay for the same any Impost or Duty whatever:— But Goods in Bales or other large Packages unusual among Indians, shall not be considered as Goods belonging bonda fide to Indians.

No higher or other Tolls or Rate of Ferriage than what are, or shall be payable by Natives, shall be demanded by either side;— And no Duties shall be payable on any Goods which shall merely be carried over any of the Portages or Carrying Places, on either side for the purpose of being immediately reimbarked and carried to some other Place or Places.— But, as by this stipulation it is only meant to secure to each Party a free Passage across the Portages on both Sides, It is agreed, that this Exemption from Duty shall extend only to such Goods as are carried in the usual and direct road across the Portage, and are not attempted to be in any manner sold or exchanged during their Passage across the same and proper Regulations may be established to prevent the possibility of any Frauds in this respect.

As this Article is intended to render in a great degree the local advantages of each Party common to both, and thereby to promote a Disposition favourable to Friendship and good Neighbourhood, It is agreed, that the respective Governments will mutually promote this amicable intercourse, by causing speedy and impartial Justice to be done, and necessary protection to be extended to all who may be concerned therein.

Article 4th:—

Whereas it is uncertain whether the River Mississippi extends so far to the Northward as to be intersected by a Line to be drawn due West from the Lake of the Woods, in the manner mentioned in the Treaty of Peace between His Majesty, and the United States, It is agreed, that measures shall be taken in concert between His Majesty's Government in America, and the Government in America, and the Government of the United States, for making a joint Survey of the said River from One Degree of Latitude below the Falls of St. Anthony to the principal Source or Sources of the said River, and also of the parts adjacent thereto;— And that, if on the Result of such Survey it should appear, that the said River would not be intersected by such a Line as is above-mentioned, The Two Parties will thereupon proceed by amicable Negotiation to regulate the Boundary Line in that quarter, as well as all other Points to be adjusted between the said Parties, according to Justice and mutual convenience, and in conformity to the Intent of the said Treaty.

Article 5th:

Whereas Doubts have arisen what River was truly intended under the name of the River St. Croix, mentioned in the said Treaty of Peace, and forming a Part of the Boundary therein described, that Question shall be referred to the final Decision of Commissioners to be appointed in the following manner. Vizt.—

One Commissioner shall be named by His Majesty, and One by the President of the United States by and with the Advice and Consent of the Senate thereof, and the said Two Commissioners shall agree on the choice of a Third, or, if they cannot so agree, they shall each propose one Person, and of the Two names so proposed, One shall be drawn by Lot, in the Presence of the Two original Commissioners;— And the Three Commissioners so appointed shall be sworn impartially to examine and decide the said Question, according to such Evidence as shall respectively be laid before them, on the part of the British Government, and of the United States.— The said Commissioners shall meet at Halifax, and shall have powers to adjourn to such other Place or Places as they shall think fit:— They shall have Power to appoint a Secretary, and to employ such Surveyors or other Persons as they shall judge necessary— The said Commissioners shall, by a Declaration under their hands and Seals, decide what River is the River St. Croix intended by the Treaty— The said Declaration shall contain a Description of the said River, and shall particularize the Latitude and Longitude of it's Mouth, and of it's Source;— Duplicates of this declaration and of the statements of their

Accounts, and of the Journal of their proceedings shall be delivered by them to the Agent of His Majesty, and to the Agent of the United States, who may be respectively appointed and authorized to manage the Business on behalf of the respective Governments;— And both Parties agree to consider each Decision a final and conclusive, so as that the same shall never thereafter be called into Question, or made the Subject of Dispute or Difference between them.

Article 6th:

Whereas it is alledged by divers British Merchants, and others His Majesty's Subjects, that Debts to a considerable amount, which were bona fide, contracted before the Peace, still remain owing to them by Citizens or Inhabitants of the United States, and that, by the operation of various lawful impediments since the Peace, not only the full recovery of the said Debts has been delayed, but also the Value and Security thereof have been in several instances impaired and lessened, so that by the ordinary course of Judicial proceedings the British Creditors cannot now obtain, and actually have and receive full and adequate Compensation for the Losses and Damages, which they have thereby sustained; It is Agreed, that in all such Cases, where full compensation in such Losses and Damages cannot, for whatever Reason, be actually obtained, had and received by the said Creditors in the Ordinary Course of Justice, The United States will make full and complete Compensation for the same, to the said Creditors; But it is distinctly understood that this Provision is to extend to such Losses only as have been occasioned by the lawful impediments aforesaid, and is not to extend to Losses occasioned by such Insolvency of the Debtors or other causes, as would equally have operated to reduce such Loss if the said impediments had not existed, nor to such Losses or Damages as have been occasioned by the manifest Delay or Negligence or wilful omission of the Claimant.

To the purpose of ascertaining the Amount of any such Losses and Damages, Five Commissioners shall be appointed and authorized to meet and act in manner following Viz^t:— Two of them shall be appointed by His Majesty; Two of them by the President of the United States, by and with the Advice and consent of the Senate thereof;— And the Fifth by the unanimous Voice of the other four;— and if they should not agree in such Choice, then the Commissioners named by the Two Parties shall respectively propose One person and of the Two names so proposed, One shall be drawn by Lot, in the presence of the Four original Commissioners.— When the Five Commissioners thus appointed shall first meet, they shall, before they Proceed to Act, respectively take the following Oath or Affirmation, in the Presence of each other, which Oath or Affirmation being so taken, and duly attested, shall be entered on the Record of their Proceedings,— Viz^t:— I A.B. One of the Commissioners appointed in pursuance of the 6th. Article of the Treaty of Amity, Commerce and Navigation between His Britannick Majesty and the United States of America, do solemnly swear (or affirm) that I will honestly, diligently, impartially and carefully examine and to the best of my Judgement, according to Justice and Equity decide all such Complaints, as, under the said Article, shall be preferred to the said Commissioners; and that I will forebear to act as a Commissioner in any case in which I may be personally interested.

Three of the said Commissioners shall constitute a board, and shall have power to any Act appertaining to the said Commission, provide that one of the Commissioners named on each side, and the Fifth Commissioner shall be present, and all Decisions shall be made by the majority of the Voices of the Commissioners then present.

Eighteen Months from the day on which the said Commissioners shall form a Board, and be ready to proceed to Business, are assigned for receiving Complaints and Applications, but they are nevertheless authorized in any particular Cases, in which it shall appear to them to be reasonable and just to extend the said Term of Eighteen Months for any Term not exceeding Six Months after the Expiration thereof;— The said Commissioners hall first meet at Philadelphia, but They shall have power to adjourn from Place to Place as they shall see Cause.

The said Commissioners, in examining the Complaints and Applications so preferred to them, are empowered and required, in Pursuance of the true Intent and Meaning of this Article, to take into their consideration all Claims, whether of principal or Interest, or Balances of Principal and Interest, and to determine the same respectively, according to the Merits of the several Cases, due regard being had to all the circumstances thereof, and as Equity and Justice shall appear to them to require.— And the said Commissioners shall have Power to examine all such Persons as shall come before them, on Oath or Affirmation, touching the Premises.— And also to receive in Evidence according as they may think most consistent with Equity and Justice, all written Depositions, or Books, or Papers, or Copies or Extracts thereof; Every such Deposition, Book, or Paper, or Copy or Extract being duly authenticated, either according to the Legal Forms now respectively existing in the Two Countries, or, in such other manner as the said Commissioners shall see cause to require or allow.

The Award of the said Commissioners, or of any Three of them aforesaid, shall in all Cases by final and conclusive, both as to the Justice of the Claim; and to the Amount of the Sum to be paid to the Creditor or Claimant.— And the United States undertake to cause the Sum so awarded to be paid in Specie to such Creditor or Claimant, without Deduction; and at such Time or Times, and at such Place or Places, as shall be awarded by the said Commissioners, and on condition of such releases or assignments to be given by the Creditor or Claimant as by the said Commissioners may be directed.— Provided always that no such Payment shall be fixed by the said Commissioners to take place sooner than Twelve Months from the Day of the Exchange of the Ratifications of this Treaty.

Article 7th:

Whereas Complaints have been made by divers Merchants, and others Citizens of the United States, that during the Course of the War in which His Majesty is now engaged, they have sustained considerable Losses and Damage, by reason of irregular or illegal Captures or Condemnations of their Vessels and other Property, under Colour of Authority or Commissions from His Majesty, and that from various circumstances belonging to the said Cases, adequate compensation for the Losses and Damages so sustained, cannot now be actually obtained, had and received by the ordinary course of Judicial Proceedings, It is Agreed, that in all such Cases, where adequate Compensation cannot for whatever Reason, be now actually obtained, had and received by the said Merchants and others in the ordinary Course of Justice, full and complete Compensation for the same will be made by the British Government to the said Complainants:— But it is distinctly understood, that this Provision is not to extend to such Losses or Damages as have been occasioned by the manifest Delay or Negligence, or wilful Omission of the Claimant.

That, for the purpose of ascertaining the Amount of any such Losses and Damages, Five Commissioners hall be appointed and authorized to act in London, exactly in the manner directed with respect to those mentioned in the preceeding Article, and after having taken the same Oath or Affirmation, (mutatis mutandis). The same Term of Eighteen months is also assigned for the reception of Claims, and they are in like manner authorized to extend the same in particular Cases;— They shall receive Testimony, Books, Papers and Evidence in the same Latitude, and exercise the like Discretion and Powers respecting that Subject, and shall decide the Claims in Question, according to the Merits of the several Cases, and to Justice, Equity, and the Laws of Nations.— The Award of the said Commissioners, or any such Three of them as aforesaid, shall, in all cases, be final and conclusive, both as to the Justice of the Claim, and to the Amount of the Sum to be paid to the Claimant; And His Britannick Majesty undertakes to cause the same to be paid to such Claimants in Specie, without any Deduction, at such Place or Places, and at such Time or times as shall be awarded to the said Commissioners, and on Condition of such releases or Assignments to be given by the Claimant, as by the said Commissioners may be directed.

And Whereas certain Merchants and others, His Majesty's Subjects complain, that, in the course of the War, they have sustained Loss and Damage, by reason of the Capture of their Vessels and Merchandize taken within the Limits and Jurisdiction of the States, and brought into the Ports of the same, or taken by Vessels originally armed in Ports of the said States:— It is Agreed, that in all such cases, where Restitution shall not have been made, agreeably to the tenour of the Letter from M^r. Jefferson to M^r. Hammond, dated at Philadelphia Sep^{tr}. 5th: 1793, a Copy of which is annexed to this Treaty,[1] the Complaints of the Parties shall be and hereby are referred to the Commissioners to be appointed by Virtue of this Article, who are hereby authorized and required to proceed in the like manner relative to these, as to the other Cases committed to Them.— And the United States undertake to pay to the Complainants or Claimants, in Specie, without Deduction the Amount of such Sums as shall be awarded to them respectively, by the said Commissioners, and at the Times and Places which in such Awards shall be specified, and on Condition of such Releases or Assignments to be given by the Claimants, as in the said Awards may be directed;— And it is further Agreed, that not only the now existing Cases of both Descriptions, but also all such as shall exist at the Time of exchanging the Ratifications of this Treaty shall be considered as being within the Provisions, Intent and Meaning of the Article.

Article 8th:

It is further agreed, that the Commissioners mentioned in this and in the Two preceeding Articles, shall be respectively paid in such manner as shall be agreed between the Two Parties, such agreement being to be settled at the time of the Exchange of the Ratification of this Treaty. And all other Expences attending the said Commissions shall be defrayed jointly by the Two Parties, the same being previously ascertained and allowed by the Majority of the Commissioners.— And in case of Death, Sickness or necessary Absence, the place of every Commissioner, respectively, shall be supplied in the same manner as such Commissioners was first appointed, and the new Commissioners shall take the same Oath or Affirmation, and do the same Duties.

Article 9th:

It is agreed, that British Subjects who now hold lands in the Territories of the United States, and American Citizens who now hold Lands in the Dominions of His Majesty shall continue to hold them according to the Nature and Tenure of their respective Estates and Titles therein, and may grant, sell or devise the same to whom they please, in like manner as if they were Natives, and that neither They nor their Heirs or Assigns shall, so far as may respect the said Lands, and the legal Remedies incident thereto, be regarded as Aliens.

Article 10th:

Neither the Debts due from individuals of the One Nation to Individuals of the other, nor Shares nor Monies which They may have in the Publick Funds, or in the Publick or Private Banks, shall ever in any Event of War, or National Differences, be sequestered or Confiscated; It being unjust and impolitick, that Debts and Engagements contracted and made by Individuals having Confidence in each other, and in their respective Governments, should be destroyed or impaired by National Authority, on account of National Differences and Discontents.

Article 11th:

It is Agreed between his said Majesty and the United States of American, that there shall be a reciprocal and entirely perfect liberty of Navigation and Commerce between their respective People, in the Manner, under the Limitations, and on the Conditions specified in the following Articles.

Article 12th:

His Majesty consents it shall and may be lawful, during the Time herein after limited, for the Citizens of the United States to carry to any of His Majesty's Islands and Ports in the West Indies, from the United States, in their own Vessels, not being above the Burthen of Seventy Tons, any Goods or Merchandizes being of the Growth, Manufacture or Produce of the said States, which it is, or may be lawful to carry to the said Islands or Ports, from the said States, in British Vessels, and that the said American Vessels shall be subject there to no other or higher Tonnage, Duties or Charges than shall be payable by British Vessels in the Ports of the United States, and that the Cargoes of the said American Vessels shall be subject there to no other or higher Duties or Charges than shall be payable on the like Articles if imported ₍there₎ from the said States in British Vessels.

And His Majesty also consents that it should be lawful for the said American Citizens to purchase, load and carry away in their said Vessels to the Unites States, from the said Islands and Ports, all such Articles being of the growth, Manufacture or Produce of the said Islands, as may now by Law be carried from thence to the said States in British Vessels, and subject only to the same Duties and Charges on Exportation, to which British Vessels and their Cargoes are or shall be subject in similar Circumstances.

Provided always that the said American Vessels do carry and land their Cargoes in the United States only, it being expressly agreed, and declared, that during the continuance of this Article, the United States will prohibit and restrain the carrying any Molasses, Sugar, Coffee, Cocoa or Cotton in American Vessels either from his Majesty's Islands, or from the United States, to any part of the World except the United States—reasonable Sea Stores excepted.— Provided also, that it shall and may be lawful, during the same Period, for British Vessels to import from the said Islands into the United States, and to export from the United States to the said Islands, all Articles whatever being of the Growth, Produce or Manufacture of the said Islands, or of the United States, respectively, which now may by the Laws of the Said States, be so imported and exported; And that the Cargoes of the said British Vessels shall be subject to no other or higher Duties or Charges, than shall be payable on the same Articles, if so imported or exported in American Vessels.

It is agreed that this Article, and every matter and Thing therein contained, shall continue to be in force during the continuance of the War in which his Majesty is now engaged, and also for Two Years from and after the Day of the Signature of the Preliminary or other Articles of Peace by which the same may be terminated.

And it is further agreed, that, at the expiration of the said Term, the Two Contracting Parties will endeavour further to regulate their Commerce in this Respect, according to the situation in which His Majesty may then find himself with Respect to the West Indies, and with a view to such Arrangements as may best conduce to the mutual Advantage and Extension of Commerce.— And the said Parties will then also renew their Discussions, and endeavour to agree whether in any, and what Cases, Neutral Vessels shall protect Enemy's Property;— and in what cases, Provisions and other Articles not generally contraband, may become such;— But in the mean time their Conduct towards each other in these Respects, shall be regulated by the Articles herein after inserted on those Subjects.

Article 13th:

His Majesty consents that the Vessels belonging to the Citizens of the United States of America shall be admitted and hospitable received in all the Sea Ports and Harbours of the British Territories in the East Indies:

And that the Citizens of the said United States may freely carry on a Trade between the said Territories and the said United States, in all Articles of which the Importation or Exportation, respectively to or from the said Territories shall not be entirely prohibited;— Provided only, that it shall not be lawful for them, in any Time of War between the British Government and any other Power or State whatever to export from the said Territories, without the Official Permission of the British Government there, any Military Stores, or Naval Stores, or Rice.— The Citizens of the United States shall pay for their Vessels when admitted into the said Ports no other or higher Tonnage Duty than shall be payable on British Vessels when admitted into the Ports of the United States:— And they shall pay no other or higher Duties or Charges on the Importation or Exportation of the Cargoes of the said Vessels, than shall be payable on the same Articles when imported or exported in British Vessels.— But it is expressly agreed, that the Vessels of the United States shall not carry any of the Articles exported by them from the said British Territories to any Port or Place except to some Port or Place in America, where the same shall be unladen; and such Regulations shall be adopted by both Parties, as shall from time to time be found necessary to enforce the due and faithful Observance of this Stipulation.— It is also understood that the Permission granted by this Article is not to extend to allow the Vessels of the United States to carry on any part of the Coasting Trade of the said British Territories, but Vessels going out with their original Cargoes, or Part thereof from One Port of Discharge to another are not to be considered as carrying on the Coasting Trade;— Neither is this article to be construed to allow the Citizens of the said States to settle or reside within the said Territories, or to go into the interior Parts thereof, without the Permission of the British Government established there;— And if any Transgression should be attempted against the regulations of the British Government in this respect, the Observance of the same shall and may be enforced against the Citizens of America, in the same manner as against British Subjects or others transgressing the same Rule;— And the Citizens of the United States whenever they arrive any Port or Harbour in the said Territories, or if they should be permitted in manner aforesaid, to go to any other Place therein, shall always be subject to the Laws, Government and Jurisdiction of whatever Nature, established in such Harbour Port or Place according as the same may be:— The Citizens of the United States may also touch for Refreshment at the Island of S^t. Helena, but subject to all Respects to such Regulations as the British Government may from Time to Time establish there.

Article 14th:

There shall between all the Dominions of his Majesty in Europe, and the Territories of the United States a reciprocal and perfect Liberty of Commerce and Navigation.— The People and Inhabitants of the Two Countries respectively, shall have Liberty, freely and securely, and without Hindrance and Molestation, to come with their Ships and Cargoes to the Lands, Countries, Cities, Ports, Places and Rivers within the Dominions and Territories aforesaid, to enter into the same, to resort there, and to remain and reside there, without any limitation of Time: Also to Hire and Possess Houses and Warehouses, for the purposes of their Commerce; and generally, the Merchants and Traders on each side, shall enjoy the most complete Protection and Security for their Commerce; but subject always as to what respects this Article, to the Laws and Statutes of the Two Countries, respectively.

Article 15th:

It is Agreed that no other or higher Duties shall be paid by the Ships or Merchandize of the One Party in the Ports of the other, than such as are paid by the like Vessels or Merchandize of all other Nations.— Nor shall any other or higher Duty be imposed in one Country on the Importation of any Articles the Growth, Produce or Manufacture of the other, than are or shall be payable on the Importation of the like Articles being of the Growth, Produce or Manufacture of any other Foreign Country. Nor shall any Prohibition be imposed on the Exportation or Importation of any Articles to and from the Territories of the Two Parties respectively, which shall not equally extend to all other Nations.

But the British Government reserves to itself the right of imposing on American Vessels entering into the British Ports in Europe a Tonnage Duty equal to that which shall be payable by British Vessels in the Ports of America:— And also such Duty as may be adequate to countervail the Difference of Duty now payable on the Importation of European and Asiatic Goods when imported into the United States in British or in American Vessels.

The Two Parties agree to treat for the more exact Equalisation of the Duties on the respective navigation of their Subjects and People in such Manner as may be most beneficial to the Two Countries.— The Arrangements for this purpose shall be made at the same time, with those mentioned at the Conclusion of the 12th: Article of this Treaty, and are to be considered as a part thereof.— In the Interval it is agreed that the United States will not impose any new or additional Tonnage Duties on British Vessels, nor increase the now subsisting Difference between the Duties payable on the Importation of any Articles in British or in American Vessels.

Article 16th:

It shall be free for the Two Contracting Parties respectively, to appoint Consuls for the Protection of Trade, to reside on the Dominion and Territories aforesaid; and the said Consuls shall enjoy those Liberties and Rights which belong to them by reason of their Function:— But, before any Consul shall act as such, He shall be in the usual forms approved and admitted by the Party to whom He is sent;— and it is hereby declared to be lawful and proper, that, in case of illegal or improper Conduct towards the Laws or Government, a Consul may either be punished according to Law, if the Laws will reach the case, or be dismissed, or even sent back, the offended Government assigning to the other Their Reasons for the same.

Either of the Parties may except from the Residence of Consuls such particular Places, as such Party shall judge proper to be so excepted.

Article 17th:

It is Agreed, that, in all Cases where Vessels shall be captured or detained on just Suspicion of having on board Enemy's Property, or of carrying to the Enemy any of the Articles which are Contraband of War, The said Vessel shall be brought to the nearest or most convenient Port, and if any Property of an Enemy should be found on board such Vessel, that part only which belongs to the Enemy shall be made Prize, and the Vessel shall be at Liberty to proceed with the remainder, without any Impediment.— And it is agreed, that all proper Measures hall be taken to prevent Delay in deciding the Cases of Ships or Cargoes so brought in for Adjudication, and in the Payment or Recovery of any Indemnification adjudged or agreed to be paid to the Masters or Owners of such Ships.

Article 18th:

In order to regulate what is in future to be esteemed Contraband of War, It is Agreed, that, under the said Denomination shall be comprised all Arms and Implements serving for the purposes of War, by Land or Sea;— such as Cannon, Muskets, Mortars, Petards, Bombs, Grenades, Carcasses, Saucisses, Carriages for Cannon, Musket-rests, Bandoleers, Gundpowder, Match, Saltpetre, Ball, Pikes, Swords, Head pieces, Cuirasses, Halberts, Lances, Javelins, Horses[,] Horse furniture, Holsters, Belts, and, generally, all other Implements of War, as also, Timber for Ship Building, Tar or Rosin, Cooper in Sheets, Sails, Hemp and Cordage, and generally whatever may serve directly to the Equipment of Vessels, unwrought Iron, and Fir Planks only excepted, and all the above Articles are hereby declared to just Objects of Confiscation, whenever they are attempted to be carried to an Enemy.

And Whereas the Difficulty of agreeing on the Precise Cases in which alone Provisions and other Articles, not generally Contraband, may be regarded as such, renders it expedient to provide against the Inconveniences and Misunderstandings which might thence arise, It is further Agreed, that, whenever any such Articles so becoming Contraband, according to the Existing Law of Nations, shall for that reason be siezed, the same shall not be confiscated, but the Owners thereof shall be speedily and completely indemnified; and the Captors, or, in their default, the Government under whose Authority they act, shall pay to the Masters or Owners of such Vessels, the full value of all such articles, with a reasonable Mercantile Profit thereon, together with the Freight, and also the Demurrage incident to such Detention.

And Whereas it frequently happens, that Vessels sail for a Port or Place belonging to an Enemy without knowing that the same is either besieged, blockaded or invested, It is agreed, that every Vessel so circumstanced, may be turned away from such Port or Place;— But She shall not be detained, nor her Cargo if not contraband, be confiscated, unless after Notice, She shall again attempt to Enter:— But She shall be permitted to go to any other Port or Place She may think proper:— Nor shall any Vessel or Goods of either Party, that may have entered into such Port or Place, before the same was beseiged, blockaded or invested by the other, and be found therein, after the Reduction or Surrender of such Place, be liable to Confiscation; but shall be restored to Owners or Proprietors thereof.

Article 19th:

And that more abundant Care may be taken for the Security of the respective Subjects and Citizens of the Contracting Parties, and to prevent their suffering Injuries by the Men of War or Privateers of either Party, All Commanders of Ships of War and Privateers, and all others the said Subjects and Citizens shall forebear doing any Damage to those of the Party, or committing any Outrage against them, and if they act to the contrary, they shall be punished, and shall also be bound in their Persons and Estates, to make Satisfaction and Reparation for all Damages, and the Interest thereof, of whatever Nature the said Damages may be.

For this Cause all Commanders of Privateers, before they receive their Commissions, shall here after be obliged to give before a competent Judge, sufficient Security by at least Two responsible Sureties, who have no Interest in the said Privateer, each of whom, together with the said Commander, shall be jointly and severally bound in the Sum of Fifteen hundred Pounds sterling, or, if such Ship be provided with above One Hundred and Fifty Seamen or Soldiers in the Sum of Three Thousand Pounds Sterling, to satisfy all Damages and Injuries which the said Privateer or her Officers or Men, or any of them may do or commit during their Cruise, contrary to the Tenour of this Treaty, or to the Laws and Instructions for regulating their Conduct:— and further, that in all Cases of Aggressions the said Commission shall be revoked and annulled.

It is also agreed, that whenever a Judge of a Court of Admiralty of either of the Parties shall pronounce Sentence against any Vessel, or Goods, or Property belonging to the Subjects or Citizens of the other Party, a formal and duly-authenticated Copy of all the Proceedings in the Cause, and of the ∧said∧ Sentence, shall, if required, be delivered to the Commander of the said Vessel, without the smallest delay, He paying all legal Fees and Demands for the same.

Article 20th:

It is further Agreed, that both the said Contracting Parties shall not only refuse to receive any Pirates into any of their Ports, Havens or Towns, or permit any of their Inhabitants to receive, protect, harbour, conceal or assist them in any manner, but will bring to condign Punishment, all such Inhabitants as shall be guilty of such Acts or Offences

And all their Ships, with the Goods or Merchandize taken by them, and brought into the Port of either of the said Parties shall be siezed, as far as they can be discovered, and shall be restored to the Owners, or their Factors or Agents duly departed, and authorized in Writing by them, (proper Evidence being first given in the Court of Admiralty for proving the Property.) even in case such Effects should have passed into other Hands by Sale, if it be proved that the Buyers knew or had good Reason to believe or Suspect that they had been piratically taken.

Article 21st:

It is likewise Agreed, that the Subjects and Citizens of the two Nations, shall not do any Acts of Hostility or Violence against each other, nor Accept Commissions or Instructions so to act, from any Foreign Prince or State, Enemies to the other Party;— nor shall the Enemies of one of the Parties be permitted to invite, or endeavour to enlist in their Military Service, any of the Subjects or Citizens of the other Party; and the Laws against all such Offences and Aggressions shall be punctually executed.— And if any Subject or Citizen of the said Parties respectively, shall accept any Foreign Commission or Letters of Marque for arming any Vessel to act as a Privateer against the other Party, and be taken by the other Party, it is hereby declared to lawful for the said Party to treat and punish the said Subject or Citizen having such Commission or Letters of Marque, as a Pirate.

Article 22nd:

It is expressly stipulated, that neither of the said Contracting Parties will order or authorize any Acts of Reprisal against the other, on Complaints of Injuries or Damages, untill the said Party shall first have presented to the other a Statement thereof, verified by competent proof and Evidence, and Demanded Justice and Satisfaction, and the same shall either have been refused, or unreasonably delayed.

Article 23d:

The Ships of War of each of the contracting Parties shall at all Times be hospitably received in the Ports of the other, their Officers and Crews paying due Respect to the Laws and Government of the Country;— The Officers shall be treated with that Respect, which is due to the Commissions which they bear; and if any Insult should be offered to them by any of the Inhabitants, all Offenders in this Respect, shall be punished as Disturbers of the Peace and Amity between the Two Countries.

And His Majesty consents, that, in case an American Vessel should by stress of Weather, Danger from Enemies, or other Misfortune, be reduced to the Necessity of seeking Shelter in any of His Majesty's Ports, into which such Vessel could not, in ordinary Cases, claim to be admitted, She shall, on manifesting that Necessity to the Satisfaction of the Government of the Place, be hospitably received, and be permitted to refit, and to purchase all the Market Price, such Necessaries as She may stand in need of, conformably to such Orders and Regulations as the Government of the Place having respect to the Circumstances of each Case, shall prescribe.— She shall not be allowed to break Bulk, or unload the Cargo, unless the same should be, *bona fide*, necessary to Her being refitted;— Nor shall She be permitted to sell any part of Her Cargo, unless so much only as may be necessary to defray Her Expences, and then, nor without the express Permission of the Government of the Place:— Nor shall be obliged to pay any Duties whatever, except only on such Articles as She may be permitted to sell for the Purpose aforesaid.

Article 24th:

It shall not be lawful for any Foreign Privateers, (not being Subjects or Citizens of either of the said Parties.) who have Commission from any other Prince or State in Enmity with either Nation, to arm their ships in the Port of either of the said Parties, nor to sell what they have taken, nor in any other manner to Exchange the same; nor shall they be allowed to purchase more Provisions than shall be necessary for their going to the nearest port of that Prince or State, from whom They obtained their Commissions.

Article 25th:

It shall be lawful for the Ships of War and Privateers belonging to the said Parties respectively, to carry whithersoever they please, the Ships and Goods taken from their Enemies, without being obliged to pay any Fee to the Officers of the Admiralty or to any Judges whatever, nor shall the said Prizes, when they arrive at and enter the Ports of the said Parties, be detained or siezed;— neither shall the Searchers or other Officers of those Places visit such Prizes, (except for the Purpose of preventing the carrying of any Part of the Cargo thereof on Shore, in any Manner contrary to the established Laws of Revenue, Navigation or Commerce.): nor shall such Officers take Cognizance of the Validity of such Prizes; but they shall be at Liberty to hoist Sail and depart as speedily as may be, and carry their said Prizes to the Place mentioned in their Commissions or Patents, which the Commanders of the said Ships of War or Privateers shall be obliged to Shew:— No Shelter or Refuge shall be given in their Ports to such as have made a Prize upon the Subjects or Citizens of either of the said Parties; but, if forced by Stress of Weather, or the Danger of the Sea, to enter therein, particular Care shall be taken to hasten their Departure, and to cause them to retire as soon as possible;— Nothing in this Treaty contained, shall however, be construed or operate contrary to former and existing Public Treaties with other Sovereigns or States:— But the Two Parties agree, that while they continue in Amity, neither of them will future make any Treaty that shall be inconsistent with this or the preceeding Article.

Neither of the said Parties shall permit the Ships or Goods belonging to the Subjects or citizens of the other to be taken within Cannon Shot of the Coast, nor in any of the Bays, Ports or Rivers of their Territories, by Ships of War or others, having Commissions from any Prince Republic or State whatever;— But, in case it should so happen, the Party whose Territorial Rights shall thus have been violated, shall use His utmost Endeavours to obtain from the Offending Party, full and ample satisfaction for the Vessel or Vessels so taken, whether the same be Vessels of War or Merchant Vessels.

Article 26th:

If at any Time a Rupture should take Place, (which God Forbid,) between His Majesty and the United States, the Merchants and others of each of the Two Nations residing in the Dominions of the other, shall have the Privilege of remaining and continuing their Trade, so long as they behave peaceably, and commit no Offence against the Laws, and in case their Conduct should render them suspected, and the respective Governments should think proper to order them to remove, the Term of Twelve Months from the Publication of the Order, shall be allowed them for that purpose to remove with their Families, Effects and Property:— but this Favour shall not be expanded to those who shall Act contrary to the established Laws; and, for greater certainty, It is declared, that such ruptures shall not be deemed to exist while Negotiations for accommodating Differences shall be depending, nor untill the respective Ambassadors or Ministers, of such there shall be, shall be recalled, or sent home on account of such Differences; and not on account of personal Misconduct according to the nature and Degrees of which, both Parties retain their Rights, either to request the recall, or immediately to send home the Ambassadors or Minister of the other, and that without Prejudice to their mutual Friendship and good understanding.

Article 27th:

It is further agreed, that His Majesty and the United States, on mutual requisitions by them respectively, or by their respective Ministers or Officers authorized to make the same, will deliver up to Justice, all Persons who being charged with Murder or Forgery, committed with the Jurisdiction of the either, shall seek an Asylum within any of the Countries of the other; Provided, that this shall only be done, on such Evidence of Criminality, as, according to the Laws of the Place where the Fugitive or Person so charged shall be found, would justify his Apprehension and commitment for Trial, if the Offence had there been committed:— The Expence of such Apprehension and Delivery shall be borne and defrayed by those who make the Requisition, and receive the Fugitive.

Article 28th:

It is agreed, that the First Ten Articles of the Treaty shall be permanent, and that the subsequent Articles except the Twelfth, shall be limited in their Duration to Twelve Years, to be computed from the Day on which the Ratifications of this Treaty shall be exchanged, but subject to this Condition, That whereas the said Twelfth Article will expire by the Limitation therein contained, at the End of Five Years from the signing of the Preliminary or other Articles of Peace which shall terminate the present War in which His Majesty is engaged, It is Agreed, that proper Measures shall, by concert, be taken to bringing the subject of that Article into amicable Treaty and Discussion so early before the Expiration of the said Term, as that new Arrangements on that Head, may by that Time be perfected and ready to take Place;— but, if it should unfortunately happen, that His Majesty and the United States should not be able to agree on such new Arrangements, in that Case, all the Articles of this Treaty, except for the first Ten, shall then cease and expire together.

Lastly,— This Treaty, when the same shall have been Ratified by His Majesty, and by the President of the United States, by and with the Advice and Consent of their Senate, and the respective Ratifications mutually exchanged, shall be binding and obligatory His Majesty and on the said States, and shall by them respectively executed and observed with punctuality and the most sincere Regard to good Faith:— And— Whereas It will be expedient, in order the better to Facilitate Intercourse and obviate Difficulties, that other Articles be proposed and added to the Treaty, which Articles, from want of Time and also Circumstances cannot now be perfected; It is Agreed, That the said Parties will, from Time to Time readily treat of and concerning such Articles, and will sincerely endeavour so to form them, as that they may conduce to mutual Convenience, and tend to Promote mutual Satisfaction and Friendship: And that the said Articles, after having been duly ratified, shall be added to and make a Part of this Treaty.—

In Faith whereof We, the Undersigned Ministers Plenipotentiary of His Majesty the King of Great Britain, and the United States of America, have signed this present Treaty, and have caused to be affixed thereto the Seal of our Arms.

Done at London, the Nineteenth Day of November, One Thousand, Seven Hundred and Ninety Four.

Grenville   John Jay[2]

DS and LbkC, NNC: JJ Lbk. 8.

1. TJ to George Hammond, 5 Sept. 1793, *PTJ*, 27: 35–38. See also JJ's Project for a Treaty with Great Britain, 30 Sept., note 23, above.

2. For the evolution of the text of the treaty, see the editorial note "Negotiating the Jay Treaty, above; JJ's Draft for a Convention and Treaty of Commerce, 6 Aug., and notes; Grenville's Draft Treaties of Amity and Commerce, 30 Aug., and notes; and JJ's Project for a Treaty with Great Britain, 30 Sept. 1794, and notes, all above.

From Grenville

Downing Street Nov[r]. 19th. 1794

Sir,

I have the honour to transmit to you the Papers which you have already seen relative to the Claims of certain Persons having Rights of Remainder, or other Interests in Estates confiscated in America during the late War, but whose Rights or Interests according to Justice and the established Laws under which those Estates were held, could not be affected by such Confiscation.

I have no doubt both from the Justice of the Case itself and from what has passed between us respecting it, that if on enquiry in America it should appear that any impediments to the prosecution of such claims in the ordinary Course of Justice have existed or still exist, these Cases will be considered as being completely within the principle of the Article in the Treaty signed between us this day, respecting the British Creditors.— But as you did not possess sufficient Information respecting the particulars of this business to be enabled to enter fully into it, I have transmitted to you the Papers relative to it, and I shall be obliged to you, if when you have received further Information upon it, you will acquaint me in what situation you conceive the Parties interested in it to stand with respect to the means of recovering their Rights in the ordinary Course of Justice. I also transmit to you for a similar purpose, an application which I have received from a particular Class of British Creditors whose Case is there Stated.[1]

I cannot conclude this Letter without repeating to you the very great satisfaction I have derived from the open and candid manner in which you have conducted on your part the whole of the difficult Negotiation which we have now brought to so successful an Issue, and from the disposition which you have uniformly manifested to promote the Objects of justice, conciliation and lasting Friendship between our two Countries.

These Dispositions are perfectly reciprocal on the part of this Government and I am happy in any Opportunity of expressing them to you and of renewing to you the sincere assurances of the very great personal esteem and regard with which I have the honour to be Sir Your most obedient humble Servant

Grenville

John Jay Esqr &c^a &c^a &c^a

LS, UkWC-A (EJ: 00045). C, with enclosures, DNA: Jay Despatches, 1794–95 (EJ: 04340). Enclosures: D, John Wilmot, Office of American Claims, to George Rose, 13 Aug. 1790, covering documents: "I send you Extracts of some Papers and ~~Reports~~ relative to the Claim of Colonel Morris and his Children.— The other Cases of a similar Nature are those of Lord Fairfax and Mr. Martin, and you will see the Attorney General's Opinion applies to all of them."; Attorney General R. R. Arden's Opinion in the case of Roger and Mary Morris, 31 Mar. 1787; Extracts from the Report of the Commissioners of American Claims, 7 Apr. 1786; 5 Apr. 1788; 15 May 1789; Extract from the Decision of the Commissioners of American Claims, on the Claim of Col. Roger Morris and Mary his Wife; Samuel and George Martin; Decision on the Claim of the Right Honorable Robert Lord Fairfax, on behalf of himself and of Frances Martin Widow his Sister, and of Denny Fairfax D.D. Philip Martin Esqr. and Thomas Martin Esqr., his Nephews, and their three Sisters his Nieces, Claim £98,000; Copy of a letter written by John Wilmot Esqr. & George Rose Esqr., 24 Jan. 1792; Memorial of 19 American Loyalists living in Great Britain and elsewhere to Grenville, 9 Oct. 1794. Endorsed: "No. 23 and 25. / Jay, J.—20 Nov. & 6 Decr. 94; rec^d. March 22. 95."; [in clerk's hand] "recorded page 173."; E, ASP: FR, 1: 505–9. WJ, 1: 334.

1. JJ forwarded Grenville's letter under cover of JJ to ER, 20 Nov. 1794, ALS, marked "Dupli-cate", DNA: Jay Despatches, 1794–95 (EJ: 04339), in which he commented that the applicants were "*American loyalists*" whose claims, he asserted, were not covered as British creditors under the peace treaty.

To Rufus King

London 19 Nov[r]. 1794

Dear Sir

I sent by the Packet the Fruit of my negociation—a Treaty— I wish I could go with it, as well that I might again be in my own Country, as that I might answer Questions on the Subjects. The Draft has undergone several Editions, with successive alterations additions &c[a].— this shews that Time and Trouble have not been spared[1]— I have just finished a hasty Letter to M[r] Randolph[2]— it will be thought slovenly, but I cannot help it— The Packet must go—

If I entirely escape censure I shall be agreably disappointed. Should the Treaty prove, as I believe it will, beneficial to our Country, Justice will finally be done— if not, be it so—[3] My mind is at Ease— I wish I could say as much for my body—but the Rheumatism will not permit me— Health & Happi-ness to you my good friend Yours sincerely

John Jay

The hon'ble Rufus King Esq[r]

ALS, NHi: King (EJ: 00754). Marked: "Dup". Addressed: "The hon'ble/Rufus King Esq[r]/Philadel-phia". Endorsed. Dft, NNC (EJ: 06708); *WJ*, 2: 238; *HPJ*, 4: 136.

1. See the editorial note "Negotiating the Jay Treaty," above.

2. See JJ to ER, 19 Nov. 1794, above.

3. In a letter of the same date to AH, JJ remarked "If this Treaty fails, I dispair of another. If satis-factory, care should be taken that public opinion be not misled respecting it—for this Reason the sooner it is ratified and published, the better." ALS, UkWC-A (EJ: 00049); C, DLC (EJ: 10771); *PAH*, 17: 390–91.

From Peter Jay Munro

New York 19th. Nov[r]. 1794

Dear Sir,

I had the pleasure of writing to you last night, under an Impression, that the Rosina (or Rosanna)[1] would have sailed early this morning, but her being detained, affords me an opportunity of writing you a longer Letter.

I am much indebted to you, for the Information respecting M^rs. White, and entirely acquiese, in the Truth of your Observations to her Son. My Ideas relative to a Reconciliation are well known to you. I feel a Reluctance, to live familiarly with persons, whom I neither love, nor respect. Forgiveness and Reconciliation are distinct; the former is enjoined, but not the latter. If a Reconcilement of hearts could be effected, I would willing agree to it, but a mere agreement to see each other, and to say nothing of what has past, can seldom be useful, and sometimes may be dangerous. If the old Lady really regreted her absurd conduct towards us, I would not oppose a reconciliation, but while she entertains the Sentiments, she hath cherished for some years past, she cannot disoblige me, but by returning to this Country.²

I spent two days with Major Lyons last week— his acc^t. is still unsettled, (owing to his not being prepared) he promises, he will be ready upon the tenth of next Month, when he is to meet me at Rye for that Purpose.—

He says that the work at the mill, has interfered with his business. Hay to the amount of about 150 loads, was cured without being wet by rain— M^r. Green the Mill-Wright, has changed the Mare he bought of the major, for the other handsome Mare.

In my Opinion, John deserves credit for the manner, in which the work at the mill is executed. The machinery appears to me, to be of better materials, and to be better put together, then that in the mill of M^r. Ramsay at Kings bridge, w^h. I examined, for the express purpose of forming a Judgment upon this Subject— The house itself appears well built, and is of good Timber, the foundation, as far as I can judge, cannot be made better than it is. The Dam has proved a heavy work, from what I can learn, and see, it hath been executed with Judgment and Care, and will probably last an Age. It still wants about four feet and an half in height— part of it is planked and gravelled. It is said, it will be finished in one fortnight, but I think it will require longer time, one floor of the mill house is laid— Six Yoke of oxen are employed, and the Major obliges his *Bulls* to lend their assistance— No money appears to be uselessly expend, but equal Care has not been taken of Time. I have been much embarrassed with John, who immediately after your Departure, took offense, and has made it a point to be from home, when I am at the mill— A Conversation he had with Aunt Jay, and some Feathers I observed ab^t. the major ∧convinces me∧ the true reason is to avoid an examination of his Acc^ts.— I have forborn to do any thing, which might tend to give him a distaste to a work, which I consider of much Importance to you, or to lessen his Ideas of his own Responsibility for it. I requested the Maj^r. to acquaint him, that if he will make out his Acc^t. ag[ains]^t. you for boarding the workmen, and let me have it, it shall be paid. The Major will probably marry in a short time, then, and not till then, will his business be conducted with regularity.[3]

I cannot account for your ~~not~~ having rec[d]., but one Letter from me by the 14th. of Sept[r]. I have written to you in *every* Month except *May*; and my Letters were regularly put into the Letter-bags at the Coffee house, either by M[r]. Towt or myself.— Uncle *Fady* says, that one of the vessels, by w[h]. we wrote was carried into France. I learn that the *Leeds* w[h]. carried a Letter from me of the 11th. of Oct[r].[4] has put back in New London into Distress; As a Paragraph of that Letter, related to your business, I will transcribe it—

"M[r]. Van Horne has rec[d]. of M[r]. Grant, the balance due upon the Jamaica bonds, for which he had taken good Notes. Your proportion of this balance is ab[t]. £400.1.6; of this Sum Aunt Jay Yesterday rec[d]. £395. the remaining £5.1.6 I chose to leave with M[r]. Van Horne for the Sake of keeping the Acc[t]. open—[5] Stagg has discharged the Judgm[t]. against him— King hath paid his note.— I have this Day given M[r]. Kelly a power of Atty to negociate your business in Vermont."[6]

The Letters, w[h]. I have had the Pleasure to ₍write₎ you, were of the following dates, viz[t]. The 15th. June—the 25th. July (I being then setting out for Albany, whence I did not return untill the 14th. of Aug[t].) the 30th. Aug[t].—the 18th. Sept[r].—the 11th. Oct[r].—the 16th. Oct[r]. & the 18th. Nov[r].—[7]

On the 17th. of Oct[r]. I set out for Albany a second Time, and did not return before the 17th. Instant— I visited the Lands in Washington County, they are well worth the sum I mentioned in a former Letter— the Tenants are willing to pay that price for them— a Deed is all that is wanting—

Our families are well— Your Sally talks faster than my Peter, but both talk enough for their Age—[8] William grows a fine Boy—I am Dear Sir Your aff[te]. Nephew

P. Jay Munro.

The Hon. John Jay

ALS, NNC (EJ: 09372). Endorsed: "... rec[d] 7 Feb. 1795 / an[d]. 21 Do / ab[t]. mill— acc[ts]. &c". Dft, NNMus (EJ: 00434).

1. The local press announced that the *Rosanna*, George Nichols, would sail for London from New York in mid-November. *Daily Advertiser* (New York), 4 Nov. 1794.

2. For JJ's interaction with the Whites, see JJ to PJM, 14 Sept. 1794, above.

3. For PJM's handling of JJ's business affairs, see PJM to JJ, 15 June 1794, above, and the editorial note "John Jay's Mission to London," above. For the Jays' business dealing with Samuel and John Lyon, see JJ to SLJ, 13 Mar. 1795, and note 5, below.

4. PJM to JJ, 11 Oct. 1794, Dft, NNMus (EJ: 00429).

5. For more on JJ and Augustus Van Horne's transactions with the Grants, see PJM to JJ, 15 June 1794, and note 1, above.

6. For more on JJ's Vermont land holdings, see JJ to Isaac Tichenor, 21 Oct. 1799, Dft, NNC (EJ: 08997).

7. PJM to JJ, 15 June, above; 25 July, not found; 30 Aug., Dft, NNMus (EJ: 00426); 18 Sept., Dft, NNMus (EJ: 00428); 11 Oct., Dft, NNMus (EJ: 00429); 16 Oct., above; and 18 Nov. 1794, Dft, NNMus (EJ: 00433).

8. For the question of whose child would speak first, see JJ to PJM, 14 Sept. 1794, above.

From John Sloss Hobart

New York 20th. Novr. 1794

My dear Sir

I embrace this opportunity to introduce to your notice Mr John Aspinwall, who will have the honor to deliver this letter— he is the youngest son of the late Mr. John Aspinwall of Flushing, and is going to reside for some years in Britain with the best of all possible recommendations for a merchant, a fair irreproachable character and plenty of *cash*—[1]

I drank a glass of porter and smoaked a pipe with Mrs. Jay on Saturday evening, master William took a Segar and attempted to play Papa, but his stomach was too weak, he sunk under the operation and was as sick as if he had been 500 leagues at Sea— You will naturally conclude what was the subject of our conversation— Haveing just seen an account that Mr. Bayard was appointed to go to London with power to pledge the U.S. for certain expenditures[2] under your direction induced us to dispair of seeing you before the next summer, indeed I am scarce ever in company ~~whose~~ but the most interesting, if not the first, questions are when will Mr. Jay return? will he be in season for the next election? &c. We are amused with various accounts respecting the situation of your negotiations, all of which concur in the prospect of a fortunate termination tho' they vary as to the progress made, it is expected the *speach* will aford some light on the subject in the course of a day or two—

you will be surprised to learn that I have not removed to Throggs Neck, but being obliged to build my house intirely new, it is only now habitable, and we are packing up in order to remove there next week— This circumstance added to the frequent interruptions occasioned by official applications obliges me to conclude this letter much sooner than I at first intended.

Mrs. Hobart desires to be respectfully remembered to you I am with great sincerity Your most Affect hble. Servt.

Jno: Sloss Hobart

Honble John Jay Esqr.

ALS, NNC (EJ: 05677).

1. John Aspinwall (c. 1705–74) was a successful sea captain and merchant. His son John (1774–1847), merchant and shipowner, was born after his father's death. In 1794, he joined his brother Gilbert's firm, which imported and sold at wholesale dry goods. Barrett, *Old Merchants of N.Y.*, 337.

2. See SLJ to JJ, 11 Nov. 1794, above, note 1, for news of Bayard's departure.

From Grenville (private)

Dover Street, Nov[r]. 21st. 1794.

Dear Sir,

I think I owe it to the confidence established between us to communicate to you *privately* the Copy of a Dispatch which I send by this packet to M[r]. Hammond. You will certainly understand that what he is expressly restrained from stating ministerially in America, is not meant to be so stated to you by me. But you will recollect that I have frequently conversed with you upon these points, & I am sure you will feel with me how Important they are to the great Object which we have been labouring to establish. If the Channels of communication are tainted by passion & prejudice, what passes thro' them will necessarily imbibe a portion of the same spirit, & after having successfully conciliated great Interests & important differences we shall see our work overthrown by the influence of personal animosities & individual contest.

If the stile of M[r]. Hammond has ever partaken of the same irritation which shows itself in all the letters he has lately received from the State Department[1] in America I think I can safely answer for his readily & chearfully adopting a language better suited to what is now I trust the situation of our two Countries— When I say this to you I do it in the confident hope that a similar resolution will be adopted by your Government, & it will then certainly be very immaterial to us whether Sentiments of friendship are conveyed to us in friendly language thro' the channel of M[r] Randolph or of any other person.

You will best judge of the use to be made of this letter, and to you I leave it with perfect confidence, Feeling that when M[r]. Hammond is directed to converse on this subject with persons disposed to promote a good understanding between the two Countries such a communication ought naturally to begin with you who have (as I hope) so much contributed to that object by the Treaty which we have so recently signed. I am &c[a].

Grenville

Honble M[r]. Jay &c &c &c

C, UkLPR: FO 95/512 (EJ: 05014). Marked: "Copy / Private and Confidential".

1. For ER's repeated complaints about Hammond, see ER to JJ, 29 May, cited at JJ to ER, 6–8 July

1794, above; ER to JJ, 11 Aug., C, NHi: Jay (EJ: 00606); C, DNA: Jay Despatches, 1794–95 (EJ: 04304); C, NHi: King (EJ: 04436); 18 Aug., C, DNA: Jay Despatches, 1794–95 (EJ: 04306); C, NHi: King (EJ: 04438); 30 Aug., C, NHi: Jay (EJ: 00611); C, DNA: Jay Despatches, 1794–95 (EJ: 04309); C, NHi: King (EJ: 04441); 5 Sept., C, NHi: King (EJ: 04442); 12 Sept. 1794, C, NHi: Jay (EJ: 00608); C, DNA: Jay Despatches, 1794–95 (EJ: 04310); C, NHi: King (EJ: 04443); *ASP: FR*, 1: 482–83, 484, 485.

To Edmund Randolph

London 21 Novr. 1794

Sir

On the 19th Inst. a Treaty was signed—[1] the next Day it was, together with my letters to You, N°. 21—22—& 23.[2] despatched to the Packet at Falmouth, which had been detained.—[3]

I now send You duplicates of them all, by M^r. Blaney, a Gentleman of Virginia, recommended to me by Gov[erno]^r. Lee.[4] The earliest advices from you will be expedient. There are articles in this Treaty which will give Strength to our applications to other Powers for Extensions of Commerce— much use may be made of them—

I daily become more convinced of the general friendly Disposition of this Country toward us— Let us cherish it— Let us cultivate Friendship with all nations— By treating them all with Justice and Kindness, and by preserving that *Self Respect* which forbids our yielding to the Influence or Policy of any of them we shall, with the divine Blessing, secure Peace union and Respectability—[5]

I feel very sensibly the Confidence that has been reposed in me, as well as the Responsibility that resulted from it— If this Treaty should prove beneficial, I shall not regret my anxiety and Efforts to render it so. The Canada article strikes me as one of the best in it— if discreetly managed, important Benefits will in my opinion be derived from it— very much ought not to be written on these subjects.

That the termination of these perplexing Differences should be effected during your administration of the foreign Department, cannot fail to give you pleasure— it will afford some compensation for the Trouble you have had; and relieve you from the disagreeable correspondences, to which such Differences so frequently give occasion—

Accept my thanks for the many interesting Communications & marks of attention I have rec^d. from you in the Course of the negotiation, and be assured that I am, with every corresponding Sentiment Sir your most ob[edien]ᵗ. & most hble Servᵗ.

John Jay

The Hon'ble Edm. Randolph, Esqʳ. Secretary of State &c &c

ALS, DNA: Jay Despatches, 1794–95 (EJ: 04341). Marked: "Nᵒ. 24—". LbkC, NNC: JJ Lbk. 8.

1. See JJ to ER, 19 Nov. 1794, above.

2. Here JJ is referring to three letters recently sent to ER: "No. 21" is 17 Nov., ALS, marked "Duplicate", Jay Despatches, 1794–95 (EJ: 04335); LbkC, NNC: JJ Lbk. 8; "No. 22" is 19 Nov., above; and "No. 23" is 20 Nov. 1794, ALS, marked "Duplicate," Jay Despatches, 1794–95 (EJ: 04339); LbkC, NNC: JJ Lbk. 8.

3. For the efforts to send copies of the signed treaty to Congress, see the editorial note "Aftermath of the Jay Treaty: Responses, Ratification, and Implementation," below.

4. For Blaney, see JJ to AH, 11 Sept.; and JJ to ER, 19 Nov. 1794, both above.

5. JJ quoted this paragraph in his letter to Robert Goodloe Harper of 19 Jan. 1796, below, which was widely reprinted in the newspapers, and also strongly attacked by opponents of the Jay Treaty. For an example of an attack on JJ's statement, see *Publius*, "For the Argus, Number VI", *Argus, Greenleaf's New Daily Advertiser* (New York), 2 Apr. 1796.

To John Adams

London 21 Nov. 1794

Dear Sir

From the Day of my appointment to this mission, my Attention has been much withdrawn from my Friends, and confined to the Business which brought me here; & which has at last been terminated by a Treaty.[1] In future I shall have more Leisure to attend to my Friends, and to my own affairs—

Both your Sons arrived here in good Health— I wrote to my friend John lately, but as yet have not had a Letter from him— I ascribe this to his Prudence— In such Times and under such Circumstances much ought not to be written— Holland is in a sadway—[2]

It may seem extraordinary, but the fact appears to me to be, that this Nation has never been more united in any War than in this. Circumstances may press them to listen to Propositions of Peace, but not without Reluctance. If the War should continue, I think we may easily avoid being involved in it.

I write in too much haste to make this Letter interesting, by Remarks on the Treaty— they might be entertaining, but to you not necessary— with sincere Esteem and Regard I am Dear Sir Your Friend & hble Servᵗ

John Jay

His Excellency John Adams Esqʳ.

ALS, MHi: Adams (EJ: 06425).

1. The treaty was signed 19 Nov.

2. JQA and his brother Thomas Boyleston Adams arrived in London on 15 Oct., on their way to The Hague. They delivered dispatches to JJ. While in London, JQA discussed the treaty with JJ, as he describes in his diary. The brothers left London after 28 Oct. and arrived in the Netherlands on 30 Oct. JQA Diaries, 15–30 Oct. 1794, vol. 21, MHi: Adams; JQA Diaries Digital, http://www .masshist.org/jqadiaries/php/doc?id=jqad21_27 (accessed Aug. 2019). JJ's letter to JQA has not been found. See also the editorial notes "John Jay's Mission to London" and "Negotiating the Jay Treaty," both above.

To Sarah Livingston Jay

London 21 Novr. 1794

My dear Sally

I have within a few Weeks past written to you by the Eagle—by the Packet—and by Capt. Burril bound to New York—[1] This letter will go by the way of Virginia, under cover to the Secretary of State—

It will give you Pleasure to be informed that my mission has been successful— A Treaty was yesterday signed, and will be transmitted under the same cover with this Letter— I hope it will give Satisfaction to our Country in general. My further stay here not being very necessary, I exceedingly regret that I cannot immediately return to you—but the Season is too far advanced— I have not Health enough for a winters Voyage—[2] I have been for some Time past troubled with the Rheumatism— Having been advised to wear vests of fleecy Hosiery under my Shirt, I have had some made, and think them useful— for some Days past I find myself better, and I ascribe it to that Circumstance—

my Letter by the New York Ship was intended to be given to M^r. Blaney, who talked of going a passenger in her— he has since changed his mind— He is mentioned in that Letter.

Peter is well, and has written to you by the NYork Vessel— He is now attending the Tryal of Mr Tooke—[3] He has many advantages here, and is not a little indebted to you for them— my Love to the children &^{c}. Yours sincerely,

John Jay

Let Yaff forward the enclosed.

M^{rs}. Jay

ALS, NTucW (EJ: 02854). Addressed: "M^{rs}. Jay / Broadway / New York". Endorsed: ". . . rec^d. March / 9th. '95".

1. Letters not found. The Brig Eagle arrived in New York from London on 24 Dec. Daily Advertiser (New York), 24 Dec. 1794.

2. This passage was quoted in an address "To the Electors of the State of New York" by JJ's supporters Nicholas Cruger, Robert Troup, and Josiah Ogden Hoffman, dated 17 Apr. 1795, as evidence that JJ did not plan to wait until after the ratification of the treaty to return to America. This piece was intended to offset rumors spread by JJ's election opponents that he would not return on time to assume the post of governor. Also cited as evidence was a letter to Frederick Jay of 21 Nov. (not found), an extract of which had already been published in the newspapers announcing the signing of the Jay Treaty. See, for example, *New-York Daily Gazette*, 31 Jan.; *Independent Gazetteer* (Philadelphia), 4 Feb. 1795; one to a friend in the city dated 22 Nov. 1794, (not found); and another to SLJ of 5 Dec. 1794, ALS, PC: Kenneth W. Rendell (EJ: 06566). See also *Herald* (New York), 22 Apr. 1795. JJ arrived in New York on 28 May as the votes were being counted.

3. John Horne Tooke (1736–1812), a radical politician tried for treason in 1794 but later acquitted. PAJ recorded attending the trial from 17 to 22 Nov., feeling that "From the evidence which I heard I am of opinion that Tooke was not guilty of *high Treason*, but that that he certainly *was* guilty of very high Misdemeanor—". PAJ Diary, A, AD, NNC.

From John Quincy Adams

Amsterdam November 21. 1794.

Dear Sir

The enclosed Letter, accompanied a packet which I intended to have sent by M^r: Vall-travers; but having since immediate opportunities to America from hence I shall not trouble you with my dispatches at present.[1]

It is here said that on the meeting of Parliament the King of Great Britain is to mention in the speech from the throne the signature of a Convention for the settlement of the differences with America. This intelligence is extremely grateful to the merchants engaged in the American Commerce here, who are anxiously solicitous for the event of your negotiation, and whose curiosity is proportionable to their anxiety.[2]

A peace to their own Country is equally an object of speculation among them: in a political view they are in great need of it, but it comes quite as near their hearts as merchants. I believe however they say Peace, when there is no Peace nor any likelihood for it. So peculiarly unhappy and perilous is the condition of the Country, between the power of France and Britain, that either is competent to destroy, and neither to protect it.

Passive obedience now characterizes the people of this city. The leaders of the popular commotion which was So immediately crushed, are partly fled, and the rest have been sentenced to six years confinement in the work house, (a punishment usually reserved for the vilest malefactors,) and perpetual banishment afterwards. The remonstrants have surrendered their arms at command, and the measure is universally censured as rash and premature, by the people who must cordially wish it had been successful.

The 50 guineas for which you were so obliging as to give me an order, upon Messrs Cazenove, our bankers here have agreed to charge to my account. It will therefore be no further troublesome to you. Please to accept the renewal of my thanks for the supply.[3]

I write by the Post, and can therefore have no dependence upon the security of a seal; for which reasons I can only repeat the assurances of the most respectful attachment, with which I have the honour to be, Dear Sir, your very humble & obedient Servant,

John Q. Adams

His Excellency John Jay

ALS, NNC (EJ: 09688). Endorsed.

1. For Vall-travers, see JQA to JJ, 14 Nov. 1794, above.

2. George III announced the treaty in his speech on the opening of Parliament, 30 Dec. 1794. "I am happy to inform you, that I have concluded a treaty of amity, commerce, and navigation, with the United States of America, in which it has been my object to remove, as far as possible, all grounds of jealousy and misunderstanding, and to improve an intercourse beneficial to both countries." Cobbett, *Parliamentary History of England*, 31: 960–61.

3. In London, JQA found himself "rather short in the necessary article of cash," as funds had not arrived from the American bankers in Amsterdam. JJ was able to lend him 50 guineas. See JJ to ER, 5 Mar. 1795, LS, DNA: Jay Despatches, 1794–95 (EJ: 04293); JJ Account as Envoy Extraordinary to Great Britain, 26 Nov. 1795, NNC (EJ: 09227); JQA Diaries, 28 Oct. 1794, vol. 21, MHi: Adams; *JQA Diaries Digital*, http://www.masshist.org/jqadiaries/php/doc?id=jqad21_53 (accessed Aug. 2019); and the editorial note "John Jay's Mission to London," above.

To Grenville (private)

Royal Hotel—Pall Mall—22 Novr. 1794—

My Lord

I have had the pleasure of recieving the Letter, which your Lordship did me the Honor to write Yesterday; enclosing a copy of one that you had written to M^r. Hammond—[1] marks of confidence from those who merit it, are grateful to the human mind— they give occasion to Inferences, which by soothing self Love, produce agreable Emotions.

Being aware that our mutual Efforts to restore good Humour & good will between our two Countries, should be continued beyond the Date of the Treaty; I am happy that our Sentiments in this Respect coincide—

The Letters I have written to America, with the two Copies of the Treaty, which are already dispatched; leave me little to add on the Subject of your Lordship's Letter. They are indeed concise: for I had not Time to amplify. They will be followed by others less general, and more pointed. There are men among us to whom those Ideas will be familiar, and who will not omit to disseminate them. Their opinions and Example will have Influence; but it will be progressive, not sudden and general. The Storm I hope & believe will soon cease, but the Agitation of the Waters will naturally take some Time to subside— no man can with Effect say to them, ["]Peace be still["]² By casting *oil* upon them, they will doubtless be the sooner calmed— Let us do so—

I have a good opinion of M^r. Hammond— nay more, I really wish him well— The asperities however which have taken place, lead me to apprehend,³ that official Darts have frequently pierced thro' the official characters, and wounded the *men*. Hence I cannot forbear wishing that Mr Hammond had a better place; and that a Person well adapted to the existing State of Things ‸was‸ sent to succeed him.⁴ I make this Remark on the most mature Reflection, and found it on those active Principles in human Nature which, however they may be repressed, cannot easily be rendered dormant, except in Cases of greater magnanimity than Prudence will usually allow us to calculate upon.

It is not without Reluctance that I give this Remark a Place in this Letter— I class M^r. Hammond among those who I think are friendly to me— I have experienced his Attentions and Hospitality— not an unkind Idea passes in my mind respecting him— public and common Good is my object & my motive.—

That official Letters and Documents have been prematurely & improperly published in america is evident. I have not been sparing of animadversions on this Head, and flatter myself that more circumspection in future will be used—

The Consuls and other public officers and agents in the two Countries, will have it much in their power (especially in america, from the nature of the Governm^t. and State of Society) to promote or to check the Progress of Conciliation & Cordiality. I have but imperfect Knowledge of those now in the United States, except Sir John Temple, whose Conduct and Conversation appeared to me to be conciliatory.⁵ I have been informed very explicitly that M^r. Hamilton the Consul in Virginia is not esteemed, and that his private Character is far from being estimable— I mention this only as meriting Inquiry—⁶

There being no french Merchants Ships in the American Seas, the Privateers must either prey on neutral Vessels, or return without Spoil— Hence they become exposed to Temptations not easy for them to resist— The Privateers of two hostile Nations have no Desire to seek and to fight each other— Between mere Birds of Prey there are few Conflicts. If they were recalled, their Crews might be usefully employed in Ships of War or of Commerce.— Pardon the Liberty of these Hints— they occurred to me, and I let my Pen run on—perhaps too far.[7]

Permit me to assure you my Lord that my[8] Endeavours to cultivate amity & good will between our Countries and People, shall continue unremitted; and that they will not cease to be animated by your Lordship's Cooperation—

To use an Indian Figure—may the Hatchet be henceforth buried forever, and with it all the animosities which sharpened, and which threatened to redden it—[9] with the best wishes for your Happiness, and with real Esteem & Regard I am My Lord your Lordships most ob[t]. Serv[t]

John Jay

The Right Honorable Lord Grenville

ALS, UK-BL: Dropmore, Ms 59049. Marked: *"private"*. Endorsed. Dft, with numerous excisions only the most significant of which have been noted, NNC (EJ: 08504); *WJ*, 1: 340–42; *HPJ*, 4: 145–47; Hist. Mss. Comm., *Fortescue Manuscripts*, 3: 534–36.

1. See Grenville to JJ (private), 21 Nov. 1794, above. The enclosed letter from Grenville to Hammond, has not been found.

2. Mark 4: 39.

3. Here, in the draft, JJ excised "conflicts between the ministers, have exasperated the men—" before interlineating "official Darts have frequently pierced thro the official characters, and wounded the men."

4. In the margin in the draft, JJ added the following sentences until the words "the public and common good is my object and my motive." and marked them for inclusion here. The passage contains several excisions, largely illegible, but including the words "His dismissal is far from a Desire . . . on the contrary His promotion w[d] give me pleasure—public & mutual". Grenville recalled Hammond in September 1794, but appointed him under-secretary at the Foreign Office in November 1795. Hist. Mss. Comm., *Fortescue Manuscripts*, 3: xxxiv.

5. Here in the draft JJ excised "Lady Temple is an amiable woman generally esteemed—".

6. John Hamilton (d. 1816), British consul at Norfolk, Virginia, was a Scottish-born North Carolina merchant who became a Loyalist and served during the war of independence as commander of the Royal North Carolina Regiment. He went to London after the war where he sought and obtained some compensation for his losses. He was appointed consul at Norfolk in 1790 and served until the outbreak of the war of 1812, when he was recalled to England.

7. JJ added this paragraph in the margin in the draft and marked it for inclusion here.

8. Here, in the draft, JJ excised "Diligence in building on the Foundation which the Treaty has laid for mutual Friendship" before interlineating "Endeavours to cultivate amity and good will between our Countries and people".

9. Here, in the draft, JJ heavily excised seven lines which cannot be deciphered.

To Noah Webster

London 22 Nov[r] 1794

Sir

Since my arrival here the news papers have been sent you by almost every vessel to New York, that carried Letters from me— I hope you have rec[d]. them; tho' from the little attention with which such Packets are sometimes treated, it is possible that all of them may not have come to your Hands—[1]

These papers were the Morning Chronicle, the best *opposition* Paper, and the *Times*, which is the best *ministerial* Paper, for so they are distinguished here. I have rec[d]. two parcels of your Heralds, and wish all the papers in our Country were as well conducted.[2]

Two parcels are now sent to You— They will inform you of the present State of Affairs in Europe— there are many Conjectures about Peace— more Time is necessary to produce such Indications as may enable one to judge with tolerable precision on that Subject

our Affairs are settled by a Treaty, signed the 19th. Inst:—but it is probable you will have heard of it before this Letter will reach you: for the public prints having announced it, the Intelligence will pass to am[eric][a]. by various Conveyances, some of which may be more speedy than this— with the best wishes for your Prosperity I [*closing and signature cut out*]
Noah Webster Esq[r].—

AL, NN (EJ: 01033). Endorsed. Dft, NNC (EJ: 08917).

1. No letters from JJ to Webster earlier than this date have been found.

2. The *Morning Chronicle and London Advertiser*, founded in 1769 and published by James Perry (1756–1821) from 1789, was the leading opposition Whig paper. The leading pro-Pitt paper, *Times* (London), founded in 1785 as *Daily Universal Register* and known as the *Times* since 1788, was published by John Walters (1738/39–1812). Despite their partisan politics, both papers were known for their high editorial standards. Karl W. Schweizer, "Newspapers, Politics and Public Opinion in the Later Hanoverian Era," *Parliamentary History* 25 (2006): 42–43, 46.

Webster published the Federalist-leaning *American Minerva*, later *New-York Commercial Advertiser* (1797), from 1793 until its sale in 1803. Webster also published a semi-weekly edition of this paper titled *Herald; a Gazette for the Country* from 1794 to 1797.

To John Adams

London 24 Nov. 1794

Dear Sir

I wrote you a few Lines last Week—[1] This Morning I was favored with two Letters from your Son of the 14 & 20th. of this Month—[2] Parents are gratified by hearing of or from their children— The former Letter was Dated at the Hague— the latter at Amsterdam— He had been rec^d. and acknowledged by the States General, and on the 14th had "a gracious audience of the Stadtholder".— In his last Letter there is this Paragraph— "It is here said that on the Meeting of Parliam^t. the King of Great Britain is to mention in the Speech from the Throne, the Signature of a Convention for the Settlem^t. of the Differences with america. This Intelligence is extremely grateful to the Merchants engaged in the American Commerce here, who are anxiously sollicitous for the Event of your Negociation; and whose Curiosity is proportionable to their anxiety"— Before your Son left us I submitted to his Consideration the Draft of the Treaty, as it then stood—[3] with real Esteem and Regard I am Dear Sir Your Friend & Servt

John Jay

His Excellency John Adams Esqr.

ALS, MHi: Adams (EJ: 06426).

1. See JJ to JA, 21 Nov. 1794, above.

2. See JQA to JJ, 14 Nov., ALS, UkWC-A (EJ: 00047), and 21 Nov. 1794, ALS, NNC (EJ: 09688). See also JJ to JQA, 24 Nov. 1794, below.

3. JQA spent the mornings of 20, 21, and 22 Oct. discussing the treaty with JJ and Thomas Pinckney. In his diary, JQA recorded: "It is far from being satisfactory to those Gentlemen; it is much below the standard which I think would be advantageous to the Country, but with some alterations, which are marked down, and to which it seems there is a probability they will consent it is in the opinion of the two plenipotenitaries, preferable to a War, and when Mr Jay asked me my opinion, I answered that I could only acquiesce in that idea." JQA Diaries, 22 Oct. 1794, vol. 21, MHi: Adams; JQA Diaries Digital, http://www.masshist.org/jqadiaries/php/doc?id=jqad21_42 (accessed Aug. 2019). See also the editorial note, "Negotiating the Jay Treaty," above.

To John Quincy Adams

London 24 Nov. 1794

Dear Sir—

I was this morning fav^d. with yours of the 14 & 21 of this month, and congratulate you and your Brother on your arrival at the place of your Destination—[1]

On the 19 Inst. a Treaty between his Britannic Majesty and the united States was signed: whereby their Differences are terminated, & their Commerce regulated in a Way which I hope will prove satisfactory to both Parties—

As this Treaty is not yet ratified, it would be improper to published it.— The curiosity of many respecting its Contents must therefore remain for some time ungratified It however contains a Stipulation which need not be kept secret vizt. That it is not to be construed or operate contrary to existing Treaties between either of the Parties & other Powers—

Accept my thanks for the Information conveyed in your Letter— You are perfectly right to be circumspect in what you write thro' the Post Offices: Tho' I must say that since my arrival here I have had no Reason to complain— but this ought not to abate our Prudence—[2]

The Desire of Peace appears to me to gain ground— Commerce must feel its wounds—&c &c To reconcile great opposing Plans and Interests—to preserve Dignity from Humiliation, and to cause a great Variety of discordant Circumstances to harmonize is no easy Task— They who perform it well deserve Commendation—

I have rec^d. a Letter from Mr Valtravers requesting me to appoint him a private Sec^y with or without a Salary, in order that he may come to London, and by that appointment be shielded against some Suit or action which he apprehends would be brought against him. as your Letter has a post mark on it, I presume it did not come by him, and that he may have postponed his Journey in Expectation of my answer. Be so obliging when next you see him, to let him know that my Secretary does not require Assistance; and that to give him an appointment merely as a Cover, would not in my Opinion be proper—[3]

The Issue of the Insurrection in Am[eric]^a. still remains unknown here. I heard to Day that a Vessel had arrived from Maryland, but as yet no Intelligence by her has reached me. If she should have brought any thing interesting, I will write it to you— Remember me to your Brother— with great Esteem & Regard I am Dear Sir Your most ob^t Servt.

John Jay

The honb. John Q. Adams Esqr. minister of the U.S. at the Hague—

ALS, MHi: Adams. Endorsed: ". . . Rec^d 28th. / Answ^d 2^d. Dec^r". Dft, NNC (EJ: 09690). For JQA's reply, see 2 Dec. 1794, below.

1. JQA to JJ, 14 and 21 Nov. 1794, both above. JJ sent a detailed summary with extensive quotations of these letters to JA on 24 Nov., above.

2. In his letter of 21 Nov., JQA remarked "I write by the Post, and can therefore have no dependence upon the security of a seal".

3. For Vall-travers's request to be appointed secretary to JJ, see his letter to JJ, 28 Oct., ALS, NNC (EJ: 07214). JQA informed JJ of his intention to give letters and a packet meant for the Secretary of State to Vall-travers to deliver to JJ in London. For this letter and more on Vall-travers, see JQA to JJ, 14 Nov., above.

From John Quincy Adams

The Hague December 2. 1794.

Dear Sir.

On my return here at the close of the last week from Amsterdam I received your favour of the 24th: ultimo:[1] and request you to accept my thanks for the communications it contains. By public report I had already heard not only that the Treaty was signed, but the pretended purport of many articles of its contents. I had already felt myself obliged ∧to leave∧ ardent, and in some instances inquisitive curiosity in the same suspence in which I found it upon this subject. Upon the state of the negotiation when I left London, I could give our friends here no other information, than what resulted from public report in that place, from which all I had collected was that the affair was in a probable train of settlement. Since the receipt of your Letter I have taken the liberty to mention the stipulation which you observe requires not to be kept secret.

The desire of Peace among all the friends and supporters of the Government in this Country is animated to the highest degree, by the prevailing opinion of an irresistible necessity. The task of essentially contributing to reconcile opposing interests, to preserve Dignity from Humiliation and to harmonize discordant circumstances, is in the public opinion once more assigned to the same person, who in that opinion has recently performed it with so much ability. The hopes which have been indulged in this particular are at this moment however restrained by the general idea, that an allied government is irrevocably determined upon the experiment of another campaign.

I have been informed since my return from Amsterdam that M^r: Valltravers is gone to England. He made ~~the~~ a similar application to that mentioned in your letter, to me, for which he assigned the same reason. I told him that such an appointment from me, would certainly afford him no protection in England; and even if it could, a compliance ~~to~~ ∧with∧ his request on my part was inconsistent with my ideas of propriety.[2]

I received this day from Amsterdam a Baltimore Newspaper of 30th. September. It contains no intelligence of consequence.[3]

The armies in this Country do not at present appear to be very active. The Duke of York is here. There appears to be some difficulty about the reception of british troops into the cities. It is said the magistracy of Amsterdam have taken a resolution against the measure as it respects that capital. I am, with every Sentiment of respect and attachment, Dear Sir, your very humble & obedient Servant,

John Q. Adams.

His Excellency John Jay Envoy Extraordinary of the United States. London.

ALS, NNC (EJ: 09685).

1. See JJ to JQA, 24 Nov. 1794, above. The stipulation he refers to is "That it [the treaty] is not to be construed or operate contrary to existing Treaties between either of the Parties & other Powers—". For JQA's opinion of the negotiations, see JJ to JA, 24 Nov. 1794, note 3, above; and the editorial note "Negotiating the Jay Treaty," note 35, above.

2. For Vall-travers's request to be appointed secretary to JJ, see his letter to JJ, 28 Oct. 1794, ALS, NNC (EJ: 07214), and JJ's letter to JQA, 24 Nov. 1794, above.

3. Probably either the *Baltimore Daily Intelligencer* or *Edward's Baltimore Daily Advertiser*.

From John Trumbull

[[London,] 10th. Decr. 1794.]

Sir

In consequence of your directions, I spoke to Mr. Burges of the propriety of making some acknowledgement on your part to the Two Clerks who wrote the Copies of the Treaty;—and in consequence of our conversation I have this morning enclosed Ten Pounds to Him, with a Request that He will divide it to the Two, according to their Merits.[1]

This Conversation introduced the general Subject of Presents, when Mr. Burges informed me that it was the established Custom here to present to the Foreign Minister who concluded a Treaty. the Portrait of the King, elegantly set, "and on this Occasion" added He, "I have by Lord Grenville's direction, already given Orders to the Kings Jeweller to have the Picture, and Box which is to enclose it, finished immediately;— It is also customary to make a proportional present to the Secretary of such minister;—and these are given on the Exchange of the Ratifications."— I answer'd "that I believed it to be otherwise with us;—and that the Officers of the United States were even prohibited to receive Presents of any kind, from any foreign Prince or State."

I submit to your Judgement, how far my answer was right;— and how far it was intended by the Constitution to prohibit the ministers of the United States receiving Presents of this Nature.[2] I am with every Sentiment of Respect Your most Obliged Servant

Jno. Trumbull

Mr. Jay

ALS, NNC (EJ: 07201). Addressed: "Mʳ. Jay / &c. &c. &c." Endorsed: "... abᵗ. presents." *HPJ*, 4: 148.

1. See JJ Account book, 1794–95, 14, D, NNC.

2. Article 1, section 9, clause 8 of the Constitution stated "And no Person holding any Office of Profit or Trust under them, shall, without the Consent of the Congress, accept of any present, Emolument, Office, or Title, of any kind whatever, from any King, Prince, or foreign State." However, it was soon recognized that refusing such gifts would be a diplomatic liability. JJ consulted with Thomas Pinckney on the subject. Pinckney, in a letter of 10 Apr. 1795 [ALS, NNC (EJ: 09464); C, ScHi (EJ: 02604)], wrote that before he went to London, TJ told him that he could accept such gifts, as "the acceptance of the present can have no influence on the conduct of the minister" because, among several reasons, it was given to all foreign ministers indiscriminately and after negotiations were completed. In TJ's view, to refuse such gifts, "might be considered as an offensive peculiarity in the ministers of the United States." See also GW's diary entry, 29 Apr. 1790, *PGW: Diaries*, 6: 70–72. According to his son William, JJ thought it more prudent to adhere to the Constitution and respectfully decline the gift. *WJ*, 1: 347–48. JJ had encountered this problem before in 1786 as Minister for Foreign Affairs, when the Spanish king gifted him the horse Hermoso. See Introduction; JJ to Diego de Gardoqui, 1 Mar. 1786; JJ to Charles Thomson, 2 Mar. 1786; and the editorial note "Negotiations with Gardoqui Reach an Impasse," *JJSP*, 4: xxviii, 304–6, 365.

To John Quincy Adams

London 13 Decʳ. 1794

Dear Sir

I am much obliged by your Letter of the 2ᵈ. of this month—[1] your Letter to Mʳ. Randolph goes by the *aurora* to New York. we have had several late arrivals from thence & from Ph[iladelphi]ᵃ.— In the *Adriana* from the latter Place Mʳ. Samˡ. Bayard came passenger, He is appointed by the Governmᵗ. to superintended the Prosecution of Claims & appeals in the Capture Causes.—[2] The Insurrection in Pennsylvania was dissipating fast, and Govᵗ. will derive Strength from its Suppression. The general Irritation had considerably abated. Specie and Emigrants were daily arriving— Trade brisk, and the prices of all our Productions unusually high. It was believed that there would be a large majority of fœderal Representatives returned to Congress. Mʳ. Smith of Sº. Carolina was re-elected. notwithstanding the Efforts of our Jacobins, affairs in general had assumed a more favorable aspect.[3]

Appearances here indicate another Campaign. The Issue of it cannot fail of being important in its Consequences. If the united States preserve peace and Tranquility, they will have Reason to be thankful.— I become daily more and more convinced that the best Disposition towards us prevails here.—

Remember me to your Brother, and be assured of the Esteem and Regard with which I am Dear Sir Your most obed^t. & h'ble Servt

John Jay

The Hon'ble John Q: Adams Esqr—

ALS, MHi: Adams. Addressed: "The Hon'ble / John Q: Adams Esqr. / minister of the United States of / america at / The Hague". "His Exc^y John Jay / London 13 Decr 94 / Rec^d 9 Jany 95 / Answ^ed Do Do". Dft, NNC (EJ: 09691); HPJ, 4: 149.

1. JQA to JJ, 2 Dec. 1794, above.

2. Samuel Bayard arrived in England several days earlier, bringing news and letters to JJ. See JJ to ER, 10 Dec. 1794, ALS, DNA: Jay Despatches, 1794–95 (EJ: 04343).

3. Republicans gained the majority in the House of Representatives in this election, with 59 total seats. William L. Smith (1758–1812), Federalist and close ally of AH, was reelected with 51.7% of the vote. Michael J. Dubin, *United States Congressional Elections, 1788–1997* (Jefferson, N.C., and London, 1998), 10–11.

Peter Jay Munro to Peter Augustus Jay

N. York ~~19th.~~ ₐ278^thₐ Decr. 1794.

D^r. Peter,

The Election for Representatives in Congress is just closed—in Albany M^r. Glen in Saratoga M^r. Van Allen & in Dutchess M^r. Bailey are unquestionably re-elected— The issue [of] the elections [in] Ulster & Orange will probably prove unfavorable to the foederal Candidate. Eight[1] days before the election it was proposed that old Chief Justice Morris sh^d. be set up in opposition to M^r. Cortlandt, in W. Chest^r & Rich[mon]^d prefering him to our other Candidate[2] I acquiesed in the nomination & M^r. Har~~r~~ison, M^r.ₐP^h[ilip].ₐ Livingston & myself wrote him a Letter upon the Subject, w^h. brought him to town. A Conference ensued that ended in his agreeing to become a Candidate. M^r. Harison Went to the Yonkers and Col^o. Fish to Richmond, and secured the Interest of M^r. Cortlandt & Judge Ryerson— expresses were sent to every Part of the County, and as I had suffered myself to engage in the Cause I was prevailed on to go into the County—[3] few men are more unpopular than the late Ch[ief]. Justice and I doubt whether his direct Influence could have procured him 100 votes.[4]

By dint of exertion[5], we have been enabled to divide the ₐformerₐ County—[6] and had the latter given the stipulated Number of votes our success w^d. have been certain. at present it is problematical—but appearances *rather* favor M^r. Morris. The exertions made at this election serve as preparations for our Grand election next Spring, and this Idea had great weight in engaging me to take active part[7] on this occasion. A Letter from your side of the Water declaring the Certainty of your return, and ascertaining the precise time of embarcation is highly necessary— from what I c^d. see and learn in the upper part of the state and from Col. Burr's electioneering Agent there (who mistook me for M^r. Prevost) it will be impossible for Clinton, Burr & the Chan[cello]^r. to prevent Uncle Jay's election.

In N York E^d. Livingston was [in] Opposition to M^r. Watts. The event is very precarious— On Long Island Saml. Jones was the federal Candidate his election is doubtfull. In Columbia Gilbert is re-elected.

Hamilton has given notice of his intended Resignation & it is said Knox & Wolcott also resign.[8]

Present my ∧best∧ Respects to Uncle Jay, tell him that we are all well and that on the 23^d. Ins^t. the mill at Bedford began to grind. Adieu Dr Cousin—

P.J.M.

Dft, NNMus (EJ: 00440). Endorsed. This text is elaborately reworked and contains multiple interlineations and excisions, largely stylistic, that have not been noted. Significant excisions are indicated in the endnotes.

1. Here PJM excised "six" and replaced it with "Eight".

2. Here PJM excised "this was truly with me was truly ag^t. the Grain, however as I preferred him to Mr. P^h. Livingston & no other candidate could be thought of".

3. Here PJM excised "Never did I find a man who filled an important public office so entirely destitute ∧of∧ friends willing to support him ∧as the late C^h. Justice. I even∧ and I".

4. Of the candidates for Congress mentioned above, the following were elected or reelected; Henry Glen (1739–1814), Federalist, who served from 1793 to 1800; John Evert Van Alen (1749–1807), Federalist, who served from 1793 to 1798; Ezekiel Gilbert, Federalist, who served from 1793 to 1796; Theodorus Bailey (1758–1828), Republican, who served 1793 to 1796 and from 1799 to 1802; Edward Livingston (Republican), who served 1795 to 1800; Philip Van Cortlandt (Republican), who served 1793 to 1808. Federalists Samuel Jones, Richard Morris, state chief justice (1779–90), and John Watts (1749–1836), who served in Congress in 1793–94, were not elected.

On the campaign for Richard Morris, see *Daily Advertiser* (New York), 17 Dec. 1794; and the *Albany Gazette*, 16 Feb. 1795, which asserted: "Westchester & Richmond—Gen. Van Cortlandt is re-elected.— The contest in the district was so well managed by the parties that the successful candidate had but about 20 votes ahead of his competitor, Richard Morris, Esq."

5. Here PJM excised "in some towns".

6. Here PJM excised "At Bedford 231 votes were taken & at Rye 120—Greeneburgh 111[?]".

7. Here PJM excised "in the support of M^r. Morris than he imagines. I will ensure Uncle Jay a majority of six hundred votes in that the County ∧of W. Chester∧ if that comes ∧continues∧ if he is then a candidate—".

8. Here PJM excised "Aunt Jay & William have gone to Rye to pass the Hollidays at Rye— The Mill at Bedford was set agoing began to grind on the 23^d Inst.— The *Sansom* has sailed ∧at last∧ two or three a few Days ago this time she carrys".

Peter Augustus Jay to Sarah Livingston Jay

London 2ᵈ. January 1795

Dear Mama

I had yesterday the pleasure of recᵍ. your letter of the 15 Novʳ.[1] upon my return to town from a very pleasant journey to Edinburgh, where I have been for the purpose of becoming a witness to a deed to Cousin P. Munro from his Father.[2] As I went in the Mail Coach which travels without ceasing even in the night, I stopped a day at York to recover from the fatigue & see the curiosities of the place. Another day was spent in the same manner between Durham and Newcastle, & yet I reached Edinburgh (400 miles distant from London) in 4 1/2 days. While there I was introduced to most of the remarkable people, & heard a sermon from Dʳ. Blair—[3] Dʳ. Adair our fellow passenger to England, who had been some days in London, returned with me to Edinburgh & was exceedingly useful to me indeed; he means to return with us in The spring in order to settle in America.[4] You will perhaps expect me to give you a description of Edinburgh, but this I assure you is utterly impossible, as it is entirely different from any thing of it's kind. One part however which has been lately built is an exception. It is called the New Town & far exceeds in beauty any thing I have seen— I remained there about ten days—

A Circumstance which you mention in one of your letters afforded us very great pleasure you say that you have not had occasion for the Doctor since our departure— We have been equally favored— Papa has indeed been several times indisposed but never seriously & excepting a little Rheumatism is now perfectly well— As for myself I have not experienced a single hour of sickness even of the slightest kind since I landed at Falmouth—

As our letters are to go by the Packet & it is now high time to put them in the Post Office, I shall not be able to write to my Uncles or to sisters, I must therefore beg you to wish them all ∧in∧ my name a merry Christmas & Happy New Year— With my earnest prayers that you may enjoy very, very, many of both I remain, Your Affectionᵗᵉ. Son,

Peter Augustus Jay

Mʳˢ. S. Jay

ALS, NNC (EJ: 06052). Addressed: "Mʳˢ. Jay / Broadway / *New York*". Endorsed, by SLJ: ". . . recᵈ. 23ᵈ. April Do 1795"; second endorsement in different hand: "P.A. Jay / 2 Janʸ. 1795." Dft, CSmH (EJ: 11228).

1. SLJ to JJ, 15 Nov. 1794, ALS, NNC (EJ: 13700).

2. For PAJ's journey to Edinburgh, see PJM to JJ, 16 Oct. 1794, and the editorial note "John Jay's Mission to London," both above.

3. Hugh Blair (1718–1800), of Edinburgh, was a noted minister of the Church of Scotland and former professor of rhetoric and belle lettres at the University of Edinburgh. Blair's multivolume publications, *Sermons* (Edinburgh, 1777), and *Lectures on rhetoric and belles lettres* (London, 1783), proved highly popular on both sides of the Atlantic.

4. James Makittrick Adair (1728–1802), Scottish physician and reformer. An acquaintance of John Sinclair and Edward Newenham, Adair owned lands in the U.S. and wished to immigrate. He accompanied the Jays on their voyage to Great Britain. See RK to JJ, 2 May, ALS, NNC (EJ: 06688), and Robert Morris to JJ, 2 May 1794, ALS, NNC (EJ: 07024), both introducing Adair. See also James Adair to JJ, 19 Dec. 1794, ALS, NNC (EJ: 05403), in which he notifies JJ of PAJ's safe arrival and recommends barristers for the Admiralty cases.

To Samuel Bayard (First Letter)

[[London] 5ᵗʰ. Day of Janʸ [1795]]
To Samuel Bayard Esqʳ.

Whereas the Secretary of State of the united States of america hath officially informed me that the President of the said united States has been pleased to appoint you agent to manage claims and appeals in Cases of irregular or illegal Captures or Condemnations of american Vessels or other Property under Colour of authority or Commissions from his britannic majesty and whereas it will be necessary to the Prosecution of the said Claims & appeals that the usual Security for costs in each Cause be given and whereas Henry ~~Mr. Bird~~ Merttins Bird, Benjamin Savage, and Robert Bird¹ ₐtrading under the firm of Bird Savage and Birdₐ have offered to become Sureties ₐjointly or separately as may be requiredₐ in the usual Sums and Form for the payment of such Cash as may be legally decreed against any such Claimants ~~and~~ ₐorₐ appellants ₐ[*In margin at bottom of page and marked for insertion here*] and also for the payment of such sum or sums of money which they may be called upon to advance for the prosecution of such claims and appealsₐ on the Faith and Engagement of the said united States to indemnify them for any Losses or Damages which they may sustain thereby.² And whereas I am empowered and instructed to authorize you to execute Bonds and make Engagements (under my Direction) to effectuate the said purposes now therefore I do hereby authorize you, in your Capacity of agent aforesaid to pledge the Faith of the said United States to the said Bird Savage and Bird that the said united States shall and will well and truly indemnify and keep harmless the said Bird Savage and Bird and each and every of them, and their respective Heirs Ex[ecutor]ʳˢ. and adm[inistrato]ʳˢ. from and against all Damages Cash and Charges which they shall ~~legally~~ sustain or ₐnecessarilyₐ be put to, by Reason of their becoming Sureties as aforesaid and will well and truly repay to them their Heirs Ex[ecuto]rs. or adm[inistrator]rs. whatever Sums of money they or either of them shall be ~~legally~~ obliged to pay on that account ∧together with Interest for the same∧—[3] Given under my Hand and Seal this 5th Day of Jany Sealed & Delivered In the Presence of[4]

Dft, NNC (EJ: 12835). C, embedded in JJ to ER, 7 Jan. 1795, DNA: Jay Despatches, 1794–95 (EJ: 04345); LbkC, embedded in 7 Jan. 1795, JJ to ER, NNC: JJ Lbk. 8; *ASP: FR*, 1: 513.

1. Henry Merttins Bird (1755–1818), his younger brother Robert Bird (b. 1760), and Benjamin Savage (b. 1750), originally of South Carolina, were partners in the London mercantile and banking firm Bird, Savage & Bird, which they established in 1782.

2. JJ also drafted an instrument authorizing Bayard to pledge the faith of the United States to the firm of Bird, Savage and Bird to indemnify them for any losses or damages sustained. Much of this text is quoted within it. Dft, NNC (EJ: 12834); C, embedded in JJ to ER, 7 Jan. 1795, DNA: Jay Despatches, 1794–95 (EJ: 04345); LbkC, NNC: JJ Lbk. 8. *ASP: FR*, 1: 513–14. JJ composed further detailed procedural instructions to Bayard of the same date, below.

3. Here in the margin, JJ placed the following note: "here attend to the first Quere in the draft of Mr Bayard's engagement".

4. In the copies, the signatories for this certification are listed as JT and PAJ.

To Samuel Bayard (Second Letter)

[London, 5 January 1795]

To Samuel Bayard Esqr. appointed by the President of the United States of America, Agent for Claims and Appeals &c &c &c

It Having been made my Duty to give you Instructions relative to your Agency, I think it expedient to give you the following for the present, and will add to them as circumstances may require.

Agreeable to the Advice which you have already received from me You will procure a proper Register, and enter in it the Title of every Cause, and note the different Papers which belong to it, and minute from time to time every Step and Proceeding in the Cause

You will I think find it useful to class all the Cases according to their discriminating and governing principles *and* Merits;— considering the Number and Variety of Cases, this cannot be hastily accomplished; much Examination Care and Judgment will be indispensable to performing it with Accuracy;— but without such a Classification there will be Danger of Confusion:— Order facilitates every kind of Business.

Make a correct Statement of One or Two Cases of each Class for the Consideration and Opinion of Counsel,— take their Opinions in Writing and send them to the Secretary of State.

With respect to such of the Classes as in their Opinion may be prosecuted with a prospect of Success, put all the Cases of such Classes as speedily as possible into a State for Decision:—but select one or two to take the lead, for formal argument; To the End that the Decrees in those Cases may become Rules whereby to decide all others under similar Circumstances;— there can be no use in expending Time and Money in causing long Briefs and laboured Arguments to be prepared in a great many Causes, whose Merits are essentially alike.

If any one or more of the Classes cannot in the Opinion of Counsel be prosecuted with a prospect of Success, you will nevertheless file the Claims and Appeals, but not proceed further, untill you shall have sent the Opinions to the Secretary of State, and received his instructions, provided there be time:— Otherwise it will be best to give One or Two of the strongest Cases a strenuous Trial, even through the last Resort; and in the mean time take care that none of the others go against you by Default.

You will find, that in many of the Cases, necessary Documents and Proofs are wanting:— in such Cases state the Defects immediately to the Secretary of State: and (when opportunities offer) write also to the Claimants or Owners; point out very particularly what you want, and the manner in which the Business should be done, and if you have doubts, consult your Counsellors:— You know that Commissions for examining Witnesses abroad may be had, and may be expedient in Cases where extra Proofs may be had, and be permitted:— By all means avoid Delay, and take care to be particularly, perspicuous and explicit in your Communications

Money will from time to time be wanted to defray the Expences incident to the Suits;— Mention this to the Secretary of State, in order that proper Measures for the purpose may be taken without Loss of Time;— The Fund I am preparing for those Expences will not be adequate;—

In some of the Cases the Claimants or Owners will probably constitute Agents of their own to manage them;— should papers respecting such Cases be in your hands, you will deliver them to such Agents, taking their Receipts for the same;— cultivate a good understanding with such Agents;— be useful to them, and endeavour to dispose them to be useful to you.

You will regularly inform the Secretary of State of your Progress and Prospects in the Business: and I think it would be well to submit to his Consideration the Expediency of sending you a formal Appointment together with such instructions as may be deemed proper.

Whenever an application to the Government here would in your Opinion be advisable, and on every other Occasion when you may desire Advice and Aid, you will apply to me, or in my absence to M^r. Pinckney.

You have undertaken an arduous task,—great Responsibility is attached to it;— Although you have able Counsellors in S^r. W^m. Scott and Doctor Nicholl,[1] yet unremitted Attention and Diligence on your part will be absolutely necessary to your giving even a moderate Degree of Satisfaction to the many persons whose important Interests are confided to your Care and Management;— You will always find me ready to assist you, in so conducting your Agency, as to render it beneficial and satisfactory to them, and honourable to yourself.[2] Given under my Hand and Seal at London the Fifth day of January in the Year of Our Lord, One Thousand Seven Hundred and Ninety five.

C, embedded in JJ to ER, 7 Jan. 1795, DNA: Jay Despatches, 1794–95 (EJ: 04345); LbkC, embedded in JJ to ER, 7 Jan. 1795, NNC: JJ Lbk. 8; Typescript, NNC (EJ: 12531). *ASP: FR*, 1: 514.

1. See William Scott to JJ, and William Scott and John Nicholl to JJ, both 10 Sept. 1794, above; and Sterling, "Letters of Samuel Bayard," 418–19.

2. Bayard faced a daunting task when he took up his informal appointment as American agent for claims and appeals in London in early 1795. The admiralty courts and Lords of Appeal, he observed, were marred by dilatory process, undue prejudice, and government interference, causing Bayard to doubt whether these bodies would award just compensation to American merchants and shipowners. A heated exchange between Bayard and British officials over the Court's handling of the ship *Betsey* nearly derailed the efforts of the recently established claims commission. Mounting expenses also proved burdensome as Bayard took on more legal counsel to deal with the heavy caseload. Despite these difficulties, the work of the commission carried on, and in late July 1797, Bayard could report with some satisfaction that upwards of £56,000 had been awarded to American claimants. For more on Bayard's role as the American agent in London, see Sterling, "Letters of Samuel Bayard," 408–24. The impact of the *Betsey* case is discussed in Perkins, *First Rapprochement*, 55. The high cost of attorney's fees is discussed in Bayard to JJ, 27 Jan. 1795 (EJ: 04352); embedded in JJ to ER, 31 Jan. 1795 (EJ: 04351); *ASP: FR*, 1: 515. Bayard outlined his strategy for facilitating the successful conclusion of legal claims in Bayard to JJ, 31 Mar. 1795, below.

From David Hartley

Bath Jan^ry 5 1795

Dear Sir

I have been requested by some very intimate friends who are now in france, to make application to you to assist them in procuring a pass port to quit France. I will explain the case to you, but I must previously explain the ground of the application personally to you. The parties are M^r & Mrs Miniconi. Mrs Miniconi is the Daughter of the late Mr Wm Neate a merchant of London, & jointly with her Sisters proprietress of land & of debts due to her late father in America. The husband of one of her Sisters (Mr Chapman) is now in America for the purpose of settling all the concerns of property, derived from the late Mr Neate to his daughters. But all such views & propositions must be suspended from final conclusion, as long as Mrs Miniconi & her husband are detained in france. Upon these grounds the case falls in to the American department. The favor for w^h I apply to you, is that you will be so good as to recommend the case to the American Minister at Paris. My friends did apply some time ago to Mr Morris the late American Minister at Paris, from whom they received a very polite & friendly answer regretting that his departure from Paris, w^h was precisely at the period of the application, deprived him of the power of giving them the assistance wch he expressed himself very desirous to have given.[1]

The case is this. Mr Miniconi is the grandson of an Italian gentleman who married an English lady. My friend the present Mr Miniconi, has married one of the daughters of Mr Neate, Miss Phillis Neate. All her properties & claims are therefore become his property & claims. Mr Miniconi, who has very considerable property, hired a country seat at Caudebec in Normandy, before the Revolution. During a considerable period of the Revolution, his friends in England heard nothing of him But we have lately received letters, that he is still resident at his house in France, and at liberty. I understand that they have no request to make on the score of personal liberty, but the permission of a passport for themselves & their Servants, to go into Switzerland. It is certainly to be understood that M^r & Mrs Miniconi are influenced by a strong desire to rejoin their friends after an anxious absence of many years, on account of various family concerns, wch have been suspended during the years of their absence. The special application thro the American channel arises from their landed property & claims in America. I am very much connected in friendship with them, & with all their friends and connections. I shall be very much obliged to you if you can procure a passport for them, & their Servants, in any manner that you may think the most adviseable. I go into Berkshire tomorrow. Be so good as to favour me with a line to Bucklebury near Newbury Berks. Pray remember me kindly to Mr Trumbull, & M^r P Jay & all friends. I am Dear Sir Your sincere friend & humble Sev^t.[2]

D Hartley

To His Excellency John Jay Esqr &c &c &c

ALS, NNC (EJ: 05671). Endorsed.

1. William Neate (1717–75), wealthy London merchant in the American trade. He and his wife Christina (1722–1800) had four daughters, Christina Chapman (1750–1823), Mary Neate (1755–

1830), Jermima Powell (1758–1836), and Phillis Meniconi (1759–1821). Phillis was married to Charles Meniconi (d. 1796). Christina's husband was Henry Chapman (1744–1798). Will of William Neate in *Abstract of Wills on File in the Surrogate's Office: City of New York* (New York, 1904), 37 (13): 210–13.

2. For JJ's reply, see JJ to Hartley, 8 Jan. 1795, below. See JJ to James Monroe, 28 Aug. 1794, above, and the editorial note "John Jay's Mission to London," and note 31, above, for other instances of JJ's inquiries in France for missing persons.

From John Sloss Hobart

New York 7ᵗʰ Janʸ 1795

My dear Sir

Having heard this morning that the Adriana is to sail in a day or two for London I embrace the opportunity of my being in town to wish you and the family with you the compliments of the season. I paid my respects to Mʳˢ. Jay on coming to town, and found her in good health and sprits having just returned from a visit to our Friends at Rye, but I suppose you'll hear the particulars of that from herself— however, *since I am up* I have to regret that the canvassers did not make a board yesterday as it prevents me from giving you the result of our election of Representatives to congress, in the western counties it is supposed Judge Cooper has succeeded, Mʳ. Russell from Washington, Glen Gilbert and Bailey are supposed to be reelected, the cidevant Ch. Justice has run Cortlandt hard if not beat him— Watts or Ed[war]ᵈ Livingston for NYork Jones or Havens for Longisland in the doubt-full gender—¹ Govʳ. Clinton has been in bad health for some months past, and is at present so much indisposed, that, I am told, he has apprised the Legislature who were ∧to meet∧ at Poughkeepsie the day before yesterday, of the very great improbability of his being able to meet them *there*, they must therefore come *here*— I should not be surpized if this circumstance should induce the Northern folks to insist on bringing forward Mʳ. Yates as a candidate at the ensuing election for governor, as they would by that fix the government at Albany without the formality of removing a Governor— the public mind is much distracted at present on that subject—² the uncertainty of the time of your return occasions much perplexity— many will contend stoutly for holding you up as the candidate your absence notwithstanding, while others, and those not a few, are fearfull *that* will be an insuperable objection with the bulk of mankind³

This much for the politics and parties of the State. The changes that have taken place and are expected at court you will hear from other hands—

Professor Kent has commenced his course of lectures, the introductory lecture has been printed at the request of the Trustees of the college. he gave me two copies one of which by his desire I inclose to you—[4] You will be pleased to hear that I am at last fixed at Throggs Neck, tho' my house is not yet furnished. I experience a growing attachment to the place, and flatter myself with a pleasing close to life, it will heighten the enjoyment of the good things, with which I am surrounded if a gracious providence will permit the friend I most respect and esteem to return home and sometimes participate with me in it— Adieu yours most sincerely and affectionately

Jn°. Sloss Hobart

M[r]. Ch. Justice Jay

ALS, NNC (EJ: 05678). Addressed: "His Excellency John Jay Esquire / Envoy Extra. and Minister Plenipotentiary / from the U.S. of America to the King of / Great Britain". Endorsed: ". . . rec[d]. 13 march / an[d]. D°. D° 1795". JJ's reply not found.

1. In New York's 1794 elections for the U.S. House of Representatives, Federalist William Cooper defeated his main opponent, Republican John Winn, in District 10 by a vote tally of 2,462–1,417. Federalist John Evert Van Alen trounced Republican Thomas Tredwell (1743–1831) in District 7, 1,109–298. Republican John Williams (1752–1806) defeated Federalist Ebenezer Russell (1747–1836) in District 9, 1,297–1,079. Republican Edward Livingston defeated Federalist John Watts in District 1, 1,843–1,638. Republican Jonathan Havens (1757–99) defeated Federalist Samuel Jones in District 2, 815–494. Republican Theodorus Bailey defeated Federalist David Brooks in District 4, 1,449–1,090. Federalist Ezekiel Gilbert defeated Republican John Bay in District 6, 1,168–441. Federalist Henry Glen defeated Republican Abraham Yates by a wide margin in District 8, 677–20. Republican Philip van Cortlandt defeated former New York Chief Justice Richard Morris in a close race in District 3, 991–972. A New Nation Votes (accessed Aug. 2018).

In a letter to PAJ, PJM informed his cousin (and therefore JJ) of his efforts on behalf of the Federalists, in part to prepare for JJ's candidacy for governor. In addition, he shared the latest political gossip, commenting about Morris that "few men are more unpopular than the late Ch. Justice and I doubt whether his ~~own~~ direct ~~interest~~ ˰Influence˰ could have procured him 100 votes." PJM to PAJ, 28 Dec. 1794, Dft, NNMus (EJ: 00440).

2. Albany became the permanent state capital under JJ's governorship in March 1797. See the editorial note "The Capital Moves to Albany," below.

3. In his letter to PAJ, PJM wrote "A Letter from your side of the Water declaring ~~with precision~~ the Certainty of your return, and ascertaining the precise time of ~~your~~ embarcation is highly necessary." In February 1795, Federalist election committees in New York City and Albany nominated JJ as their candidate for governor, while the Democratic-Republicans nominated New York Chief Justice Robert Yates of Albany as their candidate. Young, Democratic Republicans, 433–34.

4. Enclosure not found, but see An introductory lecture to a course of law lectures, delivered November 17, 1794. By James Kent, Esquire, professor of law in Columbia College. Published at the request of the trustees (New York, 1794; Early Am. Imprints, series 1, no. 27183).

From William Short

Madrid Jan. 7th. 1795

Sir

I had the honor of recieving by the last English mail your letter of the 24th. of Novr.[1] & have to return your many thanks for the communication you are so good as to make me, of the signature of a treaty with H[is]. B[ritannic]. M[ajesty]. The progress of this negotiation has been flawed, with an attentive & anxious interest, by all the observing part of Europe, & more peculiarly of course by all the agents of the U.S. employed in Europe Had you not been prevented by the considerations you mention, from corresponding with me on the subject, you may be assured therefore Sir, of the extreme pleasure it would have given me, & which wd. have been heightened by the consideration that it would have contributed to the public service, under the circumstances in which I was placed. I am much flattered by what you are pleased to say of my character, & really gratified to find that the cause of your silence proceeded from your knowlege of the infidelity of the post-office, which certainly doesn't admit of confiding to it under the mere sanction of a seal, anything that requires secrecy.— I consider it so desirable to have the honor of your correspondence that I felt some difficulty in restraining myself from greeting you (on learning through the English gazettes your arrival at London) & solliciting it— My full persuasion however that if you concieved it proper you would not omit it, & my desire at the same time not to importune you, if you should not think it proper, induced me to remain silent.— I wait with extreme impatience to learn the effect which this treaty shall have produced in the U.S. & think it a very fortunate circumstance that it will have found the Congress in session. It would give me great satisfaction to be able to communicate to you the particulars & present circumstances of the business entrusted to me here— the conveyance of this letter, by post, will shew the impropriety of attempting it.— It is a matter of considerable speculation here to ascertain what will be your future object— As it is a publick conjecture, & adopted by many, I have no difficulty in informing you that it is said you are destined to & perhaps at present at, Paris—to negotiate a general peace— My conjectures are not the same— however this opinion is adopted here by some, who have been generally more early & better informed of what has related to you since your arrival in London than I have been.

M. de Gardoqui & the Mess. d'Yranda are both flattered by your remembrance & the former particularly begs me with much warmth to return you his best & sincerest compliments— You know the arduous ministry with which he has been charged for the last three years— He has sustained it with much good fortune & much longer than was or could have been expected.— I have the honor to be, Sir, with perfect respect & esteem, your most ob^t. & h^ble Ser^t.

W: Short

The hon^ble. John Jay Esqr &c &c &c.

ALS, NNC (EJ: 07138). Addressed: "The Honb^le / John Jay Esqr. / &c. &c. &c." Endorsed.

1. JJ to Short, 24 Nov. 1794, Dft, NNC (EJ: 08918). In his letter, JJ explained that he would have sent more detailed news of his negotiations were it not for "the infidelity of the Post Office in Spain and most other Countries." He also assured Short that the treaty contained a clause that it not "be construed or operate contrary to our existing treaties with other Powers; and thereby leaves them without any Right to be displeased with it—"

To David Hartley

London 8 Jany 1795

Dr Sir

I have been fav^d. with your letter of the 5th. Instant,[1] stating the Case of M^r. and M^rs. Miniconi, who are in France, and requesting me to take measures to procure a Passport for them and their Servants— In my opinion I cannot better promote your wishes in this Respect, than by sending a Copy of Your Letter to M^r. Munro at Paris, & requesting his friendly attention to the Subject of it—[2] this shall be done by the first opportunity.—

Accept my Thanks for the Pamphlet you was so obliging as to send me—[3] It does not appear probable to me that Europe is very speedily to be blessed with a general and lasting peace, or that the period has ∧yet already∧ arrived when Reason and virtue will ~~regulate direct~~ ∧govern∧ the Conduct of the mass of mankind— ~~the tract~~ There is much Reason to believe that the majority of men are neither reasonable nor virtuous; and hence it has happened, that so many Systems which were calculated on the supposed Prevalence of Reason and Virtue, have proved delusive.

~~There is no Doubt but that~~ the Time ∧doubtless∧ will come, and is ~~gradually~~ approaching, when a new order of Things will be introduced, and when as the human Passions and Vices cease to predominate, the checks necessary to controul them will become proportionably less necessary— To see things as being what they are, to estimate them accurately, and to act accordingly, are Requisites no less essential ~~in politics~~ to sound Politics than to sound Philosophy or Religion

These are general Remarks, and not ~~intended to be applied~~ ₐmade with Reference₍ₐ₎ to the political Questions agitating in this ~~Country~~ ₐKingdom₍ₐ₎, and with which (~~as~~ ₐbeing₍ₐ₎ a citizen of ~~a neutral~~ ₐanother₍ₐ₎ Country) it would not become me to interfere with the best wishes for your Health and Happiness I am Dʳ Sʳ Your Friend & obᵗ Servᵗ

David Hartley Esqʳ.

Dft, NNC (EJ: 05672).

1. See Hartley to JJ, 5 Jan. 1795, above.

2. On 8 Jan. 1795, JJ wrote Monroe, enclosing Hartley's letter. He noted "The uniform attachment to our Country which Mʳ Hartley has always manifested, will I am persuaded, recommend the Subject of his Letter to Your Attention—". Dft, NNC (EJ: 09624).

3. The pamphlet sent may have been Hartley's *Argument on the French Revolution and the Means of Peace* (Bath, 1794).

From John Quincy Adams

Hague January 9 1795.

Dear Sir

Mʳ. M'Evers[1] has just delivered me your favours of the 13ᵗʰ: and 14ᵗʰ: of last month,[2] and I take the earliest opportunity to acknowledge the obligation, which delay, might prevent me from transmitting.

Mʳ. Schermerhorn[3] some time since handed me also a letter of introduction from you.[4] Please to accept my thanks, Sir, for the acquaintance with these Gentlemen. I shall esteem myself fortunate in any opportunity to render them a service to which your recommendation so fully entitles them.

Nothing could be more grateful to my feelings than the intelligence from America, which you are pleased to communicate. The suppression of the Insurrection, the return of conciliatory dispositions, the growing prosperity of commerce, and the prevalence of national principles, demonstrated by the re-election of good men for the ensuing Legislature, are all promising indications, that our Country will yet be flourishing, united and happy.

The friendly dispositions, of which the result of your late negotiation, and your observations since that period have tended to confirm your opinion, give us an additional ground of satisfaction. It may be expected that the Treaty, has by this time arrived in America. It is my cordial wish and hope, that it will be received with a temper similar to that which formed and acceded to its arrangements; with that combination of firmness and of generosity which is so well calculated to terminate with honour our foreign differences, and which has so happily succeeded in suppressing internal dissension.

The value of Peace and Neutrality is no where more forcibly felt, than at this moment in the Country where I am. Its situation becomes more and more critical from day to day. In the terrible agitation between the dismal alternative of Conquest or civil War, it feels at the same moment all the terrors of a torrent rushing from without, and a Volcano bursting from within.

The alarm at this place is great. The emigrants who have the means are hurrying away. The british Ambassador has gone to meet the future Princess of Wales; the Spanish, Portuguese and Prussian Ministers are gone. But the Stadtholder and his family still remain, determined it is said to stay at all Events, and partake of the common destiny. There is yet no intelligence from the Commissioners gone to Paris. Some hopes are still entertained of their success, which are strengthened, by the moderate and rainy weather, which will impede for the moment, the further progress of the french armies.

Requesting you to present my cordial remembrance to Col^l: Trumbull and to your Son, I remain, with every Sentiment of Respect and Attachment Dear Sir, your very humble and obed^t. Servt:

John Q. Adams

His Excellency John Jay &c &c &c

ALS, NNC (EJ: 09686). Endorsed: "Rec^d 14 Jan 1795". WJ, 2: 242–43 (extract); HPJ, 4: 154–56.

1. James McEvers (1763–1817[?]), partner in the New York merchant firm of Le Roy, Bayard & McEvers, who represented Dutch banking interests in land purchases made in New York. LPAH, 3: 611–12, 619–20n31. JJ communicated with Le Roy, Bayard, & McEvers in 1799 about the possibility of purchasing 3,000 stands of muskets for equipping the New York state militia. See the editorial note "Defending New York," below, and JJ to Bayard, LeRoy, and McEvers, 11 Nov. 1799, ALS, N (EJ: 01029).

2. JJ to JQA, 13 Dec. 1794, above, and 14 Dec., not found. JQA's diary entry for 9 Jan. 1795 includes "Letters M^r. M'Evers, letter from M^r. Jay." JQA Diaries, vol. 20, MHi: Adams; JQA Diaries Digital, http://www.masshist.org/jqadiaries/php/doc?id=jqad20_15 (accessed Aug. 2018).

3. Ryer Schemerhorn, probably of the Schemerhorn family of Schenectady. Schermerhorn was a merchant from New York who spent several years in the Netherlands. JQA to James Monroe, 8 Feb. 1795, MHi: Adams: JQA Lbks.

4. JQA's diary entry for 5 Dec. 1794, mentions "Visit from Mr. Schermerhorn with Letter from Mr. Jay." Letter sent by JJ not found. While at The Hague, JQA provided Schemerhorn with a letter of introduction when he visited James Monroe. JQA Diaries, vol. 22, MHi: Adams; JQA Diaries Digital, http://www.masshist.org/jqadiaries/php/doc?id=jqad22_45&year=1794&month=12&day=05&entry=entryshort&start=0 (accessed Aug. 2018).

From William Wilberforce

[Pal[ace]y[ar]d [Westminster] Tuesday [27 January 1795]]

My dear Sir

Understanding from the Bish[o]p of London[1] that you have not receiv'd any copy of the Sierra Leon Report,[2] allow me to beg your acceptance of one & & to send a Copy also for your Son & M[r]. Trumbull—[3] I trust you will think the latter part very interesting— I am dear Sir your oblig'd & faithful servt

W Wilberforce

William Wilberforce, by Charles Howard Hodges, published by John Rising and Thomas Harmar, after John Rising, published 1 February 1792. Mezzotint. (© National Portrait Gallery, London)

ALS, NNC (EJ: 90434; EJ: 09276). Addressed: "John Jay Esqr. / &c— &c &c". Although the letter is dated [27 Jan.], the endorsement reads "... 28 Jan. 1795".

1. Beilby Porteus (1731–1809).

2. *Substance of the report delivered by the Court of Directors of the Sierra Leone Company to the General Court of Proprietors, on Thursday the 27th March, 1794* (London, 1794).

In 1792, Wilberforce, Porteus, and other members of the Clapham Sect founded the Sierra Leone Company and established a colony in Sierra Leone, to be populated by free black settlers from Great Britain, Nova Scotia, and Jamaica.

3. Porteus also sent JJ a copy of the report. See Porteus to JJ, 28 Jan. 1795, ALS, NNC (EJ: 06911).

From John Dalrymple

Ed[inbu]^r[gh] 1st: Feby 1795

Sir

I have the honour to inclose you a printed paper[1] which will explain itself. When M^r. ~~Jay~~ ^Lear^ secretary to Gen: Washington was in ^Scotland^ he was some days at my castle in the Country[2] ~~this country I discovered it to him and he.~~ I informed him of the discovery and he thought ~~the discovery~~ ^it ~~would~~^ would be of great consequence to America I therefore offered to communicate my Arts to him and to teach him to make the Articles from the Yeast with his own hands The Articles were spirits from corn Spirits ^and^ from Molasses or Sugar, Worts, small beer, Seamen's beer, Strong Beer, ~~and~~ porter and Bread.

My terms were Oath of Secrecy with a high penalty on the breach of it. 2dly: After the trial made by his own hands, he was to be at liberty either to begin or not as he thought proper, and he was liberty to stop when he thought proper Lastly I was to have half the profit but not a penny unless he gained a certain Number of per cents which would probably be left to himself. ~~to fix~~ ^~~be thought proper to fix~~^ He was in a hurry to go to London, but agreed to come back and I to teach him my Arts. But I afterwards received a Letter from him in Ireland, that as there seemed danger of a breach between America and England he did not think it honorable to take advantage of my discovery, when a Breach between the Nations may disappoint one of the effects of ~~my~~ the agreement; A mark of Delicacy and honour, which I assure you makes me very partial to him, Added to the steady Sense, and enlarged views which I saw in him.

The danger between America and England being now over, thanks to the Almighty Gen: Washington and you, I wish to renew the treaty. But I forgot the Name of the house in the City of which he is a partner. I must therefore intreat you to deliver the Inclosed paper to that house, after reading it carefully yourself, and also to communicate to them the letter which I am now writing

The profits are beyond all Measure. 1ˢᵗ: With regard to distilling One Gallon of yeast powder ∧[illegible] each [illegible] which sells here at 2/ p lb∧ does the work of 500 Gallons of Dunder,³ which I believe is your ferment in America. ∧But the profit is extravagant it could be made in Ame:[rica] for six pence per pound∧ With regard to its merit, I refer you to Dʳ. Higgins'⁴ report in the inclosed paper.

With regard to beer, a Quarter of Malt or half a Quarter ~~and~~ ∧with∧ half a hundred Weight of Molasses or a quarter hund: Wᵗ of Raw Sugar, will make ~~136 lb of Wort cake each of which will make~~ ∧136∧ ∧136 lbs of Wort cake each pound of which∧ ~~will make 3 barrels of strong Beer or Porter used proportionally~~ 136 lb Wortcake, which sells at ~~a pence~~ ∧a shilling∧ ~~pence~~ a pound, but could be made in America for four pence I believe in my conscience that as much wort cake could be made at Washington town, as would serve all America and half of Europe with Beer.

With regard to hops, I got a ~~bit of~~ wood from Jamaica which cost almost nothing, and made an Infusion from it, which made part of the Wort Cake. And this infusion can be got from Jamaica or made there into cake. And I doubt not there are other bitter woods in ~~the West Indies~~ ∧America∧ which would do as well You may ask Botanists and let me know the Names of the Plants. But if you have hops in America this would be needless: for ~~they may be made~~ then the Hop cake may be made in America in the places where the hops grow, and sent to Washington town in that state, by which 98 percent of freight ~~may~~ ∧would∧ be saved: to which is to be added this other advantage, that far more ∧and better∧ infusion, and consequently Hop cake can be got from hops in a green state, than in a dry state. But the British laws force the raiser of hops to sell them in a dry state, which the American Laws do not do

This leads me to a great object, and a sure way to make a great fortune indeed if the Americans had Barley and hops, because then, both could be made either together or separately into cake, and sent to Britain. ∧But∧ the Wort cake would not serve distillers cause the duty is too high ~~and~~ on foreign Materials, nor the public Brewer because he is prohibited to use it. But ~~it may b~~ those who Brew in private families may use what Materials they please ∧either wort cake or hop cake∧ Now the brewing by private families in England is one third of the public Brewery and consequently consumes three Millions of Quarters of Malt ∧and a third of the hops used∧ and those who use it the wort cake ∧all of it∧ would pay neither Malt tax nor Excise ∧nor Hop duty∧

and only 33 perCent ad valorem upon importation, which last would serve the English Revenue because at present private families pay no Excise

I have heard that you have little Barley in America but a vast quantity of wheat. Wheat will malt and make Beer as easily as Barley. I do not know whether the British would drink it but one half of Europe ~~would~~ ₐwillₐ drink it because they do so now

If you can serve your own fortune by Joining Mr ~~Jay~~ Lear's house I should be very happy. I beg that Mr ~~Jay~~ ₐLear'sₐ house and you will do me the honour to Answer this letter

I shall send you another copy of the printed paper to morrow which I beg you will forward to Genl. Washington the most ₐgreat &ₐ virtuous character of this Age

You and I were once at Madrid together upon the same errand[5] I hope we shall be better acquainted.

The post running off I have no time to make a fair copy of this letter I have the honour to be with the highest respect your most obedient humble Servant

John Dalrymple

ALS, NNC (EJ: 05544). Addressed: "Edinr. Sixth February 1795 / His Excellency Mr Jay / American Ambassador / London". Note: "R Dundas." Franked: "Free". Endorsed: ". . . note abt. Beer Cakes—".
Dalrymple wrote again to JJ on 6 Feb. 1795, ALS, NNC (EJ: 05549). JJ replied to both letters on 14 Feb. 1795, below.

1. Printed enclosure not found, but possibly his *Letter from Sir John Dalrymple, Baronet, one of the Barons of the Exchequer in Scotland, to the Lords of Admiralty* (Edinburgh, 1795). Dalrymple sent another printed enclosure—probably the same one—to JJ with a request that it be forwarded to GW. Dalrymple to JJ, 6 Feb. 1795, ALS, NNC (EJ: 05549); JJ to Dalrymple, 14 Feb. 1795, below. See also JJ to GW, 25 Feb. 1795, ALS, DLC (EJ: 10642); Dft, NNC (EJ: 08455); C (of extract), NHi: Henry V. O'Reilly (EJ: 00691); *PGW: PS*, 17: 577–80; *WJ*, 243–45; *HPJ*, 4: 160–62 (extract).

2. Tobias Lear (c. 1762–1816), served as GW's private secretary from 1784 to 1793. In 1793, he formed his own company, T. Lear & Co., with Tristam Dalton, the former U.S. senator from Massachusetts, and James Greenleaf, the U.S. consul at Amsterdam. Lear's firm worked alongside GW's Potomac Company promoting land speculation in Washington, D.C. Lear travelled to Europe in a largely unsuccessful attempt to promote his business venture.

3. Dunder is defined as "the lees or dregs of cane-juice, used in the West Indies in the fermentation of rum". *OED*.

4. Bryan Higgins (1741–1818), Irish physician and chemist, who ran a School of Practical Chemistry in London during the 1770s and mid-1790s. Higgins went to Jamaica in 1796 to improve the production of sugar and rum. *ODNBO*.

5. JJ encountered Dalrymple during his diplomatic mission in Spain. Dalrymple attempted to interest the Spanish court in Lord Rochford's peace plan, which sought to prevent American independence via a confederation of England, France, Spain, and Portugal. See *JJSP*, 2: 4n9, 62, 63, 87, 88n4, 132–33, 137–38n11, 140, and 143n4.

To Edmund Randolph

London February 2nd. 1795.

Sir.

It occurs to me that I have omitted to inform you that after signing the Treaty, I took the three first opportunities which offered of writing to our Minister at Paris, "that it contained an express declaration that nothing contained in it, should be construed or operate against existing Treaties between the United and other powers.["]¹

The following are Copies of those Letters—

No. 1

London 24th. November 1794²

Sir

It gives me pleasure to inform you that a Treaty between the United States and his Britannic Majesty was signed on the 19th. instant.

This Circumstance ought not to give any uneasiness to the Convention:— The Treaty expressly declares that nothing contained in it shall be construed or operate contrary to existing Treaties between the United States, and other Powers:—I flatter myself that the United States, as well as well as all their ministers, will upon every Occasion manifest the most scrupulous regard to good Faith:— and that those Nations who wish our Prosperity³ will be pleased with our preserving Peace and a good understanding with Others. I have the Honour to be &c &c &c

The Honble. James Munro Esqr. Minister of the United States at Paris

2.

London 25th. November 1794.⁴

Sir.

By a Letter written and sent a few days ago, I had the pleasure of informing you, that on the 19th. Instant the principal Business of my Mission was concluded, by a Treaty signed on that Day.

It contains a Declaration, that it shall not be construed nor operate contrary to our Existing Treaties.— As therefore Our Engagements with other Nations remain unaffected by it, there is Reason to hope that our preserving peace and a good understanding with this Country, will not give uneasiness to any other.— As the Treaty is not yet ratified it would be improper to publish it.— It appears to me to be upon the whole fair, and as equal as could be expected.— In some Respects both Nations will probably be pleased, and in other displeased.— I have the Honor to be with Great Respect &c &c &c— The Honble. Mr Munro &c &c Paris

3. ~~Sir~~

London 28th. November 1794.[5]

Sir.

Within this week past; I have written to you Two Letters, to inform you, that on the 19th. instant a Treaty between the United States and his Britannic Majesty was signed:— The Design of this Letter is chiefly to introduce to you Mr Pleasants of Philadelphia, whose Connexions there are respectable;— I have not the pleasure of being personally acquainted with this Gentleman, but as a Fellow Citizen I wish to do him friendly offices; and I am persuaded that a similar disposition on your part will ensure to him such a degree of Attention as Circumstances may render proper.

As M^r: Pinckney has a Cypher with our ˄other˄ Ministers in Europe, either He or I will shortly use it, in communicating to you, the principal Heads of the Treaty confidentially:— You need not hesitate in the mean time to say explicitly that it contains nothing repugnant to our Engagements with any other Nation.— with the best wishes to your Health and Prosperity I have the Honor be &c &c &c

To the Honble. James Munro Esqr. &c &c &c Minister of the United States to the French Republic

Considering that the Declaration in question need not be kept secret, but, on the contrary that advantages would result from its publicity, I also authorized a respectable American Merchant here, who had Correspondents in France, to mention it in explicit Terms;— My Letters to M^r. Short[6] and M^r. Adams[7] conveyed the like information;— It appeared to me proper to take these early measures to obviate any disagreeable apprehensions which the French Convention might perhaps otherwise entertain;— whether our Minister at Paris received those letters I have as yet no Information from him.— From Mr Short[8] and Mr Adams[9] I have received Answers. I have the Honor to be, with sentiments of Respect & Esteem— Sir— Your most obedient and humble Servant.

John Jay

The Honble. Edm^d Randolph Esqr. Secretary of State. &c &c.

LS, DNA: Jay Despatches, 1794–95 (EJ: 04354). Marked: "N°. 29." LbkC, NNC: JJ Lbk. 8; ASP: FR, 1: 516–17.

1. See JJ to James Monroe, 19 Feb. 1795, below.

2. C, DNA: Jay Despatches, 1794–95 (EJ: 04355); RC, DLC: Monroe; *ASP: FR*, 1: 516; *Monroe Papers*, 3: 158.

3. This phrase reads "who wish us well" in the file copy.

4. C, DNA: Jay Despatches, 1794–95 (EJ: 04356); RC, DLC: Monroe; *ASP: FR*, 1: 516; *Monroe Papers*, 3: 160.

5. C, DNA: Jay Despatches, 1794–95 (EJ: 04357); FC, NNC (EJ: 09623); C, NN: Monroe (EJ: 01070); *ASP: FR*, 1: 516.

6. JJ to William Short, 24 Nov. 1794, Dft, NNC (EJ: 08918).

7. JJ to JQA, 24 Nov. 1794, above.

8. Short to JJ, 7 Jan. 1795, above.

9. JQA to JJ, 2 Dec. 1794, above.

To Sarah Livingston Jay

London, 3 [and 6] Feb. 1795

My dear Sally

My last to you was of the 2 Jany by the Packet—[1] since which I have not had the pleasure of rec^g any Letters from You; nor have any opportunities of writing to you since offered, that I know of—

This has hitherto been one of the most severe winters known in this Country for many Years.[2] There has been so much Snow and Frost, that for a Fortnight Sleighs might have been used. The weather has nevertheless been gloomy— the clouds of Smoke w^h. constantly hover over the city will not permit to enjoy much Sunshine, even when the Sky is free from other clouds. You know how much I enjoy Sunshine, and consequently how much I must regret this unceasing Gloom. I shall nevertheless enjoy the Day, whether dark or otherwise, that I shall set Sail for Nyork— for altho' I have every Reason to be satisfied, which a Stranger can well have, yet like "a Bird that wanders from its nest"[3] I am anxious to return to mine The first of March you will suspend writing to me—but I shall continue writing to you by every opportunity during my Stay here.

On Monday next Peter and I purpose to go out of Town to pass some Days at a Gentleman's Country Seat. I hope to return before Capt Kemp will sail— if so—he will bring you a Letter from me[4]

I am very sollicitous to recieve Letters from you— A vessel from New York is daily expected— I am impatient for her arrival.

I have rec^d. two Letters from M^{rs}. Ridley of old Dates.[5] I promise myself the pleasure of writing to her by one of the first York Ships. Remember me to her and our other Friends. I hope Maria has rec^d. my Letter—⁶ My Love to all the children— Yours very affectionately,

John Jay

M^rs. Jay

turn over

London 6 Feb. 1795

My dear Sally

Yesterday I had the satisfaction of ~~you~~ re⁵. yours of the 5—17—and 20 Decr. and this morning yours of the 18 Nov^r.—also M^r. Munro's of 4 and 20 Dec^r.—one from Judge Hobart of 20 Novr. one from R. Morris of Jersey of 21 Novr. and one from M^rs. Munro of 15 Dec^r.—⁷ These Letters having arrived in a moment of Business I have only given them as yet a cursory reading— I am preparing Dispatches by the packet, and am pressed for Time— I Thank you most cordially for writing so frequently— Your Letters give me great Satisfaction— Continue to manage ~~all~~ my pecuniary matters as you and Peter may think most adviseable— I have not Time now to be particular— Adieu my d^r Sally ever Yours

John Jay

Mrs Jay

ALS, NNC (EJ: 08065).

1. JJ to SLJ, 2 Jan. 1795, ALS, NNC (EJ: 08064). See also, PAJ to SLJ of the same date, above.

2. See John Kington, "The Severe Winter of 1794/95 in England," *Weather* (Dec. 1994): 419–20; and PAJ to SLJ, 7 Mar. 1795, below. The frosts lasted from December to March, with January being the coldest month.

3. Paraphrase of Proverbs 27: 8.

4. On Monday, 9 Feb., JJ and PAJ left to visit Clement Cottrell Dormer, Master of the Ceremonies (who received foreign diplomats and dignitaries, presenting them to the court) for George III's court, at his country house Rousham House, in Oxfordshire. They stayed until 14 February. PAJ wrote of the "little jaunt" to his mother: "I think [it] will be useful to papa, for tho' the Treaty is finished, he has still much Business to do, occasioned by constant applications of every kind, so that he seems still to be possessed by his old fortune or rather misfortune of being obliged to do the business of others for which his trouble is his only reward." PAJ to SLJ, 8 Feb. 1795, ALS, NNC (EJ: 06053). See also the editorial note "John Jay's Mission to London," above.

5. Letters from Catharine L. Ridley not found.

6. JJ to Maria Jay, 9 Dec. 1794, ALS, NNC (EJ: 05939).

7. SLJ to JJ, 18 Nov., ALS, NNC (EJ: 06565); 5 Dec., ALS, NNC (EJ: 13075); C, NNC (EJ: 06566); 17 and 20 Dec. 1794, not found; PJM to JJ, 4 Dec. 1794, Dft, NNMus (EJ: 00435), and 20 Dec. 1794, ALS, NNC (EJ: 00439); C, NNC (EJ: 09374). John Sloss Hobart to JJ, 20 Nov. 1794, above; Robert Morris (of New Jersey) to JJ, 21 Nov. 1794, ALS, NNC (EJ: 07025). Mrs. Munro could be either Margaret White Munro or Eve Jay Munro, 15 Dec. 1794, not found.

Memorandum to John Trumbull

[London, 5 Feb. 1795]

M.r Sibbald of upper Harley Street, is sollicitous to obtain Information ~~of~~ relative to M.r Hesilriggs late of Boulogne in France, sent to arras by order of the Convention with other English Gentlemen— Endeavour to learn whether he be dead or alive

Deliver M.r Collets Letter[1] to M.r Dubignon

Endeavour to learn whether the wife and Family of M.r the Swedish Consul at Marseilles are well— M.r Codman[2] promised to make ~~the~~ Enquiries ab.t them—

Baron Nolkin[3] who for many Years was Minister of Sweden here, is very ~~sollicitous~~ ∧desirous∧ that James Macrea Esq. ∧in arrest at abbeville∧ Should be permitted to leave France— He married a Daughter of the Barons Lady— He fled to France in consequence of having killed a Gentleman here in a Duel—and has been *outlawed*— for this Reason the Baron thinks he might be liberated—as that Circumstance w.d oppose his returning to this Country—

I told the Baron I doubted his being released— Endeavour to ascertain whether ~~on that Ground~~ his Release can ∧probably∧ be obtained—

Jer. Osborne Esq.r at Bristoll has written to me that M.r John Pigot of Brockley in Somersetshire is lately dead, and left a large Fortune— that his eldest Son ∧John Pigot∧ resided much at Paris— The Family have not heard of him for 2 Y.rs: past— he was then at Paris[4]

If you ~~can~~ ∧sh.d hear where he is∧, inform him of his Fathers Death and of the anxiety of his Friends to hear of him— Inform M.r Osborne of the Result

~~Discover from~~ ∧Enquire of∧ M.r Munro whether any Thing has been done in Consequence of my Letter to him about Miss Banister, and ~~if I sh.d be gone~~ ~~let~~ ∧write to∧ M.r Charlmers ~~home~~ at Chelsea—[5]

write to me by every good opportunity, but write nothing that in Case of publicity ~~woul~~ would cause Inconveniences to any Body—

J.J.

DftS, NNC (EJ: 13084). Endorsed. JT commissioned Johann Gotthard von Müller to engrave his painting "The Battle of Bunker Hill." He received JJ's permission to travel to Stuttgart via Paris to check on the project, travelling in a private capacity, but also meeting with James Monroe in order to relate the contents of the treaty, as well as carrying out the above business. See JJ to Monroe, 19 Feb. 1795, below. For more on JT's prints, see JJ to SLJ, 13 Mar. 1795, JT to JJ, 6 Mar., and PAJ to JJ, 1 Aug. 1798 (first letter), all below.

1. See Guy Collet to JJ, 8 Dec. 1794, ALS, NNC (EJ: 08561). Collet had been a prisoner of war for four years and had no contact with his family for fourteen months.

2. Probably Richard Codman (1762–1806), a Boston merchant, who lived in Paris.

3. Baron Gustaf Adam von Nolcken (1733–1813), Swedish Ambassador to Great Britain.

4. For more on the Pigot affair, see Jeremiah Osborne to JJ, 12 Jan. 1795, ALS, NNC (EJ: 07035), and JJ to Osborne, 13 Jan. 1795, Dft, NNC (EJ: 08925).

5. See JJ to Monroe, 28 Aug. 1794, and the editorial note "John Jay's Mission to London," both above, for more instances of missing persons in France.

To Edmund Randolph

London 6 Feby 1795

Sir

I was yesterday honored with yours of the 3^d. Decr last.[1] our Vessels here being confined by Ice, I think it best to send you some Dispatches by the Packet.

In considering the Treaty, it will doubtless be remembered that there must be two to make a Bargain. We could not agree about the Negroes. was that a good Reason for breaking up the negociation? I mentioned in a former Letter[2] that I considered our admission into the Islands as affording compensation for the Detention of the posts, and other Claims of that nature— in that way we obtain Satisfaction for the Negroes, tho' not in express words.

We are not obliged by Treaty to permit France to sell Prizes in our ports: By denying that priviledge to all we adhere to the Line of Impartiality: and without being assured of Impartiality on our part, Britain would not have granted us what she has. I wish the Season had permitted me to accompany the Treaty, for I think I could give you satisfactory answers to every Question that can arise from it— I have the Honor to be with Respect & Esteem Sir your most ob^t. Servt

John Jay

The Honble Edm. Randolph Esq Sec^y of State &c.

ALS, DNA: Jay Despatches, 1794–95 (EJ: 04301). LS, marked "*Duplicate*", ibid; LbkC, NNC: JJ Lbk. 8; *ASP: FR*, 1: 518.

1. See ER to JJ, 3 Dec. 1794, NNC: JJ Lbk. 8 (EJ: 00619); *ASP: FR*, 1: 509.

2. Possibly JJ to ER, 13 Sept. 1794, above.

To John Dalrymple

Royal Hotel—Pall Mall 14 Feb 1795

Sir

The Letter wʰ. you did me the Honor to write on the first Day of this month,[1] came to Hand as I was abᵗ. making an Excursion into the Country or it shᵈ. have been answᵈ. immediately. I returnᵈ. this afternoon— accept my thanks for these interesting Communications— I have read with pleasure the printed paper that was enclosed, and agreable to yʳ. Request, shᵈ. without Delay communicate it, together with yʳ. Letter, to Mʳ. Lear's Partners in this City,[2] but really Sir! I do not know who they are, and as yet I am at a Loss to whom to apply for Information respecting them.

Your offer to explain the arts in question to Mʳ. Lear was friendly, and I consider myself greatly obliged by your extending that offer to me; but as my official occupations demand all my Time I think I ought not to permit any Concerns of this kind however advantageous to divert me from them—

I was this moment honᵈ. with your's of the 6ᵗʰ. Inst.[3] The printed paper that was enclosed in it, shall be forwarded to President Washington by the first opportunity—[4]

Excellent Hops and Barley are produced in ~~the~~ america, but not in large Quantities— There is no Doubt however but that the Quantity ~~of both~~ will be augmented in proportion as the Demand for them may be increased— in the Northern States much Cyder is used.[5]

It will always give me pleasure to cultivate your acquaintance, and to have opportunities of manifesting the great Respect with wʰ. I have the Honor to be Sir yʳ most Oᵇ Servᵗ

C, NNC (EJ: 08929).

1. See Dalrymple to JJ, 1 Feb. 1795, above.

2. Enclosures not found; the "printed paper" is possibly *Letter from Sir John Dalrymple, Baronet, one of the Barons of the Exchequer in Scotland, to the Lords of Admiralty* (Edinburgh, 1795). For JJ's trip to Clement Cottrell Dormer's house, see JJ to SLJ, 3–6 Feb., above.

3. See Dalrymple to JJ, 6 Feb. 1795, NNC (EJ: 05549).

4. See ibid., and Dalrymple to JJ, 1 Feb. 1795, note 1, above.

5. Dalrymple continued to write JJ on the topics of yeast cakes and powder, wort cakes for the brewing of beer, and the distillation of salt water. See Dalrymple to JJ, 4 and 9 Mar., 1795, ALS, NNC (EJ: 05545; EJ: 05547); and 8 Apr. 1795, ALS, NNC (EJ: 05548).

To Grenville

[London, 15 February 1795]

The undersigned Envoy of the U.S. of America, has the honor of representing to the R[t]. Honorable Lord Grenville, his B[ritannic]. Majesty's Secretary of State for the Department of foreign affairs

That the united States have long been, and still are engaged in war with certain Tribes of Savages; and that their repeated Endeavours to restore peace, have hitherto proved fruitless

That certain Circumstances, which he has had the Honor to communicate to his Lordship, ~~wer~~ have occasioned alarming apprehensions that those Savages are urged to persevere in the war, by Enducements and Expectations proceeding from ~~the~~ some of his majestys officers and agents in Canada—

That Altho The Justice Humanity and Dignity of his Majesty oppose every Idea that a warfare so peculiarly cruel, can be countenanced by his ~~Ins~~ Instructions; yet the undersigned thinks it his Duty, to submit to the wisdom of his Majesty, whether mutual considerations do not render it expedient to extinguish those apprehensions by such assurances, and to prevent their Revival by such measures, as may be adequate to those Purposes—

Dft, NNC (EJ: 08514).

To James Monroe

London 19th. February 1795

Sir

On the 5th. of this month I had the Honor of writing to you a Letter[1] in answer to yours of the 17 ult:[2] by M[r]. Purviance, who is still here waiting for an opportunity to return, and who will be the Bearer of that Letter—[3]

You will recieve this by Col. Trumbull, who for some Time past has been waiting for an opportunity to go, thro' Paris, to Stutgard, on private Business of his own.[4] He did me the favor to accompany me to this Country as my Secretary. He has been privy to the negociation of the Treaty between the United States & Great Britain, which I have signed; and having copied it, is perfectly acquainted with its Contents. He is a Gentleman of Honor understanding and accuracy, and able to give you satisfactory Information relative to it. I have thought it more adviseable to authorize and request him to give you this Information personally, than to send You written Extracts from the Treaty, which might not be so satisfactory— But he is to give you this Information in perfect confidence that you will not impart it to any Person whatever; for as the Treaty is not yet ratified, and may not be finally concluded in its present Form and Tenor, the Inconveniences which a premature Publication of its Contents might produce, can only be obviated by Secrecy in the mean Time. I think myself justifiable in giving you the Information in Question, because you are an american minister, and because it may not only be agreable, but perhaps useful— I have the Honor to be with great Respect Sir your most obed^t. & h'ble Servt

John Jay

The Hon'ble James Monroe—Esqr. Minister of the United States of America to the Republic of France

ALS, NNPM: Presidents of U.S. (EJ: 02846). Endorsed: ". . . by Mr. Trumbull, recd. 20 march, note Mr. T. did not leave England before Mr. P. & it was not expected he wd. from [what] he told Mr. P." ACS, DNA: Jay Despatches, 1794–95 (EJ: 04297); *ASP: FR*, 1: 518; *Monroe Papers*, 3: 237–38.

1. JJ to Monroe, 5 Feb. 1795, Dft, NNC (EJ: 09625; EJ: 90058); C, PHi (EJ: 01128); C, DNA: Jay Despatches, 1794–95 (EJ: 04296); C, embedded in JJ to ER, 5 Feb 1795, DNA: Jay Despatches, 1794–95 (EJ: 04290); LbkC, NNC: JJ Lbk. 10; *ASP: FR*, 1: 517; *HPJ*, 4, 137–39; *Monroe Papers*, 3: 222.

2. Monroe to JJ, 17 Jan. 1795, C, DNA: Jay Despatches, 1794–95 (EJ: 04299); RC, NNGL (EJ: 90541); SR (extract): Sweet Catalog 141 (EJ: 12933); *ASP: FR*, 1: 517; *Monroe Papers*, 3: 206.

3. John Henry Purviance (1763–1820), son of Baltimore merchant Samuel Purviance Jr. Purviance was Monroe's secretary and interpreter during his French mission (1794–96, 1803). *Monroe Papers*, 3: 165n5.

On 24 Nov. 1794, JJ wrote Monroe, informing him that the treaty had been signed and that "This Circumstance ought not to give any uneasiness to the Convention," as it was explicitly stated in the treaty that it would not violate or negate existing treaties. In JJ's letter of 25 Nov., he repeated this assurance, but warned "As the Treaty is not yet ratified it would be improper to publish it." He reiterated this point in his letter of 28 Nov., adding that as Thomas Pinckney had a code used with other ministers, JJ would send "the principal Heads of the Treaty confidentially:—." JJ enclosed copies of these letters in his to ER, 2 Feb. 1795, above.

In his letter of 17 Jan., Monroe wrote JJ that the news of the treaty did indeed cause alarm in France, and that as he did not have the key to the code, he was sending his secretary, Purviance, to London. More importantly, Monroe observed that the French would be not satisfied with anything less than a copy of the treaty. JJ's strongly worded reply of 5 Feb. 1795, reassured Monroe that the treaty would not violate the treaty with France. He declared his intention of sharing the particulars of the treaty in "*perfect Confidence*" but pointed out that it would be improper to make the whole public before ratification, as "It does not belong to Ministers who negotiate Treaties, to publish them even when perfected, much less Treaties not yet compleated and remaining open to alteration or Rejection;— such Acts belong exclusively to the Governments who form them". For Monroe to JJ, 17 Jan., and JJ to Monroe, 5 Feb. 1795, see above notes 2 and 3. See also JJ to GW, 25 Feb. 1795, letter and note 4, *PGW: PS*, 17: 577–80.

4. For JT's trip to Paris and Stuttgart, see JJ Memorandum to JT, 5 Feb. 1795, above. JJ had JT memorize the treaty, but not to impart its contents until Monroe promised not to share the information with the French. Monroe declined, based on his previous agreement with the Convention. JT, in his words, "became obnoxious to the French rulers." A private note from Monroe hinted to

JT that it would be advisable to leave France. JT determined he would not leave before he had completed his private business (purchasing paintings from impoverished estates) unless ordered to by the government. No direct order came. Trumbull, *Autobiography*, 184–86.

To Lady Elizabeth Amherst

[R. Hotel, Pall Mall, 20 Feb. 1795]

Mr Jay presents his best Compliments and returns his many thanks for the Print of Lord Amherst which her Ladyship has done him the honor to send — [1] it will be give pleasure to his Lordships numerous friends in America, and Mr Jay will always regard it as a valuable and interesting addition to his little Collection as well from the high respect he entertains for ₐL. Amherstₐ her L as a mark of ₐher Ladyships obligingₐ this attention with Wh. her Ladyship is pleased to humor him — [2]

Dft, NNC (EJ: 12850). JJ wrote this in reply to a letter from Lady Amherst, 20 Feb. 1795 (EJ: 05448).

1. This print was most likely a version of the mezzotint James Watson (c. 1740–90) made after Reynolds's 1765 portrait of Amherst. The last edition of this print came out in 1795 or 1796 by J. & J. Boydell.

2. This gift and theater invitations (she had a box in the Drury Lane theater) initiated a relationship between the Jays and the Amhersts. See also Lady Amherst to JJ, 2 Feb. 1795, ALS, NNC (EJ: 05447); Lady Amherst to JJ, 4 Mar. 1795, ALS, NNC (EJ: 05449); and the editorial note "John Jay's Mission to London," above.

To Grenville

Royal Hotel Pall Mall London 24 Feb. 1795

My Lord

I take the Liberty of communicating to your Lordship *informally* Extracts from two Letters vizt.

Postscript of to a Letter from Mr. Boudinot formerly President of Congress, in & now a member of the House of Representatives to Mr. Bayard, dated 18 Decr. last — [1]

"Since writing the above foregoing we have recd. Letters from Genl. Wayne, who has established some strong Posts at the Miami Towns. The Indians appeared very desirous of Peace, and had sent in a Request of this nature, but had since been sent for by Governor Simcoe, and dissuaded from this Measure; he having assured them of assistance from their Father the King of Great Britain. The post at the Rapids does not appear to have been evacuated."

However Whatever may be the true Complection of this Intelligence it appears to have been and believed by Mr Boudinot, who is a worthy Man, and one who sincerely desires ~~of~~ to see a good understanding subsist between the two Countrys— Permit me my Lord to express my Sollicitude that ~~none of the disagreements~~ [*illegible*] some [*illegible*] measures may be ~~adopted~~ ∧taken to∧ ~~that put an End~~ remove the Impressions made ~~an~~ by ~~the Reports of this Kind, and which have been the being necessary~~ [*illegible*] ∧the ~~cause~~ general and prevailing Belief that ∧∧to∧∧ such unfriendly Interpositions ~~have~~ the Continuance of the Indian War is imputable—∧

Extract of a Letter from ~~Messr.~~ ∧Mr∧ Russel Sturges[2] of Boston—dated 1 Jany last—

"The Bermudians take and condemn our Vessels, without the least Colour of Law or Justice. Yesterday arrived Captns. Grosur and Taylor who were Masters of rich Vessels of D. Shear, Swan, Putnam, and Scott, which were condemned but 15 Days past, with many others; without any other Reason given in the Condemnation than these Words 'I decree them good and lawful Prizes to the Captors.'"

"J. Green"[3]

Your Lordship knows my Sentiments and Feelings on this Subject— I flatter myself they concur with your own With great Respect and Esteem I have the Honor to be ~~my Lo~~ Your Lordships most obt. Sevt.
The Rt. Honb. Lord Grenville—

Dft, NNC (EJ: 08507).

1. Elias Boudinot of Elizabeth, N.J., a member of the House of Representatives, 1789–95. Boudinot was Samuel Bayard's uncle by marriage.

2. Russell Sturgis (1750–1826), Boston-based merchant involved in the China trade.

3. Probably John Green (1736–96), former naval officer and captain of the *Empress of China*, the first American ship to trade with Canton. Newspaper accounts of ship captures in Bermuda reported, among others, seizures of the Schooner *Patty*, John Taylor, master, owned by Daniel Scott of Boston, and the Schooner *Industry*, John Grozer, master, owned by David Spear Jr. and Joseph Ripley of New York. See *Dunlap and Claypoole's American Daily Advertiser* (Philadelphia), 4 Dec. 1794 and 8 Jan. 1795, and *Gazette of the United States* (Philadelphia), 4 Dec. 1794.

To Samuel Bayard

Royal Hotel—Pall Mall—5 March 1795

Dr. Sir

I was this Eveng favd. with your's of to Day,[1] enclosing a memorial presented to the Lords Commissioners on the 14th. Ult. and a proposed Letter to Mr. Falkener urging an answa to it—informing me that the Lords had not met since, but are to meet on Saturday next; & requesting my advice whether

that Letter could with propriety be deliv^d. before the Lords have had an opportunity of giving an answer—

This is already Thursday— M^r. Falkener may in my opinion with propriety
be requested, either by Letter or verbally, to remind the Lords ~~tomorrow~~ ₍on
Saturday₎, of the memorial, & the Importance of an answ^r. to it— I presume
nothing more was intended by the Letter, tho' by its observing that no answer had yet been given, it seems to imply that the Lords have *omitted* to give
one— The Letter may easily be altered so as to be free from that Implication,
and from every appearance of Impropriety— Yours,
Saml. Bayard Esqr.

Dft, NNC (EJ: 12532; EJ: 12843). Endorsed.
   1. Letter not found.

Aftermath of the Jay Treaty:
Responses, Ratification, and Implementation

Once the treaty was signed on 19 November, Jay hurriedly sent dispatches
to George Washington, Edmund Randolph, and others giving brief
explanations of the treaty negotiations and terms of the treaty.[1] Although
he kept the terms of the treaty secret, he then wrote American diplomats in
Europe (Thomas Pinckney, James Monroe, William Short and John Quincy
Adams) of the successful conclusion, and authorized them to assure the European powers that there was nothing in the treaty that contradicted earlier
treaties with France or other nations.[2] Jay also responded to the comments
and queries he received from Washington and Randolph after the treaty was
signed.[3] Considering his health too precarious to chance a winter voyage, Jay
resolved to wait until he received news of the arrival of the treaty and planned
to return in the early spring.[4]

Rushed efforts to get copies of the signed treaty on board the last few de-
parting ships before winter so that they would arrive while Congress was still
in session proved unavailing. Two copies were inadvertently placed on the
same English packet, the *Tankerville*, which was captured by a French privateer, while the ship transporting the third text, carried by David Blaney aboard
the *Thomas* (Captain Vickery), was long held offshore by westerly winds.[5]
Jay had little opportunity to provide further information before returning to
America. He received Edmund Randolph's criticisms and questions about his
negotiations of 3 December, and answered them briefly on 6 February, while

on 2 February, Jay sent Randolph copies of his correspondence with James Monroe, assuring him that the treaty did not violate the terms of the alliance with France. He wrote Washington on 25 February and 6 March answering criticisms. On 8 March, Randolph sent a hasty note announcing the arrival of the treaty, assuring Jay it would be kept secret until the opening of Congress in June, and requesting information on the oral discussions held with Grenville. However, Jay had no opportunity to reply before his return.[6]

Blaney had finally landed in Virginia with the treaty in late February and travelled overland to Philadelphia where he arrived four days after the end of the congressional session on 3 March 1795. Washington called for a special session of the Senate to meet in June to ratify the treaty. He and his cabinet resolved to keep the terms of the treaty secret until the Senate reassembled.[7] Thus, when Jay arrived in New York on 28 May, little solid information was publicly available about the treaty, and he was given a warm welcome in New York where he awaited news of his election as governor.[8] Jay reported his arrival, but stated his health did not immediately permit him to travel to Philadelphia; he agreed to travel to the capital to answer questions in time for the opening of Congress.[9] He left New York on 8 June accompanied by senators Rufus King and Jacob Read. Little information is available about Jay's activities in Philadelphia, but he did not testify before Congress. He remained until 17 June when he left for New York.[10]

Responses to the Treaty

After cabinet discussion of what information Washington would and would not present, the president sent the treaty to the Senate for ratification on 8 June along with copies of Jay's instructions and correspondence during the negotiations.[11] Senators were pledged to secrecy and were not allowed to divulge the terms of the treaty until after the session. The procedures and votes of the Senate but not the debates are recorded in the Senate Executive Journal. The Senate had a Federalist majority so prospects for ratification were good, but even supporters of the treaty opposed Article 12 because they considered the trade concession in the West Indies as vitiated by a prohibition of reexportation from the United States of commodities from all the islands of the West Indies, not just British ones, and that it interfered with a burgeoning export trade in American cotton.[12] At the suggestion of Hamilton and King, the cabinet decided that rather than reject the whole treaty, the U.S. would propose suspending Article 12 until it could be renegotiated, and to go forward with ratification of the rest.[13] Although Aaron Burr moved to postpone consideration of the treaty and submitted a list of further modifications of the treaty to eliminate or alter every concession made to Great Britain, his proposals were voted down on 23 June by a vote of 12–10.[14] Republicans moved to seek compensation for the removed slaves, but failed by a vote of 15–12. The Senate then approved ratification of the treaty by a vote of 20–10. A last vote to reopen discussion on slave compensation failed in a 14–15 vote.[15]

Republicans then sought to appeal to public opinion to deter Washington from signing the treaty. Although the secrecy requirement was removed following ratification in the Senate, that body ruled that no copy was to be published or given out to the public. Hamilton and King persuaded Washington and Randolph that the treaty should be published to avoid triggering public suspicion, but before that could happen various senators leaked copies of it. Pierce Butler of South Carolina sent a copy to Madison, and Stevens T. Mason of Virginia released another. Benjamin Franklin Bache's paper, the *Aurora*, published a summary on the treaty on 29 June before the official copy came out, and three days later published a full text in pamphlet form. Bache then set off for New York and New England spreading copies and commentary and arousing enough opposition to trigger mob action in Boston.[16]

Treaty opponents then mobilized public opinion in town meetings throughout the United States and sent resolutions and petitions to Washington to dissuade him from ratifying the treaty. Burnings of Jay in effigy, ritual beheadings, and burnings of copies of the treaty occurred in many cities, while 4th of July celebrations provided occasions for critical toasts and speeches.[17] New York's pro-French Republicans, under the leadership of some of Jay's Livingston relatives, particularly Robert R., Brockholst, Edward, Peter R., and Maturin Livingston, were among the staunchest opponents of the treaty. Robert penned articles under the pseudonym "Cato" and sent a letter to Washington condemning the treaty,[18] while Brockholst wrote articles as "Decius" and "Cinna" and was a leader of the anti-treaty town meeting held in New York in July at which Hamilton was pelted with stones.[19] It was Edward, a member of the House of Representatives, who, after ratification, introduced a resolution demanding that Washington submit copies of Jay's instructions and correspondence regarding the treaty to the House in an effort to block funding for its implementation. Washington refused on constitutional grounds to comply.[20]

Following his visit to Philadelphia, Jay played at most a behind-the-scenes role in public defense of the treaty. He left that task largely to Hamilton and King, who penned 34 articles under the signature "Camillus." According to John Adams, citing King, Jay collaborated with them in the defense, but without himself writing any pieces.[21] Only after the treaty was ratified did Jay defend his character from personal attack, denying that he was pro-British and anti-French in an appendix to a pamphlet printed by Senator Robert Goodloe Harper of South Carolina to defend his vote for the treaty to his constituents.[22] Jay later also defended himself against allegations of excessive expenses as negotiator and charges that he had personally retained substantial amounts of the funds.[23]

Jay had correctly anticipated some of the points of opposition to the treaty, but had missed how controversial other items would prove. He had known that French officials and their supporters would bitterly oppose it despite his efforts to persuade the French that nothing in the treaty contradicted previous treaties.[24] He also expected and received southern opposition on the issue of repayment of British debts and on his failure to obtain compensation for slaves removed by the British during the war of independence. Britain would not consider the issue of compensation for the slaves, he argued, and it was not worth losing the opportunity for a treaty by insisting upon it. Jay claimed that access to the British West Indies and evacuation of the posts were intended as partial offsets for the failure of compensation.[25] Jay realized the time that would elapse before the western posts were evacuated would raise complaints, but insisted the British would not agree to an earlier date for commercial reasons and because they needed time to smooth relations with allied Indians in the area who were incensed by British abandonment of them.[26]

Jay failed to anticipate the opposition to trade provisions with the West Indies, believing the limitations he accepted to be temporary and that the few concessions he obtained were an opening wedge for better terms in future. He regarded them as the beginning of the end to British navigation policy. He suggested the restrictions on reexportation of West Indian products to Europe could be bypassed by landing goods on neutral West Indian islands and shipping them from there. He supported the prohibition on the sequestration of debts in wartime as useful because the threat of sequestration was discouraging British trade and investments in the United States. Considering the arbitration panels to be set up under the treaty an effective way of settling both debt claims and compensation for ships and cargoes seized by the British, he was surprised by the anger that more immediate compensation had not been obtained without the prior necessity of complicated and expensive judicial procedures. Jay had sought to obtain such direct payment from the British government, but Grenville faced strong political pressures against it and the measure was ultimately blocked. Jay also failed to anticipate the rage against his apparent concessions regarding the American policy that free ships made free goods; he faced claims he had tacitly abandoned American neutrality principles and paved the way for the intensified seizures of cargos the British adopted without warning early in April 1795.[27]

Opposition to the treaty was exacerbated by news that the British had renewed seizures of cargoes of provisions to France and its colonies under a secret Order in Council adopted 25 April 1795. This was perceived as a revival of the hated Order in Council of 6 November 1793 that had sanctioned the seizure of ships carrying the products of French colonies or provisions or supplies to them. Opponents argued that Jay's concessions on neutral rights had emboldened British officials to renew their attacks on American shipping.[28]

Ratification

It was this renewal of seizures that led Washington to postpone ratification of the treaty. Randolph suggested that Washington should state he would not ratify until the new Order in Council was rescinded. Washington had Randolph prepare a memorial to British minister George Hammond to that effect. But soon made aware of Randolph's disgrace in response to British exposure of French minister Fauchet's captured dispatches that implied (at least as translated) that Randolph sought money from the French in return for his support, Washington decided to go forward with ratification. He signed the treaty on 14 August 1795. Confronted with the letter four days later, Randolph resigned from office. Washington also considered, but did not adopt, Hamilton's proposal to delay exchange of the ratifications in Europe until the seizures were discontinued. In his seventh state of the union address on 8 December 1795, Washington promised to lay the treaty before Congress for appropriations as soon as the British response was received.[29]

There were differences of opinion on British motivations for the renewal of ship seizures. George Hammond told Washington that, following U.S. final repayments to France of revolutionary war debts, the French used the funds to make extensive purchases of provisions. Grenville claimed that the French were desperate for provisions and disguised their purchases as neutral property. He proclaimed that he would stop them from doing so. John Trumbull on the other hand contended the French had adequate food supplies and the British needed the food supplies for themselves. Although the British were seizing the provisions as enemy property not as contraband, they treated the captures legally as if they were contraband and paid for them as specified under the terms of the Jay treaty. This seemed to confirm to the treaty opponents that the Jay treaty tacitly recognized provisions as contraband, in contradiction of American policy on neutral rights and the terms of some of its treaties with other powers.[30]

The exchange of ratifications in Great Britain was postponed somewhat by a series of mishaps: the absence of Thomas Pinckney, then in Spain as special envoy; the belief that Chargé d'affaires William A. Deas lacked sufficient status to conduct the exchange; the failure of John Quincy Adams to reach England in time to participate, necessitating Deas's having to conduct the exchange by the instructed October 1795 deadline; and problems with Deas's sending of the texts of the final treaty, only a copy of which reached the United States, not a signed original. These events delayed plans to implement the treaty. Washington was finally able to inform Congress of the ratification at the end of February 1796.[31]

The Republicans had one last chance to block the treaty. Washington had to ask for an appropriation of $90,000, to pay for the salary and expenses of the arbitration commissioners. On 29 February 1796, Washington declared the treaty in effect, but did not yet request funding. Without consulting Madison, Edward Livingston then introduced a resolution demanding documentation of the treaty instructions and negotiations. Following the decision by a Federalist caucus to oppose this demand on the grounds that the House of Representatives had no authority over treaties, the Republicans submitted a resolution declaring the right of the House to sanction or refuse treaties which contained stipulations affecting any of the powers vested in the House, particularly appropriations. Washington continued to refuse to submit the documents, and the Republicans, having realized they had enough votes, determined to defeat the treaty.[32]

The Federalists then mobilized public opinion and exerted various forms of personal pressure on individual congressmen. Philip Schuyler in New York, John Marshall in Virginia, and James McHenry in Maryland roused supporters in their respective states. The bank presidents in Philadelphia reportedly threatened to deny discounts to those who did not sign Federalist petitions, while insurance companies, facing the possibility of war, declined to provide ship insurance policies. The British in turn asserted they would not withdraw from the posts unless the treaty was implemented. The Federalists did not claim that the British would declare war if the treaty was not signed, only that they would adopt policies like retaining the posts, increasing seizures and impressments, and stirring up western Indians, that would ultimately provoke war. Gradually, the Federalists reduced the number of supporters for Republican measures in the House.[33]

Republicans continued to insist there would be no military conflict between the two nations. The United States would return to its embargo and nonintercourse policies. Since Britain and the West Indies were dependent on American markets and supplies, Republicans argued, Britain could not resort to war. The British need for bread would prevent it.[34] Federalists disagreed that the U.S. possessed that much leverage and feared the outbreak of war would split the union. Fisher Ames of Massachusetts gave a famous, widely circulated oration on that theme, and dramatically presented the risk of frontier violence should war erupt. Albert Gallatin, Republican leader in the House, then favored withdrawing the anti-treaty resolutions, but opted for suspending the treaty until the British stopped interfering with neutral nations. However, the vote for treaty implementation passed by a vote of 51–48.[35]

Washington credited the public petitions for the victory, while historians variously credit the petitions, oratory, senatorial threats, and personal pressure placed on delegates. Washington asserted that the treaty would bring twenty years of peace, which, combined with increases in population and resources, would then enable the U.S. to bid defiance to any nation on earth. Republicans thought the U.S. already strong enough to defy Britain, and that it did not need to purchase peace with what they considered national humiliation.[36] Partisan battles over the treaty therefore continued, and contributed to the establishment of the American party system. Such conflicts were especially heated during the Quasi-War with France, and during the presidential elections of 1796 and 1800 and the gubernatorial election of 1798 in New York, then calmed down until the termination of the treaty in 1805. Then the failure to renew or replace the treaty led to the Embargo of 1807, the Nonintercourse Act of 1809, and ultimately to the War of 1812.[37]

Implementation of the Treaty

Following ratification came the task of implementing the treaty. Evacuation of the British-held posts progressed smoothly in 1796, greatly increasing support for the treaty. Washington queried Jay, among others, for advice on instructions to the diplomat who would be assigned to renegotiate Article 12 regarding West Indian trade. Jay responded on 3 June 1796 by suggesting efforts to raise the tonnage limits specified by Article 12 from 70 to 100, but warned that British anger at American popular opposition to the treaty and support for France made the times unpropitious for further negotiations. He also recommended further consideration of Lord Loughborough's proposals regarding rights of aliens and rules of evidence in inheritance cases involving citizens of both nations.[38] Jay also continued to correspond with Grenville, warning him that British resumption of ship seizures and the impressment of American seamen were jeopardizing the improved Anglo-American relations they sought to achieve when negotiating the treaty. He also corresponded with Rufus King when he became minister to Great Britain, and with Americans involved with the arbitration commissions, especially John Trumbull, Christopher Gore, and Samuel Bayard, to keep abreast of how effective procedures for implementing the treaty were, and to give advice as needed.[39]

With the support of the new British minister to the United States, Robert Liston, the first of the commissions to accomplish its mission was the commission to settle the St. Croix River portion of the boundary with Canada. This commission consisted of David Howell of Rhode Island, Egbert Benson of New York, and Thomas Barclay of Annapolis, Nova Scotia. It met in St. Andrews, New Brunswick, on 4 October 1796, secured surveyors to make an extensive survey of the disputed region, and adjourned until August 1797. Meeting then in Boston, the commission took testimony from John Adams and obtained a written deposition from Jay on what they intended when they negotiated the peace treaty. After further examination of documents and witnesses, the commission again adjourned until October 1798 by which time it had received copies of the surveyors' map. After meeting daily for ten days, on 25 October the commissioners signed a unanimous award indicating that the Schoodic River was the intended boundary.[40]

Efforts to settle American ship claims in British courts at first went badly, but after the treaty was ratified, Grenville, Lord Loughborough, and other British officials intervened to limit illegal seizures and gave more assistance to challenges to prize court decisions. They supported the right of the commission established to arbitrate cases of British seizures to determine its own jurisdiction. The ability of the commissioners to challenge decisions based on current English law if they were contrary to the law of nations was affirmed by Loughborough, who affirmed that "the construction of the American gentlemen is correct. It was the intention of the high contracting parties to the treaty, to cloth the commission with power paramount to all the maritime courts of both nations— a power to review, and (if in their opinion it should appear just) to reverse the decision of any or of all the maritime courts of both."[41] British commissioners John Nicholl and John Anstey, and American commissioners Christopher Gore of Massachusetts and William Pinkney of Maryland, and John Trumbull of Connecticut, who was selected by lot as the fifth commissioner, were allowed not to restore prizes but rather to award compensation for damages despite the decisions in British admiralty courts. The commission's deliberations then worked well until interrupted by the breakup of the third commission—the one established in Philadelphia to review the claims of British debtors.[42]

The American commissioners in Philadelphia, Thomas Fitzsimons and James Innes[43] (later replaced by Samuel Sitgreaves) were outnumbered 3 to 2 by those selected by the British (Thomas Macdonald and Henry Pye Rich) and John Guillemard, an Englishmen residing in America chosen by lot as the fifth commissioner. When the commissioners failed to reach acceptable compromises on the legal ground rules, especially the question of whether it was necessary to have previously brought a claim before the courts, and how to determine whether a defendant was capable of repaying a debt, the American commissioners withdrew from the commission, rendering it unable to vote. The breakup of the debt commission in July 1799 led in retaliation to the temporary shutdown of the claims commission until the dispute was resolved by a new convention signed by Rufus King and Lord Hawkesbury in January 1802 under which the United States government agreed to a lump sum payment of £600,000 ($2,664,000) to be divided among British debt claimants. The seizure commission was then reinstated. When the claims commission concluded its business on 24 February 1804, it had awarded $11,650,000 to American claimants for ships and cargoes seized by the British and $143,428.14 to British claimants for losses derived from French privateers armed or operating from American ports in violation of American neutrality.[44]

1. JJ to ER, and to RK, both 19 Nov. 1794, above; JJ to AH, 19 Nov. 1794, ALS, DLC: Hamilton (EJ: 10771); DftS, UkWc-A (EJ: 00049); *WJ*, 2: 237–38; *HPJ*, 4: 135; *PAH*, 17: 390–91; and JJ to GW, 19 Nov. 1794, ALS, DLC: Washington (EJ: 10638); Dft, NNC (EJ: 08454); *WJ*, 2: 236–37; *HPJ*, 4: 133–35; *PGW: PS*, 17: 173–75.

2. See JJ to Thomas Pinckney, 19 Nov. 1794, Dft, NNC (EJ: 09471); and Pinckney to JJ, 20 Nov. 1794, above; JQA to JJ, 21 Nov. 1794, above; JJ to William Short, 24 Nov. 1794, Dft, NNC (EJ: 08918); JJ to ER, 2 Feb. 1795, enclosing copies of JJ's letters to James Monroe, of 24, 24 and 28 Nov. 1794, above; Short to JJ, 7 Jan. 1795, above; Monroe to JJ, 17 Jan. 1795, ALS, NNC (EJ: 90541); C, DNA: Jay Despatches, 1794–95 (EJ: 04299); *Monroe Papers*, 3: 207; JT to JJ, 23 July 1795, below.

3. ER to JJ, 3 Dec. 1794, LS, marked Duplicate, NHi: Jay (EJ: 00619); NNC: JJ Lbk. 8; *ASP: FR*, 1: 509; and 15 Dec. 1794, LS, NHi: Jay (EJ: 00620); *ASP: FR*, 1: 509–12; JJ to ER, 7 Jan. 1795, LS, DNA: Jay Despatches, 1794–95 (EJ: 04345); *ASP: FR*, 1: 512; and JJ to ER, 2 and 6 Feb. 1795, both above; GW to JJ, 18 Dec. 1794, ALS, NNC (EJ: 07257); Dft, DLC: Washington (EJ: 10639); LbkCs, DLC: Washington; *PGW: PS*, 17: 286–89; JJ to GW, 25 Feb. 1795, ALS, DLC: Washington (EJ: 10642); Dft, NNC (EJ: 08455); and E of first four paragraphs, NHi: Henry V. O'Reilly (EJ: 00691); *PGW: PS*, 17: 577–80; and JJ to GW (private), 6 Mar. 1795, below.

4. JJ to SLJ, 21 Nov. 1794, above.

5. See Grenville to JJ, 11 May 1795, below; ER to JJ, 8 Mar. 1795, below; *Lloyd's List* (London), 28 Nov. 1794, and 21 Apr. 1795; *Boston Gazette*, 23 Mar. 1795. For the *Tankerville*, see Grenville to JJ, 11 May 1795, below.

6. See ER to JJ, 8 Mar. 1795, below.

7. Blaney to JJ, 20 Sept. 1795, ALS, NNC (EJ: 05504). For GW's summons of the Senate to meet on 8 June, see GW to JA, 3 Mar. 1795, *PGW: PS*, 17: 609.

8. For JJ's arrival and election, see John Jay's Address upon his Arrival in New York, 28 May 1795, below; Report on the Address of the Committee of Canvassers to John Jay and his Reply, with a Copy of the Certificate of his Election, 8 June 1795, below.

9. ER to JJ, 26 Apr. 1795; and JJ to ER, 28 May, and 1 June 1795 (two letters), all ALS, DNA: Jay Despatches, 1794–95 (EJ: 04295; EJ: 04294; EJ: 04292); *ASP: FR*, 1: 519.

10. On JJ's trip to Philadelphia, see *Dunlap and Claypoole's American Daily Advertiser* (Philadelphia), 11 June 1795; *Argus, Greenleaf's New Daily Advertiser* (New York), 20 June 1795.

11. On the discussion of what documents to send to the Senate and on GW's message to the Senate forwarding the treaty, see *Executive Journal*, 1: 177–91; *Annals*, 4: 653–86; *PGW: PS*, 18: 200–202; and, for the documents submitted to the Senate, see *Annals*, 4: 2370–2534; and *ASP: FR*, 1: 470–520.

12. For a summary of the arguments against the treaty and Senate opposition to Art. 12, see Combs, *Jay Treaty*, 152–58.

13. For the endeavors of AH and RK to gain senate approval for treaty ratification without the inclusion of Art. 12, see AH to RK, 11 June, and to William Bradford, 13 June 1795, *PAH*, 18: 370–73, 373–76; King, *Life and Correspondence of Rufus King*, 2: 14; Perkins, *First Rapprochement*, 31.

14. On Burr's role on the ratification issue and his resolutions on revising the treaty of 22 June 1795, see *PAB*, 1: 211–14, 218–21; Combs, *Jay Treaty*, 161; and Perkins, *First Rapprochement*, 31–32.

15. For the Senate votes, see Perkins, *First Rapprochement*, 32.

16. On the publication of the treaty, see Combs, *Jay Treaty*, 162; and Perkins, *First Rapprochement*, 33.

17. See Combs, *Jay Treaty*, 162–63; and Perkins, *First Rapprochement*, 33–34.

18. For RRL's 16 essays as "Cato", drafts of which are in NHi: Livingston, see *Argus, Greenleaf's New Daily Advertiser* (New York), 15, 17, 22, 25, 31 July; 7, 11, 17, 22, 26, 29 Aug.; and 2, 10, 16, 23, 30 Sept. 1795; and Carey, *American Remembrancer*, 1: 114–22, 147–74, 219–52; 2: 3–13; 3: 63–67. For RRL's letter to GW and the reply, see RRL to GW, 8 July 1795, and GW to RRL, 20 Aug. 1795, *PGW: PS*, 18: 300–303, 569–70.

19. On the role of Brockholst Livingston, see James Duane to JJ, 31 July 1795, below; and *PAH*, 18, 477 and note 13. For the five "Decius" essays, see *Argus, Greenleaf's New Daily Advertiser* (New York), 10, 11, 13, 14 and 16 July 1795, and Carey, *American Remembrancer*, 2: 18–40, 154–59. For the six "Cinna" pieces, see *Argus, Greenleaf's New Daily Advertiser*, 4–5, 11, 15, and 18 Aug. 1795, and Carey, *American Remembrancer*, 3: 75–101, 219–52. On their authorship, see RRL to Monroe, 25 Aug. 1795, ALS, DLC: Monroe; *Monroe Papers*, 3: 426–27. On the New York town meeting, see James Duane to JJ, 31 July 1795, and notes, below; King, *Life and Correspondence of Rufus King*, 2: 16–17; and Perkins, *First Rapprochement*, 33–34.

20. On Edward Livingston's role in the House of Representatives' efforts to block implementation of the treaty, see Perkins, *First Rapprochement*, 39.

21. See the "Introductory Note: The Defense No. 1," *PAH*, 18: 475–79, and for the "Camillus" essays, see *PAH*, 18–20: passim. For JA's statement on JJ's involvement, see King, *Life and Correspondence of Rufus King*, 2: 12–13.

22. JJ to Robert Goodloe Harper, 19 Jan. 1796, and notes, below.

23. On JJ's expenses, see JJ to TP (private), 19 Apr. 1797; and JJ to the Public, 25 Apr. 1797, both below.

24. On the French response to the treaty, see RK to JJ, 10 Jan. and 6 Feb. 1797, both below; TP

to JJ (private), 23 Jan. 1797, and JJ to TP (private), 31 Jan. 1797, both below; and the editorial note "John Jay and the Response to the XYZ Affair in New York," below.

For JJ's expectations and for his other responses to criticism of the Jay Treaty, see JJ to GW (private), 6 Mar., to Henry Lee, 11 July, to TP (private), 17 Aug., to GW (private), 3 Sept., to James Duane, 16 Sept. 1795, and to Daniel Coxe, 4 Apr. 1796, all below; JJ to ER, 1 June 1795, ALS, DNA: Jay Despatches, 1794–95 (EJ: 04294); *ASP: FR*, 1: 519; JJ to Peter Thacher, 26 May 1796, Dft, NNC (EJ: 08961); JJ to John Drayton, 6 Sept. 1797, below. JJ continued to comment on the legal aspects of implementing the Jay Treaty, but declined to reveal details of his negotiations to other than authorized officials. See JJ to Abraham Cuyler, 13 Nov. 1795, below.

25. For JJ's comments on the opposition based on the issues of slave compensation and British debts, see JJ to Duane, 16 Sept. 1795, below.

26. For JJ's comments on western posts and Indian affairs, see ibid.

27. On access to West Indian trade, see JJ to GW (private), 6 Mar., and (private), 3 Sept. 1795, both below. For JJ's views on the treaty's ban on sequestration of debts, JJ to ER, 19 Nov. 1794, above, and Combs, *Jay Treaty*, 154. On opposition to the need to go through British courts first before appealing to the arbitration commission, see Combs, *Jay Treaty*, 152. Samuel Bayard, however, reported that following news of the ratification of the Jay Treaty, British courts responded more favorably to American claims. See Bayard to JJ, 25 Feb. 1796, below.

28. On the renewal of ship and provision seizures, see JT to JJ, 23 July 1795, below; and Combs, *Jay Treaty*, 164–70; Charles R. Ritcheson, *Aftermath of Revolution: British Policy toward the United States, 1783–1795* (Dallas, 1969), 299, 354; Sterling, "Letters of Samuel Bayard," 414–16; and *PTJ*, 28: 391, 392n.

Josiah T. Newcomb argues that the Order in Council of 25 Apr. 1795, was, contrary to American perception, not similar to that of 8 June 1793. The first order was based on the Rule of War of 1756 and provided for the confiscation of all neutral vessels bound for French ports with cargoes of corn, flour, or meal. The order of April 1795 was based on the ancient right of Consolato del Mare or law of the sea and called for the seizure of enemy property disguised as neutral goods on neutral ships. Newcomb asserts, and Bradford Perkins, among other historians, agrees that the promulgation of the April order almost led to the defeat of the Jay Treaty in the United States. See Newcomb, "New Light on the Jay Treaty," *American Journal of International Law*, 28 (1934): 687–88; Bemis, *Jay Treaty*, 156; Perkins, *First Rapprochement*, 35–36.

29. For ER's recommendation to postpone ratification, see ER to GW, 12 July 1795, *PGW: PS*, 18: 312–326; for AH's recommendation to postpone exchange of ratifications if the order remained in effect, see AH to Wolcott, 10 Aug. 1795, *PAH*, 19: 111–12. On ER's dismissal and its impact on ratification, see TP to JJ (private), 14 Aug. 1795, and JJ's reply (private) of 17 Aug., both below; and Combs, *Jay Treaty*, 166–70. For ER's resignation, see ER to GW, 19 Aug. 1795, *PGW: PS*, 18: 563–65. On GW's difficulty finding a replacement for ER as Secretary for Foreign Affairs, and the ultimate appointment of Timothy Pickering, see Perkins, *First Rapprochement*, 37. On TP's role as Secretary of State, see Gerard Clarfield, "Postscript to the Jay Treaty: Timothy Pickering and Anglo-American Relations, 1795–1797," *WMQ* 23 (January 1966): 106–20.

30. On the motivations for the renewal of ship seizures, see JT to JJ, 23 July 1795, below; Tench Coxe to TJ, 30 July 1796, *PTJ*, 28: 421–23; Combs, *Jay Treaty*, 163–65; and Perkins, *First Rapprochement*, 34–36.

31. On the delays in the exchange of ratifications, see JJ to GW (private), 26 Jan.; RK to JJ, 29 Jan.; and JA to JJ, 31 Jan. 1796, all below; and Perkins, *First Rapprochement*, 37–38.

32. On the actions in the House of Representatives following promulgation of the ratified treaty

in February 1796, see *Annals*, 5: 426–783, 940–1292; King, *Life and Correspondence of Rufus King*, 2: 39–45; *PJM*, 16: 247–48, 286–87; *PTJ*, 29: 9–11, 55–57; and GW to JJ, 31 Mar., and JJ to GW (private), 18 Apr. 1796, both below; Perkins, *First Rapprochement*, 39–40; and Combs, *Jay Treaty*, 171–80. On the instructions given to JJ, see the editorial note "The Jay Treaty: Appointment and Instructions," and AH to JJ, and ER to JJ, both 6 May 1794, *JJSP*, 5: 609–21, 631–36, 636–47. For GW's refusal to send the instructions and reports on the negotiations to the House, see GW to the House of Representatives, 30 Mar. 1796, *PGW: PS*, 19: 635–38.

33. On Federalist mobilization of support, see Perkins, *First Rapprochement*, 40–42; and Todd Estes, "Shaping the Politics of Public Opinion: Federalists and the Jay Treaty Debate," *Journal of the Early Republic* 20 (Fall 2000): 393–422. On the Federalist fear of war, and Republican insistence that rejection of the treaty would not lead to war, see Combs, *Jay Treaty*, 182–84. For JJ's perception of British determination to continue the war with France and unwillingness to make concessions that Britain thought would jeopardize the war effort, see JJ to GW (private), 6 Mar. 1795, below.

34. On the view that food supplies from the United States were essential to the economies of Britain and the British West Indies, see Combs, *Jay Treaty*, 183.

35. On Fisher Ames's speech, see Todd Estes, "'The Most Bewitching Piece of Parliamentary Oratory': Fisher Ames' Jay Treaty Speech Reconsidered," *Historical Journal of Massachusetts* 28 (Winter 2000): 1–22; and Sandra Gustafson, *Eloquence Is Power: Oratory and Performance in Early America* (Chapel Hill, N.C. and Williamsburg, Va., 2000), 235–46. For the text of the speech, see *The Speech of Mr. Ames in the House of Representatives of the United States, When in Committee of the Whole, On Thursday, April 28. 1796* (Philadelphia, 1796; *Early Am. Imprints*, series 1, no. 47701); and Seth Ames, ed., *Works of Fisher Ames*, 2 vols. (Boston, 1854), 2: 1142–82. On the reasons the House ultimately voted funding for implementing the treaty, see Combs, *Jay Treaty*, 183–89. For the suggestion that a vote on funding for the building of Washington, D.C., was tied to the vote for the implementation of the treaty, see Kenneth R. Bowling, *Creation of Washington, D.C.: The Idea and Location of the American Capital* (Fairfax and Lanham, Va., 1991), 232–33 and 278n53; *PJM*, 16: 247, 286; *PTJ*, 29: 9–11, 55–57.

36. For GW's statement on the importance of the period of peace, see GW to Charles Carroll, 1 May 1796, *ALS*, ViMtvL; and Combs, *Jay Treaty*, 187. On the Republican contention that the U.S. was already strong enough to confront Great Britain, see Combs, *Jay Treaty*, 188–89.

37. See the editorial notes "John Jay Wins Reelection as Governor in 1798" and "John Jay and the Response to the XYZ Affair in New York," both below; and Combs, *Jay Treaty*, 188. On the Jay Treaty and the 1796 presidential election, see Jeffrey L. Pasley, *The First Presidential Contest: 1796 and the Founding of American Democracy* (Lawrence, Kans., 2013), esp. 101–81.

38. On the successful transfer of posts, see Perkins, *First Rapprochement*, 47–48. For alien rights, property ownership, and inheritance, see Article Proposed by the Lord Chancellor (Loughborough), [c. 9 Oct. 1794], above; JJ to Loughborough, 9 Oct. 1794, above; JJ to GW (private), 3 Sept., and (private), 4 Sept. 1795, both below; and JJ to TP, 6 June 1796, below.

39. For JJ's correspondence with Grenville, especially on the issues of ship seizures, relations with Indians, and impressments, see JJ to GW (private), 3 Sept. 1795, below; JJ to Grenville, 1 May 1796, and 4 June 1797, both below; Grenville to JJ, 17 Mar. 1796, below; and 9 July 1796, NNC (EJ: 08549). For JJ's correspondence with Samuel Bayard, agent for settling the ship claims, see Bayard to JJ, 6 Jan. 1796, ALS, NNC (EJ: 12535); C, enclosed in JJ to GW, 25 Mar., 1796, below; 25 Feb. 1796, below; 16 May 1796, below; 11 Oct. 1796, ALS, NNC (EJ: 12542); JJ to Bayard, 25 Mar. 1796, below.

For JJ's correspondence with JT as a member of the commission, see JT to JJ, 7 Sept. and 16 Dec. 1796; 20 July and 7 Aug. 1797, 20 Sept. 1798, all below; 25 Mar., ALS, NNC (EJ: 07211); LbkC, DLC:

Trumbull (EJ: 10359); and 3 June 1799, ALS, NNC (EJ: 07212); LbkC, DLC: Trumbull (EJ: 10360); JJ to JT, 20 Oct. 1796, LbkC, N: Governor's Lbk. 1 (EJ: 03050); and 27 Oct. 1797, below, and 6 June 1800, ALS, Harlan Crow Library. See also Christopher Gore to JJ, 24 Oct. 1796, and 13 Nov. 1797, below; RK to JJ, 29 Jan., 25 Aug. 1796, and 12 Nov. 1796; and 10 Jan. and 6 Feb. 1797, all below; and TP to JJ, 10 Oct., and JJ to TP, 14 Oct. 1795, both below. JJ's correspondence with merchant Daniel Coxe also discussed the treaty. See JJ to Coxe, 4 Apr. 1796, and Coxe to JJ, 30 Nov. 1796, both below.

40. On the St. Croix commission, see TP to JJ, 16 July 1796, with enclosed TP to AH of the same date, above; JJ's Testimony regarding the St. Croix River, [21 May 1798], and notes, below; Moore, *International Arbitrations*, 1: 1–44; Moore, *International Adjudications*, 1: 1–514; 2: 1–406; Perkins, *First Rapprochement*, 48–53; Lillach, "Jay Treaty Commissions," 265–68. See also JJ's Project for a Treaty with Great Britain, 30 Sept. 1794, above, note 17.

41. Francis Wharton, ed., *A Digest of the International Law of the United States taken from Documents Issued by Presidents and Secretaries of State and from Decisions of Federal Courts and Opinions of Attorney-Generals*, 3 vols, (Washington, D.C., 1888), 3: 329a.

42. On the activities of the debt commission in Philadelphia and the ship claims commission in London, see Moore, *International Arbitrations*, 1: 271–98, 299–349, 3: 18, 95–97; Moore, *International Adjudications*, 3: 1–517; 4: 1–551; Trumbull, *Autobiography*, 191–98; Fewster, "British Ship Seizures," 428–52; Perkins, *First Rapprochement*, 53–56, 117–19: Bemis, *Jay's Treaty*, 439–41; Lillach, "Jay Treaty Commissions," 268–76, 276–80; *PTJ*, 30: 623–25; Samuel Bayard to JJ, 25 Feb. 1796, below; Grenville to JJ, 9 July 1796, cited above; RK to JJ, 25 Aug., 12 Nov. 1796, 10 Jan. and 6 Feb. 1797, all below; JT to JJ, 7 Sept. and 16 Dec. 1796, below; Christopher Gore to JJ, 24 Oct. 1796, below; 13 Nov. 1797, below; and 26 Feb 1798, ALS, NNC (EJ: 08479; EJ: 08484); TP to JJ (private), 13 Dec. 1797, below; and JJ to TP, 23 Dec. 1797, below; Gore to JJ, 12 Jan. 1802, ALS, NNC (EJ: 08485). See also JJ's letters of recommendation for Gore of May 1796, Dfts, NNC (EJ: 08957). For Bayard's complaints about the British lack of cooperation regarding ship claims in the immediate aftermath of the signing of the treaty, and his reports on the greater British support given following ratification, see Sterling, "Letters of Samuel Bayard," 408–24; JJ to GW, 25 Mar., enclosing Bayard to JJ, 6 Jan. 1796, below; and Bayard to JJ, 16 May 1796, below; and 11 Oct. 1796, ALS, NNC (EJ: 12542).

43. James Innes (1754–98) of Virginia.

44. See the Convention Regarding Articles 6 and 7 of the Jay Treaty and Art. 4 of the Definitive Treaty of Peace signed at London January 8, 1802, in Hunter Miller, ed., *Treaties and other international acts of the United States of America* vol. 2 *Documents 1–40: 1776–1818* (Washington, D.C., 1931): 488–91. On the awards given on debt claims and ship seizures, see Trumbull, *Autobiography*, 237–38; Perkins, *First Rapprochement*, 213n19; Fewster, "British Ship Seizures," 452; Lillach, "Jay Treaty Commissions," 275, 280.

For 19th-century Jay correspondence on the Jay Treaty, see PAJ to JJ, 14 Jan. 1809, ALS, NNC (EJ: 06139), and 26 June 1812, ALS, NNC (EJ: 06165); and JJ to PAJ, 17 Jan. 1809, Dft, NNC (EJ: 06140).

To George Washington (private)

London 6th—March 1795

Dear Sir

My last to you was written on the 25th. ult:[1] and is gone in the Ohio, Capt. Kemp, who sailed last week for New York.[2] It was not untill after my Dispatches were sent to him, that I had the Pleasure of recieving your's of the 18th of December last—[3]

After considering all that I have seen and heard on the Subject, it is my opinion that the common and popular (not official) Language and Conduct of america relative to great Britain, manifested such a Disposition, as to create serious apprehensions in this Country, that we should join with the French in the war— That these apprehensions gave occasion to secret Designs, calculated on such an Event— that in Proportion as your Views and Counsels became developed, these apprehensions gradually subsided— That my mission was regarded as a strong Proof of your Desire to preserve peace, and that the perfect and universal Confidence reposed in your personal character, excluded every Doubt of your being sincere— that this Government are not yet entirely convinced, that a pacific and conciliatory System will be supported by the Inclination and correspondent Conduct of the great Body of the People. various Circumstances however induce me to believe, that the Cabinet ultimately determined to give conciliation a fair Experiment, by doing us substantial Justice; and by consenting to such arrangem^ts. favorable to us, as the national Interests and habitual Prejudices would admit. To relax the navigation act, was to alarm these Prejudices; and therefore was a measure which required caution and circumspection, especially in the first Instance— To break the Ice was the Difficulty—to enlarge the aperture afterwards would be more easy; and it will probably be done, if we should be reasonably temperate and prudent— to admit us into their East and West India Dominions, and into all their continental american Territories, under any modifications were were decided Deviations from their former Policy, and tended to shock ancient Prejudices— Yet these things have been done— none but a strong administration would have ventured it— These are offerings to conciliation; and include, tho' not confessedly, Satisfaction to our claims of Justice—

What passed at Paris on M^r. Munroe's arrival, I am persuaded made a strong and disagreable Impression;[4] and had not your private character prevented those Transactions from being imputable in any Degree to your orders, I do believe that the System of conciliation would have been instantly abandoned— What would have succeeded it, cannot be easily conjectured— certainly no Treaty so favorable to us as the present, would then have been attainable— whatever the american opinion of it may prove to be; The Administration here think it very friendly to us, and that it could not, in the present moment have been made more so, without exciting great Discontents & uneasiness in this country—

The present Situation of Great Britain may to us and others appear to be perillous, but the ministry seem to have no such Fears. They have been uniformly bent on prosecuting the war with Vigour, and since my arrival I have observed no change in that Resolution— Even a distinguished Leader in the Opposition lately told me, that the French could not possibly injure the Vitals of this Country— Let it be Infatuation, or what it will, the Government and the great Majority of this nation meant and mean to continue the war. I will mention a striking anecdote—

You have doubtless heard, that the merchants concerned in the american Trade ∧gave∧ me a Dinner— The principal Cabinet ministers were present, and about 200 merchants— many Toa[s]ts were given— When "the President of the united States" was given, it was proposed to be with three cheers, but they were prolonged (as if by Preconcert, but evidently not so) to six— Several other Toasts passed with great acclamation, particularly "the wooden walls of old England". almost every Toast referable to america, and manifesting a Desire of Conciliation and Cordiality, met with general and strong marks of approbation— Towards the conclusion of the Feast, I was asked for a Toast, I gave a *neutral* one—vizt. "a safe & honorable Peace to all the belligerent powers"— You cannot concieve how coldly it was recieved, and tho' civility induced them to give it three cheers, yet they were so faint and single, as most decidedly to shew that Peace was not the thing they wished— these were *merchants*. M^r. Pinckney was struck as forceably by it as I was; and we both drew the same Conclusions from it—[5]

Except an inconsiderable number, the men of Rank and Property, and all whom they can influence, throughout the Kingdom, think the war is indispensable to their Safety. The Dread of Jacobin Politics and Jacobin Scenes, and the Expectation that the pecuniary Resources of this Country will ultimately render them superior in the contest, appear to be their prevailing motives. It was expected by some that the Loss of Holland would have damped this Spirit. it has had only a partial Effect. we find the ministry and Parliament have been stimulated by it to greater Efforts.

All the members who voted for what are called the pacific Resolutions, were not moved, as many of them certainly were, by a mere Desire of Peace, but by the Policy of professing a Readiness to make peace, in order that if spurned by the French, the nation might continue in the war with more constancy and unanimity— they did not suppose that an acceptable peace could in the present moment be obtained— This People appear to think their Constitution and Property and national character and Importance as being all at Stake; and on that Stake it be inflexibly ∧determined∧ to risque every Thing—[6]

of the great number who advocated a Reform in Parliament &c. there is a portion (but how great cannot easily be ascertained) who are so sore and mortified and vexed, that in my opinion the french Successes give them as much pleasure as pain. There are men among them whose Designs as well as whose Fortunes are desperate, as well as men who have honest Designs and good Fortunes. These People are at present kept from action by the Energy of the Government, and the unanimity of the great majority of the nation as to the necessity of the war—

The french Jacobins have greatly injured the Cause of rational Liberty. The detestable massacres impieties and abominations imputable to Them, excited in the people here the most decided Hatred and abhorrence; and ˄the˄ Government by that circumstance rendered the war popular. But the System of moderation and Justice lately adopted in France, the Suppression of the Jacobins and the strict Discipline observed in their armies, will doubtless have an Influence on the Sentiments of this Nation— I think I see Traces of this Influence already, on minds not suspected of it.

The present war System however strikes me as being less firm consolidated and formidable than it appears to be. The administration has been composed more with a view to the Conciliation of Parties, than the Efficiency of measures. I think the System is liable to Fluctuation and Derangement from a variety of Events & Circumstances opposition to Reform, as leading to Innovations, is doubtless carried too far, and may produce serious consequences— Ideas of the Rights of man, and the Inferences deducible from them, are spreading among the people. Veneration for Royalty, abstractly considered, has abated, and altho the King is popular, yet it is said that the Prince of Wales[7] and the Duke of York are not— The Prosperity of Britain results from and depends on many Causes— complicated machines are most liable to Derangement— Should there be a Scarcity of corn—want of Employment to the manufacturers, or signal Convulsions or Disasters in the East or West Indies, or in Ireland, or on the Sea, the Government would find their Task very arduous. alarm and Distress will abate pride and obstinacy; and when the multitude begin to feel severely, their passions frequently take a new and dangerous Direction.

The minister would I think have stood on stronger Ground, if he had taken the first good opportunity of saying explicitly in the House of Commons; that it was France who declared war against Great Britain, and not Great Britain against France; and that the Government was disposed and ready to make peace whenever France would do it on Terms compatible with the Honor and essential Interests of Great Britain. To put an Enemy in the wrong is to obtain great advantages— pleasing and so long continuing Lord chatham at the Head of the admiralty—[8] the putting the Duke of York at the Head of the army—[9] the improper Liberties taken with neutral nations, for which the Danes & Swedes on their part, are not yet satisfied— The strange Measures relative to Ireland— and many other things which strike me as Blunders, indicate a Defect either in the Cabinet or in the minister. altho' united as to the war; yet as to the mode of conducting it, the wisest Counsels may not always prevail. Upon the whole I shall be surprised, if in the course of this war Britain does not reap more Thorns than Laurels—

I have great Reason to believe that the King, the Cabinet, and nation were never more unanimous in any System than in that of Conciliation with us. even Lord Hawkesbury does not oppose it— If it should not succeed, they will naturally pass like a Pendulum to the other Extreme. This System rests principally on their Confidence in the uprightness Independence and wisdom of your Conduct. no other man whatever enjoys so completely the Esteem and Confidence of this nation, as you do; nor except the King, is any one so popular— The Idea which every where prevails is, that the Quarrel between Britain and America, was a family quarrel, and that it is Time it should be made up— for my part, I am for making it up, and for cherishing this Disposition on their part; by Justice, Benevolence and good manners on ours. To cast ourselves into the arms of this, or of any other nation, would be degrading injurious and puerile. nor in my opinion ought we to have any political connection with any foreign power—

Before I came here, I had no Idea that the King was so popular as he is, his Reign having been marked by national Calamities produced by reprehensible measures. But his Popularity is owing to his private, rather than his official character. as a man, there is much in him to commend; and I have not heard any vice imputed to him. as a domestic man, affectionate and attentive to his Queen and children, and affable to all about him, he is universally esteemed— Few men are so punctual in all things— He patronizes the Arts and Sciences— He pays uncommon attention to agriculture and delights in his Farms— He lays out about ten thousand pounds a Year in improving and embellishing the royal Estates— He is industrious, sober and temperate; and has acquired much various Knowledge and Information. He converses with Ease, and often with adroitness, and has an uncommon memory— they who ought to know him, concur in these accounts. That he is a great & a wise King, I have not heard asserted. That he does (to use a vulgar Expression) *as well as he knows how*, seems not to be doubted; but yet some say, that he occasionally is cunning, instead of being wise— I have heard him described as being a great man in little Things; and as being generally well in ₌ten₌tioned, pertina-cious, ₌&₌ persevering—

I hope M^r. Pinckney will not be long absent— [10] he stands well here, and I think him a discreet and meritorious minister. Had M^r. Short from Madrid, or M^r. Adams from Holland, been directed to take charge of our Affairs here in the mean Time; perhaps it would have been well.

I congratulate You and our Country, on the bloodless Issue of the Insurrection— it is very reputable to the Government and to the People, and exalts both in the Estimation of this and other nations.

The Tranquility of the present Session of Congress is a pleasing circum-stance; but I suspect it has proceeded more from their having had nothing to differ about, than from a spirit of Forbearance or a Desire of unanimity— The Result of my negociations will doubtless produce fresh Disputes, and give occasion to much Declamation; for I have no Idea that the Treaty will meet with antifœderal approbation. Besides, men are more apt to think of what they wish to have, than of what is in their power to obtain— How far a Rejection of such a Treaty would put the United States in the wrong? whether it is consistant with our Honor, Engagements and important Inter-ests? whether it is preferable upon the whole to a War? are Questions which require much cool and deliberate Consideration; as well as more Information than many who ₌will₌ decide upon them possess— I regret not having had Time to make my Letter, which accompanied the Treaty, more full;[11] so as to have particularized and explained the Reasons which relate to the several ar-ticles in it— Then I had not Leisure— to have done it since, would have been too late, as the Fate of the Treaty would probably be decided before [~~illeg-ible~~] subsequent Letters could arrive. I still have thoughts of reducing them to writing; and yet there are some among them which should not be published, lest the future measures which they also respect, should thereby be marred— I allude, for Instance, to the free navigation of the S^t. Lawrence—

M^r. Randolph does not see the West India article in the same Light that I do— [12] it breakes the Ice—that is, it breakes in upon the Navigation act— The least Stream from a mass of water, passing thro' a Bank, will enlarge its Passage— The very article stipulates that the arrangements to succeed it shall have in view the *further Extension* of commerce; this should not be too nicely [~~be~~] discussed in american or English newspapers; for tho' liberal and en-lightened People will admit such Extensions of Commerce to be beneficial to both Countries, yet all ancient Prejudices must be delicately managed— there are many Men who have less wisdom than power, and more Integrity than political Information— The Restriction not to carry certain articles to

Europe &cᵃ. is confined to the U.S. and the *british* Islands— from *other* places we may freely carry them— Deposits of french & Spanish Sugars &cᵃ may be made in the Dutch Danish or other Islands, & thence carried where we please. English Sugars Cotton Cocoa and Coffee will probably not be more than our Consumption requires, and all *Cotton* brought into our Country should be there manufactured—

The Paragraph in Baches paper[13] has no Foundation in Truth. not a single Syllable has ever passed between any of the ministers and myself on the Subject of our taking any part between France and Great Britain, either as mediators or otherwise. I have neither directly nor indirectly suggested or conveyed any such Ideas to them, nor they to me— with as little Truth have some of the newspapers in this City, announced that the minister had contracted with me for a supply of corn from the United States, at a reduced Price—[14] The Gazettes in both Countries abound in Fabrications; and if to publish only what they believe to be true, is a moral Duty, many Printers have much to answer for— In this Country they generally take Sides with, or against the ministry; and publish any thing whether true or otherwise, that suits their Parties— Some of them in America are doing the same thing. it is one of the Evils incident to the Freedom of the Press, and the use made of it by bad men and hireling writers—

Thus my dear Sir I have passed part of this Day very agreably in writing you this long Letter; and the pleasure is encreased by the opportunity it affords me of assuring you how cordially and sincerely I am your obliged & affectᵗᵉ Friend & Servᵗ

John Jay

The President of the United States

ALS, DLC: Washington (EJ: 10644). Endorsed. Marked "private" in the top left corner. C, NNC (EJ: 08456); *WJ* (extract), 2: 245–52; *HPJ* (extract), 4: 162–71; *PGW: PS*, 17: 618–27.

1. JJ to GW, 25 Feb. 1795, ALS, DLC: Washington (EJ: 10642); Dft, NNC (EJ: 08455); and E of first four paragraphs, NHi: Henry V. O'Reilly (EJ: 00691); *PGW: PS*, 17: 577–80.

2. The ship *Ohio*, John Kemp, sailed from London and reached New York on 23 April. *Daily Advertiser* (New York), 23 Apr. 1795.

3. GW to JJ, 18 Dec. 1794, ALS, NNC (EJ; 07257); Dft, DLC: Washington (EJ: 10639); LbkCs, DLC; *PGW: PS*, 17: 286–89.

4. On Monroe's speech in France and the British response, see JJ to ER, 13 Sept., and ER to JJ (private), 12 Nov. 1794, both above.

5. Two similar reports but with different commentary at the end covering the dinner given to JJ on 17 Dec. 1794, and some of the toasts given, appeared in American newspapers, including *New Hampshire Gazette* (Portsmouth), 17 Feb., and *American Minerva* (New York), 20 Feb. 1795; *PGW: PS*, 17: 625. The first commented on the Indian wars as principally supported by the British so that their withdrawal of assistance would have a tendency to restore peace. It was reprinted in *Greenleaf's*

New York Journal, 25 Feb., and *Albany Register*, 2 Mar 1795. The second expressed satisfaction that "so friendly a meeting" took place so soon after the time "when apprehensions were entertained that the two countries would be involved in all the horrors of war." It was reprinted in the *Philadelphia Gazette*, 21 Feb., *Worcester Intelligencer, or Brookfield Advertiser*, 3 Mar., *Rutland Herald*, 9 Mar., *Hampshire & Berkshire Chronicle* (Springfield), 23 Mar., and *Hampshire Gazette* (Northampton), 25 Mar. 1795.

6. JJ may be referring to resolutions passed in Parliament amending motions respecting peace made in the House of Commons by Charles Gray and in the House of Lords by Francis Russell, Duke of Bedford, on 26 and 27 Jan. 1795. After pledging support for vigorous prosecution of the war, the amendments asserted that the House relied "with equal confidence on his majesty's intention to employ vigorously the force and resources of the country in support of its essential interests; and on the desire, uniformly manifested by his majesty, to effect a pacification, on just and honourable grounds with any government of France, under whatever form, which shall appear capable of maintaining the accustomed relations of peace and amity with other countries." See Cobbett, *Parliamentary History of England*, 31: 1193–1279, esp. 1211–12, 1253; and *PGW: PS*, 17: 625n5.

7. George Augustus Frederick, Duke of Wales, (1762–1830), later George IV, was unpopular due to his extravagant and dissolute lifestyle, and poor relationship with George III. *PTJ*, 14: 430.

8. John Pitt, 2nd Earl of Chatham, was appointed First Lord of the Admiralty in 1788 and served until December 1794. Noted for his disorganization, laziness and lateness, he was blamed in part for the failure of the siege of Dunkirk in 1793.

9. Frederick Augustus, Duke of York (1763–1827), second son of George III, was the general commanding the difficult Flanders campaign in 1793–94; he was promoted to field marshal in February 1795 and made acting commander in chief of the British Army in April 1795.

10. Pinckney was then negotiating a treaty in Spain.

11. JJ to GW, 19 Nov. 1794, ALS, DLC: Washington (EJ: 10638); Dft, NNC (EJ: 08454); *WJ*, 2: 236–37; *HPJ*, 4: 133–35; *PGW: PS*, 17: 173–75. See also JJ to ER, 19 Nov. 1794, above.

12. For ER's criticism of the proposals for Art. 12 regarding trade with the West Indies, see ER to JJ, 15 Dec. 1794, NHi: Jay (EJ: 00620); *APS: FR*, 1: 509–12.

13. The clipping GW enclosed from Benjamin Bache's *Aurora* (Philadelphia), 13 Dec. 1794, reported on "good authority" that JJ had requested permission from the French government to communicate directly by packet with Monroe in Paris. It asserted that "This demand is thought by some to be indicative of a desire by the British court of commencing a peace negociation with the French, in which Mr. Jay should be the mediator."

14. *Lloyd's Evening Post* (London), 20–23 Feb. 1795, for example, reported that JJ had signed a contract with William Pitt under which "America is to furnish at a reduced price, an immense quantity of corn during the ensuing season." *PGW: PS*, 17: 627.

To Sarah Livingston Jay

London 6th. March 1795

My dear Sally

The Letters which Capt. Kemp will deliver to you leave me little to write at present— He will doubtless arrive before this can reach you, and I now write not because I have any thing new or interesting to add, but in Compliance with my invariable Rule to write by [*illegible*] every Vessel for New York, unless indeed when two sail together[1]

In the course of this month, towards the latter part of it I expect to recieve advices respecting the Treaty, together with Instructions relative to the Conclusion of my Business here. my Impatience to recieve them encreases as the Time approaches— not a moment shall then be lost in dispatching what may remain to be done—[2]

altho sensible of what I am to suffer ᴧby sicknessᴧ on the ocean, yet I look forward with pleasure to the Day when I am again to embark on it; trusting that the same kind providence which brought me here, will restore me to my Family; and give me an opportunity of thanking you personally for your many affectionate Letters, and unceasing attention to our mutual Concerns— I frequently anticipate with Satisfaction the pleasing moment, when I shall again take my place by our own fire Side, and with William on one Knee and Sally on the other, amuse you with a Variety of Information— I wish Maria may then be at Home, that we may be all together— If that should not be the Case I must take an early opportunity of making her a visit, for however inconvenient it might be so soon after my arrival, my Sollicitude to see her would not permit me to omit it—[3] my affection for all the Children is as yet very equal, and nothing but a Difference in their Behaviour will ever make it otherwise— adieu my dear Sally. Yours affecˢ & sincerely

John Jay

Mʳˢ. Jay

ALS, NNC (EJ: 08066).

1. The *Ohio*, commanded by John Kemp, landed at Sandy Hook 23 Apr. 1795. *Daily Advertiser* (New York), 23 Apr. 1795. See also JJ to GW, 6 Mar. 1795, above.

2. The treaty did not reach the U.S. until 7 Mar. 1795, four months after it left Great Britain. See the editorial note "Aftermath of the Jay Treaty: Responses, Ratification, and Implementation," above.

3. Maria Jay attended the Moravian Seminary at Bethlehem, Pa. See SLJ to JJ, 11 Nov. 1794, above.

Peter Augustus Jay to Sarah Livingston Jay

London 7 March 1795.

Dear Mama

I had pleasure of writing to you by the Ohio a few days ago. The Ellice is to sail tommorrow and will carry this[1]

We begin now to be a little anxious to hear the fate of the Treaty, which must by this Time have been decided— It has doubtless been productive of much declamation clamor and abuse— And I presume a certain party in New York with a worthy Senator at their head have been the most forward to reprobate and Oppose it— Let them however remember that should it thro' their machinations be rejected, upon their heads will be all the Bloodshed and Calamities which must ensue— We are the more anxious for the Arrival of the Treaty, since ~~it~~ ₐthatₐ is now the only Obstacle to our return— We shall sail in the very first Good Vessel after receiving it.[2]

It is surprizing to hear that the winter in America has been so very mild— It would seem that all the cold weather ~~in America~~ had crossed the Atlantic— The oldest people here do not recollect so uniformly severe a season— All the Snow has not yet disappeared—

The prices of every thing in this City are enormous, so high that ₐI dareₐ not repeat them— The Poor have suffered by them beyond belief—[3]

M^rs. Church & M^rs. Lowe desire to be remembered to you— Be so kind as to give my Love to M^rs. Ridley and Munro & to my sisters, and little Wig—[4] I am my dear mama Your affectionate Son

Peter Augustus Jay

M^rs. Jay

ALS, NNC (EJ: 06054). Addressed: "Mrs. Jay— / Broadway / New York / By the Ellice Capt. Hervey". Endorsed: ". . . received the 7th. May".

1. For the *Ohio*, captained by John Kemp, see JJ to SLJ, 6 Mar. 1795, above. The *Ellice* (*Allice*), captained by Hervey (Harvey), arrived in New York on 7 May. *Daily Advertiser* (New York), 8 May 1795. See also JJ to SLJ 6 Mar., above, and 13 Mar. 1795, below; and Robert Troup to AH, 11 May 1795, *PAH*, 18: 342.

2. For the concern over the arrival of the treaty, see JJ to SLJ, 6 Mar. 1795, above, and the editorial note "Aftermath of the Jay Treaty: Responses, Ratification, and Implementation," above. The senator PAJ refers to is Aaron Burr.

3. For the harsh winter, see JJ to SLJ, 3–6 Feb., above. Commodity prices increased as a result of the inclement weather, with coal reaching the price of £4 per ton.

4. "little Wig" refers to William Jay.

From Edmund Randolph

Department of State March 8. 1795.

Sir

At 7 o'clock yesterday evening, M^r. Blaney delivered to me the very important dispatches, which you had consigned to his care. He arrived at Norfolk eight days ago, after having been beaten off from the capes of Virginia for some weeks by strong winds. His charge was in good order, and the seals and Envelope were unviolated.[1]

The Amiable for Liverpool having dropped down the Delaware, there is a chance of putting this letter on board of her until five o'clock, but no later.[2] You will not therefore expect much more from me, than the acknowledgment of the treaty.

The last evening and this morning the President has been employed in perusing your dispatches; and they will occupy his attention, until he shall have come to some definitive judgment. Altho' it is so extremely uncertain, whether you will be in England when this letter shall reach it, I should be happy to give you his opinion if he had been able in so short a time to mature it.

The Senate will meet, as I have stated to you in another letter by the Amiable, on the 11th. of June next.[3] In the mean time the treaty will remain unknown thro' the President or myself to any person upon earth.

I will only add, that the particulars of your *oral* negotiations would be of infinite value, in shewing what was unattainable— Be assured however, that whether they arrive or not in time, you shall find the same unvaried candor, which has been hitherto pursued: and especially in the documents, accompanying the treaty to the senate. It at present seems just, that no letters from this department, which we had reason to suppose would not reach you before the treaty should be concluded, will should be laid before them.

As this letter will be addressed to other gentlemen besides yourself, I shall only add my wishes for your happy return, and that I have the honor to be Sir, yr. mo. ob. serv.

Edm: Randolph

John Jay esqr.

ALS, NcU: Preston Davie (EJ: 11935).

1. David Blaney, delivered the Treaty aboard the ship *Thomas*, Captain Vickery.

2. The ship *Amiable*, Captain Thompson, left Philadelphia bound for Liverpool on 7 Mar. *Gazette of the United States* (Philadelphia), 11 Mar. 1795.

3. ER is possibly referring to his letter of 20 Sept. 1794, C, DNA: Jay Despatches, 1794–95 (EJ: 04324); C, NHi: King (EJ: 04455).

To Sarah Livingston Jay

London 13th. March 1795

My dear Sally.

On the 22d. Feby. I wrote to you by Capt. Kemp, who will also bring you a few lines enclosing a Bill of Lading and Invoice of some Ale & Porter, which I have sent you by him—[1] Capt. Hervey of the Ellice went away last Saturday— he also has a Letter for you.[2] Since the Ohio sailed, no Letters

from you have come to Hand— as you will have ceased writing the first of
this month, I cannot expect the pleasure of recieving many more Letters from
you; but in exchange for it, I shall have that of being with you in the Course
of a few months— By the first of April I hope my final orders respecting the
Treaty will arrive; & I shall then take the earliest opportunity of embarking—
so that before the first of July I shall be at Home— indeed at *present* I think it
will be sooner— but as the Sailing of Vessels is uncertain, it is impossible to
calculate exactly—

You will find herewith enclosed Duplicates of the Bill of Lading and Invoice for the porter and ale sent you by Capt. Kemp—[3] I think it best to send
them, tho' I do not apprehend they will be necessary— I hope to find those
articles safe in our cellar, and yet to have the Satisfaction of partaking of them
with you and our Friends— I suppose Judge Hobart will be so occupied in
the Improvement of his Farm, that you will see him but seldom,[4] and as Benson delights in Poughkeepsie, he will not be frequently in New York— so we
separate and scatter— But our little Family are growing up around us— Let
us resign, to what we cannot alter; and enjoy whatever Good Providence may
bless us with—

In one of your Letters, you mention having written to me, and enclosed
a Letter from Maj^r. Lyon— it never came to Hand— I think I heard that
the Vessel by which it was sent, sprung a Leak, and put back— What finally
became of her I do not know— I mention this that, if the Maj^r. should say
anything of my not having answ^d. that Letter, he may know the Reason—[5] As
the Time of my Return approaches, I think more of our Concerns at Bedford
&c^a. unless I should be assigned to the Fall circuit, I hope before next winter
to put those affairs in Train; and take measures for doing what remains to
be done— much of our Lives is spent— a few Years of Leisure and Tranquility are very desireable— Whether they will fall to ~~us~~ our Lott cannot be
known— as they are the objects of my wishes and Desire, so shall they be of
my Endeavours— If they come, let us enjoy them; if not, let us be resigned
Content is in our Power, let it also be in our Inclination—

Col. Trumbull is gone ~~the~~ to France on his way to Stutgard where ₐheₐ
has some plates engraving— He cannot ascertain the Time of his Return
precisely—[6] In the mean Time Peter will act as his Deputy Secretary; and I
believe very well— I think he has derived advantages from being here; and
that your Expectations on that stead, will not be disappointed— He is nevertheless desirous to return, and will carry with him no acquisitions, which you
would wish him to leave behind— Remember however, that the best way to
avoid Disappointment, is not to expect too much

Remember me to M^rs. Ridley— I shall not write to the children by this vessel, having written to them by Capt. Kemp— a much longer absence from you all, would give my Patience a very severe Trial— I often think of those french Emigrants who left their Families in France; and who have Reason to think my Situation, compared with theirs, very desirable— so things figure by Comparison— Peet prefers new York to London, & is anxious to be at Home again.[7] Adieu my Dear Sally Yours very affectionately

John Jay

Mrs Jay

The Minerva from N York lately arrived—[8] She brought a great number of Letters— some of them mention that the conclusion of the Treaty was known in am^r but I cannot learn that it had arrived— no Letters by that vessel have as yet come to my Hands— perhaps the Capt. or some passengers may have some for me as Capt. Haley will leave Town in the morning, I shall not have an opportunity of writing by him after this Evg— I have postponed it to the last, that, in Case of rec^g. Letters from you by the Minerva, I might mention it— If you have not written by her, I am persuaded the omission was not intentional— Adieu—

Tell M^r. Munro that I have just rec^d. his Letter of 28 Decr. last[9] I have written to you also by Capt Hervey

ALS, NHi (EJ: 12311). C, NNC (EJ: 08067).

1. Letter not found, but referenced in JJ to SLJ, 6 Mar. 1795, above.

2. JJ probably refers to his letter 6 Mar. 1795, above.

3. Enclosed financial documents not found.

4. See John Sloss Hobart to JJ, 20 Nov. 1794, ALS, NNC (EJ: 05677).

5. Specific letter by SLJ not found. SLJ was involved in a dispute with Samuel Lyon, the estate manager at Bedford, and his son John Lyon (1770–1820) over their poor workmanship. SLJ specifically complained about their failure to build a mill on the Bedford property and to properly break horses, leading the senior Lyon to offer his resignation. See SLJ to JJ, 2 Aug. 1794, above; SLJ to Samuel Lyon, 9 Aug. 1794, ALS, NNC (EJ: 09181); 14 Nov. 1794, ALS, NNC (EJ: 09179); SLJ to JJ, 22 Oct. 1794, ALS, NNC (EJ: 06561); 15 Nov. 1794, Dft, NNC (EJ: 09180); Samuel Lyon to SLJ, 10 Nov. 1794, ALS, NNC (EJ: 09238); PJM to JJ, 19 Nov. 1794, ALS, NNC (EJ: 09372); Dft, NNMus (EJ: 00434); 20 Dec. 1794, ALS, NNC (EJ: 09374); Dft, NNMus (EJ: 00439).

6. JT was not only having plates engraved, but verbally delivering the treaty to Monroe in Paris. See JJ Memorandum to JT, 5 Feb., and JJ to James Monroe, 19 Feb. 1795, both above, and JT to JJ, 6 Mar., and PAJ to JJ, 1 Aug. 1798 (first letter), both below.

7. Peet (Pete or Peter) Williams, the enslaved servant who accompanied JJ during his stay in London.

8. The Minerva, Captain Crowninchild, arrived in Gravesend from New York on 10 Mar. 1795. Lloyd's List (13 Mar. 1795).

9. PJM to JJ, 28 Dec. 1794, Dft, NNMus (EJ: 00441).

To Grenville

Royal Hotel. Pall Mall 21 March 1795

my Lord

on Tuesday next I am to dine with Mr. Vaughan at Hackney—[1] Having hitherto availed myself of only one Invitation from that Gentleman, an Appology would not be kindly recieved—

on Thursday and Friday I am not engaged, but as the one may be more convenient to your Lordship than the other, I forbear naming either—

It is very desireable that some measures to facilitate the Business in question should be concerted— the parties interested would be gratified, & the united States obliged— If america was set right as to the affair of the Indians; and relieved from West India Judges and Privateers, not better than Indians, ill Humour, having nothing to feed upon, would dye away— A discerning minister, true to your Lordships conciliatory views, and possessed if possible of your Prudence and self command, cannot be too early at Philadelphia— I am convinced my Lord! that unless your Vigilance & Interposition extend to whatever may affect the Relations between the two Countries, all will not go and continue well— with every Sentiment of Esteem I am my Lord Your Lordships most obt. Servt.

John Jay

The Right Honorable Lord Grenville

ALS, UK-BL: Dropmore, Ms 59049 (EJ: 03503). Endorsed. Dft, NNC (EJ: 08509); Hist. Mss. Comm., *Fortescue Manuscripts*, 3: 38–39.

1. Probably Samuel Vaughan Sr. (1720–1802), a resident of Hackney, in Middlesex. For JJ's contacts with the Vaughan family at this time, see William Vaughan to JJ, 28 Mar., ALS, NNC (EJ: 08149), and 28 July 1795, ALS, NNC (EJ: 08150).

From John Trumbull

Paris March 24th. 1795.

Dear Sir

I landed at Havre the Sunday after I left you, and have been in this City some days.

Mr. John Pigot of whom you requested me to enquire, has heard of his Father's Death, has obtained a passport to leave the Country, and will soon be with his Friends.[1]

I have met Mr. Catellan[2] our Consul at Marseilles who is particularly acquainted with the Swedish Consul there and informs me that He and all his Family are very well,

The Condition of the English Women and Children who were arrested at the commencement of the War, is now perfectly easy and many have been permitted to return:—

I have not ascertained the actual situation of several whose friends requested information, but am informed that there remains no objection to writing: in short one great object of the Government appears to be to bury in Oblivion the wretched Scenes which are past and to reestablish Justice and Humanity. The Proceedings against the Four accused members appear to be firm but temperate; and although the atrocities of Jacobinism are completely detested; the City is tranquil, and waits with confidence the Decision of the Government.

M[r]. Codman[3] is not in Town, but I am told He has obtained and forwarded to you, the papers which were requested.— I have written to him:[4] & when I receive his answer I shall know whether any thing remains to be done on this Subject.

There are Letters from New York by way of Falmouth so late as the 17th. February, but I learn no political News, I hope you have by this time an account of the probable Fate of your Labours— what Explanations I have had an opportunity of making on this Subject appear to be satisfactory.

I enclose a Line for M[rs]. Church,[5] and have the Honor to be with all Respect Dear Sir Your most obedient Servant and friend

Jn°. Trumbull

ALS, NNC (EJ: 07202). Addressed: "The Hon[ble]. John Jay Esq[r]. / &c &c &c / Royal Hotel Pall Mall / London / *Mr. Ward*." Stamped: "Clock/AP 3/D5 EVEN." Endorsed: ". . . rec[d] 3 apr—1795".

1. See JJ Memorandum to JT, 5 Feb., and JJ to James Monroe, 19 Feb. 1795, both above.
2. Estienne (Stephen) Cathalan Jr. of Marseilles.
3. Probably Richard Codman. See JJ Memorandum to JT, 5 Feb. 1795, above.
4. Letter not found.
5. Enclosure to Angelica Schuyler Church not found.

To Grenville

Royal Hotel—Pall Mall—31 March 1795

my Lord

As it was expected that my mission should terminate with the Business which gave occasion to it, I should have been the Bearer of the Treaty which I had the Honor of negociating with your Lordship, if my Health had been equal to a winter's voyage—[1]

The Season having now become mild and favorable, I have engaged a Passage,[2] and expect to embark in a Vessel that will sail from Bristoll on the 12th. of april at furthest—[3]

Permit me therefore to request that I may have the Honor of taking Leave of their Majestys the first opportunity that may offer— The Sense I entertain of their Condescension, and of the Kindness I have experienced during my Residence here, will remain unimpaired by absence; and be assured my Lord! that I shall always be happy in every opportunity of manifesting those Sentiments of Respect and Esteem with which I have the Honor to be Your Lordships most obedient & most h'ble Servant

John Jay

The Right Honorable Lord Grenville

Dft, NNC (EJ: 08510).

1. See JJ to SLJ, 21 Nov. 1794.

2. Two weeks earlier, JJ had written to Grenville: "All the Vessels bound from hence to New York have sailed except one, which will be ready *early* in April; and I purpose to return in her, unless some unexpected Circumstances should occur to prevent me— as that may *possibly*, tho' not *probably* be the Case, I think it best to be silent on the Subject for the *present*; but the attention due from me to your Lordship, induces me to apprize you of it." JJ to Grenville, 15 Mar. 1795, ALS, UK-BL: Dropmore, Ms 59049 (EJ: 03499); Hist. Mss. Comm., *Fortescue Manuscripts*, 3: 34.

3. JJ sailed from Bristol on the *Severn*, Captain Goodrich, on 12 Apr. and arrived at New York on 28 May. *Argus, Greenleaf's New Daily Advertiser* (New York), 29 May 1795.

From Samuel Bayard

Hatton street. 31. March. 1795.

Dear Sir—

Agreeably to your request as conveyed to me by your note of the 28 instant,[1] I have now the honor to send you a statement "of the number & description of the classes into which I have divided the cases."

It is necessary however previously to mention that in conformity with your instruction "by all means to avoid delay," my first attention has been directed to the entry of appeals & the taking out of process, in all these cases in which the papers would authorize the step. & in which the legal time of appeal was about to expire. By this precaution there has been a considerable saving of time & expence.

The next principal object of regard was to ascertain those cases in which from a deficiency of information no proceedings can yet be had. It appeared to me of importance to forward a list of these as early as possible to the Secretary of State, that our Government & citizens might without loss of time he enabled to furnish the documents that may be necessary for obtaining justice in the same. These two objects are now nearly accomplish'd. I have reason to believe that by yourself Sir, I shall be able to forward to the Secretary of State, the last process that can at present be issued in the cases now under my care.

My next attention will be directed to having our causes prepared for a hearing. In doing which the classifications you have recommended will regularly be made—

From the examination I have already given the cases, I find they will chiefly be comprehended ~~under~~ as to their principles & merits, under the following classes—

1. Where our vessels have been taken & condemn'd under the orders of the 6. of Nov^er. 1793.

2. Under *colour* of those of the 8th Jan^r. 1794.

3. Under pretence of being French property—or—as belonging to American citizens resident within the Territories of France.

4. Under pretence of trading with blockaded places

5. Where both vessel & cargo—or only one of them has been restored, but without costs of damages.

It is proper to mention that a decree has lately been made by the Judge of the Admiralty, in a case that falls within the principle of the first class: which so far as it goes is favourable to American claimants. But as the Captors have appealed from this sentence it remains to be determin'd finally by the Lords of Appeal whether they will affirm or annul the same—

In regard to the last of the above classes, I think some arrangement will be made which will save the expence, delay, & trouble of an appeal. In each of the above classes the opinion of Counsel will be taken agreeably to your instructions, where that has not been done already, before further proceedings are had. Where there is a reasonable ground to expect success I shall take care, that as far as lies in *my* power, the strongest cases shall be first brought forward for argument & decision. If in the opinion of Counsel success in any be doubtful, I shall forward such opinion to the Secretary of State, as you direct Sir. & wait his instructions in regard to the prosecution of abandonment of the suit. I have the honor to be with perfect respect & esteem Dear Sir Your obd^t. and hble. serv.

Sam. Bayard

Honble. John Jay Esqr.

ALS, NNC (EJ: 12842).

1. Letter not found, but see JJ to Bayard, 5 Jan. 1795 (Second Letter), above.

To Yranda

London 5 Ap. 1795

Sir

The President of the United States being desirous to conciliate the Interests of our two Countries has for that purpose appointed mr. Pinckney Envoy extraordinary ~~from the U.S.~~ to his Catholic Majesty, ~~and He Per and~~ He is so obliging as to take charge of this Letter— Permit me to introduce him to you—

There ~~have been~~ ^sometimes are^ occasions ~~when in writing Letters of introduction so appeared to me~~ ^on which it is^ proper to observe a Degree of Circumspection and Reserve in writing Letters of ~~Recommendation~~ ^this kind^. but the present is not one of them—

For this Gentleman I entertain the most cordial ~~Esteem and~~ Esteem, ~~and~~ ^& Regard^ His Temper and Manners are amiable, and in his Integrity and Honor I have perfect Confidence[1]

Be assured that I have not ceased to remember the Hospitality and friendly attentions with wh. you honored me when at Madrid, and that I shall always preserve & cherish those Sentiments of Respect and Consideration with w^h. I have the Honor to be Sir y^r most ob^t. & most hble Servt

The marquis D Yranda

Dft, NNC (EJ: 08190).

1. In November 1794, GW appointed Thomas Pinckney, then minister to Great Britain, as envoy to negotiate with Spain to resolve disputed issues between the two countries, including the boundaries between the United States and Spanish Florida and American rights to navigate the Mississippi River. The resulting Treaty of San Lorenzo was signed on 27 Oct. 1795, and ratified by the U.S. Senate on 25 Feb. 1796. For more on Pinckney's appointment, see GW to ER, 19 Aug. 1794, *PGW: PS*, 16: 586–97; and related documents, *ASP: FR*, 1: 533–34.

To Grenville

Royal Hotel—Pall Mall—7 Ap. 1795—

My Lord

Your obliging Letter of today[1] was this Moment handed to me— a uniform Observance of the ^usual^ respectful Attentions to Sovereigns & other Magistrates, ~~which custom has established,~~ tends to impress & preserve a proper Respect for these Stations as well as Persons. It is the common Interest of all Governm^ts. to make those marks of Respect easy to all, & indispensable to all— I percieve and feel the Impropriety of returning to america with-

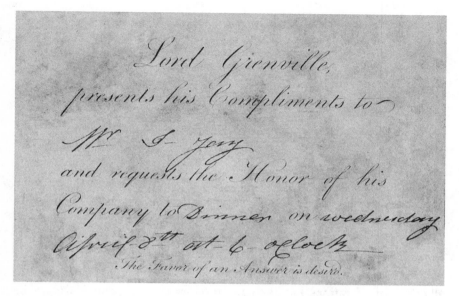

Preprinted invitation card from Lord Grenville to John Jay for dinner on 8 April 1795. (Rare Book & Manuscript Library, Columbia University in the City of New York)

out having taken Leave of his Majesty in the accustomed manner—[2] ~~from personal as well as official Considerations~~

your Lordships undertaking to make the necessary Explanations to the King, and your ~~confidence in~~ ₐbeing persuaded thatₐ they ~~his~~ will be satisfactory, relieves me from the Sollicitude I sh^d otherwise experience—[3]

It w^d. really give me pleasure to dine, for the last Time in London, with y^r Lordship— and yet the many little things to be done and attended to on the Eve of Departure, will not permit me— but at the appoint^d. Hour on Thursday I will wait on y^r. Lordship at y^r Office—[4] with the best wishes for y^r Health & Happiness I have the Honor to be y^r. Lordship's most ob Serv The R^t. Hon'ble L^d. Grenville

Dft, NNC (EJ: 08512).

1. Grenville to JJ, 7 Apr. 1795, ALS, NNC (EJ: 08550).

2. In addition to Grenville's letter, JJ had received a note that morning from James Burges, the under-secretary of state for foreign affairs, requesting that JJ present his credentials so that a meeting with George III could be scheduled prior to JJ's departure for New York. Burges to JJ, 7 Apr. 1795, ALS, NNC (EJ: 05518).

3. JJ did meet with George III before he left London. Grenville wrote the following day and explained that the king is "unwilling that you should go without His seeing you" and therefore instructed that JJ should be brought the next day to the "Queens House exactly at twelve." JJ was both "gratified and obliged" that Grenville was able to reschedule a meeting, and promised to be

"punctual to the Hour". Grenville to JJ, 8 Apr. 1795, ALS, NNC (EJ: 08546); JJ to Greenville, 8 Apr. 1795, ALS, NNC (EJ: 08515).

4. Grenville had offered to host a farewell dinner for JJ; Grenville also requested that JJ stop by his office for a final visit if he could not attend the dinner.

From Grenville

Dover Street May 11, 1795

My Dear Sir

I cannot resist the desire I feel of availing myself of the opportunity of the first packet since your departure, to express to you how happy you would make me by allowing me occasionally to recall to your recollection in this manner one who will always entertain for you the most sincere esteem & friendship— I am particularly anxious to hear of your safe arrival, & that you have found your family & friends well. These are points paramount to all other considerations, but I know your return to your Country will not be fully satisfactory to you unless you have also found the state of public affairs such as to promise the continuance of good order & tranquility. That it may be so no one more sincerely wishes than myself, and it would be a great satisfaction to me to hear it from you.

Since you left us the news of the arrival of the treaty in America has reached us. We were singularly unfortunate in the loss of the Tankerville packet.[1] By a ~~strange~~ strange negligence the November & December mails from hence were both put on board that ship without our having any notice of it from the Post office, so that while I thought we were sending duplicates by two different conveyances, we were in fact sending them by the same Vessel. My letters to Govr. Simcoe which I have frequently mentioned to you, & my des[patche]^s to Mr Hammond on the subject of the treaty were on board the same ship: so that this accident has thrown us far back in the arrangem^t of many material points. I hope however that with attention, and a continuance on the part of the two Governments of the same disposition which actuated all our communications & negotiations here, the great work which we have begun will be carried to its full extent.

I have not been inattentive to the points which remain to be settled here. One of the most material is I flatter myself at length in a train of being well arranged, I mean that which relates to the Adm[iralt]^y. Courts in the West Indies, which it is in contemplation immediately to diminish in point of number, so as to have them only at Jamaica, Barbados, Grenada, ₳Antigua₳ & Martinique. Knowing as I do how much evil has been produced by the multiplication of these Courts I look to this reduction with very sanguine hopes. But I hope the regulation will not stop there, but that the effect of it may lead to render the practice of those which still remain, more correct, & cautious than I fear it has hitherto been.

The impossibility of our receiving the ratification of the treaty till quite the end of July ~~has~~ leaves us no chance of being able to propose to Parliament during the present session those matters connected with the treaty in which the interference of the Legislature is necessary. I know that this delay will be misconstrued on your side of the Water, but it is unavoidable. I requested Mr Pinckney before he went to Spain to write to America on this point in order that the explanation of it might not rest merely on the communications of our Minister there. You will be able to speak with still more knowledge & effect to the same point. Whatever does not depend on the repeal or alteration of existing Laws will be immediately executed on the receipt of the ratification.

The public papers and the communications will inform you fully of the state of affairs in Europe. The dispositions of the people in France are evidently turning very fast towards the establishment of some settled state of order which may relieve them from the miseries of their present anarchy. In a similar situation in this Country we experienced the advantage of a known & moderate form of Government, under which the Nation had before been happy & to which therefore it returned with enthusiasm & almost with unanimity. The want of such a standard to resort to is now as far as I can judge the great obstacle to the restoration of order in France, & consequently of Peace in Europe. Mild as their old government was in its practice it was attended with many circumstances the renewal of which creates great apprehension & uneasiness, & there is no authority of sufficient weight to prescribe the form & limits of any change. Some of the Belligerent Powers are as you will have seen too impatient to wait the results of this doubtful issue. To others all idea of Peace which shall not give better security than the signature of the Committee of Safety, or the ratification of the Convention seems delusive & dangerous: and to this sentiment I profess myself strongly inclined. You are happy in America if you can avoid as I trust you will the dangers of the War & of the Peace. With the sincerest wishes for your prosperity, believe me Sir, Your most attached & faithful humble Servant

Grenville.

Honble. Mr. Jay.

ALS, NNC (EJ: 08547). Endorsed: "... an[swere]d. 1 May 1796—". C, UK-BL: Dropmore (EJ: 03502). Hist. Mss. Comm., *Fortescue Manuscripts*, 3: 68–69. *WJ*, 2: 253–55; *HPJ*, 4: 173–76. For JJ's delayed reply, see his letter of 1 May 1796, below.

1. The *Tankerville* packet sailing from Falmouth to Halifax, Nova Scotia, was captured and sunk by a French privateer. Its crew was sent to Barbados on a prize taken from the Spanish. *Aurora General Advertiser* (Philadelphia), 18 Apr.; *American Minerva* (New York), 23 Apr.; and *Gazette of the United States* (Philadelphia), 6 May 1795. The copy of the treaty carried by David Blaney, who sailed on the *Thomas*, Capt. Vickery, landed at Norfolk before reaching Philadelphia on 7 Mar. 1795, after the adjournment of Congress. See Blaney to JJ, 20 Sept. 1795, ALS, NNC (EJ: 05504).

John Jay's Address upon His Arrival in New York

[New York, 28 May 1795][1]

Fellow-Citizens, those marks of your attention to me are highly grateful— I can never forget them—and the recollection of them will give a new motive to do, what shall be agreeable to you, and conducive to the general welfare. I thank you for your kind reception, and am happy to be again in my own country, and in the midst of you, my friends and fellow-citizens.[2]

PtD, *Greenleaf's New York Journal*, 30 May 1795. JJ's speech, with varying accounts of his arrival, was printed in the following: *Weekly Museum* (New York), 30 May; *Dunlap's American Daily Advertiser*, and *Gazette of the United States* (both Philadelphia), 30 May; *Columbian Centinel* (Boston), 3 June; *New-Jersey Journal* (Elizabethtown), 3 June; *Washington Patrol* (Salem, N.Y.), 3 June; *Carlisle Gazette*, 3 June; *Political Gazette* (Newburyport), 4 June; *Rising Sun* (Kingston), 5 June; *Impartial Herald* (Newburyport), 6 June; *Boston Gazette*, 8 June; *Western Star* (Stockbridge), 9 June; *American Spy* (Troy), 9 June; *Medley or Newbedford Marine Journal*, 12 June; and *North-Carolina Journal* (Halifax), 15 June 1795. For reports of JJ's arrival, without his speech, see *Connecticut Courant* (Hartford), 1 June; *American Telegraph* (Bridgeport), 3 June; *Litchfield Monitor*, 3 June; *Hampshire Gazette* (Northampton), 3 June; *Catskill Packet*, 6 June; *Oracle of the Day* (Portsmouth), 9 June; *Georgia Gazette* (Savannah), 18 June; and *Augusta Chronicle*, 20 June 1795.

1. This report of JJ's address was preceded in *Greenleaf's New York Journal* under a 30 May dateline by the following account of JJ's arrival:

THE ship Severn, Capt. Goodrich, in 49 days from Bristol, and the ship Joseph, Capt. Stone, in 61 days from Liverpool, arrived at this port on Thursday, between twelve and one, P. M. JOHN JAY, Esq. Chief Justice of the United States, late Envoy Extraordinary to the Court of Great-Britain, and candidate for the chair of Governor of the state of New-York— and Mr. WILLIAM CONSTABLE, merchant of this city—came passengers in the Severn. Reports having been made, that Mr. Jay was in the Severn; a number of citizens hurried down to the wharf to welcome his arrival, who escorted him to his house in Broad-Way, amid repeated acclamations of joy. At 6 o'clock the bells were rang, and the battery and ship guns were fired to his honor.

Mr. JAY, on his arrival, made the following speech to the citizens who were assembled to welcome his arrival on Thursday:-

2. The address is followed in *Greenleaf's New York Journal* by the following commentary:

There is every appearance, from the complexion of the canvass, that Mr. Jay will be elected Governor; in which view his arrival at this juncture is considered as peculiarly happy; debates on the indefinite expressions, in case of absence, will be then avoided. Mr. Jay leads the Southern district with a majority of 988 votes—this, however, does not decide the election, for Orange, Ulster, Columbia, Washington, Clinton, Saratoga, and Montgomery, will give decided (though indefinite) majorities for Mr. Yates, and it is *possible* Mr. Jay will yet lose his election.

Accounts of British spoliations upon American property disseminated throughout America, from authentic documents, are *truly melancholy*— The treaty *to prevent which* will probably be *made known* after the 8th of June next.

For the final election results, see Report on the Address of the Committee of Canvassers to John Jay and his Reply, with a Copy of the Certificate of his Election, 8 June, and notes, below.

Various newspapers also reported a meeting of the Union Society on 28 May at Hunter's Hotel, at which

in consequence of the happy arrival of their much respected fellow citizen JOHN JAY, Esq. and considering this event as connected with the peace happiness and best interest of their country, they proceeded to celebrate the occasion by adjourning the ordinary business of the society, and drinking the following toasts: 1st. Health, prosperity and general esteem to our valuable fellow citizen and firm patriot JOHN JAY. 2d. Peace throughout the world. 3d. Moderation and firmness to all councils of the American Union—May her sword reluctantly drawn be the terror of the unjust. 4th. Switzerland, Holland, and free Republics. 5th. The United States, and the steady friends of its excellent continuation. 6th. Free elections and fair canvassing. 7th. Success to the honest citizens of France in their glorious struggle to obtain a free efficient and republican government. 8th. Distraction to the internal enemies of France who under the mask of patriotism destroy the freedom of opinion and promote measures of anarchy and terror. 9th. Destruction to the external enemies of France who under the mask of Religion Humanity and the love of order, pursue plans of piracy, invasion, cruelty and blood. 10th. The Liberty of the Press—May public virtue awe its licentiousness. 11th. May all who retire in free governments from exalted stations; retire with the plaudits and the laurels of an Alexander Hamilton. 12th. All citizens who associate to cherish the pure spirits of republicanism and social order. 13th. President GEORGE WASHINGTON.

See *American Minerva*, and *New-York Advertiser*, 29 May; *Herald: a Gazette for the Country*, *New-York Gazette*, and *Daily Advertiser* (all New York) 30 May; *Argus, Greenleaf's New Daily Advertiser* (New York), 1 June; *Gazette of the United States* (Philadelphia), 1 June; *Dunlap's American Daily Advertiser* (Philadelphia), 2 June; *Federal Intelligencer* (Baltimore), 6 June; *Impartial Herald* (Newburyport), 6 June; and *Richmond Chronicle*, 7 June 1795.

Report on the Address of the Committee of Canvassers to John Jay and his Reply, with a Copy of the Certificate of his Election

[New York, 8 June 1795]

On Saturday at noon the joint Committee of Canvassers assembled at the office of the Secretary of State, and from thence accompanied by the Secretary, proceeded to the house of Mr. Jay; when Mr. Hoffman, in behalf of the committee, presented to Mr. Jay the certificate of his election to the Office of Governor: preceding it by an Address which (as nearly as the noise attending the large and respectable assemblage of citizens would enable us to hear) was as follows—

"That he was assigned by the committee appointed to canvas the votes taken at the last election for Governor, Lt. Governor, and Senators, to deliver him the Certificate of his election; in doing which he felt real pleasure. That by it, the people of the State of New-York called him to the chair of Government.["]

"That, selected as the organ of their voice, the committee united in the most unbounded confidence in his virtue and patriotism; and trusted that under his administration the welfare of the State would be promoted, and the people live *united*, happy and free."

Mr. Jay replied by expressing to the Committee "his gratitude for this proof of the confidence of his fellow citizens as intimated in the certificate which he had then the honor to receive:— That he should endeavor by his continual exertions to answer as far as in his power the hopes which the committee had been pleased to express of his administration; and no pains should be spared to promote the public good and to advance the prosperity and harmony of the people of this state— That the general satisfaction he saw prevail on the fair and impartial conduct of the committee in their canvas, while it reflected honor on them, would furnish an example deserving of imitation."

A very numerous body of Citizens then presented their congratulations to Mr. JAY on his election.

On the arrival of the committee at Mr. JAY's, a Federal salute was fired from the Battery, and in the afternoon the committee dined with Mr. JAY at his house.

The following is a true copy of the Certificate, taken from the Original:

State of New-York, to wit.

WE the subscribers being the joint committee appointed by the Senate and Assembly, in pursuance of the act entitled "an act for regulating elections,"[1] to canvas and estimate the votes taken at the last election for Governor, Lieutenant Governor and Senators, having met for that purpose, at the office of the Secretary of State, on the 1st Tuesday of May last, and there on that day, and on the ten next succeeding days (Sunday excepted) canvassed and estimated the votes taken for Governor, Lieutenant Governor and Senators, at the said last election; Do upon said canvas and estimate, determine and declare that JOHN JAY, was by the greatest number of votes at the said election chosen Governor of this State, and that STEPHEN VAN RENSE-LAER, was by the greatest number of votes at the said election, chosen Lieutenant Governor of this State: and that Samuel Jones, Joshua Sands, and

Philip Livingston, were severally and respectively by the greatest number of votes, at the said election, in the Southern District of this State, chosen Senators in the said Southern District; the said Philip Livingston being chosen in the room of Matthew Clarkson, and that Thomas Tillotson, and Abraham Schenck, were severally and respectively, by the greatest number of votes at said election, in the Middle District of this State, chosen Senators in the said Middle District: and that Ebenezer Russell and Ambrose Spencer, were severally and respectively chosen by the greatest number of votes, at the said election, in the Eastern District of this State, chosen Senators in the said Eastern District: the said Ambrose Spencer, being chosen in the room of John Williams, and that Philip Schuyler, was by the greatest number of votes, at the said election, in the Western District of this State, chosen a Senator in said Western District.[2]

Given under our hands at said office of the Secretary of this State in the City of New-York, the sixth day of June, in the nineteenth year of the Independence of this State, and in the year of our Lord one thousand seven hundred and ninety-five.

Signed

Peter Vandervoort	Selah Strong
Jacob Radclift	John Schenck
Hosea Moffit	J. Van Schoonhoven
Jos. Ogden Hoffman	Michael Myers
Matthew Scott	Reuben Hopkins
Abel Smith	John D. Coe[3]

PtD, *Daily Advertiser* (New York), 8 June 1795. Reprinted: *Gazette of the United States* (Philadelphia), 9 June; *Dunlap's American Daily Advertiser* (Philadelphia), 10 June; *Wood's Newark Gazette* (E), 10 June; *Greenleaf's New York Journal* (E), 10 June; *Connecticut Courant* (Hartford), 15 June; *Mohawk Mercury* (Schenectady), 16 June; *Columbian Centinel* (Boston), 17 June; *Political Gazette* (Newburyport), 18 June; *United States Chronicle* (Providence) (E), 18 June; *Albany Gazette*, 19 June; *Oracle of the Day* (Portsmouth), 20 June; *Washington Patrol* (Salem, N.Y.) (E), 24 June; *New-Hampshire Gazette* (Portsmouth), 30 June; and *American Minerva* (Cooperstown), 1 July 1795.

1. *An act for regulating elections. Together with an act for regulating town-meetings. Passed by the representatives of the people of the state of New-York, at their tenth session. 1787* (New York, [1787]; *Early Am. Imprints*, series 1, no. 20572); *N.Y. State Laws*, (1777–97) 1: 316–31.

2. Elected to the 1795 New York State Senate were Federalist Samuel Jones who received 2,766 votes; Federalist Joshua Sands (1757–1835), state senator, 1792–97, collector for the Port of New York, 1797–1801, and congressman 1803–5, 1825–27, who received 2,856 votes; Federalist Philip Livingston who received 2,584 votes; Republican Thomas Tillotson, state senator from 1791 to 1799, who received 2,739 votes; Abraham Schenck of Fishkill, state senator from 1796 to 1799, who received 2,701 votes; Federalist Ebenezer Russell of Washington County, state senator from 1796 to 1803, received 4,752 votes; Ambrose Spencer (1765–1848), assemblyman, 1793–95, and senator,

1795–1804, New York attorney general, 1802–4, associate justice of the Supreme Court of New York, 1804–19, and state Chief Justice, 1819–22, who received 2,734 votes; and Federalist Philip Schuyler who received 4,433 votes. *A New Nation Votes* (accessed Aug. 2018).

3. The members of the Committee of Canvassers were state assemblymen Peter Vandervoort of Kings County; Jacob Radclift (Radcliff) (1764–1844), Federalist, Dutchess County; Hosea Moffit (1757–1825), Federalist, Rensselaer County; Josiah Ogden Hoffman, Federalist, New York City and County; Matthew Scott of Columbia County; Abel Smith of Westchester; and state senators Selah Strong (1737–1815) and John Schenck (1740–1831) of the southern district; Jacobus Van Schoonhoven (1744–1814) and Michael Myers (1753–1814) of the western district; and Reuben Hopkins (1748–1822) and John D. Coe (1755–1824), Federalist, of the middle district.

INDIAN AFFAIRS UNDER JAY'S GOVERNORSHIP

Like his longstanding predecessor, George Clinton, Jay used the governor's office to carry out policies that favored state growth over the needs of the Haudenosaunee (Iroquois) and other Indian groups residing in present-day central and western New York and neighboring Canada. Motivated primarily by the goals of financial gain, commercial development, and expanded white settlement, Jay's administration continued state-sanctioned practices that diminished Indian landholdings and sovereign status.[1] Yet even as Jay executed acts and laws that proved detrimental to Indian autonomy, he demonstrated a firmer commitment to constitutional principles and federal jurisprudence than had Clinton and he initiated and passed laws that created a more efficient system for the disbursement of annuities and the provision of resources. In his handling of Indian affairs, Jay was not immune to expressing prejudiced sentiments; on occasion, he identified certain Indian groups as "savages" and censured them for not adopting "civilized practices".[2] Jay was guided in his tasks by a belief that Indian communities deserved "benevolence and protection," and therefore he sought to use his limited executive power to curb the worst abuses inflicted on them.[3]

When Jay took office in July 1795, commissioners appointed by the state legislature were in the midst of talks with leaders from the Haudenosaunee nations. Authorized by an act passed a few months earlier, the commissioners—Philip Schuyler, John Cantine, John Richardson, and David Brooks[4]—traveled from Albany to the Finger Lakes region in order to negotiate land purchases with the Oneida, Onondaga, and Cayuga tribes.[5] Schuyler invited Jay to accompany the New York delegation as he anticipated that the presence of the new governor would produce more favorable terms.[6] Even though Jay did not attend the proceedings, Schuyler and his colleagues nonetheless obtained major concessions at the resulting Treaty of Cayuga

Ferry. The Cayuga reached an agreement with the state commissioners on 27 July, and the Onondaga did likewise on the following day. In exchange for a payment of $1,800 and an annuity of the same amount, the Cayuga representatives ceded a tract of land that left their people with little but their reservation. The Onondaga leaders sold their rights to Salt Lake and surrounding lands in exchange for a cash payment of $700 and annuities amounting to the sum of $1,090 and a hundred barrels of salt.[7] The New York commissioners had successfully treated with their Cayuga and Onondaga counterparts, but their negotiations stalled with the Oneida. A council was reconvened at Albany in September, and the Oneida envoys now agreed to part with three tracts of 132,000 acres in exchange for a payment of $2,952 and an annuity of the same amount.[8]

Prior to the treaty provisions being finalized between the Haudenosaunee and New York, federal officials challenged the validity of the negotiations. Such meetings, they observed, contravened provisions contained in the U.S. Constitution and the Indian Trade and Intercourse Act of 1793. The Constitution forbade individual states from entering into a treaty or alliance with other nations and granted treaty-making power solely to the president with the advice and consent of the Senate, while the 1793 act disallowed land purchases from either Indian persons or nations unless such transactions received the approval of an appointed federal commissioner.[9] William Bradford Jr., the U.S. Attorney General, invoked both the Constitution and the 1793 Act in a letter to Timothy Pickering that cited the illegality of land purchases.[10] For his part, Pickering, who served as Secretary of War, the department then responsible for overseeing Indian affairs for the federal government, expressed confidence that the new governor would invalidate any resulting agreements reached with the Haudenosaunee. "All difficulties on these subjects will cease," Pickering assured Israel Chapin Jr., the federal superintendent to the Six Nations, "as soon as Mr. Jay's administration commences.[11] Pickering was due for disappointment, however, as the governor begged off taking any official action to disrupt the negotiating process. Given his former position as the nation's foremost jurist and his current one as New York's chief executive officer, as well as his leading role in drafting the state constitution, Jay deemed it inappropriate that he should now formulate an opinion that undermined New York's legal code and system of governance. Jay felt duty-bound to follow the state's constitutional proviso[12] that empowered the legislature (and not the governor) to oversee "every Convention or Contract with Indian Tribes mediated by the state."[13] Turning his attention to the bill that culminated in the Treaty of Cayuga Ferry, Jay noted that this "act is silent" regarding the national government's supervision and approval of New York's Indian affairs.[14] The governor offered a final justification with observations that the bill had passed while Clinton held office and that the conference had already begun before Jay learned of the commissioners' itinerary and that the arrangements had already been made for the Haudenosaunee delegations.

Federal officials acquiesced to Jay's judgement and deferred from further hindering New York's efforts to secure land titles from the Haudenosaunee. The recent defeat of the Western Confederacy at the Battle of Fallen Timbers and the subsequent signing of the Treaty of Canandaigua had weakened the Haudenosaunee's strategic significance in the eyes of the United States government, as it was less likely the Six Nations would form a military alliance with the weakened Ohio Indians. The subsequent passage of the Jay Treaty and the Treaty of Greenville nullified the dual British and Indian threat and further diminished the diplomatic leverage of the Haudenosaunee nations. These developments on the northern borderlands most certainly influenced Pickering when he advised the president that "the intervention of the General Government has not been thought requisite" for talks between New York state and the Oneida, Onondaga, and Cayuga.[15] Washington concurred with Pickering's assessment and declared that his administration would sanction the outcomes resulting from the regularly scheduled talks, as had occurred with the Onondaga and Cayuga. The president added the caveat that Pickering should seek the counsel of others "with a regard to the Constitution and laws" if the talks stalled or were otherwise postponed.[16] The national government therefore might have initiated measures to block or overturn the Oneida land cessions since the terms of that agreement were not finalized until mid-September. Pickering and his colleagues opted, however, to take no such action.

Whereas the Indian treaties signed by New York in the summer of 1795 largely bore the imprimatur of the previous administration, subsequent negotiations demonstrated Jay's willingness to implement policy initiatives and assume a more active role in shaping and overseeing the state's Indian affairs. Future negotiations held during his administration would now mostly comply with existing federal guidelines. A federal commissioner was present at the three main Indian treaties signed between 1796 and 1798, and each of these agreements were submitted for approval by the U.S. Senate and then forwarded to the president for ratification. Jay also recognized that the stabilization and security of the region came at the expense of Haudenosaunee power, and he sought to use this development for the purpose of creating more harmonious relations between Indians and whites. "It appears to me," he informed the state legislature in his fourth year as governor, "that in proportion as they become less and less able or inclined to assert or defend their rights by arms, we should... become more and more disposed to protect them by law and measures conducive to their security and comfort."[17] The governor also sought to establish an efficient system for processing the payments and distribution of materials to Indian nations. Under his instigation, lawmakers passed a bill that established a set date and process for paying annuities to the Haudenosaunee.[18]

Soon after taking office, the new governor received notice from Philip Schuyler and Egbert Benson of the necessity for scheduling a conference in the upcoming months with the Mohawk living at Akwesasne.[19] The Akwesasne Mohawk, who belonged to the Seven Nations of Canada, had approached the state government in February 1794 and March 1795 with title claims to land located in northern New York. Seeking to both extinguish these claims and purchase territory from the Akwesasne community, the state legislature voted in April to commence negotiations and allocated the governor a budget of three thousand pounds to cover the treaty expenses.[20] Jay proposed that a conference be held in mid-September at Fort George, located at the southern end of Lake George. Addressing the Akwesasne's representatives as brothers, he extended an invitation to them and expressed a hope that the participants will "meet with Hearts and Minds well disposed to each other."[21] Jay and his subordinates also set about the tasks of compiling official records, arranging accommodations and provisions for the Akwesasne delegation, and appointing Egbert Benson, Abraham Ten Broeck, and James Watson to represent New York's interests at the proceedings.[22] Pickering informed Jay that the president had instructed Jeremiah Wadsworth to attend as U.S. commissioner and further explained that the proceedings must comply with the Indian Trade and Intercourse Act of 1793. Accordingly, the state agents could negotiate only for the price of Mohawk territory and that any resulting land cession to New York must "be in the form of a treaty or convention" that would then be ratified by the president after a consultation with the U.S. senate.[23] The parties met as planned at Fort George, but did not come to terms and reach a satisfactory settlement.

Subsequent talks with the Seven Nations of Canada, albeit with delays, occurred the following year. Leaders of the Akwesasne nation visited the governor in February while traveling to Philadelphia to meet with the president.[24] On their return journey, the delegates stopped once more in New York City. Jay and the state legislature seized this opportunity to reconvene the diplomatic sessions that had failed at Fort George.[25] The governor wrote to James McHenry, who had replaced Pickering as Secretary of War, and requested that a federal commissioner be named to oversee the proceedings, even recommending Abraham Ogden and Elisha Boudinot as prospective candidates.[26] Jay urged McHenry to make haste, explaining that the Akwesasne representatives were anxious to return to their community. An official meeting was not forthcoming, however, as questions arose regarding the authority and status of the Mohawk delegates. Important documents authorizing their mission for the Akwesasne nation had apparently been left behind in Philadelphia, leaving Jay unsure as to the legitimacy of the proceedings.[27] The Mohawk leaders departed for home before these issues could be fully resolved.

The conference in New York City was therefore postponed until May. Representatives from the Akwesasne Mohawk were now joined by those from the Kahnawake (Caughnawaga) Mohawk of southern Quebec for continued deliberations. For the New York delegation, Jay called on Richard Varick to serve alongside Benson and Watson as state agents.[28] Federal officials requested that Wadsworth reprise his role in representing the national government. When Wadsworth declined the posting, Abraham Ogden, one of Jay's original recommendees for the position, stepped in as commissioner.[29] Under the watchful eye of Ogden, the parties opened talks on 23 May and wrapped them up eight days later. In exchange for ceding their territorial claims, the Seven Nations of Canada received a payment of £1,233.6.8 and an annuity in the amount of £213.6.8.[30] In a later speech before the legislature, Jay conceded that the Indians' declaration of land title was "not unquestionable," but he found that an amicable agreement was "more consistent with sound policy."[31] Jay also expressed confidence that the "justice and moderation" displayed by New York's government at the recent treaty would serve to improve relations with Indian nations residing outside the state.[32]

The governor had good reason to be concerned about other Indian groups making territorial claims on New York. Soon after he had met with the Akwesasne deputies in February 1796, Jay received a visit from a delegation of four leaders representing the Mohawk community that resided in the Bay of Quinté region near Kingston, Ontario.[33] As the state government was paying for the visitors' food and lodging expenses, Jay urged the legislators to waste no time in making a decision.[34] A month later, the legislature issued a joint resolution that vetoed the possibility of negotiating with these Mohawk in the near future. New York's lawmakers explained that the "undefined" nature of the land claims rendered a meeting impossible, and that a state-led investigation would first have to verify the validity of these claims before a conference could take place.[35]

The Bay of Quinté Mohawk delegation was joined in mid-March by two representatives who came to see the governor on behalf of the Mohawks who inhabited the territory along the Grand River between Lakes Ontario and Erie.[36] Prior to their defeat at the hands of patriot forces during the revolutionary war, these Mohawk communities had lived in New York in the towns of Canajoharie, located on the southern bank of the Mohawk River, and Tiononderoge, located eastward at the confluence of the Mohawk River and Schoharie Creek. At the close of the conflict, they resettled in Upper Canada on land grants offered by Governor Frederick Haldimand in reward for their loyal service. The Mohawk now returned to New York seeking compensation for their lost territory. Joseph Brant, a key leader of the Grand River community, sought Jay's advice about how the Mohawk land claims should be presented. The governor counselled on proper procedure and recommended that the Mohawk should grant "two or three deputies with full and well authenticated powers to state those Claims with accuracy and to make a final settlement with the State Respecting them."[37] Jay concluded his letter by assuring Brant that the Mohawk title claims would receive the fullest attention and a fair and just hearing from the state government.

The talks commenced in late March 1797 in Albany, now designated as the permanent seat of state government.[38] The Mohawk delegation, including Brant, discussed terms with Abraham Ten Broeck, Egbert Benson, and Ezra L'Hommedieu, the agents representing New York. Isaac Smith was appointed by President Adams to serve as U.S. commissioner and oversee the proceedings.[39] Under the terms of the final settlement, the Mohawk representatives agreed to cede their claims to territories in New York in exchange for a payment of $1,000 with an additional $600 to cover travel expenses.[40]

The state of New York had an opportunity to purchase more territory from the Oneida nation in 1798. A delegation of Oneida leaders travelled to Albany to negotiate a land sale in February of that year.[41] The legislature wasted little time in passing a law that authorized the governor to appoint three commissioners to treat with the Oneida in the state capital.[42] Jay accordingly named Egbert Benson, Simeon DeWitt, and John Tayler to determine the land parcels and negotiation terms of the prospective transactions.[43] Upon learning that the Oneida wished to sell thirty thousand acres within their reservation for a sum of $500—$300 of which would be advanced to them—and a perpetual annuity of $700, and that an allowance would be made for seven Oneida families to continue residing on the land, Jay appointed a new trio of commissioners to hold final talks at the Oneida village of Kanonwalohale on 1 June.[44] He also sent the report and related documents to Pickering along with a request that the Secretary of State ask President Adams to appoint a federal commissioner to the talks.[45] The state agents, Benson, Tayler, and L'Hommedieu, along with the federal appointee, Joseph Hopkinson, set out on 25 May to conduct negotiations.[46] The signed treaty adhered to the terms previously decided upon in Albany.[47]

Members of the Cayuga nation expressed interest in selling off their remaining parcels of land to New York. In March 1799, the state legislature passed a bill permitting the governor to purchase available Cayuga land.[48] Later that year, Israel Chapin Jr. contacted Jay about the possibility of buying a Cayuga tract of "reserved Land."[49] Jay declined to take immediate action, however, explaining that acquiring the tract was not "an important Object to the State."[50] Moreover, Jay noted that the Cayuga were divided as to whether the land should be offered for sale, and he would only approve of the business if the entire community agreed to the purchase and if the land could be bought at a fair price.[51] In May 1800, Chapin Jr. again approached the governor with the suggestion that New York State purchase the Cayuga tract. Upon learning that most of the Cayuga had migrated westward, Jay agreed to a purchase of the land on reasonable terms, but apparently did not follow through with the transaction while in office.[52]

Private entities as well as state agencies carried out land transactions with Iroquois groups. Such was the case in September 1797, when the Seneca residing in western New York ceded millions of acres located west of the Genesee River to Robert Morris and the Holland Land Company. Thomas Morris,[53] Robert Morris's son, conducted negotiations with Seneca leaders, and Jeremiah Wadsworth, the United States Indian Commissioner, oversaw the proceedings. In the resulting Treaty of Big Tree, the Seneca parted with much of their homeland for the sum of $100,000.[54]

Issues of sovereignty and landholding also shaped relations between the state government and the Christian Indian communities of New Stockbridge and Brothertown that resided among the Oneidas in central New York.[55] Both groups sought assistance from state officials in asserting their rights to land ownership. Jay's administration handled these affairs solely within the confines of the state judicial system and therefore sought neither advice nor approval from federal authorities.

The residents of New Stockbridge twice petitioned the governor to help them secure the title to their tract comprising six square miles.[56] A three-person commission—Egbert Benson, Ezra L'Hommedieu, and James

Watson—was appointed by Jay in February 1797 to investigate the Stock-bridge claims.[57] The state legislature then enacted a statute the following month that reaffirmed Stockbridge ownership and that threatened prosecution for trespassing on their land.[58] Despite the passage of this law, the problem of white encroachment on Stockbridge territory persisted. In February 1799, John Murray Jr., the Quaker philanthropist, wrote to Jay on behalf of the Stockbridge tribe with a request that the government follow the dictates of "Justice, humanity & sound policy" and thereby redress the group's grievances.[59]

The Brothertown Indians likewise requested state assistance for resolving their territorial disputes with New York lessees and speculators. A pair of statutes passed in 1795 and 1796[60] organized a town government for Brothertown and appointed Samuel Jones, Zina Hitchcock,[61] and Ezra L'Hommedieu as commissioners to sort out the contending claims. The subsequent commission report that was submitted to the Senate greatly reduced the geographic size of the Brothertown community. In exchange for cash annuities, livestock, farming tools, cloth, and a schoolhouse, the inhabitants of Brothertown were effectively stripped of 60 percent of their land.[62]

The governor also played a pivotal role in evaluating missionary efforts among the Oneida. The Presbyterian clergyman Samuel Kirkland[63] had been ministering to the Haudenosaunee for nearly three decades and in recent years had established the Hamilton Oneida Academy. The Society in Scotland for Promoting Christian Knowledge, the agency funding Kirkland's endeavors, received complaints throughout the 1790s that he was neglecting his spiritual duties.[64] In response, the Society appointed two Boston-based ministers, Jeremy Belknap and Jedidiah Morse, to investigate the status of the Oneida mission. Since he and Morse were unfamiliar with the region, Belknap first contacted Jay in May 1796, seeking advice on travel, accommodations, and Indian affairs.[65] As the governor looked favorably upon the benevolent work undertaken by the Society in Scotland, he gladly obliged Belknap's request for information. In addition to suggesting travel routes, he offered to provide letters of introduction to Philip Schuyler, Stephen Van Rensselaer, James Duane, and Hugh White[66] and put the inspectors in touch with Egbert Benson, Samuel Jones, and James Dean,[67] all officials who had previously negotiated with the Oneida on behalf of the state.[68] Based on the findings submitted by Belknap and Morse, the Society in Scotland opted to terminate the funding for Kirkland's activities.[69]

With Kirkland no longer leading the mission, the question arose as to who would assume responsibility for the spiritual welfare and religious education of the Oneida community. Writing on behalf of the Society in Scotland, both Jedidiah Morse and Peter Thacher, a Congregationalist minister and Secretary for the Society's Boston branch, recommended that New York's government should take on the duties of promoting Christianity among the Indians. Morse and Thacher further suggested that a new minister should be hired and that his salary should be deducted from the cash annuities provided by the state.[70]

Jay praised the work of the Oneida mission, yet nonetheless questioned whether ministerial efforts had done enough to sufficiently "civilize or christianize" the residents.[71] The Oneida, he asserted, had thus far rejected practices involving permanent homes, private property, masculine labor, and a farm-based economy."[72] Since the Oneida persisted in defying attempts at their acculturation, the governor concluded that state lawmakers would probably not approve funding for future missionary activities.[73]

---

1. For an overview of New York State's relationship with its Indian neighbors during the decades of Clinton's governorship, see Graymont, "New York State Indian Policy," 438–65.

2. See for instance, JJ to Thacher, 25 Apr. 1797, below.

3. JJ's Address to the New York State Legislature, [1 Nov. 1796], below. JJ expressed a similar paternalistic concern for Indians in a letter written a decade earlier. Although tacitly acknowledging that Indian land should eventually be claimed for white settlement, JJ criticized the U.S. government for mishandling its Indian affairs and lamented that "Indians have been murdered by our People in cold Blood and no satisfaction given, nor are they pleased with the avidity with which we seek to acquire their Lands." JJ to TJ, 14 Dec. 1786, Dft, NNC (EJ: 05880); FC, DNA (EJ: 02483); PTJ, 10: 596–99.

4. John Cantine (1735–1808), Democratic-Republican state senator representing the Middle District; John Richardson of Onondaga County, served as a judge on the Onondaga court of common pleas, represented the Western District in the state senate, and was a member of the state assembly from Onondaga County; David Brooks (1756–1838), Federalist member of the New York State Assembly and judge of Dutchess County.

5. "An ACT for the better Support of the Oneida, Onondaga, and Cayuga Indians, and for other Purposes therein mentioned," 9 Apr. 1795, N.Y. State Laws, 18th sess. (1795), 43–46. For more on the commissioners and their negotiations, see Schuyler to JJ, 9 June 1795, and JJ to TP, 13 July 1795, both below.

6. Schuyler to JJ, 9 June 1795, below.

7. Report of Special Committee to Investigate the Indian Problem of the State of New York, Appointed by the Assembly of 1888 (Albany, 1889), 224–28.

8. Ibid., 241–49.

9. U.S. Constitution, Art. I, § 10, Art. 2, § 2; "An Act to Regulate Trade and Intercourse with the Indian Tribes," 1 Mar. 1793, Stat., 1: 329–32.

10. Bradford to TP, 16 June 1795, ALS, NHi: Henry V. O'Reilly.

11. TP to Chapin Jr., 29 June 1795, ALS, NHi: Henry V. O'Reilly.

12. For JJ's views on Art. 37 of the New York State Constitution, see his letter to TP, 13 July 1795, below.

13. Ibid.

14. Ibid.

15. TP to GW, 21 July 1795, C, MHi: Pickering; *PGW: PS*, 18: 389.

16. GW to TP, 27 July 1795, C, MHi: Pickering; *PGW: PS*, 18: 433.

17. JJ's Message to the New York State Senate, 2 Feb. 1799, *NYGM*, 2: 433.

18. JJ's Address to the New York State Legislature, [1 Nov. 1796], below; "An ACT to provide for the Payment of the Annuities to the Indians, stipulated to be paid by this State," 1 Apr. 1797, *N.Y. State Laws*, 20th sess. (1797), 183.

19. Schuyler to JJ, 9 June 1795, and Benson to JJ, 13 June 1795, both below.

20. "An ACT for the Payment of Certain Officers and Government and other Contingent Expences," 9 Apr. 1795. For more on the Akwesasne delegations that visited New York in 1794 and 1795, and their subsequent negotiations with the state government, see *N.Y. Senate Journal*, 17th sess. (1794), 44, 54, 84, and 18th sess. (1795), 40, 49, 50, 52, 58; *NYGM*, 2: 352–53.

21. JJ to the Indians of St. Regis, 10 Aug. 1795, below.

22. JJ to Benson, Ten Broeck, and Watson, 3 Sept. 1795, LbkC, N: Governor's Lbk. 2 (EJ: 03204). Ten Broeck filled in for Richard Varick, the original appointee who could not attend due to the sitting of the Mayor's Court in New York City. JJ to Benson, Ten Broeck, and Watson, 17 Aug. 1795, LbkC, N: Governor's Lbk. 2 (EJ: 03202); JJ to Ten Broeck, 3 Sept. 1795, LbkC, N: Governor's Lbk. 1 (EJ: 02990).

23. TP to JJ, 1 Sept. 1795, ALS, NNC (EJ: 09481). See also JJ's Message to the New York State Senate, 23 Jan. 1796, *N.Y. Senate Journal*, 19th sess. (1796), 20; *NYGM*, 2: 368. For more on the federal government's involvement with the negotiations between New York State and the Akwesasne Mohawk, see JJ to TP, 18 July 1795, C, DLC: Washington (EJ: 12501); TP to GW, 21 July 1795, *PGW: PS*, 18: 389, 390–91n2.

24. *Greenleaf's New York Journal*, 23 Feb. 1796, and *American Minerva* (New York), 24 Feb. 1796.

25. JJ's Message to the New York State Senate, 22 Feb. 1796, *NYGM*, 2: 372–73.

26. JJ to McHenry, 13 Apr. 1796, below.

27. JJ to McHenry, 22 Apr. 1796, LbkC, N: Governor's Lbk. 1 (EJ: 03003), and 28 Apr. 1796, below.

28. JJ to Benson, Varick, and Watson, 12 May 1796, LbkC, N: Governor's Lbk. 2 (EJ: 03230).

29. JJ to McHenry, 16 May 1796, LbkC, N: Governor's Lbk. 2 (EJ: 03012).

30. *At a treaty, held at the city of New-York, with the nations or tribes of Indians denominating themselves "the Seven Nation of Canada"* ([New York?], [1796?]; *Early Am. Imprints*, series 1, no. 47996), 2; *ASP: Indian Affairs*, 619.

31. JJ's Address to the New York State Legislature, [1 Nov. 1796], below.

32. Ibid. The Akwesasne Mohawk later requested an accurate survey of their lands by the New York government. *N.Y. Assembly Journal*, 16 Feb. 1799, 22nd sess., 2nd meeting (1799), 119; JJ's Message to the New York State Assembly, 16 Feb. 1799, *NYGM*, 2: 435.

33. *Greenleaf's New York Journal*, 23 Feb., and *American Minerva* (New York), 24 Feb. 1796. Both the Akwesasne and Kahnawake Mohawk came into direct dispute with other Mohawk groups of Upper Canada over their respective land claims in New York. See, for instance, Gouverneur Morris to JJ, 14 July 1799, ALS, NNC (EJ: 06977).

34. JJ's Message to the New York State Senate, 22 Feb. 1796, *NYGM*, 2: 372–73.

35. *N.Y. Assembly Journal*, 24 Mar. 1796, 19th sess. (1796), 152; *N.Y. Senate Journal*, 24 Mar. 1796, 19th sess. (1796), 84; *NYGM*, 2: 377.

36. Aaron Hill (Kanonaron) and Henry Aaron Hill (Kenwendeshon) represented the Grand River Mohawk. See JJ's Message to the New York State Senate, 29 Mar. 1796, below.

37. JJ to Brant, 1 Aug. 1796, below.

38. A two-member Mohawk legation had already arrived in New York City. The governor sent the pair on to Albany where their room and board would be less expensive and where the next convening of the state legislature was scheduled to be held. During their stay in Albany, the Mohawk delegates were looked after by Dirck Ten Broeck. "New York State Postal Expenses," 2 May 1797, DS, N (EJ: 00972); JJ to Ten Broeck, 10 Dec. 1796, LbkC, N: Governor's Lbk. 1 (EJ: 03055); Ten Broeck to JJ, [14 Dec. 1796], below.

39. TP to JJ, 11 Mar. 1797, CS, MHi: Pickering (EJ: 04823).

40. *Diary* (New York), 5 Apr. 1797; *ASP: Indian Affairs*, 636.

41. *New-York Gazette*, 6 Mar. 1798; JJ's Message to the New York State Assembly, 22 Feb. 1798, *NYGM*, 2: 412. In a letter to his uncle, PAJ noted the frequent visits of various Indian delegations that came to discuss land issues with the governor: "A large number of Indians from diff Tribes who have been at Albany have ~~greatly~~ given him much additional Trouble." PAJ to Peter Jay, 17 Mar. 1798, ALS, NNC (EJ: 09163).

42. "An ACT authorizing the Governor to appoint Commissioners to treat with the Oneida Indians, for the purchase of Parts of their Lands," 26 Feb. 1798, *N.Y. State Laws*, 21st sess. (January 1798), 280; *Commercial Advertiser* (New York), 7 Mar. 1798.

43. JJ to Benson, DeWitt, and Tayler, 27 Feb. 1798, LbkC, N: Governor's Lbk. 2 (EJ: 03276).

44. JJ to Benson, L'Hommedieu, and Tayler, 22 May 1798, LbkC, N: Governor's Lbk. 2 (EJ: 03281).

45. JJ to TP, 23 Apr. 1798, LbkC, N: Governor's Lbk. 1 (EJ: 03144).

46. TP to JJ, 5 May 1798, CS, MHi: Pickering (EJ: 04853).

47. *ASP: Indian Affairs*, 641.

48. "An ACT relative to the Lands of the Cayuga Indians, 8 Mar. 1799, *N.Y. State Laws*, 22nd sess., 2nd meeting (1799), 614–15; Council of Revision Approval, 8 Mar. 1799, D, PHi (EJ: 01173).

49. Chapin to JJ, 10 Aug. 1799, not found; JJ to Chapin, 28 Aug. 1799, ALS, NHi: Henry V. O'Reilly (EJ: 00697).

50. Ibid.

51. Ibid.

52. Chapin to JJ, 19 May 1800, not found; JJ to Chapin, 1 June 1800, ALS, NHi: Henry V. O'Reilly (EJ: 00698); JJ to the New York State Senate, 7 Mar. 1801, PtD, [New York State], *Journal of the Senate of the state of New-York: at their twenty-fourth session, began and held at the city of Albany, the fourth day of November, 1800* (Albany, 1800 or 1801; *Early Am. Imprints*, series 2, no. 1039), 62.

53. Thomas Morris (1771–1849), lawyer and New York state assemblyman, 1794–96.

54. The Seneca maintained eleven tracts in western New York. Taylor, *Divided Ground*, 313–17; Laurence M. Hauptman, *Conspiracy of Interests: Iroquois Dispossession and the Rise of New York State* (Syracuse, 1999), 91–92.

55. The Stockbridge community was an intertribal group composed of mostly Mohicans from the border region of New York and Massachusetts who moved to Oneida country following the disruption of the revolutionary war. The Brothertown Indians were another intertribal group, composed of Mohegans, Pequots, Mauntauk, and Narragansett, from New England and Long island, who also migrated westward to Oneida lands in the 1780s.

56. *N.Y. Senate Journal*, 11 Jan. 1796, 19th sess. (1796), 9; *Argus, Greenleaf's New Daily Advertiser* (New York), 27 Jan. 1796; JJ's Message to the New York State Assembly, 14 Mar. 1796, *NYGM*, 2: 373–74; JJ's Message to the New York State Assembly, 2 Apr. 1796, ALS, (EJ: 00689); *NYGM*, 2: 379; *N.Y. Senate Journal*, 25 Feb. 1797, 20th sess. (1796–97), 71.

57. JJ to Benson, L'Hommedieu, Watson, 1797 Feb., LbkC, N: Governor's Lbk. 2 (EJ: 03254).

58. "An ACT supplementary to an Act entitled, "an Act for the Relief of the Indians residing in New Stockbridge and Brothertown," 23 Mar. 1797, *N.Y. State Laws,* 20th sess. (1797), 103–4.

59. Murray to JJ, 26 Feb. 1799, ALS, NNC (EJ: 09615).

60. "An ACT relative to Lands in Brothertown," 31 Mar. 1795, 18th sess. (1795), 28–29; "An ACT for the Relief of the Indians who are entitled to Lands in Brothertown," 4 Mar. 1796, 19th sess. (1796), 13–16.

61. Samuel Jones, Recorder of New York City, 1789–97, state senator, 1791–99, and state comptroller, 1797–1800; Zina Hitchcock (1755–1832), of Kingsbury, state assemblyman, 1789–93, and state senator 1793–1803.

62. JJ to Gerard Bancker, 15 Aug. 1796, LbkC, N: Governor's Lbk. 2 (EJ: 03239); Edmund Prior and Thomas Eddy to JJ, 15 Oct. 1796, LbkC, N: Governor's Lbk. 2 (EJ: 03244); JJ to Prior and Eddy, 17 Oct. 1796, LbkC, N: Governor's Lbk. 2 (EJ: 03245); JJ to Bancker, 17 Oct. 1796, LbkC, N: Governor's Lbk. 2 (EJ: 03246). For more on New York's administration of the Brothertown community, see JJ to John Eliot, 8 Oct. 1799, ALS, MHi: Misc. (EJ: 04798); Dft, NNC (EJ: 08995); Printed: "Letter from his Excellency Governor Jay, corresponding member of the Historical Society, to its Corresponding Secretary," *Collections of the Massachusetts Historical Society. For the year M,DCC,XCIX* (Boston, 1800; *Early Am. Imprints,* series 1, no. 37930), 146–49; JJ to Samuel Jones, 29 Oct. 1799, LbkC, N: Governor's Lbk 2 (EJ: 03296); and JJ to the Superintendents of the Affairs of the Brothertown Indians, 29 Oct. 1799, ACS, N (EJ: 01016); LbkC, N: Governor's Lbk 2 (EJ; 03297).

63. Samuel Kirkland (1741–1808) graduated from Princeton in 1765 and began working as a missionary to the Haudenosaunee. Kirkland helped persuade the Oneida and Tuscarora to side with the patriot cause during the war of independence and negotiated land sales between the Indians and New York in the postrevolutionary era.

64. Taylor, *Divided Ground,* 370–71.

65. Belknap to JJ, 14 May 1796, ALS, NNC (EJ: 05482).

66. Hugh White (1733–1812) emigrated from Middletown, Conn., to New York in 1784 and served as justice of the peace for Montgomery County and then as a judge of the court of common pleas for Herkimer County.

67. James Dean (1748–1823) worked as an Indian missionary and government agent during the war of independence before serving as a judge of the court of common pleas for Herkimer County.

68. JJ to Belknap, 20 May 1796, ALS, MHi: Belknap (EJ: 04770); Dft, NNC (EJ: 08960); Belknap to JJ, 27 May 1796, ALS, NNC (EJ: 05483); JJ to Belknap, 30 May 1796, ALS, MHi: Belknap (EJ: 04771); Belknap to JJ, 15 June 1796, ALS, NNC (EJ: 08633).

69. Belknap and Morse, "Report on Oneida and Mohekunuh Indians"; JJ to John Eliot, 8 Oct. 1799, cited in note 62, above; Taylor, *Divided Ground,* 371–74.

70. Thacher to JJ, 19 Apr. 1797, below; Morse to JJ, 21 Apr. 1797, below.

71. JJ to Thacher, 25 Apr. 1797, below.

72. Ibid.

73. Ibid.

From Philip Schuyler

Albany June 9th. 1795

Dear Sir,

On wednesday last, being then in Herkemer County, I had the pleasure to be advised of your safe Arrival. Accept of my most cordial congratulations on the happy occassion, and on the confidence, evinced by the people, in electing you their Governor.

At the last session of the Legislature, the person Administring the government, was by law authorized, to treat with, and adjust certain claims, made by Indians resident in Canada, to lands within this state, and Agents were appointed, to confer with a deputation of those Indians, then in New York, to whom the faith of the state was pledged, that a conference should be held with their constituents on the subject of the claim, in the course of the present year.[1] Apprehensive that Mr. Clinton may forget, to make you the necessary communications on the Occasion, has induced me to this information.

I suspect that the claim of the indians in question, and which I understand is very extensive, is ill founded, believing that the Mohawks and other tribes of the six nations, were the original proprietors of All the lands south of the river St. Lawrence, and West of lake Champlain and the river Sorrel, and have ceeded the same to the crown of Britain thro the Medium of the government of the late Colony.[2]

Whether such a cession has been made can only be determined by a recourse to the records and files in the Secretarys office, and probably It will be requisite to go as far back in ˄a˄ research as towards the close of the last century. Judge Benson was one of the agents who conferred with the deputy˄ation˄ abovementioned, and can inform you what measures ˄If any,˄ were taken relative to this Object If ~~any,~~, perhaps the Minutes of the commissioners for Indian affairs, under the late Colony, and who resided in this city, may afford some information on the Subject, whether these minutes are in the secretarys office, or where, I am not advised— perhaps too, Coldens History of the six nations, may thro some light on this affair.[3]

The Person administring the government, together with Messrs. John Cantine David Brooks John Richardson and myself, were during the last session of the legislature, appointed commissioners, to negociate the purchase of part of the lands, reserved to the use of the Oneida, Onondaga and Cayuga tribes, In Consequence of which, It was agreed to meet those tribes at Onondaga on the 15th. of next month, and notice has been given them, then and there to convene, and It was determined that the Commissioners, Governor Clinton excepted, were to meet in this city on the first day of next month, to proceed on the Journey to Onondaga. The requisite arrangements for supplying the indians with provisions &c. during the conference, have been made, and the necessary stores for the Accommodation of the commissioners provided.[4]

Persuaded that advantages will result from your personal attendance at the conference, permit me to intreat the pleasure of your company on the tour, If not prevented by more important avocations. A pair of Camp stools, a Matress and bedding will only be requisite for you to bring along, during your stay here, you will of course be with me —

June 17th. Part of the above was written on the day of Its date, when a sudden indisposition of my daughter Mrs. Rensslaer,[5] required my Attendance, in going to visit her, my horses ran away, and threw me out of the Carriage with such violence, that two of my ribs are much injured, and otherwise so grieviously bruised, that I have not been able to stir out of my room since. I have however hopes that I shall be able to make the Journey to Onondaga. I am Dear Sir with every sentiment of respect and Esteem Your Excellencys most Obedient Servt.

Ph: Schuyler

His Excellency John Jay Esqr &c.

ALS, NNC (EJ: 07131). Endorsed: "Gen. Schuyler / recd. 26 / and. 27 June / 1795 / abt. Indian affairs—".

1. "An ACT to amend an act entitled an act relative to the Indians resident within this State," 5 Mar. 1795, *N.Y. State Laws*, 18th sess. (1795), 14.

2. For the subsequent talks held between New York state and the Akwesasne Mohawk, see the editorial note "Indian Affairs under Jay's Governorship," above.

3. Cadwallader Colden, *The History of the Five Indian Nations depending on the Province of New-York in America* (New York, 1727; *Early Am. Imprints*, series 1, no. 2849).

4. The New York State legislature appointed Schuyler, John Cantine, John Richardson, and David Brooks as Indian commissioners with instructions to negotiate land sales with the Oneida, Onondaga, and Cayuga. "An ACT for the better support of the Oneida, Onondaga and Cayuga Indians, and for other purposes therein mentioned," 9 Apr. 1795, *N.Y. State Laws*, 18th sess. (1795), 43–46. For more on these talks, see the editorial note "Indian Affairs under Jay's Governorship," above.

5. Margarita (Margaret) Schuyler, who was married to Stephen Van Rensselaer.

From Egbert Benson

[Poughkeepsie. June 13th. 1795]

D^r: Sir!

I congratulate You on Your Election, but for much the same Reason as the Turkish Governor not long since, when he could hold out no longer, surrendered to the Russians, he perceived it had been so decreed from the Beginning— Not caring any thing however about the Will, either of the Fates or of the Electors, I am extremely happy You have returned to Us, and I shall be made more so, when I find it generally beleived and declared that what You have done was *about* right—

The Object of this Letter is principally to inform You of a Matter of Business which I beleive must be attended to as soon as possible after You enter in the Administration of the Government— I was one of the Agents appointed to confer with the S^t: Regis Indians who came down during the last Sessions of the Legislature, and our Speech to them, their Answer and our Reply, having been sent by the Governor with a Message,[1] are in the Hands of Mr: Ker,[2] the Clerk of the Assembly, from whom You can have them— These Indians have lately set up a Claim to all the Lands between the two northern Lakes and the River S^t. Lawrence and almost as far south as Fort Edward, and We have promised to meet and treat with them about it early in the ensuing Fall, so that it will be necessary for You, before the last of July at farthest, to dispatch Your Message to them ascertaining the time and place; and with respect to the latter I should suppose it need not be more distant than Lake George; Fort Edward perhaps would be the most convenient—[3] If You should determine to substitute Agents to hold the Treaty, and that it will be most advisable I should be one, or if You should go Yourself and conceive it usefull that I should be with You, I am content, but of this I must be apprized by the first day of the next Term, as We shall then make a Distribution of the Circuits, and most probably one of them will be assigned to Me— You will find the requisite Authority, and Provision for the Expence, in the last Law of the Session—[4] There must be a Commissary to procure Provisions Presents &c^a., and I will only mention to You, that M^r: John Tayler[5] of Albany has been employed in that Capacity at all our late Treaties with the Indians, so that he is not only to be considered as a Sort of *Incumbent*, but I question whether You will find a more fit Person— This however You will receive as mere Intimation[6]—

M^r: S. Jones[7] was also one of the Agents, and any farther Information which You may wish on the Subject can be obtained from him— You will know from M[r]: King whether an Application has been made to the President, and an Appointment of a Commissioner to hold the Treaty under the Authority of the United States has taken place— Vide their Statute of the 1st: March 1793 for regulating Trade and Intercourse with the Indian Tribes[8]— There is the *Rub* with Your Predesessor, and I would not trust him to make a full and seasonable Communication of this Business to You— Yours sincerely

Egb[t]. Benson

ALS, NNC (EJ: 05497). For JJ's reply, see his letter of 27 June 1795, Dft, NNC (EJ: 05497).

1. Documents not found. See George Clinton to the New York State Senate, 7 March 1795, *N.Y. Senate Journal*, 18th sess. (1795), 49, 50; *NYGM*, 2: 352–53.

2. Oliver L. Ker (d. 1796) was appointed clerk of the New York State Assembly, 7 Jan. 1794. *Albany Register*, 13 Jan. 1794.

3. JJ to the Indians of St. Regis, 10 Aug. 1795, below.

4. "An ACT relative to the Indians resident within this State, 27 Mar. 1794, *N.Y. State Laws*, (1777–97), 3: 157–58.

5. John Tayler (1742–1829), Albany merchant, member of the state assembly (1777–81, 1785–87), and City Recorder for Albany (1793).

6. For the meetings held between New York State and Akwesasne Mohawk, see the editorial note "Indian Affairs under Jay's Governorship," above.

7. Samuel Jones, state senator (1791–99) and recorder for New York (1789–96).

8. "An Act to Regulate Trade and Intercourse with the Indian Tribes," 1 Mar. 1793, *Stat.*, 1: 329–32.

From William Cushing

Scituate June 18th. 1795

Dear Sir,

I heartily congratulate you, on your return to your own country, after the fatigues of the Seas, & your exertions abroad for its prosperity, I hope, without injury to your health. What the treaty is, ∧is∧ not come to us with authenticity; but whatever it be, in its beginning, middle or end, you must expect to be mauled by the Sons of bluntness and ——, one ∧of∧ the kinds of rewards which good men have for their patriotism. ∧Peace & American interest are not the objects with Some.∧ I cannot so heartily relish the gubernatorial office, which is presented to you and with so much advantage in the choice. It will doubtless be for the good of N.Y., as well of the public in general, & what is of some consequence, more for your ease & comfort, than rambling in the Carolina woods in June. If you accept, as the Newspapers seem to announce, I must, though reluctantly, acquiesce.

I was in hope to get clear of going to Phil[adelphi]a. this hot Season, but suppose it will not to do, to risque the want of a quorum, unless you give me permission to Stay at home. A Virginia cause was continued to August term, for your presence,[1] whether that will be consistent with your situation, I know not. The middle circuit will of course fall to me next; In the Summer or fall I expect the pleasure of calling to pay my respects to you.[2]

Mrs Cushing joins in sincere regards & Respects to you, Mrs Jay & Mrs Ridley & family— Yours &c. affectionately

W^m. Cushing

ALS, NNC (EJ: 05542). Addressed: "The honorable / John Jay Esqr / Chief Justice of the Supreme Court of the / United States / New York". Endorsed. HPJ, 4: 176–77.

1. *Ware v. Hylton*, on which see *JJSP*, 5: 221–22, 512–34; and *DHSC*, 7: 203–357.

2. Associate Justice of the Supreme Court William Cushing did not visit JJ when he passed through Albany en route from Massachusetts to attend the Supreme Court session in Philadelphia, explaining "that not being able to get lodging where I wished, & there but just time to cross the ferry before night, I thought it prudent to get over to pursue my journey early in the morning, the season being hot & disagreable to me, & the time being scant to reach philadelphia in season". Cushing to JJ, n.d. July 1795, ALS, NNC (EJ: 05571).

To Egbert Benson

NYork 27 June 1795

My good Friend,

[*illegible*] ∧[*illegible*]∧ after my Return from Ph^a., and just as I was about setting out for Rye ∧from whence I returned last Ev^g∧ your Letter of the 13 Ins^t,[1] which had been sent on to Ph^a., was delivered to me— It gave me pleasure to recieve it, but I should have been ∧more∧ pleased to have seen the writer. God only knows, [*illegible*] whether my Removal from the Bench to my present Station will be conduce to my comfort or not— It is a question The Dye is Cast, and nothing remains but for me to consider ∧but how∧ to fulfill in the best manner the Duties incumbent on me, without any Regard to personal consequences— In doing this I shall often need the advice of you and others in whose Judgment & Integrity I rely confide—

I thank you for the Information contained in your Letter, and agreeable to you will pay early attention to it— You will soon hear from me on the Subject Yours sincerely & aff^y—

The Honb. Egbert Benson Esqr.

Dft, NNC (EJ: 05498). Addressed: "The Honble / John Jay /Philadelphia / gone to New York". Stamped: "17/IV 15." Note: "forw^d. 90/20." Endorsed: "13 June & ans^d. 27 June 1795 / Indians".

1. See Benson to JJ, 13 June 1795, above.

To George Washington (private)

New York 29 June 1795

My dear Sir

The enclosed contains my Resignation of the office of chief Justice—[1] I cannot quit it, without again expressing to You my acknowledgments for the Honor you conferred upon me by that appointment; and for the repeated marks of Confidence & Attention for which I am indebted to You.

It gives me pleasure to recollect and reflect on these circumstances—to indulge the most sincere wishes for your Health and Happiness—and[2] to assure you of the perfect Respect Esteem and Attachment with which I am Dear Sir Your obliged & affectionate Friend and Servant

John Jay

The President of the United States

ALS, DLC: Washington (EJ: 10646). Letter marked "private" in top left corner. Dft, NNC (EJ: 08458). The letter contains the enclosure, JJ to GW, 29 June 1795, LbkC, N: Governor's Lbk. 1, (EJ: 03317). *PGW: PS*, 18: 272.

1. JJ's enclosed resignation reads as follows:

Having been elected Governor of the State of new York, & the first Day of next month being assigned for my entering on the Execution of that office, it is proper that I should, and therefore I do hereby resign the office of chief Justice of the united States.

The repeated marks of national confidence with which I have been honored, have made deep and lasting impressions on my ~~Heart~~ Mind and Heart. Permit me to assure You Sir! that no change of Situation will ever abate my Attachment to the united States, or to You— I have the Honor to be &c &c:

2. Here in the draft, JJ excised "for opportunities of".

To Henry Lee

New York 11 July 1795—

Dear Sir

Accept my cordial thanks for the friendly Congratulations expressed in your obliging Letter of the 30 of last month, which I rec[d]. Yesterday—[1]

It was obvious to me when I embarked on my late mission, that so many Circumstances combined to render *pacific* arrangements with Great Britain unwelcome to certain Politicians and their Partizans both here and elsewhere, that their approbation of any Treaty whatever with that nation, was not to be expected.—

Apprized of what had happened in Greece and other Countries, I was warned by the Experience of ages, not to calculate on the Constancy of any popular Tide, whether favorable or adverse, which erroneous or transitory Impressions may occasion—

The Treaty is as it is; and the Time will certainly come when it will very universally recieve exactly that Degree of Commendation or Censure, which to candid and enlightened minds, it shall appear to deserve. In the mean Time I must do, as many others have done before me—that is—regretting the Depravity of some, and the Ignorance of a much greater number, bear with Composure and Fortitude the Effects of each. It is as vain to lament that our Country is not entirely free from these Evils, as it would be to lament that our Fields produce weeds as well as Corn.— Differences in opinion, and other causes equally pure and natural, will unavoidably cause Parties— but *such* parties differ widely from Factions, and are probably no less conducive to good Government, than moderate Fermentation is necessary to make good Wine.—

My good Friend! we must take men and things as they are; and enjoy all the good we meet with. I enjoy the good Will, to which I am indebted for your Letter; and I enjoy the occasion it affords me of assuring you of the Esteem and Regard with which I am Dear Sir your &cᵃ., &cᵃ.—

[To Major General Lee at Strafford, Virginia]

LbkC, NNC: JJ Lbk. 10 (EJ: 12870). *WJ*, 1: 369–70; *HPJ*, 4: 178–79.

1. Letter not found, but JJ is probably mistaken in his date attribution and is actually referring to the letter that Lee sent him on 3 June 1795. ALS, NNC (EJ: 06778), contains the endorsement "Majʳ Gen. H. Lee / 3 June 1795 / anᵈ. Jul".

Henry Lee III (1756–1818), known popularly as Light-Horse Harry Lee, commanded cavalry and light troops during the war of independence. Lee was a delegate in the Constitutional Convention and continued his service to Virginia as a Federalist politician, serving as governor (1791–94), and as a member of the House of Representatives (1799–1801).

To Timothy Pickering

New York 13 July 1795

Sir,

On the 6ᵗʰ. I was favoured with yours of the 3ᵈ of this month together with the papers mentioned to be inclosed with it.[1]

My information relative to the Indian affairs of this State being imperfect, it has not been in my power to answer your letter with sufficient accuracy at a more early day.

Whether the Constitution of the United States warrants the Act of Congress of the 1. March 1793 and whether the act of this State respecting the business now negociating with the Onondaga and other Tribes of Indians, is consistent with both or either of them, are Questions which on *this* occasion I think I should forbear officially to consider and decide.[2]

It appears to me from the 37 article of the New York Constitution that every Convention or Contract with Indian Tribes meditated by this State, must be directed and provided for by Legislative Acts; and consequently that the Governor can take no measures relative thereto, but such as those acts may indicate or permit.[3]

You will perceive from an act of this State (of which you doubtless have a Copy) passed the 9. April 1795 that the negociations in question are therein particularly directed and specified and that it commits the management of the business to five Agents viz. The Governor for the time being, General Schuyler, John Cantine, David Brooks and John Richardson, or any *three* of them. As to any intervention or concurrence of the United States the act is silent and I do not observe anything in it which by implication directs or authorizes the Governor to apply for such intervention or which implies that the Legislature conceived it to be either necessary or expedient.[4]

The arrangement of this business was finished, before I came into office General Schuyler by a letter to me dated the 9. of *last* Month but which I did not receive till the 26th says "It was agreed to meet those tribes at Onondaga on the 15 of *next* month and notice has been given them then and there to convene and it was determined that the Commissioners (Governor Clinton excepted) were to meet in this City (Albany) on the first day of next Month to proceed on the Journey to Onondaga. The requisite arrangements for supplying the Indians with provisions &c. during the Conference have been made and the necessary Stores for the accommodation of the Commissioners provided."[5]

The importance of harmony between the United States and this is obvious. I am persuaded of the Presidents Disposition to promote it; and I assure you my wishes point constantly to the same object—[6] I have the honor to be with great respect Sir Your most obed.t & hble Serv.t

(signed) John Jay

The Honble Timothy Pickering Sec.y at War

C, DLC: Washington (EJ: 10650). Marked "(Copy)" below signature.

1. Letter and enclosed papers not found.

2. JJ is here referring to U.S. Constitution, Art. I, § 10, Art. 2, § 2 and "An Act to Regulate Trade and Intercourse with the Indian Tribes," 1 Mar. 1793, *Stat.*, 1: 329–32.

3. Article 37 of the New York Constitution reads: "And whereas it is of great importance to the

safety of this State that peace and amity with the Indians within the same be at all times supported and maintained; and whereas the frauds too often practiced towards the said Indians, in contracts made for their lands, have, in divers instances, been productive of dangerous discontents and animosities: Be it ordained, that no purchases or contracts for the sale of lands, made since the fourteenth day of October, in the year of our Lord one thousand seven hundred and seventy-five, or which may hereafter be made with or of the said Indians, within the limits of this State, shall be binding on the said Indians, or deemed valid, unless made under the authority and with the consent of the legislature of this State." *N.Y. State Laws*, (1777–97), 1: 13–14.

4. "An ACT for the better Support of the Oneida, Onondaga, and Cayuga Indians, and for other Purposes therein mentioned," 9 Apr. 1795, *N.Y. State Laws*, 18th Sess. (1795), 43–46.

5. Schuyler to JJ, 9 June 1795, above.

6. For more on the federal mediation involving negotiations between the State of New York and the Haudenosaunee, see the editorial note "Indian Affairs under Jay's Governorship," above.

From Samuel Huntington

Norwich July 14th. 1795.

Sir

John Brainard Esqr. Sheriff of the County of New Haven, will have the honour of delivering this letter to your Excellency; & with the other papers which he will lay before you, You will observe I have appointed him my Agent to take two Criminals who have fled from Justice in this State & are said to be in the State of New York—

I request your Excellency to give the bearer the necessary Aid & Authority to take those two Criminals Messrs Chandler & Punderson if to be found in the State of New York and bring them to Connecticut for Trial.—[1]

I am sensible that the papers are not attended with all the exact formalities, to bring the Case within the Act of Congress[2] so as to enable me to make a peremptory demand to have those Criminals delivered up immediately, but am satisfied at the same time that your Excellency will readily give the necessary aid to promote Justice & a due execution of the Law in a sister State: a delay will probably, in this case, give the Culprits opportunity to escape from condign punishment. With sentiments of perfect Esteem & Respect I have the honour to be your Excellency's humble Servant

Saml. Huntington

His Excellency Governor Jay.

LS, NNC (EJ: 05763). Addressed: "His Excellency Governor Jay / New-York". Endorsed: ". . . and."

1. A grand jury of the Connecticut Superior Court held in Litchfield County for the summer term of 1795 issued an indictment charging James Chandler and Akimaar C. Punderson with the crime of forgery. When the accused fled to neighboring New York to avoid judgement, the governor of Connecticut sought JJ's assistance with apprehending the fugitives. The pair successfully

evaded authorities for over six months, however, forcing Oliver Wolcott, Huntington's successor, to make another request for extradition. In response to Wolcott, JJ issued a warrant for the capture of Chandler and Punderson. Wolcott to JJ, 30 Jan. 1796, below; JJ to Wolcott, 19 Feb. 1796, LbkC, N: Governor's Lbk. 2 (EJ: 03216); 20 Feb. 1796, C, NN: Wolcott (EJ: 13103); JJ to the New York Officers of Justice, 20 Feb. 1796, N: Governor's Lbk. 2 (EJ: 03215).

Fugitives fleeing justice between states remained a mutual cause of concern for New York and Connecticut officials. In December 1798, JJ warned that neither state should be allowed to "become an asylum for fugitives from the justice of the other". Moreover, New York experienced this same problem with other states, particularly those sharing her border. For instance, in late 1799, the governor of Pennsylvania requested JJ's assistance with apprehending a horse thief who had fled from northeastern Pennsylvania to New York. JJ to Jonathan Trumbull Jr., 4 Dec. 1798, LbkC, N: Governor's Lbk. 1 (EJ: 03198); JJ to the Sheriff of Cayuga County, 28 Dec. 1799, LbkC, N: Governor's Lbk. 2 (EJ: 03302). See also JJ to James Wood, 11 Dec. 1797, LbkC, N: Governor's Lbk. 1 (EJ: 03108); and JJ to Josiah Ogden Hoffman, 11 Dec. 1797, LbkC, N: Governor's Lbk. 1 (EJ: 03109).

2. "An Act respecting fugitives from justice, and persons escaping from the service of their masters," 12 Feb. 1793, *Stat.*, 1: 302–5.

From John Trumbull

London 23^d. July 1795.

Dear Sir.

It is with the most real pleasure that I congratulate you on your safe Arrival in America, the Cordial Reception you have met from your fellow Citizens, and the flattering testimony they have given of their Respect and Esteem by Electing you to the first Office in their Gift.— may you long and happily enjoy the Reward of your labours.

I returned to this place from France, three Days ago;— while in that Country I only wrote to you twice, the last of which was a few days ago, enclosing the Project of a new Constitution,[1] and sent by the Nancy Capt. Butler to your Port.[2]

On my Arrival in Paris I found much Curiosity Jealousy and Prejudice on the Subject of the Treaty;— the Gentleman to whom I had your permission to communicate under certain injunctions, found himself embarrassed by a previous engagement inconsistant with those injunctions; and as I did not feel myself justifiable in the smallest departure from the instructions you had given me, He ultimately determined not to receive from me the proposed information;— That I should be there, be seen frequently with Him, and He remain ignorant on ~~subject~~ such a subject, would have encreased the Jealousies which already existed; and for this there was no remedy but in observing the utmost Distance and Coldness:— Of course the whole weight of Suspicion and Ill Will was accumulated upon me, and my situation became very awkward and unpleasant.— I thought it however prudent to remain as long as my Business required, contenting myself with repeating on all occasions that the Treaty contained nothing contrary to the engagements of pre-existing Treaties; and that whenever the contracting Governments should see fit to make it public, I had no doubt but it would meet the approbation of all reasonable men.[3]

We are now in hourly expectation, of hearing the Result of the deliberations of the Senate, as we have Accounts down to the 15[th]. June, and know that the Asia was to sail from Phil[adelphi]a. about the 20[th]:[4] with M[r] Allen's and M[r] Hammond's Families:—[5] I hope the late Orders for bringing in neutral Ships bound with Provisions to France, and the continued Captures on the Coast of America, will not prove the source of new misunderstandings.— I yesterday breakfasted with S[r]. W[m]. Scott,[6] and had some conversation on this Subject: I ventured to say to him that, having just arrived from France I could assure him that as a measure of military Policy the bringing in of Neutral Ships was utterly useless, as great quantities of foreign Corn had been received, and the Harvest was begun in the South;— that if the want of bread here operated as a Reason for the measure, I was sorry it had not been announced in another way, as we should have been equally ready to sell to this Country as to any other; that I dreaded the Effect this Measure might have upon the public Mind in America, for ∧although∧ I trusted it would not prevent the ratification of the Treaty, yet the loss falling upon the same important Class of men who had already suffered so severely, I did apprehend, that unless great Dispatch in the settlement of this Business and great liberality in payment, were experienced, it would have the Effect to counteract in a very great Degree that Return of Amity and mutual kindness which I had supposed to be the great object of the Treaty; and to render all that had been done, a mere palliative and momentary business.

Sir William Assured me, ["]that the necessities of the Country were to a certain degree the Cause of the existing Orders;— that, at the same time Government considered themselves as in the Exercise of one of the Rights of War common to all Nations, and which they should not think of contesting, were We or any other Nation to exercise the same hereafter, in similar circumstances, with respect to the Ships of this Nation:— that Government had instructed him (and He should most faithfully and with pleasure execute those instructions) to give all possible Dispatch to the Business, as well as the utmost latitude to Payments, consistant with Reason." in the mean time our People are very much dissatisfied both here and on the Continent.[7]

A Body of Emigrant Troops have lately been landed in Quiberon Bay, from whose cooperation with the disaffected people of La Vendee and Britanny much has been expected;— but I believe little will be done; we already hear of several Repulses, and additional Troops are known to be on their March from the North & East of France, where hostile operations are at present Suspended.[8]

The Public Opinion of France, no longer contrould by the Guillotine and patriotic Baptisms, is now as loudly pronounced against the Atrocious consequences of Jacobinism, as that of England or America ever were; and if they now Err in their criminal prosecutions, it is by employing a formality & caution which one can scarce refrain from Blaming, when exercised towards such a wretch as Joseph Le Bon, or Fouquier Tinville.[9]

The Constitution of which I sent you a Copy, is still under discussion; several amendments (as We think them) have been, and it is probable that others will be adopted; and I am not without a Hope, & even an Expectation that within a few months we shall see a Form of Government in operation in France, which altho' not altogether meeting our Opinions of Wisdom, will yet be a prodigious approach towards it;— and such a Declaration of Intentions towards other Nations, as will shew more Moderation than might have been expected from a People covered with so many Victories.

The Scarcity of Bread is real in this Country as well as on the Continent: Wheat has been sold here at 12/4 the Bushel, and the qu[arte]ʳ. loaf, which a little before you left England was at sixpence, is now at twelvepence halfpenny.— The Prospect of Crops in those parts of the Continent where I have been, as well as here, is good, provided the Weather should soon change, and give us a few Weeks of Heat;— but should the Rains & Cold which have long prevailed, continue much longer, the Corn will be much injured, and I see not, in that case, what is to be ₍prevent₎ a general famine.

My Plate at Stutgard I found not so nearly finished, as I had hoped, & of course the publication cannot take place this Winter; I Shall send in a few days to Mʳ. Penfield an impression of it in the State it was last January, as well as a finished one of Montgomery, from which my friends I hope will be induced to have a little longer patience: they cannot be so much hurt at the Delay as I am.—[10] I beg my Respects to Mʳˢ. Jay and Peter— as well as to Mʳ. Benson, King, Hobart &c. & am with all Respect Dʳ. Sir, Your H[umble] Servant

Jnᵒ. Trumbull

ALS, NNC (EJ: 07204). Endorsed: "... anᵈ. 10 nov." *HPJ*, 4: 179–82.

1. JT to JJ, 24 Mar. 1795, above; 2 July 1795, ALS, NNC (EJ: 07203), enclosed French Constitution adopted by the Directory on 22 Aug. 1795 not found.

2. The ship *Nancy*, Captain Butler, arrived in New York from Le Havre-de-Grâce on 24 Aug. after a voyage of 49 days. *Greenleaf's New York Journal*, 25 Aug. 1794.

3. The "Gentleman" was James Monroe, Minister to France. For JT's full account, see Trumbull, *Autobiography*, 184–87. See also JJ to Monroe, 19 Feb. 1795, above.

4. Philadelphia newspapers reported that the *Asia* was scheduled to sail for Hamburg via England on 19 June, and that it reached Deal on 19 Aug. *Philadelphia Gazette*, 10 June; *Aurora General Advertiser*, 12 Oct. 1795.

5. George Hammond, minister to the United States, 1791–95, left that post in August 1795. On 20 May 1793, he married Margaret Allen (d. 1838), the daughter of former Loyalist Andrew Allen, the attorney-general of Pennsylvania.

6. William Scott, Baron Stowell.

7. On the impact of the British renewal of seizures of ships and provisions bound for France and its colonies on the American response to the Jay Treaty, see the editorial note "Aftermath of the Jay Treaty: Responses, Ratification, and Implementation," above.

8. Battle of Quiberon, 23 June–20 July 1795. On 23 June, over 3,000 counterrevolutionary troops, transported by British warships, landed on the Quiberon peninsula, intending to support the Chouannerie and Vendée revolts in Western France. Republican forces, led by General Louis Lazare Hoche, repelled the attack and prevented the retreating counterrevolutionaries from reaching British ships. Approximately 700 prisoners were executed. Tony Jacques, *Dictionary of Battles and Sieges* (Westport, 2007), 3: 832.

9. Joseph Le Bon (1765–95), French priest turned politician and member of the Convention, who was sent on a mission to the departments of the Somme and Pas-de-Calais in 1793–94, and Antoine Quentin Fouquier-Tinville (1746–95), a public prosecutor in 1793–94. Both men were infamous for the extent of their prosecutions and executions during the Terror, and, during the Thermidorian reaction, were tried and executed in 1795.

10. For more on JT's prints, see JJ Memorandum to JT, [London, 5 Feb. 1795], above.

From James Duane

Schenectade 31st July 1795

Dear Sir.

Among your numerous and respectable friends none can participate with more sensibility in events which concern your happiness than myself. I felicitate with you on your safe arrival, on the success of your arduous mission, and on the distinguished manner in which you have been elected to the chief seat of this government. May every blessing attend you in your domestic concerns and your public administration which an indulgent Heaven can bestow!

A mind less firm might be a little discomposed, at the clamours which have been artfully excited against the treaty by too many *merely*, thro' that medium, to wound your peace and reputation: but conscious of your own rectitude, justly sensible of your eminent services, and assured of the esteem and attachment of a great majority of the people, and especially of the wise and virtuous Citizens, I am fully perswaded that you feel yourself superior

to the feeble darts of Envy and despise the entreagues of malice and disappointed ambition. When we remember that it was the fate of so many illustrious Heroes and Patriots in all ages of the world, we are almost led to conclude
that this species of persecution is inseperable from distinguished merit, and
that it rages with a degree of fury proportioned to the excellency of the Character it aims to destroy. What a horrid image of human Depravity. I wish most
earnestly to pay you my respects personally but can not reconcile it to myself
to visit my native city in the degraded situation to which it is reduced by the
late convulsive and most unprovoked tumult—a tumult which has shaken
the very foundation of all rational liberty and good government—in which
Terror and force were substituted in the place of order and deliberation; convened not to examine but, avowedly, to condemn; not to advise or recommend but to execute, silencing those Patriots who came prepared to give and
receive information with stones, and then in a Phrenzy committing a treaty
which had been sanctioned by two thirds of the Senate to the flames. If these,
as we learn, are the facts alas what reason shall we have to blush for our Capi-
tol when this intemperate procedure shall be recorded in the page of history.[1]

I flatter myself that our worthy Governour will find a time before long to
receive the congratulations of his friends in the county of Albany who have
uniformly rendered the tribute due to his merit. May I not hope that on such
a desireable occasion you will remember your friends in Duanesburgh who
have proved themselves not unworthy of a share of your attention. Schenectade might be considered as a stage: it deserves no more from you or
me—and my lodge your quarters: for I have not yet been able to build at
Duanesburgh for want of materials my son's house having hitherto employed
all my exertions. We wish your amiable Lady and my young friend Mr Jay may
accompany you. It woud make this family peculiarly happy.

I have desired my friend Mr Bowers[2] to pay you 1609. dollars ∧30 Cents∧
as a Fifth dividend being 9/ in the pound computed on the principal of the
bonds due to the late Judge Chambers and his Lady from Mr Du Bois. you
have already received a sum equal to the whole of the principal. This is a most
tedious trust and has given, and continues to give me infinite trouble. I wish
to see the end of it without distressing the purchasors who, tho' they have not
been punctual, there is reason to believe have in general made all the exertions in their power and will pay interest for the forbearance.

A dispute exists between Doctors Livingston and Jones executors of our
late uncle Mr Philip Livingston, and myself as acting trustee for Mr Du Bois's
creditors. We adjusted the demand within about £ Messrs Harrison and
Cosine gave an opinion in favor of the Doctors with respect to the ballance

in question, but apprehending it was on an imperfect statement I sent one comprehending all the circumstances to the latter gentlemen with a diferent conclusion. It did not produce conviction and we agreed to refer the decision to professor Kent chosen on my part and on their's Mr Hoffman. The case I stated the Doctors promised to return or to furnish a copy of it as I had no draft. Mr Bowers will present it to you. I wish you to peruse it and if you think my opinion well founded, your son will be so obliging as to deliver it to Mr Kent and request him To apprize Mr. Hoffman of his readiness to confer on the subject— any elucidation it may require you will be pleased to add. Were I present I coud offer nothing to strengthen the equity on our side. If the merits, in your Judgement, lie with the Doctors the creditors will be contented and it need not be pursued further. Altho' the sum is not of much moment I thought our relations pressed too hard. They make an enormous advantage by the rise of the lands on the purchase money which, till very lately, they could not raise out of the embarrassed estate of their testator; and being of this opinion I did not find myself at liberty to gratify them.[3]

With every sentiment of affectionate attachment and esteem for yourself and the sincere respects and best wishes of this family for Mrs Jay young Mr Jay and the young Ladies— I have the honor to be—Dear Sir your Excellency's most obedient and very humble Servant,

Ja^s: Duane

His Excellency Governor Jay
Schenectade 3^d September.—
Mr Bowers having extended his excursion much farther than I expected has occasioned the delay of this Letter—

ALS, NNC (EJ: 05565). Endorsed: ". . . re^d. & an^d. Septr. 1795". LbkC, in JJ's hand, NNC: JJ Lbk. 10 (EJ: 12887). For JJ's reply, see his letter of 16 Sept. 1795, below.

1. Duane is apparently responding to accounts of town meetings held in New York following the Senate's ratification of the Jay Treaty. Handbills and announcements printed in New York newspapers called for a meeting of the citizens at noon on Saturday, 18 July, "for the purpose of joining our fellow citizens of Boston, who last Monday [13 July] unanimously adopted resolutions expressive of their detestation of *the treaty* with Great Britain" and "conjuring them to come forward like freemen, and declare the treaty a disgraceful one, ruinous to our commerce, &c." Federalists led by AH sought to block such actions. On Friday evening a small group of merchants met at Tontine Hall with James Watson in the chair. AH and RK addressed them. The group developed a plan of opposition and distributed handbills challenging the town meeting to discussion and urging full attendance. In response to these notices a large crowd of both Republicans and Federalists assembled on Saturday at Federal Hall where AH, supported by RK, Josiah Ogden Hoffman, Richard Harison, and others, tried to address the crowd, but were interrupted by a call for selecting a chairman for the meeting. William Stephens Smith was elected chair. Republican Peter R. Livingston attempted to

address the chair but was interrupted by AH, whereupon, following a procedural vote, Livingston was chosen to speak but could not be heard due to the "confusion" at the meeting. A motion was made to split the meeting so that those who disapproved of the treaty should go to the right and those who approved should go to the left. AH again attempted to speak but could not be heard over the hissings and hootings of the crowd. Some accounts further stated the AH was hit in the head by stones thrown by the crowd.

Brockholst Livingston then argued that since the treaty had already been published and was available to everyone, he presumed the assembly had already made up its mind and there was no need to procrastinate the object of the meeting, which was to express the group's opinion on the treaty. He did suggest that if there were some present who had not reached a decision they could go to a nearby church where a treaty opponent would debate the treaty article by article with AH, but that effort failed. A group of about 500 then split off, proceeded to The Battery, formed a circle, and burnt a copy of the treaty in front of the governor's house. AH introduced a resolution at the main meeting stating it was unnecessary to give an opinion on the treaty; it was noisily rejected by the crowd. A motion was then carried for appointing a committee to draft resolutions expressing disapprobation of the treaty. The meeting adjourned to await the report of the committee.

On Monday, 20 July, the citizens reassembled at noon and confirmed the selection of membership of the committee; Brockholst Livingston introduced resolutions opposing the treaty which were approved by the crowd, reportedly of 5,000–6,000 people, and immediately sent by express to GW. The conflicts at these meetings also resulted in a proposed duel between AH and Republican James Nicholson, which was ultimately averted. For accounts of the meetings and for the resolutions, see the *Argus, Greenleaf's New Daily Advertiser* (New York), 17, 18, 20, 21, and 25 July 1795; William S. Smith, "To the Citizens of New York", 18 July, broadside, DLC; *PAH*, 18: 485–89nn31–33; and RK to Christopher Gore, 24 July 1795, *Life and Correspondence of Rufus King*, 2: 16–17. On the proposed duel, *PAH*, 18: 501–2; and *PGW: PS*, 18: 370–82. See also *New-York Gazette*, 20 July; *Dunlap's American Daily Advertiser* (Philadelphia), and the *Philadelphia Gazette*, both 21 July; *Gazette of the United States* (Philadelphia), 21 and 23 July; *Aurora General Advertiser* (Philadelphia), 22 July; *New-Jersey Journal* (Elizabethtown), 22 July; *Connecticut Gazette* (New London), 23 July; *Albany Register*, (24 July); *Federal Intelligencer* (Baltimore), 24 July 1795. These Accounts were later repeated in more distant newspapers, especially in New England.

2. Probably Henry Bowers Jr., whose daughter Mary Ann (1773–1828) married James Chatham Duane (1769–1842) in 1792. "Judge Chambers and his Lady" were JJ's uncle John Chambers (1710–64) and aunt Ann Van Cortlandt Chambers, sister of JJ's mother. JJ was the executor of their estate. Duane was the agent for the creditors of the loyalist Peter Dubois, former New York City Magistrate of Police under British occupation. Edward P. Alexander, *A Revolutionary Conservative: James Duane of New York* (N.Y., 1966), 36.

3. Philip Livingston, "The Signer" was the brother of William Livingston, SLJ's father, and Duane's father-in-law, Robert Livingston. Dr. Livingston was John Henry Livingston, LL.D., and Dr. Jones was Thomas Jones, physician, both of whom were married to daughters of Philip. A third administrator was Henry Brockholst Livingston. *PAH*, 26: 474–76. The other New York lawyers consulted were Richard Harison, John Cozine, and Josiah Ogden Hoffman.

From Lansdowne

Bowood Park 31ˢᵗ July 1795

Dear Sir

I know that Sir Francis Baring has the honour to be well known to you, which of course is enough to reccommend his Son to you, but I flatter myself a Line from me will be no disservice to him, especially if I am to judge by the comparative weight, which your reccommendation will always have with me; he is in truth a most respectable young Man, & I have no doubt, if he lives, will prove a Man of the first emminence.[1]

I was exceedingly sorry at the suddenness of your departure from London which quite surprised me; I have been however indisposed almost ever since ~~which~~ with the Gout, which has still left my hand so lame, that I am obliged to avail myself of that of another, which I hope You will excuse; the course of our public Affairs is as little calculated to relieve the mind, as the unseasonable weather we have experienced is to relieve the Body; Mʳ Baring is very capable, indeed more so, than anybody I know, to give You the State of things both here & upon the Continent; My Son writes to me from Genoa, that he has heard there, that our old Friend Mʳ Reyneval has been called upon at Paris, & much consulted, but I do not find any tendency to peace upon our parts, but much the contrary, if any thing can evince the folly of the War, it is the Catastrophe which has lately taken place at Quiberon.

I beg my compliments to your Son, who I shall always remember with pleasure.[2] I am with great Respect & esteem Dear Sir Your most faithfull humble Servᵗ.

Lansdown

LS, NNC (EJ: 08182). For JJ's response to Lansdowne, see his letter of 7 Jan. 1796, Dft, NNC (EJ: 08177).

1. Francis Baring, 1st Baronet (1740–1810), merchant banker and partner in Barings Bank (later John & Francis Baring & Co. and Baring Brothers & Co.) whom JJ had met in London during the Jay Treaty negotiations. Baring was close politically and personally to Lansdowne. In 1795, Baring and his associates in Hope & Co. sent Baring's second son, Alexander, later first Baron Ashburton (1773–1848), aged 22, to the United States to purchase land from William Bingham as an investment. The younger Baring arrived in November 1795. In February 1796, he purchased 1,225,000 acres of land in Maine for £107,000, one-quarter for the Barings and three-quarters for the Hopes. He remained in the United States until 1801, providing commercial intelligence for his father. On 23 Aug. 1798, Alexander married Bingham's daughter Ann Louisa (1782–1848), and his brother Henry (1777–1848) married Bingham's daughter Maria in 1802. Barings and Hope & Co. were instrumental in funding the Louisiana Purchase. *ODNBO*.

2. PAJ, who met Lansdowne during the Jay Treaty mission to London. See, for example, PAJ Diary B, 11 Jan. 1795, AD, NNC.

To the Indians of St. Regis

[New York 10 Augt. 1795]

Brothers

I send you this Message to fulfil the Promise which the Agents for the State who met you in this City last Winter then made to you.

Brothers

This promise was that we would meet You on the Business of the Lands which you say belong to You.

Brothers

I now inform you that we will meet you and hold the proposed Treaty at Fort George at the South end of Lake George on the Eighteenth day of September next.[1]

Brothers

I hope that we shall then meet with Hearts and Minds well disposed to each other and in the mean time I wish you Peace

John Jay

LS, marked "Duplicate", PC: Cowan Auctions.

1. For the conference held between New York state and the Akwesasne Mohawk, see the editorial note "Indian Affairs under Jay's Governorship," above.

JOHN JAY AND THE YELLOW FEVER EPIDEMICS

Almost immediately upon his return to the United States and his election as governor of New York, Jay would have to deal with a deadly threat: yellow fever. The disease would return to New York yearly throughout Jay's tenure, with epidemics in 1795, 1796, 1798, 1799, and 1800. In his actions and correspondence, Jay revealed his belief that government should act proactively to protect citizens, not just from war, but from other threats such as disease. In particular, *preventative* public health efforts were instituted to reduce local causes (then believed to be filth and "miasma"), at the same time that the traditional practice of quarantine was employed.

Yellow Fever

In the seventeenth and eighteenth centuries, yellow fever, also known as Yellow Jack, was a yearly visitor to the Caribbean and the American South, and appeared with regularity in the North. New York, susceptible as a port city, had outbreaks in 1702, 1731, 1742, and 1743. In 1793, Philadelphia experienced a major epidemic, marking the beginning of the disease's thirty-year appearance in the northern states. Lasting from July to November, the 1793 epidemic killed approximately 10 percent of Philadelphia's population.[1]

The yellow fever virus is spread between humans by the mosquito, *Aedes aegypti*. In the 1790s, however, the disease was ascribed to either direct contagion or environmental causes (infectious). The direct contagion theory held that the disease originated elsewhere, and was spread by direct contact with infected people and things. The environmental theory held that the disease was domestic in origin, produced by a confluence of certain conditions—humidity, rotten animal flesh, stagnant water, filth—which created the conditions (particularly miasmas, or bad air) for the disease to spread. Proponents of the direct contagion theory believed that quarantine and the banning of social and business intercourse with infected places was the proper response to an outbreak of the disease. Proponents of the environmental theory believed that the disease could be held in check by public sanitation work, such as the cleaning up of public areas, paving streets, and draining cellars.[2]

The Epidemic of 1795

New York City served as the state capital in 1795, and was rapidly growing, in both population and commercial importance. In 1790 the population was approximately 33,000; by 1800, it had grown to 60,000.[3] Foreign immigration began to contribute significantly to this increase, in addition to those who came from the rural United States. Housing was inadequate; multiple families crowded into formerly single-family dwellings. Sanitation was almost nonexistent, with waste and garbage flowing in the streets.[4]

New York had suffered a mini-epidemic in 1791, with 100 deaths. The city responded to Philadelphia's 1793 epidemic with quarantine and a measure to enforce the City's law against nuisances. By proclamation, New York's governor, George Clinton, citing a 1784 quarantine law, banned all intercourse with Philadelphia. Despite this measure, the City of New York did contribute funds to the relief effort. Clinton's proclamation became the model for similar measures passed in the ensuing two years under his and Jay's administrations.[5]

The events of 1793 resulted in the creation of the Health Committee (later Commission), a quasi-governmental public health group. On 13 September 1793, in tandem with the governor's proclamation, a citizen's committee for the city, chaired by Comfort Sands, appointed a seven member committee consisting of Robert Bowne (chair), John Broome (chair),[6] Robert Lenox, Nathaniel Hazard, White Matlack, Dr. Samuel Bard, and the Health Officer for the Port of New York Dr. Malachi Treat (appointed 10 January 1792). The Health Committee would be tasked with employing doctors to assist in the inspection of ships and inspectors to monitor the docks and ferry landings. At the next Common Council meeting of 16 September, Mayor Richard Varick and the Council appointed an additional Health Committee charged with helping the "Committee appointed by the Inhabitants" consisting of four aldermen (Isaac Stoutenburgh, John Campbell, Gabriel Furman, and Theophilus Beekman) and three members of the Common Council (assistant aldermen Frederick Stymeets, Nicholas Carmer, and George Janeway). According to their own minutes, the two Committees acted as one.[7] The Health Committee at this point supported the theory of direct contagion, and lobbied heavily for strict quarantine laws, such as a 27 March amendment to the Act of 1784—a measure that expanded the quarantine to all ships entering New York, employed a salaried health officer, and designated Governors Island as a quarantine station with the additional appointment, if needed, of physicians for Albany and Hudson.[8] During the 1794 fever season, Governor Clinton would appoint the Health Committee (membership intact) as a state commission funded by that amendment.[9]

Rumors of yellow fever in the West Indies again reached New York the following summer. Jay, having just assumed the role of governor, would have to work quickly, with the infrastructure already established by the City and left behind by Governor Clinton. On 20 July, Malachi Treat, one of three Health Officers appointed to inspect ships, examined three sick sailors on the brig *Zephyr*, just arrived from Port-au-Prince. During the course of her journey, the ship's boy had died of fever. The three sailors soon recovered, but Treat (who had autopsied the boy's body) took sick on 22 July and died eight days later. Treat's death gave fuel to the contagion model, justifying the quarantine strategy. At the same time, sailors aboard the ship *William*, in from Liverpool, fell ill, as did several people in the neighborhood. While the disease appeared to be confined, rumors of an epidemic were not, and on 8 August, the chairman of the city's Health Committee, John Broome, was forced to act. He issued a statement that all measures were being taken to confine the fever: quarantine and cleaning up of "nuisances." A quarantine center was established in a makeshift hospital and almshouse at Belle Vue farm to receive fever victims, on land leased from Brockholst Livingston, located several miles outside the city on the East River. The city later purchased the land in 1798.[10] In mid-August, as a precautionary measure, Jay declared the New

York ports closed to all vessels from the West Indies and the Mediterranean. With the exception of Treat, who had died, and Matlack, "who was absent," Jay kept all of Clinton's appointees on the Health Committee, replacing Treat with his former pupil, William Pitt Smith, as Health Officer.[11] It is notable that a good number of Clinton appointees were Republicans, most notably Broome (who on the same day the ill-fated Treat boarded the *Zephyr*, joined Brockholst Livingston's Citizen's Committee against the Jay Treaty), but either for the sake of practicality, collegiality, or political prudence, Jay chose continuity, with fever season looming. Matlack, seen by some as a rabid anti-Federalist and Jay Treaty opponent, may have been absent for political reasons, or, like many citizens of means, may have fled the disease.[12]

Throughout August, the Health Committee continued to deny that there was an epidemic. The public, however, refused to ignore the reports of further deaths, and on 21 August, the Health Committee was forced to admit that there had been twelve deaths from the fever. Three days later, they declared that an epidemic did exist, but limited its impact to the area surrounding the docks on the East River. By September, the city was in full panic, and almost all those citizens who had the means to leave New York, did so.[13]

In late August, Pennsylvania Governor Thomas Mifflin issued a proclamation "interdicting the customary intercourse" between New York and Philadelphia (and Norfolk where the disease also appeared).[14] Previous to this ban, the management of the nascent epidemic had been the concern of the Mayor and City Council. The extent of Jay's power in this situation was questionable. The governor could suggest legislation, but he lacked the power of veto. He was a member of the Council of Revision, but that body possessed little real power to override the legislature. Moreover, much of the state was highly suspicious when the governor sought to exercise authority. Executive power, as used by Clinton, grew more out of influence and party interest than specific powers. Jay, as a Federalist, was a proponent of a strong executive as a check on legislative power, but he had to act carefully. As the issue of interstate commerce involved the state executive, the ban forced Jay to act more directly.

Jay wrote John Charlton of the city's Medical Society on 4 September, to gather, in conjunction with the College of Physicians, the Health Committee, and the City Council, information regarding the supposed epidemic: "This Proclamation, by exciting alarms & apprehensions throughout this and the neighbouring States, and in foreign Countries, naturally tends to produce Embarrassments to the Commerce of this City and to interrupt that Intercourse with the Country, which is at all times necessary to the convenience and Interests of both." Jay was anxious to have the quarantine lifted, as it could prove disastrous to the city's, and therefore state's, economy, especially if other states followed suit. However, he was unwilling to suppress information that would sacrifice public health. "If such a Disease does really exist and prevail here, it should candidly be admitted and made known, that the Dangers resulting from it may be guarded against." The resultant reports stated that eighty-nine deaths had been reported and that all precautions had been taken to contain the disease. Jay sent copies of the reports to Governor Mifflin on 9 Sept., concluding "I flatter myself it will appear to your Excellency from these Documents that it is not necessary to suspend the Intercourse between this City and Philadelphia, and that therefore the Prohibition in Question will be revoked." Despite his efforts, the ban continued through October, as the disease spread and the numbers of ill and dead increased.[15]

Jay did his best to serve as an example to others and quell panic. He turned down an invitation by the French Consul to a "republican entertainment" on the grounds that it would be inappropriate, thus avoiding a potentially indelicate political situation. On 3 October, he declined John Blanchard's offer to let the Jay family evacuate to Blanchard's home in Meadow Ridge, New Jersey. He believed the epidemic was waning and would send "Mrs. Jay and the Children" (but not himself) to the country only if the danger grew worse.[16]

By the end of October, the epidemic had begun to abate. Thomas Mifflin rescinded the ban on intercourse, and sent along $7,000 as aid to the city (repaying the kindness New York City paid Philadelphia in 1793). By November, the Health Committee reported 732 total deaths. The cost to the city, in terms of both direct expenses and lost commerce, was enormous.[17]

Jay issued a general call for a day of Thanksgiving for 26 November. This proclamation is suffused with Jay's religious beliefs, saying that the late sickness only serves to remind the populace that all, good and bad, is in the hands of the "Supreme Ruler of All Nations."[18] This seemingly benign recommendation (not even an order) brought forth an immediate flood of criticism from political opponents. Jay's title of "Commander in Chief of the State of New York" was mocked for pretense and seen as indicative of an ambitious executive.[19] References were repeatedly made to the Jay Treaty. One author suggested that the Treaty was responsible for God's wrath, and inquired, "Would it not do well for the Clergy to add their most fervent petitions, that the Almighty Ruler of the Universe would be pleased to turn the heart of our enemy, the King of Great Britain—that he would extend his gracious protection to our unhappy brethren who are daily falling into the hands of British pirates, and save our commerce from future depredations."[20] Opposition papers also mocked Jay's pious tone which "possesses such genuine ingredients of the whining cant of religious hypocrisy as render him worthy of a cardinal's hat, and will even fit him for the Papal Dignity in time."[21] Jay's defenders responded by railing against the spirit of party: "It outrages all senses of decency—all regard for virtue and religion. The proposed ejaculation on the treaty, is open profanity. To countenance such shameful scurrility, is a proof of public depravity."[22]

Subsequent Yellow Fever Outbreaks

Governor Jay prepared for future outbreaks in 1796 by making more appointments, notably Dr. Richard Bayley as Health Officer of the Port of New York in February. Bayley would be instrumental throughout Jay's time in office.[23] The governor also addressed the fiscal failures of the previous year with Broome of the New York City Health Committee and with the legislature in January.[24]

On 1 April, the state legislature passed "An Act to Prevent the Bringing In and Spreading of Infectious Diseases in this State."[25] This act provided for the position of a health officer for the city of New York, the appointment of seven commissioners for the health department, the quarantining of vessels with sick passengers or sailing from foreign ports, and empowered the Governor to issue orders of quarantine. With the act came a new, separate Health Commission appointed by the governor consisting of Robert Bowne (chair) and John Campbell from the original Health Committee, Jay's protégé Francis Childs, as well as John B. Coles, William De Peyster, Jr., John Murray, Sr. (who would succeed Bowne as chair), Henry Will, and a William Robinson, all with business connections, several with Federalist affiliations.[26]

The 1796 act was amended in February 1797 to provide for the cleaning of streets, the regulation of tanners, glue, and soap makers, the inspection of ships sailing from Cape May, and to allow for the collection of fines. It was further amended by two state laws passed on 6 and 30 March 1798; this legislation contained provisions that extended the powers of the commissioners, granted the mayor the power to declare quarantine, appropriated funds for the lazaretto on Bedloe's Island, and required the removal of sick passengers to said lazaretto.[27]

The act of 1 April, like the 1794 act, other legislation passed in Pennsylvania, and the past quarantine proclamations of Clinton, Mifflin, and Jay, tested certain constitutional boundaries concerning interstate commerce and international relations. The governors had to some degree been overstepping their authority. With that in mind, as well as the expense of paying for quarantine, Jay wrote to Secretary of State Timothy Pickering two weeks after the passage of the act, concerning the governor's role in policing ports, and the need for federal aid in such areas as quarantining war ships from other nations that were at war (Britain and France) in the same quarantine anchorage.[28] This correspondence was followed by the introduction by Samuel Smith[29] of Maryland of a bill which proposed strong discretionary powers to the federal government in the quarantining of ports. Smith's proposal inspired a state's rights debate, the result being a modified federal law, passed on 27 May 1796, that empowered the president "to direct revenue officers and the officers commanding forts and revenue cutters, to aid in the execution of quarantines, and also in the execution of the health laws of the states," but ultimately left jurisdiction with the governors.[30] Clinton had already established somewhat of a precedent by unilaterally extending his authority over the Port of New York to the shores of New Jersey and Connecticut. The Federal act, besides providing for federal assistance, also tacitly approved the governors' control of their ports beyond interstate boundaries and naval authority in times of emergency. By June, Jay was receiving aid from the President via Secretary of War James McHenry.[31]

Through the remainder of 1796, Jay explored both explanations of yellow fever and the means of abatement. He corresponded with Benjamin Rush, on the domestic nature of the disease.[32] Jay ordered a new sickhouse or "lazaretto" to be built on Bedloe's (now Liberty) Island, after first considering some buildings left by the French, on advice of Samuel Bard, after ruling out housing the sick on Governors Island near the garrison.[33] Jay successfully recommended state legislation to strengthen measures to remove nuisances, asking that domestic as well as foreign causes of the disease be addressed. He also requested and received of Bayley a detailed report on the proper arrangements for the lazaretto on Bedloe's Island, including transportation.[34] The 1796 outbreak was mild (247 cases and 69 deaths), and officials believed that they had chosen the correct course. The fever season of 1797 would be even milder: twenty to twenty-five deaths.[35]

In April 1797, Jay issued a proclamation quarantining ships from the Mediterranean and West Indies. Citing his expanded powers granted by the Act of 1796, the Governor added Turkey and North Africa based on general reputation, as he had in 1795, but this time with stronger legislative backing.[36]

When the capital was moved to Albany in 1797, Jay remained in touch with members of the Health Committee and the Medical Society, often through Richard Varick, and encouraged all to report any signs of possible epidemics and suggest measures to be taken to prevent them. Jay also traveled frequently to the City, despite the risks. The abovementioned amendment to the quarantine act brought with it the complete replacement of the 1796 Health Commission with a smaller commission in February 1797 consisting of Alderman John Oothout (chair), Jacob Abramse, and Ezekiel Robins.[37]

As the fever season began, Oothout informed Jay that the fever had appeared in Philadelphia, and recommended that all ships from that city be quarantined and examined before entering the port. Jay responded by signing a quarantine proclamation the very next day, on 17 August 1797.[38]

While continuing this program of addressing the contagion vector of the disease, Jay also supported the infectious (environmental) theories of his Health Officer. Bayley approached the disease as one from the Rush camp and continued to report on issues of public sanitation during and after the 1797 outbreak. He and Oothout, who was also concerned particularly with the infectious dangers of rotten provisions, worked with the mayor and the Common Council to address these environmental issues. Jay hedged his bets as far as the rival theories were concerned and supported addressing both vectors.[39]

The health officer and commissioners of health entered the 1798 season confident that their measures were working. Ships were inspected and not allowed into port until thoroughly cleaned. Streets were cleaned, ground filled in, poor drainage attacked, offensive odors removed, and obnoxious industries monitored. As New York prepared for possible war with France by building fortifications on Bedloe's Island, the Health Commissioners were allowed to use Bellevue as a substitute location for tending to those stricken with yellow fever. Oothout and Bayley continued to be energetic in the pursuit of public cleanliness and kept the governor up to date on the efforts. Jay's preparation also consisted of surrounding himself with family and friends, working with nephew Peter Jay Munro, Matthew Clarkson (who also served on the Military Committee), and Jay's former law clerk Robert Troup. But 1798 saw the worst outbreak of the yellow fever in New York yet.[40]

The beginning of August saw the appearance of several cases; Varick and members of the common council increased enforcement of public health laws.[41] Severe rainstorms in mid-August resulted in pools of standing water and flooded basements. Oothout issued a circular, notifying merchants who reputedly stored rotten provisions that they must dispose of them immediately. In a report to Varick, Oothout proposed a regular garbage pick-up and the draining of Lispenard's meadow. Inspections of cellars were increased, as was the use of quick lime. By September, the number of deaths had reached 950, affecting even the wealthier parts of the city. Many who could flee the city did so, including the sheriff. Jay, noting the severity of the epidemic, even suggested his son escape to Rye.[42] Peter Augustus Jay later wrote his father, "I have lost a greater number of acquaintances within a few weeks than in all the former Visitations of the fever."[43] The poor were starving, necessitating the establishment of soup kitchens by the Health Committee. Landlords evicted tenants who could not pay rent, leaving many homeless. The city's officials were stymied; they had done what was successful in past years, yet the disease grew. By the time the fever had run its course in November, 1,524 were dead from yellow fever, with an additional 562 from hunger and secondary infections.[44]

Privately, Jay despaired. In a letter to Jedidiah Morse, he admitted, "I believe that Pestilence may proceed from natural causes and that it often does. Intemperance, Filth &c. will doubtless produce Diseases as Cause and Effects. But New York *never* was so clean and neat as it has been for this year past, and yet an alarming fever prevails in it. If 'Famine and Plague, Tribulations and Anguish have heretofore been sent as scourges for amendment' why not now."[45] Publicly, he called for action, urging Oothout to take all measures necessary for combatting the disease: "altho the Fever will probably cease before the middle of next month, yet every exertion should be made to remove whatever may engender or encrease its extension or its virulence: and I flatter myself that the powers vested in you by Law for those purposes will continue to be executed not only with prudence but also with promptitude and firmness."[46] However, Mayor Varick commented privately that "The two Sets of Health Commissioners have almost surfeited the Common Council. The first did nothing or less than nothing; & the last might have done *more* last Summer earlier & probably saved the lives of hundreds: they were *good* & *honest* but extremely timid & unenergetic men. The Health Committee did 4 times as much. . ."[47] Varick was referring to the chaos of having overlapping jurisdiction and terms of the reappointed Clinton and Jay Commission and the 1 April 1796 State Commission, which may have offered opportunity for corruption or inaction. Such opinions probably reflect feelings of helplessness more so than any accurate assessment of Bayley's or Oothout's abilities—by all accounts, they were capable men as flummoxed by their inability to contain the disease as Varick. This frustration seems rooted in the idea that the public officials should be able to do *something*; the failure of that effort must lie in men. Varick, nevertheless, asked for more money. Oothout himself had resigned in January 1799,[48] making a new appointment necessary.

Jay responded to Varick and his own misgivings by reorganizing the department. Alderman Gabriel Furman, a veteran of the original Health Committee(s), was appointed in Oothout's place at Varick's recommendation. Bayley's former apprentice James Tillary[49] would work with the Health Office as Resident Physician of the Port of New York, in a move toward hiring professionals, in accordance with the Act of 25 February 1799. "An ACT to amend an act entitled 'An act to provide against Infectious and Pestilential diseases'"[50] created the office of Resident Physician, placed a Health Commissioner on Staten Island, and two other Commissioners in New York City, and also regulated boarding houses and hotels. Other acts from the same session regulated the treatment of provisions, based on a report on yellow fever coauthored by Tillary favoring environmental causes.[51]

If the causes of the disease remained obscure, Jay could concentrate his efforts on the human malefactors who could be seen. In a letter from Varick reporting intelligence from Robert Troup, Jay learned that the Sheriff of New York, Jacob John Lansing, had left the city, fearing the fever. Varick describes him as "in plain English a poor dastardly Moneymaking Devil, unfit to hold the Office for this City."[52] In his reply, Jay commented that "the Removal of the Sheriff from the City is in my opinion improper— be so obliging as to inform me whether he remains out of Town, or whether he returns to it daily, or how often at stated or uncertain periods—and whether he pays any and what Degree of *personal* attention to the Duties of his office—"[53] Lansing's dereliction of duty in a time of public distress seems to have been particularly offensive to Jay, and he pursued the case, making inquiries of Robert Troup. He asked that Troup investigate the reports, and if true, to recommend a replacement. He requested the same of his nephew Peter Jay Munro, noting in both letters the "humane and commendable behavior" of one of the deputies and inquiring of his other abilities as a possible candidate.[54]

As the epidemic weakened in November, Jay endeavored to understand why it had inflicted such severe consequences, despite all the best efforts. He praised the members of the Health Committee as having not only done honor to themselves, but to their governor. He requested that they continue to investigate reports that "putrid provisions" had contributed to the severity of the epidemic, and "let nothing be omitted to ascertain the names of the Inspectors by whom those provisions were inspected and branded."[55]

The final two epidemics of Jay's administration saw the deaths of 356 in 1799 and 67 in 1800. Yellow fever would continue to return to New York in varying degrees of severity, with the last major epidemic in 1822.

The abovementioned act of 25 February 1799 continued Jay's policy of quarantine and sanitation, although with a greater and more defined role for the public sector.[56] Yellow fever also brought to the foreground such problems as the lack of a reliable water supply in New York City. Several schemes were proposed, including damming the Bronx River, or even the Harlem River.[57] But not until a bipartisan alliance between Alexander Hamilton and Aaron Burr was proposed did the City get a waterworks project going. Legislated in Albany, the Manhattan Company would create a rather poorly built wooden water main system fed from an uptown reservoir. Burr "hijacked" the legislation, seizing opportunity from sickness and filth, and transformed the waterworks into what became the anti-Federalist Manhattan Company Bank.[58]

The yellow fever epidemics forced public officials to rethink how governments act: from reactive to proactive. Even quarantines were transformed from a simple closing of ports, to legislated policies with explicit procedures. The role of government was being reshaped in the face of epidemics. Public health was transformed from private philanthropy to public policy. If it was the government's responsibility to take care of its citizens, then Jay, as governor, saw it as his responsibility to make sure that this was carried out.

1. K. David Patterson, "Yellow Fever Epidemics and Mortality in the United States, 1693–1905," *Social Science & Medicine* 34 (1992): 855–65.

Of those infected by yellow fever virus, 75–85 percent recover after four to six days. However, others enter into the acute phase of the disease within twenty-four hours, in which the patient becomes jaundiced, suffers from severe abdominal pain, vomiting, and bleeding from the eyes, ears, nose, and stomach, producing black bile and black stools. The kidneys then fail, and approximately half of those in the acute phase die in ten to fourteen days. Those who survive suffer no organ damage, and all survivors (of the lesser and more severe manifestation of the disease) gain permanent immunity. "Yellow Fever," *Centers for Disease Control and Prevention* https://www.cdc.gov/yellow fever/index.html (accessed Apr. 2018).

2. Thomas A. Apel, *Feverish Bodies, Enlightened Minds: Science and the Yellow Fever Controversy in the Early American Republic* (Stanford, 2016), Introduction, 1–10.

It should be noted that eighteenth century sources often use the term "infectious" when referring to what modern medicine calls "contagious," as seen in the quarantine legislation of the 1790s.

3. Ira Rosenwaike, *Population History of New York City* (Syracuse, 1972), 202.

4. Yellow fever was at the center of the creation of public sanitation and public works, starting in 1799 and after. The cleaning of the streets and waterways was formerly left to private individuals. Hendrik Hartog, *Public Property and Private Power: The Corporation of the City of New York in American Law, 1730–1870* (Ithaca, 1983), 131–33.

5. *MCCNYC*, 2: 34. The proclamation quotes directly from the quarantine act of 1784: "Whereas, by statute, entitled, 'An act to prevent bringing in, and spreading of INFECTIOUS DISTEMPERS in this state,' it is enacted, 'That all vessels of whatever kind they may be, having on board any person or persons infected with the YELLOW FEVER, or any other contagious distemper, or coming from any places infected with such contagious distemper, shall not come into any of the ports or harbours of this state, or nearer the city of New York than the island commonly called Bedlow's Island.' And whereas it is represented to me, that the city of Philadelphia is now infected with a contagious distemper; wherefore I DO, by these Presents, strictly forbid and prohibit all vessels, coming from Philadelphia aforesaid, and all other vessels coming from any other place infected

with any contagious distemper, or having on board any person or persons infected therewith, from entering any of the ports of this state, or to approach nearer to the city of New York than the said island called Bedlow's Island . . . ." *New-York Journal*, 14 Sept. 1793.

Clinton's quarantine proclamation of 1794, quoted in full in JJ's 1795 proclamation, used nearly the same language, substituting New Orleans and the West Indies as the areas under interdiction. Clinton's proclamation was worded to fit exactly that of the "Act to prevent bringing in, and spreading of INFECTIOUS DISTEMPERS," which was passed 4 May 1784, and reprinted two days previously. This act was based on "An Act to prevent the bringing in and spreading of infectious Distempers in this Colony," legislation passed on 24 Mar. 1758, in response to small pox and yellow fever, and revived in 1762. JJ's proclamations, likewise, kept to established precedent and legislative acts. *Daily Advertiser* (New York), 26 Aug. 1794; "Proclamation Regarding Quarantine," 27 Apr. 1797, below; *N.Y. State Laws*, (1777–97), 1: 117–19; *Diary* (New York), 11 Sept. 1793; *Laws of New-York, from the year 1691, to 1773 inclusive* (New York, [1774]), 368–69, 432–33.

6. Bowne served as chair at the first meeting on 13 Sept., and Broome was chair of the expanded Health Committee at the 16 Sept. 1793 meeting and thereafter.

7. Committee of Health, "Minute Book"; *MCCNYC*, 2: 33–34. See also Shrady, "Medical Items," 419. Robert Bowne (1744–1818), Quaker merchant, Federalist, founder of the printing firm Bowne & Co., founding director of the Bank of New York and Mutual Assurance Co., member of the New York Hospital, New York Chamber of Commerce, and the Manumission Society; John Broome (1738–1810), merchant and politician; Gabriel Furman (1756–1844), Alderman, 1st ward (1792–99), became Health Commission chair in 1799; Robert Lenox (1759–1839), merchant and philanthropist, President of the New York Chamber of Commerce, Alderman, 2nd Ward (1795–97); Theophilus Beekman (1749–1807), merchant, Alderman, Montgomery Ward, 5th Ward (1789–96); Nathaniel Hazard (1748–98), merchant; Samuel Bard, physician and founder of the first New York Hospital and the medical school at Columbia University; Isaac Stoutenburgh (1738–99), Alderman, 4th (West) Ward (1789–95), New York State Senator (1778–87), Commissioner to build first state prison; John Campbell (1740–98), Alderman, 6th Ward (1792–96); Frederick Steymets (Stymets, Stymeets) (1750–95), member of the Corporation, Assistant Alderman, 1st Ward (1792–95); Nicholas Carmer, Assistant Alderman for the 3rd (East) Ward (1791–1801); George Janeway (1741–1826), Assistant Alderman, 6th Ward (1792–96). For appointments of the second committee, see *MCCNYC*, 2: 34, and 19: 729–31. For the rest of the Committee, see "Proclamation on Yellow Fever," 13 Aug. 1795, note 4, below.

8. See Duffy, *History of Public Health*, 101. The full title of the law was "An Act to amend the act, entitled, an act to prevent the bringing in and spreading of infectious Distempers in this State". Charles Dekay Cooper (1769–1831), physician, Republican, and future Secretary of State of New York (1817–18), was appointed to the Albany post at this time. *Daily Advertiser* (New York), 21 June 1794; *N.Y. State Laws*, (1777–97), 3: 144–45.

9. Committee of Health, "Minute Book," 22 Aug. 1794.

10. Duffy, *History of Public Health*, 102; Heaton, "Yellow Fever," 68–70; and Burrows and Wallace, *Gotham*, 357. For an account of the *Zephyr* incident, see the Health Committee Report, 8 Sept. 1795, enclosed in JJ to the Governor of Pennsylvania (Thomas Mifflin), 9 Sept. 1795, below.

Belle Vue had been the property of Lindley Murray, who, on leaving New York, sold it to a Thomas Smith in 1786. The farm came into the hands of Henry Brockholst Livingston, who was leasing it for £90 a year with an agreement to sell for £1,800, which the City offered to assume without meeting Livingston's desired price of £2,000. The Common Council began negotiating in earnest in late 1795, and the sale was settled in April 1798 for £1,800, after Livingston had received several years of rent. Monaghan, *Murrays of Murray Hill*, 88; *MCCNYC*, 2: 100–101, 202, 431–33; Claude

Edwin Heaton, "The Origins and Growth of Bellevue Hospital,"*Academy Bookman* 12 (1959), 6–7; Burrows and Wallace, *Gotham*, 502–3.

11. Anderson, *Physician heal thyself*, 182.

12. Duffy, *History of Public Health*, 127; Committee of Health, "Minute Book"; "Proclamation on Yellow Fever," 13 Aug. 1795, below.

On John Broome's political activities, see New York Citizens to GW, 20 July 1795, *PGW: PS*, 18: 370–82.

Charles Adams (1770–1800), son of John and Abigail Adams, and a New York lawyer, discussed Matlack's political involvement with the Livingston Republicans and a related political meeting: "At the first gathering of Citizens on thursday the Cloven foot was discovered and The Democratic Society stood exposed to view The weather cock politics of the Livingstons is not unknown to you They were active in the scene The first Orator was a Mʳ White Matlack an excommunicated Quaker who for lesser crimes had long since been read out of their Society and who since by fraudulent bankruptcies defrauding widows and filching the poor pittance of the Orphan had sufficiently brazened his face for advocating a total neglect of payment of our debts to England the favorite subject upon which he discanted. The Livingstons came next The detestation of Hamilton and all his proceedings begged in head and ears Indian Wars Algerine depredations British impositions Generosity of France all these were consequences of The Chancellors dissappointment in not obtaining the place of Secretary of the Treasury—" Charles Adams to JA, 5 Mar. 1794, *Adams Family Correspondence*, 10: 98–101.

13. Duffy, *History of Public Health*, 103; Burrows and Wallace, *Gotham*, 357.

14. *Philadelphia Gazette*, 1 Sept. 1795.

15. See JJ to Thomas Mifflin, 9 Sept. 1795, enclosing JJ to John Charlton, 4 Sept., Charlton to JJ, 5 Sept., JJ to John Broome, 6 Sept., JJ to Richard Varick, 6 Sept., Broome to JJ, 8 Sept., New York City Committee on Health to JJ, 8 Sept., and Richard Varick to JJ, 8 Sept. 1795, below.

16. JJ to the French Consul, 19 Sept., and to John Blanchard, 3 Oct. 1795, both below.

17. See Mifflin to JJ on lifting the quarantine, 21 Oct. 1795, printed in Davis, *Brief Account*, 52–53; JJ to Mifflin, 29 Oct. 1795, ALS, PHi (EJ: 01129). On the donation, see *MCCNYC*, 2: 181–82; Duffy, *History of Public Health*, 104. On the death toll, see Heaton, "Yellow Fever," 71.

18. Proclamation for a Day of Thanksgiving, 11 Nov. 1795, below. See also John Sloss Hobart to JJ, 18–19 Nov. 1795, below, for a humorous take on the controversy.

19. See for instance, "Juvenus", "For the New-York Journal, &c.," *Greenleaf's New York Journal*, 9 Dec. 1795; Proclamation for a Day of Thanksgiving, 11 Nov. 1795, note 1, below.

20. *Argus, Greenleaf's New Daily Advertiser* (New York), 14 Nov.; *Aurora General Advertiser* (Philadelphia), 17 Nov.; *Hampshire Chronicle* (Springfield), 23 Nov.; *City Gazette* (Charleston), 31 Dec. 1795.

21. *Aurora General Advertiser* (Philadelphia), 14 Nov.; *Richmond Chronicle*, 24 Nov. 1795.

22. *Otsego Herald* (Cooperstown), 26 Nov. 1795.

23. Richard Bayley (1745–1801), Connecticut born, trained first under John Charlton (and married Charlton's sister Catherine), then under William Hunter in London. A founder of the New York Dispensary, he became professor of anatomy and surgery at Columbia, and researched yellow fever during the 1795 epidemic. Bayley published an account of the epidemic in which he emphasized environmental causes and medical meteorology. Appointed first health officer of the Port of New York in 1796, he authored the Quarantine Act of 1799. He died of yellow fever in 1801. Mayor Richard Varick initially thought Bayley "notwithstanding his oddities. . . an excellent public officer." *An account of the epidemic fever which prevailed in the city of New-York* (New York, 1796; *Early Am. Imprints*, series 1, no. 30041); Varick to JJ, 10 Jan. 1797, ALS, NNC (EJ: 09292).

24. See JJ to Broome, 29 Jan. 1796, LbkC, N: Governor's Lbk 1 (EJ: 02988); JJ's Message to the New York State Assembly, 15 Jan. 1796, below.

25. *N.Y. State Laws*, 19th sess. (1796), 28–30; *Argus, Greenleaf's New Daily Advertiser* (New York), 14 Apr.; *Daily Advertiser* (New York), 25 Apr. 1796. This act repealed similar New York City laws of 1784 and 1794, and solidified and extended the powers given to the governor and the committee.

26. Shrady, "Medical Items", 419; John Butler Coles (1760–1827), flour merchant, Alderman, 2nd Ward (1797–99), 1st Ward (1799–1802), New York State Senator (1799–1802), became involved in the waterworks scheme of Joseph Browne; William De Peyster Jr. (1735–1803), son of William De Peyster Sr., and Margareta (Roosevelt) De Peyster, served on the board of managers of the almshouse; John Murray Sr. known as "Presbyterian" John Murray, brother of Robert Murray, uncle of "Quaker" John Murray who married Catherine Bowne, Robert Bowne's daughter; John Sr. and Bowne both served as directors of the Bank of New York in the 1780s and '90s; Henry Will (1734– c. 1802), pewterer, election inspector for the 5th Ward (1794 and 1796), New York state assemblyman (1789–92); William Robinson, probably William I. Robinson of the firm Wm. & S. Robinson, merchant shipping. See Gerhard Koeppel, *Water for Gotham* (Princeton, 2000), 67–68; Monaghan, *Murrays of Murray Hill*, 105, 107. For the commission's work, see Richard Bayley and the Health Office to JJ, 31 Dec. 1796, printed in Bayley, *Letters*, 30–36.

27. *N.Y. State Laws*, 20th sess. (1797), 24–27; *Greenleaf's New York Journal*, 18 Feb. 1797; *Albany Register*, 10 Apr. 1797. There followed an act to provide for the payment of the commission and the health officer, *N.Y. State Laws*, 20th sess. (1797), 158–61. *Greenleaf's New York Journal*, 2 May; *Argus, Greenleaf's New Daily Advertiser* (New York), 3 May 1798.

28. JJ to TP, 14 Apr. 1796, below.

29. Samuel Smith (1752–1839), Republican representative from Maryland (1793–1803, 1816–22), U.S. senator (1803–15, 1822–33), general of the Maryland militia, and vice-president of the Maryland State Colonization Society (1828).

30. "An Act relative to Quarantine", 27 May 1796. *Stat.*, 1: 474. As Congress debated the bill, Robert Brooke (c. 1760–1800), Republican governor of Virginia, made a proclamation of quarantine three days before the passage. Governor Mifflin was subsequently in correspondence with TP about similar concerns, such as situations in which a merchant captain would avoid quarantine by unloading in New Jersey, where the governor may have followed a different medical theory. "Proclamation," *Columbian Mirror* (Alexandria), 7 June 1796; *Philadelphia Gazette*, 23 June 1796; Mifflin to TP, 25 June, (enclosing proclamation), 27 June 1796, (enclosing report by the port's resident physician James Mease [1771–1846] on New Jersey incidents), both ALS, MHi: Pickering.

For more on this act and the subsequent debate, see Simon Finger, *The Contagious City: Politics of Public Health in Early Philadelphia* (Ithaca, 2012), 135–41; Joseph Jones, *Outline of the History, Theory and Practice of Quarantine* (New Orleans, 1883), 10–14.

31. Orders were given to Lieutenant William Wilson, commander of Fort Jay (1796–97) on Governors Island, to assist in the enforcement of the quarantine and health laws of New York State. In the management of the port, JJ also had to appeal to President Washington in reconciling the U.S. customs inspectors and his health officers. James McHenry to William Wilson, 22 June 1795, LbkC, N: Governor's Lbk. 1 (EJ: 03022); JJ to TP, 19 Sept. 1796, LbkC, N: Governor's Lbk. 1 (EJ: 03037); LS, MHi: French (EJ: 04774).

32. Rush to JJ, 2 Aug. 1796, below.

33. For preliminaries, see JJ to John Charlton, 22 Apr. 1796, below; JJ to Alderman [Isaac] Stoutenburgh, 7 June 1796, LbkC, N: Governor's Lbk. 1 (EJ: 03020); JJ to Richard Varick, 7 June 1796, below. For detailed planning, see JJ to John Murray, 13 July 1796, LbkC, N: Governor's Lbk.

1 (EJ: 03024); JJ to Richard Varick, 18 July, LbkC, N: Governor's Lbk. 1 (EJ: 03025); JJ to Richard Bayley, 18 July, LbkC, N: Governor's Lbk. 1 (EJ: 03026). For the completion, see JJ's Address to the New York State Legislature, [1 Nov. 1796], below.

34. Richard Bayley to JJ, n.d. Dec. 1796, enclosing Bayley to JJ, n.d., ALS, NHi (EJ: 00891); Bayley, *Letters*, 13–28, in which letter is dated 28 Nov. 1796.

35. Duffy, *History of Public Health*, 105. JJ reassured his family that the fever was not as bad as feared or reported. See JJ to Ann Jay, 3 Aug. 1796, ALS, NNC (EJ: 05930); 8 June 1796, below; JJ to SLJ, 4 Aug. 1796, below.

36. Proclamation regarding Quarantine, 27 Apr. 1797, below.

37. John Oothout (1739–1804), Chairman of the first Board of Health, 1798, 1799, New York state assemblyman (1800), Alderman, 2nd Ward (1802–3); Jacob Abramse (c. 1743–1820) had been appointed Commissioner of the almshouse in 1795, and served as inspector of elections in 1799 for the 4th Ward; Ezekiel Robins (d. 1808), member of the New York Manumission Society, New York state assemblyman (1797–99, 1800–1803). The commissioners were appointed per Act of 10 Feb. 1797, see note 27, above. Shrady "Medical Items," 419; *MCCNYC*, 2: 200, 432, 499; *Longworth's American Almanack*, 57.

38. John Oothout to JJ, 16 Aug. 1797, LbkC, N: Governor's Lbk. 2 (EJ: 03268). The mid-August proclamation read as follows:

By His Excellency John Jay Esquire
Governor of the State of New York &c. &c.
A Proclamation

Whereas it appears to me as well from the Representation of the Commissioners of the Health Office of the City of New York, as from other Evidence, that an infectious Disease does at present unhappily exist and in some measure prevail in the City of Philadelphia and which is said to have been lately brought there from the West Indies Now therefore in pursuance of the Authority vested in me by the Act of the Legislature of this State entitled "an Act to prevent the bringing in and spreading of infectious Diseases in the State" I do order and declare that (until this order be revoked) all Vessels arriving in this Port from Philadelphia shall ₍be₎ subject to Quarantine. And of this the Health Officer, the Commissioners of the Health Office, the Master and Wardens of the Port, the Pilots, and all others whom it may concern are to take notice and govern themselves accordingly—.

Given under my Hand and the privy Seal ₍of₎ the State the seventeenth day of August 1797
John Jay

By His Excellency's Command David S. Jones Priv. Sec'y

"A Proclamation," 17 Aug. 1797, LbkC, N: Governor's Lbk 2 (EJ: 03269); *Minerva* (New York), 18 Aug.; *Greenleaf's New York Journal*, 19 Aug. 1797.

39. Duffy, *History of Public Health*, 105–6; Bayley to JJ, 1 Dec. 1797, Bayley, *Letters*, 63–69.

40. Duffy, *History of Public Health*, 105–7, 131–33; this document, note 10, above. See also JJ to John Oothout and the Health Office, 20 Nov. 1798, below.

41. Oothout to JJ, 10 and 28 Aug. 1798, Bayley, *Letters*, 76–77, 80–81.

42. Varick to JJ, 24 Sept. 1798, below; Duffy, *History of Public Health*, 106–8; Bayley, *Letters*, 76–83. On leaving or avoiding the city, see JJ to PAJ, 2 Sept. 1798, below; JJ to PJM 18 Sept. 1798, ALS, NNMus (EJ: 00460), where he says, "they only ought to visit it [New York City] who may find it to be their duty"; and JJ to Clarkson, 1 Oct. 1798, ALS, NNYSL (EJ: 02870), in which Clarkson is allowed to postpone inspection and keep his family safe.

43. PAJ to JJ, 24 Sept. 1798, Dft, NHi: Jay (EJ: 03591).

44. Duffy, *History of Public Health*, 108–9. See also Heaton, "Yellow Fever," 72–74; and Hardie, *Account of the Malignant Fever*, 5–48, for a detailed summary.

45. Paraphrase of 2 *Esdras* 16: 19. JJ to Jedidiah Morse, 4 Sept. 1798, Dft, NNC (EJ: 09535); C, NN: Bancroft (EJ: 01078). See also Morse to JJ, 19 Nov. 1798, ALS, NNC (EJ: 09548).

46. JJ to John Oothout, 4 Oct. 1798, below.

47. Richard Varick to JJ, 21 Feb. 1799, ALS, NNC (EJ: 09297).

48. John Oothout to JJ, 25 Jan. 1799, ALS, NHi (EJ: 00652).

49. James Tillary (1751–1818) studied medicine at Edinburgh and was appointed surgeon in the British Army. Tillary came to New York during the war of independence and apprenticed with Richard Bayley, Wright Post, and Richard Kissam. He was appointed a surgeon at New York Hospital in 1792 and served as a trustee for the College of Physicians & Surgeons, 1807–11. Anderson, *Physician heal thyself*, 184.

50. The act amends the Clinton Act of 1793. *N.Y. State Laws*, 22nd sess. 2nd meeting (1799), 587–95; *New-York Gazette*, 16 Apr. 1799.

51. For more on the Furman and Tillary appointments, see Shrady, "Medical Items," 420. See also Richard Varick to JJ, 19 Feb. 1799, ALS, NNC (EJ: 09296); John Rodgers to JJ, 26 Feb. 1799, ALS, NNC (EJ: 08653); JJ to Rodgers, 4 Mar. 1799, Dft, NNC (EJ: 08987); and JJ to Rodgers, 16 Mar. 1799, C, NNC (EJ: 08988), in which John Rodgers (1727–1811), Presbyterian minister, advocated, unsuccessfully, to get his son John R. B. Rodgers of Columbia College the post of resident physician. See also D. O. Thomas, ed., *The Correspondence of Richard Price*, vol. 2 (Cardiff, 1991), 234n5. On rotten provisions, see JJ's Message to the New York State Senate, [18 Feb. 1799], *N.Y. Senate Journal*, 22nd sess., 2nd meeting (1799), 48; *NYGM*, 2: 435–36.

52. Richard Varick to JJ, 24 Sept. 1798, below. J.J. Lansing was sheriff from 29 Sept. 1795 to 28 Dec. 1798; *PAH*, 26: 99.

53. JJ to Richard Varick, 3 Oct. 1798, below.

54. JJ to Richard Varick, 13 Oct. 1798, ALS, CtY-BR (EJ: 05230); JJ to Robert Troup, 20 Nov. 1798, ALS, CtY-BR (EJ: 12337); and JJ to PJM, 20 Nov. 1798, ALS, NNMus (EJ: 00462). In the letter to Troup, JJ notes that the sheriff may have "retired I think to Bergen [New Jersey]," which took him not only out of his county of jurisdiction, but out of state.

55. Richard Bayley, in his report to the City Council of 21 Jan. 1799, listed the causes of the late epidemic as "Deep Damp Cellars and Filthy Sunken Yards . . . Unfinished Water Lots . . . Public Slips . . . Sinks and Privies . . . Burial Grounds . . . Narrow Streets . . . Sailors Boarding Houses and Tipling Houses . . . Digging Up Made Ground . . . Putrid Substances . . . Water . . . Tents." An expanded version of this report was published as Bayley, *Letters*. This was followed by the Medical Society of the State of New York (1794–1807), *Report of the committee, appointed by the Medical Society, of the State of New-York, to enquire into the symptoms, origin, cause, and prevention of the pestilential disease, that prevailed in New-York during the summer and autumn of the year 1798* (New York, 1799; *Early Am. Imprints*, series 1, no. 35933). Both volumes pointed to the old enemies of filth, poverty, refuse, miasmas, and bad weather, but came no closer to understanding yellow fever and its spread. Instead, they provided a blueprint for urban reformers for the next century.

56. See John Charlton to JJ, 19 Dec. 1799, ALS NNC (EJ: 08671).

57. John B. Coles was involved in this scheme. He sought to build water-driven flour mills. See note 26, above.

58. See PAJ to JJ, 3 May 1799, ALS, NNC (EJ: 06083); Dft and Tr, PC of John Jay Dubois (EJ: 09965). See also Brian P. Murphy, "'A Very Convenient Instrument': The Manhattan Company, Aaron Burr, and the Election of 1800," *WMQ* 65 (Apr. 2008): 233–66.

Proclamation on Yellow Fever

[New York, 13 Aug. 1795]
By His Excellency John Jay Governor
of the State of New York &ca &ca.—
A Proclamation.

Whereas his Excellency the late Governor of this State did on the twenty second day of August last issue a Proclamation[1] in the words following Viz "Whereas there is reason to apprehend that New Orleans, and several of the W. India Islands, are infected with contagious distempers:—In order therefore to prevent the introduction of the same into this State, I do by these presents strictly prohibit and forbid all Vessels coming from New Orleans aforesaid, or from any of the said Islands or other place infected with any such contagious distemper, or having on board any person or persons infected therewith, from coming nearer to any of the Wharves or Shorts of this harbour, or any port or harbour within this State, than one Quarter of a Mile, or of landing any person or goods whatsoever, coming or imported in such Vessel, or of putting the same on board any other Vessel within this State, or the neighbouring states of New Jersey or Connecticut, until such Vessel shall have been examined by the Health officer, and by him reported to be free from any such contagious distemper; and I do hereby require the Branch Pilots and their Deputies to be vigilant and attentive in the discharge of the Duties enjoined on them by Law in this respect. And I do further by these presents appoint John Broome, Isaac Stoutonburgh, John Campbell, Theophilus Beekman, Gabriel Furman, Doctors Samuel Bard and Malachi Treat and Robert Bowne, Nicholas Carmer, Robert Lenox, Nathaniel Hazard, George Janeway, White Matlack, and Frederick Stymets, or a Major part of them, to do and execute every such lawful Act and thing as may be necessary to prevent the introduction of such contagious distempers into this City.["][2]

And Whereas there is at present reason to apprehend that all the Islands in the West Indies are more or less infected with contagious distempers and that from them the Floridas are in danger of receiving and communicating the same before seasonable notice thereof can here be had, and proper precautions taken. And Whereas it is well known that the Countries in the Levant are seldom if ever free from pestilential distempers— Wherefore to guard against and prevent as far as possible the introduction of the said Distempers into this State I do pursuant to the powers vested in me by law, strictly prohibit and forbid all and every Vessels and Vessel arriving in this State from any of the said Islands, Countries and places, And Also all Vessels arriving in this State from any other Island Port or Place, which at the time of their sailing was infected with any such Distemper. And Also All Vessels without exception arriving in this State with any sick persons or person on board—to approach nearer to the City of New York than Governors Island, or nearer to that Island, or to any part of the Shores of this State than half a Mile; or to landing any person or goods coming or imported in such Vessel, either in this State, or in the neighouring States of Connecticut or New Jersey; or to put any person or goods so coming or imported on board of any other Vessel either in this, or in the said neighbouring States— Until such Vessel shall previously have been examined by the Health Officer, and by him be regularly reported to be entirely free from any such Infectious Distempers, and also from the Contagion thereof.[3]

And I do further expressly order and direct that all such of the said Vessels above designated, as shall come to this Port through the Sound, shall forthwith pass and be carried to, and come to Anchor at the same and no other place than that which is assigned for the Anchorage of those of them which arrive through Sandy Hook—

The Branch Pilots and their Deputies, and all other persons whom it may concern, are hereby strictly enjoined and required to be vigilant and attentive in the discharge of the Duties incumbent on them by Law in these respects.

And as the aforenamed Malachi Treat has lately died, and the said White Matlack is absent, and it being proper that their places should be filled, I do therefore appoint Doctor William Pitt Smith and Andrew Van Tuyl Esquire in their stead; and do associate them with the other persons who in and by the said above recited proclamation are named and appointed for the purposes therein mentioned.[4] Given under my Hand and the Privy Seal of the State at the City of New York on the 13th. day of August in the Year of our Lord 1795. And in the twentieth year of the Independence of the United States—

John Jay

By the Governor John H. Remsen. Private Secretary.[5]

LbkC, N: Governor's Lbk. 2 (EJ: 03201). PtD, *Daily Advertiser* (New York), 14 Aug.; *Philadelphia Gazette*, 17 Aug. 1795.

1. *Daily Advertiser* (New York), 26 Aug. 1794, and *American Minerva* (New York), 27 Aug. 1794.

2. Here ends the text of Clinton's proclamation.

3. For the rationale and operation of quarantines during the yellow fever epidemics, as well as the progress of the disease in New York City at this time, see the editorial note "John Jay and the Yellow Fever Epidemics," above.

4. Dr. Malachi (Malachy) Treat (c. 1750–95), surgeon and physician, former Physician General

for the Northern Department during the war of independence, trustee and faculty member of Columbia University (1787–95), the Health Officer of the Port of New York (from 1792), and physician of the New York Hospital. On his job-related death, see the editorial note "John Jay and the Yellow Fever Epidemics," note 10, above. White Matlack (1745–1824), a Quaker abolitionist and member of the NYMS, was involved in steel manufacturing. Andrew Van Tuyl (1751–1826) was a merchant and Alderman, 3rd Ward (1794–96). Both Treat and Matlack had been appointed by George Clinton. William Pitt Smith (1760–96), son of William Smith, served in the Continental Army and was professor of Materia Medica at Columbia. Smith succeeded Treat as Health Officer.

5. John H. Remsen (c. 1770–98) was the brother of Henry Remsen, former under-secretary to the Minister for Foreign Affairs. John Remsen, a "junior" lawyer and one of 17 notary publics in New York City, was appointed JJ's secretary in 1795. He would leave JJ's service in 1796. See JJ to John H. Remsen, 12 May 1796, below. He was involved in the New York Tontine Coffee House, the forerunner of the New York Stock Exchange. He died of yellow fever on 14 Sept. 1798, at age 28. See Hardie, *Account of the Malignant Fever*, 125. See AH to JJ, 17 Sept. 1798, on the need to replace Remsen as notary. ALS, NNC (EJ: 05631); *PAH*, 22: 181–82.

From Timothy Pickering (private)

Philadelphia Augt. 14. 1795.

Sir

No man can be more anxious for the fate of the treaty with Great Britain than you; and ∧the∧ wanton abuse heaped upon you by the enemies of their country, gives you a right to the earliest possible relief. The treaty will be ratified. This day the President finally sanctions a memorial announcing it to the British minister, M^r. Hammond. The ratification will conform to the advice & consent of the Senate, unembarrassed with any other condition.

Permit me to suggest to your consideration the expediency—perhaps I should say the necessity—at this time of general ferment, when the grossest falsehoods, the most infamous calumnies are industriously disseminated to render suspected and odious the real friends to their country—of a solemn public declaration of the President, of the principles of his administration— & of his appealing to the train of actions which have marked his whole life, for the purity and patriotism of his conduct on the present occasion. Something of the kind seems due to himself, and to the early, determined & uncorrupted patriots who have supported him.[1]

The post is on the point of departure; which obliges me to conclude abruptly. With great & sincere respect I am yours

Timothy Pickering

P.S. I do not feel myself at liberty to have this exposed to any of your friends except Col^o. Hamilton & M^r. King.

ALS, NNC (EJ: 09480). Marked: "Private". C, MHi: Pickering (EJ: 04825); *WJ*, 1: 371–72; *HPJ*, 4: 182–83.

1. For JJ's reply to this letter and his response to TP's suggestion that GW should make a public statement on the treaty ratification, see JJ to TP, 17 Aug. 1795, below.

To Timothy Pickering (private)

New York 17 Aug.ᵗ. 1795

Sir

Accept my Thanks for your obliging Letter of the 14ᵗʰ. Inst: —[1] The friendly motives which induced You to communicate to me the Information contained in it, will be remembered. The Presidents Firmness on this Occasion adds new Honors to his Character, and confers new obligations on his Country.

Of the Expediency of an address I am not perfectly satisfied, altho' I think it would in many Respects be useful. It appears to me to be a good *general* Rule ∧that the President∧ should very rarely come forward except *officially*. A Degree of Reserve seems requisite to the Preservation of his Dignity and authority. ~~I have~~ any address would be exposed to indecent Strictures. Many of our Presses are licencious in the Extreme, and there is little Reason to presume, that Regard to Propriety will restrain such parties, ∧&∧ so hostile to the Constitution and Government, from acting improperly— My opinion of the Existence Views and Practices of the Leaders of these Parties, is not of recent Date; and nothing in their present Conduct strikes me as singular, except their more than ordinary Indiscretion. Industrious they are, and will be, and no activity or Means will be spared to gain a Majority in Congress, at their ensuing Session. To render this attempt abortive, the proposed Address would doubtless conduce. The Presidents Speech may indeed comprize his Sentiments and Remarks on the Subject; but then by that Time the Mischief may be advanced and ripened.— a more early Address, by correcting public opinion, would render it a check on some Representatives, who might otherwise favor the opposition. There are Men who will go with the Stream, whatever its Course may be—and there are others who will act right, when they see no advantage to themselves in acting wrong. Snares and Temptations will be spread— In a word—there are pros & Cons about the address—but it is a point on which I should confide in the Presidents Judgment, which very seldom errs—

Ancient as well as very modern History teach us Lessons, very applicable to the present Times; and point out the necessity of Temper Activity and Decision.

I think that the president, with the Blessing of Providence, will be able to carry his Country safe thro' the Storm,[2] and to see it anchored in peace and Safety. If so, his Life & Character will have no Parallel.

If on the contrary—the Clubs and their associates should acquire a decided ascendency, there would be Reason to apprehend that our Country would become the Theatre of Scenes resembling those which have been exhibited by their Brethren in France; and that to justify themselves, their utmost Malice & art will be employed to misrepresent and vilify the Government and every Character connected with it—

If the Intelligence be true, that the french are forming a Constitution & Governm[t]. similar to ours, that Government will naturally discountenance such Schemes and politics as may be hostile to it; and consequently will become cautious how they promote attacks on ours—

For my own part, I neither despair nor despond— God governs the World, and we have only to do our Duty wisely, and leave the Issue to him— I have the Honor to be with Respect & Esteem Sir Your obliged & ob[t] Serv[t]

John Jay

The Honble Timothy Pickering Esq[r].

ALS, MHi: Pickering (EJ: 04766). Marked: "private". Endorsed: ". . . On the Treaty". LbkC, NNC: JJ Lbk. 10 (EJ: 12868), missing pages 3 and 4 of letter. *WJ*, 1: 375–77; *HPJ*, 4: 191–94.

1. TP to JJ, 14 Aug. 1795, above.

2. LbkC missing text hereafter.

To William Livingston

New York 21 Aug[t]. 1795—

Dear Sir

I was this moment favored with yours dated the 16 July, instead of 16 Aug[t]., when I presume it was written.[1]

The two Papers that were enclosed in it viz[t]. the Copy of your Letter of the 16 Aug[t]. to B. Livingston and M. Clarkson Esq[r]., and of the Certificate of Doc[r]. J. Griffith of the same Date, respecting the State of your Health, shall be immediately transmitted to Judge Hobart, agreable to your Request.[2]—

As to the Subject of your Letter, and of those Papers, I can only in general Terms express my Regret, that you have been reduced to Distresses and mortifications which your Talents & Education enabled You to avoid, and from

which they still offer to extricate you whenever you may be pleased to permit
them—

On this Head Remarks might be multiplied, but they are obvious—and
must occur to You as readily as they do to me— with the best wishes for your
Happiness here & hereafter I am, Dr Sir, &^c.—

LbkC, NNC: JJ Lbk. 10 (EJ: 12867). "To W^m. Livingston Esqr. Newark" written in JJ's hand at top
of letter. William Livingston (1754–1817), SLJ's brother and eldest son of William Livingston, was
an alcoholic and had become alienated from his family. See JJ to Matthew Clarkson, 13 Sept. 1799,
ALS, NNYSL (EJ: 02863); Dft, NNC (EJ: 09799); and Clarkson to JJ, 23 Sept. 1799, ALS, NNC
(EJ: 09800).

1. Letter not found.

2. Documents not found. B. Livingston is Henry Brockholst Livingston, William Livingston's
younger brother. M. Clarkson is General Matthew Clarkson, William Livingston's cousin. Dr. John
Griffith (1736–1805) of Rahway, N.J., was a founder of the Medical Society of New Jersey.

From Edward Newenham

[Dublin— 1st Sep^t 1795]

My Dear Sir—

I congratulate you on the Treaty, which does honor to you & both Nations; some Malevolent People here, abuse it in Print & Coffee house
Conversation— they say that Mr Pitt deserves impeachment for Signing a
Treaty so disadvantageous to these Nations— they hint that he was bribed
to do it— for my Part I have Carefully read it, & consider it as an honourable
& advantageous Treaty to both Countries; I received the first Impression of
it from Philadelphia & had it immediately printed here—[1]

This Letter will be delivered to your Excellency by Isaac Weld Esqr. son of
a particular friend of mine; he is going to Visit your Happy Continent on a
Tour of Pleasure and Amusement; he has no acquaintance in America, therefore I beg leave to Introduce him to your Protection & advice for his Travelling, with such Letters of Introduction, as you may honor him with to other
states, as I suppose he will visit a great part of the 17 states[2]—

It is said, that many persons have fled from this Kingdom to America; if
such should ever get into your Company, do not give much Credit to the Account they will give you of the present state of Ireland; for we are flourishing
in Trade & Agriculture, & the Defenders are nearly Quelled; the riots are only
among the Lowest order of the People, who are soon made obedient to the
Laws; no Protestants are concern'd in these riots— We have a Good Lord
Lieutenant & a Spirited Council—upright Judges & honest Juries; bold &

Zealous Magistrates, & Union among all Protestants of Property in Land or Trade— our Harvest has been great & well saved— our fruit has also been in plenty except Apples; M^rs: Montgomery sent me some of your New York Apples, which were a *Treat* to us;—

I do not talk of Politics, as you have them more authentic, than I can give them; My wish is a good Constitution to France, & a safe & honourable to England; I do not Entirely approve of the Constitution agreed to by Convention; it never can stand as now worded— & this Executive Council will become a Band of Tyrants. The Proclamation of him that Calls himself Lewis the 18th is ill Calculated to make Friends; He ought have in the first Instance declared for a Limited Monarchy—& promised a Reform of all Abuses— this might have Effect[3]—

Lady Newenham joins me in Sincere respects to your Excellency & M^rs. Jay, whose Civility, in France, she does not forget— I have the Honor, to be, My Dear Sir with sincere Esteem Your most faithfull & obliged Hb^le Servt.

Edward Newenham

PS— I have just got a Letter from my Daughter at Marsailles— She & all her family are safe & well—[4] Last Night my youngest Daughter was married;[5] I have now 5 Daughters & 3 Sons Married— I hope soon to hear from you, with a few New York Papers— I congratulate you on y^r Honourable Election— Mr Welds father & Grandfather were warm friends to American Freedom—[6]

ALS, NNC (EJ: 09593).

1. Newenham informed GW in mid-August that he had seen the Treaty in Bache's *Aurora General Advertiser* of Philadelphia (29 June) and then published it "in one of our Irish papers." 15 Aug. 1795, *PGW: PS*, 18: 551.

2. Isaac Weld (1774–1856), the Dublin-born topographical writer and artist. His purpose, aside from adventure, was to "ascertain whether in case of future emergency, any part of those territories might be looked forward to, as an eligible and agreeable place of abode" for the Irish. Weld wrote about his journey to America in *Travels through the States of North America and the Provinces of Upper and Lower Canada, during the Years 1795, 1796, and 1797* (London, 1799). It is not recorded whether or not he visited JJ. Weld visited TJ and GW, and wrote an unflattering account of his visit to Mount Vernon. See Anthony Gerna to TJ, 2 Sept. 1795, *PTJ*, 28: 441–42; Bryan Fairfax to GW, 28 Apr. 1799, *PGW: RS*, 4: 29–33.

3. Following the death in June 1795 of Louis XVI's son Louis Charles, whom French monarchists considered Louis XVII, Louis Stanislaus Xavier, Count of Provence, younger brother of Louis XVI, was declared Louis XVIII by the French princes in exile. He prepared a manifesto, known as the Declaration of Verona, which called France back to the traditional monarchy. During his long exile he did espouse more moderate policies, and in 1814, after Napoleon's defeat, the great Powers placed him in power. He was deposed in March 1815 after Napoleon's escape from Elba, then restored again in July 1815, and reigned until his death in 1824.

4. Newenham's surviving children were Sarah Elizabeth (1757–c. 1825), married Major Alexander

Graydon (1734–1812); Margaretta, married Francis Philippe Fölsch von Fels; Edward Worth (1762–1832), married Elizabeth Persse; Elizabeth (b. 1763), married Rev. John Wallace c. 1784; William Thomas (1766–1843), married Barbara Lynam c. 1787; Grace Anna (b. 1768), married John Browne c. 1789; Robert O'Callaghan (1770–1849), married Susanna Hoare on 24 Mar. 1795; Rachael (1775–1832), married Rev. John Hoare on 31 Aug. 1795; Alicia (1774–1855), married Rev. Walter Shirley on 26 July 1796; and Burton (1776–1858), married Maria Burdett c. 1797.

Newenham had been concerned for the safety of his daughter Margaretta, whose husband was the Swedish consul in Marseilles. He asked JJ for help in ascertaining her situation. See Newenham to JJ, 15 June, ALS, NNC (EJ: 09589); JJ to Newenham, 26 June, Dft, NNC (EJ: 09591); and Newenham to JJ, 7 Dec. 1794, ALS, NNC (EJ: 09592). See also the editorial note "John Jay's Mission to London," JJ to James Monroe, 28 Aug. 1794, and JJ's Memorandum to JT, 5 Feb. 1795, all above, for other cases of JJ making inquiries about foreigners detained in France.

5. Newenham refers to Rachael's marriage.

6. Isaac Weld's father (d. 1824) and grandfather (1710–78) were also named Isaac, after Isaac Newton, a friend of his great-grandfather, Dr. Nathaniel Weld (1660–1730). Both the elder Isaac Welds were dissenting ministers, and Weld's father was a friend of Charles James Fox. *ODNBO*.

To George Washington (private)

New York 3ᵈ Septʳ. 1795

Dear Sir

I have been honored with yours of the 31 of last month.[1]

The article in the Treaty to which you allude[2] vizᵗ. the *last* was proposed by me to Lord Grenville, because it seemed probable that when the Treaty should for some time have gone into operation, Defects might become manifest, and further arrangements become desireable which had not occurred to either of us, because no plan of an article relative to *Impressments*, which we could devise, was so free from objections, as to meet with mutual approbation;— and because the Lord Chancellor's proposed article, relative to alienism & other interesting objects, was of such magnitude, that I did not think any Stipulations respecting them should be ventured, untill after that article had recieved the most mature Consideration of our Government.

I think that in endeavouring to obtain a new Modification of the 12 article, an Extension of the Tonnage from 70 to 100 Tons should be attempted, for altho this was strenuously pressed before, yet I can see no Inconvenience in repeating it by way of Experiment, not insisting on it as an ultimatum. In my opinion it would also be expedient that the new article should *specify* the particular Commodities which our vessels shall be permitted to carry from the united States to the british Islands and import from the latter into the former.

As to the Impresment of Seamen, the forming of any very satisfactory arrangement on that Head will I fear continue to prove an arduous Task. in my opinion Great Britain should at present agree not to take any Seamen from our Vessels on the *ocean*, or in her *Colonial* ports, on account of the *Injuries* thence resulting to our navigation— It would be difficult to support a Position, that she ought to agree not to seek for and take her own Seamen on board of any merchant vessels in the ports of Great Britain or Ireland.

In the India, or 13 article, "It is expressly agreed that the Vessels of the United States shall not carry any of the articles exported by them from the said british Territories to any port or place except to some port or place in *america*, where the same shall be unladen." I would propose that after the word *America*, be added, *or to some foreign port or place in asia*— There is indeed nothing in the article as it now stands which restrains the India Company's Government from continuing to permit our Vessels to carry Cargoes from India to China, but it would be better if possible to establish this as a *Right* by express agreement.

For my own part I regard the present Moment as unfavorable for Negociations with Great Britain. Altho she has Reason, not only to approve but to admire the Conduct of our Government; yet while it appears doubtful to her, whether the Sentiments and Disposition of the great Body of our people are pacific and friendly or otherwise, it seems natural to suppose it will be her Policy to be reserved. To multiply Engagements with and Facilities to us, under such Circumstances might be ascribed to her apprehensions; and as her Governmᵗ. will doubtless percieve this Risque, I suspect they will be strongly inclined to avoid it.

Besides, I should doubt the policy of introducing into the Negociation *at present*, either so many or such Propositions as may defer the ultimate Ratification so late, as to prevent orders to evacuate the posts by the 1 June next from being sent in due Season. The commercial part of the Treaty may be terminated at the Expiration of two Years after the War; and ˄in the˄ mean time a State of things more auspicious to negociation will probably arrive, especially if the next Session of Congress should not interpose new obstacles— God bless you my Dear Sir— believe me to be with perfect Respect Esteem & Attachmᵗ. Your obliged & affecᵗᵉ. Servᵗ

John Jay

The President of the U.S.

ALS, DLC: Washington (EJ: 10652). Marked: "private". LbkC, NNC: JJ Lbk. 10 (EJ: 12866); *WJ*, 2: 257–59; *HPJ*, 4: 189–91; *PGW: PS*, 18: 627–28. JJ sent GW a follow-up reply the next day, see (private), 4 Sept. 1795, below.

1. GW to JJ, 31 Aug. 1795, ALS, NNC (EJ: 07259); DftS, DLC: Washington (EJ: 10651); *PGW: PS*, 18: 614–16.

2. JJ here refers to Art. 28 that called for a periodical review of the Treaty and the proposal of additional articles; he is specifically responding to the following comment by GW: "The object of this letter is, to pray you to aid me with hints relative to those points which you conceive to be fit subjects for the further friendly negociations on the W.I. trade with G. Britain, agreeably to the recommendation of the Senate; and which appears to have been in contemplation by the concluding part of the Treaty signed by yourself and Lord Grenville." For more on the discussions on revising the Treaty, see the editorial note "Aftermath of the Jay Treaty: Responses, Ratification, and Implementation," above.

To George Washington (private)

New York 4 Sep. 1795

Dear Sir

Since mine to You of Yesterday[1] I have occasionally turned my thoughts to the subject of it—

I presume that the Treaty is ratified agreable to the advice of the Senate— and that if G. Britain consents to the Suspension of the 12 art: (which I believe will be the Case) the Treaty will thereupon be ratified on her part and become final. Of Consequence that the modification contemplated of the 12 art: together with every other additional Engagement which it may be judged useful to negociate, will be a posterior Work; and the new articles as they shall be agreed upon will from time to time be added to the Treaty.

under this View of the Business I find that my Letter requires Explanation—

I take it that the Treaty will first be ratified by Great Britain, and put out of question, before any new propositions be offered or even mentioned; so that no new matter may be introduced that could afford occasion for, or invite Hesitation or Delay.

That being dispatched, the Question which presents itself is what new Propositions will it be adviseable to bring forward into negociation? on this point I see no Reason to change the Sentiments expressed in my Letter.

on reading the Lord Chancellors article (a Copy of which was transmitted with my Letter to Mr Randolph of the 19 Novr. last)[2] you will find that a part of it, which respects the mutual admission of Evidence &c., is of considerable Importance, and is calculated, in the Language of the *last* article "*to facilitate Intercourse & obviate Difficulties*"[3] would it not be well to submit this article to the Consideration of the Attorney General and some of the Judges before any Instructions on the Subject matter of it, be given to our negociator.

while I was in London I heard Lord St. Helens[4], who had been at Madrid in a public Character speaks most handsomely of Mr. Short. I am enduced to mention this in order to counteract the Effect of some uncivil things that have been written respecting that Gentleman from Madrid. with perfect Respect Esteem and Attachm^t I am Dear Sir your obliged & affec^t. Servt.

John Jay

The President of the U.S.

ALS, DLC: Washington (EJ: 10653). Marked: "private". LbkC, NNC: JJ Lbk. 10. (EJ: 12869); *PGW: PS*, 18: 634–35.

1. JJ to GW, 3 Sept. 1795, above.

2. Article Proposed by the Lord Chancellor (Loughborough), [c. 9 Oct. 1794], above. See also JJ to ER, 19 Nov. 1794, above; and JJ to Loughborough, 9 Oct. 1794, above.

3. Quote taken from Art. 28.

4. Alleyne Fitzherbert, Baron St. Helens, diplomat who served as ambassador to Spain from 1790 to 1794, then to The Hague, from where he was forced to flee the approaching French in January 1795. *ODNBO*. For more on the discussions on revising the Treaty, see the editorial note "Aftermath of the Jay Treaty: Responses, Ratification, and Implementation," above.

To the Governor of Pennsylvania (Thomas Mifflin)

New York 9 Septr. 1795—

Sir

Your Excellency's Proclamation of the 31 of last month, prohibiting all Intercourse between this City and Philadelphia,[1] induced me to write the following Letter to the President of the medical Society in this City—

(here was inserted the preceding letter)[2]

To John Charlton

New York 4 Septr. 1795

Sir

By a Proclamation of the Governor of Pennsylvania dated the 31 of last month, all Intercourse between this City and Philadelphia is prohibited for the Term of one month, or untill that Prohibition shall be revoked

The Reason assigned for this Prohibition is thus expressed in the Proclamation "Whereas the Board of Inspectors of the Health office of Philadelphia, have reported to me, that it appears from authentic Information to them exhibited, that an infectious or contageous Disease exists in the City of New York in the State of New York, and that there is Reason to believe that a similar Disease exists in the Town of Norfolk in the State of Virginia, so that the Safety and Health of the Citizens of Pennsylvania require stoppage of Intercourse with the said infected Places" Therefore &^ca.—

This Proclamation, by exciting alarms and apprehensions throughout this and the neighbouring States, and in foreign Countries, naturally tends to produce Embarrassments to the Commerce of this City and to interrupt that

Intercourse with the Country, which is at all Times necessary to the convenience and Interests of both. Hence it becomes important to examine and ascertain with Precision, whether any and what Degree of Credit is due to the Information alluded to in the abovementioned Report of the Inspectors of the Health Office of Philadelphia. No infectious or contageous Disease can exist & prevail in this city without the Knowledge of the Gentlemen who practice Physick in it; and as the greater part of them are members of the medical Society over which you preside, I request the favor of you to summon a meeting of the Society, and to lay before them this Letter.

They will oblige me by reporting to me in writing an accurate Statement of such Facts and Observations as may in their opinion be necessary to the forming a right Judgment relative to the Existence nature and Extent of the Disease in Question. If such a Disease does really exist and prevail here, it should candidly be admitted and made known, that the Dangers resulting from it may be guarded against. If on the contrary, the Reports concerning it are ill founded, care should be taken to prevent their continuing to gain Credit.

Altho the Truth of the frequent Reports made and published by the Health Committee has not been impeached, yet ₐasₐ the before mentioned Proclamation appears to be grounded on Information more alarming than what those Reports afford, I think it adviseable to inquire whether it is warranted by any Facts within the Knowledge of the members of your Society— I have the Honor to be &ᶜᵃ.

To this Letter I recᵈ. the following answer.

[From John Charlton]

"New York Septʳ. 5 1795

Sir

The Communication which you were pleased (thro' our President) last Evening to lay before the medical Society, we consider of a nature the most serious & important: and the Information you desire, we offer with great Respect, and under Impressions the most scrupulously conscientious—

About six weeks ago, in a particular part of this city, being very low & having an Eastern Exposure, a Fever has been observed to exist, marked by the violence of those Symptoms which are acknowledged to characterize that of the malignant Sort. This Fever in a short Time attacked a considerable number of Persons, in Proportion to the Space which it occupied, and proved fatal to more than is usual with us, and which (previous to the salutary and heavy Rains we have lately had, and the consequent cloudy and cool weather) assumed an aspect, which called for and justified every prudent Exertion that could be made to investigate its origin, and check its Progress—unfortunately however, the Sensibility of the public mind on a Subject of this nature, giving Reality to apprehension, converted the necessary Efforts for Security and Prevention, into Sources of Fear and Terror. Hence probably have arisen most of the exaggerated Reports which at first alarmed our own Citizens, and being sent abroad, have excited the apprehensions of our neighbours; and given origin to measures more timed, as they respect themselves, and more injurious to us, than the nature of the case in any wise justified—

The collective opinion of this Society, as the Result of attentive observation is with Regard to the contageous nature of this Disease, most of the members are of opinion that it is not contageous; and all agree that it is so little so, as to afford no apprehension of its being communicated from man to man, out of the Sphere of its original and local atmosphere—

As to its origin Suspicions have been entertained by a few Physicians, that it may have been imported, whilst at the same Time there are many among us, who consider it as little more than that Species of Fever, which has more or less prevailed in this City at the same Season for several Years past; rendered, by the extraordinary Heat, and some local Sources of malignity, more violent and fatal than usual—

If the Board of Inspectors of the Health office of Philadelphia have recieved any Information respecting the Disease in question, other than that from the Health Committee of this City, which they deemed *authentic*, we are extremely sorry that they should have been influenced by it, from a Persuasion that such Information was equally unfounded as unauthorized—

We assure your Excellency that we have no Disposition to disguise or conceal Facts, nor do we hesitate to declare our opinion, that the alarm which has gone abroad has been unreasonably great and quite disproportionate to the actual State of the Disease, which as we have already observed, has been confined to a very inconsiderable Portion of the City. It affords us great Pleasure to be able to assure Your Excellency, that this Complaint is fast diminishing, and that the general Health of our City has been throughout the Summer, and continues at this moment unusually good.— We have the Honor to be &c. &ca. By order of the medical Society,

(signed) John Charlton President

New York Septr. 5 1795
His Excellency John Jay &c &c &c."

The committee of Health in this city was appointed for the express purpose of guarding against the Introduction and Progress of infectious Distempers, and they have manifested great vigilance and attention in the Discharge of their Duty. As they possess the best means of Information, and will always communicate it with accuracy and Candor, I wrote the following Letter to them—

[To John Broome]³

"New York 6 Septr. 1795—

Sir

The alarming and exaggerated Reports in circulation, that a dangerous and infectious Distemper prevails in this City, will be corroborated by the Proclamation of the Governor of Pennsylvania, prohibiting all Intercourse between us and Philadelphia.

I think it prudent to obtain from you and others, and transmit to the Governor of that State, authentic and conclusive Information relative to the question— whether any such Distemper does exist and prevail here?

The Reports which you have from Time to Time published, are for the most part concise and summary, and it is not necessary that they should in common be otherwise— on the present occasion, it may be useful to report to me a more particular and circumstantial Statement— I have the Honor to be &^{ca}.

John Broome Esqr Chairman" &^{c}

In pursuance of this Letter I rec^d. one from the chairman enclosing the Report mentioned in it.— they are as follows—

[From John Broome]

"New York Septr. 8 1795

Sir

I took the earliest opportunity to lay your Letter of the 6th. Inst: before the Health Committee, when they made immediate arrangements to comply with your Excellency's wishes— This you will find contained in the enclosed Report, which after mature Deliberation was adopted by the Committee— it is as particular & circumstantial a Statement as they have it in their Power to make: and which they believe is very near a real State of Facts— I have the Honor to be &^{c}.

(signed) John Broome chairman"

[Health Committee Report]

[New York, 8 September 1795]

"Sir

In answer to your Excellency's Letter of the 6 Instant, requiring from us a particular and circumstantial Statement of such Facts, relative to the Disease, which has lately made its appearance in this City, as have come to our Knowledge— we beg Leave to submit the following—

on the 20 Day of July, Doctor Malachy Treat,[4] the late Health officer of this Port, visited the Brig Zephyr from Port au Prince; on board of which he found three Persons ill of Fever, and the Corpse of one who died that morning. The Doct^r. calls the Fever in his Report, *a bilious remitting Fever*. The Brig was ordered to ride Quarantine. on the 22^d. Day of July Doct^r. Treat was taken ill, & died on the 30th. of a Fever marked by a Yellow Skin, Hermorrhages, vomiting of black matter resembling Coffee Grounds, and all such Symptoms as characterize Bilious Fever of the malignant kind.— on the 25th. Day of July, four Persons from on Board the Ship William from Liverpool, which arrived here several weeks before (all the Crew having previous to that Day and during the Voyage, been perfectly healthy) were taken ill of Fever attended with similar Symptoms, and all died within 7 Days. This Ship lay at a wharf at the point of Dover Street, in the South-easterly part of this City, which lies exceedingly low, is much of it made Ground, has an eastern Exposure, and (from the Street's having been raised about 3 Years ago, which threw the Lotts and Yards into Hollows of considerable Depth) is almost unavoidably liable to great collections of Offal and Filth of all kinds. It is a part of the Town very much crouded by poor Inhabitants, and contains a great number of lodging Houses, in which Seamen and Strangers of the poorer Class commonly resides; and from all these Causes, is unquestionably the most unhealthy part of this City, and ever has suffered most from the regular autumnal Diseases, as well as from any new and uncommon Complaint— From all which Circumstances we entertain no doubt but that the Seamen of the Ship William contracted the Disease of which they died *here*, and did not introduce it into this City. A little before and immediately after the Attack of the Seamen of the Ship William, which first called the Attention of this Committee, several other Persons in Water & Front Streets, and in the neighbourhood of Dover Street, were seized with Fever, which especially in those Cases which proved mortal, was marked by severe vomitings, a Yellow Skin Hermorrhages, and in some Cases a vomiting of black matter resembling Coffee Grounds, and which generally terminated within seven Days—and proved fatal to more in Proportion to the number seized than is usual in the ordinary Complaints of this Season, in this City—

From that Time the Disease continued to spread in that neighbourhood, extending itself to a few Houses lower down towards Peck's Slip, to one or two in Pearl Street, & Cherry Street, but principally upwards towards the Ship Yards— the number of Deaths encreasing slowly until the 9 august, from which to the 11th. inclusive, 13 died. From that Day the number of Deaths reported to us have gradually decreased, so that 9 only are reported to have died within the last five Days; and in all from the 30th. of July to this Day, 89 have been reported to this Committee. 44 persons in all have been sent to Belle-vue Hospital, of which the greatest number have been Seamen and Strangers, who have arrived in this city, sick of various complaints: and of this number several in the very last Stages of their Diseases.— 20 have died, 16 have been discharged cured, & 18 remain in the House, most of them convalescent.

The number of Deaths includes all the Cases which to our Knowledge have happened between the 26 July, and the 7th. of September inclusive, either in this City, at the New York Hospital, or at the Hospital at Belle-vue, arising from Fever in the least approaching to the Character of this Disease—

And as this Committee have made every Exertion in their Power to obtain the necessary Information, they do not hesitate to say, that this Statement is sufficiently *correct* to afford the Basis of every public measure which may be thought necessary for our own Safety, or for the Security of our neighbours. By order of the Committee—

(signed) John Broome Chairman"

This Report, and the one from the medical Society, have been communicated to the Mayor and Corporation of the City, to whom on the 6th. Instant I wrote the following Letter

[To Richard Varick]

"New York 6 Septr. 1795

Sir

The Suspension of all Intercourse between this City & Philadelphia is inconvenient to them as well as injurious to us. The Information which induced their Health office to apply to their Governor for his Suspension was doubtless such, as in their opinion justified that measure. There nevertheless is Reason to believe, that more credit was inadvertently given to it, than it deserved.

Whether a contageous Disease does exist and prevail in this City, is a question to which a satisfactory answer can only be formed from correct Statements of well authenticated Facts, and the opinions of men well informed and meriting Confidence—

on the present occasion I think it adviseable, to obtain such Statements and opinions, and to transmit them to the Governor of Pennsylvania. If it should appear from them, that the usual Intercourse between this City and Philadelphia may be resolved without any Danger to the latter, the Prohibition which suspends it will of course be revoked—

I have requested and recieved from the medical Society of this City their Report on this Subject, and when to this is added the Publication of the medical Gentlemen who compose the Society called The College of Physicians, the Sentiments of the Faculty relative to it will be ascertained.

As the Common Council of the City is composed of magistrates and other members from the different wards, and as a dangerous infectious Distemper cannot be presumed to prevail here, without exciting their notice and attention, I request from them a Statement of such Information as they may possess, together with their opinion relative to this interesting Subject—

These Documents, with the Report of the Health Committee will afford to the Governor of Pennsylvania the best and most authentic Evidence that the nature of the Case will admit of; and such as cannot fail to reduce the many exaggerated Reports that are in circulation to the Standard of Truth— I have the Honor to be &ca.—

The Hon'ble Richd. Varick Esqr. Mayor of the City of New York"

In answer to this Letter I received one from the Mayor, enclosing an Extract from the minutes of the Board on this Subject— They are as follows—

[From Richard Varick]

"New York Septr. 8 1795

Sir

I have the Honor to inform your Excellency that on this Day I laid before the Common Council of this City, your Letter of the 6th. Instant, together with the Copy of the Report of the medical Society of this City on the Subject of the Disease said to exist in this City, which accompanied it—and also a copy of the Report of the Health Committee of this Date to your Excellency on the same Subject—

In answer to your Letter, I am requested by the common Council to inform you, that they have duly considered these Reports, and that they do believe that the Facts contained in them are, according to the best Information they have been able to obtain, correct and true; and further, that from the Information recieved by the individual members of the Board, it is their opinion that a much greater Degree of general Health prevails in this City at present than is usual at this Season of the Year— a certified Copy of this Resolution of the Board upon that Subject, I do enclose to your Excellency— I have the Honor to be &ca.

City of New York ss At a common Council held on Tuesday 8th. Day of Septr. 1795 Present—

Richard Varick Esqr. Mayor

Gabriel Furman— John Campbell— Theophilus Beekman— Wynant Van Zandt— Isaac Stoutenburgh— Andrew Van Tuyl— Nicholas Bayard Esqrs. Aldermen

Garret Harzin George Janeway Fred^k. Stymets Mangle Minthorn Nich^s. Carmer Assistants.[5]

The Mayor laid before the Board a Letter from His Excellency the Governor of the sixth Instant on the Subject of the Proclamation issued by the Governor of Pennsylvania, suspending all Intercourse between this City and Philadelphia, and the said Letter together with a Report made to his Excellency on the fifth Instant by the medical Society in this City, and also a Report made to his Excellency by the Health Committee of this City on this Day, were respectively read, and duly considered And thereupon Resolved that Mr Mayor be requested to inform His Excellency the Governor, in answer to his Letter, that the Board do verily believe that the Facts contained in the said respective Reports, are according to the best Information this Board have been able from time to time to obtain, correct and true; And further, that from the Information recieved by the individual members of this Board, it is the opinion of this Board, that a much greater Degree of General Health prevails in this City at present than is usual at this Season of the Year—
Extract from the minutes.

(signed) Robt. Benson Clk"[6]

Your Excellency will find (herewith enclosed) a Paper containing a Letter from the President of a Society of medical Gentlemen in this City, called the College of Physicians, to the chairman of the Committee of Health—

Thus Sir! I have laid before you, and submit to your Consideration, a Collection of Facts and opinions which merit Credit and Respect.—

I flatter myself it will appear to your Excellency from these Documents that it is not necessary to suspend the Intercourse between this City and Philadelphia, and therefore that the Prohibition in Question will be revoked.[7] I have the Honor to be &^{ca}.

His Excellency Ths. Mifflin Esqr. Govr. of Pennsylvania

LbkC, NNC: JJ Lbk. 10 (EJ: 12883). PtD, *Philadelphia Gazette*, 24 Sept.; *New-York Gazette*, 28 Sept. 1795.

1. On 26 Aug., Mifflin asked the inspectors of the Philadelphia Health Office and inspecting physician about conditions in New York. On 31 Aug. they reported that there was indeed yellow fever in New York and Norfolk. Mifflin's proclamation of 31 Aug., issued "with a sincere regret for the unhappy occasion," banned all intercourse between Philadelphia and New York and Norfolk, by land or water, and issued a fine of three hundred dollars for violators. The ban was to be in place for one month, or "until such prohibition shall be by Proclamation lawfully revoked." *Pennsylvania Archives*, Series 9, vol. 2, pt.1: *Executive Minutes of Governor Thomas Mifflin, 1794–96*, ed. Gertrude MacKinney (Harrisburg, 1931), 1005, 1008, 1009–10; *Philadelphia Gazette*, 1 Sept.; *Dunlap's American Daily Advertiser* (Philadelphia), 2 Sept; and *Independent Gazetteer* (Philadelphia), 5 Sept. 1795. For the

1795 yellow fever epidemic and JJ's response to it, see John Jay's Proclamation on Yellow Fever, 13 Aug. 1795, and the editorial note "John Jay and the Yellow Fever Epidemics," both above.

2. In the letterbook, Charlton's letter was recorded before the letter to Mifflin.

3. Chairman of the New York Health Committee. For identification of the original Health Committee members, see editorial note "John Jay and the Yellow Fever Epidemics," and note 7, above.

4. On the death of Malachi Treat, see the editorial note "John Jay and the Yellow Fever Epidemics," note 10, and "Proclamation on Yellow Fever," note 4, both above.

5. Several members of the Common Council listed comprised the majority of the Health Committee. Aldermen Wynant Van Zandt Jr. (1767–1831), a merchant, and Nicholas Bayard (1736–98), and assistant aldermen Garret Harzin and Mangle Minthorn (1737–1821), were not on the Health Committee.

6. *MCCNYC*, 2: 176–77. Robert Benson was the brother of Egbert Benson.

7. On 17 Sept. 1795, Mifflin replied to JJ, stating that he had referred JJ's letter and enclosures to the Board of Inspectors and the Board of Physicians, who stated that, although the fever had abated somewhat, they advised the continuance of the ban. Mifflin noted, "It could certainly be no alleviation of their sufferings, that the inhabitants of Philadelphia should be exposed to the same affliction; and your excellency will readily allow, that every embarrassment, as well foreign as domestic, that may be the effect of a suspension of the intercourse between the two cities, will operate equally against both." *Gazette of the United States* (Philadelphia), 25 Sept. 1795; Davis, *Brief Account*, 44–45.

On 26 Sept., the *Aurora General Advertiser* (Philadelphia) reported the "lengthy correspondence" between JJ and Mifflin, commenting ". . . the desertion of New-York is a corroborating proof of its malignancy. The New-Yorkers in the beginning of this month blamed us much for our precipitancy, the present state of the disorder fully exonerates us from the charge." On 21 Sept., Mifflin issued another proclamation, continuing the prohibition of intercourse between Philadelphia and New York for another month. One month following the proclamation, Mifflin wrote JJ informing him that the ban had been lifted, congratulating him on the positive change in New York's health. *Greenleaf's New York Journal*, 26 Sept. 1795; *Pennsylvania Archives*, 1016–18; Davis, *Brief Account*, 52–53; *Philadelphia Gazette*, 27 Oct.

In his reply of 29 Oct., JJ wrote, "This Information is rendered the more acceptable, by the Sentiments of Benevolence and Sympathy which accompany it. Good offices under the Pressure of calamities, endear Societies as well as Individuals to each other; and they deserve well of mankind in general, who by infusing into the bitter cup of adversity, the Blessings of Beneficence and Humanity, promote the Influence and operation of this great Truth, *that the relative Duties & Interests of Men are inseparable—*" ALS, PHi: Gratz (EJ: 01129); LbkC, NNC: Governor's Lbk. 10 (EJ: 12885).

To Richard Harison

New York 14 Sept. 1795

Dear Sir

The more I reflect on the attempts made in the ports of the united States to fit out Privateers for foreign Service, the more I am impressed with the Importance of suppressing a Practice so disreputable to a neutral nation— The Report of the Wardens of this port, and Mr Armstrongs Letter[1] induce reason‸able‸ ground to presume that such attempts are now making in this

Port; and if successful, that they will be repeated. The Information contained in those Papers, together with such as may result from your further Enquiries, may produce Evidence sufficient to warrant the proceedings proper on such occasions— in that Case, nothing on my part shall be wanting to afford any aid which Circumstances may require—[2] with Sentiments of Esteem and Regard I am Dear Sir your most ob[t]. Serv[t]

John Jay

Rich[d]. Harrison Eq[r]. Attorney General of the U.S. for New York District—

ALS, NHi: Harison (EJ: 00766). Endorsed. Dft, NNC (EJ: 12833).

1. Neither document has been found.

2. For more on the outfitting of privateers in the port of New York City, see the case of *La Vengeance* in JJ to TP, 8 June 1797, below.

To James Duane

New York 16 Sept[r]. 1795—

Dear Sir

I read your kind and affectionate Letter of the 31 July[1] last with great Satisfaction and Sensibility, and I thank you for it. It is pleasing to see Friendship like an Evergreen, bid Defiance to the vicissitude of Seasons.—

The opposition to which you allude, except as to its Degree of malignity, was not unexpected. When the mission to England was pressed upon me, it was percieved that there were Parties who would endeavour to wound the Government through the Sides of the Envoy; and either depreciate his Success, or censure his want of it.

It had long been obvious that negociations relative to the Posts, would unavoidably extend to the Complaints of Great Britain relative to the Debts; and that every Idea of paying them, would be offensive to the Southern States.

The attempts of the French to plunge us into the war, were well known; and it was equally plain that they would not cease to be hostile to an amicable settlement of our Differences with Great Britain.

The Constitution still continued to be a Rock of offence to the antifœderalists, and the funding System, by affording Support to the Government, had become exceedingly obnoxious to that Party— It was evident then

That a Treaty with Great Britain, by preventing War, would disappoint the Southern Debtors of the Reciepts in full, with which they flattered themselves from a War—

That it would displease the French—by less[en]ing our supposed Dependence on them for Protection against Great Britain—by diminishing their Influence in our Councils—and by making us Friends with their Enemies—

That it would discontent the antifœderalists—by disarming them of their affected complaints against the Government on account of the Posts, and Commerce &cᵃ. and by giving additional Strength to the administration—&c. &cᵃ.—

Hence there was Reason to apprehend that a Treaty with Great Britain would become a Signal to the antifœderalists, the Debtors and the French, to unite their Efforts to prevent its taking Effect—and to embarrass its Execution ∧if ratified∧—and to conduct their opposition in the manner most injurious to the Constitution, and to the Administration, and to all the men who are attached or give Support to either— That with the Parties would naturally be associated the Jacobin Philosophers, the disorganizing Politicians, and the Malcontents of various Descriptions. Together with the many who have little to lose and much to covet; and those who regard war as speculation, and prefer Spoil and Plunder to patient Industry and honest Gains. To these also may be added, the numerous Herd of those who blindly follow their Leaders; who judge without understanding, who believe without Evidence, and who are to their Demagogues, what some other animals are to their Riders—

On the other Hand—the highest Confidence was reposed in the wisdom and Firmness of the Government, and in the Virtue and good Sense of the great mass of our People, who (especially in the eastern and middle States) possess a Degree of Information and Steadiness, not to be found in other Countries. This Confidence I then entertained, and still retain. I persuade myself it will be justified by the Event; and that the Delusion which certain Spirits are spreading, to decieve the People, will not infect the sound part of the nation. If however this persuasion should prove to be ill founded, we may expect to see our Country afloat on a Sea of Troubles— But having been conversant with Difficulties we are apprized that it is more proper as well as more useful to turn our Faces, than our Backs to them.

As to the Treaty— it must and will speake for itself— it has been maliciously slandered, and very ably defended—but no calumny on the one hand, nor Eloquence on the other, can make it worse or better than it is— At a future Day it will be generally seen in its true Colors and in its proper point of View—

Strenuous Efforts will be made to gain and mislead a majority of the House of Representatives, at the ensuing Session of Congress; and if they succeed, many Perplexities and Embarrassments may be expected. but Perplexities and Embarrassments are incident to human affairs; and while *moral* Evil remains in the World, it will constantly generate *political* ones.

M^r. Bowers has been so obliging as to call and pay me the money mentioned in your Letter, but he omitted, and I forgot to ask him for, your Statement of the Case between you and Doct^rs. Livingston and Jones— I will remind him of it— It gives me pleasure to learn from him, that your Health is perfectly re-established; and that your amiable Family enjoy that inestimable Blessing— May you and they long continue to enjoy it— Whenever I visit Albany, I shall certainly make an Excursion to Duanesburgh.— your Family are taking deep Root there; and they have my best wishes that they may there *be* and *remain "like a Tree planted by the Water Side, whose Leaf shall not wither"*—[2] I am Dear Sir Your obliged & obed^t Servt

John Jay

James Duane Esqr

ALS, CSmH (EJ: 05287). Addressed: "James Duane Esqr. / Schenectade". Endorsed: "Answered". LbkC, NNC: JJ Lbk. 10 (EJ: 12877); *WJ*, 1: 375–77; *HPJ*, 4: 191–94.

1. See Duane to JJ, 31 July 1795, above.

2. Paraphrase of Psalm 1: 3. In his reply of 29 Dec. 1795, ALS, NNC (EJ: 05566), Duane remarked "It displays the just Sentiments by which your Life has been uniformly conducted and which ˄will˄ hand down your name to posterity unsullied and venerated, in spite of the malevolence of your envenomd adversaries, who feel that they sink into contempt in proportion to your elevation." He also discussed the conflict over the DuBois estate, asking JJ's advice. See also his letter of 31 July 1795, above.

To the Consul of the French Republic
(Jean Antoine Bernard de Rozier)

[Saturday Even^g. 19 Septr. 1795—]

The Governor is very sensible of the polite attention which induced the consul of the French Republic,[1] and the French Citizens to invite him to their "republican Entertainment" on Tuesday next. He would with great Pleasure dine with them on that Day, but while general anxiety Distress & alarm pervade his native City, it will not be in his power to command that Degree of Hilarity which becomes such convivial Scenes—[2]

LbkC, NNC: JJ Lbk. 10 (EJ: 12897).

1. Jean Antoine Bernard de Rozier (d. 1799), the French vice consul in New York, 1795–98. *DHSC*, 7: 545n3. See Pierre-Auguste Adet, the French minister to the U.S., introducing Rozier to JJ, 26 June 1795, ALS, NNC (EJ: 08563); JJ's reply of 8 July 1795, ALS, NHyF (EJ: 03532); LbkC, N: Governor's Lbk. 1 (EJ: 03318).

2. The city was in the midst of an acknowledged yellow fever epidemic; see the editorial note "John Jay and the Yellow Fever Epidemics," above.

To John Blanchard

New York 3 Oct.r 1795

Dear Sir

I was this moment fav[ore]d. with your's of the first of this month;[1] & very sincerely thank You for your friendly offer to accommodate my Family, in Case the Disorder prevailing here should make it adviseable to remove them. As the Disorder seems to abate I flatter myself that measure will not be necessary. our Situation affords us considerable Security against the Disorder, and I think it best that my Family should remain here, lest their Removal should increase the alarm which is already too great— If indeed the Danger should become very imminent, it would doubtless be right for M.rs Jay & the Children to leave me, and go into the Country—[2]

I am glad you have reminded me of my Mare and Colt. While I had the Circuits to ride, and consequently many long Journies to make, that excellent Mare was important to me— but as I now have Rest from those Fatigues, I feel very much disposed to give her Rest also; and have therefore concluded to let her pass the Remainder of her Days in breeding, and in nursing her Foals. If the one she now has is not already weaned, I should prefer letting it suck thro' the winter— would it be convenient to You to keep them both untill april next? I had Thoughts of sending them to my farm; but it occurs to me that untill the Colt is a little gentled, and used to the Halter, there would be some Risque in crossing the Ferry—[3] I am D.r Sir &c.a

LbkC, NNC: JJ Lbk. 10 (EJ: 12875).

1. Letter not found. John Blanchard (c. 1730–1811) was a prosperous merchant who had served as a captain in the Continental Army and lived in Elizabethtown (serving as alderman and then justice of the peace) before retiring to what is now Chatham Township, N.J. *Princetonians*, 173.

2. During the yellow fever epidemic of 1795, many New Yorkers fled the city for the country. See the editorial note "John Jay and the Yellow Fever Epidemics," above.

3. JJ rode several horses during his tenure on the circuit court, and mentions them and his concern for their welfare in his diary and letters. *JJSP*, 5: 243, 259, 278. This mare may have been a descendant of a mare belonging to JJ's father, of which he wrote Richard Peters, "Of her Stock I have *always* had Saddle Horses— those which I selected for that purpose, remained mine as long as they lived—" JJ to Peters, 16 Oct. 1811, ALS, PHi (EJ: 01159); Dft, NNC (EJ: 11524).

From Timothy Pickering

Department of State Octr. 10. 1795.

Sir,

The inclosed copy of my letter of the 6th instant to William Lewis & William Rawle Esquires[1] will apprize you of the object of this address. Their answer, which is also inclosed, does not, I confess, correspond with my ideas of the meaning of the seventh article of the treaty which you negotiated with Lord Grenville. I always conceived that the principal ground of our complaints of spoliations was, the capture of our vessels under the orders of the Privy Council of Great Britain, especially the order of the sixth of November 1793, as being repugnant to the laws of nations: but one opinion expressed by those gentlemen amounts to an abandonment of this ground, and an admission of consequences beyond even the present claims of the British admiralty courts: it would put an end to our commerce with the French West India Islands, by subjecting all our vessels, in the present course of that Trade, to *legal* captures, by the British on one hand & by the French on the other. To admit that opinion would be to renounce, as it strikes me, the great object which was the *immediate* cause of your extraordinary mission: Hence I cannot but conclude that the opinion mentioned requires a review.

Again, if the business of the Commissioners to be appointed under the seventh article, applies merely to ascertain the amount of compensations in cases of insolvency of the captors, in the very few instances in which, upon their principles, restoration is to be expected, the provision for effecting it seems to me vastly disproportioned to the object. And where are they to apply, if their powers are so circumscribed, "the law of nations"; and with what pertinency can their decisions be mentioned as "in all cases final & conclusive, both as to the *justice of the claim*, and the amount of the sum to be paid to the claimant"?

In the case of the Betsey, lately decided in the High Court of Appeals (of which you will have seen some account in the news-papers) it would seem, from M^r. Bayard's information, that the chief ground for affirming the sentence of the Vice-Admiralty Court in Bermuda was, that George Patterson, the owner of the vessel, and partner with his brother William in the property of the cargo, *had taken his residence in Guadaloupe.* This appeared by G. Patterson's letter to his brother, found on board the Betsey: for although he went to Guadaloupe in her, & she was taken when returning from that first voyage, yet he *remains at Guadaloupe, and proposes that his brother should send her to him there with another cargo.*[2]

Further, M[r]. FitzSimons[3] informs me, that an American ship loaded at Guadaloupe with *sugar* &c. and bound to Amsterdam, having been taken, and tried by ∧a∧ British admiralty court, was acquitted.

This and other cases show that the British do not mean *now* to take the broad ground assumed in the order of the sixth of November; but which the opinion referred to would allow them to repossess.

But I will not trouble you with any further observations. You see, Sir, what are my views in addressing you: they are expressed in my letter to M[r]. Lewis & M[r]. Rawle. Your explanation of this subject, to which no one is so competent will be gratefully received by me; and cannot fail to afford much satisfaction to the President.[4] I hope you will find time to write next week; the President I think will be here on Friday. I am with very great respect Sir, your obed[t]. servant

Timothy Pickering

His Excellency Governor Jay

ALS, NNC (EJ: 09483); LbkCs, MHi: Pickering (EJ: 04826); DNA: Domestic Letters, 8, 432–34.

1. TP to Lewis and Rawle, 6 Oct. 1795, C, NNC (EJ: 09482); LbkC, DNA: Domestic Letters, 8: 430–31. The copies of the opinion sent by Lewis and Rawle on the role of the spoliation commission to be established under the Jay Treaty have not been found.

2. Accounts derived from the London newspapers of the verdict of the High Court of Appeals in London of 25 July 1795 affirming the verdict of the Bermuda admiralty court on the seizure of the ship *Betsey*, Capt. William Furlong, owned by George and William Patterson of Baltimore, appeared in several American newspapers in October 1795. See, for example, *Philadelphia Gazette*, 3 Oct. 1795.

In his letter to Lewis and Rawles cited in note 1 above, TP stated that the report of the case and a letter of 29 July 1795 from Samuel Bayard regarding it were to be laid before the committee of merchants in Philadelphia at a meeting to be held the following week. He was therefore seeking legal opinions on the applicability of the 6th and 7th articles of the Jay Treaty on the course on which claims under those articles must proceed. He queried whether cases must first be brought to the British court of appeals, or whether they could be appealed directly from the vice-admiralty courts. If the first was affirmed, TP contended that every decision of the Court of Appeals could be examined by the commissioners on the spoliation commission if the American claimants were dissatisfied. He argued that as an independent nation the United States had a right to contest the principles or rules of law guiding British courts, and that the commissioners could negotiate on the differences between the two parties. On the spoliation commission, see the editorial note "Aftermath of the Jay Treaty: Responses, Ratification, and Implementation," above. For the dispute over the power of the spoliations commission to question decisions of the High Court of Appeals, see Moore, *International Arbitrations*, 1: 324–28.

3. Philadelphia merchant and former congressman Thomas FitzSimons was chairman of the merchants' committee in Philadelphia. On 2 Oct. TP sent FitzSimons a copy of Bayard's letter and the report on the decision on the *Betsey* case seeking the committee's suggestions for advice to send

Bayard. He wrote again on 14 Oct. sending FitzSimons information on British handling of Danish captures that he said countered the interpretations given by Rawle and Lewis. See TP to FitzSimons, 2 and 14 Oct. 1795, LbkCs, DNA: Domestic Letters, 8: 427; 9: 2.

4. For the reply, see JJ to TP, 14 Oct. 1795, below. Bayard submitted the *Betsey* case to the spoliation commissioners when they first met in October 1796. See Bayard to JJ, 11 Oct. 1796, ALS, NNC (EJ: 12840).

To Timothy Pickering

NYork 14 Octr. 1795

Sir

I was Yesterday ∧afternoon∧ honored with yours of the 10 Inst. enclosing ∧a∧ copy of your Letter to Messrs. Lewis and Rawle and ∧of∧ their opinion on the points stated in it.—[1] Notwithstanding my Respect for the Talents & Candor of those Gen^t. ~~I do not~~ ∧yet I do not hesitate to say that∧ the Cognizance and Powers given to the Commissioners designated in the 6 and 7 articles of the Treaty are ∧in my opinion∧ vastly more comprehensive than those Gentlemen consider them— indeed I cannot concieve how it was possible to give ~~them~~ ∧Com[missione]^{rs}∧ greater Latitude, consistantly with Reason and common Sense, than by authorizing ∧them∧ to "decide the claims in question according to the merits of the several cases and to *Justice Equity* and the *Laws of Nations*["]— If it be asked what are the Claims and cases which they are authorized ∧so∧ to decide—let it be answered in the ~~words~~ ∧Language∧ of the Treaty— all claims ~~of~~ for, and cases of, Losses and Damages ~~by Reason of illegal~~ ∧caused by∧ irregular or illegal captures or condemnations of american vessels or other Property under colour of authority or commissions from his B.[2] Majesty, and in which cases adequate compensation cannot for *whatever Reason* be now actually obtained had and rec^d. in the ordinary Course of ~~judicial Proceedings~~ Justice—

The Duty of the Commissioners is two fold— ∧first∧ to decide on the merits ∧of all∧ claims ∧made∧ in such Cases, according to Justice Equity and the Laws of Nations, and secondly to ascertain ~~the~~ and *award* the amount of the Losses and Damages sustained by ∧those∧ Claimants in whose favor they decide the merits of the case to be—

~~If acts contrary~~ ∧as on the one Hand no∧ Legislative or judicial ~~acts contrary~~ ∧acts in this country, repugnant∧ to the Treaty of Peace [*illegible*] ~~should deprive~~ ∧and prejudicial to∧ British Creditors ~~of their Rights under that Treaty The Commrs~~ ~~Hands of commissioners are not to be restrained~~ ∧by those act∧ ~~from doing~~ ∧can restrain the Com^{rs} under the 6 art: from doing Justice to those creditors∧ Justice[3] ~~by those acts~~ ∧to those Creditors∧

If ˄so˄ on the other ˄Hand˄ ˄no˄ Royal Instructions, or Decisions of Courts ˄given˄ made ~~and~~ ˄or˄ executed contrary to the Laws of Nations ~~to Jus-tice or Equity should have occasion~~ᵈ ˄and causing˄ Losses and Damages to American Citizens ˄can restrain˄ the Comʳˢ under the 7 art ~~are not restrained from thereby~~ from doing ~~Justice~~ ˄that Right to the claimants wʰ. Justice Eq-uity & the Laws of Nations may prescribe˄ ~~Compleat and~~ perfect Justice to all parties is the object of both ˄the˄ articles, and the Comʳˢ are empowered to do it, ˄as˄ in ~~wor~~ Terms as explicit and comprehensive as the English Lan-guage affords

I would with great pleasure take up and consider this subject at large and give you a formal opinion upon it— But ~~circumstanced as I am~~ But ~~it does not appear to~~ me ˄I must doubt the utility ~~to~~ or˄ expediency in the present Moment, ~~to~~ ˄of˄ bringˢ forward to the ~~public~~ ˄Merchants or other Descrip-tion of people˄ any opinions of mine ~~on any parts of~~ ˄relative to these or other articles of˄ the Treaty—⁴

on recieving your Letter I took the Liberty of communicating ~~it~~ ˄this morning˄ to Col. Hamilton ˄the opinion of Mʳ Lewis & Mʳ Rawle˄ and with his Permission enclose open for your Inspection a Letter from him to Mʳ Woolcot, in which you will find his sentiments on the points in Question—⁵ I have the Honor to be with great Respect & Esteem Sir yʳ most obᵗ. & hble servᵗ

The Honle. Timʸ Pickering Esqʳ

Dft, NNC (EJ: 09484). LbkC, NNC: Lbk. 10 (EJ: 12874).

1. See TP to JJ, 10 Oct. 1795, above, and notes.

2. The LbkC reads "brittanic".

3. This word does not appear in the LbkC.

4. Here in the manuscript the following section is crossed out: "A spirit of Delusion and Decep-tion arising from the Fermentation of impure Politics and mischievous machinations is spread ~~and spreading~~ thro the County; ~~and~~ I trust it will finally be dissipated by the wisdom and Firmness of the Government and by the Virtue and good Sense still remaining among the People— In the meantime However circumspection is necessary, and the most guarded Prudence must accompany ~~so~~ vigorous Measures—".

5. See AH to Oliver Wolcott Jr., 13 Oct. 1795, PAH, 19: 314–18.

To Edward Bancroft

New York 30 Octʳ. 1795

Dear Sir

On my Return two Days ago from a little Excursion into the Country I had the pleasure of recieving your Letter of the 24 of Augᵗ. last;¹ and thank you very sincerely for the friendly congratulations and Sentiments expressed in it—

Your Son soon after his arrival at Philadelphia, and also M^r. J. Vaughan wrote to me relative to the object of his coming to this Country;[2] but the State of the Health of this City was then such, as to render it prudent for him to postpone his Journey here until the prevailing Disorder should so far abate as to leave no Room for just apprehensions of Danger. within these ten Days past, it has been rapidly diminishing, and in the course of another week will probably disappear—

It will I assure you always give me pleasure to have opportunities of being useful to any of your Family. The Profession which your Son had chosen is a good one; and one that will always find an ample and tolerably fertile field in the united States. I believe however that in all of them it is overstocked,—in this it certainly is—but that obstacle is not insuperable by a man of Talents Prudence and Industry—[3]

The opposition and Ferment excited here was not unexpected; but the Treaty presented only the *occasion* not the motive for it. French Influence & Intrigues had long been strenuously operating to plunge us into the war— The Debtors wished for them to give them Receipts in full—and the anti-fedœralists enlisted and were enlisted by both. These Parties are combined, and will make every Effort to acquire an ascendancy in the House of Representatives at the ensuing Session of congress— The President is firm and wise, and much is to be expected from the good Sense of the majority of the People.

Peace in Europe would be useful to us, and so would the Establishment of any Tolerable Constitution in France. In these Times it is difficult to predict what will happen, from what has happened—but Providence governs the world & we have only to do our Duty— M^rs. Jay and my Son are on a Visit to my Brother at Rye— I am &c^a.—

LbkC, NNC: JJ Lbk. 10 (EJ: 12873).

1. Edward Bancroft to JJ, 24 Aug. 1795, not found, but see Bancroft's letter to John Vaughan, 15 Aug. 1795, E, NNC (EJ: 08151), which was probably enclosed in John Vaughan to JJ, 17 Oct., ALS, NNC (EJ: 08152).

2. Samuel Bancroft to JJ, 15 Oct., not found, but referenced in JJ to Samuel Bancroft, 16 Oct. 1795, ALS, MHi: Waterston (EJ: 04767); Dft, NNC (EJ: 08946). JJ's draft correspondence contains the following note at the bottom of the letter: "Govr. Jay presents his Comp^ts. To M^r J[ohn]. Vaughan, and agreeable to the Request of M^r. S[amuel] Bancroft takes the Liberty of committing the enclosed Letter for Gentleman to Mr. Vaughans Care NYork 16 Octr 1795".

3. Samuel Forrester Bancroft (1775–99), the second son of Edward Bancroft, attended Dr. Wil-

liam Rose's London academy, alongside his elder brother, Edward Nathaniel (1772–1842). Continuing his education, Samuel enrolled in science courses at the University of Montpellier and eventually earned a degree from Trinity College, Cambridge. Samuel settled on law for his future vocation, and his father consulted with JJ about the feasibility of his studying and setting up a practice in the United States. Although Edward wanted AH to direct Samuel's legal training, he feared that his twenty-year-old son would succumb to profligacy and dissipation if situated in a large city. Edward therefore favored a rural environment for Samuel, and specifically requested that Tapping Reeve (1744–1823), who founded a law school in Litchfield, Conn., oversee his preparation for the bar.

JJ found young Bancroft to possess an imprudent character and agreed with his friend's assessment that Samuel should train under Reeve, free from the distractions of New York and Philadelphia. Samuel's name, however, does not appear on the student register of the Litchfield School, so it is doubtful that he attended. Regardless, Samuel's legal aspirations proved short-lived as he was soon transformed into a criminal fugitive. Accused of raping a young girl in Philadelphia in December 1796, Samuel fled the United States, eventually reaching the safety of England the following year. See Edward Bancroft to John Vaughan, 15 Aug. 1795, E, NNC (EJ: 08151); JJ to Samuel Bancroft, 16 Oct., ALS, MHi (EJ: 04767); Dft, NNC (EJ: 08946); Vaughan to JJ, 17 Oct., ALS, NNC (EJ: 08152); 7 Nov. 1795, ALS, NNC (EJ: 08153); JJ to Vaughan, 21 Jan. 1796, below; JJ to Edward Bancroft, 22 Apr. 1796, NNC, Dft (EJ: 08954); and JJ to the New York State Officers of Justice, 15 Dec. 1796, below. See also Schaeper, *Bancroft*, 241, 243–44.

Proclamation for a Day of Thanksgiving

[New York, 11 November 1795]

By His Excellency
John Jay Esquire
Governor and Commander in Chief of the State of New York[1]
A Proclamation:

Whereas the Great Creator and Preserver of the Universe is the Supreme Sovereign of Nations, and does, when and as he pleases, reward or punish them by temporal Blessings or Calamities, according as their National Conduct recommends them to his Favor and Beneficence, or excites his Displeasure and Indignation.

And Whereas in the course of his Government, he hath graciously been pleased to shew singular kindness to the People and Nation of which this State is a constituent Member— By protecting our Ancestors in their first Establishments in this then Savage Wilderness; by defending them against their Enemies— by blessing them with an uncommon degree of Peace Liberty and Safety, and with the civilizing light and influence of his Holy Gospel— By leading us (as it were by the Hand) through the various Dangers and Difficulties of the late Revolution, and crowning it with Success— by giving us Wisdom and Opportunity to establish Governments and Institutions auspicious to order Security and rational Liberty— by preserving us from being involved in the Wars and other grievous Calamities which at this moment afflict and distress many Nations— by restoring Peace between us and the Hostile Indians who infested our Borders— by constantly favoring us with fruitful Seasons; and in general by giving us a greater portion of public welfare and Prosperity than to any other People—

And Whereas it hath pleased him, by permitting sickness to prevail and be fatal to the Lives of many in our principal City, and in sundry Places in this and other States, and by the extensive Alarms and Embarrassments which attended it, to remind us that Prosperity and Adversity are in his Hand, and that in all our pursuits we are to remember, that he is the Cause and Giver of all the Good that was, that is, or that will be. And Whereas our Almighty Sovereign in Addition to his other Mercies hath lately stayed the Hand of the destroying Angel, and by thus manifesting and multiplying his Benefits to us as a People, calls upon us as a People to manifest our Gratitude to him—

Wherefore, and particularly on this occasion it appears to me to be the public duty of the People of this State collectively considered, to render unto him their sincere and humble Thanks for All these his great and unmerited Mercies and Blessings— And Also to offer up to him their fervent Petitions to continue to us his Protection and favor, to preserve to us the undisturbed Enjoyment of our Civil and Religious Rights and Priviledges, and the valuable Life and usefulness of the President of the United States— To enable all our Rulers Councils and People to do the Duties incumbent on them respectively with Wisdom and fidelity— To promote the extension of true Religion, Virtue and Learning— To give us All Grace to cultivate National Union Concord and Good Will; And Generally, to bless our Nation, and All other Nations in the manner and measure most conducive to our and their best Interests and real Welfare.

Whether the Governor of this State is vested with Authority to appoint a day for these purposes, and to require and enjoin the Observance of it, is a Question which, circumstanced as it is, I consider as being more proper for the Legislature than for me to decide. But as the People of the State have constituted me their Chief Magistrate, and being perfectly convinced that National Prosperity depends, and ought to depend, on National Gratitude and Obedience to the Supreme Ruler of All Nations, I think it proper to recommend and therefore I do earnestly recommend to the Clergy and others my fellow Citizens throughout this State to set apart Thursday the twenty sixth day of November instant for the Purposes aforesaid and to observe it accordingly.

Given under my Hand at the Government House in the City of New York on the eleventh day of November in the Year of our Lord One thousand Seven hundred and ninety five, and In the twentieth Year of the Independence of the United States.[2]

(signed) John Jay

LbkC, N: Governor's Lbk. 2 (EJ: 03205). PtD, *American Minerva* (New York), 12 Nov.; reprinted: *Argus, Greenleaf's New Daily Advertiser* (New York), *Daily Advertiser* (New York), and *Philadelphia Gazette*, 13 Nov.; *Aurora General Advertiser* (Philadelphia), *Dunlap's American Daily Advertiser* (New York), *Gazette of the United States* (Philadelphia), and *Greenleaf's New York Journal*, 14 Nov.; *Independent Gazetteer* (Philadelphia) and *Telegraphe and Daily Advertiser* (Baltimore), 18 Nov; *Albany Register*, 20 Nov.; *American Mercury* (Hartford), and *Daily Advertiser* (New York) (supplement), 23 Nov. (EJ: 13155); *Richmond Chronicle*, 23 Nov.; and *Massachusetts Mercury* (Boston), 24 Nov. 1795.

1. *Greenleaf's New York Journal* took particular exception to JJ's title as Commander in Chief, claiming on 9 Dec.:

Many bold and original traits in the public agency of Gov. Jay, shew his towering genius far above that ordinary levil: a brilliant example of which is the new and manifest title he hath assumed at the head of his late proclamation for a thanksgiving.

"*His Excellency John Jay, Esq. Governor and Commander in Chief of the State of New-York;*" not of the militia, but of the State, and consequently of all its authorities.

From the arbitrary nature of all military authority, the militia must necessarily be commanded by a single chief, and we have no reason at present to doubt, that when an old military commander is made first magistrate in a nation, he will retain the relish and habit of his wonted domination: but I have till now been so ignorant as to suppose that, *of the State of New-York, the Law was Commander in Chief*, neither the enacting or administering of which was left to any single man.

What suprizes me most is, that as Governor Jay is now in military command, and as *his beloved President* is an *old commander* (who alone has saved the country) the Governor's federal loyalty could so daringly assume the presidential prerogative, when at the same time his superfine modesty seems to have given him qualms at presuming without other authority to merely recommend a thanksgiving day.

JUVENUS.

County of Columbia, 22 Nov. 1795.

2. For the reaction to the Proclamation, see John Sloss Hobart to JJ, 18–19 Nov. 1795, below, and the editorial note "John Jay and the Yellow Fever Epidemics," above.

To John Sinclair

New York 12 Nov[r]. 1795

D[r]. Sir

Since my arrival my Time has been so much occupied by public Concerns, as that neither my Friends nor private affairs have rec[d]. from me the Degree of attention that was due to them. Accept my thanks for the Letters and Papers with which you have favored me. They shall be the Subject of another Letter—[1]

You may remember my mentioning to you that common Salt had been used with Success as a manure for *Flax*, and my promising to procure and transmit to You more particular Information respecting the Quantity or Proportion of Salt which was found to be most proper.

I have taken some Pains to ascertain this, but from the Result of my Inquiries there is Reason to presume that further Experiments accurately made, are necessary to afford a satisfactory answer to the Question, and the more so, as the nature of the Soil, and perhaps the Season, do not appear to me to have been sufficiently regarded; and which may possibly account for certain proportions of Salt succeeding much better in some Instances than in others. A Gentleman in New England has published some Facts, from which it appears that the Subject merits attention— he says

"In June 1786 I salted one Bed of my onions, one Bed of my Carrots, and one Bed of my early Turnips—laying the Salt under the Surface, in the Centers of the Intervals between the Rows, at some Distance from the Roots; that the Salt might have Time to be dissolved and altered before the fibrous Roots should reach it. The Carrots of the salted Bed evidently grew much larger and better than the Rest; but I could not percieve that the Salt was at all beneficial to the onions, or to the Turnips. . . . According to M^r. Ford's Experiment in salting *Flax* Ground, Salt seems to be highly beneficial to that Crop. He spreads the Salt at the Time of sowing the Seed; and thinks that the Quantity of Salt should be *double* to that of the Seed. From three acres in Flax salted, he had fifty Bushells of Seed, and an excellent Crop of Flax. M^r. Elliot tells us of *five* Bushells of Salt being applied to *one* acre of *Flax*, which is a much larger Proportion; and that it had an extraordinary Effect; and also of a crop of wheat being encreased by Salt."[2]

A Gentleman from Dutches County in this State passed last Evening with me. Speaking of apples, the one half part of each of which was sweet, and the other half part tart or sour, he told me there were Trees which produced such apples in or near his neighbourhood— that he had examined and tasted the apples, and that many others had done the same. He told me that on Inquiry he had been informed that the method of obtaining such apples was as follows vizt.

Take two Scions or Grafts, one from a *sour*, and the other from a *sweet* apple Tree— divide or split with a sharp Knife each Graft into two parts or halfs, taking Care to pass the Knife thro' the centre or middle of as many Buds as were in a Line with each other— then take one half of the sweet Graft and join it to a half of the sour Graft; in such a manner that two or more of the half Buds in each do exactly meet and fit each other. Then carefully wind round them woorsted or woolen Thread to keep them together, and having thus become one Graft, cut it so as that the Bark of the Wedge part of it, which enters the Stock or Tree engrafted, being partly of both kinds, may recieve the Sap of the Stock on both Sides. If this artificial Graft takes and grows, which frequently happens, the two parts of which it consists will gradually unite and incorporate & become a Tree whose Fruit *on the Branches shooting from the united Buds* partaking of both natures, will be on one Side sweet and on the other sour.

He particularly examined an apple of this kind, which on one Side exactly resembled a winter apple called here the Rhode Island Greening, but on the opposite Side was of a different Color and appearance. He was assured that this apple was from a Tree composed in the manner before mentioned, of Grafts from a Rhode Island Greening, & a common sweet apple Tree.—[3]

You will recieve herewith enclosed the first volume of the memoirs of the american academy. In the 386 page you will find an account of an apple Tree which produced Fruit of this singular kind, so that however marvelous the Story of these apples may seem, you will see that I do not speake without Book—[4]

With the best wishes for the Success of your excellent Institution and for your personal welfare, I have the Honor to be Dear Sir your most ob^t. & hble Servt

Sir John Sinclair Bar[one]^t. President of the Board of Agriculture London—

LbkC, NNC: JJ Lbk. 10 (EJ: 12872). PtD, *Communications to the Board of Agriculture; on subjects relative to the husbandry: and internal improvement of the Country* (London, 1797), 1: 361–62; John Sinclair, *An account of the systems of husbandry adopted in the more improved districts of Scotland* (Edinburgh, 1814), 2: 182–83.

1. Sinclair and JJ had met in London and continued to correspond. See Sinclair to JJ, 6 July 1794, above; JJ to Sinclair, 8 July 1794, Dft, NNC (EJ: 08890); JJ to John Sloss Hobart, 12 Aug. 1794, above; John Sloss Hobart to JJ, 20 Nov. 1794, above. For Sinclair's response, see his letter of 14 Mar. 1796, below. For more on their correspondence, see the editorial note "John Jay's Mission to London," above.

2. This section is quoted from Samuel Deane, *The New-England farmer; or, Georgical dictionary: containing a compendious account of the ways and methods in which the most important art of husbandry, in all its various branches, is, or may be, practiced to the greatest advantage in this country* (Worcester, 1790; *Early Am. Imprints*, series 1, no. 22450), 239. C, n.d., in WJ's hand, NNC (EJ: 09137).

3. This section containing the above three paragraphs was later printed in Thomas G. Fessenden, *The New England Farmer, and Horticultural Journal* (Boston: 1825), 3: 202, citing JJ as the source; and *The Genesee Farmer*, 9 Aug. 1834, with JJ referred to as "an American Statesman" writing in a "British publication on Agriculture."

4. Peter Whitney, "An Account of a singular Apple-Tree, producing Fruit of opposite Qualities; A Part of the same Apple being frequently Sour, and the Other sweet." *Memoirs of the American Academy of Arts and Sciences: to the end of the year [1783]* vol 1. (Boston, [1785]; *Early Am. Imprints*, series 1, no. 18900), 386–87.

To Abraham Cuyler

New York 13 Nov[r]. 1795

Sir

I was this morning favored with your's of the 5th. of this month,[1] mentioning M[r]. Harison's opinion that the Debts in question were not recoverable by Virtue either of the Treaty of Peace, or of the Treaty of amity between the United States and Great Britain—

As to M[r]. Harison's opinion, I do not hesitate to say that I concur in it— But whether the Subjects of it were or were not discussed in the Course of the late negociation I must decline giving you the Information you request, notwithstanding the Respect and friendly Sentiments with which I have the Honor to be Sir &c. &c.

LbkC, NNC: JJ Lbk. 10 (EJ: 12876).
1. Letter not found.

From John Sloss Hobart

Throggs Neck 18th.[–19] Nov[r]. 1795

Dear Sir

I intended to have acknowledged the receipt of your favor by M[r]. Munro,[1] while at Albany; but he did not return from Washington before I set out for home; I was obliged by your hint respecting the corn, and availed myself of the opportunity to procure a supply of seed against another year, should it come to hand, I shall have enough for myself and a friend.

I have read with pleasure your Excellency's proclamation for a day of thanksgiving and prayer; the causes are well assigned, and the petitions well adapted.[2] Every body will agree that we have received great and undeserved mercies, as a society, from our Creator, and that ∧it∧ is fit and proper we should, as a society, acknowledge, and implore the continuance of them. But by whose authority shall the times and seasons for the purposes, be pointed out?—

I wot[3] that in good olden time it was the peculiar province of holy church, and so continued till Henry the 8th, of *pious* memory, made a kind of Hotch pot business of it, by uniting the ecclesiastical and civil power in his own hands; his example has been followed by his successors to the present day, they issue their proclamations appointing days for public fasting, humiliation and prayer, in times of public calamity, and for public thanksgiving and praises upon signal instances of public mercies. It may be said their proclamations are authoritative, ours only recommendatory— but I ask, if the recommendation does not partake of the nature of a *conge d'elire*?[4] and who will be hardy enough to neglect an acknowledged duty when recommended from such high authority?— Am I mistaken—Or do my glasses magnify too much— when I fancy I see the cloven foot of *monarchy* in this business? Alass!— where are the direfull effects of this extraordinary envoyship to end? The benefits of our commerce transferred to Britain— The usurpations of its monarchy transferred to us— Nor is this all— The poor clergy are by the constitution confined to the care of souls: they may not intermeddle with the political concerns of the community: the door is forever barred against them; let who may be rulers; they *must* be subject. And shall the poor pittance of power, arising from the authority of calling their congregations together, to observe particular days for religious purposes, be thus wrested from them. It is in vain to say that no interference with their authority is intended; for whether intended or not, it may happen that our civil Governor may recommend a thanksgiving to be celebrated on the same day which our spiritual Governors had set apart for fasting— The case I observe has actually hapened in the present instance— And I applied yesterday to the casuistry of the parson of the parish to decide for me between them, and tell which ought to be obeyed, he, good man, entered an *advisari*, and may eventually take it *ad referendum*. It seems, this power ought to be exercised by the spiritual or the civil rulers solely. It is an *hereditament* of which they cannot be seized as *tenants in common*, unless there should be formed such an intimate *alliance* between church and state, as to prevent all possibility of interference.[5]

If Camillus can dispose of these objections to the proclamation, in as handsom a manner as he has those to the treaty;[6] I shall tremble for the fate of my country, when you are sent on an extra mission to the court of Rome, lest the same spirit of immitation might produce a Bull constituting another *Defender*, Tho' I trow not of the faith.[7]

But to be serious, once more, As the church in this town is unfit for the celebration of divine service, should the weather continue favorable, and business will admit of my absence from home, I propose to go to town to church on Thanksgiving day, when I shall have the pleasure of paying my respects in person to M^rs. Jay and the family— In the meantime please to present my respectfull compliments to them, and believe me Yours most sincerely

Jn°: Sloss Hobart

His Excell^y Govr. Jay

19th. I find since writing the above by the daily Advertiser, that the Proclamation no more than the Treaty, is to escape the shafts of envy and malevolence.[8]

ALS, NNC (EJ: 05680). *WJ*, 1: 386–88; *HPJ*, 4: 195–96. Both published versions excised the first and last paragraphs.

1. Letter not found.

2. See JJ's Proclamation, 11 Nov. 1795, calling for a day of Thanksgiving in response to the abatement of the yellow fever epidemic, above.

3. Wot: archaic variant of "to know," used here for literary effect. *OED*.

4. Congé d'élire: a royal warrant given to a diocese to elect the person to their vacant see. *OED*.

5. JJ's call for a day of Thanksgiving met with attacks from the anti-Federalist press, mainly from *Argus, Greenleaf's New Daily Advertiser* (New York) and the *Aurora General Advertiser* (Philadelphia). These attacks often referenced the Jay Treaty. Hobart seems to be responding in particular to the piece in *Argus, Greenleaf's New Daily Advertiser* (New York) of 18 Nov. that was reprinted in the *Aurora General Advertiser* (Philadelphia) of 20 Nov.:

> Governor Jay's proclamation for a day of thanksgiving is considered as a party production and as such has disgusted multitudes of people. That the United States have many blessings for which they ought to express their gratitude to the Divine Being is undoubted. The Religious Societies perform this duty every Sunday; but that the Governor should particularly enjoin us to pray for the valuable & useful life of the President at the very moment 9 persons in 10 are exasperated at his late conduct in ratifying an infamous treaty is not very delicate especially as his excellency or coadjutor Camillus, was the treaty maker. We may pray for the President, as we ought for all our Rulers, and indeed for all men; but we are not bound to honor them with epithets, to which they are not entitled.
>
> The Governor's qualms about the constitution excite our risibilty. It is a pity he had not been equally scrupulous about the constitution of the United States when negotiating his celebrated treaty. This is straining at a gnat, and at the same time swallowing a camel!!!

6. *Camillus* was the pen name used by AH and RK in their newspaper essays defending the Jay Treaty. For more on the *Camillus* essays, see "Introductory Note: the Defence No. 1," *PAH*, 18: 475–79.

7. The *Aurora General Advertiser* (Philadelphia) of 14 Nov. commented, "this correspondent is of opinion, that his late proclamation possesses such genuine ingredients of the whining cant of religious hypocricy as render him worthy of a cardinal's hat, and will even fit him for the Papal Dignity in time." For more on the reception of the Proclamation, see the editorial note "John Jay and the Yellow Fever Epidemics," above.

8. See "COMMUNICATIONS" in *Argus, Greenleaf's New Daily Advertiser* (New York), 18 Nov. 1795.

To Edmund Burke

New York 12 Dec[r]. 1795

Sir

The last time I had the pleasure of seeing you we ~~conversed among other things, and speaking of the apples of this Country~~ I promised to send you ~~a few~~ ∧some apple∧ Trees ~~of some of the best Sorts~~—[1] Fifty Trees ~~have been put~~ ∧of five different Sorts are now∧ on Board the Rosanna Cap[t]. John Pollard,[2] whose Rec[eip][t]. for them you will find herewith enclosed Ten of these Trees are in the New Town Pippin ~~which~~ you ~~are acquainted~~ know what they are— Ten ~~other~~ are what we call Spitzenberghs, from the Name of the Man in whose orchard the first Tree of the kind was found ~~The Fruit is~~ The apple is red, large and fair, it keeps untill January, and we esteem it next to the New Town pippin— Ten are of a kind called Rhode Island Greenings, from being of very green when ripe, and from having been first produced in Rhode Island— it is a very good apple, tho' in my opinion inferior to the two first— Ten are Summer Pippins—a very large fair Yellow apple, ~~& in Perfection late in autumn and but seldom sound and good beyond December— a mild tart agreeable apple~~—Ten ~~of bear Summer apples~~ ∧which bear∧ large and sweet ∧apples, which are ripe soon after Harvest∧ As these Trees are from a Nursery man in whose Care I have confidence I presume no mistakes have been committed—[3]

The great majority of our orchards consisting of Trees ~~the that~~ which have never been engrafted, ~~the~~ ∧afford a∧ variety of apples ~~in this Country is~~ so great as not to be enumerated— among them are many that are excellent, and a great Many that are worth but little— ~~The Climate and the contiguous States is very friendly to this Fruit, *and*~~

~~How these Trees will succeed in England or how far their Fruit may be changed by the Climate Experience only can decide— It seems to me it appears probable that the warm Summer~~ With great Respect and Esteem, and with the best wishes for your Health and Happiness I have the Honor to be Sir Y[r] most ob[t]. & hble Serv[t]

The Honble Edm. Burke Esq[r]

Dft, NNC (EJ: 12824).

1. JJ had become acquainted with Burke in London during his negotiations for the Jay Treaty. See the editorial note "John Jay's Mission to London," above. PAJ's Memoranda & Statement of Accounts, dated 11 Sept. 1794, records "When we return to America to send a Barrel of Shag Bark nuts to Lord Inchiquin & some Newton Pippin Trees to M[r]. Burke—", AD, NNC.

2. The *Rosannah* cleared the port of New York on 12 Dec. bound for London. *Argus, Greenleaf's New Daily Advertiser* (New York), 12 Dec. 1795.

3. JJ sent Burke American varieties of apple trees, with three of the four New York varieties. The Newtown Pippin was developed on Long Island and became well-known as an excellent cidering and eating apple. This variety was also famously grown by GW and TJ, and its cultivation in Virginia gave rise to its alternate name, the Albemarle Pippin. The Esopus Spitzenbergh, another New York apple, is also known for being an all-round apple. Rhode Island Greenings, also known as Orange Pippins, first appeared in the 17th century. The Summer Pippin's alternate names of Champlain, Haverstraw, and Nyack point to its origin in New York State. U. P. Hendrick, *Cyclopedia of Hard Fruits* (New York, 1922), 29, 34, 36, 54.

DEFENDING NEW YORK

The defense of the city and port of New York consumed the state government throughout the tenure of Jay's governorship. The threat posed by French naval forces to New York's vulnerable maritime trade coupled with the bitter memory of British occupation during the previous war meant that the fortification and armament of New York City remained high priority issues. Yet delays and disputes continuously plagued defensive measures as authorities and agencies at the municipal, state, and national levels squabbled over issues of land ownership, administrative jurisdiction, and resource allocation. As New York's chief executive, Jay did his best to mediate the complex and often competing agendas of the involved parties. Despite Jay's endeavors, difficulties nonetheless persisted that undermined his efforts to establish a comprehensive and viable defense system for New York City and its adjoining waterscape.

Before Jay held the post of governor, the previous administration under George Clinton had worked to secure New York's harbor in the midst of a national war scare.[1] As New York and much of the country braced for a seemingly imminent conflict with Britain in 1794, federal attention focused on the lack of adequate coastal fortifications along the eastern seaboard. A committee report undertaken by the House of Representatives found New York City woefully unprepared to withstand a seaborne attack, and therefore recommended erecting fortified works, mobilizing troops, and acquiring artillery pieces for the metropolis as well as Paulus Hook and Governors Island.[2] The difficulty of implementing such measures was remarked upon by Washington, who noted that the defense of New York City posed a particular challenge for military engineers.[3]

In response, Congress passed two acts[4] in March for the protection of the nation's ports and harbors; these statutes implemented what later became known as the nation's First System of Coastal Fortifications.[5] That same month, the New York legislature supplemented the federal funding with an appropriation of thirty thousand pounds and established a seven-person committee to oversee defense preparations.[6] Charles Vincent, who was appointed as temporary engineer, developed an ambitious plan for fortifying the inner and outer harbors; he called for the construction of defensive positions to cover the Narrows—the body of water separating Staten Island from Brooklyn—and also commenced an earthworks square-shaped fort on Governors Island that was later named Fort Jay in 1798.[7] The heavy costs associated with labor and materials, however, hindered progress and forced Vincent and his colleagues to scale back their plans.[8]

The prospect of war reaching American shores receded with the signing of the Jay Treaty, and the interest in carrying out military preparations likewise diminished. When Clinton left office in June 1795, his administration left the newly elected governor a legacy of partially constructed earthworks and an insufficient number of cannon to properly defend the port. Despite the public's curbed enthusiasm for expensive military projects, Jay advocated for their completion. In an inaugural address before the state legislature in January 1796, he laid out a comprehensive defensive agenda, contending that the nation must be prepared to "resist and repel hostilities" through the coordinated efforts of state and federal authorities.[9] He then emphasized the commercial necessity of fortifying the port of New York by reminding state lawmakers that it was the sole location "through which the great mass of our exports and imports pass."[10]

Throughout 1796, the planning of harbor defenses moved forward, while the actual work proceeded slowly. An early appropriations bill allocated five thousand pounds for fortifying Oyster, Bedloe's (Bedlow's), and Governors Islands.[11] Matthew Clarkson, one of the commissioners overseeing fortifications, presented Jay with a survey of the state of defenses for the three harbor islands along with recommendations for improvement.[12] Joseph François Mangin, a French architect and military engineer who had replaced Vincent as chief engineer, developed his own plan for fortifying the port.[13] The state government, however, lacked the necessary resources to implement these defensive measures. The New York delegation in Congress led by Edward Livingston sought relief by requesting additional federal monies. They pointed out that the state had already laid out $200,000 for defense yet it had received only $17,522 from the national government. Jay's hopes for federal and state cooperation were dashed as the motion was soundly defeated by a vote of 64–14. Opponents to the measure argued that no additional federal funding

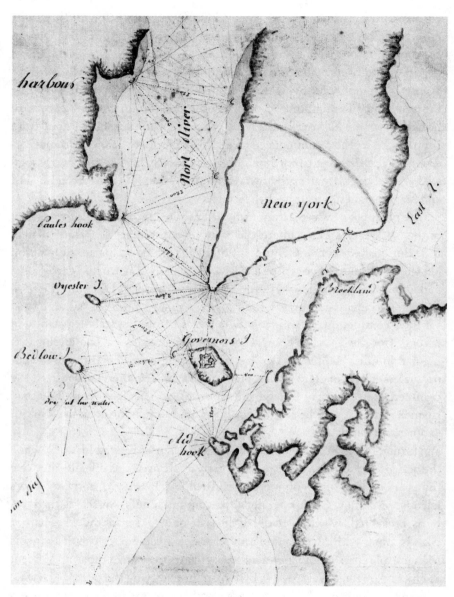

Detail of "A Chart of Newyork harbour," a map of New York Harbor defenses, date unknown. (RG 77, Fortifications Map File, Dr. 142 Sheet 92; National Archives and Records Administration)

would be forthcoming until New York state agreed to both cede the property upon which the fortifications stood to national authorities and discharge its outstanding debts due to the United States.[14] As the year drew to a close, the governor reiterated that fortified positions must be installed for the state's "one port" and lamented that they remained in a state of disrepair.[15]

Financial shortcomings in the following year further delayed any substantial progress on harbor defenses. When Jay learned from Philip Van Cortlandt that the House of Representatives had passed a resolution to take up the issue of fortifications in New York City, he wrote to the State Committee on Fortifications and requested that the members provide Van Cortlandt with an accurate report on the status of defensive preparations. The governor further recommended that state commissioner Ebenezer Stevens and Mangin should travel to Philadelphia to meet with members of Congress in order to influence a more favorable outcome.[16] Stevens proved an ideal appointee as the commissioner already served as an agent for the Department of War. Stevens's mission to the nation's capital failed, however, to convince Congress to appropriate the requisite funds.[17] Jay commiserated with John Williams, the representative for the state's Ninth Congressional District, that the trickle of federal aid had dried up and "that no measures very effectual will be taken by the present Congress".[18] The setback, however, did not shake the governor's conviction that the defensive projects were vital for the long term security of New York City and the United States. "The nation will have reason to be dissatisfied," he confided to Williams, "if after so long an Interval of peace and Prosperity, war should find us in a defenceless state."[19]

Fears of a French attack were stoked by a massive fire that struck the Wall Street area in early December 1796, and by other fires that devastated other port cities. Many frightened residents suspected arson and that pro-French saboteurs set the blazes to spread confusion and foment Jacobin terror.[20] Such fears were seemingly confirmed several months later by John Clarke, a Republican sympathizer from New York, who had served aboard the French privateer La Vengeance. Clarke confessed to Jay that while serving aboard ship, he heard mention of a series of fires that had been deliberately set. More disturbing was Clarke's confession "That the Destruction of all our sea port Towns ∧and Frigates∧ is mediated—[and] that a French Fort Fleet will ∧is expected to co-operate with Incendiaries in that Design."[21]

As tensions mounted between France and the United States during the summer of 1797, Federalists in the nation's legislature once again took up the issue of putting American ports in a state of military preparedness. The Department of War estimated that $200,000 was needed to fulfill this objective, with nearly half of the sum earmarked to fortify the three islands located in New York's inner harbor.[22] Congress eventually allocated $115,000 for maritime fortifications located throughout the nation and permitted state governments to credit the amounts they spent on defensive measures against the debt owed to the United States.[23] New York's access to federal funding, however, was not guaranteed, due to unresolved issues over territorial jurisdiction and unpaid debt.

Expectant of federal aid, Jay wrote to Secretary of War James McHenry and enquired about how the funds for coastal defense would be divided among the respective states.[24] The secretary's response was not encouraging; sums had been provided for "indispensable Repairs to the "Banks and Fort at Mud Island [near Philadelphia]", but no present action had been taken and no plans were yet in place to apply these funds to the defense of New York.[25]

Regardless of the inactivity displayed by the Department of War, Jay remained resolute in his commitment to shoring up fortifications. With negotiations between the United States and her former ally at a standstill, he perceived that the two countries were drifting towards war and that such a conflict would prove disastrous for New York. "A compleat State of Defence at Home," he wrote to Pickering, "appears to me to be the only solid Foundation on which to rest our Hopes of Security; and I regret that more has not been done towards it."[26] Jay then touched on the issue of popular opinion regarding France, noting that the "public Reports and Letters," such as those submitted by Pickering and other officials were instrumental in cultivating support for government policies.[27]

Jay's remarks on the relationship of circulating news and mobilizing public support were borne out by developments during the spring and summer of 1798. As New Yorkers learned of the reception and treatment that the American commissioners received at the hands of Talleyrand and the Directory, their debates over improving defenses and how they would be financed took on greater urgency.[28] The ensuing diplomatic uproar heightened the perceived vulnerability of New York's port to a possible French raid or invasion. This sentiment intensified with the appearance of a congressional report on coastal fortifications showing that the Department of War had neglected the protection of New York City, while leaving a considerable amount of the allocated funds unexpended.[29]

State officials and private citizens in New York were dissatisfied with the national government's response and articulated their grievances and frustrations through a flurry of resolutions, petitions, memorials, and correspondences. The New York Chamber of Commerce complained about the poor condition of the city's defenses to the state assembly, who in turn asked for an updated status and a financial accounting from the governor.[30] Seeking to comply with the Assembly's charge, Jay contacted Commissioner Stevens, Secretary of War McHenry, and Secretary of State Pickering for advice and news. In addition, Stevens was directed to travel to the state capital and present his findings in person before the legislative session drew to a close.[31] Jay also delivered a threefold message to the Assembly members: first, he promised to pass on the latest plans and estimates of harbor defenses; next, he offered reassurances that the national government recognized New York's commercial significance and would thereby provide material and monetary assistance to secure the city and port; and finally, he suggested that the delegates remain in session until they drew up a budgetary plan for fortifications and military stores.[32]

Stevens did not attend the legislative session in Albany because he was, at the behest of the Chamber of Commerce, once again pleading the case for New York before federal officials in Philadelphia.[33] The commissioner shared Jay's concerns that New York City's immense wealth and property "*invite invasion*" and feared that such an event would devastate state trade and national revenue. Stevens offered a sobering assessment of New York's vulnerability, noting that the fortifications on Governors Island and elsewhere remained incomplete and that not "One piece of Ordinance fit for Service" was to be found in Manhattan. With its defenses in disarray, the city would be at the mercy of a single "Twenty Gun privateer". In a telling admission, he hinted that this crisis arose because no clear policy had been established for assigning and coordinating defensive duties. Due to this defect within the federal system of governance, Stevens observed that "it is to be apprehended that the reciprocal reliance on each other which exists on the part of the United States and of this State, arising from circumstances which it is unnecessary to mention, will be the means of preventing either from paying that Attention which is necessary to the defence of this important place".[34]

The subsequent report submitted by Stevens along with another sent by Congressman Livingston did little to assuage Jay's fear that there would be no federal grants for fortifications. Stevens had spoken with both the congressional Committee for the Protection of Commerce and the Defence of the Country and with President Adams. Although the former had assured him that the existing proviso mandating land cessions would be repealed, the president had insisted that he would not recommend that New York receive twenty thousand dollars for military arms and equipment until it agreed to hand over the disputed properties to the United States.[35] Livingston confirmed Stevens's evaluation, passing on the unwelcome news that New York City would in all likelihood not be a beneficiary of an upcoming appropriations bill for coastal defenses.[36]

As funding for New York appeared inextricably linked with ceding territorial jurisdiction, the state legislature took what it hoped would prove an important step in defusing the issue. In early April, lawmakers passed a measure authorizing a commission, comprised of the governor, lieutenant-governor, chancellor, chief justice of the state supreme court, and mayor of New York City, to enforce land cessions on Staten Island and the nearby harbor islands to the United States for the purpose of securing the city and port.[37] The governor wasted little time in informing McHenry of this development and asked the secretary of war which "particular Spots or Parcels of Ground the United States would prefer for these Purposes."[38]

Congress spent two days in April debating the issue of fortifying ports before passing a bill on 3 May.[39] The law appropriated $250,000 for defenses, but did not specify how the amount would be divided among the different locations. The bill repealed the requirement that states must relinquish the property upon which the fortified positions were built, while allowing those indebted to the federal government to be issued a credit for the amount they spent on defensive projects.[40]

While Congress passed its defense bill, the citizens of New York City developed their own initiatives to insure the safety of their community. A committee from the local Chamber of Commerce, which included Ebenezer Stevens, penned a memorial to the Common Council asking for the sum of $40,000 to be raised to supply the city with "18 or 20 heavy Cannon mounted on field Carriages." The committee had considered raising this sum through a "private Contribution," but rejected this option on the grounds that it would place "unequal berthens" on a few private citizens "while the whole of the Community reap the benefit." The Common Council advised the governor to request additional federal support from President Adams. Specifically, the Council desired that an executive order be issued that would requisition artillery pieces held at West Point for the city's defense.[41] Mayor Richard Varick sent the Council's memorial and resolution to Jay, who in turn forwarded the documents to the secretary of war. The governor added a reminder to McHenry of the state's commitment to the populace, observing that "if it be desirable that the people should look up to the National Government for protection, it certainly is equally desirable that they should not be disappointed."[42]

Most New Yorkers by this time approved of measures designed to improve the safety of their persons and property. The intense partisanship that shaped local debates over the militia and other military matters were largely absent when it came to fortifications.[43] Although rare, dissenting voices were not entirely silent. For instance, Varick commented that the recent memorial presented by the Chamber of Commerce was met "with a very cold Reception and some unfriendly Remarks" by Jacob De La Montagnie, an alderman and Republican.[44] Nor was the governor immune from public criticism. During the reelection campaign of 1798, a piece appearing in a Republican-leaning newspaper accused Jay and fellow-Federalist Commissioner James Watson of displaying incompetence and mismanaging the defensive duties assigned to them. The anonymous writer further leveled an implicit charge of cowardice against the governor, by noting that Jay, a commissioned militia officer, had fled from the enemy to Kent, Connecticut, during the Revolutionary War.[45]

Jay refused to publicly respond to such allegations, and he also avoided openly condemning Republicans for blocking the progress of New York's defenses. Nonetheless, his personal correspondence did contain several rebukes against the New York legislature. In a letter to Varick, the governor criticized state lawmakers for not following his earlier advice that they remain sitting in session until a defensive budget was successfully drawn up.[46] Jay's communications with Stevens further reveal his frustration with the state legislature. This body, he complained to the commissioner, lacked a "serious disposition" and therefore had missed an opportunity to lay out efficient plans for financing and constructing New York's defenses.[47] The recent law passed by the legislature to build a state arsenal was likewise censured by Jay who accused the bill's supporters of allocating insufficient sums for the project and of relying too heavily on future funding.[48] Jay completed his critique with a warning that "untill we become more united in our Councils, and less influenced by Considerations in which the public has little Interest, our affairs will not be wisely managed."[49]

Stevens concurred with Jay's assessment that the legislature's misconduct and lack of action would demoralize the populace. He therefore encouraged the governor to journey from Albany, which had been designated as the state capital in 1797, to the threatened port city.[50] Such a move would allay the general mood of anxiety that gripped New York City. "Visit us," Stevens urged, as "we are without a leader, or head, to step forward and purpose vigorous exertions".[51] Stevens also advised that Jay directly contact Adams and other officials in Philadelphia about committing funds for New York fortifications. Stevens had already spoken with the "Heads of the Departments on military matters," but he insisted that *"your writing* would have the most effect, and would be most likely to accomplish the end."[52] The governor, however, had already contacted McHenry weeks earlier, seeking information on the status of federal grants.[53] The Secretary assured Jay that the security of New York was "important to the union," but stopped short of offering concrete support. McHenry then reminded Jay that the War Department had received several "varied calls of the same Nature, each important and claiming attention."[54]

Each faltering effort by the government to secure New York City was now met with growing discontent by the local populace. In early June, the citizenry took matters into its own hands by organizing several committees with a collective design to pressure state and federal officials to commit more resources and energy to fortifying New York's port and harbor. Committees representing New York's seven wards, along with a Committee from the Chamber of Commerce, and a delegation of military officers who had served in the revolutionary war, assembled at City Hall on 8 June. Commissioner Matthew Clarkson presided over the proceedings as participants appointed Alexander Hamilton, Aaron Burr, and Ebenezer Stevens to the Military Committee, a three-person board responsible for overseeing local defensive arrangements.[55]

As representatives of New York's civic committees, Clarkson and the Military Committee lacked formal authority, but this circumstance did not stop them from galvanizing both those in political office as well as the general populace to action. Less than a week after the gathering at City Hall, Clarkson passed on the meeting's agenda to the Common Council. The Council responded that same day with a resolution calling for a loan of $50,000 for the city's defenses.[56] The Military Committee also consulted with the secretary of war when he traveled to New York City in mid-June for the purpose of surveying the harbor. McHenry asked the members for advice on the specific placement of batteries and whether an outer ring of defenses centered on Sandy Hook and the Narrows would be preferable to the current plan of fortifying the islands in the inner harbor.[57] Later that month, the joint committees held another meeting and passed a resolution urging residents to assist with defensive efforts by registering for volunteer labor in their respective wards. Those suffering from "bodily indisposition" had the option of contributing ten shillings as payment for "procuring persons to perform such parts of the duty as may require instruction and practice."[58] Peter Augustus Jay informed his friend in early July that volunteers had nearly finished constructing a battery designed for some forty to fifty artillery pieces and further remarked upon the "Spirit of Resistance" that New Yorkers now displayed against the French enemy.[59]

In addition to these measures, Clarkson wrote to the governor urging him to convene an early session of the state legislature so that lawmakers could take up the work of New York's fortifications.[60] Whereas Jay conceded the merit of Clarkson's recommendation, he nonetheless refrained from taking immediate action. Such an important decision, Jay insisted, required that he first travel southward and personally assess the state of defenses and plans for their improvement. Moreover, Jay contended that it would be premature for the legislators to debate the issue of fortifications before McHenry had even presented his findings to Congress and other federal officials.[61] With a mind to coordinate the various defensive efforts of the governmental and nongovernmental agencies, Jay forwarded his correspondence with Clarkson to Varick and requested that the mayor and the Common Council share their views on the measures proposed by the civic committees.[62] The Council responded with a resolution endorsing an early convening of the state legislature. The Council members further resolved to explore the feasibility of raising more funds for defense, and declared that "the essential Interests of the Community, induce them to unite with the Committee of the Citizens".[63]

After much deliberation, the governor concluded that the ongoing diplomatic crisis left him little choice but to employ his executive authority and order an early meeting of the state legislature. Accordingly, on 2 July, Jay issued an official proclamation instructing the members of New York's Assembly and Senate to convene for a special session in Albany on 9 August.[64] In his speech before the legislature, Jay warned of an impending conflict with France and raised the suggestion that the assembled lawmakers should implement a new taxation scheme to help cover the expense of fortifying New York City.[65]

Jay's calls for legislative action did not fall on deaf ears. On 27 August, lawmakers passed a bill that appropriated $150,000 for repairing and completing fortifications on Manhattan, Governors Island, Bedloe's Island, Oyster Island, and Long Island. Jay was now empowered to directly appoint subordinates who would plan and oversee the construction of fortified works. The team that Jay assembled included experienced individuals like Ebenezer Stevens, who would serve as superintendent of fortifications, Matthew Clarkson, who would assist with financial matters, and Joseph F. Mangin, who would continue as the City's chief engineer. These three officials would report directly to Alexander Hamilton, who in addition to serving as Inspector General of the American army, would soon take on the responsibilities of directing New York's military in concert with Jay.[66]

The new law therefore granted the governor a good deal of authority over defensive matters, yet it also called for close coordination with the president of the United States and his advisors. Whereas Jay bore responsibility for sanctioning the defensive plans to be devised and implemented, he could only authorize the expenditure of funds pending approval from Adams, and therefore needed to consult with Hamilton, the designated federal appointee in charge of supervising harbor fortifications.[67] The resulting arrangement by which the state monies allocated for New York City's defenses were managed by the national government presented local, state, and federal officials with potential disputes over administrative authority and financial resources. Even Hamilton, ever wary of his public reputation, expressed misgivings about taking on such a delicate position. Adams sought to overcome feelings of mistrust and potential conflict by assuring Jay that his administration would not overstep its jurisdiction and would work in close cooperation with New York authorities in matters of defensive preparation.[68]

Whereas the unfolding events of the XYZ affair intensified sectarian divisiveness and rancor in New York City, the efforts to build up harbor defenses during the summer of 1798 offered a notable exception to this trend. Most local Federalist and Republican leaders set aside their political differences and cooperated on resolving the problems of inadequate fortifications and insufficient armament. For instance, rivals Aaron Burr and Alexander Hamilton served together on the recently formed Military Committee. Burr had already chaired a five-person committee in the state assembly that reported on the budget for New York's defense, and he continued to mobilize his colleagues in support of appropriations by working alongside the City's Military Committee.[69] He even traveled to the nation's capital to promote the cause of New York's defenses before federal officials.[70] In this capacity, Burr acted as an effective liaison, coordinating efforts between civic groups in New York City, the state legislature and governor's office in Albany, and the national government in Philadelphia. Hamilton had such great faith in Burr's ability to oversee fortifications that he recommended Burr to serve as his successor as superintendent of harbor defenses.[71]

In late October, Jay laid out a course of action for Hamilton and his fellow appointees. He first called for a thorough and accurate survey of the port to be followed by a drafting of plans of fortified positions. Jay urged his subordinates to work quickly so that the defensive proposals could be submitted for approval by the president and the secretary of war before the next meeting of the state legislature in January.[72]

To facilitate the survey's completion, Jay directed Clarkson to cover related expenses by drawing on the Bank of New York for the amount of $500 and instructed Hamilton to coordinate with Clarkson, Burr, and Stevens on the subsequent plans for fortifications.[73] Jay expressed a desire to attend the proceedings, but "An unexpected and painful Complaint (the Piles)" prevented him from leaving Albany for New York City. Jay further excused his absence with an admission that he lacked a firm understanding of military science and would therefore rely on the judgement of those possessing technical expertise.[74]

In addition to providing funds for the construction of fortified works, the recent defense bill also made a generous allowance for procuring and storing artillery, small arms, and munitions.[75] The shortage of weaponry and military stores had plagued the state's defense efforts since Jay first came to the governor's office. In his opening address before the state legislature in January 1796, Jay quoted New York's Constitution on the necessity of maintaining a "proper magazine of warlike stores" and spoke of ending the state's dependence on foreign sources of weaponry by encouraging the growth of domestic arms manufacturing.[76]

By the fall of 1798, Jay recognized that the state's scarcity of weapons and war materials could not be resolved without overseas assistance.[77] He contacted Rufus King, the American minister to Britain, with a request that King contract for muskets to equip the New York militia.[78] Although the weapons were not available from British sources, less expensive muskets "made on the English model" could be had from sources in Hamburg. Joseph Pitcairn, the American consul in Hamburg, would make the purchasing arrangements for "Three thousand Muskets with Steel ram rods and Bayonets."[79] That spring Jay instructed King to place the order and also directed Matthew Clarkson to handle the financial transactions in New York, allotting $10,000 to cover the costs of a thousand stands of arms with the remainder to be paid at a later date.[80] Pitcairn successfully negotiated for 2,500 muskets with accoutrements at the rate of twenty-six shillings and six pence per stand of arms and arranged for the cargo to be transported by the American ship *Prosper* and the Danish ship *Margaretha Elizabeth*.[81] The two vessels sailed from the port of Hamburg with the *Prosper* arriving in New York in August and the *Margaretha Elizabeth* in October 1799.[82] Stevens reported that the arms had rusted from an exposure to salt water during the voyage, but he reassured the governor that this damage could be repaired at minimal cost.[83]

Finding small arms to defend New York no longer posed a problem for Jay, but he still faced the difficulty of financing the city and harbor defenses. The implementation of fortification plans submitted by Hamilton and his subordinates stalled because the recent defense bill lacked adequate provisions for resolving matters of monetary requests, transfers, and reimbursements. For instance, Stevens informed Hamilton in late November 1798 that Mangin was awaiting payment for his engineering services and that many of the hired laborers and tradesmen also required compensation. Stevens further mentioned that the devastating impact of the yellow fever epidemic upon the local economy made it imperative to pay employees in a timely manner.[84]

The Military Committee and the Corporation of New York City frequently called upon the governor to help settle the financial problems they encountered arising from defense expenditures. When the city of New York exceeded its summer budget of $50,000 for fortifications, Mayor Richard Varick contacted Jay for assistance, pleading that "there must be a new provision by law to relieve us."[85] Lawmakers in Albany, however, could offer little relief as they first had to decide whether to accept the federal funding offered in a recent Congressional bill. The terms of the bill stated that the sums expended on defensive appropriations would be used to pare down the debt that New York owed the United States and included the provision that the places of fortification must be ceded to the federal government.[86] The legislature delayed making a decision, however, even though Jay warned the state senate in March 1799 that continued deliberation would cause "embarrassments" to President Adams.[87]

Without the benefit of further federal assistance and with defense costs running over budget, the legislature voted in April to stop work on existing and new fortifications and to remit funds for any outstanding expenses incurred by these same projects.[88] In the months following this legislation, Hamilton reported that progress on the defensive works "proceeds heavily" and inquired about the availability of additional state funding.[89] Several mechanics and laborers remained unpaid, and Stevens warned that he "should not be surprized should they one & all commence a suit against me."[90]

The passage of two pieces of state legislation in February and March 1800 revitalized the efforts to secure the city and harbor of New York. After months of wavering over whether they should comply with federal statutes, state lawmakers finally ceded Bedloe's, Governors, and Oyster Islands to the United States and approved a $20,000 appropriation to be spent on fortifications over the next five years.[91] Jay welcomed these developments, commenting to Clarkson that "The unavoidable Delays which have retarded the measures to be taken for fortifying the port of New York are I hope now at an end."[92] The governor envisioned setting up an administrative apparatus for overseeing defense matters similar to the one established some two years earlier. He would seek the approval of President Adams and Samuel Dexter, the new Secretary of War, for major proposals, while state and local officials would closely coordinate with federal authorities on the placement and construction of fortifications.[93] Seeking trusted subordinates to continue the project, the governor tapped Stevens to purchase materials, hire laborers, and superintend the work, and asked Clarkson to take charge of the financial accounts.[94] For the role of chief engineer, Jay followed the advice of Samuel Dexter and selected Jean Xavier Bureaux de Puzy, a French émigré politician who had served on Lafayette's staff.[95]

Yet Jay's enthusiasm was misplaced. As his tenure in office drew to a close, the prospect of making significant progress toward the completion of fortifications grew increasingly remote. The recent defense initiatives outlined by the governor were not fully implemented, and Hamilton, Stevens, and Clarkson—his trusted and experienced colleagues—were worn down by fatigue and frustration and expressed doubt that they would continue in their duties. Clarkson pointed out to Jay the difficulties of working within a complex bureaucratic system while being deprived of just compensation. Clarkson also revealed his concern that rumors were circulating of Jay's imminent retirement. If the governor did not intend to seek another term in public office, Clarkson avowed that he would step down from his post.[96] Moreover, by late 1800, the threat of a French assault on New York City and the American seaboard had diminished considerably with ongoing negotiations and the subsequent signing of the Treaty of Mortefontaine. While the construction of harbor defenses never entirely ceased, state lawmakers now saw little advantage to be gained by appropriating funds for defensive measures amid this shifting political climate.

1. Clinton to the New York State Legislature, 7 Jan. 1794, and 3 Jan. 1795, *NYGM*, 2: 333, 349; *Albany Gazette*, 9 Jan.; *Columbian Gazetteer* (New York), 16 Jan; *Catskill Packet*, 21 Jan. 1794; *American Minerva* (New York), 13 Jan.; *Daily Advertiser* and *Herald* (both New York), 14 Jan.; *Mott and Hurtin's New-York Weekly Chronicle*, 15 Jan. 1795.

2. *ASP: Military Affairs*, 1: 63.

3. Bartholomew Dandridge Jr. to Henry Knox, 28 Mar. 1794, *PGW: PS*, 15 459.

4. "An Act to provide for the Defense of certain Ports and Harbors in the United States," and "An Act making Appropriations for the Support of the Military Establishment of the United States, for the Year One Thousand Seven Hundred and Ninety-Four," 20 and 21 Mar. 1794, *Stat.*, 1: 345–46, and 346–47.

5. The First System of Coastal Fortifications spanned 1794–1807 and constituted a system more

in name than in actual practice. Although the federal government provided troops, funding, and resources, there was little centralized planning and coordination between national and state authorities. Robert S. Browning III, "Shielding the Republic: American Coastal Defense Policy in the Nineteenth-Century" (Ph.D. diss.: Univ. of Wisconsin–Madison, 1981), 18–19.

6. "An Act authorizing the Erection of Fortification, within this State," 26 Mar. 1794, *N.Y. State Laws*, (1777–97), 3: 133–136. The committee members were George Clinton, Matthew Clarkson, James Watson, Richard Varick, Nicholas Fish, Ebenezer Stevens, and Abijah Hammond. A law authorizing payment to the commissioners for fortification work was passed a year later. "An Act making further Provision for Fortifications within this state," 6 Apr. 1795, *N.Y. State Laws*, 18th sess. (1795), 30.

7. *ASP: Military Affairs*, 1: 77–81; *Daily Advertiser* (New York), 19 Oct.; *Gazette of the United States* (Philadelphia), and *Philadelphia Gazette*, both 20 Oct.; *American Mercury* (Hartford), 25 Oct.; *Albany Gazette*, 29 Oct 1798.

8. Arthur P. Wade, "Artillerists and Engineers: The Beginnings of American Seacoast Fortifications, 1794–1815" (Ph.D. diss.: Kansas State Univ., 1977), 18–19.

9. JJ's Address to the New York State Legislature, 6 Jan. 1796, below.

10. Ibid.

11. "An Act for the Payment of certain Officers of Government, and other contingent Expences," 11 Apr. 1796, *N.Y. State Laws*, 19th sess. (1796), 46.

12. JJ to John Williams, 28 Jan. 1796, LbkC, N: Governor's Lbk. 1 (EJ: 02987); *Greenleaf's New York Journal*, 8 Mar. 1796; JJ's Message to the New York State Assembly, 10 Feb. 1796, *NYGM*, 2: 370–71.

13. JJ to McHenry, 19 Apr. 1796, LbkC, N: Governor's Lbk. 1 (EJ: 02999).

14. *Annals*, 4: 1360–73. The issue of paying off New York's debt to the national government continued to influence the debates over federal aid for New York's fortifications. See JJ to John Williams, 24 Feb. 1797, below.

15. JJ's Address to the New York State Legislature, [1 Nov. 1796], below.

16. *Annals*, 4: 1672; JJ to Van Cortlandt, 4 Jan. 1797, LbkC, N: Governor's Lbk. 1 (EJ: 03057); JJ to Matthew Clarkson, Richard Varick, and the Commissioners for Fortifying the Port and City of New York, 4 Jan. 1797, below.

17. Stevens to JJ, 12 Feb. 1797, letter not found, but referenced in JJ to Stevens, 24 Feb. 1797, ALS, NHi: Stevens (EJ: 00686).

18. JJ to Williams, 24 Feb. 1797, below. The letters of Williams and Stevens were taken under consideration by legislators in Albany. JJ's Message to the New York State Assembly, 19 Jan. 1797, ALS, NyRyJHC; *Albany Gazette*, 30 Jan. 1797; *N.Y. Assembly Journal*, 20th sess. (1796–97), 60, 66.

19. JJ to Williams, 24 Feb. 1797, below.

20. For more on the fires that occurred in New York City and elsewhere, see JJ to TP, 8 June 1797, and note 4, below.

21. For more on Clarke's confession and his service on *La Vengeance*, see ibid., and note 2, below.

22. *ASP: Military Affairs*, 1: 117–18.

23. *Annals*, 5: 298–324; "An Act to provide for the further Defence of the Ports and Harbors of the United States," 23 June 1797, *Stat.*, 1: 521–22.

24. JJ to McHenry, 17 July 1797, LbkC, N: Governor's Lbk. 1 (EJ: 03086); JJ to McHenry, 14 Sept. 1797, letter not found, but referenced in McHenry to JJ, 19 Sept. 1797, C, NNC, enclosed in JJ to Clarkson, 4 Oct. 1797; C, NNC (EJ: 12306); LbkC, N: Governor's Lbk. 1 (EJ: 03094).

25. McHenry to JJ, 19 Sept. 1797, C, NNC, enclosed in JJ to Clarkson, 4 Oct. 1797; C, NNC (EJ: 12306), LbkC, N: Governor's Lbk. 1 (EJ: 03094).

26. JJ to TP, 13 Nov. 1797, ALS, MHi: Pickering (EJ: 04784); *WJ*, 1: 284–85; *HPJ*, 4: 233–34.

27. Ibid.

28. For more on the XYZ Affair and the subsequent hostilities with France, see the editorial note "John Jay and the Response to the XYZ Affair in New York," below.

29. *Commercial Advertiser*, and *Greenleaf's New York Journal* (both New York), 14 Mar.; *Spectator* (New York), 17 Mar. 1798; *Annals*, 5: 1246–48.

30. *N.Y. Assembly Journal*, 21st sess. (January 1798), 241, 246–47. The Assembly received six additional petitions from New York residents, and Stevens referenced at least one of them in a letter to the governor. *N.Y. Assembly Journal*, 21st sess. (January 1798), 255; Stevens to JJ, 22 Mar. 1798, ALS, NHi: Jay (EJ: 00871). The Chamber of Commerce memorial was also presented before Congress on 26 Mar. where it was referred to the Committee for the Protection of Commerce and the Defence of the Country. *Annals*, 5: 1312.

31. JJ to Stevens, 20 Mar. 1798, with enclosure of the New York State Assembly, 19 Mar. 1798, ALS, NHi: Stevens (EJ: 00870); LbkC, N: Governor's Lbk. 1 (EJ: 03132); JJ to McHenry, 20 Mar. 1798, with enclosure of the New York State Assembly; 19 Mar. 1798, LbkC, N: Governor's Lbk. 1 (EJ: 03130); JJ to TP, 20 Mar. 1798, LbkC, N: Governor's Lbk. 1 (EJ: 03131). JJ noted that he forwarded his letter to TP in case McHenry "should be absent or otherwise prevented from answering it soon".

32. JJ's Message to the New York State Assembly, [21 Mar. 1798], below. For the governor's intelligence update, see JJ's Message to the New York State Assembly, 5 Apr. 1798, *NYGM*, 2: 418–19.

33. Comfort Sands to JJ, 4 Apr. 1798, ALS, NHi: Jay (EJ: 00897).

34. Stevens to JJ, 22 Mar. 1798, ALS, NHi: Jay (EJ: 00871).

35. Stevens to JJ, 3 Apr. 1798, ALS, NHi: Stevens (EJ: 00872).

36. Livingston to JJ, 31 Mar. 1798, ALS, NHi: Jay (EJ: 00896). For the governor's reply, see JJ to Livingston, 9 Apr. 1798, LbkC, N: Governor's Lbk. 1 (EJ: 03138).

37. "An Act to Cede the Jurisdiction of Certain Lands in this State to the United Laws," 6 Apr. 1798, *N.Y. State Laws*, 21st sess. (January 1798), 535.

38. JJ to McHenry, 7 Apr. 1798, LbkC, N: Governor's Lbk. 1 (EJ: 03137).

39. *Annals*, 5: 1380–83, 1393–1402.

40. "An Act supplementary to the Act providing for the further Defence of the Ports and Harbors of the United States," 3 May 1798, *Stat.*, 1: 554–55.

41. The memorial and resolution are found in "Papers relative to the Defence of the City of New York 1798," n.d., C, NHi: Jay (EJ: 00899). See also *MCCNYC*, 28 and 30 Apr. 1798, 2: 433, 435–36.

42. Varick to JJ, 2 May 1798, ALS, NHi: Jay (EJ: 00898); JJ to McHenry, 7 May 1798, LbkC, N: Governor's Lbk. 1 (EJ: 03153).

43. See the editorial note "Militia Matters in New York State," below.

44. Varick to JJ, 2 May 1798, ALS, NHi: Jay (EJ: 00898).

45. *Greenleaf's New York Journal*, and *Argus, Greenleaf's New Daily Advertiser* (both New York), 21 Apr. 1798. The episode referred to by the newspaper essay occurred in October 1777 while JJ presided as chief justice of the newly constituted State Supreme Court in Kingston. JJ and Sally, and other government officials, had to flee the state capital to Kent, Conn., upon learning that the British were approaching. These troops commanded by John Vaughn were heading up the Hudson in support of Burgoyne's forces near Saratoga. During their stay in Kent, the Jays boarded with Joel Bordwell and his family. See JJ to Charles De Witt, 8 Oct. 1777, Tr, NKiSH (EJ: 12088), and Bordwell to JJ, [2 Oct. 1787], *JJSP*, 4: 551–52. For another newspaper piece critiquing JJ's decision to flee Kingston, see the editorial note "Militia Matters in New York State," below. For more on newspaper criticisms of JJ's reelection campaign, see the editorial note "John Jay Wins Reelection as Governor in 1798," below.

46. JJ to Varick, 7 May 1798, LbkC, N: Governor's Lbk. 1 (EJ: 03154); JJ's Message to the New York State Assembly, [21 Mar. 1798], below.

47. JJ to Stevens, 26 May 1798, below.

48. "An Act relative to the Public Building in the City of Albany, and for erecting an Arsenal in the City of New-York," 30 Mar. 1798, *N.Y. State Laws*, 21st sess. (January 1798), 418–19. JJ had previously warned lawmakers that they needed to pass legislation authorizing the construction of a state arsenal in New York City. On 10 Aug. 1798, the governor informed the state assembly that the existing bill did not provide enough funds for building the arsenal. A modified bill passed later that month empowering JJ to determine the costs, terms, and location of the arsenal's construction. JJ's Address to the New York State Legislature, [2 Jan. 1798], below; "An Act for the further Defence of this State, and for other Purposes," 27 Aug. 1798, *N.Y. State Laws*, 22nd sess. (August 1798), 548.

49. JJ to Stevens, 26 May 1798, below.

50. On Albany becoming the state capital, see the editorial note "The Capital Moves to Albany," below.

51. Stevens to JJ, 30 May 1798, below.

52. Ibid.

53. JJ to McHenry, 7 May 1798, LbkC, N: Governor's Lbk. 1 (EJ: 03153).

54. McHenry to JJ, 15 May 1798, copied in JJ to Stevens, 4 June 1798, ALS, NHi: Stevens (EJ: 00904).

55. *Greenleaf's New York Journal*, 13 June 1798. For an overview of the formation of the various committees, see Clarkson to JJ, [10 June 1798], note 1, below, and *PAH*, 21: 483–84n2.

56. *MCCNYC*, 13 June 1798, 2: 446–47. The Bank of New York authorized the loan of $50,000 and distributed the funds in $10,000 increments. *MCCNYC*, 25 June, 31 July, 20 Aug., 10 Sept., 2 Oct. 1798, 2: 452, 458, 462, 467, 473. The following year, the state treasury reimbursed New York City for the amount of the loan. *MCCNYC*, 14 Oct. 1799, 2: 577.

57. McHenry to AH, 4 June 1798, *PAH*, 21: 484; McHenry to JJ, 6 June 1798, C, NHi: Jay (EJ: 00873); *New-York Gazette*, 13 June 1798; McHenry to the Military Committee of New York City, 13 June 1798, *PAH*, 21: 513–15. The Military Committee recommended that the defensive positions for New York City remain centered at Governors, Bedloe's, and Oyster Islands. AH, Burr, and Stevens to McHenry, [14 June 1798], *PAH*, 21: 515–17.

58. *Commercial Advertiser*, and *New-York Gazette* (both New York), 20 June 1798. See also *Spectator* (New York), 4 July 1798.

59. PAJ to Augustus Brevoort Woodward, 8 July 1798, ALS, NNC (EJ: 90166).

60. Clarkson to JJ, [10 June 1798], below.

61. JJ to Clarkson, 14 June 1798, below. JJ followed his own advice and arrived in New York City on 23 June. JJ to William North, 25 June 1798, below.

62. JJ to Varick, 27 June 1798, enclosure not found, LbkC, N: Governor's Lbk. 1 (EJ: 03161), and version including Varick to JJ, 29 June 1798, and fragment of JJ to Clarkson, 14 June 1798, CS, NNC (EJ: 09842).

63. Meeting of the Common Council of New York City, 27 June 1798, C, NNC (EJ: 09840), *MCCNYC*, 29 June 1798, 2: 452–53.

64. Proclamation Summoning an Early Session of the New York State Legislature, [2 July 1798], below.

65. JJ's Address to the New York State Legislature, [9 Aug. 1798], below.

66. For more on AH's appointment, see the editorial note "Hamilton takes Command," below.

67. "An Act for the further Defence of this State, and for other Purposes," 27 Aug. 1798, *N.Y. State Laws*, 22nd sess. (August 1798), 547–49.

68. JA to JJ, 17 Oct. 1798, ALS, NNC (EJ: 05437); copy of document in JJ's hand included in JJ to AH, 24 Oct. 1798, ALS, DLC: Hamilton (EJ: 10783).

69. Phineas Bowman, Adam Comstock, Gaylord Griswold, and Amos Hall, served with Burr on the Assembly committee. *N.Y. Assembly Journal*, 21st sess. (January 1798), 185; See also Burr to Stevens, 20 July, 8 and 10 Aug. 1798, and the editorial note "New York Defense in the Quasi-War," *PAB*, 1: 348, 349, 349–50, 344–48.

70. AH to Oliver Wolcott, 28 June 1798, *PAH*, 21: 521–22.

71. For more on AH's recommendation of Burr, see the editorial note "Hamilton takes Command," and note 16, below.

72. JJ to AH, 24 Oct. 1798, includes copy of JA to JJ, 17 Oct. 1798, ALS, DLC: Hamilton (EJ: 10783); LbkC, N: Governor's Lbk. 1 (EJ: 03176); *PAH*, 22: 211–12.

73. JJ to Clarkson, 5 Nov. 1798, ALS, NNYSL: Jay (EJ: 02873); LbkC, N: Governor's Lbk. 1 (EJ: 03181); JJ to AH, 5 Nov. 1798, ALS, DLC: Hamilton (EJ: 10785); LbkC, N: Governor's Lbk. 1 (EJ: 03183); *PAH*, 22: 225–26.

74. JJ to AH, 5 Nov. 1798, ALS, DLC: Hamilton (EJ: 10785); LbkC, N: Governor's Lbk. 1 (EJ: 03183); *PAH*, 22: 225–26. AH replied two weeks later that the survey of the port was completed, but that he had not consulted with professional engineers. AH to JJ, 19 Nov. 1798, ALS, DLC: Hamilton (EJ: 10788); *PAH*, 22: 251–52. For JJ's reply, enclosed in a letter to Matthew Clarkson, see JJ to AH, 26 Nov. 1798, LbkC, N: Governor's Lbk. 1 (EJ: 03190); ALS, DLC: Hamilton (EJ: 10789); *PAH*, 23: 265–66; JJ to Clarkson, 26 Nov. 1798, C, NNYSL: Jay (EJ: 02868).

75. The bill allocated $165,000 for arms, ammunitions, and an arsenal. "An Act for the further Defence of this State, and for other Purposes," 27 Aug. 1798, *N.Y. State Laws*, 22nd sess. (August 1798), 548.

76. JJ's Address to the New York State Legislature, 6 Jan. 1796, below. For New York's ongoing efforts and continuing problems with obtaining arms and ammunition, see Stevens to JJ, 6 Jan. 1798, below.

77. JJ continued to advocate for domestic manufacturers to supply the state with weapons. In February 1799, he wrote to the state assembly about constructing an arsenal in Albany. In his remarks, the governor recommended that mechanics should be hired for the purpose of crafting firearms for the militia and concluded that "To depend on foreign supplies for the articles necessary for our own defence does not appear to be prudent." *Albany Gazette*, 1 Mar.; *Commercial Advertiser* (New York) (supplement), and *Whitestown Gazette*, 4 Mar.; *Spectator* (New York), 6 Mar. 1799; *N.Y. Assembly Journal*, 21 Mar. 1799, 22nd sess., 2nd meeting (1799), 133–34; JJ's Message to the New York State Assembly, 21 Mar. 1799, *NYGM*, 2: 436–37; Contract for construction of Albany Arsenal between JJ and Phillip Hooker and Elisha Putnam, 29 Apr. 1799, D, N (EJ: 03713).

78. JJ to RK, 30 Sept. 1798, ALS, NHi: King (EJ: 00705); LbkC, N: Governor's Lbk. 1 (EJ: 03171); copy found in RK to Joseph Pitcairn, 18 Dec. 1798, ALS, OCHP: Pitcairn (EJ: 01534).

79. RK to JJ, 7 Dec. 1798, ALS, NNC (EJ: 06701); C, NHi: King (EJ: 00877); C, NNC (EJ: 08630); copy located in RK to Pitcairn, 18 Dec. 1798, ALS, OCHP: Pitcairn (EJ: 01534). JJ mentioned that he included an extract in his letter to Matthew Clarkson dated 18 Apr. 1799, but the extract has not been found.

80. JJ to RK, 17 Apr. 1799, ALS, NHi: King (EJ: 00704); Dft, NNC (EJ: 06712); JJ to Clarkson, 18 Apr. 1799, LS, NNC (EJ: 09789); Dft, NNC, (EJ: 09798); C, NHi: Misc. Mss Jay (EJ: 10075); LbkC, NHi: King (EJ: 04479). For Clarkson's response, see his letter to JJ, 23 April 1799, C, NNC (EJ: 11461).

81. RK to JJ, 19 Apr. 1799, C, NHi: King (EJ: 00878); Pitcairn to JJ, 21 May 1799, C, NNC (EJ: 08659); RK to JJ, 31 May 1799, C, NNC (EJ: 08631); C, NHI: King (EJ: 00880); Dupl, NNC (EJ:

11460); invoice covering 4 May–9 July 1799 by Pitcairn, 9 July 1799, Dupl, NNC (EJ: 08663); Pitcairn to JJ, 13 Aug. 1799, ALS, NNC (08867).

82. *Massachusetts Mercury* (Boston), 13 Aug. 1799; Clarkson to JJ, 21 Oct. 1799, ALS, NNC (EJ: 09790); C, NNC (EJ: 09802).

83. Stevens to JJ, 5 Sept. 1799, C, NHi: Stevens (EJ: 03614). JJ had another opportunity to purchase muskets manufactured in Hamburg in November 1799 when the mercantile firm of Le Roy, Bayard, & McEvers proposed to sell him 3,000 stands of arms for use by the state militia. JJ, however, declined the offer. JJ to Messrs Le Roy, Bayard, & McEvers, 11 Nov. 1799, C, NN (EJ: 01029).

84. Stevens to AH, 29 Nov. 1798, *PAH*, 22: 266–67. For the yellow fever epidemic, see the editorial note "John Jay and the Yellow Fever Epidemics," above.

85. Varick to JJ, 10 Jan. 1799, ALS, NNC (EJ: 09295).

86. "An Act respecting Balances against certain States, by the Commissioners appointed to settle the Accounts between the United States and the several States," 15 Feb. 1799, *Stat.*, 1: 616–17.

87. JJ's Message to the New York State Senate, 22 Mar. 1799, *NYGM*, 2: 440; *N.Y. Senate Journal*, 22nd sess., 2nd meeting (1799), 94.

88. "An Act for the Payment of certain Officers of Government, and other contingent Expences," 3 Apr. 1799, *N.Y. State Laws*, 22nd sess. 2nd meeting (1799), 843, 844. For an overview of the expenses for fortifications and defenses and the payment of debts owed to the United States, see the report by Samuel Jones, *N.Y. Assembly Journal*, 16 Jan. 1800, 23rd sess. (1800), 10–16.

89. AH to JJ, 29 July 1799, ALS, NNC (EJ: 05633); C, DLC: Hamilton (EJ: 10791); *PAH*, 23: 291–92; JJ to AH, 3 Aug. 1799, ALS, DLC: Hamilton (EJ: 10792); Dft, NNC (EJ: 05651); *PAH*, 23: 302.

90. Stevens to AH, 21 Oct. 1799, *PAH*, 23: 544.

91. "An Act to cede to the United States the Jurisdiction of certain Islands situate in and about the Harbour of New-York," 15 Feb. 1800, *N.Y. State Laws*, 23rd sess. (1800), 7; "An Act complying with the Act of Congress respecting Balances reported against certain States by the Commissioners appointed to settle the Accounts between the United States and the several States, 23 Mar. 1800, *N.Y. State Laws*, 23rd sess. (1800), 114–17; *N.Y. Assembly Journal*, 6 Mar. 1800, 23rd sess. (1800), 144–45; TP to JJ, 5 May 1800, C, MHi: Pickering (EJ: 04847). A longstanding dispute over ownership rights delayed the transfer of Oyster Island to federal authorities until June 1808.

92. JJ to Clarkson, 21 Aug. 1800, ALS, NNYSL: Jay (EJ: 02860).

93. Dexter to JJ, 28 June 1800, C, NNYSL: Jay (EJ: 02857); C, DLC: Jefferson (EJ: 10221); *N.Y. Assembly Journal*, 5 Nov. 1800, 24th sess. (1800–1801), 8; JJ's Message to the New York State Assembly, 5 Nov. 1800, *NYGM*, 2: 469.

94. JJ to Clarkson, 21 Aug. 1800, ALS, NNYSL: Jay (EJ: 02860).

95. For more about the hiring of de Puzy and his role in improving New York's fortifications, see McHenry to JJ, 10 May 1800, MiU-C: McHenry; *Papers of the War Department 1784 to 1800*, http://wardepartmentpapers.org/document.php?id=39547 (accessed Jan. 2018); McHenry to Hamilton, 12 May 1800, *PAH*, 24: 476–77; DLC: McHenry; Dexter to JJ, 28 June 1800, C, NNYSL: Jay (EJ: 02857); JJ to Clarkson, 21 Aug. 1800, ALS, NNYSL: Jay (EJ: 02860); Dexter to JJ, 30 Aug. 1800, ALS, MB (EJ: 02671); JJ to Clarkson, 1 Oct. 1800, NNYSL: Jay (EJ: 02861).

96. Clarkson to JJ, 27 Aug. 1800, ALS, NNC (EJ: 09791); C, NNC (EJ: 09803).

Address to the New York State Legislature

[New York, 6 January 1796]

Gentlemen of the Senate and Assembly,

PERMIT me to avail myself of this first opportunity, which has occurred, of expressing through you to my constituents, the high sense I entertain of that esteem and confidence which prompted them to place me in the station I now fill. Fully apprized of the duties which it imposes upon me, my best endeavours shall be exerted to fulfill them; and I flatter myself, that in the course of my administration, the sincerity of this assurance will be found to rest on better evidence than professions can afford.

To regard my fellow-citizens with an equal eye—to cherish and advance merit—wherever found—to consider the national and state constitutions and governments, as being equally established by the will of the people—to respect and support the constituted authorities under each of them—and in general, to exercise the powers vested in me, with energy, impartiality and prudence, are obligations of which I perceive and acknowledge the full force.

I concur in the sentiments and adopt the language of our excellent and illustrious President, in observing that "we could not have met at any period, when more than at the present, the situation of our public affairs afforded just cause for mutual congratulations;"[1] and I make this observation with the greater pleasure, as in the general welfare of the union, this State participates so largely.

The rapid increase of our population—the flourishing state of our agriculture and commerce—the extension of our external and internal navigation—the progress of learning and science, so essential to rational liberty and good government, and the uncommon degree of wealth and plenty, which follow the footsteps of industry and the arts of peace, in all their walks, unite with numerous other blessings, in affording us abundant reason to rejoice, to be content, and to be grateful.

But although national prosperity can neither be attained nor preserved without the favour of Providence; so neither can it be attained or preserved without the subordinate instrumentality of those means, which providence provides, and reason directs us to use.

There is no state of human happiness, public or private, so perfect or secure, as to dispense with that constant care and superintendence, which all our affairs require; and which you will now find it expedient to extend to several interesting objects.

It has been often and justly observed, that in order to preserve peace, every nation should not only treat others with justice and respect, but also be in constant readiness to resist and repel hostilities. Imbecility invites insult and aggression: and the experience of ages proves, that they are the most secure against war, who are the best prepared to meet it. Although it belongs to our national government to provide for the defence of the United States, and although that great object will doubtless continue to receive as well as to claim their attention, yet it is also highly interesting, that nothing properly depending on us be omitted to give efficacy to their laws and measures.

Having but one port through which the great mass of our exports and imports pass, the importance of fortifying it has been generally seen, and considerable progress has been made in executing the plans formed under the direction of the general government for that purpose. Much yet remains to be done and if from the details which will be laid before you, it shall appear that further aids on the part of this state would be proper, I am persuaded they will be readily afforded.[2]

Difficulties have been experienced in importing from foreign countries sufficient quantities of arms and ammunition, and the present scarcity of those articles in general, and of one of the most essential of them in particular, is a disagreeable circumstance.

It certainly is very desirable that we should not depend on foreigners for the means of defence, and therefore that the manufactures necessary to furnish these supplies, should be encouraged and patronized by the legislature. The constitution of this State expressly directs that "a proper magazine of warlike stores, proportionate to the number of inhabitants, be forever, at the expense of this State, and by acts of the legislature, maintained and continued in every county in this State."[3] They who formed this constitution, had been taught by severe experience, that the day of alarm and battle was not the best season for seeking and procuring these important stores.

Laws and regulations, however carefully devised, frequently prove defective in practice, and as the regulation of the militia pursuant to the act of Congress, merits constant attention, it may be useful to enquire whether experience has pointed out the necessity of any amendments which, consistently with that act, may be made in our law on this subject.[4]

There is an article in the constitution, which by admitting of two different constructions, has given rise to opposite opinions, and may give occasion to disagreeable contests and embarrassments. The article, I allude to, is the one which ordains that the person administering the government for the time being, shall be president of the council of appointment and have a casting voice, but no other vote; and with advice and consent of the said council, shall appoint all the officers, which the constitution directs so to be appointed.[5] Whether this does by just construction, assign to him the exclusive right of nomination? is a question, which though not of recent date, still remains to be definitively settled. Circumstanced as I am in relation to this question, I think it proper merely to state it, and to submit to your consideration the expediency of determining it by a declaratory act.

The more the principles of government are investigated, the more it becomes apparent, that those powers and those only, should be annexed to each office and department, which properly belong to them. If this maxim be just, the policy of uniting the office of the keeper of the great seal, with that of governor, is far from being unquestionable. The powers of the former not being necessary to the latter. It seems, on general principles, more proper that important acts, made or agreed to by the governor, should be validated and rendered binding on the state by an officer, who did not officially participate in them, than by himself.

Important cases occasionally arise, in which a competent knowledge of the law, and that kind of discretion which results from it, are necessary to decide, whether the sanction of the great seal ought to be given or to be withheld, and although persons not possessed of those acquirements, may administer the government very ably in other respects, yet in that respect they would be liable to commit mistakes not easy to correct.

One great object of which a people free always enlightened and governed by laws of their own making, will never lose sight, is that those laws be, so[6] judiciously applied and faithfully executed as to secure to them the peaceable and uninterrupted enjoyment of their rights. To this end it is necessary, and sound policy certainly requires, that the dispensation of justice should invariably be committed to the men the best qualified to perform that very interesting task. With this policy the present situation of the Chancellor and of the Judges of the Supreme Court does not appear to me to correspond. Their salaries, not being more than adequate to their current expenses, yield little or no surplus to form a provision for their families. Instead of the tranquillity, the domestic comforts and the exemption from anxious cares, which sensibility claims for declining years, they must, when those years arrive, retire to private life, without having received from their country the means of enjoying it. These circumstances have no tendency to invite able and distinguished lawyers, few of whom possess ample patrimonies, to exchange their lucrative practice, for seats on the bench, and yet by such men only should those seats be filled. Permit me, therefore to submit to your consideration, whether justice, public good, and the honor of the state, do not strongly recommend, that some provision be made for such of these judicial officers as, having long and faithfully served their country in that capacity, come to the age, at which, according to an article in the constitution, their commissions expire.

There is another subject, also belonging to the judiciary department, respecting which some legislative provision has become very requisite. So great is the extent and population of the state, and so numerous and frequent are our courts, that the Attorney General cannot possibly manage all the prosecutions (existing at the same time in different counties) which demand his care and attention. It continues to be worthy of consideration, how far the severe penalties prescribed by our laws in particular cases admit of mitigation, and whether certain establishments for confining, employing, and reforming criminals, will not immediately become indispensable.[7]

The measures which have been taken pursuant to the laws respecting the management of our affairs with certain of the Indian tribes, together with the results of those measures, and a variety of documents on that and other subjects, will be communicated and laid before you.[8]

While on the one hand we all lament the distresses occasioned by the sickness which lately prevailed in this city, it becomes us, on the other hand, to acknowledge with gratitude that divine interposition by which its extent and duration were so limited. The expenses which that uncommon and unexpected calamity made indispensable, exceed the sum assigned by law for such purposes; and the precautions which in the city of Albany it was judged prudent to take, in order to prevent the inhabitants from being involved in the like calamity, demanded expenditures which yet remain to be provided for.

These accounts will be laid before you; together with those which respect the application of the moneys granted for the relief of the refugees from St. Domingo, residing here. The situation of these unfortunate people still continues to be truly distressing and to interest our compassion.[9]

The wisdom of our laws has ordained that every place shall maintain its own poor: but it appears to me proper to remark, that by the events of the desolating war between many of the European powers, and by the advantages which this country offers to emigrants, a great number of persons are induced to come to this state, without other resources than what the benevolence of our citizens or other adventitious circumstances may furnish. As these people do not properly belong to any particular place in this or the neighbouring states, would it not be right to consider those of them, who may be real objects of charity, as the poor of the state, and to provide for them accordingly.[10]

The intimate connection that subsists between our agriculture, commerce, and navigation, strongly recommends the policy of facilitating and multiplying the means of intercourse between the different parts of the state. This topic embraces many others, which will not escape your discernment, and which, on investigation, will be found to be highly interesting. Indeed the improvements of which our local situation and civil policy are susceptible, are so various, as to afford you an arduous and complicated, but still not an unpleasing, task. It is a task which cannot be properly performed without much time, application, and well-digested information, for it will always be found more difficult, and also more useful, to legislate well, than to legislate much.

There is reason, however, to expect, that, in the course of the session, considerable progress will be made; and that the benefits resulting to our fellow-citizens, from your attention to their interests, will afford additional proofs, that their confidence cannot be so discreetly placed, as in the wisdom and patriotism of their real and responsible representatives. That wisdom and patriotism will, I am persuaded, give to your deliberations all the advantages which accompany moderation and concord; and you may rely on my readiness to co-operate with you in every measure for augmenting and securing to our constituents, the numerous blessings they derive from the happy state of peace, liberty and safety, which by the favor of Heaven, we enjoy.

JOHN JAY.

PtD, *Argus, Greenleaf's New Daily Advertiser, Daily Advertiser,* and *American Minerva* (all New York), 7 Jan.; reprinted, *Philadelphia Gazette,* and *Herald* (New York), 9 Jan.; *Aurora General Advertiser* (Philadelphia), 12 Jan.; *Federal Gazette,* and *Telegraphe* (both Baltimore), 14 Jan.; *Albany Gazette,* 15 Jan.; *Gazette of the United States* (Philadelphia), 16 Jan.; *Impartial Herald* (Newburyport), 9 Feb. 1796; *N.Y. Assembly Journal,* 19th sess. (1796), 4–7; *N.Y. Senate Journal,* 19th sess. (1796), 4–6; *NYGM,* 2: 358–66. For the legislature's response and JJ's reply, see *N.Y. Assembly Journal,* 12 and 13 Jan. 1796, 19th sess. (1796), 19–20, 22; *N.Y. Senate Journal,* 12 and 13 Jan. 1796, 19th sess. (1796), 10–11, 12.

1. GW opened his address before Congress on 8 Dec. 1795, with the following statement: "I trust I do not deceive myself while I indulge the persuasion that I have never met you at any period, when, more than at the present, the situation of our public affairs has afforded just cause for mutual congratulation, and for inviting you to join with me in profound gratitude to the Author of all Good, for the numerous and extraordinary blessings we enjoy." *Annals,* 4: [10]; *PGW: PS,* 19: 221.

2. For the efforts to fortify and arm New York City during JJ's governorship, see the editorial note "Defending New York," above.

3. JJ is citing Art. 40 of the state constitution, *N.Y. State Laws,* (1777–97), 1: 14.

4. For JJ's efforts to reform the state militia, see the editorial note "Militia Matters in New York State," below.

5. Article 23 of New York's Constitution reads: "That all officers, other than those who by this constitution are directed to be otherwise appointed, shall be appointed in manner following, to wit;

The assembly shall, once in every year, openly nominate and appoint one of the senators from each great district, which senators shall form a council for the appointment of the said officers, of which the governor for the time being, or the lieutenant governor, or the president of the senate, when they shall respectively administer the government, shall be president, and have a casting voice, but no other vote; and with the advice and consent of the said council shall appoint all the said officers; and that a majority of the said council shall be a quorum; And further, the said senators shall not be eligible to the said council for two years successively." *N.Y. State Laws*, (1777–97), 1: 11.

6. The Senate and Journal volumes read as "be always so".

7. JJ's reform endeavors on the pardon system, state prison, and penal codes are discussed in the editorial note "Crime and Punishment in Federalist New York," below.

8. The eighteenth session of the state legislature passed the following acts involving Indian affairs: "An Act to amend an Act, entitled an Act relative to the Indian Residents within this State," 5 Mar. 1795; "An Act relative to Lands in Brothertown," 31 Mar. 1795; "An Act for the better Support of the Oneida, Onondaga, and Cayuga Indians and for other Purposes therein mentioned," 9 Apr. 1795. *N.Y. State Laws*, 18th sess. (1795): 14, 28–29, 43–45. For more on the state's relationship with Indian groups, see the editorial note "Indian Affairs under Jay's Governorship," above.

9. For the yellow fever epidemic, see the editorial note "John Jay and the Yellow Fever Epidemics," above.

French Saint-Domingue (now Haiti) was the richest colony in the Caribbean, producing sugar, coffee, and indigo, and was a main source of trade with the U.S. The French Revolution divided white planters (*grands blancs*), many seeing it as their opportunity to wrest power from the metropole, while others remained loyal to the crown. Working-class whites (*petits blancs*) saw a chance to gain more land and power. *Gens de couleur* (free people of color, most often of mixed race) saw a chance to gain equal political rights (granted in 1792). And the nearly half a million enslaved people saw an opportunity to gain their freedom. The first wave of refugees came after the slave revolts of 1791. War between France and England broke out in early 1793, with some planters and exiles taking up arms for the English. In response, the French minister Sonthonax ordered the enslaved freed in exchange for their aid in defense against the British and white royalists. On 20 June 1793, thousands of freed slaves attacked and burned the capital Cap François or Le Cap, the richest city in the Caribbean. Approximately ten thousand people, white, *gens de couleur*, and slaves, left on ships, seeking sanctuary in the U.S., particularly in Charleston, Norfolk, Philadelphia, and New York (all cities with trading ties to the island). Most soon found themselves in financial trouble. Aid was provided by Congress, state, local, and private means. Furstenberg, *When the U. S. Spoke French*, 54–59; and Ashli White, *Encountering Revolution: Haiti and the Making of the Early Republic* (Baltimore, 2010), 70–78. See also JJ's Address to the New York State Legislature, [1 Nov. 1796]; JJ to Richard Lawrence, 23 Jan. and 9 Feb. 1797, and 6 Jan. 1798; and Lawrence to JJ, 27 Jan. 1797, all below. For a description of the state of the refugees, see Germaine Pierre De Crosses to JJ, 25 Jan. 1792, ALS, NNC (EJ: 08569), and Susannah Livingston Symmes to SLJ, 29 July 1793, AL, NNC (EJ: 13204).

10. On 9 Jan. 1796, a special committee "relative to providing for emigrants as the poor of the state" was formed, consisting of Ezra L'Hommedieu, Selah Strong, and Reuben Hopkins. *N.Y. Senate Journal*, 19th sess. (1796), 9. On the large numbers of refugees and emigres coming to the U.S. throughout the 1790s, see note 9 above, and Furstenberg, *When the U.S. Spoke French*, 35–88.

Message to the New York State Assembly

New York 15 January 1796

Gentlemen

You have already been apprized that the Sum granted by the Act respecting infectious Distempers, proved incompetent to the Expences (of which an Account is preparing) occasioned by the late calamitous Sickness in this City. And also that the precautions taken in Albany against the introduction of it into that City caused Expenditures which yet remain to be provided for.[1] To the end that the Legislature may have full Information on the latter Subject, I now lay before you the following Papers vizt.

N°. 1. A Copy of a Letter from the Mayor of Albany to me.

2. A copy of my Answer to it.

3. A Copy of his Reply, together with the 12 Accounts mentioned in it.—

John Jay

CS, N (EJ: 00975). Enclosures: Abraham Yates to JJ, 2 Nov. 1795, not found; JJ to Yates, 17 Dec. 1795, LbkC, N: Governor's Lbk 1 (EJ: 02981); and Yates's reply, not found; *NYGM*, 2: 366–67.

1. The 1794 amendment to the 1784 quarantine law, signed by Clinton, provided for a Health Officer and necessary expenditures to protect Albany from "distempers." See the editorial note "John Jay and the Yellow Fever Epidemics," above.

To Robert Goodloe Harper

New York 19th. Jany 1796

Sir

A Friend of mine lately sent me your address to your constituents relative to the Treaty.[1] I have read it with Pleasure— Had all the publications on that Subject been written with ~~with~~ equal Knowledge and Attention, or with equal Candor and Decorum, more Truth would have been disseminated, and less Irritation excited.[2]

I observe in it the following Paragraph—vizt. "Objections both personal and constitutional have been made to M^r. Jay. He has been said to be prepossessed in Favor of Britain, and an avowed Enemy to France. If this had been true, it would have been a sufficient reason for rejecting him—but it is not true. I can contradict it, and do, on my own knowledge. I heard M^r. Jay express in public and private, and those who have been much more and much longer acquainted with him, assure me that he always has expressed the utmost Pleasure in the french Revolution, and the warmest wishes for its Success. the greatest Dislike for the former Government, and Sentiments of the highest Esteem and Respect for the Nation"

I am much obliged to you Sir for this vindication, but it being summary and in general Terms, and comprehending only one of the Points, I think it best in order to obviate ˄all˄ further Questions, to state particularly my Sentiments relative to them both.

It has for obvious Reasons been judged convenient to represent me as being strongly attached to the Interests of Britain, and as being equally hostile to those of France. Before I take notice of either, I will premise—that as it is my Duty, so it is my Inclination and Resolution never to be a Partizan of any foreign Court or Nation; but to be and remain with those independent and genuine americans who think it unwise and improper to meddle in foreign Politics; and who regard all foreign Interference in our Counsels, as derogatory to the Honor and dangerous to the best Interests of the united States.

Not being of british Descent, I cannot be influenced by that Delicacy towards their national Character, nor ~~feel~~ that ~~Interest in~~ ˄Partiality for˄ it, which ˄~~not being unnatural,~~˄ might otherwise be supposed ˄not to be ~~unatural˄~~ unnatural. I nevertheless continue to concur in and to express those Sentiments of Esteem for that nation which are expressed, and I believe with great Sincerity, in the early Journals of Congress.[3]

It is not from the Characters of this or that administration, or prevailing Party in the Government, that the character of a Nation is to be inferred. A true Judgment of it can no otherwise be formed, than by observing the general Tenor of their Dispositions and Conduct viewed under all their Circumstances, and in all their Relations, during a long Course of Time. It certainly is chiefly owing to Institutions Laws and Principles of Policy & Government originally derived to us as british colonists, that with the Favor of Heaven the People of this Country are what they are.

Notwithstanding the Tendency which all arbitrary Governments and particularly the long Reign of such a monarch as Louis the fifteenth, have to debase and corrupt their Subjects, the People of France continued to be highly distinguished by their Talents and by their Progress in the arts both of Peace and of War. ~~I experienced their Hospitality and~~ ˄It is true that I˄ returned from that country to this, ~~not only~~ ˄with opinions unfavorable to their court; but not only˄ without a wish unfriendly to them, but on the contrary with Sentiments of goodwill and Regard. That I have from early Life expressed a strong Dislike to the former arbitrary Government of France is well known— the more I became acquainted with it, the more it appeared to me to be a Government always dreadful in Theory; and always more or less ∧so∧ in Practice, according to the characters of those by whom its powers were exercised—

In the Revolution which put a Period to it, I did cordially rejoice, I mean the one which limited the Power of the King & restored Liberty to the People. The ~~able and~~ patriotic Assembly which concerted and accomplished that Revolution, and the People and Army who concurred in and supported it, did themselves immortal Honor; and impressed me, (altho my Judgment did not accord with all[4] their Acts) with great Respect and Esteem for them, and with the warmest wishes for the ultimate Success and Perfection of the Constitution and Government which they established—

The Successors of that memorable Assembly ~~found occasion in the improper Conduct of the king to~~ produced another Revolution. They abolished the Constitution and Government which had been just established, and brought the King to the Scaffold.

This Revolution did not give me pleasure. I derived no Satisfaction from the ~~misfortunes~~ ∧disastrous Fate∧ of a Prince who (from whatever motives) had done us essential Services, and to whom we had frequently presented the strongest assurances of our attachment and affection. This Revolution had in my Eye more the appearance of a woe than a Blessing.— It has caused Torrents of Blood and of Tears, and been marked in its Progress by atrocities very injurious to the Cause of Liberty, and offensive to morality and Humanity. But this Revolution having abolished the monarchy, declared France a Republic, and recieved the general Concurrence of the nation, a new Constitution became indispensable: and as, in case this Revolution should be overthrown by the combined powers, they would doubtless dictate what that new Constitution should be, (an Interference not to be submitted to) I wished Success to the Revolution so far as it had for its Object, not the disorganizing and managing of other States, which ought neither to be attempted nor permitted, but the exclusive ordering of all internal affairs, and the Establishm[en][t]. of any Constitution which the Nation should prefer. It gives me Pleasure to find that one has lately been so established; and I sincerely wish it may be the means of giving permanent Peace Liberty and good Government to France.—[5]

As to the Issue of the War—I am far from desiring that either France Britain or Germany, or any other Power, should acquire a decided Preponderancy in Europe. In my opinion it would conduce more to the Welfare and Peace of those nations, and also of the united States, that they should remain in capacity to limit and repress the ambition of each other.

I will conclude this letter with an Extract from one which I wrote to the late Secretary of State, dated at London on the 21 November 1794[6]—viz.[t]

"I daily become more and more convinced of the general friendly Disposition of this Country towards our's— Let us cherish it.— Let us cultivate Friendship with all nations.— By treating them all with Justice and Kindness, and by preserving that Self Respect which forbids our yielding to the Influence or Policy of any of them, we shall, with the Divine Blessing, secure Peace union and Respectability"— with Sentiments of Esteem & Regard I have the Honor to be Sir Your most ob[t]. & hble Serv[t]

Robert Goodloe Harper Esq[r]

Dft, NNC (EJ: 90212; EJ: 12778). Endorsed. *WJ*, 2: 261–65, with notation "This letter was published by Mr. Harper, at Mr. Jay's request"; *HPJ*, 4: 198–203. For the printed texts, see below. On the relationship of this letter to the defense of the Jay Treaty, see the editorial note "Aftermath of the Jay Treaty: Responses, Ratification, and Implementation," above.

1. Robert Goodloe Harper (1765–1825) was a member of the U.S. House of Representatives from South Carolina, 1795–1801. Failing reelection in 1800, he moved to Maryland, where he practiced law, served in the War of 1812 as a major general, and was a Federalist senator from Maryland and an unsuccessful Federalist vice-presidential candidate in 1816. Joseph Cox, *Champion of Southern Federalism: Robert Goodloe Harper of South Carolina* (Port Washington, 1972), 61–65, 80n13.

Harper sent periodic reports on his congressional activities to his constituents. His address dated 17 Dec. 1795, justifying his support of the Jay Treaty and responding to the vociferous attacks on it in South Carolina, especially one by John Rutledge, included a defense of JJ and his role in negotiating the treaty. *An Address from Robert Goodloe Harper, of South-Carolina, to His Constituents, containing his Reasons for approving the Treaty of Amity, Commerce and Navigation, with Great-Britain* was printed in Philadelphia at the end of 1795 and reprinted in Boston in 1796 (*Early Am. Imprints*, series 1, nos. 28802, 30538). Harper's address succeeded in placating his constituents, who, following a meeting of the leading citizens at the county court house on 2 Apr. 1796, responded with an address confirming their support, despite their continued reservations about the treaty. They also reelected Harper for two more terms. See the address of Newberry County, S.C., to Harper, 12 Apr. 1796, printed in the *South Carolina State Gazette* (Charleston), 6 May, *City Gazette* (Charleston), 12 May, and *Minerva* (New York), 26 May 1796.

The unidentified friend who sent JJ a copy of Harper's address was probably RK, but no letter forwarding it has been found. On 19 Jan. 1796, JJ sent RK his letter to Harper and a copy of it originally intended for publication by John Fenno in the Philadelphia-based *Gazette of the United States*, ALS, NHi: King (EJ: 00866). In letters to RK (not found), Harper advised against publication of JJ's letter in the newspapers and suggested addition of a note in a new edition of his address. Instead JJ proposed, and RK and Harper agreed to, the inclusion of the letter in an appendix to the pamphlet. See JJ to RK, 19 Jan., ALS, NHi: King (EJ: 00866); 27 Jan., ALS, NHi: King (EJ: 00867); and 2 Feb. 1796, ALS, NHi: King (EJ: 00868); RK to JJ, 29 Jan., below; and Harper to JJ, 30 Jan. 1796, ALS, NNC (EJ: 08640); and King, *Life and Correspondence of Rufus King*, 2: 55–56.

Harper's address and JJ's letter were printed by Thomas Bradford in a pamphlet published in Philadelphia in February 1796 under the title *An address from Robert Goodloe Harper, of South Carolina, to his constituents, containing his reasons for approving of the treaty of amity, commerce, and navigation, with Great Britain. To which is annexed a letter from Governor Jay to the author, printed from the original* (*Early Am. Imprints*, series 1, no. 30540). In March it was published by James Rivington in a New York edition by printers Thomas and James Swords (*Early Am. Imprints*, series 1, nos. 30539, 47796). Several newspapers, including the *Salem Gazette*, *Rural Repository* (Leonmister), *Courier of New Hampshire* (Concord), and the *South Carolina State Gazette* (Charleston), also published it in serial form. For notices of the publication and sale of the pamphlets, see, for example, *Aurora General Advertiser* (Philadelphia), 12, 18 and 19 Feb.; *Massachusetts Mercury* (Boston), 12 and 23 Feb.; *Gazette of the United States* (Philadelphia), 17 Feb.; *Columbian Centinel* (Boston), 13 and 24 Feb.; *Federal Gazette & Baltimore Daily Advertiser*, 19, 23, 25 Feb., 2 and 3 Mar.; *American Minerva*, 5–25 Mar. 1796.

Following publication of the pamphlet, JJ's letter was reprinted in numerous newspapers, largely in northern states, including the *Gazette of the United States* (Philadelphia), 16 Feb.; *American Minerva* (New York), 18 Feb.; *Independent Gazetteer* (Philadelphia), 20 Feb.; *Herald* (New York), 20 Feb.; *Federal Gazette & Baltimore Daily Advertiser*, 23 Feb.; *New-Jersey Journal* (Elizabethtown), 24 Feb.; *Massachusetts Spy* (Worcester), 24 Feb.; *Federal Orrery* (Boston), 25 Feb.; *Albany Gazette*, 26 Feb.; *Impartial Herald* (Newburyport), 26 Feb.; *Columbian Centinel* (Boston), 27 Feb.; *Connecticut Courant* (Hartford), 29 Feb.; *State Gazette* (Providence), 29 Feb.; *Hampshire Gazette* (Northampton), 2 Mar.; *Oracle of the Day* (Portsmouth), 2 Mar.; *Rural Repository* (Leominster), 3 Mar.; *Virginia Gazette* (Richmond), 4 Mar.; *Amherst Village Messenger*, 8 Mar.; *New Hampshire and Vermont Journal* (Walpole), 8 Mar.; *Courier of New Hampshire* (Concord), 14 Mar.; *North-Carolina Journal* (Halifax), 14 Mar.; *Otsego Herald; or Western Advertiser* (Cooperstown), 24 Mar.; *Federal Mirror* (Concord), 26 Apr. 1796. Pieces supporting the sentiments expressed in JJ's letter and Harper's address appeared in the *Salem Gazette*, 1 Mar. and *Oracle of the Day* (Portsmouth), 2 Mar. 1796.

Some responses to JJ's letter challenging his positive portrayal of Great Britain appeared in the newspapers, particularly the "The Mask Thrown Off," in the *Aurora General Advertiser* (Philadelphia), 4 Mar. 1796; "An Enemy to Oppression," *Argus, Greenleaf's New Daily Advertiser* (New York), 8 Mar.; *Aurora General Advertiser* (Philadelphia), 17 Mar.; and "Publius," nos. 1–6, in *Greenleaf's New-York Journal*, 29 Mar., 1 Apr. and 5 Apr.; and *Argus, Greenleaf's New Daily Advertiser* (New York), 29, 30, 31 Mar., and 2 Apr. 1796. Such comments also interpreted JJ's letter as indicating he was in fact a royalist, at best a supporter of limited monarchy, and not of a representative republic.

2. This sentence does not appear in the published text.

3. Probably a reference to pieces like the "Address to the People of Great Britain," 21 Oct. 1774, drafted by JJ, on which see *JJSP*, 1: 95–107; *JCC*, 1: 82–90.

4. The word "all" was omitted in the version of JJ's letter printed in the *American Minerva* (New York), an error reported as a source of confusion by "A Federalist" in that newspaper on 4 Mar.

5. For additional comments on the French Revolution, see, for example, JJ to David Hartley, 14 Dec. 1789; to AH, 11 Apr. 1793; and to Grenville, 7 Sept. 1794; and, for the background, the editorial notes "John Jay and the Issue of Neutrality" and "John Jay and the Genet Affair," *JJSP*, 5: 479–90, 546–61; JJ to Ferdinand Grand, 1 Mar. 1790, Dft, NNC (EJ: 12787); and to PAJ, 25 Nov. 1797, ALS, NNGL (EJ: 90551).

6. See JJ to ER, 21 Nov. 1794, above.

To John Vaughan

New York, 6ᵗʰ ∧21∧ January 1796

Sir

My Friendship for Doct. Bancroft has enduced me to ~~turn my attention~~ consider with great attention the Plan most adviseable to adopt relative ~~to the placing of~~ ∧preparing∧ his Son ~~in a Lawyers office,~~ ∧for the Profession of the Law∧ and ~~for~~ especially the place where.[1]

The Doctʳ., for whose Judgmᵗ. I have great Respect, appearing to prefer some Place at a Distance from our Capital, ~~was~~ is a Circumstance which has embarrassed me—for ∧in an∧ in my opinion the Capital affords ∧in many Respects∧ most advantages ~~to To~~ Not choosing to ~~give~~ ∧risk∧ a ~~hastily~~ Opinion ∧in∧ a matter of so much Importance∧ I have hitherto permitted your last Letter ~~to~~ on this interesting Subject to remain thus long unanswered ∧for∧— ∧[In margin] it was not until the ~~return of the Judges from their Circuits &~~ their assembling ∧∧of the houses∧∧ at the Term wʰ. commenced here on the 19 Inst. that I cᵈ. decide with ~~proper~~ ∧∧sufficient∧∧ certainty that a Gent[leman]. wʰ. had studied ~~out of~~ and been admitted to practice in another State, cᵈ. be admitted ~~to into the courts of~~ ∧∧practice in∧∧ this State. I am now assured that a proper Door is left open for them∧ ~~After well considering all the and viewing them it in all the Lights in which I could place it~~ ∧After ∧∧having∧∧ well considered the Subject∧ I ~~finally~~ concur in ~~the Doctʳˢ. Opinion, and & in~~ your Idea respecting ~~his Sons~~ ∧Mr. Bancrofts∧ being placed with Mʳ. Reeves,[2] ~~where~~ ∧with whom∧ I think he ~~would do well to~~ ∧shᵈ.∧ remain untill he ∧shall∧ become qualified to practice the Law and ~~shall obtain a License to practice ∧it∧ in~~ ∧be admitted to the Bar in∧ that State— He may afterwards t remove here ~~or elsewhere according to Circumstance~~; for a ∧prudent∧ Man of ∧distinguished∧ Talents & professional skill ~~and Prudence~~ will find no Difficulty in establishing himself advantageously in ~~whatever part~~ ∧any part∧ of our Country he may prefer ~~to~~. I am Dʳ Sʳ your most obᵗ. & hble Servᵗ

Mr. John Vaughan Phᵃ.—

Dft, NNC (EJ: 08154). Endorsed: ". . . abᵗ. Mʳ Bancroft".

1. On 7 Nov. 1795, John Vaughan wrote to JJ, communicating Edward Bancroft's wishes for his son Samuel's education and proposing that Samuel be placed first with Tapping Reeve of Litchfield, Conn., and then AH. This plan would enable the younger Bancroft to be qualified for the bar in both Connecticut and New York. ALS, NNC (EJ: 08153). This letter was presented to JJ by the younger Bancroft. For more on plans about Bancroft's legal training and his subsequent fugitive status and flight to England, see JJ to Edward Bancroft, 30 Oct. 1795, and notes, above; and JJ to the New York State Officers of Justice, 15 Dec. 1796, and notes, below.

2. Tapping Reeve, founder of the Litchfield Law School, and Conn. state supreme court justice.

To George Washington (private)

New York 26 Jany 1796

Dear Sir

The British Ratification of the Treaty not having arrived and consequently the time for appointing the Commissioners mentioned in it not being come, I have this long postponed replying to yours of 21 last month.[1]

It certainly is important that the Commissioners relative to the Debts, and also the Captures, be men the best qualified for those places.

Probably it would be adviseable to appoint one Lawyer and one Merchant for each of them. The capture Cases are to be decided in London. From much that I have heard, and the little I have observed of M^r. Higginson[2] of Boston I am induced to think him as a Merchant, the best qualified of any I am acquainted with, and the Mass of the Captures being from the Eastern & middle States, it perhaps would be most satisfactory that the Commissioners should be from those Countries; with him I should be inclined to join Mr King or M^r. Dexter,[3] or perhaps Mr Smith of S^o. Carolina.[4]

For the Debts, it seems to me best to take some sensible Merchant north of the Potomack, and particularly of Philad^a., if one of acknowledged Weight and Character could be found willing to serve— if not I should think of Col. Wadsworth, or some other like him and associate with him Judge Paterson, or Mr Benson, or Mr Marshall.

I am really very much at a Loss about Sir John Sinclair's Plan—[5] it pleases me and I wish that our Country would offer Bounties for useful Discoveries whenever made.

Perhaps no Inconvenience could arise from recommending such a Measure to Congress in general Terms, without having any Reference whatever to Great Britain—but even this I think had better be postponed untill the Treaty Business shall have been dispatched— With perfect Respect Esteem & attachm^t. I am Dear Sir your obliged & affect^e. Servt.

John Jay

The President of the U.S.—

ALS, DLC: Washington (EJ: 10657). Marked: "private". Dft, NNC (EJ: 08460); C, MH (EJ: 05359); PGW: PS, 19: 385–86.

1. GW to JJ, 21 Dec. 1795, ALS, NNC (EJ: 07260).

2. Stephen Higginson was a merchant and shipmaster, and the naval officer at the Port of Boston.

3. Samuel Dexter was a Massachusetts lawyer.

4. William Loughton Smith was a South Carolinian lawyer who served in the House of Representatives from 1789 to 1797, and a close ally of AH.

5. For more on the correspondence between JJ and Sinclair on agricultural affairs, see Sinclair to JJ, 31 Mar. 1795, ALS, NNC (EJ: 07141); 29 Mar. 1797, ALS, NNC (EJ: 08635); 15 July 1797, ALS, NNC (EJ: 07147); JJ to Sinclair, 1 Apr. 1795, Dft, NNC (EJ: 08936); 12 July 1797, below; 7 Nov. 1797, Dft, NNC (EJ: 08975). See also the editorial note "John Jay's Mission to London," above.

From Rufus King

Philadelphia 29. Jan. 1796

Dear Sir

M[r]. Harper concurs in the idea of printing by way of note, your return Letter to him,[1] and by this post will transmit a copy to M[r]. Morris for that purpose—

We are yet without the ratification from England,[2] & I am not wholly free from an apprehension that the instructions given to M[r]. Deas[3] may have been so misconceived by him, that a still further Delay may happen before we can receive it— Three original Ratifications by the President were sent by different Vessels to Mr. Deas; and he was instructed in case of the Ratification by his Br[itish]. Maj[esty]. without delay to transmit by different conveyances, *three copies thereof.* A copy or transcript of the original, Ratification made by M[r]. Deas has been transmitted by him, and his Letter is silent respecting an intention of sending an Original—[4]

From the Deranged state of the Office of State for some time past, this Subject appears not to have been attended to, and it was not until the Receipt of Deas's Copy of the Ratification, that his instructions were resorted to in order to ascertain what he had been directed to do on this Subject—

By Letters from M[r]. Adams, he probably arrived in London early in Nov[r]. though the sole Business for which he was ordered there, will have been completed before his arrival (for he has not been instructed respecting the further Negotiation relative to the 12—Art[ic]le.) yet it is hoped that on looking into the Business, and perceiving that an original Act of Rat[ificatio]n. has not been sent, he will correct the Error. With sincere Respect & Esteem I am &c.

Rufus King

ALS, NNC (EJ: 06689). Endorsed: ". . . an[swere]d 2 Feb 1796".

1. See JJ to Robert Goodloe Harper, 19 Jan. 1796, and notes, above.

2. TP frequently wrote to Deas during the winter of 1795–96, informing him that the American government had yet to receive the ratified treaty. TP to Deas, 27 Feb., and 9 Mar. 1796, MHi: Pickering.

3. Instructions to Deas not found.

4. William Allen Deas of South Carolina (1764–c. 1820) was chargé d'affaires in Great Britain during the absence of Thomas Pinckney in Spain. TP had drafted the instructions for the official

exchange of ratifications of the Jay Treaty. Because Deas was not considered of sufficient rank, TP ordered JQA, American minister at The Hague, to travel to London to handle the business. To permit news of the ratification to arrive by the time Congress assembled in December, Deas was authorized to act if JQA did not arrive by 20 Oct. On 28 Oct. 1795, Deas informed TP that Great Britain had ratified the treaty on that day and enclosed a copy of the British instrument of ratification. TP to JQA, 25 Aug. 1795, MHi: Pickering; Deas to TP, 28 Oct. 1795, DNA: RG 59, Despatches from United States Ministers to Great Britain, 1791–1906, vol. 3, November 29, 1791–May 4, 1797. Deas's dispatch is endorsed as received on 28 Dec. 1795.

JQA arrived in London on 11 Nov. and took up negotiations with Grenville on impressment, evacuation of western posts, and neutral rights, until Pinckney's return in mid-January 1796. JQA returned to the Netherlands in May 1796. *Adams Family Correspondence*, 11: 32, 33n4. Instructions regarding renegotiation of Art. 12 on trade with the West Indies were later given to RK when he was appointed minister to Great Britain, but only temporary and partial concessions were obtained while the war between Britain and France continued. Perkins, *First Rapprochement*, 73–76.

The original British instrument of ratification, sent by Thomas Pinckney, did not arrive until 22 Apr. 1796. TP to Pinckney, 23 Apr. 1796, LbkC, RG 59, Diplomatic and Consular Instructions of the Department of State, 1791–1801, vol. 3, June 5, 1795–January 21, 1797. See *PAH*, 19: 496; Perkins, *First Rapprochement*, 37–38; TP to RK, 8 June 1796, MHi: Pickering.

From Oliver Wolcott

Litchfield January 30th. 1796

Sir

In consequence of the death of our late Worthy Governor,[1] the duties of that office have devolved upon me, as Lieu[t]. Governor of the State. And I therefore take the liberty to inclose to your Excellency, the Copy of a Bill, authenticated by George Pitkin Esq[r]. the Clerk of our Superior Court, found by the G[rand]. Jury of Litchfield County, against Ahimaaz C. Punderson and James Chandler for having commited a fraud upon the Treasury of this State, and who as I am informed have for several Months past secreted themselves within the State of New York— one of whom I am well assured, was a few days ago, in Dutchess County, and there associated with persons of the most suspicious Characters— I have therefore to request Your Excellency that agreeable to a Law of Congress,[2] You would issue Your Warrant, to apprehend these men, and that they be delivered to the Order of the Executive of this State, that they may be brought to a legal Tryal— And as they are the fugitives from Justice, I wish that Your Warrant might be directed to every Officer of your State, qualified to serve the Same, and that You will please to transmit it to me, that I might appoint some person to advise relative to the Execution, so as to insure its success—

We have no right to expect that Your Excellency will issue a Warrant unauthorised by Law, at the same time You will permit me to observe, that I conceive that our Criminal Law, as relative to our local Relations, must be extremely precarious in its operation, as it now is, a person may commit the most atrocious felony, and he has only to step over the line of the State, and he is perfectly secure, till a Bill shall be found against him, which by the unfrequency of our Judicial Session, may be several Months after the Crime has been committed, and the perpetrator of it, fully known. In consequence, his escape, is rendered easy and secure into any part of the World—

The National Constitution establishes a right relative to this Subject, but imposes no restraint upon the internal police of a State— Connecticut therefore continues in force, an Ancient law, the substance of which is, that if any person convicted of a Crime for which a Corporal punishment may be inflicted, or shall flee from a prosecution of this Nature from another State into this, the person charged with an Original Order, or having legal authority within the State from which such fugitive fled, to apprehend him, may apply to any magistrate within this State, and obtain a Warrant to arrest such person, and to bring him before any Magistrate, and if upon an examination such Magistrate shall be convinced that such person is a fugitive from Justice, he shall remand him, to some proper Officer within the State from which he fled, to be by him disposed of—

I shall engage the post to deliver Your Excellency this Letter as soon as he shall arrive at New York, and if it shall not be inconvenient, I wish that Your Warrant may be transmitted upon his Return, otherwise that it might be deposited in the post Office—[3] I am Sir with respect and esteem, Yours Excellency's Most Obedient and humble Servant,

(signed) Oliver Wolcott

Governor Jay—

LbkC, N: Governor's Lbk. 2 (EJ: 03214). An enclosure entitled "Copy of the Indictment" appears in the document following the final signature. It contains the indictment of Punderson and Chandler that was drawn up by the Litchfield County Superior Court on 27 Aug. 1795.

1. Samuel Huntington, governor of Connecticut, 1786–96. Huntington had made a similar request six months earlier. See Huntington to JJ, 14 July 1795, above.

2. "An Act respecting fugitives from justice, and persons escaping from the service of their masters," 12 Feb. 1793, Stat., 1: 302–5.

3. For JJ's response to Wolcott's request, see JJ to Wolcott with enclosure, 19 Feb. 1796, LbkC, N: Governor's Lbk. 2 (EJ: 03216); 20 Feb. 1796, C, NN: Wolcott (EJ: 13103); JJ to the New York Officers of Justice, 20 Feb. 1796, N: Governor's Lbk. 2 (EJ: 03215).

From John Adams

Philadelphia January 31. 1796

Dear Sir

D'Ivernois continues to send Us his Speculations,[1] which I value the more for giving me an Opportunity to congratulate you, upon the Durability and impenetrability of the Anvil, while so many hammers are wearing themselves out by their Strokes upon it. The Treaty is not arrived and Congress will do nothing with spirit till they have vented themselves upon that. But all their Hammers will be as brittle as the multitude which We have already seen fly to Pieces.[2]

I envy you the society of your Family and nothing else. If I did not consider the whole Universe as one Family, I Should envy you still more.[3] I am, dear Sir very Sincerely and faithfully yours,

John Adams

His Excellency Governor Jay

ALS, NNC (EJ: 05434). JJ replied on 2 Feb. 1796. ALS, MHi: Adams.

1. François D'Ivernois (1757–1842) was a Genevan economist and politician in exile in England and ardent opponent of the French Revolution who corresponded with and sent copies of his writings to JA, TJ, GW, and others. He had recently proposed to have the deposed professors of the University of Geneva staff a national university in Washington, D.C., and sent copies of his works *La Révolution française à Genève; Tableau historique et politique de la conduit de la France envers les Genevois depuis le mois d'octobre 1792, jusqu'au mois de juillet 1795* and *Réflexions sur la guerre En réponse au Réflextions sur la Paix*, both London, 1795. *PTJ*, 28: 268–69, 275–78, 280–81, 306–9, 600; *PGW: PS*, 17: 564–69; *Adams Family Correspondence*, 11: 81–83, 83n3.

In his reply of 2 Feb., cited above, JJ commented "D'Ivernois is very industrious— I hear no more of his plan of transplanting the University of Geneva into the united States. He is a sensible diligent man, and I suspect his Correspondence with Mr Gallatin has done no Harm—".

2. In his reply of 2 Feb., JJ stated "It gives me pleasure to find that in your opinion no great mischief will be done by the combustible Materials in Congress— If like Doct^r. Youngs Squib, they only 'burn hiss and bounce, waste paper, stink and dye' all will be well. The Tide has changed and begins to run strong— I hope it will be observed and used, or as they say in Massachusetts, *improved.*—". The quotation is from English poet and dramatist Edward Young's *The Love of Fame*, Satire 3, line 65.

3. To this JJ replied: "To be with my Family is a Comfort, and yet I have too much to do with public affairs to be comfortable— You can retire from the Senate to your Country Seat, and pass six months of Otium cum Dignitate ['leisure with dignity'— see Cicero, *Pro Sestio*, XLV: 98]— We have both had busy lives, and I apprehend that in the Fluctuation of human affairs, I am not to expect to enjoy the Tranquility and Repose which all wish for, but which few find until they pass to that Country where the weary rest from their Labours—and where parties and Politics have no admittance. I suspect that young nations like young people are apt to burn their Fingers; and that we have much wisdom to learn, and to pay for— I think I see in this Country the Seeds of Trouble; and that our political machine will in more Senses than one get out of order— But be

these things as they may, I believe it to be wise to do all the Good we can, and to enjoy all the Good we meet with—."

From Samuel Bayard

London 25. Feb[y] 1796

Dear Sir

I had the honor of writing you by the January Packet in answer to your favour of Nov[r]. last.[1] By the present conveyance (The Hope Cap[t]. Haley)[2] I have the pleasure to forward you the 3 last parts of Madame Rolands work—& a letter from M[r] Burke to the Duke of Bedford which made its first appearance yesterday—[3] It is perfectly of a peice with all the productions of this extraordinary man— It bears the marks of that glowing eloquence— that extravagance of censure—that acrimony of invective—& with all of that feeling heart ∧& well informed mind∧ which have so long characterized its celebrated author— I have no doubt but you will derive pleasure from the perusal of it—

I have had the pleasure of reading your speech delivered at the opening of the legislature of New York. It has been received with much approbation here—particularly by Such ∧as are∧ attach'd to our ∧form of∧ govern[men][t].—& to those who administer it— The answers of both branches of the legislature, expressive of the just sense they entertain of your patriotism, your talents & services were also much prais'd. Interested as I know you must feel in every thing relative to the appeals under my care, I cannot withhold some information on this topic.[4]

On saturday last was brought to a hearing the first of those, that were instituted by me— I am sorry to add the decision was not favourable, altho' I could ∧not then∧—nor can I yet perceive any *just* reason why it should not be—

In the Court of Admiralty on the other hand we have had as favourable a decision as we could wish in the first of the Martinique cases. Should the Judge continue *uniform* in his opinion I trust we shall ∧have∧ equal success in the rest— But this hope can scarcely be indulged without presumption— the result of experience— Sir J. M. is seldom long of the same sentiments on any subject.

I look with stronger hope to the Commissioners under the treaty— I shall anxiously wait for their appointment & arrival— They surely will be the means of terminating our disputes with G[reat]. B[ritain]. amicably if it ∧is∧ intended they should be ∧so∧ terminated—[5]

To secure the performance of justice—it is necessary that we should be in a condition to enforce our demands— In this recur it highly gratifying to find both the President & yourself advising those cautionary measures which while they regard internal security have a tendency to ensure respect to our rights from foreign powers—& to prevent a resort to the last dreadful alternative.

I hope the ruling powers of this nation may discern justly the interest they have in the good opinion of & uninterrupted intercourse with, the U. S. & that in consequence they will take those measures of justice & sound policy—that will preserve the two nations on a footing of peace & good understanding with each other— M^rs. Bayard begs her best regards may be presented to yourself and M^rs. Jay— I remain Dear Sir Your most obed^t. serv^t

Sam. Bayard

ALS, NNC (EJ: 08641).

1. Letter not found.

2. The *Hope* under Captain Haley sailed from Gravesend on 25 Feb. and arrived in New York on 26 Apr. *Argus, Greenleaf's New Daily Advertiser* (New York), 25 Apr.; *Greenleaf's New York Journal*, 26 Apr. 1796.

3. Probably the last three sections of the English translation of Madame Roland's *Appel à l'impartialité Postérité* published in London as *An Appeal to Impartial Posterity, by Citizeness Roland ..: Or, A Collection of Pieces Written by Her During Her Confinement In the Prisons of the Abbey, And St. Pélagie* . . . (1795). Marie-Jeanne Philippon Roland (1754–93), a prominent Girondist, was guillotined during the Reign of Terror in November 1793. Burke's publication was *A Letter from the Right Honourable Edmund Burke to a noble lord on the attacks made upon him and his pension in the House of Lords, by the Duke of Bedford and the Earl of Lauderdale*, early in the present sessions of Parliament (London, 1796).

4. See JJ's Address to the New York State Legislature, 6 Jan. 1796, above.

5. On Bayard's efforts and those of the claims commission appointed to settle American claims against British ship seizures, see the editorial note "Aftermath of the Jay Treaty: Responses, Ratification, and Implementation," above. Sir J.M. refers to James Marriott (1730–1803), judge of the High Court of Appeals for Prizes, 1778–98. On the Martinique cases generally, see Fewster, "British Ship Seizures," 426–52, and, for the role of Judge Marriott, ibid., 440–41.

To Henry Brockholst Livingston

New York 26 Feby. 1796

Sir

I was this morning fav^d. with your's of the 21 Inst:[1] requesting me ~~as one of the Commissioners of the Land Office~~ to inform you, if you are not entitled to a Grant of Lands for your military Services?

~~Officially~~ circumstanced as I am in Relation ~~to the Legislature and~~ to the Land Office, I doubt the propriety of my expressing any opinion on the merits of claims which ~~as a~~ ∧if pursued I may as one of the∧ Commissioners of that Board ~~I may~~ ∧probably∧ be ~~officially~~ called upon ∧officially∧ to consider and decide. ~~I really think it would be adviseable for you to consult some distinguis~~ But for this Consideration, I would with pleasure examine the Laws which respect your Case, and give you my opinion upon it— I have the Honor to be &c.

Col. H. B. Livingston

Dft, NNC (EJ: 09640).
1. Letter not found.

To John Lowell

New York 29 Feb. 1796

Dear Sir

I have been fav[ore]ᵈ. with your's of the 15 Inst:¹ by Mʳ Parkman, and am much pleased with him and his fellow Traveller Mʳ. Coolidge.² Their Representation of the State of Things in Massachusetts, corresponds with the Hints on that Head suggested in your Letter. There is too much Intelligence in the northern States to admit of their being greatly and long decieved and misled; and I hope the same Remark will in Time become equally applicable to all the others. Considering the nature of our Governments, a Succession of Demagogues must be expected; and the strenuous Efforts of the wise and virtuous will not cease to be necessary to frustrate their artifices and Designs. They will always be hostile to merit, because merit will always stand in their way; and being actuated by Every ambition or avarice, and not unfrequently by them ∧all∧, will be diligently at work, while better men take their Rest.

It seems strange, but so it is in all Republics, that many excellent men, who are happy in their Families and Fortunes, and in the Esteem and Society of their Friends; who enjoy their Villas and their Gardens, and neglect not to guard their Trees and Vines from Caterpillars, and their favorite Plants and Flowers from nipping Frosts, and yet omit attending to the political Grubs, who are constantly & insidiously labouring to wound and prey upon the Roots of all their temporal Enjoyments. Several Gentlemen of this Description with us, becoming alarmed have been very useful, and I presume this has been more or less the Case in other States— Be pleased to present Mʳˢ. Jay's and my best Compliments to Mʳˢ. Lowell, and be assured of the Esteem & Regard with which I am Dear Sir your most obᵗ. & hble Servᵗ.

John Jay

The Hon'ble Judge Lowell

ALS, NHi: Jay (EJ: 02959). Addressed: "The Hon'ble / J. Lowell Esqr / Judge of Massachusetts District / Roxbury / near / Boston". Endorsed. LbkC, NNC: JJ Lbk. 10 (EJ: 12871); C, SR: C.F. Libbie & Co. (27 Jan. 1903) (EJ: 11271); WJ, 2: 265–66; HPJ, 4: 204–5.

1. Letter not found.

2. Samuel Parkman (1751–1824) and Joseph Coolidge (1747–1820), both merchants of Boston.

From William Hamilton

New York March 8. 1796

Honoured Sir

Be pleased to pardon my presumption in presuming to take the liberty of thus writing to you but I would not have gone so far had I not Believed you to be a person that would listen to the meanest persons who would wish to address themselves to you being confident that you will not refuse to hear my simple address. I have therefore attempted to write the following. I am dear Sir one of those whom the generality of men call Negroes my forefathers or ancestors from Africa but I am a native of New York worthy Sir when I behold many of the sons of Africa groaning under oppression some laboring with difficulty to get free & others having to bear the yoke I cannot help shedding a silent tear at the miserable misfortunes Providence hath brought upon them. But should I blame Heaven for this when it appears from the Sacred truths of the King of Heaven that his displeasure toward the perpetrators of this evil deed or rather these evil deeds when in the spirit or Prophesie Solomon beheld as I am inclined to believe these days he cried out and I returned & beheld all the oppression done under the sun & beheld all the tears of the oppressed & they had no comforter & into the hand of the oppressor was given power & so they had no comforter Therefore I praised the dead that were already dead more than the living that were yet alive how falsely & contradictory do the Americans speak when this land a land of liberty & equality a christian country when almost every part of it abounds with slavery & oppression how offended would the gentlemen be that is told by another that this is not a land of Liberty & equality when he is asked again is this a free state with respect to the negroes he has to answer no kind Sir does not every or is not every one that keeps slaves that are Negroes continually stealing but Dear Sir does not every [one] know that these slaves were stolen from their own Country or deceived a means no better & brought here & sold I mean in this Continent or some part of Christendom. When their purchasers buy them they know they were stolen property therefore they were equal to thieves Agreeable to this they know that they [the] indisputable right of these Africans & their children is liberty & freedom but those that keep them slaves take it from them & they also take it from them against their will for none are willing to be slaves just like a robber he robs them because it is in his power to do it and see that negroes are kept slaves for nought what harm have they done the Americans have they every injured them in the least why will they not let the oppressed free or are they brutes that they should be Slaves

> Is there as ye sometimes tells us
> Is there one who reigns on High
> Does he bid them buy and sell us
> Speaking from his throne the sky.[1]

Has God appointed us as their slaves I answer No his word says that stealeth a man and selleth him shall surely be put to death. I have already shewn that every slaveholder is stealing mens labor & liberty some men say that Negroes are like Brutes & ought to be slaves but these are unreasonable men— but may they

> Deem our nation brutes no longer
> Till some reason they can find
> Worthy of regard and stronger
> Than the colour of our kind

The intent of my writing to you was this to know whether there can be no measures taken for the recovery of the objects of pity is it not high time that the scandal of this country should be taken away that it might be called a free nation indeed & in truth is it not time that negroes should be free is it not time that robery should cease is it not that the threatening of heaven should be taken away. may kind heaven smile upon this nation incline them to do unto all men as they would all men should unto them may Negroes be manumitted may heaven diffuse its choise blessings on your head may you open your mouth & jud[g]e righteously & plead the cause of the poor & needy may your family be blessed from above So no more at present but remain your humble servant

William Hamilton

NB an answer from you will be very acceptable by the person who gives you this.[2]

ALS, NNC (EJ: 07312). Addressed: "To his excellency John Jay Esqʳ / Governor of the State of New York". Endorsed: "William Hamilton a / black man / 8 March 1796". William Hamilton (1773–1836) was a carpenter and community activist. He was the first president of the New York African Society for Mutual Relief, and a member of the Phoenixonian Society, and the Philomath Society. He opposed the American Colonization Society's efforts to relocate blacks. Many of his public addresses were published. *Encyclopedia of African-American Culture and History* (Detroit, Mich., 2006).

1. The poem quoted is William Cowper's 1788 "The Negro's Complaint," *Scots Magazine* 54 (January 1792), 32; *Town and Country Magazine* 24 (April 1792), 185; *Gentleman's Magazine* (December 1793). See also Joseph Jones, "The 'Distress'd' Negro in English Magazine Verse," *Studies in English* 17 (8 July 1937): 88–106.

2. No answer to this letter has been found. Under JJ's governorship, the state legislature did pass a law on 29 March 1799 that gradually phased out the practice of slavery. "An Act for the gradual abolition of slavery," 29 Mar. 1799, *N.Y. State Laws*, 22nd sess. (1799), 721–23.

Proclamation regarding a Protest at the New York State Assembly

[New York, 11 March 1796]

By His Excellency John Jay Esquire. Governor of the State of New York &cᵃ. &cᵃ. &cᵃ.—

A Proclamation

Whereas the Honorable the House of Assembly now in Session were pleased on the tenth day of this month to declare and resolve in the words following, to wit,

["]Whereas the Deliberations of this House were interrupted by the tumultous Shouts and clamors of People within the Bar of the same on the ninth day of March instant.[1] And Whereas an Attempt to controul the proceedings of the Representatives of this State by any particular Set of them is a Violation of all Order and would tend to the Destruction of a free and equal Government if the same were tolerated in as much as it would render the Great Body of the People of this State subject to the passions which might influence the Conduct of Individuals in a particular part of it.

And Whereas the People of this State have received an outrageous Insult thro' the Medium of their Representatives from the aforesaid persons which insult ought out to remain unpunished—

Therefore resolved (if the Honorable the Senate concur herein) that his Excellency the Governor be requested to issue his Proclamation commanding all Magistrates and other Officers of this State to make every exertion for the apprehending of every person or persons guilty of the above Offence and take such other legal Steps as he may think necessary to bring all persons offending in the premises to condign punishment to the end that the Representatives of the People when deliberating for the public Good may not in future be exposed to interruption and insult—"[2]

And Whereas the Honorable the Senate did on the same day concur in the said Resolution—[3] Now therefore in pursuance thereof I do hereby command All Magistrates and other Officers of this State, and particularly in the City of New York, to make every exertion for the apprehending of any person or persons guilty of the abovementioned Offence, and to give immediate Notice thereof to the Attorney General of the State, to the end that proper Measures may thereupon be taken and pursued for bringing the said Offenders to condign punishment; it being of the utmost importance to the preservation and enjoyment of national Liberty and Good Government that the Representatives of the People when deliberating for the public Good should never be interrupted or insulted with Impunity—

Given under my Hand and the Privy Seal of the State at the Government House in the City of New York on the eleventh day of March in the Year of our Lord One Thousand seven hundred and ninety six, And in the twentieth Year of the Independence of the United States—

(signed) John Jay

By His Excellency's Command John H. Remsen Private Sec[y]

LbkC, N, Governor's Lbk. 2 (EJ: 03220); PtD, *American Minerva* (New York), 12 Mar.; *Argus, Greenleaf's New Daily Advertiser* (New York), 14 Mar.; *Aurora General Advertiser* (Philadelphia), 16 Mar. 1796.

1. The fracas that disrupted the meeting of the New York State Assembly in March 1796 stemmed from a series of events that began four months earlier with a dispute between Gabriel Furman, a merchant and alderman of New York City, and member of the Health Committee, and Thomas Burk and Timothy Crady, two recent Irish immigrants who worked on a ferry operating between Manhattan and Brooklyn. Although Burk and Crady were subsequently convicted in the Court of General Sessions and sentenced to two months imprisonment, with an additional twenty-five lashes for Crady, they managed an escape from jail and fled to neighboring Pennsylvania. William Keteltas (Kettlas) (1765–1812), a Republican lawyer who had moved from Poughkeepsie to New York City, viewed the proceedings against the pair as a miscarriage of justice and petitioned the state assembly to impeach Mayor Richard Varick and the other magistrates who had tried the case. When his petition was dismissed in mid-February 1796, Keteltas responded by penning editorials that accused lawmakers of unfairly shielding Varick and his Federalist colleagues while persecuting him for daring to defy their authority. Federalists in the legislature sought to sanction Keteltas, ordering him to appear before the Assembly to answer charges of slander. On the appointed day, a large crowd of supporters accompanied Keteltas to the assembly chamber and disrupted the proceedings, leading JJ to issue the above proclamation. This would not be the last time that Keteltas would be embroiled in controversy. During the gubernatorial election of 1798, he campaigned on behalf of Livingston in Dutchess County and was set upon and assaulted by political rivals. For an overview of these events, see Young, *Democratic Republicans*, 476–85, and the editorial note "John Jay and the Response to the XYZ Affair in New York," below. A Republican editor reported that upon learning of the disturbance involving Keteltas before the state assembly, the governor made his way on foot to the legislature dressed in his militia uniform and armed with a sword. *Argus, Greenleaf's New Daily Advertiser*, 10 Mar.; *Greenleaf's New York Journal*, 11 Mar. 1796. See also the diary entry of 9 Mar. by Alexander Anderson, a medical student at King's College and physician at Bellvue. *Diarium commentarium vitae Alex. Anderson ann. 1793-[99]*, vol. 2, NNC.

2. *N.Y. Assembly Journal*, 19th sess. (1796), 125.
3. *N.Y. Senate Journal*, 19th sess. (1796), 66–67.

From John Sinclair

Board of Agriculture Whitehall March 14. 1796

Sir

Your favor on the use of Salt as a Manure, & on an extraordinary Sort of Apple, was read to the Board of Agriculture at its last Meeting.[1] The Communication was deemed very valuable, particularly the experiments on Salt, which seems in various Cases to have had a decided effect. Should any farther information on this, or similar Topics occur to you, we shall be very happy if you would, at your Leisure, communicate it. We have received various letters tending to the same purport from the Vicinity of our Salt Works, & calling for a Repeal, or new arrangement, of the Duties on refuse Salt.— With great Regard, I remain, Sir, Your faithful & obedient Servant

John Sinclair

His Excellency John Jay &c &c &c—New York

NB. We beg leave at the same time to return you our best thanks for your obliging Present of the 1st. Volume of that interesting Publication, The Memoirs of the American Academy of Arts and Sciences.

ALS, NNC (EJ: 07145). Endorsed.

1. See JJ to Sinclair, 12 Nov. 1795, above. For more on their correspondence and work for agricultural improvement, see JJ to GW (private), 26 Jan. 1796, note 5, above.

From Grenville

Cleveland Row March 17 1796.

Dear Sir

I cannot let Mr Liston go without taking the occasion of his departure to recommend him to you, and to express my hope that his character & conduct will be found well calculated to continue & promote that harmony which it was the object of our labours to establish.[1] I have, since you left us, taken one occasion to renew to you my assurances of the sincere esteem & friendship with which your whole conduct has impressed me, and of the high sense which I entertain of your virtues & talents. It is a great satisfaction to one when in the course of so many unpleasant discussions as a public man must necessarily be engaged in, he is able to look back upon any of them with as much pleasure as I derive from that which procured me the advantage of friendship & intercourse with a man valuable on every account. You I trust saw enough of me to know that these expressions are not on my part compliments of course, but that they proceed from sentiments of real esteem & regard.

I need not tell you with how much pleasure on every account I have learnt that the public in the United States is recovering from the delusion into which they had been led and that justice is now done by the Country at large, as it was before by well informed & well principled men to the uprightness & ability of your conduct. I on my part should have thought that I very ill consulted the interests of my own Country if I had been desirous of terminating the points in discussion between us on any other footing than that of mutual justice & reciprocal advantage, nor do I conceive that any just objection can be stated to the great work which we jointly accomplished, except on the part of those who believe the interests of Gr. Britain & the United States to be in contradiction with each other, or who wish to make them so.

It would be a great gratification to me to learn occasionally that you are well, and that you retain a friendly recollection of one who is with the greatest sincerity Most truly & faithfully Your obedient Humble Servant

Grenville

ALS, NNC (EJ: 08548). FC, UK-BL: Dropmore, MS 59049; *WJ*, 2: 267–68; *HPJ*, 4: 205–6.

1. Robert Liston (1742–1836) replaced George Hammond as British minister to the U.S. He served from March 1796 to 1800.

To George Washington

[NYork 25 March 1796]

Govr. Jay presents his respectful Compliments to the President of the United States, & takes the Liberty of sending the enclosed Copy of a Letter which he this Day rec^d. from Mr S. Bayard.

London, 6$^{th.}$ Jan^y: 1796—

Dear Sir

I am honored with your favour of the 11 Novr. for which I beg you will accept my acknowledg^{ts}: the one enclosed for Col: Trumbull I sent immediately to Mr. Deas, who has almost daily opportunities to Paris where Col: T. was by the last accounts received of him—[1]

It is with sincere satisfaction that I inform you of the favourable disposition which has *lately* been evinced both in Court of appeals and of admiralty, in cases where our citizens are concerned. A change of policy has evidently taken place, owing I have reason to think to the ratification of the Treaty by the President.[2] In those suits instituted against Sir J. Jervis and Sir C. Grey in the Court of Admiralty, the Judge has declared that he will allow the captors no further time to bring in their papers, but will grant an Order for the restitution of the property seized and sold by these Officers at Martinique, St. Lucie and Gaudaloupe & claimed by us, in the course of the present month.[3]

The Court of Appeals also have recently displayed a spirit widely different from that in the case of the Betsy Capt: Furlong.— They have reversed the sentences of the Vice Admiralty Courts in 2 Cases that were argued before them on the 21 Dec[r]. & reprobated in pointed terms the irregular Conduct of the Judges by whom these sentences were passed.

Added to the circumstance of the Presidents having ratified the treaty notwithstanding the clamor raised against it— this change of measures must be ascribed in a degree to the steps taken in consequence of the decree in the Betsy. I early expressed my sentiments fully, but with coolness and moderation to Sir W. Scott, D[r]. Nicholl and to M[r]. Sansom & such of the merchants as I knew had a connection and interest with ministry— Thro' M[r]. Adams also I convey'd the information to Lord Grenville which I had rec[d]. from the Sec[y]. of State—namely that our Gov[t]. had learned this decision "with disappointment & chagrin. These Steps have had their effect and I trust that in future we may not experience any avoidable delays nor that our cases will be so decided as to excite further complaints—"[4]

The Courts of Admiralty and Appeals have adjourned during the holidays soon after the expiration of which we shall probably have decrees in several important cases, that will influence the determination of many others.

Mrs. Bayard joins me in wishing yourself, Mrs. Jay and Son the compliments of the Season—together with continued health and happiness. I am Dear Sir with sincere respect and esteem Your most Obed[t]. and humble Serv[t].

(signed) Sam[l]. Bayard

[His Excellency John Jay Esq[r].]

AL, DLC: Washington (EJ: 10658), enclosing a copy in JJ's hand of Samuel Bayard to JJ, 6 Jan. 1795. The ALS of Bayard's letter is in NNC (EJ: 12535). *PGW: PS*, 19: 589–90. For JJ's reply to Bayard, see his letter of 25 Mar., below.

1. JJ's letter to Bayard of 11 Nov., and his letter to JT have not been found.

2. For Bayard's earlier criticism of the Jay Treaty and the British courts' handling of the spoliation claims cases prior to the final ratification of the treaty, see Sterling, "Letters of Samuel Bayard," 408–24. Bayard reported in July 1795 that "Since Mr. Jay's departure however there has been a striking change in the conduct of the Judge of the Admiralty and of the other authorities toward American

citizens. All we have lately seen is rather adverse than friendly." Ibid., 419. For the background, see the editorial note "Aftermath to the Jay Treaty: Responses, Ratification, and Implementation," above.

3. On the legal and political complications involved in the ship captures made under the auspices of Lt. Gen. Charles Gray and Vice Adm. John Jervis, British commanders in the West Indies, see Fewster, "British Ship Seizures," 426–52.

4. According to Bayard, JQA, directed to England to facilitate the final ratification of the treaty, though he was not in the end needed for that purpose, was "endeavouring to come to some understanding with Lord Grenville on the principles that are to govern the majority of the cases." Bayard to Elias Boudinot, 12 Dec. 1795, in Sterling, "Letters of Samuel Bayard," 422.

To Samuel Bayard

New York 25 March 1796

Dear Sir

I had this afternoon the pleasure of recieving your obliging Letter of the 6th. Jany last, and am happy to learn from it that the Decrees in the Capture Cases will probably be satisfactory— This Information appeared to me to be interesting, and therefore I have communicated it to the President:[1] altho I presume you have written fully to the Secretary of State about it, either by the packet or some other Vessel— The Letters enclosed for your Friends were immediately sent to the Post office according to your Request—[2]

Untill within a few Days past we had been for months without any Intelligence from Europe— Our accounts now are as recent as could be expected, & I wish they were equally pleasing— The public papers afford us but little Reason to conclude that Peace will be reestablished this Winter; on the contrary, there seems to be Room to apprehend that another Campaign will prolong the Miseries of War.

This Letter will probably go by the Packet, whose sailing being always uncertain, and sometimes sudden, I think it best to be prepared— If any other vessel should sail before her bound to London I will enclose some printed papers for you—

Be so good as to remember me to our American Friends in London— Mrs Jay joins with me in requesting you to present our best Comp[limen]ts. to Mrs. Bayard— With the best wishes for your & her Health— I am Dear Sir your most obt. & h'ble Servt

John Jay

Saml. Bayard Esqr

ALS, MHi (EJ: 04769). Endorsed: ". . . rec'd 14. May. & answ'd— / the 16 May by the Harriot".

1. See Bayard's letter of 6 Jan. 1796, enclosed in JJ to GW 25 Mar., above.

2. Letters not identified, but for excerpts from Bayard's private correspondence at this time, see Sterling, "Letters of Samuel Bayard," 408–24.

Message to the New York State Senate

New York, 29 March 1796

Gentlemen,

It appears to me that the concurrent resolution of the two houses of the Legislature of the twenty-fourth instant[1] respecting the Mohawk Indians now in town applies only to the four who were mentioned in my message,[2] and who as the resolution states have not adequate powers to make any settlement respecting the claims of their constituents to certain lands in this State.[3]

But besides these four, there are two others here, viz. Aaron Henry Hill the son of Brandt, and Aaron Hill the son of Capt. David.[4] I understand from Mr. Chapin[5] the superintendent of the United States for Indian affairs that pursuant to the advice of one or more of the late commissioners of this State, they were deputed, and fully authorized by the Mohawks to come to this city and to treat and finally conclude of and concerning their claims to lands in this State.

These two deputies came here some weeks ago in company with the superintendent and with him went on to Philadelphia without having made any communications to me relative to the object of their deputation.

About a fortnight ago they returned here and sometimes came to me in company with the other four; but on no occasion made known to me the nature and extent either of their claims or of their authority. I learn of the superintendent that they expected their business here would be brought on by a member of the Legislature.

Under these circumstances I think it advisable to ask the direction of the Legislature, whether I am to consider the concurrent resolution as extending to these two as well as the other four.

The superintendent, with whom they expect to return, has been so obliging as to furnish me with a statement of the presents which are usually made to Indians on such occasions; this statement including an account of their expenses will accompany this message.[6]

John Jay

PtD, *N.Y. Senate Journal*, 19th sess., (1796), 92. NYGM, 2: 378–79.

1. *N.Y. Assembly Journal*, 19th sess. (1796), 152; *N.Y. Senate Journal*, 19th sess. (1796), 84; NYGM, 2: 377.

2. JJ's Message to the New York State Senate, 22 Feb. 1796, NYGM, 2: 372–3.

3. For the visit by the four-member Mohawk delegation from the Bay of Quinté to New York City, see the editorial note "Indian Affairs under Jay's Governorship," above.

4. The Hills were a leading Mohawk family hailing from Tionoderoge in the Mohawk Valley. Like the Brants they supported Great Britain during the war of independence and relocated to the Haudenosaunee settlement at Grand River in Upper Canada, maintaining strong friendship and kinship ties with the Brant family.

Due to the Mohawk practice of using same names or variants of the same for family members, JJ confused and misidentified the Mohawk delegates visiting New York City. "Aaron Henry Hill the son of Brandt" is probably Aaron Hill (Kanonaron) also known as "Little Aaron," the son of Aaron Hill (Oseragighte). Aaron Hill (Kanonaron) was identified as "Aaron Hill Jr." in the Senate records. "Aaron Hill the son of Capt. David" is probably Henry Aaron Hill (Kenwendeshon) (1770–1832), the son of David Hill (Karonghonte, Karonyonte) (d. 1790), grandson of Aaron Hill (Oseragighte) and nephew of Aaron Hill (Kanonaron). Henry Aaron Hill (Kenwendeshon) married Christina Brant (Aoghyatonashera) (b. 1742), the daughter of Joseph Brant, in 1795. Henry Aaron Hill (Kenwendeshon) was identified as "Henry A. Hill" in the Senate records. The editors wish to thank Professor Jamie Paxton of Moravian College for providing this information.

5. Israel Chapin Jr. (1764–1833).

6. Statement not found.

From George Washington

Philadelphia 31ˢᵗ. Mar 1796

Accept, my dear Sir, my thanks for your note of the 25ᵗʰ. Instant—enclosing a copy of Mʳ. Bayards letter to you.—[1] The purport of it is pleasing; but the conduct of the British armed Vessels in the West Indies, is intolerable beyond all forbearance.

My answer, given yesterday, to the House of Representatives' request of Papers, will, I expect, set a host of Scribblers to work:—but I shall proceed steadily on, in all the measures which depend on the Executive, to carry the British Treaty into effect.—[2]

This reminds me of the name of Pickman,[3] who, sometime ago you mentioned as a Commissioner;[4]—but upon enquiry of his countrymen, it was found he was unfit—& Mʳ Benson declines.—[5] Let me pray you to send the enclosed to Colᵒ. Hamilton[6]—& be assured of the Affectᵉ. Regard of

Gᵒ: Washington

His Excellʸ Jnᵒ. Jay

ALS, NNC (EJ: 07261). Endorsed. *PGW: PS*, 19: 641–42; *WJ*, 2: 267; *HPJ*, 4: 206–7.

1. JJ to GW, 25 Mar. 1796, above.

2. GW to the House of Representatives, 30 Mar. 1796, *PGW: PS*, 19: 635–38. The address was printed in *Claypoole's American Daily Advertiser*, and the *Philadelphia Gazette* (both Philadelphia) of 31 Mar., and the *Argus, Greenleaf's New Daily Advertiser* (New York), on 2 Apr., and subsequently in many other newspapers. On the resolution of 24 Mar. from the House of Representatives re-

questing copies of JJ's instructions and correspondence regarding the Jay Treaty and GW's refusal to submit the records of the Jay Treaty negotiations, see *PJM*, 16: 254–63, 290–301; *PAH*, 20, 64–69, 103–4, and the editorial note "Aftermath of the Jay Treaty: Responses, Ratification, and Implementation," above.

3. On JJ's recommendation of Pickman, see Pickman to JJ, 7 July, ALS, NNC (EJ: 07168), and 27 Nov. 1795, ALS, NNC (EJ: 07169); JJ to Pickman, 14 Dec. 1795, Dft, NNC (EJ: 08949); JJ to GW, 14 Dec. 1795, ALS, DLS: Washington (EJ: 10654); Dft, NNC (EJ: 08461); GW to JJ, 21 Dec. 1795, ALS, NNC (EJ: 07260); Dft, DLC: Washington (EJ: 10656). Benjamin Pickman Sr. (1740–1819), a Salem merchant who suffered heavy losses by underwriting ships that were captured, was seeking appointment as one of the American commissioners to settle British debts. The name "Pickman" is excised from the texts of the *WJ* and *HPJ* volumes.

4. The following sentence is excised from the *WJ* and *HPJ* volumes.

5. JJ had recommended Benson as one of the commissioners to consider British debt claims in his letter to GW of 26 Jan. 1796, above.

6. GW to AH, 31 Mar. 1796, *PGW: PS*, 19: 640–41; *PAH*, 20: 103–5.

To Daniel Coxe

NYork 4 Ap 1796

Dʳ Sʳ

On the 28 ~~of last month~~ ₐUlt:ₐ I had the pleasure of recᵍ your friendly Letter of the 14 of Novʳ. last by Mʳ Bewsher who arrived at Norfolk on the 16 of last Month & from thence sent it to me by post—[1] on his arrival here it will give me pleasure to manifest my Respect for your Recommend[atio]ⁿ. by attentions to him—

The Letter ~~that~~ you enclosed for General Schuyler was immediately delivᵈ to him, and you will find his answer to it herewith enclosed—[2]

Accept my thanks my Dʳ. Sir for the friendly Congratulations expressed in your Letter. The opposition ~~made~~ to the Treaty was no Surprize upon me— I was prepared to expect and to meet it. as you doubtless have seen our public papers, the moderation and Firmness of the President as well as the Sentiments expressed by the ~~par~~ greater part of the State Legislatures ~~a~~ cannot be unknown to you. The Transactions relative to this Treaty will form an interesting page in our History— ~~I have Reason to hope that the opposition~~ Be pleased to present my ~~best~~ compliments to Mʳˢ. Coxe— with the best Wishes for ~~your~~ ₐtheₐ Health and Happiness ~~and~~ of yourself & Family I am Dʳ Sʳ your most obᵗ. & hble Servᵗ

Danˡ Coxe Esqʳ

Dft, NNC (EJ: 08953). New Jersey-born Daniel Coxe (1741–1826) of London, cousin of Tench Coxe, was a prominent Loyalist lawyer and landowner whose property was attainted in 1778–79. He lived in Philadelphia and then New York, and served in the British Army during the war of independence before fleeing to England in 1783. While in London, Coxe joined several philanthropic societies and served on the Common Council for Tower Ward. In 1798, he edited and distributed Robert Goodloe Harper's pamphlet *Observations on the Dispute between the United States and France*. Coxe's inheritance claim on the New Jersey estate of his deceased aunt was argued before the U.S. Supreme Court in 1804. Pennsylvania Society of Colonial Governors, *Pennsylvania Society of Colonial Governors*, vol. 1 (Philadelphia, 1916), 152; *Oracle and Public Advertiser* (London), 22 Dec. 1795; *True Briton* (London), 19 June 1798; William Cranch, *Reports of Cases argued and adjudged in the Supreme Court of the United States, in February Term, 1804, and February Term, 1805*, 2nd ed. (New York, 1812), 279–336.

1. Daniel Coxe to JJ, 14 Nov. 1795, ALS, NNC (EJ: 05532). Possibly Joseph Bewsher, a prize-winning student of mathematics at Cambridge University in 1789.

2. Coxe's letter to Schuyler regarding lands in New York, and Schuyler's reply, have not been found. See, however, Coxe's letter to JJ of 30 Nov. 1796, below.

To Lady Elizabeth Amherst

[New York, 12 Ap. 1796]

Mr Jay presents his respectful comp^{ts}. to Lady Amherst, and returns many thanks to her Ladyship for the prints which she did him the Honor to send. it was not untill last week that they came to his Hands. The Respect entertained in this Country for his Lordships Character & Services renders them ∧very∧ interesting.[1]

Among the agreable ~~Hours~~ ∧moments∧ which Mr Jay passed in London his Recollection often dwells ∧~~with pleasure~~∧ on those for which he is in-debted ~~to~~ ∧to the obliging attentions of∧ Lord and Lady Amherst— His Son retains similar Sentiments and Impressions, and they both unite in the best wishes for the Health and Happiness of Lord and Lady Amherst, and of the young Ladies—[2]

Dft, NNC (EJ: 12539). Endorsed: ". . . in an^r. to 24 Sep. 1795". *HPJ*, 4: 207.

1. Lady Amherst sent JJ ten proof prints of the Boydell engraving of the 1766 Joshua Reynolds portrait of Lord Jeffrey Amherst on 24 Sept. 1795, ALS, NNC (EJ: 05454). She noted that this was a reengraving of the portrait (an initial one was done in 1766). She also sent ten loose inscriptions to be pasted on the prints or on their backs when framed. In February 1795, Lady Amherst had given JJ a print of the original engraving while he was in London. See Lady Amherst to JJ (ALS, NNC (EJ: 05448), and JJ to Lady Amherst, Dft, NNC (EJ: 12850), both of 20 Feb. 1795.

2. JJ met the Amhersts while on the Jay Treaty mission in 1794–95. For his relationship with them, see the editorial note "John Jay's Mission to London," above. The "young Ladies" were the Amhersts' nieces, Elizabeth and Harriet, who lived with them.

Jeffery Amherst, 1st Baron Amherst, by James Watson, published by John and Josiah Boydell, after Sir Joshua Reynolds, ca. 1796. Mezzotint. (© National Portrait Gallery, London)

To Lord Jeffrey Amherst

NYork 12 Ap. 1796

My Lord

The Letter you did me the Honor to write on the 27 Septr. last was ∧here∧ delivered to me a few weeks ago by Mr Austin — [1] He was He was unfortunate in his voyage, and yet happy in surviving the many disast~~erous occurrances~~ ∧[disast]ers∧ he met with — He seems an amiable young man, and is now on his way to Canada — [2]

Our Legislature being in Session I have endeavoured but without Success to obtain from the members of the County in w^h. your Lands are Situated,

Information respecting them. In consequence of a Conversation I had on the Subject with Genl. Schuyler, who assured me it w^d give him pleasure to have opportunities of being useful to y^r. Lordship I this Day wrote him a Letter of w^h. the following is a Copy

(here insert it)[3]

The General expects to set out for Albany the Day after Tomorrow, and on his arrival there will immediately take the measures mentioned in the above Letter— on ~~recs~~ being informed by him of the Result, I shall ~~immediately~~ ∧without Delay∧ communicate it to y^r. Lordship—

In this Country my Lord, and particularly in the part of it settled by people from New England, there is a general Disinclination to holding Lands on Lease— There being much Land to be sold and for moderate Prices Freeholds are preferred; ~~as~~ it ~~being~~ is not uncommon for two or three Crops to pay the first Cost of the Land— some of our Land Holders have disposed of Farms in fee, reserving a Rent Charge periodically increasing— others have given ~~very~~ long Leases, the Rent increasing at given periods ~~& a Fine reserved on Sales or Transfers~~ Except in our Cities Rents ~~in this Country~~ ∧as yet∧ bear no proportion to the Value of the Land rented, and in general such Lands are neither well managed nor the Rents well paid— These Inconveniences result from the State of Things & of Society in this Country; and ~~I presume~~ ∧they∧ will ∧probably∧ continue ~~to operate~~ while ~~such~~ immense Tracts of Wilderness remain to be occupied—[4]

My son is very sensible of the Honor your Lordship does him, and joins with me in requesting the favor of your Lordship to present our respectful comp^{ts}. to Lady Amherst and the Young Ladies,[4] ~~and~~ with Great ∧& sincere∧ Respect and Esteem I have the Honor to be my L^d. Y^r. Lordships most ob^t. & faithful Servt

The R^t Honb. L^d. Amherst

Dft, NNC (EJ: 12540: EJ: 12851). Enclosure: JJ to Philip Schuyler, 12 Apr. 1796, below.

1. Lord Amherst to JJ, 27 Sept. 1795, ALS, NNC (EJ: 05455). Amherst first requested JJ's assistance in securing his land in Tryon Co., N.Y., while JJ was in London. See Lord Amherst to JJ, 7 Mar. 1795, ALS, NNC (EJ: 05450); JJ to Lord Amherst, 5 Apr. 1795, Dft, NNC (EJ: 12533); and Lord Amherst to JJ, 6 Apr. 1795, ALS, NNC (EJ: 05452). In his letter, Amherst enclosed a copy of the 14 Apr. 1769 royal grant giving him 20,000 acres in N.Y. State (enclosure not found). *Calendar of N. Y. Colonial Manuscripts, Indorsed Land Papers* (New York, 1864), 472–73, 530, 598, and 601.

2. Lt. Col. Henry Austen was appointed cornet in the 60th Foot in 1795. He served in the West and East Indies, Canada, and Ireland during the rebellion of 1798. *The Royal Military Calendar* (London, 1815), 3: 278.

3. JJ to Philip Schuyler, 12 Apr., below.

4. In a codicil to his will, dated 24 July 1794, Lord Jeffrey Amherst left his nephew William Pitt

Amherst "the Estate I am possessed of in the Government of New York consisting of twenty four thousand Acres which were of no Value till the Treaty was made with Mr Jay and I give it on the same condition as I have given him the Jesuits Estate in Canada". Article 9 of the Jay Treaty allowed for British subjects to "grant sell or devise the same to whom they please, in like manner as if they were Natives." Will of The Right Honorable Jeffery Lord Amherst of Saint James's Square, Middlesex, Uk-KeNA, PROB 11/1295/156. Amherst died in 1797. Lady Amherst to JJ, 29 Aug. 1797, ALS, NNC (EJ: 05456), and JJ to Lady Amherst, 19 Dec. 1797, Dft, NNC (EJ: 12857). JJ continued to advise William Pitt Amherst on his estates into the 1820s.

To Philip Schuyler

NYork 12 Ap. 1796

Dr. Sir

In pursuance of what passed between us the Day before Yesterday, I now enclose the Boundaries of the Tract granted to Ld. amherst. It has been so long neglected, that I shd. not be surprized if a number of Intruders have settled on it. I think with You that the best Way of obtaining correct Information will be to employ a Surveyor to visit it, and to instruct him to ascertain and report whether any and what persons have taken possession of any and what parts of it. Be so obliging as to employ the Surveyor you named to me; or any other that you may think proper. I will be responsible for the Expence, and will always be ready to pay it on yr. Certificate.[1]

It will be necessary to the managemt. of this Estate that Ld. Amherst shd. have an Attorney residing up the River— on yr. Return be so good as to think of and recommend to me some person whom I could ~~mention~~ with Confidence mention to Ld. Amherst—[2] I am &ca.

The Honb. Genl. Schuyler

Dft, NNC (EJ: 09358). Enclosed in JJ to Lord Jeffrey Amherst, 12 Apr. 1796, above.

1. In his reply, Schuyler explained that a Mr. Winne had been engaged, but had not yet begun the survey. 11 Nov. 1796, below.

2. Schuyler made several suggestions, but ultimately John Evert Van Alen, a surveyor and member of Congress, was engaged. He was succeeded by his nephew Evert (1772–1854), a surveyor and civil engineer. See JJ to John Evert Van Alen, 25 May 1797, ALS, N (EJ: 00978); Van Alen to JJ, 31 May 1797, ALS, with enclosed proposal, NNC (EJ: 07216: EJ: 07215); JJ to Lord Amherst, 3 June 1797, Dft, NNC (EJ: 06710); and JJ to Van Alen, 19 Dec. 1797, ALS, N (EJ: 00979). For the younger Van Alen, see William Pitt Amherst to JJ, 10 Sept. 1807, ALS, NNC (EJ: 05466); JJ to William Pitt Amherst, 5 Jan. 1808, Dft, NNC (EJ: 12858); and William Pitt Amherst to JJ, 2 Apr. 1808, ALS, NNC (EJ: 05467).

To James McHenry

New York 13th. April 1796.

Sir,

The Letter which You did me the Honor to write,[1] respecting the claim of the St. Regis Indians to Lands in this State together with the Report of the Secretary of State on that Subject were immediately laid before the Legislature;[2] and give occasion to a Concurrent Resolution of which the enclosed is a Copy.[3]

But as the Chiefs of those Indians who were with You have represented to me that they are fully authorized to terminate all Questions arising from the said Claim, by an amiable Settlement with this State; it has been judged adviseable to hold a Treaty with them here and again endeavour to bring all differences to a friendly and final Conclusion.—

Permit me therefore to request that the President will be pleased to appoint as soon as it can conveniently be done, a Commissioner on the part of the United States to hold the said Treaty. A proper person may doubtless be found in Philadelphia who would immediately come on to this place— Perhaps Mr. Abraham Ogden[4] of New Ark, or Mr. Elisha Boudinot of Elizabeth Town would if appointed consent to serve— We are anxious to avoid delay for as these Chiefs are now here, it is very desireable that so good an opportunity of treating with them may not be lost. I understand from them that their full powers to treat were given in Writing signed by the principal Men of their Constituents, and were left either with You or the Secretary of State.—[5]

Be pleased Sir to favor me with such Information on this head as you may possess. I have the Honor to be With Great Respect Sir Your Most Obedt & h'ble Servt.

(Signed) John Jay

The Honorable James Mc.Henry Esqr. Secretary of War

LbkC, N: Governor's Lbk. 1 (EJ: 02995).

1. Letter not found.

2. JJ's Message to the New York State Senate, 26 Mar. 1796, *N.Y. Senate Journal*, 19th sess. (1796), 88; *NYGM*, 2: 376. TP wrote to McHenry on the land claims of the Seven Nations of Canada on New York State on 18 Apr. 1796 (MHi: Pickering). See also JJ's Message to the New York State Assembly, 26 Mar. 1796, *N.Y. Assembly Journal*, 19th sess. (1796), 159.

3. The resolution introduced in the New York State Senate on 24 Mar. 1796, and passed that same day, called for an evaluation of the land claims made by the Akwesasne Mohawk. *N.Y. Senate Journal*, 19th sess. (1796), 84.

4. Abraham Ogden (1743–98) of Newark, New Jersey, served in the New Jersey Assembly in 1790 and as U.S. attorney for the state from 1791 to 1798. Ogden was appointed by GW as Commissioner to negotiate with the Seven Nations of Canada in May 1796.

5. For more on New York's treaty negotiations with the St. Regis Indians, see the editorial note "Indian Affairs under Jay's Governorship," above.

To Timothy Pickering

New York 14 April 1796.

Sir

An Act of the Legislature of this State to prevent the bringing in and spreading of infectious Diseases in this State, authorizes the Governor to assign the Stations where vessels made subject to Quarantine shall come to Anchor and remain, until visited by the Health Officer and reported to be free from Infection.[1]

As difficulties and embarrassments of a delicate nature would arise in case it should be made a question whether a *State* Law can extend to Vessels belonging to *Sovereign Powers*— I submit to your Consideration the expediency of obviating them by an Order of the President directing that all such Vessels arriving in any of the United States shall take only such Stations, and refit only ∧at∧ such places, and on such proof of their requiring it, as shall be ordered and required by the Government of such State.—

Besides the danger of infection to which We may be exposed by those Vessels, such a Regulation would tend to prevent the Inconveniencies which often arise from the Indiscretion of their Crews, especially when Ships of War belonging to belligerent Powers happen to be placed near to each other in a neutral Port.

Whatever Orders touching such Vessels may heretofore have been sent to my Predecessor, I will thank you for Copies of. I have some of them, but am not certain that I have them all. I have the Honor to be with great Respect & Esteem Sir Your Most Obt. & h'ble Servt.

(Signed) John Jay

The Hon'ble Timothy Pickering Esqr.—Secretary of State—

LbkC, N: Governor's Lbk. 1 (EJ: 02996).

1. "An Act to Prevent the Bringing In and Spreading of Infectious Diseases in this State." *N.Y. State Laws*, 19th sess. (1796), 28–30; *Argus, Greenleaf's New Daily Advertiser* (New York), 14 Apr. 1796. For details of quarantine laws, see the editorial note "John Jay and the Yellow Fever Epidemics," above.

From Walter Robertson

[[New York] 15 Ap^l. 1796]

Mr Walter Robertson presents his respects to the Governor & begs leave to inform him that he is very desirous of having his portrait, for the purpose of being engraved as a comparison to two prints of the President and Co^l. Hamilton. Mr Robertson has already sketched the Governors features from an unfinished portrait of Mr Stewart's and now takes the liberty of requesting to know at what time his Excellency could make it convenient to honor him with a sitting either at the Government House or at his house N° 3 Stone Street.[1]

AL, NNC (EJ: 07076). Addressed: "His Excellency / The Governor". Endorsed by John Jay: "M^r. Walter Robertson / 15 ap. 1796 / miniature painter". *WJ*, 2: 207–8. See JJ's reply of the same day, below.

    1. Walter Robertson (c. 1750–1802) was an Irish born miniature painter and engraver. He became associated with Gilbert Stuart in London and Dublin. Bankruptcy caused him to accompany Stuart to New York in 1793, planning to engrave and paint miniature versions of Stuart's portraits, most notably that of Washington. See SLJ to JJ, 2 Aug. 1794, above, and Carrie R. Barratt and Ellen G. Miles, *Gilbert Stuart* (New York and New Haven, 2004), 123, 135. See also JJ to PAJ, 16 Apr. 1798, below.

To Walter Robertson

[New York, 15 April 1796]

The Govr presents his Comp^ts. to Mr Robertson & would with great pleasure comply with his Request, ~~and is so far constantly engaged~~ but the Session being just concluded so many public affairs remain to be dispatched that he fears ~~it~~ he will not for some time yet be sufficiently at Leisure— The Govr. has two Portraits drawn by Stewart, one of which is finished,[1] and Mr Robertson may at any Time and as often as he pleases have access to him and if a Leisure hour sh^d. intervene it shall be at Mr Robertsons Service

Dft, NNC (EJ: 08952). Endorsed: "To Mr Robertson / Painter / Stone St. / Ap. 1796".

    1. The finished portrait refers to the one of a pair painted by Stuart of JJ in London in 1783–84, both retrieved and completed by JT. See the editorial note "An American in England" and JJ to Gilbert Stuart, 22 Feb. 1784, *JJSP*, 3: 491, 561. The unfinished portrait refers to the portrait of JJ in his judicial or academic robe. Stuart began the portrait early in 1794, before JJ left to negotiate the treaty with Great Britain. In his absence, a frustrated SLJ kept after Stuart to finish the portrait, with PJM posing for the body. As late as 1808, PAJ described the portrait as unfinished, probably referring to the drapery of the robe. See SLJ to JJ, 2 Aug. 1794, above, especially note 3; PAJ to JJ, 8 July 1808, ALS, NNC (EJ: 06131); and Barratt and Miles, *Gilbert Stuart*, 120–23. See also JJ to PAJ, 16 Apr. 1798, below.

John Jay, by Ellen Sharples
(probably after James Sharples),
c. 1795. Pencil on paper. (© Bristol
Culture/Bristol Museum & Art
Gallery)

To George Washington (private)

New York. Monday 18 Ap. 1796

Dear Sir

You can have very little Time for private Letters, and therefore I am the more obliged by the one you honored me with on the 31 of last Month.[1] I was not without apprehensions that on Inquiry it might not appear adviseable to gratify M[r] Pickman's wishes,[2] for altho' Integrity and amiable manners are great yet they are not the only Qualifications for office —[3]

Your answer to the Call for Papers, meets with very general approbation here.[4] The prevailing party in the House of Representatives appear to me to be digging their political Grave. I have full Faith that all will end well, and that France will find the United States less easy to manage than Holland or Geneva.

This Session of our Legislature is concluded, and nothing unpleasant has occurred during the course of it. I think your measures will meet with general and firm Support from the great Majority of this State — There is no Defection among the Fœderalists — as to the others they will act according to

Circumstances— These contentions must give you a great Deal of Trouble, but it is apparent to me that the conclusion of them, like the conclusion of the late war, will afford a Train of Reflections which will console and compensate ∧you∧ for it— attachment to You as well as to our Country urges me to hope and to pray that you will not leave the work unfinished. Remain with us at least while the Storm lasts, and untill you can retire like the Sun in a calm unclouded Evening. May every Blessing here and hereafter attend You. I am Dʳ Sir, your obliged & affectᵗᵉ Servᵗ

John Jay

The President of the U. S.

ALS, DLC: Washington (EJ: 10659). Marked: "private". Dft, NNC (EJ: 08462); Tr, MH: Sparks; *WJ*, 1: 393; *HPJ*, 4: 208–9.

1. For the letter of 31 Mar. 1796, see above.

2. For more on the consideration of Pickman as an American commissioner to settle British debts, see GW to JJ, 31 Mar., and note 3, above.

3. This sentence was excised from the *WJ* and the *HPJ* volumes.

4. For more on GW's response regarding the House resolution calling for the release of the instructions to the American minister in Britain, see GW to JJ, 31 Mar. 1796, and note 2, above.

To John Charlton

[N. York 22 April. 1796.]

Dʳ. Sir

I take the liberty of enclosing a Plan of a Lazaretto shown by Dʳ. Bard with his Letters to me on the subject—¹ Be so obliging as the lay them before the Medical Society, and request them to favor me without delay with their opinion and Plan of such a Building as they may judge the best calculated for the purpose; in case the one offered by Dʳ. Bard should be thought defective.— This is a subject which I do not understand, and therefore am solicitous to avail myself of the knowledge of those whose profession and information have naturally led them to Inquiries of this Kind— I am Dʳ Sir Your most Obᵗ Servᵗ.

(signed) John Jay

Doctʳ. Charlton President of the Medical Society

LbkC, N: Governor's Lbk. 1 (EJ: 03001).

1. A plan for building a lazaretto on Bedloe's Island, which was acted upon in 1797. See the editorial note "John Jay and the Yellow Fever Epidemics," above; and JJ to Richard Varick, 7 June 1796, below.

To James McHenry

New York 28th. April 1796.

Sir

I have been honored with Yours of the 25th. Instant—[1] The Chiefs have just left me— They insist on their having plenary powers, & seem much to regret that the Instrument expressing those powers cannot be found— The Interpreter as well as the Chiefs are certain that it was presented to the President.

For my own part I perceive no reason to doubt, but on the contrary I beleive that they are authorized to come to a final Settlement with us— As the Treaty is to be held under National Authority, it is of importance that the National Government be satisfied that they treat only with Persons duly authorized— If the President is content to proceed, I am— if he should hesitate, the Interpreter and One of the Chiefs will return and obtain a New Instrument—but this will consume much time, and they are very impatient to finish their Business and go Home in order to attend and assist at some Great Council Fire soon to be held. How far it would be expedient to conclude with them *provisionally*, I am not clear— to ratify or not to ratify is a question which would enable and perhaps induce mischievous Men among those Indians to give further trouble to the President and to us.—[2]

As to Col. Wadsworth—[3] I really think the Business of holding the proposed Treaty cannot be committed to any Gentleman more worthy of Confidence.— I have the Honor to be With Great Respect Sir Your Mo[st] Ob[t] & H'ble Serv[t].

(Signed) John Jay

The Hon'ble James Mc.Henry Esqr. Secretary at War

LbkC, N: Governor's Lbk. 1 (EJ: 03003).

1. Letter not found.

2. For New York's treaty negotiations with the Akwesasne Mohawk, see the editorial note "Indian Affairs under Jay's Governorship," above.

3. Jeremiah Wadsworth declined serving as U.S. commissioner and was replaced with Abraham Ogden whom JJ had recommended in an earlier letter. See JJ to McHenry, 13 Apr. 1796, above.

To Grenville

New York 1 May 1796

My Lord

The great Questions which have agitated this Country since my arrival, may I think be considered as determined: I will therefore no longer postpone thanking your Lordship for the Letter which you did me the Honor to write on the 11th. of may last; respecting which I shall omit saying any thing further by this opportunity.[1]

The Treaty will go into operation, and be supported by a great majority of the People— a majority comprizing the greater part of the men most destinguished by Talents worth and weight. Strenuous Efforts[2] were made and persisted in to mislead the people by all the various means which art unrestrained by Principle very readily devises. The English and Irish Emigrants joined the opposition; & what seems more singular is, that the french Republicans and the french Refugees so far forgot their animosities, as to concur in resisting the Restoration of good will between Great Britain and the united States.—

anxious that the present current of public opinion in favor of a pacific & conciliatory System, may not be checked by fresh obstacles, permit me my Lord to submit to your Consideration the Prudence as well as Justice of strong measures to prevent as far as possible those very exceptionable Impressments and other Severities which too often occur. They may give occasion, and I am persuaded will continue to give occasion, to more clamor than Facts will justify; but it is certainly true, that much just cause for complaint does exist, and that there are persons here who would rejoice if there was much more. There is Reason to believe that certain Individuals in the british Service have been irritated by the improper Things said and published in this Country, to indiscreet acts of Resentment; not considering, and probably not suspecting, that they were said and published for the Purpose of Provocation. It is to be wished that they had recollected that these things were not said and published by our Government—nor by those who desire to promote, and who do promote Peace and Harmony with Great Britain—nor by those who are actuated by Zeal for the Honor and Interest of their *own* Country.

We have aimed at and laboured for the Restoration of mutual Justice and mutual good will between our Countries. The greatest Difficulties are surmounted and perseverance with prudence and Temper on both Sides will ensure Success. Would not orders to discharge all impressed americans, and enjoining a just and friendly conduct towards the People of this Country, cherish their Confidence; and manifest that Disposition to Conciliation, which repeated Instances of Violence and Severity enable designing men (and with great appearance of Reason) to draw into Question?[3] Would not friendly assurances on these Points to our Government tend greatly to impress the public with still more favorable opinions of the Propriety and Policy of their Measures; and consequently diminish the Credit and Influence of those who seize every occasion of impeaching *their wisdom*, and your Sincerity? These Men have indeed for the present missed their object, but they have not abandoned their Designs— I mean the Leaders, not the Rank and File of the Party—among the latter are many misled honest Men, who as they become undecieved, will act with Propriety—

Pardon my Lord! the Liberty I take in these Observations— I write freely, because I confide fully in your Candor; and because I flatter myself that you confide in mine— I have not Leisure at this moment to be more particular— This Letter will soon be followed by others— With great and Sincere Esteem and Regard I have the Honor to be my Lord Your Lordships most Obed.t & h'ble Servant

John Jay

The Right Honorable Lord Grenville

ALS, UkLPR (EJ: 04922). Marked: "Copy". FC, in JJ's hand, NNC (EJ: 08513); *WJ*, 2: 268–70; *HPJ*, 209–11.

1. Grenville to JJ, 11 May 1795, above.

2. File copy has "Endeavours" instead of "Efforts."

3. In his reply, Grenville praised the quality of the members of the spoliation commission and expressed hope that the British commissioners going to America for the settlement of British debts will be equally satisfactory. He then wrote the following regarding impressment:

With respect to the impressments I am confident that such orders as you speak of have been more than once repeated. I speak from general impression not having had opportunity to ascertain the fact since I received your letter. But I think I can answer for it that they shall be renewed. In this Country much of the detail of that business has fallen within my own knowledge. And I can say positively that I do not think one instance can be brought where a seaman has not been discharged who could produce, I do not say proof, but any probable or plausible ground for supposing him a native Citizen of the United States, or a resident there at the time of the separation from this country: In some instances the conduct observed has been so favorable that within the last week before I received your letter two men were discharged, one on producing a certificate of an American consul here which did not recite on what grounds, or from what proof it was given, but merely asserted the fact that the bearer was an American Citizen, and the other on producing a paper neither certified nor attested, but purporting to be a discharge from an American Regiment of militia, a paper which even if genuine may as you will easily see have passed into twenty hands before it was produced here.

I saw in the proceedings of the last session of the Congress some steps taken toward a regular establishment for the granting Certificates. If such an establishment were formed with proper & sufficient checks to prevent it being abused the effect would be to do away the greatest part of our difficulties on the subject. But I much fear that the ideas prevalent in America on the subject of emigration will prevent this ever being well & satisfactorily done.

I have been led to this discussion by what you say of the advantage which might arise from giving orders which I am confident have been repeatedly given— the assurances of Mr Liston on the subject will also I trust be such as you seem to desire.

Grenville to JJ, 9 July 1796, ALS, NNC (EJ: 08549); *WJ*, 2: 274–77; *HPJ*, 4: 220–22.

To Robert Liston

[Friday Morning 8 oC[loc]^k. 6 May 1796]

The Govr. presents his Comp^ts. to Mr Liston— The enclosed affidavit of Rich^d. Van Dyke respecting certain Americans whom he mentions to have been impressed, and to be now detained on Board *the Assistance*, was delivered to the Governor last night.[1]

Mr Liston will readily percieve the Influence w^h. such Complaints never fail to have on public opinion and Sensibility, and how strongly Justice as well as prudence recommend that the merits of them be ascertained, and right done, without Delay—

The Govr. purposing to have the Honor of paying his Respects to M^r & M^rs. Liston in the Course of this Day, had concluded to take that opportunity of communicating & conversing on ∧the Subject of∧ this aff[ai]^r.— but as public Business makes it necessary for him first to visit one of the Islands in the Harbour, where he may perhaps be detained untill one or two oC[loc]^k. he on further Reflection thinks it better to avoid Delay, and to transmit it at this early Hour—[2]

Dft, NNC (EJ: 08956). Robert Liston, who served as the British minister plenipotentiary to the United States, and his wife Henrietta Marchant Liston (1752–1828), sailed from Portsmouth, England, in March 1796 on the HMS *Assistance*, a fifty-gun ship captained by Henry Mowat. Liston received the above letter from JJ upon his arrival in New York City.

1. The HMS *Assistance* stopped and boarded the *Amphion* under command of Capt. Williams, and removed two of the sailors, reported as American-born, and eight passengers. *Minerva* (New York), 16 May 1796. See also Liston to John Temple, 6 May 1796, ALS, NNC (EJ: 06782).

2. In her travel diary, Henrietta Marchant Liston recorded her impression on first meeting the Jays: "We met here the present Governor Mr. Jay, formerly American Minister to Great Britain & the *framer* of the British Treaty, his appearance is rather singular, in dress & manners strikingly like a Quaker. His eye is penetrating, his conversation sensible & intelligent; his deportment grave & though his Political Character is *firm & decided*, there seems to be a general indecision in his manner of expressing his Sentiments. I visited Mrs. Jay, who, as wife to the Governor was entitled to it, otherwise it is the fashion here, as in England, that Strangers *receive* the first visit. Mrs. Jay's claim was strengthened by her being confined to her Chamber with a hurt on her Leg. I found her young &

pretty, & more affable than is common amongst her Country Women." Louise V. North, *The Travel Journals of Henrietta Marchant Liston: North America and Lower Canada, 1796–1800* (Lanham, Boulder, New York, London, 2014), 4.

To the Tammany Society

[New York 11ᵗʰ. May 1796.]

The Governor has taken into Consideration the request signified to him by a Committee of the Tammany Society in this City "That he would order the Flags on Governor's Island, and also on the Battery, to be hoisted on the day of their Anniversary, vizᵗ. the 12 May Instant."—[1]

It appears to him that if such a Compliment be paid to the Tammany, it ought not to be refused to any other of the numerous Societies in this City and State. Arbitrary Preferences would be partial and unjust; and to discriminate on any principle of comparative Utility or respectability, would be a Task too invidious to be undertaken for an object like the present. He doubts the policy and prudence of making such marks of public Respect, more general than they now are; and thinking it his duty to observe the Limits which Usage and acknowledged propriety prescribe, he presumes that his declining to give the Orders in Question will, on being maturely considered, meet with approbation.—[2]

The President and Members of the Tammany Society in the City of New York—

LbkC, N: Governor's Lbk. 1 (EJ: 03009). *HPJ*, 4: 213.

1. The Tammany Society's request has not been found. Founded in 1786, the Tammany Society of New York City was incorporated on 12 May 1789.

2. A 1796 city directory lists forty-two social, benevolent, trade, professional, and ethnic societies (including fourteen Masonic lodges). The entry for the Tammany Society, or Columbian Order notes that this organization "was founded on the true and genuine principles of republicanism, and holds out as its objects, the smile of charity, the chain of friendship, and the flame of liberty; and in general, whatever may tend to perpetuate the *love of freedom*, or the political advantages of this Country." John Low, *The New-York directory, and register for the year 1796* (New York: 1796; *Early Am. Imprints*, series 1, no. 30706), 57.

Established as a fraternal organization, the Tammany Society of New York City became increasingly politicized during the mid-1790s, and its membership largely affiliated with the city's Democratic Society and Republican Party. Jerome Mushkat, *Tammany: The Evolution of a Political Machine, 1789–1865* (Syracuse, 1971), 8–26.

To John H. Remsen

NYork 12 May 1796

Dʳ Sir

As I see you every Day, it may seem singular that I shᵈ communicate to you by Letter any thing wʰ I might with more Ease be mentioned to you in Conversation. In times when it is so common for Men and Measures to be misrepresented, more than ordinary Caution is adviseable; and that Consideration induces me to commit to paper, what I shᵈ otherwise say to you personally ~~in conversation~~ on the following Subject—[1]

I daily experience so many Inconveniences from not having a Secʸ constantly with me, that I must endeavour to have one who could devote his whole time to the Business of that place. Your professional and more lucrative occupations do not permit ~~me~~ you to do this; and the Interest I have in yʳ. Welfare forbids me to regret your being more proffitably employed.

The Character given ∧me∧ of you when you came into the office, has ~~wholey~~ been verified by your Conduct, wʰ. has not only afforded me Reason to be satisfied, but justly entitled you to that Esteem and Regard, and to those friendly wishes for your Happiness and Prosperity with wʰ. I am Dʳ Sir, your most obᵗ. & h'ble Servᵗ

John Remsen Esqʳ.

Dft, NNC (EJ: 08959).

1. For biographical information on Remsen, see Proclamation on Yellow Fever, 13 August 1795, note 5, above. For Remsen's reply, see John H. Remsen to JJ, 14 May, below. Remsen was replaced as private secretary by David S. Jones. See Proclamation regarding Quarantine, 27 Apr. 1797, note 3, below.

From John H. Remsen

[New York 14ᵗʰ. May 1796.]

Respected Sir

When You appointed me your Private Secretary You honored me very unexpectedly, & altho' it was a flattering distinction, I sincerely confess it was not without some reluctance, for the reason hereafter mentioned, that I accepted the Appointment. Shortly before, the Directors of the Bank of the United States committed to my Charge their Law and Notarial Business, the duties of which combined with those of my profession, I apprehended would not well accord with those of the Secretaryship; but Young & sanguine I undertook the important task of performing the Duties of each Appointment, hoping by industry & perseverance to accomplish, what on mature reflection & after the greatest exertion I find to be impracticable.— By reason of a considerable Access of Law and Notarial Business, notwithstanding an economist of time, I found my duties too weighty, & concluded to resign my Secretaryship Immediately on the rising of the Legislature, a measure at that time I was induced to relinquish, tho' with great reluctance, through the persuasion of my Friends.—

On retiring from the Office duty and still more strongly inclination commands me to express my most grateful Acknowledgments for the Appointment—for that indulgence & Aid You have so chearfully afforded me, & attention with which You have honored me—and also for that testimonial you have been pleased to grant me of your approbation of my Character & Conduct, which, coming from Your Excellency, I esteem truly valuable.—

The good opinion, Sir, you entertain of me I shall make it my study to cherish, & to evince my Gratitude whenever Occasions shall present.—[1] I have the Honor to be Your Excellency's Obliged & Most Ob.t Serv.t

John H. Remsen

His Excellency John Jay Esq.r

ALS, NNC (EJ: 07073). Addressed: "His Excellency / John Jay Esquire". Endorsed.
   1. Remsen was replying to JJ's note of 12 May, above.

From Samuel Bayard

London 16. May 1796.

Dear Sir

Your favour of the 25. March[1] reached me on saturday last (the 14.th inst.). It came I presume by the packet—or it would probably have been accompanied by the "printed papers" you were so obliging as to propose sending me—[2] Every information from the U. States is exceedingly interesting at all times—but peculiarly so when our national affairs are in so critical a posture as they were ~~when~~ at the date of the latest accounts from America—

I had occasion to call on M.r Hammond this morning, & from ʌhimʌ received intelligence of so late a date from Philad.a as the 17 April— Congress were then it seems engaged in debating the resolution laid on the table by M.r McClay—[3] It *cannot* be that the House of Representatives would be so *mad* as to adopt such a resolution— It is *impossible* they would expose us to the horrors of war when we are on the eve of settling all differencies ∧with G. B.∧ amicably.

The decisions of the Lords of Appeal have of late been as favourable as we could expect— They have reversed *several* sentences of condemnation grounded on the orders of the 6 Novr. 93.— they have determined to restore all property seiz'd ∧& condemned∧ by virtue of these orders if not *otherwise* liable to Condemnation— And yet in a late case (the Sally—Choate M[aste]^r.) they have declar'd these orders to be perfectly conformable to the laws of nations—& the revocation of them by those of the 8. Jany. 94. to have been made entirely from a spirit of amity & concession to the U. States— Under the circumstances which attended the Commencement of the present war they hold that Captors were authorized with or without these orders of the 6. Novr. to *seize* neutral vessels trading *generally* with the French West Indies, but they say altho' the *seizure* was justifiable, the condemnation might not be unless the property on examination proved to be Enemy's—

On the whole however I think there is a wish with the Lords of Appeal to do us as full justice as their prejudices in favour of Captors & ∧of∧ *their* rights will permit— But where *they* fail to do us ample justice the Commissioners under the treaty may be resorted ∧to∧—& I trust with confidence— D^r. Nicholl has been nam'd as one—& I hear a M^r. Antley is the other, on the part of this Country— A better or fitter man could not have been selected than the former—& so far as I know the latter may be an equally suitable man—

Agreeably to your instruction I have endeavoured to keep the Secretary of State fully & correctly informed of ~~all~~ whatever is important respecting the claims and appeals under my care, but have to regret that I [*illegible*] ∧have∧ not heard so often in reply as perhaps the interests of those in whose behalf I act, would require— Mrs Bayard joins in best regards to yourself & M^rs. J. with Dear Sir your ob^t. serv^t.

Sam Bayard

ALS, NNC (EJ: 12841).

1. JJ to Bayard, 25 Mar. 1796, ALS, MHi (EJ: 04760).

2. In his letter of 25 Mar., JJ wrote, "This Letter will probably go by the Packet, whose sailing being always uncertain, and sometimes sudden, I think it best to be prepared— If any other Vessel should sail before her bound to London I will enclose some printed papers for you—".

3. Samuel McClay (1741–1811) was a Pennsylvania Republican and member of the House of Representatives (1795–97). McClay proposed on 14 Apr. to abolish the treaty that JJ had negotiated with the British government since the Royal Navy was still seizing American merchantmen and impressing American sailors. McClay withdrew his motion, but then requested that his resolu-

tion be read before the House. *Annals*, 5: 969–71, 974. See also JM to James Monroe, 18 Apr. 1796, RC, DLC: Madison; *PJM*, 4: 9–11, and note 3.

From Timothy Pickering

Department of State 4ᵗʰ. June 1796.

Sir,

In the last Article of the British Treaty, concluded between you and Lord Grenville on the 19ᵗʰ: of November 1794, it is agreed that there shall be added to it other Articles which for want of time and other circumstances could not then be perfected. As it is intended to authorize Mʳ. King to enter into further negotiations with Great Britain, I shall feel myself greatly obliged by your informing me what were the subjects of the Articles above referred to; besides the impressing of our seamen, which is indeed one of the highest importance; and the questions mentioned in the 12ᵗʰ: Article, whether in any and what cases neutral vessels should protect enemy's property; and in what case provisions and other Articles not generally contraband, may become such.

Mʳ: King's instructions must be formed in the ensuing week;[1] I hope, therefore, you will excuse my requesting the favour of an early answer. I have the honor to be, with great respect, Sir, Your most obedient Servant,

Timothy Pickering

His Excellency Governor Jay New York

ALS, NNC (EJ: 09488). C, MHi: Pickering (EJ: 04827). For JJ's reply to TP, see his letter of 6 June, below.

1. See TP to RK, 8 June 1796, ALS, MHi: Pickering.

To Timothy Pickering

New York 6 June 1796

Sir

I was this Moment favored with your's of the 4 Instant.[1] under the last article any further arrangements which might become desireable or mutually beneficial may be made in an easy & convenient Manner— it enables the parties to bring into negociation any Propositions of that kind which they may think proper.

You will observe that the 3ᵈ article admits us to navigate in *small* vessels trading bona fide between Montreal and Quebec, under such Regulations as

shall be established to prevent the Possibility of any Frauds in this Respect—
These Regulations are yet to be made—

An Article which should have for its object the Prevention of Indian Wars,
was the Subject of much Conversation between Lord Grenville and myself—
perhaps it would be useful to resume it—

Disputes and Trespasses between american and british Traders may happen in the Indian Country— would it be improper to agree that if they
occurred on our Side of the Line they should be cognizable by us; and if on
their Side of the Line by them. The Expediency of some specific arrangement on this Head may merit attention—

Among the papers of my Correspondence with the late Sec^y. of State there
is an article, drawn by the L^d. Chancellor, which among other Things respects
the Proofs of Deeds & wills &^{c}. and how papers shall be authenticated in the
one Country to be admitted in Evidence in the other— this is an important
Subject—

Purposing to go out of Town in the Morning, and having many little matters to dispatch in the mean Time, I am obliged to write in Haste. I have the
Honor to be with great Respect Sir Your most ob^t. Servt.

John Jay

The Hon'ble Timothy Pickering Esqr Sec^y of State

ALS, MHi: Pickering (EJ: 04772). Addressed. Endorsed: ". . . subjects of further negotiation."
Franked: "FREE". Dft, NNC (EJ: 09489). The Dft contains several lengthy and largely illegible
excised passages that have not been noted.

1. See TP to JJ, 4 June 1796, above.

To Richard Varick

New York 7th. June 1796

Sir

Considering the Works erected on Governors Island and the obvious objections to having a Lazaretto near a Garrison I am solicitous to procure some
other place for that purpose

You are apprized of the difficulty or rather impossibility of purchasing
from individuals any ground in a convenient situation for a Lazaretto on account of the popular prejudices against having such an establishment in their
neighbourhood

As Bedloe's Island which belongs to the Corporation has heretofore been used and considered as a proper place for the purpose I think it would be agreeable both to the State and to the Citizens of New York that it should be purchased by the State and the intended Lazaretto built there in preference to Governors Island in case the French intend soon to remove from it as I have understood they purpose to do— for I have no desire to interfere with any arrangements between the Corporation and them relative to it—. Be pleased therefore to lay this Letter before the Corporation and to inform me whether they will sell it to the State and at what price— considering that this city is more immediately interested in the precautions necessary to be taken against the introduction of Contagious Disorders by Vessels arriving in this port than the more distant parts of the State, I flatter myself that the Terms will be moderate, and such as the Legislature would approve of my acceding to—[1] I have the Honour to be with great Respect— Sir your most obt. & H'ble Servt.

(signed) John Jay

The Honble. the Mayor of the City of New York

LbkC, N: Governor's Lbk. 1 (EJ: 03021). *HPJ*, 4: 217–218.

1. The City Corporation granted the island (for the price of 5 shillings) to the State a week later, and ordered the French government to remove from the island the next month. *MCCNYC*, 2: 248, 257. See the editorial note "John Jay and the Yellow Fever Epidemics," above.

To Ann Jay

New York 8 June 1796

My dear Nancy

I had this moment the Pleasure of recieving your Letter of the 5th. of this month.[1] Your Mama and Brother have lately written to You, and a little Bundle was sent at the same Time— You will probably recieve them before this Letter will come to your Hands.

Your apprehensions relative to a Fever prevailing here are not well founded. I have no Information nor Reason to beleive, that any Credit is due to the Reports which you have heard on that Subject.[2]

When you return you will find the Grounds within our Enclosure here much altered— they have been levelled, and excepting a little part reserved for a Garden, the Rest is laid out for Grass; and I hope the next Spring to surround the whole with Trees. A Well is now digging near the Kitchen door, so that the Inconveniences we have experienced in that Respect will soon be at

Ann Jay, by Charles B. J. Févret de Saint-Mémin, 1797. (From *The St.-Mémin Collection of Portraits* [New York, 1862]; Rare Book & Manuscript Library, Columbia University in the City of New York)

an End. Your Brothers & Sisters are well, and your Mama is recovering from the Effects of the accident she met with much faster than was expected; for she again walks with Ease, tho' I think rather more than is adviseable, considering that her Foot is not yet quite restored to its former State—[3]

If nothing should occur to detain me, I expect to go to Rye tomorrow, and on my Return shall flatter myself that further Letters from you to some of us, will by that Time have arrived.

I am my dear Nancy Your aff^te. Father

John Jay

Miss Ann Jay

ALS, NNC (EJ: 05929).

1. Letter not found.

2. See the editorial note "John Jay and the Yellow Fever Epidemics," above.

3. SLJ accompanied by her daughter Maria took the waters at Lebanon Springs, for relief from their respective maladies, and as a means of avoiding the yellow fever that beset New York City. See JJ to SLJ, 25 July 1796, and note 1, below.

To the Bishop of London (Beilby Porteus)

New York 18 June 1796

My Lord

On my Return from England I ~~took the earliest opportunity of~~ communi- ~~cating~~ catinged to Mr Randolph the Memorandum ∧w^h∧ your Lordship had given me relative to your Estate in Virginia— he very readily ~~understood~~ ∧prom- ised∧ to make the necessary Inquiries and to write to you ~~Lordship~~ respecting the Result of them— Thinking that the Business could not be in better Train, I omitted to take a Copy of the Memorandum—[1]

It appears to me not improbable that the disagreable Circumstances w^h. ~~he~~ ∧Mr Randolph∧ has since experienced,[2] have diverted his Attention from the Subject, and that you remain uninformed whether any thing and what has been done— If this Conjecture should prove well founded, be pleased to send me another memorandum, and I will with great pleasure take ~~care that~~ measures for procuring ∧& transmitting to you∧ the Information you desire— I have the honor to be with great Respect & Esteem Your Lordships most ob^t. & most hble Servt.

The Right Rev^d. the Lord Bishop of London—

Dft, NNC (EJ: 08876).

1. Beilby Porteus was Lord Bishop of London (1787–1809), and an Anglican reformer and abolitionist. Porteus was born in Virginia, where his parents were planters, who returned to England. Porteus and JJ met in London during the Jay Treaty negotiations, and continued to correspond. See the editorial note "John Jay's Mission to London," above.

2. Porteus informed JJ that ER had not provided him with the information he sought and restated his query. Porteus to JJ, 10 Oct. 1796, ALS, NNC (EJ: 04907). His elder brother, Edward Porteus (d. 1752), had remained in America and owned a farm named St. Mathews near Port Tobacco, Md. Edward Porteus left the property to his widow, and upon her death, it was to pass to his brother. The Bishop wished to know if his sister-in-law were still alive, and if not, what was the condition and value of the estate. He emphasized that he had a copy of his brother's will. JJ sought assistance from James McHenry, explaining that McHenry's "acquaintance with Persons and affairs in Maryland" would enable him to give JJ aid in the matter. JJ to McHenry, 6 June 1797, Dft, NNC (EJ: 08972); no reply has been found. Article 9 of the Jay Treaty allowed for British nationals to inherit lands in the U.S. For another such case, see JJ to Lord Jeffrey Amherst, 12 Apr. 1796, above.

From William Henry Clinton

Portland Place June 20th 1796

Sir

From the ill state of my Fathers Health, (whom I have since had the Misfortune to lose) I was introduced by Colonel Stevenson to Mr Pinckney to state to him some Claims of my Father for Property in the State of New York, & which was said to be confiscated by that State. I gave to Mr Pinckney some Memorandums, which he obligingly promised me he would communicate to your Excellency, as you was then in England, & request that you would give it some Attention; I could not expect, as your Excellency then held the Office of Chief Justice of the United States, that you should have given any Opinion on the Circumstances stated to you, that might in the least commit you in future, should it ever come before you in your judicial Capacity. Lest the Multiplicity of Business should have obliterated from your Excellency's Recollection, the Statements, which were submitted to you by Mr. Pinckney, I beg leave to trouble you with a Repetition of them, as copied from my Fathers Papers.[1]

Sir Henry Clinton's Father when in America, bought two Estates in the Colony of New York, the one in Ulster County of four thousand Acres, the other in Dutchess or Orange County of two thousand Acres— The late Governor Clinton of the State of New York had been employed previous to the War in America by Sir Henry Clinton to get these Estates surveyed and estimated; the Ulster Estate was then valued at Fifteen shillings Pr. Acre, & he was actually in Treaty in Sir Henry Clintons Name with the Tenants of the other, for the Sale of it.—[2]

On my Fathers writing to Governor Clinton on the Subject of his Property, he received from him an answer, of which the following is the Substance, "that the Estates were confiscated that one of them had been sold, & that his Friends did not think it for his Interest to repurchase it at the price which had been given; that Sir Henry Clintons name had been put into the Bill of Attainder, as being thought an American born" which was a Mistake— The State of York had passed an act to restore to British born subjects their Property, which has not in this Instance been complied with. Sir Henry Clinton has repeatedly claimed his Property, as may be seen by his Correspondence with Governor Clinton. A Gentleman from New York offered to purchase one of the Estates of Sir Henry Clinton (in the Year 1792) & was so satisfied on the subject of Recovery, that he said he would be at the sole Expence, as he hinted that the Persons who bought the Estate had done it for a Trifle & on Speculation, that if the Estates were not Claimed & restored to Sir Henry Clinton by a certain Period, they would apply to the Legislature to confirm them in the purchase, under pretence that we had not given up the Forts; I make no Comments on the 5th Article of the Definitive Treaty, conscious that your Excellency is free from Prejudice or Animosity, & that when this Case shall come before the Legislature, I shall meet with impartial Justice & your Protection.— As Congress promised to recommend to all the separate States the Restitution of british Property that might have been with-held under different pretences, & being so with-held would prevent the United States in their diplomatic Character from fulfilling of the Treaty, I should conceive, if the Property should appear to have been unjustly detained, that the Congress of the united States possess full powers to decide Questions, which regard the national Honor, & the national Interests, & as all Treaties are confined to the Senate House they must possess with the Power of making them, the power of enforcing the Execution of them. I am yet willing to believe that it is the interested conduct of some Individual & not the Legislature of New York, which has created all the supposed Difficulties.[3]

My Brother Lieut. Coll: Clinton, who is at present in the West Indies,[4] will I hope call at New York on his Return to pay his Respects to your Excellency, & receive any communications you may please to give him. Mr Hammond has obligingly written to Mr Bond requesting him to interest himself in this matter. I beg your Excellency's Pardon for giving you this trouble, & have to regret that my professional Duties as Aide de Camp to the Duke of York prevent my going to New York at present to remove any Difficulties, that might be stated, & to personally assure Your Excellency of the Respect with which I am Yr most Obedt. Servt,

W.H. Clinton

His Excellency John Jay Esqr.

ALS, NNC (EJ: 05526). Endorsed: ". . . recd 20 June / and 18/19 Septr. 1796 / sent answr to H. White / who recd this Letter from / his Brother in London". Also reads "Recd 18 Sepr. 1796" in top left hand corner of first page. FC, MiU-C: Clinton (EJ: 04930); Dft, MiU-C: Clinton (EJ: 04932).

1. Papers not found. Henry Clinton (1730–95), son of colonial governor of New York George Clinton (1686–1761), was born in England, but raised from the age of thirteen in New York. He entered the military in 1745 and saw his first action during the Seven Years' War. During the war of independence, he served under Howe until elevated to commander-in-chief in 1777. William Henry Clinton (1769–1846) and his brother Henry Clinton (1771–1829) both followed their father into the military, becoming generals, and serving through the Napoleonic Wars.

2. After the death of George Clinton, Henry Clinton attempted to establish the boundaries of the tracts in Ulster Co., N.Y., and near Danbury, Conn. He employed the future Governor George

Clinton (no relation), who continued to survey after he passed the bar in 1764. John P. Kaminski, *George Clinton: Yeoman Politician of the New Republic* (Madison, 1993), 14. William B. Willcox, *Portrait of a General: Sir Henry Clinton in the War of Independence* (New York, 1964), 20–21.

3. For the resolution of Congress regarding the restitution of confiscated property, see *JCC*, 26: 30–31. For the confiscation of Loyalist and British property, see *JJSP*, 1: 582, 583, 603, 607n2, 619, 620n5, 639, 705, and 706n4; *JJSP*, 3: 202–3, 207, 209n7, 209n10, 212, 216, 223–24, 261–62, 263n5, 270–71, 396, 408n2, 426, 464, 535n4, 545n1, and 549n9; and *JJSP*, 4: 36, 324n3, 362n2, and 431n3.

4. In September 1795, the younger Henry Clinton served with the 66th regiment in the West Indies as a lieutenant-colonel. For JJ's reply, see JJ to William Henry Clinton, 19 Sept. 1796, below.

CRIME AND PUNISHMENT IN FEDERALIST NEW YORK

Years of experience as chief justice for the New York Supreme Court of Judicature (1777–79) and the Supreme Court of the United States (1789–95) had instilled Jay with a certainty that the just practice of law was necessary for maintaining good governance and social harmony. Jay affirmed this belief in his inaugural address before the state legislature: "One great object of which a people, free, enlightened and governed by laws of their own making, will never lose sight is, that those laws be always so judiciously applied and faithfully executed, as to assure to them the peaceable and uninterrupted enjoyment of their rights."[1] The principle of administering justice in a manner both equitable and consistent had guided his judicial decisions in the previous two decades and continued to do so during his two terms as New York's chief executive.[2]

In his bid to uphold the efficacy of New York jurisprudence, Jay urged legislators to overturn or at least improve upon the most serious defects therein. As with his predecessor George Clinton, Jay focused much of his efforts on ameliorating the state's draconian criminal laws through the application of Enlightenment principles.[3] "It continues to be worthy of consideration," he remarked to state senators and assemblymen in January 1796, "how far the severe penalties prescribed by our laws in particular cases admit of mitigation; and whether certain establishments for confining, employing and reforming criminals will not immediately become indispensable."[4] Two months later, lawmakers moved by the "dictates of humanity and the principles of justice" altered the criminal laws of the state so that the "punishment of crimes should be proportioned to the different degrees of guilt of the offenders."[5] Prior to the passage of this bill, those convicted in New York of committing sixteen different felonies, including forgery, burglary, and arson, would receive a death sentence.[6] However, under the new law, only treason, murder, and theft from a church were still categorized as capital offenses.

Further provisions in the statute called for the construction of two state penitentiaries in New York City and Albany.[7] Penal reformers such as Thomas Eddy anticipated that confinement would serve as more than merely a primary form of punishment; in their eyes, imprisonment, along with a steady regimen of discipline, labor, and religious practice, would create an environment suitable for rehabilitation in which offenders would recognize and contemplate their past mistakes.[8] Whereas construction on New York City's Newgate Prison began in the summer of 1796, a lack of adequate funding forced legislators to cancel the Albany project after several months.[9] Located on the east bank of the Hudson River, Newgate Prison comprised four acres containing cells, workshops, dining facilities, hospital, gardens, yards, and guard towers.[10] With the completion of the prison in November 1797, the governor issued a proclamation announcing that the institution was now "ready for the Reception of Prisoners" from throughout the state.[11]

The implementation of penal reform measures met with mostly positive responses. Samuel Bayard wrote from London congratulating the governor on his successful collaboration with state lawmakers. The resulting legislation, he asserted, was "erasing from our laws every vestige of blood — & [was] in the mild & benevolent spirits of the religion we possess." Bayard predicted that a system of justice based on principles of "repentance & amendment" rather than those of "legal revenge, disgrace, and punishment" would have a unifying impact on the state and diminish existing political and social divisions.[12] Not all New Yorkers, however, shared Bayard's enthusiasm. Jay acknowledged that most citizens supported penal reform, yet he also observed much resistance in Albany and throughout the northern counties.[13]

The state of New York granted its governor broad discretionary powers for pardoning criminals, making Jay a central figure in reforming the penal code.[14] Article 18 of the New York Constitution authorized the chief executive to pardon and commute the sentences of all convicted criminals, excepting those found guilty of treason and murder. In the latter two cases, the governor could grant a reprieve until the next sitting of the legislature and also recommend that lawmakers show mercy to the condemned.[15] The more recent statute passed in March 1796 further empowered the governor to commute a death sentence to a term of imprisonment in the state penitentiary with conditions of hard labor or solitary confinement.[16]

Jay reviewed recent capital punishment cases in the months prior to the passage of the reform bill. Between November 1795 and April 1796, he issued several stays of execution.[17] On the advice of Robert Yates, the chief justice for the state supreme court, Jay granted reprieves to three men found guilty of burglary and forgery, thereby delaying their death sentences until state legislators could introduce a new penal code.[18] Yates alerted the governor to a similar situation three months later regarding another trio convicted of forging promissory notes.[19]

Jay viewed the power to pardon as a crucial instrument for carrying out his executive duties and one that demanded his adherence to the "steady Principles of Sound Policy combined with those of Benevolence" when determining whether someone was deserving of clemency.[20] Such responsibility, he averred, was "to be considered as a *trust* to be executed, not according to my will and inclination, but with sound discretion, and on principles which reconcile mercy to offenders, with the interests of the public."[21] Jay therefore recognized the necessity of disregarding his personal views when taking up the question of pardons. In such matters, he asserted, "Prudence and Discretion" must dictate the governor's decision-making process. Jay further confided that "very few Convicts would be long imprisoned" if he made judgments based on his own "wishes or Feelings."[22]

The governor's response to forgery cases involving Israel Stone and Stephen Belknap, both of whom hailed from Connecticut, sheds further light on how he handled the pardon process. Facing life imprisonment, Stone relied on powerful allies residing in his hometown of Litchfield—such as Tapping Reeve, Uriah Tracy, and Benjamin Tallmadge—to secure his release through the intercession of Governor Oliver Wolcott.[23] Stone possessed a manner and temperament commensurate with that of "other young Men of his rank in life" the petitioners explained to Wolcott, so his participation in such a crime could only occur under the influence of "evil counsellors".[24] They made an additional appeal based on the status of Stone's family and friends within the community, emphasizing that his father, Jonah Stone, possessed an "upright Deportment & respectable Character".[25] Wolcott forwarded the document to Jay, adding his own recommendation for clemency.[26] Although respectful of Wolcott and his fellow advocates, Jay remained unconvinced that a pardon should be issued for Stone. The nature of forgery, Jay observed, entailed "a very great Degree of cool deliberate Wickedness," and unlike most other crimes, it does not result from acts of "Passion, Ebriety or Precipitation."[27] He further noted a disturbing trend in the rising number of forgery cases, warning that such an increase will prove especially harmful to a "Commercial Nation" like the United States.[28] Speaking to the issue of Stone's social status, Jay remarked that many forgers shared the same "decent and reputable" background as Stone and considered it an injustice to "look with a more favorable Eye on those who become criminal in spite of a good

Education and of good Examples than on those Offenders who from Infancy have lived destitute of such advantages."[29]

Like Stone, Stephen Belknap of Norwalk was given a life sentence for his forgery activities. Belknap received further punishment for taking part in an escape with other inmates from the New York City jail in April 1798. Upon his recapture shortly thereafter, authorities added eighteen-months of hard labor to his current sentence and transferred him to the newly built state prison.[30] Belknap pinned his hopes for a gubernatorial pardon on the efforts of Norwalk's leading citizens. In a petition sent three months after his jail break, Belknap's supporters pleaded for leniency by highlighting that his father had suffered a grave wound while serving as an officer in the war of independence and was now reduced to an invalid status.[31] Neither social connections nor family conditions, however, swayed the governor in his decision not to issue a pardon. Moreover, given Belknap's participation in the recent jail break, Jay saw little reason to look favorably upon one whose "offence included disrespect to the laws, opposition and defiance to their authority, and a most unjustifiable combination to break from their control by force of arms, and without regard to the blood and lives of faithful officers and innocent citizens."[32] The governor further pointed out that releasing Belknap would potentially undermine both the authority of "civil magistrates and ministers of justice" who carried out the law and the public belief that pardons and the recently enacted penal reform would establish a more secure and more just society.[33]

Whereas anyone had the right to submit a petition to the governor, the episodes involving Stone and Belknap highlight the fact that those seeking pardons frequently turned to persons of prominence and authority to plead their cause. In several instances, Jay declined pardon requests from persons with whom he was well acquainted, including Alexander Hamilton, Philip Schuyler, and Stephen Van Rennselaer.[34] Jay certainly had no intention of offending or alienating his close friends, relatives, and political allies, yet he understood that his duties as an elected state official took precedence over other considerations. Such was the case in August 1798 when Hamilton wrote to Jay on behalf of Janus Ross, "a very simple lad" with "respectable connections" in his home state of South Carolina.[35] Ross had attempted to pass a forged check after mismanaging funds loaned to him by a family friend. Jay refused to grant amnesty, however, and explained to Hamilton that since "the Power to pardon is a *Trust*" conferred upon him by the people and the state of New York, it should "be exercised in Principles of sound Discretion, combining Policy Justice and Humanity."[36]

In deciding whether or not to issue a pardon, Jay often solicited advice from the magistrates who deliberated on the specific court case under review. For instance, in October 1797, Jay requested that Richard Varick and James Kent consult and advise as to whether a pardon should be granted to Peter Heaton.[37] Two years later, George Barneswell appealed on behalf of his teenage son who had been convicted of manslaughter. Since the crime was the unfortunate result of a "ᴀplayfulᴀ Indiscretion" and was deemed accidental in nature, Jay assured Barneswell that his son's punishment would probably only be severe enough to leave a "suitable Impression on the public mind".[38] Nonetheless, the governor was determined to "form a correct opinion on the subject," and delayed making a final decision until he had first discussed the issue with the judge who had presided over the trial.[39]

Jay received many pardon requests on behalf of inmates serving their sentences at the state penitentiary. When deciding these cases, he regularly sought out information about the prisoner's conduct and character from the staff overseeing the institution. One such petition was submitted in December 1797. Two months previous, Thomas Sterling Jr. had received a year-long sentence for stealing a gold watch. Prior to issuing a pardon in February 1798, Jay inquired about how Sterling had "conducted himself during his Imprisonment" and asked for other pertinent "Facts and Circumstances."[40] He followed a similar course of action that same month for the case of John Garret. At the behest of John Lansing Jr., the newly appointed chief justice of New York's Supreme Court, the governor looked into the possibility of reducing Garret's life term to seven years with hard labor. Jay requested a report on Garret's stay at Newgate from Isaac Stoutenbourgh, the chairman of the prison's board of inspectors. The governor anticipated that the prospect of an early release would motivate Garret and other inmates to exemplary behavior.[41]

Proponents of penal reform in New York agreed with the governor that the use of pardons would have a positive impact on convicted felons. Robert Bowne,[42] an inspector at Newgate Prison, professed confidence that pardoning would encourage "Industry, Sobriety, and general good Behaviour" among the imprisoned population.[43] In his published account of the institution, Thomas Eddy shared Bowne's assessment and noted with approval that the governor had sought the advice of Newgate's board of inspectors when considering whether a prisoner was deserving of pardon.[44]

The governor's confidence that pardoning would improve the status of inmates, as well as his optimism concerning the efficacy of penal reform, would be tested during his final years in office. Beset by overcrowding and unsanitary conditions, Newgate Prison experienced a series of escapes and uprisings. In June 1799, a planned breakout by fifty to sixty armed prisoners was disrupted by the rapid mobilization of local militia forces.[45] The situation worsened the following summer when the militia was again called out to subdue rioting inmates; in a separate incident, fifteen prisoners successfully escaped and made their way to New Jersey.[46] In an attempt to prevent future disturbances, authorities called for the formation of a "State Prison Guard" to provide permanent security at the penitentiary.[47] Jay expressed his frustration with these developments in an address to the state assembly. Noting that the pervasiveness of escapes from Newgate had created a sense of "anxiety and uneasiness" among the public, he criticized the current "mild system of punishment" as failing in its purported goals and counselled legislators to create harsher penalties for those attempting to flee from the prison.[48]

1. JJ's Address to the New York State Legislature, 6 Jan. 1796, above.

2. The charges that JJ delivered before jurors in New York State and on the Eastern Circuit convey his measured stance in matters of justice and his insistence on equal treatment for all before the law. See Charge to the Grand Jury of Ulster County, 9 Sept. 1777, *JJSP*, 1: 480–81, and John Jay's Charge to the Grand Juries of the Eastern Circuit, 12 April–20 May 1790, *JJSP*, 5: 238.

3. Clinton frequently voiced criticisms against New York's harsh penal code during his later years in office. Clinton to the New York State Legislature, 7 Jan. 1794, and 6 Jan. 1795, *NYGM*, 2: 335–36, 349–50; *Albany Gazette*, 9 Jan.; *Columbian Gazetteer*, 16 Jan; *Catskill Packet*, 21 Jan. 1794; *American Minerva* (New York), 13 Jan.; *Daily Advertiser* and *Herald* (both New York), 14 Jan.; *Mott and Hurtin's New-York Weekly Chronicle*, 15 Jan. 1795.

While in London a few years earlier, Jay viewed a model of Jeremy and Samuel Bentham's proposed model prison, the Panopticon, and probably discussed the topic of penal reform with them. JJ to John Sloss Hobart, 12 Aug. 1794, and notes 4–5, and 9, above.

4. JJ's Address to the New York State Legislature, 6 Jan. 1796, above.

5. *Greenleaf's New York Journal*, 1 Mar. (extract of draft); *Daily Advertiser* (New York), 9 Apr.; *Albany Gazette*, 19 Apr. 1796; "An Act making Alterations in the Criminal Law of this State, and for erecting State Prisons," 26 Mar. 1796, *N.Y. State Laws*, 19th sess. (1796), 20–24, quoted material located on page 20.

6. "An Act for Punishing Treasons and Felonies, and for the better regulating the Proceedings in Cases of Felony," 21 Feb. 1788, *N.Y. State Laws*, (1777–97), 2: 73–80.

7. "An Act making Alterations in the Criminal Law of this State, and for erecting State Prisons," 26 Mar. 1796, *N.Y. State Laws*, 19th sess. (1796), 22–24.

8. For the intellectual currents shaping penal reform of this era, see Benjamin Rush to JJ, 9 July 1796, below, and W. David Lewis, *From Newgate to Dannemora: The Rise of the Penitentiary in New York, 1796–1848* (Ithaca, 1965), 1–28.

9. JJ to PJM, 21 Jan. 1797, below; "An Act to suspend the powers of the Commissioners for erecting a State Prison in the County of Albany," 3 Feb. 1797, *N.Y. State Laws*, 20th sess. (1797), 19–20. For the controversy surrounding the placement of the prison in Albany, see JJ to the Commissioners for Erecting a State Prison in the County of Albany (Philip Schuyler, Abraham Ten Broeck, Jeremiah Van Rensellaer, Teunis J. Van Vechten), 1 Aug. [17]96, LbkC, N: Governor's Lbk. 1 (EJ: 03032).

10. Eddy, *Account of the State Prison*, 17–20.

11. Proclamation on the Completion of the State Prison, 25 Nov. 1797, below. In March 1797, PAJ reported to his father that much progress had been made on the penitentiary: "I walked out this afternoon to look at the new Prison it is considerably advanced and seems to be excellent workmanship— It is expected that it will be ready next Autumn to receive the convicts who may then be in Goal." PAJ to JJ, 10 Mar. 1797, ALS, NNC (EJ: 06057).

12. Bayard to JJ, 11 Oct. 1796, ALS, NNC (EJ: 12840); C, NNC (EJ: 12542).

13. JJ to PJM, 21 Jan. 1797, below.

14. In addition to noting the influence of granting pardons for capital punishment crimes at the state level, JJ also recognized the significance of this policy for national affairs. For GW's seventh annual address to Congress, JJ wrote a section on the necessity to "extend clemency and pardon" to John Mitchell and Philip Vigol (Weigle; Wigel), two whiskey rebels found guilty for treasonous activity and who had their death sentences commuted by GW. GW had earlier consulted with JJ in 1790 on whether he should pardon or commute the sentence of Thomas Bird, a mariner hailing from Bristol, England, who had been found guilty of murdering his ship's captain off the African coast. JJ also advised GW the following year concerning a possible pardon for Clarkson Freeman who was charged with counterfeiting U.S. securities. Draft of George Washington's Seventh Annual Address to Congress, [28 Nov.-7 Dec. 1795], *PAH*, 19: 464n18. See also Philip Vigol Stay of Execution, [16 June 1795], *PGW: PS*, 18: 242–43. For the Bird case, see Thomas Bird to GW, 5 June 1790, *PGW: PS*, 5: 478–81; GW to JJ, 13 June 1790, *JJSP*, 5: 260–61; *PGW: PS*, 5: 517; JJ to GW, 13 June 1790, *JJSP*, 5: 261; *PGW: PS*, 5: 518. For the Freeman case, see William Lewis to GW, 7 Mar. 1791, *PGW: PS*, 7: 521–22; JJ to GW, 11 Mar. 1791, *PGW: PS*, 7: 543–47.

15. *N.Y. State Laws*, (1777–97), 1: 10.

16. "An Act making Alterations in the Criminal Law of this State, and for erecting State Prisons," 26 Mar. 1796, *N.Y. State Laws*, 19th sess. (1796), 24.

17. The governor continued to grant stays of execution in the latter years of his term. See, for example, those issued in the cases of Benjamin Holmes and John Pastano. JJ's Address to the New York State Senate, [29 Jan. 1800], ALS, MHi: Washburn (EJ: 04799); PtD, *New-York Gazette*, 10 Feb.; *Spectator* (New York); 12 Feb. 1800. *NYGM*, 2: 454.

18. Rosewell Herd and Abner Stockwell, convicted of burglary in Montgomery County, and Jessup Darling, convicted of forgery in Columbia County, were all scheduled to be executed on 18 December 1795. Yates to JJ, 18 Nov. 1795, LbkC, N: Governor's Lbk. 2 (EJ: 03206); JJ to Yates, 30 Nov. 1795, ALS, StEdNL-M (EJ: 09235); JJ to the Sheriff of Montgomery County, 30 Nov. 1795, LbkC, N: Governor's Lbk. 2 (EJ: 03319); 30 Nov. 1795, LbkC, N: Governor's Lbk. 2 (EJ: 03207); 2 Mar. 1796, LbkC, N: Governor's Lbk. 2 (EJ: 03219); 7 Apr. 1796, LbkC, N: Governor's Lbk. 2 (EJ: 03224); JJ to the Sheriff of the Columbia County, 30 Nov. 1795, LbkC, N: Governor's Lbk. 2 (EJ: 03208); 2 Mar. 1796, LbkC, N: Governor's Lbk. 2 (EJ: 03218); 7 Apr. 1796, LbkC, N: Governor's Lbk. 2 (EJ: 03225).

19. Jo. Webb, who used the alias Josiah Stiles, Isaac Storr Hutchinson, and Noah Gardiner were sentenced to death by the supreme court of judicature in January 1796. The governor issued stays of execution before the sentences could be carried out in February and March. All three eventually received pardons and had their sentences commuted to life imprisonment. Yates to JJ, 5 Feb. 1795, LbkC, N: Governor's Lbk. 2 (EJ: 03213); JJ to the Sheriff of the City and County of New York, 11 Feb. 1796, LbkC, N: Governor's Lbk. 2 (EJ: 03210); 11 Feb. 1796, LbkC, N: Governor's Lbk. 2 (EJ: 03211); 11 Feb. 1796, LbkC, N: Governor's Lbk. 2 (EJ: 03212); 7 Apr. 1796, LbkC, N: Governor's Lbk. 2 (EJ: 03221); 7 Apr. 1796, LbkC, N: Governor's Lbk. 2 (EJ: 03222); 7 Apr. 1796, LbkC, N: Governor's Lbk. 2 (EJ: 03223); JJ to Lewis A. Scott, 30 Apr. 1796, LbkC, N: Governor's Lbk. 1 (EJ: 03005); 30 Apr. 1796, LbkC, N: Governor's Lbk. 2 (EJ: 03320); 30 Apr. 1796, LbkC, N: Governor's

Lbk. 2 (EJ: 03229); Carolyn Strange, *Discretionary Justice: Pardon and Parole in New York from the Revolution to the Depression* (New York, 2016), 45–46.

20. JJ to Wolcott, 20 Oct. 1797, below.

21. JJ to the Justices and Selectmen of the Town of Norwalk, Conn., 2 July 1798, *WJ*, 1: 398; *HPJ*, 4: 246.

22. JJ to John Williams, 1 July 1799, Dft, NNC (EJ: 08991); *WJ*, 1: 400.

23. Petition to Oliver Wolcott, 15 Sept. 1797, ALS, NNC (EJ: 07276).

24. Ibid. Tallmadge followed up with personal appeals on behalf of Stone. See Tallmadge to JJ, 29 Sept. 1797, ALS, NNC (EJ: 07159); JJ to Tallmadge, 20 Oct. 1797, LbkC, N: Governor's Lbk. 1 (EJ: 03100); Tallmadge to JJ, 1 Dec. 1797, ALS, NNC (EJ: 07160); C, NHi: Tallmadge (EJ: 00654).

25. Petition to Oliver Wolcott, 15 Sept. 1797, ALS, NNC (EJ: 07276).

26. Wolcott to JJ, 19 Sept. 1797, ALS, NNC (EJ: 07277); this letter appears on the same document as Petition to Oliver Wolcott, 15 Sept. 1797, ALS, NNC (EJ: 07276).

27. JJ to Wolcott, 20 Oct. 1797, below.

28. Ibid. JJ held strong convictions on the crime of forgery. In August 1798, he admitted to AH that "It is with me a question whether any Person convicted of *Forgery* ought to be pardoned at *present*, when offences of that kind abound." While serving as the chief justice of the United States Supreme Court he had emphasized the dangers that forgery posed to the young republic. JJ to AH, 30 Aug. 1798, ALS, DLC: Hamilton (EJ: 10782); *PAH*, 22: 170; *HPJ*, 4: 250; Charges to the Grand Jury, Circuit Court for the District of Vermont, [Bennington, 25 June 1792], *JJSP*, 5: 425–27.

29. JJ to Wolcott, 20 Oct. 1797, below.

30. *Argus, Greenleaf's New Daily Advertiser* (New York), 30 Apr.; *Weekly Oracle* (New London), 5 May; *Commercial Advertiser* (New York), 13 June; *Federal Gazette & Baltimore Daily Advertiser*, 15 June; *Greenleaf's New York Journal, Spectator*, and *Weekly Museum* (all New York), 16 June; *Weekly Oracle* (New London), 23 June 1798.

31. *WJ*, 1: 396–97.

32. JJ to the Justices and Selectmen of the Town of Norwalk, Conn., 2 July 1798, *WJ*, 1: 398; *HPJ*, 4: 247.

33. Ibid.; *WJ*, 1: 398–99; *HPJ*, 4: 247–48.

34. AH to JJ, 27 Aug. 1798, below; Schuyler to JJ, 7 Sept. 1797, ALS, N (EJ: 00981); Van Rensselaer to JJ, 12 July 1796, ALS, NNC (EJ: 07224).

35. AH to JJ, 27 Aug. 1798, below.

36. JJ to AH, 30 Aug. 1798, ALS, DLC: Hamilton (EJ: 10782); *PAH*, 22: 170; *HPJ*, 4: 250.

37. JJ to Varick, 5 Oct. 1797, below.

38. Barneswell to JJ, 12 Dec. 1799, letter not found, but mentioned in JJ to Barneswell, 23 Dec. 1799, Dft, NNC (EJ: 09000).

39. JJ to Barneswell, 23 Dec. 1799, Dft, NNC (EJ: 09000).

40. JJ to the Inspectors of the New York State Prison, 23 Dec. 1797, LbkC, N: Governor's Lbk. 1 (EJ: 03113). For related documents, see JJ to Scott A. Lewis, 7 Feb. 1798, LbkC, N: Governor's Lbk. 1 (EJ: 03120); and JJ to Isaac Stoughtenburgh, 10 Feb. 1798, LbkC, N: Governor's Lbk. 1 (EJ: 03121).

41. JJ to Stoutenburgh, 27 Feb. 1798, LbkC, N: Governor's Lbk. 1 (EJ: 03125).

42. Robert Bowne, Quaker merchant and founding member of the NYMS.

43. Bowne to JJ, 10 Apr. 1800, ALS, PHi: Dreer (EJ: 01172).

44. Eddy, *Account of the State Prison*, 67.

45. *Weekly Museum* (New York), 15 June; *Albany Gazette*, 17 June 1799. For reports on how individual prisoners responded to the riot, see Bowne to JJ, 10 Dec. 1799, ALS, NNC (EJ: 08672). Local officials increased the security at Newgate Prison by appointing a brigade of twenty firemen who

were to be "properly armed & accoutred" in order to "quell or suppress any conspiracy or insurrection." *MCCNYC*, 2 Dec. 1799, 2: 585.

46. *Prisoner of Hope* (New York), 7 June 1800. See also the activities of the state assembly for 9 Feb. 1801, *N.Y. Assembly Journal*, 24th sess. (1800–1801), 66.

47. Matthew Clarkson to JJ, 12 Mar. 1801, ALS, NNC (EJ: 09795); Richard Varick to JJ, 12 Mar. 1801, ALS, NNC (EJ: 09305); Eddy, *Account of the State Prison*, 29.

48. See the activities of the state assembly for 17 Mar. 1801, *N.Y. Assembly Journal*, 24th sess. (1800–1801), 196; JJ's Message to the New York State Assembly, 17 Mar. 1801, *NYGM*, 2: 478.

From Benjamin Rush

[Philadelphia July 9th: 1796:]

Dear Sir!

The bearer of this letter is Caleb Lownes—a respectable Merchant[1] of our city, and a gentleman to whom the science of Morals, and humanity owe great obligations.— He visits your city in Order to impart to the Commissioners for building your penitentiary house, the result of his experience in the Construction and government of our own. Your station, but what are more, your principles & feelings will I am sure induce you to afford him the patronage of your name.— May the success of his mission add to the honor of your Administration of the Government of New York!—[2]

With best wishes for your public and private happiness, and Comp[limen]ts: to Mrs Jay in which my dear Mrs Rush joins I am Dr Sir your sincere friend

Benjn: Rush

ALS, NNC (EJ: 09453).

1. Caleb Lownes (1754–1828), a Philadelphia Quaker and merchant, served as a charter member of the Philadelphia Society for Alleviating the Miseries of Public Prisons and sat on the Board of Inspectors for the Pennsylvania State Prison, a converted jail located on Philadelphia's Walnut Street that opened in 1795.

2. Lownes's endeavors to reform Pennsylvania's penal code influenced similar measures proposed by Thomas Eddy (1758–1827), a fellow Quaker merchant and philanthropist residing in New York City. Working closely with state senators Philip Schuyler and Ambrose Spencer, Eddy helped to craft the bill passed in March 1796 that diminished the use of capital punishment and established Newgate Prison. He then served as the first agent, or warden, for the institution. Eddy, *Account of the State Prison*, 11–13. For more on the establishment of this institution, see the editorial note "Crime and Punishment in Federalist New York", above, and Proclamation on the Completion of the State Prison [25 Nov. 1797], below.

Interstate cooperation regarding penal reform and the rise of state prisons continued during JJ's administration. In mid-1800, James Monroe, then governor of Virginia, requested information regarding Newgate Prison. JJ to Robert Bowne, 2 June 1800, ALS, NNC (EJ: 09005); JJ to Monroe, 3 June 1800, Dft, NNC (EJ: 09006); JJ to Monroe, 14 June 1800, C, CSt (EJ: 05145).

From Timothy Pickering

Philadelphia July 16. 1796.

Sir

Some doubts having arisen on the mode of executing the 5th article of the British treaty, relative to the river S^t. Croix, I wrote this morning a letter to Colonel Hamilton on the Subject, and requested him to converse with you. But he may chance to be absent; and as M^r. Howell will in the course of two or three days be returning to Rhode Island through your city, I thought it expedient to communicate the affair directly to you, and without delay, as M^r. Howell will be happy to receive your mature ideas concerning it. I therefore take the liberty to inclose to you a copy of my letter to Col^o. Hamilton; being with sincere respect and esteem, Sir, your most ob^t. serv^t.

T. Pickering

His Excellency John Jay Esqr.

[ENCLOSURE]

Timothy Pickering to Alexander Hamilton

Philadelphia July 16. 1796.

Dear Sir,

M^r. Howell, the Commissioner for settling the S^t. Croix boundary, has been here this week, and started the following questions.

1. "How far will it be proper for M^r. Howell to use his discretion in refusing to draw lots for the third Commissioner, in case the British Commissioner shall persist in proposing a Gentleman on his part who may be, in M^r. Howell's opinion, not an indifferent person?"

2. "In case inhabitants of Massachusetts are thought objectionable on the part of the British, will not all inhabitants of New Brunswick and Nova Scotia be also, if not equally, objectionable?"

3. "Whether the authority of the Commissioners can be legally executed, unless the three Commissioners sign the declaration required of them by the Treaty?" In other words, whether if any two of the Commissioners agree, they can finally decide the question?

I had previously received from M^r. Sullivan (the Agent for the United States) a letter stating the interview between M^r. Howell and M^r. Barclay at Boston; in which it appeared that Mr. Barclay considered the appointment of a Commissioner from Massachusetts would be improper, because there was not one from New Brunswick. Yet (Judge Sullivan remarks) Nova Scotia, where M^r. Barclay resides, may be considered as a party, seeing he said that he could not take any steps towards the appointment of a third Commissioner, until he consulted Sir John Wentworth, the Governor of that province, on the subject, as well as the Governor of New Brunswick. Judge Sullivan further remarks, "that the lands in New Brunswick he considers as owned by proprietors in Nova Scotia, as those in Vermont are by proprietors in New Hampshire; and that, therefore, Commissioners in New Brunswick would be as eligible as ˄in˄ Nova Scotia."

But the most unpleasant part of Judge Sullivan's information is, "That though the third Commissioner is to be nominated and chosen or drawn by the two original Commissioners, Mr. Barclay does not consider himself as acting judicially in the business, or as equally responsible to both Nations on the point; but considers the appointment as a matter of negotiation between the parties, *and that any advantages that which may be gained will be honourable*". Mr. Howell also informed me that Mr. Barclay did avow this extraordinary opinion: and if it were a just one, as founded on the Treaty, it had been better to decide the question by the cast of a die: but it is so repugnant to the oath which each Commissioner is to take, it is impossible that it should be the true construction of the article. I suppose it was chiefly the avowal of this principle on the part of Mr. Barclay, that led Mr. Howell to propose his first Quere: for while he should propose for the decision of the choice of the third Commissioner by lot, a Gentleman belonging to another State than Massachusetts, in order to obtain a *disinterested judge*, it would be with extreme repugnance that he would admit the name of an inhabitant of New Brunswick or Nova Scotia, on account of the direct interest of the former, and the probable interest of the latter, as above suggested by Judge Sullivan; especially as Nova Scotia already furnishes one of the Commissioners. If then it will consist with good faith to refuse to draw lots, on so partial a nomination by Mr. Barclay, it is desirable that it might be done. In a report made to Congress by Mr. Jay, in April 1785, on this subject, he proposed that his Britannic Majesty should name his half of the Commissioners, "being inhabitants of any of his dominions except those which are situated in and to the west and south of the gulph of St. Laurence, and that the United States should name the other half from any of their Counties, except Massachusetts". The whole number of Commissioners then contemplated by Mr Jay was 6. 8. 10. or 12.

The 3rd Question asked by Mr. Howell is in itself, as well as for the reasons contained in the preceding observations, highly important. The words in the Article are—"The said Commissioners shall by a declaration under their hands and seals decide what river is the river St. Croix intended by the Treaty": Not the said Commissioners or *any two of them agreeing*. What is the legal construction of this article on this point? No such question arises on the 6th. and 7th. Articles, any three of the five Commissioners being competent to a decision, the fifth Commissioner being present. On one hand if *unanimity* be necessary, it will enable either party to counteract any flagrant partiality; on the other, it may defeat a great object of the Article—putting a final end to a dispute that might have disagreeable consequences. Permit me to request your attention to this subject, and that you would converse with M[r]. Jay upon it. In the course of two or three days I expect M[r]. Howell will call on you both at New York.[1] I am very respectfully and affectionately yours,

(Signed) T. Pickering

ALS, NNC (EJ: 09490); C, MHi: Pickering (EJ: 04828). Enclosure: TP to AH, 16 July 1796, ALS, DLC: Hamilton; C, NNC (EJ: 09492); C, MHi: Pickering; *PAH*, 20: 255–57.

1. For reply, see JJ to TP, 20 July 1796, below.

To Timothy Pickering

New York 20 July 1796

Sir

I had last Evening a Conversation with Col. Hamilton on the Subject of your Letter to him of the 16th. Instant—a Copy of which was enclosed in yours to me of the same Date—[1] He will I presume state to you particularly our opinions on the three Questions mentioned in it—

It appears to me adviseable that, prior to the Nomination by either Party of a third Commissioner, M[r] Howell should endeavour to agree with M[r]. Barclay on such Principles as would exclude exceptionable persons—such for Instance—that no person personally interested in Lands that may be affected by the Decision should be appointed—that no Person interested as a Freeholder or Inhabitant liable to Taxes in, or holding an Office under the Province or State between which the Line to be settled must run, shall be appointed—that no Person known to have given and advocated a decided opinion in favor of either Claim shall be appointed &c:

If M[r] Barclay should nominate for the Ballot a person *personally* interested, I think M[r] Howell would be justifiable in refusing to proceed in the Business— That Exception resulting from obvious Principles of Equity and Fairness— each Party has equal and reciprocal Latitude, but both should aim at Impartiality and Justice—

I think the nature of the Transaction indicates that the award of two out of three will be definitive notwithstanding the Dissent of the third—

If M[r] Barclay consider himself as a Manager, and not as an impartial Judge between the Parties, and thinks that any advantages which may be gained would be honorable, he certainly has a very incorrect Idea of his Duty. If he has made any such Declarations they should be well substantiated, for in my opinion they go to his Disqualification. If he should persist in such opinions, and in the Business of appointing a third Commissioner should act accordingly I think Mʳ Howell would be right in declining to proceed— In that Case the Facts should be accurately ascertained in order to become the Subject of a proper Representation to the British Court— Care should, and doubtless will be taken that all the Proceedings on our part should bear unequivocal Marks of Candor; and that neither Captiousness nor light or invidious Suspicion or Insinuations be imputable to our Commissioner ∧or our∧ Agent— I have the Honor to be with real Respect & Esteem Sir Your most obᵗ. & hble Servᵗ.

John Jay

The Honb. Timothy Pickering Esqʳ. Secʸ of State

ALS, MHi: Pickering (EJ: 04773). Addressed. Stamped: "N. York JULY 21". Endorsed: "Mʳ. Jay July 20. 96 / St. Croix." Dft, NNC (EJ: 09491).

1. See TP to JJ, 16 July 1796, with enclosed TP to AH of same date, above. On the St. Croix commission, see the editorial note "Aftermath of the Jay Treaty: Responses, Ratification, and Implementation," above.

From John Trumbull

Rochefort 21ˢᵗ. July 1796.

Dear Sir.

Your Favor of the 12ᵗʰ. December,[1] is the last I have had the Honour to receive from you, this I received and answered on the 6ᵗʰ. March;—[2] I have since received a number of Letters from America, through Mʳ Pinckney, which convince me that I have not been so entirely forgotten by my friends as I supposed.

I embark this Afternoon for the North, having terminated the Business which has kept me here since November in a manner that I hope will prove successful— This goes by a Brig to Baltimore which I have loaded with Brandy, and as I suppose tippling is not out of fashion, I hope to be well paid for the trouble of sending it

The Prospect, or rather the Certainty of the Crop of Wheat &c. in this Country is most abundant.— Since I am here the Assignats have followed their elder brother Continental Money to the Grave, and given a fine Subject, for a French M^c.Fingal—[3] they are succeeded by *Mandats* at 30 for 1—which like our 40 for 1 Money, have but a feeble & sickly existence, and will soon follow the others of the Family to Oblivion—[4] As all these illusory Systems Vanish, & Coin reappears, plenty follows.—& you may now buy—nay I do buy for my Vessels excellent Beef at 5 1/2 sous p^r. pound.—best Ship Bread at 40^{lt} p^r C^t.[5] & all other provisions in proportion.— Many of our Countrymen suffer extremely by this change—& I am told that late in May, Flour was still sold in New York at 13 or 14 Doll[ar]^s pr Barrel, while in no Port of Europe could two thirds of that price be found.— As your State wins or loses more on these Occasions than any other, I take the liberty to write this to you in the hope that our friends at least will beware of harm.

The Armies of France are every where successful— a considerable part of Italy is in their possession— at home Good Order and Quiet reign to a considerable Degree,— the various Schemes of public Credit, which necessity has dictated must occasion however much Evil so long as the continuance of the War requires such immense Expenses— I believe the Government are sensible of this, & sincerely desirous of Peace as the only means of restoring entirely, what ought to be the End of all Government, Domestic & Individual Prosperity & enjoyment. I beg you to present my respect to M^{rs}. Jay, and to accept the Assurances of my sincere Respect & friendship.

Jno. Trumbull

ALS, NNC (EJ: 07205). Addressed: "His Excellency John Jay Esqr / Governor of the State of / New York / New York"; with notation: "By the Eliza Johnson / Capt. Crozier / to Baltimore". Marked: "Ship 29 / Paid". Endorsed. The brig *Eliza Johnson* carrying brandy and captained by Crozier, left the Charente River in France on 12 Aug. and arrived in Hampton Road on 16 Sept. and Baltimore on 24 Sept. 1796. *Claypoole's American Daily Advertiser* (Philadelphia), 26 Sept.; *Gazette of the United States* (Philadelphia), 27 Sept.; *Boston Gazette*, 3 Oct. 1796.

1. Letter not found.

2. ALS, SR: "Forest H. Sweet, 'Autograph Letters', List no. 108, item 146" (EJ: 13617).

3. On the collapse of the Continental currency, and the new emission currency issued to replace it at a rate of 40 for 1, see Circular Letter from Congress to their Constituents, [13 Sept. 1779], and notes, *JJSP*, 1: 667—78. The satirical epic poem *M'Fingal* (or McFingal), written by JT's cousin John Trumbull, poet, satirist, and polemicist, was first published in 1776 in one canto, but republished in 1782 with three additional cantos, the fourth of which, entitled *The Vision*, included critical commentary on paper money. *M'Fingal: a modern epic poem, in four cantos* (Hartford, 1782; *Early Am. Imprints*, series 1, no. 17752).

4. Assignats were a form of paper currency backed by the value of confiscated lands issued by the National Assembly in France from 1789 to 1795. Over time the assignats lost most of their value, and in March 1796 the Directory replaced them with mandats, a currency in the form of land warrants. Assignats were exchangeable for mandats at a rate of 30 for 1, but mandats also quickly failed, and France returned to metallic currency. JJ's circular letter cited in note 2 above was translated into

John Trumbull, self-portrait, c. 1802. Oil on canvas. (Yale University Art Gallery)

French and published in France in 1795, apparently as part of the debate there on paper money. *JJSP*, 1: 678n1.

  5. That is, forty livres tournois per hundredweight.

To Sarah Livingston Jay

New York 25 July 1796

My dear Sally

I hope this Letter will find you at Lebanon in better Health than when you left us— The Passage, the Journey, Change of air, and Leisure will all aid the Waters in the Recovery of your Health—[1] While I was from Home this morning M^rs. Ridley was informed of a Sloop just about to sail for Kinderhook and in Haste wrote you a few Lines. It is said that another will sail this Evening and by her this Letter is intended to go. Sallys Face is better—

William is well— I am as usual— The Staten Island Boy is now here, and appearances are in his favor— he seems to be willing and handy—about 16 Years old and rather short for that age— I have no Letters from Nancy since your Departure— Tomorrow or next Day I hope to make a Visit to our Friends at Rye; unless as has often been the Case, some unexpected circumstance should occur to prevent me. We have nothing new. You will probably see some of Mr Van Schaacks Family— remember me to them—and also to M^{rs}. Cortlandt— We have sent her aunt notice of this opportunity, who together with the Children are well— You shall hear from me by every opportunity; and I need not tell you how much pleasure frequent Letters from you will give to My Dr Sally Your aff[ectiona]^{te}

John Jay

My Love to Maria

ALS, NNC (EJ: 08069).

1. SLJ and Maria Jay spent twenty-seven days in Lebanon Springs at the bathhouse run by Isaac Terboss. PAJ accompanied his mother and sister on the trip from New York City. SLJ took the therapeutic waters to treat a leg injury, and Maria went to treat a facial ailment. See JJ to Ann Jay, 8 June 1796, above; SLJ to Catharine Livingston Ridley, 28 July [misdated 29 July], ALS, NNC (EJ: 06471); 29 July 1796, below; JJ to SLJ, 31 July, ALS, NNC (EJ: 08070); 4 Aug. 1796, below; Bill from Isaac Terboss, 22 Aug. 1796, D, NNC.

Sarah Livingston Jay to Catharine Livingston Ridley

Lebanon 29th. July [17]96.

My D^r. Catharine,

I did myself the pleasure of writing to you yesterday[1] by M^r. Francis Huger,[2] since which Hetty, who is dissatisfied with our Land-Lady has determined to go to New York— She will on Monday set out for Albany in the stage that runs from this place to that, & from thence will take the stages to New York— As there would be an impropriety in my remaining without a Maid, I wish Peter to engage a berth for Eliza either in an Albany stage or Sloop as he thinks best— if in a Sloop he can recommend her to the Captain's care, & request him to procure a Seat for her in the stage from Albany here.

Except the propriety there is in my having a Maid there is very little use for one until we take our passage; so that Eliza will be quite equal to any thing I want with one— The sooner however she can come the better, & if that little box should have arrived from Baltimore I should be glad she would bring it with her— If Peter can find the travelling backgammon table M^{rs}. Cortlandt would be very glad she could bring that with her likewise—[3] Give my love to M[r]. Jay & Peter & remember me to inquiring friends— Adieu! Yours sincerely—

S. Jay

ALS, NNC (EJ: 08121). Endorsed.

1. SLJ's letter of 28 [mistakenly dated 29] July, ALS, NNC (EJ: 06471).

2. Probably Francis Kinloch Huger (1773–1855), physician, artillery colonel, and son-in-law of Thomas Pinckney, recently back from an attempt to free Lafayette from an Austrian prison with Dr. Julius Erich Bollman (1769–1821).

SLJ noted in her letter of 28 July, that "M[r]. & M[rs]. Huger & an younger brother of M[r]. Huger's arrived here, how long they are to stay is uncertain. The young Gentleman will take charge of this letter as he leaves this place this afternoon & will pass thro' New York in his way to Philadelphia."

3. SLJ and Maria Jay visited Lebanon Springs for health reasons. SLJ updated her sister on their respective conditions: "Whether I shall be benefited by coming here or not is yet uncertain. Not the least irruption has appear'd since I left home, tho' I frequently feel those sensations which used to precede the irruption. I shall at any rate rejoice on Maria's account, for the sore upon her nose which had made its appearance before we left home puts on an appearance so like poor Mamma's, & proves so obstinate that I believe nothing less than these Springs would have cur'd it. yesterday I thought it better, but today the scab was swashed off in the Bath & I perceive a humor from it which threatens to be tedious. another sore of the same nature has appeared upon her finger." SLJ to Catharine Livingston Ridley, 28 [mistakenly dated 29] July, ALS, NNC (EJ: 06471). For more on the visit to Lebanon Springs, see also JJ to SLJ, 25 July 1796, and note 1, above, and 4 Aug. 1796, below.

To Joseph Brant

New York 1st. August 1796

Sir

I was favored the Day before Yesterday with your Letter of the 24th. June[1] respecting Compensation from this State for Lands Claimed by the Mohawks— Not possessing sufficient Information I cannot at present form a Judgment of the Merits of those claims, whatever they may be I think it would be advisable for the Claimants to unite in appointing and sending here at the next Session of the Legislature, two or three deputies with full and well authenticated powers to state those Claims with accuracy and to make a final settlement with the State Respecting them.— Claims of this kind become more and more obscure by time, and they ought always to be determined while the Facts on which they depend remain capable of being ascertained and proved in a satisfactory manner.— The Young men who were here did not appear to possess either the Information or the Powers necessary to a conclusive Settlement—[2] I do not as yet know whether Justice demands any thing or what for the Claimants from this State but I assure you and them that nothing on my part shall be wanting to cause what may be right to be done — For altho' the state ought firmly to Reject and resist all spurious Claims, yet every consideration of Justice and sound Policy, which I believe to be inseperable, demands that all Claims which on Examination appear to be well founded, should be readily and fairly satisfied — [3] I have the Honor to be with sentiments of Respect Sir Your most Ob.^t & H'ble Servt

(signed) John Jay

Capt. Jos: Brandt

LbkC, N: Governor's Lbk. 1 (EJ: 03031).

1. Letter not found.

2. Aaron Hill (Kanonaron) and Henry Aaron Hill (Kenwendeshon) visited JJ in New York City in March. See JJ's Message to the New York State Senate, 29 Mar. 1796, above.

3. For New York's negotiations with the Mohawk of Upper Canada, see the editorial note "Indian Affairs under Jay's Governorship," above.

From Benjamin Rush

[Philadelphia 2nd August 1796.]

Dear Sir,

Permit me to request your Acceptance of a Copy of a medical Work which I have just published.[1] It contains some new proofs of the domestic Origin of the yellow fever in our Country, and of Course cannot fail of being interesting to the *first* Citizen of the state of New York. Until the domestic Origin of the yellow fever in the United States be admitted, we shall always hold, the health, commerce, and population of our Cities by the precarious tenure of rainy and cool summers.— There is no truth in any science more obvious ^than this,^ and nothing more true, than that it may be prevented with as much ease and certainty as any of the common evils of life.

Mr Lownes[2] (who speaks with great Gratitude of your Civilities to him) informs me that you have lately devoted some of your leisure hours to the Study of the prophesies of the Old testaments. You will find by the Conclusion of my book that I have not been indifferent to them. D^r: Hartley's "Observations on man" have opened many delightful views upon those subjects.[3] Winchester upon the prophesies which are yet to be fulfilled, is full of great & interesting matter.[4] If you have y ^not^ read that work, you have a sublime pleasure yet to come. He is at all times ingenious, and for the most part, I believe his Opinions are consonant of the natural & simple meaning of the

Scriptures. My dear Mrs Rush joins in most respectful Compliments to Mrs Jay with Dear Sir your sincere, and Affectionate friend

Benjn: Rush

Govr. Jay

ALS, NNC (EJ: 09454).

1. Benjamin Rush, *Medical inquiries and observations: containing an account of the bilious remitting and intermitting yellow fever, as it appeared in Philadelphia in the year 1794. Together with an inquiry into the proximate cause of fever: and a defence of blood-letting as a remedy for certain diseases* (Philadelphia, 1796; *Early Am. Imprints*, series 1, no. 31144). Rush was one of the leading proponents of the infectious (environmental) cause of epidemics. See the editorial note "John Jay and the Yellow Fever Epidemics," above.

2. Probably Caleb Lownes.

3. In the conclusion of his work, Rush notes that yellow fever may fulfill Biblical prophecy, and that the disease may, according to David Hartley (1705–57), allow for "the propagation of Christianity throughout the world by *natural* means," also quoting his ideas about training missionaries in medicine, 256–57. See also David Hartley, *Observations on man: his frame, his duty, and his expectations* (London, 1749).

4. Elhanan Winchester, *A course of lectures, on the prophecies that remain to be fulfilled. Delivered in the borough of Southwark, as also, at the chapel in Glasshouse-Yard, London 1789* (Norwich, [1794–95]; *Early Am. Imprints*, series 1, nos. 29907 and 28110).

To Sarah Livingston Jay

New York 4 Augt. 1796

My dear Sally

I wrote you a few Lines some Days ago—[1] M^rs^. Danbery will be the Bearer of them; but I understand she is still here, & will not set out untill Tomorrow or the next Day— M^rs^. Ridley has also written by her, and sent you one or two umbrellas

Your kind Letters of the 27 & 28 of last Month[2] have come to Hand, and I thank you for them very sincerely— It gives me pleasure to assure You that the town is perfectly free from the Yellow Fever, so that no Credit is due to any Reports to the contrary—[3] indeed I understand from those who have the best opportunities of being informed, that the city is more than commonly healthy at this Season of the Year— Little Sallys Face is again as smooth as ever, and altho she is I think somewhat ~~thinner~~ leaner than she was, yet she is ʌinʌ very good spirits.

William and Peter are well, and often talk of you. I had a Letter two Days ago from Nancy, assuring me that her Complaints continue to abate and her Health to improve— she expresses a strong Desire to be frequently informed respecting you & Maria.

Our Cousin Mr Augustus Van Horne died last Sunday Evening—[4] He was not supposed to be so near his End— M^r. & M^rs. Cruger[5] are going to the Eastward, and it is probable you will have the pleasure of seeing them at the Springs—[6] I wish I could say as much relative to myself— Business does not cease to forbid my being long absent from the City.

M^rs. White's Family is still afflicted with Sickness— her Son is far from well; and has had one or more Fits which give alarm—

I wish I could join with you in listening to the murmuring Brook you mention; but my busy Life allows me few of the pleasures which Leisure and Retirement afford— Adieu my Dear Sally Yours very affectionately

John Jay

Remember me to M^rs. Cortlandt & Maria.

ALS, NNC (EJ: 10022).

1. Probably JJ's letter of 31 July, C, NNC (EJ: 08070).

2. Letters not found.

3. See the editorial note "John Jay and the Yellow Fever Epidemics," above.

4. Augustus Van Horne died on 2 Aug. *Argus, Greenleaf's Daily Advertiser* (New York), 4 Aug. 1796.

5. Nicholas Cruger and Ann Markoe Cruger.

6. SLJ and Maria were then taking the waters at Lebanon Spring. See JJ to SLJ, 25 July, and SLJ to Catharine Livingston Ridley, 29 July 1796, both above.

To John Lowell

New York 24 Augt. 1796

Dear Sir

Your Letter of the 1st. Instant[1] was last Week left at my House—presuming from that Circumstance that your Son was in town,[2] I sent my Son to enquire for him at our principal Lodging Houses, and at other Places—but without Success. I regret ˄my˄ not having had the Pleasure of seeing him, and evincing by friendly attentions my Esteem and Regard both for You and for him—

It is happy for the United States that so great a part of the People are able to discern their true Interests. The Nature of our Government demands from the virtuous and enlightened unceasing Vigilance and Effort—not merely that Good may be done, but that Mischief may be prevented. How far we may prudently calculate on there being constantly a due portion of this vigilance & Effort Experience is yet to decide—

The general Tranquility we at present enjoy exceeds what might have been expected. I wish it may be durable— we shall be more free from Danger, when a greater proportion of our People become well informed— Schools Colleges and Churches are in my opinion absolutely essential to Governments like ours.

The Desire of *Destinction* operates most powerfully in this Country as an Incitement to the Acquisition of Wealth— it will perhaps become a Characteristic in our national Character; and in many Respects produce Evil— But altho' many things are not exactly as we wish, we have nevertheless abundant Reason to be thankful— With the best Wishes for the Health and Happiness of Yourself and Family I am Dear Sir Your most ob.^t & hble Servt

John Jay

ALS, NHi (EJ: 02963).

1. Lowell to JJ, 1 Aug. 1796, ALS, NNC (EJ: 06915).

2. When Lowell's eldest son, John Lowell Jr., travelled to Philadelphia on private business, he planned to visit New York on his return trip to Boston for the purpose of meeting JJ. Lowell noted that he would feel "wounded if a Son of yours, should visit our State without giving me an Opportunity of seeing him," and further informed JJ that his son "will render himself agreable by being able to give you a correct State of the Politics of our Part of the Union." Lowell to JJ, 1 Aug. 1796, ALS, NNC (EJ: 06915).

From Thomas Pinckney

London 25th. August 1796

Dear Sir,

In compliance with the request contained in your favor of the 18th. of June[1] by Mr King I inclose an acknowledgement of my having received from you the sum of £1185..16.0 towards the fund for prosecuting the claims of our Citizens in cases of capture. I have likewise to acknowledge the receipt of your favor by M^r. Gore;[2] & while I express my satisfaction in the appointments which have lately been made of our public Agents to this Country, I am happy to have it in my power to congratulate You upon the Office of the fifth Commissioner having fallen to our friend Col. Trumbull.

M^r. King not having arrived in time for me to embark with a reasonable prospect of reaching home before the Autumnal Equinox, I have deferred my departure till that stormy season shall have passed. On my arrival in America I shall doubtless learn whether there will be a probability, as suggested in your last favor, that I may be of utility there, in a line compatible with the circumstances in which I may then find myself—'till then I can only say that my disposition in general prompts me to render what services may be in my power when not inconsistant with the duties I owe to my young family or repugnant to my feelings of propriety.

Accept, dear Sir, my best wishes for your health & prosperity and believe me to be with perfect esteem and respectful regard Your faithful & most obedient Servant,

Thomas Pinckney

His Ex^y. Mr Jay

ALS, ScHi (EJ: 03484). C (fragment), NNC (EJ: 09466). Addressed: "His Excellency / John Jay Esquire / &c^a. &c^a. &c^a / New York". Endorsed: ". . . Rec^d. 16 Octr by D^r. Edwards".

1. JJ to Pinckney, 18 June 1796, Dft, NNC (EJ: 09473).

2. Probably a letter of introduction for Christopher Gore, one of the newly appointed commissioners for maritime claims under the Jay Treaty. JJ to Pinckney, 10 May 1796, Dft, NNC (EJ: 08957).

From Rufus King

London August 25. 1796

Dear Sir

All that I have yet seen here, corresponds with the information you gave ∧us∧ respecting the temper and inclinations of this Government— My own experience authorises no conclusions— The Commissioners on the part of G[reat]. B[ritain]. in the Capture Questions are as unexceptionable as we could have expected— they are both esteemed enlightened, candid, and honorable, men— our Commissioners are equally reputable; and the completion of the Board which this day took place, by a decision by lot in favor of our Countryman Col^o. Trumbul, places this Business in a satisfactory Situation— It was not to have been expected that the Commissioners would agree in the fifth Man; next to this it was of great importance that they should agree on the two names to be thrown into the Urn— Our commissioners agreed to Doct. Swabry named by the british Commissioners, and they agreed to Col. Trumbull named by our commissioners—[1]

At present I perceive no reason to suppose that any Delays, which are improper will happen in the further progress of this important Business. With perfect Respect & Esteem I am D^r. Sir Your ob. Serv

Rufus King

P.S. M^r. Pinckney will embark in about four weeks—
M^r. Jay &c. &c. &c.

ALS, NNC (EJ: 06690). Note: "Liverpool 31 Aug^t / In the Diana His M[ost].O[bedient].S[ervant]. / J. Maury." Endorsed: ". . . rec^d 21 Oct. / ans^d. 21 Octr. 1796." The ship *Diana* captained by Samuel

Pile, sailed from Liverpool and arrived in Philadelphia on 21 Oct. *Philadelphia Gazette*, 21 Oct. 1796. James Murray (1746–1840), a Virginia merchant residing in Liverpool, served as the longstanding U.S. consul in that city from 1790 to 1829.

1. On the maritime claims commission, see the editorial note "Aftermath of the Jay Treaty: Responses, Ratification, and Implementation," above.

To Thomas Mifflin

New York 6th September 1796

Sir

I have been favored with your Excellency's Letter of 27th July containing a number of Papers respecting certain Intruders on the Lands of Pennsylvania, and intimating a wish that such measures may be taken as our Law should warrant to restrain and punish their assembling in or retreating to this State— I should have written to you sooner but waited for the Result of certain Enquiries which were making in those Quarters.[1]

The union of the States has introduced Relations between each of them far more intimate and diversified, than those which exist between distinct nations. Hence has been produced a State of things not contemplated in all its Combinations, by the Law of Nations or by the Common Law, nor does this subject appear to me to have been as yet minutely attended to, ~~nor~~ ∧or∧ provided for either by our National Legislature or by the Legislatures of the different States.

The union having occasioned new relative Duties and Interests between its members, considered even in their separate & individual capacities, new Laws are necessary to define and enforce the performance of those duties— The Case stated in your Letter appears to belong to this Class, and there is Reason to doubt whether the law of this State as it now stands can take Cognizance of it, especially if the Persons alluded to conduct themselves with caution— But these however are Questions which it is not within my Department to express any opinion upon. I nevertheless assure you with great Truth, that I shall always be ready to do whatever may properly depend upon me, on any occasion that may occur, to restrain and punish those who attempt to disturb the Peace or violate the Rights of any ∧of∧ the other States.

I expect that our Attorney General will return to Town in about Ten Days— If you think it proper, I will put these papers into his hands, with directions to do whatever may be proper on the subject of them— I mention this because as you communicated them to me in *Confidence*, I feel a Hesitation about making this or any other use of them without your permission.

I have the Honor to be with great Respect your Excellency's most obedient and humble Servant,

John Jay

His Excellency Thomas Mifflin Esqr. Governor of the State of Pennsylvania

LS, NNGL (EJ: 90535). Endorsed: "1796 6th. September: From / His Excellency / John Jay Esqr. / Governor of the State of / New York in answer to / Govr. Mifflins Letter respecting / Intrusions on Penn^a: Land by / Connecticut Claimants". LbkC, N: Governor's Lbk. 1 (EJ: 03036).

1. Letter not found. Mifflin's endorsement of JJ's letter indicates that his letter referred to his concerns over residents of Connecticut who claimed title (and disputed title held by settlers from Pennsylvania and New York) for land in the "Connecticut Gore," the territory on the New York–Pennsylvania border.

The controversy over these lands arose due to a title dispute between New York and Connecticut over a strip of land in what is now Steuben County, N.Y. The land, 8 miles wide (north–south) and 240 miles long (east–west) was above the New York–Pennsylvania line and below the Massachusetts-Connecticut line (if extended). Connecticut claimed title to this land, like the Western Reserve, under its 1662 "sea-to-sea" charter. Settlers from New York, Pennsylvania, and Connecticut settled in the area. In 1795, Connecticut sold the Gore to Jeremiah Halsey and Andrew Ward, in exchange for the duo finishing the new state house in Hartford. Halsey and Ward formed the Connecticut Gore Land Company and began granting titles to settlers. On 8 Feb. 1796, JJ wrote to the New York State Senate that "certain persons under pretence of title from a neighbouring state. . . were by improper practices endeavouring to draw into question the jurisdiction, and to excite opposition to the lawful authority of this state over this tract." JJ directed the state attorney general, Josiah Ogden Hoffman, to investigate, and he presented those papers to the legislature. In response, the legislature issued a resolution to protect New York's claims. However, the Gore Company upon hearing this, preempted New York's action by bringing their own ejectments against the New York claimants in U.S. Circuit Court for the District of Connecticut, arguing that the land in question was under Connecticut's jurisdiction. Justice Cushing presided, with the Connecticut claimants represented by James Sullivan and Theophilus Parsons. The New York defendants were represented by Hoffman and AH. Indeed, the legal case of the New Yorkers was entirely directed and paid for by New York State. Concurrently, New York and Connecticut attempted to resolve the matter out of court. Matters of borders and of legal jurisdiction, state and federal, were clearly the larger issues at stake in this dispute. Eventually, after much negotiation and a separate suit between the two states before the Supreme Court, Connecticut ceded claim to the Gore in exchange for the Western Reserve lands (now northeastern Ohio). DHSC, 8: 178–270 and LPAH, 1: 657–73; N.Y. Senate Journal, 19th sess. (1796), 34, 44, 45, 50–51, 68. See Josiah Ogden Hoffman to JJ, 14 Dec. 1797, below; JJ to Jonathan Trumbull Jr., 4 Dec. 1799, Dft, NNC (EJ: 08998); and JJ's Address to the New York State Legislature, 28 Jan. 1800, ADS, PHi: Gratz (EJ: 01135); PtD, New-York Gazette, 3 Feb.; Argus, Greenleaf's New Daily Advertiser and Spectator (both New York), 5 Feb.; Massachusetts Mercury (Boston), 7 Feb.; Newburyport Herald, 7 Feb.; Greenleaf's New York Journal, 8 Feb.; Universal Gazette (Philadelphia), 13 Feb. 1800; N.Y. Assembly Journal, 23rd sess. (1800) [28 Jan. 1800], 5–7; N.Y. Senate Journal, 23rd sess. (1800) [28 Jan. 1800], 4–6; NYGM, 2: 448–54.

From John Trumbull

London September 7th. 1796.

Dear Sir

I returned to this Country a few days since, from an Excursion which was protracted to a much greater length than I at first intended or foresaw:— It will I am sure, give you pleasure to know that there is every probability of my being tolerably rewarded for the trouble I have had.

On my Arrival here, I had the pleasure to find, among many Letters from my friends, your several favors of the 10th. Novr. 13th. Jany. 12th. May and 18th. June, for which I beg you to accept my thanks;— You must at the same time receive my Apology for a sort of Petulance, which I fear escaped me in one of my Letters to you written at Rochefort.—[1] I had (until then) received *no* Line from you after your Arrival in America, and few from any of my friends.— I was ignorant how many of your and their favors waited my arrival here;— and I sometimes felt keenly the mortyfying fear of being forgotten.

Dr. Edwards will deliver you this, He will also communicate to you the State of a discussion which was pending when He left Paris, between the Government of France, and our Minister there:— I Trust that the Treaty will have the same fate on this Side of the Ocean as it has had on your's, and derive Advocates and Friends from every new Discussion.— So far as I learn, Mr. Monroe has conducted the Argument so properly as to have almost driven his Opponent from the Field, and I have real hope that Honor will derive to his Country and himself, from this Source;— It is not an easy thing however for a Man to act the part of Advocate for Measures to which He is personally adverse.[2]

You will know that I have most unexpectedly become once more an Agent in this Business of the Treaty, having been by the Concurrence of Choice and Destiny named the 5th. Commissioner under the 7th. Article:—[3] I could hardly have been called to a Situation more unlooked for than this;— I feel its Delicacy and Importance, and the imperfect preparation for its Duties which I derive from the general Nature of my pursuits for many Years past.— But the general Principles of Justice and Equity I hope are sufficiently established in my Mind, to prevent the Danger of any gross Errors: and, the Law of Nations so far as relates to this Subject, is neither so Voluminous or Intricate, but that the degree of Attention which I have sometimes given to other subjects, applied to this, will, I trust render me Sufficiently master of it.— It will however be almost impossible so to Conduct as not to offend alternately, some of both Parties; and I must trust to the Candour of the dispassionate to do me Justice in believing, that if I should be thought to Err, my Errors will, at worst be those of Judgement only, from which the best and the Wisest can claim no Exemption.

I am happy to learn that so great, and to you so pleasing a Change has taken place in the Opinions of the People of your State— it is natural.— public Opinion is generally correct, so far as Information is just; and to produce this change, nothing further was necessary, than that you should be better and more universally known. I beg you will present my best respects to Mʳˢ. Jay, to whom as well as to yourself I most heartily wish all Happiness, Being most truly, Dear Sir Your friend & Servant,

Jnᵒ. Trumbull

ALS, NNC (EJ: 07206). Endorsed. LbkC, DLC: Trumbull (EJ: 10355).

1. Letters not found. A JJ letter to Noah Webster sent in mid-January 1796, mentioned that a letter for JT was enclosed. JJ to Webster, 13 Jan. 1796, Dft, NNC (EJ: 08950).

2. Dr. Enoch Edwards (1751–1802) of Pennsylvania. Edwards carried letters from James Monroe documenting his defense of the Jay Treaty in France in correspondence with French minister of foreign affairs Charles Delacroix. See *PTJ*, 29: 230; *PJM*, 16: 387.

3. For JT's role on the spoliation claims commission, see the editorial note "Aftermath of the Jay Treaty: Responses, Ratification, and Implementation," above.

To George Washington

New York 19 Septʳ 1796

Dear Sir

It occurs to me that it may not be perfectly prudent to say that we are never to *expect* Favors from a Nation, for that assertion seems to imply that Nations always *are*, or always *ought* to be moved *only* by interested motives. It is true that disinterested Favors are so rare, that on *that account* they are not to be expected between nations; and if that Sentiment turned on that Reason vizᵗ. their being so *uncommon*, the assertion would then be so limited by that Reason, as not to be liable to misconstruction. I think it would be more safe to omit the word *expected* and retain only the words *not to be calculated upon*, which appear to me to be quite sufficient— Permit me to submit this to your Consideration and believe me to be with perfect Respect Esteem & attachment, Dear Sir your obliged & obᵗ. Servᵗ.[1]

John Jay

The Presid. of the U.S.

ALS, DLC: Washington (EJ: 10661).

1. When GW intended to retire in 1792, he had JM draft a farewell address, but as GW was persuaded to remain in office, he did not then use it. However, in 1796 upon his determination to retire, GW drafted a new address based in part on JM's draft but with additional commentary. He sent it to AH for review, and AH prepared a new draft, to which he made further revisions after discussing the text with JJ, before forwarding it to GW. AH also revised the original draft and returned it to GW, but the president decided to work from AH's original revision, and after conferring with cabinet members, sent his revised text dated 17 Sept. to David C. Claypoole for publication in the *American Daily Advertiser* (Philadelphia) on 19 Sept. JJ then sent this final suggestion to GW that he rephrase one passage in the address, but it arrived too late to be included.

The paragraph in question as printed in the published version of the Farewell Address read as follows: "Harmony, liberal intercourse with all nations, are recommended by policy, humanity, and interest. But even our commercial policy should hold an equal and impartial hand; neither seeking nor granting exclusive favours or preferences; consulting the natural course of things; diffusing and diversifying by gentle means the streams of commerce, but forcing nothing; establishing (with powers so disposed, in order to give trade a stable course, to define the rights of our merchants, and to enable the government to support them); conventional rules of intercourse, the best that present circumstances and mutual opinion will permit, but temporary, and liable to be from time to time abandoned or varied, as experience and circumstances shall dictate; constantly keeping in view that 'tis folly in one nation to look for disinterested favours from another; that it must pay with a portion of its independence for whatever it may accept under that character; that, by such acceptance, it may place itself in the condition of having given equivalents for nominal favours, and yet of being reproached with ingratitude for not giving more. There can be no greater error than to expect or calculate upon real favours from nation to nation. 'Tis an illusion, which experience must cure, which a just pride ought to discard." Following the deaths of AH and GW, JJ was at various times called to testify as to their relative roles in the authorship of the address. See especially JJ to Richard Peters, 29 Mar. 1811, FC, NNC (EJ: 12797); C, PHi (EJ: 04050).

See also the Introductory Note and text to AH to GW, 10 May; GW to AH, 15 May; AH, Abstract of Points to Form and Address [16 May–5 July 1796]; AH to GW, 30 July 1796; and AH, Draft of Washington's Farewell Address," *PAH*, 20: 169–73, 174–78, 178–83, 264–65, 265–88; *PGW: PS*, 10: 349–54, 478–84; Carol M. Brier, "John Jay and George Washington's Valedictory," parts 1 and 2, *Supreme Court Historical Society Quarterly* 32 (2010), no. 1: 6–9, and no. 2: 6–9; and *Washington's farewell address, in facsimile, with transliterations of all the drafts of Washington, Madison, & Hamilton, together with their correspondence and other supporting documents; edited, with a history of its origin, reception by the nation, rise of the controversy respecting its authorship, and a bibliography by Victor Hugo Paltsits* (New York, 1935).

To William Henry Clinton

New York 19 Septr. 1796

Sir

I rec^d. Yesterday the Letter which you did me the Honor to write on the 20th. of June last,[1] relative to Lands held by the late Sir Henry Clinton in this State, and which during the late War were confiscated by an act of the Legislature. At that Time I was in Europe, and have little Information respecting the

Principles on which several of the Persons affected by that act, were named in it— There is Room to doubt whether the Reason for inserting Sir Henry Clintons name was the one you mention vizt his being supposed to have been born in america— Gov^er. Tryon was also named in that act, altho' well known not to have been a native of this Country.[2] In Times like those, the irascible Passions usually operate forceably; and it happened in the course of that contest, that they were too often unnecessarily inflamed.

It is natural for You to enquire whether there be any and what Degree of Probability that the Property in Question would, on application to the Legislature of this State, or to the Governm^t. of the united States, be restored?— as this State is *interested* in the question, my official Situation constrains me to be reserved— it is a question in Regard to which I have no personal Interest; having never purchased nor in any way been the Proprietor of any confiscated Property whatever.

as to the article in the Treaty of Peace to which you allude— permit me to remind you of the Destinction between a *Recommendation* and a *Stipulation* to restore. I think Sir! you would do well to state the Case to some able Counsellors, and be guided by their opinion as to the Merits of your Claim to Restitution. If your Brother should, as you expect, call here in his Way from the West Indies, he will have an opportunity of obtaining candid and judicious opinions and correct Information on every Point that may be deemed material; and my Endeavours to render New York agreable to him shall not be wanting.[3]

Whatever occasions may heretofore have subsisted between the two Countries for Crimination and Complaint, it certainly is desirable that they should not be incautiously revived or brought into View; but on the contrary, that the Impressions they made should be succeeded by those which mutual Justice Kindness and friendly Attentions always produce—[4] I have the honor to be with great Respect, Sir your most ob^t. & h'ble Servt.

John Jay

Col: W. H. Clinton aide de Camp to His Royal Highness the Duke of York

ALS, MiU-C (EJ: 04931). Endorsed: ". . . Governor Jay / to / Col^o. Clinton / In answer to Col. C. / letter of June 20th. 1796 / respecting the late / Sir H. Clinton *American Property / Original*". Dft, NNC (EJ: 08966).

1. See William Henry Clinton to JJ, 20 Jun. 1796, above.

2. In his reply of 8 Aug. 1797 [ALS, NNC (EJ: 08651)], Clinton wrote that while he was inclined to agree with JJ on this point, "were there not papers, which state that Fact among others." The elder Clinton had spent part of his youth in New York while his father was colonial governor. On the rights of "real British subjects" to property, see Extracts from JJ's Report on Violations of the Treaty of Peace, *JJSP*, 4: 431n3.

3. Clinton's brother, Henry Clinton, was captured by the French while sailing from San Domingo, where he had served with the 66th regiment. He returned to England in 1797.

4. In his reply of 8 Aug., Clinton wrote, "I hope that the Justice of my Claim will be admitted from my refutation of such pretence as may have been set up against my Father, & then have no doubt but that both Countries will consent to Arbitration. I can have no Objection to the Decision of your Excellency & Mr. Bond, being certain that the Interests of an Individual as well as those of the State will be considered, and that the Amity which subsists between the two Countries will point out some means of doing justice to both: under these Circumstances therefore I shall wait a favorable Opportunity to pursue my Claim."

From Christopher Gore

London 26. Septr. 1796

My dear Sir

Since my arrival in this country, your letters have procured me many civilities & attentions—[1] From the Lord Chancellor[2] I have received very markt & pleasing attention— And both he, & Lady Loughborough are very particular, in their enquiries after your health & happiness—

You will have learnt before this reaches you, that your late Secretary is the fifth commissioner— After it was understood that we could not agree on a person to fill this office, the commissioners on the part of the U. States, gave to those on the part of this Government, several names from which they might select, one the most agreeable to them, to be the object of ballot— The British Commiss[ioners] did the same to us— The B[ritish]. C[ommissioners]. consulted Lord Grenville on the names handed them— His Lordship said he did not know these gentlemen, but that the situation, in which Mr Trumbull had been placed by you, renderd him worthy of their confidence, & that respect to you woud induce him to prefer that name to any other— This was accordingly selected by them—& Doctor Swabeyes by the American Commissioners— Mr Trumbull's name was drawn—

I am happy in the belief that both Mr T[rumbull]. & Mr P[inckney]. are solicitous to preserve inviolate the honor of our nation, as well as secure redress for those individuals, whose claims will be the principal subject of consideration—

Doctor Nicholl & Mr Anstey appear to be candid and just men—and altho' it is not improbable, that, in the course of our business, there may be a difference on some points, yet I entertain no doubt, that these gentlemen will always be disposed to do what, in their opinion, shall be conformable to the law of nations, to justice, & equity— This is not less the duty of the Amer[ican]. Comm[issioners]. and I trust will be equally the object of their enquiry, and the end at which they will aim—[3]

I pray you to present the sincere respects, and regards of Mrs Gore & myself to Mrs Jay, & Mrs Ridley, and to be assurd that I remain with the most perfect respect & regard your faithful friend & obed Serv.

C. GORE

ALS, NNC (EJ: 08481; EJ: 08476). Endorsed: "... rec^d. nov 1796".

1. For JJ's letters of introduction on behalf of Gore, see JJ to Thomas Pinckney, 10 May 1796, Dft, NNC (EJ: 08957).

2. Alexander Wedderburn, Lord Loughborough.

3. On the work of the maritime claims commission, see the editorial note "Aftermath of the Jay Treaty: Responses, Ratification, and Implementation," above.

To Henry Glen

New York 11 Octr. 1796

Dear Sir

I have had the Pleasure of recieving your Letter of the 5th. ult:[1] mentioning that the British Garrisons had retired from Oswego and Niagara, and that our Troops were in Possession of those Posts— I am happy to learn that this Business was conducted in a manner so satisfactory to both Parties— The officers on both Sides deserve Credit for the Decorum & Propriety which they observed on the occasion— It is to be hoped that mutual Care will be taken to avoid every thing that may cause Irritation or Disgust, and that the People on each Side of the Line will remember that it is the Interest, as well as the Duty of Neighbours, to live in a neighbourly manner— This State may always derive advantages from a friendly Intercourse with Canada, in perhaps a greater Proportion than any of the other States; and therefore it should and doubtless will be our Policy to facilitate it by such Improvements as to Roads and Canals, as the State of Things may from Time to Time indicate—when you meet with Judge Duane[2] be so good as to present my best Comp^ts. to him— I am Dear Sir your most Ob^t & hble Servt

John Jay

Henry Glen Esqr

ALS, Harlan Crow Library. (EJ: 10755). Addressed: "Henry Glen Esqr / Schenectady—" Endorsed. Henry Glen, a Schenectady merchant, was appointed Assistant Deputy Quartermaster General and state commissioner for Indian affairs during the war of independence. Following the conflict, he sat in the New York State Assembly (1786–87, 1810) and in the U.S. House of Representatives (1793–1801).

1. Letter not found.

2. James Duane, then residing in Schenectady.

From Christopher Gore

London 24. Octbr. 1796

My dear Sir

I have the pleasure to inform you, that we have begun our operations, under the treaty with this country— It is impossible to prophecy, with any certainty, what will be the temper, and disposition, with which some points will be met.

To decide causes, that have been determined by the Lords Commissioners of appeal, & perhaps reverse their decisions, will affect the sensibility of some men— To draw within the jurisdiction of the boards, causes, before the same have been thro' the different courts, will affect not only the sensibility of pride, but perhaps a stronger passion the love of property. Such a decision would very materially lessen the profits of Doctors Commons—[1] On the other hand, it is but candid, for us to reflect that in making decisions of the latter kind, if such should be made, we may be influenced by a desire of saving to our country, & its citizens the great sums that are necessary in carrying causes thro' the admiralty courts—

The first point will come up in a cause, that is now before the Board—the other will possibly not be agitated very soon— I take the liberty of sending you, by Capt Fox, a poem written by our brother Comm[issioner] Mr Anstey,[2] a pamphlet on manners, & Mr Burke's letter on the subject of making peace with France—[3] With my best respects to Mrs Jay, in which Mrs Gore sincerely unites, I remain my dear Sir, with the highest respect, & esteem, Your faithful Friend and obed. Servt.

C. GORE

His Excellency John Jay Esqr.

ALS, NNC (EJ: 08482; EJ: 08477). Endorsed.

1. Doctors' Commons, also called the College of Civilians, was a society of lawyers practicing civil law in London. On the work of the Maritime claims commissioners, see the editorial note "Aftermath of the Jay Treaty: Responses, Ratification, and Implementation," above.

2. Probably Anstey's *The Pleader's guide, a didactic poem, in two books, containing the conduct of a suit at law, with the arguments of Counsellor Bother'um, and Counsellor Bore'um, in an action between John-a-Gull, and John-a-Gudgeon. For Assault and Battery, at a late Contested Election by the late John Surrebutter, Esq. Special Pleader, and Barrister at law* (London, 1796).

3. Edmund Burke, *Two letters addressed to a member of the present Parliament, on the proposals for peace with the regicide directory of France* (London, 1796).

Address to the New York State Legislature

[New York, 1 November 1796]

Gentlemen of the Senate & Assembly

When it is considered how greatly the Happiness of of every Nation depends on the Wisdom with which their Government is administered, the occasion which has called you together at this early Season, cannot but be regarded as unusually important.[1]

The Period fixed for the Election of a President of the United States is approaching, and the Measures preparatory to it in this State, are now to be taken. In every possible Situation of our National affairs—whether of Peace or War, of Tranquility or Ferment, of Prosperity or Misfortune, this object will not cease to demand the utmost Care and Circumspection.

Hitherto the Embarrassments arising from Competitions, and from the Influences incident to them, have not been experienced. They have been excluded by the uniform and universal Confidence reposed in that illustrious Patriot, who, being distinguished as the Father and Ornament of his Country by a Series of great & disinterested Services, was also eminently qualified, by an uncommon assemblage of Virtues and Talents, for that important and exalted Station.

But that extraordinary Man, having with admirable Wisdom & Fortitude conducted the Nation thro various Vicissitudes and unpropitious Circumstances, to an unexampled Degree of Prosperity, is now about to retire— Mankind has not been accustomed to see the highest Military & Civil Powers of a Nation so recieved, used and resigned, as they have been in this glorious Instance. Every Reflection and Sentiment connected with this interesting Subject, will naturally arise in your Minds— May the same benevolent, wise, and over-ruling Providence which has so constantly and remarkably sustained and protected us, preside over the Public Deliberations and Suffrages.

It gives me Pleasure to inform you, that at a Treaty, held in this City, under the authority of the United States, a final agreement has been concluded between this State, and the Indian Tribes who call themselves the Seven Nations of Canada.[2] Altho their Title to the Territory they claimed, was not unquestionable; yet it was judged more consistent with Sound Policy, to extinguish their claims and consequently their Animosities, by a satisfactory Settlement, than leave the State exposed to the Inconveniences which allways result from Disputes with Indian Tribes. Besides, considering our Strength and their comparative Weakness, every appearance of taking advantage of that Weakness, was to be avoided.

The Claims of the Mohawks to certain other Lands still remain to be adjusted,[3] but there is Reason to expect that these may ∧also be∧ amicably settled; and that the Period is not far distant, when the Indians on our Borders, having convincing Proofs of our Justice and Moderation, will by good offices and a Friendly Intercourse, be led to rely on our Benevolence and Protection, and to view our Prosperity as connected with their own.

I submit to your Consideration whether the Payments to be annually made to the different Tribes who are entitled to them by Contracts with the State, should not be so ordered, as that they may be *punctually* paid in a uniform manner, and at a *fixed* Expence.[4]

Difficulties were experienced in executing the benevolent Intentions of the Legislature respecting a Lazaretto in the vicinity of this City. Ground conveniently situated, could not be purchased; and the placing it on Governors Island, where it could not have been erected at a proper distance from the Garrison, was liable to strong objections. These Difficulties have been removed by the Liberality of the Corporation of the City. They have gratuitously conveyed Bedlows Island to the State, for this & such other Public uses as the Legislature may from time to time direct. Certain Buildings, erected there by the French Republic, have been purchased; and prepared to serve the purpose of a Lazaretto for the present— but as additions & alterations will be necessary, and as Precautions should be taken to prevent that Island from being further Diminished by Encroachments of the Water, the appropriation of some money for these objects will be requisite.

The measures prescribed by Law to prevent the bringing and spreading of infectious diseases in this State, have been taken and faithfully executed. It is however to be lamented, that Cases of the like Fever, with that which in the last Year proved so fatal to this City, have occurred, and there is at present very little Reason to doubt whether that Disease may be generated here. The Subject of Nuisances therefore, having become important to the Safety as well as ∧to∧ the Comfort of our Fellow Citizens, well deserves the Notice and Interposition of the Legislature.[5]

Precarious is the Peace & Security of that People who are not prepared to defend themselves. Permit me to observe that this State has but one Port, & that, important as it is to the whole State, its Situation cannot yet be deemed Secure. The Fortifications that were begun are still unfinished, and it appears to me to merit Consideration, whether this Port can otherwise be secured, than by skilfully fortifying the Passage at the Narrows.[6] It cannot be too frequently recollected that seasons of Peace & Prosperity are the most favorable for Measures & Works of this kind.

Considering the Funds which the State possesses—the appropriations which have been and will be made for various Public uses—the Accounts consequent to such Appropriations—and the evident utility of so arranging and conducting our Fiscal affairs, as that the Funds may be advantageously managed, Accounts with Individuals regularly settled, and the Ballances due to or from them punctually paid—I think it my Duty to suggest whether more adequate Provision for these Objects should not be made.

Altho our Taxes have for Years past been inconsiderable, and altho there is at present no Prospect of our being pressed by any necessity to encrease them, yet it is to be presumed from the Vicissitudes which attend human affairs, that at some future Period, more ample Contributions may become indispensable:— Would it not therefore be prudent, at this calm & tranquil Season, to adopt & establish such Rules & Regulations for Taxation, as being perfectly consistent with the Principles of Justice and rational Liberty, and gradually acquiring the advantages of Experience & usage, may relieve this delicate Subject from many of the perplexing Questions about Principles, Mode & Manner, which at all Times are difficult, & which are particularly embarrassing in Times of Anxiety & Agitation—?

The distressed Situation in which the french Refugees from S^t. Domingo arrived here, induced the Legislature to provide for them in a very benefi- cent manner. The Sums allotted for their support have been expended, and the accounts audited and settled— Many of those unfortunate Persons have left the State; but it is represented to me that a Number of Old Persons and Children are still here, & in a Situation so destitute & wretched, that I cannot forbear mentioning it to you. They cannot with Propriety be considered as the Poor of any particular District— their fate is peculiar, as well as distress- ing; and they appear to me as having become by the Dispensations of Provi- dence the Poor of the State.[7]

It often happens that Persons not urged by Circumstances equally press- ing, come into the State from distant Parts, and in many Instances become burthensome to it. This Subject seems to call for some Regulations, especially as the Law heretofore passed relative to it, has ceased to operate.

I ought not to omit informing you, that the Hon'ble M^r. King having been appointed Minister Plenipotentiary to the Court of Great Britain, & accepted that Place, his Seat in the Senate of the United States has become Vacant.[8]

In the Course of your Deliberations on the Affairs of the State, and the means of preserving & encreasing the Public Welfare, many interesting Subjects will rise into View— such as these among others: The Manner in which the Salt Springs may be rendered the most useful, and the Woods in the Neighbourhood of them best preserved—[9] the Facilities & Encouragement that may be proper towards obtaining an accurate Map of the whole State—[10] The Necessity of rendering the Laws respecting Roads & Bridges more effectual—[11] and of revising & amending those which relate to the militia,[12] & which direct the Inspection of certain of our Staple Commodities—[13] as these & various other objects derive Importance from their Relations to the General Welfare, they will I am persuaded recieve a proportionate Degree of your Attention: And I assure you that it is no less my Desire, than it is my Duty, to cooperate with you in guarding & promoting the Prosperity & Happiness of our Fellow-Citizens.

John Jay

DS, ICHi (EJ: 03505). Endorsed: "Governors Speech to the / Legislature Novem. *1st 1796* / Senate Copy". *Herald* (New York), 2 Nov.; *Register of the Times* (New York), 4 Nov.; *Claypoole's American Daily Advertiser* (Philadelphia), 4 Nov.; *Greenleaf's New York Journal*, 8 Nov.; *Gazette of the United States (Philadelphia)*, 9 Nov.; *Wood's Newark Gazette*, 9 Nov.; *Salem Gazette*, 11 Nov.; *Andrew's Western Star* (Stockbridge), 21 Nov. 1796; *Albany Chronicle*, 2 Jan. 1797, and other newspapers; *N.Y. Assembly Journal*, 20th Sess. (1796–97), 5–6; *N.Y. Senate Journal*, 20th Sess. (1796–97), 4–5; NYGM, 2: 379–85.

For the responses of the state legislature and JJ's replies, see *Philadelphia Gazette*, 8 Nov.; *Aurora General Advertiser* (Philadelphia), 10 Nov.; *Register of the Times* (New York), 11 Nov.; *Andrew's Western Star* (Stockbridge), 21 Nov., and other newspapers; *N.Y. Assembly Journal*, 20th Sess. (1796–97), 11–12; *N.Y. Senate Journal*, 20th Sess. (1796–97), 10, 11.

1. A state law passed on 26 Mar. 1796 called for the legislature to convene on 1 Nov. for the purpose of choosing the presidential electors. *N.Y. State Laws*, 19th sess. (1796), 26.

2. For New York's treaty with the Akwesasne and Caughnawaga Mohawk communities, see the editorial note "Indian Affairs under Jay's Governorship," above.

3. For New York's treaty with the Mohawk of Upper Canada, see the editorial note "Indian Affairs under Jay's Governorship," above.

4. "An ACT to provide for the Payment of the Annuities to the Indians, stipulated to be paid by the State," was passed on 1 Apr. 1797. *N.Y. State Laws*, 20th sess. (1797), 183.

5. The state legislature passed on 30 Mar. 1797, "An ACT for the establishment and support of a Lazaretto," *N.Y. State Laws*, 20th sess. (1797), 158. For more on the yellow fever epidemic and the building of the lazaretto, see the editorial note "John Jay and the Yellow Fever Epidemics," above; JJ to Charlton, 22 Apr. 1796, above; JJ to Alderman Stoutenbourgh, 7 June 1796, LbkC, N: Governor's Lbk. 1 (EJ: 03020); JJ to John Murray, 13 July 1796, LbkC, N: Governor's Lbk. 1 (EJ: 03024); Richard Bayley to JJ, December 1796, ALS, NHi (EJ: 00891) containing letter of 28 Nov. 1796 and report on the lazaretto.

6. For the various plans to fortify New York's inner and outer harbors, see the editorial note "Defending New York," above.

7. On 2 Nov. 1796, a committee was formed in the Senate to consider the bill, "An act for the support of the St. Domingo French refugees in the City of New-York." It passed the Senate and the Assembly on 11 and 17 Jan., respectively. On 21 Jan. 1797, the Council of Revision deemed that "it does

not appear improper" that the bill become law. *N.Y. Senate Journal*, 20th sess. (1796–97), 7, 25, 28, 29; *N.Y. Assembly Journal*, 20th sess. (1796–97), 6, 32, 55, 65; and *N.Y. State Laws*, 20th sess. (1797), 360. See also JJ's Address to the New York State Legislature, 6 Jan. 1796, notes 9–10, above; JJ to Richard Lawrence, 23 Jan. and 9 Feb. 1797, and 6 Jan. 1798; and Lawrence to JJ, 27 Jan. 1797, all below.

8. After RK stepped from his senate seat to take on the role of U.S. minister to Britain, John Laurance (Lawrence) succeeded him as U.S. senator after winning a special election held by the New York State Assembly. *N.Y. Assembly Journal*, 20th sess. (1796–97), 18–19.

9. On 1 Apr., the state legislature passed "An ACT concerning the salt springs in the county of Onondaga," *N.Y. State Laws*, 20th sess. (1797), 206–12.

10. On 28 Mar., the state legislature passed "An ACT in addition to an act entitled an act for the further direction of the Commissioners of the Land Office, and for other purposes therein mentioned, *N.Y. State Laws*, 20th sess. (1797), 126–28.

11. In order that "direct communications be opened and improved between the western, northern, and southern parts" of New York, the state legislature established three lotteries in order to raise the sum of $45,000. See "An ACT for opening and improving certain great roads within this state," *N.Y. State Laws*, 20th sess. (1797), 136–43, quote on 136.

During the twentieth session of the state legislature, lawmakers passed additional bills to build bridges over the Cayuga Lake, Rosendal Kill, and the Mohawk River, and to construct and repair roads in Orange Town and between Albany and Schenectady. *N.Y. State Laws*, 20th sess. (1797), 23–24, 133–36, 187–203, 213, 220–22.

12. For more on the efforts to reform the state militia, see the editorial note "Militia Matters in New York State," below.

13. The state legislature passed "An ACT to continue in force an act entitled 'An act for enreasing the compensation to the measurers of grain and inspectors of flour and meal in this state'" on 30 Mar., and "An ACT making alterations in the inspection laws of this State" on 3 April. *N.Y. State Laws*, 20th sess. (1797), 158, 217–19.

From Philip Schuyler

Albany November 11th 1796

Dear Sir

Your favor of the 11th ult[1] which I received soon after its date, was mislaid, and It did not Occur to me until two days ago that I had not answered It—

I believe the appointment of Mr Smith[2] to the Sheriffs Office in Washington was a prudent Measure, and will probably afford general satisfaction.

From the best information I can procure, neither of the two characters, whom you mention, as soliciting the office of assistant Attorney, are competent to the proper discharge of Its functions. Mr John Henry[3] would be perfectly Adequate but he will not take It. A Mr Bears, Son in Law to Mr Sturges[4] of Connecticut has been some Years in practice in this city, he is a man of sense, having considerable abilities, and a good citizen, what his law knowledge is I really do not know, If that is Adequate, he would be a proper character for the office,—

Soon after my return from New York I requested Mr Winne[5] a Surveyor to examine Lord Amhersts lands and to report to me,[6] he informed me that he was to make surveys in the Summer in the vicinity of his lordships lands, and that he would then view them. Sickness prevented him from doing the one or the other, but during the last term of the Supreme Court I saw him, when he assured me that he was speedily going to that part of the Country, would examine the lands, and give me a detailed Account of them, the moment I receive It, shall transmit It.

My health is good, but a troublesome Ulcer in my thigh does not render it prudent for me to be from home, hence I believe I shall not Attend the legislature at the present session, or If at all not until towards the close of the year. I am Dear Sir with great truth Your Excellenceys Affectionate Humle. Servant,

Ph: Schuyler

His Excellency Governor Jay &c.

ALS, NNC (EJ: 09348).

1. Letter not found.

2. Dr. Philip Smith (c. 1762–1807) of Easton served as sheriff of Washington County from September 1796 to February 1798. *Albany Gazette*, 7 Oct. 1796; *N.Y. Civil List*, 212.

3. Possibly John V. Henry (c. 1767–1829), an attorney of Albany. Henry served as a Federalist member of the state assembly (1800–1802) and as state comptroller (1800–1801).

4. William Pitt Beers (1766–1810), an attorney of Albany, was married to Ann Sturges Beers (1765–1837), the daughter of Jonathan Sturges (1740–1819), an attorney, jurist, and politician from Fairfield, Connecticut.

5. Probably Jacob Winne (1760–1805[?]), surveyor and state assemblyman from Albany County (1800–1801). Winne surveyed Rensselaerwyck Manor in 1789 and did some surveying for Schuyler in 1792–93.

6. On the surveying of Amherst's property, see JJ to Lord Jeffrey Amherst, and JJ to Schuyler, both 12 Apr. 1796, above.

From Rufus King

London Nov. 12, 1796

Dear Sir

I take the Liberty to introduce to you Mr. Macdonald and Mr. Rich the british commissioners in the Debt Questions;[1] the former is a Barrister of Eminence, and Mr. Rich, who has for many years past resided in Holland, is a merchant of irreproachable Character— both are Esteemed to be men of fair & honorable Reputation— That such Characters are appointed on this Occasion may be considered as proof of the Disposition of this Government to cultivate a good understanding and Harmony between the two

Countries—with sincere respect & Esteem I have the honor to be Dear Sir Your ob[edient]. & faithful Ser[vant]

Rufus King

His Excellency M^r. Jay

ALS, NNC (EJ: 06691). Endorsed. Tr, misdated 12 Nov. 1790, NNC (EJ: 11287).

1. Thomas MacDonald and Henry Pye Rich (1737–1809) were appointed as the British commissioners to settle British debt claims under Art. 6 of the Jay Treaty, on which see the editorial note "Aftermath of the Jay Treaty: Responses, Ratification, and Implementation," above.

From Daniel Coxe

London, John Street, Berkeley Square Novr. 30th. 1796

Dear Sir,

I take the Opportunity of the Viscount d'Orleans sailing for New York, to acknowledge the receipt of your favor by M^r. Gore,[1] to whom, from having been out of Town the Summer, and but very lately returned to it, I have not yet been able to pay him all that attention which your introduction entitles him to,— that pleasure I expect soon to have.

The stay of the Viscount d'Orleans will, I beleive, be but short at New York, but should he have occasion or opportunity to pay his Respects to You, I beg leave to speak of him as a French Gentleman of very amiable & genteel Character, formerly in the Naval Service of France, who has some Business to transact in America relative to Property— He has been much in my Family as a Visitor. As Names sometimes confound & may prejudice, it may be proper to say that he is not connected with the Family of that Name, whose Character & Memory has been so distinguished for worthlessness in France & the world, as to render it almost proverbial—[2]

General Washingtons late Address on his Resignation has just reached us, and causes much regret among the Friends to America here, that a Character so distinguished, and so necessary to the support of its Union and Political Interests, should, at a moment so critical as the present, and before Peace is restored to Europe, and in which America, remote as she is, must eventually be greatly interested, retire from the Helm. His *public* Reasons are, no doubt, unanswerable & honorable to himself, and his *private* ones ʌperhapsʌ still more so; but a change of such magnitude at *this* time, fills us with some apprehensions, unless, without meaning to flatter, *You* were the Character to succeed him. But we have not the consolation to hear that *You* are a Candidate, and fear lest it may, from improper influence, fall into the hands of a Person who may not so truly study the real Interest of America in a reciprocal union of it as Your liberal spirits has evinced in conducting the late Treaty—[3]

Give me leave, Sir, through You, as any opportunity may present, to thank Gen[l]. Schuyler for his polite attention in answering my Letter to him, under cover to You, respecting the Weston-hook Lands— I wish I could derive more solid advantage to myself from the Interest I hold in that Patent than he afords me to expect— The Proprietors on the spot seem strangely to neglect a valuable Interest, so much so, that at this distance from it, I would willingly accept of £1000 sterling for my 5/8th of 1/9th of about 80 or 90,000 Acres which I understand were left clear to the Proprietors on the dispute & Compromise with M[r]. Ransellear, tho', perhaps, *now* much settled by the New Englanders—[4] M[rs]. Coxe unites with me in best Regards to You M[rs]. Jay & Family— I have the honor to be with real Respect and Regard Your Excellency's most Obedient and most humble Servant,

Dan[l]. Coxe

His Excellency John Jay Esqr &c &c &c

ALS, NNC (EJ: 05533). Endorsed: ". . . rec[d] 10 march 1797".

1. See JJ's letter of introduction of Christopher Gore to Coxe, 9 May 1796, Dft, NNC (EJ: 08957).

2. Individual not identified. The "family of that Name" to which Coxe refers is probably that of Louis Philippe, duc d' Orléans (1773–1850), son of Louis Philippe Joseph d'Orléans (1747–93). Forced into exile in 1793, he sailed from Hamburg to the United States, arriving in Philadelphia in October 1796.

3. For JJ contributions to GW's farewell address and his reflections on his retirement from public service and the presidency, see JJ to GW, 19 Sept. 1796, and his Address to the New York State Legislature, [1 November 1796], both above.

4. See JJ to Coxe, 4 Apr. 1796, above. The Westonhook patent was awarded in March 1705 by Edward Hyde, Viscount Cornbury, governor of New York, to Pieter Schuyler and eight other patentees including Dirck Wessels Ten Broeck, Jan Janse Bleecker, John Abeel, Ebenezer Wilson, Peter Fauconier, Dr. Daniel Cox, Thomas Wenham, and Henry Smith of New York. Although the boundaries were ill defined, the land was east of the Hudson and south of Albany. Since it bordered Connecticut and Massachusetts those state also had claims to some of the land, and New England settlers moved into the area. For background on the competing claims over the Westenhook patent, see *LPAH*, 3: 324–35; and Brooke, *Columbia Rising*, 173–80.

From Dirck Ten Broeck

[Albany 14. December 1796]

I have the honor to acquaint your Excellency that I have procured two rooms in the house of M[r]. Rooseboom, for your accommodation in this place this winter, and am in hopes the exertions of the family will contribute much to your ease, and comfort, both M[r]. & M[rs]. Rooseboom asuring us that nothing shall be wanting on their part to make every ∧thing∧ agreeable to you. I shall be highly gratified, in finding the result, correspond with my wishes on this subject—[1]

On Monday last, I dispatched a Sledge for the Cask of porter, you had consigned to my care, (by Capt. Fryers sloop), which arrived here last Evening, I have had it put into Mr. Roosebooms cellar; the Sloop got up no farther than Loeningburgh.[2]

Your Excellencies letter of the 10th. instant,[3] was handed to me last Eve by the two Mohawk Indians, (accompanied by another of the Chiefs of that Nation being the father of *John*, who handed me the letter)— agreeable to your directions I've procured decent Lodgings for them, and shall have an eye toward them, for fear they should make too free with the *strong waters* of their Host—[4]

It is with singular satisfaction I can now inform you, that the Citizens of Albany are making every exertion to accommodate the Gentlemen of the Legislature, and I feel satisfied that their exertions will not be in vain—

The rooms in our Court house, have been put in ample order for the reception of both Branches of the Legislature, & I conclude, we shall find ourselves comfortably & conveniently situated—

Any commands your excellency shall please to honor me with, will be punctually attended to, & executed to the best of my ability—I am Sir—with respect, & esteem, your Mo[st]. obedt. Servt. &c.

Dirck Ten Broeck

ALS, NNC (EJ: 07162). Endorsed. *HPJ*, 4: 222–23.

1. For JJ's accommodations in Albany, see the editorial note "The Capital Moves to Albany," below.

2. Lansingburgh, N.Y., a town located approximately twelve miles north of Albany on the east bank of the Hudson River.

3. JJ to Ten Broeck, 10 Dec. 1796, LbkC, N: Governor's Lbk. 1, (EJ: 03055).

4. The Mohawk delegation is discussed in the editorial note "Indian Affairs under Jay's Governorship," above.

To the New York State Officers of Justice

[New York, 15 December 1796]

By His Excellency John Jay Governor of the State of New York &ca &ca

To all & every the Sheriffs Constables & other Ministerial officers of Justice within the said State—

Whereas pursuant to a Statute of the Congress of the U.S.: in such case made and provided, his Excellcy Thomas Mifflin Governor of the Common-w[ealt]ʰ. of Penns[ylvani]ª. has transmitted to me an Affidavit made by Sarah Anderson Spinster before Hilary Baker Mayor of the City of Philade∧l∧phia whereby a certain Bancroft, whos chri∧s∧tian name appears from another affidavit to be Samuel, stands charged with having in the month of December insᵗ. at the City of Philadelphia committed a Rape on the Body of Fanny Sibbald an Infant of the Age of Eight Years; and whereas the said Governor of Pennsylvania hath represented to me that according to information by him received the said Samuel hath fled into this State; whereupon the said Governor hath applied to me to cause the said Samuel Bancroft to be arrested and Secured untill a person shall be appointed by the sᵈ. Governor of Pennsª. to receive him and bring him to Pennsª. that he may be there dealt with according to Law.[1] Now therefore in pursuance of the Statute before mentioned I do hereby order & require such of you within the Limits of whose authority the said Samuel may be found to arrest & secure him and deliver him to the Goaler of any Goal or Prison in this State nearest to the place where such arrest shall be made and the Goaler of the said Goal is hereby commanded to receive the said Samuel Bancroft & him safely keep in the said Goal untill he shall be thence delivered according to Law.

Given under my hand & the privy Seal of the State this 15 day of December 1796 and in the 21ˢᵗ Year of the Independence of the U.S.

(signed) John Jay

By the Governor
David S. Jones, Private Secʸ.

LbkC, in hand of David S. Jones, N: Governor's Lbk. 2 (EJ: 03252). Printed in several newspapers, including *Minerva* (New York), 15 Dec.; *Daily Advertiser*, and *Herald* (both New York), 17 Dec.; *Philadelphia Gazette*, 19 Dec.; *Connecticut Journal* (New Haven), 21 Dec.; *Federal Gazette* (Baltimore), 21 Dec.; *Salem Gazette*, 23 Dec.; *Weekly Oracle* (New London), 24 Dec.; *Albany Gazette*, 26 Dec.; *Newport Mercury*, 27 Dec.; *Norwich Packet*, 29 Dec. 1796; *Western Centinel* (Whitestown, N.Y.), 4 Jan. 1797.

1. On Edward Bancroft's request for JJ to arrange his son's legal education, see JJ to Bancroft, 30 Oct. 1795, and notes, and JJ to John Vaughan, 21 Jan. 1796, both above. The plans came to naught in December 1796 when officials in Philadelphia charged Samuel with raping eight-year-old Fanny Sibbald, probably the daughter of shipping merchant, George Sibbald. Samuel escaped and was believed to have fled to either New York or New Jersey. In response to Pennsylvania's request, JJ issued this warrant for Bancroft's arrest on 15 December. However, Bancroft found passage on a ship bound for the Caribbean and eventually returned to the safety of England. Samuel apparently concealed his fugitive status and disgraced past. He married into a wealthy British family in December 1798, and died of an unknown cause within a year of his marriage. Schaeper, *Bancroft*, 243–44.

From John Trumbull

London Dec[r]. 16th. 1796.

Dear Sir.

I had the honour of writing to you on the 7th Sept[r] by D[r]. Edwards,[1] since when I have received none of yours.

The Official communications of the American Commissioners conveyed by this Ship, state that Objections have been made on the part of this Government, by their Agent, to the Jurisdiction of the Board in certain cases:— And they explain the Nature and Extent of those Objections: as well as the Opinion of the British Commissioners on the previous question whether there be a power in the Board to decide on such Objections, or even to entertain any question relative to their Jurisdiction.

You will of course know from the Government the precise State of this Business, and it is therefore unnecessary (as it might perhaps be improper) for me to say anything further on the Subject, or to give any Opinion of the Shape which the Business may hereafter assume:— But the whole is so very unexpected to me, that I cannot refrain from reminding you of the Advice which you formerly gave to some of your friends on an important occasion—"to hope for the best but vigilantly to prepare for the worst"—[2] I am &c

By the Pegasus Frigate[3] with the British Commissioners to NYork

LbkC, DLC: Trumbull (EJ: 10379).

1. JT to JJ, 7 Sept. 1796, above.

2. On the spoliation claims commission in London, see the editorial note "Aftermath of the Jay Treaty: Responses, Ratification, and Implementation," above. On the challenges made in Britain to the jurisdiction of the claims commission, see Moore, *International Arbitrations*, 1: 324–29. The arguments arose during deliberations on the case of the Ship *Betsey*, Captain Furlong. The British agent before the commission, Nathaniel Gostling, argued that the commissioners could not overrule the decisions of the British High Court of Appeals; and that it had no jurisdiction over cases that were still pending before the appeals court, or over cases that had not been appealed to the courts, since in those instances remedy could be had in the normal course of law. Such rules would have eliminated virtually all cases coming before them. The American commissioners contended that decisions of the Court of Appeals could not be considered final if they were based on orders in council that violated the law of nations. When JT as fifth commissioner agreed with the two American commissioners, the two British commissioners withdrew, thus bringing the proceedings to a halt.

On 16 Dec., RK discussed the stalemate with Grenville, who feared great opposition in Britain to overturning decisions made by the Court of Appeals. RK contended the commission could not overturn the court decisions and restore prizes but could authorize compensation, payable by the

British government. Grenville referred him to the Lord Chancellor Loughborough who had participated in the treaty negotiations. Loughborough criticized statements made by American claims agent Samuel Bayard that the court decisions were illegal and unjust, but also declared Gostling's general demurrers of jurisdiction "absurd", and recommended both take their statements back. On 26 Dec., RK, Pinckney, Gore, and JT met with Loughborough, who declared court decisions were final but compensation could be sought; that in cases where ships were restored but compensation for freight and damages was not awarded, claimants could seek compensation through the commission; and that when appeal was not made to the courts before a set deadline for justifiable reasons, such cases too could be appealed to the commission. The commission could thus review court procedures; it could not reverse court decisions, but could redress injustices by awarding compensation. Loughborough also stated that in future the commissioners could decide whether cases were within their competency.

In January 1797, Grenville told RK that he had informed the British commissioners "that they should proceed in examining and deciding *every question* that should be brought before them, according to the conviction of their Consciences" in doing which they would examine cases already decided, and award on them and on all others, according to the Provisions of the Treaty which it would likewise be their "duty to consider and interpret." The commission then reassembled and began to make awards in April 1797. *PAH*, 20: 506, note 3.

3. HMS *Pegasus*, a twenty-eight gun frigate, commanded by Capt. Ross Donnelly.

To Matthew Clarkson, Richard Varick, and the Commissioners for Fortifying the Port and City of New York

Albany 4th: January 1797

Gentlemen

I received Yesterday a letter from General Van Cortlandt of the 26 ult[1] with a Resolution of the House of Representatives of the 16 ult. appointing a Committee[2] relative to Fortifications of which the enclosed are Copies —.[3]

You will perceive from these Papers the Importance of conveying to the Committee accurate Information respecting the State of our Fortifications and the Expediency of Additional Works to render our Harbour secure — It is desirable that the Committee should make such a Report to Congress as may induce them to provide more ample Supplies for these Objects, than they have hitherto done; and in my opinion it would be useful to employ the Engineer Mr Mangin and Col. Stephens to wait on the Committee at Philadelphia and communicate to them in Detail all the Information that may be requisite to enable them to understand the Subject perfectly —[4] I think I sent to Col. Morton[5] a Statement of the Expenses which would probably be incurred in finishing the Works —

As it will be prudent to avoid Delay, I think it will be best to make the necessary communications immediately, and I will write by the Post to Mr Van

Cortlandt that the Committee will soon receive them from you — [6] I have the Honor to be Gentlemen your most obed^t. & humb^e. Servt.

John Jay

[Genl. Clarkson, R. Varick & others — Comm^{rs}. for fortifying the City & Port of N.Y.]

LS, NNYSL (EJ: 02859). LbkC, N: Governor's Lbk. 1 (EJ: 03056).

1. Letter not found, but referenced in JJ to Van Cortlandt, 4 Jan. 1797, LbkC, N: Governor's Lbk. 1 (EJ: 03057). Philip Van Cortlandt represented New York's 3rd District in the House of Representatives.

2. *Annals*, 4: 1672. The seven-person committee consisted of Abraham Baldwin (Ga.), Isaac Coles (Va.), Nicholas Gilman (N.H.), William Lyman (Mass.), John Patten (Del.), Mark Thomson (N.J.), and Philip Van Cortlandt (N.Y.).

3. Enclosures not found.

4. For more on Mangin and Stevens's activities, see the editorial note "Defending New York," above.

5. Jacob Morton (1762–1836), Federalist lawyer and militia officer who represented the city and county of New York in the state assembly.

6. JJ to Van Cortlandt, 4 Jan. 1797, LbkC, N: Governor's Lbk. 1 (EJ: 03057).

From Rufus King

London Jan 10. 1797

Dear Sir

You probably will have heard before this Letter gives you the information, that the Directory have refused to receive General Pinckney, who on presenting his Letter of Credence was informed by La Croix in behalf of the Directory, "qu'il ne reconnoitra et ne recevra plus Ministre plenipotentiaire des Etats unis jusqu'apres le redressement des Griefs demandé au Gouvernment Americaine, et que la republique francaise est en droit d'en attendre."[1]

The Redacteur[2] which I send you contains the Speech that subsequent to this Answer, Mr. Monroe made to the Directory, and likewise their Reply — [3] by a recent Letter[4] I am informed that it is uncertain whether General Pinckney will be allowed to remain at Paris; cards of Hospitality had been refused to him, though granted to all americans who visit paris — in case he is obliged to leave the Territories of the Republic, he will go to Amsterdam, and wait the instructions of Government — I forbear to make any comments upon this Conduct of the Directory, or upon the Equally extraordinary Notes presented to our Government, which have been received by the late arrivals —

It will be satisfactory to you to learn that there is good reason to conclude that certain embarrassments wh. have been thrown in the way to obstruct the Proceedings of the Board of Com[missione]ʳˢ. have been entirely removed— Much moderation, prudence, and candor have been requisite on this Occasion, & I add with pleasure, that I have found no cause to complain of the influence of any improper views or principles on the part of the administration— I think I am not sanguine in my expectations that this Business will henceforth proceed in a satisfactory manner— The commissioners have before them a Case, where the sentence of condemnation by the V. Ad[mirality] Court has been affirmed by the H. C. of Appeals. it is a strong case in every respect—and I think will be decided in our favor on all the Points, and what is of great importance There is a probability that the Decision may be unanimous—

I send you Ludmalmesbury's Correspondence;[5] as yet we have seen no similar Publication by the Directory— with perfect Esteem & Respect I am very sincerely yrs

Rufus King

PS. I fear I have expected too much in supposing a *probability* of Unanimity in the Commissioners—

His Exʸ Mʳ Jay—

ALS, NNC (EJ: 06692). Addressed. Stamped. Endorsed: ". . . ansᵈ. 3 May 1797."

1. Translation: "that it will not recognize or receive any Minister plenipotentiary from the United States until after the redress of the grievances demanded from the American Government that the French Republic has a right to expect." This extract also appears in Delacroix to Monroe, 11 Dec. 1796, *Monroe Papers*, 4: 132.

2. Newspaper not found. For more on the *Rédacteur*, see JT to JJ, 20 Sept. 1798, note 4, below.

3. The speech delivered by Monroe to the Directory on 1 Jan. 1797, and the reply of the same date by Paul Barras, President of the Directory, is found in *Massachusetts Spy* (Worcester), 5 Apr.; *Albany Chronicle*, 10 Apr.; *Amherst Village Messenger*, 11 Apr.; *Rising Sun* (Keene), 11 Apr.; *Sun* (Dover), 12 Apr.; *Rural Repository* (Leominster), 13 Apr. 1797; Monroe, *A view of the conduct of the executive, in the foreign affairs of the United States, connected with the Mission to the French Republic, during the Years 1794, 5, & 6* (Philadelphia, [1797]; *Early Am. Imprints*, series 1, no. 32491), 397–99; *Monroe Papers* 4: 138–39. Copies were printed in various American newspapers at Monroe's request. Monroe to JM, 1 Jan. 1796 [1797], *PJM*, 16: 442–44; *Monroe Papers*, 4: 140.

4. Letter not found.

5. James Harris, *Official Copies of the Correspondence of Lord Malmesbury, Minister Plenipotentiary to the French Republic, and the Executive Directory of France: Containing Copies of the Letters of Lord Grenville, Comte Wedel Jarlsberg, Messrs. Barthelemi, Wickham, &c. &c. relative to the Negotiations for Peace* (London, 1796). James Harris (1746–1820), the earl of Malmesbury, held unsuccessful peace negotiations with the French Republic from 1796 to 1797.

From Jedidiah Morse

Charlestown Jany. 14 1797

Dear Sir,

Soon after I had the honour of receiving your Letter wh[ic]h accompanied the Laws of N York,[1] I wrote you by a vessel bound to N. York & accompanied my Letter with a Sett of the last Edit[io]n of my Geog[raph]y. in boards for your acceptance. It was as long ago as October last. I hope they reached you safely.[2]

The *hint* you dropped when I last saw you, relative to my undertaking to write the history of the American Revolution, has led to a train of reflections on the subject. I own I felt so unequal to the work, That I was confounded at the suggestion of the idea ∧of undertaking it∧. Nor do I on consideration feel more confidence in my own abilities. I am willing, however, to undertake what any man of common judgement & industry may do, & that is, *to collect materials* for such a work. This would indeed naturally coincide with the attention wh[ic]h I am bound to pay to my other publications. But in order to collect to advantage, it would be best to have at first a well digested plan, as far as one could be formed, of the work into wh[ic]h the materials are to be compiled— There ought to be certain leading points & objects to guide the enquirer after information, that he may know what he is about, & the progress he is making.— Now, sir, as you have acted an important & conspicuous part through the whole of the Revolution, I know of no person more capable ∧than yourself∧ of guiding an Enquirer to the several objects that ought principally to engage his attention, ~~then yourself,~~ & to the sources where he may obtain the best information. If you will oblige me, sir, with your directions, as to the great points of enquiry—& such observations as may occur as to ~~tha~~ a plan of the Work, I shall be happy, as I have opportunity, to direct my attention to the subject, & to prepare something, if my life & health sh^d. be preserved, for some future historian of our country. If my abilities bore any proportion to the love I bear to my country, & the zeal I have for its honour & happiness, I should not for a moment hesitate engaging in the compilation of its History.

Some original & very valuable Letters have lately fallen into my hands, wh[ic]h throw much light on the transactions at Paris during the negotiation of the Peace of 1783, & wh[ic]h if publickly known would, I apprehend, greatly change the public opinion respecting the French nation—& do away *entirely all obligations to gratitude* for their assistance in our revolution. Pardon me if I say, the *people* of the United States, are [*mutilated*] but little acquainted with what they owe to the *discernment* & *firmness* of their Ministers (Dr. F[ranklin] *excepted*) who negotiated that Peace.—

I presume, sir, on your goodness, to excuse both the *matter* & the *length* of this letter. I am, Sir, with very great & sincere respect & esteem your most obd^t Servt

Jed^h. Morse

Gov. Jay.

ALS, NNC (EJ: 09546).

1. See JJ to Morse, 9 Aug. 1796, C, CtY-BR (EJ: 05216).

2. See Morse to JJ, 24 Oct. 1796, ALS, NNC (EJ: 09545). *The American universal geography, or, A view of the present state of all the empires, kingdoms, states, and republics in the known world, and of the United States in particular. In two parts . . . The whole comprehending a complete and improved system of modern geography. Calculated for Americans. Illustrated with twenty-eight maps and charts . . .* (Boston, 1796; *Early Am. Imprints*, series 1, nos. 30823, 30824). For JJ's acknowledgment of Morse's earlier letters and his reply to the current one, see his letter of 28 Feb. 1797, below.

To Peter Jay Munro

Albany 21 Jany. 1797—

Dear Peter

I was Yesterday favored with your's of the 14th. of this month.[1] I congratulate you and M^rs. Munro on the Addition lately made to your Family, and am happy to learn that her Health is re-establishing so fast.[2]

The Demeanour of a certain Person[3] was probably assumed for the Purposes you allude to— He sometimes calculates with more Reliance on Probabilities than they warrant.

Affairs here go on smoothly— Albany deserves Credit for attentions to the Legislature— they are in general well accommodated & well satisfied— our new *penal* Code does not appear to me to be popular in *this* part of the Country, whatever it may be in others.[4] I begin to apprehend that appropriations *competent* to the finishing of the State Prisons this Year, will not be made at present: for the State of our Treasury presents objections to it—[5] When you see or write to our Friends at Rye, remember me to them— I am Dear Peter, your aff^te. uncle,

John Jay

Peter Jay Munro Esqr

ALS, NNMus (EJ: 00447).

1. PJM to JJ, 14 Jan. 1797, Dft, NNMus (EJ: 00446).

2. Frances Munro (1797–1869) was born on 9 Jan. 1797, the fourth child and third daughter of Peter Jay and Margaret White Munro.

3. Samuel Lyon.

4. The public responses to New York's revised penal code are discussed in the editorial note "Crime and Punishment in Federalist New York," above.

5. For more on the establishment of the state penitentiary in New York, see Benjamin Rush to JJ, 9 July 1796, above; Proclamation on the Completion of the State Prison, 25 Nov. 1797, below; and the editorial note "Crime and Punishment in Federalist New York," above.

To Richard Lawrence

Albany 23ᵈ. Januʸ. 1797

Sir

It gives me pleasure to inform you that the Legislature has been pleased to appropriate 2500 Dollars for the Relief of the French Refugees in our City, whose complicated Distresses recommend them so strongly to our Beneficence & humane Attentions.[1]

You will find herewith enclosed a Warrant on the Treasurer for 1000 Dollˢ. and a Copy of the Act lately passed on this Subject. The Directions and Intent of it, must be carefully observed and pursued in the Distribution of this Money— No new Comers into the City (altho they be real Refugees from Sᵗ. Domingo) are objects of this Law— such of them only as were and have continued to be Residents in the City of New York at and from the time of the passing of the former Laws for their Relief, are to be considered as within the Intent and Meaning of the present act. This should be particularly attended to, lest Persons of the like description in other States should be tempted by the prospect or hope of sharing in this Bounty to remove to and reside in New York.

I have no Reason to suppose that any provision has been made by the french Republic or others for these unfortunate sufferers; if however *that* should be or become the case, stop your hand, and inform me of it immediately.

I flatter myself that you will readily undertake this Business, and will conduct it in the most careful manner and on the most moderate Terms. The Sum granted is not large, and great circumspection & Prudence will be necessary in the Application of it.—[2] I am &ᶜᵃ

(signed) John Jay

Mʳ. Richᵈ. Lawrence

LbkC, N: Governor's Lbk. 1 (EJ: 03061).

1. "An ACT for the support of the St. Domingo French Refugees in the City of New-York," 20 Jan. 1797, *N.Y. State Laws*, 20th sess. (1797), 11–12. For the pay warrant, see JJ to Gerard Bancker, 22 Jan.

1797, LbkC, N: Governor's Lbk. 1 (EJ: 03253). See also JJ's Addresses to the New York State Legislature, 6 Jan. and [1 Nov. 1796], both above.

2. Richard R. Lawrence (1765–1822) was a Quaker merchant, and philanthropist, and member of both the Manumission Society and the Society of New York Hospital, as well as a commissioner of the Alms-House. On 28 Nov. 1796, the Common Council ordered that "a Loan of 300 Dollars be made to Richd Lawrence one of the Commiss^rs [of the] Alms House to be applied towards the Relief of certain indigent refugee families from St Domingo. And that Mr Mayor issue his Warrant on the Treasurer for payment thereof." *MCCNYC*, 2: 306. For Lawrence's membership in the NYMS, see *JJSP*, 4: 538. For the response to the refugee crisis, see JJ's Addresses to the New York State Legislature, 6 Jan. and [1 Nov. 1796], both above; JJ to Lawrence, 9 Feb. 1797, and 6 Jan. 1798, and Lawrence to JJ, 27 Jan. 1797, all below.

From Timothy Pickering (private)

Philadelphia Jany. 23. 1797.

Sir,

You will have seen the President's message to Congress relative to French affairs.[1] The letter to M^r. Pinckney to which the President refers, I now do myself the honor to inclose.[2] I have taken the liberty to use your name in the investigation of the French claims to our gratitude—and your sentiments also; sometimes quoting, but in other cases not distinguishing by the usual marks; the selection I was making not easily admitting of it: this you will excuse.—[3] I have long thought that our transactions with the French at the commencement of our revolution—during its continuance—and at its close, ought to be made known by authentic documents, for the purpose of repelling unjust demand, detecting imposture and establishing truth. I therefore seized with eagerness the present opportunity of giving to our citizens at large *some information* concerning them: but the subject requires a history. I have the honor to be with sincere respect sir, your most ob^t. servant,

Timothy Pickering

His Excellency / John Jay Esqr.

ALS, NNC (EJ: 09494). Marked: "(private)". C, MHi: Pickering (EJ: 04822).

1. For JJ's response to this letter, see JJ to TP (private), 31 Jan. 1797, below.

2. On 20 Jan. 1797, GW wrote both houses of Congress about Franco-American relations. GW directed TP, his secretary of state, to draft an open letter to Charles Cotesworth Pinckney, the minister plenipotentiary to France, explaining and defending American foreign policy, including the controversial Jay Treaty. GW submitted a copy of TP's letter of 16 January 1797 with his address to Congress. Both GW's address and TP's letter were printed in newspapers throughout the country, and subsequently in pamphlet form. *ASP: FR*, 1: 559–76. For an example of newspaper publication of this material, see *Gazette of the United States* (Philadelphia), 21 Jan. 1797; for pamphlet publication, see *A letter from Mr. Pickering, secretary of state, to Mr. Pinckney, minister plenipotentiary at Paris, in answer to the complaints communicated by Mr. Adet, minister of the French republic, against the*

United States of America (Richmond, 1797; *Early Am. Imprints*, series 1, no. 33064), and *A letter from Mr. Pickering, secretary for the Department of State of the United States—to Mr. Pinckney, minister plenipotentiary of the United States of America, at Paris* (Stockbridge, 1797; *Early Am. Imprints*, series 1, no. 33065).

3. For TP's discussion in his letter of the alleged American ingratitude to France, and French motivation for aiding the U.S. during the Revolution, he quoted or paraphrased many of JJ's comments on French conduct during the peace negotiations in 1782; see *ASP: FR*, 1: 569–73. On deteriorating relations with France, see the editorial note "John Jay and the Response to the XYZ Affair in New York," below.

To Francis Ley

Albany, 26 Jany 1797

Sir

I was by the last post favored with yours of the 23^d. ult[1] mentioning that you purpose to publish, by Subscription, a work on the Subject of preserving Houses from external Fire, and the Means of removing Goods from such as may be in Danger from it. That you would bestow one half of the Subscription money on the Sufferers by the late Fire at Savannah, and that one Copy shall be sent to those whose Subscriptions equal or exceed the Expense of publishing the Work.[2]

You request me to remit ~~to Savannah for the Sufferers~~ ˄the amount of what may be˄ subscribed to the Presid^t. of the Bank of the U.S. at Charleston, the one half to be remitted to Savannah for the Sufferers, and the other half to remain in the Bank until the Copies due for Subscriptions shall be delivered— The Certificate (of which a Copy was inclosed) that the Plans described in the work *"are new ingenious and useful"* derives great Weight from the Characters of the Gentlemen who subscribed it.

It gives me pleasure to learn that Discoveries so interesting to Society have been made. but Sir! permit me to observe that the Singularity of your *present plan* for a Subscription, will I suspect rather retard than promote its Success. It is not pleasant, but it is candid, to say that as I do not approve of, so I cannot recommend it. I will nevertheless encourage every proper measure for the Relief of the Havannah[3] Sufferers and I will also promote every proper & Customary plan for enabling Authors to publish ingenious works and Inventions; which if really useful to the public, cannot fail of being profitable to themselves—[4]

Mr Francis Ley— Charleston—

Dft, NNC (EJ: 08968).

1. See Francis Ley to JJ, 23 Dec. 1796, ALS, NNC (EJ: 06780). Francis Ley, a Charleston shopkeeper, ran a dry goods store in the city. He supported the incorporation of the Charleston Water

Company in 1799. Jacob Milligan, *The Charleston Directory. By Jacob Milligan, Harbour Master. September 1794* (Charleston, [1794]; *Early Am. Imprints*, series 1, no. 27320), 24; *Acts and Resolution of the General Assembly, of the State of South-Carolina. Passed in December, 1799* (Charleston, 1800; *Early Am. Imprints*, series 1, no. 38533), 25.

2. Savannah experienced a devastating fire on the night of 26 Nov. 1796. One local newspaper reported that "Two Thirds of the City appear in ruin" and estimated that three hundred homes were destroyed by the blaze. *Columbian Museum*, 29 Nov. 1796.

3. JJ mistakenly wrote this instead of "Savannah"

4. No publication by Ley has been found.

From Richard Lawrence

New York 1st. mo[nth] 27th 1797.

Esteemed Friend

Thine of 23d inst. forwarded by the Mayor I have just received, with the warrant for 1000 Dollars and a Copy of the Act, and in observing the Contents am induced to make the following remarks—[1] I am Sensible of the propriety of thy observation on the necessity of economy in the distribution of this Money; and shall therefore carefully observe the same; and assure thee it is not an Object of profit to be subjected to the importunities of this distres'd people and so frequently interrupted in my regular Business for the small Commission heretofore Charged of five pr Cent; but at thy request and a desire to be useful to suffering humanity shall again undertake it and hope to render a Satisfactory statement of its expenditure—

I sincerely regret the denial of releif to any who may have come here since the passing of the former Act, even tho' now resident amongst us and equally objects of our compassion; particularly on account of four families within my present knowledge, who have come here since that time and whose necessities are really urgent; two of them particularly on Account of ill health, they have all resided in our City for some time past— I therefore hope thee will consider again whether they do not come within the intent of the last law; am aware any who may come after it are exempted—[2] I may also inform thee have found a necessity of anticipating the present appropriation by advancing a considerable sum to purchase fire Wood, Blankets, and some Cloathing for the most needy, the first just before and the latter Articles at the time of the extreme Cold weather we had some time ago, in this I hope to have thy approbation, and waiting thy Answer when Convenient remain respectfully Thy friend

Richard Lawrence

ALS, NNC (EJ: 06775). Addressed: "John Jay / Governor of the State of New York / at present in the City of/Albany". Endorsed: "rec^d. 3 Feb. / Rich^d. Lawrence / 27 Jan^y / rec^d 3 / ans^d. 9 Feb 1797".

1. See JJ to Richard Lawrence, 23 Jan. 1797, above. For the refugee crisis, see JJ's Addresses to the New York State Legislature, 6 Jan. and [1 Nov. 1796], both above, and JJ to Lawrence, 9 Feb. 1797 and 6 Jan. 1798, both below.

2. For JJ's reply and opinion on this point, see JJ to Lawrence, 9 Feb. 1797, below.

To Timothy Pickering (private)

Albany, 31 Jany 1797—

Sir

Accept my Thanks for your obliging Favor of the 23^d. Instant,[1] enclosing a Copy of your interesting Letter to M^r. Pinckney,[2] which is read here with great avidity and satisfaction— it enables our Citizens to form a correct Judgment of the Conduct Claims and Complaints of France, relative to this Country; and to appreciate the wisdom, abilities and virtue with which our Govern^t is administered. Adet's indiscreet note[3] afforded a fair opportunity for these Explanations, and had he foreseen the use you have made of it, he would doubtless have been more circumspect. It is not clear to me that the overbearing and violent conduct of France towards the united States, is to be regarded as a misfortune— as to a war with that People, I neither desire nor expect it— The *necessity* however of these appeals to the Public is to be regretted.

Among my Letters from Spain, I ~~hav~~ remember to have written one, stating in *Cyphers* a Conference with the Minister— it affords a singular Proof of the views and Designs of France at an *early* Period of our Revolution.[4] The Facts were communicated to me in conversation, but were accurately committed to Paper *immediately* on my returning home. That Part of the Letter may perhaps yet remain in Cyphers— The Facts alluded to should be carefully kept secret during the Life Time of the Minister— a Disclosure *in the present State of Things* would probably prove very injurious to him. Being at a Distance from my Papers, I cannot give you the Date of that Letter— I think it was written to the then Sec^y for foreign Affairs; and I presume is to be found in the Book in which my Correspondence with him is recorded— I have the Honor to be with sincere Respect & Esteem Sir your most ob^t & h'ble Servt

John Jay—

The Hon'ble Timothy Pickering Esqr.

ALS, MHi: Pickering (EJ: 04775). Addressed. Marked: "private". Endorsed: ". . . On my long letter of Jan^y / 17. to Genl. Pinckney / Look for the letter written / by M^r. Jay from Spain / shewing the early designs / of France toward the / U. States". Dft, NNC (EJ: 09495).

1. TP to JJ (private), 23 Jan. 1797, above.

2. JJ refers to the letter that TP directed to Charles Cotesworth Pinckney, the newly appointed minister to France, of 16 Jan. 1797, a copy of which was among the documents GW sent Congress with his address of 19 Jan. 1797 on relations with France. TP's letter was published in the *Gazette of the United States* (Philadelphia) on 21 Jan. 1797, and subsequently in many other newspapers, as well as in pamphlet form. See TP to JJ (private), 23 Jan. 1797, note 2, above.

3. Adet's "indiscreet note" refers to either Pierre Auguste Adet (1767–1848), the French minister, to TP, of 27 Oct. 1796, or, more likely, his longer note to TP of 15 Nov. 1796. While the 1796 presidential election was in progress, Adet sent a notice to the secretary of state on 27 Oct. announcing that France in accordance with its decree of July 1796 intended to treat neutral nations in the same way as they allowed other nations [i.e., Great Britain] to treat them; it would disregard the provision of the treaty of commerce with the United States of 1778 that "free ships make free goods" and would now seize American ships along with those of other neutral nations that were carrying British property.

When GW learned of Adet's letter and publication, he wrote AH on 2 Nov. for advice on how to respond to Adet. He asked AH to show his letter to JJ— "As I have a very high opinion of Mr. Jay's judgment, candour, honor and discretion (Tho' I am not in the habit of writing so freely to him as to you)"— and to let him have their joint opinion.

AH replied on 4 Nov. that he had sent GW's note to JJ and conferred with him "last night" (3 Nov.), stating that "Mr. Jay & myself are both agreed also, that no immediate publication of the reply which may be given ought to be made—for this would be like joining in an appeal to the Public—would countenance & imitate the irregularity & would not be dignified— nor is it necessary for any present purpose of the Government. Mr. Jay inclined to think that the reply ought to go through Mr. Pinckney to the Directory with only a short note to Adet acknowleging the reception of his paper & informing him that this mode will be taken. I am not yet satisfied that this course will be the best. We are both to consider further and confer. You will shortly be informed of the result." AH and JJ also recommended responding to the disrespect Adet had shown the government in publishing his letter by receiving Adet at his levies with "a *dignified reserve*, holding an *exact medium* between *offensive coldness* and *cordiality*. The *point* is a nice one to be hit, but no one will know better how to do it than the President."

In the interim GW wrote AH on 3 Nov. that, in response to information from TP on the state of public opinion, it was considered necessary to make an immediate response and that he would see its publication in newspapers of that date (*Aurora* and *Claypoole's American Daily Advertiser*, both of Philadelphia).

TP's letter, dated 1 Nov., asserted that the Franco-American treaty confirmed the policy that "free ships should make free goods," and therefore that France had no right to seize neutral American vessels trading with the British. TP also noted that the British had issued no new orders regarding the seizure of American ships carrying French goods, but that such seizures were within the law of nations. He concluded by chiding Adet for making his original note public, arguing that "it was properly addressed to its government, to which alone pertained the right of communicating it in such time and manner, as it should think fit to the citizens of the United States."

Adet briefly replied on 3 Nov., and then published in the *Aurora* (Philadelphia), and subsequently other newspapers, a long note dated 15 Nov. announcing that the Directory had ordered him to suspend his diplomatic functions and reiterating French complaints against the Jay Treaty and alleged neutrality violations since 1793, particularly cases regarding privateers and prizes. A note printed in the *Aurora* following Adet's letter insinuated that a Federalist victory could bring about a war with France. See the *Aurora* for 31 Oct., and 5 and 15 Nov. 1796.

Federalists then contended that Adet's purpose was to embarrass GW and the Federalists and influence the election in favor of TJ. They argued that Adet sought to terrorize the United States into electing TJ, and that, like Genet before him, Adet was trying to appeal to the people against the authority of GW and his government. They criticized France for interfering in American political affairs and seeking to manage its government as they had done to such other client states as Switzerland, Holland, and the Italian states. AH continued to disapprove of TP's publication of his response to Adet and criticized him as showing too much "warmth" and "sharpness" to be effective. Under the pseudonym "Americanus," AH published his own answer to Adet in December 1796, and again recommended sending a letter addressed to Pinckney countering Adet's charges. TP completed that letter on 16 Jan. 1797. See *ASP: FR*, 1: 559–88; AH to Oliver Wolcott Jr., 1, 9 and 22 Nov. 1796, *PAH*, 20: 361–66, 378–80, 411–14; GW to AH, 2, 3 and 21 Nov. 1796, *PAH*, 20: 362–66, 366–67, 409–11; AH to GW, 4, 5, 11, and 19 Nov. 1796, *PAH*, 20: 272–73, 374–75, 389–90, 408–9; Wolcott to AH, 17 Nov. 1796, *PAH*, 20: 398–400; "The Answer," signed "Americanus," *Minerva* (New York), 8 Dec. 1796; *PAH*, 20: 421–34; JM to TJ, 5 Dec. 1796, *PTJ*, 29: 215.

For other examples of Federalist responses to Adet's writings, see "Brutus," *Gazette of the United States* (Philadelphia), 3 Nov. 1796; "The Times, No. XVI," *Minerva* (New York), 8 Nov. 1796; "The People's Answer," *Connecticut Courant* (Hartford), 14 Nov. 1796; William Willcocks, *Minerva* (New York), 3, 5 and 26 Dec. 1796, and *Weekly Advertiser* (Reading), 7 Jan. 1797. For the French refusal to receive Pinckney, and the further decline in Franco-American Relations, see the editorial note "John Jay and the Response to the XYZ Affair in New York," below.

4. Conversation not identified. Possibly a reference to JJ's notes on a Conference with Floridablanca of 23 Sept. 1780, enclosed in JJ to the President of Congress, 6 Nov. 1780; *JJSP*, 2: 265–75, esp. 268–69. JJ's encoded conversation with Montmorin as French ambassador to Spain, described in JJ to RRL, 28 Apr. 1782, *JJSP*, 2: 761, is probably not the conversation referred to, since Montmorin had died in 1792.

From Rufus King

February London Feb. 6. 1797

Dear Sir,

I thought it probable that the Directory after refusing to receive General Pinckney would have permitted him to remain at Paris till they should have received News from America of a date so late as to give the Result of the Election for President. I have been mistaken; whether the information already received on that Subject, which I presume has not been satisfactory, or the Elevation that has followed the prodigious Successes lately obtained by Buonaparte in Italy, has wrought the change, I cannot decide, but I have learnt this morning that the General has been ordered by the Directory to leave Paris, and the Territories of the Republic, and that in consequence thereof he was to depart for Amsterdam on the 31st. ulto.— this is a Step more extraordinary and decisive than I had supposed likely to happen—

If we give full credit to the french accounts of their late victories, & I believe them in the main, the Fate of Mantua, so long suspended by the Defense
of Wurmser,[1] must be decided, and all Italy must according to present appearances submit to the arms of France— you will readily perceive the possible
consequences of such an Event, but I will not add any Reflections upon this
interesting & perplexing Topic.

Our affairs here are as well as we can expect them to be— I mean in
particular those which depend upon a liberal and candid execution of the
Treaty— Difficulties from a Quarter from whence it was natural to look
for them, have for a Time arrested the Proceedings of the Com[issione]rs.
these by moderation and prudence have been effectually removed, and
the Business proceeds in a Satisfactory manner— Some cases have been
decided—and among them a leading one, being the Case of the Patersons
of Baltimore— A Ship and Cargo belonging to them were condemned in
the W[est]. Indies—[2] This Sentence of Condemnation was affirmed by the
H[igh]. Court of Appeals— Application has been made to the Board of
Commissioners, who have pronounced (Nicholl[3] only dissenting) that they
had Jurisdiction of the Cause, and that upon its merits the Claimants were
entitled to receive from the Treasury of the King, full & complete Compensation for their Loss & Damages—

The conduct of the Gov[ernment]. has upon this occasion been candid
and correct— the Difficulties which have occurred have led to a pretty full
consideration of the Provisions of the 7. Art[icle]. and I had the Satisfaction
to find that we agreed in our Constructions— very respectfully, yr. ob. Ser

Rufus King

Mr. Jay

ALS, NNC (EJ: 06693). Endorsed.

1. Dagobert Sigmund von Wurmser (1724–97) commanded the Austrian forces during Bonaparte's siege of Mantua. With his troops running low on food and stricken by disease, Wurmser
surrendered Mantua to the French on 2 Feb. 1797.

2. On the case of the Brigantine *Betsey*, Captain Furlong, owned by George Patterson of Baltimore, and her cargo, owned by George and William Patterson, see Moore, *International Arbitrations*, 3: 2838–57; 4: 4205–16; and *International Adjudications*, 4: 81–89, 179–290; and Perkins, *First
Rapprochement*, 55. Wealthy Baltimore merchant William Patterson (1752–1835) was the father of
Elizabeth Patterson, future first wife of Jerome Bonaparte, brother of Napoleon. George Patterson
was his brother. In April 1797 the spoliations commission awarded the Pattersons £6317.1.4½ in
damages.

3. Dr. John Nicholl, one of the British members of the spoliations commission.

To Richard Lawrence

Albany, 9 Feb. 1797

Sir

I have been fav^d. with yours of the 27 of last month.[1] I wish ~~it was in our power and consistent with Prudence to~~ ∧we could∧ give Relief to all who ~~may be~~ ∧are∧ in need of it— but if this State should ~~attempt to~~ provide for all ~~the~~ French Refugees without *Distinction*; those who reside in other States where the like Provision is not made, ~~who~~ would remove to our City for the Purpose of sharing in our Bounty— The present act like the Former ~~means to provide~~ & ∧has Respect∧ only ~~for~~ ∧to∧ those whom Providence cast upon *us*, and not ∧to∧ those whom Providence cast on *other States* ~~who ought to take care of them~~—If ~~the~~ therefore four Families you mention came to New York from any of the other States, they certainly are not Objects of the act. As to the anticipations you mention, I see at present no Objections to them—[2]

There is in New York a free black man named Peter Williams— he formerly lived with Mr. Amar, and afterwards with ∧Mr∧ B. Moore, Tobacconists— he has set up and follows that Business— I do not know in what part of the City he lives. I have purchased of M^r. Cor[neliu]^s Glen, a negroe woman named Dinah, ~~who~~ whom after serving me faithfully a certain Time, ~~will be~~ ∧I intend to∧ manumitted. She is a neice of Peter Williams. She has a child going on two Years which M^r. Glen offers to give her, in Case she makes proper Provision for it by the first of May next. She ~~is persuaded that~~ ∧hopes & believes∧ her uncle will take it— she has written to him on the Subject by the post, but rec^d. no answer— she is anxious and uneasy and fears some accident has happened to the Letter— Will you be so good as to send for Peter Williams & to inform him of these Circumstances, and to communicate his answer to me.[3] I make no appology for giving you this Trouble, because under similar Circumstances I would chearfully do the same Thing on your Request. With real Esteem I am Sir Your ob^t Servt

John Jay

M^r. Richd Lawrence

Dft, NNC (EJ: 08969).

1. Richard Lawrence to JJ, 27 Jan., above.

2. In a letter sent later to Lawrence, JJ revised his opinion, noting that "if they arrived at New York from beyond Sea, and not from one of the United States, I think considering their Distress" these four families could be helped. JJ to Lawrence, 24 Feb. 1797, LbkC, N: Governor's Lbk. 1 (EJ: 03064).

For the refugee matter as a whole, see JJ's Addresses to the New York State Legislature, 6 Jan. and [1 Nov. 1796]; JJ to Lawrence, 23 Jan. 1797; and Lawrence to JJ, 27 Jan. 1797, all above; JJ to Lawrence, 24 Feb. 1797, LbkC, N: Governor's Lbk 1 (EJ: 03064), and 6 Jan. 1798, below.

3. JJ's letter of 24 Feb. thanks Lawrence for obtaining the information from Williams, but does not reveal what that was. Both Blase Moore and Peter Williams (c. 1755–1823) are listed as a "tobacconist" in the 1797 city directory. *Longworth's American Alamanack*, 251, 334. Williams had been owned by a Loyalist who trained him as a tobacconist. He was sold to the John Street United Methodist Church congregation, working as the sexton, and eventually bought his freedom. In 1796, he and other African American congregants left the church due to discrimination, and founded the Mother African Methodist Episcopal Zion Church. His son, the Reverend Peter Williams Jr., would become the first African American Episcopal minister and a leading abolitionist.

From an 1808 letter written by PAJ to his father, it appears that Peter Williams did not purchase his niece and her child: "P.S. Dinah a negro woman who lived with you at Albany called here a short time ago & told me that you had sold her & her child for a limited time to one Inman, & that you told her at the time of the sale that at the expiration of her service she was to receive a sume of Money from Inman. Inman she says sold her to one Camp & her Child to M[rs]. Breeze at Utica. Her time has expired & she now works for herself. But Camp refuses to pay her any thing & her Child is still held as a slave. I promised her to inquire of you if these were the facts in order that if they were true I might write to her former Master in her behalf." 21 Jan. 1808, ALS, NNC (EJ: 06126). JJ's reply has not been found.

To John Williams

Albany 24 Feb. 1797

Sir

Accept my Thanks for your Letters of the 15 and 17 Instant, which together with a Copy of the Report of the Committee respecting the Fortifications of Ports & Harbours, I rec[eive][d]. this morning.[1] It appears to me probable that no measures very effectual will be taken on this Subject by the present Congress — but it is to be hoped that the succeeding one will attend to it. The Nation will have Reason to be dissatisfied, if after so long an Interval of peace and Prosperity, war should find us in a defenseless State —[2]

As to the Ballance claimed from this State — sound Policy certainly requires, that this delicate Business should be conducted to a final Settlement in the Manner most just and conciliatory. Asperity on either Side can produce nothing but evil; nor will the Temper of this State be rendered flexible by harsh Resolutions. I flatter myself that mutual Respect will be observed on both Sides; and that this affair will yet be amicably and satisfactorily terminated —[3] It would give me pleasure to be ascertained that M[r] Pinckney has been properly rec[eive][d]. by the Directory.[4] I do not despair of it; especially as it is probable that their exceptionable conduct towards this Country, has been calculated on Representations, which being ill founded, must soon cease to operate — I have the Honor to be Sir Your most ob[t]. & h'ble Serv[t]

John Jay

ALS, N (EJ: 04367). Addressed: "General John Williams / in Congress / Philadelphia". Franked "ALBANY NY FREE". Endorsed. In addition to working as a physician, John Williams held various state political and military appointments for New York during the Revolution and the years thereafter. Williams served as a Democratic-Republican representative for the 9th District in the 4th Congress (1795–97) before switching his allegiance to the Federalists while serving in the 5th Congress (1797–99).

1. Letters not found. JJ is probably referring to a Congressional report that came out on 10 Feb. 1797, on the status of fortifications in the nation's harbors and ports, including New York. *Report of the committee appointed to the sixteenth of December last, to enquire into the actual state of the Fortifications of the ports and harbours of the United States; and what further provision is necessary to be made on the subject. 10th February 1797, ordered to lie on the table 11th February 1797* (Philadelphia, 1797; *Early Am. Imprints*, series 1, no. 32988).

2. For Congressional debates over funding New York's fortifications, see the editorial note "Defending New York," above.

3. House members serving in the 4th Congress debated the issue of state debt owed to the federal government throughout late December 1796 and early January 1797. Much of the discussion focused on the state of New York, which possessed the lion's share of the debt, amounting to over two million dollars. *Annals*, 4: 1747–62, 1767–87, 1789–1816.

4. For responses to the French Directory's treatment of Pinckney, see RK to JJ, 10 Jan. 1797, above.

To Jedidiah Morse

Albany 28 Feby 1797

Dear Sir

I have been fav[ore]^d. with yours of the 14 ult. and also with the one which accompanied the Set of your Geography, for which be pleased to accept my Thanks.—[1]

It gives me Pleasure to learn that you will endeavour at least to *prepare* for a History of the American Revolution. To obtain competent and exact Information on the Subject, is not the least arduous part of the Task— it will require much Time patient Perseverance and Research.

As the Revolution was accomplished by the Councils and Efforts of the *union,* and by the auxiliary Councils and Efforts of *each individual* State or Colony; it appears to me that your Enquiries will necessarily be divided into those *two* Departments— the *first* will of course include *foreign* affairs, and both of them will naturally divide into two others vizt. the *civil* and the *military*— Each of these you know comprehend several distinct Heads, which are obvious.

So much of our Colonial History as cast Light on the Revolution viewed under all its aspects, and considered in all its *anterior* Relations will be essential. I think our colonial History is strongly marked by discriminating Circumstances relative to our political Situation and Feelings at *three*

different Periods— 1ˢᵗ. down to the Revolution under King W[illia]ᵐ.—
2ᵈ. from thence to the Year 1763— and 3ᵈ. from that Year to the *union* of the
Colonies in 1774— Want of Leisure will not permit me to go into Details—

As to Documents— the public and *private* Journals of Congress— the
Papers mentioned or alluded to in them—such as certain Reports of Committees, Letters to and from civil and military officers, ministers, Agents State
Governors &cᵃ.—the proceedings of the standing Committees for *marine,
commercial, fiscal, political* and foreign affairs—all merit attention— There
are also Diaries, and Memoirs, and private Letters which would give some
aid and Light to a *sagacious* and *cautious* Inquirer— for Experience has convinced me that they are entitled to no other Respect or attention than what
they derive from the well established Characters of the writers for Judgment
accuracy and Candor—

As to Characters, I have throughout the Revolution known some who
passed for more than they were worth—and others who passed for less.—
on this Head great Circumspection is particularly requisite—

It is to be regretted, but so I believe the Fact to be, that except the Bible,
there is not a true History in the World— Whatever may be the ‸virtue‸
Discernment and Industry of the Writers, Truth and Error, tho' in different
Degrees, will imperceptibly become and remain mixed and blended untill
they shall be separated forever by the great and last refining Fire— With real
Esteem & Regard I am Dʳ Sir your most obᵗ Servᵗ.

John Jay

The Revᵈ.

ALS, PHi: Gratz (EJ: 01130). Addressed. Stamped: "ALBANY NY". Endorsed: " . . .hoping he will
write / a history of Amer. Revo. / lution—& specifying the proper Sources / of information". Dft,
NNC (EJ: 12775); *WJ*, 2: 278–80; *HPJ*, 4: 223–25. The Dft contains lengthy, often illegible, excisions
that are not recorded here. For the reply, see Morse to JJ, 21 Apr. 1797, below.

1. See Morse to JJ, 14 Jan. 1797, above, and 24 Oct. 1796, ALS, NNC (EJ: 09545).

Report of the Regents to the New York State Legislature

[Albany, March 6th, 1797]

REPORT of the REGENTS of the UNIVERSITY, made to the
Legislature, the 9th of March, ult. and entered on the Journals of both
Houses.

To the HONORABLE *the* LEGISLATURE,
The Regents of the University
Respectfully report,

That during the year past, *Columbia* and *Union* Colleges, and *Erasmus-Hall, Johnstown, Cooperstown, Canandarqua, Oxford, Hamilton-Oneida, Cherry Valley, Union* in Stone Arabia, *Clinton, Washington* and *Lansingburgh* Academies, have been visited by Committees of the Regents; and from the reports of the Committees, the following appears to be the state of these seminaries respectively.— *Columbia* College consists of two faculties, the faculty of arts and the faculty of physic. In the faculty of arts there are seven professors— one of the mathematics, natural philosophy, astronomy, geography and chronology, one of the Greek and Latin languages, and Grecian and Roman antiquities, one of the Oriental languages, one of natural history and agriculture, one of the French language, one of law, one of logic and moral philosophy, and one of belles-lettres; and in the faculty of physic there is a dean and six professors— one of midwifery, who is also clinical lecturer in the New-York hospital, one of the theory and practice of physic, one of surgery, one of anatomy, and one of botany and materia medica: there are ninety-four students in the faculty of arts, and about thirty in the faculty of physic. The only compensation to the Medical Professors are the fees of tuition; and the salaries of the President and of the Professors in the faculty of arts remain nearly the same as at the time of the last annual report. The President, in his report to the committee who visited the College,[1] states it to be in general in a flourishing state— that strict order and discipline are maintained— that by arranging the students after each examination according to their respective merits in their classes, such a general emulation has been excited, as in a great measure to supersede the necessity of punishment— that from the learning & reputation of the professors, from the increasing number of students, from their progress in their studies, from the general plan and good government of the institution, and from the number of grammar schools in and near the city, under able and reputable teachers, he has reason to expect, that a few years will greatly enhance the growing fame of the college, at least double the number of its students, and raise it to a pitch of exalted prosperity; he however, suggests, that it labors under the greatest difficulties for the want of a convenient library, a suitable hall for public exhibitions, a sufficient number of lecture rooms, and proper apartments for the arrangement and use of the philosophical and chymical apparatus; and requests the attention of the Regents to the situation of the Faculty of Physic, whose emoluments are by no means a compensation for their assiduous and learned labors, and that a fostering public aid is requisite to promote this useful and rising medical institution on which the lives and health of our citizens so essentially depend.[2] *Union* College— From the report of the Committee of the Trustees, it appears that the property of the college consists in various articles, to the following amount, namely:

	Dolls.	Cts.
Bond and mortgages, producing an annual interest of 7 per cent.	21,301	6
Subscriptions and other debts due on the books of Treasurer	4,983	10
Cash appropriated for the purchase of books	1,356	45
House and lot for the President	3,500	
Lot for the scite of the College	3,250	
House and lot heretofore occupied for the Academy, a donation from the consistory of the Dutch Church	5,000	
Books, &c. in the possession of The Trustees, and on the way From Europe	2,381	99
Cash appropriated by the Regents, for the purchase of books in the hands of the committee	400	
Legacy by Abraham Yates,[3] jun. Esq. of Albany	250	
	42,422	60

And 1604 acres of land. The faculty of the College at present consists of the President and one Tutor, and the salary of the former with an house for his family is 1100 dollars, and of the latter 665 dollars per annum, with an additional allowance at present of 250 dollars, on account of the extraordinary price of the necessaries of life. There are thirty-seven students, eight in the class of languages, twenty in the class of history and belles-lettres, six in the class of mathematics, and three in the class of philosophy. The course of studies is, the first year Virgil, Cicero's orations, Greek testament, Lucian, Roman antiquities, arithmetic and English grammar— the second year, geography and the use of the globes, Roman history, history of America, and the American revolution, Xenophon, Horace, criticism and eloquence— the 3d year, the various branches of mathematics, and vulgar and decimal fractions,

& the extraction of the roots—geometry, algebra, trigonometry, navigation, mensuration, Xenophon continued, and Homer; and the 4th and last year, natural philosophy, the constitution of the United States and of the different states, metaphysics, or at least that part which treats of the philosophy of the human mind, Horace continued and Longinus; and during the course of these studies, the attention of the classes is particularly required to elocution and composition in the English language; a provision is also made, for substituting the knowledge of the French language instead of the Greek, in certain cases, if the funds should hereafter admit of instituting a French professorship; all which together with the system of discipline, is contained in a printed copy of the laws and regulations for the government of the College, and which accompanies this report.[4] The trustees further report, that the officers of the College discharge their duty with ability, diligence and fidelity, and that the students generally have exhibited specimens of their progress in science, at the examinations, which are public, and statedly three times a year; that the recent institution, or the entire want of grammar schools and academics, in the different towns and counties most convenient to Schenectady, considerably impedes for the present the increase of students in the College, which has hitherto been indebted for its principal supplies to the grammar schools in that place, and to the academy in Salem, in Washington county; that there are, however, indications which evince, that in proportion to the establishment and proper management of schools and academies to the northward and westward, this seminary will become an institution of immense importance to the interest of science, in this part of the United States; and they beg leave to represent, agreeably to their statement of the last year, that an alteration in some of the articles of their charter would be of considerable service to the College, as it regards the number of trustees requisite to form a quorum for business and the exercise of discipline by the officers of the College, without the necessity of summoning a meeting of the trustees for the purpose;[5] and finally, that it would essentially promote the interest of that part of the country, if the Legislature would patronize with further donations this infant seminary; the want of means to endow professorship, obliges the present officers to attend to too many branches of science, insomuch so that the President has during the present year, instructed the classes in history, chronology, antiquities, geography, natural and moral philosophy, criticism, logic, constitutions of the United States and of the different states and languages. *Erasmus Hall*— In this Academy there are one hundred and six scholars, all of whom, except from the city of New-York, are from the West indies or distant parts of the United States— the branches of education are the same as heretofore reported, and three of the scholars are studying the principles of natural philosophy, and thirty learning the French language, in connection with their other studies, and all of them give the most satisfactory specimens of progress and accuracy in the several branches in which they were examined, and the institution under the same principal and teachers, continues to support its high reputation. *Clinton* Academy has sixty three scholars, three of whom are taught Latin and Greek, three mathematics, six English grammar, and fifty-one reading and writing; in addition to which, there are thirty scholars in arithmetic and English grammar, who attend in the evening only. *Johnstown* Academy has forty-four scholars, sixteen of whom are taught mathematics, sixteen spelling, and twenty-seven reading and writing, comprehending fourteen who are taught arithmetic. The building consists only of one room of a convenient size, and [the] teacher is paid out of the tuition money. This Academy has no funds, owing to which, and to a want of attention in those to whom the direction and superintendance of it is intrusted, it is not so flourishing as when visited the preceding year. *Cooperstown* Academy— The building which is sixty-six feet long, forty feet broad, and two stories high, is nearly finished, and in erecting it the whole of the property, except two shares in the Albany Banks, has been expended. *Canandarqua* Academy— The donations in land and subscriptions in money to this Academy, are estimated to amount upwards of 30,000 dollars, and it is expected it will be respectable and useful. *Hamilton-Oneida* Academy is in a worse situation than it was the preceding year— The building is covered, but there is no prospect it will be further completed; the funds being wholly expended, and the property already taken in execution to satisfy debts still due. *Union* Academy in Stone-Arabia— The trustees of this Academy have hitherto employed a person to teach as in an ordinary school only, in a small house, belonging to a one of the churches there, the teacher lately died, and no other has since been procured; materials however have been prepared for erecting a building in the course of the ensuing summer. *Oxford* Academy, has sustained a considerable injury by the resignation of the late principal,[6] but it is expected he will soon resume his charge, and his talents and attention afford prospects of very great usefulness. *Cherry-Valley* Academy— The building is convenient, two stories high, 60 feet long and 30 feet broad, and nearly finished— the subscriptions amount to 3100 dollars, of which 2815 dollars have been received, and the additional sum of 1587 1-2 dollars has been lately been subscribed for the purpose of employing teachers. The present principal appears to possess talents and industry, and is allowed a salary of 400 dollars, and there is an assistant teacher, who has a salary of 200 dollars per annum. The number of scholars amount to eighty, of whom twenty are taught Latin, and the rest arithmetic and reading English— The prospect that this Academy would become useful, was such as induced the committee to pay to them the sum allotted to it by the Regents, as a donation to purchase books. *Washington* Academy has thirty scholars, ten of whom are taught Latin and Greek, two mathematics and book-keeping, and the remaining eighteen, English grammar, writing and arithmetic, and during the last year five students were admitted into Union College from this Academy— No alteration, with the respect to the estate or compensation to teachers, or the mode of instruction, has taken place since the last report. *Lansingburgh* Academy has forty scholars, who are instructed in the English language and grammar— The trustees have provided a convenient building, consisting of two rooms on the first and three on the second floor, but as yet unfinished; and they contracted with a person to teach the Latin language; and from the increase of Lansingburgh and the other towns in the vicinity, and the zeal of the trustees, the committee was induced to pay to them the sum appropriated by the Regents during the last year. It is only necessary for the Regents to request the attention of the Legislature to the real and personal property vested in the Regents by law, and they respectfully suggest the propriety of enabling the Regents to make such disposition thereof, by sale or otherwise, as that an annual income may result to the University, to be disposed of by the Regents, in their discretion, for promoting literature. By Order of the Regents,

> JOHN JAY, Chancellor.
> By command of the Chancellor,
> David S. Jones, Secretary.

PtD, *Albany Gazette*, 10 Apr.; *Albany Chronicle* 17 and 24 April (cont.); *Minerva* (New York), 18 Apr.; *Herald* (New York), 19 Apr.; *Argus, Greenleaf's New Daily Advertiser* (New York), 20 Apr.; *Mohawk Mercury* (Schenectady), 9 May 1797; *N.Y. Assembly Journal*, 20th sess. (1796–97), 145–48; *N.Y. Senate Journal*, 20th sess. (1796–97), 83–86.

1. Report issued by President William Samuel Johnson not found.

2. During JJ's governorship and the years preceding it, Columbia College (formerly King's College until 1784) depended on state funding to maintain its operating budget. Between 1785 and 1792, Columbia received 10,552 pounds in one-time grants and from 1792 to 1799, it received an annual gift of 750 pounds from the State Legislature. "An Act to encourage Literature by Donations to Columbia College, and to the several Academies in the State," 22 Apr. 1792, *N.Y. State Laws*, (1777–97), 2: 479–80; "An Act for the payment of certain officers of government and other contingent expences," 11 Apr. 1796, *N.Y. State Laws*, 19th sess. (1796), 46; Robert A. McCaughey, *Stand Columbia: A History of Columbia University in the City of New York, 1754–2004* (New York, 2003), 71–72.

3. Abraham Yates Jr., who served as Mayor of Albany, state senator, and member of the Continental Congress, died on 30 June 1796.

4. Laws and regulations of Union College not found.

5. The charter for the institution was amended on 30 Mar. 1797 to enable the faculty to impose disciplinary measures upon students. Franklin B. Hough, *Record of the University of the State of New York during the Century from 1784 to 1884* (Albany, 1885), 152n2.

6. Probably Uri Tracy (1764–1838). A native of Norwich, Conn., Tracy moved to Oxford in 1791 and became the first principal of the local Academy in 1794. Henry J. Galpin, *Annals of Oxford, New York: with Illustrations and Biographical Sketches of some of its Prominent Men and early Pioneers* (Oxford, N.Y., 1906), 54–55.

THE CAPITAL MOVES TO ALBANY

When state lawmakers adjourned mid-session in November 1796, they left New York's City's Federal Hall with an agreement to reconvene a few months later in Albany.[1] Since the formation of New York's government in 1777, the state legislature had shifted its meeting sites between Kingston, Poughkeepsie, Albany, and New York City, and had thereby relocated the state capital sixteen times within a twenty year period.[2] The removal of the seat of government up the Hudson River in early 1797, however, proved more than just a temporary transfer of power, as legislators passed subsequent acts in the following months that solidified Albany's status as the permanent capital.[3] Although the official record offers little explanation for this shift in policy, Albany's rise in political prominence vis-à-vis New York City occurred due to a combination of factors, the most significant being the republican belief that situating the state legislature in a central location produced a fairer and more efficient system of representation.[4] The decision also reflected Albany's rising status as a communications and commercial center, as well as concerns over New York City's vulnerability to yellow fever outbreaks and naval attacks. Moreover, many communities residing in the hinterland and northern section of the state shared an anxiety that their downstate rival was amassing too much political influence and power.[5]

As the year drew to a close, the members of the state senate and assembly travelled to Albany for their scheduled meeting. Since Jay would also perform his official duties in Albany, he likewise made the journey northward, arriving by sleigh on New Year's Eve.[6] Albany's city hall, the old *Stadt Huys*, had been converted for use by the legislature when the session opened on 3 January, and Jay noted with approval that the local residents were welcoming and well prepared to receive the influx of visitors.[7] The move itself, however, was far from a welcome development. As one of Jay's colleagues noted, "the Governor is well but rather out of temper with the abrupt adjournment of our Legislature to meet in January next, and at Albany."[8] Jay's transition to his new accommodations was eased through the assistance of Dirk Ten Broeck who procured him two rented rooms and arranged for a cask of porter to be delivered to his quarters.[9] Jay found the new lodgings pleasant enough, but nothing could replace the domestic comforts of the Government House, his residence in New York City. As he confessed to his wife who remained behind with their younger children, "I shall not, and cannot, forget that I am not at home."[10]

It was a long and at times winding path that state lawmakers followed in granting Albany the coveted status of New York's capital. After hearing a proposal brought to the assembly floor in mid-January, members of both houses debated the contentious issue for nearly two months before passing legislation that ultimately secured the city's political prominence.[11] The resulting omnibus bill contained several provisions, including the erection of a public building in Albany for housing the papers of the state legislature, the records and offices of the secretary of New York, and the clerk of the State Supreme Court. The bill also called for the relocation of the offices of the state treasurer and comptroller to either Albany or nearby Watervliet, a division of the duties of the clerks of the State Supreme Court between Albany and New York City, and the sitting of the State Court of Probate in Albany.[12]

Although newspapers were largely silent on the move to Albany, it seems to have elicited a mixed response from New Yorkers. For instance, Elihu Hubbard Smith, a physician in New York City, welcomed the shift as a positive development for the state. As he commented to a friend, "The removal of the Seat of Government & the Public Offices, to Albany—which is now provided for, will, probably, preserve the union of the different parts of the State, some years longer, than it might, otherwise, have continued."[13] Yet Smith also noted that the physical shift of the capital portended a political shift of power; "The only danger arises, he warned, "from the ardent temper of the many young men who represent the western & northern Counties."[14] Robert Troup shared the latter sentiment, commenting that the eventual removal of the "seat of government" to Albany was proof that "The northern and western interests are much too powerful for us."[15]

Jay had correctly assumed that the state legislature would continue to meet in Albany, but he was less sure as to whether other government agencies would remain in New York City or be relocated elsewhere.[16] Upon hearing that Albany had been selected to serve as the state capital, Jay forwarded the news to Sally, explaining, "the Bill fixing the Seat of Govt. here has become a Law— it provides that the Legislature shall convene, here and that the

Treasury, Secretary's and other offices shall be removed to this place as soon as the arrangem[ts]. Necessary for the Purpose shall be made."[17]

While lawmakers were debating the placement of the state capital, Jay also faced the uncertainty of where he and his family would reside for the duration of his term in office. Initial reports from the *Studt Huys* suggested that the governor's presence would not be required at future legislative sessions. Jay informed Sally in mid-February, "I shall be left to reside in New York," and communicated soon after that, "Nothing has as yet occurred which indicates a fixed Opinion that the Governor ought to reside at this Place."[18] A few weeks later, however, Jay overheard rumors that Albany would indeed become the permanent abode for the state's chief executive officer and that the legislature might also cover the expenses of his family's accommodations. "I find there is much Conversation," he wrote to his wife, "about providing a House here for the Governor."[19] Although he doubted whether any decisions would be made during the current session, state lawmakers did manage to pass a resolution defraying the cost of his housing before they adjourned in early April.[20]

Upon returning to New York City at the end of the legislative meeting, Jay would take much comfort knowing that he and Sally no longer faced the daunting prospect of a prolonged separation. The several months prior to moving proved a busy period for the Jays. In addition to planning and making preparations for their new home, they had to arrange for the rental and upkeep of their properties in New York City. James Caldwell,[21] an Albany merchant and entrepreneur, leased the Jay family his stately three-story brick house located on State Street, a main thoroughfare.[22] Jay also relied on the support of Albany's John Tayler, the Indian agent and recently appointed justice of the Court of Common Pleas, who lived nearby at 50 State Street. Tayler aided Jay with various endeavors: he made sure that the stables and carpentry for the new house were completed on time; that a sleigh was built for use by the family during the winter months; that firewood was supplied in the yard; and that "M[rs] Jays determination as to the carpet" was made known to Caldwell.[23] Tayler also helped to organize and store the furniture and sundry goods that Jay shipped up the Hudson aboard sloops hired for that purpose.[24]

At about the same time that the governor and his family arrived at their new residence on 20 September, Jay sent additional freight to Albany, along with four "Man servants", two horses, and one cow on a vessel captained by John Bogart.[25] Although it took Sally a little time to adjust to her new surroundings, the members of the household were largely content with their new arrangements.[26] In October, Jay commented that he and his family "are pretty well settled," but noted nonetheless, that "if we had a little more room we should find ourselves very comfortable."[27]

1. *N.Y. Assembly Journal*, 20th sess. (1796–97), 20–21, 30; *N.Y. Senate Journal*, 20th sess. (1796–97), 13, 22, 23.

2. *N.Y. Civil List*, 110–16. New York City proved the most prominent location for the state legislature in recent years with eleven of the previous sixteen meetings held there since 1784.

3. With the organization of the state government in 1777, JJ recommended that the first session of the legislature be held in Albany. His suggestion met with resistance, however, from lawmakers, largely from the southern counties, who balked at the high expenses that would accompany a residency in Albany and who also objected to the eventual possibility that Albany might acquire the status of state capital. See JJ to Philip Schuyler, 20 June 1777, *JJSP*, 1: 436–37.

4. Rosemarie Zagarri, "Representation and the Removal of State Capitals, 1776–1812," *Journal of American History* 74 (Mar. 1988): 1239–56.

5. John Sloss Hobart raised the possibility in early 1795 that "Northern folks" in New York State would support Abraham Yates Jr., the mayor of Albany, as a gubernatorial candidate with the expectation that his election would result in the capital being moved to Albany. Hobart to JJ, 7 Jan. 1795, above. See also Burrows and Wallace, *Gotham*, 354.

6. JJ to SLJ, 1 Jan. 1797, ALS, NNC (EJ: 08072).

7. JJ to PJM, 21 Jan. 1797, ALS, NNMus (EJ: 00447).

8. Robert Troup to RK, 16 Nov. 1796, King, *Life and Correspondence of Rufus King*, 2: 110.

9. Dirck Ten Broeck, Albany attorney, state assembly member, and son of Abraham Ten Broeck (1734–1810), the mayor of Albany. JJ lodged with the Roseboom family in Albany, probably either the household of Hendrick Roseboom of the 1st Ward or that of Jacob Roseboom of the 3rd Ward. *Heads of Families at the First Census of the United States Taken in the Year 1790: New York* (Washington, D.C., 1908), 12, 14; Dirck Ten Broeck to JJ, 14 Dec. 1796, ALS, NNC (EJ: 07162).

10. JJ to SLJ, 1 Jan. 1797, ALS, NNC (EJ: 08072).

11. Gaylord Griswold (1767–1809), representing Herkimer County, introduced the bill entitled, "An Act for establishing the permanent Seat of Government" on 14 Jan. *N.Y. Assembly Journal*, 20th sess. (1796–97), 52; *Argus, Greenleaf's New Daily Advertiser* (New York), 23 Jan.; *Greenleaf's New York Journal*, and *Herald* (both New York), 25 Jan. 1797. See also *Diary* and *Minerva*, (both New York), 14 Feb. 1797. For more on the legislative process of naming Albany as the seat of government, see Albert B. Corey, "Your State Historian Speaking: How Albany Became the Capital of the State," *New York History* 27 (Jan. 1946): 122–24.

12. "An Act for erecting a public Building in the County of Albany, and for other Purposes therein mentioned," 10 Mar. 1797, *N.Y. State Laws*, 20th sess. (1797), 61–65.

13. Smith, *Diary*, 292.

14. Ibid.

15. Robert Troup to RK, 16 Nov. 1796, King, *Life and Correspondence of Rufus King*, 2: 110.

16. JJ to SLJ, 12 Jan. 1797, SR, Diana Rendell Catalogue, no. 6, June 1986.

17. JJ to SLJ, 10 Mar. 1797, below. Although the transfer of the capital to Albany was a decision made solely by the state legislature and did not involve the executive branch, JJ's opponents nonetheless accused him of orchestrating the move for political gain. In November 1797, PAJ wrote to his

father with news that "The Democratic Agents have already began to electioneer in Westchester—Among the ingenious accusations they have preferred against you are those of removing the Seat of Government to Albany." PAJ to JJ, 26 Nov. 1797, ALS, NNC (EJ: 06060).

18. JJ to SLJ, 12 Feb. 1797, ALS, NNC (EJ: 08073); JJ to SLJ, 28 Feb. 1797, ALS, NNC (EJ: 08074).

19. JJ to SLJ, 10 Mar. 1797, below.

20. *N.Y. Assembly Journal*, 20th sess. (1796–97), 192, 193.

21. James Caldwell of Watervliet (1747–1825).

22. Inventory of JJ's Property, 8–9 Nov. 1798, below; *Albany Centinel*, 29 Sept. 1797.

23. Tayler to JJ, 26 May 1797, ALS, NNC (EJ: 07161). John Tayler played an active civic role in the Albany and state community, serving in the Assembly (1777–87), as Canal Commissioner of New York (1792), as Recorder of Albany (1793), and in the Senate (1802, 1804–13). Tayler later served as Lieutenant Governor of New York (1811, 1813–14) and as acting Governor (1817).

24. JJ hired the services of the sloop *Albany*, Anthony Van Santwood, and an unnamed sloop, Thomas Nash. "Mr. Van Santwoods rec^t. For things taken on board his sloop", n.d., DS, NNC; "Thomas Nash's Rec^t. For things taken on board his Sloop, 15 Sep^{br}. 97", DS, NNC.

25. *Albany Centinel*, 29 Sept.; *Albany Chronicle*, 2 Oct. 1797; "Rec^t. from Cap^{tn}. Bogart for passages freight &^{c}. 30th. Dec^{br}. 1797", DS, NNC. John Bogert (1761–1853), a Hudson River skipper who carried items between Albany and New York City, logged three additional voyages for JJ on 12 and 23 Oct., and 17 Nov. 1797. The following spring, PAJ shipped more household goods to his family in Albany aboard Capt. Lansing's sloop. PAJ to JJ, 26 Apr. 1798, below. Stefan Bielinski, *Captain John Bogert*, https://exhibitions.nysm.nysed.gov/albany/bios/b/jobogert6121.html (accessed Aug. 2019).

26. Commenting on the family's move to Albany, PAJ reported in March 1798 that "Mama is more pleased with it than she expected to be— except the trouble occasioned by a great ˄deal˄ of Company & very bad markets she is pretty pleasantly situated." PAJ to Peter Jay, 17 Mar. 1798, Dft, NNC (EJ: 90163). For the family move, see also SLJ to PAJ, 27 Sept. 1979, ALS, NrRyJHC.

27. JJ to PJM, 14 Oct. 1797, ALS, NNMus (EJ: 00450).

To Sarah Livingston Jay

Albany 10 March 1797

My dear Sally

I was this afternoon fav^d. with yours of the 5th. Instant,[1] enclosing the ~~mes~~ Letter[2] ~~from~~ mentioned but omitted in your last. my last to you was written on the 5th of this month.[3] in it I informed You that I had rec^d. yours of the 25th. Ult:[4]

For two Days past we have had severe cold weather— no Water to be seen in Streets— all hard frozen— so that unless much Rain should speedily fall, the River will probably continue in its present State longer than was expected.[5]

I am not certain that I gave Peter Directions to send nails to Bedford for John Nichol's House—[6] If not—let him ask our Carpenter how many nails

3000 Shingles require. some will be wanted for the Sides and Floor of the House. A Quantity for these purposes should be seasonably sent— perhaps some person going from New York to Bedford would take charge of them.

The Bill fixing the Seat of Gov^t. here has become a Law—[7] it provides that the Legislature shall convene here, and that the Treasury, Secretary's and other offices shall be removed to this place as soon as the arrangem^{ts}. Necessary for the Purposes shall be made. With Respect to the Govr. the Law is silent. there are opinions however that he ought to reside here— What Influence these opinions may have on the next Legislature cannot be foreseen—[8]

It gives me pleasure that Peter and Polly consented to stay with you as long as they did, and that they were in such good Health & Spirits— of your attentions to them I am well persuaded. and so I am convinced they are— another month will I hope put an End to our separation; and that I have then have the Satisfaction of finding you and the children well. My Love to them— I am dear Sally Yours very affectionately

John Jay

Mrs Jay— Saturday Morn^g.—It snows very fast— turn over

This Letter arriving at the Post Office after the mail was closed I have opened it to acknowledge the Rec^t. of yours[9] by M^r. Glen,[10] who delivered it to me this morning. as it informed me that You and the Children were well it is interesting and I thank You for it— This is a fine warm Day, and the snow which fell yesterday is melting very fast— I find there is much Conversation about providing a House here for the Governor; but I rather doubt its being done this Session— When next you write to our Friends at Rye remember me to them. Remember me also to M^r & Mrs^s. Munro. I hope her Health is re-established and the little one doing well—

ALS, NNC (EJ: 08075). Addressed: "M^{rs}. Jay / Government House / New York". Stamped. Endorsed: "J. Jay / 10 March 1797".

1. Letter not found.

2. Letter not identified.

3. Letter not found.

4. Letter not found.

5. A local paper reported a few days later that the ice in the Hudson River had recently began to flow, thereby opening up the waterway to navigation. *Albany Gazette*, 16 Mar. 1797.

6. The 1800 federal census lists John Nickoles as heading a six-member household in Bedford.

7. "An Act for erecting a public Building in the County of Albany, and for other Purposes therein mentioned," 10 Mar. 1797, *N.Y. State Laws*, 20th sess. (1797), 61–65.

8. For more on the legislature and the state government's relocation to Albany, see the editorial note "The Capital Moves to Albany," above.

9. Letter not identified.
10. Probably Henry Glen.

From Peter Thacher

Boston April 19 1797

Sir

The board of commissioners in Boston from the society in Scotland for propagating christian knowledge have directed me to address your excellency, upon a subject which is important to the interests of christianity and of the society whom they represent.

This society have, for a number of years past, supported a mission to the Oneida indians who live in your state. M^r. Kirkland, who has been their missionary, is now about to quit that employment.[1] We are informed that your state has purchased large tracts of land from these indians and annually pay them a considerable sum of money. Under these circumstances we feel a difficulty in recommending to the society in Scotland to continue their mission to the Oneidas. We cannot but suppose that they are able from the annuities of your government to support a minister ~~from~~ ∧for∧ themselves, and that if part of their money was given him, it would be expended more for their ~~advantage~~ real benefit than they expend it themselves. The fund at the disposal of the society was raised for the purpose of sending missionaries among indians who were in pagan darkness, and who were unable to procure the gospel for themselves. The indians of Oneida are in neither of these predicaments, and we cannot therefore suppose that they are entitled to any part of it. They are surrounded on every side with white inhabitants and are under the protection of a rich and powerful government. Your excellency will excuse us therefore for suggesting to you the propriety of your state's supporting a missionary among them, and the unsuitableness of his being paid by persons in a foreign country. It is important to the state of New York that these indians should be civilised and that their morals should be such as may render ∧them∧ harmless and useful to society. Some of these observations will apply also to the indians of New Stockbridge who are under the care of the Rev^d. Mr Sargeant,[2] whose salary is as yet paid by the scotch society.

Our particular situation, as well as our solicitude for the indians who have been for some time in a sense under our care, must be our apology for troubling your excellency on these subjects, and for requesting you to take them under your consideration and to adopt such measures as to your wisdom may seem meet.

With the highest respect and the warmest personal friendship and esteem for your excellency, I subscribe myself, Sir Your most obedient, humble servant

Peter Thacher, Secretary to the / board of commissioners, Boston

ALS, NNC (EJ: 07165). Addressed. Stamped. Marked: *"Paid 20"*. Endorsed: ". . . 19 Apr. / and 25 apr 1797". Jedidiah Morse referenced this letter in his correspondence to JJ of 21 Apr. 1797, below. For JJ's reply, see JJ to Thacher, 25 Apr., below.

1. For more on Kirkland and his mission to the Oneida, see the editorial note "Indian Affairs under Jay's Governorship," above.

2. John Sergeant Jr. (c. 1747–1824) lived among the Mohican community of New Stockbridge. Sergeant followed the calling of his father, John Sr. (1710–49), a Congregationalist minister, who established a mission for the Mohican Indians in Stockbridge, Mass. Unlike Kirkland, the younger Sergeant set up schools within the neighboring Oneida villages. See Taylor, *Divided Ground*, 369.

To Timothy Pickering (private)

New York 19 April 1797—

Dear Sir

I enclose one of Greenleafs Papers, printed the 15 of last month. You will find in it some Statements and Remarks on the Expences of the british Treaty—[1]

Some Gentlemen on whose Judgments I rely, and among them Col. Hamilton, think it adviseable that some notice be taken of this publication— a certain Description of People make a Handle of it—

I enclose a Paper on the Subject, which I think might with Propriety be certified by the Comptroller and Auditor of the Treasury, and published either under your or Mr. Wolcot's Signature, in one or more of your Papers.[2] Be pleased to consult with him about it, and do therein what you may judge to be most proper— For my own part, I doubt the Expediency of further or more particular Details. our general Election is at Hand, and therefore it is obvious that the sooner this is done the better on that Account with sincere Esteem and Regard I am Dear Sir your most obt Servt

John Jay

The Honble Timothy Pickering Esqr

ALS, MHi: Pickering (EJ: 04777). Marked: *"Private"*.

1. From a Correspondent, *Greenleaf's New York Journal*, 15 Mar. 1797. Using figures derived from U.S. Treasury accounts and published by TP in the New York–based *Diary or Loudon's Register* on 11 Mar. 1797, the correspondent had criticized the expenditures involved in negotiating the Jay treaty, especially the costs of JJ's sailing "in state", and estimated the costs of prosecuting claims against the British at $200,000 dollars, and of losses by French captures predicated on and sanctioned by the

British treaty at $6,000,000. The piece was also printed in the *Aurora General Advertiser* of Phila-
delphia on 16 Mar. 1797. This was followed eight days later with a letter written by "A Citizen" to the
printer of the *Gazette of the United States*, another Philadelphia newspaper, estimating the costs of
JJ's mission at over $36,000 and inquiring what became of the money. "A Citizen" also appeared in
Stewart's Kentucky Herald of Lexington on 18 Apr. 1797.

Similar charges resurfaced in 1799–1800. See the *Constitutional Telegraph* (Boston), 5 Oct. 1799,
Kentucky Gazette (Lexington), 16 Jan.; and *American* (Baltimore), 22 Nov. 1800.

2. For JJ's response to such charges, first published in the *Gazette of the United States* (Philadelphia) on 25 Apr., and the accompanying certificate by Register of the Treasury Joseph Nourse of 24
Apr. 1797, see below.

For JJ's expenses, see also JJ to ER, 5 Mar. 1795, DS, DNA (EJ: 04293); JJ to Oliver Wolcott Jr.,
19 Nov. 1795, Dft, NNC (EJ: 08948); JJ to Thomas Pinckney, 18 June 1796, Dft, NNC (EJ: 09473);
Certificate of Auditor Account, signed by Richard Harrison, Joseph Nourse, and John Steele, 22–27
Oct. 1796, AD, NNC (EJ: 09839).

From Jedidiah Morse

Charlestown April 21st. 1797

Respected & Dear Sir,

I should have acknowledged the receipt of your obliging & acceptable Letter of the 28th of Feby.[1] earlier, but for the great & unremitting attention I have
been obliged to pay to my Gazetteer[2] wh[ic]h is in the press.

The plan of a History of our Revolution wh[ic]h you, Sir, have suggested,
is certainly natural, plain, concise, comprehensive & judicious— & your directions, as to the objects of enquiry, in order to complete the plan, are as excellent as the plan itself.— I feel my self much obliged, assisted & encouraged
in the undertaking by the whole of your excellent Letter.— As my leisure &
opportunities permit, I shall be assiduous in collecting & arranging materials,
preparatory to the execution of the general plan.— Any aid from you, Sir,
either by advise, or documents printed or MS. would be gratefully received.

When I was last in N. York, on my return from Oneida, in conversation
with Mr Jones[3] on the subject of Indian affairs, he suggested to me that such
was the concern of the Commissioners for Indian affairs, for the welfare of
the Indians under their care, & their ability, (in consequence of the sale of
a part of their ∧(the Indians)∧ lands,) to support missionaries, or Ministers
among them, that if the Society of Scotch Commissioners in Boston would
find & recommend proper persons for the Mission, they would be cheerfully
supported & paid by the State of New York— Such, as nearly as I can recollect, were his ideas suggested to me on the subject— They struck me forcibly
& very agreeably— I thought a plan of the kind ~~would~~ might be of essential
service to the Indians, If the Society in Scotland could ~~have~~ be informed that

the Missions wh[ic]h they have supported hitherto, would be continued by the State of N York, they would direct their funds, wh[ic]h hitherto ˄have˄ been appropriated to this purpose, to some other use.— The Society in Scotland, by their last Letters, have dissolved their connexion with Mr Kirkland, & his mission, of course ceases. Mr Sarjeant is still held in esteem by the Society as an honest, & faithful man— & if N. York sh^d. not support him, it is probable the Society will, as his mission is considered of use & importance to the Stockbridge Indians. D^r. Thacher ˄our Secretary˄ by order of the board, has written you, Sir, on this Subject—[4] & before we communicate any thing decisive on the Subject of these Missions, ~~we should~~ to the Society in Scotland, we shall wait your answer.— Should you, Sir, & your Commissioners for Indian affairs, think it expedient to continue the Missions among these Indians, & conclude to support them, the Society here would use their best endeavours, if desired, to find out, & recommend suitable persons for the purpose.[5] With great & real esteem, I am, Sir, very respectfully your most obd^t. Servt

Jed^h Morse

Gov. Jay.

ALS, NNC (EJ: 09547); C, CtY-BR (EJ: 05213).

1. JJ to Morse, 28 Feb. 1797, above.

2. *The American gazetteer, exhibiting, in alphabetical order, a much more full, and accurate account, than has been given, of the states, provinces, counties. . . Published according to act of Congress* (Boston, 1797; *Early Am. Imprints*, series 1, no. 32509).

3. Samuel Jones.

4. See Peter Thacher to JJ, 19 Apr. 1797, above, in which Thacher suggested that the state of New York assume the financial burden of maintaining the mission among the Oneida led by Samuel Kirkland. For JJ's reply to Thacher, see 25 Apr. 1797, below.

5. For more on the missionary efforts by the Society in Scotland for Promoting Christian Knowledge and the state of New York, see the editorial note "Indian Affairs under Jay's Governorship," above.

To Peter Thacher

N York 25 Ap. 1797

Sir

I was this morning fav^d. with yours of the 19th. Inst:[1] stating the Reasons which render it doubtful whether the Society in Scotland ~~ought in future~~ ˄would˄ ˄˄will˄˄ think it adviseable˄ to be at the Expence of continuing ˄a˄ mission at ~~Oneida if~~ among the Oneida Indians; and suggesting the Propriety ~~of maintaining one~~ ˄at the Expense of this state˄ in that ~~Tribe at the~~

~~Expense of this State for the Benefit of those Tribes and of the Indians of New Stockbridge~~ ∧of its being done in future by this State∧

The Motives which induced that ~~respectable~~ ∧benevolent∧ society to establish the missions in question were certainly laudable; but Sir ~~it has long been my opinion~~ ∧I thi∧ is there not Reason to apprehend^d that until the Savages can be prevailed upon to dwell in fixed Habitations, to have separate Property, & to depend more on ~~Cultivati~~ Husbandry than on the chase for Subsistence, little Success will attend the best Endeavo^{rs} to civilize ~~and~~ ∧or∧ to christianize them? measures for ~~the~~ operating this change in their Way of ~~Life~~ ∧living∧, are now executing under the Patronage of the State; and the Quakers are zealously pursuing the same object. ~~considerable~~ ∧some∧ Progress has been made ~~and is making~~— much Expence has been ∧& will be∧ incurred, ~~and it appears however that [illegible] was not [illegible]~~ ∧But it is not yet certain∧ that even this ~~benevolent and~~ judicious Experiment will ~~succeed~~ perfectly succeed. The Indian Men regard Labour as degrading, and fit only for women & Slaves— Prejudices associated with a Sense of Honor are not easily overcome.

This State has provided for a School, but I ~~doubt~~ ∧think it questionable∧ whether the Legislature will provide for ~~a~~ ∧any∧ Missionaries among the Indians ~~especially~~ ∧at present, especially∧ as former Experience does not afford very strong arguments in favor of it[2] ∧It seems to be a prevailing opinion that until these Savages shall have made ~~greater~~ ∧∧some more∧∧ Progress towards∧ a civilized State ∧no∧ great or permanent ~~change~~ alterations in their opinions or manners ~~of savages or Indi a Tribe of mis~~ ∧Indians∧ could be accomplished by missionaries however zealous indefatigable and disinterested—[3] with very sincere Respect & Esteem I am Sir your most ob. & hble Servt

"The Rev^d. Doct^r. Thatcher—"

Dft, NNC (EJ: 08970).

1. Thacher to JJ, 19 Apr. 1797, above.

2. The following section contains six lines of deleted and illegible text.

3. For more on the missionary efforts among the Oneida, see the editorial note "Indian Affairs under Jay's Governorship," above.

To the Public

[Philadelphia, 25 April 1797]

To the PUBLIC.

In Greenleaf's paper printed at New-York in March last there was a publication of which the following is an extract, viz.

"It is curious to estimate the expences which the British Treaty has cost the United States. The account may be stated as follows.

	Dolls.	*Ct.*
"1794 7th May—The United States advanced for Mr. Jay's outfit.["]	18,000	
"Of this Mr. Jay must have *saved* the whole, as his expences in going to Europe were provided for, as will be seen in the next article.["]		
"23d June—To pay Jay's passage to Europe,["]	3,708	51
"As good a passage might have been had for 30 guineas—but the Envoy must sail in state. Thus is public money trifled with.["]		
"16th Sept.—To pay incidental expences attending Jay's mission.["]	10,000	
"A moderate sum truly for incidental expences. How could this have been expended?["]		
"1795, 8th April—To defray sundry expences in negociating a treaty with Great Britain["]	5,000	—"[1]

This deceitful statement, besides the design of casting reproach on the administration of the late President Washington, and exciting, anew, unfounded prejudices against the British treaty, was specially calculated to impair the public confidence in Mr. Jay's prudence or integrity, or both. In justice to that gentleman and the government, it ought to be made known, that he undertook the mission to Great Britain without any compensation for his services, and the trouble and inconvenience of a voyage across the Atlantic; and that the expences of the mission (which of course the government must have defrayed) instead of 36,708 dollars and 51 cents, as above falsely stated, were no more than 12,000 dollars and 36 cents, exclusive of the hire of the vessel which carried him to Europe. This appears by the following official certificate of the Register of the Treasury:—[2]

TREASURY DEPARTMENT.

Register's Office, April 24, 1797.

I certify that it appears from the files and records of this office that the monies advanced to his excellency John Jay, esquire, on account of his mission to great Britain, in 1794, amounted to no more than 18,000 dollars, and that the said sum has been fully accounted for as follows:

	Dolls.	*Cts.*
By expences in England, including £275 sterling paid for the salary of his secretary colonel Trumbull; the sum of £63 sterl. paid in retaining fees on behalf of American captured vessels; loss in exchange; his passage from England to New York; and his expences from thence to Philadelphia and back to New York—amounting in the whole to	12,000	36
By payment to John Quincy Adams, esq. minister resident at the Hague, £52 10s. sterling, for which he is accountable, being equal to	233	33
By payment to Thomas Pinckney, esquire, minister plenipotentiary at London, by an order in his favor on the banker's employed by Mr. Jay, the payment of which order is acknowledged by Mr. Pinckney £1185 16s sterling. equal to	5,270	22
By money refunded into the treasury of the United States	496	09
Dollars	18,000	

JOSEPH NOURSE, Register

As to the expenses of Mr. Jay's passage to England, it is well known that an embargo, by Congress, at the time existed, and therefore that the government was constrained to hire and dispatch a vessel in ballast, on that urgent and interesting occasion.

It would be equally easy to give satisfactory answers to the malignant strictures contained in the publication here referred to: but the clear detection of the deceit and falsehood of the parts already noticed, renders in unnecessary. It would, moreover, consume too much time to attend to all such unfounded and unworthy accusations against the federal government and its officers. The people have, for years past, been witnesses to the industry with which the government and the real friends of the United States have been unceasingly calumniated. An examination of the facts would (as in the present case) expose the calumnies, and prove them as groundless and infamous as their authors are wicked and detestable.

A FRIEND TO TRUTH.

PtD, *Gazette of the United States* (Philadelphia), 25 Apr., with the accompanying certificate by Register of the Treasury Joseph Nourse of 24 Apr. 1797; reprinted *Minerva* (New York), 27 Apr.; *New-York Gazette*, 29 Apr. 1797; E, *Greenleaf's New York Journal*, 29 Apr.; *Herald* (New York), 29 Apr.; *Porcupine's Gazette* (Philadelphia), 1 May; *Albany Gazette*, 5 May, 1797, and in other newspapers published outside of New York; Dft, n.d., NNC (EJ: 09222). The draft does not include the Register's certificate. However, in his letter to TP (private), of 19 Apr. 1797, above, in which he forwarded a copy of his text, JJ suggested his defense would be strengthened by certification by the comptroller and auditor of the treasury. Several passages of JJ's draft contain major excisions, largely illegible, and differ substantially from the final text as published. These passages are quoted in the endnotes below. Minor changes in wording, spelling, punctuation, capitalization and the like are not noted.

At least since the time of Silas Deane's disgrace following failure to adequately support and settle his accounts in public office during the war of independence, JJ was extremely careful to document his expenses and settle his accounts promptly. Although he generally ceased to respond to political attacks on himself or his actions, JJ was prompt to dispute any charges or intimations of financial malfeasance or lack of integrity. See the editorial notes "John Jay's Presidency of the Continental Congress," and "Silas Deane: A Worrisome Correspondent," *JJSP*, 1: 549–51; 2: 243–46.

For JJ's explanations of his expenses while in England and the documents on the settlement of his accounts in 1795 and 1796, see JJ to ER, 5 Mar. 1795, LS, DNA: Jay Despatches, 1794–95 (EJ: 04293); JJ to Oliver Wolcott Jr., 19 Nov. 1795, Dft, NNC (EJ: 08948); JJ Account as Envoy Extraordinary to Great Britain, 26 Nov. 1795, NNC (EJ: 09227); Account of David Blaney, 7 Jan. 1796, C, NNC (EJ: 08407); JJ to TP, 25 Jan. 1796, Dft, NNC (EJ: 09487); JJ to Thomas Pinckney, 18 June 1796, Dft, NNC (EJ: 09473); Certificates of Settlement of JJ's Account, of Richard Harrison, Auditor, 22 Oct., of John Steele, Comptroller, 25 Oct., and of Joseph Nourse, Register, 27 Oct. 1796, DS, NNC (EJ: 09839).

Accusations of misappropriation continued to dog JJ. After the *Albany Register* reprinted this letter on 15 Aug., JJ discussed the matter at length, noting: "Calumny my dear Sir! has been an Engine of Partys in all countries, and particularly in elective Governments. It is an Evil which, originating in the Corruptions of human nature, is without Remedy, and consequently is to be borne patiently. The Esteem of the wise and Good is valuable; and to acquire and preserve it, is all that ambition ought to aim at.—" JJ to Henry Van Schaack, 23 Sept. 1800, Dft, NNC (EJ: 09432); *WJ*, 1: 415–17; *HPJ*, 4: 275–78. For the continued criticism against JJ, see Bird, *Press and Speech Under Assault*, 133.

1. Both here and in the draft JJ omits broader charges raised by "*a* CORRESPONDENT" in *Greenleaf's New York Journal* of 15 Mar. 1797 about the total costs of JJ's alleged failures with regard to the Jay treaty apart from the question of his personal advances and expenditures. These allegations read as follows:

20th Nov.—To obtain papers relative to British captures   16,012 83

Mr. Pickering, from whose account the preceding items are taken, estimates the costs of prosecuting the American claims in England at 25ol. sterling each cause, or 50,000 dollars per annum. If these claims only continue 4 years, which is a short time, the sum will amount to   200,000

If Great Britain ever intended to make America compensation for illegal captures, why all this preliminary expence and waste of money? Could not the commissioners have determined upon their illegality as well as the Court of Appeal? No man but Jay would have consented to so stupid, so ruinous an article.

The loss by French captures predicated on and sanctioned by the British treaty, amounts at least to   6,000,000

Total dolls.   6,252,721 34

This is a very moderate calculation of the expence to which this country has been put to obtain a treaty, to get rid of which the United States would now willingly pay ten times that sum. No estimate is made of the expense of the Senate and House of Representatives while employed in canvassing this vile instrument, nor of the salaries of the different commissioners nor of the war which in consequence of it we shall have on our hands with France. The country people are astonished what becomes of the public money. We have only to make a few more such treaties, and their very farms must be sold to pay the expences attending them.

2. The equivalent of this paragraph and the remainder of JJ's draft reads as follows:

This Statement was doubtless contrived and published with Design ~~to create an opinion to the Prejudice of~~ ∧~~impeach~~ impair the public Confidence in∧ Mr. Jays Prudence or Integrity or both—

In ~~the~~ Justice ~~due~~ to that Gentleman ~~makes it proper to be~~ ∧it ought to be made∧ known that he undertook the mission to Great Britain without any Compensation for his services ∧& Trouble∧; but ~~his~~ ∧the∧ actual Expences ∧attending it∧ were to be ∧provided for &∧ paid by the public—

To enable him to defray these Expences he ~~had~~ ∧was furnished with∧ Bills to the amount of 18'000 Dollars, for which he was to account.

On his Return he accordingly rendered an account supported by proper vouchers, and that account has been regularly settled at the Treasury—

It appears from it that the whole of his Expenses charged to the United States, including ∧Loss on Exchange and∧ his passage ~~to new york~~ from England to New York— ∧and∧ his Expences from thence to Philadelphia, and back to New York, and including, also 275£ Sterling paid for ∧the∧ salary of his secretary Col. Trumbull, ~~amounting to~~ together with the £63 Sterling paid ~~to~~ in Retaining Fees on Behalf of american owners of Vessels captured—amounts to which sum being deducted from--   18000

12000.36

left a Ballance remaining to the U.S. of   5999.64

For the character[?] and [illegible] ~~of accounting of and settling this Balance, his~~ ∧This Ballance being duly accounted for and settled, Mr. Jays∧ Account with the United States was ~~finally~~ closed— ~~for~~ The before mentioned Sum of 18,000 Dollars ~~was~~ ∧being∧ the only ~~Treasury~~ [illegible] Money [illegible] ∧which had been advanced to him—∧

As to the Remark made on the Expences of Mr Jays Passage to England--it is well known that an Embargo at that Time existed, and therefore that the Government was constrained to hire, ∧& dispatch a∧ ~~an empty~~ Vessel ~~for that pressing~~ ∧in Ballast on that urgent & interesting∧ occasion—

It is ~~eas~~ equally easy to give satisfactory answers to the other malignant charges contained in that illiberal Publication but to pay particular attention to all ~~the~~ ∧such∧ scandalous accusations ~~which~~ against the fœderal Government and its officers, would consume more time than ought to be employed on such objects. especially as the People have for Years past been witnesses to the Industry with which foreign and domestic machinations have not ceased to calumniate ∧our∧ the Government and real Friends of the united states—

Proclamation regarding Quarantine

[New York, 27 April 1797]

By his Excellency John Jay
Governor of the State of New York &ca. &ca.
A Proclamation—

Whereas by an Act of the Legislature of this State Entitled "An Act to prevent the bringing in and spreading of infectious Diseases in this State" passed the first Day of April 1796,[1] it is among other things enacted,

"That all Vessels arriving in the Port of New York from Ports beyond the Sea, having on board forty Passengers— All Vessels arriving in the said Port, having on board a Person sick with a Fever— All Vessels arriving in the said Port, on board of which a person may, during the time such Vessels were at the foreign Port from which they last sailed, or during their Passage from thence to the Port of New York, have died of a Fever— All Vessels arriving in the said Port, from Places where at the time of their Departure an infectious disease prevailed—shall be subject to Quarantine of course—.["]

"That it shall be lawful for the Person administering the Government of this State, from time to time whenever and as he shall judge adviseable, to issue his Proclamation declaring what other Vessels, to be described as coming from the Countries, Islands or Ports therein to be mentioned, shall also be subject to Quarantine— that it shall in like manner be lawful for him to issue his Proclamation assigning and limiting the Places or Spaces where all Vessels subject to Quarantine, shall on their arrival within the said Port, be brought to Anchor and remain until they shall have been visited and examined by the

Health Officer, and by him reported, to some one of the Commissioners of the Health Office, to be free from Infection—"

And Whereas the Coasts and the Islands of Turkey and of Africa on and in the Mediterranean are frequently visited by Infectious Diseases; and the like Calamities are common to some of the West-India Islands, whence there is danger of their being communicated to the American Continent— Now therefore in virtue of the Powers vested in me by the said Act I do order and declare, that all Vessels arriving in the Port of New York, from any Port, Place or Island in the Mediterranean, or from any Port, Place or Island in the West Indies, or from any Port, Place or Island whatever in America lying to the Southward of Georgia, shall be subject to Examination by the Health Officer, and to Quarantine if he shall judge it necessary, and that they shall not be excused therefrom on account of their having touched at an intermediate Port without having discharged their Cargoes at such intermediate Port— and Whereas by an Act of the Legislature of this State, passed the 10th. Day of February 1797 Entitled "an Act to amend an Act entitled an Act to prevent the bringing in and spreading of infectious Diseases in this State",[2] it is enacted "that all Coasting Vessels coming from any Place south of Cape May altho not subject to Quarantine, shall be liable to Examination, if the Health Officer shall deem it expedient, by some fit Person to be deputed by him", I do also order and declare that every Coasting Vessel arriving in this Port from any Place south of Cape May, and which on such Examination shall be found to be so circumstanced as that in the Judgement of the Health Officer she ought to perform Quarantine, such Vessel shall be subject to Quarantine accordingly—. And I do further order & direct that all Vessels subject to Examination by the Health Officer and to Quarantine and arriving in the Port of New York, either thro the Sound or thro Sandy Hook shall be brought to anchor only at some convenient Place near Governors Island, to the Southward of such a right Line from Long Island to the Jersey shore as will touch the northern Extremities of Governors Island and of Ellisons Island, but such Vessels shall not be brought to anchor at a less Distance from any land whatever, within the Harbour than one Quarter of a Mile—. And I do expressly prohibit and forbid the Branch Pilots and their Deputies to bring any of the said Vessels so arriving in this Port to anchor at any other Place or Places in the Harbour of New York—.

> Given under my Hand and the privy Seal of the State, at the City of New York, on the 27th. Day of April 1797—.

By his Excellency's Command David S. Jones Private Secretary[3]

LbkC, N: Governor's Lbk 2 (EJ: 03259). PtD, *Diary* (New York), 29 Apr. 1797; *Minerva*, and *Advertiser* (both New York), 29 Apr.; *New York Gazette*, 1 May; *Greenleaf's New York Journal*, and *Herald* (both New York), 3 May; *Albany Gazette* (extract), 5 May; *Register of the Times* (New York), 5 May 1797.

1. "An ACT to prevent the bringing in and spreading of Infectious Diseases in this State," 1 Apr. 1796, *N.Y. State Laws*, 19th sess. (1796), 28–30. For the yellow fever epidemics, actions by the state government, and the controversy over quarantine, see the editorial note "John Jay and the Yellow Fever Epidemics" above.

2. "An ACT to amend the act entitled 'an act to prevent the bringing in and spreading of infectious diseases in this State,[']" 10 Feb. 1797, *N.Y. State Laws*, 20th sess. (1797), 24–27. In addition to including coasting vessels, the amended law gave the health commissioners increased power to regulate the tanning trade.

3. David S. Jones (1777–1848) was the son of state senator and recorder Samuel Jones. After graduating from Columbia College in 1796, he was appointed JJ's private secretary, a position which he held for two years. In a letter of 31 July 1798 [ALS, DLC: Hamilton (EJ: 10781)], JJ wrote AH recommending the younger Jones, noting I was not only satisfied but pleased with his Temper Disposition & Behaviour, and that I have perfect confidence in his Integrity and Honor."

Militia Matters in New York State

New York had fielded a militia since colonial times and continued to rely on this institution as the state's primary military force during Jay's governorship. Whereas Washington, Hamilton, Pickering, and other Federalist leaders favored a more permanent and centralized military akin to a standing army, the Whiggish fear that such a force posed a fundamental threat to republican liberty ushered in an American military system based on a series of state militias and a small standing army, with both federal and state authorities exerting control over militia forces.[1] The individual states managed the daily affairs—organization, armament, discipline—of their respective militias during peacetime, and the Constitution of 1787 granted Congress the power to mobilize these troops for federal service in times of invasion and insurrection.[2] The 1792 Militia Acts further cemented the central place of the state forces within the nation's military establishment.[3]

New York's constitution called for the existence of an active militia, in peacetime as well as in war, that was to "be armed and disciplined, and in readiness for service."[4] The state required militia service of able-bodied white men between the ages of eighteen and forty-five and expected them to provide their own firearms and accoutrements, attend unit musters, and subject themselves to military justice. Two types of units filled out the ranks of the state militia—common militiamen and volunteer corps; the former served mostly as infantry, and the latter fulfilled more specialized roles in grenadier, light infantry, rifle companies, cavalry and dragoon troops, and artillery batteries.[5] All of these militia units served within one of four territorial divisions—Southern, Middle, Eastern, and Western—that were created to correspond with the state's administrative districts.[6] In addition to mustering for company and regimental exercises three times a year, the troops were called upon for inspections, drills, and marches on civic holidays and special occasions.

As governor and commander-in-chief, Jay recognized that the militia of New York, along with those of her sister states, provided the nation's defensive foundation.[7] In an opening address before the state legislature in January 1798, Jay called upon lawmakers to do their duty and improve upon the existing militia laws, reminding them, "The maxim that every nation ought to be constantly prepared for self-defence, is founded on the experience of all ages."[8] Shortly thereafter in a letter to one of New York's congressional delegates, Jay expressed support for a new militia bill, remarking that "The Nation should take care of itself, and by its own acts do whatever (within the Limits of the Constitution) may be necessary to the National Welfare."[9] He therefore sought to ensure that New York's militiamen were properly equipped, trained, and organized, and that they were led by proficient and reliable officers. In his first address delivered before the state legislature, Jay emphasized the correlation between national security and a well-regulated militia and prodded lawmakers to reexamine and improve upon the existing militia laws so that they complied with federal regulations.[10] His endeavors to institute reforming measures such as this one rarely went unchallenged, however, as a host of political, structural, and administrative obstacles threatened to derail the governor's vision of establishing the militia as a cohesive and effective defensive force.

The intense partisanship of New York politics that arose in response to events of the mid-1790s—the Whiskey Rebellion, Jay's recent treaty with Britain, and the radicalization of the French Revolution—adversely affected Jay's plans for improving the state militia.[11] A number of the volunteer companies formed throughout New York were defined by the ethnic composition and the political allegiance of their membership. The governor expressed concern that such affiliations posed a danger to the young republic in their capacity to promote Jacobin ideology and thereby undermine bonds of social unity and national loyalty. The episode involving the short-lived Hibernian Volunteers of New York City underscores Jay's anxiety that militia units were susceptible to radical politics. Founded in January 1796 by young men of Irish lineage, the New York Hibernian Volunteers swore "to assist in the defence and Protection of the United States and its Constitution & Laws, against all enemies whether Foreign or Domestic."[12] The unit disbanded some two months later, ostensibly due to a disagreement with the governor over the company's designated uniform, which included a grass green short coat decorated with a shamrock on the facings and a helmet ornamented with an Irish harp alongside an American eagle.[13] Whereas Jay disapproved of the uniform's color and emblems, he had other reasons for not supporting the Hibernian Volunteers who wished to enroll in the state militia. Despite the loyalty oath taken by the members, the governor was undoubtedly alarmed by the prospect that the Volunteers were actually an extension of the United Irishmen movement and fearful that the true objective of the company was to incite violence and espouse radicalism in New York City.[14]

The politicization of the militia remained an issue that rankled Jay for much of his tenure in office. The militia as an institution, he believed, should remain strictly apolitical and refrain from expressing any partisan notions, whether in favor of Federalists or Republicans. For instance, in May 1798, the officers of the militia brigade for New York City and County convened for the purpose of sending an address to President Adams in support of his measures against French aggressions. The governor learned of this event from his son, Peter Augustus, who served as an officer in the brigade.[15] Peter Augustus chose not to attend the meeting because he deemed it inappropriate that his fellow officers should "undertake in our Military Capacity to control, condemn, or even approve the Measures of the Government or any particular Branch of it."[16] Jay shared his son's assessment that it was wrong for the assembled militiamen to delve into political affairs.[17]

Politics turned personal during Jay's reelection bid when an Albany newspaper inserted a letter that assailed him for lacking the fortitude required of a military leader.[18] Prominent among the denunciations was the claim that the governor had committed an act of cowardice some twenty years earlier in failing to "defend his country" against British soldiers who attacked and destroyed the town of Esopus [Kingston], New York, in 1777.[19] Such behavior reflects poorly on "the character of the Captain General of our militia," the author asserted, further warning readers that "[Y]our towns may be burned—your country desolated" if another such invasion occurred under Jay's current leadership.[20]

The selection of militia officers proved another controversial issue that beset Jay's administration. New York's governor shared the power of naming officers and assigning ranks with the Council of Appointment.[21] The passage of federal statutes that expanded the nation's armed forces and the corresponding need for institutional reform at the state level, however, hindered Jay's ability to effectively manage militia matters. Longstanding military customs further challenged the governor's authority by calling into question the process and legitimacy of formal militia appointments.

Jay and his colleagues therefore had to deliberate carefully over how they awarded commissions and granted promotions. Such decisions were made more difficult due to the fact that officers' commissions were highly prized items in the honor-obsessed milieu of Federalist New York. Being named as an officer in the state militia was a distinction sought by many, for it publicly affirmed one's reputation as a trustworthy and virtuous citizen. Even with the expansion of the officer corps during the Quasi-War, there remained more candidates than postings, and those passed over for commissions and promotions often complained of unfair treatment by the governor and the state apparatus. For instance, in the spring of 1798, Jay wrote to Melanchton Lloyd Woolsey, a former lieutenant-colonel who had served in Clinton County, asking him to return to militia service. Woolsey had recently resigned his commission upon learning that one of his leading subordinates had lost out on a promotion to an officer whom Woolsey believed to be less deserving.[22]

The problems associated with officer seniority and appointments proved more than a minor irritant involving one or two individuals. In the spring of 1797, the officers of the elite Regiment of Artillery for the City and County of New York threatened to resign en masse over the refusal of the state government to promote their commanding officer, Sebastian Bauman, to the rank of brigadier general.[23] In a pair of memorials sent to the governor the previous year, the officers laid out their arguments in favor of Bauman's advancement, explaining that they could not abide for an officer of lesser seniority to be promoted over him. This action, the officers protested, set a dangerous precedent of disallowing any of them to rise above the rank of lieutenant colonel. The memorialists expressed confidence that the government would resolve the affair according to the "principles of private and official honor," but warned that they would quit the Artillery Regiment if their grievances were not redressed.[24] The governor counselled patience, informing the officers that a recently passed militia law[25] called for artillery and cavalry units to be formed into their own brigades and promised that this matter would soon receive his full attention.[26] At a meeting held at Hunter's Hotel in early May, members of the Regiment of Artillery agreed not to resign their posts before lawmakers had an opportunity to devise a solution at the subsequent legislative session.[27] The officers then sent a third memorial to Jay in early January 1797 proposing that artillerymen should have same system of promotion as their counterparts in the infantry.[28] Jay forwarded the message to legislators in Albany along with a personal note urging them to revise the militia laws.[29] The reform measure stalled in committee, however, as state lawmakers opted to wait for the passage of a new congressional militia bill before taking further action.[30] Disappointed that they had not received proper satisfactions through official channels, Bauman and his fellow officers tendered their resignations that spring.[31] They also compiled several documents related to the affair into a printed pamphlet with the intent of justifying their conduct before the court of public opinion.

The Bauman episode created a dilemma for state officials. Without a commandant or subordinate officers, the Regiment of Artillery would lack a viable command structure and therefore be incapable of performing its defensive duties. Fearful that such a situation would render New York City and its port more vulnerable to maritime attack, the Council of Appointment devised a solution to avoid the lengthy process of appointing a new set of officers. Accordingly, the council refused the proffered resignations; only Bauman stepped down as commandant while the other officers were persuaded to remain at their posts.[32]

Finding a suitable replacement for Bauman proved a more difficult prospect. The post was offered on at least two occasions to Ebenezer Stevens, who had considerable experience serving with artillery units during the war of independence and who was currently in charge of procuring ordinance and supplies for the state artillery.[33] Jay urged Stevens to accept the appointment, noting that in the likelihood of a conflict with France, the public depended on the artillery for protection. Moreover, Stevens had previously drawn up plans for expanding and reorganizing the Artillery Regiment and was the governor's chosen man for carrying them out.[34] Stevens made clear that he could not command the officers who remained with the regiment because they resented "the Idea of being superseded" and he did not think it proper to "hurt their feelings."[35] Instead of serving as colonel for the regiment, Stevens suggested that an entirely new corps of artillerymen be raised in New York City and placed under his command. To strengthen the bonds of loyalty and camaraderie among the ranks, Stevens further recommended that members should be permitted to elect the remaining officers.[36] Although Steven's proposal had the backing of many local citizens, the governor doubted that his measure would receive legislative support, observing that the issue of whether militiamen should vote for their superiors was not "free from doubt."[37]

Stevens eventually relented and agreed to assume command of the Regiment of Artillery. He could not in good conscience refuse to serve when "all his fellow Citizens are anxious" that he do so.[38] Stevens acknowledged that his earlier refusal to lead the Artillery Regiment was essentially a matter of honor that dated back to the formation of the unit in the previous decade. Stevens explained that he had tried without success to serve as its first commandant, asserting that due to his seniority in rank, the appointment should have been rightfully his. Although Philip Schuyler and Alexander Hamilton had both supported his claim, Governor Clinton had seen fit to pass him over in favor of Bauman. Stevens confessed to Jay that this rough treatment at the hands of the state government had "wounded my military pride."[39] Stevens's honor would now be restored by his new command and by an act of the state legislature that passed a few weeks thereafter. In addition to doubling the size of the Artillery Regiment so that it contained eight companies organized into two battalions, the bill conveyed the rank of brevet brigadier general upon the regimental commandant.[40]

With the prospect of a Franco-American conflict seeming ever more likely, Adams and other statesmen recognized the need to augment the nation's militia forces and make them more combat effective. In June 1797, Congress authorized the creation of a rapid deployment force of eighty thousand militiamen, with New York responsible for supplying 7,923 troops.[41] The following year, legislators in Philadelphia approved the formation of a Provisional Army, an additional militarized force numbering ten thousand men.[42] Lawmakers anticipated that the quotas imposed by the recent legislation would be met through the raising of volunteer companies in communities throughout the United States. In response to the latter law, a host of new military units arose in New York City and throughout the state.[43] James Watson remarked on this phenomenon to Jay: "It will occur to your Excellency that the volunteer companies, of all descriptions, now forming are composed of persons respectable for their property, understanding, and virtues. Formed into a Legion under good Commanders they will always be found ready to defend their County, its liberties, and laws."[44]

The governor advised that more reform measures were needed to accommodate the incoming companies and he played an active role in determining which units would be accepted into New York's militia establishment and whether they should be unified in a single corps.[45] In these matters, he consulted regularly with Alexander Hamilton, who oversaw the defenses of New York City, Matthew Clarkson, who commanded the southern division of the state militia, and James M. Hughes, who led the Brigade for the City and County of New York.[46]

The formation of several new companies in the Spring and Summer of 1798 once again raised the question of how would their command structure be organized.[47] Peter Augustus informed his father that many local militia officers were distressed by the rumor that the governor intended to staff a new regiment with officers who had no previous command experience.[48]

This issue proved particularly divisive in New York City where the brigade commanded by Hughes clashed with the newer volunteer companies over the awarding of commissions. The volunteer militiamen expected that they would be able to elect their officers, while members of the regular militia preferred the promotion of officers who had seniority of service.[49] Peter Augustus reported that the brigade officers were contemplating whether they should contact the Council of Appointment "on the Subject of the proposed nomination of persons to Captains Commissions who are now in the Ranks."[50] The governor and the Council of Appointment tended to uphold the system that allowed new companies to choose their own leaders. Hamilton pointed out this method of appointment created greater cohesion within the unit, even asserting that "To attempt to place them under the present Militia officers is to annihilate them."[51] Hamilton further ventured that the militia officers who voiced opposition were in fact part of an "antifederal scheme" intended to discredit the government and that they "can easily be replaced, with as good or better" if they chose to resign in protest.[52]

Whereas the governor shared Watson's optimism that the rise in volunteers reflected the patriotic and respectable sentiment of New Yorkers, Jay also shared Hamilton's apprehension that Republican operatives would exploit the expansion of the militia to their political advantage. As he had with the Hibernian Volunteers, Jay probably played a role in disbanding the Washington Infantry, a volunteer company raised in the summer of 1798 for men of Irish heritage. Soon after their formation, the Washington Infantry suffered a double blow with the troops decimated by yellow fever and the officers refused commissions by the Council of Appointment.[53] Other potential threats materialized that summer. Jay heard of "a new company of Democrats" forming in the city that had elected Edward Ferris, a "dramshop" owner, as their commanding officer. Ferris had allegedly declared that if the French invaded the city, he would join with the enemy.[54] Although Ferris seems ultimately not to have received a commission, other men who were deemed as politically unsuited were successful militia appointees. William Whitehead, a cabinetmaker, was one such figure. In the spring of 1798, Whitehead received a lieutenancy and commanded the Rising Sun Company of the Second Regiment of New York City, a unit known for its Republican sympathies.[55] Whitehead's political credentials, which included posts within the local Democratic Society, Tammany Society, and the General Society of Mechanic and Tradesmen, furthered the suspicions of Brigade officers who favored Federalist policies.[56] Even the Artillery Regiment formerly commanded by Bauman was affected by partisan mistrust; Peter Augustus remarked that the unit was severely understrength due to its being led by "Jacobinical Officers."[57]

Evidence of militia partisanship extended beyond New York City. The governor received reports from Peter Augustus that the recent military appointments in nearby Westchester County were causing unease among local officials. At least half of the militia officers, including those who would soon be appointed to Micajah Wright's recently established Troop of Horse, were described as "disaffected" and of harboring Republican sentiments.[58] Indeed, these anxieties seemed well founded, as Jay's son informed him shortly thereafter that "one of the most violent Jacobins in the County" had been commissioned as a coronet in Wright's Troop.[59] At times, Peter would offer advice to his father on those officers in the Westchester militia who were politically reliable and deserving of promotion.[60]

Maintaining discipline among the militia troops was an ongoing problem during Jay's administration. Those enlisted personnel and officers who engaged in improper behavior were commonly punished with fines or had their commissions revoked. Even generals were not immune from obeying military regulations; for instance, Patrick Campbell, who led a militia brigade in Herkimer County, was removed from command in March 1797 after being found to be "intemperate and inattentive to the duties of his said office."[61] The influx of volunteers the following year made it much more difficult to uphold disciplinary standards. When the Council of Appointment learned that a company of light infantry from Westchester County had frequently not appeared for their parade inspections, it responded by dissolving the unit and revoking the officers' commissions.[62] The frequency of such incidents alarmed the governor and persuaded him to issue a call for revising New York's military code.[63] At Jay's urging, state lawmakers passed a militia bill that forbade the sale of alcohol at musters, established court-martials for dereliction of duty, and imposed stiff fines upon those found guilty.[64]

---

1. The nation's regular military forces were reorganized in 1796 from the Legion of the United States to the United States Army, which was limited to 3,359 men. The creation of the Additional Army in July 1798 expanded the regular army to 14,421 men. "An Act to ascertain and fix the Military Establishment of the United States," 30 May 1796, *Stat.*, 1: 483–86; David A. Clary and Joseph W. A. Whitehorne, *The Inspectors General of the United States Army: 1777–1903* (Washington D.C., 1987), 69; "An Act to augment the Army of the United States, and for other purposes," 16 July 1798, *Stat.*,

1: 604–6. For an overview of Federalist thought regarding the roles of the militia and a standing army, see Richard H. Kohn, *Eagle and Sword: The Federalists and the Creation of the Military Establishment in America, 1783–1802* (New York and London, 1975).

2. U.S. Constitution, Art. I, § 8.

3. "An Act to provide for calling forth the Militia to execute the laws of the Union, suppress insurrections and repel invasions," and "An Act more effectually to provide for the National Defence by establishing an Uniform Militia throughout the United States," 2 and 8 May 1792, *Stat.*, 1: 264–65, and 271–74. These statutes were updated three years later with "An Act to provide for calling for the Militia to execute the laws of the Union, suppress insurrections, and repel invasions; and to repeal the Act now in force for that purpose," 28 Feb. 1795, *Stat.*, 1: 424–25.

4. *N.Y. State Laws*, (1777–97), 1: 14.

5. Lyle D. Brundage, "The Organization, Administration, and Training of the United States Ordinary and Volunteer Militia, 1792–1861," (Ph.D. Diss.: Univ. of Michigan, 1958), 22.

6. *An act, to organize the militia of this state. Passed the 9th of March, 1793* (New York, [1793]; *Early Am. Imprints*, series 1, no. 25897); "An Act to organize the Militia of this State," 9 Mar. 1793, *N.Y. State Laws*, (1777–97), 3: 58–68. New York's militia was reorganized in 1799 to five divisions. "An Act further to amend the Laws relative to the Militia of this State," 30 Mar. 1799, *N.Y. State Laws*, 22nd sess., 2nd meeting, 739–47.

7. JJ may have had brief experience commanding troops as a militia officer during the war of independence, being appointed a colonel of the 2nd New York City Militia Regiment in 1775. Militia Commission of John Jay, 3 Nov. 1775, D, NNC (EJ: 07361). During the ratification debates held in Poughkeepsie during the summer of 1788, JJ argued against a proposed amendment that sought to limit the federal government's authority over the state militia. See the editorial note "John Jay at the New York Ratifying Convention," and Extract from Melancton Smith's Notes of Debates, [21 July 1788], *JJSP*, 5: 10, 50.

8. JJ's Address to the New York State Legislature, 2 Jan. 1798, below.

9. JJ to John Williams, 12 Jan. 1798, ALS, N (EJ: 04368).

10. JJ's Address to the New York State Legislature, 6 Jan. 1796, above.

Lawmakers responded by passing a bill that offered inducements to those who enrolled in volunteer companies, established a uniform court martial system for them, and created a means of payment for their "necessary equipments, music and cloathing." "An Act to amend the Act entitled An Act to organize the Militia of the state," 11 Apr. 1796, *N.Y. State Laws*, 19th sess. (1796), 51–52, quote on 52; *Argus, Greenleaf's New Daily Advertiser* (New York), 18 Apr.; *Greenleaf's New York Journal*, 19 Apr.; *Albany Gazette*, 2 May; *Mohawk Mercury* (Schenectady), 3 May 1796.

11. For an overview of how these events shaped the political climate of New York and the nation, see Elkins and McKitrick, *Age of Federalism*.

12. "N.Y. Hibernian Volunteers".

13. Ibid.

14. JJ wrote to TP on 21 Dec. 1798, below, warning of the threat posed by the United Irishmen to New York.

15. As an officer, PAJ enjoyed a rapid rise in the militia ranks. He was appointed as an ensign in Jacob Morton's 3rd Regiment in April 1796, and then promoted to lieutenant two years later. PAJ aspired to hold a joint appointment as adjutant in a legion of light troops that was being organized in the spring of 1799. Soon thereafter, he was serving as one of the adjutants for Morton's 6th Regiment, a new militia formation, and quickly advanced to the rank of captain in Hughes's Brigade. In this unit, he served as brigade major and inspector. *Daily Advertiser* (New York), 19 Apr. 1796; Commission for PAJ, 11 Apr. 1798, PtDS, NNC (EJ: 12776); *Argus, Greenleaf's New Daily Advertiser* (New

York), 21 May 1798; PAJ to JJ, 10 Apr. 1799, ALS, NNC (EJ: 06079); JJ to PAJ, 15 Apr. 1799, ALS, NYKaJJH (EJ: 09983); JJ to PAJ, 26 June 1799, ALS, NYKaJJH (EJ: 09984); *New-York Gazette,* 13 July 1799; *Albany Centinel,* 19 July 1799; Hastings and Noble, *Military Minutes,* 1: 357, 450, 489, 538.

16. PAJ to JJ, 13 May 1798, below.

17. JJ to PAJ, 17 May 1798, below.

18. *Albany Register,* 20 Apr. 1798. See the editorial note "John Jay wins Reelection as Governor in 1798," below.

19. *Albany Register,* 20 Apr. 1798. For more on this episode, see the editorial note "Defending New York," note 45, above.

20. *Albany Register,* 20 Apr. 1798.

21. Articles 23 and 24 of the state constitution covered the issue of official appointments. *N.Y. State Laws,* (1777–97), 1: 11.

22. Melanchton Lloyd Woolsey (1754–1819) of Plattsburgh. JJ to Woolsey, 7 May 1798, Dft, NNC (EJ: 08979). Woolsey had been appointed as commandant for the Clinton County Regiment in March 1788. Hastings and Noble, *Military Minutes,* 1: 142. Woolsey returned to his post and was soon promoted to brigadier general in August 1798 when the Clinton County militia was expanded to brigade strength. Hastings and Noble, *Military Minutes,* 1: 456.

23. The artillery unit had been formed by Bauman at company strength in 1784, before expanding into a battalion and later a regiment some two years later. Emmons Clark, *History of the Seventh Regiment of New York. 1806–1889,* (2 vols.; New York, 1890), 1: 36–37; Hastings and Noble, *Military Minutes,* 1: 110. For the refusal of the Council of Appointment to promote Bauman, see Hastings and Noble, *Military Minutes,* 1: 329–30.

24. *Statement of the Officers of Artillery,* 15–20, 21–23, quote on 23.

25. "An Act to amend the Act entitled An Act to organize the Militia of the state," 11 Apr. 1796, *N.Y. State Laws,* 19th sess. (1796), 51–52; *Statement of the Officers of Artillery,* 24 (extract).

26. JJ to the Officers of the Artillery Regiment, 3 May 1796, LbkC, N: Governor's Lbk. 2 (EJ: 03010); *Statement of the Officers of Artillery,* 23.

27. *Statement of the Officers of Artillery,* 24–25.

28. Ibid., 25–26.

29. Ibid., 28; JJ's Message to the New York State Assembly, 16 Feb. 1797, *NYGM,* 2: 388–89.

30. JJ to Bauman, 15 Apr. 1797, LbkC, N: Governor's Lbk. 1 (EJ: 03073); *Statement of the Officers of Artillery,* 27–28; *Minerva* (New York), 15 Mar., *Argus, Greenleaf's New Daily Advertiser, Daily Advertiser,* and *Diary* (all New York), 16 Mar., *Greenleaf's New York Journal* and *Herald* (both New York), 18 Mar. 1797.

31. Bauman to JJ, [15 May 1797], below; *Statement of the Officers of Artillery,* 29–30, 30–31; *Diary* and *Herald,* (both New York), 17 May; *Register of the Times* (New York), 19 May; *Aurora General Advertiser* (Philadelphia), 19 May; *Albany Chronicle,* 22 May, *Otsego Herald* (Cooperstown), 1 June 1797. Bauman forwarded copies of the pamphlet to the president and vice-president. Bauman to JA, 29 May 1797, ALS, MHi: Adams; Bauman to TJ, 29 May 1797, *PTJ,* 29: 403.

32. *Commercial Advertiser* (New York), 20 Apr.; *Greenleaf's New York Journal,* 21 Apr.; *New York Gazette,* 23 Apr. 1798; Hastings and Noble, *Military Minutes,* 1: 454.

33. JJ to Stevens, 21 Apr. 1797, LbkC, N: Governor's Lbk. 2 (EJ: 03257); Hastings and Noble, *Military Minutes,* 1: 454.

34. JJ to Stevens, 26 May, 1798, below.

35. Stevens to JJ, 30 May 1798, below.

36. Ibid.

37. JJ to Stevens, 4 June 1798, ALS, NHi: Stevens (EJ: 00904). Enclosure: James McHenry to JJ, 15 May 1798, C in JJ's hand.

38. Stevens to JJ, 11 Aug. 1798, C, NHi: Stevens (EJ: 00874); Hastings and Noble, *Military Minutes*, 1: 470. At the time of his appointment, Stevens also accepted the post of commissary of military stores for New York. Hastings and Noble, *Military Minutes*, 1: 461.

39. Ibid. For JJ's reply to Stevens, see 11 Aug. 1798, ALS, NNC (EJ: 00678).

40. "An Act to augment the number of artillery-men in the city and county of New-York and to regulate the same," 27 Aug. 1798, *N.Y. State Laws*, 22nd sess. (August 1798), 550–52. Stevens was formally appointed by brevet to brigadier general in April 1799. *Commercial Advertiser* (New York), 18 Apr.; *Daily Advertiser* (New York), 19 Apr. 1799; Hastings and Noble, *Military Minutes*, 1: 470. To fill the officers' vacancies within the expanded regiment, JJ, David Van Horne, the adjutant general of the state militia, and James M. Hughes, the brigade commander, opted to promote some of the unit's long serving noncommissioned officers and matrosses. JJ to Matthew Clarkson, 10 Jan. 1799 (misdated 1798), ALS, NNYSL: Jay (EJ: 02869); Hastings and Noble, *Military Minutes*, 2: 470–71.

41. *Daily Advertiser, Minerva, Diary*, and *Greenleaf's New York Journal* (all New York), 1 July, *Herald* (New York), 5 July 1797; "An Act authorizing a detachment from the Militia of the United States," 24 June 1797, *Stat.*, 1: 522.

42. "An Act authorizing the President of the United States to raise a Provisional Army," 28 May, 1798, *Stat.*, 1: 558–61.

43. See for instance, the notice for the Federal Rangers in the *New-York Gazette*, 14 June 1798.

44. Watson to JJ, 11 Aug. 1798, ALS, NNC (EJ: 08652).

45. JJ urged the state legislature to pass reform measures to better accommodate the enlarged militia force. In March 1799, lawmakers in Albany heeded the governor's advice and passed a comprehensive militia bill for cavalry and artillery units. JJ and his colleagues opposed the formation of volunteer companies from existing militia regiments, fearing that such moves would "promote disorganization, and subvert subordination." Although a bill had passed both the state senate and assembly allowing this activity, the Council of Revision soon vetoed it. JJ's Addresses to the New York State Legislature, 2 Jan. and 9 Aug. 1798, both below; JJ's Message to the New York State Senate, 22 Mar. 1799, *NYGM*, 2: 439–40; *Albany Centinel*, 26 Mar. 1799 (extract); *N.Y. State Laws*, 22nd sess., 2nd meeting (1799), 739–47; *N.Y. Assembly Journal*, 20th sess. (1796–97), 206–8; *N.Y. Senate Journal*, 20th sess. (1796–97), 129; *Albany Centinel*, 5 Jan.; *Albany Gazette* and *Albany Register*, both 8 Jan.; *Greenleaf's New York Journal*, 17 Jan. 1798; *N.Y. Assembly Journal*, 21st sess. (January 1798), 10; *NYGM*, 2: 403.

46. JJ to AH, 30 Aug. 1798, ALS, DLC: Hamilton (EJ: 10782); *PAH*, 22: 169–170; *HPJ*, 4: 250; AH to JJ, 8 Sept. 1798, ALS, NNC (EJ: 05630); JJ to Clarkson, 7 Nov. 1798, LbkC, N: Governor's Lbk. 1 (EJ: 03186); 13 Nov. 1798, ALS, NNYSL: Jay (EJ: 02867); JJ to Hughes, 13 Nov. 1798, ALS, PC: Robert S. Johnson (EJ: 05123); LbkC, N: Governor's Lbk. 1 (03187).

47. The passage of the militia bill organizing cavalry and artillery units in March 1799 further muddled the question of who had authority over officer appointments. By late 1800, the governor and attorney general were tackling the issue of whether brigade majors in the cavalry would be chosen by the brigade commander or by the council of appointment. Josiah Ogden Hoffman to JJ, 14 Nov. 1800, ALS, N (EJ: 00993).

48. PAJ to JJ, 27 Mar. 1798, ALS, NHi: Jay (EJ: 13080).

49. *Argus, Greenleaf's New Daily Advertiser* (New York), 31 July, 8 Aug. 1798.

50. PAJ to JJ, 10 Aug. 1798, ALS, NNC (EJ: 06072); Dft, NNC (EJ: 11464).

51. AH to JJ, 27 Aug. 1798, below.

52. Ibid. JJ shared AH's assessment that the dissenting militia officers who resigned their commissions had political motives for doing so. JJ to AH, 30 Aug. 1798, ALS, DLC: Hamilton (EJ: 10782); *PAH*, 22: 169–170; *HPJ*, 4: 250.

53. "N.Y. Hibernian Volunteers."

54. PAJ to JJ, 10 Aug. 1798, ALS, NNC (EJ: 06072); Dft, NNC (EJ: 11464). A city directory lists Edward Ferris as a grocer residing on 60 Roosevelt Street. *Longworth's American Almanack*, 177.

55. Hastings and Noble, *Military Minutes*, 1: 449; *Argus, Greenleaf's New Daily Advertiser* (New York), 21 May; *Greenleaf's New York Journal*, 23 May and 11 July 1798; *Longworth's American Almanack*, 332.

56. PAJ to JJ, 10 Aug. 1798, ALS, NNC (EJ: 06072); Dft, NNC (EJ: 11464); *Argus, Greenleaf's New Daily Advertiser* (New York), 2 July 1798; *Longworth's American Almanack*, 84.

57. PAJ to JJ, 10 Aug. 1798, ALS, NNC (EJ: 06072); Dft, NNC (EJ: 11464).

58. PAJ to JJ, 29 Dec. 1798, below; Hastings and Noble, *Military Minutes*, 1: 463.

59. PAJ to JJ, 16 Mar. 1799, ALS, NNC (EJ: 06077). For more on the politicization of regular militia units, see the episode involving George I. Eaker, in PAJ to JJ, 13 May 1798, below.

60. PAJ to JJ, 22 Feb. 1800, Dft, NNC (EJ: 11459).

61. Hastings and Noble, *Military Minutes*, 1: 390.

62. Ibid., 469–70.

63. JJ's Message to the New York State Senate, 22 Mar. 1798, *NYGM*, 2: 439–40; *N.Y. Senate Journal*, 22nd sess., 2nd meeting (1799), 91–92.

64. "An Act further to amend the Laws relative to the Militia of this State," 30 Mar. 1799, *N.Y. State Laws*, 22nd sess., 2nd meeting (1799), 739–47.

From Sebastian Bauman

[15 May 1797]

To his Excellency John Jay Esqr. Governor and Commander in chief of the Militia of the State of New York &^{c} &^{c}

I am sorry that circumstances have finally brought me to quit and give up my Military Commission, which I cannot hold any longer without the greatest degradation, inadmissable and incoherent with the Character of a Soldier.

The Appointment of Brigadier General Hughes[1] who was a junior Officer, and to whom I am now as it were subordinate, altho' I am the oldest Officer, is a subject too keen to a man of sensibility, my being an Artillery Officer may cloak that business over, but cannot justify the Act, as I stated once before. Innovation of this kind distroys every Military order and subordination, the only guide and safe guard to a Community in time of public danger. To superceed an Officer when once commissioned in what is called the fighting department without any cause of impeachment, is an Act of injustice and the greatest injury possible a Military Officer can receive, for it implys a tacit desire for him to resign Impressed with these sentiments I cannot hold any longer that Commission which the State intrusted me with in the year 1786[2]—and I do herewith resign the same—

The Honorable the Council of appointment may judge the propriety or impropriety of this measure, but they cannot suppose that under the circumstances above recited, I should risk my life and reputation in a Military capacity, and continue Equipt and ready at the call of my Country, to perform the duty and fatigue of a Soldier without a share in the honor of regular promotion the only recompence a grateful Country can bestow on Military atchievements, would be acting against the rule of Common sense and shew how little regard I had for my Country when I had none for myself.

The Officers of the Regiment I had the honor to command seem likewise sensible of their discouraging situation have also resign'd their Commissions which I herewith inclose,[3] accompanied with a letter addressed to me stating their reason for so doing—[4] I am Sir Your Excellency's most Ob^t. & Very Humble Servt.

S. Bauman

ALS, NN: Emmet (EJ: 01071). PtL, *Statement of the Officers of Artillery*, 30–31. The manuscript is undated; a dateline is located in the published version.

1. James M. Hughes (1756–1802) of New York City commanded the Brigade of the City and County of New York in the state's militia establishment. One of the original members of the Society of Cincinnati, Hughes had served as an aide-de-camp to Horatio Gates at Saratoga.

2. Hastings, *Military Minutes*, 2: 110.

3. *Statement of the Officers of Artillery*, 29–30. Whereas the Council of Appointment accepted Bauman's resignation, it refused to do so for the other officers of the Artillery Regiment.

4. For an overview of the Bauman affair, involving the resignations of Lt. Col. Bauman (Beauman) (1739–1803) and his subordinate officers from the Regiment of Artillery for the City and County of New York, see the editorial note "Militia Matters in New York State," above.

To Grenville

New York 4 June 1797

My Lord

A long Interval has passed between the Date of my last Letter, and that of this— they would have been more frequent, had they been exposed to less Risque of Interception. My Respect and Esteem for your Lordship remain unabated; and I yet flatter myself with the pleasure of becoming a better Correspondent. It will give you satisfaction to know that Letters I have rec^d. from M^r. King and M^r. Gore make *Honorable Mention* of the Candor and good Faith of your Governm^t?— they both appear to be well pleased, and I am glad of it. The Proceedings of the Congress now in Session will doubtless be sent to You. There appears to be a general Disposition to pacific measures throughout the Country— if it procures peace, so much the better—if not, we shall be the more united. To put our adversaries in the wrong, is always a valuable Point gained—especially as the Forbearance necessary for the purpose, will not be in the present Instance be prompted by Fear, nor produce Dejection— In every Event some malcontents are to be expected; and it is remarkable that *Patriots* born in british Dominions are very distinguishable among those who the most invariably oppose our Goverm^t. & its measures. They appear to be as little disposed to promote good will between our two Countries, as the French— indeed they seem to like our Goverm^t. as little as they did their own— I have the Honor to be with great Respect Esteem and Regard my Lord Your Lordships most ob^t. Servt

John Jay

PS. I recollect to have observed to your Lordship in a Letter written while I was yet in London, that the Conduct & Conversation of your Consul here, appeared to me to be conciliatory. I have since become convinced that the Professions & circumstances which led to that opinion, merited but little confidence— it is therefore proper for me to correct that mistake—[1]
The Right Hon'ble Lord Grenville

ALS, UK-BL: Dropmore (MS 59049); Dft, NNC (EJ: 08516); *WJ*, 2: 281–82; *HPJ*, 4: 226–27.

1. The consul mentioned is John Temple. JJ wrote in November 1794 that Temple's "Conduct and Conversation appeared to me to be conciliatory." See JJ to Grenville (private), 22 Nov. 1794, above. For Grenville's response to JJ's current letter, see RK to JJ, 16 Aug. 1797, below.

To Timothy Pickering

New York 8 June 1797

Sir

~~Read the enclosed Letter first~~ To understand this Letter it will be necessary ~~to r~~ *first* to read the enclosed, ~~this being a sequel to~~ that— ~~which I forward now because~~‸which was intended for this mornings post but‸ the mail was closed when my Sec^y brought ~~the enclosed~~ ‸it‸ to the ~~Post~~ office—[1]

The Capt. Clarke in Question is well known in this City— During the late War he served in the American army— ~~Since the Re~~ He has since been ~~well~~ considered and with Reason as one of Genets Partizans and agents—a violent Democrat and Gallican ~~I have~~ He is said to be subtle, active, ~~and~~ ‸factious,‸ unprincipalled, ~~and was in many Respects valuable for Enterprizes an [Irish?] good man and needy~~ ‸and needy— I have had no opportunity of judging from my own observation how far this character of him is just—‸[2]

The Vessel in which he came, arrived last Evening—about 10 ~~o~~ OCK. last night Mr. Pollocks Letter was delivered to me by the Capt I ~~immediately~~ sent him for Clarke, but ~~before~~ he had come on shore and was not to be found. ~~I wanted to see him before he could see any Persons who might change have influence over him—~~

He was with me this morning—but his Communications were much the same with those mentioned by M^r. Pollock— He professes that the ~~very injurious~~ unjustifiable Conduct ~~of the French~~ ∧France∧ to ~~his~~ ∧our∧ Country urges him to make these Discoveries [~~in question?~~], and to do whatever may be in his power to frustrate the~~se secret~~ Designs of the French ag^t. us

I ~~think~~ ∧suspect∧ with M^r. Pollock that ~~he~~ ∧Clark∧ probably knows more thatn he at present is inclined to ~~reveal~~ reveal— He has a Letter for you which he purposes to deliver himself—³ He says that while on board the Revenge he heard the Fires *which afterwards* happened in this City, spoken of as Fires that would certainly happen— and that the ~~very~~ ∧particular∧ Houses and Stores were mentioned.⁴ ~~He is positive~~ That the Destruction of ~~all~~ our sea port Towns ∧and Frigates∧ is meditated— that a French ~~Fort~~ Fleet ~~will~~ ∧is expected to∧ co-operate with Incendiaries in that Design— That Efforts will be made to gain Canada by Conquest or Revolution—and that they depend on substantial aids from Vermont ~~and~~ Kentucky &c^a. ~~& Tennessee &c^a—~~ That he has Reason to think a watchful Eye sh^d. be kept over Genet, having often heard him spoken of in a Way ~~which led him to that opinion—~~ ∧that excited his apprehensions∧

He deals much in generals—and as to the particulars he details, they neither afford nor are accompanied with Evidence sufficient to justify the arrest of any Individuals— He says he will endeavour & expects to obtain more certain Information— and thinks that with proper *Secrecy* and Management, much may be discovered.

The Capt. Expects the money for ~~his~~ ∧Clarks∧ Passage according to Mr Pollocks Stipulation & the sooner that is done the better; lest Clarke ~~finding~~ suspecting any Hesitation of that point, may become less Zealous than he now appears to be— I do not believe that Clark w^d. committ himself as he has done to Mr Pollock, to me, and to our Att^y Genl. ~~G~~ who was present this morning, for the sake s merely of this Passage Money which is only 50 Dol.—⁵ He must have other ~~views~~ ∧motives∧— He may ~~b~~ ∧be∧ ~~influenced~~ ∧actuated∧ by his ~~Dispute with the Capt. Of the French Privateer~~ ∧personal~~ Resentments∧—by some remaining Love for his Country—by the Hope and Expectation of Reward, and ~~probably~~ ∧perhaps∧ by each of these Considerations—

It appears to me prudent ∧not∧ to pay, ∧not only∧ his passage, ~~to pay~~ ∧but∧ his Expenses to Phᵃ.—⁶∧to treat him kindly but with Circumspection—∧ to employ him as ~~his~~ Circumstances may indicate, and not to damp his Hopes ~~whatever they may be~~ ∧of Reward∧— He may ~~be nothing more than a cunning~~ ∧relative to this Business be an∧ Impostor, and he may ~~not~~ ∧not∧ ~~in this Business~~ ∧He may∧ be sincere and in earnest and consequently ~~very~~ useful. These are ~~Que~~ Doubts which can only be decided by fair Experiment.

I was to have gone into the Country this morning, ~~but mus~~ but this Business will detain me untill Tomorrow— During my absence I expected Mʳ Hoffman our attorney Genˡ. would attend to ~~what might further be necessary to be done respecting~~ ∧it∧ ~~—and Clark is to see him again privately tomorrow— For him to come frequently & publicly to the Offices of Govᵗ might excite Suspicion~~ ∧it∧. ∧Finding however that∧ Mʳ Hoffman ~~however is~~ ∧being∧ ∧was∧ obliged to go to Albany in a few Days, it was concluded between us that Mr. Harizon the Attorney Genˡ ∧of the US∧ for this District should be made acquainted with all the Particulars— While Mʳ Hoff[m]an remains in Town they will act in Concert— After his Departure I ~~hope~~ ∧presume∧ Mʳ. Harison will readily attend to it. I expect to be absent ∧abᵗ∧ ten Days— in the mean Time ∧to avoid Delay∧ be pleased to ~~instruct~~ ∧give∧ Mʳ. Harison such Instructions as you may think proper—~~when I return I wil~~ I have the Honor to be with great Respect & Esteem Sir Your most ob. & hᵇˡᵉ. Servᵗ
The Honb. Timothy Pickering Esq / Secʸ of State

Dft, NNC (EJ: 09497). Endorsed: ". . . abᵗ. a Capᵗ. Clarke".

1. Probably P. J. Pollock to TP, 23 May 1797, MHi: Pickering. Procopio Jacinto Pollock, son of Oliver Pollock, was nominated by GW for the post of consul at New Orleans and confirmed by Senate in March 1797. GW to U.S. Senate, 2 Mar. 1797, DNA: RG 46—Senate; *Senate Executive Journal*, 4th Cong., 2nd sess., 228, 232. See Horace Edwin Pollock, *Pollock genealogy: a biographical sketch of Oliver Pollock, Esq., of Carlisle, Pennsylvania, United States commercial agent at New Orleans and Havana, 1776–1784: with genealogical notes of his descendants: also genealogical sketches of other Pollock families settled in Pennsylvania* (Harrisburg, 1883), 19–20.

2. John Clarke sailed from New York on 22 Oct. 1796, aboard the French privateer *La Vengeance* (*Revenge*), Captain Berard (Berrard). Clarke claimed he served as an "inspector of ship papers", but Berard countered that he had served as a commissioned officer. Following a dispute with Berard, Clarke wished to return to New York, and asked Pollock for a letter to serve as protection from prosecution. Pollock to TP, 23 May 1797, and TP to Richard Harison, 13 June 1797, both MHi: Pickering.

La Vengeance had sailed with a French crew from Santo Domingo and brought into New York, *La Princessa de Asturias*, a Spanish prize valued at $200,000 in the summer of 1795, where the legality of the capture was challenged by the Spanish consul on the grounds that the privateer had been previously armed in New York in violation of American neutrality. The privateer was under investigation for possible neutrality violations by Richard Harison, the United States Attorney for the District of New York, who also played a major role in contesting the legality of the Spanish prize. When Adet, the minister of the French Republic, complained in the press that the U.S. justice system had acted unfairly in ruling against Berard, TP requested that Harison send him information about the proceedings that could be used to sway public opinion and vindicate the court's decision. See the notes in support of the *La Vengeance* from Adet to the U.S. Secretary of State of 15 Nov., published in several American newspapers, including *Argus, Greenleaf's New Daily Advertiser* (New York), 23 Nov. 1796. See also TP to Harison, 1 Oct. 1795, and 10 and 15 Dec. 1796, all MHi: Pickering. For more on the diplomatic communications regarding *La Vengeance* case, see *ASP: FR*, 1: 564, 584–85, 621–29.

3. See Pollock to TP, 23 May 1797, MHi: Pickering.

4. Large fires suspected as arson occurring in New York, Baltimore, Philadelphia, Savannah, and Morrisville, Pa., were reported in the various newspapers in late 1796. In particular a huge fire in New York on 9 Dec. 1796 consumed a block of stores and houses in the Wall Street area, affecting nearly fifty buildings with an estimated value of about $70,000. Additional cases of attempted arson at individual houses in New York were also reported. Some rumors attributed the fires to a group of incendiaries, possibly foreign, or to "a Negro plot". See *Greenleaf's New York Journal* 9 Dec.; *Argus, Greenleaf's New Daily Advertiser* (New York) and *New-York Gazette*, both 10 Dec.; *Daily Advertiser* (New York), 12 Dec.; *Minerva* (New York), 14 Dec.; *Columbian Centinel* (Boston), 17 Dec.; *Claypoole's American Daily Advertiser* (Philadelphia), 19 Dec. 1796; Abigail Adams to JA, 31 Dec. 1796, *Adams Family Correspondence*, 11: 472–75; Angelica Church to AH, 20 Jan. 1797, *PAH*, 20: 471–73; and Robert Troup to RK, 28 Jan. 1797, King, *Life and Correspondence of Rufus King*, 2: 136–37.

5. The brig *Diadem* under Captain Collin left Havana and spent two weeks at sea before reaching New York on 7 June. TP instructed Harison to pay fifty dollars to Collin for giving passage to Clarke from Havana to New York. *Minerva* (New York), 8 June, and *Daily Advertiser* (New York), 9 June 1797; TP to Harison, 13 June 1797, and TP to Hoffman, 15 June 1797, both MHi: Pickering.

6. For additional correspondence related to payments for Clarke and information received regarding him, see TP to Harison, 13 June 1797, and to Hoffman, 15 June, 1797, both MHi: Pickering. Clarke did not immediately travel to Philadelphia, and what further information he provided, if any, has not been determined.

From Timothy Pickering (private)

Philadelphia June 8 [179]7:

Sir,

The manner in which you have noticed my letter to General Pinckney, at its first publication, and recently in your letter of the 27th ult.[1] has given me the truest satisfaction; while the reproaches of the whole body of democrats, of *French Devotees*, excite no other sensation than that of regret for the mischief their lies and misrepresentations produce thro' the country. I am well informed that in Virginia, great pains have been taken to make the people believe, "that my letter to Genl. Pinckney is one tissue of misrepresentation and falsehood." M^r. Edward Livingston, by his spee[ch] in the House of Representatives, doubtless intended [to] confirm and extend the belief of that base assertion, by the manner in which he spoke of my statement of the convention of the armed neutrality.[2] I understood that M^r. Harper replied satisfactorily to M^r. Livingston, but I do not recollect seeing his *arguments* in the case. I confess the 9th article of the convention of the armed neutrality is singularly constructed; the latter clause in it importing the permanency of that agreement; but inconsistently with the first clause, which clearly declares its being entered into for the war then existing, and that it was to serve as a *basis* to future engagements. This, connected with the *history* of the armed neutrality, especially of the measures of the king of Sweden for the express purpose of rendering the principles then adopted, permanent rules, by the agreement of all the maritime powers, at the conclusion of the war, satisfied me that the convention was in reality *temporary*, and designed to continue only during that war. And thus I stated it in my letter. If the statement is erroneous it is more than I know; and I am sure that neither you nor any gentleman who know me will think the error was designed. I should however be extremely obliged, if you can find leisure to examine the question, by your favouring me with your opinion, and glancing at the facts and reasons on which you found it. I am, with great sincerity your respectful & ob^t. serv^t.

Timothy Pickering

His Excellency John Jay

ALS, NNC. (EJ: 09498). Marked: "(private)". Letter is torn at the date line.

1. See JJ to TP, 27 May 1797, ALS, MHi: Pickering (EJ: 04778); Dft, NNC (EJ: 09496).
2. For Livingston's speech before the House of Representatives on 24 May, see *Annals*, 7: 115–35.

From John Trumbull

29 Berner's Street, London June 10th. 1797.

Dear Sir

You will permit me to present to your acquaintance the Bearer of this Letter. M^r. Neimsiwits a Polish Gentleman the Friend & Companion of the unfortunate Kosciusko.[1]

Mr Neimsiwits was a member of the constitutional Assembly of Poland;— was afterwards wounded by the Gen^ls. side:—and carried with him a Prisoner to Petersburg, where, so long as the Empress lived, He was confined & treated in the most rigorous manner;—being set at Liberty by the present Emperor. He goes with his friend to America, and hopes there to find an hospitable Asylum.

I beg leave to commend him to your protection and friendship— and am Dear Sir Your much obliged friend & servant,

Jno: Trumbull

His Excell^y John Jay Esqr. &c &c &

ALS, NNC (EJ: 07207). Addressed: "His Excellency / John Jay Esqʳ / Govʳ. of the State of New York / New York". Endorsed.

1. Former Continental army officer Tadeusz Kosciusko, the leader of a Polish uprising against Russia, was captured in October 1794 at the Battle of Maciejowice. In 1796, following the death of Catherine the Great, Czar Paul I pardoned Kosciusko, who them emigrated to the U.S. Kosciusko later returned to Europe and lived in Switzerland until his death in 1817. His aide Julian Ursyn Niemcewicz (1758–1841), Polish playwright, poet, novelist and translator, accompanied him to America. In 1800 Niemcewicz married SLJ's cousin Susan Livingston Kean, widow of Congressman John Kean, but returned to Poland after Napoleon's invasion in 1807. He subsequently became secretary of the senate and president of the constitutional committee of Poland and engaged in his literary activities. During the failed November uprising of 1830–31 against Russia, Niemcewicz went to London as the Polish envoy to Britain unsuccessfully seeking aid, and remained in exile, first in Britain, then in France, until his death in Paris in 1841.

To John Sinclair

N York, 12 July 1797

Dʳ Sir

I was Yesterday favᵈ. with yours of 29 March last[1] enclosing three Copies of your account of the origin &cᵃ. of the Board of agriculture — for wʰ. accept my Thanks[2]

This Publication is in many Respects interesting — It shews how much may be accomplished by the Talents ~~Zeal~~ & Perseverance of patriotic Individuals; and how ~~much~~ ∧greatly∧ the Success of the best Institutions depends ~~of~~ on the application and Zeal of their Directors.

When the mass of Information acquired ∧& ~~which is~~ still accumulating∧ by the Board shall be∧ ~~come perfectly arranged~~ ∧methodized &∧ compressed, and the Results rendered obvious to the Public, ~~it is to be expected that~~ the Progress of Improvements will ∧Doubtless∧ ~~be~~ be ~~exceedingly accelerated~~ ∧come more & more rapid∧ especially ~~by~~ ∧after∧ the Return of Peace & general Tranquility.

The Husbandry of our northern and middle States has within ten Years past ~~improved~~ ∧advanced∧ far beyond the Expectations of the most sanguine — A Farmer on Long Island last Year paid above twenty Guineas for the hire of a Young Bull for one Season — and a calf of this Spring was lately sold in west Chester for ~~fifty Guineas~~ ∧250 Dol∧ — I mention these Prices to shew the spirit which prevails relative to the Breed of horned Cattle, for ~~as to Horses~~ ∧altho∧ our attention ~~may to them the~~ [qu?] ~~still more~~ ∧to Horses is∧ greater than to other animals ∧yet it∧ originates in various ~~motives~~ ∧Inducements∧ some of wʰ. have no immediate Reference to ~~Li~~ Husbandry.

Formerly the Subject of Manures was much ~~neg~~ neglected; at present our Farmers are becoming attentive to it— In several Places green Sea weed is raken in great Quantities from the Bottoms of coves and Inlets ∧along the Sea Shore∧— Shells are collected and immense Quantities of Fish are taken— for the sole purpose of manure— The planting of the Locust Tree ~~is~~ increases— it is the most durable Timber we have and I think is worth your Notice— it grows well in England— I ~~seen~~ ∧have some young∧ Trees there which appeared to thrive well—

~~The Proceedings of your Board begin to be known here and will excite~~ ~~more Curiosity and Interest, in future than at present— Political Events and~~ ~~Questions have for some time past almost engross^d. the~~ ~~attention thoughts~~ ~~of our People— and~~ ∧they∧ ~~have an inauspicious Influence on the arts of~~ ~~Peace~~—I have the honor to be with great Respect and Esteem D^r S^r your most ob^t Ser^t

Sr John Sinclair Bar[one]^t.

Dft, NNC (EJ: 08973). Endorsed: ". . . in an[swe]^r. to 29 march last".

1. Sinclair to JJ, 29 Mar. 1797, ALS, NNC (EJ: 08635). For more on their correspondence, see the editorial note "John Jay's Mission to London, 1794–95," above.

2. Sinclair, *Account of the Origin of the Board of Agriculture, and Its Progress for Three Years After Its Establishment* (London, 1796).

Sinclair founded the Board or Society for the Encouragement of Agriculture and Internal Improvement (commonly known as the Board of Agriculture), a voluntary organization dedicated to agricultural experimentation, in 1793. JJ was made an honorary member in March 1795. See Sinclair to JJ, 31 Mar. 1795, ALS, NNC (EJ: 07141), and JJ to Sinclair, 1 Apr. 1795, Dft, NNC (EJ: 08936).

On 15 July 1797, Sinclair wrote JJ, enclosing his address to the Board and some agricultural surveys, requesting that JJ provide them with agricultural news from America. ALS, NNC (EJ: 07147). JJ noted in his reply, "We in this Country are as yet so far behind You in these excellent arts, that we can ~~afford but little~~ [*illegible*] ∧can cast only a few ~~interesting~~ mites into your Treasury.∧— You will teach us useful Lessons, ~~and more~~ in agriculture, & they will cost us nothing; which is more than we can say ~~as~~ for [*illegible*] some of the other Lessons we are learning." JJ to Sinclair, 7 Nov. 1797, Dft, NNC (EJ: 08975).

To Timothy Pickering

New York 15 July 1797

Dear Sir

I herewith return the Book which you was so obliging as to send me.[1] Whether the Convention of armed Neutrality was limited in its Duration to that of the war then subsisting, or remained in force after the Return of Peace? is a question to which the inaccurate manner in which the 11th. article[2] is expressed, appears to have given occasion.— The original (which is not translated with perfect Precision) is in these words— vizt.

Cette Convention, arrêtée et conclue pour tout le Tems que durera la Guerre actuelle, servira de Base aux Engagemens que les Conjonctures pourroient faire contracter dans la Suite des Tems, et à l'Occasion des nouvelles guerres maritimes par lesquelles l'Europe auroit le Malheur d'etre troublée. Ces *Stipulations doivent* au Reste être regardées comme permanentes, et feront Loi en matiere de Commerce et de navigation, et toutes les fois qu'il s'agira d'apprecier les droits des Nations neutres.—[3]

On considering this article, it appears to me that a Distinction is made between the Convention considered as a *defensive alliance*, & the *Principles* which are declared in it— that the Term or Duration of the *defensive alliance* is limited to that of the war, and did expire with it— but that the *Principles* ~~having been~~ in question, having been adopted and insisted upon by the Parties as just and reasonable, were to be constantly and uniformly regarded by them as such. According to this Construction the two clashing Clauses of the article will be reconciled, and in my opinion the nature of the *other* Stipulations, will justify confining the operation of the latter Clause to those Stipulations only, which declare the Principles contended for.

It was evidently the Design of the Parties to bring on a general Discussion of the Laws of Nations relative to the Rights of *neutral* Nations touching Commerce and Navigation; and if possible to accomplish a general Recognition of these Principles as a part of those Laws.— several Passages in the State papers printed with the Convention manifest such a Design. upon the whole—it is my opinion

(1) That the *Alliance* between the Parties to the Convention, was formed for the mutual *Defence* of the neutral Rights asserted in it, *during* the war *then* subsisting, and no longer. and this is to me the more clear, from our hearing nothing of the Convention during the *present* war— especially as the Spoliations by Britain on Denmark, would doubtless have induced the latter to claim the Benefit of it, if it had remained in full force—

2[d]. That the Principles alluded to were permanently adopted by the *Parties* to the Convention—

3 That they implicitly admitted that those Principles had not as yet become a part of the existing & acknowledged Laws of Nations— I have the Honor to be with great Respect & Esteem D[r] Sir your most obed[t] Serv[t]

John Jay

The honble Timothy Pickering

ALS, MHi: Pickering (EJ: 04780). Endorsed: "Gov[r] Jay—July 15. 1797 / Construction of the 11th article / of the convention of the armed/neutrality". Dft, NNC (EJ: 09499).

1. On 10 July 1797, TP sent JJ a history of the Convention of the Armed Neutrality, commenting,

"You will have the goodness to return the book as soon as convenient, it being the property of the public." ALS, MHi: Pickering (EJ: 04824).

2. Here JJ mistakes the 11th Art. for the 9th.

3. "This convention shall be in full force as long as this present war shall last; and the engagements contained therein shall serve as the basis for all future engagements and treaties that circumstances may cause to be concluded on the outbreak of fresh maritime wars which may hereafter unfortunately disturb the tranquility of Europe. As to the rest, all that has been stipulated and agreed upon, shall be considered as permanent and shall constitute the law to be aplied in matters pertaining to commerce and navigation, as well as in cases involving the rights of neutral nations." James Brown Scott, ed., *The Armed Neutralities of 1780 and 1800* (New York, 1918), 303–4.

From John Trumbull

London 20th: July 1797.

Dear Sir

On the 9th. instant, Mr. King put into my hands your Letter of the 3d. June, containing duplicate of one dated 20th. October[1] the original of which never came to hand.— I beg you to accept my thanks for both, and particularly for the wise reflexions & Counsel contained in that of October:— Experience has shewn that my apprehensions of delicate and high responsibility, were not unfounded;—in truth the real difficulties of my Situation, and the Magnitude and Nature of Questions which it has fallen to me to decide, have far outgone even what I at first apprehended. I have made those decisions in the most careful and conscientious manner; and I hope that neither this Nation, nor any Individual has suffered Injury; nor my Native Country, my friends or myself disgrace; by what I done.

The History of our Proceedings is I understand, regularly communicated by the American Commissioners to their Government:— and as those Papers will of course be open to your observation, I will not enter into any Detail.[2]

Lord Malmsbury is at Lisle treating for Peace, with Commissioners from the French Republic;— I hope—though I cannot say that I *firmly expect* that their Negotiation will have a more favorable Issue than the last.

I look with anxiety for the proceedings of our Councils which I wish may unite Firmness with Moderation, and consist more in Deeds than in Words.— The Gentlemen who are appointed joint Commissioners with Mr. Pinckney will I hope have the Happiness to succeed in Averting from our Country, *once more* the worst of Evils.[3]

I beg you to present my best Respect to Mrs. Jay. and most cordial remembrance to M^r: Benson, M^r. and M^rs. Church.—Peter—and other friends I am with the highest Respect. Dear Sir Your obliged friend & Servant

Jno: Trumbull

His Excellency John Jay Esq. & &

ALS, NNC (EJ: 07208). Addressed: "His Excellency John Jay Esqr. / Governor of the State of / New York." Note. "By the Factor / Capt. Kemp". Endorsed: ". . . rec^d 17 Sep 1797". LbkC, DLC: Trumbull (EJ: 10356); C, NNC (EJ: 12819), attached with JT's letter of 7 Aug., below.

The ship *Factor* under John Kemp, sailed from Falmouth on 5 Aug. and arrived in New York on 11 Sept. *Lloyd's List* (London), 8 Aug.; *Minerva* (New York), 11 Sept, 1797.

1. JJ's letter of 3 June 1797 enclosing a copy of his letter of 20 Oct. 1796, has not been found. For the draft of his letter of 20 Oct., see DftS, NNGL (EJ: 90543).

2. On the role of the claims commission on which JT served, see the editorial note "Aftermath of the Jay Treaty: Responses, Ratification, and Implementation," above. The official correspondence of the commissioners is in Records of Boundary and Claims Commissions and Arbitrations, 1716–1994.

3. On the commissioners to France, see the editorial note "John Jay and the Response to the XYZ Affair in New York," below.

To James Sullivan

New York 28 July 1797

Sir

I have been favored with your's of the 30th. of last month,[1] informing me of the necessity of my being at Boston on the 14th. of august next, to give Testimony to the Commissioners appointed to determine what River was intended, by the River S^t. Croix in the Treaty of Peace.

If on further Consideration my personal attendance should be judged indispensable, I shall certainly think it my Duty to attend— But really Sir! when I reflect on the nature of my Evidence, it appears to me that my affidavit, or answers to written Interrogatories, would be sufficient and Satisfactory—

My Testimony would amount to this— vizt.—that in the negociations for Peace, the River S^t. Croix, as forming part of our Eastern Boundary, came into Question—That several Rivers in those Parts were said to have that name—That much was urged and argued on that Topic—that mitchels map was before us, and frequently consulted for geographical Information—that both Parties finally agreed, that the River S^t. Croix laid down on that map, was the River S^t. Croix which ought to form a Part of that Boundary—

It may be asked—Did You at that Time understand that the River S^t. Croix, laid down on Mitchels Map, was then so decidedly and permanently adopted and agreed upon by the Parties, as *conclusively* to bind the two

Nations to that Limit, even in *Case* it should afterwards appear that Mitchel had been *mistaken*; and that the *true* River S^t. Croix was a different one from that which he had delineated on his Map by that Name?—

To this Question I answer—That I do not recollect nor beleive that such a case was then put or talked of—² with the best wishes for your Health & Happiness I have the Honor to be Sir Your most obed^t. & h'ble Servt

John Jay

Jam^s. Sullivan Esqr.

ALS, MHi (EJ: 04781). Addressed: "Jam^s. Sullivan Esqr / counsellor at law / Boston". Endorsed. LbkC, N, Governor's Lbk 1 (EJ: 03088); *HPJ*, 4: 228–29.

1. Letter not found.

2. For the affidavit JJ prepared for the commissioners appointed to determine which river was intended as the northeastern boundary, see Testimony regarding the St. Croix River, [21 May 1798], and notes, below. The commissioners' questions were enclosed in Sullivan to JJ, 4 May 1798, ALS, NHi: Jay (EJ: 04480; EJ: 10087).

To John Vaughan

New York 31 July 1797

Dr Sir

I have been fav^d. with yours of the 11th. Instant,¹ in which you mention having rec^d. from your Brother for me a Portrait of the late President, engraved from a painting of Stewart;² and that You had sent it to the Care of M^r. Constable—³

I have since rec^d. it and am much obliged by this mark of your Brothers attention, as well as by your Care respecting it. When next you write to your Brother be pleased to present to him my Thanks— I am impatient to hear of Benjⁿ., and the more ∧so∧ as we had Reason to expect he would before This Time have arrived in America—⁴ I am Dr Sir, Your most ob^t. Servt

John Jay

Mr John Vaughan

ALS, PPAmP: John Vaughan (EJ: 02569). Duplicate, NNC (EJ: 08169).

1. Letter not found.

2. Engraving not found. The engraving was probably based on either Stuart's 1796 life-size portrait of GW held by the Marquis of Lansdowne or his earlier portrait of 1795.

3. Probably Dublin-born William Constable, a wealthy merchant and land speculator of New York. Constable travelled to Europe for the purpose of selling land that he had acquired in northern New York.

4. For the written exchange between JJ and Benjamin Vaughan, see Vaughan to JJ, 18 Aug. 1797, ALS, NNC (EJ: 12463, EJ: 13011); Dft, PPAmP: Benjamin Vaughan (EJ: 02582); TR, NNC (EJ: 13012); and JJ to Vaughan, 31 Aug. 1797, below.

From John Trumbull

London August 7th. 1797.

Dear Sir

Lest *Kemp*, by whom the original of the above was sent, should be taken, I have written duplicate — [1]

Our Awards had all been drawn payable at the Treasury here on the First of July: — for want of proper previous arrangements, they remained *unpaid*, at the date of the foregoing: — Of course, as there was I believe only one, in which the Board had been unanimous — and many ∧in∧ which there had been but a majority — I was not a little anxious, until the payments were made:

That has taken place some days since; and many unpleasant questions are now at rest: —

Two ∧other∧ Questions I foresee, which will rest on my feeble Shoulders: one of which is most important — This Business is not conducted as I hoped it would have been; — but I trust that my Nerves will not fail me, should they even be put to more severe trials, than they have been.

Of the vast Mass of Business which is before the Courts of this Country, The Lords of Appeal have decided in not more than thirty Causes; — the Martinico Cases have not yet been decided in the high Court of Admiralty: — And in April next, the Eighteen Months named in the Treaty, for the reception of Claims expires: — You see the question which will then arise: — I hope it will be justly and equitably decided.[2] I am Dear Sir With the highest Respect Your Obliged friend & servant

Jn° Trumbull

C, NNC (EJ: 12819), attached with JT's letter of 20 July, above. LbkC, DLC: Trumbull (EJ: 10357). In the upper-lefthand margin of the LbkC is the note "John Jay Esqr. / &c &c / New York. / by the Belvidere".

1. Copies of JT's letters of 20 July and 7 Aug. were sent from London by the ship *Belvidere*, captained by Solomon Ingraham.

2. On the work of the claims commission, see the editorial note "Aftermath of the Jay Treaty: Responses, Ratification, and Implementation," above. On the Martinique cases, see also Fewster, "British Ship Seizures," 426–52.

From Rufus King

London Augt. 16th. 1797

Dear Sir,

I had the pleasure to receive your Letter by M^r. Flemming; that for Lord Amherst was but just in time to be delivered before his Death.—[1] From the very great Reserve that every where exists concerning the negotiations in Italy and at Lisle, it is not easy to form a satisfactory opinion respecting their termination; indeed the great struggle that exists between the Directory and the two Councils, seems for sometime past to have withdrawn the public attention from those negotiations, and to have fixed it at Paris— Portugal has concluded a peace with France, and I hope that our Commissioners may likewise be able to adjust the misunderstanding between us and them. I have heard that M^r. Talleyrand, who succeeds La Croix in the office of foreign affairs, has expressed himself in a Friendly manner on the subject of American affairs.[2]

We must not expect with too much confidence that we shall escape a war; (and ought to prepare for a disappointment in our sincere desires to remain in Peace;) the security and the Fate of Genoa and of Venice should admonish us of our Duty; and the wisdom and many Precautions of Switzerland, which alone have hitherto preserved them, should also encourage us to meet the expences of a necessary State of defence.—

There seems to have been a satisfactory Persuasion that the preliminary articles with Austria was the Harbinger of a general Peace; and our Representatives may have compromitted the public welfare by an injudicious œconomy on the Subject of National Defence.— With sincere respect & attachment, I have the Honor to be, Dear Sir, Your faithful & obd^t Servt.

Rufus King

P.S. I was asked confidentially by the person to whom you wrote ~~before~~ if I could explain the occasion of the Postscript of y^r. Letter; I answered in the negative, adding that it was plain that you had changed your opinion, that you was not accustomed to do so except upon Sufficient grounds, and that your present Opinion agreed with my own— he replied that he certainly had no partiality in favor of the Character in Question, and if any fact or circumstance could be named, that w^d. authorize his interference, that there would be no Objection to ~~remove~~ displace—[3]

LS, with PS in the hand of Rufus King, NNC (EJ: 06695); Tr, NNC.

1. See JJ to RK, 3 June 1797, ALS, NHi: King (EJ: 00709), introducing Pierre Fleming of New York; and JJ to Amherst, 3 June 1797, Dft, NNC (EJ: 06710).

2. On the relationship between the American commissioners to France and Talleyrand, see the editorial note "John Jay and the Response to the XYZ Affair in New York," below.

3. See the postscript to JJ to Grenville, 4 June 1797, criticizing the conduct of John Temple, the British consul based in New York City. Dft, NNC (EJ: 08516).

To Jeremy Belknap

New York 17 Augt. 1797

Dr Sir

I have been fav^d. with yours of the 24 June.[1] It gives me pleasure to find that your biographical work advances. If it does not proceed too fast, it will be very interesting— especially as it will have ~~the~~ ∧an∧ advantage which all works of that kind cannot boast, vizt. of judicious selection and candor.

I wish I could comply with your Request in a full & satisfactory manner— but the History of the Dutch Governm^{nt}. in this State, is involved in much obscurity— even the traditional accounts which remain are very imperfect. There are extant one or two dutch authors who I am told ∧have∧ given an account of the early settlem^t. by the Dutch— when last at Albany I heard them spoken of, and I took some pains to persuade a Gentleman to translate them and some other papers which were represented to me as worthy of attention—but I cannot as yet flatter myself that it will be done. Your Letter will enduce me to renew my Efforts and Enquiries when I return there the ensuing Fall. Of the Dutch Governors little is at present known. Of Stuyvesant we know somewhat more than of the others. You will find Papers relative to some of his official Acts in Smiths History of New Jersey—and in Hazard's collection of State papers—[2] I shall continue my Enquiries and let you know the Result of them—[3] I am Dear Sir Your most ob^t. Servt.

John Jay

The Rev^d. Doct^r. Belknap

ALS, NNC (EJ: 04782). Addressed: "The Rev^d. Doct^r. Belknap / Boston". Marked: "post p^d." Stamped: "PAID 20." Endorsed.

1. Belknap to JJ, 24 June 1797, ALS, NNC (EJ: 05479). Belknap was instrumental in forming on 24 Jan. 1791 the Massachusetts Historical Society, in order to preserve and disseminate historical records. JJ was elected a member of the organization in June 1792 (*JJSP*, 5: 394n21, 395nn30–32). Belknap's three-volume *History of New Hampshire* (Philadelphia, 1784–92; *Early Am. Imprints*, series 1, nos. 18344, 21366, and 24088), and his two-volume *American biography: or, An historical account of those persons who have been distinguished in America as adventurers, statesmen, philosophers, divines, warriors, authors: Comprehending a recital of the events connected with their lives and actions* (Boston, 1794, 1798; *Early Am. Imprints*, series 1, nos. 33393 and 26637) established his reputation as a respected historian. Belknap had previously solicited information from JJ on New York history in 1795. Belknap to JJ, 9 Nov. 1795, ALS, NNC (EJ: 05481).

2. Samuel Smith, *The history of the colony of Nova-Caesaria, or New-Jersey: containing, an account of its first settlement, progressive improvements, the original and present constitution, and other events, to the year 1721. With some particulars since and a short view of its present state* (Burlington, 1765; *Early Am. Imprints*, series 1, no. 10166). Smith (1720–76) was a Quaker merchant and politician. Ebenezer Hazard, *Historical collections; consisting of state papers, and other authentic documents; intended as materials for an history of the United States of America* (Philadelphia, [1792–94]; *Early Am. Imprints*, series 1, no. 27105). Hazard was a Philadelphia publisher, editor of historical documents, businessman, and Postmaster-General of the United States (1782–89).

3. JJ later followed up with Belknap on the subject of Dutch records in New York: "As to the Dutch manuscripts I have taken great pains to get Extracts and Translations of such as I had understood from Mr Yates (our late Ch. Justice) were interesting. I have endeavoured to prevail on that Gent^n. to undertake it, but without Success— one of the most material manuscripts he says is missing and not to be found— He being engaged in other matters & not very industrious, my Expectations are not sanguine— there is no person here, nor I believe in the *State*, so capable of this Business in every Respect except Industry, as he is. I also desired a Gentleman at N York to search the Records there, and extract what might be interesting to the object of your work. He gave me Reason to expect he would do it, but it still remains undone. Unfortunately we have few men of Leisure, and very few indeed of any Description who *well* understand the Dutch Language, and are qualified for Researches of this Kind—". JJ to Belknap, 12 June 1798, ALS, MHi: Belknap (EJ: 04789).

To Benjamin Vaughan

NYork 31 Augt. 1797

Dear Sir

I had this afternoon the pleasure of recieving your favor of the 18 Inst.—[1] M^rs. Jay joins with me in sincerely congratulating you & your amiable Family on your arrival in this Country— May your Expectations of Happiness in it be perfectly realized. The Reasons which have determined you to settle on the Kennebeck, I can easily concieve are cogent; but I flatter myself you will sometimes find Leisure for Excursions this way—

I presume that our political Sentiments do not differ essentially— To me it appears important that the american Governm^t. be preserved as *it is*, untill mature Experience shall *plainly* point out very useful amendm^ts. to our Constitution—that we steadily repel all foreign Influence and Interference; and with good faith and Liberality treat all Nations as Friends in peace, and as Enemies in War—neither meddling with their affairs, nor permitting them to meddle in ours— These are the primary objects of my Policy— The secondary ones are more numerous—such as—To be always prepared for War— to cultivate Peace—To promote Religion, industry, Tranquility, and useful Knowledge; and to secure to all the quiet Enjoym^t. of their Rights, by wise and equal Laws irresistably executed. I do not expect that mankind will, before the millenium, be what they ought to be, and therefore in my opinion every political theory which does not regard them as being what they *are*, will probably prove delusive.—

It will give me pleasure to recieve the publication[2] you mention—being from your Pen it will I am persuaded be interesting— Be pleased to present our best Comp^{ts}. to Mrs Vaughan and your Sister— I am, D^r. Sir your affect^{te}. & hble Servt

John Jay

Benjn. Vaughan Esqr.

ALS, PPAmP: Benjamin Vaughan (EJ: 02561); Dft, NNC (EJ: 08155); *WJ*, 2: 282–83; *HPJ*, 4: 230–31. After a three-year residence in France and Switzerland (1794–97), former British diplomat Benjamin Vaughan obtained a passport to join his family in the United States, and settled in Hallowell, Maine.

1. Vaughan to JJ, 18 Aug. 1797, ALS, NNC (EJ: 12463; EJ: 13011); Dft, PPAmP: Benjamin Vaughan (EJ: 02582); Tr, NNC (EJ: 13012).

2. In his letter of 18 Aug., Vaughan promised to send when printed an essay on the "*life of a peasant*, who was alike memorable for his industry, sense, knowledge in farming, & virtue, and whose example may be essentially useful to this country." Based on the life of a well-known Swiss farmer named Kliyogg, this work was copublished in 1800 by Vaughan with Benjamin Edes (1732–1803) of Boston. [Hans Kaspar Hirzel], *The Rural Socrates: or An account of the celebrated philosophical farmer, late living in Switzerland, and known by the name of Kliyogg* (Hallowell, 1800; *Early Am. Imprints*, series 1, no. 37617).

To John Drayton

NYork, 6 September 1797

D^r. Sir:

~~on reading~~ The Letter which you was so obliging as to write to me on the 21 July 1795,[1] ~~it appeared however prudent to delay~~ excited no other Surprize than that certain Gentlemen had forgotten the Respect which they owed ~~both~~ to themselves ~~and~~ ∧as well as∧ to me

It was foreseen that *any* Treaty with Great Britain would be ~~violently~~ opposed by the *Debtors* to that Country, by ~~the Enemies of~~ the Antifœder∧al∧ists, and by the Partizans of *France*— I returned from England expecting and prepared to meet with Censure and Calumny; but not from certain ∧Individuals∧ whom I had always believed to be incapable of such Conduct—

So little Impression have these Circumstances made on my mind, that I do not regret the Part I have acted, ∧nor have I published a single Line to defend it—∧ Public Opinion will gradually become correct, & if it should not; I know the time will come when all the Libels & Lies in the world will perish, and leave Truth untarnished and undisguised by Error—

The motives which produced your Letter are rendered obvious by the

Sensibility which ˄pervades it˄— I thank you for it Sincerely; and I should it have done it more early, had it not appeared to me adviseable to suspend our Correspondence, untill the agitations alluded to, should have subsided— It will give me pleasure to be informed that this Letter has come safe to yᵣ Hands— I am Dʳ Sir your affᵗᵉ. & hble Servᵗ

John Drayton Esqʳ

Dft, NNC (EJ: 08974). The Dft contains extensive excisions, most of which are either illegible or insignificant and are not recorded here.

1. Drayton to JJ, 21 July 1795, not found. Drayton was a member of the South Carolina House of Representatives. For controversies involving Drayton that may have deterred JJ from answering his letter, see Drayton to JJ, 29 Jan. 1794, and notes, *JJSP*, 5: 584–88.

From Timothy Pickering

Trenton Sept. 9. 1797.

Sir,

Perhaps you may think the rude and insolent letter of the Chevalier de Yrujo to me, dated the 11th of July,[1] not entitled to an answer, especially as the documents which had been made public proved to every well informed man and attentive reader that his observations were either futile or unfounded. But I thought it would be necessary to make some remarks on his letter, to be eventually communicated to Colᵒ. Humphreys at Madrid;[2] and if the Spanish minister's letter should be laid before Congress, it seemed proper that those remarks should accompany it, & both, if Congress pleased, be published together. For this purpose a direct answer to the Chevalier would be a convenient form. I had another motive to write the answer— The minister plumed himself on his letter; and some of our miscreant citizens had paid him compliments, to raise his ideas of his contemptible performance.

The Answer being lengthy, and having occasion for a number of copies, I concluded to get it *printed*, altho' it is *not to be published*, unless Congress should order it, in the way above mentioned. I now take the liberty to present you with a copy.[3]

As nobody more accurately understands our dispute with Spain relative to the Mississipi, than your Excellency, I was peculiarly gratified by your approbation of the manner in which I had treated that Subject in my former correspondence with the Spanish minister. I am with the truest respect, Sir, your obᵗ servant,

T. Pickering

His Excellency John Jay Esq.

ALS, NNC (EJ: 09500). For JJ's reply, see his letter of 11 Sept. 1797, below.

1. *ASP: FR*, 2: 87–88. Yrujo's letter also appeared in newspapers, including *Aurora General Advertiser*, *Porcupine's Gazette*, and *Philadelphia Gazette* (all Philadelphia), 14 July 1797. Spanish minister Carlos Martínez de Yrujo y Tacón, marqués de Casa Yrujo (1763–1824), alleged in his letter that British and American incursions on Spanish possessions occurred along the Mississippi.

2. TP to Humphreys, 18 July 1797, MHi: Pickering.

3. TP enclosed a copy of *Letter from Mr. Pickering, secretary of state, to the Chevalier de Yrujo, envoy extraordinary and minister plenipotentiary of His Catholic Majesty to the United States of America. August 8th, 1797* ([Trenton?, 1797]; *Early Am. Imprints*, series 1, no. 33067).

From Rufus King

[London Sep. 9. 1797]

Dear Sir

What we know of the negotiations between france Austria and England, gives little encouragement to hope that their issue will be pacific— The internal Situation of france is alarming; instead of a Reconciliation between the Directory & the Councils, the breach appears to grow wider— Both sides court the Armies, and a civil war seems to be organizing itself— I send you a posthumous work of M[r]. Burke's[1]—likewise the copy of Lord Malmesburys first negotiation—[2] The result of the second shall be likewise forwarded as soon as it is public— I wish I could say that I had any expectation that it will Differ from the former— very truly and respectfully I have the honor to be D. Sir, Yr. Ob. ser

Rufus King

J. Jay Esq[r].

ALS, NNC (EJ: 11466). Endorsed: ". . . an[d]. 14 nov / 1797".

1. Edmund Burke's *Three memorials on French affairs, written in the years 1791, 1792, and 1793* (London, 1797).

2. For the publication on Lord Malmesbury's negotiations, see RK to JJ, 10 Jan. 1797, note 5, above.

To Timothy Pickering

New York 11 Sept[r]. 1797—

D[r] Sir

I was this morning fav[d]. with yours of the 9 Inst.[1] and have just finished reading your answer to the Chevaliers indiscreet & improper Letter— If no Faction hostile to the true Interests of this Country existed in it, I presume that the proper way to treat that Gentleman would be to insist on his Recall and to refuse to do Business with him— under present Circumstances, Prudence requires that more than ordinary pains be taken to preserve public opinion from the Errors into which that Faction so industriously labor to mislead it. On this Principle I approve of your treating that Letter with more attention than it really deserved. While such continues to be the State of Things, the aggressions of Foreigners ought not to be concealed from the public Eye; and perhaps we should now have fewer aggressions to complain of if our Delicacy and Forbearance and Silence had not encouraged Doubts of our Self Respect— The answer is not too long— in my opinion it is always best to do Business thoroughly or not at all— It is a great point to keep, and to *shew* one's adversaries to be, in the wrong—and this point you have gained with Respect both to Adet and the Chevalier— It gratifies me not a little to see American ministers act like Americans on independent and american Ground, uninfluenced and undisgraced by foreign management— with sincere Esteem I am D[r] Sir Your most ob[t]. Serv[t]

John Jay

The Hon'ble Timothy Pickering Esq[r].

ALS, MHi: Pickering (EJ: 04783). Addressed: "The Hon'ble Timothy Pickering Esq[r]. / Trenton". Franked: "Free". Endorsed: ". . . / rec[d]. 15th. / on the letter from and / to Yrujo.— & on Adet's".

1. See TP to JJ, 9 Sept. 1797, above.

James Sharples Receipt to Sarah Livingston Jay

Sep[r] 27th 1797

Rec[d] of M[rs] Jay 150 Dollars for a Group of Portraits

J Sharples[1]

ADS, NNC (EJ: 13219). Endorsed by SLJ: "M[r]. Sharpless's / rec[t]. for a Group / of portraits /27th. Sep[br]. 1797".

1. James Sharples (c. 1751–1811), English-born portrait painter who immigrated to the United States in 1794 with his wife, painter Ellen Wallace Sharples (1769–1849) and children Felix (b. 1786), James Jr. (1788–1839), and Rolinda (c. 1793–1838). The family settled in Philadelphia and New York, but travelled throughout the east coast, executing portraits and miniatures, in charcoal and pastels. Other sitters included the Washingtons, the Adamses, AH, TJ, GM, Lafayette, the Madisons, and other political leaders. Profiles were created using a physiognotrace, a device that enabled the profile of the sitter to be exactly copied.

Portraits of the Jays known to exist are of JJ, collection of the Bristol Museum, attributed to Ellen Sharples; SLJ with WJ and Sarah Louisa Jay, collection of the John Jay Homestead; and PAJ, collection of the New-York Historical Society. It is believed that portraits were done of Maria Jay and Ann Jay, but the location of these is unknown. Katharine McCook Knox, *The Sharples, Their Portraits of*

Sarah Livingston Jay and children, by James Sharples, c. 1789. Pastel on paper. (John Jay Homestead State Historic Site, Katonah, NY; New York State Office of Parks, Recreation, and Historic Preservation)

George Washington and His Contemporaries (New Haven, 1930), 101; and Kathryn Metz, "Ellen and Rolinda Sharples: Mother and Daughter Painters," *Woman's Art Journal* 16 (1995): 3–11.

To Richard Varick

Albany 5th. October 1797

Dr. Sir

I have received a Petition from Peter Heaton, stating that he had been convicted of Larceny, at a Court of Quarter Sessions held in the City of New York on the 10th. July last and sentenced to Six Months Imprisonment at hard Labor in Bridewell— The prayers for a Pardon and his Petition is supported by a number of very respectable Subscribers— Be so good as to converse with the Recorder[1] on the Subject and inform me whether the Case is so circumstanced as that a Pardon would be proper—[2] I am &ca.

John Jay—

The Hon'ble Richard Varick Esqr.

LbkC, N: Governor's Lbk. 1 (EJ: 03095).

1. James Kent.

2. For more on JJ's policies regarding the issuing of pardons, see the editorial note "Crime and Punishment in Federalist New York," above.

To Oliver Wolcott

Albany 20th. October 1797

Sir,

It was not untill Yesterday that I recieved (under cover from Col. Talmadge) the Letter which your Excellency did me the Honor to write on the 19th. of last Month, with the one addressed to you by several Gentlemen of Litchfield[1] requesting your Interposition with ^me^ for the Pardon of Israel Stone,[2] who is now under Sentence of confinement for Life on Conviction of Forgery—.

To your Excellency it cannot be necessary to observe, that the Power to pardon, is a Trust which in its Exercise ought to be regulated by the steady Principles of Sound Policy combined with those of Benevolence. I hold it to be my Duty to grant Pardons whenever they may be consistant with the public Good; and to refuse them in all Cases of manifest Guilt, in which they may be opposed by the public Good—.

Israel Stone is convicted of Forgery. This is a Crime which never has Passion, Ebriety or Precipitation to plead in its Excuse— on the contrary it always indicates some Degree, and not unfrequently a very great Degree of cool deliberate Wickedness— The injurious Consequences of this Crime to Society, particularly in a Commercial Nation, are obvious—. of all atrocious Offences we find that this has become the most common and prevalent— there are at this moment a number of Persons in Prison who are charged with it and who are yet to be tried.—

It was apprehended that the late Law of this State to mitigate Punishments in Cases of Forgery and many other Felonies, might at least for a Time, tend to encourage Offenders— for the fear of Death being taken away, the fear of Imprisonment for Life, which alone remains, would naturally be diminished not only by the Hopes of escaping either Detection, or Arrest or Conviction; but also by that of eluding perpetual Confinement—. If to these Hopes should be added that of easily and speedily obtaining Pardons, by the Mediation or for the sake of worthy Relations and Friends, our present mild System would probably soon prove so severe on the public, as to render the Prudence of continuing it very questionable—.

It is the Interest of Benevolence and Humanity, that this System should realize the Expectations formed from it, but it certainly cannot have even a fair Experiment, unless much care be taken to enable mild Punishments to produce by their Certainty a Portion of that dread which capital ones impress by their ~~Certainty~~ ^Severity^—.

Israel Stone is not the only Forgerer in our Prisons whose former Character was fair, who was probably seduced, and whose Parents and Friends are respectable— there are several of this Description. So greatly does this Crime prevail, that the Heinousness and Turpitude of it seems to have abated in the Opinion of too many; more Persons belonging to decent and reputable Families have disgraced and ruined themselves by this, than by any other Crime— Justice however cannot look with a more favorable Eye on those who become Criminal in spite of a good Education and of good Examples than on those Offenders who from Infancy have lived destitute of such valuable advantages.—

These Remarks and Reflections together with the Conclusions resulting from them convince me that the proper Time or Season for pardoning this Offender is not yet come and therefore that on this Occasion I can neither gratify my own wishes nor those of the respectable Gentlemen who have humanely interested themselves in his Behalf—.[3]

They who are Parents can easily concieve what must be feelings of this mans Father[4] and Family— I pity them sincerely— and I assure you that nothing but a strong Sense of my Duty restrains me from giving them the Consolation which they desire; and which it is very natural that Persons so circumstanced should be anxious to obtain and happy to receive—.[5] I have the Honor to be with Respect & Esteem your Excellency's most obed[t]. Serv[t].

(signed) John Jay

His Excell[y]. Oliver Wolcott Esq[r]. Governor of Connecticut—

LbkC, N: Governor's Lbk. 1 (EJ: 03099).

1. Wolcott to JJ, 19 Sept. 1797, ALS, NNC (EJ: 07277). Petition to Oliver Wolcott, 15 Sept. 1797, ALS, NNC (EJ: 07276), in the same document as Wolcott's letter sent to JJ. The document was signed by Tapping Reeve, Uriah Tracy, Reuben Smith (1732–1804), Benjamin Tallmadge, Julius Deming (1755–1838), and John Allen (1763–1811).

2. Israel Stone (1775–1842) of Litchfield, Conn., was convicted of forgery in January 1797 and

sentenced to life imprisonment in the state penitentiary. *Diary* (New York), 31 Jan.; *Weekly Monitor* (Litchfield), 8 Feb.; *New York Magazine* (Feb. 1797), 107.

3. In addition to delivering the Wolcott letter and Litchfield petition, Benjamin Tallmadge wrote JJ, stating that Stone had been the unwilling dupe of a "few designing Men." The governor replied to Tallmadge and Wolcott, and explained why he was unwilling to grant a pardon for Stone. The following year, Stone escaped from the prison hospital and fled to Connecticut. JJ called on state authorities to spare no effort in apprehending him, and asked Jonathan Trumbull Jr., then governor of Connecticut, to assist with Stone's recapture and extradition. After six years as a fugitive, Stone apparently voluntarily turned himself over to authorities and served out his life sentence. Tallmadge to JJ, 29 Sept. 1797, ALS, NNC (EJ: 07159); Tallmadge to JJ, 1 Dec. 1797, ALS, NNC (EJ: 07160); C, NHi: Misc. Mss. Tallmadge (EJ: 00654); *New-York Gazette*, 13 June; *Carey's United States Recorder* (Philadelphia), and *Philadelphia Gazette*, both 14 June; *Albany Gazette*, 22 June; *Georgia Gazette* (Savannah), 19 July; *Argus, Greenleaf's New Daily Advertiser* (New York), 5 Sept.; *Commercial Advertiser* (New York), 7 Sept.; *Daily Advertiser* (New York), 10 Oct. 1798; JJ to Isaac Stoutenburgh, 30 Oct. 1798, LbkC, N: Governor's Lbk. 1 (EJ: 03180); JJ to Josiah Ogden Hoffman, 22 Nov., LbkC, N: Governor's Lbk. 1 (EJ: 03189); 4 Dec. 1798, LbkC, N: Governor's Lbk. 1 (EJ: 03197); JJ to Jonathan Trumbull Jr., 4 Dec. 1798, LbkC, N: Governor's Lbk. 1 (EJ: 03198); *New-England Palladium* (Boston), 2 Mar.; *Columbian Museum* (Savannah), 3 Mar.; *City Gazette* (Charleston), 12 Mar. 1804; "Annual Account of Prisoners in the State-Prison," in [New York State], *Journal of the Assembly of the state of New-York; at their twenty-eighth session, begun and held at the city of Albany, the sixth day of November, 1804* (Albany, [1805]; *Early Am. Imprints*, series 2, no. 9014), 125.

4. Jonah Stone (c. 1749–1825) of Litchfield.

5. For more on Stone's case and JJ's use of pardons, see the editotial note "Crime and Punishment in Federalist New York," above.

From Peter Augustus Jay

New York 24th October 1797—

Dear Papa

On Saturday Cæsar put on board Capt Hanson's Sloop several Articles which Mama requested me to send viz a Jug of Oil, the Racks for the Spit a Box of Rush-lights & the Safe— in the latter was a Bag containing Salt Petre Isinglass &c and also a small Pot of Ointment for you which Doctor Charlton[1] had given me a day or two before,— The enclosed Letter[2] accompanied it, but I thought it would go more speedily & with greater Safety by the Post— I was at that time so hurried as to be able to write but a very few lines—

I have received of General Clarkson for Mama £100—& at the Bank Doll: 59 3/100 for Interest on your Stock viz $15 on the 6 pr Cts & 44 3/100 on the 3 pr. Cts— I shall somehow pay Mr. Roosevelt another £100 on his Bond.[3] Your Directions are to pay him not only the Principal but also the interest up to the Day of Payment. Would it not answer every Purpose to make an Indorsement on the Bond acknowledging the Receipt of the Interest due at that Period, since if it be now paid to him, it will instantly become due again to you. I only mention this for your Consideration & unless you direct the Contrary shall act agreable to my Instructions—

M[r] Munro has had two Conversations with Judge Benson[4] on the subject of my Admission as an Attorney from which it appeared not only that there was no certainty of succeeding in an Application for that purpose But that the Judge himself entertained great Doubts upon the Subject And also that thro' Ignorance of a late rule of Court we had suffered the first week of Term to elapse in Deliberations during which only, Motions for Examinations can be made— I do not Know whether I ought to regret this Disappointment— Though I am very desirous to be in a situation to maintain myself & to releive you from any further expence on my account yet I am sure this Consideration would have no weight in inducing you to advise an Examination before I could pass it with Credit, especially as it appears to me of great importance that the first impressions made by a young practitioner should be favorable— In this Respect I hope to be much better prepared at the next term than I am at present—

Be pleased to give my love to Mama & Sisters & to thank Maria for her Letter which I received today & hope soon to have the pleasure of answering— I am your Affectionate Son

Peter Augustus Jay

Gov[r]. Jay

ALS, NNC (EJ: 06058).

   1. John Charlton.

   2. Letter not found.

   3. Probably Nicholas J. Roosevelt (1767–c. 1854), of New York City. See JJ Account Book (Lbk), 1787–1830, D, NNC; PAJ to JJ, 29 Dec. 1798, below; and 5 Apr. 1801, ALS, NNC (EJ: 08370).

   4. Egbert Benson, associate judge of the supreme court of New York.

To John Trumbull

Albany 27 Oct[r]. 1797

Dear Sir

I rec[d]. three Days ago by the post, your Letter of the 7 August, in which was a Copy of the one you had written on the 20 July, and the original of which I had recieved and read with Pleasure.[1]

The Difficulty and Delicacy of your Task my good Friend! are obvious, ~~and~~ ʌbutʌ I flatter myself the Reputation to be derived from it, will soften the Trouble & anxiety it gives You. It was not to be expected that the Judgments of the Commiss[rs]. would not frequently differ, for the best Judges sometimes vary in opinion from each other; but it is to be expected as well as wished, that their Decisions may bear the Test of the severe Examination, which they will certainly at one Time or other undergo.

I am glad the Payments you allude to have been made; and I hope the Business will continue to be conducted with such Prudence as well as Justice and Equity, as that no obstacles may arise from Disgust or Irritation on either Side. The Delays of the Court of Admiralty do not surprize me. I have no Faith in any *british Court of admiralty*; tho I have the greatest Respect for and the highest Confidence in their Courts of *Justice*; in the number of which those Courts do not deserve to be ranked— I do not extend this Stricture to the Lords of appeal—

The question you hint at is interesting, perhaps a mode might be devised for making and recieving claims *de bene esse*—but if any thing of that kind should be done, it should be on more mature consideration than that on which I suggest it,— it is a Thought which just occurs to me, and which I have not examined[2]

I am settled here with my Family at least for the winter— The Legislature have determined that this City shall be the Seat of Governm[r]. and that the principal public offices shall be here.[3] our Friend Benson is in New York in bad Health; and there is some Reason to fear that his Disorder (a Weakness in his Bowels) will be tedious, and perhaps never *perfectly* cured. When a young Man he was indisposed with it for several Years.

As to Politics, we are in a better state than we were, but we are not yet in a sound State— I think that nation is not in a sound State whose Parties are excited by objects interesting only to a foreign Power— I wish to see our People more americanized, if I may use that Expression. Untill we feel and act as an independent nation, we shall always suffer from foreign Intrigue.

whether peace in Europe would ensure peace to america, is a Question on which Doubts are entertained. In my opinion it will depend on Circumstances, and not on any Right or wrong about the matter.

Remember me to our Friends M[r] King and M[r]. Gore. I owe Letters to them and to others—but the Fate of Letters has been so precarious, that I have written much fewer than I should otherwise have done— I am Dear Sir yours Sincerely

John Jay

Col. John Trumbull

ALS, N (EJ: 11256). Addressed: "Col[l]: John Trumbull / London". Endorsed: ". . . Rec[d]. London January 9th / Ans[d]. March 6th." Dft, NNC (EJ: 13085); *WJ*, 2: 283–84; *HPJ*, 4: 231–33.

1. JT to JJ, 20 July and 7 Aug. 1797, both above.

2. In his letter of 7 Aug., JT had raised the question of what to do if the slow pace of decisions in the British admiralty courts meant few cases could be referred to the claims commission before the deadline for submission of appeals. For the work of the commission, see the editorial note "Aftermath of the Jay Treaty: Responses, Ratification, and Implementation," above.

De Bene Esse: Conditionally; provisionally; in anticipation of future need. A phrase applied to proceedings that are taken ex parte or provisionally, and are allowed to stand as well done for the present, but which may be subject to future exception or challenge, and must then stand or fall according to their intrinsic merit. *Black's Law Dictionary Online*.

3. See the editorial note "The Capital Moves to Albany," above.

From Timothy Pickering

Trenton Oct. 28 1797.

Sir,

Last evening I received the inclosed letter[1] for you from Mr. King. With His dispatches by the Wm. Penn[2] I received a copy of the treaty of commerce & navigation between G. Britain & Russia, concluded the 21st of February last.[3] There is no provision, *that free ships shall make free goods.* The articles of contraband are confined to those immediately relating to war, and do not comprehend naval stores & ship timber. But my principal inducement to mention this treaty is, to inform you of a subsequent declaration on the 11th of May, to explain a passage in the 9th article, which says "the subjects of the High Contracting Parties shall not pay higher duties upon the importation & exportation of their merchandize, than are paid by the subjects of other nations:" The declaration is, "that by the words *other nations,* European nations alone are to be understood."— This exception must doubtless have been made to enable G. Britain to favour the trade of the *United States.*

Since Talleyrand has been appointed Minister for foreign affairs, a Major Mountflorence[4], Chancellor to our Consul General Skipwith[5] (but a very different man from his principal) waited upon him. Talleyrand received him very cordially, enquired politely after General Pinckney, and added, "he hoped soon to have the pleasure of seeing him in Paris."— Talleyrand has dismissed all the officers in his department, except Mr. Giraudet[6] the secretary general, who treated Genl. Pinckney with so much politeness, before he was ordered to leave Paris. Mr. Otto[7] & Mr. La Forest[8] are both at present employed in that department. Both these persons have been in America, & I presume you will know their characters; tho' I do not, but from transient information.

Some of our Jacobin papers asserted that Mr. Thos. B. Adams, the President's son, who in the current year made an excursion from the Hague to Paris, was ordered to leave France. This is not only utterly false, but he was on the contrary treated with distinguished respect. The day before he ^was^ returning, he rec'd a polite invitation to dine with Carnot (the Director) was civilly treated, & urged to endeavour to reconoile the two countries. He was also admitted, & had a seat assigned him, at the ceremony of drawing the lot for the new director. I am very respectfully Sir your ob^t. servant

T. Pickering

His Excellency John Jay.

ALS, NNC (EJ: 09501).

 1. Probably RK to JJ, 16 Aug. 1797, above.

 2. The *William Penn* under Captain Josiah left London in late August and arrived in Philadelphia on 27 Oct. *Aurora General Advertiser* (Philadelphia), 24 Oct.; *Gazette of the United States* (Philadelphia), 27 Oct. 1797.

 3. For more on this treaty signed at St. Petersburg, see RK to AH, 27 June 1797, note 6. *PAH*, 21: 116.

 4. James Cole Mountflorence (d. 1820).

 5. Fulwar Skipwith (1765–1839).

 6. Charles-Philippe-Toussaint Guiraudet.

 7. Louis-Guillaume Otto.

 8. Antoine René Charles Mathurin de La Forêt.

From Rufus King

London Octr. 31. 1797

Dear Sir

 Our Envoys have been at Paris from the first of the month— during the last fortnight there has been no Person from France by whom I could have heard from them— Col. Trumbull is at Paris on his Return from Germany, and we expect him here in a day or two; we shall be better able after his arrival than at present to form an Opinion concerning the issue of our Negociation— It remains still uncertain whether the war with Austria will recommence— The Preparations on both sides are immense—but the continuation of the negotiations at Adina, and the Prolongation of the armistice, induce many to believe that a definitive Treaty of Peace is likely to be soon concluded— The Treaty between France & Portugal has not yet been ratified by the latter, tho the time allowed for that purpose has elapsed. further time for Deliberation it is understood has been given by France— The Option of a war with france or England situated as Portugal is, is embarrassing—

 The inclosed Newspaper gives you the Dec[larati]on of this Government on the Rupture of the late Negotiations at Lisle: Parliament meets next week when, we hear, the correspondence will be given to the Public—[1]

 The late naval Victory[2] has very considerably allayed the public concern respecting invasions and it will also contribute to raise and support the national Fortitude— General La fayette is at length free. The enfeebled Health of mad: la fayette did not permit them to encounter a winter's passage to america, they have therefore taken Quarters in a Village of Holstein about 60. miles from Hamburgh— An Austrian Prison is no Place of profit; and France is not just now in the practice of making remittances; the Consequence is plain— I have therefore offered to supply the General with money, he accepts the Offer— These supplies I shall continue as his occasions may require; I am without Authority, but for many reasons I think the President would approve of this Conduct— With Perfect Respect & Esteem I am Dear Sir Yr. ob. & faithful Serv[t]

Rufus King

John Jay Esq[r].

ALS, NNC (EJ: 06696). Endorsed. Tr, NNC. Enclosure not found.

1. For the Declaration of the British government concerning the collapse of negotiations at Lisle, see *Oracle and Public Advertiser* (London), 31 Oct. 1797. For the publication of the records of Lord Malmesbury failed negotiations at Lisle, see *State papers relative to the negotiation for peace; containing the declaration of the court of Great Britain; the official correspondence between Lord Malmesbury and the Commissioners of the French Directory at Lisle; and His Majesty's speech on opening the present session: together with The Addresses of the Lords and Commons, and His Majesty's Most Gracious Answers* (London, 1797); *Lord Malmesbury's embassy: Official Records, in the negotiation at Lisle presented to the two Houses of Parliament, Containing the whole state papers which passed between the British and French plenipotentiaries, &c.* (Edinburgh, 1797). The correspondence also appeared in British and later in American newspapers. For a previous publication on the negotiation, see RK to JJ, 10 Jan. 1797, and note 5, above.

2. A Royal Navy squadron under Adam Duncan decisively defeated a Dutch naval force commanded by Jan de Winter at the Battle of Camperdown on 11 Oct. 1797.

To Peter Augustus Jay

Albany 2[d]— nov[r]. 1797

Dear Peter

Your Letter of the 28 ult: was delivered to me this morning—[1] mary had strong Claims to the Care and Kindness of our Family. I wish you had been sooner informed of her Illness, that every assistance in our Power to afford, might if requisite, have been rendered. It is a consolation however to reflect, that you found her comfortably circumstanced as to accommodations; and that she had not been without medical aid. The Attentions paid to her by M[r]. Munro, D[r]. Charlton and yourself give me great Satisfaction. She was the last of our *old* Family Servants, and I greatly regret the Indiscretions & consequent Troubles of her latter Years. few Servants and few Families deserved better of each other than they did—so greatly does right Conduct on the one Side, tend to produce it on the other—

The Sum you have given for the Franklin, does not exceed the Price I expected.[2] I this morning gave Cap.[t] Bogart a Letter for you— it contains more commissions— He will not probably sail before Saturday or Sunday— This is *Thursday* night.

The Rule of Court you mention is not a bad one: but will it not so far affect you as to prevent your practicing both as an Att[orne]y & a Counsellor? but whether it does, or does not, is a question which I do not think very interesting.

The amount of the Dam[age]s assessed in Leguen's cause renders it very important to the Parties; and there being a special verdict seems to indicate that it turns on some nice Points, which I am glad you have heard ably discussed.

You did well not to send by the post the *large* Packet from S.[r] John Sinclair—[3] The custom house officer might have acted more delicately; and his Principal will doubtless tell him so. The Expectation of seeing You here in January will make me look forward to that month with more than common pleasure— Your mama is recovering from a bad Cold— The Rest of us are well— I am D.[r] Peter your very aff.[te] Father

John Jay

M.[r] Peter Augustus Jay—

ALS, PC (EJ: 11350). Reply not found but SLJ reported that JJ did receive a letter of an unknown date from PAJ in early November. SLJ to PAJ, 7 Nov. 1797, ALS, NNC (EJ: 10006).

1. PAJ to JJ, 28 Oct. 1797, Dft, NyRyJHC. PJM reported that Hannah, Mary's daughter, reported to him that her mother was stricken with smallpox. Doctors were called for, but there was little hope for survival.

2. JJ expected the Franklin stove at his Albany residence on 7 Nov, but its arrival was delayed by icy conditions on the Hudson River. SLJ to PAJ, 6 Nov. 1797, ALS, NNC (EJ: 10006). See also PAJ to JJ, 28 Oct. 1797, Dft, NyRyJHC; JJ to PAJ, 25 Nov. 1797, below.

3. For case involving Leguin and the package sent by Sinclair, see PAJ to JJ, 28 Oct. 1797, Dft, NyRyJHC. Sinclair sent JJ on 15 July 1797 a copy of his address before the British Board of Agriculture and the agricultural surveys carried out by the society. ALS, NNC (EJ: 07147). See also JJ to Sinclair, 12 July 1797, note 2, above.

From Rufus King

London Nov. 12. 1797

Dear Sir

By M.[r] Seton I sent you the Dec[larati]on of this Government on the rupture of the Negociation at Lisle—[1] I now send you Lord Malmesburys correspondence with a number of News Papers—[2] The treaty between Portugal & France has been annulled by the latter, because it had not been ratified by the former within the time first prescribed for that Purpose, tho it is asserted that this time had been prolonged, and had not expired, when after the news of the definitive treaty with Austria, the Directory declared it void.

Portugal will be attacked by France unless Spain shall succeed in her endeavours to avert the Blow— If portugal is attacked the Revolution of Spain will probably be completed by the same Army— The Congress at *Rastat*[3] which is now about meeting, will it is supposed bring to light Engagements hitherto kept secret, between the Emperor and France, and likewise between France and Prussia. Whether they will succeed in restoring Peace to Germany is thought by some persons problematical, tho if Prussia, Austria, and France have previously arranged their Pretensions, the others who are interested will be obliged to concur— The Leaders of the Opposition in this Country do not attend Parliament— I think I am not mistaken in the Opinion, that the failure of the late negociation has had a *great influence* in uniting this nation, still more than they before were united, in the Belief that the firm prosecution of the war is necessary to the national welfare and existence—

Our Envoys on Sunday last, after having been a month at Paris, had not made such progress in their Business as to enable them to decide with much confidence concerning the issue of their missions— in the mean Time our Vessels continue to be captured by the french Cruisers, and the Tribunal of Cassation (the members of which have been reformed since the 18th. fructidor) after having for some Months before the arrival of our Envoys suspended giving Judgment in Amern Causes, are passing Decrees, which confirm the Condemnation of our Ships for the want of a Role d'Equipage—[4]

My Knowledge of the interior of the Negociation is too imperfect to authorize me to give any Opinion respecting its Result, but judging from Facts and Circumstances which are collected from news Papers, and other such channels of information, [*illegible*] my Hopes have been weakened since the arrival of our Envoys—[5] With sincere respect & Esteem I am Dear sir Yr ob. & faithful Sert.

Rufus King

John Jay Eqr.

ALS, NNC (EJ: 06697). Endorsed. Tr, NNC (EJ: 01131).

1. See RK to JJ, 31 Oct. 1797, above.

2. See RK to JJ, 31 Oct. 1797, note 1, above.

3. The Congress of Rastatt met in southwestern Germany between November 1797 and April 1799 for the purpose of negotiating a peace between France and the Holy Roman Empire.

4. The Cour de Cassation is the highest court of criminal and civil appeal in France, with the power to overturn the decisions of lower courts. It considers decisions only from the point of view of whether the lower court has applied the law correctly; it does not review the facts of a case or retry it. A role d'equipage is the list of a ship's crew; the muster roll.

5. For relations with France at this time, see the editorial note "John Jay and the Response to the XYZ Affair in New York," below.

From Christopher Gore

London 13 Novr. 1797.

My dear Sir,

I have the honor to acknowledge the receipt of your friendly letter of June last—[1]

Since that time you have doubtless heard, how far our board has progressed, in the business of their commission. There is little prospect of our doing much more in relation to claims, on the Brit. Govt, until next April; when the term of 18 M[onth]s, limited, by the article, for the reception of complaints, except in extraordinary cases, will have expired— The Lords Commiss[ion]ers of appeal have not decided, definitively, more than three or four causes, within the last year.

The dec[larati]on of his Britannic Majesty, stating the causes of the failure of the late negotiation for peace, has been fully confirm'd to the mind of almost every man, by the correspondence of Lord Malmsbury—[2]

France is said to be very tranquil at present—and perfectly silent on the late revolution there, as well as on the naval victory of Admiral Duncan.[3]

All foreign newspapers are stopt by the postmaster—And little is known in that country, but what the Directory choose to Communicate—

Some predict another struggle, on the motion for excluding all nobles, & their relations— Barras was of the nobility, and to his patronage, Buonaparte in some measure, owes his greatness— The latter is expected in Paris—and we hear that the former will not be content with the order, tho' he is personally excepted—

Our ministers were in Paris last Sunday— We do not learn that any thing has yet been done by them, with the Govt. of France. I pray you to present my best respects, with Mrs Gore's, to Mrs Jay, & to believe to be very respectfully your friend, and obed servant,

C. Gore

ALS, NCC (EJ: 08483; EJ: 08478). Endorsed.

1. Letter not found.

2. See RK to JJ, 31 Oct. and 12 Nov., both above.

3. For Duncan's victory at the Battle of Camperdown, see RK to JJ, 31 Oct. 1797, note 2, above.

To Rufus King

Albany 14 Novr. 1797

Dear Sir

Since my last of the 7th. Inst:[1] I have been fav^d. with your's of the 9th. Sept^r.[2] with the two Pamphlets which you was so obliging as to send with it, and for which accept my thank's. The one by M^r. Burke I have read, and find Remarks in it which will deserve attention — The other I had seen —

A late arrival has brought Intelligence of the Explosion at Paris — it opens a wide Field for Speculation and Conjecture — It is difficult for a demoralised People to have any stable Government — human Laws can reach only a small Portion of human actions. I am anxious to know how our Com[missione]^{rs}. have been recieved. to me it does not appear certain that the new Revolution will injure us: but the cloud is too thick to be penetrated — It seems that France is to be purified by Fire; if so, she is not yet ready to leave the Furnace. we hear that L^d. Malmsbury has returned to England; and yet I should not be surprized if something like a Peace should be patched up this winter between France and *Austria* — I suspect the Emperors Resources to be exhausted so much, as that it will not be in his power to provide for the Expence of *such* a campaign next Year as would become his Dignity and Interests — but this is all Guess work —

Benson is here, and means to *remain* here — he is better, but not well; and I fear his future Days will be passed in a kind of middle State between sick & well —[3]

Tichenor is Governor of Vermont, and it is said will do his best to fœderalize it — The cause of good Governm^t. gradually gains Ground, and the Clergy very generally promote it — Remember me to our Friends Trumbull and Gore — Yours Sincerely

John Jay

The Honb. Rufus King Esqr.

ALS, NHi: King (EJ: 00707).

1. JJ to RK, 7 Nov., ALS, NHi: King (EJ: 00708); Dft, NNC (EJ: 06711).

2. RK to JJ, 9 Sept., above.

3. Egbert Benson was serving on the St. Croix boundary commission (1796–98). It met in Boston

in 1797, then adjourned until 1798, pending completion of relevant surveys. He did attend the 1798 session at Providence. See Moore, *International Arbitrations*, 1: 1–43.

Proclamation on the Completion of the State Prison

[25 November 1797]

By His Excellency John Esqr.
Governor of the State of New York
A Proclamation

Whereas by an Act of the Legislature of this State Entitled "an Act making Alterations in the Criminal Law of this State and for erecting State Prisons"[1] Boards of Commissioners[2] were instituted and appointed for erecting and building the State Prisons, which in and by the said Act were directed to be built in the City of New York, and in the County of Albany—

And Whereas in and by the said Act, it was further enacted "that the Person administering the Government of this State for the Time being, as soon as either of the said State Prisons is ready for the Reception of Prisoners, shall issue a Proclamation giving public notice thereof, and directing the Sheriffs of the several Counties, to convey the Prisoners in the Goals of their Counties to the State Prison wherein such offenders are to be imprisoned, and that thereupon the said Sheriffs shall ˄forthwith˄ safely convey such Prisoners to such Prison["]—

And whereas by a subsequent Act entitled "An Act to suspend the Powers of the Commissioners for erecting a State Prison in the County of Albany"[3] the said Powers were accordingly suspended, and the thirty fourth Section of the before-mentioned Act was repealed, and it was also enacted "*that the State Prison to be built in the City of New York shall be considered as the State Prison for the whole State.*"[4]

And Whereas the State Prison in the City of New York is ready for the Reception of Prisoners—

Now therefore I do hereby give public notice thereof accordingly, and do hereby direct the Sheriffs of the several counties of this State, to convey to the said State Prison in the City of New York, such of the Prisoners in their respective Goals as are adjudged and Sentenced to be imprisoned in the State Prison: And hereof the said Sheriffs and the Keeper of the State Prison, and all others whom it may concern, are to take Notice and govern themselves accordingly—[5]

Given under my Hand and the privy Seal of the State at the City of Albany, on the twenty fifth Day of November in the year of our Lord one thousand

Seven hundred and ninety Seven: and in the twenty Second year of the Independence of the United States of America—

John Jay

By His Excellency's Command David S. Jones Private Secretary

LbkC, N: Governor's Lbk 2 (EJ: 03274). PtD, *Albany Register*, 1 Dec.; *Commercial Advertiser* (New York), 2 Dec. 1797.

1. *Greenleaf's New York Journal*, 1 Mar. (extract); *Daily Advertiser* (New York), 9 Apr.; *Albany Gazette*, 19 Apr. 1796; *N.Y. State Laws*, 19th sess., (1796), 20–24.

2. Philip Schuyler, Abraham Ten Broeck, Daniel Hale, Jeremiah Van Rensselaer, and Tunis T. Van Vechten served on a board of commissioners for building the state prison in Albany and were authorized to purchase a four-acre lot for this purpose. "An Act making Alterations in the Criminal Law of this State, and for erecting State Prisons," 26 Mar. 1796, *N.Y. State Laws*, 19th sess. (1796), 22. For more on the work of these commissioners, see JJ to Schuyler, Ten Broeck, Van Rensselaer, and Van Vechten, 1 Aug. 1796, LbkC, N: Governor's Lbk. 1 (EJ: 03032); JJ to PJM, 21 Jan. 1797, above; *Albany Chronicle*, 6 Feb; *Diary*, and *Minerva* (both New York), 7 Feb.; *Herald* (New York), 8 Feb. 1797; JJ's Message to the New York State Senate, *N.Y. Senate Journal*, 20th sess. (1796–97), 41; 21 Jan. 1797, *NYGM*, 2: 387.

3. *N.Y. State Laws*, 20th sess. (1797), 19–20.

4. Ibid.

5. For the construction and early use of Newgate Prison, see the editorial note "Crime and Punishment in Federalist New York," above.

To Peter Augustus Jay

Albany 25 Novr. 1797

Dear Peter

Your Letter of the 17th. Inst.[1] came to hand Yesterday. On my Return from Schenectady the Day before, I rec^d. yours by Capt. Bogart— the Ice still detains his Sloop below—

M^r. Church may change the Glass at my Expence, but I should prefer having it done in the Spring ˄rather˄ than during the Winter, for I think it would *then* be better done. Let the carriage way by the Gate be paved with square Stone as you propose; and that either by the workmen of the Corporation, or others, as on Enquiry you may find most advantageous. I am satisfied with M^r. Green's arrangem^t for paying his Bond.

We are much obliged by M^{rs}. Cortlandt's ready and friendly Attention to your Sister's Cloak— if the Money you advanced should be insufficient, pay the Balance—or in other words, settle the Account. I doubt your having an opportunity of sending them by water— If not bring them with you, unless a very good opportunity of sending them should sooner offer— Delay is generally better than Risque— Your Punctuality and attention give us all much Pleasure. Little Sally is delighted with your Letter—[2] Wm. seems a little hurt at what he thinks a Preference in favor of Sally— he has been dictating to Mama a Letter to You, which one of these Days will be finished and sent to You.[3]

I wrote to You lately by Mr. Wills—[4] among other things for another Franklin, which I ˄now˄ suspect the Ice will not permit any of the Sloops to bring here.[5]

The Impressions made at New York by the late Proceedings of the Directory are similar to those which I find are made here, and probably throughout the U.S. in greater or lesser Degrees. That Transaction justifies Conclusions which strike me as being important—vizt. If the great and influential Leaders of the vanquished Party are perjured Traitors, it evinces that an extensive and corrupt Defection exists in France. If they are innocent, it follows that the Govt. of that Country is possessed by Men who do not deserve the Confidence either of that or of any other Country . . . In either case, there must be in the Republic an unprecedented & unparalled ~~Degree~~ ˄want˄ of virtue—

Remember to pay Capt. Farquhar what I owe him— I also owe yr. uncle Fœdy above £100, and he doubtless wd. be glad to recieve any part of it on acct.— Pay ˄him˄ as you find yourself in cash, and by no means expose yourself to Inconveniences on that head— You can depend only on what you have in Hand— future Payments like most other future things may be prevented or delayed by Contingencies not in our power to foresee or obviate— Your uncle can have no Reason to complain of Delay, even if he shd. not be pd. this winter. I am Dr Peter your affte. Father

John Jay

Mr Peter Augustus Jay

ALS, NN: Jay Family (EJ: 02934; EJ 09999). Addressed: "Mr. Peter Augustus Jay— / Government House / New York". Stamped: "ALBANY NOV 25". Endorsed: ". . .recd 29 Nov". C, NNGL (EJ: 90551).

    1. Letter not found.

    2. Letter not found.

    3. Letter not found.

    4. Letter not found.

    5. For more on JJ's acquisition of a Franklin stove, see his letter to PAJ, 2 Nov. 1797, and note 2, above.

From Peter Augustus Jay

New York 26 Nov.[r] 1797

Dear Papa

I have been amused for a week past with daily promises by the Agents of two Furnaces respecting the Stove you wrote for, there being none of that Kind to be had ready made— As I am informed the River is closed for a Distance below Albany, and as from the weather it is doubtful whether it will again be open I do not think it will be prudent to wait any longer— You had better therefore provide one in Albany—[1]

A few nights ago a Part of the stone floor of the Porch before the Gov[t] House fell thro'. Upon Examination the timber on which it was laid appeared perfectly rotten— As it was dangerous to leave it in that Situation I employed Bourdet to repair it, which is now nearly done— It was necessary to put new Plank under about one third of the whole Floor & I fear that the Rest will require the same Reparation in the Spring—

Yesterday being the Anniversary of the Evacuation was celebrated by the Military—[2] But there was much less Parade on the Occasion than has been usual—[3]

It is said that late Intelligence has been received from Amsterdam of the favorable Reception of our Envoys at Paris—

The Democratic Agents have already begun to electioneer in Westchester— Among other ingenious accusations which they have preferred against you are those of removing the Seat of Government to Albany[4]—of creating the new Office of Comptroller & of Abolishing all Justices courts in New York & thereby preventing the Poor from recovering their debt Debts—

From all I have been able to observe I augur well concerning the Election of Governor— But from the inactivity and indecision of the Friends of Government I fear there is some reason to apprehend a new Defeat in the Choice of Representative—

Uncle Fady is very unwell— Miss Dunscomb [who] is with him has been so ill that her recovery was dispaired of but is now much better— D[r]. Titford has purchased the farm at Bedford for £2500 & the Storehouse for 5200 dollars— M[rs]. Jay has agreed to sell her right of Dower in them to the Trustees for whatever D[r]. Kemp shall determine to be its Value The Price given by D[r]. Titford is to include this Sum— I am your affectionate Son

Peter Augustus Jay

Gov[r]. Jay

ALS, NNC (EJ: 06060).

1. For more on JJ's attempts to procure a Franklin stove, see his letters to PAJ, 2 Nov., and note 2, and 25 Nov. 1797, both above.

2. Evacuation Day marked the end of the seven-year British occupation of New York City. The anniversary of the British leaving the city on 25 November was celebrated as a civic holiday.

3. For local press coverage of the planning and events for the sixteenth anniversary of Evacuation Day, see *Daily Advertiser* (New York), 23 Nov.; *Greenleaf's New York Journal*, 25 Nov.; *Diary*, and *New-York Gazette* (both New York), 27 Nov.; *Argus, Greenleaf's New Daily Advertiser* (New York), 28 Nov. 1797.

4. For the removal of the state capital to Albany, see the editorial note "The Capital Moves to Albany," above

From Timothy Pickering (private)

Philadelphia Dec[r]. 13. 1797.

Sir,

Yesterday, in conversation with M[r]. FitzSimons (who, you will doubtless recollect, is one of the commissioners on the claims of British debts) he mentioned two questions of vast importance which were presented at the threshold of the business: one, ∧on∧ which side lay the *onus probandi* respecting the solvency or insolvency of the debtor—the other, whether interest should or should not be allowed during the war.

He remarked, that from the decided abilities of M[r]. M[c]Donald, one of the British Commissioners, he saw clearly that his opinion would govern his colleague; and he was *fearful* that another, on whom British attachments would naturally operate, would be *powerfully influenced*, if not decided, by the same opinion. Under these circumstances, he expressed his strong solicitude to obtain all possible light on the two leading questions above mentioned, and particularly to be possessed of your reasoning on the question of interest, in the judicial decision given by you in Virginia— His anxiety seemed the greater on account of the absence of his colleague, Col[o]. Innes,[1] who left this city in August, has been dangerously sick, and is not yet so far recovered as to be able to travel; and so much time has already been lost, it may not be practicable to postpone a determination of those two questions, much longer.

The free correspondence with which you have honoured me, induced me to tell M[r]. FitzSimons that I would write you on the subject, and request to be favoured with your argument on the question of interest. I presumed there would be no impropriety in your making the communication, or I should not have asked it: it may be under any injunction that you may think proper.

If you have time to suggest your ideas on the other question, Whether the

British creditor must prove the insolvency, or the American Government the solvency, of the debtor, at any given times, I know they would be gratefully received.[2] I am very respectfully Sir, your obt. servt.

Timothy Pickering

His Excellency John Jay.

ALS, NNC (EJ: 09503). Marked: "Private".

1. James Innes of Virginia.

2. On the debt commission in Philadelphia, see the editorial note "The Jay Treaty: Responses, Ratification, and Implementation," above. For the response, see JJ to TP (private), 23 Dec. 1797, below.

From Josiah Ogden Hoffman

New York Decr. 14. 1797

Sir

I concieve it my Duty to state to Your Excellency the Situation of and proceedings in the two Suits instituted against Mary Lindsley and others, and against Abraham Miller, by Samuel Fowler and Jonathan Lyman Citizens of the State of Massachusets for the Recovery of Lands situate within the Counties of Steuben and Tioga in this State, to which the Plaintiffs claim Title by Virtue of and under Grants from the State of Connecticut—.[1]

These Suits were commenced in the Circuit Court of the United States for the District of Connecticut— A Judgement by Default was obtained in the Suit against Abm. Miller— it has been waived and a Plea accepted— Pleas to the Jurisdiction of the Court are now interposed in both Suits averring that the Lands in Controversy are *in fact* within the State of New York, and that the Circuit Court of the United States for the District of New York, and the Courts of the State of New York have exclusive Jurisdiction of the Subject-Matter of Controversy— The Truth of this Plea is contested by the Plaintiffs and Issue is joined thereon—.

For the Purpose of trying this Issue Col. Hamilton and myself attended at the Circuit Court of the United States for the District of Connecticut, held at Hartford on the Eighteenth day of September last, the great Object of the Plaintiffs appeared to be to obtain a Trial by a Jury composed of the Citizens of the State of Connecticut. To prevent a Measure so adverse to the unbiassed Administration of Justice, and so hazardous to the Interests of this State, we thought proper to challenge the array of the Jury, and assigned two Reasons for Causes of such Challenge. 1. that the Deputy Marshal who had arrayed the Pannel of the Jury was a Citizen, Inhabitant, and Freeman of the State of Connecticut. 2. that he was a Claimant under the State of Connecticut of part of the Lands contained in the above mentioned Grant—

These causes of Challenge were severally insisted on as valid; and after a very lengthy Argument the Court thought proper to disallow the first, and to admit the last. By this Decision the Trial of the Cause in the State of Connecticut is merely postponed; and if the Judgement of the Court, which at that Time presided, should be hereafter confirmed, a Connecticut Jury will be competent to the Trial of the Question. Of the Legality of this Decision, the Counsel associated with me, and myself entertain, as we think well founded Doubts; but on a Question so extremely important to the Interest of this State, a Confidence in our own Judgement ought not to induce us to hazard a renewal of a Discussion which may lead, in the Event of a concurrence of Opinion by the next court, to a prejudiced hearing of the present Controversy—.

The principal Reason assigned by the Court for disallowing the first cause of challenge was, that the Laws of the United States had not made any provision for the Trial of a Cause Situated as this is, except by a Jury of the District from whose Court the Process had issued—. If no such provision really does exist, the propriety of one is manifest and the Interests of this State are so deeply implicated in the Subject, as to entitle it to the immediate Attention of its Government—.

In all Controversies similar to the present, it must be essential to a fair Decision, that the Supreme Court of the United States should possess the power of ordering the removal of the proceedings from the respective Circuit Courts in the several Districts, into the Supreme Court, to the End that a Jury may be summoned to try the cause, from a District of the United States not interested in the Controversy; or that some other adequate provision should be made for a Trial exclusive of the Jury of either State interested or concerned— A Representation of this Subject on the part of our Government in such a mode as shall be deemed the most eligible, to the Congress of the United States, it is presumed from its obvious Equity and Propriety, would certainly produce the desired effect, and thereby ensure to this State, a just and ample Decision of the present Question—.[2]

The Expences attending the Defence of these Suits have already been and will continue to be very considerable. From the Zeal of the opposite Party, we are to calculate on every possible exertion to promote their Success— They have employed, at very great Expence, Counsel of the first repute, and they appear to prosecute their Claim with great ardour and much apparent Confidence. From these Considerations I judge that the charges in the further Defence of this Business: will be rather enhanced than diminished: and I submit to your Excellency the propriety of some Legislative provision specially defining the Allowance to Witnesses— I have hitherto nearly confined myself to the Payment of their Actual Expences— they claim an additional Allowance, and it appears to me just that a reasonable one should be made to them—.[3] I have the Honor to be Your Excellency's most obedient Servant,

(signed) Josiah Ogden Hoffman

His Excellency John Jay Esq.

LbkC, N: Governor's Lbk. 1 (EJ: 03199). Heading: "Copy of the Attorney General's Letter".

1. For a full discussion of the legal points of these cases, as well as documents, see *DHSC*, 8: 178–270, *Fowler v. Lindsley*; *Fowler v. Miller*; *New York v. Connecticut*. *DHSC*, 1:1, *Fowler v. Lindsley*: in Docket, 521; in Fine Minutes, 308, 310, 315, 316; in Inventory of Case Papers, 585, 585n; in Notes for Docket Entries, 535; in Original Minutes, 463, 464, 467, 470, 471. *Fowler v. Miller*, same. *N.Y. v. CT*: in Docket, 523–24, 526, 528; in Fine Minutes, 317, 318, 320, 325; in Inventory of Case Papers, 585; in Original Minutes, 472, 473, 474. The New York plaintiffs were served with a writ by the Connecticut Circuit Court in September 1796, when JJ wrote to Hoffman, asking that he consult with AH and Richard Harison on the matter (JJ to Hoffman, 28 Sept. 1796, LbkC, N: Governor's Lbk. 1 [EJ: 03043]). Miller had requested JJ's assistance in the matter. See Miller to JJ, 24 Dec. 1796, LbkC, N: Governor's Lbk. 1 (EJ: 03060), and JJ to Josiah Ogden Hoffman, 23 Jan. 1797, (LbkC, N: Governor's Lbk. 1 (EJ: 03059). For the Connecticut Gore controversy in general, see *LPAH*, 1: 659–72; JJ to Thomas Mifflin, 6 Sept. 1796, above; JJ to Jonathan Trumbull Jr., 4 Dec. 1799, Dft, NNC (EJ: 08998); and JJ's Address to the New York State Legislature, 28 Jan. 1800, ADS, PHi: Gratz (EJ: 01135). For full citation, see JJ to Thomas Mifflin, 6 Sept. 1796, note 1, above.

2. JJ presented Hoffman's letter to the N.Y. Senate and N.Y. Assembly on 10 Jan. 1798. See *N.Y. Senate Journal*, 22nd sess. (August 1798), 20–21, and *N.Y. Assembly Journal*, 22nd sess. (August 1798), 38–39; *Albany Centinel*, 16 Jan.; and *Greenleaf's New York Journal*, 27 Jan. 1798. On 18 Jan., the Senate issued the following: "*Resolved*, as the sense of this Legislature, That for the due administration of justice, and in order to carry into effect the wise provision of the National Constitution upon this subject, it is necessary that a Law should be passed by the Congress of the United States, directing the mode of removing the aforementioned suits, and all others of a similar nature for trial, from the Circuit Court of the District, in which they may have been commenced, into the Supreme Court of the said United States, or at least making provision for the trial thereof by a jury taken from some District or Districts, other than those which comprehend the States that are interested in the question to be determined, with suitable precautions to secure the eventual controul of the said Supreme Court." *N.Y. Senate Journal*, 22nd sess. (August 1798), 21. See also JJ to Hoffman, 10 Jan. 1798, LbkC, N: Governor's Lbk. 1 (EJ: 03116).

3. New York State handled the legal fees for this case. See JJ's Message to the N.Y. Senate, 28 Mar. 1799, *N.Y. Senate Journal*, 22nd sess., 2nd meeting (1799), 109; and "An Act for the payment of certain Officers of Government, and other contingent expences," *N.Y. State Laws*, 22nd sess., 2nd meeting (1799), 837–44, particularly 843. For payments to Hoffman, see JJ to Gerard Bancker, 23 Dec. 1796, LbkC, N: Governor's Lbk. 2 (EJ: 03255); JJ to Samuel Jones, 6 Sept., LbkC, N: Governor's Lbk. 2 (EJ: 03270), and 30 Oct. 1797, LbkC, N: Governor's Lbk. 2 (EJ: 03271); and JJ to Hoffman, 25 Oct. 1797, LbkC, N: Governor's Lbk. 1 (EJ: 03102). Hoffman claimed that his financial difficulties at this time resulted in part from his expenses for this case. See JJ to Hoffman, 22 Oct. 1798, below, and Hoffman to JJ, 31 Oct. 1798, C, NNC (EJ: 08470).

To Timothy Pickering (private)

Albany 23 Decr. 1797

D^r. Sir

I have been fav^d. with yours of the 13 Inst:—[1] Having no Reason to expect that I should have occasion for any papers respecting causes tried before me in the Sup[reme] Court of the U. S. I left them at New York.

The written argument You allude to, did not comprehend the Question of *Interest*— it not being in Controversy among those on the Demurrer. On that Subject I made notes, but no formal written opinion or argum^{ts}.—not having those notes nor the necessary Books with me, I could not speedily do Justice to that point.

The Doubt "on which Side of the Question lays the onus probandi respecting the Solvency or Insolvency of the Debtor" appears to me to be a very extraordinary doubt— It is a well settled and universally rec^d. *maxim* that the Plaintiff or Demandant must shew his Right to the Thing he demands—and that he who claims to recover under a Statute or a Treaty must shew that his Case is within the Provisions of it.

The Creditor before he can charge the U.S. must shew

That *such a Debt* as is provided for by the Treaty of Peace, was *then* and still remains, in the whole or in part, actually due and payable to him; and that the amount due to him cannot now be actually obtained had and rec^d. in the ordinary Course of Justice[.] If the Debtor be insolvent, he must shew that the *Losses* he sustained by that Insolvency, were occasioned by Mislawful Impediments which took place contrary to the Treaty of Peace—

The *Insolvency* of the Debtor and the *Losses* resulting from it to the Creditor, are to be distinguished.

It is not to be presumed that any Debtor is insolvent— it must be shewn.

It is not to be presumed that an Insolvency, when proved to exist; was caused by the lawful Impediments in question— they were favorable to the Debtor.

The Creditor cannot charge the U. S. unless he further shews

That the Debtor was generally believed and reputed to be solvent, when the Impediments complained of took place.

That he did whatever a prudent and attentive Creditor should do (under such Circumstances) to recover or secure the Debt— That the Debtor took advantage of those Impediments to frustrate his Endeavours— That afterwards the Debtor by misconduct or misfortune, became insolvent, and therefore that the Governm^t. which interposed or permitted those Impediments is justly chargeable, not with the Insolvency but with the *Losses* occasioned by it to the Creditor.

That this opinion is well founded I percieve no Reason to Doubt and I would place it in various and strong points of Light, if the approaching Session of the Legislature, and of the Council of appointm^t. and some unfinished Business of the last Council of ~~appointment~~ ∧Revision∧ did not crowd such a variety of affairs upon me, as scarcely to allow Leisure for these hasty Lines— I am Dr Sir, yours sincerely,

John Jay

The Hon'ble Timothy Pickering Esqr.

ALS, MHi: Pickering (EJ: 04785). Addressed: The Hon'ble Timothy Pickering Esqr. Marked: "Private". Endorsed: ". . . rec^d. Jany 2 1798 / confirmation of the 6th article / of the British Treaty— relating / to British debts". Dft, NNC (EJ: 09504).

1. TP to JJ (private), 13 Dec. 1797, above.

Address to the New York State Legislature

[Albany, 2 January 1798]

Gentlemen of the Senate and Assembly,

IT must afford sincere and cordial satisfaction to our Fellow Citizens, to see the Representatives whom they have freely chosen, thus peaceably and calmly assemble, to deliberate on their common concerns, and to concert the measures most conducive to their common prosperity.

Nor will they derive less satisfaction from the reflection, that at this moment the Representatives of the Nation, of which this state constitutes an important member, are in like manner convened, and in harmony proceeding to consider and provide for our national interests.

This is an eventful and interesting period; and very important and impressive are the circumstances and considerations which render union, prudence and energy essential to the welfare, if not to the safety of the United States. May the great Author and Giver of good counsels, dispose and enable our governments and people to fulfil their respective duties wisely.

During the last Summer, an extraordinary occasion induced the President to convene the Congress— Their acts and Journals will be laid before you for your information. Among the acts there is one of which it is proper to make particular mention.

It is entitled "An Act authorizing a Detachment from the Militia of the United States."[1] By it the President is empowered to require of the Executives of the respective states, to take effectual measures, at such time as he shall judge necessary, to organize, arm and equip and hold in readiness to march at a moment's warning, the proportion of eighty thousand men assigned to them respectively.

In pursuance of this act, the President has been pleased to direct, that the quota of troops assigned to this state, should be held in readiness; and orders have been accordingly given, and in numerous instances have been complied with in a manner very honorable to the militia of this state.

It will not escape your observation, Gentlemen, that by this act the Executives of the several states are not only to organize, but also to *arm* and *equip* the detachments required of them. When on this, or any future occasion, such detachments shall be called to the field, it is not to be expected that they will be found completely armed and equipped. There will doubtless be deficiencies; and to me it appears proper, that the necessary supplies should be seasonably provided, and that they be managed in the manner best calculated to guard against waste and misapplication.[2]

On reviewing the internal affairs of the state, you will, I think, find it necessary to amend some of our existing statutes.

The act making alterations in the criminal law, and substituting the punishment of imprisonment, instead of death, for certain felonies, appears to me to have omitted either expressly to declare, or impliedly to decide, whether in any and what respects the convictions in those cases extinguish or affect civil rights and relations.[3]

The restriction in the act respecting Assistant Attornies General, which limits the appointments to counselors at law *resident* in the respective districts, has been and still is in one of the districts productive of inconvenience and embarrassment.[4]

The laws respecting quit-rents might in my opinion be amended by a provision, enabling the holders of land subject to it, to acquire at any time an exoneration from that charge, on just and reasonable terms. To me it appears advisable, that the proprietors of land throughout the state, should by the gradual operation of such a provision, be eventually placed in this respect on a similar and equal footing.[5]

Imperfections in the militia laws are frequently experienced; and the relation which this subject bears in the defense of the nation in general, and of this state in particular, places it in an interesting point of light.— The maxim that every nation ought to be constantly prepared for self-defence, is founded on the experience of all ages— it is true at all times, and under all circumstances— it is by the constitution of the state expressly recognized and adopted, and in strong terms enjoined as a duty on the Legislature. It deserves, therefore, to be considered whether the provisions made by the existing laws for this object, are sufficiently ample and adequate.[6]

Under color and cover of the act for defraying county charges, taxes are often so unequally assessed on unimproved wood land, and with such inexcusable waste and destruction collected, as to require legislative interposition. Every system of taxation is certainly defective and exceptionable, which does not afford the best checks which human prudence and human laws can devise, against partiality, fraud and oppression. That government cannot cease to attract and to preserve confidence and attachment, which leaves no rights without protection, no grievances without redress.

It is considered as a rule to which there are few exceptions, that when a law is treated with manifest and general disrespect and disobedience, it should either be repealed, or more competent means to enforce it be devised; a tolerated violation of one law naturally leading to and encouraging the infraction of others.

Altho' the obligation to observe and obey equal and constitutional laws, plainly results from our social compacts, and makes a part of the moral law, yet the statute prohibiting usury and limiting the interest of money, is notoriously and daily violated, and that, not only by those on whom such considerations have little influence, but even by too many of those whose characters and conduct are in other respects fair and correct.

There is also much reason to regret that more respect is not generally paid to the injunctions of the act relative to Sunday— If the Sabbath be, as I am convinced it is, of divine appointment, this subject ought not to be regarded with indifference.[7]

In a state so progressive as ours, new cases and exigencies will frequently arise, and require legislative provision.

At least two arsenals for the reception and safe keeping of military stores are thought to be necessary—one at New-York and another at this place. For the one at New-York, the corporation of that city have liberally and gratuitously granted to the people of the state a large, and valuable lot of ground and the Commissioners have my approbation to erect an arsenal on it.[8]

The situation of Albany, considered in relation to the other counties, to security and to the facility of transportation by land and water, seems to point it out as a proper place for an arsenal; and on a larger scale than the one proposed for New-York. If these ideas should meet with your approbation, the means of realizing them will of course be attended to.

The value and importance of the military stores, which will from time to time belong to the state, require that they should be well preserved, and also securely kept— Both these considerations unite in suggesting, whether these purposes can be so properly and œconomically effected as by a competent number of guards, carefully selected, organized and regulated. The utility of this measure becomes more apparent, on considering that it may be made subservient not only to the security and business of the arsenal, but also to the security of the state-prison; every escape from which, however caused, will in a degree counteract the purposes of that benevolent institution. Sound policy dictates that our present mild punishments should be made to produce by their *certainty* and *duration,* a portion of that dread which sanguinary ones impress by their *severity.*[9]

I forbear, Gentlemen, to press your attention to the great interests of Learning, Public Justice, Agriculture and Commerce; being persuaded that nothing will be omitted to render the Session useful to our Fellow-Citizens and honorable to their Representatives.

John Jay

PtD, *Albany Centinel, Albany Gazette,* and *Albany Register,* 5 Jan.; *Daily Advertiser* and *Commercial Advertiser* (both New York), *Northern Centinel* (Salem, N.Y.), 8 Jan.; *Greenleaf's New York Journal, Spectator,* and *Time Piece* (all New York), *Claypoole's American Daily Advertiser,* and *Porcupine's Gazette* (both Philadelphia), 10 Jan.; *Otsego Herald* (Cooperstown), 11 Jan.; *Federal Gazette* (Baltimore), 12 Jan.; *Federal Gazette* (Boston), 16 Jan. (extract); *Universal Gazette* (Philadelphia), 18 Jan. 1798; *N.Y. Assembly Journal,* 21st sess. (January 1798), [5–6]; *N.Y. Senate Journal,* 21st sess. (January 1798), 4–6; *NYGM,* 2: 397–402.

For legislative replies and JJ's responses to the replies, see *Albany Chronicle,* and *Albany Gazette,* 8 Jan.; *Commercial Advertiser* (New York), 12 Jan; *Argus, Greenleaf's New Daily Advertiser* (New York), and *New-York Gazette,* 18 Jan.; *Greenleaf's New York Journal,* and *Spectator* (New York), 20 Jan. 1798; *N.Y. Senate Journal,* 21st sess. (January 1798), 10–11; *N.Y. Assembly Journal,* 21st sess. (January 1798), 27.

1. "An Act authorizing a detachment from the Militia of the United States," 24 June 1797, *Stat.,* 1: 522.

2. For the efforts of the state government to properly equip its military forces, see the editorial note "Defending New York," above.

3. "An ACT relative to the Civil Relations of Persons sentenced to Imprisonment for Life," passed 29 Mar. 1799, declared felons sentenced to life imprisonment as "civilly dead to all intents and purposes in the law." *N.Y. State Laws,* 22nd sess., 2nd meeting (1799), 689.

4. "An ACT to amend the act entitled 'An act making provisions for the more due and convenient conducting public Prosecutions at the Courts of Oyer and Terminer and Gaol Delivery, and General Sessions of the Peace,'" passed 8 Jan. 1798, annexed New York City and County to the district composed of Suffolk, Queens, Kings, Richmond, and Westchester Counties. *N.Y. State Laws,* 21st sess. (1798), [243].

5. Lawmakers crafted reform legislation for quitrents in "An ACT concerning Quit-Rents" and "An ACT to exonerate certain persons from paying arrears of quit-rent," the former passed 16 Mar., and the latter 5 Apr. 1798. *N.Y. State Laws,* 21st sess. (1798), 307–11, 511–13.

6. For the passage of militia reform legislation during JJ's administration, see the editorial note "Militia Matters in New York State," above.

7. Lawmakers outlawed the sale of "strong or spirituous liquors, ale or porter" on Sunday, the Christian Sabbath. "An ACT to amend the act, entitled 'An act for suppressing immorality,' passed the 23d day of February, 1788," 3 Apr. 1798, *N.Y. State Laws*, 21st sess. (1798), 467–68, quote on 467.

8. For the construction of an arsenal in New York City and Albany, see the editorial note "Defending New York," above.

9. For security issues in the state penitentiary and JJ's views on issuing pardons, see the editorial note "Crime and Punishment in Federalist New York," above.

To Richard Lawrence

Albany 6 January 1798

Sir

Be so good as to inform me of the present Condition and number of the St. Domingo Refugees that if they require further Assistance, ~~to~~ the Necessity and Extent of it may appear with a proper Degree of Certainty— It will also be proper that your Account of the Expenditures made for them during the last year be exhibited and settled before I make any Communications to the Legislature on the Subject—for such Communications should be made & accompanied with full Information respecting the actual State of the Business—[1] I am Sir your most obedt Servt

John Jay

Mr. Richard Lawrence

LbkC, N: Governor's Lbk. 1 (EJ: 03115).

1. On 2 Jan. 1798, a payment of £400 for the support of the refugees was recorded. Lawrence's reply to JJ of 16 Jan. 1798, as noted by JJ's report of 25 Jan. 1798 to the Assembly, has not been found. In his report, JJ noted that "sum of money appropriated by the Legislature the last year for the support of the French Refugees from St. Domingo, residing in the city of New York, being nearly expended, I think it my duty to apprize you of this circumstance, and submit to your consideration the propriety of making a further and seasonable provision for those unfortunate individuals." *N.Y. Assembly Journal*, 21st sess. (January 1798), 67, 71; *NYGM*, 2: 405. JJ made a similar communication to the Senate on 13 Mar. 1798, noting that the "distressed situation of those unfortunate refugees being known to the Legislature, it cannot be necessary nor delicate to press their attention to considerations which their own humanity and benevolence will naturally suggest." *N.Y. Senate Journal*, 21st sess. (January 1798), 88; *NYGM*, 2: 413. It appears that Lawrence, in his capacity as a commissioner of the Alms House, was also receiving funds to aid refugees from the Common Council. *MCCNYC*, 2: 436, 438, 442. See also JJ's Addresses to the N.Y. State Legislature, 6 Jan. and [1 Nov. 1796]; JJ to Richard Lawrence, 23 Jan. and 9 Feb. 1797; and Lawrence to JJ, 27 Jan. 1797, all above.

From Ebenezer Stevens

New York 6 January 1797ʌ8ʌ

His Excellency John Jay
Dear Sir,

I have the honor to enclose Your excellency a return of the field artillery ammunition and small arms which I have received from the Commissioners appointed by the Legislature to procure the same and also of the issues therefrom to the different counties agreeable to your Excellency's orders—[1] I beg leave to inform your Excellency that fifty cases small arms recently missorted were damaged and incurred so much rust as made it absolutely necessary to employ a suitable person to clean and repair them— Mr Allen the person employed has done the needful and they are now in good order— The expense of which if it amounts to five per cent must be paid by the Underwriters but if less it will not amount to an average and in that Case the State must reimburse me— Your Excellency will permit me to observe that it is necessary to have the remainder of the small arms rubbed, oiled, and repacked— it cannot be any great expense and will preserve them for two or three years— I would also recommend five thousand Cartridge boxes that are water proof to be contracted for, which will cost at least ten thousand dollars if properly made and that one hundred rounds of Cartridges be provided for each piece, put up in proper order— I know there is sufficient powder and I beleive lead for the purpose, but with respect to the latter Mr Hunter can inform You— Of the eighty pieces of heavy artillery contracted for at Salisbury[2] twenty one have been brought to Governors Island and I beleive the remainder are nearly finished— Your Honor will see the propriety of having all those guns mounted as Commissioners have procured suitable and properly seasoned timber for that purpose which is now on Governors Island— I would recommend six of them being mounted on travelling field carriages for the use of this island, to prevent Ships going up the North or East river in case of a War and that Shot be provided for both the field and heavy artillery. Mr Mangin has furnished me with a plan for the intended arsenall at Potters field,[3] which I will send your Excellency the first opportunity, and has added his observations and explanations for the arrangement and completion of the (*whole*) Same—which I think judicious of which the whole or part can be put in execution, as may be judged proper. Some place is undoubtedly wanted for the artillery and military stores which are deposited at present in wretched hovels that make them continually in need of repairs and being so Very Valuable ought not to be without a proper place for their reception and preservation— Should the Legislature resolve to erect such a building it will be necessary to appoint a Maj[or] Gen of ordnance and Military stores and make suitable provision for defraying incidental charges— And as it is essentially requisite that some person should be appointed to instruct the different Companies in the proper use and management of field artillery and the implements attached thereto, I beg leave to recommend John McLean[4] (who was a Sergeant with me during the late war) as a person perfectly capable of this important task. He was requested by several companies the last summer to undertake a journey for the purpose of instructing them as they were conscious of inexperience which frequently endangers the lives of many and, in consequence of their repeated request did at his own expense undertake a journey to Ulster and Orange Counties and communicate instruction to the Corps of Artillery there. There are nine pieces of iron ordnance laying on Skids at the Battery— Six of them are six pounders and the other three are four pounders much eaten by the rust, and if Your Excellency thought fit to recommend to the legislature to have them sold it would be a good reason season to dispose of them— they cannot be of any use to the State as their Calipers[5] vary and are irregular—

It is essential that the legislature grant your Excellency a sum of money annually to be applied to the repairs of the Ordnance and military stores of every kind and defraying other contingent expenses, such as transporting Artillery, Ammunition &c. to the different Counties. Gov[r]. Clinton always had a grant of money for this purpose.[6]

I have presumed from the confidence Your honor has been pleased to place in me to make these representations and wishing You the Compliments of the Season Remain

Ebenezer Stevens

ALS, NHi (EJ: 00685). Endorsed. E, NHi: Stevens (EJ: 00684).

1. In March 1794, the New York State Legislature appointed Matthew Clarkson, James Watson, and Benjamin Walker (1753–1818) to a newly formed commission for the purpose of purchasing "field-artillery, arms, accoutrements, and ammunition," to be used by the state militia. These same appointees apparently remained at their posts during JJ's administration. In April 1797, JJ instructed that Ebenezer Stevens be the person responsible for the materials obtained by the commissioners. "An ACT to provide Field-artillery, Arms, Accoutrements, and Ammunition, for the Use of the Militia of this State," 22 Mar. 1794, N.Y. State Laws, (1777–97), 3: 222–23; Benjamin Walker to JJ, 20 Sept. 1796, LbkC, N: Governor's Lbk. 2 (EJ: 03241); JJ to Stevens, 21 Apr. 1797, LbkC, N: Governor's Lbk. 2 (EJ: 03257).

2. The cannon foundry in Salisbury, Conn., provided artillery pieces for New York State.

3. JJ notified Richard Varick in June 1797 that he was in favor of erecting an arsenal for New York City in Potter's Field. JJ to Varick, 30 June 1797, LbkC, N: Governor's Lbk. 1 (EJ: 03085).

4. John McLean (1755–1821) served in the New York 5th regiment during the war of independence, and oversaw powder stores in New York City during the post-Revolutionary era. In 1800, he was appointed as a first lieutenant in Stevens's Regiment of Artillery. McLean later went on to serve as commissary general for the state of New York. *MCCNYC*, 2: 89, 377; Hastings and Noble, *Military Minutes*, 1: 527.

5. A compass used to measure the caliber of shot. *OED*.

6. For more on military procurement in New York, see the editorial note "Defending New York," above.

From Richard Varick

New York January 10, 1797[8]. 7 OClock P.M.[1]

Sir

I have the Honor of once more troubling Your Excellency & perhaps calling a Moments Attention from more important public Concerns, to inform You of a Measure proposed to the Common Council of this City this Day by the Recorder & myself & by them unanimously adopted, to wit,

We have discovered by Experience that the public Business of the Sessions could not be dispatched in four Terms only of 7 Days; & none of the Magistrates have for some Time past appeared Willing to sit & try any Man at a *Justices* or *Bridewell Court*. And I having expressly declared that I will much rather *resign my Office* than again sit in a Court where *Myself & my Brethren* may stand accused before the Assembly of this State by the *Perjury* of *any Rascal* in the Community or be the Object of private Prosecution thro the *contemptible & officious Zeal* of even an *Alexander Hamilton* himself; the Recorder & myself agreed during the late Sessions to apply to the Common Council & induce them to apply to the Legislature at this Sitting for two additional Terms for our Sessions to wit, on the 1st. Tuesdays in April, June, August, October, Decr. & February, so as to avoid New Years day, the 1st. Day of May & 4th. July.—

2.— That a public prosecutor may be appointed for this City only &

3rdly. That the Bridewell may by Law be declared the Criminal Goal of this City & the prisoners be subject to the Keeper of the Bridewell, whereby we shall avoid great Expences in Maintaining Pris[one]rs. & the Expence of Watchmen to secure the Sheriffs Debtors & give Room to those who are imprisoned for Debt.[2]

The Representation to the Legislature was prepared & agreed to without Difficulty & will go up by this Conveyance to Mr. Comptroller to come into the Senate under his Auspices & that the Bill may be drawn by his correct Hand.—[3]

In Case we shall obtain a District Attorney I think it but a Discharge of my public Duty to mention to Your Excellency, that Mr Colden[4] has for 3 or 4 Sessions conducted M^r. Hoffman's Business & to the entire Satisfaction of the Court. His *Zeal, Application* & *Information* on the subject of public prosecutions is not to be surpassed by those of Any Gentleman at the Bar & as a Gentleman & Citizen he has equal Claims to any of the Younger Gentlemen of the Bar.

It would also be very eligible if the present Health Commissioners, especially Oothout and Abramse could be prevailed on to continue in Office.— The State will probably make *some* Compensation to them & they have a Claim ‸on‸ & I doubt not but they will receive some Compensation for their Services from the Corporation.— We have been silent hitherto lest our Conduct may stifle the *Generosity* of the Legislature. What I have expressed with Respect to the Commiss[ione]^rs. of Health more strongly applies with Respect to D^r. Bailey, who notwithstanding his Oddities, has many very valuable Traits of an excellent public Officer. He dose do his Duty, where others are *Mealy mouthed* I shall urge the Corporation to consider his Merits & services after the State have first paid his Actual Expenditures & compensated his public Services to the Community at large exclusive of this City, which I hope will be better considered than last hinted.[5]

The Corporation have agreed with Mangin our Engineer & Goerck, two of the City Surveyors[6] for an accurate Map, from present Measuration of all the City to the Whitestone, with *Elevation* &c^a. for $3,000, so that I hope soon to hear if not to see, of something effectual being projected about the Canal from the Hudsons River to the fresh Water Pond. It *works heavily* & I cannot envy the Appointment by the State of Commissioners to regulate that Part of the City.

I am persuaded that Your Excellency will be as weary of reading my two Letters[7] as I am at this Moment of writing I therefore beg leave to close by Requesting My Respects to M^rs. Jay & the Ladies & by Wishing You all the Compliments of this Season & many very happy Years—

Rich. Varick

His Excellency The Governor.

ALS, NNC (EJ: 09292).

1. Varick misdated this letter "1797".

2. The three provisions were approved by the Common Council on 10 Jan. 1798. *MCCNYC*, 2: 428–29.

3. The state legislature addressed these issues by passing a pair of laws on 2 Mar. 1798: "An ACT concerning the Court of General Sessions of the Peace, and the Gaol for Offenders, in and for the

city and county of New-York," and "An ACT more effectually to discover and apprehend offenders in the city of New-York," *N.Y. State Laws*, 21st sess. (January 1798), 280–82, 282–86.

4. Cadwallader D. Colden (1769–1834), was appointed as district attorney for New York's 1st District in 1798.

5. Oothout resigned in 1799; the rest stayed on. On the Health Commissioners and the Health Officer, as well as concerns about water supply, see the editorial note "John Jay and the Yellow Fever Epidemics," above.

6. Joseph F. Mangin and Cassimer T. Goerck worked as city surveyors in New York. *Longworth's American Almanack*, 189, 292.

7. Second letter has not been found.

Message to the New York State Senate

[Albany, 22d Feb. 1798]

Gentlemen,

I think it my duty to lay before you a petition[1] and a number of affidavits,[2] from which it appears, that in the town of Livingston, combinations of disorderly person have been formed to obstruct the course of justice and by force to exclude certain proprietors from the possession of lands which have been adjudged to them by the courts, and laws of the land; that the service of legal process is frequently and violently resisted, and that the sheriff and his deputies have in the discharge of their official duties been opposed, in a manner and to a degree very offensive to justice and subversive to good order.[3]

The first and obvious principles and objects of civil society, certainly demand that individual citizens be, without partiality, protected in the enjoyment of their property and other rights; and the honor and dignity of the State require that the authority of its laws be maintained, and the respect due it government preserved.

These circumstances and reflections induce me to recommend to your consideration, whether such extraordinary and daring combinations, do not call for more prompt and efficacious means of repressing them than our laws at present afford.[4]

John Jay

PtD, *Poughkeepsie Journal*, 6 Mar.; *Commercial Advertiser* (New York), 7 Mar.; *New-York Gazette*, 10 Mar. 1798; *N.Y. Senate Journal*, 21st sess. (January 1798), 66; *NYGM*, 2: 411–12.

1. Petition of John Livingston on behalf of himself & the Infant Heirs of Robert Livingston Deceased—Henry Livingston and Henry W. Livingston to the New York State Senate, [Livingston, 17 Feb. 1798], ALS on microfilm, N: Correspondence and Legislative action files (Series A1818).

2. Affidavits of Jacob Gaul and David Ingersoll, both 13 Feb. 1798, LS, NNC (EJ: 09850 and EJ: 09848); Peter Loucks and John Melius, both 15 Feb. 1798, LS, NNC (EJ: 09854 and EJ: 09853); James Lester and Nicholas Kline, both 16 Feb. 1798, LS, NNC (EJ: 09851 and EJ: 09852); John L.

Latham, 17 Feb. 1798, LS, NNC (EJ: 09849); John A. Baker and John Noyes, both 19 Feb. 1798, LS, NNC (EJ: 09847 and EJ: 09855).

3. The vast landholdings of Robert Livingston in the Hudson Valley were partitioned among four of his sons following his death in 1790. As explained by the above petition and affidavits, the section of the estate inherited by Henry Livingston was soon embroiled in conflict as tenants and local residents laid claim to the property. Throughout the first half of the 1790s, the tenants resisted largely in a peaceful manner by submitting petitions to the state legislature and by defending themselves in court against Livingston's attempts to evict them from the land. Matters worsened in the spring of 1797 as the tenants engaged in acts of ritual violence—physical assault, arson, intimidation—against the Livingston family, surveyors, officers of the law, and those tenants and lessees who complied with landlords. The Livingstons therefore sought assistance from the state, sending JJ a petition along with affidavits detailing the actions taken against their estate. See the affidavits listed in note 2, above; Henry Livingston to JJ, [c. 25 Jan. 1800], ALS, NHi (EJ: 00648); Brooke, *Columbia Rising*, 218–22; Humphrey, *Land and Liberty*, 129–35.

4. Upon learning of the disturbances at Livingston Manor, the state legislature issued a joint resolution in February authorizing JJ to mobilize the militia of Columbia County and surrounding areas to end the insurgency. Shortly thereafter, the governor complied and issued a proclamation ordering the militia to suppress any dissent and bring the protesters to judgement before a Court of Oyer and Terminer. Despite the efforts by New York authorities to restore law and order, it took some time before the insurgency finally fizzled out. Acts of resistance continued well into 1799, and Henry Livingston wrote again to the governor in early 1800 complaining of a tenant conspiracy against him and his family. *N.Y. Senate Journal*, 21st sess. (January 1798), 68; *N.Y. Assembly Journal*, 21st sess. (January 1798), 164–65; Proclamation on the Livingston Land Riots, [1 Mar. 1798], below; Henry Livingston to JJ, [c. 25 Jan. 1800], ALS, NHi (EJ: 00648); JJ's Address to the State Legislature, 28 Jan. 1800, ADS, PHi: Gratz (EJ: 01135), for full citation, see JJ to Thomas Mifflin, 6 Sept. 1796, above; Brooke, *Columbia Rising*, 222–23; Humphrey, *Land and Liberty*, 135–36.

Proclamation on the Livingston Land Riots

[Albany, 1 March 1798]

By His Excellency John Jay Esqr. Governor of the State of New York—

A Proclamation

Whereas it is the Duty and the Interest of the Citizens of this State, to respect obey and support the Constitution Laws and Government, which they have established for their own Security and Welfare— And it is also the Duty of those to whom the Execution of the Laws is confided, to exercise the Authorities vested in them with Fidelity and Decision— And Whereas both Houses of the Legislature of this State did on the 23^d. and 24th. Days of last Month concur in a Resolution expressed in the words following vizt.

"Whereas it appears by sundry Affidavits accompanying a Message from his Excellency the Governor,[1] that the regular Administration of Justice has been interr∧upt∧ed by numerous Combinations of Individuals in the Town of Livingston in the County of Columbia, and that the Deputies of the Sherif of the said County have been prevented from executing the Duties of their Offices in attempting the same—

Resolved that his Excellency the Governor be, and he is hereby requested to cause the Laws of the State to be enforced in the said Town of Livingston in the County of Columbia and to call out such Part of the Militia of the said County, or of any of the adjacent Counties, as he may think necessary for that purpose; and that the Legislature will make Provision therefor."[2]

And Whereas it is not improbable that divers of the Offenders have unwarily been misled and deceived by designing and interested Individuals, and if apprized of the Criminality and Consequence of their Conduct would return to a proper Sense of their Duty now therefore I have thought it proper to issue this Proclamation, and to exhort, to warn, and to command the said Offenders to forebear committing the like violences in future. And I do strictly enjoin and require the Judges, the Justices, the Sherif and all other Ministers of Justice in the s[d]. County to be vigilant and active in preserving the Peace of the free course of Law and Justice in the said Town—

To the End that means proportioned to the Exigencies of the cases may be seasonably afforded, I have directed the Adjutant General to transmit Orders to certain Commanders of Regiments and the Corps of Horse (who will be named to the Sherif) that they do respectively, and whenever the Sherif of the said County shall apply for the same, detach under the Command of a discreet officer, so many men well armed and equipped as Circumstances may in the Opinion of the said Sherif require; which Detachment or Detachments are forthwith to march and to aid and assist the said Sherif and the Magistrates in suppressing according to Law any Riots and unlawful and tumultuous Proceedings, and in apprehending all person concerned therein, or who shall do and offer any violence to the Sherif or his Deputies, or to any of the magistrates in the Execution of their official Duties— The said Detachments while on such Service will be allowed full Pay and Rations.[3] And I do hereby direct the Sherif of the said County whenever any such offenders shall be apprehended to inform me of it immediately, that a Commission of Oyer and Terminer may thereupon be issued, and the said offenders be without Delay prosecuted, and if convicted, be brought to exemplary Punishment—. Given under my Hand and the privy Seal of the State at Albany the first Day of March 1798 and in the 23[d]. year of the Independence of the United States— By His Excellency's Command David S. Jones Private Secretary

LbkC, N: Governor's Lbk. 2 (EJ: 03277); *Albany Centinel*, 6 Mar.; *Commercial Advertiser* (New York), *Mohawk Mercury* (Schenectady) and *Massachusetts Mercury* (Boston), all 13 Mar. 1798; *Northern Centinel* (Salem, N.Y.), 19 Mar. 1798.

1. See JJ's Message to the New York State Senate, 22 Feb. 1798, above.

2. *N.Y. Senate Journal*, 21st sess. (January 1798), 68; *N.Y. Assembly Journal*, 21st sess. (January 1798), 164–65.

3. JJ sent copies of the proclamation to John Noyes, the sheriff of Columbia County, with instructions to distribute them in public venues. JJ also enclosed a copy of his orders for local militia commanders and requested that Noyes keep him informed of events in the town of Livingston. The governor sent a similar message to John Livingston, the brother of Henry. JJ to Noyes, 3 Mar. 1798, LbkC, N: Governor's Lbk. 1 (EJ: 03126); JJ to Livingston, 1 Mar. 1798, LbkC, N: Governor's Lbk. 1 (EJ: 03127).

From John Trumbull

72 Welbeck S[t]. London March 6th: 1798

Dear Sir

The last letter which I have had the honor to receive from you is dated in Albany the 27th. Oct[r]. and the last which I wrote to you was of the 10th. December.—[1] Our Commissioners have not ˄been˄ received to an Audience in Paris, nor has any Negotiation with them been fairly opened:— Decrees more offensive than all the acts of which they had to complain have been passed under their Eyes,—and to me it appears, that we are in fact at war.[2]

I have at length the satisfaction of informing you, that my two American Plates are finished, and in a style perfectly satisfactory to me;— I had hopes of sending out their Impressions to my Subscribers by this Convoy, but it has been impossible to print a sufficient number to deliver to all, & as I can make no distinctions, I must suffer the whole to wait another Convoy when they will all be sent.[3]

In the mean time I have shipped on board the Mary Cap[t]. Allyn a Case directed for you of which the Bill of Lading is inclosed to D. Penfield, Esq[r]. with directions to convey it to you, & which contains a pair of Proofs of these Prints, of which I beg you will do me the honour to accept.—[4] I have to regret that the Talents which I had to employ in this work, were not more equal to the dignity of the Subject;—and that the times in which I live are so little favorable to its successful continuation With the highest respect I am Dear Sir, Your obliged Servant & Friend

Jn[o]. Trumbull

ALS, NNC (EJ: 07209). Addressed: "His Excellency John Jay Esq[r]. / Governor of the State of New York / New York / By the Mary / Cap[t]. Allyn". Stamped: "NEW YORK". Endorsed: ". . . ans[d] 26 May 1798"; *HPJ*, 4: 235–36.

1. JJ to JT, 27 Oct. 1797, above.

2. See the editorial note "John Jay and the Response to the XYZ Affair in New York," below.

3. JT hoped to capitalize, like his teacher Benjamin West, on his paintings of revolutionary war subjects by selling engraved prints by subscription. In April 1790, he offered the first two engravings, of the death of General Warren at Bunker's Hill and the death of Montgomery at Quebec. These were to be engraved by Johann Gotthard Müller (1747–1830) of Stuttgart. JT recollected in his *Autobiography* that his subscribers included "the president, vice-president, ministers, seventeen senators, twenty-seven representatives, and a number of the citizens of New York." However, the plates were not finished until 1797, and the final engravings not published until 1798. Perhaps due to the long delay, the project was not a financial success. JT wrote to GW on the same date, sending him his proofs [JT to GW, 6 Mar. 1798, DLC: Washington]. GW did not receive his prints (four sets) until February 1799. Trumbull, *Autobiography*, 164, 216, 218–19. See also, JJ's Memorandum to JT, 5 Feb. and JJ to SLJ, 13 Mar. 1795, both above, and PAJ to JJ, 1 Aug. 1798 (first letter), below.

4. Bill of lading not found. Daniel Penfield (1759–1840), a friend of the Trumbull family, was a merchant, revolutionary war veteran, and real estate speculator. Trumbull, *Autobiography*, 337.

Message to the New York State Assembly

[Albany, 21 March 1798]

GENTLEMEN,

IN pursuance of your resolution of the 19th instant,[1] I have taken measures to be informed of the present intentions of the government of the United States, relative to putting the city and port of New-York in a respectable state of defence—, on receiving that information, it shall be immediately communicated to you.

As the constitution of the United States has committed to our national government the power, and the means, & the duty of providing for the national defence, it is to be expected, as well as hoped, that due attention will be paid to the security of a city and port so obviously and essentially important, not only to this State, but to the United States.

But at this juncture, when prudence forbids delay, it, in my opinion, deserves to be considered, whether it would be advisable for the Legislature to adjourn, until they see this great object provided for; and whether existing circumstances do not justify a confidence that the United States will cheerfully assume the expense of such judicious measures as this State may take for that purpose.[2]

Urgent considerations also recommend that our supply of arms and stores be seasonably augmented, and made ample, and that no time be lost in perfecting those military arrangements and establishments to which menacing circumstances admonish us to attend— on these subjects, the Legislature already possess much information, and I expect soon to furnish you with additional details; at present, it may be proper to observe, that, according to an estimate made the last year, about sixty thousand dollars will be necessary to finish the fortifications on the three Islands in the harbour of New-York.

JOHN JAY

PtD, *Albany Centinel*, 23 Mar.; *Albany Chronicle* and *Albany Register*, 26 Mar.; *New-York Gazette*, *Daily Advertiser*, and *Time Piece* (all New York), 28 Mar.; *Philadelphia Gazette* and *Gazette of the United States* (Philadelphia), 29 Mar.; *Aurora General Advertiser* (Philadelphia), 30 Mar.; *Federal Gazette* (Baltimore), and *Spectator* (New York), 31 Mar.; *Delaware and Eastern-Shore Advertiser* (Wilmington), 2 Apr.; *Telegraphe and Daily Advertiser* (Baltimore), 3 Apr.; *Massachusetts Mercury* (Boston), 4 Apr.; *Connecticut Gazette* (New London), 11 Apr. 1798; *N.Y. Assembly Journal*, 21st sess. (January 1798), 255; *NYGM*, 2: 413–14.

1. On 19 Mar. the New York State Assembly resolved: "That his Excellency the Governor be requested to cause to be laid before the House an estimate of the sums necessary, and means to be adopted for putting the city and port of New-York in a respectable state of defence, and that he be also requested to inform this House whether there be ground to expect the cooperation of the government of the United States in defraying the expence attending this object." *N.Y. Assembly Journal*, 21st sess. (January 1798), 246.

2. The assembly adjourned on 6 Apr.; JJ called it back into special session on 2 July and addressed the new session on 9 Aug. See, below, and, for the background, the editorial note "John Jay and the Response to the XYZ Affair in New York," below.

From Timothy Pickering

Philadelphia, April 9. 1798.

Dr Sir,

The dispatches from our envoys in Paris being published this morning, I do myself the pleasure to inclose you a copy.[1] Unless the corruption of the French Government and their unjust, tyrannical, rapacious and insulting conduct towards the U. States shall rouse the indignant spirit of the *people*, our independence is at an end. The leaders of the opposition in Congress, while thunderstruck with the exhibition of these dispatches, acknowledged the justice and moderation & sincerity of the Executive in his endeavours to accommodate our differences with France: but to all appearance, they will still oppose efficient measures even of defence—certainly by sea,—and perhaps by land. Galatin professes to believe that our envoys have entered on a negociation, & that a treaty has ere this time been conducted. Mr. Jefferson says there is no evidence that the Directory had any knowledge of Talleyrands unofficial negociations! I am with great respect your obt. servant

T. Pickering

Governor Jay

ALS, NNC (EJ: 09505). *HPJ*, 4: 236.

1. See *Message of the president of the United States, to both Houses of Congress, April 3d. 1798* (Philadelphia, 1798; *Early Am. Imprints*, series 1, nos. 34812 and 34813). On 5 Apr. Congress ordered publication of five hundred copies of JA's message, together with the dispatches from the envoys to the French Republic. For the background, see the editorial note "John Jay and the Response to the XYZ Affair in New York," below.

To Timothy Pickering

Albany 10 April 1798

Sir,

Altho' your Letter of the 15 ult.[1] has lain thus long unanswered, it has not been forgotten. The one which came enclosed in it,[2] in Behalf of the Tuscaroras, was on the 26 ult: laid before our Legislature with a Message, of which the enclosed is a Copy—[3] Nothing material however has been done in pursuance of it—an opinion having prevailed, that our intended purchase of the Oneidas should first be compleated.[4] David[5] arrived here last Week, and delivered to me a Copy of that Letter. I told him how matters were circumstanced, and assured him of my Disposition and Intention to promote the object you recommend.

The *Dispatches* have given occasion to much Speculation & many Conjectures, as well as to their Contents, as the Reasons why they were not wholly or partially communicated to the Congress. Some of our Friends regret that they were with held untill they were asked for—but cogent Reasons doubtless existed. They now are where no Secrets ever were or will be kept—unless judicious Extracts from them (if not the whole) should be published by Authority, it would not be extraordinary if a thousand Stories half true and half otherwise, should be spread thro' the Country, and be adopted or rejected as they might happen to suit this or that Party. Some Circumstances said to be detailed in them, are already circulating— by some they are believed to be genuine, by others they are ridiculed—[6]

The public Mind is at this moment prepared by Sollicitude Suspense and Curiosity, to recieve deep Impressions. Our affairs require very delicate management, and I flatter myself that none of our measures will be injured by Precipitation on the one hand, nor by Indicision on the other— With great Respect & Esteem I am Sir Your most obt. Servt.

John Jay

The Honb. Timothy Pickering Esqr.

ALS, MHi: Pickering (EJ: 04786). Addressed: "The Hon'ble Timothy Pickering Esq". Endorsed: "Gov. Jay / April 10. 1798 / rec^d. 17. – Tuscaroras / Envoys Dispatches."

1. Letter not found, but the enclosed letter of the same date is cited below.

2. See TP to JJ, 15 Mar. 1798, FC, MHi: Pickering (EJ: 04852).

3. Enclosed copy not found. For JJ's message to the New York State Senate, see *NYGM*, 2: 410–11. Two leaders of the Tuscarora stopped in Albany in mid-February 1798 in transit to Philadelphia for a meeting with JA and TP. TP discussed the faithful service of Nicholas Cusick (Kanatijogh; Kaghnatsho) (1758–1840) and other Tuscarora during the war of independence and sought JJ's assistance with creating a homeland for them. TP further suggested that the Tuscarora, most of whom lived near Niagara, should be settled among either the Oneida or the Seneca communities in New York and that these groups should be encouraged by the state government to grant a portion of their property to the Tuscarora.

4. For more on the land transactions between New York and the Oneida, see the editorial note "Indian Affairs under Jay's Governorship," above.

5. Possibly David Fowler (1735–1807), Montaukett Indian leader of the Brothertown community, brother-in-law of Samson Occum (1724–92).

6. JJ had not yet received the printed texts of the dispatches from the envoys to France that TP sent on 9 Apr. See TP to JJ, 9 Apr. 1798, above, and for the background, the editorial note "John Jay and the Response to the XYZ Affair in New York," below.

John Jay Wins Reelection as Governor in 1798

By late 1797 the Republicans were mobilizing to build on their rising electoral strength in New York City and the opposition to the Jay Treaty to challenge Jay's reelection for governor and replace him with his former long-time friend turned Republican opponent, Robert R. Livingston. As Federalist physician and author Elihu Hubbard Smith reported to Senator Uriah Tracy of Connecticut on 29 Nov. 1797: "In our own State, the political campaign is soon to open. Lately, we have recovered more courage, & think that there is less to fear from the change in the Representation—from this city in particular, than was originally apprehended. A very stren[u]ous effort, however, will certainly be made, at the ensuing election, to substitute Chancellor Livingston for Mr. Jay: perhaps with effect. The adherents of the first are confident of success—but nothing certain can be augured from their expectations."[1]

The campaign for Jay's reelection formally opened in March 1798 as various local committees of Federalists met to nominate him for governor. The first to meet was a large Federalist group that included many members of the legislature. Chaired by Leonard Gansevoort, it assembled in Albany on 6 March, nominated Jay for governor and Stephen Van Rensselaer for lieutenant governor, and appointed a committee to support their election. The election committee composed a circular letter dated 9 March and addressed

"To the Electors of the State of New York" that was printed in newspapers throughout the state.[2] Republicans met in New York City, in Albany and elsewhere in March and nominated Livingston as their candidate for governor and Van Rensselaer for lieutenant governor. They too formed an election committee to support their candidates that prepared a circular letter attacking the earlier Federalist circular as improperly composed by a "legislative committee" and depicting Jay and his treaty as the cause of conflict with France. It further condemned his administration for appointing only its supporters and for removing opponents from office.[3]

Although not as personal and bitter as the previous Jay campaigns, the 1798 campaign was an intense one because it was viewed as a referendum on John Adams's defense policy toward France and the response to the XYZ Affair.[4] As negotiator of the Jay Treaty, to which Republicans attributed French hostility to the United States, the governor was attacked for his inveterate opposition to France and his alleged support for war with that country, and blamed for the taxes raised to provide for state defense. Livingston on the other hand was depicted as a peacemaker and longtime supporter of France. Most opposition to Jay's reelection focused on these issues.[5]

The campaign itself was generally peaceful, though newspapers reported the beating of one Livingston supporter, William Keteltas, in Herkimer. Federalists subsequently printed a broadside allegedly found in Keteltas's possession labelled "War! War! War!," that depicted Jay as a warmonger.[6] At the same time Jay's fitness to serve as commander-in-chief for the state was challenged as newspapers recalled his flight from Esopus to Connecticut during a British attack in 1777.[7]

Complaints about other aspects of his earlier life and career also were resurrected. One was the charge that he had refused to accept paper money in payment of debts during the 1780s, in defiance of state legal tender laws. Allegations that Jay had asserted there should be only two classes, the rich and the poor, made during the 1792 campaign, were revived. Republicans induced Jay's former law clerk and agent John Strang to sign two affidavits on 23 March 1798. One stated the Jay had sent Strang to Westchester in 1792 to warn Daniel Horton against making such statements.[8] The second reproduced a model bond Jay developed on his return from Europe in 1784 that stipulated that every loan payment should be "in good gold or silver coin, and not in paper, or other fictitious money, notwithstanding that the same should be made legal tender by act or acts of the legislature of the state of New York."[9] Strang's affidavits were published in the newspapers and circulated as broadsides.

In response to Strang's allegations of Jay's statement regarding rich and poor, the governor directed Peter Augustus Jay to locate copies of the deposition he had obtained and published in 1792 denying that the deponents had ever heard him make such a statement. Once found, these were published in the newspapers to disprove Strang's charge. Jay's supporters also denied that his bond specifying payment in specie defied tender laws, but contended it merely sought to hold his debtors to honorable repayment of the true value of their loans. They also asserted that the bonds were developed in Jay's capacity as an executor for his father's estate, which had lost 10,000 pounds during the war to depreciation of the currency, and as trustee for the funds of his blind brother and sister, Peter and Nancy Jay.[10]

In the course of challenging Jay's defenses, his opponents also revived references to old family disputes and depictions of Jay adopted by his estranged brother-in-law Brockholst Livingston. Jay's alleged vindictiveness and refusal to forgive his brother (James Jay, or possibly Frederick), and brother-in-law, Brockholst, were raised, as well as his purported greed and preoccupation with money as shown by his determination to be paid in specie.[11] To charges that Strang was a traitor to his former benefactor, it was alleged that Jay in fact had failed to pay Strang for services performed. Strang was at this time in financial difficulty; he was arrested for debt and then released under a state insolvency law in 1799. His accounts recorded Jay family debts to him, the legitimacy of which the family denied.[12]

The election was held the end of April, but canvassing of the votes to obtain the official count lasted until mid-June 1798. Newspapers reported votes from the various districts as they came in, and by mid-May most newspapers reported Jay was the probable winner, though Republicans did well in the congressional and legislative elections.[13] Once Jay's election was declared on 12 June, celebratory receptions were held in Albany and, as Jay traveled to New York City, also in Poughkeepsie. Jay reached New York City on 23 June and met with federal officials on defense policy.[14]

1. Smith, *Diary*, 395.

2. On the meeting of 6 Mar. and circular letter of 9 Mar. by JJ's supporters, see *Daily Advertiser* (New York), 17 Mar. 1798.

3. On the meetings and circular letter of RRL's supporters, see *New-York Gazette*, 15 Mar. and 23 Apr.; *Time Piece* (New York), 21, 23, 30 Mar.; *Greenleaf's New York Journal*, 31 Mar., 7, 12, 14, 17, 18, 21, 23 24, 25, 26 and 27 Apr.; *Albany Register*, 30 Mar. and 2, 6, and 9 and 16 Apr.; *Albany Chronicle*, 2 and 9 Apr.; *Poughkeepsie Journal*, 10 Apr. 1798; and *Commercial Advertiser* (New York), 23 and 26 April; and PAJ to PJM, 19 Feb. 1798, Dft, NNC (EJ: 90162). See also "Verity"'s attack on the pro-Jay circular letter in the *Albany Register*, 2 Apr. 1798. According to PAJ, JJ's supporters produced another circular letter in response to the Republican circular, then decided against disseminating it. PAJ to JJ, 15 Apr. 1798, below.

4. Personal enmity and rivalry, however, was not entirely absent on RRL's part in the contest for the governorship. Writing from Albany to AH, Philip Schuyler remarked that Livingston was "Assiduous in blackening Mr Jays Character." Schuyler to AH, 31 Mar. 1798, *PAH*, 21: 387–88. Abigail Adams remarked on this display to her eldest son: "An insatiable Ambition devours the Chancellor. To see Mr. Jay stand higher in the publick estimation and Elected chief over him; fills him with the same sensations, which Milton put into the mouth of the Arch fiend. 'Better to Reign in hell, than serve in Heaven.'" Abigail Adams to JQA, 27 May 1798, MHi: Adams.

5. For instance, Livingston and his political allies warned that the 1794 Treaty and subsequent Federalist policies would bring the United States and Britain into a close relationship that was sure to cause an "impending rupture" with France. Schuyler to AH, 31 Mar. 1798, *PAH*, 21: 387–88.

6. For the attack on William Keteltas (Ketteltas) at Herkimer, N.Y., see his letter of 26 Apr., originally printed in the *Albany Register* of 30 Apr., and reprinted in *Greenleaf's New York Journal* of 9 May 1798. See also *PAH*, 21: 468–69. For the broadside he purportedly circulated, see *Crisis. To the People of New York. War! War! War!* ([New York] and [Albany] [1798]; *Early Am. Imprints*, series 1, nos. 48406 and 33277). For additional attacks on JJ's role in the Jay Treaty and the consequent conflict with France, and for support for RRL as the peace candidate, see also "A Republican," in the *Time Piece* (New York), 20 Apr., and "Victory," 24 Apr. 1798, in the *Time Piece* (New York), 25 Apr. 1798. Other disruptive activities responding to the XYZ Affair and defense measures, such as those at the Society for Free Debate, were also believed to be related to the election campaign.

7. For publications challenging JJ's military knowledge and courage and mentioning his flight to Connecticut in 1777, see "An Elector," *Albany Register*, 20 Apr., *Greenleaf's New York Journal*, and *Argus, Greenleaf's New Daily Advertiser* (New York), 21 Apr. 1798. "An Elector" included a broad range of attacks on JJ's career and governorship. He condemned JJ's anti-immigrant and anti–religious freedom proposals during the state constitutional convention. He also took JJ to task for his disobedience to his instructions to consult France during the peace negotiations. "An Elector" further cited hostile British actions since the signing of the Jay treaty, before criticizing certain of JJ's actions as governor, such as requesting an act declaratory of his powers with regard to appointments, his proposal for pensions for judges, and his appointment of former Tories to office.

8. On the depositions of JJ's Westchester neighbors of 1792, and Strang's affidavit regarding them, see *Albany Centinel*, and *Albany Gazette*, both 27 Apr.; *Northern Centinel* (Salem, N.Y.), 7 May 1798. For the deposition as published in 1792, see Joshua Purdy, Ezekiel Halstead, and Daniel Horton to the Public, [5 Apr. 1792], and note 1, *JJSP*, 5: 388–89. For JJ's directions to locate the 1792 depositions, see JJ to PAJ of 6 Apr. 1798, ALS, NNC (EJ: 90216).

9. For the bond and Strang's affidavit regarding its use, see PAJ to JJ, 19 Apr. 1798, below; *Greenleaf's New York Journal*, 4 Apr. 1798. See also "Investigator," *Albany Register*, 23 Mar. 1798; and "Philo-Investigator" in *Albany Register*, 30 Mar. 1798, which depicted JJ as brooding "over his good gold and silver coin with all the solicitude of a miser."

For JJ's statement as President of Congress of 13 Sept. 1779 expressing confidence that paper money would be redeemed that was cited by "Investigator" to contrast with his statement on tender laws in 1784, see *JJSP*, 1: 667–78.

10. For defenses of JJ's postwar policies on paper money, see "A.B." in the *Albany Centinel*, 3 Apr.; and "Obscure Individual" to "Mr. Investigator," *Albany Centinel*, 6 Apr.; "Monitor" to "Philo-Investigator", *Albany Centinel*, 13 Apr., and *Albany Register*, 16 Apr. See also "Tickler"'s reply to "Monitor," in *Albany Register*, 23 Apr.; and "A Tickling for the Tickler," in *Albany Centinel* and *Albany Gazette*, both 27 Apr., and the *Albany Register*, 30 Apr. 1798.

11. For references to the Jay family conflicts, see "A Tickler" replying to "Monitor," *Albany Register*, 23 Apr., and "A Tickling for the Tickler," *Albany Register*, 30 Apr. 1798.

12. For allegations that JJ was no benefactor to Strang, but in fact his debtor, see "A Tickler," *Albany Register*, 23 Apr. 1798. For Strang's insolvency and allegations of Jay family indebtedness to him, see JJ to PAJ, 7 Dec. 1799, ALS, NNC (EJ: 10030); PAJ to JJ, 26 Nov. 1799, ALS, NNC (EJ: 06088); and 21 Aug. 1800, ALS, NNC (EJ: 06095); Dft, NyKaJJH (EJ: 09974). Just when Strang and JJ became estranged is unclear. "Monitor" claimed that Strang abused and forfeited JJ's confidence, was dismissed, and was seeking revenge. *Albany Gazette*, 13 Apr. 1798.

13. For the various local election returns published in May and June, see, for example, *Greenleaf's New York Journal*, 30 Apr., 5, 15, and 30 May, 6, 9, 13, and 27 June; *Daily Advertiser* (New York), 5, 6, 7, 8, and 11 June; and *Spectator* (New York), 9 May and 13 June 1798. On 13 June the *New-York Gazette* reported that JJ had won reelection with a majority of 2,380 votes. For a more detailed breakdown of the state's voting patterns for the 1798 gubernatorial election, see *A New Nation Votes*, https://elections.lib.tufts.edu/catalog/tufts:ny.governor.1798 (accessed July 2018).

On Republican legislative and congressional victories, see PAJ to JJ, 7 June 1798, ALS, NNC (EJ: 06068); and Abigail Adams to Thomas Boylston Adams, 21 July 1798, ALS, MHi.

14. For the celebrations and JJ's travel to New York City, see Address from the People of Poughkeepsie to JJ, 18 June 1798; and JJ to William North, 25 June 1798, both below.

From Peter Augustus Jay

New York April 15th 1798

Dear Papa

I had the pleasure of rec^g: your Letters of the 6th, 7th, & 9th. inst on Friday, & another which accompanied the Pardon for M^r. Meeks's Man yesterday—[1] I shall immediately attend to the different directions contained in them— Most of the Prints are already very neatly boxed; the Cases containing Copies of the U. S. Laws I have put on board Bleeckers Sloop (the same in which Maria came down) & taken the enclosed Receipt— She is to sail tomorrow— I will be obliged to you to mention which of the Books are to be left with me in Order that I may have Boxes made accordingly—Ruckel is waiting to fill up more Lots, but wishes to proceed with those he has already undertaken before he fixes upon the Terms, I shall however endeavor to bring him to some Agreement—

I feel much disappointed about Popes House— There is only one Applicant & he refuses to give more than £30 unless a back building is to be added this Summer in which Case he would pay £40— I see Bills on the doors of a great many Houses near it—

M^r. Munro has found the original of the Affidavit you mention; inclosed is a Copy—[2]

The Committee appointed to promote your Election had framed & *signed* a circular Letter in answer to that published by their Opponents—[3] But after reconsidering the Measure, they determined that it was unnecessary &

that their Triumph would be greater to succeed without ~~it~~ having descended to any Altercation, & therefore suppressed— This was told me by M^r. Cruger, who is a Member of the Committee & who differed in opinion from his Colleagues—

Capt: Brett arrived yesterday & brought Maria a Letter from Mamma.[4] His Sloop did not come up to the dock till Night, so that I have not yet got the trunks from on Board— My Love to Mamma Sisters & William— I am your Affectionate Son

Peter Augustus Jay

Govr. Jay

ALS, NNC (EJ: 06063). Stamped: "New York / April / 16." Endorsed: ". . . rec^d: & an^d. 15 19 ap. 1798". Dft, NNC (EJ: 10034). Enclosures not found.

1. JJ to PAJ, 6 Apr., ALS, NNC (EJ: 90216). Letters of 7 and 9 Apr., and one relating to a pardon for Mr. Meek's man, not found. In his letter of 6 Apr., JJ informed PAJ that there was a bill before the state assembly that would probably pass to rent out Government House, the public residence in which JJ and his family lived before moving to the new capital at Albany in September 1797. Many of the family belongings remained in their former house, and JJ directed PAJ to prepare to empty the premises. For the legislative decision on 5 Apr. to rent out Government House, see *N.Y. Senate Journal*, 21st sess. (January 1798), 130, 140; *N.Y. Assembly Journal*, 21st sess. (January 1798), 323–24.

2. On the affidavit JJ requested in his letter of 6 Apr., see Joshua Purdy, Ezekiel Halstead, and Daniel Horton to the Public, 5 Apr. 1792, *JJSP*, 5: 388–89; and, for the background, see the editorial note "The Disputed Election of 1792", *JJSP*, 5: 353–59. For the relevance to the 1798 campaign, see the editorial note "John Jay Wins Reelection as Governor in 1798," above.

3. On the committee to support JJ's election of which Nicholas Cruger was a member, and on the circular letter of RRL's supporters, see the editorial note "John Jay Wins Reelection as Governor in 1798," above.

4. No letter has been found from SLJ to Maria Jay dating from early 1798.

To Peter Augustus Jay

Albany 16th. April 1798

Dear Peter

I have rec^d. your's of the 10th.—[1] M^r. Tiebout the Engraver,[2] is desirous of publishing a Print from my *last* Portrait by Stuart, and I have given ~~him~~ ^s^ ^Brother^ a Letter to you mentioning my having consented to his having the Loan of that Picture for that purpose. I now repeat it that you may not at *present* have the Trouble of putting it up in a Case.

The moment the Election is over speak to Hallet[2] about selling my Coach, with or without the Harness, for the Stable I have here is too small to recieve that & the other Carriages I have, & I can here do without it.—[3] I say, *after the*

Election is over, because our adversaries would not omit to make even such a Circumstance the Subject of animadversion.

I herewith send, wrapped up in a Paper tied with red Tape, a pair of Slips or Galoshoes, which I had made here last winter, to supply the Place of those I had then inadvertently left at NYork— I send them for your Uncle Peter— That little Bundle together with this Letter will be committed to the Care of the Comptroller,[4] who expects to sail Tomorrow.

Nobody here on our Side seems to doubt the Success of the Election, & there prevails a Degree of Confidence and Security, which may expose it to Hazard— for my own part I am neither sanguine nor anxious.[5]

How deep and how general the Impression ~~made~~ expected from the Publication of the Dispatches from Paris will be, is yet to be decided. I should not be surprized if the leading Partizans of France should see nothing in them to inculpate the *Directory* or *nation*. A strong Delusion seems to be spread over this Country— whether it will now be wholly or how far dissipated, is difficult to calculate or even conjecture.[6]

If there be, as there probably is, some new and interesting Pamphlet, I think you would do well to send a Copy to Genl. Schuyler. Remember us to your Cousin Munro and Maria. I am your affe[ctiona]^te. Father,

John Jay

Mr Peter Augustus Jay

ALS, PC (EJ: 07347).

1. Cornelius Tiebout (c. 1777–1832), a New York–born engraver, learned engraving as an apprentice to the silversmith John Burger, publishing maps, subject plates, and line portraits after 1789. In 1793, he went to England for training in stipple engraving. While in London, he engraved and published a portrait of JJ in April 1795, after the Stuart/Trumbull portrait. He returned to New York in November 1796. After 1799, he moved to Philadelphia, working there until 1825, after which he moved to Kentucky, where he died. The above proposed engraving was never made. See David McNeely Stuaffer, *American Engravers upon Copper and Steel* (New York, 1907), 1: 271–72; Carrie R. Barrett and Ellen G. Miles, *Gilbert Stuart* (New York, 2004), 123; SLJ to JJ, 2 Aug. 1794, and note 3; and Walter Robertson to JJ and JJ's reply, both 15 Apr. 1796, all above.

2. Probably James Hallet, a former coachmaker in New York City. *Daily Advertiser* (New York), 23 Feb. 1792; *New-York Gazette*, 5 Aug. 1797.

3. For more on the sale of JJ's coach, see JJ to PAJ, 19 Apr. 1798, below; and 26 Jan. 1799, ALS, NyKaJJH (EJ: 09978).

4. Samuel Jones.

5. See the editorial note "John Jay Wins Reelection as Governor in 1798," above.

6. On the publication of the dispatches from the envoys to France, see TP to JJ, 9 Apr. 1798, above, and the editorial note "John Jay and the Response to the XYZ Affair in New York," below.

To Timothy Pickering (private)

Albany 19 Ap. 1798

D^r S^r.

I am very much gratified by your friendly attention in sending me the Copies of the Dispatches from, and of the Instructions to, our Envoys at Paris, which came enclosed in your Letters of the 9 and 11 Instant.[1]

The Demands and Language of the French Government will form an extraordinary Page in modern History; and however palliated or expounded, cannot fail to excite the Indignation of honest Men in this and every other Country. More Time than has as yet elapsed, is necessary to ascertain their general Effect on the public mind— for my own part I suspect there is too much Reason to infer from *certain Declarations* that some of the Leaders of the antifœderal party will continue to be impelled by private Interest as well as party Zeal to adopt and persevere in reprehensible Measures— many well meaning People err for want of knowing the Truth—but there are others to whom this Remark is not applicable—

The Instructions are in my opinion ably drawn, and do Honor to the administration. The publication of them will certainly promote if not effect unanimity. With great Esteem & Regard I am Dr Sr Your most ob^t. Servt.

John Jay

The Honble Timothy Pickering Esqr

ALS, MHi: Pickering (EJ: 04787). Marked: "private". Addressed: "The Hon'ble Timothy Pickering". Endorsed: ". . . rec^d. 25th / Dispatches from / & Instructions to / our Envoys in Paris."

1. On the instructions to and dispatches from the envoys to France, see TP to JJ, 9 Apr., above, and the editorial note "John Jay and the Response to the XYZ Affair in New York," below. TP to JJ of 11 Apr. not found.

From Peter Augustus Jay

New York 19 April 1798

Dear Papa

I yesterday rec^d. your Letter of the 16th inst:[1] & the Bundle which accompanied it— The latter shall be sent to Rye by the Boat—

I am almost sorry you intend to dispose of the Coach,[2] & should prefer parting with the Chariot which in a few years more will be unfit for use, or at any Rate a constant Bill of Cost— Besides that the former will probably sell for much less than its Value— I shall however pursue your Directions with Respect to it—

Your Picture is already cased. But no great inconvenience can arise from opening it provided M^r. Tiebout will take it as it is to his own house—³

I wish much to know what part of the Furniture is to be sent to Albany. M^r. Munro I believe has room for all the Articles, and M^r. Cruger has sent to inform me that I might put what I pleased in his Store—

A Meeting has been held at Bedford where D^r. Hale was nominated as Representative in Congress, and Maj^r. Lyons, M^r. Teed, Saml. Youngs, M^r. Mead & M^r. Robart as Members of Assembly— M^r. Barker has since been substituted in the place of the last who declined— I fear that not more than one or two will succeed of the whole Number nominated—⁴

I hear that Handbills are circulating thro' the County containing Strang's Affidavit & form of an Obligation, but with little or no Effect—⁵

Maria & all our Friends are well— Please to remember me affectionately to Mama & Nancy— I am your affectionate Son

Peter Augustus Jay

Govr. Jay—

ALS, NNC (EJ: 06064). Addressed: "His Excellency / Governor Jay— / Albany—" Endorsed: ". . . ans^d. 25 ap 1798".

1. See JJ to PAJ, 16 Apr. 1798, above.

2. Ibid., for JJ's instructions to sell his coach.

3. Ibid., for Tiebout's plans to engrave a print of the JJ portrait by Gilbert Stuart.

4. For the meeting held at Bedford on 16 Apr., see *New-York Gazette and General Advertiser*, 20 and 23 Apr., and *Commercial Advertiser* (New York), 21 Apr. 1798. Dr. Mordecai Hale was the local Federalist candidate for Congress, and Samuel Lyon, JJ's estate manager, and Charles Teed, Samuel Youngs, Enoch Mead, and John Robart were Federalist candidates for the assembly. Barker was probably John Barker, an incumbent assemblyman for Westchester. Of this group, only Charles Teed (variously spelled Tridd, Tidd), an incumbent, was elected. The other winners for the assembly for Westchester were Abel Smith, Elijah Lee, William Adams, and Israel Honeywell. See the *Spectator* (New York), 6 June; *Hudson Gazette*, 12 June. 1798.

5. On John Strang's affidavit of 23 Mar. with a copy of a model bond developed by JJ as trustee for the Peter Jay estate in 1784 specifying repayment of loans in specie rather than paper money regardless of state legal tender laws, see the editorial note "John Jay Wins Reelection as Governor in 1798," above.

From Peter Augustus Jay

New York 26 April 1798

Dear Papa

I have this Afternoon put on board Capt Lansings Sloop 15 Barrels of Wine, 1 Case of Flasks with d^o Nine Boxes of Prints & Pictures & small Articles of Glass & China & one small black trunk— I have sent you all the wine except two Barrels whose hoops appeared too insecure to be trusted— I will send you a List of the Contents in a Letter by Capt. Lansing—[1]

I have just returned from the Society for free Debate & tho' it is very late, I cannot forbear to mention the Occurrences that have just happened there— This Society was lately instituted, in all probability with the intention that it should be converted into a Jacobin Club. A Committee of Managers was appointed consisting with only one or two Exceptions of Violent Democrats: These preside in Rotation— Every Person who will pay a Shilling becomes for that evening a Member—[2] The Chairman for this Meeting happened to be John Swarthout,[3] one of the Antifederal Candidates as Assemblyman— Upon going into the Room almost by Accident I found it entirely filled by a great Croud of People who were listening to a Discussion of this Question "Is it ∧most∧ expedient under existing Circumstances to lay an Embargo, or to arm our Vessels in Defence of our carrying Trade?" A M͏ʳ. Davis, One Butler an irish Shoemaker, & D͏ʳ. Smith brother to the late Chief Justice of Canada, supported the propriety of an Embargo in long & inflammatory Speeches,[4] and were answered by M͏ʳ. Brown a sensible Quaker, M͏ᶜDougal a Painter and a young but really eloquent Man of the name of Howe, a Student at Princeton College—[5] It was easy to perceive from the Applauses & Hisses bestowed upon the Speakers that tho the Question had been chosen with a View to influence the Election & a great number of Democrats were present, that a vast Majority were Federalists & would decide in favor of Arming— The Chairman was in many instances evidently partial, & in all of them overruled (tho' not without much Noise & Riot) by the Society— Finding how Matters were going, he proposed that on account of the lateness of the hour, the final Decision should be deferred until the next Meeting; this being negatived he took the Question on a Motion for Adjournment which being also lost, he by Virtue of a power which he said was vested in him by the Constitution adjourned us— The Society nevertheless ~~nevertheless~~ remained & directed the Constitution to be read which was found to confer no such Authority— The Chairman was then obliged to resume the Chair & put the final Question which was carried in favor of arming by at least five to one— Having pronounced the Decision with an Appearance of extreme mortification & anger, he refused to hear any other Motion & again left the Chair— M͏ʳ. Howe then moved that a Committee should be appointed to form an Address from the Meeting to the President & Congress of the U.S. approving of the Measures which have been pursued with Respect to France & expressing a determination to support them— Col: Morton being placed in the Chair the Motion was carried And M͏ʳ. Cozine, Col: Morton

M^r. Evertson Col: Stevens & M^r. Hoffman appointed the Committee—[6] And then after a fruitless attempt by Peter R. Livingston[7] to call another Meeting to consider the Address which might be reported, & after three Cheers the Society separated—

This Circumstance induces me to give more Credit to the Assertions of our Friends who are confident that the whole of the federal ticket will be carried in this City— I am your Affect^c. Son

Peter Augustus Jay

Gov. Jay

ALS, NNC (EJ: 06065). Addressed: "His Excellency / Governor Jay / Albany". Stamped: "New York / Apr. / 27". Endorsed: "P. A. Jay— / 26 apr. 1798—". E, *HPJ*, 4: 238–40.

1. Letter not found. For more on shipments of goods up the Hudson River to the Jay family home in Albany, see the editorial note "The Capital Moves to Albany," above.

2. The Society for Free Debate was apparently modelled on a debating society by the same name in London that followed similar procedures. See Mary Thale, "London Debating Societies in the 1790s," *Historical Journal* 32 (February 2009), 57–86. It was formed in March 1798 as a public forum to debate contemporary issues. It met every Thursday at 7 PM at Hunter's Hotel, and was open to "such persons as are fond of discussion." Topics were selected at the previous meeting and announced to the public. Selection of the topic "Would it be better policy, under existing circumstances, to lay an embargo, than arm in defense of our carrying trade", placed the society into the center of national and local political controversy. Each party apparently sent many supporters, and between four hundred and five hundred people attended, by far the largest number to that point. Although the chairman for the event, John Swartwout, was a Republican and sought to promote the embargo over defense measures, the Federalists predominated, blocked proposals to postpone a decision, and obtained an overwhelmingly high vote in support of JA's defense measures. Following the meeting the Federalists formed a committee to compose an address to the president and Congress. On the formation of the society, see *Argus, Greenleaf's New York Journal*, 10 Mar. 1798. For additional depictions of the events at the meeting of 26 Apr., see *Daily Advertiser* (New York), 28 and 30 Apr.; *New-York Gazette* 28 Apr. and 1 May; "Leonidas," and a satirical account signed by "Citizen Anti-Jacobin," both in the *Commercial Advertiser* (New York), 28 Apr.; and the response to "Leonidas" by "L" in *Greenleaf's New York Journal* and the *New-York Gazette and General Advertiser*, both 2 May; the *Time Piece* (New York), 2 May; and "Z" responding to "Miltiades," in *Greenleaf's New York Journal*, 3 May 1798.

On the following Thursday, 2 May, the society met again and after discussing an "uninteresting question", the Republican group called James Nicholson to the chair and sought to reverse the decision of the previous week on the question of arming for defense, but each side so interrupted the other that little could be accomplished. According to one Republican piece, the "friends of order" (Federalists) at the meeting "menaced" the Republicans, broke the banister and benches in the gallery and some of the glass in the neighboring doors. Most Republicans departed and the meeting adjourned. The society sought to restore its reputation by publishing a statement of its true purposes and a copy of its Constitution. See *Greenleaf's New Daily Advertiser* (New York), 3 May and 5 May 1798, the latter of which included the comment that the truest criteria of the political wishes of the public would be seen in the New York election returns. See also *Carey's U.S. Record* (Philadelphia), 8 May 1798.

A piece calling for the restoration of the society on proper principles appeared on 17 May, and a notice appeared for a debate to be held on 22 May. However, after such upheaval it appears the society ceased to function, as no further notices for its meetings appeared. *Argus, Greenleaf's New Daily Advertiser* (New York), 17 May; *Commercial Advertiser* (New York), 22 May 1798.

3. John Swartwout (1770–1823), a New York City merchant and staunch supporter of Aaron Burr, was elected to the assembly in 1798. He is best known as Burr's second in his duel with AH, and for a lengthy duel with DeWitt Clinton in 1802.

4. Matthew Livingston Davis, secretary for the Society for Free Debate, a printer, and an editor of the Republican New York newspapers *Evening Post* (1794–95) and *Time Piece* (1797–98), was a friend and strong supporter of Burr, and later his editor and biographer. See Jerome Mushkat, "Matthew Livingston Davis and the Political Legacy of Aaron Burr," *New-York Historical Quarterly* 59 (April 1975), 123–48. The other pro-embargo speakers were probably one of two John Butlers, the first listed as a boot- and shoemaker, and the second as a lady's shoemaker, and Dr. James Smith, brother of former chief justice William Smith (1728–93). See *Longworth's American Almanack*, 138.

5. One of the speakers on behalf of defense measures may have been Hugh McDougall, owner of a paint and oil shop at 92 Broadway. *Longworth's American Almanack*, 237. Neither Brown, the sensible Quaker, nor Howe, the Princeton student, has been identified.

6. For the address dated 30 Apr. by the committee members Jacob Morton, Ebenezer Stevens, John Cozine, Nicholas Evertson (1766–1807), a New York City lawyer, and Josiah Ogden Hoffman expressing support for JA's measures, and JA's reply of 8 May, see *Daily Advertiser* (New York) of 10 May and *Spectator* (New York), 12 May 1798.

7. Peter Robert Livingston (1766–1847), of Rhinebeck, Dutchess County, N.Y., a state senator, 1815–22, 1826–29, assemblyman, 1823, and lieutenant governor of N.Y., 1828.

From Peter Augustus Jay

New York 6 May 1798

Dear Papa

I have at length compleated the evacuation of the Gov.[t] House & taken Possession of my Rooms at M[rs.] Wests from whence I now write—[1] The Trouble of moving which was much greater than I expected to find it, prevented my writing during the last week. I sent you a number of Articles by Capt: Dusenberry, all those that remain are at M[r.] Munro's, who has had one of his unfinished rooms floored on purpose to put them in. Both he and M[rs.] Munro have given us every Assistance in their Power. Aunt Livingston's Furniture Books &c I have sent to M[rs.] Rutgers. Had she not given me permission to do this I should have been greatly embarrassed— It was not till after every thing had been moved that we heard any ∧thing∧ from Aunt; Maria then rec[d.] a Letter from her saying that she did not Know what we would do with her things, & requesting us to send her Ivory Cabinet & a few other Articles to M[rs.] Cortlandts— Mama's Instructions came also too late But fortunately they had been in most instances anticipated— Avery has moved into the house, which I suspect he will find ill calculated for his Business—

He has lett the Stable as a pot ash Store for £100 per A[nnu]m. M^r. Munro has taken the Hay that was in Bundles, for which he is to pay whatever it cost. As I do not Know the Price you gave for it I will be obliged to Mama to send me an Account of it— Upon examining the Chair I do not think it is adviseable to repair it And as you do not want the Cart & have no place to put it in I should think it best to sell that also—

I am mortified to tell you bad News of Popes House. The Carpenter who offered £30 for it has contented himself with taking Rooms elsewhere & I have not even heard of another Tenant— You have the Consolation however (if it be such) to have Companions in Misfortune, several other houses being in the same Situation—

I have received $30 of Pingree on account of Rent & of Arnot $25 and a Dividend of $225 on your Shares in the N. York Bank And I have paid for insuring the Stone Street House $66.94—

I mentioned in a former Letter the Proceedings had at a Meeting of the Soc^ty. for free Debate—² On last Thursday the Democrats mustered their whole Strength to carry a Vote of Censure on those Proceedings— The fœderal party apprized of the Design appeared also in great force to frustrate the Attempt— The Democrats tho' the smaller Number with surprizing Impudence placed Commodore Nicholson in the Chair & by this Procedure occasioned a Scene of the greatest Noise & Confusion I have ever witnessed. The adverse parties were frequently on the point of a general Engagement. Many of our most respectable people were present; but no one was heard— If a Speaker began by addressing himself to the Chairman he was stopped by one party & by the other if he did not— After this State of Confusion had continued from before Nine till long past Eleven, the Federalists divided from their Opponents & having an evident (the not large) Majority, the Commodore adjourned the Meeting which immediately dissolved—

Last evening a Meeting of *Young Men* was held at the Assembly Room in William Street where 900 or 1000 attended & a Set of animated Resolutions were unanimously passed— I am one of a Committee to draft an Address to the President— Many Antis were present, but had the Prudence to observe a profound Silence— Every Symptom was exhibited of ardent Attachment to the Gov^t. & violent *Hatred* to France and our Democrats— If they were guilty of any fault it was in carrying Matters too far—³

Betts to a great Amount have been laid on your Election at the odds of ten to one in your favor— I am your Affect[ionate]: Son

Peter Augustus Jay

Govr. Jay

ALS, NNC (EJ: 06066). Dft, NNC (EJ: 10036).

1. Here in text, a bracket has been inserted in another hand, accompanied by this text: "ₐBegin again on 3ᵈ. page at #ₐ" and on the third page "#. . . . ." is inserted at the words "I mentioned in a former Letter. . ."

On the legislative decision to lease Government House, JJ's previous home as governor, see JJ to PAJ, 16 Apr., and note 1, above. The house was leased by John Avery, manager of the Tontine Coffee House, and used as a public boarding house. See *Porcupine's Gazette* (Philadelphia), 8 May; *Bee* (New London), 16 May 1798.

2. On the tumultuous meeting of the Society for Free Debate, see PAJ's letter to JJ of 26 Apr. 1798, above.

3. On the formation of the Young Men's group in New York and the address prepared by PAJ, see PAJ to JJ, 13 May 1798, and notes, below. On addresses of support for JA and opposition to France, see also the editorial note "John Jay and the Response to the XYZ Affair in New York," below.

To Peter Augustus Jay

Albany 10ᵗʰ. May 1798

Dear Peter

I have recᵈ. Yours of the 26 ult. The one by Capᵗ Dusenbury, and this morning that of the 6ᵗʰ. inst:—[1] a variety of affairs induced or rather constrained me to postpone writing to you until now; & I have been hitherto so constantly interrupted that it is uncertain whether I shall be able to finish this in Time for the post.

Tell Mʳ. Munro that I am very much obliged to him for assisting you so effectually in removing our Effects from the Govᵗ. House;[2] and being at the Trouble and Expence of flooring one of his unfinished Rooms for the purpose of receiving them. I am glad Mʳˢ. Rutgers consented to take the articles belonging to your aunt. altho avery has rented the Stable so well, I suspect he will be disappointed in his Expectations of Proffit from the House—

There was in the House a writing Table with many Drawers & in them I think there were Papers, which I am not certain of having taken out when I left the House— You have probably attended to this— if not—don't forget it— continue your Endeavours to rent Popes House; and be not too nice abᵗ. the Price.

I am satisfied that the broken Chairs and the Cart should be sold. as to the pressed Hay— your Cousin is welcome to have it—

You did well to mention the Details of certain proceedings of the Society for free Debate— They are interesting— I am glad a proper spirit is rising in N York— it should be encouraged, and yet so managed (if possible) as rather to conciliate than disgust and repel— The *Young Men* do themselves

Honor; but being *young* it would ∧not∧ be unnatural if they should carry some things rather too far.[3]

Of the Issue of the Election— I cannot find sufficient Data to form a decided opinion upon— I believe however that the Chancellor will not succeeded and had not his opponents been very indiscreetly secure and confident, and consequently remiss, the majority against him would have exceeded our Calculations as well as his—[4]

I sometime ago hinted to You the propriety of showing some marks of attention to General Schuyler—[5] If you could write to him something of an interesting Nature which he w^d. not probably be ∧so∧ soon informed of by others— or if you were to send him some new pamphlet &c.—the purpose would be answered— It is useful as well as proper to manifest a Disposition to remember and return Civilities— we are all well— I am Dear Peter your very aff^te. Father

John Jay

Mr Peter Augustus Jay

ALS, NNC (EJ: 90218). Addressed: "M^r. Peter Augustus Jay / at M^r. Munro's Office / New York". Endorsed: "Letter from Papa / Albany 10 May 1798 / an^d. 15 May". Stamped: "Albany May 11 98". Additional Notes: "15 / rec^d. 15 May".

1. For PAJ's letters to JJ of 26 Apr. and 6 May 1798, see above.

2. On the evacuation of JJ's property from Government House, his home as governor while in New York City, see PAJ to JJ, 15 Apr. 1798, and note 1.

3. On the formation of the Young Men's group in New York, see PAJ's letters of 26 Apr. and note 2, and 6 May, both above, and 13 May 1798, below.

4. For the outcome of the election, returns for which were beginning to be listed in newspapers, see the editorial note "John Jay Wins Reelection as Governor in 1798," above.

5. Letter not found.

To Timothy Pickering

Albany 13 May 1798

D^r. Sir

It is said that the Naturalization Act is to be revised and amended.[1] Permit me to suggest an idea which I have for many years deemed important. We doubtless may grant to a Foreigner just such a portion of our Rights & Priviledges, as we may think proper. In my opinion it would be wiser to declare explicitly, that the Right & Priviledge of being elected or appointed to, or of holding and exercising any office or place of Trust or power, under the United States, or under any of them, shall not hereafter be granted to any

Foreigner— But that the President of the U. S. with the consent of the Senate, be nevertheless at Liberty to appoint a Foreigner to a military office— I am Dear Sir Your most ob.[t] Serv.[t]

John Jay

The Honble Timothy Pickering Esq.[r]

ALS, MHi: Pickering (EJ: 04788). Dft, NNC (EJ: 90219); *WJ*, 1: 407; *HPJ*, 4: 241.

1. The original Naturalization Act of the United States, adopted on 26 Mar. 1790 (*Stat.*, 1: 103), limited naturalization to free white persons of good character and stated that children of U.S. citizens born abroad would be considered as "natural born citizens," except for those whose "fathers had never been resident in the United States". It required a two-year residence in the United States and one year in the state of residence before applying for citizenship. That act was replaced by the Naturalization Act of 1795 (*Stat.*, 1: 414), which extended the residence requirement to five years in the United States.

On 2 May 1798 Harrison Gray Otis of Massachusetts had proposed a resolution in the House of Representatives denying future naturalized citizens the right to hold any office of honor, trust, or profit, and Christopher G. Champlin (1768–1840) of Rhode Island had objected that this might bar service of foreigners in the army and navy and such a limitation should only apply to civil offices. James Goodhue Harper of North Carolina advocated limiting citizenship in future exclusively to those born in the country. Neither measure was adopted (See *PTJ*, 30: 301n; *Annals*, 8: 1568–69). The Naturalization Act adopted on 18 June 1798 (*Stat.*, 1: 566–69), one of the Alien and Sedition Acts enacted at that time, extended the residence requirement for citizenship to fourteen years. The Naturalization Act of 1802, adopted 14 Apr. 1802 (*Stat.*, 2: 153), returned the residence requirement to five years. For JJ's fear of foreign influence and longtime opposition to officeholding by the foreign born, see the editorial notes "John Jay and the Constitutional Convention of 1787", and note 11, *JJSP*, 4: 465, 466–67n11; and "John Jay and the Response to the XYZ Affair in New York," below.

From Peter Augustus Jay

New York 13 May 1798

Dear Papa

It is now some time since I had the pleasure of hearing from you— this I attribute to your having been at Schenectady where I perceive by the Papers you was present at the Commencement—[1]

M.[r] Seth Marvin[2] some time ago applied to me to purchase your Share of Lot N.[o] 18 in Cheesecocks Patent (containing as he says 195 Acres) for which he offered 24/pr. Acre, but it appeared during our Conversation that he had given 30/per for the adjoining Lot. I promised to write to you on the Subject & he was to call the end of this Month to know the Result—

Maria is very anxious to go to Rye & I am no less so not having been there since Christmas— If possible I shall go with her the last of this Week— When we last heard from there Dinah was dangerously ill— her Death would be a serious Misfortune to Uncle—

I have obtained a Copy of a Calculation made by the Livingstons, by which the Chancellor is to succeed by a Majority of 940— they nevertheless refuse to bet on the event of the election at a smaller difference than ten to One—[3]

In my last Letter I mentioned that there had been a Meeting of Young Men, & that I was one of a Committee to draft an address to the Pres.: This Meeting was called by an Individual without any previous preparation & conducted with all the Inconsideratiness of Youth— And the Committee composed of persons accidentally nominated, contained only one who had the smallest Interest among the Mechanics or lower Class of People. They all live in the same Neighborhood & are prohibited by an express Resolve from Soliciting Signatures

It was agreed that each Member should Draft an Address & it is perhaps an additional proof of their Indiscretion that mine was preferred— I was obliged to draw it in Haste & already perceive in it, when it is too late to remedy them, a Number of Defects— This Circumstance shews the Wisdom of the Advice you have often given me to cultivate Composition with more Assiduity— Great pains have been industriously & too successfully taken to prevent the Mechanics from signing it— They are led to believe that it is equivalent to an Inlistment— We have however upwards of Six hundred Subscribers &, among them all the young men of Respectability in the City—[4]

On Friday Evening there was another Meeting when it was agreed that Measures should be taken in Concert with General Hughes[5] to acquire Military Knowledge— This may serve as a temporary Expedient to preserve our present Enthusiasms, but I have too little Opinion of youthful Constancy to expect from it any permanent Benefit—

On the same Evening the Officers of the Brigade assembled at the Request of General Hughes & with only Six Dissentients agreed to address the President— This Step appeared to me so contrary by to the Principles by which military men ought to be governed that I could not prevail on myself to join in it— To undertake in our Military Capacity to control, condemn, or even approve the Measures of the Government or any particular Branch of it, I supposed a very pernicious Example— I take it to be our Duty to obey implicitly every Command of our Rulers however inexpedient or to resign our Commissions— There was no one whom I could consult on the Occasion— But being determined ∧not∧ to act contrary to my own Conviction & unwilling on many Accounts to oppose the Address after the Meeting had been called, I thought it most prudent to stay away from it—[6]

In Philadelphia, black Cockcades are much worn as marks of Attachment to Government— a few have been introduced here & it has become a Question how far it is expedient to adopt them— Numbers of those who have hitherto been unfriendly to us, especially the more timorous who love to swim with the tide are desirous of changing Sides as far as their pride will allow them— But they cannot yet agree to wear the Badge of a Party to which they have always been Enemies— The Propriety of widening the existing Differ[ences/*torn*] between the Parties & in a Degree shutting the Door again[st] Converts seems to be Questionable— On the other Hand it is w[*torn*] that the Crisis has arrived when the friends of their Country ought to separate from its Enemies, that every Man ought to declare his Sentiments & be treated according as they are proper or otherwise— that the Badge will be a Bond of Union among those who wear it, & a Pledge which they cannot forefeit without Disgrace & finally that it will infuse fear into the disaffected— Col: Hamilton approves of the Cockade but neither he nor any Gentleman of Note puts it on & unless they do it will never become general— However trifling this Subject may appear, it may not be unimportant in its consequences—& I should therefore be very happy to Know your Sentiments respecting it—[7]

You have doubtless heard already of the Death of Mr James Jones & the Papers will inform you of all the Circumstances of that unfortunate event—[8] My Love to Maria & Nancy— I am your very Affect: Son

Peter Augustus Jay

Govr. Jay

ALS, NNC (EJ: 06067). Addressed: "His Excellency / Governor Jay/Albany". Stamped: ". . . May/ 14". Endorsed: "P.A. Jay / 13 May / an^d. 25 May / 1798 / wrote p^r post 25 May—". Dft, NNC (EJ: 11347). No letter from JJ to PAJ of 25 May has been found, but much of JJ's letter of 17 May, below, appears to reply to this letter.

1. JJ attended the commencement for Union College in Schenectady on 2 May 1798. See *Albany Centinel*, 8 May; *Commercial Advertiser* (New York), 12 May 1798.

2. Col. Seth Marvin of Orange County, New York.

3. For JJ's victory over Robert R. Livingston in the gubernatorial election of 1798, see the editorial note "John Jay Wins Reelection as Governor in 1798," above.

4. For an account of the meeting of the Young Men of the City of New York on 5 May 1798 and the appointment of PAJ to a committee to prepare an address to the president, and for notices of the circulation of the address for signatures, see *Commercial Advertiser* (New York), 7 and 8 May; and the *New-York Gazette*, 10 and 11 May 1798. PAJ's discussion of the quality of his address may have been prompted by a newspaper piece criticizing it as excessively long and poorly worded; and proposing an alternative text that appeared in the *New-York Gazette* of 12 May. Nevertheless, it was his that was adopted, signed and delivered to JA. On the early meetings of the group, see the *Commercial Advertiser* (New York), 7, 10 and 18 May; *Daily Advertiser* (New York), 7 and 22 May; and *New-York Gazette*, 14, 15, and 24 May 1798. For published copies of the address and JA's reply of 26 May, both of which were read to the assembled Young Men's group on 31 May, see the *Commercial Advertiser* (New York), 31 May; *New-York Gazette*, 1 June; *Daily Advertiser* (New York),

2 June; *Argus, Greenleaf's New Daily Advertiser* (New York), 4 June; *Spectator* (New York), 6 June; *Philadelphia Gazette*, 12 June; *Columbian Centinel* (Boston); and *Virginia Herald* (Fredericksburg), 20 June 1798.

Such groups and their addresses of support originated in Philadelphia and spread to other cities, including Boston and Baltimore, and Reading, Pa.; all the addresses and JA's replies were widely published. In New York the Young Men's group also sought military training and practiced military exercises first at the Battery and subsequently on the green of Columbia College. That all did not go smoothly at first is indicated by an admonition for greater disciple and punctuality published by a committee of the Young Men's group. The Young Men also planned and paraded as a group in a Fourth of July celebration held at the Battery. See *Philadelphia Gazette*, 20 June; *Federal Gazette* (Baltimore), 25 June; and *New-York Gazette*, 18 and 28 June 1798. For JJ's comments on the Young Men's group, see JJ to PAJ, 17 May 1798, below.

5. James M. Hughes commanded the Brigade for the City and County of New York.

6. For JJ's agreement with PAJ that the military should not make political addresses to the president or otherwise involve itself in politics, see his letter to PAJ of 17 May 1798, below. For more on JJ's views of the state militia, see the editorial note "Militia Matters in New York State," above.

7. Federalists supporting defense efforts against France often wore black cockades, while French supporters traditionally wore tricolor ones. For references to the use of the black cockades by Philadelphia's Young Men's group and discussions of the desirability of promoting use of the black cockade, see *Albany Centinel*, 15 May; *Mirror* (Concord, N.H.), 22 May; *New-York Gazette*, 28 June 1798. According to PAJ, the New York Young Men's group voted that only those undergoing military training should wear the black cockade. See PAJ to JJ, 7 June 1798, ALS, NNC (EJ: 06068); Dft, NNC (EJ: 10052). Ultimately, a black cockade with an eagle in the center was adopted as an insignia for the U.S. army, and also later worn by the New York state militia. See *PGW: RS*, 3: 192, 261; *PAH*, 22: 246, 361; 24: 127; "An Act further to amend the Laws relative to the Militia of this State," 30 Mar. 1799, *N.Y. State Laws*, 22nd sess., 2nd meeting (1799), 747. For JJ's comments on the cockades, see his letter to PAJ of 17 May 1798, below.

8. James Jones, brother of Dr. John Jones, was killed in a duel by JJ's estranged brother-in-law, Henry Brockholst Livingston, after confronting Brockholst over his publication of a mocking article in the *Argus, Greenleaf's New Daily Advertiser* (New York), of 11 May falsely alleging that Jones, a man nearly 60 years old, had attended the meeting of Young Men. See "A Fair Statement," *Commercial Advertiser* (New York), 11 May; *Greenleaf's New York Journal* and *Spectator* (both New York), 12 May; *Time Piece* (New York), 14 May; *Centinel of Freedom* (Newark), 15 May; *New-Jersey Journal* (Elizabethtown), 15 May; *Guardian; or New–Brunswick Advertiser*, 15 May; *American Mercury* (Hartford), 17 May; "A Fair Statement of the late unfortunate Rencontre at New York," *Boston Price-Current*, 17 May; *Albany Centinel*, 18 May; *Salem Gazette*, 18 May; and *Oriental Trumpet* (Portland), 23 May 1798. Brief notices appeared in the *Massachusetts Mercury* (Boston), 15 May; *Newport Mercury* , 15 May; *Bee* (New London), 16 May; *Minerva* (Dedham), 17 May; *Chelsea Courier* (Norwich), 17 May; *Columbian Museum* (Savannah), 18 May; *Vermont Gazette* (Bennington), 18 May; and *Oracle of the Day* (Portsmouth), 19 May 1798, and subsequently in several other newspapers. The statement by Jones's friends ran in the *Gazette of the United States* (Philadelphia), 14 May 1798.

Here in the Dft, PAJ excised the following paragraph: "I am sorry to observe among the last appointments in the Militia several of the violent oppositionists— These men are grateful only to ₜₕₑ Colonels who recommended them & exert all the influence derived from their Commissions to injure the hand that bestowed them— The Adjutant you have appointed to Col: Boyd's Reg^t: ~~deliv~~ I am told delivered an Oration last night to the Tammany Soc^y. containing Principles wh. w^d. have been thought inflammatory, even during the time of our ~~most~~ democratical fervor—"

The above paragraph refers to the Anniversary Festival the Tammany Society or Columbian Order held on Saturday 12 May at the Great Wigwam on Nassau Street, corner of George Street. There a "Long Talk" was delivered by George I. Eaker, and various highly political toasts were given. Eaker's appointment by the New York Council of Appointment as adjutant of the Second Regiment commanded by Lieut. Col. William Boyd, appears in a published notice dated 17 May in the *Argus, Greenleaf's New Daily Advertiser* (New York), of 21 May 1798. PAJ's appointment as a lieutenant of the Third Regiment appears on the same list. See also Hastings and Noble, *Military Minutes*, 449.

For the announcement and reports of the Tammany Society meeting in New York newspapers, see *Argus, Greenleaf's New Daily Advertiser* (New York), 12 and 16 May, *Commercial Advertiser* (New York), 16 May, *Daily Advertiser* (New York), 17 May, *New-York Gazette and General Advertiser*, 17 May, *Time Piece* (New York), 18 May, and *Greenleaf's New York Journal*, 19 May 1798. For a Federalist criticism of the toasts given at the meeting, see "A Man," in *New-York Gazette*, 22 May 1798. George I. Eaker (c. 1774–1804) was a New York Republican lawyer and orator who fatally shot AH's son Philip Hamilton in a duel in November 1801. *PAH*, 25: 435–38.

To Peter Augustus Jay

Albany 17 May 1798

Dear Peter

Your Letter of the 13 came to hand this morning—[1] The Intermissions between the Interruptions I have since had, have be∧en∧ so short, that I could not bestow much consideration on some of the Matters stated in it, and which demand mature and deliberate Reflection.

After having examined certain papers relative to the Land which Marvin desires to purchase, I will write to you on the subject— I cannot do it to day.

It is very proper that both you and Maria should visit our friends at Rye— you have been too long absent from there.

The Calculation and nature of the Bets you mention, cannot easily be accounted for— If they really believe they have succeeded, its an artifice to make money—[2]

The young men might have managed better—but they will learn— perhaps a *standing* Committee composed of members judiciously selected from the different classes of Citizens, would if proposed and agreed upon, afford an opportunity of so extending the circle as to comprehend those who remain out— If such an Idea should be adopted, some soothing and preparatory measures will doubtless be expedient. no act should be equivalent to an Enlist^mt^. and unless the address really bears that Construction, an explanatory Resolution by the standing committee, expressing the Sense in which they understand it, would probably remove that objection.

no becoming and proper means should be omitted to satisfy convince and attract the mechanics &ᶜ— of whom are armies composed?

To assemble for the purpose of military discipline, will ∧not only∧ in that view be useful—but also in others, if the *privates* attend— They may then be taught other Things besides the manual Exercises, & to see things as they really are—

For military men, in that capacity, to approve or censure the measures of Govᵗ. by acts of their Body assembled to deliberate on those subjects, cannot in my opinion be proper—[3]

I am as yet at a Loss how to advise respecting the Cockades— perhaps for the present it might not be amiss for the military to adopt them—and for the standing committee of the young men to recommend them to the members of their *Society*, but not until measures have been taken to render it as comprehensive as possible— I give these Remarks as hints not as opinions— under *present* circumstances perhaps the elderly and meer mohair Citizens should not be pressed to wear cockades by *mohair* citizens I mean those who are not included within any *military* description—[4] They who from honest motives are in the Act of passing, or preparing to pass, from one party to another have more than ordinary sensibility and are not to be roughly handled—[5]

I am a little sollicitous to see the address of our young Citizens— The next Ph[iladelphi]ᵃ. Papers will probably contain it—[6]

The Citizens of this place assembled yesterday and tho both parties attended, there was no opposition to the Resolutions proposed & carried[7]

We are all well— I wrote to you by the last post—and your mama wrote to maria by the Lᵗ. Govʳ.[8] I am Dr. Peter your affᵗᵉ. Father

John Jay

ALS, NNC (EJ: 90220). Addressed: "Mʳ. Peter Augustus Jay— / at Mʳ. Munro's— Broadway / New York". Endorsed: "Letter from papa / Albany 17 May 1798 / anᵈ. 6 June". Various mathematical calculations are also written on the address page. For PAJ's reply of 7 [not 6] June, see ALS, NNC (EJ: 06068); Dft, NNC (EJ: 10052).

1. PAJ to JJ, 13 May 1798, above.

2. For RRL's ultimate defeat, see the editorial note "John Jay Wins Reelection as Governor in 1798," above.

3. For JJ's engagement with the state militia, see the editorial note "Militia Matters in New York State," above.

4. "Mohair" is military slang for a civilian; that is a man in the civil line, a townsman, or tradesman, derived from the mohair buttons worn by persons of those descriptions or any others not in the army; the buttons of military men being always of metal. *OED*, citing the 1785 work Francis Grose, *A Classical Dictionary of the Vulgar Tongue* vol. 1 (London, 1785).

5. On the rise of Young Men's groups supporting JA's defense program in the aftermath of the XYZ affair, see PAJ's letter to JJ of 13 May 1798, and note 4, above.

6. For citations to the text of the address of the New York Young Men's Society, drafted by PAJ, see PAJ to JJ, 13 May 1798, note 4, above.

7. On the general meeting of the Citizens of Albany on 16 May, chaired by Albany Mayor Abraham Ten Broeck, and the resolutions carried, see *Albany Centinel*, and *Argus, Greenleaf's New Daily Advertiser* (New York), and *Daily Advertiser* (New York), all 22 May 1798. The meeting authorized a committee to prepare an address to President Adams expressive of the sentiments conveyed in the resolutions. The address pledging "to sustain with energy the Constituted Authorities of our Country against all the machinations of its enemies, whether foreign or domestic" was signed by about eight hundred freeholders and electors and transmitted to Henry Glen for presentation to the president. See *New-York Gazette*, 31 May 1798.

8. For JJ's previous letter, see JJ to PAJ, 10 May 1798, above. SLJ's letter to Maria Jay has not been found.

Testimony regarding the St. Croix River

[New York, 21 May 1798]

The answer of John Jay, who, was one of the Commissioners by whom the Treaty of Peace between Great Britain & the United States was negotiated, to the Interrogatories put to him at the Instance of the Agent on the part of the United States, by the board of Commissioners for ascertaining the River St. Croix, intended in and by the said Treaty.

The said John Jay having been duly sworn answers & says— that in the course of the said Negotiations, difficulties arose respecting the Eastern extent of the United States— That Mitchels map was before them & was frequently consulted for Geographical information. That in settling the Eastern boundary line (described in the Treaty) and of which the River St. Croix forms a part, it became a question which of the rivers in those parts, was the true River St. Croix; it being said that several of them had that name. That they did finally agree that the River St. Croix laid down on Mitchel's Map, was the river St. Croix which ought to form a part of the said Boundary line.— But whether that River was then so decidedly and permanently adopted & agreed upon by the Parties as conclusively to bind the two Nations to that Limit, even in case it should afterwards appear that Mitchel had been mistaken, & that the true River St. Croix was a different one from that which is delineated by that name on his Map, is a question or case, which he does not recollect nor believe was then put or talked of— By whom in particular that map was then produced, and what other Maps, Charts, & Documents ˄of state˄ were *then before the Commissioners* at Paris, and whether the British Commissioner then produced or mentioned an act of Parliament respecting the boundaries of

Massachusetts are circumstances which his recollection does not enable him to ascertain.— It seems to him that certain Lines were marked on the Copy of Mitchel's map which was before them at Paris: but whether the map mentioned in the Interrogatory as now produced, is that Copy—or whether the lines said to appear on it are the same lines he cannot without inspecting and examining it undertake to judge—[1]

To the last Interrogatory he answers— That for his own part he was of opinion that the Easterly Boundaries of the United States ought on principles of Right & Justice to be the same with the Easterly Boundaries of the late Colony or Province of Massachusetts.— Altho' much was said & reasoned on the Subject, yet he does not at this distance of time remember any particular & explicit declarations of the Parties to each other which would authorize him to say that the part of the said line (described in the Treaty) which is formed by the River St. Croix, was mutually & clearly conceived and admitted to be also a part of the Eastern Boundary line of Massachusetts.— He doubts there having then been very clear conceptions relative to the just & precise Easterly extent of Massachusetts: for he has reason to beleive that respectable opinions in America at that time considered the River St. John as the proper Eastern Limit of the United States.

John Jay

Sworn this 21st. May 1798.— before me Egbt. Benson

(Copy.).—

C, NHi: Jay (EJ: 04481, EJ: 10086). Endorsed: "Copy of the Answer of John Jay / to Interrogations abt. the River / St. Croix— May 1798". Marked: "No. 3—"

1. On the Mitchell map and the questions regarding the northeastern boundary of the United States during the 1782 peace negotiations and subsequently during the Jay Treaty negotiations, see *JJSP*, 3: 180, 182, 185n3, 185–86, 206, 209n3 and n5, 269, 597, 597nn1–4. On the request for JJ's testimony by the commissioners appointed to determine what river was intended as the boundary, see JJ to James Sullivan, 28 July 1797, above; the interrogatory was enclosed in Sullivan to JJ, 4 May 1798, ALS, MHi: Jay (EJ: 04480; EJ: 10087).

To Ebenezer Stevens

Albany 26 May 1798

Sir,

Mr. Smith delivered to me this morning your Letter of the 21st. Inst, and I assure you he shall recieve from me whatever facilities circumstances may indicate in the Course of the Business you allude to—[1]

When the Adj[utan]t. Gen[enera]². first arrived I understood from him, that you would accept the Command of the artillery Regt. at New York. I have since rec^d. a few Lines from him informing me that you decline it.[3] This latter Information gives me as much Regret, as the former did pleasure, especially as the Importance of our artillery Corps is enhanced by the State of our public affairs, and demands that more attention should be paid to them than in Times less critical. I did flatter myself to have concerted with you a Plan for putting them on a better Footing as to organization and numbers, than they now are; & to have seen that plan executed under your Direction—

Had there been a serious Disposition in the Legislature last Winter to fortify our Port, competent Provision would have been made for it— They left the Business of the arsenal in a singular State— without adopting any Plan, they appropriated 3000 Doll^rs. to that Object.[4] The Sum in my opinion is inadequate— what is your opinion? To attempt it under the Expectation of subsequent and further Grants, is to invite the like Censure which the Commissioners for Building public offices here experienced. Untill we become more united in our Councils, and less influenced by Considerations in which the public has little Interest, our affairs will not be wisely managed. I have the Honor to be Sir your most ob^t Servt

John Jay

Col. Eben^r. Stevens—

ALS, NHi: Stevens (EJ: 00677). Addressed: "Col. Eben^r. Stevens / New York". Endorsed.

1. Letter not found.

2. David Van Horne served as the adjutant general (the senior state military officer and de facto commander of the state's military) of the New York state militia from 1793 to 1801.

3. For Stevens's reason for declining the post, see his letter to JJ of 30 May 1798, below, and the editorial note "Militia Matters in New York State," above.

4. "An Act relative to the Public Building in the City of Albany, and for erecting an Arsenal in the City of New-York," 30 Mar. 1798, *N.Y. State Laws*, 21st sess. (January 1798), 418–19. For more on government finances and the construction of a state arsenal, see the editorial note "Defending New York," above.

From Ebenezer Stevens

New York 30th May 1798—

Sir

I am honoured with your favour of the 26th. instant,[1] and sincerely thank you, for the attention paid to M^r. Smith—

I agree with you that we ought to be united in our Councils, and uninfluenced by Considerations in which the public has little interest: be assured, it is my sincere wish, that the greatest unanimity take place, for it is absolutely necessary; and no Steps should be neglected, that can contribute toward so desirable an object. I am ready to do all in my power, either in a private or public capacity, for the good of my Country—

With respect to my declining to accept the Command of the Artillery Regiment,—[2] I found the Gentlemen who were Officers under Col: Bauman,[3] did not like the Idea of being superseded, and unwilling to hurt their feelings, I took what I considered a proper step— I wish all their resignations had been accepted of, and a new regiment of Twelve Companies formed— however, I now think it will be best, to let that Corps remain for Battallion Service. The Secretary at War,[4] writes me, that he has ordered Eight twelve pounders from Albany, to be placed under my directions for the defence of this City— A number of the Citizens are willing to enroll themselves under my command, who may be depended on in case of danger— this Body may be patronized by the Legislature at their next Session, I would recommend their Choosing their own Officers, and when they are known as a Body, their Commissions may be given them. If we are ever Visited by an Enemy, it will be for the sake of plunder: and heavy artillery or Field Carriages, will be the best means of defending the City. Captain Fry's[5] orders ought to be altered, for by his present orders, he has no right to fire a Gun on an Enemy, without they fire on him. I sincerely wish your Excellency would Visit us, we are without a leader, or head, to step forward and propose vigorous exertions, though our situation is so very critical. Our Citizens I verily believe, are ready to a man, with their Lives and Fortunes for their Country's defence—but some one of Influence to arrouse them, is highly necessary. It appears to me very needful, that some person should be invested with power to use the means of defence, in your Excellency's absence, if necessity requires it— But this can be done, when you come here, which I hope will be soon, as it will give me an opportunity of conversing with you on many subjects that would be serviceable to our defenceless City— I think that if a subscription was set on foot, plenty of money might be raised to place our heavy artillery in a capacity of being useful, which I am sorry to say are without Carriages or Shot; and of course, of no service whatever— I imagine, if you were to write the president, what our wants are, it would have a good effect; he told me he would be happy to receive your Letter, when I was in Philadelphia.[6] Is not part of the Sum appropriated by Congress for the Defence of the Sea ports, intended for us? perhaps on your application, it might be advanced immediately?— I am now in Correspondence with the Heads of the Departments on military matters, and have strongly recommended immediate measures for our defence; but *your writing* would have the most effect, and would be most likely to accomplish the end— I have done a number of nothing Jobs, and been a Servant to the Public on various occasions and yet, when a Commission is to be given by Government; it is given to those kind of Men, who never would show their heads in case of actual danger— I have a large Family, and it is natural for me to employ my services, where I may expect some return of profit the United States ought to have an Agent here, I believe I could fill it with as much advantage to them as any person, and I candidly confess to you, that it would be pleasing to me to fill that Office, but I have never been thought of, except on cases of emergency, and secondary matters, which took up much of my time, was troublesome, and no way profitable— I am ready to serve Government, and it is in my power to be very useful to them in the artillery department— But I have digressed from the subject of your Enquiry, and must beg your Excellency will excuse me— Our Corporation have voted me One thousand Dollars to procure Timber &c to mount some Eighteen pounders on Field Carriages for the Defence of this City,[7] I expect to receive an order from the Secretary at War, for 5 Iron Eighteen pounders to be delivered me, that are now on Bedlows Island; which will be mounted on Travelling Carriages, for this Island. And with respect to the Three thousand Dollars appropriated by our State Legislature for building an Arsenal, the Sum is too small;[8] and so incompetent for the object, that it would be wrong to attempt it— nothing but the censure you so justly observe could be expected.

I think we ought to have no more military stores here, than are actually wanted, and I suggest the Idea, whether the artillery here, or a part of it, had not better be at Albany in some Storehouse, to prevent them from being injured, for in their present State, without ammunition, or being in the Care of the Companies of Militia for whom they are intended, and of cause cannot be delivered till those Companies are formed, they might as well be there as here, and would be safer in my opinion. perhaps the very attempt to remove them, may excite our Citizens to a consideration of our defenceless State, and strike them with the necessity of providing the means of self protection. Col: Baumans late Regiment have their Complement of Artillery, & as those I am to take the Command of, will want a Gun-house— Suppose you appropriate the Three thousand Dollars or a part of it to that Object, and the remainder in Shot and powder. I would recommend this object to take place, and hope when our Legislature meet again, they will do more for us, than they did the last session— I lament my being absent, when I was wanted at Albany— I have the Honor to be Your Excellency's Most obed[t]. & faithful Serv[t]

Eben. Stevens

P.S. I mean the Three and Six pounders which are intended for the Brigade Companys of artillery throughout the State, by moving them to Albany, as they cannot be of any service here,— and if left till danger is to be apprehended, it would alarm the City by their removal, this would supersede in a great measure, the necessity of this money being lain out to begin an arsenal,—but the heavy artillery will want to be covered from the weather— His Excellency Governor Jay—Albany

ALS, NNC (EJ: 08648). Endorsed: ". . . rec^d. & an^d. 4 June 1798".

1. JJ to Stevens, 26 May 1798, above.

2. For the episode involving Stevens and the command of the Regiment of Artillery for the City and County of New York, see the editorial note "Militia Matters in New York State," above.

3. Sebastian Bauman, the former commandant of the Artillery Regiment, resigned his commission upon being denied a promotion to brigadier general.

4. James McHenry.

5. Frederick Frye (1761–1828) of Andover, Mass., served in the Corps of Artillerists and Engineers and commanded a company of federal troops stationed on Governors Island.

6. Stevens had met with congressional leaders and with President Adams in the spring of 1798 to discuss the status of fortifications for New York City. Stevens to JJ, 22 Mar. 1798, ALS, NHi: Jay (EJ: 00871), and 3 Apr. 1798, ALS, NHi: Stevens (EJ: 00872). See also the editorial note "Defending New York," above.

7. MCCNYC, 30 Apr. 1798, 2: 436.

8. "An Act relative to the Public Building in the City of Albany, and for erecting an Arsenal in the City of New-York," 30 Mar. 1798, N.Y. State Laws, 21st sess. (January 1798), 418–19.

From Matthew Clarkson

[New York June 10th. 1798.]

Sir,

The Citizens of New York, anxious and disquieted on account of the imperfect state of defence of this port and City, and fearing from the great and complicated objects which engage the attention of the General Government at this juncture, that measures for their security may not be executed as promptly as the danger may require:—have been induced to appoint Committees to devise and pursue such measures, in aid of those of the Government, for that object, as should appear to them expedient and necessary.[1]

These Committees have accordingly met, and consulted, and are about to adopt some expedients towards the end of their trust. But aware that whatever they may be able to Accomplish must be very inadequate, desirous that as speedily as possible, the necessity of their charge may be superseded by the more effectual care of the Government, and considering that the purpose for which they have been appointed is obviously of primary importance to the State at Large, also, that Events have recently occurred, making a very material change in the public Situation, which were not in the view of the Legislature at their last session, it has appeared to them proper, and adviseable, in reference to the object contemplated by their fellow Citizens, that the Legislature of this State, should be convened at some early day.[2]

Under this impression, and in the name of the Citizens of New York, in whose behalf they act, the said Committees beg leave to submit to Your Excellency's consideration the expediency of a special, and speedy Convention of our Legislature, and respectfully to request that the measure, if it shall not appear to You improper may be carried into effect.

In taking this step, they trust that justice will be done to the motives, that it will be well understood, that no officious, interference with Legal discretion is intended, and that the extraordinary nature of the conjuncture (in a case more immediately within the observation of our Citizens) will be conceived to divest this application of any thing which could be supposed to form an inconvenient precedent.

On behalf, and by Order of the Committees, I have the Honor to be, with great respect, Your Excell^y's Most obed^t· Servt.

M. Clarkson Chairman

Dupl LS, NNC (EJ: 11465). Marked: "(*Duplicate*)". Endorsed: ". . . Fortifying N York &c.—". C, undated, N (EJ: 02970), letter attested by "Jas: Fairlie Sec^y.—". C, undated, with attached fragment of JJ's reply of 14 June, NNC (EJ: 09841). For the reply, see JJ to Clarkson, 14 June 1798, below.

1. According to press accounts, sixty former army and naval officers met at Gaultier's tavern on 5 June and appointed Clarkson as chair for the proceedings. The assembly appointed a committee to "devise and pursue in concert with our fellow citizens at large, such measures as may be judged expedient for the security of the port and city of New York." The bipartisan committee consisted of Col. Alexander Hamilton, Col. Aaron Burr, Col. Ebenezer Stevens, Col. Marinus Willet, Maj. Nathaniel Pendleton, Gen. Matthew Clarkson, and Col. Hamilton Fish. On 6 June the committee met with a committee from the Chamber of Commerce and recommended that citizens of each ward meet and appoint three persons from each ward as a committee to meet with the two other committees to devise defense measures. All the committees convened on 8 June, again with Clarkson as chairman, and appointed a Military Committee (AH, Burr, and Stevens) to provide cannon and ammunition and another committee to handle the finances involved. See *Greenleaf's New York Journal*, 6 June; *Philadelphia Gazette*, 8 June; *Aurora General Advertiser* (Philadelphia), 8 June; *Spectator* (New York); 9 June; *Albany Register*, 11 June; *Greenleaf's New York Journal*, 13 June; Supplement to the *Connecticut Gazette* (New London); 13 June; *Albany Gazette*, 15 June 1798.

For the bipartisan nature of the committee appointed on 5 June, see letter by "MONTGOMERY", *Daily Advertiser* (New York), 11 June 1798. For a notice concerning the appointment of John Blagg, Ezekiel Robins, and John Cozine as the committee representing the 3rd Ward, see *Commercial Advertiser* (New York), 8 June; *Greenleaf's New York Journal*, 9 June 1798. For the response of New York City's Common Council, see *MCCNYC*, 13 June 1798, 2: 446–47. See also the editorial note "Defending New York," above.

2. On 2 July, JJ issued a proclamation calling for an early session of the state legislature. See Proclamation Summoning an Early Session of the New York State Legislature, [2 July 1798], below.

To Matthew Clarkson

Albany 14 June 1798

Sir

I was this morning favd. with yours of no date[1] in which as Chairman of the Committees lately appointed by the Citizens of New York you communicate to me their request that the Legislature of the State be speedily convened.

There certainly is much weight in the reasons you assign for this request, and I am persuaded that it originates in the best motives— The policy of keeping our City & Port in a constant and respectable state of defence is obvious, and that their present exposed and defenceless situation affords just cause of alarm is in my opinion equally evident.

It is to be regretted that this subject has not met with all the attention due to its importance— but Regrets can cast no light upon the present Question—which is—shall the Legislature be convened and this business again submitted to their consideration?

This question is not free from difficulties and much may be said for and against the expediency of the proposed measure— the wisdom of adopting or of declining it will as in most other doubtful cases, be probably judged of and decided by future events. I purpose to set out ₍for N York₎ early in the next week, and until my arrival there shall postpone forming a conclusive opinion on the subject. The Secy. at War[2] will by that time have visited New York and the measures of the Genl. Government as to fortifying the Port cannot long remain undecided or unknown— Besides if the Fortifications must be suspended until aid be furnished by the Legislature, the best of the season proper for such work will be lost— if means can be provided to keep the work going on until the season is over, the expence and inconvenience of a special session may be avoided—[3] On these points I wish to obtain more perfect information than I at present possess. I have the Honor to be Sir Your most obt. Sert.

Majr. Genl. Clarkson.

LbkC, N: Governor's Lbk. 1 (EJ: 03160). C, incomplete, written on the bottom of an undated copy of Clarkson to JJ, 10 June, NNC (EJ: 09841).

1. See Clarkson to JJ, 10 June 1798, above.

2. James McHenry.

3. JJ called for a special session on 2 July 1798. See below.

Address from the People of Poughkeepsie

[Poughkeepsie, 18 June 1798]

To his Excellency John Jay—

Sir—

The inhabitants of Poughkeepsie are not in the habit of assembling to testify their respect for the constituted authorities of their Country, or their attachment to the persons whom the suffrages of their fellow-citizens have called to the exercise of important duties. They have been accustomed, on the contrary, to observe the operations of Government in silence, and to indulge without expressing the pleasure arising from a belief of faithfulness in the conduct of their public officers. But when they view the severe aspect of the storm which threatens to overwhelm the peace & happiness of the United States, and when they retrospect, also, the part which your Excellency acted in the drama of American Independence—their feelings & their judgments constrain them to declare to you the satisfaction they experience on the event of your re-election to the office of Chief magistrate of this State. They wait on you, Sir, to assure you of their joy on this occasion, and to impart those cordial emotions which become them as citizens and as freemen, on your arrival in their village.[1]

The regard which we tender your Excellency is a tribute due to useful talents and to well-tried patriotism. We present it with sincerity.

We pray a realization of our wishes, that the God of Nations may continue your services to America through the times of peril which await her, and that you may enjoy a full reward in the confidence and approbation of your Country.—

Signed by order of the meeting—

*W*ᵐ. *Emett* Chairman

Peter W. Radcliff Secʳʸ.

DS, NNC (EJ: 09846). Endorsed: "address from Poughkeepsie / 1798 / to Govʳ Jay".

1. According to the *Albany Register*, of 25 June 1798: "On Tuesday last, as Mr. JAY passed through Poughkeepsie on his way to New-York, he received a flattering address from a number of the citizens of that place, congratulating him on his re-election to the office of governor."

From Henry Glen

Philadelphia 22ᵈ. June 1798.—

Dear Sir

This a Companies an other Communication sent by message by the president of the United States to Both Houses of Congress on the 18ᵗʰ. Instand—

we received this morning a message from the President with two Letters the One from Mʳ. Gerry & the Other from Messʳ Talleyrand What has been passᵈ Between them Since the Departure of Generalˢ Marshall & Pinckney which I shall Forward to you as Soon as they are printed.[1] I have done all whats necesary to be done in Regard of Mʳ. Van Rensselier. According to your request in your letter I Callᵈ Immeiadʸ [Immediately] on the Secʸ. of war & showᵈ. him your letter to me he Gave for Answer that due Atention would be paid to the Accommadation[2] I am Sorry to See this morning the names of the Members who are Relected to Congress I find Messʳˢ. Williams & Broock out & two men in their Room who I do not like a Judge Thompson from Still water in the Room of Mr Williams & a Mr. Baley from Dutches County in the Room of Mr. Broock[3] Our new Senater Comes On Very well[4] General Marshall was receivd in Great style into this City he was meat about 6 Miles from the City by the Secʸ of State & Mʳ Bingham in the latterˢ Coach &c. & three Companys of Light horse & Thousand spectators Bells in the City Ringing which is Not a small[?] number Great was the sight Next morning the Members of Congress in a Body whent to see him at his Loadging. On Saturday he is to dine with the Members of Congress there is a dinnir Providing for the purpose.[5] I am afraid we will have to Go to war with our faithfull alies. I am Dʳ Sir yours Sincerely—

H Glen

The Honᵇˡᵉ John Jay Esqʳ

ALS, NNC (EJ: 08649). Henry Glen, a Schenectady merchant, former deputy quartermaster general, and former commissioner on Indian affairs, was a delegate to the House of Representatives from 1793 to 1801.

1. For JA's message of 18 June submitting a dispatch from the envoys extraordinary to the French Republic, and his message of 21 June, submitting a letter from Elbridge Gerry of 16 Apr., with copies of Talleyrand to Gerry, 3 Apr., and Gerry's reply of 4 Apr. 1798, see *Annals*, 7: 581, 585–86; 8: 1971–72, 2029–31. Congress ordered five hundred of each to be printed. They were printed along with JA's earlier message on the XYZ Affair in *Instructions to the envoys extraordinary and ministers plenipotentiary from the United States of America, to the French republic, their letters of credence and full powers, and the dispatches received from them relative to their mission. Published by the secretary of state, in conformity to the resolutions of Congress, of the 22d June 1798* (Philadelphia, 1798; *Early Am. Imprints*, series 1, no. 34838).

2. See JJ to Glen, 2 June 1798, Dft, NNC (EJ: 08978), regarding a position as sailing master on one of the new U.S. armed vessels for Killian Henry Van Rensselaer (1769–1801). At this time AH also wrote to TP on Killian's behalf. Killian was the son of Henry Killian Van Rensselaer (1744–1816), a revolutionary war general, and brother of Solomon Van Rensselaer (1774–1852), an army officer who was wounded while serving with Anthony Wayne against the Ohio Indian Confederacy and future congressman (1819–22), whom JJ appointed Adjutant General in 1801. Killian obtained a commission as lieutenant in the Navy on 7 Jan. 1799. He was killed in a duel with a British officer in Hispaniola in March 1801. *Executive Journal*, 1: 302–3; *PAH*, 21: 494, 495nn2–4; Catharina Van Rensselaer Bonney, *A Legacy of Historical Gleanings* (2 vols.; Albany, 1875), 1: 155–56.

3. In New York's 1798 congressional election for District 5 (Dutchess County), the Republican candidate Theodorus Bailey defeated the incumbent Federalist David Brooks by a tally of 1,502 to 1,192 votes. In the same election for District 7 (Clinton, Saratoga, and Washington Counties), Republican John Thompson (1749–1823), unseated Federalist John Williams by a tally of 2,197 to 1,569 votes. *A New Nation Votes* (accessed Aug. 2019).

4. William North. See JJ to William North, 25 June 1798, and note 1, below.

5. John Marshall (1755–1835), who had recently returned from France, was received with great fanfare in Philadelphia for his role as envoy in the XYZ affair. See *Federal Gazette* (Baltimore), 20 June (supplement), and 23 June 1798 (supplement).

To William North

NYork 25 June 1798

Dʳ. Sir

On my arrival here the Day before Yesterday I had the pleasure of receiving your Letter of the 22 Instant, enclosing the Presidents last communication for which accept my thanks— the others which I recᵈ. just before I left Albany being in my Trunk which I expect this morning, I cannot now answer particularly—[1]

In my opinion it would be both just and proper to declare the Treaty with France to be void— but I think it would be more advisable to direct Reprizals than to declare war at *present*, for the public mind does not appear to me to be quite prepared for it— of this however you are better informed & therefore can judge better than I can— should it be the case, the Jacobin Leaders will continue to persuade their deluded followers that the Govᵗ. is chargeable not only with Precipitation but with a *desire* to prevent an accommodation which they affect to believe practicable, notwithstanding the Treatment of our Envoys &cᵃ &cᵃ

Whenever the mass of our People are convinced that the war would be just necessary and *unavoidable*, they will be content that it should be declared, and will support it vigorously— but I doubt whether that conviction however well founded, is as yet so prevailing and general as it ought to be; and as it would be, but for the arts practised to retard and prevent it. To me there seems to be Reason to apprehend that there are characters to whom Revolution and Confiscation would not be disagreable— nothing should be omitted to frustrate their Endeavours to decieve— every thing should be done to inform the People and cause them to see Things as they are— Mr. Gerry's remaining in France is an unfortunate Circumstance—it tends to prolong vain Hopes—to cherish old Divisions, and to create new ones. He was doubtless actuated by the best Intentions, but I think he committed a mistake.[2] If both Houses should concur in opinion that a Declaration of War would be *seasonable,* I hope the minority against it, may not be so considerable as to give Countenance to a contrary opinion— There are attempts to make mischievous use of Talleyrands Letter—[3] I am Dr Sir yours sincerely

John Jay

P.S. Ought War to be declared by such thin Houses?

The Honb. Wm. North Esqr

ALS, NNGL (EJ: 90523). Addressed: "The Hon'ble Wm. North Esqr / in the Senate of the U.S. / Philadelphia". Franked: "Free"; Dft, NNC (EJ: 12772); *HPJ*, 4: 244–45.

1. For JJ's appointment of William North to the Senate seat vacated by John Sloss Hobart, see JJ to North, 4 May and 7 May 1798, LbkCs, N: Governor's Lbk. 1 (EJ: 03150, EJ: 03152); and JJ to North, 7 May, ALS, NNC (EJ: 90217); and, for the replies, North to JJ, 5 May, LbkC, N: Governor's Lbk. 1 (EJ: 03151); 7 May, ALS, NNC (EJ: 13046). For North's letter of 22 June, see ALS, NNC (EJ: 12773); and, for his previous letter, see North to JJ, 9 June 1798, ALS, NNC (EJ: 13014).

2. See the editorial note "John Jay and the Response to the XYZ Affair in New York," below.

3. Possibly a reference to Talleyrand's memoir on Franco-American relations given to the envoys on 18 Mar. 1798, a copy of which Talleyrand had sent to Benjamin Bache, who published it in the *Aurora* on 16 June before the government had officially received a copy. Bache also printed the envoys' reply to Talleyrand in installments starting on 20 June. JJ's remark may also refer to Talleyrand's letter to Elbridge Gerry of 3 Apr. 1798, which Bache published on 23 June. It referred to the departure of Pinckney and Marshall from France and to the "obstacles which their known opinions have interposed to the desired reconciliation" and stated his desire to resume communications with Gerry. See Stinchcombe, *XYZ Affair*, 119; *Aurora* (Philadelphia), 16, 18, 19, 20, 21, 22, 23, and 25 June 1798.

JOHN JAY AND THE RESPONSE
TO THE XYZ AFFAIR IN NEW YORK

John Jay's summoning of a special session of the New York state legislature in July 1798 initiated his formal response to the deteriorating relations with France and the public furor over the French demands for bribes, loans, and United States assumption of liability for losses resulting from French seizures of American ships and cargoes that came to be known as the XYZ affair.

In 1797 the French government under the Directory, having interpreted the Jay Treaty as an American alliance with Great Britain, authorized the seizure of all ships carrying British goods. Over three hundred American ships were seized, primarily in the West Indies. John Adams appointed Charles Cotesworth Pinckney of South Carolina to replace James Monroe as minister to France, but when he arrived in November 1796 the French government refused to recognize or admit him. Pinckney retired to Amsterdam to await further instructions. Adams learned of this in March 1797 and called a special session of Congress to meet on 15 May 1797 to consider further negotiations and respond to the French ship seizures. In an address to Congress on 16 May, Adams called for "a fresh attempt" at negotiation "to adjust all our differences with France," together with "effectual measures of defense". Federalists were supportive, but Republicans were opposed to any defensive actions against France as a threat to peace. In July 1797 Adams added Elbridge Gerry of Massachusetts and John Marshall of Virginia to Pinckney as a commission to seek further negotiations, and Congress adjourned. Adams went home to Massachusetts and did not return to Philadelphia until November 1797 after the yellow fever epidemic abated.[1]

By the time the commissioners arrived in Paris in October 1797, Talleyrand had become foreign minister, and an anti-American faction had seized power in the Directory. Talleyrand sent to the commissioners private agents who demanded as the price for opening negotiations a douceur or bribe for Talleyrand of $250,000, a low-interest loan of $10 million in compensation for Adams's alleged insult to France in his speech before Congress of 16 May 1797, and American assumption of compensation to American merchants for French seizures of ships and cargoes. While such demands were not uncommon in Europe, the American commissioners considered the proposals not merely corrupt but a demand for tribute and an insult to American dignity and independence. They refused to make any payments in advance of negotiations. Discussions were broken off on 1 November, and Pinckney and Marshall returned to the United States, while Gerry, in an effort to avoid immediate war, remained in France in the hope of reopening negotiations.

The commissioners' dispatches explaining the situation, most of which were in code, arrived in Philadelphia on 4 March 1798. Adams sent the unencoded dispatch dated 8 January to Congress on 5 March, and on 19 March sent a message reporting the failure of the mission to Congress and calling for defense measures. He revealed that the Directory had declared all French ports closed to neutral shipping and that any ship carrying English goods was subject to French capture.[2] However, even after the more comprehensive reports on the French demands were deciphered, Adams decided not to reveal the details to Congress because of their inflammatory nature. Republicans in Congress, convinced that Adams sought war with France, assumed that he was withholding information favorable to France. On 2 April, they demanded that copies of Adams's instructions to the commissioners and of all their dispatches be submitted to Congress. Adams complied on 3 April and forwarded additional material on 4 May.[3]

The news of the behavior of the French agents infuriated Congress, and once communicated to the public, aroused much of the nation, and prompted hundreds of addresses in support of Adams from state and local governments and other public bodies.[4] Both Congress and various states began taking action to strengthen American defenses and thwart the influence of France and its supporters. Congress authorized the arming of American merchant ships and the acquisition of twelve frigates for a revived United States navy, created a provisional army of ten thousand men, and made other military appropriations for harbor fortifications and cannon foundries. On 7 July 1798 Congress annulled the Treaty of Alliance with France of 1778, and authorized attacks on French warships in American waters. Federalists questioned the loyalty of pro-French Republicans, resulting in the passage of the Alien and Sedition Acts, measures that Adams had not proposed but did sign when passed. The period of residence required for citizenship was raised from five to fourteen years, and Congress required the registration of aliens and authorized the president to expel any foreigner considered dangerous. False, scandalous, and malicious writings against the government were made punishable by fine and imprisonment.[5] What became known as the Quasi-War with France was fought between American and French vessels, largely in the Caribbean. Some Republicans, particularly Albert Gallatin and Thomas Jefferson, continued to insist that the demands of the French agents, whose names were withheld in the dispatches sent to Congress, and referred to simply as X, Y and Z, did not represent official French government policy.[6]

Jay, like most Federalists, and indeed much of the nation, was indignant about the news of French actions. On 21 March 1798, he questioned the wisdom of adjourning the legislature until more was known about the seriousness of the situation and defense measures were taken. However, when no further news arrived quickly, the legislature adjourned on 6 April.[7] Correspondence with Timothy Pickering and others kept Jay informed of the foreign affairs news as it arrived.[8] Not until after Jay had secured reelection and received additional information from federal officials did he take official action on the threat. On 2 July he summoned the legislature to meet at Albany on 9 August to take action for the defense of New York.[9]

In the interim, however, he had privately expressed his reaction to the

XYZ affair. In a letter to Pickering of 13 May 1798 discussing the proposed revisions to the naturalization act, Jay reiterated his customary fear of foreign influence and suggested barring all foreigners from holding state or national office, appointed or elective, although he would allow presidential appointment of foreigners to military positions with the consent of the Senate.[10] His private correspondence informed him of the responses to the XYZ affair in New York, including the preparation of public addresses by various organizations, generally Federalist, supporting Adams and condemning French policy.

Once the legislature convened Jay referred the published records related to the XYZ affair to it, and addressed it on 9 August supporting Adams and recommending defense measures to supplement those of the federal government.[11] On 10 August he submitted to the legislature a proposal from the Massachusetts legislature for a constitutional amendment barring foreigners from holding office as vice president, senator or representative.[12] The legislature responded with an address in support of Adams similar to those already adopted by other states. Jay forwarded the address to the president with an effusive cover letter praising Adams, to which Adams replied in kind.[13] The legislature also appropriated $150,000 for defense measures, including harbor fortifications and expansion of the state militia. The state senate approved the proposed amendment limiting officeholding by foreigners, but the assembly did not, and no action was taken. Jay then turned his effort to implementing the military preparations.[14]

In September Washington was appointed commander in chief and insisted on his right to choose the principal officers, including Alexander Hamilton as his second in command.[15] However, Elbridge Gerry arrived on 1 October 1798 and met with Adams on 4 October. Gerry indicated that Talleyrand was ready to negotiate. Adams hoped the new army might not be needed. He accepted the Federalist demand for appointment of a commission rather than a single envoy to conduct further negotiations. William Vans Murray, Oliver Ellsworth, and William Richardson Davie (later replaced by John Marshall) were selected as commissioners. Jay, like most Federalists, remained skeptical of French intentions, fearing French ambitions for conquest in the Americas as well as in Europe.[16] However, war fever gradually died down.

The negotiators annulled the treaty of alliance with France of 1778 and negotiated a new agreement based on the 1776 Model Treaty. The resulting Convention of 1800, also known as the Treaty of Mortefontaine, was ratified by the Senate on 18 December 1801, after a delay caused by opposition to the treaty's failure to obtain compensation for French ship seizures.

1. McCullough, *Adams*, 484–86. On the XYZ affair, see generally, Stinchcombe, *XYZ Affair*.

2. *ASP: FR*, 2: 150–52.

3. *Annals*, 7: 525, 535–36; 8: 1374–75; *ASP: FR*, 2: 153–82. A motion in the Senate calling for submission of the instructions and dispatches had been made on 20 Mar. and postponed on 3 April. JA sent copies to both houses on 4 April. The pamphlet published on 9 Apr. 1798 with congressional authorization was *Message of the president of the United States to both Houses of Congress, April 3d 1798* (Philadelphia, 1798; *Early Am. Imprints*, series 1, nos. 34812, 34813).

4. On the content and importance of the hundreds of public addresses, see Thomas Ray, "Not One Cent for Tribute: The Public Addresses and American Popular Reaction to the XYZ Affair, 1798–99," *Journal of the Early Republic* 3 (Winter 1983): 389–412.

5. See JJ to TP, 13 May, above. JJ made no public statements about the Sedition Act, did not ask the legislature for a state sedition law, and did not seek investigation or prosecution of anyone under the act. See Bird, *Press and Speech under Assault*, 415–18; and, for a discussion of JJ's general support of free speech and press, 120–33, 410–23. On the debates over and passage of the Alien and Sedition Acts and enforcement of the acts, see *PTJ*, 30: 300, 301n; *Annals*, 8: 1566–82; *Stats*, 1: 566–69; James M. Smith, *Freedom's Fetters: The Alien and Sedition Laws and American Civil Liberties* (Ithaca, 1956), 26–34; Bird, *Press and Speech under Assault*, 246–58, 310, 325–26, 399–409, 463–65.

6. Talleyrand's intermediaries included Jean Hottinguer (X), Pierre Bellamy (Y), and Lucien Hauteval (Z), along with Nicolas Hubbard (W).

7. *N.Y. Assembly Journal*, 21st sess. (January 1798), 333.

8. See TP to JJ, 9 Apr.; JJ to TP, 10 and (private), 19 Apr.; PAJ to JJ, 15 and 26 Apr. and 6 May; and JJ to PAJ, 16 Apr. 1798, all above. In June 1798, John Marshall arrived in New York and said he believed France did not want war and urged moderation. He added that Gerry, whose stay in France had been widely criticized, had remained because the French said there would be war if he did not. McCullough, *Adams*, 503.

9. On 10 June 1798, Matthew Clarkson, chairman of a committee appointed by citizens of New York, suggested that JJ convene the legislature on defense issues. JJ referred the letter to Richard Varick, mayor of New York City, for the information of the City Council. However, JJ declined to call the legislature until Secretary of War James McHenry arrived and informed him what federal plans existed for defending New York. On 22 June Henry Glen arrived in New York carrying copies of JA's address to Congress of 18 June, and of letters from Gerry and Talleyrand on what had passed since Pinckney and Marshall departed; Glen stated he expected war with France. JA asserted no new envoys would be sent to France until he had received assurances they would be received, but he did not ask for a declaration of war. See Clarkson to JJ, 10 June, and JJ's reply of 14 June 1798, both above; JJ to Varick, 27 June, LbkC, N: Governor's Lbk. 1 (EJ: 03161); C, with C of Varick's reply of 29 June, NNC (EJ: 09842); Glen to JJ, 22 June 1798, above. In a letter to Senator William North of 25 June, above, JJ approved of declaring the treaty with France void and directing reprisals against French seizures, but advised against declaring war since the public was not yet prepared for it. Although Republicans continued to believe all Federalists sought immediate war with France, AH also opposed a declaration of war at this time for the same reason JJ did. See McCullough, *Adams*, 485.

10. See JJ to TP, 13 May 1798, above.

11. See JJ's Address to the New York State Legislature, 9 Aug. 1798, below.

12. See JJ's Message to the New York State Senate, 10 Aug. 1798, below.

13. See the New York State Senate to JJ, 13 Aug. 1798, and JJ's reply of the same date, below; New York State Assembly to JJ, 14 Aug., and JJ's reply of the same date, below; JJ to JA, 21 Aug. 1798, and note 1, below.

14. For the state action on defense measures, see the editorial note "Defending New York", above.

15. See the editorial note "Hamilton Takes Command," below.

16. See JJ to JA, 3 Jan., ALS, MHi: Adams (EJ: 06428); and to Benjamin Goodhue, and notes, 29 Mar. 1799, ALS, NNYSL (EJ: 02872).

Proclamation Summoning an Early Session of the New York State Legislature

[New York, 2 July 1798]

By His Excellency John Jay Esq.

Governor of the State of New York

A Proclamation

Whereas the Government of the United States, to whom the people thereof have co‸m‸mitted the exclusive direction of their National affairs, has been pleased to publish, for the Information of the Citizens, divers important and alarming events and transactions; from which it appears, That there exist well founded apprehensions that the Directors of the French Republic have long formed and are strenuously pursuing a system of empire and aggrandizement subversive of the national Rights & Independence, not only of the greater part of Europe, but also of the United States—imposing upon them the necessity of partaking in her Wars and contributing to her expences:

That the cautious and neutral conduct which the United States and several other nations have observed towards the Republic has not been able to shield them from the operation of that System: but on the contrary that complaints against the United States have been diligently sought and alledged, and followed, not by friendly remonstrances and conciliatory overtures, but by unnecessary and unmerited marks of contempt and by injurious and repeated aggressions: That the late and present President, both of whom are eminently distinguished by uprightness and sincerity, have at two different periods sent Ministers to that Republic with ample powers and special Instructions to do their utmost endeavours to preserve peace, and bring all differences to an amicable conclusion, and on reasonable terms: That notwithstanding the accustomed respect which civilized and contending Nations usually pay, as well as owe to each other, and which requires that Ambassadors charged with overtures for peace and conciliation, should at least be received and heard and treated with civility, yet the first of those Ministers was refused to be admitted into the presence of the said Directory, and after singular delay and neglect, was dismissed in a manner very disgusting to free, independent, and friendly people:—

That although the respect which every nation owes to itself, strongly opposed the policy of giving to those directors another opportunity of again treating the United States with singular indignity, yet an earnest and prevailing desire to maintain peace with all Nations and particularly with the French Republic, induced the President to appoint three Envoys extraordinary, selected from the Three great Districts of the U. States and sent them to France with ample powers and Instructions to treat in a friendly manner with that Government, respecting all differences and Complaints, and to accomodate and settle them on terms limited only by the honor independence and essential interests of the United States:

That notwithstanding such strong desires proved by such unequivocal and uncommon efforts to preserve peace and friendship with that Republic, those Envoys were not only refused to be received and accredited but new difficulties and fresh obstacles to accomodation were interposed, by demands which no Nation ought to make, and to which no Nation ought to submit.

These facts and circumstances strongly indicated designs and systems hostile to our peace and independence; and in connection with the long continued, encreasing, and ruinous depredations on our Commerce, afford reason to expect that a more open and decided rupture will take place the moment that further delay shall cease to be convenient.

And whereas several of the more alarming of these events had not been published by order of the Government of the United States, and in an authentic manner, until after the adjournment of the last Session of the Legislature of this State, and it has become prudent to take without delay such measures relative to defence, as the present exigency requires, and which cannot be seasonably and sufficiently provided for by the United States, without the auxiliary efforts of this State: Wherefore concurring in the opinion with many of our best-informed Citizens, I think it my duty to give the Legislature of this State, an early opportunity of taking these important matters into their serious Consideration; and thereupon to do whatever may be proper and necessary in such an emergency; with firm reliance on the divine protection, and with inflexible resolution never to surrender their Independence and pay tribute to any nation whatever.

I do therefore in pursuance of the authority constitutionally vested in me hereby summon and require the members of the Senate and also the members of [the] Assembly of this State to convene and meet in the City-Hall of the City of Albany, on the Ninth day of August next; and this Proclamation (which all Printers of Gazettes in this State are hereby desired forthwith to publish in their Papers) is to be considered as due and sufficient notice.[1]

Given under my Hand and the Privy-Seal of the State, at the City of New York, on the 2nd day of July in the Year of our Lord 1798, and in the 22nd Year of the Independence of the United States of America.

(signed) John Jay

LbkC, N: Governor's Lbk. 2 (EJ: 03283). Printed: *Spectator, Daily Advertiser,* and *Greenleaf's New-York Journal* (all New York), 4 July; *Argus, Greenleaf's New Daily Advertiser* (New York), 5 July; *Gazette of the United States* (Philadelphia), 6 July; *Porcupine's Gazette* (Philadelphia), 6 July; *Federal Gazette* (Baltimore), 7 July; *Albany Gazette,* 9 July; *Alexandria Advertiser,* 11 July; *Northern Centinel* (Salem, N.Y.), 16 July 1798.

1. For the background to JJ's calling the legislature into special session, see the editorial note "John Jay and the Response to the XYZ Affair in New York," above. For the opening of the legislature, see JJ's Address of 9 Aug. 1798, below.

HAMILTON TAKES COMMAND

As calls for military action against France grew louder during the summer of 1798, Jay tapped Alexander Hamilton to take charge of the various efforts then underway to put the City of New York on a wartime footing. Although Hamilton's formal duties were those of chief superintendent of fortifications, he in fact served in a much broader capacity than this title suggests. Throughout the Quasi-War, the governor frequently sought his counsel on military matters ranging from militia appointments and reorganization to supply and provisioning.[1]

Jay and Hamilton had worked well together over the past two decades, from promoting the Whig cause in provincial New York to their grand collaboration on the *Federalist* essays.[2] Jay had long held Hamilton's partisan credentials, political astuteness, and legal acumen in high regard and now sought to harness these talents and ambitions for his own administration. In April 1798, Jay offered Hamilton, then a practicing attorney and private citizen, the senatorial seat recently vacated by John Sloss Hobart.[3] Hamilton appreciated "the mark of confidence" but respectfully declined the appointment as he did yet not "wish to sacrifice the interest of my family to public call."[4]

Within a few months, however, Hamilton reversed course and became a state appointee when he accepted the governor's invitation in late August to direct the maritime defenses of New York City.[5] Hamilton's preoccupation with the nation's military affairs explains his willingness to serve as Jay's subordinate. Moreover, his membership on the city's Military Committee already attuned him to the financial and logistical difficulties of fortifying the port. His work with this civic body thereby served as a stepping stone to his current post and enabled him to act as a more effective liaison between local leaders and the governor's office.[6]

Hamilton's military credentials and experience were further bolstered by his recent appointment as Inspector General of the United States Army. Fearing the outbreak of Franco-American hostilities, the federal government supplemented its meager forces in the Regular Army with the creation of an Additional Army in July 1798.[7] As part of the Army's reorganization, President Adams reluctantly selected Hamilton over other senior officers to take command of the troops stationed throughout the northern states and western territories, making him the dominant figure under Washington within the nation's military establishment.[8] Along with Pickering and other prominent Federalists, Jay supported Hamilton's meteoric rise, remarking that "his former military station and character, taken in connection with his late important place in the administration" made him an ideal candidate.[9] Pickering, who actively campaigned on Hamilton's behalf, noted in a letter to Washington that both he and Jay approved of an "elevated station" for Hamilton.[10] When Hamilton's posting was publicly announced, Jay was quick to congratulate him on the appointment and on attaining the rank of major general.[11] It was certainly not lost on the governor that Hamilton's promotion placed him in a unique position to support New York's military endeavors.

Although he agreed to oversee the city's defenses, Hamilton did express initial reservations about agreeing to Jay's request. His father-in-law, Philip Schuyler, warned him that holding two active appointments might prove too burdensome, as the new posting was sure to interfere with his existing duties. It was the fear of being accused of monetary malfeasance, however, that ultimately gave him pause. Hamilton had authored a pamphlet the previous year pertaining to his role in the Reynolds scandal of 1792 in which he admitted his sexual impropriety, but defended himself against charges of financial chicanery.[12] With this episode weighing heavily on his mind, he had no wish to embroil himself in another controversy involving the misuse of public funds. Sensing Hamilton's vulnerable position, Schuyler assured him that Jay did not intend "that you should be embarrassed with Accounts, [and] that proper persons would be appointed for that purpose."[13] Hamilton wanted to confirm Schuyler's guarantee so he raised the issue directly with the governor, noting "I am sincere in saying that a charge of this kind would on various accounts be unpleasant to me among the rest as likely to involve ill natured & foolish criticism. But I shall not decline the trust if you think proper to repose it provided the manutension of the money is no part of it".[14] Hamilton's anxieties of being charged with any wrongdoing, however, proved short-lived. Soon after he started as superintendent of fortifications, Hamilton was assisting Jay with the disbursement of funds. Hamilton felt secure carrying out these duties as he knew that the governor had hired an individual who would audit and keep the accounts related to defense expenditures.[15]

The burden of directing New York City's defenses eventually proved too overwhelming for Hamilton. In February 1799, he announced that following the completion of a comprehensive survey of the harbor, he would step down as superintendent and would not oversee the subsequent implementation of the fortification plans. Hamilton explained that he lacked the "energy & dispatch" to carry out these tasks and that they interfered with his other duties.[16] He recommended Aaron Burr as his successor, but Jay chose not to accept this advice and chose another person to fulfill the role of superintendent.

1. For AH's involvement with the New York militia, see the editorial note "Militia Matters in New York State," above.

2. JJ and AH's relationship during the American Revolution is discussed in AH to JJ, 26 Nov. 1775, *JJSP*, 1: 157–59; *PAH*, 1: 176–78; AH to JJ, 2 June 1777, *JJSP*, 1: 428–30; *PAH*, 1: 261–64; AH to JJ, 14 Mar. [1779], *JJSP*, 1: 607–10; *PAH*, 2: 14–19; JJ to AH, 18 Sept. 1779, *JJSP*, 1: 680–82; *PAH*, 2: 182–83. For their literary efforts to ratify the Constitution of 1787, see the editorial note *The Federalist*, *JJSP*, 4: 572–85.

3. JJ to AH, 19 Apr. 1798, ALS, DLC: Hamilton (EJ: 10775); LbkC, N: Governor's Lbk. 1 (EJ: 03139); *PAH*, 21: 433; JJ to AH, 19 Apr. 1798, ALS, DLC: Hamilton (EJ: 10776); LbkC, N: Governor's Lbk. 1 (EJ: 03140); *PAH*, 21: 434.

4. AH to JJ, 24, Apr. 1798, DftS, DLC: Hamilton (EJ: 10778); *PAH*, 21: 447.

5. JJ to AH, 30 Aug. 1798, ALS, DLC: Hamilton (EJ: 10782); *WJ*, 2: 285–86; *HPJ*, 4: 249–50; *PAH*, 22: 169.

6. For AH's involvement with the Military Committee, see the editorial note "Defending New York," above.

7. For the reorganization of the U.S. Army during the Quasi-War, see *PAH*, 22: 383–87.

8. For AH's appointment as Inspector General, see *PAH*, 22: 4–17. For AH's subsequent service during the Quasi-War, see Richard H. Kohn, *Eagle and Sword: The Federalists and the Creation of the Military Establishment in America, 1783–1802* (New York and London, 1975), 243–55.

9. JJ to TP, 18 July, 1798, below. For more on the correspondence between JJ and TP discussing AH's ascendancy, see TP to JJ, 20 July, below; JJ to TP, 26 July, below; TP to JJ, 28 July 1798, ALS, NNC (EJ: 12545).

10. TP to GW, 1 Sept. 1798, *PGW: RS*, 2: 573. TP had sent a letter in favor of AH earlier that summer. TP to GW, 6 July 1798, *PGW: RS*, 2: 386–87.

11. JJ to AH, 28 July 1798, ALS, DLC: Hamilton (EJ: 10780); *PAH*, 22: 33–34.

12. *Observations on Certain Documents contained in No. V and VI of "The History of the United States for the Year 1796," in which the Charge of Speculation against Alexander Hamilton, late Secretary of the Treasury, is fully refuted. Written by Himself* (Philadelphia, 1797; *Early Am. Imprints*, series 1, no. 32222). For more on the pamphlet and the Reynolds Affair, see *PAH*: 21: 121–44.

13. Schuyler to AH, 17 Aug. 1798, *PAH*, 22: 79–80.

14. AH to JJ, 8 Sept. 1798, ALS, NNC (EJ: 05630); *PAH*, 22: 176–77.

15. JJ to JA, 26 Sept. 1798, LbkC, N: Governor's Lbk. 1 (EJ: 03168); *HPJ*, 4: 250–51. JJ forwarded this letter to AH, 26 Sept. 1798, LbkC, N: Governor's Lbk. 1 (EJ: 03169); JA to JJ, 17 Oct. 1798, ALS, NNC (EJ: 05437); C in JJ to AH, 24 Oct. 1798, ALS, DLC: Hamilton (EJ: 10783); JA to AH, 17 Oct. 1798, ALS, DLC: Hamilton; *PAH*, 22: 200–201; JJ to AH, 24 Oct. 1798, ALS, DLC: Hamilton (EJ: 10783); LbkC, N: Governor's Lbk. 1 (EJ: 03176).

16. AH to JJ, 12 Feb. 1799, ALS, NjP: C.P. Greenough Fuller; C (incomplete), NNC; *PAH*, 22: 476–77. AH was still carrying out his duties as superintendent in the summer of 1799. See AH to JJ, 29 July 1799, ALS, NNC (EJ: 05633); C, DLC: Hamilton (EJ: 10791); *PAH*, 23: 291–92. See also AH to JJ, 12 Feb. 1799, ALS, NNC; *PAH*, 22: 476.

To Timothy Pickering

New York 18 July 1798—

Dear Sir

I this morning rec^d. the two Copies you was so obliging as to send me of the State papers published in pursuance of the Resolution of Congress of the 22^d. June. they shall be laid before our Legislature at the approaching Session—[1]

Every true American here rejoices that General Washington has accepted the Command of the army— it is an auspicious Event— Being of the Number of those who expect a severe war with France, the moment she makes peace with Britain, I feel great anxiety that nothing may be omitted to prepare for it. At the Commencement and indeed during the Course of our revolutionary war, we suffered from the Inefficiency of too many of our military officers— great care should be taken to avoid the like mistakes—former Rank cannot compensate for the want of essential Qualifications. To pass by certain Characters cannot but be unpleasant; and yet in my opinion public Good forbids their being called to the Field. we shall probably have very different Generals to contend with from those which Britain sent here last war; and we should have very different ones to oppose them from several of those who then led our Troops. I cannot conceal from you my Sollicitude that the late Sec^y of the Treasury may be brought forward in a Manner corresponding with his Talents and Services— It appears to me that his former military station and character, taken in connection with his late important place in the administration, would justify measuring his Rank by his Merit and Value.[2] pardon these Hints— I know that these matters are not within my Departm^t., but they occupy my mind continually. It is an agreable Circumstance that our President, notwithstanding the diplomatic Skill of France, stands high in the public Estimation and Confidence, and that the utmost Reliance may be reposed on his Patriotism. He has much to think of and to do; but while his measures are well matured, deliberately adopted and vigorously executed, his administration will be rendered more and more glorious by successive Difficulties— Yours sincerely

John Jay—

The Honb. Timothy Pickering Esqʳ.—

ALS, MHi: Pickering (EJ: 04790). Addressed: "Honble Timothy Pickering Esqʳ". Endorsed: "John Jay Esqʳ / July 18. 1798. / recᵈ. and / ansᵈ. 20ᵗʰ." Marked: "relative to Colᵒ. Hamilton / to be appointed to a / chief military command".

1. On 22 June Congress authorized the publication of JA's messages related to the XYZ affair and the enclosed dispatches for distribution among the various states. See the editorial note "John Jay and the Response to the XYZ Affair in New York," and note 3, above.

2. On the appointment of AH as Inspector General, see the editorial note "Hamilton Takes Command," above.

From Timothy Pickering

Philadelphia July 20. 1798.

Dʳ. Sir,

I have this moment received your letter of the 18ᵗʰ.[1] By the newspapers which go hence this morning, you will see your wishes respecting Colᵒ. Hamilton gratified.[2] At the head of the appointments, he is Inspector General with the rank of Major General. This was intended to place him next in command to Genˡ. Washington:[3] yet I feel some solicitude about the effect. Under circumstances not dissimilar, in the American War, I believe some staff officers, *not taken from the line,* were resisted in their claims to command officers of inferior rank *in the line.* I wish therefore that the act of Congress authorizing the appointment of an "Inspector General with the rank of major general," had been explicit— that the Inspector General might be appointed from among those who should be major generals; or that some mode had been devised to remove all doubt of Colᵒ. Hamilton's right to command all the major generals; under the law as it stands.

I take very kindly the communication of your sentiments in this matter; & shall feel my obligations increase with the future communication of your ideas and opinions on every subject involving the safety, the interest & the happiness of our country. But altho' I deem so lowly of my own discernment in such weighty concerns as to render such communications from you and other eminent citizens peculiarly grateful, yet on the present occasion I cannot withhold the pleasure of showing you the perfect coincidence of our thoughts, by presenting you with a copy of my letter of the 6th instant to

General Washington.[4] Col^o. Hamilton arrived here the next morning, and in the freedom and confidence with which we conversed I handed ∧it∧ to him to peruse.— General Washington's answer of the 11th.[5] I received the 16th. and sent to Col^o. Hamilton extracts[6] to show the current of the General's reasoning; concluding with an expression of my hopes, that as he (Col^o. Hamilton) had, in the war for our independence, ~~had~~ devoted his talents to enhance another's glory, so he would not withhold them now that the preservation of that independence demanded their fullest exertion. After that, M^r. M^c.Henry returned, and informed me that Genl. W. was some time balancing between the priority of Col^o. Hamilton and General Pinckney; weighing the high respectability and importance of the latter in the three southern states, against the superior talents of the former: the latter finally preponderating. *Perhaps* the observations in my letter of the 6th (which I perceive Genl. Washington did not communicate to M^c.Henry) might have turned the scale. I send you herein the General's answer, which I will thank you to return.[7]

I was rejoiced that the Senate had the fortitude to put a decided negative on the President's nomination of his son-in-law William S. Smith to be adjutant general, with the rank of brigadier.[8] When I saw that the President was *invincibly* bent on the nomination, I did not hesitate to inform a number of senators of it, and to urge their negative, for the honor and even for the safety of the army. The President did not know, that Col^o. S. was as bankrupt in fame as well as fortune;[9] and that he had totally mistaken his military talents.— I spoke to so many, and with so little reserve, that I thought it not improbable that my interference would eventually be known to the President: but I chose to hazard his displeasure rather than the approbation of that nomination. Unfortunately General Washington had arranged the name of Col^o. Smith among the candidates for the office of a brigadier.— I am aware the step I took was a delicate one; and even its propriety may perhaps be questioned:— if the candidate in question had not been so nearly connected with the President—and if the latter had not so peremptorily pronounced the eulogium of the former as a *great military character*, and in a tone to forbid any reply—[10] it would have become me to have frankly stated my opinion of his true character, and total unworthiness and unfitness to fill that important place. If in taking the other course I have done wrong, my motives I hope will make my apology with you and some others whose good opinions are peculiarly dear to me. With true respect, I am, D^r. Sir, your ob^t. servant

Timothy Pickering

John Jay Esqr.

ALS, NNC (EJ: 09508). Endorsed: ". . . ans^d. 26 D^o". C, MHi: Pickering (EJ: 04854); C, DLC: Hamilton (EJ: 10779).

1. JJ to TP, 18 July 1798, ALS, MHi: Pickering (EJ: 04790).

2. AH's appointment as Inspector General with the rank of major general was announced in the *New-York Gazette*, 21 July, and the *Albany Gazette*, 23 July 1798.

3. For more on AH's promotion, see the editorial note "Hamilton Takes Command," above.

4. TP to GW, 6 July 1798, *PGW: RS*, 2: 386–87.

5. GW to TP, 11 July 1798, *PGW: RS*, 2: 397–400.

6. TP to AH, 16 July 1798, *PAH*, 22: 22–24.

7. JJ obliged, returning GW's letter in his reply to TP. See JJ to TP, 26 July 1798, below.

8. *Annals*, 5: 624.

9. The phrase "as bankrupt in fame" has been crossed out in the Library of Congress copy. TP used a variation of this phrase and leveled a barrage of criticism against Smith in a later letter, remarking that "The President did not know that he was a bankrupt in fame as well as fortune. He had effectually concealed his swindling transactions from his father-in-law, who believes him sound in morals and a great military character the two opinions are alike incorrect." TP to GW, 1 Sept. 1798, *PGW: RS*, 2: 576–77.

10. TP might be referring here to an episode that occurred a few days earlier. According to Abigail Smith Adams, three Federalist senators—Benjamin Goodhue (1748–1814) of Massachusetts, and James Hillhouse, and Uriah Tracy (1755–1807), both of Connecticut—visited the president on 18 July and asked that he withdraw his nomination of Smith as adjutant general. JA refused their request, remarking that his son-in-law was "universally allowd to be a Brave officer, [and] that he had fought & bled in the Service of his County." Abigail Adams to William Smith, 23 July 1798, ALS, MHi: Smith-Townsend. For more on this meeting, see TP to AH, 18 July 1798, note 4, *PAH*, 22: 25–26.

While serving as minister to Great Britain, JA had written to JJ and described Smith's military accomplishments in glowing terms, noting, "Colonel Smith did me much honour in becoming my aid De Camp, after having been General Washington's, has behaved so Well since he has been here & has so many scars & tokens of gallant service to Country in the War, that to reward him as far as lay in my power, I have given him a Girl who is worthy of him." JA to JJ, 16 June 1786, LbC, MHi: Adams. The editors would like to thank Rhonda Barlow for providing the above information.

To Timothy Pickering

Albany 26 July 1798

D^r. Sir

I returned to this place Yesterday, and this morning had the pleasure of recieving your's of the 20th. Instant;[1] for which and the papers enclosed in it, accept my thanks— they give me great Satisfaction— The one you desire to be returned, shall be enclosed with this Letter.[2]

Hamilton's Rank is I fear still liable to question— your Remarks on that Head certainly have weight— Such Doubts should not be left to be brought forward or not, at some future Day, according to Circumstances— To me it appears important, that the relative Rank of Officers, and especially of General officers, should be *decidedly* ascertained known and acknowledged.

with respect to a certain Candidate,[3] I concur with you in Sentiments[4] as to the Impropriety of putting that person in the place proposed for him; and I not only approve but commend the Integrity which enduced you to oppose it. I think the president could not have been fully informed of the objections to which that nomination was liable, or he would have seen its Tendency to an Imputation of his too easily yielding to domestic Considerations; and that he would not have been entirely shielded from it by any presumption that the Generals arrangement would not have contained that name, if it ought to have been omitted— I suspect the General's Information was imperfect, and that neither of them have Reason to Regret the Decision of the Senate.

Be so good as to send me a Copy of the Acts passed during the late session of Congress, to be laid before our Legislature; and believe me to be with great and very sincere Esteem Dr Sir Your most ob^t. Servt.

John Jay

ALS, MHi: Pickering (EJ: 04791). Endorsed: "John Jay Esqr. / July 26. 1798. rec^d. 31." Dft, NNC (EJ: 09509). The draft contains numerous excisions, not all of which are recorded here.

1. See TP to JJ, 20 July 1798, above.

2. TP sent JJ a copy of his letter to GW dated 6 July 1798, and GW's reply of 11 July 1798, with a request that JJ return the latter. For more on this correspondence, see TP to JJ, 20 July 1798, above.

3. William S. Smith; JJ had written here in the Dft version, "you ‸doubtless‸ was [~~certainly very?~~] delicately circumstanced, ~~and~~".

4. JJ had written here in the Dft version, "~~Respecting that the appointment ought not~~ Sentiment ~~respecting~~".

From Peter Augustus Jay (First Letter)

New York 1 August 1798—

Dear Papa

I am happy to learn from the Newspapers that you have safely arrived at Albany— I am sorry however that the fatigue of your Journey must too soon be succeeded by the still more unpleasant fatigue of the approaching session of the Legislature— I am told by M^r. Ten Broeck[1] that the Democratic Party have a Majority of four in the lower House, & of Course that the next Council of Appointment will be an improper one— He sails today on board Capt Boyds Sloop— I shall send by the same Vessel Col: Trumbulls Prints[2] & a Bundle ~~of~~ containing Sisters Shoes & some Muslin for Mama.

At this place the Stream of public Opinion continues to run with increasing rapidity in our Favor— Several Insults lately offered to the Cockade & the Song of Hail Columbia have contributed to accelerate it— A few Evenings ago I was unluckily one of a Company who received much Abuse on Account of the latter— As this Affair has been grossly misrepresented I send you the inclosed Statement which I wrote at the Request of one of the Printers & is strictly accurate—[3] Altho I cannot reproach myself even with Imprudence in the Business, I greatly regret it; since the very Circumstance of having been engaged in a Broil with a Set of Blackguards at a late Hour of the Night has in it something disgraceful— It has however tended to increase the influence of those it was meant to injure, as I think all violent attacks upon a Party which is superior in Numbers & Enthusiasms always must—

Mrs. Bruce's Son Archibald[4] is desirous of being appointed Surgeons Mate of Col: Swartwouts Regt.[5] & I have promised to mention it to you— The Col: I am told will recommend him for the Commission—

Mr. Tiebout some time ago applied to me to obtain for him the Print you have at Albany of General Washington[6] (which he has heard is a better likeness than any he can procure here) in order to copy it for the same work in which yours is to be inserted— I do not Know whether he spoke to you when in town as he intended & therefore mention it now—

Mr. Bleecker does not think that in the present State of the funds he can dispose of your Stock in the Manner you proposed— I am Your Affect: Son

Peter Augustus Jay

Govr. Jay—

ALS, NNC (EJ: 90167). Addressed: "His Excellency / Governor Jay— / Albany—". Endorsed. Enclosure not found.

1. Abraham Ten Broeck, Albany businessman and mayor of Albany, 1779–83 and 1796–98.

2. JT's engravings of the deaths of Generals Warren and Montgomery. See JT to JJ, 6 Mar. 1798, above.

3. Enclosure not found. PAJ's account of the disturbance submitted to the local press was possibly the following:

Last Friday about half past ten in the evening 5 young men were walking on the Battery. Animated by the presence of our illustrious President, who had that day entered the city, under the display of flags, and the thunder of our cannon, amidst the glitter of swords, a forest of bristling bayonets, and the shouts and acclamations of assembled thousands, they were singing, as was common throughout the town, the Federal Song— "Hail Columbia"— A much larger number of boatmen and low fellows, from the wharves and docks immediately collected; and, instigated by the deluding demon of French Jacobinism, and no doubt by some of its mad or corrupted votaries, here approached our young men singing in opposition to them— what song do you think my countrymen? The infamous French song "Ca Ira!" Heavens, what a contrast! How honorable to those who wore the badge of Americanism— How degrading and traitorous in the others. Both parties quickly met each other, and it was not long before the *alien* crew, conscious of their superior numbers, began the dastardly attack, and first insulted, and then beat and bruised them in a most shameful manner. Mr Samuel Malcom, one of the young men seemed to be particularly singled out as the object of their infernal hatred. It was asked if he was the secretary to the president, and on having answered in the affirmative, three or four ruffians grappled him, and altho' he defended himself with great courage, yet he received considerable injury. One villain in the scuffle attempted to gouge him; at another time he was seized by the throat by two or three, and the consequence would have been fatal, had not one of his companions that instant come to his assistance. Meantime several watchmen, and a number of people assembled, and the ruffians desisted from their purpose. Yet no attempt was made to secure them; on the contrary disposition friendly to their escape was discovered.

The young men finding themselves thus unsupported thought it most prudent to retire. In consequence of this unprovoked and scandalous outrage, it was resolved next day that the young men who wore the cockade would go on the battery in the evening, and meet in a body any attack that should be made on the mark they had assumed to evince their disposition to support our government against the insolence, perfidy, ambition, and rapacity of France. A large number of opposite opinions collected:— No attack, however, was made or insults given. They sung several patriotic songs; and at the conclusion, determined to go to mr. Malcom's house and give him three cheers to proclaim in this manner their indignation at the insult offered thro' him to them all, and their fixed resolution to maintain their ground against all opposition. Accordingly, about 400 assembled in front of his house, huzzaed three times, and sung Hail Columbia. They then moved up Broadway to Trinity Church, and there dispersed.

PtD, *Daily Advertiser* (New York), 30 July 1798. Reprinted in several newspapers, including, *Porcupine's Gazette* and *Gazette of the United States* (both Philadelphia), 31 July; *Claypoole's American Daily Advertiser* (Philadelphia), 1 Aug.; *Carey's United States Recorder* (Philadelphia), 2 Aug.; *Albany Centinel*, 3 Aug.; *Massachusetts Mercury* (Boston), 3 Aug.; E, *New-Jersey Journal* (Elizabethtown), 7 Aug.; *Georgetown Gazette* (S.C.), 28 Aug 1798.

A different, though still pro-Federalist rendering, of the affair appeared in the *Farmer's Register* (Chambersburg), 8 Aug. 1798. The Democratic-Republican press responded with its own counter-narrative that interpreted events as representing a Federalist display of divisive politics, excessive party spirit, and slavishness to the executive branch; such a perspective is provided in the *Aurora* (Philadelphia), 1 Aug. 1798. A less partisan accounting appeared in *Greenleaf's New-York Journal*, 1 Aug.; *Carey's United States Recorder* (Philadelphia), 2 Aug.; and *New-Jersey Journal* (Elizabethtown), 7 Aug. 1798.

4. Archibald Bruce (1771–1819), son of Judith Bayard Bruce and William Bruce, developed an interest in mineralogy while studying at Columbia College. "Archibald Bruce" in W. E. Wilson (2016), *The Mineralogical Record: Biographical Archive* https://mineralogicalrecord.com/labels .asp?colid=1015 (accessed July 2018).

5. Lt. Col. Bernardus Swartwout commanded the 5th militia regiment for New York County. *Military Minutes*, 1: 450.

6. For Tiebout, see JJ to PAJ, 16 Apr. 1798, above. The GW print is most likely Tiebout's 1798 engraving, designed and drawn by Charles Buxton, and published by Charles Smith in N.Y. described in David McNeely Stauffer, *American Engravers upon Copper and Steel* (New York, 1907), 2: 526.

From Peter Augustus Jay (Second Letter)

New York 1 Augt. 1798

Dear Papa

I have already written to you by this Mornings Post since then, I have met Gosman[1] the Mason in the Street who told me that he had been sent for by M^r. Church to make another Vault under the Street before the front Door or else to inlarge the old one. I thanked him for the Information & told him that if the thing was to be done at all it must be on M^r. Church's Credit & not yours, but that I would be obliged to him to see me again before he should make any Beginning, which he readily promised— I wish you would be so good as to inform me whether you have any Objections to the digging of this Vault or any Directions to give concerning it—

I saw M^r. Church the Day before yesterday, but he then said not a Word on the Subject— I am Your Affect: Son,

Peter Augustus Jay

Govr Jay

ALS, NNC (EJ: 06070). Addressed" "His Excellency / Governor Jay / Albany". Endorsed.

1. George Gosman (c. 1754–1820), listed in 1798 *New-York Register and Directory* as a "mason and builder" located at 112 Liberty St.

From Timothy Pickering

Philadelphia Augt. 6. 1798.

Sir

By this day's mail I have addressed to you two copies of the laws passed at the last session of Congress.[1]

Of the ten thousand copies of the instructions to & dispatches from our envoys to the French Republic, I propose to send eight hundred to be distrib-uted in the state of New-York. They are now ready, & I shall forward them to the Collector M^r. Sands at the city of New York.—[2] For the convenience of distributing them in the mail, I have caused them to be made up into packets of 5. 10. & 15. which I have franked; and the packets will be accompanied with printed letters, in equal numbers, to regulate the distribution to individual citizens. If you will be pleased to direct M^r. Sands what number of the copies to retain for distribution in the lower counties, he will forward the residue to Albany, to be distributed as you shall think best. I take the liberty now to inclose my letter (which is circular) explaining the plan of distribution, & a copy of the circular letter to be signed & sent by the distributor with each packet:[3] The letter to the Distributor, you will have the goodness to direct to any gentleman at Albany whom you think most proper, & who will take the trouble to dispatch the packets by the mails.— I presume M[r]. Sands would take that trouble at New-York: but if there be any person there whom you prefer, and favour me with his name, I will address him accordingly; and in the mean time request M[r]. Sands, after forwarding the proportion you shall order to Albany, to retain the residue subject to future orders. I have the honor to be, with great respect, Sir, your most ob[t]. serv[t].

Timothy Pickering

His Excellency Governor Jay

P.S. I thought I should hazard a proper distribution of the dispatches, if I committed them to the governors of *some* of the States; and therefore I formed the plan before indicated, of transmitting them to one or two citizens in each state, who should send them in the packets to others, who would make the distribution to individuals: for this reason it will be necessary that the Governors whom I do address on the subject, should ∧*not*∧ notice it in any of their public acts.

ALS, NNC (EJ: 09510). Marked: "(Not official)".

1. *Acts Passed at the Second Session of the Fifth Congress on the United States to America begun and held at the City of Philadelphia, on Monday, the thirteenth of November in the year MDCCXCVII* (Philadelphia, 1798; *Early Am. Imprints*, series 1, no. 34688).

2. *Instructions to the envoys extraordinary and ministers plenipotentiary from the United States of America, to the French republic, their letters of credence and full powers, and the dispatches received from them relative to their mission. Published by the secretary of state, in conformity to the resolutions of Congress, of the 22d June 1798* (Philadelphia, 1798; *Early Am. Imprints*, series 1, no. 34838). JA appointed Joshua Sands collector for the port of New York on 26 Apr. 1797.

3. For more on the distribution of documents relating to the XYZ Affair, see TP to JJ, 2 Aug. 1798, LS, SR: Kenneth Rendell Catalog 45 (1970), item 361 (EJ: 13616).

Address to the New York State Legislature

[Albany, 9 August 1798]

Gentlemen of the Senate and Assembly—

Percieving the various Objections which opposed the holding a special Session of the Legislature, and particularly at this Season of the Year, it was not until after very mature Reflection, that I became convinced that it was my Duty to convene you.[1] The Reasons on which the opinion was founded, have been made known; and subsequent Events have not diminished their Force. Our national Affairs in Relation to France, had since the last Session assumed an aspect so serious and alarming, as to enduce the Government of the united States to communicate to the Public, the Information contained in the State Papers which will be laid before You; and thereby to apprize the Nation of the Dangers which demanded immediate Attention to their Defence and Security.[2] Altho' aware that this great Business belonged to the national Government, yet how far the Safety and essential Interests of this State required that auxiliary and correspondent measures on her Part should be taken without Delay, was a question more proper for You than for me to consider and decide; and that it might without Loss of Time be submitted to your Consideration, a special Session was indispensable—

From the disinterested and friendly Attentions early and repeatedly paid to the Government of the french Republic; and particularly in not only recognizing Its Independence and Authority at a delicate crisis; but also in paying to it, before all the stipulated periods had arrived, the whole Debt contracted under the monarchy,[3] the United States had Reason to expect that the most scrupulous Regard would have been shewn by that Republic, to all the Rights which belonged to their independent pacific and neutral Situation. But these Expectations however rational proved to be delusive. The Rulers of that Republic immediately endeavoured to take undue advantage of this friendly Disposition, and did not hesitate to practice improper arts, and to make overbearing Attempts to envolve us in their Wars and for their objects; and that without any Regard to the State of Peace and Tranquility with which Providence had blessed us, and which it was not less our Duty than our Interest to preserve and maintain, until Reasons the most cogent and indispensable should render a Recurrence to arms necessary and justifiable.—[4]

It is remarkable that from the arrival of the first Minister sent here by that Republic,[5] their Conduct towards us has been constantly becoming more and more disrespectful offensive and inimical; notwithstanding the sincere and conciliatory overtures made to them by the United States. Two Legations sent to them with ample powers and Instructions to propose and even to request an amicable Discussion and Settlement of Differences, have been treated and repelled in a manner repugnant to Justice and Decorum; and the late very reprehensible and disgusting Demands which have been made, leave no Room for us to believe or hope that peace with the United States is among the Objects of the present Directory.[6] The Intrigues and Violence by which several European Republics have been subjugated and empoverished, and by which the Peace and neutral Rights of other unoffending nations continue to be disturbed and violated, cast Light on the Designs and Views of France in their Treatment of this Country— they unite in admonishing us to guard against that System of Deception Domination and Rapine which, embracing both Europe and America, will with Respect to the latter, be still more decidedly manifested, in Case the Directory should acquire a Preponderancy on the Ocean.—

Very wisely therefore has the Government of the United States called upon the nation to prepare for Defence; and very incumbent it is on every ∧State∧ and on every Citizen to co-operate in providing for the general Security. Whether any and what measures conducive to that End, should now be adopted by this State, is a subject which deserves your serious Consideration. It is a question which comprehends several interesting Objects. The Defence of our Port, respecting which some papers will be laid before you— the Defects of the militia Laws, the want of Arsenals, ∧and of sundry articles of military Stores∧ and of appropriated Funds for contingent military Services, are with others of the like kind worthy of Attention.—[7]

While Security is in question, the Expense of providing for it is a secondary Consideration. The Objects before mentioned cannot be accomplished without more Expense than the United States can seasonably and fully provide for. I am apprized of the State of our Treasury, and that it has been greatly exhausted by appropriations heretofore made by the Legislature; but as on the one hand no money can be taken from it without legislative authority, so on the other, it can only be replenished by such means as may be prescribed by Law. It is to be regretted that too many of our Citizens seem to have inadvertently flattered themselves, that unlike all other People past and present, they were to live exempt from Taxes. To the Influence of this Error it is owing, that the State is at this moment in Debt, and paying Interest for money, which in my opinion, it would have been ∧more∧ wise to have collected by a Tax, than to have obtained on Loan. To me it appears to be for the Interest of the State, that the Principal of our Funds, unless on great and urgent occasions, should remain untouched, and that whenever our necessary Expenses exceed our Income, the Deficiency should be supplied by Taxes judiciously and impartially emposed. The Confidence I have in the good Sense of our constituents persuades me, that every Tax adopted on proper occasions, and for necessary Purposes, and on an equitable Plan, will meet with their approbation; especially when they reflect that all the officers of the Government, and every member of the Legislature must partake in its Inconveniences.—[8]

But whatever Difficulties or Differences in opinion may exist or occur relative to our domestic Expenses, it certainly becomes us unanimously and firmly to resolve, that they shall not be encreased by Tribute & Contributions to any foreign nation. The Great Sovereign of the Universe has given us Independence, and to that inestimable Gift has annexed the Duty of defending it. We may be envolved in a severe Contest, but we have no Reason to despair of Success. The United States cannot be conquered but by civil Discord under foreign Direction; and it is useful to recollect, that to this Cause all fallen Republics have owed their Destruction. History will declare to future ages, that the United States were as kind as a neutral nation could with Justice be, to the Republic of France in the Day when her Destiny was doubtful. It is to be hoped that History will also declare that when in the Day of her Power, France became tyrannical as well as triumphant, and had indecently required us to descend and take a Place among her Tributaries, the United States with great magnanimity, and not with less wisdom, spurned her Requisitions and maintained their Dignity—

Permit me to conclude by assuring you, that I shall most cordially co-operate with you in cherishing a Spirit of Union and of Patriotism; and in encouraging and enabling the Citizens of this State to take, not only a due and necessary, but a distinguished part in preserving and transmitting to Posterity our national Honor unsullied, and our national ∧Rights and∧ Sovereignty undiminished.—

John Jay—

DftS, MWA: Jay (EJ: 02615). Printed: *Albany Centinel,* 10 Aug.; *Argus, Greenleaf's New Daily Advertiser* and *Daily Advertiser,* and *New-York Gazette* (all New York), 14 Aug.; *Claypoole's American Daily Advertiser* and *Gazette of the United States* (both Philadelphia), 15 Aug.; *Greenleaf's New York Journal* and *Spectator* (both New York), 15 Aug.; *Porcupine's Gazette* (Philadelphia), 15 Aug.; *Federal Gazette* (Baltimore), 16 Aug.; *Massachusetts Mercury* (Boston), 17 Aug.; E, *Gazette* (Portland), 20 Aug.; *Northern Centinel* (Salem, N.Y.), 20 Aug.; *Guardian, or New Brunswick Advertiser,* 21 Aug.; *Western Star,* (Stockbridge), 21 Aug.; *Berkshire Gazette* (Pittsfield), 22 Aug.; *Connecticut Journal* (New Haven), 22 Aug.; *Sun* (Dover, N.H.), 22 Aug. 1798; *N.Y. Senate Journal,* 22nd sess. (August 1798), 4–5; *N.Y. Assembly Journal* 22nd sess. (August 1798), 5–6; *NYGM,* 2: 420–24.

1. See JJ's proclamation of 2 July 1798, above; and the editorial note "John Jay and the Response to the XYZ Affair in New York," above. JJ delivered this address on 9 Aug. to both houses of the legislature in the assembly room. He also presented a written copy to the assembly, which was read and referred to a committee of the whole house. The assembly ordered copies printed and three hundred to be given to the house for its use. It resolved to present a response to JJ, and appointed a committee consisting of John B. Prevost of New York City, John L. Van Rensselaer of Rensselaer County, and Nathaniel King of Chenango County. *N.Y. Assembly Journal,* 22nd sess. (August 1798), 5–7. For the assembly's response of 14 Aug., and the senate's response of 13 Aug., see below.

In addition the assembly adopted resolutions appointing committees to take up the various parts of the speech relating to the laws, the arsenals and military stores, the defense of the port of New York, and taxation, and to report their opinions to the house. *Albany Gazette,* 17 Aug. 1798; *N.Y. Assembly Journal,* 22nd sess. (August 1798), 8–9. For action taken by some of these committees, see the editorial note "Defending New York", above; and note 8, below.

2. See *Instructions to the envoys extraordinary and ministers plenipotentiary from the United States of America, to the French republic, their letters of credence and full powers, and the dispatches received from them relative to their mission. Published by the secretary of state, in conformity to the resolutions of Congress, of the 22d June 1798* (Philadelphia, 1798; *Early Am. Imprints*, series 1, no. 34838); and note 3 of the editorial note "John Jay and the Response to the XYZ Affair in New York," above.

3. For the recognition of the French Republic and the repayment of the debt to France, see JJ to GW, 23 Sept. 1791; the editorial note "John Jay and the Issue of Neutrality," and note 22; JJ's Draft of a Proclamation by George Washington, enclosed in JJ to AH, 11 Apr. 1793, and note 9; *JJSP*, 5: 336–38, 479–85, 488n22, 491–92, 493n9. JJ had supported both measures.

4. See the editorial note "John Jay and the Issue of Neutrality," *JJSP*, 5: 479–90.

5. See the editorial note "John Jay and the Genet Affair," *JJSP*, 5: 546–61.

6. For the rejection of the missions of Charles Cotesworth Pinckney, and of the American commission consisting of Pinckney, John Marshall, and Elbridge Gerry, and the demands made by Talleyrand's private agents, see the editorial note "John Jay and the Response to the XYZ Affair in New York," above.

7. See the editorial notes "Defending New York" and "Militia Matters in New York," both above.

8. According to the *Albany Centinel* of 17 Aug. 1798:

> Mr. Burr, from the committee who whom was referred that part of his Excellency the Governor's Speech which relates to taxation, reported that the mode of taxation now practiced in this State, is in the opinion of the Committee imperfect and arbitrary, and that a system of taxation on just and equal principles ought with all possible diligence be projected and adopted. That considering the great difficultly and magnitude of the subject much time and consideration will be requisite to mature and perfect it; that from the inconvenience of the season your committee apprehend that the subject cannot at this special session receive the attention and deliberation due to its intricacy and importance. The committee therefore submit to the house the following resolution.
>
> Resolved that the Comptroller be and he is hereby directed to report to this house on the first day of the next meeting of the Legislature, an uniform system of taxation for this state, together with the draft of a bill for carrying the same into operation.
>
> Resolved that this House do agree with the committee in the said report: and do adopt the proceeding resolution.

See also *N.Y. Assembly Journal*, 22nd sess. (August 1798), 18. For the report dated 1 Jan. 1799 by Samuel Jones as state comptroller, respecting a system of taxation for the state, see *N.Y. Assembly Journal*, 22nd sess., 2nd meeting (1799), 3–5. It was submitted and read on 2 Jan. 1799 and referred to the committee of ways and means. For actions on tax proposals in the lower house of the state legislature, see *N.Y. Assembly Journal*, 22nd sess., 2nd meeting (1799), 11, 44, 51, 52, 102, 130, 162, 166, 178, 182, 184, 190, 242, 243–45, 248, 257, 267–68, 288–89. The two resulting bills established the state taxation system: "An Act for the assessment and collection of Taxes," 1 Apr. 1799, and "An Act to raise a sum of Money for the use of this State by Tax, and for the further support of Government," 3 April 1799, *N.Y. State Laws*, 22nd sess., 2nd meeting (1799), 747–71, 834–36.

Address from the Inhabitants of Washington County

[Hartford, N.Y., 9 August 1798]

Address.—

Of the Inhabitants of Washington County, convened at Hartford, by public notice, on the 9th. of August. 1798.—

To his Excellency John Jay. Esqr. Governor of the State of New York.

Sir

We cheerfully embrace this opportunity of congratulating you upon your reelection to the elevated office of first ~~Majestr~~ᴧ~~at~~ᴧ~~y~~ ᴧmagistrateᴧ of this State, and we regard it a mark of discernment in our Citizens, both pleasing and encouraging that, notwithstanding the false, the foul and inflamatory publications industriously circulated to defeat their intentions, such a respectable majority of their suffrages should appear for one whose attachment to their liberties has been uniform, whose firmness in prosecuting them inflexible, and whose integrity, in every part of his official conduct, is unimpeachable.—

We have witnessed, with real pleasure, the pacific measures invariably pursued by the Executive of the United States, towards the Nations of the world; we have traced ~~the~~ ᴧwithᴧ special approbation, his prudent and perseverant attempts to conciliate the affections of the French, by adjusting existing uneasiness, and cannot conceal our emotions of indignation and regret that hitherto they have proved unsuccessful. From the distinguished abilities of our Envoys, the liberal nature of their instructions, and the ample powers with which they were vested, we indulged the flattering hope that every hostile appearance between the two countries would easily be accommodated, and a negociation speedily succeed; but on the contrary, we find that Republic wantonly depredating our commerce, insulting our citizens, endeavouring by different schemes to divide the people from their government, and what rouses in our souls the highest indignation, degrading our very country in the degradation of our Envoys at their bar. These facts we consider calling us as in a tone of thunder, to promptitude of measures, to union and energy of execution.—

We are happy that, agreeably to that firmness which has uniformly marked your public conduct, you have this day convened our Legislature to cooperate with the president of the United States, in concerting measures for our common defence. We humbly hope that they will cordially concur in every measure which your wisdom may deem useful and requisite.—

Peace we estimate as one of the most precious gifts of heaven, and with heart felt emotions of gratitude, we adore the ruler of nations for our long un-interrupted enjoyment of it; yet basely to persue this blessing at the expence of our liberty is undutiful, not only to our selves but also to that benignant *Deity*, who decreed that man should be free. The moment that an individual or a nation, passively receives the insults of oppression, they sink from that elevation of character for which they were originally destined.

Under the impressions of this great truth, while we express unlimited con-fidence in your wisdom and rectitude, we solemnly pledge ourselves at the hazard of our *property* and *Blood* to support you in every laudable measure. Signed by order and in behalf of the meeting.

John Williams Chairman

Zeb: R. Shepherd Sec^ry.

DS, NNC (EJ: 09845). PtD, *Albany Gazette*, 17 Aug.; *Gazette of the United States* (Philadelphia), 25 Aug. 1798; *WJ*, 1: 403–4. Both newspapers also printed the resolutions of the Washington County meeting, and the address sent to the president. On the preparation of such addresses, see the edito-rial note "John Jay and the Response to the XYZ Affair in New York," above. For JJ's reply of 16 Aug. 1798, see below.

Message to the New York State Senate

[Albany, August 10th, 1798]

Gentlemen,

His Excellency the Governor of the Commonwealth of Massachusetts, has in a letter dated the 12th day of last month, transmitted to me, for the purpose of being laid before the Legislature of this State, a concurrent and unanimous Resolution of the House of Representatives and of the Senate of that Commonwealth, and approved by the Governor. The object of it is to obtain an amendment of the Constitution of the United States to provide against the introduction of Foreign influence into our National Councils.

I think it my duty to lay these interesting papers before you, and to recom-mend the important subject of them to your consideration.[1]

John Jay

PtD, *Argus, Greenleaf's New Daily Advertiser* (New York), 20 Aug.; *New-York Gazette*, 20 Aug.; *Daily Advertiser* (New York), 21 Aug.; *Greenleaf's New York Journal*, 22 Aug.; *Otsego Herald* (Coopers-town), 23 Aug. 1798; *N.Y. Senate Journal*, 22nd sess. (August 1798), 6.

1. For the resolution of the Massachusetts legislature of 28 June 1798, see *Acts and Resolves of Mass., 1798–1799* (Boston, 1897), 211–12. It was widely reprinted in the newspapers; see, for ex-ample, *Greenleaf's New York Journal*, 14 July; *Universal Gazette* (Philadelphia), and *Observatory* (Richmond), both 19 July; and the *Medley or Newbedford Marine Journal*, 27 July; *Greenfield Gazette*,

6 Aug.; *Virginia Argus* (Richmond), 4 Dec. 1798. The proposed amendment stipulated: "That (in addition to the other qualifications prescribed by the said constitution) no person shall be eligible as President or Vice-President of the United States, nor shall any person be Senator or Representative in the Congress of the United States, except a natural born citizen, or unless he shall have been a resident in the United States, at the time of the declaration of independence, and shall have continued either to reside within the same, or to be employed in its Service from that period until the time of his election." Massachusetts delegates introduced the resolution in Congress on 7 and 9 July 1798, where it was ordered to lie on the table, and subsequently ignored. See *Claypoole's American Daily Advertiser* (Philadelphia), 1 Aug. 1798; *Annals*, 1: 602; 2: 2132–33; *PAB*, 1: 363–66. The resolution was also circulated among the various states, enclosed in letters from Governor Increase Sumner.

According to the Senate Journal, JJ's message and the accompanying papers were received from his private secretary, read, and committed to a committee of the whole on 10 Aug.; the resolution was adopted by the New York State Senate on 17 Aug. 1798, and sent to the state House of Representatives for concurrence. On 18 Aug., the assembly referred the resolution to a committee of the whole, but no action was taken there before the legislature adjourned. See *Albany Centinel*, 21 Aug.; *New-York Gazette*, 27 Aug.; *Gazette of the United States* (Philadelphia), 28 Aug. 1798; *PAB*, 1: 263–64; *NYGM*, 2: 424.

Before the legislature reconvened in January 1799, similar resolutions were adopted by the Connecticut and Vermont legislatures in October, by the Rhode Island legislature in November, and by the New Hampshire House of Representatives in December. However, outside New England they met with little support. Both North and South Carolina adopted resolutions condemning the principles of the proposed amendment. *PAB*, 1: 364–65; *Independent Chronicle* (Boston), 10–14 Jan. 1799.

In 1799, JJ submitted copies of similar state resolutions sent him to the legislature. These frequently were approved by the state senate but failed in the assembly. For example, Connecticut's resolution adopted in October 1798 by the Connecticut General Assembly, was printed in the *Connecticut Gazette* (New London), of 7 Nov.; *Western Star* (Stockbridge), 13 Nov.; *Amherst Village Messenger*, 17 Nov.; and the *Impartial Herald* (Suffield, Conn.), 20 Nov. 1798. Governor Jonathan Trumbull Jr. forwarded it to JJ on 3 Nov. 1798, and JJ submitted it to the legislature on 4 Jan. 1799. The senate promptly approved it. The assembly set Tuesday, 8 Jan., for consideration of the issue by the committee of the whole. A motion was introduced to concur with the senate resolution, but it was not adopted. *N.Y. Assembly Journal*, 22nd sess., 2nd meeting (1799), 6–7, 13–14.

The details of the assembly debate in the committee of the whole, in which Aaron Burr played a leading role in opposition to the measure, were printed in the *Albany Register* for 11 Jan. 1799 (reprinted in *PAB*, 1: 366–73). Burr denied the risk of foreign influence through election, contending that Americans were already sufficiently distrustful of foreigners, and that the length of residence required by U.S. laws "rendered it impossible that any person be elected to Congress but such as are of approved talents and virtue." He pointed out the appointment of foreigners to prominent military posts posed a greater potential risk for treachery but confidence was reposed in them, and that it was native-born Americans like Benedict Arnold who were treasonous in the past. Burr claimed the resolution would operate ex post facto taking away rights promised to those whom America had welcomed and to whom it had granted asylum. Also speaking against the resolution were assemblymen Adam Comstock (1740–1819) of Saratoga County, James Fairlie (1757–1830) of New York City, David Hopkins of Washington County, Erastus Root (1773–1846) of Delaware County, and Stephen Reynolds of Dutchess County.

Speaking for the resolution were Federalists Nathaniel King (1760–1840) of Chenango County, the speaker of the house, Dirck Ten Broeck of Albany, and Joseph Shurtleff (1746–1814) of Albany

County, who pointed to the failure of the U.S. House of Representatives to pass necessary defense measures, and complained that the leader in that action was foreign-born (Albert Gallatin). The measure failed by a vote of 40 for and 62 against. Republicans sought to have a preamble explaining the assembly's decision added to its message of nonconcurrence with the senate resolution, but that motion did not pass. See *N.Y. Assembly Journal*, 22nd sess., 2nd meeting (1799), 6–7, 13–14, 47–48; *PAB*, 1: 363–78.

Two new resolutions were introduced into the New York State Assembly on 17 Jan. 1799, by John Van Rensselaer. The first proposed that the president, vice president, members of Congress and of the cabinet, and the commander in chief and "first Admiral" of the navy all be natural born citizens or resident in and citizens of the U.S. on 4 July 1783, and have continued to reside in the U.S. or be employed in its service since that time. The second required electors of the president and vice president of the U.S. to designate upon their ballots the name of the person they wish to elect to either office. These resolutions, printed in the *Gazette of the United States* (Philadelphia), 25 Jan. and in the *Medley, or Newbedford Marine Journal*, 1 Feb. 1799, were tabled. *PAB*, 1: 375–76n. 21.

On 5 Feb. 1799, JJ forwarded a letter from the governor of New Hampshire dated 10 Jan. 1799, enclosing two resolutions, adopted on 26 Dec. 1798, one calling for separate ballots for president and vice-president, and one requiring that candidates for president, vice-president, senator and representative, be natural born citizens or residents at the time of the Declaration of Independence, and to have continued to reside in the U.S. or been employed in its service from that period to the time of his election. Should Congress not adopt the latter resolution, the state delegates were empowered to modify the amendment proposal to limit election for president and vice-president to natural born citizens or residents at the time of the Declaration of Independence and citizens for fourteen years by the time of their election, and stipulating that no person could be a member of Congress who was not "actually naturalized" at the time of the making of the amendment and a citizen for fourteen years at the time of election.

The New York State Senate adopted a resolution stipulating separate ballots for president and vice-president on 11 Feb. 1799, and submitted it to the assembly for concurrence. Action was postponed until 7 Mar. 1799, when a bill submitted by a house committee on "An Act providing for the election of electors for the President and Vice President of the United States" was given a reading, and a vote was taken to give a second reading, which passed, but again no action was taken. See JJ's Message to the Senate, 5 Feb. 1799, *Albany Centinel*, 8 Feb.; *Commercial Advertiser* (New York), 11 Feb.; *New-York Gazette*, 13 Feb.; *Spectator* (New York); *Otsego Herald*, 7 Mar. 1799; *N.Y. Assembly Journal*, 22nd sess., 2nd meeting (1799), 127–28, 179; *NYGM*, 2: 433.

Vermont responded to the letter sent by Massachusetts to its governor, Isaac Tichenor, who gave a speech supporting the resolution on 12 Oct. 1798 that was widely printed in New England in such newspapers as the *Vergennes Gazette*, 18 Oct.; *Federal Galaxy* (Brattleboro), 20 Oct.; *Farmer's Weekly Museum* (Walpole), 29 Oct.; *Impartial Herald* (Suffield), 13 Nov., *Thomas's Massachusetts Spy* (Worcester), 14 Nov.; *Putney Argus*, 17 Nov.; *Weekly Oracle* (New London), 19 Nov.; *Sun* (Dover), 21 Nov.; and *Amherst Village Messenger*, 1 Dec. 1798. The legislature responded with a resolution of 23 Oct. 1798, printed in the *Gazette of the United States* (Philadelphia), 21 Nov.; and *Alexandria Times*, 23 Nov. 1798. With his message to the legislature of 28 Jan. 1800, JJ again referred the resolutions from Vermont to the legislature for consideration, but again no action was taken. ADS, PHi: Gratz (EJ: 01135), for full citation, see JJ to Thomas Mifflin, 6 Sept. 1796, note 1, above.

Maryland responded with a resolution of the House of Delegates of 1 Jan. 1799, assented to by the Maryland Senate on 9 Jan. 1799. The resolution was printed in the *Philadelphia Gazette*, 13 Feb., *Albany Gazette*, 15 Feb.; *Centinel of Freedom* (Newark), 19 Feb., and the *Genius of Liberty* (Morristown), 21 Feb. 1799. On 12 Feb., JJ submitted a letter from the Maryland Council of State of 19 Jan.

1799, forwarding their resolution to the legislature. It was referred in the assembly to the committee of the whole, but again no action was taken. *N.Y. Assembly Journal,* 22nd sess., 2nd meeting (1799), 103–4; *NYGM,* 2: 434. The New Jersey legislature adopted the Maryland resolution on 19 Feb. See *New Jersey Journal* (Elizabethtown), 26 Feb. 1799. Delaware apparently also adopted the measure on 10 Jan. 1799. JJ forwarded it to the state senate on 4 Mar., where it was merely referred to the committee of the whole. See *N.Y. Senate Journal,* 22nd sess., 2nd meeting (1799), 63; *City Gazette and Daily Advertiser* (Charleston), 11 Dec. 1799. On 16 Mar. 1799, JJ forwarded to the legislature a message from the governor of Virginia of 2 Mar., enclosing a resolution adopted by the legislature on 16 Jan. 1799, opposing any retrospective action depriving persons already serving in Congress of their positions, but proposing an amendment making foreigners who did not already have rights under the constitution at the time of the passage of the amendment ineligible to take office as U.S. senator or representative, or to any office in the Judiciary or Executive Departments. *N.Y. Assembly Journal,* 22nd sess., 2nd meeting (1799), 220–21; *NYGM,* 2: 438.

Although none of these measures passed while JJ was governor, some of their objectives were achieved after JJ left office. The Twelfth Amendment was passed by Congress in 1803 and ratified by the states in 1804. In addition to requiring separate ballots for president and vice-president, the amendment specified that no person "constitutionally ineligible" to be president could be vice-president, thereby requiring the vice-president also to be a natural born citizen. See Herman V. Ames, "The Proposed Amendments to the Constitution of the United States During the First Century of Our History," *Annual Report of the American Historical Association for the Year 1896* (2 vols.; Washington, D.C., 1897), 2: 30, 4, 77–80.

For JJ's earlier support for restricting officeholding to natural born citizens, see the editorial note "John Jay and the Constitutional Convention of 1787," and note 11; and JJ to GW, 25 July 1787, *JJSP,* 4: xxiii, 465, 466–67n11, 528–29.

From the New York State Senate

[*Senate Chamber, August 13, 1798.*]

SIR,

While we regret the occasion which has induced your Excellency to convene the Legislature at this unusual season, we cannot but consider the measure as resulting from the menacing aspect of our public concerns, and dictated by a just conception of the crisis, and a solicitude on the part of your Excellency for the dearest interests of our common country.

The communications from the Executive of the United States, referred to by your Excellency have produced just alarm to every patriotic American; and beholding, as we do, in the conduct of the Executive Directory of France towards these United States, the most painful proofs of a dereliction of every principle of justice and rectitude, and of settled hostility to this country, we do not hesitate in declaring the measures of defence adopted by the General Government, in our opinion to have become indispensably necessary, and entitled to our warmest approbation.

The faithful page of history will record, the early recognition of the French Republic by our government, while the issue of her struggles was dubious; our friendship in an anticipated payment of our national debt, and our sacred observance of the great land marks of political justice, in the discharge of the various duties imposed by our neutral situation— a conduct on which the early declaration of France invited our Government to repose itself, for the preservation of peace and security.

While we view this crisis as pregnant with danger, and demanding the union of all who cherish a love of country in a patriotic display of the virtues and talents of America, we cannot believe, that in a cause so just, with resources so abundant, under the military auspices of a character alike distinguished in the cabinet and in the field, with a reliance on the great Dispenser of all earthly blessings, the republic is to be despaired of. Nor do we conceive the period to have arrived, when the annals of the United States are to be sullied forever, by the inglorious purchase of peace, in a compliance with the mercenary demands of the French government.

While history presents us, on one hand, with the successful struggles of many inconsiderable but united republics for their liberties, against the most formidable powers—and on the other, with the overthrow and subjugation of States much more considerable, but divided, we accord with your Excellency in the sentiment, that the great source of danger to be apprehended to the United States may be found in the disunion of our citizens, under the influence of foreign councils.

While a disposition on the part of France to interfere in the political concerns of other nations, is evinced by multiplied proofs, painful to humanity, in Europe as well as America, we repose ourselves with confidence on the virtue of our fellow-citizens of all classes, that they will repel with all the ardor of patriotism, those unhallowed reproaches, so fatal to our peace and independence.

On the subject of defence, and the other interesting objects recommended by your Excellency, we shall bestow all that consideration, which a regard to the protection and safety of every part of the State, and the important crisis may demand. *By Order of the Senate*

STEPHEN VAN RENSSELAER, President.

PtD, *Albany Gazette* and *Albany Centinel*, 17 Aug.; *Daily Advertiser* (New York) and *New-York Gazette*, 21 Aug.; *Greenleaf's New York Journal*, 22 Aug.; *Spectator* (New York), 22 Aug.; *Berkshire Gazette* (Pittsfield), 22 Aug.; *Philadelphia Gazette*, 22 Aug.; *Federal Gazette* (Baltimore), 23 Aug.; *Gazette of the United States* (Philadelphia), 23 Aug.; *Massachusetts Mercury* (Boston), 24 Aug.; *Teleg-*

raphe and Daily Advertiser (Baltimore), 24 Aug.; *Northern Centinel* (Salem, N.Y.), 27 Aug.; Thomas's *Massachusetts Spy* (Worcester), 29 Aug.; *Universal Gazette* (Philadelphia), 30 Aug.; and *Otsego Herald* (Cooperstown), 30 Aug. 1798; *N.Y. Senate Journal*, 22nd sess. (August 1798), 8.

After JJ's address on 9 Aug., above, was given to the legislature, the state senate appointed a committee, consisting of Thomas R. Gold, William Denning, and James Gordon, to prepare a response, and assigned discussion of the issues raised in the address to a committee of the whole. Gold presented a draft address on 11 Aug. that was referred to the committee of the whole. He read the address to the senate on 13 Aug. The senate approved it, without amendment, ordered it to be signed by President of the Senate Stephen Van Rensselaer, and presented it to JJ. *N.Y. Senate Journal*, 22nd sess. (August 1798), 7–8. For JJ's reply, see JJ's Message to the New York State Senate, 13 Aug. 1798, below.

Message to the New York State Senate

[Albany, 13 August 1798]

GENTLEMEN,

I receive this address with great satisfaction—[1] it expresses sentiments and evinces knowledge which cannot be too generally entertained and diffused. While the people of the United States have just and clear views of their true interests, it will not be possible to force or seduce them to pass under a foreign yoke; especially when, as at present, both their civil and military affairs are directed by men of tried virtue and patriotism, and who by great and eminent services have justly merited the confidence they enjoy.

JOHN JAY.

PtD, *Albany Gazette* and *Albany Centinel*, 17 Aug.; *New-York Gazette* and *Daily Advertiser* (New York), 21 Aug.; *Greenleaf's New York Journal*, and *Spectator* (New York), 22 Aug.; *Gazette of the United States* (Philadelphia) and *Philadelphia Gazette*, 22 Aug.; *Claypoole's American Daily Advertiser* (Philadelphia), 23 Aug.; *Federal Gazette* (Baltimore), 23 Aug.; *Telegraphe and Daily Advertiser* (Baltimore), 24 Aug.; *Massachusetts Mercury* (Boston), 24 Aug.; *Northern Centinel* (Salem, N.Y.), 27 Aug.; *Thomas's Massachusetts Spy* (Worcester), 29 Aug.; *Universal Gazette* (Philadelphia), 30 Aug.; and *Otsego Herald* (Cooperstown), 30 Aug. 1798. *N.Y. Senate Journal*, 22nd sess. (August 1798), 11.

1. See New York State Senate to JJ, 13 Aug. 1798, above.

From the New York State Assembly

[Assembly-Chamber, August 14, 1798.]

SIR,

Being fully convinced that your Excellency in convening this extraordinary session of the Legislature, has been solely influenced by a just and attentive regard to the public welfare, and that the measure is warranted by the very critical situation of public affairs, it is with the utmost promptitude that we meet your Excellency at this important and alarming crisis.

It is to be regretted, that the repeated, disinterested and friendly attentions of our government to the republic of France, have not produced the happy effects we had reason to expect; and that from the progress and result of the negotiations tendered by the United States to the republic of France, there is reason to apprehend that peace with us is not among the objects of the present Directory.

Admonished by multiplied examples in Europe, that civil discord, directed by a foreign hand, is the bane of republican governments, we feel persuaded that the virtue and patriotism of the great body of our fellow citizens, will repel with equal firmness the diplomatic arts, and open violence, not only of the republic of France but of all foreign nations.

Permit us to assure your Excellency, that the several important subjects submitted to our consideration, in your Excellency's speech, and the papers accompanying the same, shall receive our sincere deliberation.

The necessary appropriations for the defence of the state, for the erection of arsenals, and for a suitable supply of military implements and stores, will in a particular manner engage our immediate attention.

It is with pleasure we receive, and with great sincerity we reciprocate, your Excellency's asurances, of a determination to cherish a spirit of union and patriotism, and shall most cheerfully co-operate with you in encouraging and enabling our citizens to transmit to posterity, our national honor and our national rights unsullied and undiminished. *By order of the Assembly,*

DIRCK TEN BROECK *Speaker.*

PtD, *Albany Gazette* and *Albany Centinel,* 17 Aug.; *Daily Advertiser* (New York) and *Argus, Greeenleaf's New Daily Advertiser,* 21 Aug.; *Greenleaf's New York Journal,* 22 Aug.; *Spectator* (New York), 22 Aug.; *Federal Gazette* (Baltimore), 22 Aug.; *Philadelphia Gazette,* 22. Aug.; *Gazette of the United States* (Philadelphia), 23 Aug.; *Massachusetts Mercury* (Boston), 24 Aug.; and *Telegraphe and Daily Advertiser* (Baltimore), 24 Aug.; *Northern Centinel* (Salem, N.Y.), 27 Aug.; *Universal Gazette* (Philadelphia), 30 Aug.; and *Otsego Herald* (Cooperstown), 30 Aug. 1798. *N.Y. Assembly Journal,* 22nd sess. (August 1798), 16.

This final text of the assembly's response to JJ's address of 9 Aug., above, is the culmination of a series of drafts submitted to a committee of the whole and amended in the course of debate, a process that indicated the sensitivity of the subject and the political divisions involved with regard to the references to France. The original draft (not found) submitted by the committee appointed to prepare the address was replaced in the committee of the whole by amendment on a motion by John Van Rensselaer, one of the original committee members who composed an alternate draft. A second proposed address submitted by David Hopkins of Washington County was approved in place of Van Rensselaer's draft. A third proposed draft submitted by John B. Prevost was rejected. The committee of the whole then returned to discussing and revising Hopkins's text. The committee then reported it to the house where it was again read and agreed to. *N.Y. Assembly Journal*, 22nd sess. (August 1798), 12–17. For JJ's reply, see JJ's Message to the New York State Assembly, 14 Aug. 1798, below.

Message to the New York State Assembly

[Albany, 14 August 1798]

GENTLEMEN,

It gives me pleasure to find that you concur with me in opinion, as to the situation of our public affairs, and the expediency of convening the Legislature at this alarming crisis.[1] The utility of this measure will depend on the result of your deliberations; which will I am persuaded be such, as clearly to evince that the fear of France has not fallen upon us, but on the contrary, that we have not only sensibility to feel, but also resolution to resent, the indignities offered to our nation and government, and repel with the spirit becoming a brave and free people, every attack on our national honor and Independence.

JOHN JAY

PtD, *Albany Gazette* and *Albany Centinel*, 17 Aug.; *Daily Advertiser* (New York) and *Argus, Greenleaf's New Daily Advertiser*, 21 Aug.; *Greenleaf's New York Journal* and *Spectator* (New York), 22 Aug.; *Federal Gazette* (Baltimore), 22 Aug.; *Philadelphia Gazette*, 22 Aug.; *Gazette of the United States* (Philadelphia), 23 Aug.; *Massachusetts Mercury* (Boston), 24 Aug.; *Telegraphe and Daily Advertiser* (Baltimore), 24 Aug.; *Universal Gazette* (Philadelphia), 30 Aug.; and *Otsego Herald* (Cooperstown), 30 Aug. 1798. *N.Y. Assembly Journal*, 22nd sess. (August 1798), 19.

1. See New York State Assembly to JJ, 14 Aug. 1798, above.

To the Inhabitants of Washington County

To the Inhabitants of Washington County who convened at Hartford by public notice on the 9 Augt 1798

Albany 16 augt 1798—

Gentl^n.

The address with which you have honored me ~~by your chairman and secretary~~ contains Congratulations & Assurances which I recieve with Gratitude.[1] I view the Conduct of ~~France the French D France~~ ˄The french Directory˄ towards this Country in the same Light that You do; and observe with pleasure that your Sentiments and Resolutions ~~as~~ respecting it are such as ˄particularly˄ become ~~Americans~~ ˄the People of a County which bears the name of *Washington*˄ ˄Americans˄. It is worthy of Consideration, that we have no Liberty to acquire, but much to preserve; ~~for~~ we already possess all the Liberty that men can have, the entire and perfect Liberty of governing our-selves. [*illegible*] Every Principle of Honor and Interest calls upon us to use this Liberty wisely, and to ~~defend it at every Risque~~ ∧unite ~~us~~ in ~~resolving∧ and~~ preparing to defend ~~it at every Risque~~ ∧it∧ with the like Spirit and Perse-verance with ~~with~~ ∧which∧ it was obtained— accept my best wishes for the Prosperity of your County; and ~~it may as may ever be distinguished by the~~ noble ∧excellent∧ ~~Principles as well as~~ ∧the Example of the∧ ~~virtuous manner of Washington~~ ∧that as it bears the name so it may also ~~follow∧~~ cherish the Patriotism & other virtues which distinguish the illustrious Washington.

John Jay

Dft, NNC (EJ: 09224). *WJ*, 1: 404–5.

1. See Address from the Inhabitants of Washington County, 9 Aug. 1798, above. For the back-ground, see the editorial note "John Jay and the Response to the XYZ Affair in New York," above.

From John Cosens Ogden

[[Troy] Augt 17. / [17]98]

Sir

While the enobled situation of yourself, and the Lieut[enan]^t. Gover-nor of the State of New York, call upon you both, to give public ~~notice~~ and costly dinners to statesmen, to maintain the dignity of government, I am en-closed in the walls of a loathsome prison, because my Father-in-Law, General Wooster,[1] embarked with you, General Washington, and other military men and revolutionalists, and sacrifised his family, and those connected with them, to maintain liberty and independence for the States.

Having sought to do my duty, as a son and brother for nearly thirty years & particularly while my brothers were young, served in the army, and were qualifying themselves for honorable and virtuous life, I became involved for a small sum, on their accounts, which has been cruelly pushed, from mere ma-levolence, from one made rich and great, by those events of war which have made me, and mine poor & miserable. These brethren are dead long since.

In this situation, I am in want, and secluded, from the benefits of even that liberty, and that friendship, from distinguished Statesmen, which honor, hu-manity, their hearts and wishes dictate.

By the valor of my country men, brethren, and the relations of the family of my wife, you have become the Governor of a State, while your utmost am-bition once, would have been to be an eminent Lawyer.

My letter two days since hinted at my situation. The prisoners and the charity, not of opulent men, give me bread in Troy, while the State of New York has given the fortune of my wife, her mother, and brother, and his ~~family~~ & our children into the hands of the people of Vermont, to serve the purpose of selfishness, sacrilege, and sedition.[2]

With these facts in my possession, I reluctantly ask for a guinea, which shall be accepted gratefully and applied prudently to relieve my wants, while I [~~illegible~~] ∧transmit∧ copies of this to Gen⹁. Washington and the first men of the States.[3] A smaller sum will be received with gratitude, but your wealth, and station excused me from asking for less.

The evasions of Statesmen, Sheriffs, and Bailiffs, unless founded in justice and humanity, are of no avail with wise, brave, patriotic, and suffering citizens. They, I trust, will never see the families of their generals and of the clergy, who have done their duty amidst a plundered church, and an infidel age trampled upon in any State.

Speculators in Land, Loans, and in Independence may flourish for a while, but the people will hear the calls of humanity in a State which rob[b]ed America's good citizens, to please Vermonters, who gained speculations for themselves, and thus exposed the christian church to sacrilege and infidelity.

Humanity my Dear Governor, calls upon you, and copies of this will call upon other Statesmen, no longer to suffer the addresses of distressed widows and their families to pass without success, while distresses increase in a multiplied ration upon those whom the nation pity; Whom honor, plighted faith, and justice ought to protect. I have the honor to be Your Excellency's devoted servant,

John C. Ogden

Copy of a letter sent to Gov⹁ Jay

CS, DLC: Washington (EJ: 10663). Addressed: "General Washington / Mount Vernon, / Virginia". Endorsed. John Cosens (Cousins) Ogden (1751–1800), son of Moses Ogden of Elizabethtown, N.J., and a 1770 Princeton graduate, lived in New Haven until 1786 when he was ordained a priest in the Episcopal Church by Samuel Seabury. From 1786 until forced into retirement in 1793 reportedly upon "his mind becoming deranged," he was rector of St. John's Episcopal Church in Portsmouth, N.H. Then and thereafter as an itinerant minister and missionary he was involved in numerous disputes with Congregationalists, President Timothy Dwight of Yale and others, and published polemical pamphlets and anonymous Republican pieces in the *Aurora* (Philadelphia). In 1800 he published his last work: *A Excursion into Bethlehem & Nazareth, in Pennsylvania in the Year 1799; with a succinct History of the Society of the United Brethren commonly called Moravians* (Philadelphia, 1800; *Early Am. Imprints*, series 1, no. 38149). See Richard A. Harrison, *Princetonians, 1769–1775: A Biographical Dictionary* (Princeton, 1980), 93–98; *The Granite Monthly: A Magazine of Literature, History and State*, 36: 268–69.

1. David Wooster, of Stratford, Conn., served with the British Army in the Seven Years' War and as a brigadier general in the Continental Army, participating in the Canadian Campaign of 1775–76. He returned to Connecticut to command the state militia and was mortally wounded at the Battle of Ridgefield in April 1777.

2. Wooster had served before the war as collector at New Haven, and Ogden, who had married Wooster's daughter, Mary Clapp Wooster, granddaughter of former President Thomas Clapp of Yale, subsequently sought unsuccessfully to secure that post. Wooster, who had advanced funds to pay his troops, died insolvent, and as his papers were destroyed in a British raid on his home after his death, his family was unable to prove any of their claims and received no repayment or pension. Ogden's writings often complained of the unfairness of the treatment of him and of his wife's family compared to the success of others who rose to prominence during the Revolution and after. At the time of this letter Ogden was briefly in debtors' prison in Troy, N.Y.

3. Although Ogden had been writing GW about his various travails since 30 Oct. 1789, Tobias Lear's acknowledgment on 4 Feb. 1790 of Ogden's letter of 20 Jan. 1790 is the only response that has been found. In his appeal to GW of 4 Sept. 1798, Ogden enclosed copies of his letters to JJ of 17 and 29 Aug. and 4 Sept., and wrote: "How far you ever condescend to second such requests as the following to Governor Jay, I cannot tell. If it is consistent with your line of proceeding I know that I have only to hint at the favor." Ogden had asked JJ to help him secure the post of collector of the customs at New Haven, upon the death of the current collector. On 12 Feb. 1799 he wrote GW from Litchfield, Conn., contending that Oliver Wolcott Jr. had imprisoned him there for a small debt because he wanted the post of collector for a relative and because Wolcott had "joined with the church plunderers in Portsmouth to destroy" him. For Ogden's letters to GW, see *PGW: RS*, 3: 27–28.

On JJ's assistance to Ogden, see Ogden to JJ, 29 Aug., C in author's hand, DLC: Washington (EJ: 12505); and, for his reply to an earlier letter from Ogden (not found), see JJ to Ogden, 21 Mar. 1798, LbkC, N: Governor's Lbk. 1 (EJ: 03133).

To John Adams

Albany 21 Aug.ᵗ 1798.—

Sir

I have the Honor of transmitting to You, herewith enclosed, an address from the Senate and assembly of this State which passed and was agreed to by both Houses *unanimously*—[1]

It gives me pleasure to reflect that from this and[2] the numerous other Expressions of the public Sentiment, relative to the reprehensible conduct of France towards this Country, you may rely on the decided co-operation of the nation in the measures necessary to protect their Rights, and maintain their Honor and Independence—

I have too long known and too often been a witness to your patriotic and successful Exertions, not to be convinced that you well deserve both Confidence and Gratitude; and it is but doing them Justice to say that no Republics have given to their Patriots and Benefactors less cause of Complaint than the united States of america— I have the Honor to be with great Respect and Esteem Sir Your most obed.t. & most h'ble Serv.t

John Jay

John Adams Esq.r.— President of / the united States of america—

ALS, MHi: Adams. Endorsed: "Gov. Jay Albany Aug 21.st / inclosing an address of the/Senate & Assembly of the State / of New-York rec.d Aug 30 / ans.d 31. Aug." Enclosures: Resolutions of the New York State Senate and Assembly, 17–20 Aug. 1798, and Address to the President by the New York State Senate and Assembly, 17–20 Aug. 1798; Dft, NNC (EJ: 07472); LbkC, N: Governor's Lbk. 1 (EJ: 03164). For JA's reply to JJ, see 30 Aug. 1798, ALS, NNC (EJ: 05435).

1. The enclosed address sent to JA read as follows:

To the President of the United States of America
The Respectful Address of the Senate and Assembly of the State of New York
Sir
Persuaded that it was the Duty and Interest of the United States to preserve and cultivate Peace and a good Understanding with all Nations, we unanimously approve of the Measures you have taken for that purpose with respect to France.

The manner in which our Ministers of Peace and Conciliation have been treated and rejected by that Republic, we consider as an Infraction of the Laws and Usages of civilized Nations, and as a violation of that equality of Sovereign Rights which ought to subsist and be maintained between them. The Indignity offered to our Nation by that Treatment is greatly aggravated by Pecuniary Requisitions. On these Topics we cannot reflect without Surprise and Indignation. When to these Considerations are added, those extensive Depredations on our Commerce which no amicable Overtures for Accomodation, could induce the Directory to forbear or suspend, we think our Situation relative to that Republic so serious, as to render a general Expression of the Public Sentiment indispensible.

Being a free and independent People, we are determined to remain so. The Constitution of the United States is the deliberate work and free choice of the People, and we will at every Hazard maintain it. The Government of the United States results from the Constitution, and being Administered by Men, constitutionally chosen and appointed, shall, in all its constitutional and legal proceedings, receive our decided support. And whatever Differences of Opinion may have existed among us on local Questions, on these great Points, we neither are nor will be, *a divided People*; but on the contrary, it is our unanimous Resolution, at the risk of our Lives and Fortunes, to maintain and defend our National Honor Rights and Independence, against the French Republic and every other Nation and Power.

We are convinced of the necessity of Union among ourselves, and shall regard those as unworthy, who at this momentous juncture of our Affairs shall attempt to disseminate Discord among the People, who while united, are able to repel the Attacks of any Enemy that may dare towards our Country.

This State, Sir, will in every Event, and to every Extent, bear her full proportion of the National Burthens, in full Confidence, that due Attention will be paid to the strong claims she holds in the National Defence and Protection.

We cannot on this Occasion omit expressing the Satisfaction we derive from the fresh instance of great and disinterested Patriotism which your illustrious Predecessor has manifested. He has been, and may he long continue to be, the Instrument of great good, and the example of great virtue to his fellow Citizens. You also have strong and well founded Claims to the Gratitude of our Country. May a kind Providence enable you to add to them by such Councils and measures as will speedily secure the Blessings of Honorable Peace to our Nation, and to yourself the Honor and Satisfaction of having wisely and successfully fulfilled the Duties of your exalted and important Station.

By order and on behalf of the Senate.
Stephen Van Rensselaer
President

In Senate August 17th. 1798
In Assembly August 20th. 1798

By order and on behalf of the Assembly
Dirck Ten Broeck
Speaker—

D, MHi: Adams. PtD, *Albany Gazette*, 24 Aug. 1798; reprinted, *Commercial Advertiser* (New York), 28 Aug.; *New-York Gazette*, 28 Aug.; *Albany Centinel*, 28 Aug.; *Gazette of the United States* (Philadelphia), 28 Aug; *Greenleaf's New York Journal*, 29 Aug.; *Argus, Greenleaf's New Daily Advertiser* and *Spectator* (both New York), 29 Aug.; *Telegraphe and Daily Advertiser* (Baltimore), 31 Aug.; *Whitestone Gazette* (Utica), 3 Sept.; *Russell's Gazette* (Boston), 3 Sept.; *Connecticut Journal* (New Haven), 5 Sept.; *Connecticut Gazette* (New London), 5 Sept.; *Berkshire Gazette* (Pittsfield), 12 Sept.; *Impartial Herald* (Suffield, Conn.), 18 Sept. 1798. *N.Y. Assembly Journal*, 22nd sess. (August 1798), 20–21; *N.Y. Senate Journal*, 22nd sess. (August 1798), 16. NYGM, 2: 445–46; HPJ, 4: 248–49.

JA responded to the New York state legislature with the following:

GENTLEMEN,

I have received your unanimous address. If an address of so much dignity and authority could have received any additions from the channel of conveyance, you have chosen that which is nearest to my heart, in his Excellency John Jay the Governor of the state of New-York, of whose purity, patriotism fortitude, independence and profound wisdom I have been a witness for a long course of years. The position in the Union of the great and growing state of New-York, its incalculable advantages in agriculture, as well as commerce, renders this unanimous act of the two houses of its legislature, one of the most important events of the present year.

With the most sincere respect and cordial satisfaction, Gentlemen, I congratulate you on the decided appearance in America, of a solid national character. From the Mississippi to the St. Croix, unquestionable proofs have been given of national feelings, national principles, and national system. This is all that was wanting to establish the power of the American people, and insure the respect and justice of other nations. For all that is personal to myself, I pray you to accept my best thanks. I never have had, and I never shall have, any claims on the gratitude of my country. If I have done my duty to them, and they are convinced of it, this is all that I have desired or shall desire.

The strong claims which your state holds in the national defense and protection will have every attention that depends on me.

I thank you for the expression of the satisfaction you derive from the fresh instance of great and disinterested patriotism which my illustrious predecessor has manifested. May he long continue to be, as he ever has been, the instrument of great good, and the example of great virtue to his fellow-citizens; the last act of his political life, in accepting his appointment, will be recorded in history as one of the most brilliant examples of public virtue, that ever was exhibited among mankind.

JOHN ADAMS.

Quincy, August 31, 1798.

PtD, *Spectator* (New York), 9 Jan.; reprinted, *Federal Gazette* (Baltimore), 12 Jan.; *Columbian Centinel* (Boston), 19 Jan.; *Eastern Herald* (Portland), 28 Jan. 1799; *N.Y. Senate Journal*, 22nd sess., 2nd meeting (1799), 4; *N.Y. Assembly Journal*, 22nd sess., 2nd meeting (1799), 8; *NYGM*, 2: 446–47.

2. JJ did not include the phrase "this and" in the draft version.

From Alexander Hamilton

New York Aug 27. 1798

Dear Sir,

I was very sorry when at Albany not to have seen You. I called the day after my arrival but you were then indisposed or abroad & the rest of my stay I was very unwell.

An apprehension is excited here that in consequence of the Petitions of the Militia Officers the persons named to the new Companies will not be appointed.[1] I take it for granted that this must be a groundless apprehension as far as may depend on the Executive. For certainly the ordinary Militia Officers can on no military principles have any pretensions in relation to *new* and *extraordinary* Corps which grow up or are created. And as to expediency, nothing can be clearer. The utility of these new corps in various aspects needs no comment. Their existence depends on their being officered in the manner they themselves desire. To attempt to place them under the present Militia Officers is to annihilate them.

Ten to *One* the Opposition on the part of these Officers originates in an Antifœderal scheme. Let them by their disappointment be disgusted & resign. What then? They will have acted presumptuously or ignorantly. Many bad men will be gotten rid [of] & the best can easily be replaced, with as good or better.— Tis then a plain case. There is really not a difficulty worth the least attention.

M[r]. Gracie[2] has solicited my interposition with you for the pardon of *Janus* ∧Ross∧ lately convicted of forging a Check on the Bank— His argument is that he ∧the Culprit∧ is of respectable connections in South Carolina—quite a lad (say from 16 to 18) a very simple lad—& led to this act by the embarrassment of not being able to account for the *prudent* expenditure of a sum of money advanced him by a friend of his fathers for his own use. I confide in what M[r] Gracie says & really believe it is as favourable a case for a pardon as can easily occur.³ I remain with respect & true attachment Dr Sir Y^r Obed^t Servt

A. Hamilton

ALS, NNC (EJ: 05629). Addressed: "His Excellency / Governor Jay / Albany—". Endorsed: ". . . ans^d 30 Do. [Aug.] 1798". Stamped. *PAH*, 22: 163–65. For JJ's reply, see his letter of 30 Aug. 1798, ALS, DLC: Hamilton (EJ: 10782); *WJ*, 2: 285–86; *HPJ*, 4: 249–50; *PAH*, 22: 170.

1. In response to Congress's call in May 1798 for a Provisional Army, several volunteer companies formed throughout New York State during the summer. A dispute arose concerning officer appointments for these new units. The volunteers insisted that they should select their leaders, while many serving in the regular militia contended that those militiamen who had seniority in rank deserved to be promoted and appointed as officers. For more on this episode, see the editorial note "Militia Matters in New York State," above.

2. Archibald Gracie (1755–1829), born in Scotland, lived in Virginia and then New York where he prospered as a merchant, shipowner, and banker. Gracie served as president of the New-York Insurance Company and a director of the Bank of New York.

3. For more on the Ross case and JJ's acts of pardoning, see the editorial note "Crime and Punishment in Federalist New York," above.

From John Adams

Quincy Aug 30th 1798

Sir,

I had last night the pleasure to receive the letter your Excellency did me the honor to write me on the 21st of this month inclosing the resolutions of the Senate & Assembly of New-York, & their unanimous address.¹ I can scarcely imagine any event that could do me more honor or give me greater satisfaction. The unanimity of New York, of vast importance in the union, is a happy omen of success & prosperity to this country. I pray you, Sir, to accept of my sincere thanks, for the affectionate & obliging manner, in which you have communicated to me, this important proceeding of your legislature With great respect, esteem & affection I am always your Excellencys most obedient & most humble Servant

John Adams

His Excellency John Jay Esqr.

ALS, NNC (EJ: 05435). Endorsed.

1. See JJ's letter to JA of 21 Aug. 1798, and enclosure, above.

To Peter Augustus Jay

Albany— Sunday 2ᵈ. Septʳ. 1798

Dear Peter

I have recᵈ. your Letter of the 28 Ult.¹ and altho' I have nothing interesting to communicate, yet frequent Letters between us are both proper and agreable.

Within a few Days past many Sloops with many Passengers have arrived from NYork— accounts said to have come from them, have filled this City with alarm and anxiety. From your Letter and from one I have recᵈ. from the Health office I am persuaded that the Sickness at New York has become serious, and threatens considerable Calamities to its Inhabitants— on such occasions they who can remove themselves and their Families do well not to remain; and I am glad to find that you intended to go to Rye—where I expect this Letter will find You—²

Mʳ. Munro's broken Sulkey³ may not be a misfortune to him—unless Circumstances should occur to make it his *Duty* to visit the City, I think he should stay at Mamaroneck— They who unnecessarily expose themselves to Danger, and they who improperly avoid it are both reprehensible. Remember either to get the £100 from John Lyons or his Bond for it— if you recieve it, discharge my Note for that Sum to your uncle Peter and add the Interest due on it. I doubt your getting that money without a Jaunt to Bedford, and the Ride will not be unpleasant— when there, obtain & communicate whatever Information you may Judge interesting. We now have pleasant weather, & I find myself the better for it. The Family are all well. The little notes in your Hands should not be forgotten— Habits of Punctuality are worth more than they cost to every man, and particularly to one of your Profession. Your vacant Hours at Rye might be agreably employed in making ∧for your uncle∧ a map of the Farm, distinguishing the Fields, and noting the Springs Islands &cᵃ. I am Dʳ. Peter Your Affᵗᵉ. Father

John Jay

Remember me to our Friends at Rye—

[*in margin*] ∧W[illia]ᵐ. is delighted with his Eagle, and much the more from his having recᵈ. it from *You*. Little Attentions often make deep and durable Impressions on men as well as Children—∧

Mʳ. Peter Augustus Jay—

ALS, NNC (EJ: 11463). Endorsed: "Letter from Papa / Albany 2 Septʳ. 1798 / recᵈ. Sept. 8ᵗʰ. at Rye".
1. Letter not found.

2. See the editorial note "John Jay and the Yellow Fever Epidemics," above.

3. "Sulky": a two-wheeled carriage accommodating one person.

From John Trumbull

72 Welbeck S[t]. London Sep[tr]. 20th. 1798

Dear Sir,

I wrote you a long letter on the 10th. of December last, which with many others was lost with the Ship Fame, which foundered at Sea:[1] a similar fate may also have attended letters from you to me, since it is very long since I have had the Honour to receive a line from you;— I have written several times since.

In one of mine of last year I hinted to you a difficulty which was likely to occur in the business of the Commission on the 10th. of October—[2] We met this question, on the 10th. of April, and after much discussion and difficulty have at length succeeded to establish a Rule under which I trust that the Business will be entirely concluded within Two Years.— The Doctrine very obstinately insisted on by Doctors Commons would have rendered our Board, like their Courts, perennial.

The Government of France see that they played a bad game with our Commissioners; & finding that bullying does not succeed, have already begun to flatter; I think however in a very bungling manner.—[3] The parting proposition made to M[r]. Gerry of recalling & renewing all Commissions to Privateers in the West Indies signifies nothing, since it is not of illegal Commissions, but of improper Instructions that we have to complain.— The second measure, the Arretée taking off the Embargo which had been laid on American Ships is of as little moment and as easily seen thro:— the treatment which our Merchants had long met, had so far discouraged them from the French Commerce, that the Embargo did not affect more than 20 Ships in all the Republic, and those of little value:— It was natural therefore that they should be willing to exchange this trifling plunder for the much greater advantage which they must expect to derive from such a display of seeming liberality and Moderation accompanied as it is with such sugared Words of good will, and professions of an ardent desire for the Continuance of Harmony.— As the War will probably be renewed in Europe, we must expect to see this game played in its full extent, and with the deepest Art;— but I trust that the Fate of Venice, Switzerland &c &c who have been ruined by their silly confidence in similar professions will guard us against adding ourselves to the number of deluded Slaves.

The Friendship of that Government is infinitely more to be dreaded by us than their Arms;— distant as we are I do not fear the latter but the influence of their Intrigues appears to be as boundless and dangerous as their Ambition.

The Redacteur of the 15th. and other Paris papers of the 16th. announce in a pompous and silly message of the Directory, the safe arrival of Buonaparte with his Army in Egypt,—of his having been at Grand Cairo on the 23rd. July, and of his having continued his March— I presume to the Red Sea and India— the same papers state that the Fleet which carried him, has been attacked by Admiral Neilson in a Fort at the Mouth of the Nile, and after an obstinate defence, entirely destroyed or captured. We hope that this News coming from such Authority will prove true,— altho we have been so often deluded by similar Accounts, that we are become a little slow of Faith.[4]

Ireland has been in Arms;— happily their friends the French have been slow and feeble in their cooperation, and the Affair was nearly crushed before the arrival of the paltry reinforcement which surrendered at Discretion to Lord Cornwallis a few days ago.— no apprehension is now entertained of a renewal of the War, unless a powerful French force should again have the good fortune to Land.[5]

This Letter will be delivered to you by my friend M[r]. James Wadsworth[6] whose conduct in Europe has been very respectable, who has been lately in France, and whose Politics are I believe very right,— that is, void of all confidence in foreign *friends Lips* and disposed to see America rely for prosperity, only upon God, and her own exertions; temporary connexions founded on present Interests He will admit, but thinks with many others, that we have had sufficient experience of European friendship,— He will be an useful inhabitant of your Western Country— With him goes M[r]. West's oldest Son, with the intention of purchasing and settling in the same neighbourhood.[7] He is a young Man of many excellent qualities,—who I think chooses wisely, considering the miserable prospect of an Artist has in the present times, and who I hope will succeed and become a valuable acquisition in that quarter:— any recommendation from me of the Son of such a man, is to be sure, superfluous, yet I should feel myself wanting in Duty to his Parents as well as in friendship to him, if I did not solicit for him, your notice, advice & protection. I beg my best Respects to M[rs]. Jay, and am with the highest Regard & Esteem Dear Sir Your Obliged and faithful servant and Friend

Jn°: Trumbull

His Excellency John Jay Esq[r]. &c &c &c

ALS, NNC (EJ: 07210). Endorsed: ". . . an^d. 12 Decr. D^o. [1798]". LbkC, DLC: Trumbull (EJ: 10358).

1. A copy of JT's letter of 10 Dec. 1797 discussing the situation in France is located in JT's Lbk, NHi: Trumbull.

2. See JT to JJ, 7 Aug. 1797, above, in which he expressed concern that the term for the commission would expire before much would be accomplished.

3. On the French refusal to receive the American commissioners unless they payed bribes and the American response, see the editorial note "John Jay and the Response to the XYZ Affair in New York," above.

4. The British fleet under Sir Horatio Nelson defeated the French naval force that carried Napoleon's troops to Egypt at the Battle of the Nile, 1–3 Aug. 1798.

5. A French force of approximately one thousand troops invaded Ireland in August 1798 to assist the United Irish Rebellion, but were defeated in the Battle of Ballinamuck (8 Sept. 1798) by British forces led by Cornwallis. A second attempt by a larger French force to land in Ireland failed on 12 October.

6. James Wadsworth (1768–1844) of Connecticut was recruited by his second cousin Jeremiah Wadsworth as a land agent for development of lands in western New York acquired in the Phelps and Gorham Purchase. He promoted settlement of Genesee Valley lands both in the United States and in Europe and settled in and developed Geneseo, N.Y. His European travels, including his voyages, lasted from February 1796 to November 1798. See Henry Greenleaf Pearson, *James S. Wadsworth of Geneseo, Brevet Major-General of United States Volunteers* (New York, 1913), 1–21.

7. Benjamin West's son, Raphael Lamar West (1769–1850), painter and lithographer, arrived in the United States in 1800 with intent to settle in western New York; disappointed by his prospects, he returned to England within two years.

From Richard Varick

New York Sept. 24. 1798

Dear Sir

On Saturday Evening last (by post) I had the honor of receiving your Excellency's favor of the 17th.—[1]

It is true that the Attorney General[2] was in Custody in his own House at the suit of Brockholst Livingston, who while in Town promised to forbear & when gone the Ca. Sa[3] was issued.— The Business was adjusted last Monday & the Attorney General set off Express to Delaware Oyer & Terminer.

An Execution also issued ag^ts. Thomas Cooper[4] for the same Debts, he was not taken, but went up as an Express to Brockholst to settle it for the Attorney General & was to cross the River to Coldenham & to pass from there to Delaware County to attend the Attorney Generals Business unless Hoffman should appear at Coldenham at a certain Time.— That Execution is with drawn If Cooper is still absent it must be on Account of the fever which prevails in the Vicinity of his Office which is in Wall Street:— He is however much involved.— All this I have from Col^o. Troup Yesterday.

I sought for the Sheriff but was told that his fears had driven him across the Hudson. He told Troup that the fever prevailed in his neighbourhood, his apprehensions had brought it nearer that it actually yet has been: but he is in plain English a poor dastardly money making Devil, unfit to hold the Office for this City.[5]

The Jail is yet free from fever & so are our Alms House & Bridwell where the Health Committee & police Office are now established.— the £10. Court is shut up & from motives of Humanity to the Debtors as well as our Officers I am not sorry for it.[6]

The City is indeed much afflicted.— The Numbers of Sick cannot be less than 800 or 1000 in the different parts & in many Instances the patients do not survive 48 or 36 Hours.

The Deaths of today

20th . — 21 Men 16 Women— 3 Childn.— 34 of fever
21 . — 29 . . 14 . . . 2 . . . . 39 do.
22 . — 28 . . 14 . . . 4 . . . . 41 do.

Among the above I recollect Mr Goerck City Surveyor Mrs. Brevoort an Old Lady, Widow of Elias of Maiden Lane Mr Robt. Hyslop, Dr. Amasa Dingley & Gilbert Milligan, Archibald McLean printer.— Thomas Marwood Mercht. & George Doolit Architect who built the New York Bank.[7]

Dr Brooks is like to Die.— Dr. Gardner Jones Br. in Law to the Comptroller was taken ill on Friday Night & has laid very ill till this Morning when he is a little better: but I apprehend his Death.— Dr. John Bowne Hicks taken very violently Yesterday, but is somewhat better.—[8]

I shall write the Comptroller abt. Dr. G. Jones by next Post. I remain with Great Respect Your Excellencys most obedt Servt.

Rich. Varick

His Excellency Govr. Jay

The Mayrs. Court sat on Tuesday last & consisted of the Mayr. Sheriff Dy. Clerk, Cryer 2 Attorneys & 3 bye Standers.— Next Tuesday the Sessions are to meet & I expect no better Attendance, except the Recorder & an Ald[erma]n. to form the Court.

ALS, NNC (EJ: 09293).

1. Letter not found.

2. Josiah Ogden Hoffman.

3. "Ca. Sa." an abbreviation of the Latin legal term "Capias ad Satisfaciendum," which translates roughly as a writ commanding an officer to place a person in custody until a claim is satisfied. For a full description of the term, see William Blackstone, *Commentaries on the Laws of England in four books*, 1st Worcester ed. (Worcester, 1790; *Early Am. Imprints*, series 1, no. 22365), 3: 414–17.

4. Thomas Cooper (d. 1817) was a New York City lawyer.

5. Jacob John Lansing. See editorial note "John Jay and the Yellow Fever Epidemics," above; and JJ to James Morris, 18 Jan. 1799, Dft, NNC (EJ: 08984).

6. "An ACT to amend an act for the more speedy recovery of debts to the value of ten pounds" which amended an earlier 1787 law, was passed by the New York legislature on 9 Apr. 1795. See *N.Y. State Laws*, 18th sess. (1795), 49–50; *The ten pound act: that is to say, an act for the more speedy recovery of debts to the value of ten pounds* . . . (Lansingburgh, 1795; *Early Amer. Imprints*, series 1, no. 29195).

7. Casimir Thomas Goerck (c. 1755–98); Mrs. Brevoort was possibly Lea (Persel) Brevoort, who married Elias Brevoort (1715–75) of Maiden Lane; Robert Hyslop, merchant; Amasa Dingley, physician; Gilbert Milligan, physician; Archibald McLean, editor and proprietor of the *New York Gazette*; possibly George Doolittle, an Irish architect who emigrated to America.

8. Either David or John Wallis Brooks; John Bowne Hicks (d. 1798).

To Richard Varick

Albany 3 Octr. 1798

D^r. Sir

I have been fav^d. with yours of the 28th·ult. and am much obliged to You for the Information contained in that, & in your preceding Letters.[1] Yesterday Capt. Benson rec^d. a letter from his Brother Robt.[2] from which there appears Reason to hope that Violence of the fever at New York begins to abate—

The Removal of the Sheriff from the City is in my opinion improper— be so obliging as to inform me whether he remains out of Town, or whether he returns to it daily, or how often at stated or uncertain periods—and whether he pays any and what Degree of *personal* attention to the Duties of his office—

I must request the favor of you to forward the enclosed Letter to Mr King by the packet—[3] With great Esteem and Regard I am Dear Sir your most ob^t Servt—

John Jay

The Honb. Rich^d. Varick Esqr

ALS, DUSC (EJ: 13436). Addressed: "The Hon'ble / Rich^d. Varick Esqr— / mayor of the City of / New York". Marked: "Post paid" in JJ's handwriting and stamped "PAID". Endorsed: ". . . Ans^d."

1. Letter of 28 Sept. not found. On yellow fever and Sheriff J. J. Lansing, see Varick to JJ, 24 Sept. 1798, above; the editorial note "John Jay and the Yellow Fever Epidemics," above; and JJ to James Morris, 18 Jan. 1799, Dft, NNC (EJ: 08984).

2. Henry and Robert Benson.

3. Probably JJ to RK, 30 Sept. 1798, ALS, NHi: King (EJ: 00705), and LbkC, N: Governor's Lbk. 1 (EJ: 03171), requesting the purchase of muskets.

To John Oothout

Albany 4. Oct[r]. 1798

Sir.

I have been fav[d]. with yours of the 24. Ult.[1] and should have written to you frequently had anything sufficiently interesting occurred. All accounts from New York represent the City as being in a Melancholy situation; and great credit is to those who like you and others are doing every thing in their power to mitigate the common calamity. Altho the Fever will probably cease before the middle of next month, yet every exertion should be made to re-move whatever may engender or encrease its extension or its virulence: and I flatter myself that the powers vested in you by Law for those purposes will continue to be executed, not only with prudence but also with promptitude and firmness.[2] With Sentiments of esteem and regard I remain Sir Your most ob[t]. Serv[t]:

John Oothout Esq[r]. Chairman of the Com[rs]. of the Health Office—

LbkC, N: Governor's Lbk. 1 (EJ: 03172).

1. Letter not found.

2. JJ wrote this letter in the midst of New York's worst yellow fever epidemic. See the editorial note "John Jay and the Yellow Fever Epidemics," above. See also JJ to John Oothout and the Health Office, 20 Nov. 1798, below.

Morris S. Miller for John Jay to John Barber and Solomon Southwick

Albany 9 Oct[o]. 1798.

Gentlemen

I yesterday informed His Excellency the Governor that on applying for your account against him for the Albany Register, you observed to me that it had been sent (without being charged) to the Governor as a compliment to the first Magistrate of the State.

I am directed to signify to you, that the manner in which your Paper frequently treats the National Government and many of our most worthy and respectable public Characters will not permit him to consider or receive it as a Compliment. He therefore requests that it may in future be omitted. I am Gentlemen Your most ob[t]. & Hum[bl][e]. Serv[t].

Morris S. Miller Private Sec[y].[1]

Mess[rs]. Barber & Southwick[2]

LbkC, N: Governor's Lbk. 1 (EJ: 03173).

1. Morris S. Miller (1779–1824) of New York City. Following his service for JJ, Miller moved to Utica and became involved in local politics, sitting as president of that village (1808), serving as judge of the court of common pleas (1810–24), and representing his district as a Federalist representative in Congress (1813–15).

2. John Barber (c. 1758–1808) and Solomon Southwick (1773–1839) published the *Albany Register*, a Republican newspaper.

To Josiah Ogden Hoffman

Albany 22 Octr. 1798

Dr Sir

It is painful to say disagreable Things to ones Friends, ~~and yet~~ and it is not without Reluctance that I apprize You, that your pecuniary Embarrassments ~~have excited apprehensions that~~ are considered as being incompatible with the Attention and Independence with which the Duties of your office should be executed. This opinion has for some time past been gradually becoming more strong and more extensive, ~~and~~ Your arrest at New York, and the unsettled State of your Accounts with the public, have ~~greatly~~ ∧tended to∧ ~~confirmed~~ it —[1] It has been mentioned not only to me but also to others, that in Excuse for not paying a certain account, you alledged the want of money in the Treasury but that you w^d. endeavour to negociate the Cash warrant you rec^d. from the Comptroller; which warrant I am assured was duly paid to you by the Treasurer—

The Cordiality ∧& Friendship∧ which has so long and uniformly subsisted between our Families, will not permit me to conceal from you these disagreable Circumstances. They have made such strong Impressions, even in minds perfectly well disposed towards You, that the Question whether an Att[orne]^y. Gen[era]^l. so circumstanced should be continued in office, must speedily be considered. Whatever the Result may be, you should also be apprized, that it will certainly be insisted that the Attorney General do in future reside at the Seat of Government, and I confess to You candidly that I [~~illegible~~] ∧think it highly∧ proper & expedient, and therefore as indispensable.

I am aware of the Effect of this Letter on your Feelings— mine are very far from being gratified by it[2] ~~for~~ With the best wishes that you may soon be blessed by the Return of Prosperity I am D[ea]^r. Sir, your most ob^t. & hble Servt.

Josiah Ogden Hoffman Esqr.

Att[orne]^y Genl. of the State of NYork

N.B. Enclosed this to Mr Hale to forward—not knowing where Mr Hoffman resides at present—.

Dft, NNC (EJ: 08468). Endorsed.

1. JJ refers to both Hoffman's personal debts, contracted in land speculation, and his handling of public funds to cover expenses related to the court cases surrounding the Connecticut Gore controversy, specifically, disagreements in reimbursing General Matthew Carpenter (d. 1839) of Chemung County, N.Y., for expenses incurred as a witness. Hoffman enlisted the help of AH and Robert Troup in clearing the matter in general and his reputation with JJ in particular. In his lengthy reply to JJ of 31 Oct. 1798, Hoffman explained that his personal debts were the result of standing as surety for others. As to his arrest, Hoffman remarks that "the Cause of this Arrest was not for any debt of my own—its to the unsettled state of my Accounts with the Publick" and a disagreement with the Comptroller over when those accounts should be stated and settled and the amount owed. It is apparent from Hoffman's remarks that he believed that state comptroller Samuel Jones had insinuated that Hoffman had stolen public funds. See Stephen Van Rensselaer to AH, 6 Nov. 1797, *PAH*, 21: 310–11; John Laurance to AH, 10 Dec. 1797, *PAH*, 21: 327–28; Richard Varick to JJ, 24 Sept. 1798, above; Hoffman to JJ, 31 Oct. 1798, ALS, NNC (EJ: 08470); Troup to JJ, 5 Nov. 1798, below; AH to JJ, 8 Nov. 1798, *PAH*, 22: 226–28; JJ to AH, 10 Nov. 1798, *PAH*, 22: 233–34; JJ to AH, 12 Nov. 1798, *PAH*, 22: 236–37; JJ to Hoffman, 12 Nov. 1798, Dft, NNC (EJ: 08466); and JJ to Troup, 12 Nov. 1798, Dft, NNC (EJ: 12827). For the Connecticut Gore controversy, see JJ to Thomas Mifflin, 6 Sept. 1796, Hoffman to JJ, 14 Dec. 1797, both above; and JJ to Jonathan Trumbull Jr., 4 Dec. 1799, Dft, NNC (EJ: 08998); and JJ's Address to the New York State Legislature, 28 Jan. 1800, ADS, PHi: Gratz (EJ: 01135), for full citation see JJ to Thomas Mifflin, 6 Sept. 1796, above.

2. In his reply to JJ of 31 Oct. 1798, Hoffman took pains to defend his honor and address JJ's concerns about how his conduct affected his ability to perform his duty. "Early in life, I prescribed to myself a Rule for my political and private Conduct— I have ever intended, that the Publick Good, should characterize the one, and the other, I trust, bears no Stamp of Turpitude— The uniform consistency of my political life, has acquired me the disinterested friendship of many Characters, equally eminent in Abilities and Station— Among such, I have felt a pride in numbering yourself, and of such friendships, I was most ambitious— to be deprived of them, through deceptive Misrepresentations, or by the Insinuations of Prejudice, must prove to me, the source of unceasing Regret— You can judge then, Sir, how gratifying it will be to my pride, to be restored to that Confidence which, I flatter myself, you once professed. . ."

From Robert Troup

New York 5 November 1798

Dear Sir,

The letter which the Attorney General lately received from you in relation to his office has been shewn both to General Hamilton and to me.[1]

Notwithstanding my ardent desire to withdraw myself from all concerns of a public nature I find it impracticable in some instances, without great violence to my feelings, to avoid a communication of circumstances which have come to my Knowlege. The situation of the Attorney General furnishes an instance of this Kind; and I Know you too well to believe you capable of being displeased with any information, however unimportant, that proceeds from disinterested motives.

During the Attorney General's late arrest I gave him, at his request, all the assistance in my power; and in a short time I was made happy by his discharge. Whilst I was pursuing this object I discovered that his debts were much more inconsiderable than they were generally supposed to be: and that he was in a favorable train of negociating the settlement of such as threatened an indignity to his person. My endeavours have since been united with his to hasten the settlement; and I have good reason to conclude we shall soon be successful. Hence I cannot help persuading myself that he will not again be exposed to the severe mortification he has lately experienced.

His removal to Albany General Hamilton and I think with you to be indispensable. He concurs with us in opinion; and has come to a resolution of sacrificing his private convenience to that of the public.

From an account he has exhibited to me it appears that the State is in his debt, and I have no doubt that Carpenter's story about the warrant is a gross calumny.

These circumstances I suggest to you as worthy of consideration before you finally determine on the propriety or impropriety of submitting to the Council the question of the Attorney General's continuance in office. A measure which must deeply affect his reputation and the interest of his family! At the same time I acknowledge that no inducements should be permitted to interfere with a due respect to the honor & welfare of the State.[2]

Perhaps it may not be improper to add that it is not Known that the Attorney General, in executing any of the duties of his office, has manifested a want of attention—industry—or talents.

I cannot conclude this letter without mentioning that I have come to a candid & explicit explanation with the Attorney General on a point which has proved a source of infinite disquietude to many of your friends. It has long been thought by them that he has in several cases, where important appointments were depending, maneuvred with the members of the Council, and thus disappointed your wishes, openly expressed, in favor of better, and fitter men. This charge has been so repeatedly urged against him that I confess I have been one of those who believed it true. I told him so, but he declared it to be wholly unfounded. As I was not furnished with facts to prove the charge I proceeded to assure him that if it were true he had injured You—he had injured your friends—and he had set an example pregnant with serious mischiefs. And I added that if he persisted in the same course the inevitable consequence must be, his separation from every man who valued a virtuous and independent executive.[3] My ideas on this point perfectly accord with those of General Hamilton, and he has explained himself to the Attorney

General respecting it, in a manner equally candid & explicit.[4] With the sincerest regard I am Dear Sir, your friend,

Rob. Troup

His Excellency Governor Jay

ALS, NNC (EJ: 07196). Endorsed: ". . . an[swere]ᵈ. 12 Nov 1798".

1. See JJ to Josiah Ogden Hoffman, 22 Oct. 1798, and note 1, above, for an explanation of Hoffman's financial troubles. AH wrote a similar letter in Hoffman's defense, dated 8 Nov. 1798, *PAH*, 22: 226–28. In his letter, AH ended by warning JJ "Let me My Dear Sir caution you on the subject of the Comptroller. He is Hoffman's enemy on personal grounds & it is easy to confide too much in his candor." In JJ's reply of 10 Nov. 1798, *PAH*, 22: 233–34, he cautioned AH "Should he [Hoffman] be again humiliated by a Cause: I shall certainly think it my Duty to place the office in a Situation where it will not be exposed to such Indignity."

2. In his reply to Troup of 12 Nov. 1798, Dft, NNC (EJ: 12827), JJ emphasized his personal concern for Hoffman's situation but noted: "From my Infancy friendly Sentiments ~~towards~~ ₐrespecting ₐ that Family have been habitual to me. But my dear Sir you well know that ~~my~~ official Duties [*illegible*] must prevail whenever there ~~may be~~ ₐis a ₐ competition between them and personal Considerations. [*illegible*] An Attorney General ~~be be exposed to the weight~~ ₐought not to remain ever exposed to ₐ that ~~oppressive~~ ₐdepressing ₐ and painful ~~Influences~~ ₐkind of ascendency ₐ which Creditors have over those who enjoy personal Liberty at their will and by their Forbearance."

3. In his 12 Nov. reply to Troup cited in note 2, above, JJ responded to this point: "Whatever Interference Mʳ Hoffman may or may not have had, with the Counsels of Appointment I cannot ascertain. Certain it is ~~however~~ that a general Belief of it exists; ~~admitting it to have been the Case;~~ I never suspected him to have been actuated by ~~any~~ ₐon any occasion by ₐ motives on any occasion hostile to me".

4. In JJ's letter to Hoffman of 12 Nov. 1798, Dft, NNC (EJ: 08466), he gave him advice on how to proceed with his difficulties and expressed happiness "to learn from your Letter that they have greatly subsided; ~~and~~ ₐbut I ₐ shall be ₐstill ₐ more ~~so still be~~ ₐhappy, both for your ₐ Sake & that of the public ₐto ₐ be assured, that they have been surmounted; ₐ~~and that both for your part & that of the public~~ₐ; for I will not conceal from you that ~~th~~ not only the arrests, but the ~~mortifying overtures, mercies &~~ ₐre-iterated—Indulgencies and ₐ Forbearances of Creditors are ₐin my opinion ₐ incompatable with the authority Respectability & Independence ~~of your~~ which should ~~invariably~~ be associated with your office."

Inventory of John Jay's Property

[Albany, 8–9 Nov. 1798]

Recᵈ. of John Jay nine Lists vizᵗ.

1 a List respecting the House and Lot of Ground in the City of Albany, where he now resides

2 a List of Slaves owned by him

3 a List of Land owned by him in Tioga County—

4 a List of Land owned by him in Ontario County—

5 a List of Houses & Lots owned by him the City of NYork

6   a List of Land owned by him in Orange County—

7   a List of Land owned by him in WestChester County—

8   a List of Land owned by him in Otsego County

9   a List of land owned by him in the County of Sussex and State of New Jersey—

10   a List of Land owned by him in the County of Chittendon, and State of Vermont—

11   a List of Land purchased by him in New Hampshire

Harm^s A Wendell

Albany Nov. 1798—

1   List or account of the House and outhouses, & Lot of Ground, occupied by John Jay, in the city of *Albany*, and owned by James Caldwell of the Town of Water Vliet on the 1 Octr. 1798—

The Lott is on the Southerly Side of *State* Street, and extends to Street— It's width being various in different parts, its Dimensions cannot be so clearly described or understood as by dividing it into three parts.

The *first* part on State Street is 32 feet 6 Inches wide in front & Rear, and 86 feet in Length— The *second* part then begins, and is 61 feet wide, but after extending in Length 52 feet, becomes 68 feet wide— there the *third* part beings, and is 28 wide throughout, and 37 feet in Length.

The Dwelling House on this Lot fronts on State Street, and is 28 feet wide, and 49 feet 6 Inches in Length— it is built of Brick, and has *three* Stories. The Number & Size of the Windows is as follows

		Number	Height Feet – Inches	Width Feet – Inches
Garret		2	4 – 7	2 – 3
3^d Story		6	5 – 8	3 – 3
2^d. Story	Front	3		3 – 6
	Rear	2	6	3 – 6
1st. Story		4	6 – 6	3 – 6
Cellar	Front	1	2 – 6	1 – 6
	Rear	1	4 – 4	3 – 6

In the Rear of the House there is a Piazza or Shed, a small part of it is enclosed, and in that part are two windows of the same size vizt. 5 feet by 3 Feet— On the Lot is a Carriage House & Stable built of Wood, under one Roof— it is 32 feet wide, & 34 feet deep. There is also on the Lot a Pidgeon and Fowl House of Brick 9 Feet by 11 Feet,— a necessary House of Brick, 8 feet by 8 feet 6 Inches, and a Tenement of Wood, one story high, and 16 feet square— in it are two Windows of the same size, vizt. 6 Feet by 3 feet 6

Inches— The neighbours next to this House are Abraham Ten Eyck on the East and M^rs. Cheeseburgh on the West—[1]

Albany 8 Novr. 1798

2   List of Slaves between the ages of twelve & fifty Years owned by John Jay—on the 1st. Octr. 1798—

I have three male and three female Slaves— five of them are with me in this City; and one of them is in the City of New York. I purchase Slaves and manumit them at proper ages, and when their faithful Services shall have afforded a reasonable Retribution; but while the property remains vested in me, I consider them as being within the Intent of the Act of obedience to which this List is given—[2]

Albany 8 Novr. 1798

3   List and Description of Land owned by John Jay of the City of Albany in the County of *Tioga* on the 1 Octr. 1798—

I am the owner of *one* undivided *fourth* part of a Tract of Land containing sixteen thousand acres, on the East side of Chenengo River, being part of a larger Tract purchased by the State, of the Oneida and Tuscarora Indians, and distinguished in a map thereof filed in the Secretary's office, by being part of Township number three or Green Township—[3]

Albany 9 Novr. 1798—

4   List and Description of Land owned by John Jay of the City of Albany, in the County of *Ontario* on the 1 Octr. 1798—

I am the owner of *one* undivided *fourth* part of a Tract of Land of twenty two thousand five hundred and forty six acres and one fourth of an acre, in the said County of Ontario— Being part of a Tract granted by the State to George Scriba, and which in a map thereof deposited in the Secretary's Office is distinguished as Lott N°. 13—

Albany 9 Novr 1798

5   A List and Description of Houses and Lots owned by John Jay of the city of Albany, in the City & County of New York- on the 1 Octr. 1798—

One vacant Lot of twenty five feet by one hundred, on the Easterly Side of the Broadway, and fronting the same, and adjacent to the northerly Side of the House and Lot lately occupied by Moses Pengree— Also about Eight acres (for I have not with me the papers necessary to ascertain the *exact* Quantity) of vacant Land, of which the greater part is swamp, situate on the Easterly Side of the Broadway, between the Vacant Lot abovementioned, and the Lot of the Corporation on which water works were formerly commenced— of this parcel of Land there have been laid out six Lots of twenty five feet by one hundred feet— one of them is the Lot on which I built the small house lately occupied as aforesaid by Moses Pengree— I do not know the name of the Person to whom it has been rented for this Year— the other five Lots are occupied under Leases from me for long Terms. Also a Lot at the corner of Stone Street and broad Street, of which the great part is occupied for storing of coal, by a M^r. Arnet— therein on it a little work shop and a small Tenement, whose exact Dimensions I do not know. Also the House and Lott of Ground in the Broadway which is occupied by John B. Church Esqr., and the House and Lot of Ground in Stone Street occupied by Mr Ludlow—[4]

Albany 8 Novr. 1798—

6   List and Description of Land owned by John Jay of the city of Albany in the County of Orange on the 1 Octr. 1798—

I am the owner of certain Lots in the patent of Cheescocks, but whether & how far they are affected by the Line between Orange and Rockland I am uncertain vizt. Lot n^o.^{x} 2 part of the great mountain Lot N°. 7, containing fourteen hundred & ninety six acres, which by the Commissioners who divided it in 1789 was valued at two shillings per acre. N°.5^x part of Great Mountain Lot N°. 10 containing four hundred and Eighty acres, valued at the same Sum and Lot N°. 9 part of great mountain Lot N°. 10 containing three hundred and fifty acres, valued at one Shilling per acre— Also Lot N°. 41 containing one hundred and fifty acres, valued at ten Shillings per acre— it was occupied some Years ago by Israel Lummereaux, of whom I have not heard for several Years. When this Division was made I supposed it comprehended all the Lands in that patent devised to me and the other Devices, but I have been informed that there is a small Residue still in common. I have also an undivided Interest in common with Robert Morris Esqr. Judge of New Jersey District, and others, in a Tract adjoining to Cheescocks, but have not in my possession any Papers respecting it— I believe a very little of this Tract remains unsold— but Mr Morris who has always managed this Business can and will give satisfactory Information on the Subject—[5]

Albany 9 Nov. 1798

7   List and Description of Land owned by John Jay of the City of Albany, in the County of West Chester on the 1 Octr. 1798—

I am the owner of *one* undivided *half* part of a Lot of Land containing by Estimation Seventy acres, in the Township of Rye adjacent to the farm of Peter Jay and occupied by him—

I also own a Tract in the Township of Bedford, which ought to contain not less than seven hundred and fifty acres, but on which I have Reason to believe that considerable Encroachment has been made— Between fifty and Sixty acres of this Tract are occupied by John Nicolls— about one hundred more together with a Grist and Saw mill thereon by John Lyons; and the Residue is occupied and managed by Maj^r. Saml. Lyons—^{6}

Albany 8 Novr. 1798—

8   List and Description of a ∧a Lot of∧ Land owned by John Jay of the City of Albany in the County of *Otsego* on the 1 Octr. 1798

I am the owner of Lot N^o. thirty five in the patent of Whiteborough, which I believe is in the County of *Otsego*, containing nine hundred and fifty seven acres, confirmed to me by an act passed the 18 Feby 1789—^{7}

Albany 9 Novr 1798—

9   List or Description of Land owned by John Jay of the City of Albany, in Sussex County in the State of New *Jersey*— on 1 Octr. 1798—

I am the owner of *one* undivided *third* part of a Tract of one thousand and fifty five acres, commonly called the great Bog Meadow, situate in the Town of Newtown, and part of which may be seen from the Court House in that Town— adjoining to this meadow I have Land in severalty, which having been surveyed by, and being under the Superintendence and Care of Martin Ryerson Esqr., who lives within a few miles of the Court House, will doubt-less be more accurately described by him than it is at present in my power to do.—^{8}

Albany 8 Novr. 1798—

10— A List and Description of Land owned by John Jay of the City of Albany, in the County of Chittenden in the State of *Vermont* on the 1 Octr. 1798

I am the owner of *seven* undivided *sixteenth* parts of a Tract of Land granted by the State of Vermont on the 28 Decr. 1792 to me and John Cozine in different proportions— this Tract is situate in the County of Chittenden, in the Town of Jay, in the said State of Vermont, and contains sixteen thousand acres straight measure to the same more or less—^{9}

Albany 8 Novr. 1798

List or description of Land purchased by John Jay of the City of Albany in the Township of Fairfield in the State of New Hampshire—

In the Year 1774 I purchased of Nathaniel Cushman of Lebanon in Connecticut, and he did by Deed dated the 12 April 1774 convey to me five Rights or Shares in the Township of Fairfield in New Hampshire, as granted by the then Governor of New Hampshire by patent or Charter dated the 17 December 1771. For the property I have since paid Taxes— Since the Revolution I have been informed that the state of New Hampshire has regranted this Land— and my public Duties leaving me very little Leisure to attend to

my private Concerns, I am at a Loss to determine whether I shall ever recieve any Benefit from this purchase. I nevertheless think it my Duty to state
these Facts—

Albany 9 Novr 1798

AD, NNC (EJ: 09216). Endorsed: "Lists on acc.^t of the Real Estate / of John Jay— made according
to / the Act of Congress imposing a / direct Tax—".

On 14 July 1798 the federal government imposed the first direct tax on the owners of houses,
land, and slaves. The tax was intended to finance defense expenditures during the Quasi-War with
France. Each state was assigned a quota of the two million dollar tax. See *Stat.*, 1: 597–604. The 1798
Federal Tax lists developed for implementing the law provided ownership, rental, and descriptive
information for every house then existing, but few records are still extant for most states, including New York. See Judith Green Watson, "A Discovery: 1798 Direct Tax Records for Connecticut,"
Prologue 39 (Spring, 2007): 6–15. Harmanus A. Wendell of Albany, the recipient of JJ's lists, was
appointed one of the assistant assessors for the Albany District assigned to assess the value of property and to collect the taxes thereon as required by the law. See *Albany Gazette*, 2 Nov. 1798.

1. For more on JJ's property in Albany, see the editorial note "The Capital Moves to Albany,"
above.

2. Five of the six enslaved persons belonging to JJ can be identified with a degree of certainty:
the three enslaved women were probably Clarinda, Dinah, and Phillis, the last of whom was living in New York City. Two of three enslaved men were probably Jack and Peter. For more on the
lives of those enslaved members within John Jay's household, see Jan Horton, *Listening for Clarinda*
(Bedford, 2000).

3. For more on JJ's property in the Chenango Tract, see John Rutherfurd to JJ, 24 June 1795, ALS,
NNC (EJ: 07083), and JJ to Rutherfurd, 27 June 1795, C, NNC (EJ: 08943).

4. For more on JJ's property in New York City, see the editorial note "A Man of Property," *JJSP*,
4: 6–9.

5. For more on JJ's property in the Cheesecock Patent, see PAJ to JJ, 13 May 1798, above.

6. For more on JJ's farmstead in Bedford, see Circuit Court Diary [11 Oct.–16 Dec. 1791], and
[15 Apr.–1 June 1792], *JJSP*, 5: 339, 389; PAJ to JJ, 29 Dec. 1798, below; and 16 Mar. 1799, ALS, NNC
(EJ: 06077); JJ to PAJ, 12 Apr. 1799, ALS, NyKaJJH (EJ: 09982).

7. Goldsborough Banyer Jr. to JJ, 30 Jan. 1804, ALS, NNC (EJ: 09702).

8. For more on JJ's property in Sussex County, see Circuit Court Diary [27 July–7 Aug. 1791],
JJSP, 5: 327 and 328n6; PAJ to JJ, 27 Nov. 1800, ALS, NNC (EJ: 06098); 23 Dec. 1800, Dft, NNC
(EJ: 11452).

9. For more on JJ's property in Chittenden County, see JJ to Isaac Tichenor, 21 Oct. 1799, Dft,
NNC (EJ: 08997).

To John Oothout and the Health Office

Albany 20th. Novr 1798

Gentlemen

Those Officers who fulfill their Duties in a manner highly satisfactory &
useful do honor not only to themselves but to the Governm.^t Convinced by
repeated and concurring Accounts of the Zeal, Perseverance & Talents by

which you have rendered most important services to our suffering fellow Citizens, during the late melancholy season, I think it my duty to express to you my Warmest approbation & thanks.—.—. I have been frequently informed that the late fever did certainly derive additional malignancy from large Quantities of putrid provisions stored in the City. Let nothing be omitted to ascertain the names of the Inspectors by whom those provisions were inspected and branded.

Permit me to recommend this subject to your Attention, and to request that you will transmit to me whatever Information you may possess or acquire concerning it. I have the Honor to be with great Esteem Gen.ᵗ Your most obᵗ. Servᵗ.

John Oothout Esqʳ. Chairman of the Comʳˢ. of the Health Office[1] NYork Noʳ. 20 To Col. Troup, Genˡ. Clarkson, P.J. Munro[2]

LbkC, N: Governor's Lbk. 1 (EJ: 03188).

1. The Health Office consisted of Dr. Richard Bayley, Health Officer, and the Health Commission: John Oothout, Jacob Abramse, and Ezekiel Robins. They were tasked with policing tainted provisions, which were thought to be a possible cause of yellow fever. See the editorial note "John Jay and the Yellow Fever Epidemics," above.

2. The members of JJ's unofficial staff during the 1798 yellow fever epidemic—Robert Troup, Matthew Clarkson, and PJM—were probably copied here. Troup and Munro's copies might have accompanied the letters that JJ sent them about Sheriff J.J. Lansing. See JJ to Troup, 20 Nov. 1798, ALS, CtY-BR (EJ: 12337); and JJ to PJM, 20 Nov. 1798, ALS, NNMus (EJ: 00462). See the editorial note "John Jay and the Yellow Fever Epidemics," above and accompanying notes 48–50.

To Timothy Pickering

Albany 27 Nov. 1798

Sir,

I take the Liberty of requesting the favor of you to give the enclosed Letter to Mʳ. King, a place among your next Dispatches to him; it contains a Copy of one I wrote to him in September last, authorizing and requesting him to purchase three thousand musquets and Bayonets for this State—[1]

Accept my thanks for the interesting Pamphlet you was so obliging as to send me.[2] The Fate of Geneva affords a useful Lesson to other States, and admonishes us to guard against foreign Influence and Interference with the utmost Circumspection.

Attempts will certainly be made to abate our Vigilance, and relax our Exertions, by political opiates: and I am not without apprehensions, that our Credulity may endanger our Safety, notwithstanding what we and other nations have experienced. The French can give us only one, and that perhaps a precarious, proof of the Sincerity of their pacific Professions, vizt. a speedy honorable and conclusive Settlement of existing Differences— With great Respect and Esteem I am Sir your most obed^t. Servt.

John Jay

The Honb. Timothy Pickering Esqr.

ALS, MHi: Pickering (EJ: 04793). Endorsed: ". . . Chauvets pamphlet / The French". LbkC, N: Governor's Lbk. 1 (EJ: 03191).

1. JJ to RK, 30 Sept. 1798, ALS, NHi: King (EJ: 00705); LbkC, N: Governor's Lbk. 1 (EJ: 03171); copy found in RK to Joseph Pitcairn, 18 Dec. 1798, ALS; OCHP: Pitcairn (EJ: 01534); RK's reply of 7 Dec. 1798, ALS, NNC (EJ: 06701); C, NHi: King (EJ: 00877); C, NNC (EJ: 08630); copy located in RK to Pitcairn, 18 Dec. 1798, ALS, OCHP: Pitcairn (EJ: 01534). See also the editorial note "Defending New York," above.

2. David Chauvet, *The conduct of the Government of France towards the Republic of Geneva*. Translated from the French. By a citizen of Trenton (Trenton, 1798; *Early Am. Imprints*, series 1, no. 33510).

To Rufus King

Albany 12 Decr. 1798

Dear Sir,

The last Letter from you which has reached me is dated the 5 Augt. last—[1] Two Days ago I rec^d. the news papers you was so kind as to send me by Capt. Kemp— the Derangements caused by the late fever at New York seem to have extended to every thing in that City—

The Treaty between Austria and Naples countenanced the probability of a war between them and France; and subsequent Events do not encrease the prospect of a general peace. It appears that the Invasion of Egypt followed by Nelsons victory, has produced a Declaration of war by the Turk ag[ains]^t. France. If it be true that Oglore has not only been pardoned but promoted, the affairs of the turkish Empire must be in sad State— Russian anxiaties are dangerous Remedies for Imbecilities at Home— I suspect the Turk has much to fear.

The Directory and Buonoparte have gotten rid of each other, and they both must know and think of it— I presume therefore that Buonoparte when deciding on his present Expedition did not calculate with Certainty on aid from them, and consequently that his Expectation of Success must rest on other Circumstances— What may be his objects or his Fate cannot be known or foreseen as yet— possibly and I think not improbably, important Consequences will be the Result— One has already taken place— I mean the bringing the Turks into the war—

Britain makes a distinguished Figure, and the United States have by their late Measures compensated in some Degree for their preceding Errors— French Influence continues very active, and will not be entirely expelled— their Agents and partizans are less loud and insolent, but not less industrious and unprincipled— much will depend on the present Session of Congress, and on this head I am not free from apprehensions—

our Friend Ames was here some weeks ago— in better Health than I have seen him for Years. Benson is far from well— a weakness in his Bowels gradually diminishes his Strength, and no medicines have hitherto been of much use to him— His Spirits are good, and he is not very uncomfortable; but I fear this complaint will undermine his Constitution and bring on premature Infirmities— Hobart by the appointment of District Judge is provided for— I saw him last Summer in good Health and Spirits at West Chester; where he improves his Farm and sees his Friends with great pleasure— Gen. Schuyler whose Situation was thought desperate, has recovered wonderfully, by the use or Respiration of oxogen air, prepared and prescribed by Dᵣ. Stringer.[2] I hope London agrees with you and your Family, and it will give me pleasure to hear that Mʳˢ. Gore enjoys good Health there notwithstanding the Smoke which deprives that City of much Sunshine— As to Mʳ Gore, he is blest with robust Health—may it continue. Remember me to them & Mʳˢ. King. I am Dʳ Sir Yours Sincerely

John Jay

The Honb. Rufus King Esqʳ

ALS, NHi: King (EJ: 00706). Addressed: "The Honble / Rufus King Esq / London". Endorsed: "... and. 18 Mai 99". For RK's reply, see 18 May 1799, ALS, UkWC-A (EJ: 0008).

1. RK to JJ, 5 Aug. 1798, C, TxU-Hu (EJ: 03501).

2. Samuel Stringer (1734–1817), physician of Albany. Stringer had served as head of the Continental medical corps for the Northern Department during the war of independence.

To Timothy Pickering

Albany 21 Decʳ. 1798

Sir

I congratulate you on the addresses in answer to the Presidents Speech— so far so good. Accept my thanks for Judge Addisons address— it does him credit— Such publications are useful—[1]

Much has lately been said about Societies of united Irishmen in this Country— an original Letter was lately communicated to me, but in a way which renders Secrecy proper— thro the same channel, if not discovered or suspected, I may possibly obtain further Information. I subjoin an Extract from the Letter— it proves the Existence of such Societies, and a design to encrease them.[2] With great Respect and Esteem I remain Sir Your most obt. Servt.

John Jay

The Hon'ble Timothy Pickering

Extract

New York— 30 May 1798

"After I receive yours I will write you a long & pleasing Letter, as I have a great Deal of News. I belong to a Society of united Irishmen here, there is numbers here— could send you an *American Constitution* to form one in Albany if you pleased— we get all their proceedings from Ireland here and in Philadelphia, Baltimore and Charlestown where there is numbers. I will let you, perhaps in my next, know some of our late pleasing news. I remain with longing Expectation of your answer your Friend

P.S. I beg you may not neglect, as we want to have a Society formed in Albany—"

ALS, MHi: Pickering (EJ: 04794), containing extract. Addressed: "The Hon'ble / Timothy Pickering Esqr / Secretary of State / Philadelphia". Endorsed: ". . . United Irishmen".

1. JJ refers to TP's reply of 22 Sept. 1798 to a memorial sent to JA by the people of Prince Edward County, Va., which was widely printed. See, for example, *Gazette of the United States* and *Porcupine's Gazette* (both Philadelphia), 9 Oct.; *Daily Advertiser* (New York) and *New-York Gazette*, both 12 Oct. 1798. Of TP's reply, JA wrote "I however think the Answer excellent, and wish you had to answer all the saucy Addresses I have recd." JA to TP, 15 Oct. 1798, ALS, MHi: Pickering. See Elkins and McKitrick, *Age of Federalism*, 613. The address TP sent was Alexander Addison, *Liberty of speech, and of the press. A charge to the grand juries of the County Courts of the Fifth Circuit of the state of Pennsylvania* (Washington, D.C., 1798; *Early Am. Imprints*, series 1, no. 33267). In it, Addison defends the right of government under the Sedition Act to define strictures on free speech in order to prevent "licentiousness" which he regarded as the enemy of liberty. Scottish-born Addison (1758–1807) was the first president judge of the 5th Judicial District of Pennsylvania, located in the western portion of that state.

2. The Society of United Irishmen was formed in 1791 under the leadership of Theobald Wolfe Tone, Thomas Russell, and James Napper Tandy. Rooted in the Whig parliamentary reform movement of the 1780s, and influenced by Thomas Paine's 1791 *Rights of Man* and the French Revolution, the Society sought a more independent Irish parliament and the emancipation of the Catholics. Its membership was drawn from both Catholics and Protestants (mainly Presbyterians). British suppression after the declaration of war with France in 1793 led to the movement going underground and growing more radical, seeking independence for Ireland. The society solicited French military aid, and in 1796 and 1797, two French invasions were thwarted. In 1798, with the hope of further French aid, a rebellion initially involving thousands rose, particularly in County Wexford. However, the primary leadership was arrested, and French aid proved minimal, causing the collapse of the rebellion. While some revolutionaries were executed, others were offered jail terms, amnesty, or

emigration (both forced and voluntary). RK, as the minister to Great Britain, worked quickly to prevent the majority of the group's leadership from going to the United States. He believed, as did many Federalists, they would spread France's influence and bolster the support of Republicans.

However, many of the Society's followers had already emigrated to the U.S., beginning in the early 1790s. These were largely Presbyterians, many of the merchant class, who became involved in Republican politics. It is estimated that over sixty thousand Irish immigrants came to the U.S. during this decade, settling in New York, Philadelphia, Washington, Baltimore, and Charleston, as well as the countryside. While older Irish immigrants, including Catholics, tended to be Federalists, these new immigrants joined the Republicans, and would eventually be a force in TJ's election. In the summer of 1797, the American Society of United Irishmen was formed. Its leaders were James Reynolds, William Duane, and John Daley Burk. While never great in number, the Society soon attracted the attention of Federalists, who feared the Society's connections with revolutionary France and their support for the Republicans. Philadelphia-based William Cobbett (1763–1835), the pro-British pamphleteer and editor of *Porcupine's Gazette* (1797–99) who wrote under the pseudonym "Peter Porcupine," and John Ward Fenno, also of Philadelphia, who edited the Federalist paper *Gazette of the United States*, stirred up alarm against the Society. In 1798, Cobbett published the purported "Declaration and Constitution of the American Society of United Irishmen" *Porcupine's Gazette* (Philadelphia), 8 May 1798, and *Detection of a conspiracy, formed by the United Irishmen, with the evident intention of aiding the tyrants of France in subverting the government of the United States* (Philadelphia, 1798; *Early Am. Imprints*, series 1, no. 48395). By December 1798, the *Albany Centinel* (14 Dec. 1798), a Federalist newspaper, was commenting "We learn that meetings of United Irishmen are holding in the various capitals of the United States. Government ought to keep a vigilant eye on them." See David A. Wilson, *United Irishmen, United States: Immigrant Radicals in the Early Republic* (Ithaca, 1998), 1–3, 40–50. For JJ's concerns that the United Irishmen would infiltrate the state militia, see the editorial note "Militia Matters in New York State," above.

From Peter Augustus Jay

New York 29 Dec.ʳ 1798

Dʳ. Papa

I mentioned in my last letter[1] that I was about going to Rye in ~~the~~ your Coach. I accordingly carried it there ~~it where it will be attended to~~ ‸the next day‸ From Rye I ~~tr~~ went to Bedford ‸where‸ the Court sat ~~there~~ on the 17th—but scarcely any Business was done & ~~it the Term~~ ‸it‸ was adjourned in less than an hour after it opened— fewer people attended than I remember to have seen on a similar occasion— I dined the next Day with Judge Miller[2] who has always been extremely ~~all~~{?] civil to me. He told me he intended to take the Liberty of writing to you about the Military Appointments in the County, concerning which he seemed to ~~be~~ very uneasy— He computed the Number of ‸Militia‸ Officers who were dissaffected to the Govᵗ. at ~~more for~~ more than one half Judge Rockwell[3] says they exceed 2 thirds— ~~Several~~ The Sheriff & several other persons mentioned to me that it was much feared ‸that‸ the Officers who remained to be appointed in the new troop of wʰ.

Ab. Wright[4] is ~~a~~ Captain w^d. be of a similar Stamp—recommendations of such persons having been made to the Adj^t. Genl.[5]— I passed two Days with Maj^r. Lyons & urged him to make the necessary preparations for his house as soon as possible—which he promised— He shewed me a Letter from the person to whose ∧care∧ he had committed the Boards at Coscob declaring that they were all piled near his house & that not one of them had been stolen or injured. The Maj^r. informed me ~~that he c^d. have~~ the Sashes ∧c^d. be∧ made ~~there~~ ∧at Bedford∧ by a good workman for 5^d [dollars] a light less than half of what was asked me in the City— ∧The∧ Materials however ~~were~~ to be found by him— In the plan of the House you ~~had~~ left at Bedford only one Chimney ~~was~~ ∧is∧ marked. The Maj^r. supposed that you intended to have one at each end & said that you had left it to his own Choice whether they sh^d. be ~~cor-ner chimney or~~ in the Corner or in the middle of the Rooms— The first w^d. be more economical, but on account of their appearance he seemed inclined to prefer the latter— As I wish to give ~~as~~ an exact plan to Bourdet I w^d. be obliged to you to give me directions on these heads— John Lyon gave me ~~then~~ an Acc^t. of the Expences of making the Brick which far exceeds what I or I believe you expected— ~~He said~~ In order to account for it he s^d. that Bathrick had been wanting in Industry & made the Expence much greater than if he had ∧had∧ the original ~~conduct~~ ∧direction∧ of the business & added that as he had made an advantageous purchase of Bathricks right he w^d. be enabled to make some Agreem^t with you w^h. w^d. diminish the Amount— As he was in debt to you on account of the Mill he did not wish to receive any Money— He had made Experiments on the Lime stone & which ~~did not answer~~ proved of a ~~good~~ ∧bad∧ Quality ~~& he therefore decline making any~~ I fear this failure will occasion Embarrassments as there is ~~not~~ no one in the Neighborhood who will engage to make Lime at a reasonable price—

I spent Christmass at Rye & returned to Town in the Stage on Thursday— on my arrival I found your Letters of the 10th. 13th. & 21 inst— & to day ∧rec^d.∧ that of the 25th.[6]

I have called on M^r. Mark for the Net due on his & Mr Roosevelts Bond ~~wh~~ the latter gent. is not in town ~~but~~ ∧&∧ I expect to receive it in a few days— —[7] The Bond in my possession is for £213.0.10 & dated 9th May 1797— The Bond from John Merritt & Robert Merritt is for £44.16.1 1/4 & dated Feb 7 1792— M^r. Remsen[8] informs me that he has ~~already~~ written to you[9] on the subject of the Letter ~~directed~~ w^h. we supposed & w^h. proved to be intended for Uncle Fady[10] & that he ~~left~~ ∧has∧ desired the postmaster to send Uncle F. ~~any~~ any other Letters w^h. sh^d. be directed in a like Manner.[11] I ∧have∧ received a Letter from Uncle Aug[us]^t[us].[12] ~~together with that I forwarded to you~~ ∧of

the same date with that to you_∧— He wished to have a waistcoat & trou-
sers made by a taylor who lived near him _∧& who made him a ~~trouser~~ some
clothes last spring_∧ & as M^r. Van Winkle with whom he lodges supposed that
they would ~~be made cheaper~~ _∧cost less_∧ there than in New York I ~~wrote~~ wrote
to him; & ~~in~~ desired him to ~~have~~ let that Taylor make them _∧& sent him by
Van Winkle a flannel Waistcoat & p^r. of Mittens with a [*illegible*]_∧ I had a Coat
made directly by Codington & lined with flannel & instantly upon the Re-
ceipt of your last letter purchased a Great Coat 3 p^r milled Stockings & ~~the~~ the
Silk & ~~Cotton~~ _∧linnen_∧ handkerchiffs— I will procure the other Articles on
Monday morning & send them as you direct.

Uncle Peter[13] ~~is anx~~ has been very anxious ~~to~~ about M^r. Harisons[14] Mortgage to him— M^r. Platts[15] informs me that he has sent it to you & _∧I_∧ do not
doubt but you have rec^d. it—but Uncle w^d. be gratified to Know that it is
safe— Wishing you many a merry Christmass I am &c.

PAJ

Govr Jay

Dft, NHi: Jay (EJ: 03592). Endorsed.

1. Letter not found.

2. Probably Judge William Miller of Bedford who had served as town supervisor for Harrison's
Precinct during the 1780s. J. Thomas Scharf, *History of Westchester County, New York, including Mor-
risania, Kings Bridge, and West Farms, which have been annexed to New York City*, vol. 1 (Philadelphia,
1886), 655–56; see also JJ to Miller, 5 Apr. 1792, *JJSP*, 5: 387–88.

3. Nathan Rockwell (1737–1803) of South Salem sat on the bench of the court of common pleas
and represented Westchester County in the New York State Assembly, 1780–82, 1787–90, and 1800.
S.C. Hutchins, ed., *Civil List and Forms of Government of the Colony and State of New York* (Albany,
1870), 192.

4. Although the 1800 federal census lists an Abijah Wright (b. 1763) of Stephens Town and an
Abraham Wright (b. 1758) of North Salem, both located in Westchester county, neither individual
appears on the records of militia appointments for that county in 1798. These same records show,
however, that in 1798 Micajah Wright was appointed to command a newly raised troop of horse stationed in the upper part of Westchester County. John Lyon served as a lieutenant in Wright's unit.
Hasting and Noble, *Military Minutes*, 463, 469.

5. For more on partisanship and militia officers, see the editorial note "Militia Matters in New
York State," above.

6. JJ to PAJ, 10, 21, and 25 Dec., not found; 13 Dec., ALS, NNC (EJ: 11462).

7. For more on Nicholas J. Roosevelt's bond, see 24 Oct. 1797, note 3, above.

8. Henry Remsen Jr. of New York, financier and former under-secretary in the Department of
Foreign Affairs.

9. Letter not found.

10. Frederick Jay, JJ's younger brother, merchant and auctioneer of New York.

11. PAJ is referring to an episode in which a Liverpool merchant sent a letter to a "Mr. John Jay
Merchant at New York." JJ surmised that his name appeared in error and that the correspondence

was actually intended for his brother Frederick. See JJ to Henry Remsen, 18 Oct. 1798, ALS, DN-DAR (EJ: 05146).

12. Augustus Jay, JJ's elder brother who was mentally disabled and apparently boarded with a caretaker.

13. Peter Jay, JJ's elder brother who lived on the family estate in Rye.

14. Probably Richard Harison of New York, who served as the United States Attorney for the District of New York from 1789 to 1801.

15. Possibly Jonas Platt (1769–1834) of Poughkeepsie, a lawyer and county clerk of Herkimer County, and former member of the New York State Assembly.

Biographical Directory

Biographical information on major figures appears in the biographical directory of the volume in which that person first appears. Please see the index to find the volume and page number.

ADAMS, JOHN (1735–1826). Federalist Party leader. Friend of John Jay. Vice-president of the United States, 1789–97, and President from 1797–1801. Led the country during the Quasi-War with France, building up its naval and land forces. Signed the Alien and Sedition Acts, controversial bills sponsored by Congressional Federalists in 1798. (Please see volume 2 for full biographical listing.)

ADAMS, JOHN QUINCY (1767–1848). Massachusetts lawyer and diplomat. Eldest son of John and Abigail Adams. Minister to the Netherlands, 1794–97; minister to Prussia, 1797–1801. Supported Jay Treaty and traveled to Britain to facilitate the exchange of ratifications but arrived too late to participate. (Please see volume 5 for full biographical listing.)

BAUMAN (BEAUMAN), SEBASTIAN (1739–1803). German-born artillerist and engineer, Bauman emigrated to North America where he served in the New York militia during the Seven Years' War. At the outbreak of the war of independence, he was an infantry officer in the New York militia before being promoted to major and assigned to Lamb's Second Continental Artillery Regiment in 1777. He assumed command of the Regiment of Artillery for the City and County of New York in 1785 and held this post until his resignation in 1797 after being passed over for promotion.

BAYARD, SAMUEL (1767–1840). Philadelphia-born lawyer and judge. In October 1794, Washington appointed Bayard agent of the United States in charge of pursuing U.S. spoliation claims before British admiralty courts, a position he held for four years. He later served as presiding judge of Westchester County, appointed by Governor Jay, practiced law in New York and New

Jersey, and served as presiding judge of the court of common pleas in New Jersey, and in that state's legislature. (Please see volume 5 for full biographical listing.)

BELKNAP, JEREMY (1744–98). New Hampshire–born clergyman and historian. A graduate of Harvard, Belknap spent twenty years ministering in Dover, before assuming the pulpit of Boston's Federal Street Church in 1787. He had a leading role in founding the Massachusetts Historical Society in 1791 and served as the organization's corresponding secretary. Belknap and Jedidiah Morse visited Oneida and other Indian groups in upstate New York in 1796 and reported on the status of missionary efforts among those communities. He authored several publications on the history and natural history of New Hampshire, New England, and North America.

BENSON, EGBERT (1746–1833). Justice of the New York Supreme Court of Judicature, 1794–1801. Benson also served as a state agent in meetings with Mohawk, Oneida, and Stockbridge delegations during Jay's governorship and was one of the three commissioners appointed to settle the boundary issues involving the St. Croix River (1798). (Please see volume 1 for full biographical listing.)

BRANT, JOSEPH, OR THAYENDANEGEA (1743–1807). Mohawk leader, military chieftain, and diplomat. Mentored by William Johnson, Brant served in the Seven Years' War and attended Eleazar Wheelock's Indian School in Lebanon, Connecticut. He traveled to London with Guy Johnson at the outbreak of the war of independence seeking assistance for the Mohawk. During the war he fought alongside the British, leading volunteer forces in the northern campaigns. Working on behalf of the Six Nation communities in Upper Canada after the conflict, Brant helped to create the Mohawk reserve on the Grand River in 1784, traveled to London in 1785 seeking support for his Indian Confederacy, and sought to negotiate land settlements with the state of New York during the mid to late 1790s.

BURR, AARON (1756–1836). New Jersey–born lawyer and politician. Burr served in the Continental Army from 1775 to 1779 as a lieutenant colonel, and continued his military service after the war by commanding a militia regiment in New York. Admitted to the bar in Albany in 1782, Burr opened a practice in New York City the following year. His lengthy political career began with a seat in the state assembly from 1784 to 1785 and again in 1798–99. Burr assumed the roles of New York's attorney general from 1789 to 1790 and commissioner of Revolutionary claims in 1791 and went on to become a state leader of the Republican Party. A powerful figure in the Republican-affiliated Tammany Society of New York, he established the Bank of the Manhattan Company. Burr represented the state of New York in the U.S. Senate from 1791 to 1797. Called upon to help resolve the contested gubernatorial election of 1792, he advised that votes in Otsego and Tioga Counties should be disqualified, and thereby aided George Clinton's narrow victory over John Jay. Running as a candidate in the 1796 presidential election, Burr came in fourth place. In the subsequent election of 1800, he and Jefferson initially tied with seventy-three electoral votes each, before the House of Representatives voted in Jefferson as president and Burr vice-president. While serving in this post from 1801 to 1805, Burr lost the New York gubernatorial election in 1804. He blamed Hamilton for the defeat and eventually challenged and killed his former friend in a duel held near Weehawken in July. Although indicted for murder, Burr fled to South Carolina, and the charges were eventually dropped. Burr then headed west and became involved in various intrigues for which he was accused of treason in 1807. Chief Justice John Marshall presided over the trial and acquitted Burr of charges. After going into self-imposed exile in Europe from 1808 to 1812, Burr returned to New York and resumed his law practice. He died on Staten Island in 1836.

CAVENDISH, WILLIAM HENRY CAVENDISH-BENTINCK, 3RD DUKE OF PORTLAND (1738–1809). British politician, prime minister, 1783, 1807–9. He began his political career as a Rockingham Whig. He opposed Shelburne and was a major force behind the Fox-North coalition. After the failure of that coalition, he was a leader in the Whig opposition, but increasingly came in conflict with the more radical members of his party, such as Fox and Richard Brinsley Sheridan. His opposition to the French Revolution and support of the war against France caused him and his followers to split from the Foxites; they became known as the Portland Whigs. Pitt brought him into the cabinet as home secretary, 1794–1801.

CHAPIN, ISRAEL, JR. (1764–1833). Served as an officer in the New York State militia. When his father, Israel Chapin Sr., died in 1795, Chapin succeeded him as the federal superintendent to the Six Nations. During Jay's administration, Chapin frequently served as adviser and provided oversight for the negotiations between the Haudenosaunee and the New York State government.

CLARKSON, MATTHEW (1758–1825). Born in New York City, Clarkson served on the staffs of Benedict Arnold and Benjamin Lincoln during the war of independence. Clarkson continued his military service after the war as a state militia general and was appointed commander of the Southern District of New York in 1798. He also held numerous political offices, sitting in the state assembly (1789–90) and state senate (1793–95) and serving as U.S. Marshal for the District of New York (1791–92) and as commissioner of loans for New York. Clarkson was also active in civic and philanthropic organizations, serving as vice-president of the New-York Manumission Society, as regent of the University of the State of New York, as commissioner for Newgate Prison (1796–97), and as commissioner overseeing the defenses of New York City and harbor.

DUNDAS, HENRY, 1ST VISCOUNT MELVILLE (1742–1811). Scottish politician from a prominent legal family. Entered the English House of Commons in 1774 and became lord advocate for Scotland in 1775. He supported Pitt against the Fox-North coalition, becoming Pitt's principal man of business in the House of Commons after Pitt's ascendency, the two often acting in private. In 1791 he entered the cabinet as home secretary (1791–94). After the coalition with the Portland Whigs, he became secretary of state for war (1794–1801), a new post that gave him control of the defense of Great Britain and the colonies. Dundas was also president of the Board of Control that supervised the East India Company (1793–1801). He was an active proponent of free trade and a follower of Adam Smith. Pitt, Dundas, and Grenville were popularly known as "the Triumvirate."

EDDY, THOMAS (1758–1827). Quaker merchant of New York City. An active social reformer, Eddy served as governor of the New York Hospital, and as the first director of Newgate Prison in New York City.

GRENVILLE, WILLIAM WYNDHAM, BARON (1759–1834). British politician; son of former prime minister George Grenville and cousin of William Pitt, the younger. In 1791 Grenville became secretary of state for the foreign department, in which capacity he was the primary negotiator with Jay of the Jay Treaty in 1794. (Please see volume 5 for full biographical listing.)

HAMILTON, ALEXANDER (c. 1755–1804). Federalist Party leader of New York; U.S. Secretary of the Treasury, 1789–95. After resigning in early 1795, Hamilton returned to his law practice. He continued, however, to shape national politics, by leading efforts to secure ratification of the Jay Treaty and by preparing drafts of Washington's Farewell Address. In mid-1797, he became embroiled in a scandal concerning his affair with Maria Reynolds and wrote a lengthy pamphlet defending his actions. With the threat of a pending French invasion, President Adams appointed Hamilton as a major-general. He served as inspector-general of the U.S. Army from 1798 to 1800, commanding all troops stationed in the northern states. During the summer of 1798, Hamilton took on an additional assignment when he accepted Jay's invitation to serve as chief superintendent of fortifications for New York City. (Please see volume 1 for full biographical listing.)

HAMMOND, GEORGE (1763–1853). As British envoy to the United States, 1791–95, he strongly protested U.S. neutrality violations. Recalled on Jay's recommendation by Grenville, he became undersecretary of state for foreign affairs, 1795–1806. (Please see volume 5 for full biographical listing.)

HARISON (HARRISON), RICHARD (1747–1829). Federalist lawyer and politician of New York. Harison was appointed by George Washington to serve as the U.S. attorney for the District of New York in 1789 and held this post until 1801. During this time he investigated and prosecuted cases involving privateering and other violations of the Neutrality Act. Harison also served as recorder for New York City from 1798 to 1801. (Please see volume 5 for full biographical listing.)

HOBART, JOHN SLOSS (1738–1805). Puisne justice of the State Supreme Court of Judicature from 1777 to 1798. Hobart served a short tenure in 1798 as a Federalist in the U.S. Senate before being appointed that same year as judge of the United States District Court of New York. (Please see volume 1 for full biographical listing.)

HOFFMAN, JOSIAH OGDEN (1766–1837). Born in New Jersey, Hoffman studied law and was admitted to the bar in New York. He served in the New York State Assembly from 1791 to 1797 and in 1812–13, and as New York State Attorney General from 1795 to 1802.

HUGHES, JAMES M. (c. 1756–1802). New York City attorney and master in chancery. Hughes served as an aide-de-camp to Horatio Gates during the war of independence and later led a regiment of New York militia before assuming command of the Brigade for the City and County of New York. In the first half of the 1790s, he sat in the state assembly representing the City and County of New York. Hughes was also a founding member of the New-York Manumission Society.

JAY, PETER AUGUSTUS (1776–1843). After graduating from Columbia in 1794, Peter Augustus accompanied his father on his mission to London and served as his private secretary during the negotiations. On his return to New York City, he studied law and established a law practice with his cousin Peter Jay

Munro. He served as an officer in the state militia throughout the 1790s rising to the rank of major. (Please see volume 1 for full biographical listing.)

JAY, SARAH VAN BRUGH LIVINGSTON (1756–1802). Wife of John Jay, who managed family affairs in New York during Jay's absence to negotiate the Jay Treaty. Assisted in his election campaign of 1795. First Lady of New York during Jay's two terms as governor, 1795–1801. (Please see volume 1 for full biographical listing.)

JEFFERSON, THOMAS (1743–1826). Vice-President of United States, 1797–1801. Anti-British Republican party leader and opponent of the Jay Treaty and the Alien and Sedition Acts. Author of the Kentucky Resolution of 1798 declaring the right of a state to declare a federal law unconstitutional. (Please see volume 4 for full biographical listing.)

JENKINSON, CHARLES, FIRST EARL OF LIVERPOOL, LORD HAWKESBURY (1729–1808). British politician. Associated with George Grenville and Pitt, the Elder, earlier in his career. After the fall of the Fox-North coalition, he supported Pitt. In 1786, he was made Baron Hawkesbury and became president of the Board of Trade. In 1791, Pitt brought him into the cabinet. He was created Earl of Liverpool in 1796. Hawkesbury adhered to older mercantilist notions of economics and trade, rejecting free-trade policies and firmly opposed concessions to the Americans.

KING, RUFUS (1755–1827). After moving from Massachusetts following ratification of the Constitution, King became a Federalist lawyer and politician in New York City. He served as U.S. senator from New York, 1789–96, and was a key supporter of the Jay Treaty. He resigned his Senate seat in 1796 when Washington appointed him the U.S. minister to Britain (1796–1803). (Please see volume 5 for full biographical listing.)

LISTON, ROBERT (1742–1836). Scots-born British career diplomat. Ambassador to Spain, 1784; minister to Sweden, 1788–93; ambassador to Constantinople, 1793–94; minister to United States, 1796–1800. Worked to improve Anglo-American relations following the Jay Treaty, and assisted in the settlement of the St. Croix boundary dispute. He married Harriet Merchant of Antigua in 1796, a popular hostess who kept a diary recording the Listons' stay in America.

LIVINGSTON, EDWARD (NED) (1764–1836). Republican politician who represented New York in the U.S. House of Representatives from 1795 to 1801.

Opposed Jay's campaigns for governor. A key critic of the Jay Treaty, Livingston was active in the efforts to prevent its ratification. (Please see volume 5 for full biographical listing.)

LIVINGSTON, ROBERT R. (1746–1813). Chancellor of New York, 1777–1801. A former friend and political ally of Jay, Livingston became a Clintonian and Republican supporter in the 1790s. He opposed Jay's election in 1792 and 1795, and ran against him in 1798. Staunchly pro-French, he opposed the Jay Treaty, the Quasi-War, and the Alien and Sedition Acts. (Please see volume 1 for full biographical listing.)

MADISON, JAMES (1751–1836). Delegate to the U.S. House of Representatives from Virginia, 1789–97. Pro-French Republican Party leader in the 1790s and opponent of the Jay Treaty and the Alien and Sedition Acts. Author of the Virginia Resolution of 1798 declaring the right of a state to declare a federal law unconstitutional. (Please see volume 4 for full biographical listing.)

McHENRY, JAMES (1753–1816). Irish born physician and statesman. McHenry emigrated to the United States in the early 1770s and studied medicine in Philadelphia under Benjamin Rush. McHenry served as a surgeon during the war of independence, before being taken prisoner at Fort Washington. Released in 1778, he was appointed as a secretary to Washington from 1778 to 1780, and transferred to the staff of Lafayette, a post he held until his retirement from military service in 1781. In addition to serving in the Maryland state legislature for thirteen years, McHenry represented that state in the Continental Congress from 1783 to 1786, and was a delegate to the Federal Constitutional Convention. McHenry assumed the duties of Secretary of War from 1796 to 1800, serving in the cabinets of Washington and Adams. Under his leadership, the U.S. Army expanded and reorganized in response to the threat posed by France during the Quasi-War.

MONROE, JAMES (1758–1831). Senator from Virginia, 1790–94. Pro-French Republican party leader; opponent of Jay's appointment as envoy and of the Jay Treaty. Minister to France, 1794 to 1796. (Please see volume 4 for full biographical listing.)

MORSE, JEDIDIAH (1761–1826). Connecticut-born Congregationalist minister, geographer, educator. Three years after receiving a degree in divinity from Yale in 1786, Morse took up the pulpit of the First Parish Church in Charlestown, Mass., until 1819. Morse assisted Jay's administration by writing a report with Jeremy Belknap on the status of missionary efforts among the Oneida and other Indian communities in upstate New York. A staunch Federalist, he feared that the ideas of Jacobinism and the French Revolution threatened the stability of the American Republic. Morse gained prominence for writing several popular works on American geography.

MUNRO, PETER JAY (1767–1833). New York lawyer. Nephew of John Jay who assisted in his business and political affairs, especially during Jay's London mission. Active in Jay's gubernatorial campaign in 1795. (Please see volume 5 for full biographical listing.)

NICHOLL, SIR JOHN (1759–1838). British judge and politician. He was entered to Lincoln's Inn in 1775 and in 1785 as an advocate in Doctor's Commons, where he met his mentor Sir William Scott. An expert in maritime law, he often represented American claimants before the British admiralty courts. In 1796 he was appointed one of the British members of the spoliations commission.

PICKERING, TIMOTHY (1745–1829). Lawyer and politician born in Salem, Massachusetts. After commanding the Essex County militia regiment at the beginning of the war of independence, Pickering became adjutant general of the Continental Army in 1777 and Quartermaster General in 1780. After moving to Pennsylvania in 1786, he supported ratification of the U.S. Constitution in that state. As a leading figure of the Federalist Party, Pickering was appointed Postmaster General (1791–95), Secretary of War (1795–96), and Secretary of State (1795–1800). In addition, Pickering served as a federal agent to negotiate with the Haudenosaunee at the 1794 Treaty of Canandaigua and continued to serve as an adviser for Indian affairs during Jay's administration. Strongly anti-French, Pickering was dismissed as Secretary of State in 1800 after opposing Adams's efforts to make peace with France during the Quasi-War. As senator from Massachusetts, 1803–11, and member of the House of Representatives, 1813–17, he supported secession of New England states following Jefferson's election, opposed the embargo of 1807, and helped organize the Hartford Convention of 1814–15.

PINCKNEY, THOMAS (1750–1828). U.S. minister to Great Britain, 1792–96, and envoy extraordinary to Spain, 1794–95, where he negotiated the Pinckney Treaty, establishing U.S. boundaries with the Spanish colonies and guaranteeing American navigation rights on the Mississippi River. Member of the House of Representatives from South Carolina, 1797–1801. (Please see volume 5 for full biographical listing.)

PITT, WILLIAM (THE YOUNGER) (1759–1806). British prime minister, 1783–1801, 1804–6. Opposed the French Revolution, and led Great Britain in war against the expansionist French beginning in 1793. This war was the primary focus of his administration in the 1790s and led Pitt to seek alliances with continental European nations and to suppress dissent at home. (Please see volume 3 for full biographical listing.)

SCHUYLER, PHILIP (1733–1804). Albany landowner and Federalist politician. A state senator from 1792 to 1797, Schuyler was elected to the U.S. Senate in 1797 and served in that capacity before retiring due to ill health in early 1798. He served as a state agent and negotiated with the Haudenosaunee in the mid-1790s, using his influence to gain land concessions from the Oneida that benefited his enterprise, the Western Inland Lock Navigation Company. (Please see volume 1 for full biographical listing.)

SCOTT, WILLIAM, BARON STOWELL (1745–1836). British judge and politician. Scott made his reputation as an advocate and judge in the Admiralty and ecclesiastical courts. In 1782 he was appointed advocate-general to the Admiralty, and in 1788 became the king's advocate-general and was knighted. In this position he was the government's chief adviser on civil, canon, and maritime law, the senior crown law officer, and the Foreign Office's standing officer on international law. In 1798 he was appointed judge of the high court of Admiralty and a member of the privy council.

SINCLAIR, SIR JOHN (1754–1835). Scottish politician, member of Parliament, agricultural improver, and founder of the Board of Agriculture. Sinclair's interest in political economy and agricultural improvements, led to his major project, *The Statistical Account of Scotland* (1790–99) which gathered reports from Scottish clergy on geography, history, agriculture, population, economy, and society of each parish. In 1793, he formed the Board or Society for the Encouragement of Agriculture and Internal Improvement (commonly known as the Board of Agriculture), a voluntary organization dedicated to agricultural experimentation. Jay met Sinclair in London and continued to correspond with him on agricultural issues.

STEVENS, EBENEZER (1751–1823). Merchant and politician of New York City. Born in Roxbury, Mass., Stevens served as commanding officer of the artillery of the Northern Department and attained the rank of lieutenant-colonel during the war of independence. Stevens was an important figure in efforts to enhance the defenses of New York City and harbor, holding multiple posts at municipal, state, and federal levels that involved the planning, oversight, and implementation of fortification projects. A brigadier general in the state militia, he commanded the Artillery Regiment of the City and County of New York and acted as Commissary of military stores for New York. In addition, Stevens served in the state assembly from 1799 to 1800.

TRUMBULL, JOHN (1756–1843). Painter and diplomat. Served as Jay's secretary during his mission to Great Britain, 1794–95. Chosen as fifth commissioner on the spoliation claims commission in 1796. (Please see volume 5 for full biographical listing.)

VAN RENSSELAER, STEPHEN, III (1764–1839). Proprietor of his extensive family estate, Rensselaerswyck Manor in Albany County, New York. As a Federalist politician, he held a seat in the state assembly from 1789 to 1791 and the state senate from 1791 to 1796. After failing to win election in 1792, Van Rensselaer served as lieutenant governor under Jay from 1795 to 1801. (Please see volume 5 for full biographical listings.)

VARICK, RICHARD (1753–1831). Born in Hackensack, N.J., Varick attended King's College, but left his studies in 1775 to join the Continental Army. Varick rose rapidly in the ranks, serving on the staffs of Philip Schuyler, Benedict Arnold, and George Washington. Following the war, he held the post of recorder for the City of New York in 1784, sat as a member of the state assembly from 1786 to 1788, and served as attorney general from 1788 to 1789. In 1789, Varick began a twelve-year tenure as the Federalist mayor of New York City.

WASHINGTON, GEORGE (1732–99). President of the United States from 1789 to 1797. Supported neutrality policy. Appointed Jay special envoy to Britain in 1794 and supported ratification of the Jay Treaty with some reservations. After retiring to Mount Vernon, Washington was called back to public service in 1798 as commander-in-chief to defend against possible French invasion. (Please see volume 4 for full biographical listing.)

WATSON, JAMES (1750–1806). A native of Connecticut, Watson served as an officer during the war of independence. Relocating to New York City after the conflict, Watson commenced a successful mercantile business. As a Federalist politician, he represented his constituents in both the state assembly (1791, 1794–96) and the state senate (1796–98), before serving in the U.S. Senate from 1798 to 1800. Watson was one of the commissioners who oversaw the defensive preparations for New York City's port and harbor. In 1800, Watson resigned his Senate seat to accept an appointment as naval officer for the port of New York.

WEDDERBURN, ALEXANDER, 1ST EARL OF ROSSLYN, LORD LOUGHBOROUGH (1733–1805). Scottish peer and politician; member of the Select Society. Solicitor-general under Lord North and first lord of the Treasury under the Fox-North coalition. His opposition to the French Revolution and support of the war against France brought him into Pitt's favor. He succeeded his rival Edward Thurlow as Lord Chancellor in 1793 as part of Pitt's wartime cabinet, serving until 1801. He also acted as legal adviser to George III. Loughborough negotiated with Jay on Anglo-American legal issues during his London mission.

WILLIAMS, JOHN (1752–1806). Surgeon and politician of Salem, New York. After immigrating to New York from Britain in 1773, Williams opened a medical practice and served in the State Provincial Congress in 1775. That same year he was appointed Surgeon of New York's militia. He sat in the State's first senate from 1777 to 1779, but was temporarily expelled for embezzling militia funds before being cleared of charges. Williams resumed his political career in the state assembly from 1781 to 1782 and again in the state senate from 1782 to 1794. He also continued his militia service in peacetime, being appointed as a brigadier general in 1786. As an Anti-Federalist, Williams argued against the U.S. Constitution as a delegate representing Washington and Clinton Counties at New York's ratification convention. Williams was a member of the House of Representatives from 1795 to 1799, serving as Republican Representative during his first two years in office, and switching to the Federalist Party for his reelection.

Index

References to earlier volumes are indicated by the volume number followed by a colon and page number (for example, 1:753).

"A" (pseudonym): writings of, 63n7
"A.B." (pseudonym): writings of, 626n10
Abbeville, France: arrest at, 272
Abeel, John, 510n4
Abramse, Jacob, 352, 615, 710n1; identified, 359n37
Adair, James Makittrick, 252, 253n4; identified, 253n4
Adams, Abigail Smith, 668n10
Adams, Charles: identified, 357n12; information from, 357n12
Adams, John: addresses of, lv, 656, 659n9; addresses to, 555, 633n2, 634n6, 635, 639, 640n4, 641n4, 644n7, 658, 659n4, 679, 690–91n1, 713n1; and Alien and Sedition Acts, 657; and appointment of William S. Smith, 669; appointments of, 673n2; British treatment of, xxii; cabinet of, 725; correspondence of, 205n1, 246n1, 433nn1–3, 654, 658, 668n10; and defense measures, 624, 633n2, 658, 678; and defense of New York, 403–4, 405, 408, 411, 649n6; dispatches and instructions forwarded to Congress by, 659n3; embarrassment of, 410; identified, 719; and Indian affairs, 321, 623n3; letters from, 433–34, 693; letters to, 238–39, 244–45, 689–92; memorials to, 713n1; messages of, 622n1, 653, 653n1, 656, 659n3, 666n1; and military appointments, 663, 667; and militia matters, 558; praises JJ, 691n1; and relations with France, xxviii, 656, 660; speeches of, 712, 713n1; and St. Croix River dispute, 207; support for, lvi, 678; testimony of, for boundary commission, 286; views on family, 433; views on military preparedness, 435; visits New York City, 670n3; and XYZ affair, 621, 624, 657–58, 693

Adams, John Quincy: arrival in London, 1, 238, 239n2; correspondence and dispatches of, 204, 238, 239n2, 244–45, 245, 246n1, 246n2, 246n3, 269, 430; and exchange of ratifications, 284; funds advanced to, 241, 241n3, 548; identified, 719; information conveyed by, 443; instructions to, 431n4; and Jay Treaty, 4, 77, 82n35, 239n2, 245–46, 245n3, 279; JJ's views on, 296; letters from, 204, 205n1, 240–41, 247–48, 262–63; letters to, 245–46, 249–50; and Loughborough article, 191–92n5; mission to the Netherlands, 1, 245; negotiations of, 431n4, 444n4; reception of, 204–5

Adams, Thomas Boylston, 239n2, 245, 250, 591

Adams, William, 631n4

Adams family, 584n1

Addington, Henry, 10n19

Addison, Alexander (Judge), 712, 713n1; identified, 713n1

Adet, Pierre Auguste, 382n1, 583; complaints of, 520–21n2, 523, 524–25n3; identified, 524n3; and neutrality violations, 568–69n2; suspends diplomatic functions, 524n3

Adina: negotiations at, 592